FUNDAMENTALS OF AUTOCAD®

Steven B. Combs
Ivy Tech State College
Jay H. Zirbel
Murray State University

Prentice Hall
Upper Saddle River, New Jersey *Columbus, Ohio*

Library of Congress Cataloging-in-Publication Data

Combs, Steven B.
Fundamentals of AutoCAD / Steven B. Combs, Jay H. Zirbel.
p. cm.
Includes index.
ISBN 0-13-256439-4
1. Computer graphics. 2. AutoCAD (Compter file) I. Zirbel, Jay H. II Title.
T385.C54855 1998
604.2'0285'5369--dc21 97-27756
CIP

Editor: Stephen Helba
Production Coordination: Lisa Garboski, bookworks
Design Coordinator: Karrie M. Converse
Text Designer: Meryl Poweski
Cover Designer: Proof Positive/Farrowlyne Assoc., Inc.
Production Manager: Deidra M. Schwartz
Marketing Manager: Debbie Yarnell

This book was set in Times Roman by The Clarinda Company and was printed and bound by Courier/Kendallville, Inc. The cover was printed by Phoenix Color Corp.

Printed in the United States of America

10 9 8 7 6 5 4 3 2 1

ISBN: 0-13-256439-4

Prentice-Hall International (UK) Limited, *London*
Prentice-Hall of Australia Pty. Limited, *Sydney*
Prentice-Hall of Canada, Inc., *Toronto*
Prentice-Hall Hispanoamericana, S. A., *Mexico*
Prentice-Hall of India Private Limited, *New Delhi*
Prentice-Hall of Japan, Inc., *Tokyo*
Simon & Schuster Asia Pte. Ltd., *Singapore*
Editora Prentice-Hall do Brasil, Ltda. *Rio de Janeiro*

PREFACE

AutoCAD® is probably one of the more intimidating software packages taught in education. With its stiff computer hardware requirements and numerous commands, it can be a daunting task for both the instructor to teach and the student to learn. This book focuses on using AutoCAD as a drafting tool. Wherever possible, examples and exercises are used to provide real-world problems in an effort to make this book practical as well as functional. Included are Auto CAD's most popular 2-D drawing commands that should be covered with one-half of an academic year for high schools or one college semester.

UNIQUE FEATURES

While there are many good AutoCAD books on the market, *Fundamentals of AutoCAD* has several unique and important features, including the following:

- **Updated for AutoCAD Release 13c4 for Windows® 95/NT 4.0.** Many AutoCAD texts are based on the initial version of AutoCAD Release 13 and do not include the new commands and features released in version 13c4. Version 13c4 included several new commands and dialog boxes, which are all thoroughly covered in this text. One of the most significant features of this upgrade was support for Windows 95 and Windows NT 4.0. While the hardware and cost requirements for Windows NT 4.0 are out of reach for most educational institutions, Windows 95 offers an inexpensive alternative. The interface is similar in both operating systems, however, and gives students trained with Windows 95 the versatility to work with the Windows NT version of AutoCAD as well.
- **Unit Exercises.** Each unit contains 10 short-answer questions as well as one applied exercise that is intended to develop students' AutoCAD skills. The exercises are generic in nature and are not for any one discipline. These are not meant to be the only assignments given to students; the instructor should include additional assignments of his or her own development or consider using one of the optional workbooks that are available as supplements to this text.
- **Optional Workbooks.** Workbooks are available for specific educational disciplines: Mechanical Drafting Workbook (ISBN 013-887738-6), Architectural Drafting Workbook (ISBN 0-13-758574-8), and Electronics Drafting Workbook (ISBN 013-758566-7) are currently available. These workbooks describe the use of commands in a manner specific to a particular discipline. Discipline-specific examples and exercises are also included, giving the students more real-world experience.
- **Work Disk.** By using the work disk, students can work with commands and features immediately without having to create complex geometry. See the disk for instructions on its use.
- **Web Page.** One of the most exciting new features is a Web page for this text. On this interactive Web page, students can provide feedback to the authors, participate with other students in electronic discussion groups, test their retention with online quizzes, and link to other Web pages that contain information and news about the world of AutoCAD. Instructors can also provide feedback to the authors, participate with other instructors in discussions about curriculum, give online quizzes and have the results electronically mailed back to the instructor, and link to other Web pages that contain the latest information and news about AutoCAD and AutoCAD in education.

Organization of the Text

The text is divided into 16 units to correspond with the 16 weeks in a typical semester. Each unit is divided into sections, grouping similar commands and exercises together. Units 1 through 4 present the basic skills necessary to begin using AutoCAD. Many of the skills in these sections form the foundation for other commands, so it is imperative that students understand these units thoroughly. Units 5 through 8 expand on various drawing commands and techniques, allowing students to create complex geometry. These units ensure students can create any shape they can imagine. Units 9 through 11 introduce the various ways to select and edit existing objects. A large amount of editing is usually required throughout the course of a drawing. Editing commands not only modify existing objects, but they also create new objects. Unit 12 includes advanced drawing commands that assist in the creation of complex shapes and objects. Unit 13 presents what is traditionally thought of as the most difficult concept for new students—dimensioning an object. Unit 14 allows students to extract information from their drawings for further analysis. Unit 15 discusses how to automate the placement and creation of repetitive shapes. Finally, Unit 16 introduces the concept of isometric drawings and their creation.

Unit Layout

To assist in the learning of AutoCAD, each unit consists of the following sections:

- **Overview.** Briefly describes the material to be presented in the unit.
- **Objectives.** Different from the outline, this section presents specific skills that students should have upon completion of the unit.
- **Outline.** Outlines the entire unit and lists the commands to be presented.
- **Illustrations.** Each unit contains numerous illustrations to help in describing a specific function or command. AutoCAD is a very graphic package, and the addition of well-defined illustrations helps in clarifying difficult concepts.
- **Tutorials.** Tutorials provide the procedures necessary to utilize a command or feature. Tutorials are located in boxes and are easy to find. The segregation of these tutorials makes them easy to identify. A tutorial will walk students through a particular command or concept so they can see first-hand how a command or series of commands is used.

- **Skill Builders.** Skill Builders provide tips and shortcuts that allow for easier or faster AutoCAD operation. They are techniques commonly used by professionals.

- **For the Professional.** For the Professional introduces advanced concepts that increase students' understanding of an AutoCAD command or feature. AutoCAD was developed for the creation of engineering graphics. Many of the commands and features are based on tools or skills from manual drafting. A For the Professional is used to provide additional information that may help students' avoid problems, or offers advice that relate to the topic. This will increase students' awareness of how and why a command is used in a specific situation.
- **Summary.** The summary is a wrap-up of the unit used to reinforce retention and to promote additional thought and discussion.
- **Review.** The review consists of 10 short-answer questions that test students' retention of commands and procedures. They can be used as homework or to spark a discussion after the lecture.
- **Exercises.** These short drawing assignments are meant to incorporate many of the commands and features presented within the unit. Each assignment comes complete with a step-by-step procedure for getting started. As students progress through the units, the step-by-step procedures are decreased, and students are asked to draw from their knowledge in completing the assignments.

To the Student

Many excellent jobs are available for people with a good understanding of AutoCAD. While the textbook contains complete explanations of all the commands, nothing can take the place of practice. To become proficient in AutoCAD, you must continually work with the program and refine your skills. AutoCAD is a complicated software package. Many have likened AutoCAD to learning a foreign language. In order to understand its commands and nuances, you must practice it daily.

The Review exercises are designed to make you think. After class, try to answer each one without looking back at your notes or the book. Then, verify your answer with the text. Most of the Review items are quite simple, especially if you have done the reading and listened to the lecture.

Complete the Unit Tutorials. The tutorials present a step-by-step method for utilizing a command or feature. Often a tutorial will highlight different methods of using a command. Completing the tutorials will give you a more rounded view of AutoCAD in addition to valuable practice. If you have questions, ask your instructor for additional help.

HAVE FUN! AutoCAD is fun. You will receive great satisfaction when you figure out how to use a command or how to create a complex object or shape. Follow these steps and we are sure that your experience with AutoCAD will be a pleasurable and rewarding one.

Acknowledgments

We would like to thank the following individuals for their assistance during this project. To the team at Prentice Hall: Stephen Helba—Thanks for the trip to New Jersey and the opportunity to pitch our idea. Kim Gundling—Thank you for always checking up on us. While we know this is your job, you always did so in a way that seemed more like a personal conversation rather than a business call. Heidi Lobecker—Keep that Web page going! Without you and your team, we would not have all of the neat high-tech accessories that accompany this text. Patty Kelly—Thanks for overseeing our layout for the text and workbooks. You were a wonderful liaison with bookworks. At bookworks we would like to thank Lisa Garboski and her team for the timely layout of our manuscript. Eye appeal is a must, and we must say that you have done a wonderful job.

We would also like to thank Dixie Endsley for taking on the tough job of technical review. Your attention to detail was just what this manuscript needed. Just remember, if anything is wrong, it's your fault!

Mr. Combs would like to thank Wendy Bowles at Prentice Hall. You have to be the hardest-working "Book Rep." Thanks for lunch and for the great ideas. Thanks are also in order for Mary Kissinger. Thanks for taking all of my messages and helping me stay organized. You do a great job!

I would especially like to thank my wife Elizabeth. I spent many hours away from you while preparing this text and I promise to make each and every one of them up to you. You truly are a wonderful and supportive wife. Thanks for all of your help in collaborating on unit assignments, reviewing manuscript, making tedious editing corrections, screen captures, and providing me with excellent feedback. They say "behind every great man is an even better woman." They must have been talking about you! We are two halves . . .

I dedicate this book to my daughter Katherine. Although you are too young to read this now, thanks for being the best daughter a father could have, "pea pie."

Steven B. Combs, Ivy Tech State College, Evansville, Indiana

scombs@ivy.tec.in.us

Dr. Zirbel would like to thank his wife, Krissy, and two boys, Cory and Cody. Writing a textbook is not a trivial undertaking, and I could never accomplish such a task without your support and understanding.

Dr. Jay H. Zirbel, Murray State University, Murray, Kentucky

jay.zirbel@murraystate.edu

Contents

UNIT 1 Introduction to AutoCAD and Working with the Windows Environment 1

Overview 1

Objectives 1

Introduction 1

Outline 2

The Basics of Windows 2

Starting Windows 2
Working with the Taskbar 2
Opening and Closing Windows 5
Minimizing and Maximizing Windows 5
Working with Dialog Boxes 6
Getting Help in Windows 8

Starting AutoCAD and Understanding the Display 9

Starting AutoCAD 9
The AutoCAD Display 11

Interacting with AutoCAD 13

Issuing Commands 13
Typing Commands 13
Using Toolbars 15
Using Pull-Down Menus 16
Using the Screen Menus 18
Working with Dialog Boxes 18
AutoCAD Help System (HELP) 19

TUTORIAL 1.1: Using the Help System 20

WORKING WITH FOLDERS 22

Managing Files and Folders 22
AutoCAD File Operations 24
Creating a New Drawing 24
Opening an Existing Drawing 25

TUTORIAL 1.2: Creating a New Drawing File 26

Saving and Exiting a Drawing 27

TUTORIAL 1.3: Opening an Existing Drawing File 28

Saving a Drawing File 28

Using Savetsime 30

Closing Autocad 30

Summary 31

Review 32

Exercise One 32

UNIT 2 Creating Your First Drawing 33

Overview 33

Objectives 33

Introduction 33

Outline 34

Starting a New Drawing 34

TUTORIAL: Starting the Example Drawing 35

Saving your Work 36
Setting Display Formats and Units (DDUNITS) 36
Setting the Drawing Size (LIMITS) 37

TUTORIAL 2.1: Setting the Display Formats and Units 38

TUTORIAL 2.2: Setting the Drawing Size 40

Using AutoCAD Drafting Tools 41

Using the Grid (GRID) 42

TUTORIAL: Setting the Grid 44

Using Snap (SNAP) 44

Rotating the Snap 46

Using the Coordinate Display (COORDS) 47

TUTORIAL: Setting the Snap 48

Using Ortho (ORTHO) 49

Drawing Lines (LINE) 50

Drawing Line Segments (LINE) 50

Using the Close and Undo Options 51

Drawing Continued Line Segments 52

Cleaning up the Display (REDRAW) 52

Quitting AutoCAD 53

TUTORIAL: Using the Line Command to Create the Roof Plan 53

Understanding Objects 56

What is an Object? 56

Understanding the Drawing Database 56

Summary 57

Review 57

Exercise Two 58

UNIT 3 Viewing and Plotting a Drawing 59

Overview 59

Objectives 59

Introduction 59

Outline 60

Understanding the Display 60

Understanding the Virtual Screen 60

Refreshing the Screen (REDRAW) 61

Regenerating the Screen (REGEN) 61

Regenerating the Drawing Automatically (REGENAUTO) 62

Setting Display Options (VIEWERS) 62

Using Zoom to Control the Display 63

Zoom All 64

TUTORIAL 3.1: Using the Zoom All Command 64

Zoom Center 65

TUTORIAL 3.2: Using the Zoom Center Command 65

Zoom Dynamic 66

TUTORIAL 3.3: Using the Zoom Dynamic Command 67

Zoom Extents 70

TUTORIAL 3.4: Using the Zoom Extents Option 70

Zoom Left 70

TUTORIAL 3.5: Using the Zoom Left Command 71

Zoom Previous 71

TUTORIAL 3.6: Using the Zoom Previous Command 72

Zoom Vmax 72

TUTORIAL 3.7: Using the Zoom Vmax Option 72

Zoom Window 73

TUTORIAL 3.8: Using the Zoom Window Option 73

Zoom Scale 74

TUTORIAL 3.9: Using the Zoom Scale Option 74

Zoom In and Zoom Out 75

Panning the Display (PAN) 75

Shifting the View a Specific Distance 76

TUTORIAL 3.10: Panning a Drawing 76

Using the Aeiral View Window 77

Aerial Window Options 78

Aerial Window Menu Options 79

TUTORIAL 3.11: Using the Aerial View Window 79

Creating Views (VIEW AND DDVIEW) 82
Listing Views 83
Restoring Views 83
Deleting Views 83
Saving Views 83
TUTORIAL: CREATING AND SAVING VIEWS 84
INTRODUCTION TO PLOTTING 85
Configuring AutoCAD for Plotting (PLOT) 87
Understanding Plotting Options 88
Device and Default Information 88
Setting Pen Parameters 89
Specifying Pen Assignments 89
Specifying Paper Size 91
TUTORIAL 3.12: USING THE PLOT DIALOG BOX TO DETERMINE PAGE LIMITS 91
Specifying Plot Scale, Rotation, and Origin 92
Previewing the Plot 93
TUTORIAL 3.13: PLOTTING A DRAWING 94
SUMMARY 95
REVIEW 95
EXERCISE THREE 96

UNIT 4 BASIC CAD DRAWING TECHNIQUES 97
OVERVIEW 97
OBJECTIVES 97
INTRODUCTION 97
OUTLINE 98
SETTING DISPLAY FORMAT AND PRECISION (UNITS AND DDUNITS) 98
Units Report Format 98
Display Precision 99
Angular Measurement 100
TUTORIAL 4.1: DRAWING LINES USING THE FIVE DIFFERENT UNITS 102
WORKING WITH PHOTOTYPE DRAWINGS 102
Creating a New Drawing From a Prototype 103
Setting Prototype Drawing Options 104
COORDINATE SYSTEM BASICS 104
TUTORIAL 4.2: CREATING A PROTOTYPE DRAWING 105
Using Coordinates in AutoCAD 106
TUTORIAL 4.3: USING ABSOLUTE COORDINATES TO CREATE A SIDE ELEVATION PROFILE 109
Understanding Polar Coordinates 110
TUTORIAL 4.4: USING RELATIVE COORDINATES TO CREATE A SIDE ELEVATION PROFILE 111
TUTORIAL 4.5: USING RELATIVE AND ABSOLUTE POLAR COORDINATES TO CREATE SIDE ELEVATION PROFILE 111
TUTORIAL 4.6: CREATING PROPERTY LINES WITH COORDINATES AND A PROTOTYPE DRAWING 112
SUMMARY 113
REVIEW 113
EXERCISE FOUR 114

UNIT 5 UNDERSTANDING LAYERS AND LINE TYPES 115
OVERVIEW 115
OBJECTIVES 115
INTRODUCTION 115
OUTLINE 116
WORKING WITH LAYERS 116
Using the layer Control Dialog Box (DDLMODES) 116
TUTORIAL 5.1: ADDING LAYERS TO A PROTOTYPE DRAWING 118

TUTORIAL 5.2: CHANGING THE CURRENT LAYER 120

TUTORIAL 5.3: CONTROLLING LAYER COLOR 121

CONTROLLING LAYER VISIBILITY 122

Turning Layers On and Off 122

Freezing and Thawing Layers 122

Locking and Unlocking Layers 123

TUTORIAL 5.4: CONTROLLING LAYER VISIBILITY 124

Renaming Layers 124

Using Filters to Limit the Display of Layer Names 124

TUTORIAL 5.5: COMPLETING THE APARTMENT COMPLEX FRONT ELEVATION WITH LAYERS 125

UNDERSTANDING LINETYPES 126

What are Linetypes? 126

Listing Linetypes (LINETYPE,DDCTYPE) 126

Loading a Linetype 128

TUTORIAL 5.6: LOADING A LINE-TYPE 128

Setting the Linetype 129

TUTORIAL 5.7: SETTING THE LINE-TYPE 130

Setting a Default Linetype 130

Understanding Linetype Scale (LTSCALE) 131

TUTORIAL 5.8: ADDING HIDDEN AND CENTER LINES AND CHANGING THE LINETYPE SCALE 132

Creating you own Linetype (LINE-TYPE) 134

TUTORIAL 5.9: CREATING A LINE-TYPE 136

SUMMARY 136

REVIEW 136

EXERCISE FIVE 137

UNIT 6 CREATING BASIC GEOMETRY 139

OVERVIEW 139

OBJECTIVES 139

INTRODUCTION 139

OUTLINE 139

DRAWING RECTANGLES (RECTANG) 139

TUTORIAL 6.1: CREATING A REC-TANGLE 140

DRAWING CIRCLES (CIRCLE) 141

Drawing Circles with Center Point and Diameter 143

TUTORIAL 6.2: CREATING A CIR-CLE WITH CENTER RADIUS 143

TUTORIAL 6.3: CREATING A CIRCLE WITH CENTER DIAMETER 145

Drawing Circles with Three Points 145

TUTORIAL 6.4: CREATING A CIRCLE WITH THREE POINTS 146

Drawing Circles with Two Points 147

Drawing Circles with Tangent, Tangent, Radius 147

TUTORIAL 6.5: CREATING A CIRCLE WITH TWO POINTS 148

TUTORIAL 6.6: CREATING CIRCLES WITH TANGENT, TANGENT, RADIUS 149

TUTORIAL 6.7: DRAWING A STOVE/OVEN SYMBOL 149

DRAWING ARCS (ARC) 152

Drawing Arcs with Three Points 153

TUTORIAL 6.8: CREATING AN ARC WITH 3 POINT OPTION 153

Drawing Arcs with Start, Center, End 153

TUTORIAL 6.9: CREATING AN ARC WITH START, CENTER, END 154

Drawing Arcs with Start, End, Radius (SER) 155

TUTORIAL 6.10: CREATING AN ARC WITH START, END, RADIUS 155

Continuing an Arc from an Exist-ing Arc 156

TUTORIAL 6.11: CONTINUING AN ARC FROM AN EXISTING ARC 157
TUTORIAL 6.12: DRAWING A BREAKFAST BAR SYMBOL 158
Drawing Polygons (POLYGON) 160
TUTORIAL 6.13: DRAWING AN INSCRIBED POLYGON 162
TUTORIAL 6.14: DRAWING A HOT TUB SYMBOL WITH POLYGON, RECTANG, AND CIRCLE 163
SUMMARY 164
REVIEW 164
EXERCISE SIX 164

UNIT 7 ANNOTATING A DRAWING WITH TEXT AND HATCHING 167
OVERVIEW 167
OBJECTIVES 167
INTRODUCTION 167
OUTLINE 167
ADDING TEXT TO A DRAWING 168
Defining a Text Style (STYLE,DDSTYLE) 168
TUTORIAL 7.1: CREATING YOUR OWN TEXT STYLE 173
Entering Text with Text and Dtext 174
Changing the Style 175
Justifying Text 175
Aligning Text (ALIGN and FIT) 176
Using Special Characters in Text 177
TUTORIAL 7.2: CREATING TEXT WITH TEXT AND DTEXT 178
Entering Text with MText 180
Importing Text 181
TUTORIAL 7.3: USING MTEXT TO CREATE AND IMPORT TEXT 183
Editing Text (CHANGE,DDEDIT, AND DDMODIFY) 184
Editing MText Objects 185
TUTORIAL 7.4: EDITING TEXT AND MTEXT 187
Hiding and Displaying Text (QTEXT,TEXTQLTY, TEXTFILL) 188
Spell Checking a Drawing 188
TUTORIAL 7.5: HIDING AND SPELL CHECKING TEXT 190
FILLING AREAS WITH HATCHING 191
Creating Hatching Patterns (BHATCH) 191
Defining the Pattern Type 191
Pattern Properties 192
TUTORIAL 7.6: CREATING A HATCH PATTERN 193
Defining the Area to Hatch 194
TUTORIAL 7.7: HATCHING AN AREA OF A DRAWING 195
Advanced Hatching Options 197
Editing a Hatch (HATCHEDIT) 199
TUTORIAL 7.8: EDITING A HATCH 200
Understanding Common Hatching Problems 201
SUMMARY 201
REVIEW 201
EXERCISE SEVEN 202

UNIT 8 DRAWING ACCURATELY 203
OVERVIEW 203
OBJECTIVES 203
INTRODUCTION 203
OUTLINE 204
WORKING WITH ENTITY POINTS AND OBJECT SNAP 204
Understanding Objects Points and Object Snap 204
DRAWING WITH OBJECT SNAP MODES 212
Drawing with Temporary Objects Snap Modes 212

TUTORIAL 8.1: Using Temporary Object Snap Modes to Create a Circle—Top Window 213
Using Running Object Snap Modes (OSNAP AND DDOSNAP) 217
TUTORIAL 8.2: Using Running Object Snap Modes to Create a Divided Octagon 218
Using Multiple Running Object Snap Modes 219
TUTORIAL 8.3: Using Multiple Running Object Snap Modes 220
Using QUIck Object Snap Modes 221
Turning Running Object Snaps Off 221
Controlling Aperture Box Size 221
Using Point Filters for 2-D Construction 222
Using the .X Point Filter 223
Using the .Y Point Filter 223
TUTORIAL 8.4: Using Point Filters to Locate a Circle in the Center of a Rectangle 224
Summary 224
Review 224
Exercise Eight 225

UNIT 9 Creating Selection Sets 227
Overview 227
Objectives 227
Introduction 227
Outline 227
Methods for Creating a Selection Set 228
Picking Objects 228
Selecting Objects with the Toolbar 228
Using the Select Command 230
Selecting Objects 230
Pick-First Selection Versus Pick-After Selection 231
Using Shift to Select Option 232
TUTORIAL 9.1: Picking Points 233
TUTORIAL 9.2: Selecting Objects with a Window 234
Changing the Press and Drag Settings 235
TUTORIAL 9.3: Selecting the Last Object Created 236
TUTORIAL 9.4: Selecting with the Crossing Option 237
TUTORIAL 9.5: Selecting Objects with a Box 238
TUTORIAL 9.6: Selecting All Objects 239
TUTORIAL 9.7: Using the Window Polygon (WPOLYGON) 239
TUTORIAL 9.8: Using the Crossing Polygon (CPOLYGON) 241
TUTORIAL 9.9: Selecting with a Fence 242
Selecting Multiple Objects from the Drawing Database 242
TUTORIAL 9.10: Selecting a Single Object 243
Completing the Selection Set 243
TUTORIAL 9.11: Selecting the Previous Selection Set 243
Object Selection Cycling 243
TUTORIAL 9.12: Removing and Adding Objects to the Selection Set 244
TUTORIAL 9.13: Undoing a Selection 244
TUTORIAL 9.14: Canceling the Selection 244
Using the Object Selection Filters 245
Selecting Groups 245
System Variable that affect Selecting Objects 245
TUTORIAL 9.15: Creating an Object Selection Filter 246
Summary 247

Review 247
Exercise Nine 247

UNIT 10 Basic Editing Skills 249
Overview 249
Objectives 249
Introduction 249
Outline 250
Deleting and Restoring Objects 250
Deleting Objects 250
Restoring Accidentally Erased Objects 251
TUTORIAL 10.1: Erasing and Restoring Objects 251
Undoing Your Work 252
TUTORIAL 10.2: Working with Undo and Redo 253
TUTORIAL 10.3: Purging an Unwanted Layer 255
Removing Unwanted Objects 256
Moving, Copying, and Offsetting Objects 256
Moving Objects 256
TUTORIAL 10.4: Moving Objects 257
Copying Objects 258
Creating Objects with Offset 258
TUTORIAL 10.5: Copying Objects 259
TUTORIAL 10.6: Offsetting Objects 260
Rotating, Mirroring, Scaling, and Stretching Objects 261
Rotating Objects 261
Creating Mirror Images 262
TUTORIAL 10.7: Rotating Objects 263
TUTORIAL 10.8: Mirroring Objects 265
Scaling Parts of a Drawing 266
TUTORIAL 10.9: Scaling Objects 267
Stretching Parts of a Drawing 268
TUTORIAL 10.10: Stretching Objects 269
Editing Edges and Corners of Objects 270
Trimming Objects 270
TUTORIAL 10.11: Shortening Objects with the Trim Command 271
Erasing Parts of Objects 273
TUTORIAL 10.12: Using the Break Command 274
Extending Objects 275
TUTORIAL 10.13: Extending Objects 277
Filleting Objects 278
TUTORIAL 10.14: Rounding and Cleaning Edges with the Fillet Command 280
Chamfering Objects 281
TUTORIAL 10.15: Creating Chamfers 282
Producing Arrays of Objects 283
Rectangular Arrays 284
TUTORIAL 10.16: Duplicating Elements in a Grid Format 285
Polar Arrays 286
TUTORIAL 10.17: Duplicating Elements in a Circular Format 287
Summary 289
Review 289
Exercise Ten 289

UNIT 11 Editing with Grips 291
Overview 291
Objectives 291
Introduction 291
Outline 291
Working with Grips 291
Selecting Objects with Grips 293

TUTORIAL 11.1: Selecting Single and Multiple Grips 294
Setting Grips Options 296
Editing Block with Grips 297
TUTORIAL 11.2: Setting Grip Options 298
Using the Grip Modes 298
Stretching Objects with Grips 298
TUTORIAL 11.3: Stretching Objects with Grips 299
Moving Objects with Grips 300
TUTORIAL 11.4: Moving Objects with Grips 300
Rotating Objects with Grips 301
Scaling Objects with Grips 301
TUTORIAL 11.5: Rotating Objects with Grips 301
TUTORIAL 11.6: Scaling Objects with Grips 303
Mirroring Objects with Grips 303
TUTORIAL 11.7: Mirroring Objects with Grips 304
Copying Objects with Grips 305
TUTORIAL 11.8: Copying Objects with Grips 306
Implications of Using the Same Grip Point 306
Summary 307
Review 307
Exercise Eleven 307

UNIT 12 Advanced Drawing Technique 309
Overview 309
Objectives 309
Introduction 309
Outline 310
Indicating Locations with Point 310
Selecting the Point Style 311
Setting the Point Size (pdmode) 311
Setting Point Size Relative to Screen Size 311
Setting Point Size to an Absolute Unit 312
Dividing and Measuring an Object 312
Dividing Objects into Equal Segment 312
Using Divide to Insert Objects 313
Measuring an Object (measure) 314
Using measure to Insert Objects 316
TUTORIAL 12.1: Drawing a Stair Elevation 316
Drawing Rings, Solid-Filled Circles, and Ellipses 320
Drawing Ellipses (Ellipse) 320
Defining Endpoints and Distances 322
Defining Endpoints and Rotation 322
Defining Center and Axis Point 323
Defining an Ellipse Arc 324
TUTORIAL 12.2: Creating a Bathroom Sink Symbol 325
Drawing Infinite Lines and Free hand Drawings 326
Drawing Infinite Lines (xline) 327
Drawing Rays (ray) 331
Creating Freehand Drawings (sketch) 332
TUTORIAL 12.3: Sketching Your Initials with the Sketch Command 333
Working with Multilines 334
Defining Multiline Styles (mlstyle) 334
Creating Multilines 337
TUTORIAL 12.4: Creating Multiline Styles with Mlstyle 338
TUTORIAL 12.5: Drawing Multilines 341
Editing Multilines 342
TUTORIAL 12.6: Adding Vertices to a Multiline 350

TUTORIAL 12.7: Removing Multiline Sections 351

TUTORIAL 12.8: Making Multiline Corners 353

Using Polylines 354

Polyline Options 355

Polyline Arc Options 356

TUTORIAL 12.9: Drawing Polylines Using the Line and Arc Option 357

Drawing Boundary Polylines 358

TUTORIAL 12.10: Creating a Boundary 360

Editing Polylines 361

Closing or Opening a Polyline (pedit close and open) 362

Joining Polylines (pedit join) 362

Setting Polyline Width (pedit width) 362

Curving and decurving Polylines 362

Spline Linetype Generation (pedit 1type gen) 364

Changing the Last pedit (pedit undo) 365

Editing Polyline Vertices (pedit edit vertices) 365

TUTORIAL 12.11: Modifying a Polyline's Vertices 367

Summary 368

Review 368

Exercise Twelve 368

UNIT 13 Dimensioning a Drawing 371

Overview 371

Objectives 371

Introduction 371

Outline 372

Dimensioning Basics and Dimensioning with Precision 372

Parts of Dimension 373

Standards Organization 374

Associative and Non-Associative Dimensions 374

Creating Dimension Styles 375

TUTORIAL 13.1: Creating a Dimension Style and Changing the Dimension Geometry 379

TUTORIAL 13.2: Changing the Dimension Line Format 383

TUTORIAL 13.3: Changing the Dimension Text Format 385

Linear and Radial Dimensioning 386

Linear Dimensions 386

Aligned Dimensions 387

TUTORIAL 13.4: Creating Linear Dimensions 388

Continued Dimension Strings 389

TUTORIAL 13.5: Creating Aligned Dimensions 390

TUTORIAL 13.6: Adding Continued and Baseline Dimensions 391

Radial Dimensions 393

TUTORIAL 13.7: Adding Radius and Diameter Dimensions 394

Angular Dimensions 395

Angular Dimensions 395

Editing Dimensions 396

Relocating and Rotating Dimension Text 396

TUTORIAL 13.8: Adding Angular Dimensions 397

Modifying Dimensions and Dimension Text 398

Modifying the Dimension Object Using Object Grips 398

TUTORIAL 13.9: Modifying Dimensions 399

Additional Dimensioning Features 400

Oblique Dimensions 401

Leaders 401

TUTORIAL 13.10: Adding Leaders 402

Summary 403

Review 403

Exercise Thirteen 403

UNIT 14 MODIFYING OBJECT CHARACTERISTICS AND EXTRACTING INFORMATION FROM YOUR DRAWING 407

OVERVIEW 407
OBJECTIVES 407
INTRODUCTION 407
OUTLINE 408
MODIFYING OBJECT PROPERTIES 408
Selecting Multiple Objects for Modification 408
Changing Color and Linetype 409
Moving the Object to a Different Layer 409
Adjusting the Linetype Scale 409
TUTORIAL 14.1: USING THE CHANGE PROPERTIES DIALOG BOX 410
Changing Object Characteristics (ddmodify) 410
Setting Default Object Properties with a Dialog Box 416
TUTORIAL 14.2: USING THE MODIFY DIALOG BOX 417
Editing Text 418
Renaming Object Traits 419
Removing Unwanted Objects 420
TUTORIAL 14.3: MODIFYING OBJECT CHARACTERISTICS 420
EXTRACTING INFORMATION FROM YOUR DRAWING 422
Listing the Status of AutoCAD (status) 422
TUTORIAL 14.4: LISTING THE STATUS OF A FILE 423
Listing Object Information 424
TUTORIAL 14.5: LISTING THE OBJECT OF A FILE 425
TUTORIAL 14.6: USING THE DIST COMMAND 426
TUTORIAL 14.7: USING THE ID COMMAND 428
Calculating Area 428
Finding Area 428
TUTORIAL 14.8: USING THE AREA COMMAND 429
Adding and Subtracting Features 430
TUTORIAL 14.9: USING THE AREA COMMAND 430
Keeping Track of Time 431
TUTORIAL 14.10: USING THE TIME COMMAND 432
SUMMARY 433
REVIEW 433
EXERCISE FOURTEEN 434

UNIT 15 USING SYMBOLS AND ATTRIBUTES 437

OVERVIEW 437
OBJECTIVES 437
INTRODUCTION 437
OUTLINE 438
USING GROUPS 438
Using Blocks to Represent Symbols 439
TUTORIAL 15.1: CREATING A BATHTUB SYMBOL; 441
Listing Blocks in the Current Drawing 442
TUTORIAL 15.2: USING BLOCKS WITH THE ? OPTION 443
Creating Blocks on Layer O 443
Using Layers to Create Blocks 443
Using Byblock with Blocks 444
TUTORIAL 15.3: USING WBLOCK TO CREATE A DOOR SYMBOL 445
TUTORIAL 15.4: INSERTING SYMBOLS INTO A DRAWING 448
ADDING INFORMATION TO BLOCKS WITH ATTRIBUTES 452
Defining an Attribute 453
Attribute Tag, Prompt, and Value 453
Attribute Mode Settings 454
Attribute Insertion Point Settings 454
Attribute Text Options 455

TUTORIAL 15.5: DEFINING AND INSERTING AN ATTRIBUTE 456
Using Ddate to Edit Attributes in a Block 458
Editing Attributes with Attedit 458
Editing Attributes one at a time with Attedit 459
Editing Attributes Globally with Attedit 460
TUTORIAL 15.6: CHANGING THE ATTRIBUTES DISPLAY SETTING 461
TUTORIAL 15.7: REFINING ATTRIBUTES WITH ATTREDEF 464
Creating a Template File 465
Extracting Information 466
TUTORIAL 15.8: EXTRACTING ATTRIBUTE DATA 467
SUMMARY 468
REVIEW 469
EXERCISE FIFTEEN 469

Unit 16 CREATING ISOMETRIC DRAWINGS 473
OVERVIEW 473
OBJECTIVES 473
INTRODUCTION 473
OUTLINE 473
UNDERSTANDING ISOMETRIC AND PICTORIAL DRAWINGS 474
SETTING UP AN ISOMETRIC DRAWING 476
Setting Isometric Snap and Grip 476
Setting and Using the Isometric Plane 477
TUTORIAL 16.1: SETTING UP TO CREATE AN ISOMETRIC DRAWING 478
CREATING AN ISOMETRIC DRAWING 478
Drawing Lines on the Isometric Grid 479
Drawing Isometric Ellipses and Arcs 479
TUTORIAL 16.2: CREATING AN ISOMETRIC DRAWING 481
SUMMARY 487
REVIEW 487
EXERCISE SIXTEEN 487
INDEX 499

UNIT 1

INTRODUCTION TO AUTOCAD AND WORKING WITH THE WINDOWS ENVIRONMENT

OVERVIEW

In this first unit you will be introduced to AutoCAD, the premier Computer-Aided Design (CAD) software for personal computers. The user interface will be introduced as well as the procedure for starting, exiting, and saving files in AutoCAD. Before that can be done, it is important that you are able to operate in the Windows environment.

As you begin to create drawings in AutoCAD, there will be many times when answers or solutions will not be immediately apparent; therefore, the Windows and AutoCAD Help systems will also be presented so that you can research answers interactively.

OBJECTIVES

- Begin and Shut Down Windows
- Understand the basic functions of the Windows graphical user interface
- Load and Exit AutoCAD
- Issue AutoCAD commands
- Enter information in AutoCAD
- Develop basic file-management skills
- Use the Windows and AutoCAD Help system

INTRODUCTION

For years, AutoCAD has been the CAD software of choice for personal computers (PCs). It all began in 1982 when 16 programmers began to produce a PC-based competitor for the proprietary CAD system. Developed for the Zilog Z-80-based CP/M microcomputer, the software later was rewritten for the more popular MS/DOS operating system. In the past years it has been translated to the following operating systems: Windows, Windows NT, UNIX, MAC/OS, and AIX. Some versions have come and gone, but the operating system of choice for the current version of AutoCAD is Windows and Windows NT. This is mainly due to the fact that these two operating systems are presently the most popular among personal computer users. At the time of this writing, Windows 95 and Windows NT 4.0 are the prevalent versions of the operating systems. Each has an identical desktop metaphor that leads to very similar file-management operations. As a matter of fact, once AutoCAD is running in full-screen mode, the user would be hard-pressed to determine which version of Windows AutoCAD is running under. You should be able to accomplish the tasks and tutorials presented in this unit in either version.

There have been many versions of AutoCAD and the Windows operating systems. Each adds new features and functions that allow the user to become more productive and efficient. Now more than ever, AutoCAD and Windows are more intertwined. The user interface for both is very similar. Consisting of windows, scroll bars, pull-down menus, and other graphical user interfaces (GUIs), the two interact well with one another. A working knowledge of one will lead to a reduced learning curve for the other. This unit will present a brief introduction to these two common interfaces. You will see the similarities immediately.

This unit will assume that Windows and AutoCAD have already been installed and are operating properly. If this is not the case, please consult the installation manuals for Windows and AutoCAD for specific information on how to install the software. This unit is meant to be only a primer for Windows. It will not and should not cover all aspects of the Windows operating system. There are many good reference books that accomplish this, and you should have one in your library to answer any questions that are beyond the scope of this book.

OUTLINE

The Basics of Windows
Starting AutoCAD and Understanding the Display
Interacting with AutoCAD
Tutorial 1.1: Using the Help System
Working with Folders
Tutorial 1.2: Formatting a Disk and Creating a New Folder
AutoCAD File Operations
Tutorial 1.3: Creating a New Drawing File
Saving and Exiting a Drawing
Tutorial 1.4: Opening an Existing Drawing File
Summary
Review
Exercises

THE BASICS OF WINDOWS

Since the release of Windows, working on a computer has never been easier. In the early days of computing it was necessary to memorize cryptic commands and codes to accomplish even the easiest tasks. More advanced commands were left to software professionals or "propeller heads." Windows remedies this situation by allowing you to perform almost all commands with the click of a mouse button. Even young children can now perform simple Windows tasks. This section will introduce you to the basic elements of the Windows operating system after which you will begin AutoCAD.

STARTING WINDOWS

The first step to learning Windows is starting it on the computer. This is an easy process that differs little from computer to computer. The hardest step is finding the Power button on the computer and monitor. Once found, simply turn them on. In most cases both of these devices are connected to a power strip that has one centralized switch that controls all powered peripherals (devices attached to the computer), as well as the computer itself. When the power is applied to the computer, Windows will automatically load, and a screen similar to Figure 1.1 will be displayed on your computer. You are now presented with the Windows desktop. From here, all Windows operations can be performed.

WORKING WITH THE TASKBAR

The taskbar (Figure 1.2) is used to start and manage applications such as AutoCAD. It serves two functions—to begin applications and to display the applications currently running. The taskbar is normally located at the bottom of the desktop, although it can be at the top, right, or left. It can also be hidden from view until the edge of the desktop containing the taskbar is reached. If you cannot locate the desktop on your system, follow these steps to locate the taskbar with your mouse:

1. Look for a thin, gray line on one of the edges of the desktop.
2. If an edge cannot be seen, move the mouse until the pointer, represented as an arrow, is at the bottom of the screen. If a taskbar does not appear, try the top, left, and then right edges of the screen until the taskbar appears.
3. Moving the pointer away from the edge will once again hide the taskbar.

Use the following steps to locate the taskbar using the keyboard:

1. Press Ctrl Esc. The taskbar will be displayed with the Start button already selected.
2. To hide the taskbar, move the pointer to a blank portion of the desktop and single-click the left mouse button.

Figure 1.1
The Windows desktop.

The main feature of the taskbar is the Start. Single-clicking on this button will display another menu of options. The main options are described in Table 1.1. The two most important options are Programs and Shut Down. As discussed in Table 1.1, the Programs option will allow you to access all programs currently available. It is from here that you will start AutoCAD. You will use the Shut Down option to close Windows and turn off the computer.

Figure 1.2
The Windows taskbar.

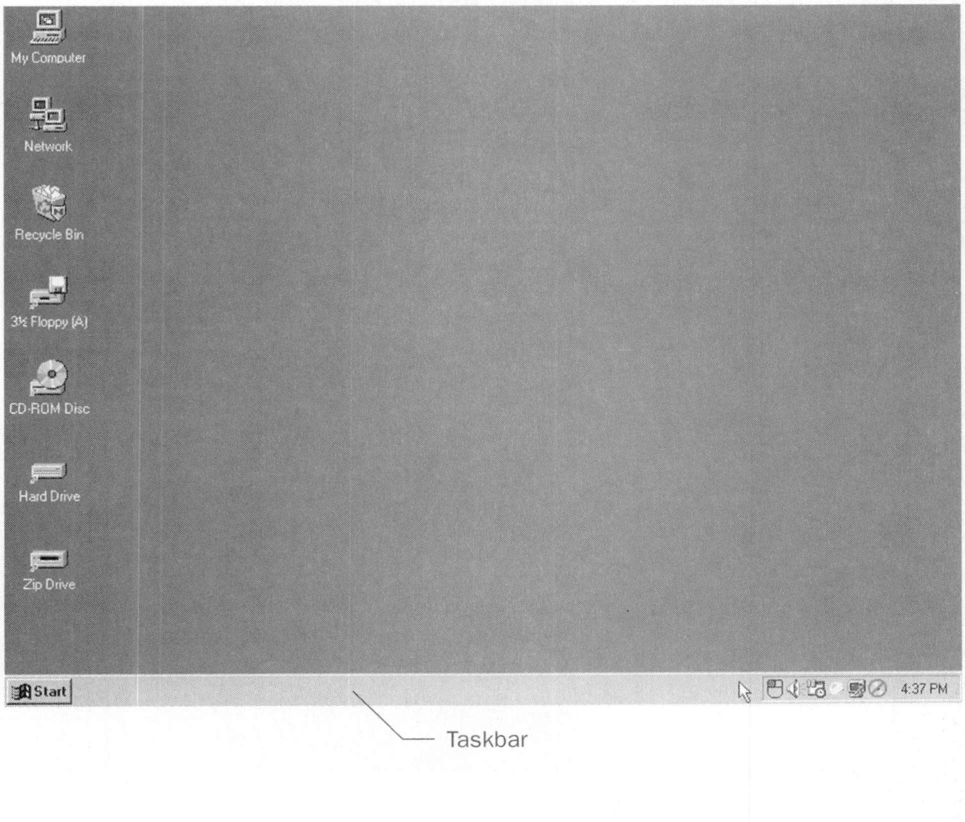

TABLE 1.1 START BUTTON OPTIONS

Option	Description
Programs	Loads software configured and available for Windows
Documents	Loads a previously created document and originating application
Settings	Changes settings concerning the Control panel, Printers, and Taskbar
Find	Finds Files or Folders and Computers on a network
Help	Loads Windows Help
Run...	Used to load applications by typing its name
Shut Down...	Used to shut down the computer or restart Windows

To shut down Windows follow these steps:

1. Move the pointer to the taskbar.
2. Select the Start button (Ctrl Esc).
3. Select Shut Down. The Shut Down Windows dialog box will appear as shown in Figure 1.3.
4. Select Shut down the computer. The radio button, the circle with the black dot, will highlight the option with a black circle.
5. Select Yes. Windows will now begin the shut down procedure.
6. When Windows informs you it is safe to turn off your computer, you can then do so.

FOR THE PROFESSIONAL

It is very important that Windows be closed properly. If the correct procedure is not followed, files can be left open on the computer and become corrupted. It will be very frustrating to lose many hours' worth of work because this simple one-minute procedure was not followed.

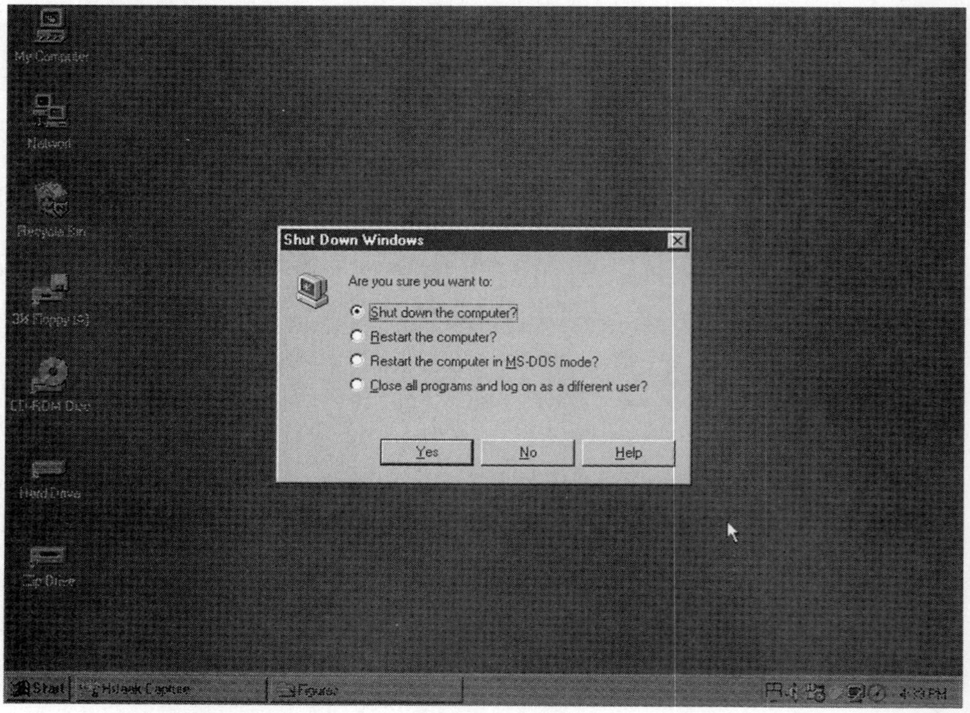

Figure 1.3
The Shut Down Windows dialog box.

Opening and Closing Windows

Windows got its name from the fact that it uses a series of windows to contain the application and application data. AutoCAD itself is a windowed application. Therefore, it is important to know how to open and close windows. In order to do so you must become familiar with icons and the title bar of a window. The title bar is found at the top of each window as shown in Figure 1.4.

Icons can be found on the Windows desktop or in the Programs option on the Start button. Icons are small pictures that represent an application, file, or folder. To open up a specific application, file, or folder window simply double-click on the appropriate icon if it is located on the desktop. Similarly, you can use the Start button to open applications, files, or folders. Once these windows are open you will need to close or minimize them later.

To close an application, click on the application Close button or double-click on the application icon identifier on the title bar. Both of these objects are shown in Figure 1.5. You also can close an application's window. Application windows contain the actual data for an application and are created when an application is started. Closing these windows does not close the application—only the file where the application data is stored. The procedure is the same as for closing applications. The only difference is that the Close button and application identifier icon are found on the top of the application window as shown in Figure 1.5.

Minimizing and Maximizing Windows

Under certain circumstances, it is advantageous to move a window out of the way, or minimize it. This allows you once again to see the desktop and work with other windows. To minimize a window, select the Minimize button as shown in Figure 1.4. When an application or application window is minimized it is placed on the taskbar as a button. To

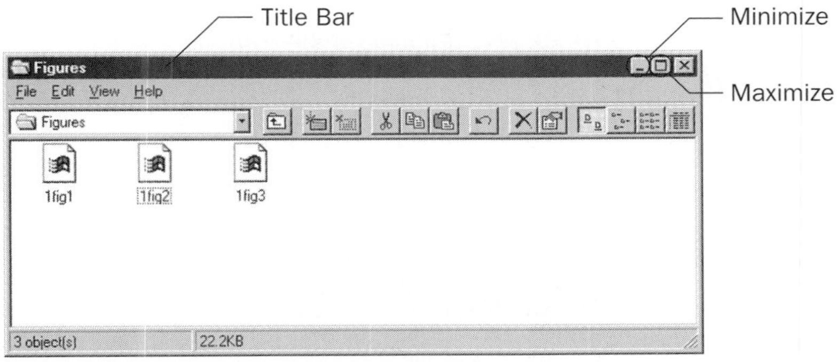

Figure 1.4
The title bar is located at the top of a window.

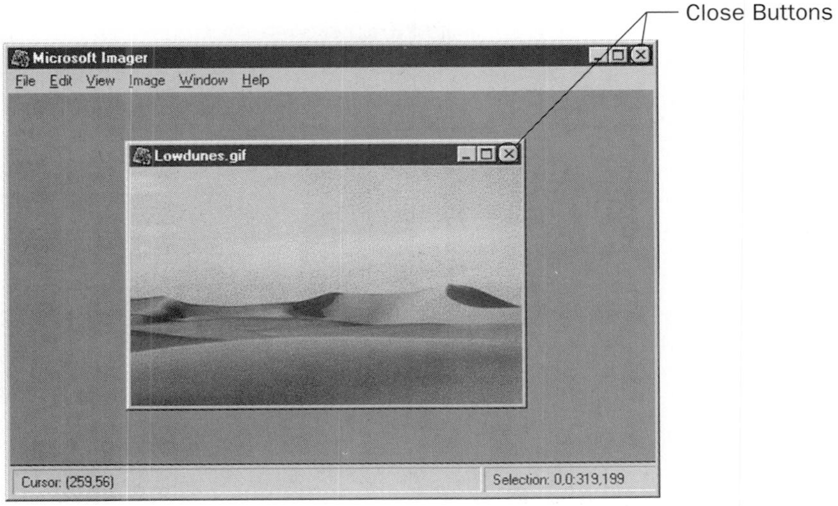

Figure 1.5
Close application windows using these buttons and icons.

restore the window to its previous position and size, select the application button on the taskbar. This feature allows you to run more than one application at a time and to switch easily between them.

Skill Builder

You can also use the Ctrl Tab keystroke combination to switch between applications.

Maximizing a window will resize the window to take full advantage of the desktop space. A maximized window will have no border and none of the desktop will be visible. To maximize a window, select the Maximize button as shown in Figure 1.4. To restore the window to its previous position and size, select the Restore button as shown in Figure 1.6.

Working with Dialog Boxes

Dialog boxes allow the application to request information from the user. A common AutoCAD dialog box is found in Figure 1.7. Dialog boxes will appear when certain commands require user interaction. There are seven components of a dialog box used for entering information. They include: edit boxes, list boxes, scroll bars, buttons, radio buttons, check boxes, and image tiles. Each component will be described in detail in this unit. These components are grouped in the dialog box by tiles. A tile is identified by a thin line dividing various sections of a dialog box. When used together, these components allow data to be entered easily into the software. The only component that requires the use of the keyboard is the edit box.

Edit Boxes Edit boxes allow the user to input information via the keyboard. They are typically used to enter names of files, layers, or text styles. These are necessary when a list of options would be too long or when characters from the keyboard have to be entered. An edit box can be found in Figure 1.8.

Figure 1.6
Use the Restore button to return the window to its previous size and position.

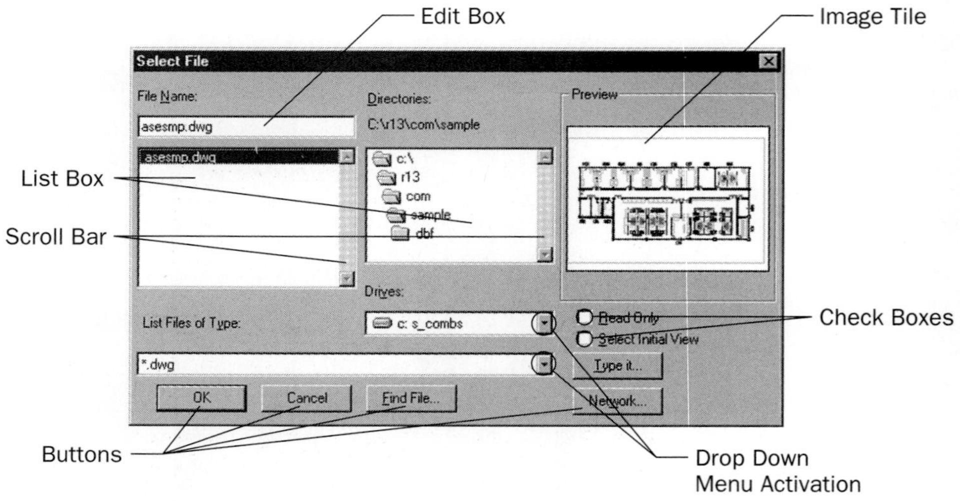

Figure 1.7
The components of the AutoCAD Select File dialog box.

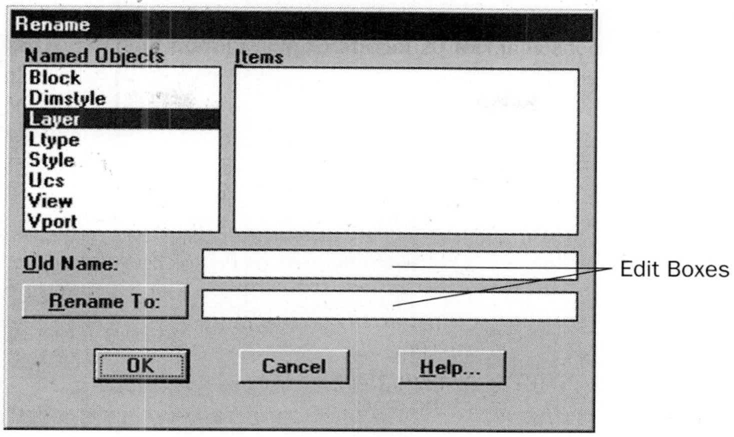

Figure 1.8
An AutoCAD edit box.

List Boxes List boxes contain a group of items that can be selected. When the list is longer than the available list area, a scroll bar is displayed. A list box is shown in Figure 1.9.

Scroll Bars A scroll bar allows you to scroll through a series of options in a list box. It consists of a slider, an up arrow, and a down arrow. A scroll bar is shown in Figure 1.9. Scroll bars are usually used in conjunction with list boxes.

Buttons Buttons are very similar to their real-world counterparts (that is, the buttons on a machine, not the ones on clothing). You simply press them to make a selection. An OK button and Cancel button are shown in Figure 1.10.

Radio Buttons Radio buttons allow dialog boxes to group a small list of similar options within a tile. To choose an option, simply click on the word or blank button. There can be only one radio button selected at a time. A tile that contains sample radio buttons can be found in Figure 1.10.

Check Boxes Check boxes are similar to radio buttons; they are selected the same way. There are two differences: You can select more than one option within the tile, and the verification of selection is not a black circle but rather an *x*. A tile that contains sample check boxes can be found in Figure 1.11.

Image Tiles A picture is worth a thousand words. There are times when a simple image representing a feature or drawing would assist you in selecting an option. That is the concept of the image tile. An image is placed within a dialog box tile. Generally used for display purposes only, some image tiles even allow you to select them on different areas to change an option or feature. An image tile can be found in Figure 1.12.

Figure 1.9
An AutoCAD list box and scroll bar.

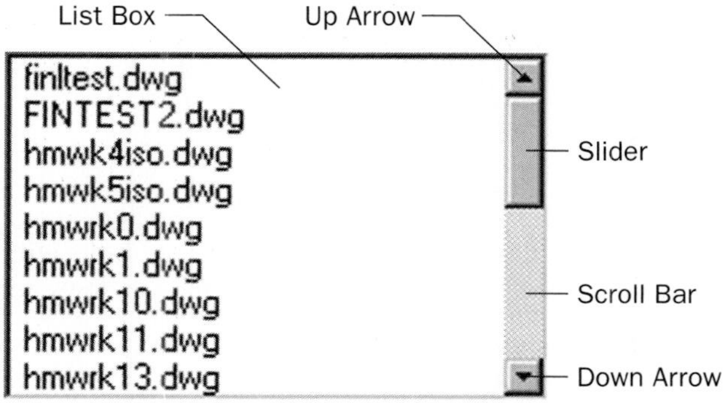

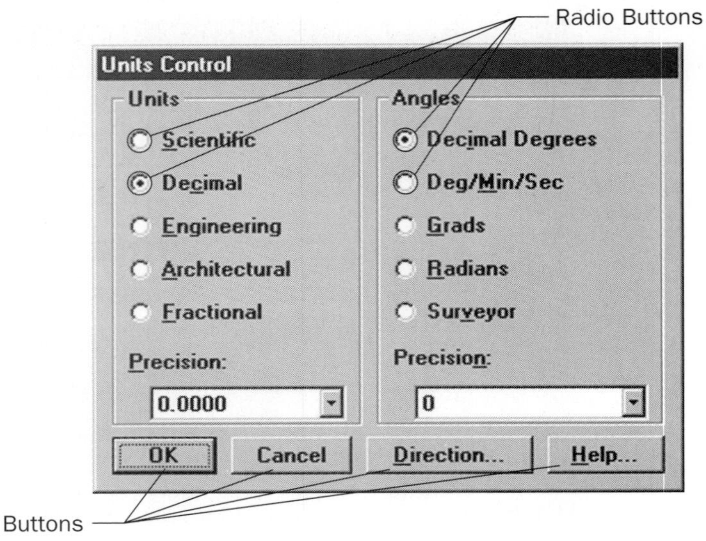

Figure 1.10
An example of the two types of buttons available in the AutoCAD Units Control dialog box.

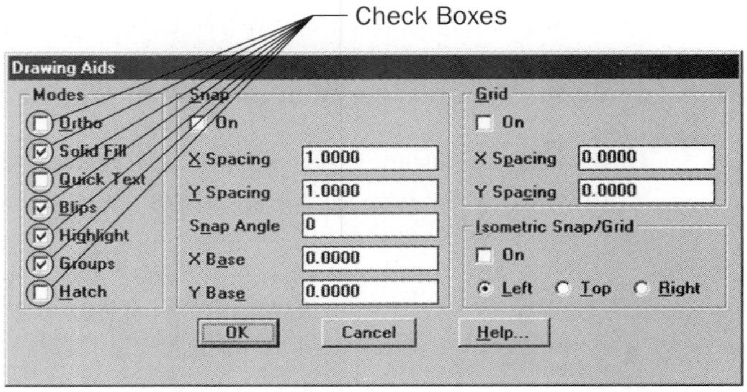

Figure 1.11
An example of a series of check boxes available in the AutoCAD Drawing Aids dialog box.

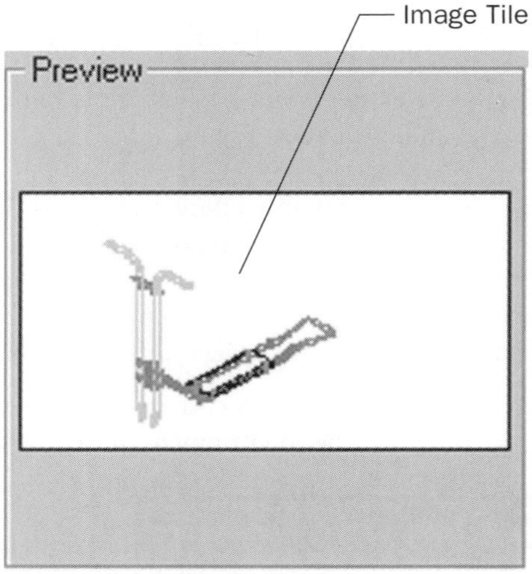

Figure 1.12
An example of an image tile found in the AutoCAD Select File dialog box.

Getting Help in Windows

Windows includes a very comprehensive Help utility that is easy to access. To access help, use the following procedure at the windows desktop:

1. Click the Start button and then select Help. The Help Topics: Windows Help dialog box appears.

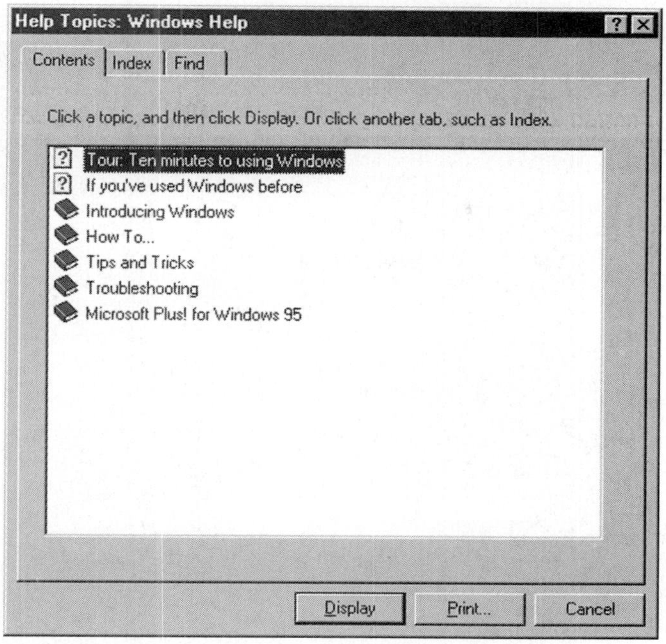

Figure 1.13
Use the Windows Help utility to find information regarding Windows topics.

2. Click on the Contents tab to receive a list of available reference books. Select the book that contains the information you need.
3. If you are unsure of which book to search, click the Index tab and review the list of available topics using the scroll bar, or type in a topic in the edit box.
4. To do an extensive search for a topic, click the Find tab and type in a topic. Windows Help will display the location of all instances for that topic.

Figure 1.13 shows the Windows Help utility.

STARTING AUTOCAD AND UNDERSTANDING THE DISPLAY

Once you have an understanding of basic Windows operations, you can start AutoCAD and begin drawing. This section will show you how to start AutoCAD and then discuss the various parts of the AutoCAD display. As you explore the display, pay close attention to the components' locations. Throughout this book you will be required to know their locations and how to interact with each part of the display.

STARTING AUTOCAD

Starting AutoCAD is simply a matter of locating it on the taskbar under the Programs options. It may be even easier. Occasionally a shortcut is placed on the desktop that allows the student to find the icon immediately. Figure 1.14 shows a Windows desktop that contains a shortcut icon as well as the location of AutoCAD on the taskbar. To load AutoCAD, use the following procedures:

1. Locate the AutoCAD shortcut icon on the desktop.
2. Double-click on the AutoCAD icon. AutoCAD will begin loading.

Or use the following procedure to start AutoCAD using the taskbar:

1. Select the Start button on the taskbar.
2. Select Programs.
3. Select the AutoCAD program group.
4. Select the AutoCAD program icon. AutoCAD will begin loading.

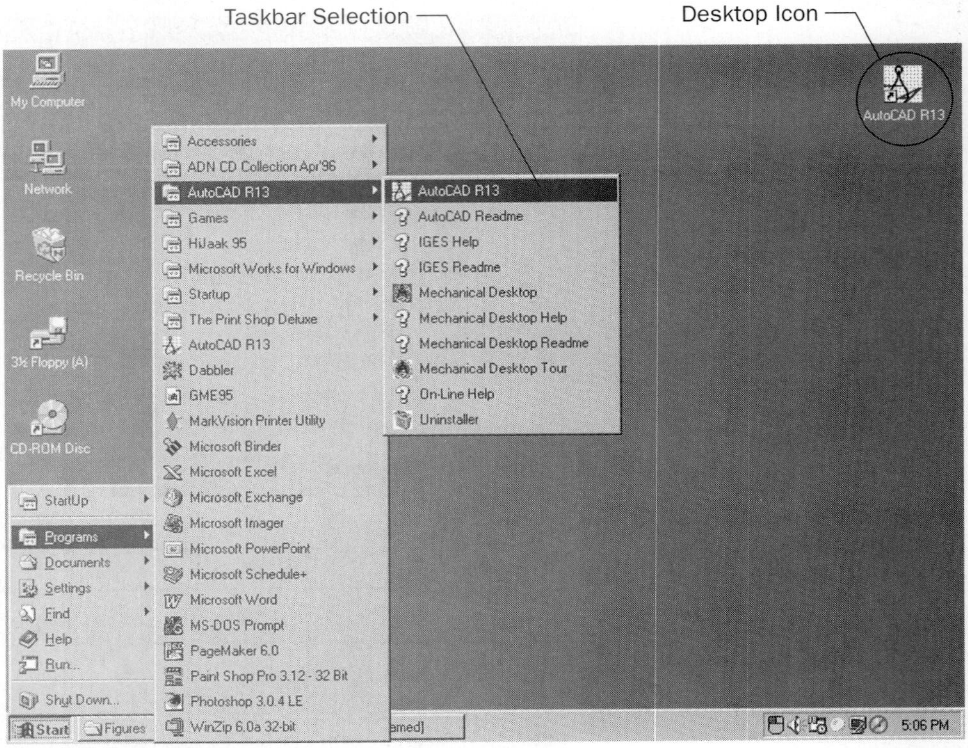

Figure 1.14
This computer allows the student to load AutoCAD from the desktop or the taskbar.

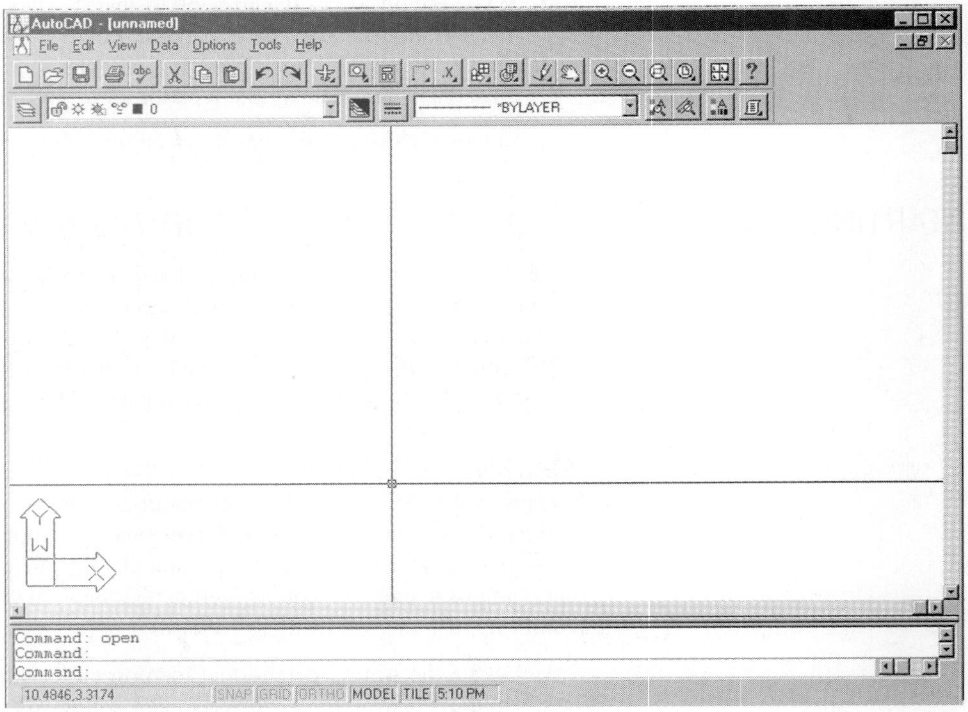

Figure 1.15
The AutoCAD display.

Once AutoCAD is loaded, the screen will be similar to Figure 1.15. Now it's time to become familiar with the parts of the AutoCAD display and their functions.

THE AUTOCAD DISPLAY

The AutoCAD display is one of the most configurable and versatile interfaces available for PC applications. As you will find in this section, AutoCAD can be configured for each individual user. This allows AutoCAD to adapt to the techniques you use when creating drawings in AutoCAD. Because of this ability, you may find that your screen will differ from those in this book. The configuration shown in this book is of the AutoCAD default settings. If certain components of the display are missing, or there are other objects not shown in this book's figures, you will soon learn how to modify your screen to match.

The AutoCAD display's primary purpose is to display a drawing. Its secondary purpose is to provide you with an interface with which to create that drawing. A tertiary purpose is to display information and statistics about the drawing, which also assists you in creating a drawing. Let's take a look at each of the major components of the AutoCAD display and its function. Figure 1.16 shows the AutoCAD display and labels the components. Use this figure as a reference to locate the components as they are introduced.

Once you can identify the parts of the AutoCAD display you will learn how to interact with AutoCAD using these components.

Title Bar The AutoCAD title bar is the same as the title bar discussed previously in this unit. Starting from left to right, it includes the application icon, the title AutoCAD, the name of the current file, the Minimize button, the Maximize/Restore button, and the Close window button. Beneath the title bar are the pull-down menus.

Pull-Down Menus The first customizable item displayed on the AutoCAD display are the pull-down menus. The menus are used to enter commands using either the mouse or the keyboard. This area is typically reserved for commands that require further options or

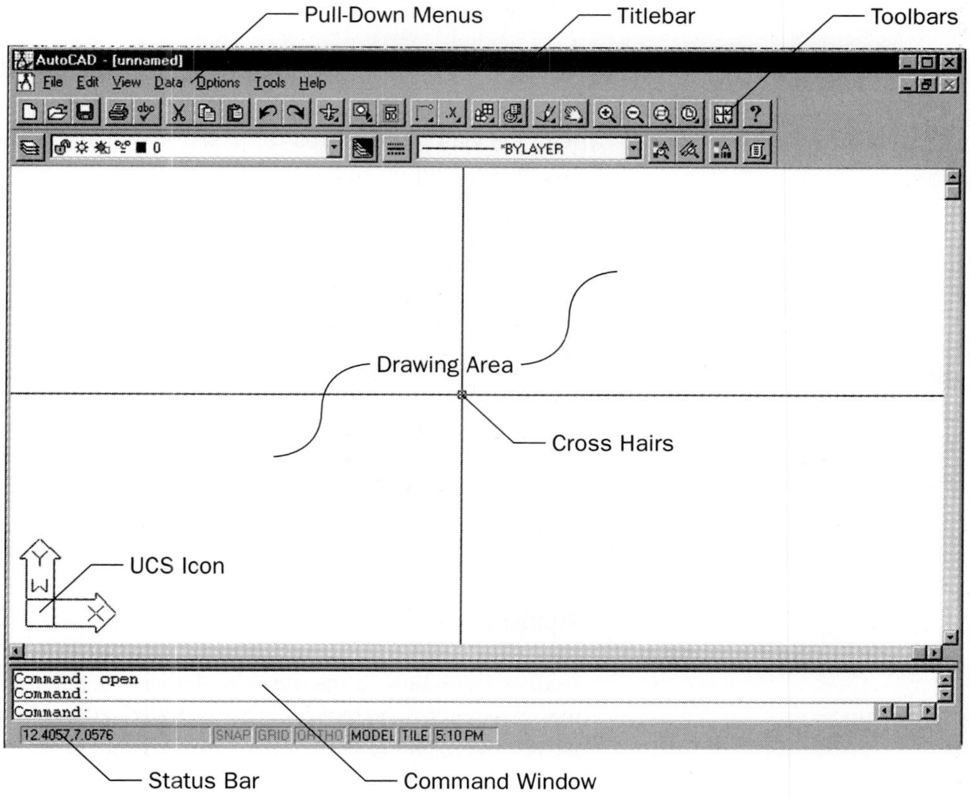

Figure 1.16
Labeled components of the AutoCAD display.

dialog boxes in their operation. Using the pull-down menu is one way to enter commands. Another is to use the toolbars.

Toolbars Toolbars contain icons or small pictures that represent a command. There are a total of 17 different toolbars. All toolbars are geared toward creating a drawing, whereas the pull-down menus are used for drawing setup and AutoCAD preferences. The purpose of the toolbar is to allow the user to issue commands in AutoCAD without using the keyboard, and while this method is very efficient, there are still many experienced users of AutoCAD who find old habits hard to break. New users however should become accustomed to these toolbars and use them as often as possible. Toolbars can be either floating, contain their own window elements, or docked, part of the AutoCAD borders.

As mentioned earlier, many experienced AutoCAD users use the keyboard to issue commands. They do this with the `Command:` prompt in the command window.

Command Window At the bottom of the AutoCAD display is the command window. This window contains two components: the command prompt and the command history. This area is used to enter commands from the keyboard. The command history provides a quick list of the previous commands issued, including those entered from the pull-down menus or the toolbars. The location of the command window can be changed as well as the length of the command history. There is yet another way to issue commands—the status bar.

Status Bar The status bar displays the status of various functions such as Snap, Grid, and Ortho. It will allow you to toggle that status. It also displays the current coordinates of the crosshairs.

Screen Menu The screen menu is the forgotten child of the AutoCAD display. It is so forgotten that AutoCAD does not display it in its default configuration. Used in previous versions of AutoCAD as an alternative to the keyboard, it is less efficient than using the toolbars and pull-downs and is provided as a courtesy to past AutoCAD users. New users will want to keep this component turned off. Turning it off will give you more space in the drawing area.

Drawing Area/View Window The drawing area/view window is used to display the drawing. Think of it as a sheet of paper. It is also used to change the view of a drawing. With the view window you can zoom in on a portion of the drawing to enhance details or pan the drawing from left to right.

UCS Icon The UCS icon is used as a visual reference to indicate the orientation of the XYZ plane. When using AutoCAD as a drafting tool, you need to be concerned only with the X and Y values because you will not be creating 3-D models. Once you become familiar with the direction of the X and Y axes, you no longer need the UCS icon displayed. Many experienced users simply turn off this icon using the **ucsicon** command.

Crosshairs To enter coordinates using the mouse, use the crosshairs. The crosshairs consist of a vertical and horizontal line. They are frequently used to visually line up items while creating them, and appear as crosshairs only when you need the X and Y coordinate reference within the drawing area. Occasionally it will change to a pickbox within the drawing area when using certain command features.

Pickbox When it is necessary to select an object to delete or modify, the crosshairs will change to a pickbox. The pickbox is represented by a small box. The size of this box can change depending on the user's preference. When used, the pickbox will appear on top of the crosshairs' intersection. The pickbox will appear only in the drawing area. When moved out of the drawing area it will change to a cursor.

Cursor The cursor is used to make selections from the pull-down nenus, toolbars, or screen menu. Represented by an arrow, it becomes the cursor when either the crosshairs or the pickbox is moved out of the drawing area.

INTERACTING WITH AUTOCAD

There are many different ways of interacting with AutoCAD. You can type commands at the command prompt, select commands from the toolbars and screen menus, and choose various drawing options from the pull-down menus. This allows for flexibility among users. Touch typists may want to take advantage of the keyboard to enter commands, while new users of computers may want to use just the toolbars and mouse. Either way, both types of users can be quite proficient.

As you read through the next few sections, you will find the `Command:` prompt and toolbar methods presented. A strong emphasis is placed on the use of toolbars. AutoCAD Release 13 for Windows includes a very comprehensive set of toolbars that will allow anyone to quickly enter commands using the mouse. Even though you can enter the commands using the mouse, there are many commands that need numeric values or coordinates. Because it's not very easy to enter these values with a mouse, you have to enter this type of information from the keyboard.

ISSUING COMMANDS

The `Command:` prompt (Figure 1.17), usually at the bottom of the AutoCAD screen, is where you enter commands via the keyboard. AutoCAD is ready to accept commands when the `Command:` prompt is empty, as shown here.

Figure 1.17
The command prompt is used to display commands as they are entered.

```
Command:
```

Entering a command from the toolbars, pull-down menus, or the keyboard, will cause that command to be placed in the `Command:` prompt, as in this example:

```
Command:line
```

Any options required by the command will be placed in the `Command:` prompt as well, as demonstrated below:

```
Command:line
From Point:
```

The line command at this time is requesting a start point or "From Point." To specify that point, you need to enter coordinates via the keyboard or use the mouse to specify the coordinates.

TYPING COMMANDS

Typing commands is the oldest method available for interacting with AutoCAD. The very first version of AutoCAD required all commands to be entered from the keyboard. And despite the advent of GUIs, many users still enter commands this way. Before you enter commands with the keyboard, you first need to become familiar with it. The first type of keys you need to be introduced to are the function keys. Generally at the top of the keyboard they look like the following:

TABLE 1.2 Function Keys Assignments

Key	Function
F1	Invokes Help
F2	Displays the AutoCAD text windows
F4	Toggles tablet mode
F5	Cycles between isoplane modes
F6	Toggles the coordinate display
F7	Toggles the grid
F8	Toggles ortho mode
F9	Toggles snap mode
F10	Activates the menu bar

TABLE 1.3 Accelerator Keys Assignments

Keys	Function
Ctrl A	Toggles group mode
Ctrl B	Toggles snap mode
Ctrl C	Copies the selection set in the drawing and places it on the Windows clipboard
Ctrl E	Toggles the isoplane mode
Ctrl L	Toggles ortho mode
Ctrl N	Creates a new drawing
Ctrl O	Opens a file
Ctrl P	Plots the current drawing
Ctrl S	Saves the current drawing
Ctrl V	Pastes the contents of the Windows clipboard in the current drawing
Ctrl X	Cuts the selection set from the drawing and places it on the Windows clipboard
Ctrl Z	Undoes the last command sequentially since the last time the file was saved

Not all function keys are operational in AutoCAD. Table 1.2 lists the operational function keys.

A series of keystrokes that works very similar to the function keys are the accelerator key assignments. Each of these keystrokes begin by holding down Ctrl and then pressing the appropriate key. Table 1.3 describes the accelerator key combinations.

The cursor keys, ← → ↓ ↑, will allow you to move the crosshairs using the keyboard instead of the mouse. They also assist in editing text on-screen and in text edit boxes. Another key that is very handy when editing text is the ←Backspace key. This key will delete characters to the left of the cursor in a text edit box or in the `Command:` prompt. Similar to the ←Backspace key is the Del key. This key will delete characters to the right of the cursor location. Use these keys to correct mistakes. Once a command is entered properly, press ↵Enter or the spacebar to execute the command.

The last key we will discuss is Esc. This keystroke will cancel any command at any stage of its execution. It will also close dialog boxes and cancel any changes made. Finally, it will back out of pull-down menu selections. This key will be used often to correct errors.

For the Professional

Versions of AutoCAD prior to Release 13 did not use Esc to cancel commands but, rather, the Ctrl C combination.

USING TOOLBARS

A new feature of Release 13, and probably the most powerful, is the addition of toolbars. Slowly becoming standard on all Windows software, toolbars are both intuitive and configurable. Consisting of an icon that represents a command, a simple click of the mouse will enter that command.

Two toolbars will automatically appear in a default configuration of AutoCAD. They are the Standard Toolbar and the Object properties toolbar. In addition to these default toolbars, AutoCAD also provides 15 additional toolbars as shown in Figure 1.18.

To access the toolbars follow the following steps:

1. Select Tools/Toolbars from the pull-down menu. Once this menu is accessed a list of toolbars will appear as shown in Figure 1.18.
2. To display the toolbar, simply select the toolbar name. The toolbar will be displayed.

Displayed toolbars can be in one of two states: floating or docked. Floating toolbars can be moved around the screen and contain a normal window title bar with the name of the toolbar displayed as shown in Figure 1.19. Docked toolbars have no border and are "docked" on the top, bottom, right, or left side of the AutoCAD display. To change from a floating toolbar to a docked toolbar, drag the floating toolbar to one of the edges of the AutoCAD screen. Once the toolbar reaches the edge, it will lose its windows properties and become part of the AutoCAD window border. To change a docked toolbar to a floating toolbar, drag the docked toolbar to the drawing area. Once it has been moved, the toolbar will once again receive its windowed properties and will include the title bar. The default Standard and Object properties toolbars are docked. Figure 1.19 shows an example of docked and floating toolbars.

You should not display all of the toolbars at all times because there is not enough space. A good user of toolbars will display just the toolbars necessary to complete the drawing at hand. To create a simple technical drawing, you will probably display only the Draw, Modify and Dimensioning toolbars. These will contain the majority of the commands needed. For special considerations, others will be displayed and disposed of depending on the need.

If the icon on the button does not give you enough information to determine its function, hold the cursor over the button for a second or two. A small yellow box, a tool tip, will pop out under the cursor with the name of the command associated with the button. Once the button is selected a few times, you will become familiar with the button and will no longer need to wait for the yellow box to verify your selection.

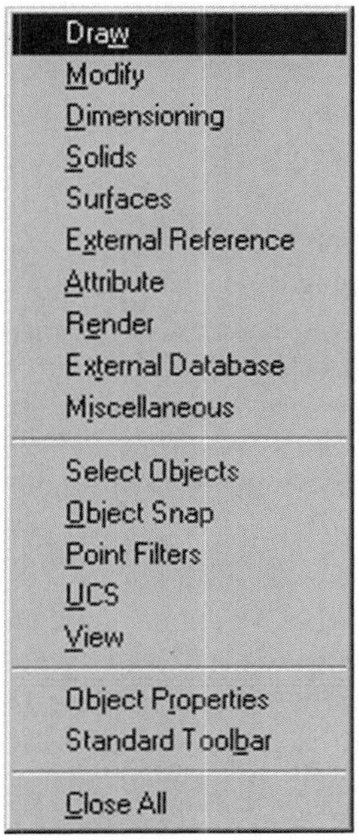

Figure 1.18
Select toolbars to display from this menu.

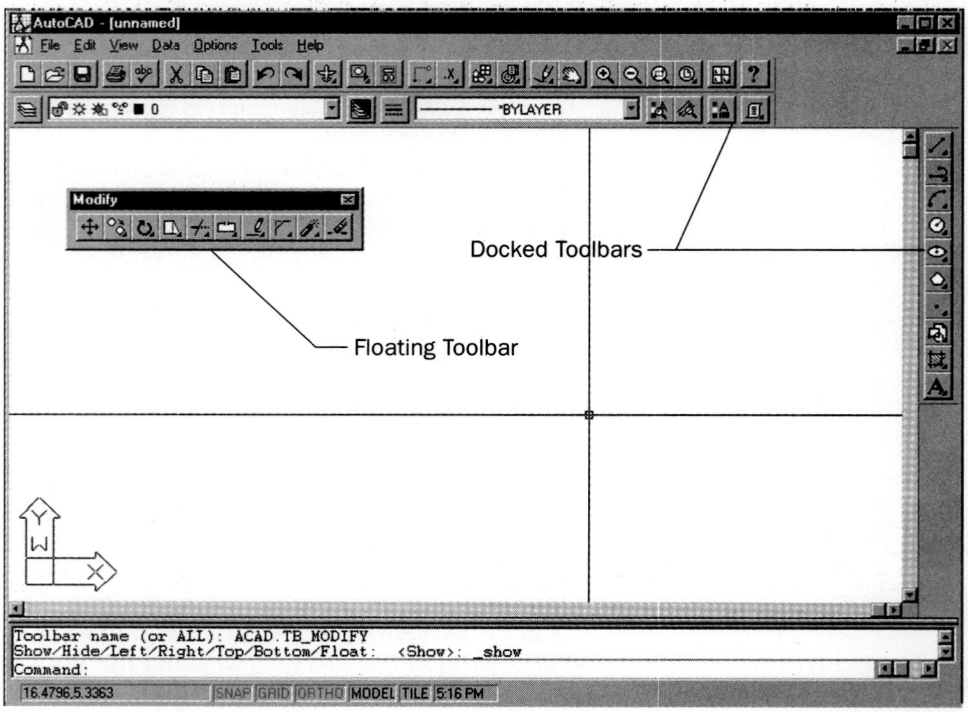

Figure 1.19
Toolbars can be either floating or docked.

Some toolbars contain either simple buttons or flyout buttons. A simple button contains only one command. A flyout button offers a choice of related commands. Follow these steps to use a flyout:

1. Identify the flyout button. Look for a small black arrow at the bottom right of the button.
2. Place the cursor over the button.
3. Click and hold the right mouse button. The flyout will appear displaying additional related commands as shown in Figure 1.20.
4. Move the cursor to the command desired.
5. Select the button. The flyout will close and that button will be displayed on the toolbar as will the command placed in the `Command:` prompt.

Toolbars are so versatile, they can be displayed from other toolbars. Use the Aerial View icon on the Standard toolbar to access additional toolbars or to quickly select a toolbar without using the pull-down menus.

Using Pull-Down Menus

Across the top of the AutoCAD screen are the pull-down menus. Typically, pull-down menus provide access to drawing set-up and file-management commands. To use a pull-down menu, complete the following steps:

1. Move the crosshairs to the top of the screen until it turns into the arrow.
2. Click on the menu heading needed. A list of available related commands drops down.
3. Select a command. Figure 1.21 shows a pull-down menu being activated.

If more options are available for a command, an arrow pointing to the right or a dialog box will appear. If a command is followed by three periods (...), a dialog box will be displayed providing more options for that command.

You may have noticed that the menu items have some letters underlined. These allow you to access the pull-down menus from the keyboard. Use the following procedure to access the pull-down menus from the keyboard:

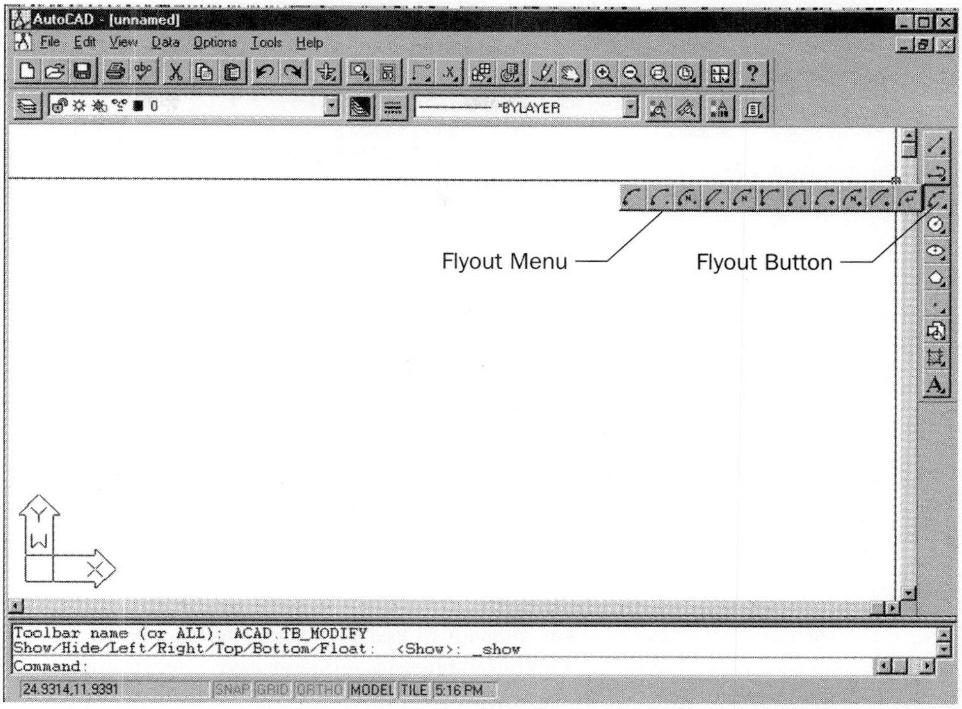

Figure 1.20
A flyout button will provide additional commands.

1. Press and hold Alt.
2. Select the underlined letter that represents the menu to be selected. For example, to invoke the File menu, you would press F.
3. Continue pressing the appropriate underlined keys until the desired command is entered.

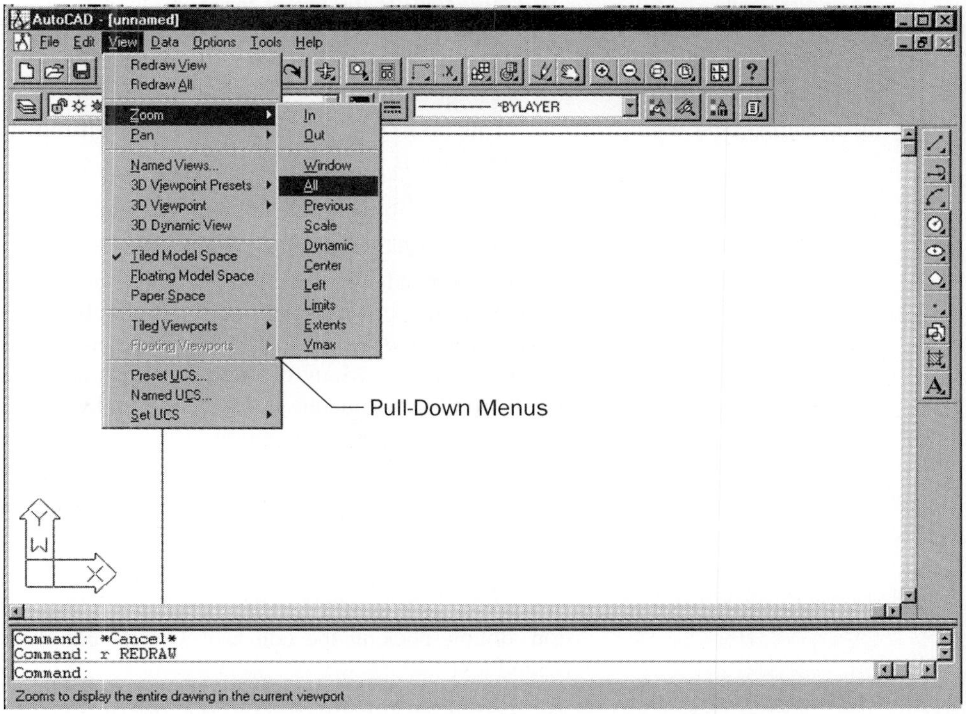

Figure 1.21
Using the pull-down menus to enter AutoCAD commands.

SKILL BUILDER

Touch typists can enter commands quickly using the keyboard. Many good AutoCAD users will use the keyboard exclusively to enter commands. A nice feature of AutoCAD is the many different ways you can interact with AutoCAD.

The keyboard equivalent for every pull-down command is not listed in this book due to space considerations. If you need to know the keystroke you must first go through the command selection with the mouse.

Using the Screen Menus

The screen menus are not part of the default AutoCAD configuration. They have since been replaced by the toolbars as the more effective way to enter commands with the mouse. When using the screen menus, you have to navigate over many screens, and users found it difficult to find their way out. These menus where provided in the past to answer the request of users who were not touch typists. It allowed commands to be entered using the mouse. In order to view the screen menus they must first be turned on from the Options/Preferences dialog box. Because some third-party AutoCAD additions still require their use, we will address their use below.

1. Turn on the screen menus using the Options/Preferences dialog box.
2. Move the cursor over the menu item to be selected or press the [0 Ins] key to activate the menu.
3. Move through the menu by moving the cursor or by pressing the cursor keys.
4. Make a selection by pressing the left mouse button or by pressing [Enter]. If an item selected is all uppercase, a sub-menu will appear. Once a menu contains a highlighted command, that command is ready to be used.
5. If you get lost in the menus and want to start from the beginning, click on the word *AutoCAD* at the top of the menu.
6. Clicking on the asterisks (****) underneath *AutoCAD* will display the object snap screen menu.

This book will not discuss where each individual command is located within the screen menus. If you need that information, consult your AutoCAD user's guide.

Working with Dialog Boxes

When commands or functions require more information than can be comfortably entered in the `Command:` prompt, a dialog box is provided. The dialog box will be displayed over the drawing area. It is composed of a series of tiles that contain various dialog box functions. Many of these functions are accessed by using the mouse. However, like the pull-down menus, look for the underlined letter. Pressing and holding [Alt] and that letter will select that option. The following sections explain the use of the dialog box functions.

Edit Boxes Edit boxes are used to input characters. To enter information in edit boxes, simply click in the edit box and begin typing. To make corrections, use [Backspace] or the cursor keys as you would with any other windows software. To highlight the whole selection, double-click in the edit box. Once highlighted, begin typing to replace the highlighted text.

List Boxes List boxes can be either fixed or pop-ups. They may or may not have a scroll bar. Use the scroll bar, as described below, to move through the list. To select an item in the list box, click on the item. Selecting an item usually causes an action, such as changing to a different drive directory or modifying a filename.

Scroll Bars Scroll bars will scroll through a list of options. To move up the list one item, click the UP ARROW. Likewise, to move down the list one item, click the DOWN ARROW. The slider can be dragged to scroll through the selection. To move up or down one page at a time, click above or below the slider box. Note that scroll bars may also be horizontal.

Buttons and Radio Buttons Buttons and radio buttons are used to make simple selections or change the status of a command. More common to all dialog boxes are the buttons. Two very common buttons are the OK and Cancel buttons found on the majority of the dialog boxes. Simply click on them to select that option.

Occasionally dialog boxes will contain radio buttons to provide the student with a quick list to choose from. You can choose only one selection. If another selection is chosen, the previous selection will be erased. To verify the selection, the button will fill with a black circle similar to the ones created with a #2 pencil on standardized tests.

Check Boxes If a dialog box can have more than one option selected within a list, it will rely on check boxes for student input. Simply select the option with the mouse and an *X* will appear in the check box to show that it is selected.

Image Tiles When an image tile is displayed in a dialog box, click on the picture to make modifications to the setting. Image tiles are usually displayed when the concept can be better described by a picture rather than a word or phrase.

Using the AutoCAD Help System (HELP)

Unlike the DOS version of AutoCAD, AutoCAD for Windows includes an excellent online Help facility. There are many times when you will ask yourself, "How do I create this shape?" You could of course thumb through the user's manual for 15 or 20 minutes looking for the command in question, or you could use the AutoCAD Help system and perform an electronic search. This search will typically be much quicker than searching manually through the user's guide. Another nice feature is the ability of the search engine to cross-reference commands with other commands and then quickly jump to that reference. To access the Help facilty use one of these methods:

- Press F1.
- Type **`HELP`** at the `Command:` prompt.
- Choose Help/Contents... from the pull-down menu.
- Click on the Help button on the Standard toolbar.

Once the help command is entered, the AutoCAD Help window will be displayed as shown in Figure 1.22. This window gives you seven buttons across the top of the screen that are always available. The Contents button will display the home contents page. Use this to return to the contents page. The Search button will allow you to do a detailed search for a command that may not be easily found by using the contents page. The Back button will allow you to return to a previous page. The History button will display another window that lists all Help topics visited in that session. The Forward and Backward buttons move through the Help topics in alphabetical order. Finally, the Glossary button displays an alphabetical list of important concepts. To end the Help system select either Cancel or the Close button described previously.

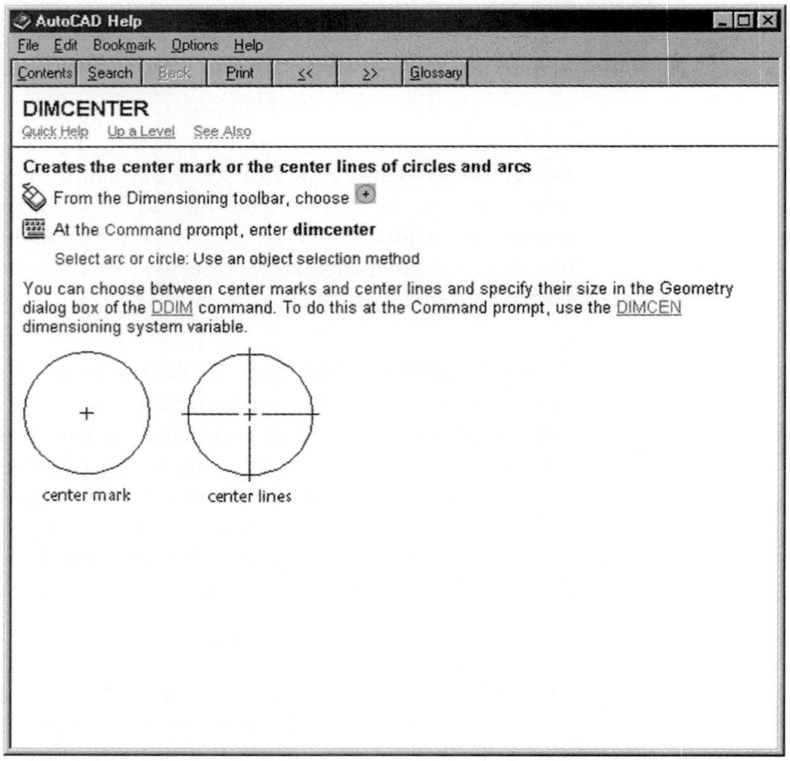

Figure 1.22
Use the AutoCAD Help window to search for commands.

Tutorial 1.1: Using the Help System

In this tutorial you will use the AutoCAD Help system to locate information on the circle command.

1. Load AutoCAD using one of the methods described in Section 2: Starting AutoCAD and Understanding the Display. The AutoCAD display will appear.
2.  Select the Help icon in the Standard Toolbar. The AutoCAD Help window will appear as shown in Figure 1.23.
3. Click on the Search button. The Help Topics: AutoCAD Help dialog box appears.
4. Click on the Find tab. The Find menu card is displayed as shown in Figure 1.24.
5. Type `circle` in the Type the words you want to find text edit box. The dialog box will present areas of help that contain this command.
6. Select the Circle command selection in the Click a topic list in tile number 3.
7. Select the Display button at the bottom of the dialog box. The information concerning the Circle command will be displayed.
8. Select File/Exit to close the Help window and return to AutoCAD.

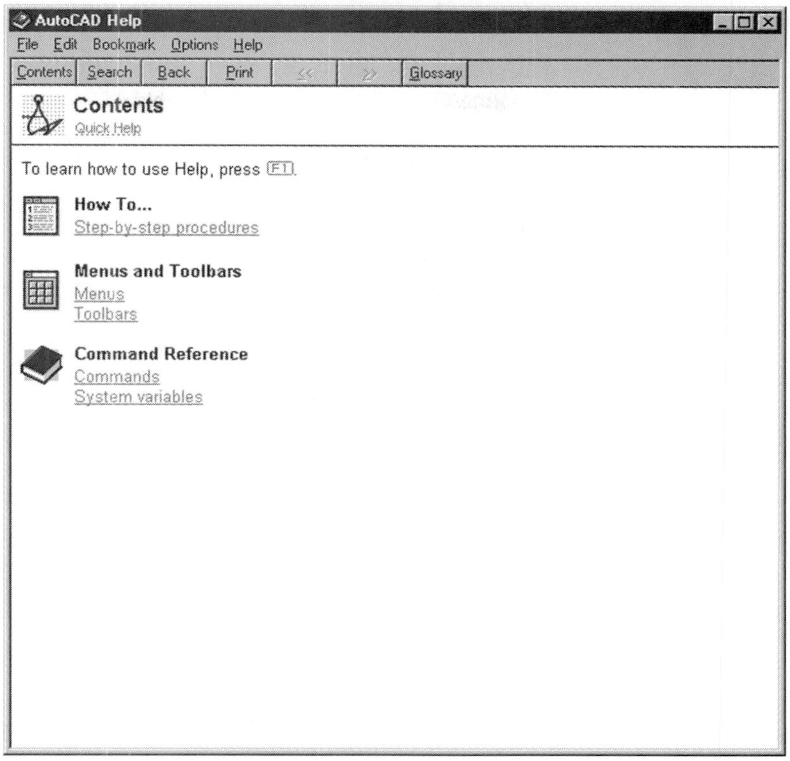

Figure 1.23
Use the AutoCAD Help window to search for more information on a command.

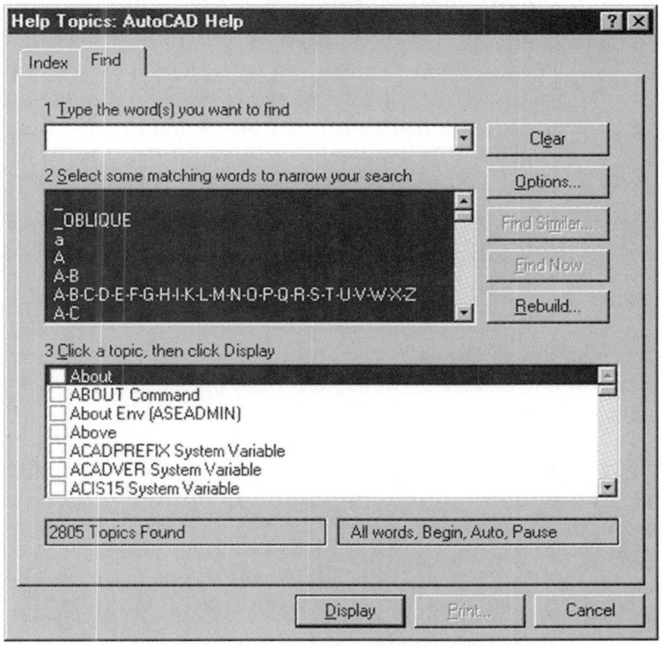

Figure 1.24
After selecting the Find tab, the information in the dialog box will change.

WORKING WITH FOLDERS

One of the most important skills of the Windows and AutoCAD student is the proper management of files. After all, if you can't save your work and edit it later, the advantages of using a computer are lost. Prior to the introduction of Windows, it was very difficult to manage and group files. Computers relied on Microsoft Disk Operating System (MS/DOS). To manipulate files you had to remember commands and then type them at a prompt. The commands themselves were not hard to remember; it was the options that were needed. For instance, to copy a file, the command was simply COPY. Not very difficult, but now you had to include the storage device label, the sub-directory or directories the file is stored in, and the name of the file, and then repeat the information for the destination location of the file. A sample COPY command is shown below:

```
C:>copy a:\autocad\drawings\homework.dwg c:\autocad\files\homework.dwg
```

As you can see, the only familiar word is possibly the copy command itself. And this is an easy command. Other commands provided even more memorization and frustration.

Windows took away all of the cryptic commands and replaced them with a GUI that allowed the same command to be completed with a few clicks of the mouse—a very welcome feature for those who cannot type. In Windows, sub-directories are known as folders, just like the folders found in your notebooks or at home. This makes working with files more intuitive.

MANAGING FILES AND FOLDERS

So just how do you create these files and folders? Well, AutoCAD does a very good job of saving your files as you will find out in the next section. It is up to you to create a proper folder to store that file in. It is also up to you to make sure that you place the correct file in the right folder. If you don't, it will be hard to locate that file at a later time. The key thing to remember is to name files and folders appropriately. Don't name files or folders based on dates or use a series of numbers. These will be hard to identify months later. Name them what they are! Windows allows you to use up to 256 letters to describe a file. A vast improvement over the old MS/DOS 8.3, or eight characters and a three-letter extension. And while this allows for a lot of latitude, you don't want to write a short essay describing the file. One to three words should be enough to describe the file as long as it is being placed in an appropriate folder. Let's look at an example.

This book assumes that you are presently in a CAD Fundamentals course. Your instructor has given you your first homework assignment. It is your job to decide where the file is going to be stored. It may be on a 3½″-floppy disk, hard drive, or on a network drive. Suppose you have been instructed to create a simple space plan for a residential home and to save the file to a 3½″-floppy disk. First off, the 3½″-floppy is known as a removable storage media. That simply means that you can remove this floppy and take it with you. While this might sound great at first, there are some limitations you should be aware of.

- Floppy disk must first be formatted to be used.
- They are typically slower than a hard drive or a network drive.
- They hold a very small amount of information.
- They can be easily damaged by excessive heat or strong magnetic fields.

The folder you create on the floppy disk will be named CAD FUNDAMENTALS. The file would probably be called HOMEWORK1 or SPACE PLAN. Many times in the classroom or in industry, you will be given the name of the file. The name will be based on some standard that ensures anyone can find that file at a later date. Let's look at the process for formatting a disk and creating a new folder in the following Tutorial.

There are many more features in Windows for managing files and folders. This section gives you just enough information to begin saving files in AutoCAD. For more infor-

Tutorial 1.2: Formatting a Disk and Creating a New Folder

In this tutorial you will format a new 3½″-floppy disk and create a new folder on that disk called CAD FUNDAMENTALS.

1. Place an unformatted high density 3½″-floppy disk in the computer. Figure 1.25 shows this step being executed on a common computer. An arrow located on the disk displays the correct direction to insert the disk.

Figure 1.25 *Insert the disk as shown.*

2. Double-click on the My Computer icon at the top left of the Windows desktop as shown in Figure 1.26. The My Computer window appears as shown.

Figure 1.26 *The My Computer icon on the Windows desktop.*

3. Single-click on the 3½″-Floppy icon. The icon will become highlighted.
4. Select File/Format... from the window pull-down menu. The Format-3½″ Floppy dialog box will be displayed.
5. Select Full in the Format type tile.
6. Click the Label text edit box in the Other options tile and enter your last name. This will identify this disk as your own should it fall into someone else's hands.
7. Select the Start button. The disk will begin formatting.
8. When the disk has been formatted, Windows will display a summary list and tell you that the format has been successful and ask you if you want to format another disk. Answer No. The dialog box will be closed. It is now time to create a new folder on the formatted floppy.
9. In the My Computer window, double-click on the 3½″ Floppy icon. The 3½″ Floppy window will appear as shown in Figure 1.27.

Figure 1.27
The 3½″ Floppy window.

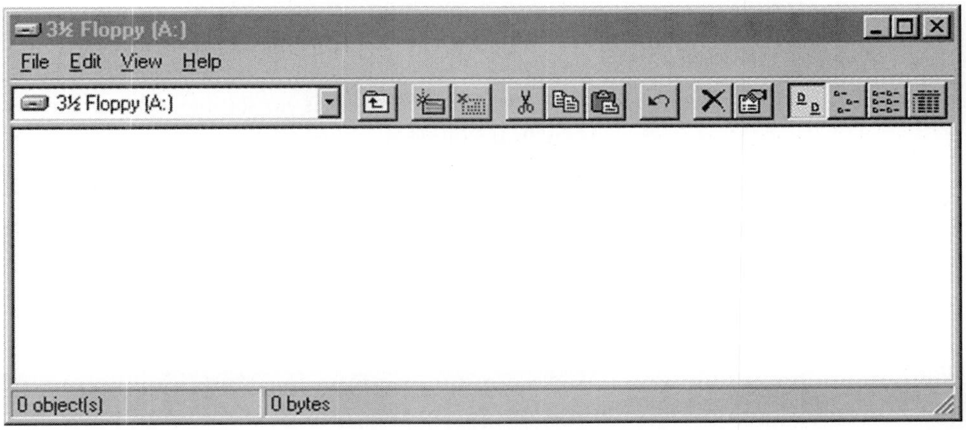

10. Select File/New/Folder. A new folder will appear in the 3½″ Floppy window. The folder name will be highlighted.
11. Using the keyboard, enter *CAD Fundamentals* and press Enter The folder will be named and the highlight will be removed. The folder can now be used to store AutoCAD files.

mation on managing files, you may wish to consult the Windows user's guide. In the next section we will discuss how to use this newly created folder to store information.

AUTOCAD FILE OPERATIONS

In the previous section you learned how to create a folder on a floppy disk to store drawing files. This folder will be used as a storage location for an AutoCAD drawing file. The next section also introduces you to probably the most important concept in AutoCAD—saving files for future use. One of the advantages of CAD over manual drafting is this ability to save drawing files electronically. This not only saves paper, but allows the file to be transferred and stored electronically so other users can make modifications. AutoCAD provides you with all of the necessary file-management commands to correctly store and create new files. This section will examine the fundamental file-operation commands.

CREATING A NEW DRAWING

The very first file operation you need to become familiar with is the New command. Before beginning any drawing you should use this command to create a new drawing file in the proper folder. There are other options that are available using this command. Let's take a look at their use. To use this command use the following procedures:

- Type **new** at the `Command:` prompt.
- Choose File/New... from the pull-down menu.
- Click on the New button on the Standard Toolbar.
- Press Ctrl N.

Once the New command has been entered the Create New Drawing dialog box will be displayed as shown in Figure 1.28. The first tile of this dialog box contains the Prototype... button with a text edit box, the No Prototype check box, and the Retain as Default check box. A prototype drawing is simply a drawing that already has been configured for the settings and defaults normally used for a particular class or assignment. For instance, this file may contain a title block that has already been created as well as units set to architectural. To select a prototype file, either enter the name in the edit box or click the Prototype... button to use a file selector to locate and select the file as shown in Figure 1.29.

When a new file is created from this prototype file, you do not have to recreate the title block from scratch or establish the units. The normal default prototype file is the acad.dwg file. This file has no settings or geometry. It is used to create a new file from scratch. If you do not wish to use a prototype file, select the No Prototype check box. If you are using a prototype file for a drawing and want to use that file as the prototype for all files, click on the Retain as Default check box.

Finally, on the Create New Drawing dialog box, there is the New Drawing Name... text edit box. This is where you will place the name and location of the new file that is being created. Clicking on the New Drawing Name... button will display the Create

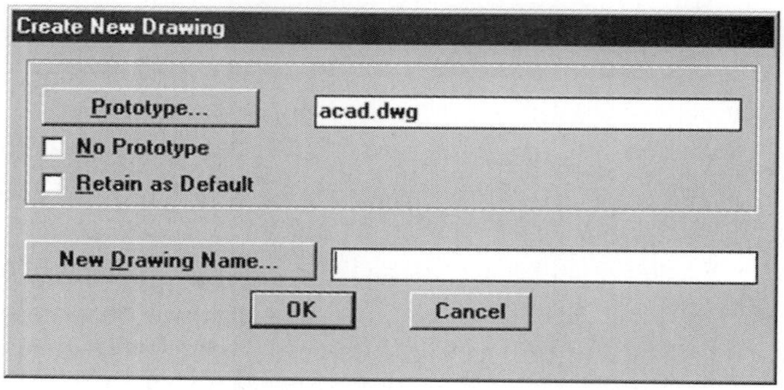

Figure 1.28
The Create New Drawing dialog box.

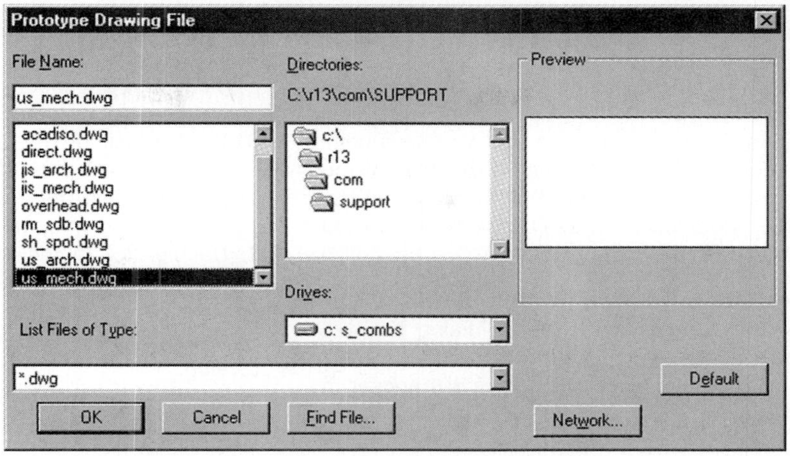

Figure 1.29
Selecting a prototype file.

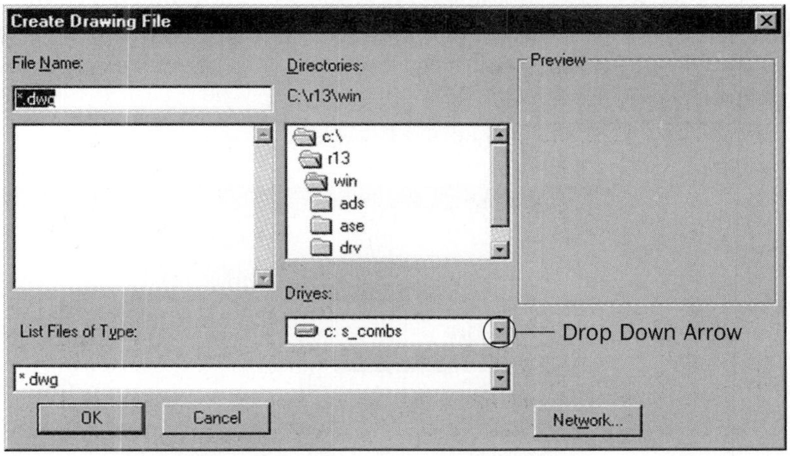

Figure 1.30
The Create New File dialog box.

Drawing File dialog box as shown in Figure 1.30. Use this dialog box to find the location to store the current drawing file as well as to give the file a name.

Opening an Existing Drawing

Once files are created in folders you will probably want to view them or modify them at a later time. To do this you will use the Open command. To use this command use the following procedure:

- Type **open** at the `Command:` prompt.
- Choose File/Open... from the pull-down menu.
- Click on the Open button on the Standard Toolbar.
- Press Ctrl O.

Once the Open command has been entered the Select File dialog box will be displayed as shown in Figure 1.31.

Choose the storage device and folder where the file is stored. Single-click on the file to display a preview of the file in the Preview tile as shown in Figure 1.31. To select the file, double-click on the name.

If you cannot locate a file, click on the Find File... button. The Browse/Search dialog box will be displayed as shown in Figure 1.32. This dialog box will display a thumbnail presentation of a series of drawings located in a folder. These thumbnails are identical to the Preview tile described above. The Size list box allows you to choose between

Tutorial 1.3: Creating a New Drawing File

In the last tutorial you formatted a floppy and created a new folder called CAD Fundamentals. This tutorial will begin where the previous one ended. Ensure that you have completed the last tutorial before continuing. In this tutorial you will create a new drawing file called PRODUCT.DWG on the floppy disk in the folder called CAD FUNDAMENTALS. You will use no prototype for this drawing file.

1. Select the **new** button from the Standard Toolbar. The Create New Drawing dialog box will appear as shown in Figure 1.28.
2. Select the No Prototype check box. An *x* will appear in the check box.
3. Select the New Drawing Name... button. The Create New File dialog box is displayed as shown in Figure 1.30.
4. Select the arrow on the Drives drop down list. The various drives attached to the computer will be displayed.
5. Select the a: drive from the list. This should be the 3½″-floppy disk. Once selected, the pop-up list will close and the folder you created in the previous tutorial will be displayed in the Directories list box.
6. Double-click on the CAD FUNDAMENTALS folder. The contents of the CAD FUNDAMENTALS folder will be displayed. Since there are no files in this newly created folder, the display will be empty.
7. Double-click in the File Name text edit box. The contents will be highlighted.
8. Type **product.** It is not necessary to add the .DWG extension. AutoCAD will automatically add this extension.
9. Select the OK button or press Enter. The dialog box will close and the Create New Drawing file will once again be displayed.
10. Select the OK button or press Enter. The dialog box will close and the drawing area will be blank.
11. Select File/Exit to exit the drawing file and close AutoCAD.

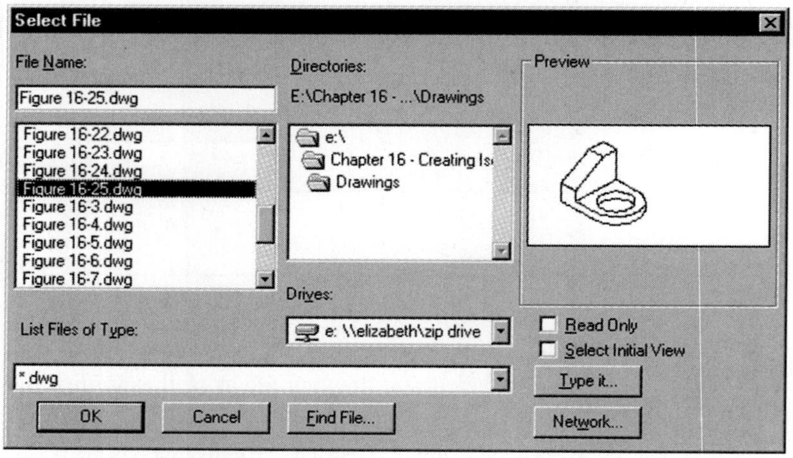

Figure 1.31
The Select File dialog box.

small, medium, or large thumbnails to be displayed in the image tile. To see thumbnails, follow the same procedures for selecting a file. Using this feature presents you with a visual way of locating files. It you look across the top of the dialog box, you will see another tab titled Search. This tab allows you to search for a drawing by name, date, or directory location.

Once the Search tab is selected, the Browse/Search dialog box will change to the one displayed in Figure 1.33. This dialog box allows you to search for a drawing by name, date, or location. Using the default settings will search the entire hard drive on the computer for AutoCAD drawing files. You can limit your search by selecting single folders or by searching only the floppy disk. When Search is selected, AutoCAD will begin searching for files that match your criteria. Once these files are found, thumbnails and the name and location of the file will appear in the image tile as shown in Figure 1.33. If you want to load one of these files, simply double-click on the image or filename.

Using Read-Only Mode

In the Select file dialog box you will find the Read-Only check box. You can use this option to open the file to view only. This will ensure that you don't inadvertently make

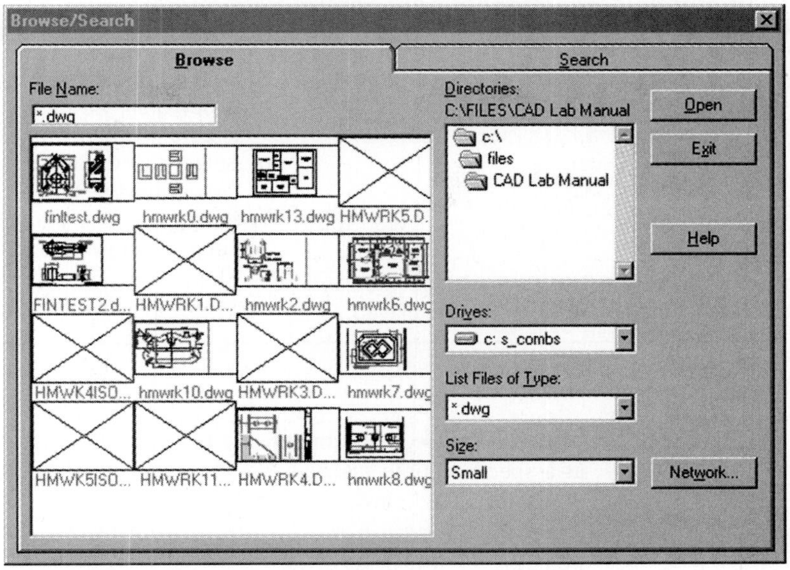

Figure 1.32
The Browse/Search dialog box with the Browse option selected.

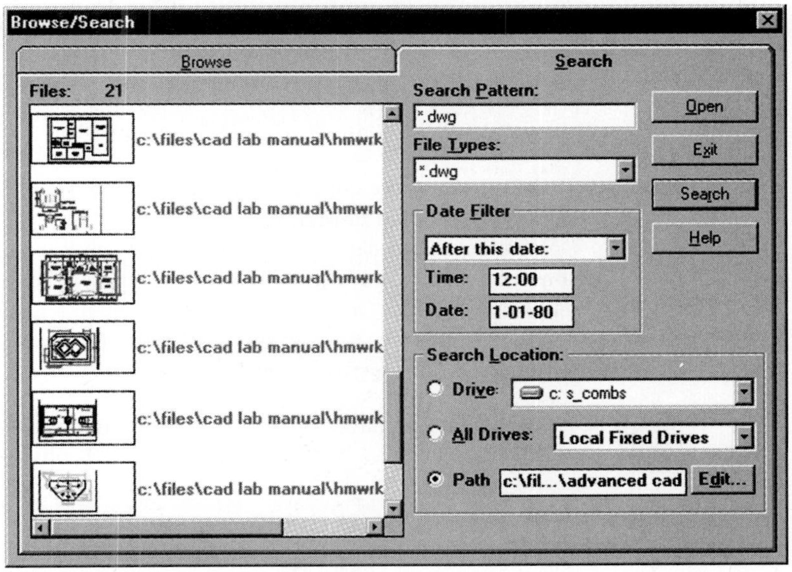

Figure 1.33
The Browse/Search dialog box with the Search option selected.

modifications to the drawing file. When opened, you will not be able to modify the drawing file. While you cannot modify the drawing, you can save it as another file using the SaveAs command. Make sure the check box is empty before loading a file that you wish to modify.

SAVING AND EXITING A DRAWING

Archiving a file for later use is referred to as saving a file. It is very important that you establish a good routine for saving drawing files. Saving should become a habit. There have been many occasions when a student has lost files and many hours of work because he or she forgot or was too lazy to save a drawing. There are many things that can cause a drawing file to be lost, such as a power outage, a circuit breaker being blown, computer hardware or software failure, or even someone just closing AutoCAD before completing the drawing. The purpose of this section is to make you aware of the commands used to save a drawing file as well as reinforce the fact that you should save often. You will also

Tutorial: Opening an Existing Drawing File

In this tutorial you will open a previously created drawing located on the Fundamentals of AutoCAD workdisk.

1. Start AutoCAD.
2. Insert the Fundamentals of AutoCAD workdisk.
3.  Select the Open button from the Standard Toolbar. The Select file dialog box is displayed.
4. Select the pop-up arrow on the Drives pop-up list. The various drives attached to the computer will be displayed.
5. Select the a: drive from the list. This should be the 3½"-floppy disk. All of the drawing files located on the root directory of the workdisk will be displayed.
6. Select the OPEN_ME.DWG. A preview will appear in the Preview image tile.
7. Select OK. The file will be loaded and displayed in the AutoCAD drawing area.

be introduced to a system variable that will allow you to automatically save a drawing file at a specified time interval. Finally, you will learn how to properly exit AutoCAD and return to the Windows desktop.

Saving a Drawing File

Saving a file in AutoCAD is a very simple process. So simple that you will wonder why anyone ever loses a file. There are actually three different commands used for saving a drawing file: the **save, qsave,** and **save as** commands. The basic command is **save.** To use this command use the following procedure:

- Type **save** at the `Command:` prompt

Once the **save** command has been entered the Save Drawing As dialog box will be displayed as shown in Figure 1.34.

Select the folder using the procedures outlined in opening a file. Then place the file name you wish to save the file as in the File Name: text edit box. Click on the OK button to save the file. Once the file has been given a name, you can use the **qsave** command to save the drawing file without displaying the dialog box. To use the **qsave** command, use one of the following methods:

- Choose File/Save... from the pull-down menu.
- Select the Save button on the Standard Toolbar.
- Press Ctrl S.

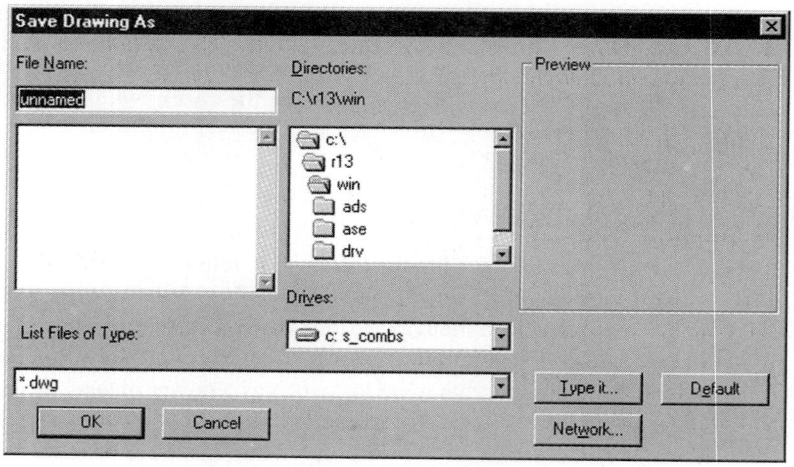

Figure 1.34
The Save Drawing As dialog box.

SKILL BUILDER

If you used the **new** command to begin a drawing, you can bypass using **save** to name the file.

When the command has been issued the drawing file will contain all objects created up to that point.

FOR THE PROFESSIONAL

The **qsave** command is a simple command that can save you hours of lost work. Use it frequently. A good rule of thumb is to use the **qsave** command as often as the amount of work you can *afford* to lose. For instance, if you can afford to lose only 15 minutes of work, save every 15 minutes. If you can afford to lose three hours of work, save every three hours and be prepared for the possibility of repeating the last three hours of drawing.

There are times when you may want to save the present file under a new folder or with a different name. This is helpful if you want to place a quick copy of the drawing file on the network or on a floppy for your instructor to grade or to be used as a backup copy in case your storage device fails. To save a file to another directory or with a new name use the **saveas** command. Enter this command using the following procedure:

- Type **saveas** at the `Command:` prompt.
- Choose File/Save As... from the pull-down menu.

When you enter the **saveas** command the Save Drawing As dialog box appears as shown in Figure 1.34. Follow the same procedures outlined in the **save** command.

SKILL BUILDER

If the **save** or **save as** commands have not been issued, the first time the **qsave** command is issued, the Save Drawing As dialog box will be displayed. Unless you need to change the name of the file, there is no reason to use any other command other than **qsave** to save your files.

While you were experimenting with this command, you may have seen the Save R12 DWG... option under the File pull-down menu. This command is used when you want to share a drawing file with someone else that owns a copy of AutoCAD Release 12. There are many people who have not upgraded to AutoCAD Release 13. This command will allow you to share files back and forth between these versions of AutoCAD. You should note that an AutoCAD Release 12 file can be read in AutoCAD Release 13 without any conversion, but you must use this command to share AutoCAD Release 13 files with AutoCAD Release 12. To use this command, use one of the following methods:

- Type **saveasR12** at the `Command:` prompt.
- Select File/Save R12 DWG... from the pull-down menu.

Once the command has been entered, the Save As Release 12 Drawing dialog box will be displayed. Other than the title, this dialog box is identical in use to the Save As dialog box found in Figure 1.34. **Be sure not to save the file with the same name as the AutoCAD Release 13 file or it will be overwritten. Use a unique name such as HMWRK12.DWG instead of HOMEWORK.DWG. This inclusion of R12 will let you know that file was saved in the AutoCAD Release 12 format.**

Using Savetime

A system variable that can assist you in saving your drawing file at a given interval is the **savetime** variable. A system variable is a command that allows you to enter information that instructs AutoCAD to accomplish tasks using certain parameters. In this case the **savetime** system variable instructs AutoCAD to create a backup copy of the current drawing file at a specified time interval. Once a value, say 15 minutes, is entered, AutoCAD will automatically save that file every 15 minutes. This system variable needs further explanation. AutoCAD will not save the drawing in the same file name you specified using the **save** or **save as** command. Instead AutoCAD saves the drawing file as AUTO.SV$. If you were to lose a file and needed to recover information you would simply rename the drawing file with a .dwg extension instead of the .sv$ extension. To enter a value in the **savetime** system variable follow one of the following procedures:

- Type **`savetime`** at the `Command:` prompt.
- Select Options/Preferences... for the pull-down menu.

The sequence for using the command from the `Command:` prompt is as follows:

```
Command: savetime
New value for SAVETIME <120>: 15
```

In the example above, a time interval of 15 minutes has been specified. To accomplish the same thing using the pull-downs follow the steps below.

1. Select Options/Preferences... from the pull-down menu. The Preferences dialog box will appear as shown in Figure 1.35.
2. If not already displayed, select the System tab. The System options will be displayed.
3. Place the time interval in the Automatic Save text edit box.
4. Ensure that the Every check box is selected.
5. Select the OK button. The dialog box will close and the new settings will take place.

Closing AutoCAD

It is fitting that the last two commands in this unit are **quit** and **end**. Both of these commands close AutoCAD. They are used when you have completed your drawing or are

Figure 1.35
*Use the Preferences dialog box to set the **savetime** value.*

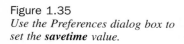

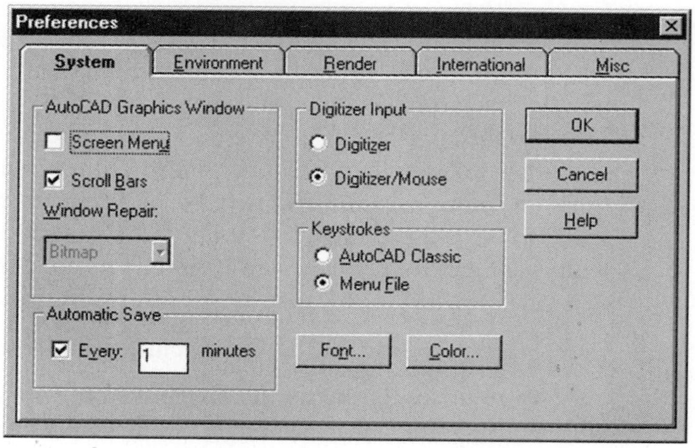

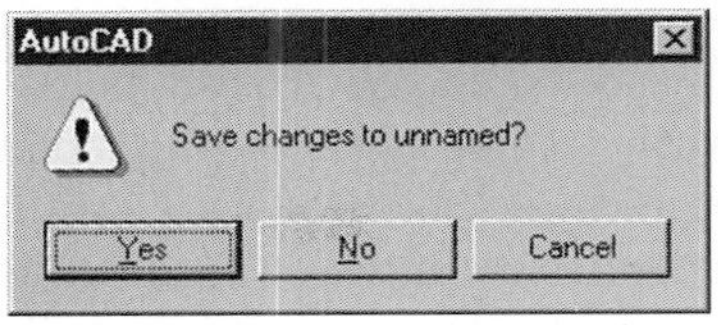

Figure 1.36
The AutoCAD question dialog box.

through with the current drawing session. The first command, **quit,** can be entered using one of the following methods:

- Type `quit` at the `Command:` prompt.
- Select File/Exit from the pull-down menus.

Once the command is entered, AutoCAD will begin its closing procedure. If you have not saved your drawing since changes were made, the AutoCAD question dialog box will be displayed as shown in Figure 1.36.

This dialog box is used to verify that you wish to save the file before closing AutoCAD. Selecting Yes will save your current drawing modification and close AutoCAD. Selecting No will not save your current drawing modifications and close AutoCAD. Selecting Cancel will cancel the command and return you to the drawing editor. If **qsave** was the command issued right before **quit,** this dialog box will not be displayed.

A command that is similar to **quit** is the **end** command. This command can be entered only at the `Command:` prompt. The **end** command combines the functions of the **save** and **quit** commands by saving the drawing file and closing AutoCAD. No dialog box will be displayed. The **end** command also performs another important function, it creates a backup file in the same folder as the original drawing file. The only difference is that the extension is .bak instead of .dwg. This backup file will not change unless you modify the original drawing file and again execute the **end** command. This allows you to have a previous copy of your drawing file in case you are not happy with the changes you have made in the current drawing session. To use the backup file, simply rename the file with the .dwg extension. When used with the **savetime** system variable discussed above, these two commands can save you many hours of duplicate drawing.

For the Professional

Good AutoCAD users have more than one copy of their drawing files. And while **savetime** and **end** can help you archive files, there is no better way to protect your work than by creating backup copies to floppy disks, tape, or removable storage devices. Once created, you should store these backups in a safe location.

SUMMARY

Windows and AutoCAD are tied together and an understanding of both of their file operation commands is essential to creating and storing AutoCAD drawing files. Both share similar features such as dialog boxes, pull-down menus, and Help systems. Learning one will help you understand the other. As you explore the AutoCAD display you will find many different ways of interacting with AutoCAD. For instance, there are four different ways you can enter the **qsave** command. No way is better than the other; AutoCAD allows each user to select the method of interaction that suits them best.

Folders are used to store drawing files. Similar to their paper counterparts, you can label folders and place many different files within them. To place files in these folders you use the AutoCAD **new** command to create drawing files and then update them frequently using the **qsave** command. When you want to review or modify these files, use the **open** command. Finally, when you are done making modifications to these files, use the **end** command to save the file and close AutoCAD. You are now ready to create your first drawing. The next unit will introduce you to these procedures.

REVIEW

1. How is the Windows operating system started?
2. Explain the difference between minimizing and maximizing windows.
3. How is AutoCAD started?
4. Explain the various ways of issuing commands in AutoCAD.
5. What are the differences between floating and docked toolbars?
6. Describe the differences and similarities between radio buttons and check boxes.
7. List and describe the benefits of an electronic Help facility such as the one found in AutoCAD and Windows.
8. Explain the difference between file folders and file names.
9. List and explain the three commands used to save an AutoCAD drawing file.
10. What is the difference between the **quit** and **end** commands?

EXERCISE 1

In this assignment you will use the steps outlined below to create a backup disk. The steps listed do not include all of the necessary steps. You may have to refer to the appropriate section in the unit to jog your memory. This backup disk is used to archive drawings and to ensure that you have a backup drawing in case you lose your workdisk or it is damaged. Once this backup disk is created, you will then begin AutoCAD and create a new drawing file. Once the file is created, you will save the drawing and exit AutoCAD. Finally, you will delete the file.

1. Format a blank High Density 3½″-floppy disk using the label *CAD_Backup.*
2. Create a new folder called *CAD Fundamentals.*
3. Start AutoCAD and create a new file called *Blank Drawing.*
4. Save the drawing file and exit AutoCAD.
5. Verify that the file was created by viewing the contents of the *CAD Fundamentals* folder on the 3½″-disk.
6. Delete the file by dragging it to the Recycle bin on the desktop.
7. Use this disk to create backup drawings of all files used in this course. Never use this disk as a workdisk!

UNIT 2

CREATING YOUR FIRST DRAWING

OVERVIEW

In the previous unit, you learned how to work in the Windows environment, how to load AutoCAD, and the components of the AutoCAD display. In this unit you will learn how to create a new drawing and then you will draw a roof framing plan. It is very important that you learn the material in this unit. Without a complete understanding of this material, you will not be able to continue through the rest of this book and become a proficient AutoCAD user. Let's begin drawing!

OBJECTIVES

- Create a new drawing.
- Set the display format and units.
- Set the drawing limits.
- Use AutoCAD drawing tools.
- Draw lines.
- Clean up the display.
- Save your drawing.
- Exit AutoCAD.
- Develop an understanding of objects.
- Develop an understanding of the drawing database.

INTRODUCTION

In manual drafting, a pen or pencil is used to draw lines, arcs, text, dimensions, and other geometry. A manual drafter may use a straightedge to draw lines, a scale to measure, a triangle to construct 30-, 60- and 45-degree lines, a compass to draw circles, and other drafting equipment. Templates of standard parts are used in certain cases to speed up the drawing process. Even the use of templates, however, is unsuccessful in speeding up the labored task of dimensioning and adding notes. If a drafter is lucky, he/she may have access to a drafting machine, and while this is a definite improvement over a T square or parallel bar, it still cannot match the speed and accuracy of AutoCAD. To complete a drawing, each geometric object is created one at a time.

AutoCAD provides tools similar to those mentioned for the creation of geometry, emulating many standard drafting tools. To draw a straight line, for example, AutoCAD provides a command that allows anyone to do so.

In this unit, several of AutoCAD's basic functions are introduced. You start by creating a new drawing and setting up the drawing environment. Several of AutoCAD's drafting tools are then introduced. These tools help speed up the drawing process.

As you go through this unit, keep in mind that there are many right ways to use AutoCAD. Many of the commands can be accessed using different methods, just as geometry can be created using different methods. This resourceful feature of AutoCAD is due to the fact that AutoCAD was designed to meet the needs of a wide variety of users, such as engineers, architects, and interior designers. Many users of AutoCAD have a preferred method of using the software. In time you will develop a style and method that works best for you.

OUTLINE

Starting a New Drawing
Tutorial 2.1: Starting the Example Drawing
Tutorial 2.2: Setting the Display Format and Units
Tutorial 2.3: Setting the Drawing Size
Using AutoCAD Drafting Tools
Tutorial 2.4: Setting the Grid
Tutorial 2.5: Setting the Snap
Drawing Lines (LINE)
Tutorial 2.6: Using the Line Command to Create the Roof Plan
Understanding Objects
Summary
Review
Exercises

STARTING A NEW DRAWING

When you first start AutoCAD, the standard AutoCAD window is displayed along with a new blank drawing. This is called the drawing editor (see Fig. 2.1). You can begin creating geometry immediately in this area.

For the Professional

You can create and edit a drawing within the drawing editor without giving the drawing a name. You are prompted for a name and have the opportunity to change the drive and/or path the first time you issue the **save** command to save the drawing in a file.

While you can create and edit a drawing within the drawing editor without giving it a name, the drawing is not saved until you store it in a file. The contents of a file can be any number of things, such as a word processing document, a spreadsheet, or an AutoCAD drawing. When you give the drawing a name and save it, a file with that name is created. This named file contains all important information regarding the drawing. When you open the file later, the drawing appears exactly the same on-screen as when you last saved it to the file.

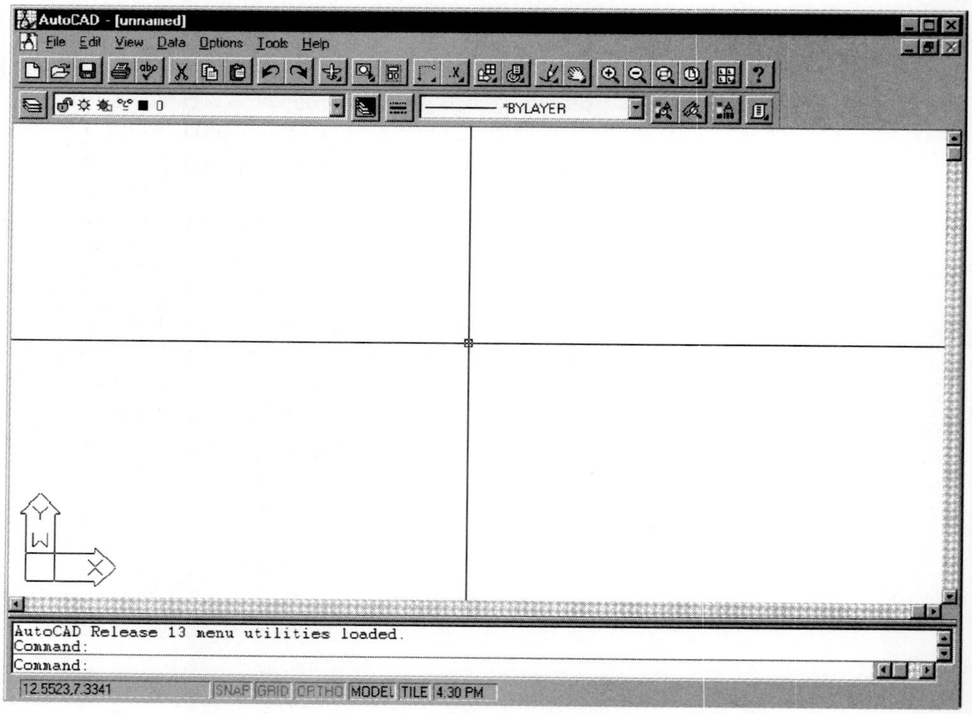

Figure 2.1
The standard drawing editor in AutoCAD 13 for Windows.

Tutorial 2.1: Starting the Example Drawing

The tutorial in this unit is a roof plan of an apartment complex. By the time you finish this unit, you will have drawn the roof plan shown in Figure 2.2.

1.  To begin your new drawing and assign a name to it, select the New button on the Standard toolbar. The Create New Drawing dialog box is displayed, as shown in Figure 2.3. Notice that the insertion point appears in the New Drawing Name edit box.
2. Ensure a disk is inserted in the A drive and enter A:\ROOFPLAN. Your screen should now look like Figure 2.4. To continue, click OK or press [Enter] to return to the drawing editor.

Skill Builder

You can access the Create New Drawing dialog box by entering **new** at the `Command:` prompt or typing [Ctrl][N].

For the Professional

It is important that you know the exact location of your drawings. If your drawings are not placed on the proper disk or in the proper directory, they may be difficult to find later. Proper file-management techniques are an essential part of working with AutoCAD.

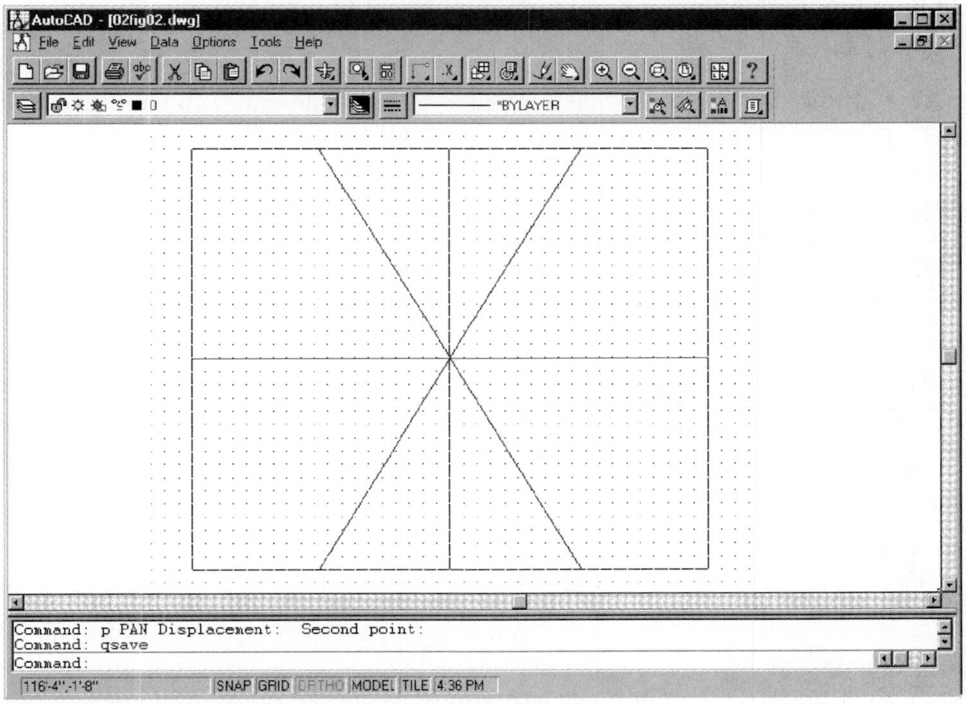

Figure 2.2
The roof plan created by completing the tutorials in this unit.

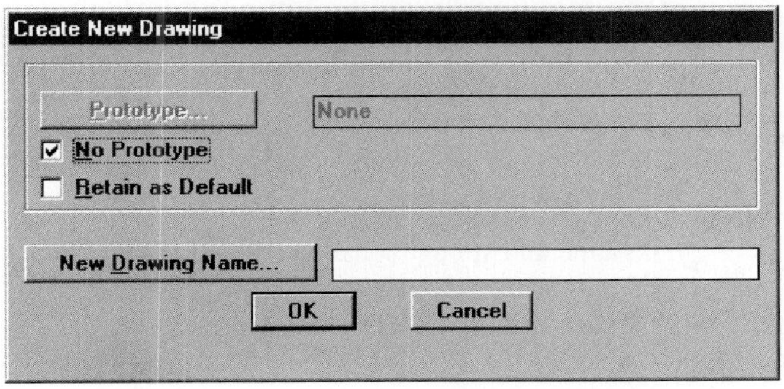

Figure 2.3
The Create New Drawing dialog box is used to start a new drawing.

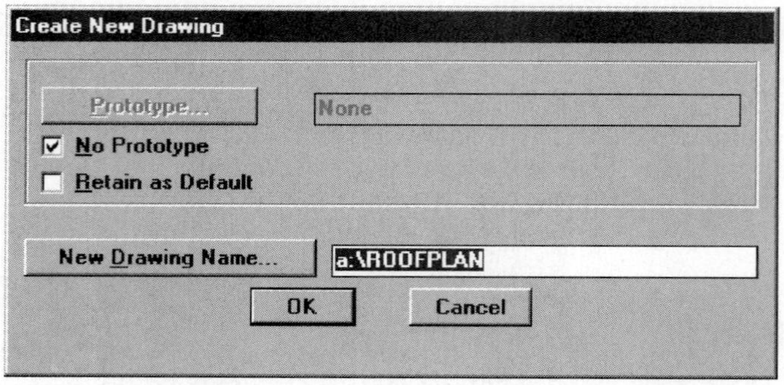

Figure 2.4
Creating the new drawing named "roof."

Saving Your Work

Remember to save your work every 10–15 minutes as you work through the tutorials. This is extremely important in the event of a power failure or some other unforeseen problem. By saving your work regularly, all the work saved before the problem is most likely usable. You can invoke the save **command** by entering **save** at the `Command:` prompt, clicking the Save button in the toolbar, choosing File/Save from the pull-down menu, or by typing Ctrl S.

For the Professional

If you want to stop working on the tutorial and continue later, you can use the End command to save your drawing, exit AutoCAD, and return to the Windows desktop.

When you enter **end** or **save**, your drawing is saved with the drawing name and a **dwg** file extension. The old version is saved as a backup with a **bak** file extension. For example, when you work on the drawing **roofplan** and enter End, the drawing is saved as **roofplan.dwg**. If you have a previous version of **roofplan** on your disk, that old version is saved as **roofplan.bak**. The extension is automatically added by AutoCAD. You enter only the file name.

If you do stop working on the **roofplan** drawing and exit AutoCAD, you need to restart AutoCAD and open the **roofplan** drawing when you are ready to continue with the tutorial. To restart AutoCAD, click AutoCAD on the Start menu. To open the **roofplan** drawing, select the **open** icon, type **open** at the `Command:` prompt, choose File/Open from the pull-down menu, or type Ctrl O. When you select the File pull-down menu, you are given a list of the most recent drawings you have worked on at the bottom of the pull-down menu. To open a drawing from this list, select the drawing name from the list or enter the number preceding its name.

At this point, you should be able to open AutoCAD successfully, begin a new drawing, and understand how to use dialog boxes. You should also know how to save a drawing, properly end a drawing, and open an existing drawing.

Setting Display Format and Units (DDUNITS)

Through careful planning before beginning a drawing, you can greatly reduce the time it takes to complete it. Setting up the drawing correctly involves several factors that affect the final accuracy and quality of the drawing. Before beginning the drawing you should determine the:

- Name and storage location of the drawing file
- Units with which the drawing is created
- Paper size on which the drawing fits
- Scale of the drawing

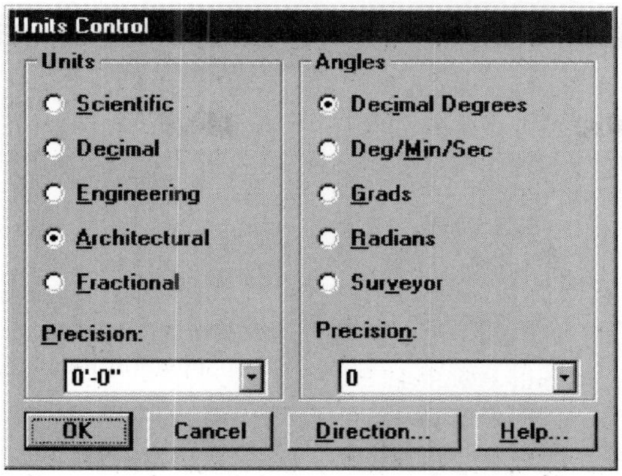

Figure 2.5
With the Units Control dialog box, you can set the units and precision.

The AutoCAD system of units lets you use real-world units of measure in your drawing, such as architectural and decimal units. By default, decimal units are used for numeric display and input within AutoCAD. These units, however, can represent anything you want. One unit on-screen can represent 1 inch, millimeter, or mile. The first task is to determine the appropriate type of measurement for your drawing.

Most drawings use a variety of sizes and scales. For example, you may want to do a drawing of a floor plan. In that case, it would be advantageous to specify feet and inches. The easiest way to set units in AutoCAD is with the Units Control dialog box. You access this dialog box when you choose Data/Units... You can also enter **ddunits** at the `Command:` prompt. Figure 2.5 shows the Units Control dialog box.

Setting the Drawing Size (LIMITS)

The first task in creating a new drawing is to determine the name and storage location of the drawing. The second task is to determine and set the units with which the drawing is created. The third task is to determine the paper size on which the drawing fits. When you compare the paper size selected to the overall geometry of the object, in most cases the geometry can't be represented at true size on standard-size paper. When you use manual drafting methods, the geometry itself is scaled accordingly to fit on the paper size selected. When working with AutoCAD, however, never scale the geometry itself; scale the limits instead.

Lines, arcs, circles, and other geometric objects should always be drawn full size within AutoCAD. If the length of a floor plan is 52′, it is drawn 624 units (inches) within AutoCAD. When you create the line, you will be able to specify the length as 52′. You will not have to convert this measurement to inches. Consequently, the size of the product determines the size of the drawing. The command that AutoCAD uses to specify the drawing area is Limits.

A drawing's limits help designate your working area. Limits can be thought of as representing the perimeter of the paper on which you create the drawing. The primary use of setting the limits is to provide a boundary to help contain the drawing within a set sheet size. When the limits are set properly, AutoCAD prevents you from drawing geometric objects outside the limits. This is similar to preventing you from drawing off the edges of a sheet of paper.

Because geometry should always be created full scale, the limits must be modified. The limits of the AutoCAD drawing area are determined by the following:

- The actual size of the geometry
- The extra space allowed for dimensions and notes
- A border and a title block
- The actual size of the paper on which the drawing will be plotted

To determine the minimum amount of space needed for a drawing, first determine the actual size of the geometry. For example, suppose that a house plan measures 46 ×

Tutorial 2.2: Setting the Display Format and Units

In the first tutorial, you set the name and storage location of the drawing file. In this tutorial, you will set the drawing units used to create the roof plan. When you change the drawing units, the coordinate display format also changes to reflect the current units. For this project, you will use architectural units with a precision of 0′-0″. Follow these steps:

1. When you initially load AutoCAD, you see the standard drawing editor. For this tutorial, you need only the Standard and Object Properties toolbars displayed. Any other toolbars should be closed at this time. Before continuing, check to make sure your screen looks like Figure 2.6.
2. From the pull-down menu, choose Data/Units.... The Units Control dialog box appears (see Figure 2.5).
3. Select Architectural in the Units section of the dialog box.
4. Click the DOWN ARROW button for the Precision option. In the pop-up list, select 0′-0″ as shown in Figure 2.7.
5. Click the OK button to accept the changes. Notice that the coordinate display format in the toolbar now includes both feet and inch measurements for both the X and Y axes.

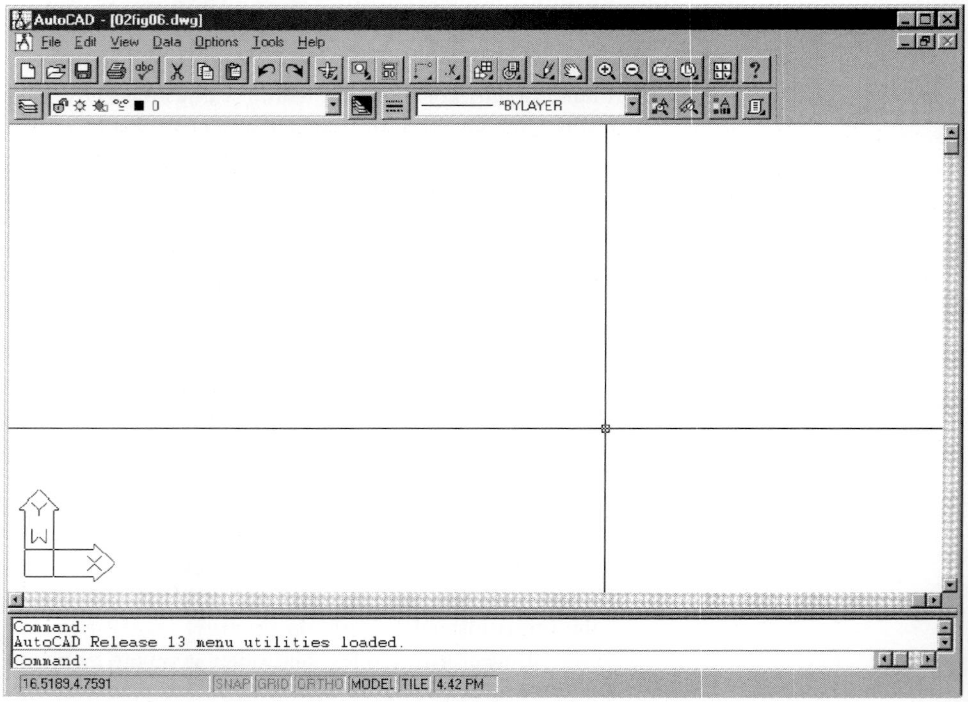

Figure 2.6
The standard drawing display used for this tutorial.

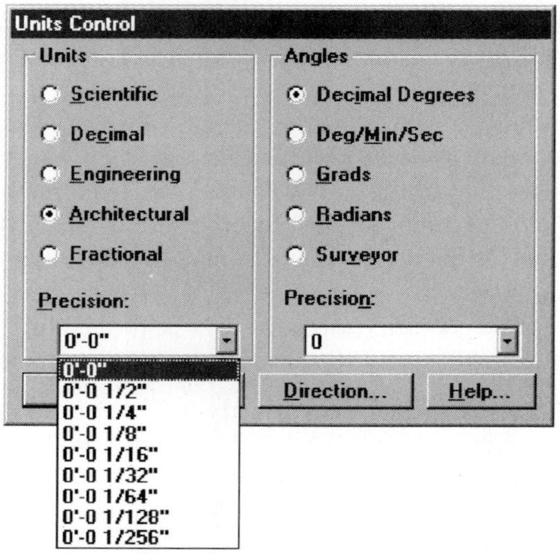

Figure 2.7
Setting the Units to Architectural and precision to 0′-0″ in the Units Control dialog box.

24 feet. Next, add any additional space needed for dimensions, notes, a border, and a title block. For this example, an additional 20 feet is needed (10 feet on each side) around the plan for dimensions, notes, and a border. Thus, this drawing needs a minimum space of 66 × 44 feet.

Once you determine the minimum space that the drawing requires, you need to decide the actual size of the paper on which the drawing will be plotted. For the preceding example, you'll use a C-size sheet of paper. A C-size sheet of paper is 22 × 17 inches. Most architectural floor plans are drawn at 1/4″ = 1′-0″. Multiplying 4′ (4 units/inch) × 22 will result in 88′ and 4′ × 17 = 68′, using a C-size paper with a 1/4″ = 1′-0″ scale, you will have a space of 88′ × 62′. Because the drawing needs a minimum space of 66 × 44 feet, it will easily fit in this 88′ × 62′ space. The drawing limits for this example should be set at 88′ × 62′.

In Table 2.1 you will find common sheet sizes and their associated limits. Use this table when you are unsure as to what size paper to use or what the limits should be set to for a given drawing. Note that the values given are for the upper-right limits. It is assumed that the lower-left limits will always be 0,0. You should also note the orientation of the paper. In the table, the values are given so that the orientation of the paper is set to portrait—the paper is taller than it is wide. If you require a landscape orientation, or the paper needs to be wider than it is tall, reverse the values. For example, for landscape orientation for an English drawing, set the upper-right limits to 11 × 8.

Sheet Size	English Limits	Metric Limits	Architectural Limits
A	8 × 11	203 × 279	32′ × 44′
B	11 × 17	279 × 432	44′ × 68′
C	17 × 22	432 × 559	68′ × 88′
D	22 × 34	559 × 864	88′ × 136′
E	34 × 48	864 × 1219	136′ × 192′

You should be aware that not all output devices can plot to the edges of a piece of paper. It may be necessary to modify these limit values slightly to create an accurate plot. Consult your output device owner's manual or your instructor for more information. We will also discuss how to obtain this information in Unit 3, "Viewing and Plotting a Drawing."

You specify limits by choosing Data/Drawing Limits or by entering **limits** at the `Command:` prompt.

The following command sequence is used to set the limits:

From the Data pull-down menu, choose Drawing Limits.

```
Reset Model Space Limits:
ON/OFF<Lower left corner><0'-0",0'-0">: 0'-0",0'-0"
```

The value displayed in the <0′-0″,0′-0″> section may indicate something different. The numbers in this section display the current value. Depending on what has been done in AutoCAD prior to beginning this tutorial, your value may be different.

This prompt sets the lower-left corner of the designated sheet size to the lower-left corner of the display screen. Responding with 0′-0″,0′-0″ places the lower-left corner at 0′-0″,0′-0″. The horizontal distance is entered first, followed by a comma, then the vertical distance. The value of 0′-0″,0′-0″ refers to the Cartesian coordinate (X & Y) values of the lower-left corner of the drawing area. Using these values places the lower-left corner of the drawing area at 0′-0″,0′-0″. The lower-left corner may be set at any location other than 0′-0″,0′-0″, however. Setting the lower-left corner to 0′-0″,0′-0″ is the most common and recommended setting.

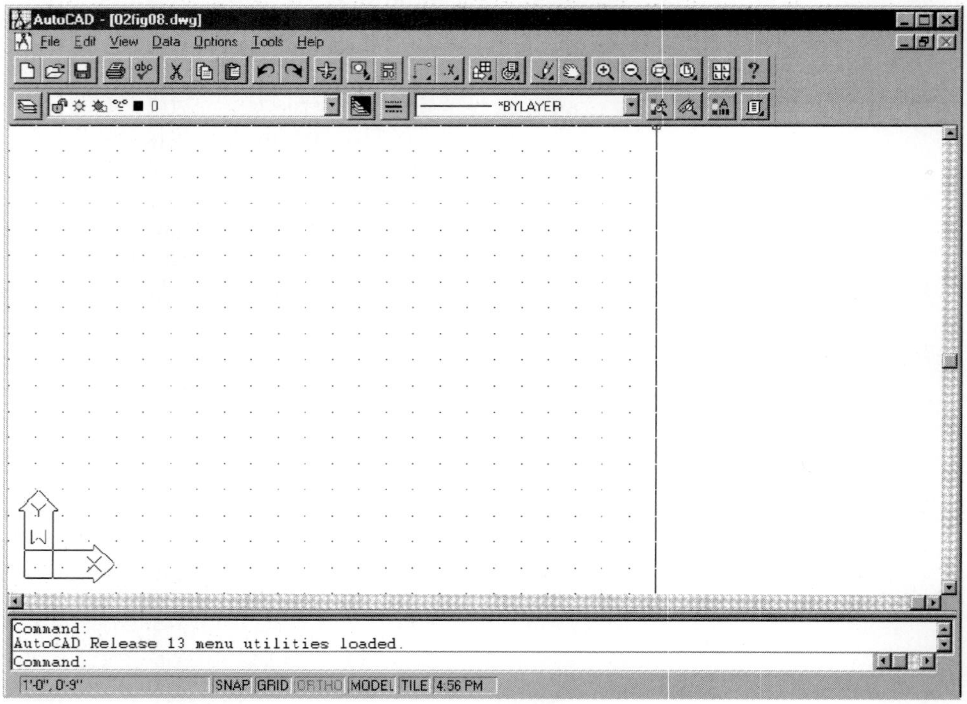

Figure 2.8
Use of the **limits** *command, with the AutoCAD default lower-left limit set to 0′-0″,0′-0″, and the upper-right limit set to 1′0″,0′,9″.*

Skill Builder

If you know that the lower-left limit is going to be 0,0 for a drawing, consider using the **limmax** system variable. With **limmax** you have to specify only the upper-right limits of the drawing area. Likewise, if you just want to modify or change the lower-left limit, use the **limmin** system variable.

The **limits** command continues with a request for the upper-right corner. The AutoCAD default for the upper-right corner is 1′-0″,0′-9″ This is a standard A-size sheet. The values entered determine the upper-right corner of the sheet size. The horizontal distance

Tutorial 2.3: Setting the Drawing Size

In the first tutorial, you set the drawing name and storage location. In the second tutorial, you set the units in which the drawing is created. The next task is to define the size of the work area with the **limits** command. The roof plan is plotted at a scale of 1/8″ = 1′. For this project, you set limits to be proportional to the size of an 8.5 × 11″ A-size sheet of paper. Since the majority of printers available for the consumer today do not print on 9 × 12″ paper, you have to set the limits to the more common 8.5 × 11″ A-size paper. The limits are set to 0′-0″,0′-0″ for the lower-left corner and 88′-0″,68′-0″ for the upper-right corner. The upper-right limits were determined by taking the size of the A-size sheet of paper and multiplying it by 4. Refer to Table 2.1 for more information. To define the size of the drawing area, follow these steps:

1. Select Data/Drawing Limits from the pull-down menu.
2. Specify the limits, using the following command sequence.
   ```
   Reset Model space limits:
   ON/OFF/<Lower left corner><0'-0",0'-0">: Enter
   Upper right corner<1'-0",0"-9">: 88',68' Enter
   ```
3. Move the crosshairs to the upper-right corner of the drawing area. Notice that the coordinate display on the toolbar indicates the upper-right corner to be smaller than the upper-right limit you just entered.
4. Select View/Zoom/All.
5. Move the cursor back to the upper-right corner of the drawing area. You should see that the coordinate display on the toolbar now indicates the upper-right corner to be greater than the default upper-right limits set for 9 × 12 paper.

(X value) is entered first, followed by a comma, then the vertical distance (Y value). Note that in Figure 2.8, the drawing limits 1′-0″,0′-9″ do not extend all the way to the right side of the screen. This is because the computer's video resolution differs from the aspect ratio of standard drawing sheet sizes.

You can change the limits at any time by executing the **limits** command. The first section of the **limits** command, ON/OFF, refers to a limits check. Using the **limits** command helps you designate your working area and avoid drawing off the paper. It is possible, however, to draw outside the limits, either deliberately or accidentally. With the limits check turned on, drawing outside the limits results in an ** Outside limits error message. With the limits check turned off, the error is not given.

USING AUTOCAD DRAFTING TOOLS

AutoCAD provides a variety of drawing aids that help in laying out the drawing and increasing speed and efficiency. These drawing aids include:

- Grid—a visual space indicator.
- Snap—an object creation precision tool.
- Coords—coordinates display toggle.
- Ortho—ensures the creation of vertical and horizontal lines.

Grid, Snap, and Ortho can be selected and changed through the Drawing Aids dialog box. You access this dialog box by choosing Options/Drawing Aids. You can also display the Drawing Aids dialog box by entering **ddrmodes** at the `Command:` prompt. You can enter the **grid, snap, coords,** and **ortho** commands directly at the `Command:` prompt. Figure 2.9 shows the Drawing Aids dialog box.

The Ortho, Snap, and Grid functions can be activated by single-clicking the appropriate box. The Snap and Grid spacing can also be set by typing the values in the boxes after X Spacing and Y Spacing (under Snap), and after X Spacing and Y Spacing (under Grid).

FOR THE PROFESSIONAL

To set the same Snap values for the X and Y spacing, type the value in the box after X Spacing and press Enter. The Y Spacing is automatically set to the same value as the X Spacing. The same procedure works for setting the grid.

The **blipmode** system variable can also be set in the Drawing Aids dialog box by clicking the Blips check box. Blips are temporary markers displayed on-screen whenever you designate a point. These marks are not printed, plotted, or saved as a part of the drawing. When Blips is off, the marker blips are not displayed. The Blips setting can be changed at any time during the drawing session.

Certain geometric objects, such as solids, have filled interiors. The Solid Fill option controls the **fillmode** variable, which can be set as well in the Drawing Aids dialog box.

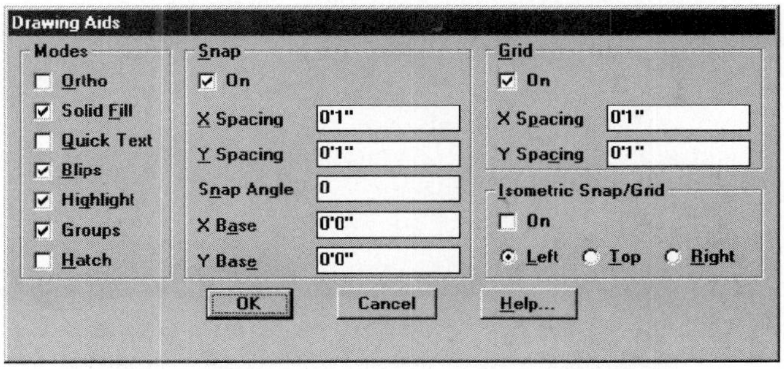

Figure 2.9
The Drawing Aids dialog box can be used to set many of the AutoCAD drafting tools.

When the Solid Fill mode is off, only the outlines of filled objects are displayed. Objects with filled interiors include traces, solids, and wide polylines. Creation and manipulation of these objects are discussed in upcoming units.

Using the Grid (GRID)

Grid paper is used by drafters, engineers, and students to assist in laying out a drawing or sketch. A similar type of grid can be used in AutoCAD. Using the **grid** command places a pattern of dots on-screen at any spacing, as shown in Figure 2.10. The grid pattern appears only within the drawing limits and helps define the drawing area. The grid is for visual reference only and is not considered part of the drawing. It does not appear in print or on any plot of the drawing.

Setting Up the Grid The grid can be changed through the Drawing Aids dialog box by typing **ddrmodes** at the `Command:` prompt. Alternatively, you can type **grid** at the `Command:` prompt. When you enter the **grid** command, a prompt appears that shows the default grid spacing and several other options:

```
Command: grid
Grid Spacing(X) or ON/OFF/Snap/Aspect <Current Value>:
```

You can press Enter to accept the default values or enter a new value. You set the dot spacing of the grid by entering a specific measurement. If the grid spacing you enter is too small to display on-screen, a Grid too dense to display message appears. If this happens, enter a larger grid spacing.

For the Professional

In many cases, the screen can display a very dense grid pattern. This can slow down the computer significantly when certain operations are performed. A very dense grid also lessens the usefulness of the grid.

Figure 2.10
The default grid shown in the standard drawing editor.

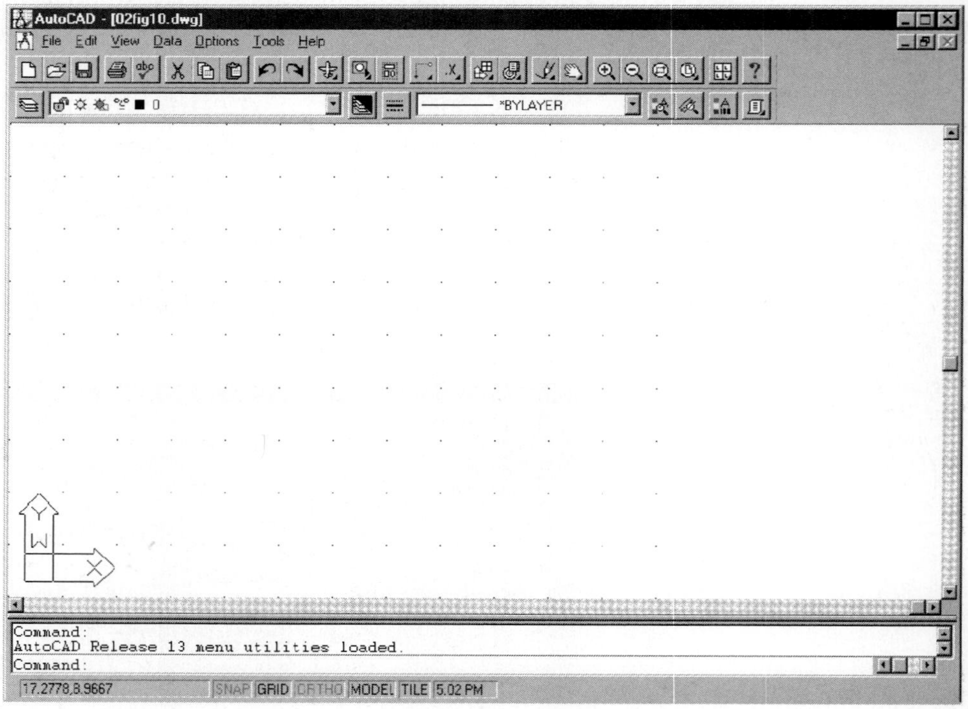

Toggling the Grid If you have a dense grid pattern on the screen, it may be advantageous to turn it off to increase the speed of your computer. Alternatively, you can toggle the grid on and off to redraw the screen. This removes any blips displayed when you create geometry. You can turn the grid on and off using any of the following methods:

- On the status bar, double-click **grid.**
- Press the F7 key.
- Press Ctrl G.
- Type **grid** at the `Command:` prompt and then type **on** or **off.**
- Access the Drawing Aids dialog box by choosing Options/Drawing Aids. Select or deselect the On check box under Grid to turn the grid on or off.

Setting the Aspect Ratio The Aspect option at the grid prompt line enables you to set different values for horizontal and vertical spacing. For example, if you want to set the horizontal grid spacing at .25 and the vertical grid spacing at 1 while in the standard drawing editor, enter the following:

```
Command: grid
Grid Spacing(x) or ON/OFF/Snap/Aspect<Current Value>: A
Horizontal Spacing(X)<Current Value>: .25
Vertical Spacing(X)<Current Value>: 1
```

Setting this aspect ratio provides the dot spacing shown in Figure 2.11. You can also set the aspect ratio by entering the appropriate values for the X and Y spacing in the Drawing Aids dialog box.

Selecting the Grid Style By invoking the Aspect option of the grid, you can display different horizontal and vertical spacing. The grid can also be rotated and aligned to geometry, and set up to define an isometric grid. To change the grid style, you must change the Snap settings.

Using a grid does not ensure accurate point selection, but instead enables you to estimate distances quickly. The grid provides only a frame of reference by which you can estimate distances in the drawing. For you to accurately pick a grid point, the grid must

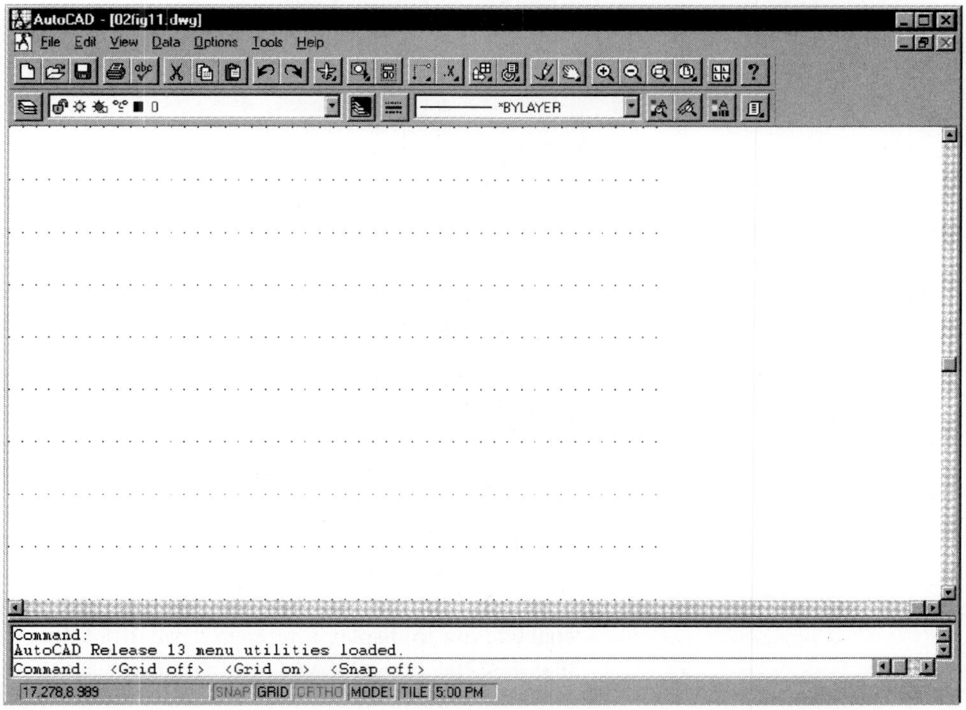

Figure 2.11
The grid can act as a drawing aid. Note the greater spacing in the vertical direction invoked with the Aspect option, as compared with Figure 2.10.

be used with another command called **snap**. The **snap** command causes the crosshairs to snap at specific intervals. If the snap spacing is set to the grid spacing, you can accurately pick a grid point. Snap is discussed later in this unit in the section "Using Snap." Grid points by themselves, however, are useful only as a visual estimating mechanism.

Tutorial 2.4: Setting the Grid

Continuing with the roof plan project, in this tutorial you will learn how to set the grid spacing to 2′ for both the X and Y axis. Once the grid spacing is established, you will then turn on the grid using the dialog box as well as toggling the grid on and off using F7.

1. Select Options/Drawing Aids... from the pull-down menu. The Drawing Aids dialog box appears.
2. Define the grid increment by entering 2′ for the X Spacing and then pressing Tab. By pressing Tab, that value assigned in the X will be applied to the Y. Check the Grid On box to activate the grid.
3. Select OK in the Drawing Aids dialog box. You should now see the grid displayed in the drawing area (Figure 2.12).
4. Press F7 to toggle the grid off.
5. Press F7 again to toggle the grid back on.

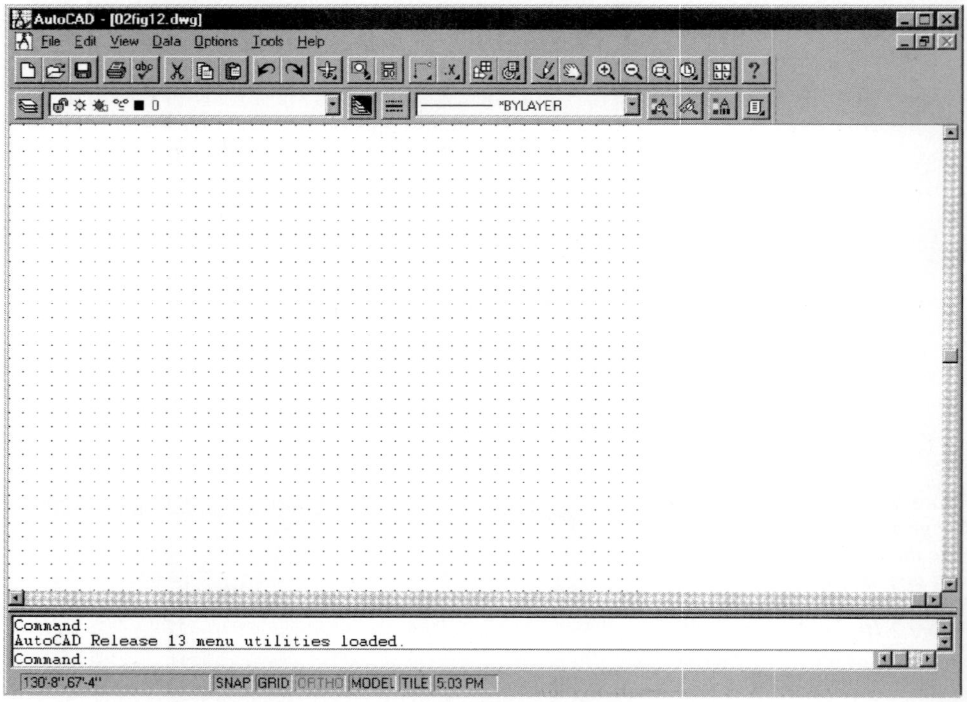

Figure 2.12
The drawing area after the limits have been set and the grid displayed.

For the Professional

You may have noticed that the grid does not extend all the way to the right of the drawing area. That area is outside the limits settings established in the preceding exercise. The grid is constrained within the limits established in an earlier tutorial.

Using Snap (SNAP)

In the earlier section, "Setting Display Format and Units (DDUNITS)," you learned how to display coordinates, distances, and angles to the precision selected. The **grid** command enabled you to display a reference pattern of dots on-screen. Even with the correct display and the grid activated, however, you can't easily move the crosshairs to an exact location on-screen.

One tool that AutoCAD uses to make creating precision drawing easier is the **snap** command. When the **snap** command is invoked, the cursor moves only in specific increments. For example, if Snap is set to 6″, you could quickly draw a line that is 1′-6″ long. You do this by picking a point on-screen and moving the crosshairs three snap increments, and then picking another point.

Setting the Snap Increment The **snap** command enables you to set the **snap** increment and control the **snap** in other ways. When you enter **snap** at the `Command:` prompt, the following information is displayed:

```
Command: snap
Snap Spacing or ON/OFF/Aspect/Rotate/Style <Current Value>:
```

At the **snap** command prompt, enter the **snap** spacing or increment. If the **snap** spacing is set to 1 foot, for example, the crosshairs move only in one-foot increments. Setting **snap** properly for the drawing you are working on can greatly increase your drawing speed and accuracy.

When beginning a new drawing, examine the overall distances and points involved in the drawing. Set **snap** to a distance that enables you to easily lay out the main features of the drawing. As you continue to work on the drawing, you can change the **snap** increment at any time to suit your current needs without affecting the drawing.

FOR THE PROFESSIONAL

It is important to understand that the **snap** increment and grid have no relationship. The **snap** spacing can be set to match the grid points, but the **snap** increment also can be set so that the crosshairs snap to points other than the grid. If the grid is displayed but **snap** is turned off, picking a grid point does not place the crosshairs exactly at that grid point's coordinate.

FOR THE PROFESSIONAL

If the **snap** increment does not seem to be affecting the movement of the crosshairs, check the **snap** setting. If **snap** is turned on and the **snap** increment is set too small, the incremental movement of the crosshairs may not be evident. To remedy this, increase the **snap** increment.

Toggling Snap At times you may want to turn **snap** off. If you need to erase an object that doesn't fall on the **snap** increment, for example, toggling the **snap** off makes it much easier to select it. You can turn the **snap** function on and off with one of these methods:

- On the status bar, double-click **snap.**
- Press the F9 key.
- Press Ctrl B.
- Type **snap** at the `Command:` prompt and then type **on** or **off.**
- Access the Drawing Aids dialog box by choosing Options/Drawing Aids... and then select or deselect the **on** check box under Snap to turn **snap** on or off.

Unlike the grid, the **snap** increment is invisible. Toggling **snap** on or off only forces the crosshairs to move to the specified increment.

Skill Builder

To set the grid at the same increment as the **snap**, use the Snap option after entering the **grid** command at the `Command:` prompt.

Setting the Aspect Ratio The normal application of the **snap** command sets equal horizontal and vertical spacing. The Aspect option at the Snap prompt line enables you to set different values for horizontal and vertical spacing. Below is an example:

```
Command: Snap
Snap Spacing or ON/OFF/Aspect/Rotate/Style <Current Value>: A
Horizontal Spacing <Current Value>: .75
Vertical Spacing <Current Value>: 1
```

You can also change the aspect ratio by entering different values for the X and Y spacing in the Drawing Aids dialog box.

Rotating the Snap

The normal pattern for **snap** is horizontal rows and vertical columns. Circumstances arise, however, when it would be beneficial to align **snap** and **grid** to an angle other than horizontal and vertical. Changing the angle of **snap** and **grid** can be beneficial when drawing an auxiliary view that is at an angle to another view in the drawing. When **snap** is rotated, you are given the option of setting a new base point. The base point is the pivot about which **snap** is rotated. The base point of the normal **snap** is 0,0, or where the lower-left corner of the limits are usually set. When drawing an auxiliary view, for example, you may want to set the base point at the location where the view begins. Once the base point is located, the rotation angle is set. The angle may range from 0–90° or 0–90°. You do this with the Rotate option.

For the Professional

An auxiliary view is any view other than the six standard orthographic views for an object—front, back, top, bottom, left, and right. An auxiliary view is usually created to show the true shape of an inclined plane or surface. To do so, the lines of sight must be perpendicular to the inclined plan. Figure 2.13 shows an example of an object with front and auxiliary view.

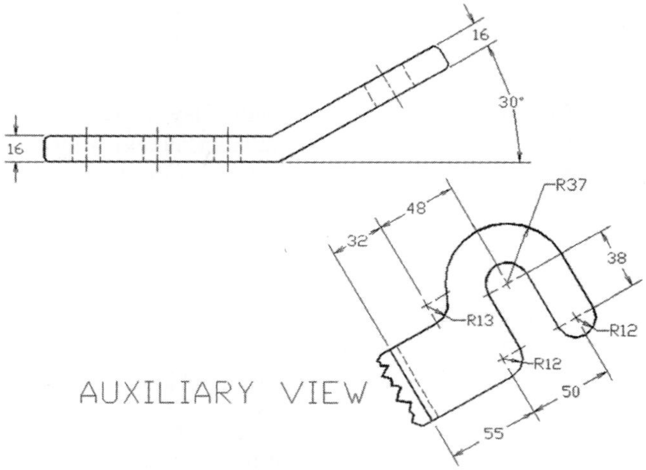

Figure 2.13
An auxiliary view is used to show the true shape of the inclined plan.

```
Command: snap
Snap Spacing or ON/OFF/Aspect/Rotate/Style <Current Value>: R
Base point <0,0>: Press Enter or pick a new base point.
Rotation Angle <0>: 30
```

The grid automatically rotates counterclockwise when a positive value is given and clockwise when a negative value is given. Figure 2.14 shows a rotated **snap** and grid used in the construction of an auxiliary view. Remember that **snap** is invisible. The grid is shown only for illustrative purposes. You can also rotate **snap** and enter a new base point in the Drawing Aids dialog box.

The **snap** Style option can set two different grid styles. The standard option is the one used up to this point. The **snap** Style also can be set to isometric, which aids in the creation of isometric drawings. Isometric drawings will be covered in more detail in Unit 16, "Creating Isometric Drawings."

An Isometric Snap can be established by using the following procedure.

```
Command: snap
Snap Spacing or ON/OFF/Aspect/Rotate/Style <Current Value>: s
Standard/Isometric <S>: I
```

snap will now be set so that you can create an isometric drawing. Isometric drawings are pictorial representations of an object. They are drawn so that all horizontal lines are created 30° off horizontal and all vertical lines are 90° off horizontal. The Isometric Snap allows you to easily create these 30° and 90° lines. An example of an isometric drawing is shown in Figure 2.15. Unit 16, "Creating Isometric Drawings," will discuss the methods used to create this isometric drawing.

USING THE COORDINATE DISPLAY (COORDS)

The coordinate display is located at the bottom of the screen in the status bar. By default, the coordinate display is on. AutoCAD dynamically displays the current location of the crosshairs in the current unit of measure. You can toggle the coordinate display on and off with one of these methods:

Figure 2.14
The **snap** *Rotate command rotates the grid to aid in the drawing of auxiliary views.*

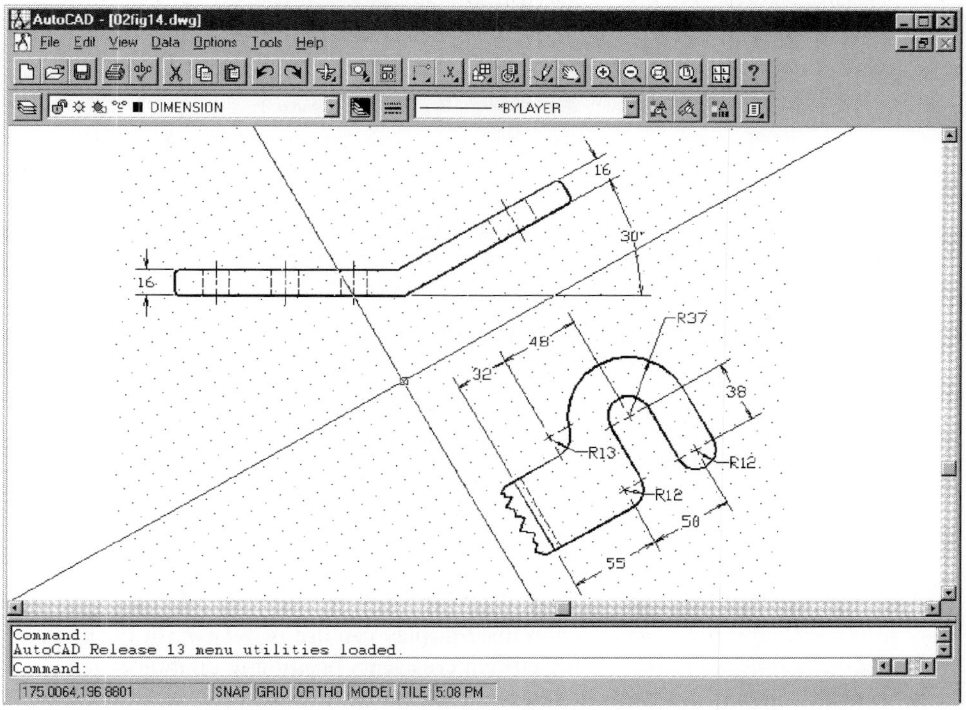

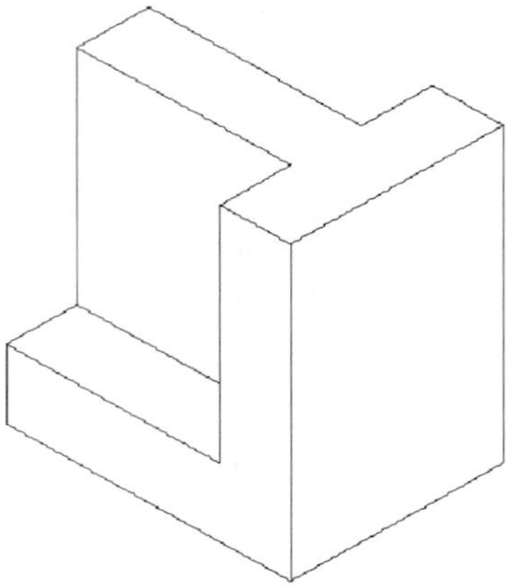

Figure 2.15
An example of an isometric drawing.

Tutorial 2.5: Setting the Snap

Continuing with the roof plan project, you are now ready to get set the Snap increment to assist in the exact placement of the starting and endpoints of lines that represent the roof framing plan. For the roof framing plan, it is beneficial to have Snap set to 1′. After setting the Snap increment, you will use the F9 function key to toggle Snap on and off.

1. Select Options/Drawing Aids... from the pull-down menu. The Drawing Aids dialog box appears.
2. Set the **snap** increment in the Drawing Aids dialog box to 1.
3. Select the **snap** check box to turn Snap on. The Drawing Aids dialog box should now look like Figure 2.16.
4. Select OK in the Drawing Aids dialog box. The dialog box will close.
5. Move the crosshairs. You will notice that it snaps at 1′ increments.
6. Press (F9 to toggle Snap off.
7. Move the crosshairs. You will notice that it no longer snaps at 1′ increments but flows smoothly across the drawing area.
8. Press F9 again to toggle Snap on.
9. Moving the crosshairs, you will also notice that the coordinate display changes in increments of 1′.

Figure 2.16
The Drawing Aids dialog box, with Snap spacing set to 1′0″ and Grid set to 2′0″.

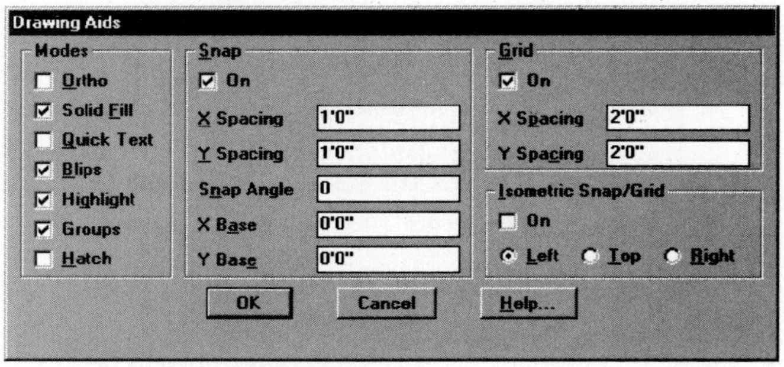

- On the status bar, double-click the coordinate display.
- Press the F6 key.
- Press Ctrl D.

When the unit of measure changes, the coordinate display changes accordingly. Figure 2.17 shows the coordinate display in the status bar.

Two modes are offered with the coordinate display. The default mode shows the absolute coordinate of the current crosshairs location. *Absolute* refers to the distance the crosshairs is from the origin, or 0,0. As you move the crosshairs, the coordinate display dynamically changes to show the current crosshairs location. The second mode that the coordinate display can use is relative. In the relative mode, the coordinate display shows the current crosshairs position in relation to the last point. The display is given in a relative polar mode.

Figure 2.17
The coordinate display in the status bar showing decimal units.

You can use the coordinate display as a display guide to aid in locating points and specific coordinates. When used in combination with the **snap** and **grid** commands, the coordinate display can speed up drawing time considerably.

Using Ortho Mode (ORTHO)

While **snap** is a useful tool for drawing horizontal and vertical lines, AutoCAD provides another tool to help you draw straight lines. With AutoCAD's **ortho mode,** you can draw lines that are perfectly horizontal or vertical. The advantage of using the **ortho mode** when drawing rectangular shapes is that all lines are guaranteed to be horizontal and vertical and all corners are guaranteed to be square.

For the Professional

The command *Ortho* comes from *orthogonal,* which means "at right angles." You may have heard the term *orthographic projection.* That projection system derives from the theory of right angles. When projecting points on a surface to another view, we often will construct either a vertical or horizontal construction line into the view that the point is to be projected. There are six primary orthographic views: front, back, top, bottom, left, and right. Figure 2.18 shows an object with the six primary orthographic views constructed.

You can toggle **ortho mode** on and off with these methods:

- On the status bar, double-click **ortho.**
- Press the F8 key.
- Press Ctrl O (the letter not the number).
- Type `ortho` at the `Command:` prompt.

When **ortho mode** is activated, it's impossible to draw a line at an angle using the crosshairs. When used in conjunction with the **snap** and **grid** commands, it makes geometry creation significantly faster and much more accurate.

Figure 2.18
Six orthographic views for an object.

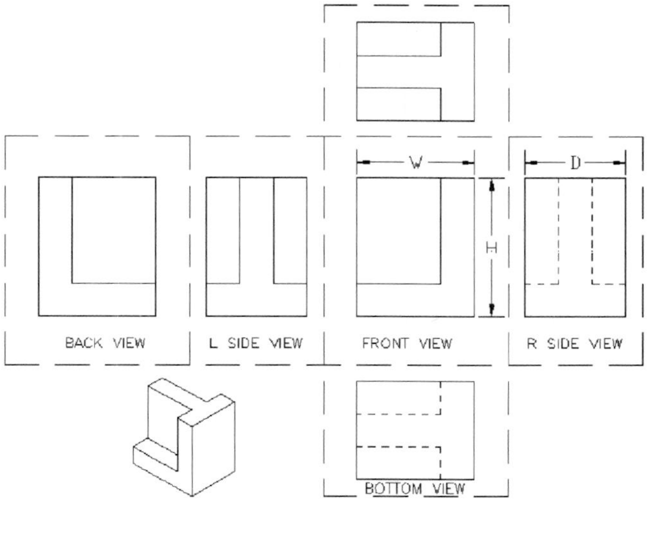

DRAWING LINES (LINE)

One of the most common geometric objects created in any form of drafting is the line. Lines are used in many areas of drafting—from object lines to construction lines. When drawing lines manually, we use a ruler to ensure that the line is straight from endpoint to endpoint. With AutoCAD, we no longer need to be concerned with whether the line is going to be straight. Everyone can draw a straight line using AutoCAD. Because lines are involved in almost every aspect of drafting, the line is the first AutoCAD object introduced.

Access the **line** command by choosing the Line icon from the Draw floating toolbar. Alternately, you could enter Line at the `Command:` prompt. The following command sequence is used for the **line** command:

Select the Line button on the Draw floating toolbar.

```
From point: Enter POINT 1
To point: Enter POINT 2
To point: ↵Enter
```

SKILL BUILDER

If the Draw toolbar is not displayed, you can access it by selecting Draw from the Tools/Toolbars/Draw.

SKILL BUILDER

If the Line icon is not displayed on the Draw toolbar, click and hold on the first button. A flyout menu will appear. Move the mouse down to the Line button and release the mouse button. The Line command will now be selected and will remain as the first button until another command in the flyout is selected.

SKILL BUILDER

You also can type the letter *l* at the `Command:` prompt as a shortcut to begin the Line command. These single letter commands are called hot keys.

DRAWING LINE SEGMENTS (LINE)

After you enter the Line command, you are prompted for two pieces of information. The first is the start point of the line; the second is the end point of the line. After you select the first point at the From point: prompt, AutoCAD responds with To point:, and you select the second point. When the second To point: prompt is given, you may stop adding lines by pressing ↵Enter. If you want to draw a series of connected lines, continue selecting as many additional points as you like. When you are drawing a series of lines, you are repeatedly prompted for the end point of the line. When finished, press ↵Enter or space bar to return to the `Command:` prompt. The following command sequence for drawing a series of lines is illustrated in Figure 2.19.

Select the Line button on the Draw floating toolbar.

```
From point: Enter POINT 1.
To point: Enter POINT 2.
To point: Enter POINT 3.
To point: Enter POINT 4.
To point: ↵Enter
```

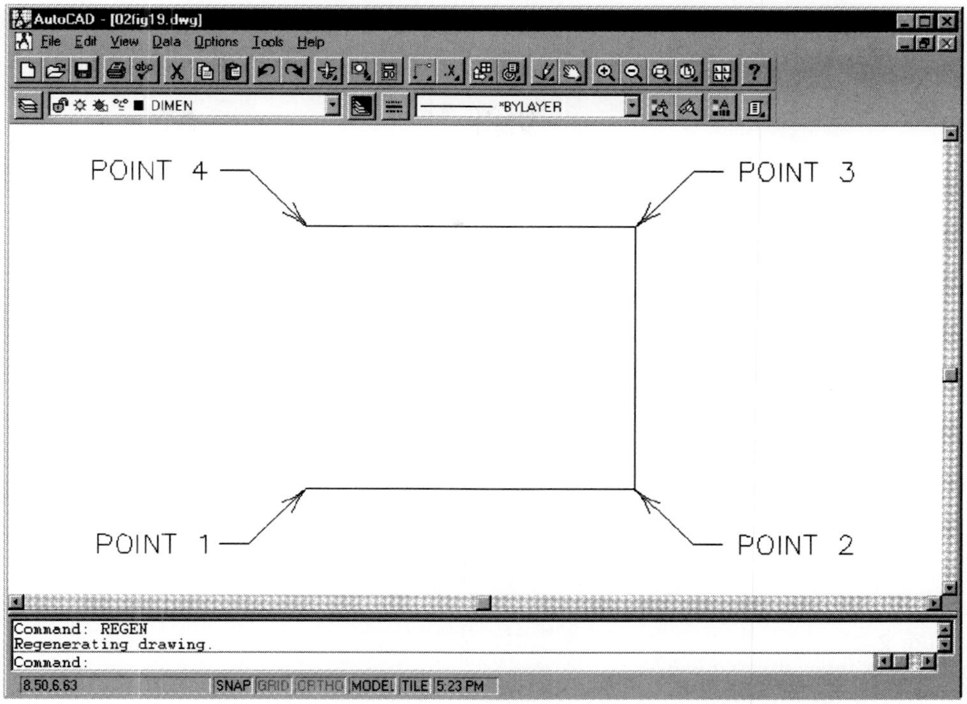

Figure 2.19
The **line** *command is used to draw a series of connected lines.*

For the Professional

Even if you are drawing a series of connected lines, each line remains a separate object.

Choosing the Line button enables you to draw one or more line segments, as described earlier. The From point: prompt is issued, and then To point: is automatically issued until you press either Enter or the space bar.

Using the Close and Undo Options

In many instances when you draw a polygon, the last line drawn ends at the beginning location of the polygon. The definition of a polygon is a series of lines that enclose an area. The Close option within the AutoCAD **line** command closes an open polygon. Close sets the To point: to the same value as the From point: in the group of line segments making up the polygon. The Close option also ends the **line** command. To use this option, type *c* or *close* at the To point: prompt. Here is the command sequence for the Close option, as illustrated in Figure 2.20:

Select the Line button from the Draw floating toolbar.

```
From point: Enter POINT 1.
To point: Enter POINT 2.
To point: Enter POINT 3.
To point: c
```

If you make an error in selecting a point location for a line, the Undo option removes the last point picked and the associated line segment. Because you are still in the **line** command, you can re-select the point. Undo can be used after picking any To point: if you don't like the last line segment drawn. It is possible to undo all the way back to the beginning of the **line** command. You can also use Undo after picking the first From point: if you don't like the start point for the line. Once you are back to the `Command:` prompt, the U command will remove all the lines drawn by the **line** command.

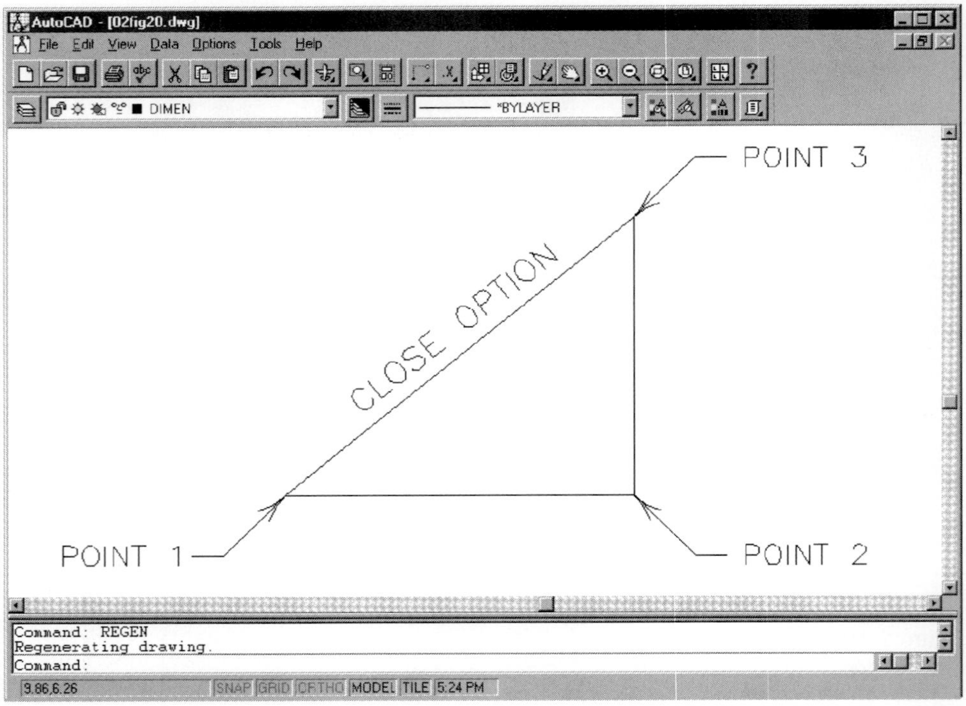

Figure 2.20
The Close option draws a line back to the From point: of the polygon.

Drawing Continued Line Segments

The **line** command also allows you to continue a line from the last point picked. If you press the space bar or Enter at the From point: prompt, the line segment continues from the last point picked. This option allows you to create adjoining line segments without drawing all the segments with one line.

Cleaning Up the Display (REDRAW)

When you use such options as Undo within the **line** command, blips may still appear on the display where points were picked. If the grid was activated when you used the Undo option, the section of the grid under the line may also appear missing. Issuing the **redraw** command when the screen has become filled with blips and missing objects cleans up the computer display. **redraw** restores the image on-screen and removes the blips and any missing parts of the grid. Use the **redraw** command with one of these methods:

- Enter **redraw** or **R** at the `Command:` prompt.
- Choose View/Redraw View.

You can issue the **redraw** command at any time when the `Command:` prompt is displayed. To redraw the screen in the middle of a command, precede **redraw** or **R** with an apostrophe ('). The **redraw** command is transparent, which means that you can use it while another command is active. The View/Redraw View pull-down selection will also invoke a transparent redraw command. Other transparent commands wil be introduced in later units.

Skill Builder

To redraw the screen quickly, press F7 twice or double-click **grid** in the status bar twice. This toggles the grid on or off, which causes the screen to redraw. The grid must be set to a value that is visible on-screen.

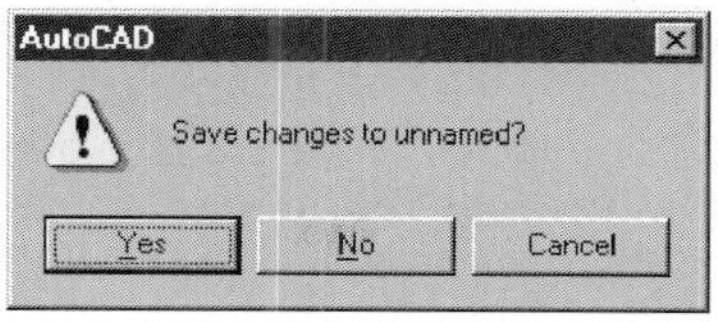

Figure 2.21
The AutoCAD dialog box enables you either to save or discard any changes you made to the drawing.

Quitting AutoCAD

To complete your AutoCAD drawing session, type *end* at the `Command:` prompt. This exits the drawing editor, saves your drawing, and returns you to Program Manager. Other options for ending your drawing session are:

- Type **quit** at the `Command:` prompt.
- Choose File/Exit.
- Select the close button on the title bar.

If either of these commands is entered before you have saved your work, AutoCAD gives you a chance to save or discard your changes. The AutoCAD dialog box is displayed, as shown in Figure 2.21.

You also can begin a new drawing or open an existing drawing without having to exit AutoCAD. To begin a new drawing while in the drawing editor, choose File/New. If this is done before you have saved your work, the AutoCAD dialog box will appear on-screen. To open an existing drawing while in the drawing editor, choose Open from the File pull-down menu. You will again be prompted with the AutoCAD dialog box if you have not saved your work.

Pressing Enter when the AutoCAD dialog box is displayed activates the highlighted Yes button. This saves the drawing as it was previously named. If the drawing has not been named, the Save Drawing As dialog box is displayed. You also can choose No if you don't want to save any changes made to the drawing since the previous save was issued. Choose Cancel if you decide that you don't want to quit and want to return to the drawing editor.

Tutorial 2.6: Using the Line Command to Create the Roof Plan

After setting the units, limits, Grid, and Snap as shown in the previous sections, you are ready to create the roof plan, as shown in Figure 2.22.

In this tutorial, you first draw the perimeter of the roof plan as shown in Figure 2.23. You begin by using the Line command. Next, you will move the crosshairs and select locations at points A, B, C, D, and back to A. You will be moving in a counterclockwise direction. Before you begin, ensure that the Snap (F9), Ortho (F8), and Coordinate (F6) display options are toggled on. Snap will allow you to select specific locations in the increments established, making it possible to choose exactly the required location. The Ortho option will constrain your lines to be vertical and horizontal only. When you are asked to create diagonal lines, ensure that Ortho is off.

If you make a mistake in selecting a point location as you work on this tutorial, type *u* at the To point: prompt. This removes the last line segment, enabling you to pick another point location and continue.

To draw the roof perimeter, follow these steps:

1. Check to make sure the Snap and Grid are on and set properly. This can be done with the Drawing Aids dialog box. To invoke the Drawing Aids dialog box, select Drawing Aids from the Options pull-down menu. Make sure the Snap and Grid check boxes are on, the Snap spacing is set to 0′4″ increments, and Grid is set to 2′0″ increments.
2. Ensure that the Ortho option is toggled on. This can be done by checking the status bar at the bottom of the screen to see if Ortho is bold. If it is not, double-click in the **ortho** box or press F8.
3. Next, ensure that the coordinate display is turned on. Check the status bar for **coords.** If it is bold, the coordinates are turned on. If it is not bold, double-click in the **coords** box or press F6.
4. Select the Line button from the Draw floating toolbar.
5. `To point:` Move the crosshairs to point A. When the Coordinate display in the status bar displays the coordinates 6′-0″,2′-0″, select that location for point A.
6. `To point:` Move your crosshairs toward point B. Notice that because Ortho has been turned on, the line being created is forced to be horizontal and only the X coordinate value in the status bar is changing. When the Coordinate display in the status bar indicates the coordinates 82′-0″,2′-0″, select that location for point B.
7. `To point:` Move your crosshairs toward point C. The line is now forced to be vertical and only the Y coordinate value is changing. When the Coordinate display in

the status bar indicates the coordinates 82′-0″,66′-0″, select that location for point C.

8. To point: Move your crosshairs to point D. When the Coordinate display in the status bar indicates the coordinates 6′-0″,66′-0″, select that location for point D.
9. To point: c Enter C to connect point D to point A, closing the perimeter of the roof plan. The Close option automatically connects point D to point A and ends the line command.

Next, create the ridge lines for the roof plan (refer to Figure 2.22). Notice that the ridge lines are composed not only of vertical and horizontal lines, but also of diagonal lines. Begin by drawing the vertical and horizontal lines as shown in Figure 2.24. First draw the vertical line from point E to point F.

1. To draw the vertical and horizontal lines, follow these steps:
2. Select the Line button from the Draw floating toolbar.
3. `From point:` Move your crosshairs to point E. Press F6 until the coordinate display in the status bar indicates 44′-0″-66′-0″. Select that location for point E.
4. `To point:` Move your crosshairs to point F. The coordinate display in the status bar should indicate the coordinates 44′-0″,2′-0″. Select that location for point F.
5. `To point:` Enter This exits the command and returns you to the Command: prompt.
6. Select the Line button from the Draw floating toolbar.
7. `From point:` Move your crosshairs to point G. The coordinate display in the status bar should indicate the coordinates 6′-0″,34′-0″. Select that location for point G.
8. `To point:` Move your crosshairs to point H. The coordinate display in the status bar should indicate the coordinates 82′-0″,34′-0″. Select that location for point H.
9. `To point:` Enter This exits the command and returns you to the Command: prompt.

To finish the roof plan, you must add the diagonal ridge lines as shown in Figure 2.25. First draw the diagonal line from point J to point K. Because these lines are diagonal, it is important that the Ortho option be turned off.

To draw the diagonal lines, follow these steps:

Turn Ortho off by pressing the F8 key once or double-clicking the word **`ortho`** on the status bar. The **`ortho`** button on the status bar should no longer be bold, indicating Ortho is turned off.

Select the Line button from the Draw floating toolbar.

- `From point:` Move your crosshairs to point J. The Coordinate display in the status bar should indicate the coordinates 24′-8″,66′-0″. Select that location for point J.
- `To point:` Move your crosshairs to point K. The Coordinate display in the status bar should indicate the coordinates 63′-4″,2′-0″. Select that location for point K.
- `To point:` Enter This exits the command and returns you to the Command: prompt.

Select the Line button from the Draw floating toolbar.

- `From point:` Move your crosshairs to point L. The Coordinate display in the status bar should indicate the coordinates 63′-4″,66′-0″. Select that location for point L.
- `To point:` Move your crosshairs to point m. The Coordinate display in the status bar should indicate the coordinates 24′-8″,2′-0″. Select that location for point M.
- `To point:` Enter This exits the command and returns you to the `Command:` prompt.

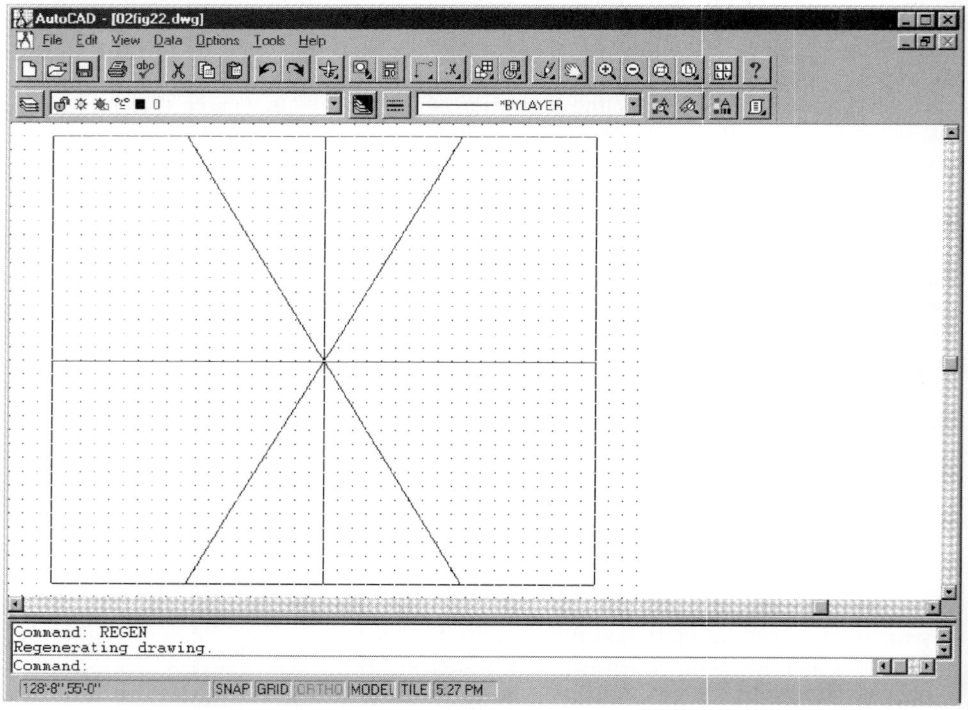

Figure 2.22
The completed roof plan.

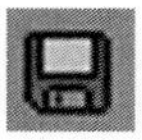

Save your drawing by selecting the Save button from the Standard toolbar. Save the drawing as **roof-planplan.dwg** in the directory of your choosing. If you are unsure where to save your drawing, consult with your instructor.

Congratulations! You have created your first AutoCAD drawing. If you are finished drawing for now and want to leave the drawing editor, type **end** or **quit** at the Command: prompt. Remember, **end** will save the drawing and exit AutoCAD and **quit** will exit AutoCAD and prompt you to save or discard your changes.

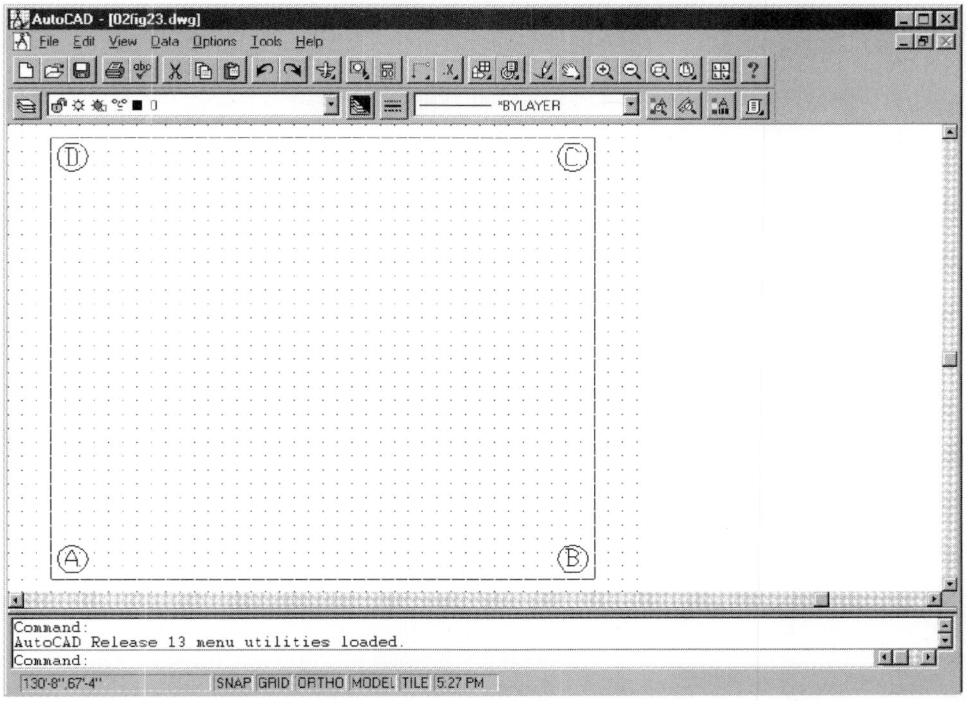

Figure 2.23
Completing the roof plan perimeter.

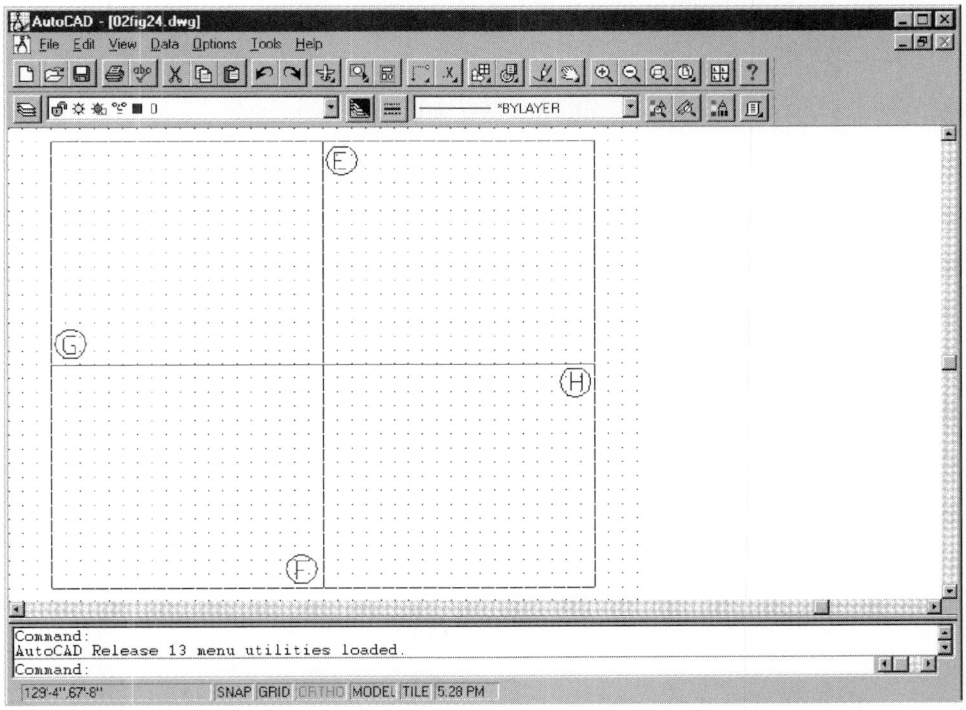

Figure 2.24
Drawing the vertical and horizontal lines for the roof plan.

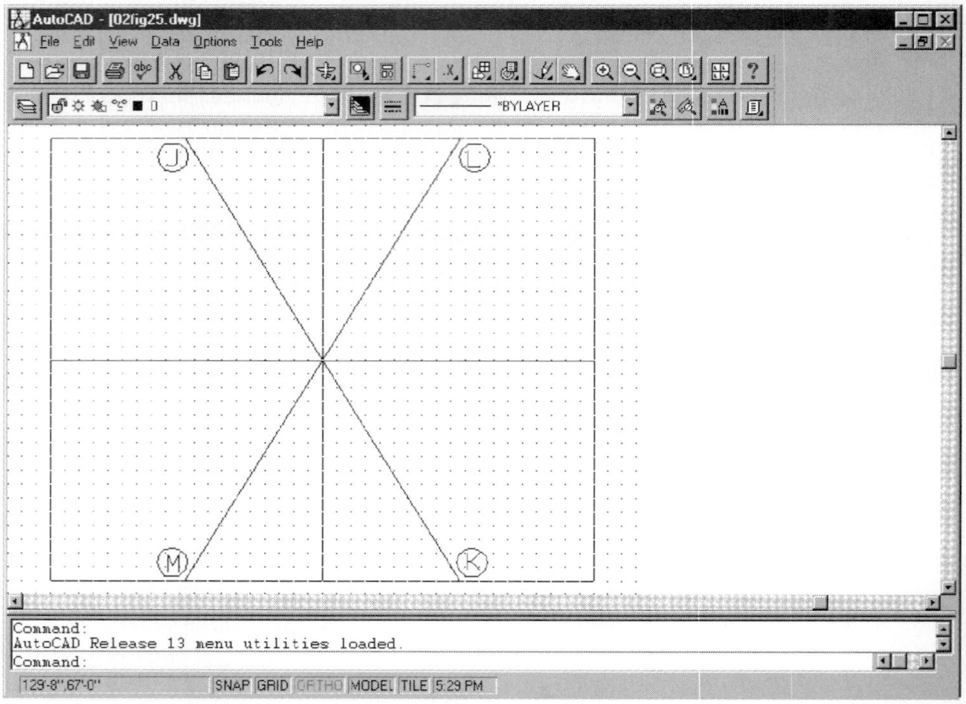

Figure 2.25
Drawing the diagonal ridge lines to complete the tutorial.

UNDERSTANDING OBJECTS

At this point we will take a break from drawing and discuss objects. We mentioned earlier that a line was an object. Before we continue creating these objects, it would be good to know the definition of an object.

WHAT IS AN OBJECT?

Everything that you create in AutoCAD is a distinct object. Later, as you learn to create other geometry such as circles, arcs, dimensions and text, you will be creating new objects. You will also create new non-graphic objects such as layers, linetypes, blocks, and dimension styles. As you progress in your AutoCAD training, you will learn how to create, erase, and rename many types of objects.

UNDERSTANDING THE DRAWING DATABASE

AutoCAD stores all objects in a drawing database. This database is stored in the saved AutoCAD file. A database is a grouping of information about objects by type. Using this database format, it is easy to modify and edit the drawing. For instance, in AutoCAD a line is defined by its starting point coordinates and its ending coordinates. This information is stored in the drawing database. With this information you can tell how long the line is and the angle of the line off horizontal. Every object you create is added to the database. When you use the **undo** command, you erase the previous entry in the database. In more advanced applications, the database can be used to determine the area of a floor plan or the circumference of a circle. The following is a listing for a drawing of a circle and a line. All of the information displayed is created by reviewing the drawing database.

```
Command: list
Select objects: Other corner: 2 found
```

```
Select objects:
          LINE      Layer: 0
                    Space: Model space
          Handle = 29
     from point, X= 12.1918 Y=  4.7647 Z=  0.0000
       to point, X=  6.3970 Y=  8.9928 Z=  0.0000
      Length =  7.1733, Angle in XY Plane =  144
     Delta X = -5.7948, Delta Y = 4.2281, Delta Z = 0.0000
          CIRCLE    Layer: 0
                    Space: Model space
          Handle = 28
        center point, X=  9.1967 Y=  7.0089 Z=  0.0000
        radius   2.1760
circumference   13.6723
          area   14.8756
```

As you can see, the drawing database can provide us with much information. Notice that a listing of the circle yields the radius, circumference, and the area.

SUMMARY

Before beginning any actual geometry creation, you must decide the following about the drawing:

- The name and storage location of the drawing
- The units the drawing will use
- The paper size on which the drawing will be output

Once you make these decisions, you can begin a new drawing and enter the path and name. Then you can set the units. Finally, you can set the limits based on the paper size and the size of the drawing. Remember to include extra space in the actual size of the drawing to account for dimensions, notes, border, and title block.

After you have made these preliminary decisions, you can set up the AutoCAD drafting tools. Use the Drawing Aids dialog box to set Snap, Grid, and Ortho. As you begin drawing, it's very important to save your work often. Once your drawing is setup, you may now create basic geometry such as lines. These lines are called *objects.* All objects are stored in the drawing database. In the next unit you will learn additional methods of entering point locations into the drawing other than using the Snap, Grid, and Coordinates.

REVIEW

1. Explain the use of limits and how they relate to paper size.
2. List the five types of units that are available in AutoCAD. What professions would use these file types?
3. What is the difference between **grid** and **snap**? How do they compliment each other?
4. Explain **ortho** mode and its operation.
5. List the function keys needed to toggle the following functions: **grid, snap, coords,** and **ortho**.
6. What settings can be made in the Drawing Aids dialog box?
7. Describe the two methods used to specify coordinates on the drawing area.
8. What two pieces of information are necessary to create a line?
9. Define what objects are and their importance to AutoCAD.
10. Explain the benefits of an AutoCAD drawing database.

EXERCISE 2

In this assignment you will create a scaled drawing of the front and side views of an antique wooden filing cabinet. Before beginning the drawing you will be required to properly set up the drawing file. Once the drawing is set up, refer to Figure 2.26. You should be able to determine the length of lines and location of lines based on the grid that is displayed.

1. Set units to decimal with a precision of 0.000.
2. Set the lower-left limits to 0,0 and the upper-right limits to 11.5,8. Remember that the lower-left limits default is 0,0. Consider using the **limmax** system variable instead of the **limits** command to save time.
   Steps 3–6 can be completed using the Drawing Modes Dialog box (DDRMODES).
3. Set **grid** to .25.
4. Set **snap** to .125.
5. Set **blipmode** to **Off**.
6. Set **ortho** mode to **on**.
7. Using Figure 2.26 as a guide, create the filing cabinet drawing using the **line** command. Remember that the **undo** and **close** options of the **line** command are available.
8. Save the drawing with the file name *filing cabinet* to a device of your choosing or to one selected by your instructor. Be sure to use the **qsave** command frequently!
9. Once completed, you may be asked either to plot the drawing (see Unit 3, "Viewing and Plotting a Drawing") or turn in the drawing electronically (on disk or through a computer network). Your instructor will provide further details.

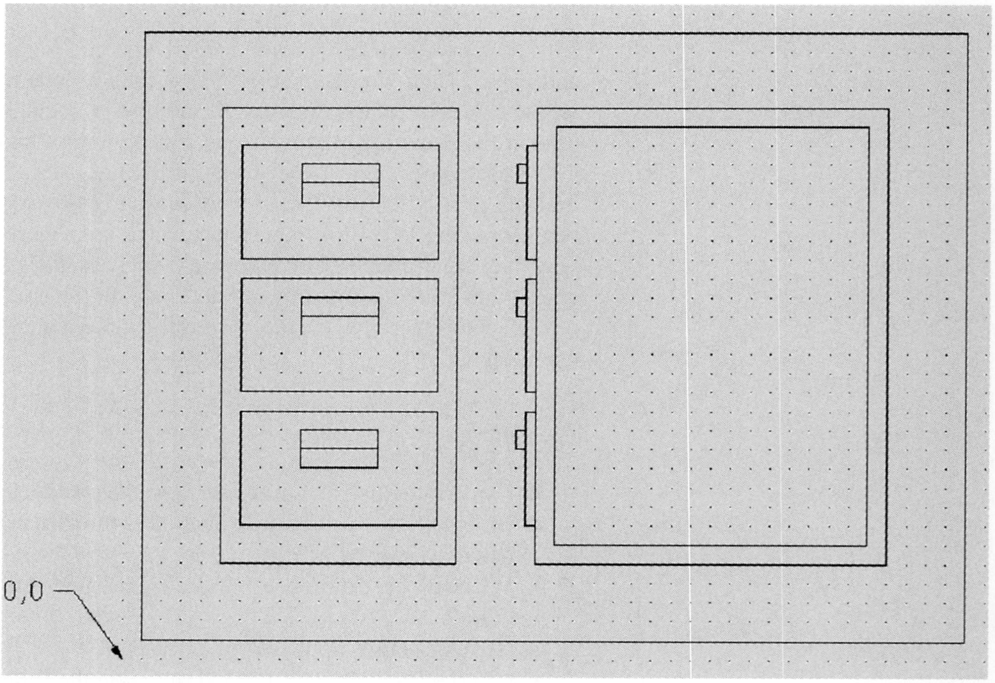

Figure 2.26
Use this drawing to assist in the creation of the filing cabinet drawing.

UNIT

3

Viewing and Plotting a Drawing

OVERVIEW

As you learn how to create drawings, you will find that there are times when you want to magnify and view certain details. While viewing the complete floor plan for an office complex, for example, you will not be able to see details concerning bathroom fixtures or electrical outlets. You need a way to "zoom in on" these areas. View commands will allow you to see those details.

It is also important that you be able to share your drawing files with others. Generally, it is not convenient to carry a computer around with you to show your drawings to instructors, family, or clients. You need a way to produce hard copy output of your files. While storing everything electronically seems like a great idea, there are still many people who prefer or require that drawings be plotted on paper.

OBJECTIVES

- Understand how AutoCAD drawings are displayed on-screen.
- Use basic View commands to assist in creating drawings.
- Understand the difference between View commands and the Aerial View window.
- Create and save various views of drawings for later use.
- Plot drawings using plot options and parameters.

INTRODUCTION

The best solution for working with drawings that have a high level of detail is to let AutoCAD increase or decrease the magnification of the drawing. AutoCAD allows you to view enlarged portions of the drawing so you can see all the details. When you have a section of the drawing magnified on-screen, you see only that section magnified.

In the creation of drawings, you often can see artifacts left by AutoCAD, such as blips, small dots on the screen, and incomplete lines. You may think that these lines were erased inadvertently. Before you begin to construct missing lines or recreate new lines, try the **regen** or **redraw** commands. You may find that your drawing is not in as bad of shape as you thought. In this unit, you're shown how these two commands are the most common and useful commands in the viewing of a drawing.

The **zoom** command allows you to enlarge or reduce the amount of the drawing displayed on-screen. You can move the portion of the enlarged drawing back and forth or up and down with the **pan** command. In the Windows version of AutoCAD, the **dsviewer** command invokes an Aerial View window that allows you to see the entire drawing in a separate window. When using **dsviewer,** you can locate the part of the drawing you want to view and move to it using the **zoom** and **pan** functions.

The **view** command allows you to create, name, and save specific views of a drawing. When you have to do additional drawing or editing operations in the area of a drawing defined by a saved view, you can quickly and easily recall the view.

Displaying a large drawing on-screen can be a tedious process. It takes time to access the Open menu, find the correct file, and load the drawing from the disk. If you need to zoom in on a specific part of the drawing, the process slows down even more. Fortunately, AutoCAD has a method to display a large drawing quickly and efficiently.

In this unit you will learn how to use AutoCAD's display commands. By viewing your drawing in different ways, AutoCAD gives you the ability to create drawings with greater speed, ease, and accuracy than is possible in manual drafting.

OUTLINE

Understanding the Display
Understanding the Virtual Screen
Using Zoom to Control the Display
Tutorial 3.1: Using the Zoom All Command
Tutorial 3.2: Using the Zoom Center Command
Tutorial 3.3: Using the Zoom Dynamic Command
Tutorial 3.4: Using the Zoom Extents Command
Tutorial 3.5: Using the Zoom Left Command
Tutorial 3.6: Using the Zoom Previous Command
Tutorial 3.7: Using the Zoom Vmax Command
Tutorial 3.8: Using the Zoom Window Command
Tutorial 3.9: Using the Zoom Scale Command
Tutorial 3.10: Panning a Drawing
Using the Aerial View Window
Tutorial 3.11: Using the Aerial View Window
Tutorial 3.12: Creating and Saving Views
Introduction to Plotting
Tutorial 3.13: Using the Plot Dialog Box to Determine Page Limits
Tutorial 3.14: Plotting a Drawing
Summary
Review
Exercises

UNDERSTANDING THE DISPLAY

AutoCAD uses a drawing database to store and display geometry in a drawing. This drawing database gives useful information about the geometry, such as endpoints, midpoints, and center points. The advantage of using a database is that it enables you to find points relative to other geometric objects, such as intersections and tangent points.

When you create a drawing in AutoCAD, you're really building a database list of the objects in the drawing rather than originating the drawing on-screen. The drawing display serves as a representation of the drawing database only. For final output, the hard copy device will provide more resolution or detail than the monitor.

UNDERSTANDING THE VIRTUAL SCREEN

When you are working on a drawing, AutoCAD maintains the drawing information in more than one format. One format uses the vector graphics information and stores the information in a database by using precise floating-point values. This format ensures high precision. The drawback, however, is that calculations involving floating-point numbers take longer than those involving integers.

Besides the vector graphics database, AutoCAD maintains information needed for the screen display. The screen display uses integer values to locate screen coordinates. Each coordinate on-screen is called a pixel. A pixel is a single point of light on-screen; each pixel is defined separately. The information required to display the pixel are the coordinates of the pixel and its color.

When AutoCAD displays an object on-screen, it converts the floating-point database values to the appropriate integer screen coordinates. Because it takes a great deal of time to convert the coordinates from the floating-point database to the screen pixel integer coordinates, AutoCAD maintains a virtual screen between your drawing and the screen.

When the drawing view is changed, AutoCAD refreshes the screen; it reads the virtual screen and changes the physical screen accordingly. The translation from the virtual screen data to the physical screen data is very fast. AutoCAD quickly recalculates changes in the physical screen from the virtual screen.

Refreshing the screen forces AutoCAD to recopy the current drawing area from the virtual screen to the physical screen. Certain display commands, such as **zoom** and **pan,** automatically refresh the screen.

For the Professional

Many video card and software developers market display drivers that enhance or alter the display. The drivers usually offer additional display-related commands and options. The display drivers usually offer trade-offs between display speed, the regularity of display refreshing, memory usage, and other display-related items. This unit discusses the display features that come with AutoCAD. Users running a third-party display list driver need to read this chapter and consult their driver's documentation.

Refreshing the Screen (Redraw)

As you continue working on a drawing, the physical screen can become corrupted or "dirty." This can be caused by adding, erasing, or modifying objects. Parts of objects can disappear when an overlapping object is removed. Small crosses, or blips, may appear on the display where points were picked. Use any of the following commands to clean up the screen after editing:

Skill Builder

A quick way to redraw the screen is to press F7. This toggles the grid on and off, causing a redraw in the process. The grid spacing must be set to a value you can see for this to work.

- Click the Redraw button on the Standard toolbar.
- Choose View/Redraw View pull-down menu.
- Enter **`redraw`** at the `Command:` prompt.

For the Professional

You can issue **redraw** as a transparent command by preceding it with an apostrophe ('). Because a transparent command can be used when another command is active, you can clean up the screen whenever you want—even in the middle of another command.

Regenerating the Screen (Regen)

When you change a drawing, AutoCAD must update both the drawing database and the virtual screen so that they match one another. However, not every change to the drawing database necessitates a regeneration. For example, when you draw a line, the drawing database, virtual display, and physical screen are updated; when you edit a line, the drawing database and virtual display are updated, but the physical screen must be refreshed with the **redraw** command. A complete regeneration is not required. When a regeneration occurs, the floating-point database values are converted to the appropriate integer—which updates the screen coordinates—and the entire drawing database is read. This can be a time-consuming process, depending on the configuration of the computer and the size of the drawing.

Several commands described in this chapter move, magnify, or shrink the image on-screen. Occasionally, these operations require that AutoCAD regenerate the entire drawing, recompiling the screen coordinates for all objects. If the display is moved or zoomed to the point where the virtual screen no longer has the necessary information to create the physical screen, then you get a regeneration. In a large drawing, this can take a long time. AutoCAD displays the message Regenerating drawing... whenever a regeneration is performed.

You can force AutoCAD to regenerate the drawing by entering Regen at the `Command:` prompt. The advantage of using **regen** is that the regenerated image is the most accurate image AutoCAD can produce. The disadvantage of using **regen** is the time it takes to regenerate.

SKILL BUILDER

Layers that are **frozen** are not included when a drawing regeneration is done; layers that are turned **off** are. When you work with large drawings, you can freeze layers that are not needed. You avoid unnecessary drawing generations and help speed up your drawing time.

Regenerating the Drawing Automatically (RegenAuto)

Certain commands cause AutoCAD to regenerate the drawing automatically. To control the regeneration and help speed up the drawing process, you can ask AutoCAD to warn you before it regenerates the screen. To access the **regenauto** command enter **regenauto** at the `Command:` prompt.

At the ON/OFF <ON>: prompt that appears, enter **off.** AutoCAD now asks permission before regenerating the drawing:

```
About to regen – proceed?<Y>
```

Setting Display Options (ViewRes)

The **viewres** (**view resolution**) command controls drawing regeneration and the appearance of curves in the drawing. The speed of Zoom and Regeneration are controlled in two ways. First, fast zooms can be turned on or off. *Fast zoom* means that AutoCAD maintains a large virtual screen so that most operations can be done at Redraw (fast) speed. If fast zooms are turned off, all Pan and Zoom operations cause a Regen. By default, the fast zoom option is turned on.

Second, **viewres** determines how fine to generate curves. When circles or arcs are small, AutoCAD uses a few straight vectors to fool your eyes into seeing a smooth curve. When circles and arcs are large, AutoCAD needs more vectors to make a smooth arc. The **viewres** circle zoom percent tells AutoCAD how smooth you want your circles and arcs to be. The higher the percentage, the more vectors AutoCAD uses to display arcs and circles. **viewres** affects only the AutoCAD screen; the database is used to plot the drawing, therefore all arcs and circles are plotted as actual curves.

The following command sequence is used to control **viewres** resolutions:

```
Command: viewres
Do you want fast zooms? <Y>:
```

This is the default setting and will enable transparent display commands, so press [Enter].

```
Enter circle zoom percent (1-20000) <100>:
```

The higher the number, the smoother the arcs and circles will appear. As the number increases, regeneration will take longer.

You may need a regular regeneration or a regeneration with a higher zoom percent to see the information you need for picking points on curves. For example, if a circle is drawn with a few big lines, you may have a hard time finding a quadrant or tangent point. Sometimes a curve may intersect with another object but not show the contact on the display if a regen is necessary or the **viewres** zoom percent is set low. Use **regen** to display the arc or circle as a curve.

USING ZOOM TO CONTROL THE DISPLAY

One of the most important functions of AutoCAD is to provide a means to let you see your drawing more clearly. The **zoom** command lets you magnify your drawing to do detailed work. You access the **zoom** command in one of the following ways:

- Select the **zoom** flyout from the Standard toolbar and select the Zoom option needed.
- Choose View/Zoom. A cascading submenu appears, listing the different Zoom options (see Figure 3.1).
- Enter `zoom` at the `Command:` prompt. The following options are then displayed:

```
All/Center/Dynamic/Extents/Left/Previous/Vmax/Window/<Scale(X/XP)>:
```

For the Professional

You can also enter **Z** at the `Command:` prompt as a shortcut to begin the **zoom** command. Likewise, the **zoom** command options each have a capitalized letter that indicates the shortcut you can enter for the option. For example, you can enter **Z** for the **zoom** command and **A** for the All option.

Skill Builder

You can issue **zoom** transparently ('Z) as long as a regen is not required.

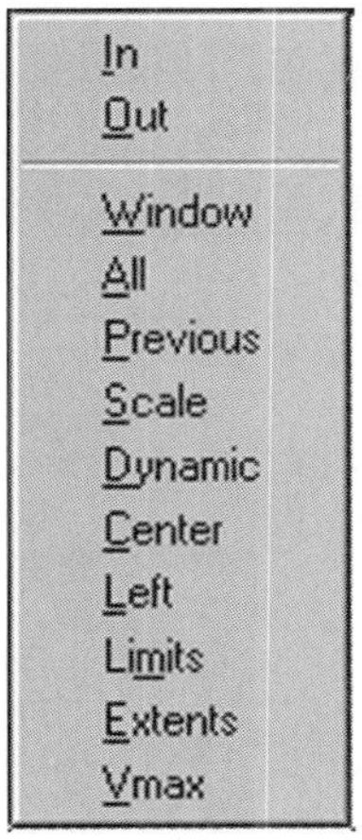

Figure 3.1
The Zoom cascading submenu.

ZOOM ALL

The **zoom all** option displays the drawing to its limits or extents, whichever is greater. The size of the drawing's limits is determined by the **limits** command, discussed in Unit 2, "Creating Your First Drawing." If you have geometry outside the limits, **zoom all** zooms beyond the limits to display everything in the drawing file (this is called the drawings extents). **Zoom all** always regenerates the drawing.

TUTORIAL 3.1: USING THE ZOOM ALL COMMAND

In this tutorial, you use the **zoom all** command to view all items found in the apartment floor plan shown in Figure 3.2. This apartment floor plan is used for all tutorials in this chapter and each tutorial continues from the one before it. To view the items, follow these steps:

1.  Select **open** from the Standard toolbar. If prompted by the AutoCAD Save Changes dialog box, select the appropriate response. The Open Drawing dialog box appears.
2. Load the 3fig02.dwg file. After the file is loaded, your screen should resemble Figure 3.2.
3.  Choose **zoom all** from the Standard toolbar Zoom flyout menu.
4. The drawing extends to the edges of the drawing area, as shown in Figure 3.3. **zoom all** always makes full use of the drawing area to display the drawing.

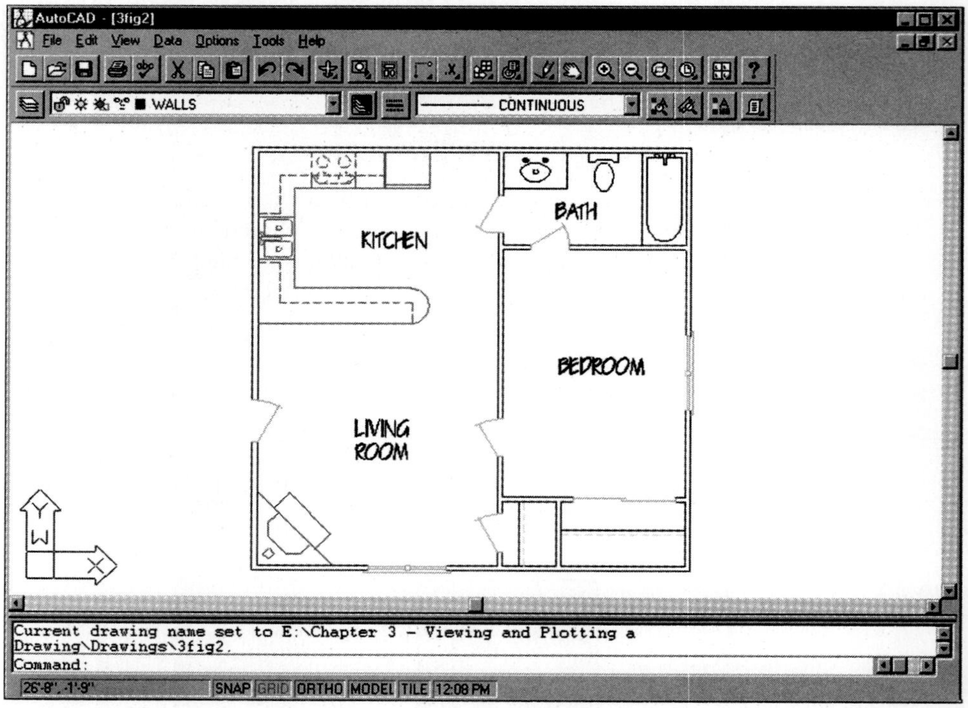

Figure 3.2
The apartment floor plan used for all tutorials in this unit.

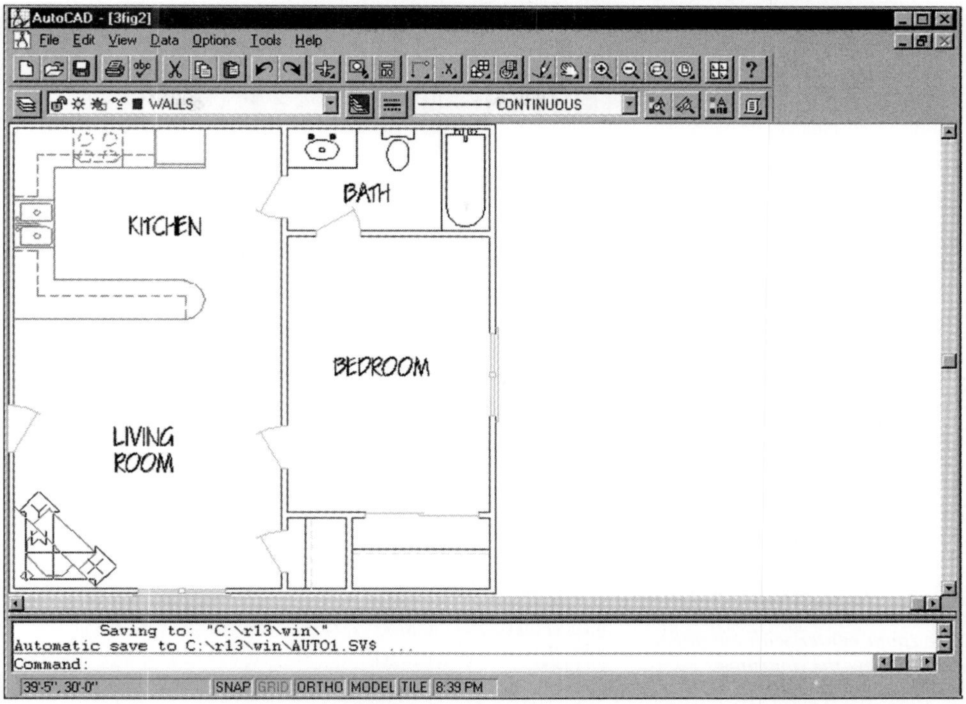

Figure 3.3
*Use **zoom all** to view the apartment floor plan.*

ZOOM CENTER

With the **zoom center** option from the Zoom flyout menu, AutoCAD creates a new view of the drawing based on a new center point. When you select **zoom center,** AutoCAD prompts for the center point of the new view. You can specify exact coordinates or use the cursor to pick a point on-screen. After specifying the center point, AutoCAD prompts you for the magnification or height of the new view.

A value followed by an *x* indicates "times" or the magnification power. A number larger than 1 zooms in; a number smaller than 1 will zoom out. If you supply a number without the *x,* AutoCAD reads the number as the height of the new view in the current units.

TUTORIAL 3.2: USING THE ZOOM CENTER COMMAND

As a reminder, this tutorial continues from the preceding tutorial. Here, you use the **zoom center** option to view the bathroom in the apartment floor plan. Follow these steps:

1.  Choose **center** from the **zoom** flyout toolbar.
2. At the Center point: prompt, pick a point in the center of the bathroom.
3. At the Magnification or Height <30′,2″>: prompt, enter *2x.* The bathroom centers in the drawing area at a scale two times larger than the previous scale (see Figure 3.4).
4.  To try a different height, select **center** from the **zoom** flyout toolbar.
5. At the Center point: prompt, move the crosshairs to the center of the bathroom and press the Pick button.
6. At the Magnification or Height <30′,2″>: prompt, enter 8′.
7. The bathroom is now centered in the drawing area with 8′ of height displayed, similar to Figure 3.5.

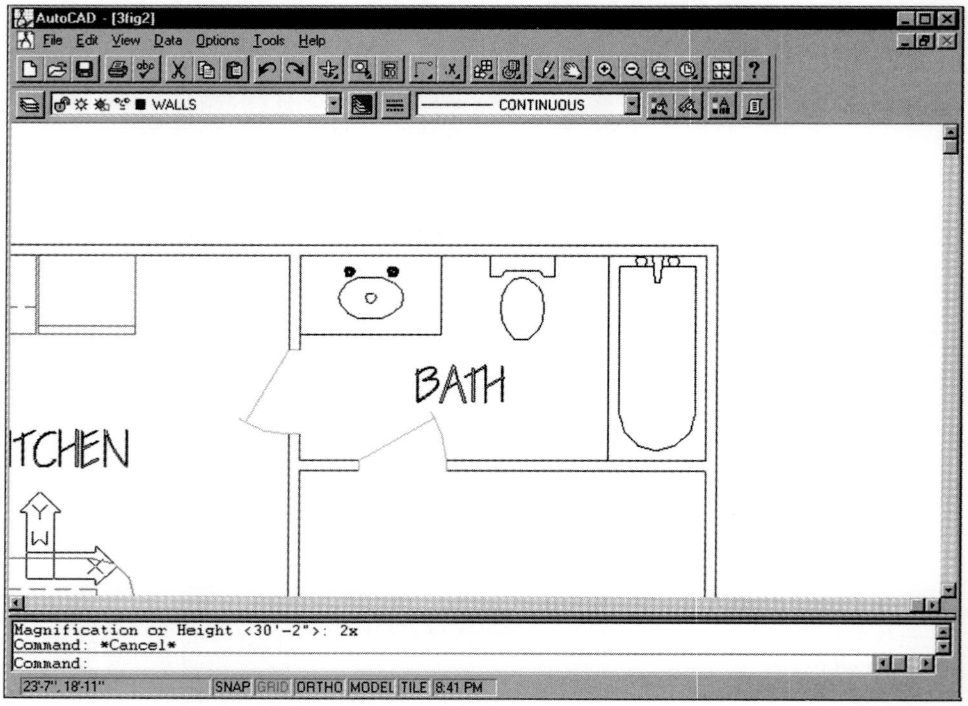

Figure 3.4
*Use **zoom center** with magnification to view the apartment bathroom.*

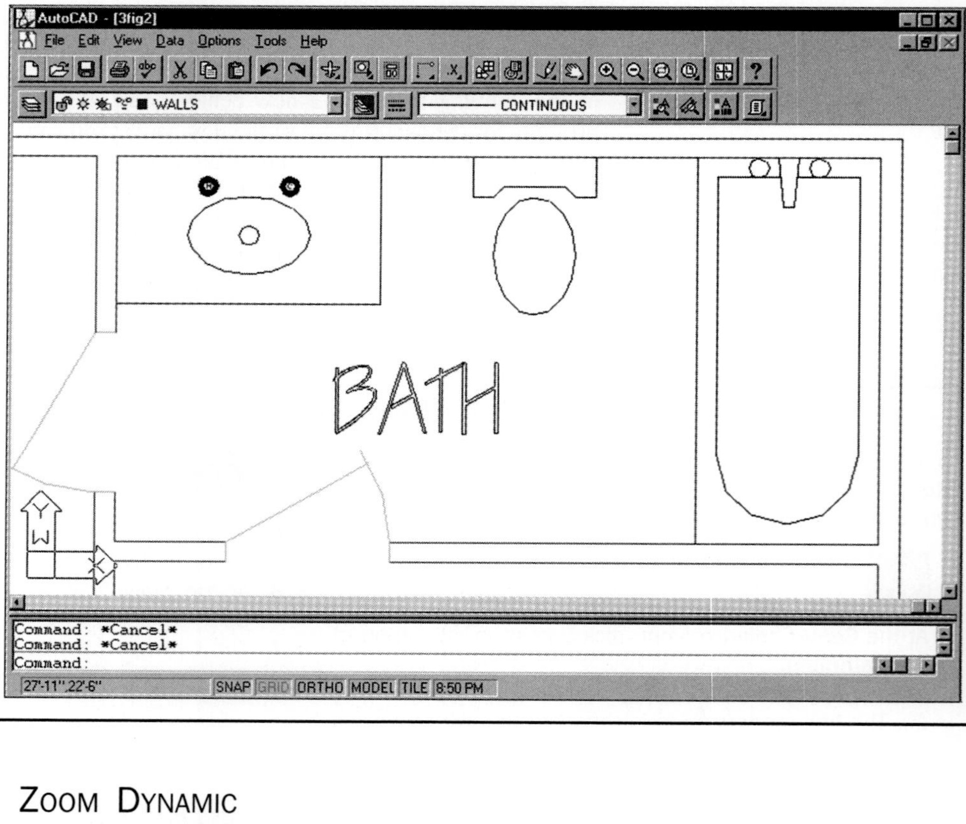

Figure 3.5
*Use **zoom center** to view the apartment bathroom.*

ZOOM DYNAMIC

The **zoom dynamic** option temporarily displays the whole drawing (as much as possible without causing a regen) and allows you to display any portion of the drawing as your next screen view. AutoCAD does this by constructing a view box. When you choose **zoom dynamic,** the screen switches to a temporary display, showing a combination of the limits, extents, current display location, future display location, virtual display boundaries, and an icon described in the following list:

- **Drawing extents.** This box displays the drawing's extents or limits, whichever is greater. This is the same area that is displayed when you use the **zoom all** option.
- **Current view.** This box (a dotted green line) shows the previous view before you selected **zoom dynamic.** If the current display is coincident with the drawing extents or limits, the green box may not be visible.
- **Generated area.** This area, indicated by four red corner angles, marks the virtual screen. This is the area you can zoom to without causing a regeneration.

If you select an area inside the four red corner angles, the next display is calculated at the faster redraw speed. If you select an area outside the four red corner angles, a **regen** is performed, slowing the next display. Try to size the View and Pan boxes inside the four red corner angles.

- **Panning view box.** This view box (a white box with an *X* in the center) represents the area that will be drawn next on-screen. An *X* indicates that this is a panning box. Place the *X* at the spot you want to be the center point of the next display. The width and height ratio of the view box matches the width and height ration of the drawing area. If you press the Pick button, the Zooming view box appears.
- **Zooming view box.** With this box (a white box with an arrow on the right side), you can increase or decrease the zoomed display. Moving the pointer to the right increases the box size. Moving the pointer to the left decreases the box size. You also can pan up or down with the zooming view box. However, you can't move the box to the left.
- **White hourglass.** When the white hourglass appears in the lower-left corner, it is a warning that the current view will cause a regeneration. As you adjust the panning and zooming view boxes, the hourglass may appear and disappear. As long as you stay in the four red corner angles, the hourglass does not appear, and AutoCAD is not forced to regenerate the drawing.

The **zoom dynamic** command is not completed until you press ↵Enter. You can select between the panning view box and zooming view box by pressing the Pick button. By using the different box options and the Pick button, you can fine-tune the display you need.

Tutorial 3.3: Using the Zoom Dynamic Command

This tutorial continues from the preceding tutorial. Here, you use the **zoom dynamic** command to view the kitchen in the apartment floor plan. Follow these steps:

1.  Choose **dynamic** from the **zoom** fly-out toolbar. Your screen changes as shown in Figure 3.6. Notice the dotted green line around the bathroom. This is the previous Zoom setting, allowing you to reference your last **zoom** command.
2. When you move the cursor, the view box adjusts to your movements. At this time, the view box is the same size as the one for the previous **zoom** setting from the preceding tutorial.
3. Move the view box so that the upper-left corner is aligned with the upper-left corner of the kitchen, as shown in Figure 3.7. The viewing area now has an arrow on the right side. This lets you know that you are ready to adjust the view box size proportionally to the drawing area.
4. Move the cursor to the right, as shown in Figure 3.8, and press the Pick button. The right arrow is replaced by an *X* in the middle of the viewbox.
5. Center the view box over the kitchen, as shown in Figure 3.9, and press ↵Enter. Your screen should now resemble Figure 3.10.

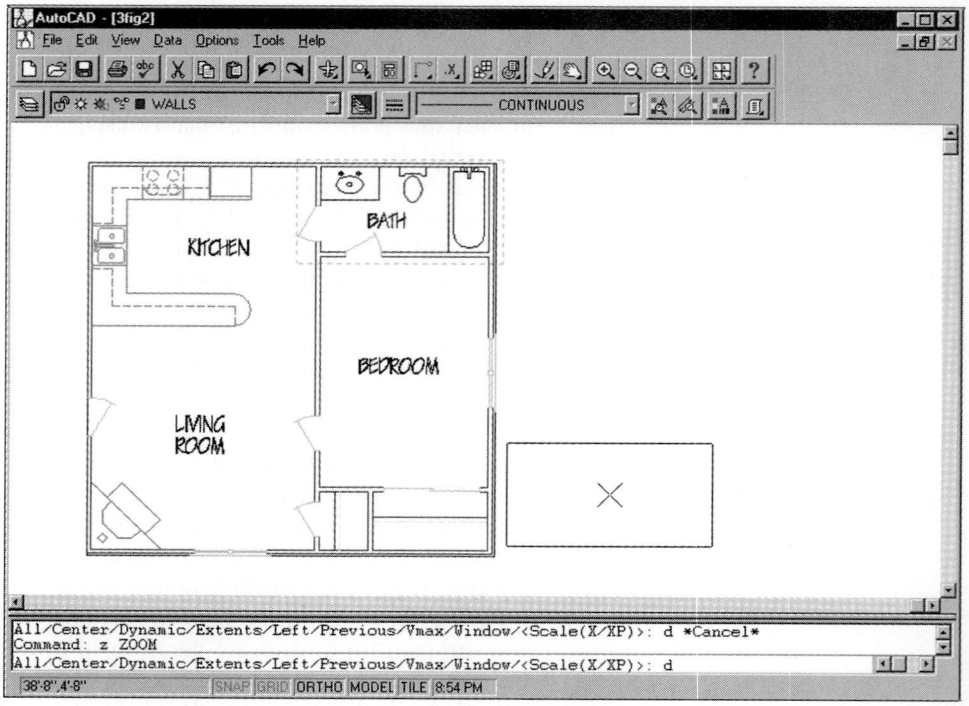

Figure 3.6
*Using the **zoom dynamic** option.*

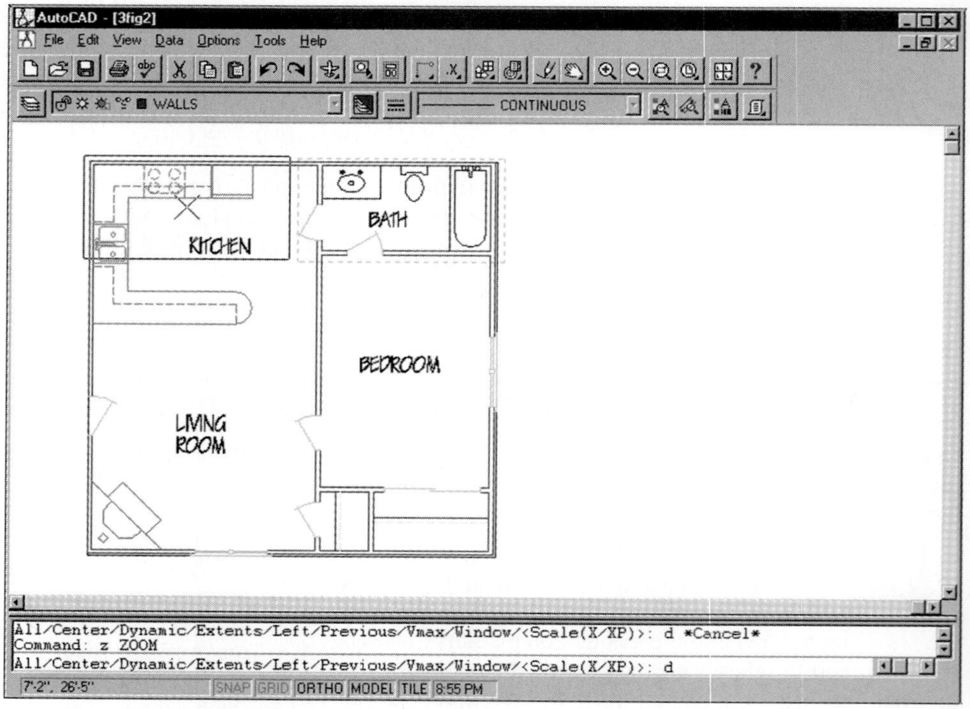

Figure 3.7
Moving the view box.

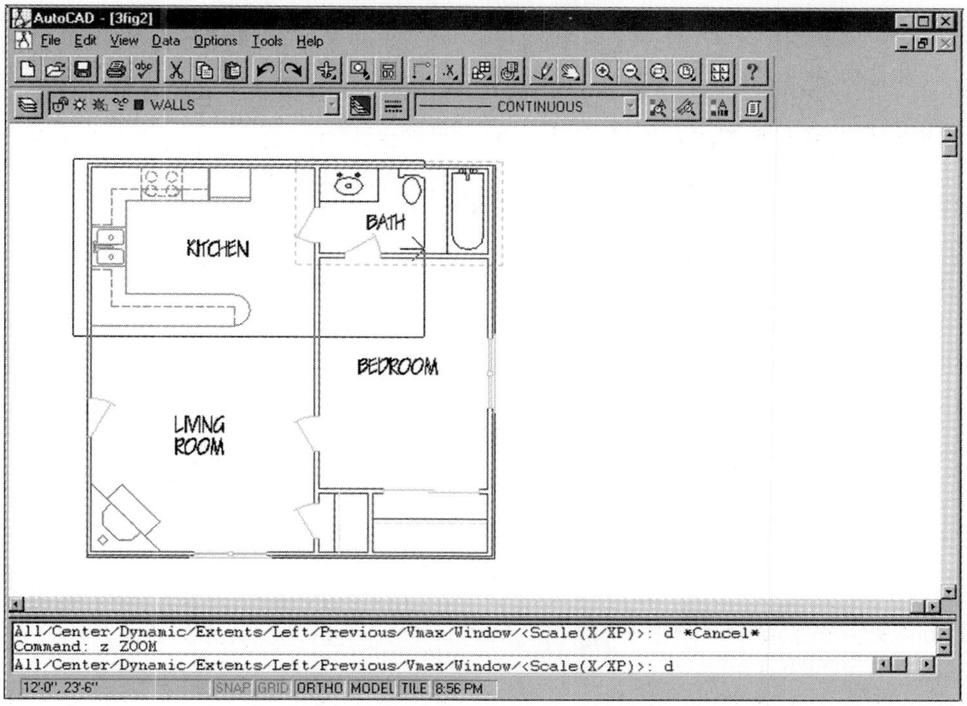

Figure 3.8
Adjusting the view box size.

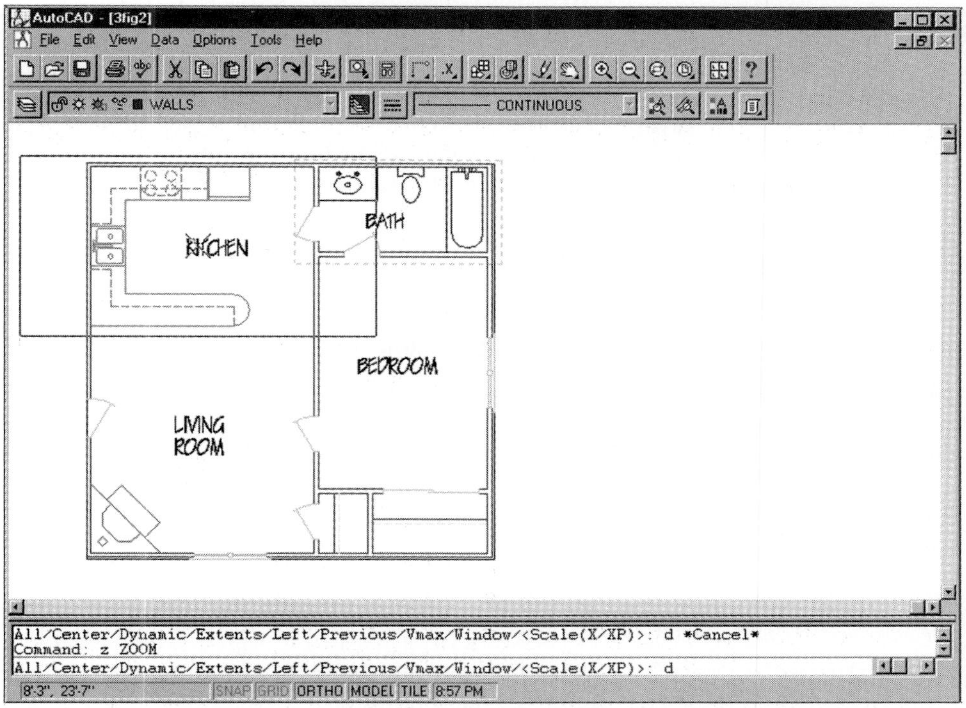

Figure 3.9
Centering the view box over the kitchen.

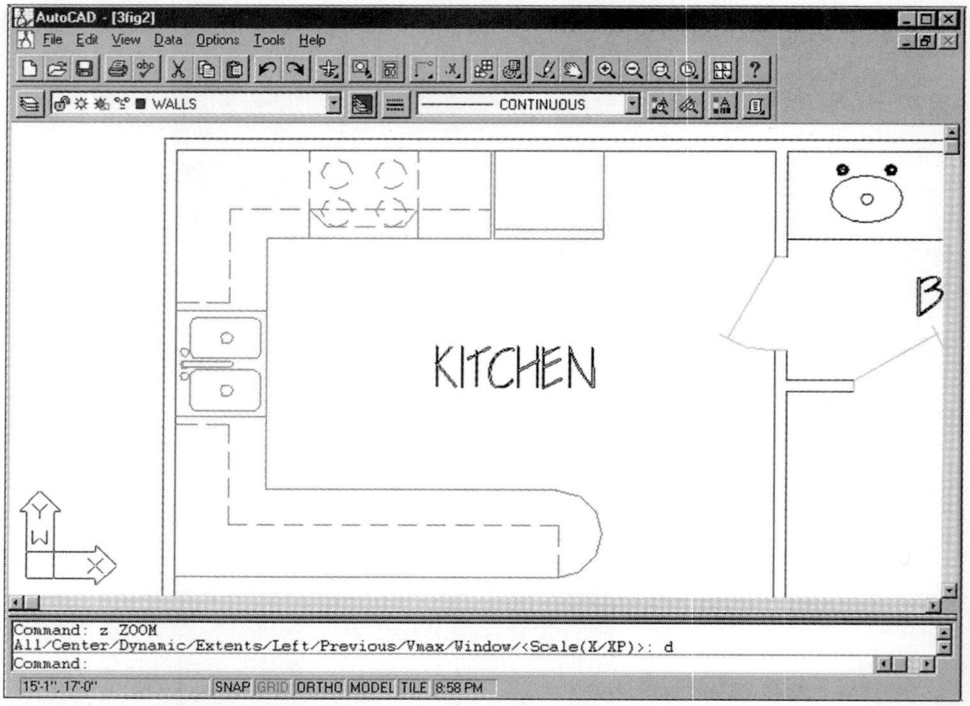

Figure 3.10
*Use **zoom dynamic** to view the kitchen.*

Zoom Extents

The **zoom extents** option zooms to the portion of the drawing that has objects. This option gives the tightest possible view of all geometry in the drawing file. **zoom extents** always causes a regeneration.

Tutorial 3.4: Using the Zoom Extents Command

Again, this tutorial continues from the preceding tutorial. Here, you use the **zoom extents** command to view the apartment floor plan. Follow this step:

1.  Choose **extents** from the **zoom** fly-out toolbar. The apartment extents are placed within the drawing area as shown in Figure 3.3. For this example, the **zoom extents** option is very similar to **zoom all.**

Zoom Left

With the **zoom left** option, you can create a new zoomed view by specifying the new location of the lower-left corner and the zoom height. The lower-left corner can be specified with coordinates or the screen crosshairs. After you specify the lower-left corner coordinates, AutoCAD prompts for the magnification or height of the new view.

As with the **zoom center** option, you can enter a value followed by an *x*. This indicates "times" the current magnification. A number larger than 1 will zoom in; numbers less than 1 will zoom out. If you supply a number without the *x*, AutoCAD reads the number as the height of the new view in the current units. Pressing (Enter) at the Magnification or Height prompt is the same as panning to the new location, because you are accepting the default current height.

TUTORIAL 3.5: USING THE ZOOM LEFT COMMAND

This tutorial continues from the preceding tutorial. Here, you use the **zoom left** command to display the closets in the apartment floor plan. Follow these steps:

1.  Select Left from the **zoom** fly-out toolbar.
2. At the Left point: prompt, move the crosshairs to the bottom-left of the closets in the bedroom and press the Pick button.
3. At the Magnification or Height <30′,2″>: prompt, enter *2x*. Your screen should resemble Figure 3.11. The **zoom left magnification** or **height** option is identical to the **zoom center** option. This option always puts the drawing to the right of the point you selected as the left point.

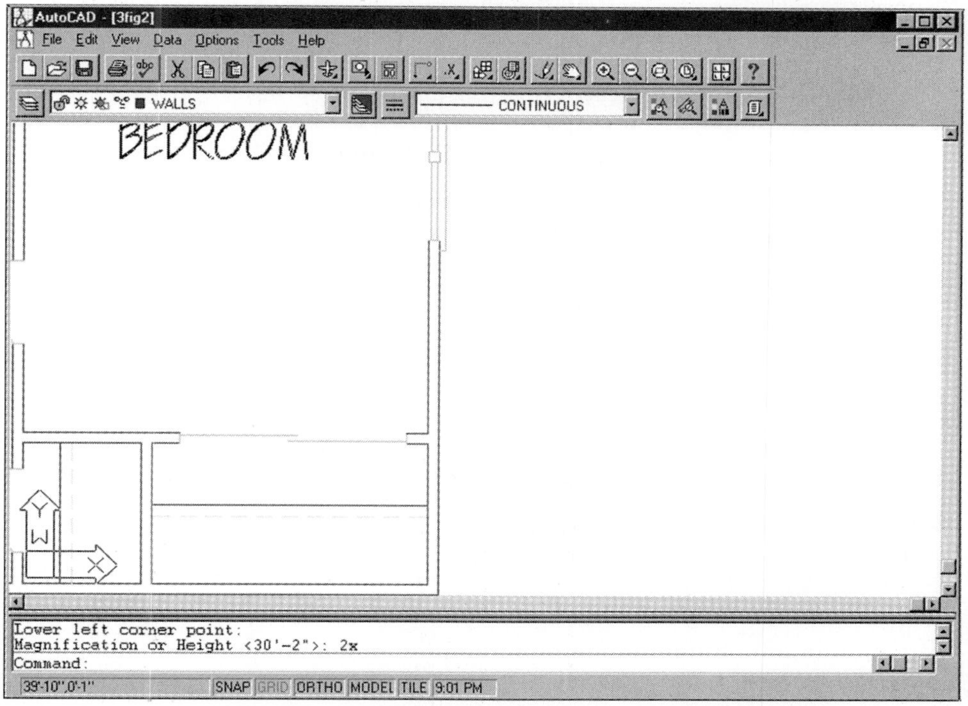

Figure 3.11
*Use **zoom left** to view the closets in the apartment floor plan.*

ZOOM PREVIOUS

Every time you zoom in or out of a drawing, AutoCAD keeps track of the previous display. AutoCAD remembers the last 10 views. Continually entering **zoom previous** causes AutoCAD to step back through the previous 10 zooms.

FOR THE PROFESSIONAL

If you erase several objects and issue **zoom previous,** the previous view is displayed, but the erased objects do not reappear.

TUTORIAL 3.6: USING THE ZOOM PREVIOUS COMMAND

This tutorial continues from the preceding tutorial. In this tutorial, you use the **zoom previous** command to view the apartment floor plan. Follow this step:

1.  Select **zoom previous** from the Standard toolbar **zoom** flyout. The screen should resemble Figure 3.3, because that was the previous zoom before the **left** option was used. **zoom previous** always reverts to the last zoom scale factor.

ZOOM VMAX

zoom vmax zooms out to the drawing's virtual screen limits. The virtual screen is the area to which AutoCAD can zoom out without regenerating the drawing. Usually, the virtual screen is larger than either the drawing's extents or limits.

TUTORIAL 3.7: USING THE ZOOM VMAX OPTION

This tutorial continues from the preceding tutorial. Here, you use the **zoom vmax** command to view the virtual screen limits of the apartment floor plan. Follow this step:

1.  Select **vmax** from the **zoom** fly-out toolbar. The drawing area zooms out to the drawing's virtual screen limits, as shown in Figure 3.12. This is the largest area to which AutoCAD can zoom or pan without calculating a regeneration.

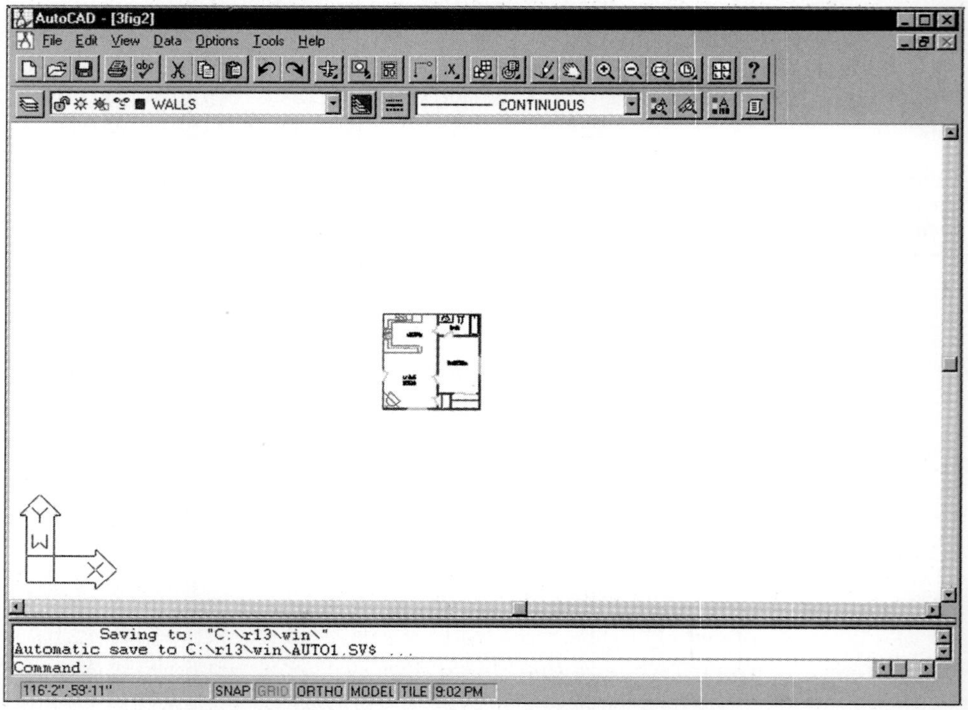

Figure 3.12
*Use **zoom vmax** to display the virtual screen limits of the apartment floor plan.*

Zoom Window

The **zoom window** icon is available directly from the Standard toolbar. A rectangular window is used to select a drawing area to display on-screen. The window grows out of the first point you select. When you press the Pick button to pick the second corner, the objects in the box enlarge to fill the screen. To use the Zoom Window from the **zoom** command's option prompt, it is not necessary to enter *w*. You can simply pick a point at the Zoom option and AutoCAD assumes you want to define a window. Be sure the point you pick is one of the four corners of the window and then select the opposite corner of the window.

Tutorial 3.8: Using the Zoom Window Command

As before, this tutorial continues from the preceding tutorial. In this tutorial, you use the **zoom window** command to view the apartment floor plan. Follow these steps:

1.  Select the **zoom window** icon from the Standard toolbar.
2. Create a window by picking two points to define it (see Figure 3.13). When the second point is picked, AutoCAD will automatically zoom. Your resulting screen should look similar to Figure 3.14.

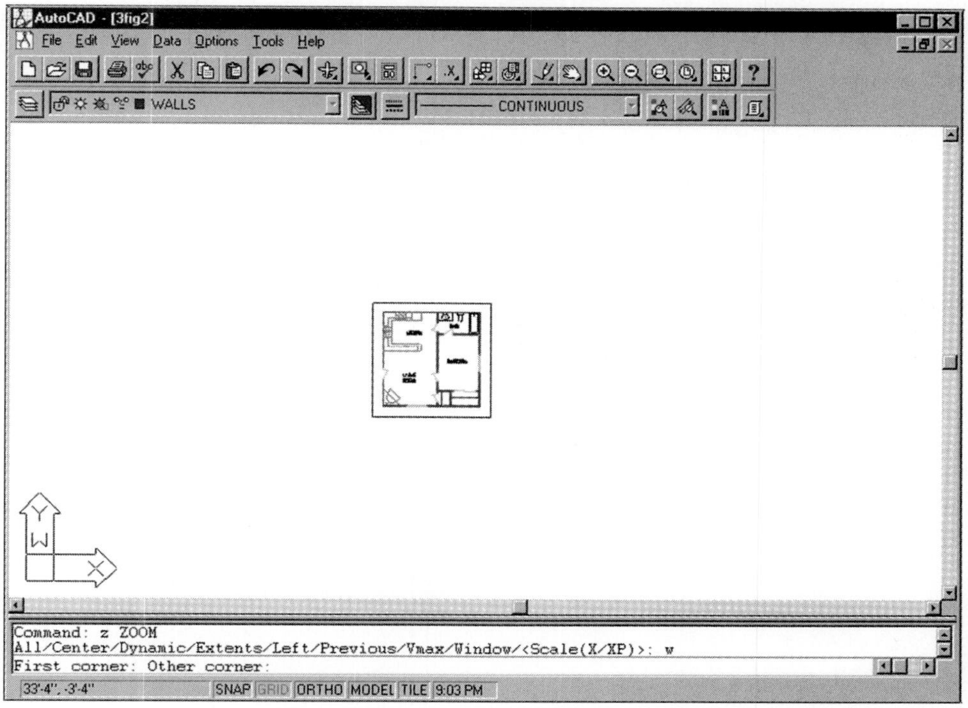

Figure 3.13
*Creating a window around the apartment floor plan with the **zoom window** option.*

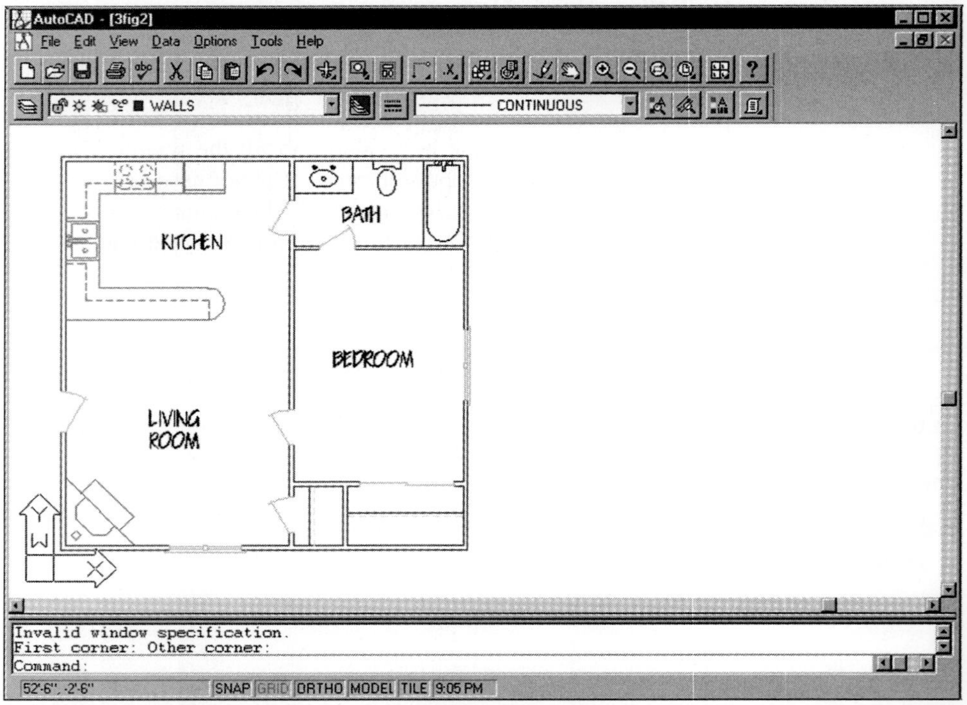

Figure 3.14
*Use **zoom window** to display the apartment floor plan.*

Zoom Scale

The **zoom scale** option enables you to zoom in and out while maintaining the same center point of the screen. Applying a magnification factor of 1 displays a view of the drawing limits. A value of less than 1 zooms out from the limits; a value greater than 1 zooms in. If you use an *x* in the scale factor, the image is magnified in relation to the current view.

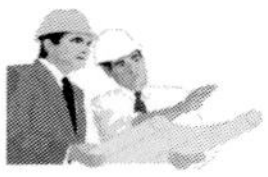

For the Professional

In most cases, you zoom the screen image at a percentage of what the current view is displaying. With no *x* after a value, the numeric size is an absolute value of the limits size (considered a Zoom Scale of 1).

Tutorial 3.9: Using the Zoom Scale Command

This tutorial continues from the preceding tutorial. Here, you use the **zoom scale** command to view the apartment floor plan at half scale. Follow these steps:

1.  Choose Scale from the Zoom fly-out toolbar.

2. At the `All/Center/Dynamic/Extents/Left/Previous/Vmax/Window/<Scale(X/XP)>:` prompt, enter .5. The drawing zooms at the absolute half (.5) scale and displays in the drawing area (see Figure 3.15).

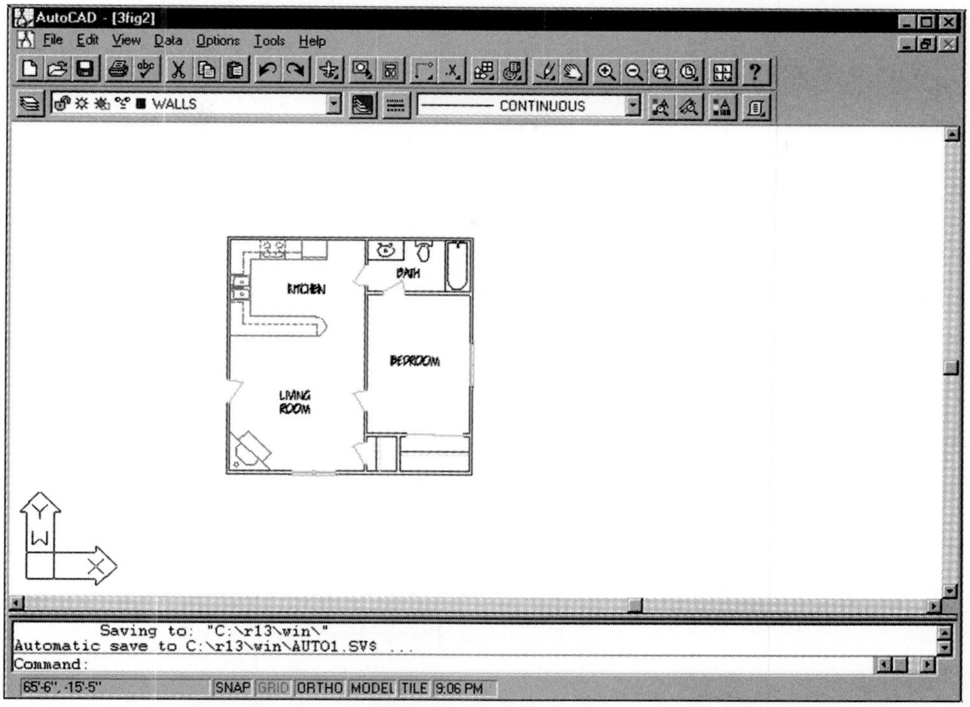

Figure 3.15
*Use **zoom scale** to display the apartment floor plan at half-scale.*

Zoom In and Zoom Out

There are two new Standard toolbar buttons available in AutoCAD Release 13: Zoom In and Zoom Out. These two buttons allow you to quickly and easily select a scale factor of two times the relative size (2x) using Zoom In and half the relative size (.5x) using Zoom Out. In normal use, you should find these buttons very useful for quickly zooming in or out to allow for a better view of the overall drawing or of smaller details.

- Clicking the Zoom In icon invokes the **zoom scale** option with a scale factor of 2x.
- Clicking the Zoom Out icon invokes the **zoom scale** option with a scale factor of .5x.

Panning the Display (Pan)

Occasionally, you may want to see a section of the drawing that is outside the current viewing screen. Panning is generally faster than zooming because you don't have to zoom out to a larger view and back in again. However, the ability to use the **pan** command is largely dependent on knowing where you want to go in the drawing. If you know you want to see a feature just to the left of the current view, you can easily pan to the left. If, however, you don't know exactly where the view is, relative to the current view, you have no choice but to zoom out and then back in at the new location or use Zoom Dynamic.

Using the **pan** command is often faster than using the **zoom** command to change views. The reason is that often you must use the **zoom** command several times to display the necessary view unless you begin with a large initial view. Furthermore, **pan** does not cause a drawing regeneration unless you pan outside the virtual screen.

With the **pan** command, you can move the current view, as seen in the viewport, very quickly. Move the current area where you are working from an initial point to a second point of displacement, and the view of the drawing changes accordingly. Use the following methods to access the **pan** command:

- Click the Pan button on the Standard toolbar. This brings up a fly-out toolbar, showing all the pan options.

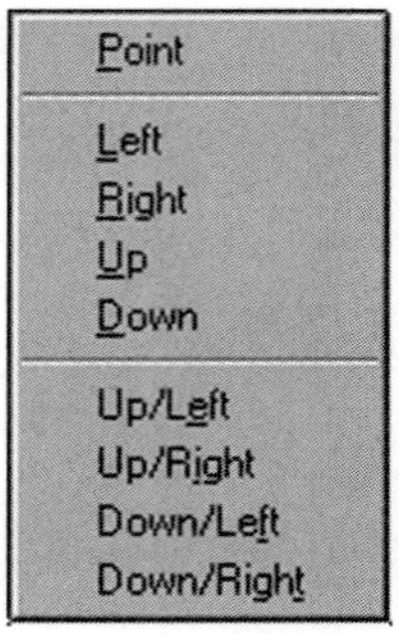

Figure 3.16
The Pan cascading submenu offering several options.

- Choose View' Pan. AutoCAD displays a cascading submenu that lists the different Pan options as shown in Figure 3.16.
- Enter **pan** or **p** at the Command: prompt or 'pan or 'p to use the command transparently during another command. AutoCAD then prompts for the pan displacement.
- Move the scroll bars at the bottom and side of the drawing area.

For the Professional

You can issue the **pan** command transparently by preceding it with an apostrophe ('). **pan** works only if the desired pan does not require a regen. Transparent pans can be done only if **viewres fast zoom** mode is on. You cannot use **pan** transparently during **zoom, pan,** or **view** commands.

Shifting the View a Specific Distance

You can also execute a pan displacement by entering a pair of coordinates at the Displacement: prompt.

For example, you can enter a coordinate as the initial displacement point and press Enter for the second point. The coordinate specifies a relative distance that the view will move. A negative value in the x-axis moves the viewport to the left. A negative value in the y-axis moves the viewport down.

The **pan** option on the Standard toolbar and pull-down menu also offers several preset pan distances. When you select a preset pan distance, the drawing pans a set amount and direction. The Pan L button (choose Left in the pull-down menu), for example, pans the drawing to the left. Refer to Figure 3.16 for the Pan cascading submenu and its preset options. Each preset option pans the current view in the preset direction by a distance that is approximately half of the value of the **viewsize** system variable. ViewSize measures the height of the current view.

Tutorial 3.10: Panning a Drawing

This tutorial continues from the preceding tutorial. In this tutorial, you use the **pan** command to shift the view of the apartment floor plan. Follow these steps:

1.  Choose **pan** from the Standard toolbar.
2. At the Displacement: prompt, enter 14′,15′.
3. At the Second point: prompt, enter 52′,15′. The apartment floor plan is shifted to the right 38′, as shown in Figure 3.17. You can also use the crosshairs to pick the points necessary to accomplish this process.
4.  Select Previous from the Zoom fly-out toolbar. The drawing reverts to that in Figure 3.9. Notice that the **zoom previous** option works not only with the **zoom** command, but also with the **pan** command.

5.  Select **pan** from the Standard Toolbar.

6. At the Displacement: prompt, move the cursor so that the coordinates displayed in the status bar are approximately 14′,15′, and press the Pick button. Don't worry about being exact.

7. At the Second point: prompt, move the cursor so that the absolute coordinates displayed in the status bar are approximately 52′,15′. Then press the Pick button. Again, don't worry if the coordinates are not exactly right. Your drawing area should now resemble Figure 3.10.

8.  Select **all** from the Zoom fly-out toolbar.

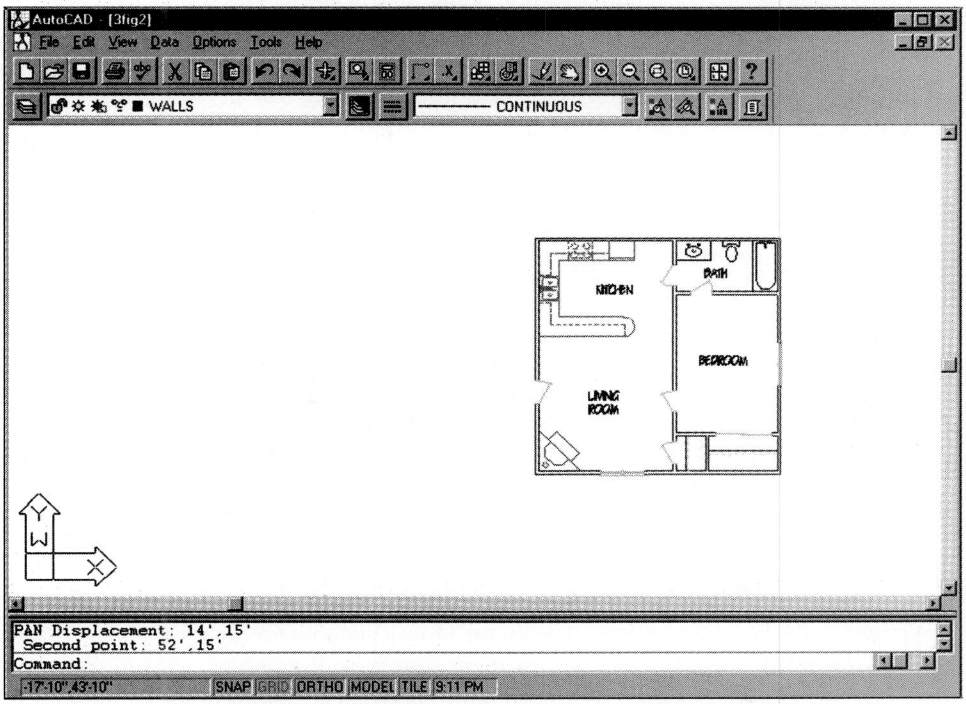

Figure 3.17
*Use the **pan** option to shift the view of the apartment floor plan.*

USING THE AERIAL VIEW WINDOW

AutoCAD for Windows offers a powerful feature for zooming and panning a drawing. The Aerial View window is a tool that allows you to see the entire drawing in a separate window, as shown in Figure 3.18. You can use the Aerial View window to quickly locate

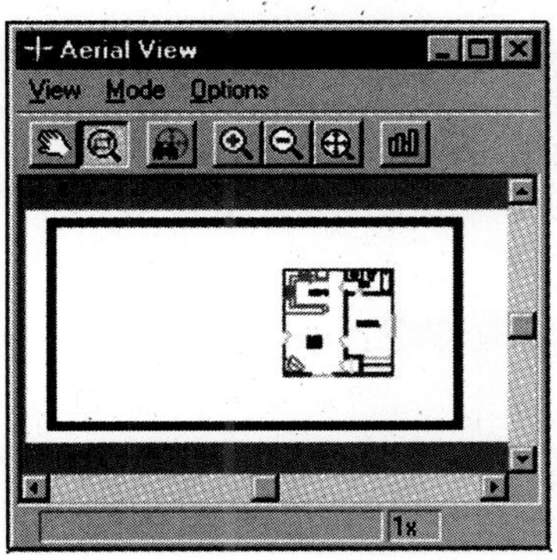

Figure 3.18
The Aerial View window enables you to quickly pan and zoom a drawing.

a view or detail of the drawing. You can change the magnification, zoom in on an area, and match the view in the graphics window to the one in the Aerial View window (or vice versa). You can access the Aerial View window in one of two ways:

- Select the Aerial View icon from the Standard toolbar.
- Enter **`dsviewer`** at the `Command:` prompt.

You can move the Aerial View window to any location on-screen by clicking the title bar, holding down the left mouse button, and dragging. You can also resize this window by moving the cursor to the edge of the window until the double arrow appears, then hold down the left mouse button and drag the edge of the window until the window is the desired size.

Aerial Window Options

Pan, Zoom Window, Locator, Zoom In, Zoom Out, Global, and Display Statistics can be directly accessed from the icons in the Aerial View window. The icon commands are described here:

- **Pan.** When you press the Pan button, a box outlined in dashes appears. This is the pan box outline, which is the same size as the current zoom box. If there is no zoom box, the pan box is the same as the aerial window. When you move the pan box to a new location and click, the main view displays what was selected in the Aerial View window.

- **Zoom.** The Zoom option uses crosshairs to create a zoom box in the Aerial View window. The crosshairs are used to select two opposite corners of the zoom box. The zoom box appears as a solid border, and the graphics window displays the area defined in the Aerial View window.

- **Locator.** This allows you to select the area of the drawing that you wish to have displayed in the Aerial View window. Select Locator from the Aerial View pull-down menu and drag the target to the drawing area. Let up on the button and the area is displayed in the Aerial View window. The amount of zoom can be changed by selecting Locator Magnification from the Options pull-down menu in the Aerial View window.

- **Zoom In.** This option automatically doubles the magnification in the Aerial View window.
- **Zoom Out.** This option reduces the magnification by one-half in the Aerial View window.

- **Global.** This option redisplays the entire drawing in the Aerial View window.
- **Statistics.** This option displays information about the display list driver in the Display Drive Info window (see Figure 3.19). This window shows how many bytes are in the display list and what percentage of the physical memory is being used to maintain the display list. The display list is part of the video driver that controls the display in AutoCAD for your graphics card.

For the Professional

It is always good to keep a good account of your memory and system resources. When both of these become low, AutoCAD and other applications may terminate and you may lose many hours of work.

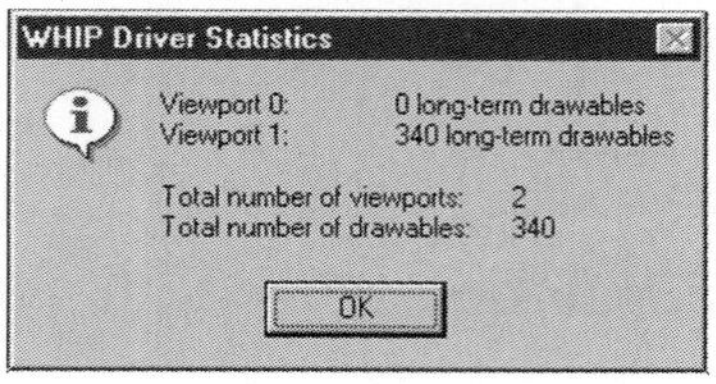

Figure 3.19
Displaying the Statistics option.

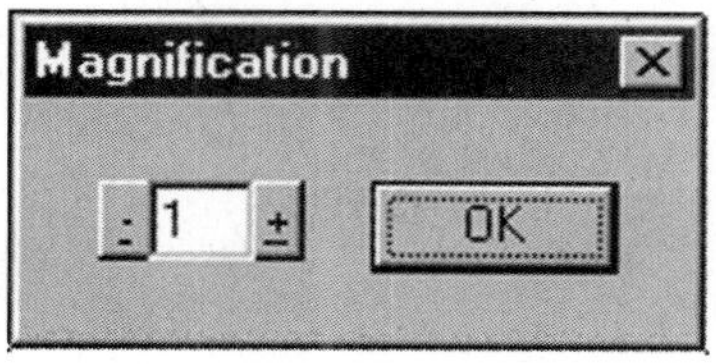

Figure 3.20
You can change the view magnification in the Magnification dialog box.

Aerial Window Menu Options

The Aerial Window menu bar contains three choices: Option, Mode, and View. The following selections are available on the Options pull-down menu:

- **Auto Viewport.** The Auto Viewports toggle option is used when multiple viewports are displayed on-screen. The default status of ON displays the active or current viewport in the Aerial View window. When this option is turned off, you must click in the Aerial View title bar to update the window to match the current viewport.
- **Dynamic Update.** When you edit a drawing, the Aerial View window is automatically updated. If the computer begins to slow down during intensive editing operations, you can turn this option off to conserve system resources.
- **Locator Magnification.** This option enables you to change the magnification. When you choose this option, the Magnification dialog box appears (see Figure 3.20). Choose the + or – button to increase or decrease the magnification.
- **Display Statistics.** This option displays information about the display list driver in a separate window. It performs the same function as the Statistics button.

The Mode pull-down menu contains the following two options:

- **Pan.** This option allows you to pan in the Aerial View. When you move the pan box to a new area and click, the graphics window displays the area you selected in the Aerial View window. This option performs the same function as the Pan button.
- **Zoom.** With this option, you can zoom in on a defined area in the Aerial View window and display it in the graphics window. Zoom performs the same function as the Zoom button.

The **view** pull-down menu contains these three options:

- **Zoom In.** This option controls the magnification of the image in the Aerial View window. Zoom In doubles the magnification.
- **Zoom Out.** This option reduces the magnification in the Aerial View window by one-half.
- **Global.** With this option, you can redisplay the entire drawing in the Aerial View window.

Tutorial 3.11: Using the Aerial View Window

This tutorial continues from the preceding tutorial. Here, you use the functionality of Aerial View. Follow these steps:

1.  If you do not have the Aerial View window displayed, choose Tools, Aerial View. The Aerial View window appears over the drawing area (see Figure 3.21).
2.  Click Pan. Move your cursor within the Aerial View window. Notice that a view box similar to the **zoom dynamic** view box appears in the Aerial View.
3. Move the view box over the kitchen in the Aerial View, as shown in Figure 3.22, and press the Pick button. Minimize the Aerial View window. Your screen should resemble Figure 3.23.
4.  To see a complete view of the kitchen, restore the Aerial View window using the task bar and click Zoom in the Aerial View window.
5. Now, still in the Aerial View window, create a window around the kitchen, as shown in Figure 3.24. The resulting drawing area should resemble that in Figure 3.25.

6.  To perform what is similar to a **zoom all,** select Global from the Aerial Window toolbar.

7. To close the Aerial View window, click the Minimize button.

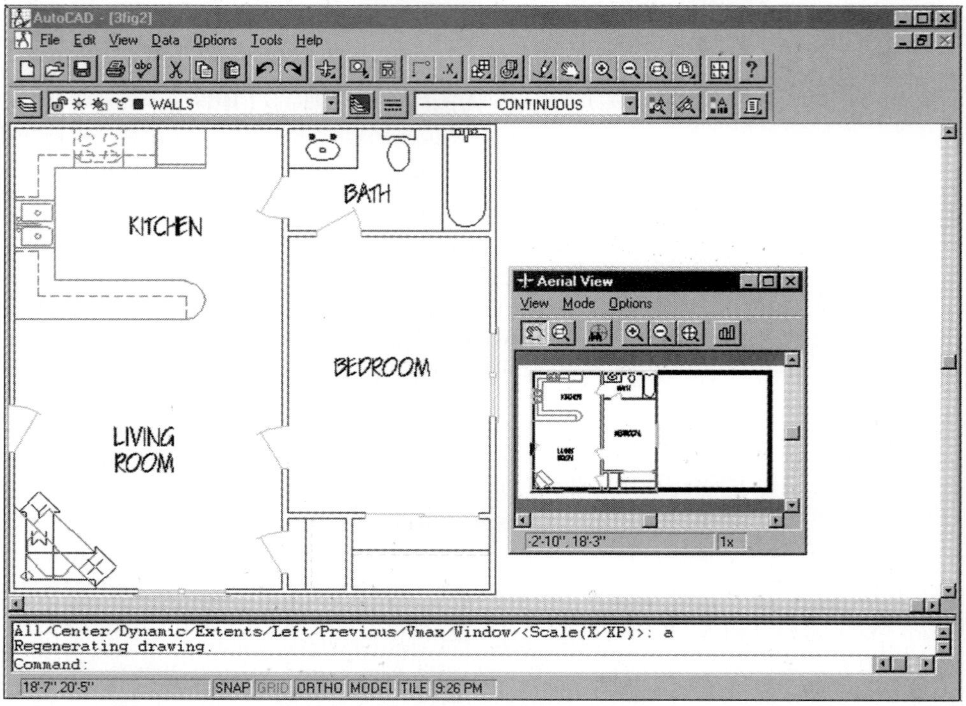

Figure 3.21
The Aerial View window.

Figure 3.22
Moving the view box within the Aerial View window to display the kitchen.

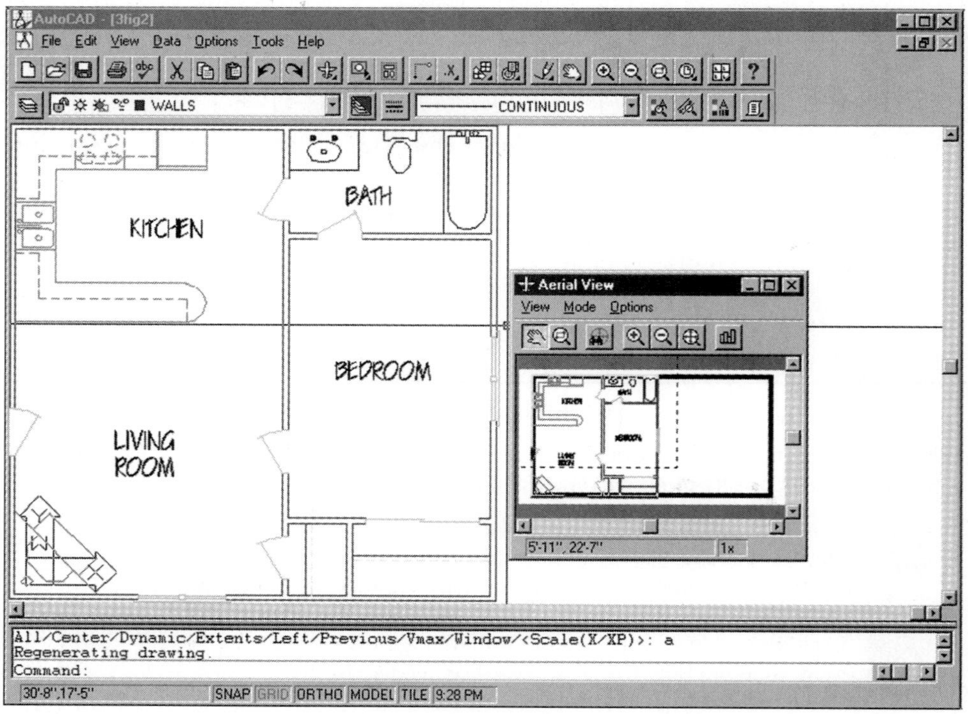

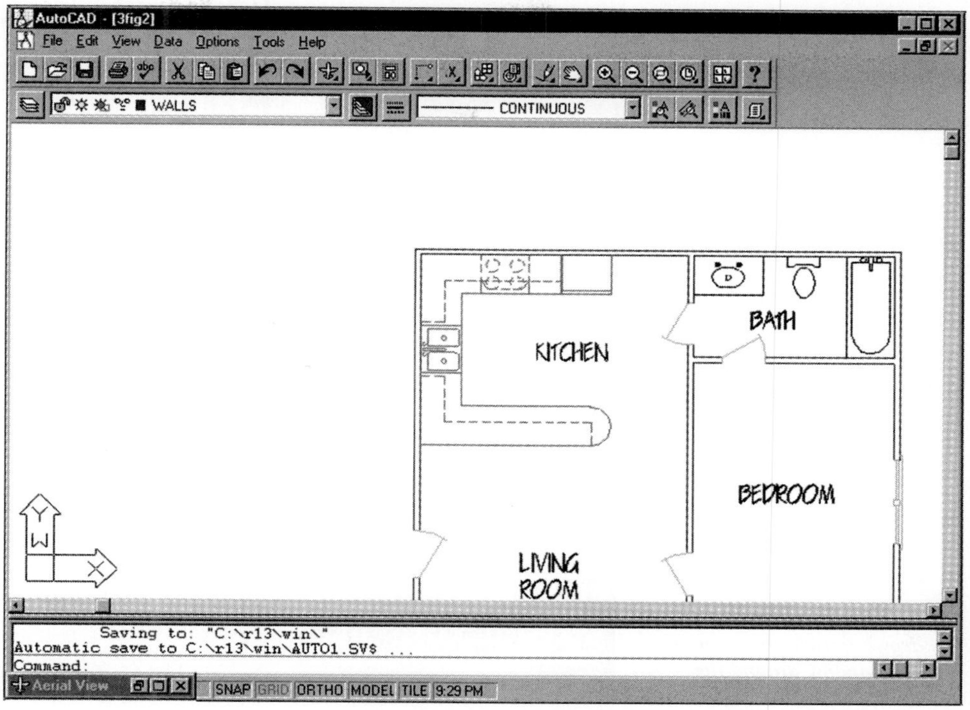

Figure 3.23
The drawing area after moving the view box to display the kitchen.

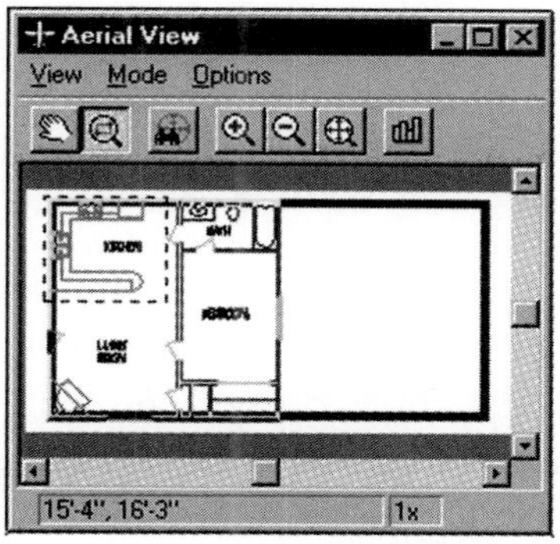

Figure 3.24
Creating a window around the kitchen in the Aerial View window.

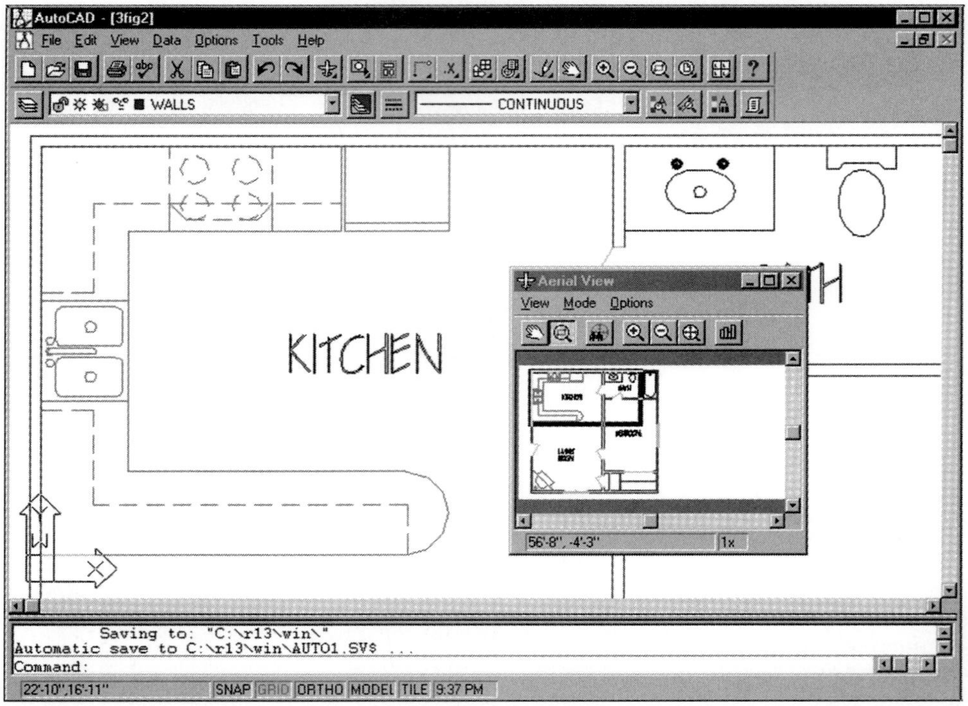

Figure 3.25
The drawing area after you created the window around the kitchen.

Creating Views (View and DDView)

Panning and zooming a small drawing takes little time, but these operations can slow down considerably when working on a large drawing. Saving views of your drawing and accessing them later can greatly increase your drawing speed; this is possible with the **view** command. A view can be a specific part of your drawing, such as the zoomed view of a room. After creating the view, you can name and save it. You can then instruct AutoCAD to display the view at any time. The **view** command is accessed in the following ways:

- Choose the Named Views from the View fly-out toolbar.
- Choose View\Named Views from the pull-down menu. The View Control dialog box is displayed (see Figure 3.26).
- Enter **`ddview`** at the `Command:` prompt. This command also accesses the View Control dialog box.
- Enter **`view`** at the `Command:` prompt. AutoCAD responds with:

`?/Delete/Restore/Save/Window:`

Figure 3.26
The View Control dialog box is used to save and restore views.

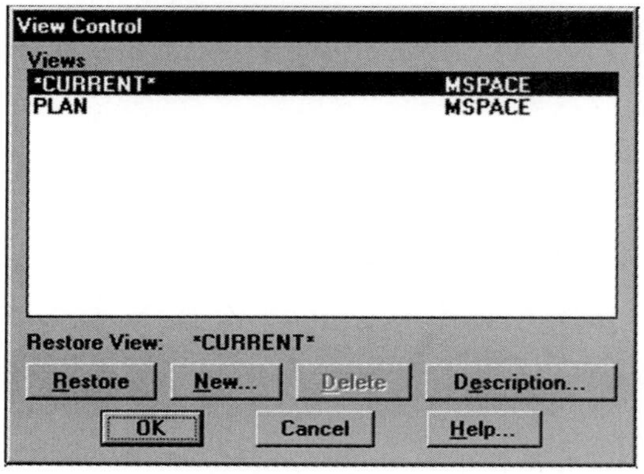

SKILL BUILDER

The Open File dialog box, used to open existing drawings, includes an option to Select Initial View. This option displays a list of views saved in the drawing and enables you to select the view you want to see displayed when AutoCAD loads the drawing. This is a fast way to open a drawing and get to a specific view.

LISTING VIEWS

Entering ? at the AutoCAD **view** prompt will list all views you created with the drawing. An alternative is to bring up the View Control dialog box using the **ddview** command. It also lists all the views saved with the drawing.

RESTORING VIEWS

A saved view can be restored to the screen at any time by highlighting the view in the View Control dialog box and choosing Restore.

DELETING VIEWS

The best method for listing and deleting views is through the View Control dialog box. To delete a view, highlight it and choose Delete. The view name is immediately removed from the list. If no view name is highlighted, the Delete option is grayed.

SAVING VIEWS

To create a new view, select the New button in the View Control dialog box. This brings up the Define New View dialog box, as shown in Figure 3.27. If the view currently on-screen is the view you want to save, enter the name in the text box and click Save View.

To create a new view, select the Define Window radio button. The Window button is now active. When you click the Window button, you return to the drawing and are asked to define a window. After you name this view and click Save View, it appears in the list as a saved view.

SKILL BUILDER

To save on regeneration time, especially with large drawings, you can save a view of the entire drawing. Issue the **zoom all** command and then save the view. You can restore this view at any time without experiencing a drawing regeneration.

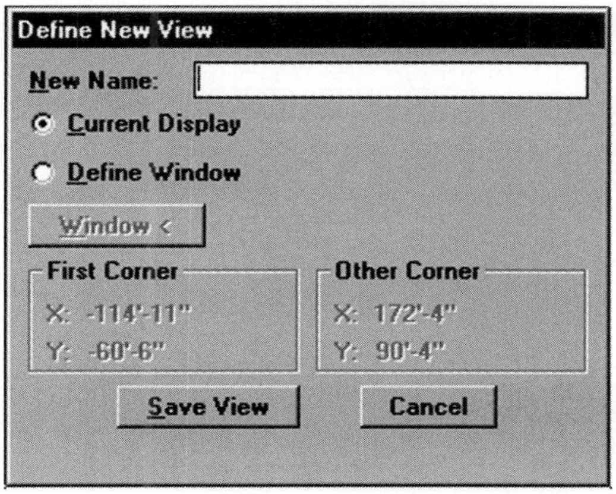

Figure 3.27
You can name and define a new view in the Define New View dialog box.

TUTORIAL 3.12: CREATING AND SAVING VIEWS

This tutorial continues from the previous tutorial. Here you use the **ddview** command to create specific views of the apartment floor plan that can be recalled at any point during the drawing. Follow these steps:

1.  Select **zoom window** from the Standard toolbar.
2. Specify the two corners of the window.
3. First corner: 16′6,22′5
4. Other corner: 30′4,30′. Your drawing area should look like that in Figure 3.28.
5.  Choose Named Views from the View pull-down menu. The View Control dialog box is displayed (see Figure 3.29).
6. Select the New... button in the dialog box. The Define New View dialog box appears (see Figure 3.30).
7. Enter *bathroom* in the New Name input box and click Save View. The View Control dialog box appears and the view BATHROOM has been added to the list.
8. Click OK to close the View Control dialog box.
9.  Select All from the Zoom fly-out toolbar. The full view of the apartment floor plan returns.
10. To return to the BATHROOM view, choose View, Named Views. The View Control dialog box is redisplayed, as shown in Figure 3.31.
11. Select the bathroom view, click the Restore button, and click OK. The bathroom view is once again displayed on-screen as shown in Figure 3.20.

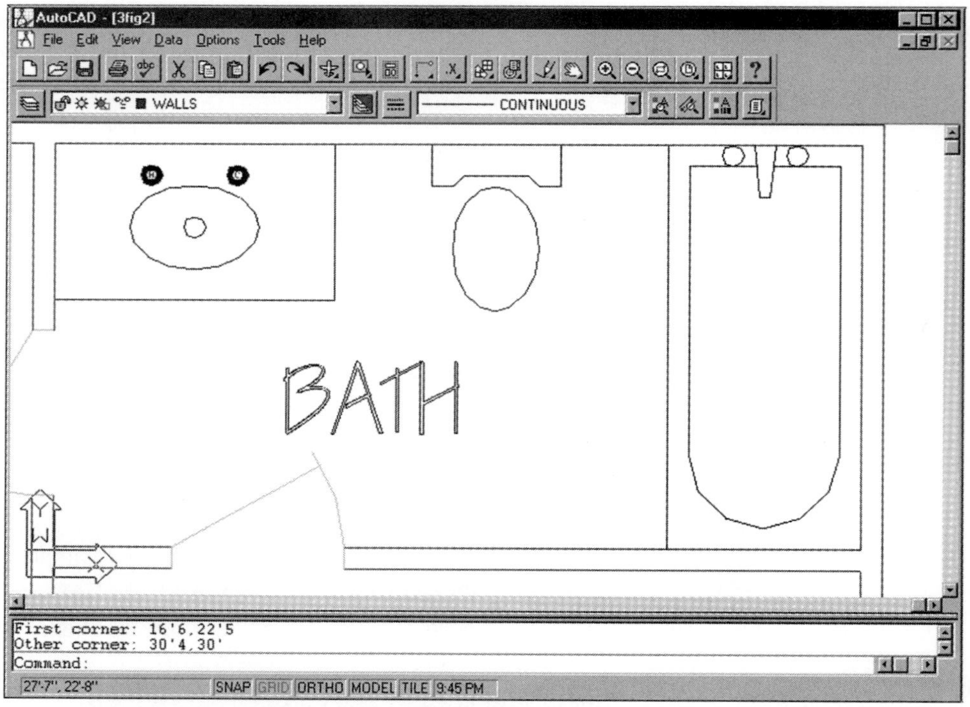

Figure 3.28
Zoom Window obtains a view of the bathroom in the apartment floor plan.

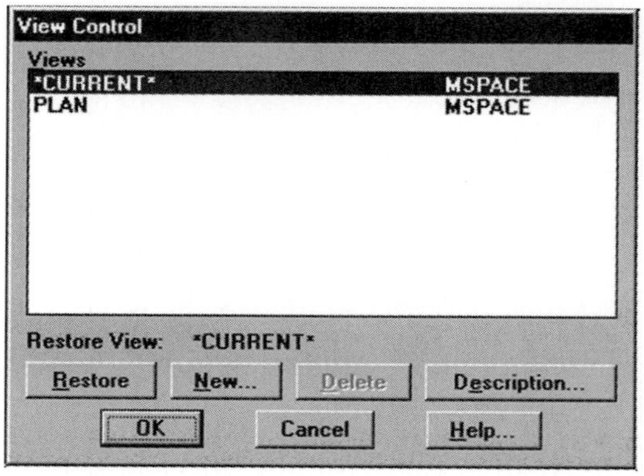

Figure 3.29
Use the View Control dialog box to create a new view.

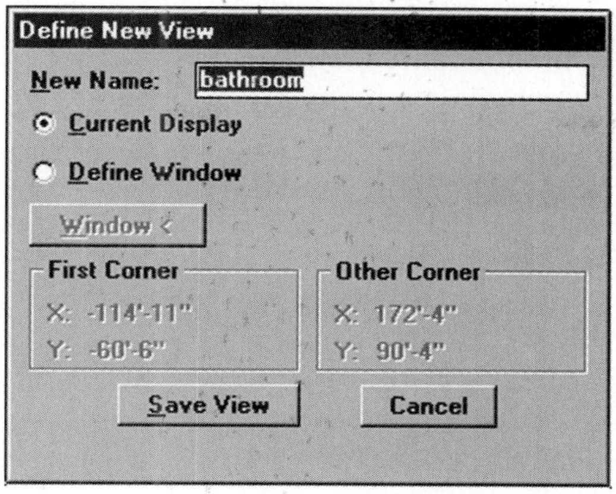

Figure 3.30
Use the Define New View dialog box to define a new view of the bathroom in the apartment floor plan.

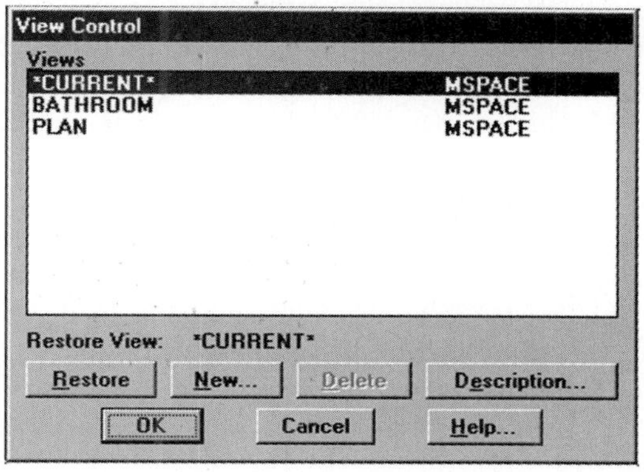

Figure 3.31
The View Control dialog box with the BATHROOM view listed.

INTRODUCTION TO PLOTTING

Plotting is an essential part of the drafting process. Having a plot, or hard copy, lets you share your drawing with others without the need for AutoCAD and a computer. Because the resolution of the plotting device is higher than that of the computer screen, a plot will allow you to catch mistakes that otherwise might not have been seen using the AutoCAD display. Also, there is nothing like having your creation on paper; it adds *permanence* to the drawing.

Before beginning plotting in AutoCAD, let's take a look at the various types of plot devices. There are generally two types of plot devices: plotters and printers. These are further subdivided into various types. Various types of plotters include pen, pencil, thermal, and inkjet. Pen plotters are the most common and operate by holding a pen in a gripper. The gripper then moves along the x-horizontal axis. Meanwhile, the paper moves along the perpendicular y-horizontal axis.

The result is a device that works similarly to a computer controlled Etch-a-Sketch. To draw a diagonal line or circle, the plotter must move both the pen and the paper at the same time and at the correct rate of speed necessary to create the shape. Some of the pros and cons of pen plotters are shown in Table 3.1.

TABLE 3.1 PROS AND CONS OF PLOTTERS

Pros	Cons
Plots on A–F size sheets of paper.	Expensive
Allows hard copy to be produced on both velum and paper.	Pens may run out before drawing is complete.
Produces output that resembles hand drawings.	Difficult to set up and configure.
Easy to specify line widths.	Drivers are not always available for all software.
Many plotters will produce black and white or color output.	

For the Professional

Inkjet plotters are becoming a popular alternative to pen plotters. They offer the advantage of speed and color with a low maintenance cycle. They are quiet and also include Windows drivers that allow them to be used with almost any software package that runs under the Windows operating system. Can you imagine a C-size plot of a favorite letter or a plot of a screen shot from your favorite computer game that could be used as a poster in your room or office?

Another common type of output device is the printer. Common types of printer technologies used to plot AutoCAD drawings are laser and inkjet. Laser printers are close cousins to the copy machine. They both use heat and toner to place the image on a piece of paper. Laser printers have computer processors and memory that will off-load the computer from having to do a large portion of the processing. This allows a laser printer to produce hard copy faster than a plotter. Laser printers are used primarily to produce only black-and-white output, although new technology and price reductions will someday put color laser printers on almost everyone's desk. For the time being, the least expensive way to get color output is by using an inkjet printer.

Inkjet printers use a cartridge that contains ink. The ink is forced through small nozzles and sprayed on the paper. The result is output that can be created in either black and white or color, based on the cartridge that is being used at the time. Thousands of colors can be created by mixing the primary colors of red, yellow, and blue. Most inkjet cartridges contain only these colors.

So, should you use a printer or a plotter for hard copy output? Ask yourself these questions:

- Do I need the best professional quality available? If yes, consider plotters for professional quality output.
- What size output do I need? If you only need A–B size output, use a printer. For larger output, use the plotter.
- Do I need color output? Here you can use both printers and plotters. The determining factor will once again be the size of the drawing.

Once you have determined the type of output device needed, you can use AutoCAD to produce the plot. AutoCAD refers to any hard copy output as a *plot.* The command to produce a plot is simply **plot**. To enter the Plot command, use one of the following steps:

- Select the Print button from the Standard toolbar.
- Select File/Print… from the pull-down menu.
- Type `plot` at the `Command:` prompt.

Skill Builder

If the Plot Configuration dialog box is not displayed when you enter the **plot** command, type `cmddia` at the `Command:` prompt. Ensure that the setting is 1. The dialog box is displayed when you enter the **plot** command.

Once the Plot command has been entered, the Plot Configuration dialog box is displayed as shown in Figure 3.32.

Before this dialog box can be displayed, AutoCAD must first be configured for the plotter that is attached to the computer or on the same network.

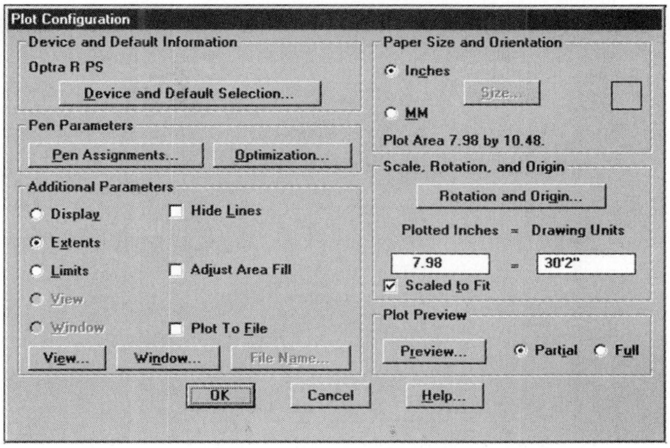

Figure 3.32
The Plot Configuration dialog box.

Configuring AutoCAD for Plotting (Plot)

For most of you, the configuration of a plotter has already been accomplished. Configuring a plotter for AutoCAD is an advanced concept. It is introduced in this book only to give you an introduction to the process. Because there are so many different plotters available on the market, this book cannot possibly cover all of them. We will cover the procedures necessary to get you started. If you have any other questions, refer to both the AutoCAD user's manual and the plotter's user's manual for more specific instructions.

To instruct AutoCAD that you want to configure a plotter, use one of the following methods:

- Select Options/Configure from the pull-down menu.
- Type **config** at the `Command:` prompt.

Once this command has been entered, the AutoCAD Text Window will be displayed as shown in Figure 3.33.

Within the window will be information concerning the configuration of AutoCAD on that particular computer. Once this window is displayed, press Enter The window will scroll more information concerning the configuration. Your window should resemble the one shown in Figure 3.34.

You will be presented with many options, such as configuring the display, digitizer, and system console. Looking at the Text Window, you will find that to configure a plotter you should choose option 5. Once you have selected option 5 you will be prompted with

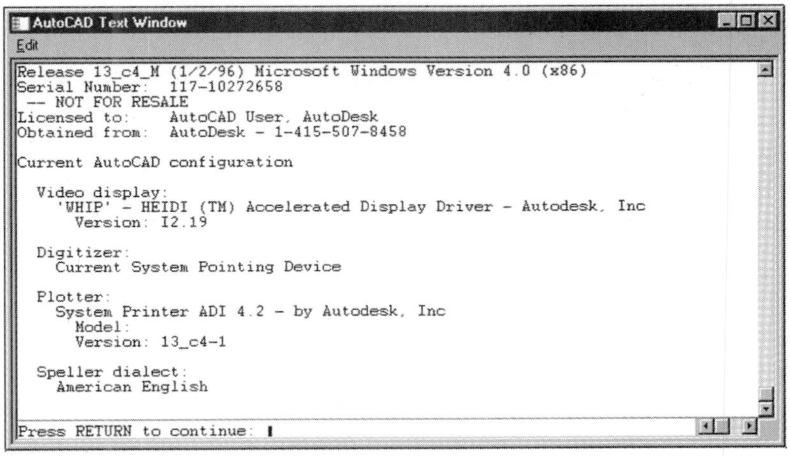

Figure 3.33
Use the AutoCAD Text Window to prompt you for information needed to configure a plotter.

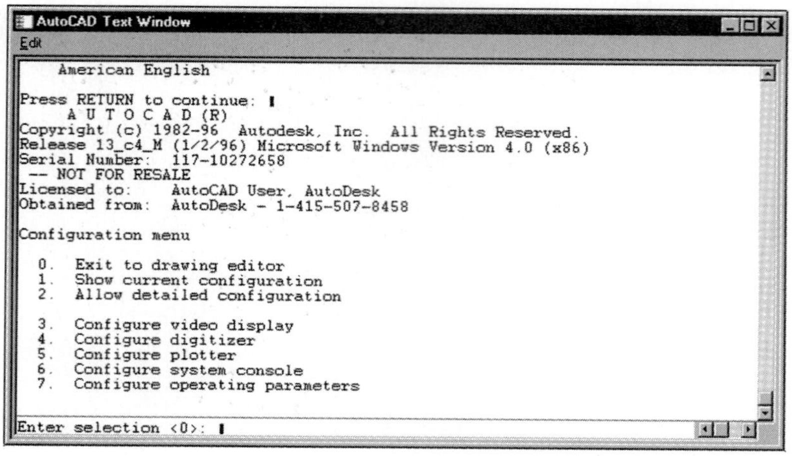

Figure 3.34
A list of configuration options.

information needed to configure a plotter. At this point you should consult your plotter's user's manual and the AutoCAD user's manual.

For the Professional

The **config** command, when not used properly, can cause AutoCAD to become inoperable. It is suggested that unless you know the command specifically, or have been instructed to do so, that you not make changes to any settings. A rule of thumb: if AutoCAD is working, don't mess with these settings.

Understanding Plotting Options

Once the plotter has been configured and you have entered the **plot** command, the dialog box found in Figure 3.32 will be displayed showing you the many different plot options that are available. You will not have to use or change all of these options each time you plot a drawing. The dialog box may look very complicated, but once you understand its components, you will find it easy to produce accurate plots. You will find that many of the options will not be needed for the types of drawings you are creating. This unit will provide an overview of all options. Less commonly used options will not be covered in depth, while options that are required the majority of the time will be covered completely.

Device and Default Information

This dialog box tile contains only a single button, the Device and Default Selection button. Pressing this button will display the Device and Default Selection dialog box as shown in Figure 3.35.

This dialog box is used to list and modify the parameters of all configured plotting devices. There are four options available in this dialog box. They, along with brief descriptions of their use, are listed below.

- Save Defaults To File...—Creates a Plot Configuration Parameters (PCP) file. Using these files will store different plot parameters so changes can be made quickly for different plot requirements.
- Get Defaults From File...—Loads the PCP file into AutoCAD.
- Show Device Requirements...—Displays a dialog box containing information regarding the current plot device.
- Change Device Requirements...—Displays a dialog box that allows you to make changes to the plot device configuration.

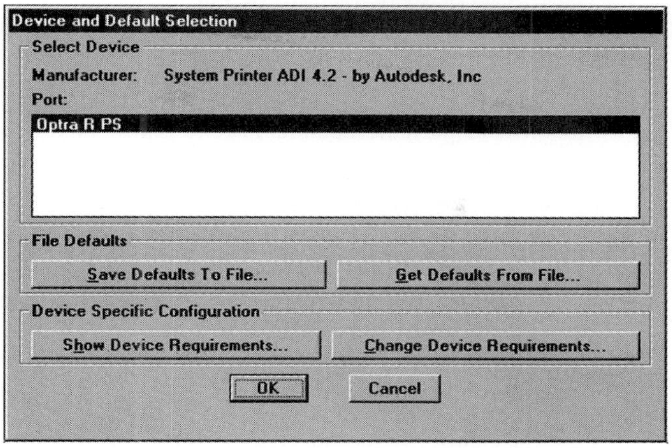

Figure 3.35
The Device and Default Selection dialog box.

Setting Pen Parameters

Used only when you are plotting to a pen or pencil plotter, the Pen Parameters tile is used to modify pen parameters. It is important to note that not all plotters support all of the options that are presented in this section. To find out what parameters you need to set for your plotter, consult the plotter's user's manual. There are two areas that can be modified in this section of the Plot Configuration dialog box, the Pen Assignments and Optimization.

Specifying Pen Assignments

When you select the Pen Assignments..., the Pen Assignments dialog box appears as shown in Figure 3.36.

This dialog box contains a list of the current pen parameter settings on the left, and a way to modify these settings on the right in the Modify Values tile. You can modify the following values:

- Color—Changes the pen assignment based on the color of the object in the drawing database. Changing this option will ensure that AutoCAD is aware of the color configuration of the pens in the plotter.
- Pen—Assigns a pen number in conjunction with the color of an object in the drawing database. When used with plotters that have a single pen, AutoCAD will pause the plot and allow you to change the pen to match the new color needed.
- Linetype (Ltype)—Assigns the linetype to the current color.
- Speed—Adjusts the speed of the pen based on the current color. Use this option if you have pens that are moving too fast, causing pens to skip. This skipping will often degrade the linetype quality.
- Width—Assigns the widths of a line to the current color. Linetype widths are important in producing technically correct drawings. Common metric line widths

Figure 3.36
The Pen Assignments dialog box.

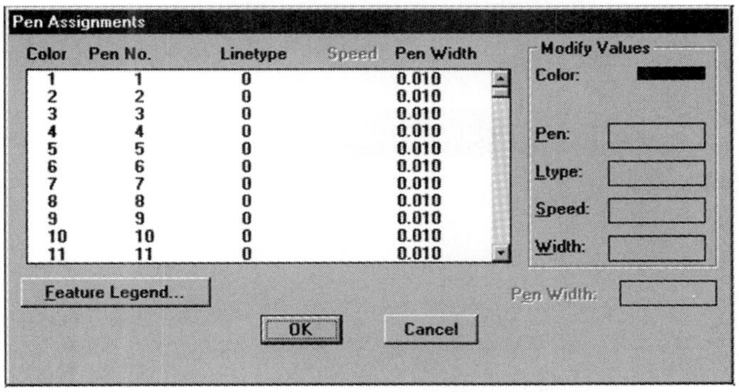

include 0.3mm, 0.5mm, 0.7mm, and 0.9mm. These line widths will vary depending on the discipline for which the drawings are being created.

One last option in this dialog box is the Feature Legend... button. Selecting this button will display the Feature Legend dialog box. This dialog box displays the available hardware linetypes, speeds, or pen widths for the configured plotter. This dialog box will vary depending on the plotting device configured for each computer.

Selecting Additional Parameters

This section of the Plot Configuration dialog box allows you to select which objects will be plotted, how hidden lines are represented on 3-D objects, how area fills will be handled, and whether the drawing will be plotted to a file. Each of these areas will be described below.

- Display—Plots the view presented in the drawing area before the plot command was entered.
- Extents – Plots all objects within the drawing file regardless of their relationship to the limits of the drawing.

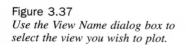

Skill Builder

Before using the Extents option, be sure to select View/Zoom/All. This will update the drawing database and ensure that all objects are included in the plot.

- Limits—Plots all objects within the drawing limits that was specified using the **limits** command.
- View—Plots a previously saved view. In order to use this option, you must first create a view using the **view** command. When you select the View radio button, you must also select the View... button. When you select this button, the View Name dialog box will appear as shown in Figure 3.37. Select the view to be plotted.
- Window—Used to plot a portion of the drawing that was defined using a rectangular window. Once you select this radio button, select the Window... button to create a rectangular window that will specify the objects to be included in the plot. Once this button is selected, the Window Selection dialog box will be displayed as shown in Figure 3.38. This dialog box allows you to specify the window using coordinates for opposite corners of the window. Selecting the Pick< button will return you to the drawing area to create a window using the mouse. If you know the exact coordinates of the window, you can enter those in the First Corner and Other Corner text input boxes.
- Hide Lines—Used to remove hidden lines from 3-D models during the plot process. This option is not used at any time when plotting 2-D drawings.
- Adjusting the Area Fill—Rarely used except for plotting printed circuit schematics, this option ensures the greatest precision possible for the current plot device. Use

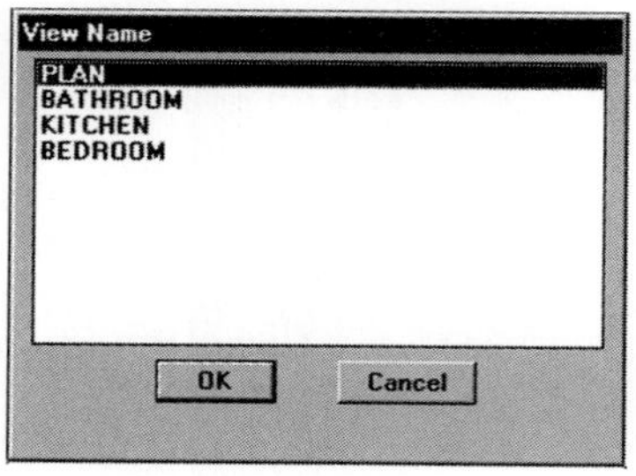

Figure 3.37
Use the View Name dialog box to select the view you wish to plot.

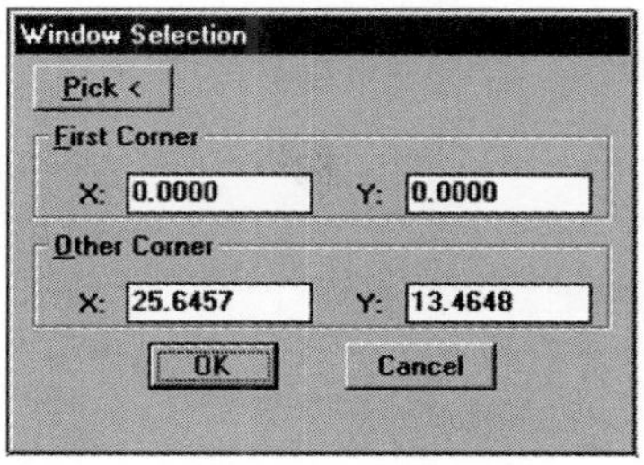

Figure 3.38
Use the Window Selection dialog box to select objects to be plotted.

this option only when you must create a drawing that is accurate to within one-half a pen width.

- Plot To File—Selecting this radio button redirects the plot from the plotter to a file. This option is occasionally used when you want to plot to a plot device that is not currently attached to your workstation but may be located on another computer that does not have AutoCAD.

Specifying Paper Size

One of the most important aspects of plotting is specifying what paper size to use. The drawing must be legible and easy to read once plotted. Rarely will you want to plot an architectural drawing on an A-size sheet of paper. Likewise, you probably won't want to waste an E-size sheet of paper on a mechanical part that is only 2″ × 3″. This portion of the Plot Configuration dialog box will allow you to specify the paper size using the following options:

- Inches—Selects inches as the plotting units. Use this option to plot drawings that have been created using foot and/or inch measurements.
- MM—Select millimeters as the plotting units. Use this option to plot drawings that have been created using metric units.
- Size...—Select this button to display the Paper Size dialog box. The dialog box will present you with a list of the available paper sizes for the currently configured plotting device. The settings in this dialog box will vary based on the plot device. You can also create a **user:** setting that will allow you to specify a portion of the available paper size. Another setting that is included with the list of available paper sizes is the **max** setting. Using this option will ensure that all of the paper is used for the plot. This setting is occasionally larger than the largest paper size listed.

Tutorial 3.13: Using the Plot Dialog Box to Determine Page Limits

A common question for new AutoCAD users is, "What should I use for my limits settings?" An uneducated response would be to set the upper-right limits to the size of the sheet of paper on which you wish to plot. For instance the limits for an A-size sheet of paper would be lower left = 0,0 and upper right = 11,8.5. Unfortunately, if you are plotting to a laser printer you will get a shock when you try to plot. A portion of your drawing will be cut off. What many do not know is that a typical laser printer cannot plot to the edges of a piece of paper. Many times up to a quarter inch may be lost on each side, resulting in a loss of one-half inch of plot area in both the horizontal and vertical edges. So how do you find out just how much of the paper the plot device can print on? In this tutorial, you will learn the procedures necessary to determine what the limits and plot extents are for a particular plotting device. Follow these steps:

1. Ensure that your plot device is properly configured.
2.  Select the Print icon from the Standard toolbar. The Plot Configuration dialog box will be displayed.
3. Select the Size... button in the Paper and Size Orientation tile. The Paper Size dialog box will be displayed as shown in Figure 3.39. If this button is greyed out, skip to step 6.
4. Select the MAX Paper size.
5. Select the OK button. You are returned to the Plot Configuration dialog box.
6. In the Paper Size and Orientation tile, the Plot Area will be displayed as shown in Figure 3.40. Use this value as the upper-right limit for a drawing that is going to be plotted at a scale of 1 Plotted Inch = 1 Drawing Unit. If you

need to plot a drawing at half scale, change the upper-right limit to 2 times the plot area. If you need to plot a drawing at double scale, change the upper-right limit to one-half the plot area.

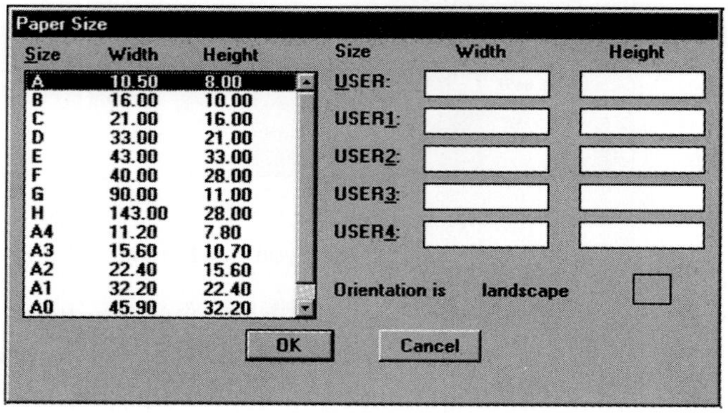

Figure 3.39
The Paper Size dialog box.

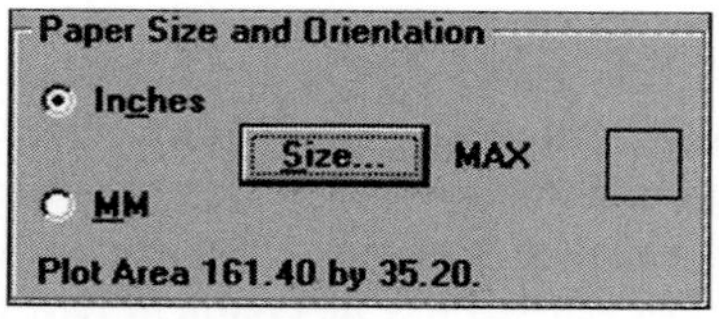

Figure 3.40
This value will be used for the upper-right limits for a drawing that will be plotted at a 1=1 scale.

Specifying Plot Scale, Rotation and Origin

After you select the paper size, you must now make decisions based on the plot scale, the rotation of the plot, and whether you should make adjustments to the plot origin. All of these options should be reviewed before creating the actual plot. To modify these values, use the Scale, Rotation, and Origin tile. You can make the following changes:

- Rotation and Origin...—Select this button to display the Plot Rotation and Origin dialog box as shown in Figure 3.41. In this dialog box you can change the Plot Rotation to either 0, 90, 180, or 270. The rotation affects how the drawing is rotated on the paper. Typically, only 0 and 90 are used on printers. Most plotters use a setting of 0, and the plot rotation is handled by the plotter. Once the plot rotation is established, you now have an opportunity to change the X Origin and the Y Origin. Consult your plotter's user's manual to see if the values need to be changed from the default as specified by the lower-left limits setting.
- The Plotted Inches = Drawing Units is probably one of the most confusing areas of the Plot Configuration dialog box for new users. It really is quite simple to understand. Plotted Inches represents an inch on the plot. Drawing Units are the number of units you specify to be represented as a single inch on the plot. For example, to plot a drawing that uses standard units at ½ scale you would use 1 Plotted Inches = 2 Drawing Units. Get it? 1 = 2 or 1 over 2 or ½. To plot a drawing at double scale,

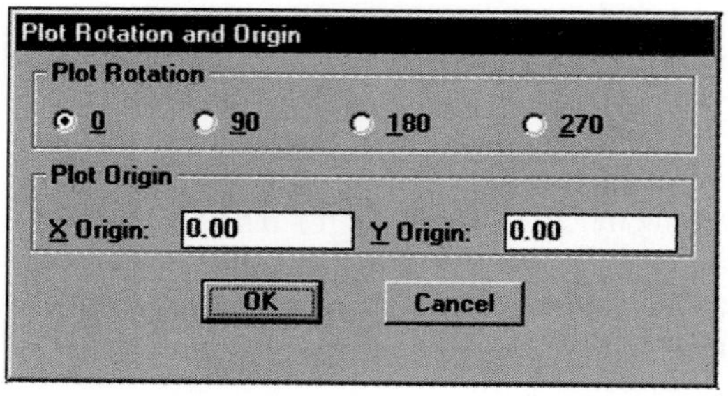

Figure 3.41
Use this dialog box to modify the rotation and origin settings.

use 2 Plotted Inches = 1 Drawing Units. To plot a drawing that uses $^1/_4'' = 1'$ you have to first make sure that units have been set to architectural and then you would use .25 Plotted Inches = 1′ Drawing Units.

- The Scaled to Fit check box allows you to plot the drawing without specifying a scale. While the plot will be proportionally correct, no scale will be assigned to the plot. AutoCAD will attempt to use as much of the available drawing area as possible.

FOR THE PROFESSIONAL

Using the Scaled to Fit option should be used only on drawings that will not be used for manufacturing. Since no scale is assigned to the plot, if a dimension were left off, the manufacturer would not be able to use a scale to determine the missing dimensions. This option is great if you want to create a quick test plot to check your work. Avoid using it on a regular basis.

PREVIEWING THE PLOT

Previewing the plot is a very important step. Using this option will allow you to visually verify that you have made the correct settings before you plot and possibly waste paper. To check your settings you have two options, Partial and Full. Once you have selected the type of preview, use the Preview... button to view the preview.

- Partial—Select this radio button and click the Preview... button to display the Preview Effective Plotting Area dialog box as shown in Figure 3.42. This dialog box displays the paper size in relation to the effective plotting area. If the plotting area exceeds the paper size, a warning will appear in the Warnings text box. If warnings are displayed, you should return to the Plot Configuration dialog box and make adjustments.
- Full—Select this radio button and click the Preview... button to display a full plot preview as shown in Figure 3.43. Another window will also be displayed with the options to Pan and Zoom as well as End the Preview. This window can be moved by dragging it to another location. Using Pan and Zoom will allow you to better view the plot preview at different locations and scale. This option will take longer to produce than the partial option.

```
Effective plotting area: 10.43 wide by 7.92 high
Position paper in plotter
Press RETURN to continue or S to Stop for hardware setup
```

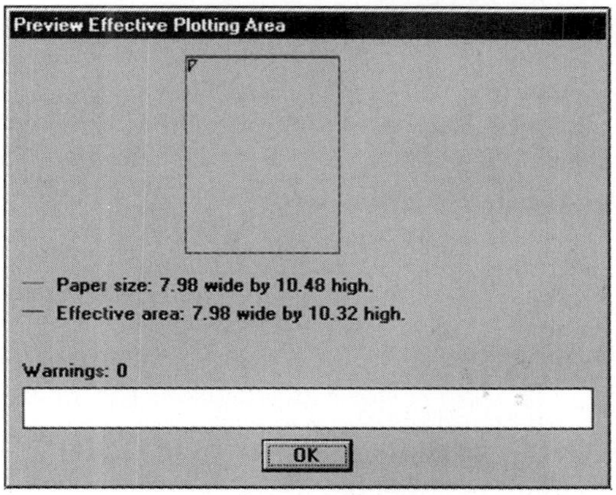

Figure 3.42
Use the Preview Effective Plotting Area to verify the plot settings.

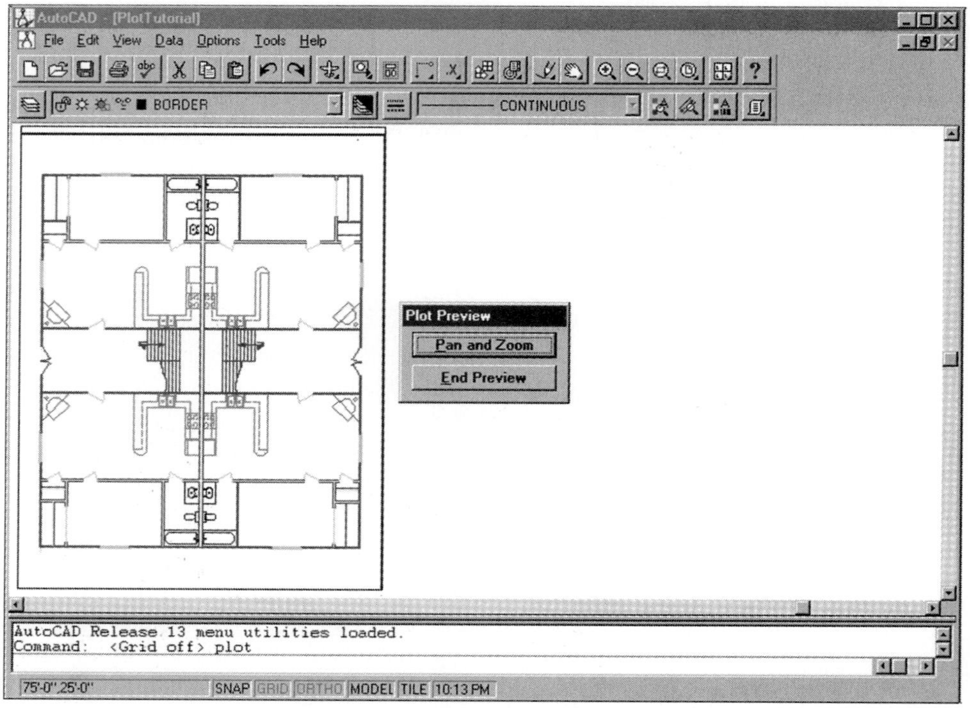

Figure 3.43
Use the Full Preview to display the complete drawing as it will appear on the final plot.

For the Professional

You should always use the **plot preview** option before plotting a drawing. Plot materials can be quite expensive and using this short technique will save you money and time.

Tutorial 3.14: Plotting a Drawing

In this tutorial you will plot the apartment complex that you have been viewing in this unit. Since there are more plotting devices than this book can possibly cover, this tutorial must make a few assumptions: your plotting device will plot an A-Size sheet of paper, and your plotting device has been properly configured.

You will plot the apartment complex at scaled to fit specifications so no particular scale or limits will be necessary. Once you have completed this tutorial, it would a good idea to research the type of plotting device you have and become familiar with its controls and functions. A good place to start would be in the plotting devices user's manual. Use the following steps to plot the apartment complex:

1.  Select Open from the Standard toolbar. The Select File dialog box appears.
2. Select the PlotTutorial.dwg file from the demo disk.
3.  Select **print** from the Standard toolbar. The Plot Configuration dialog box will appear.
4. Select the Extents radio button in the Additional Parameters tile.
5. Select the Inches radio button in the Paper Size and Orientation tile.
6. Select the Size... button in the Paper Size and Orientation tile. The Paper Size dialog box is displayed.
7. Select the MAX paper size if it is available. If not, skip to step 9.
8. Click the OK button. The Paper Size dialog box closes and you are returned to the Plot Configuration dialog box.
9. Select the Rotation and Origin... button in the Scale, Rotation, and Origin tile. The Plot Rotation and Origin dialog box will appear.

10. Select a Plot Rotation of 90.
11. Ensure that the X and Y offsets are set to 0.
12. Select the OK button to close the dialog box.
13. Select the Scaled to Fit check box in the Scale, Rotation, and Origin tile.
14. Select the Partial radio button in the Plot Preview tile.
15. Select the Preview... button. The Preview Effective Plotting Area dialog box is displayed. Check for any warnings. If there are warnings, select OK and repeat steps 1–10. If there are no warnings, continue to step 16.
16. Select the Full radio button in the Plot Preview tile.
17. Select the Preview... button. A full preview of the plot will be displayed.
18. Select the End Preview button to return to the Plot Configuration dialog box.
19. Select the OK button of the Plot Configuration dialog box. The dialog box will close and the plot will begin.
20. You may receive the following in the Command: prompt. If so you will have to press Enter to continue the plot.

FOR THE PROFESSIONAL

Plot times vary based on the size of the drawing file, computer, network print server, or the plot device.

SUMMARY

Viewing a drawing at different magnifications and different locations is very important to the proper creation of geometry. The many commands and options available are not included to confuse, but to allow you to have as many options as possible so that you can create the necessary view. Use Zoom commands to move the view closer to the geometry you are creating to get more accurate drawing results. Pan the view to move over to other sections of the drawing. It can be quite time-consuming to continually create or zoom views. Once a view is found, it may be advantageous to save that view for later use.

Once the drawing is created, it will probably be necessary to create a hard copy output of the drawing. Hard copy can be used to share your ideas as well as to review the drawing for accuracy. Many mistakes on a plot can be found that would not be apparent on the display while the drawing was being created. Be sure to verify all options in the Plot Configuration dialog box and create a plot preview before creating hard copy. These two extra steps can save you time and supplies.

REVIEW

1. What is the difference between the **redraw** and **regen** commands?
2. What is a disadvantage in using the **regenauto** system variable.
3. Discuss the use of the **zoom dynamic** command.
4. What is the difference between the **zoom extents** and **zoom all** commands?
5. Explain the **pan** command and its use.
6. Discuss the functions of the Aerial View Window.
7. Why would it be beneficial to save a view?
8. Discuss the difference between printer and plotter technology.
9. What is the difference between the full and partial preview options in the Plot Configuration dialog box?
10. Outline the procedures to determine the maximum limits for an output device connected to an AutoCAD workstation.

EXERCISE 3

In this assignment you will use plotting and viewing techniques to plot three views of the apartment complex floor plan shown in Figure 3.44. You will plot the complete drawing not to scale and a scaled view of a bathroom and apartment #2. Plot all drawings on an A-size sheet of paper.

1. Open the Apartments.dwg file from the workdisk.
2. Restore a previously saved **view** called SHEET.
3. Plot the complete drawing using the Scaled to Fit option.
4. Restore a **view** called BATH. Notice the detail that was missing when the view was at a smaller scale.
5. Use the **zoom dynamic** to enlarge the view of the sink. Now you know which is hot and which is cold!
6. Plot the bathroom, using the **view** option, at a scale of 1 plotted inch = 2 drawing units. Modify the Rotation and Origin settings to ensure that the plotted view of the bathroom is centered on the page.
7. Plot Apartment #2, using the Window option, at a scale of 1 plotted inch = 4 drawing units. Ensure that you include all wall lines for this apartment. Modify the Rotation and Origin settings to ensure that the plotted view of the bathroom is centered on the page.
8. Save a View of Apartment #2.

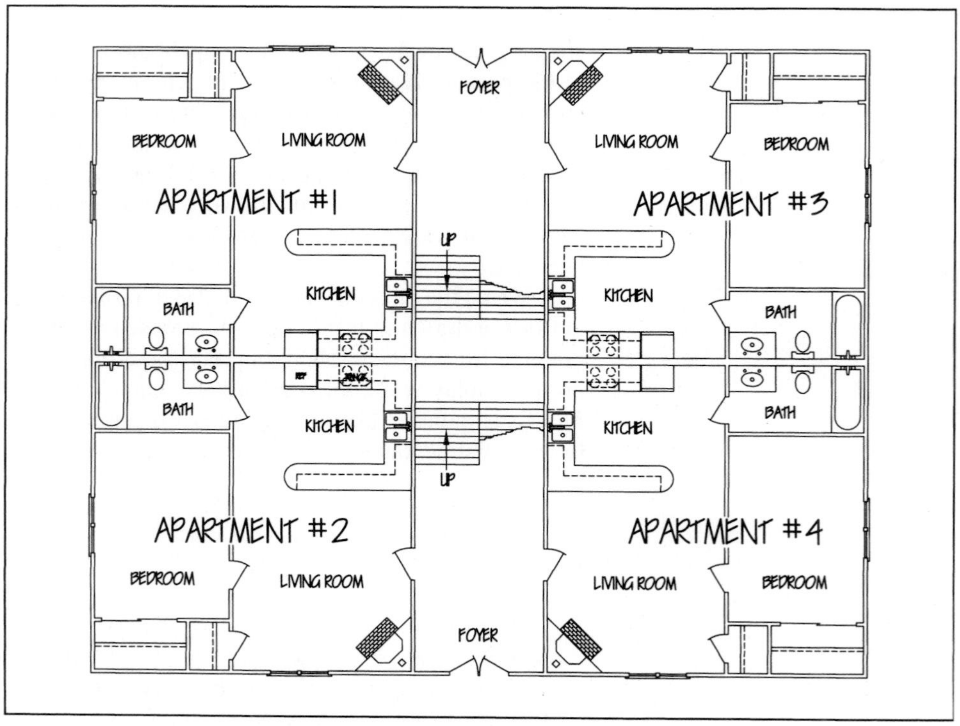

Figure 3.44
The apartment complex floor plan.

UNIT

4 Basic CAD Drawing Techniques

OVERVIEW

In this unit you will first learn how to set the type and precision of units commonly used in CAD drawings. Next you will explore the use of a prototype drawing. A prototype drawing can be used to speed up and standardize the drawing process. You will also learn how to accurately enter coordinate information into your drawing.

OBJECTIVES

- Set the display format and precision.
- Create a prototype drawing.
- Set the prototype drawing options.
- Begin a new drawing by using a prototype drawing.
- Create geometry using relative coordinates.
- Create geometry using absolute polar coordinates.
- Create geometry using relative polar coordinates.

INTRODUCTION

The manual drafter normally begins with a sheet of drafting paper. Depending upon the type of drawing to be completed, he or she will select the appropriate units. The manual drafter will use specific scales for each design project. The architect, for example, will normally use an architectural scale with dimensions given in feet and inches. The mechanical drafter will normally use a decimal scale. Like manual drafting, AutoCAD allows you to use different units in your drawing.

In many cases, the manual drafter uses a sheet of paper that contains a preprinted border and title block. The title block is frequently labeled with the company name and address and has a place for the drawing title, part number, scale, material, and drafter's name, as well as an area for revisions. The manual drafter tapes down the sheet of paper and adds the necessary views, dimensions, and so on. Using drafting paper with a preprinted border and title block ensures standardization within the company. This approach saves time because the manual drafter doesn't have to draw the border and title block with each new drawing.

AutoCAD has a feature called a *prototype drawing,* which provides a similar function to that of the preprinted border and title block used in manual drafting. A simple prototype drawing may contain values for limits, grid, and snap. A complex prototype may contain a border and title block, established text styles, and other drawing variables.

In Unit 2, "Creating Your First Drawing," you learned how to set up AutoCAD to use the snap increment and grid to accurately locate points in the drawing. Another way to specify exact points and create accurate drawings is to use coordinates. AutoCAD uses the Cartesian coordinate system for specifying exact points in a drawing. The second part of this unit discusses the two-dimensional coordinate system for locating points and lines. Four different coordinate entry methods are discussed: absolute, relative, absolute polar, and relative polar.

OUTLINE

Setting Display Format and Precision (UNITS and DDUNITS)
Tutorial 4.1: Drawing Lines Using the Five Different Units
Working with Prototype Drawings
Coordinate System Basics
Tutorial 4.2: Creating a Prototype Drawing
Tutorial 4.3: Using Absolute Coordinates to Create a Side Elevation Profile
Tutorial 4.4: Using Relative Coordinates to Create a Side Elevation Profile
Tutorial 4.5: Using Relative and Absolute Polar Coordinates to Create a Side Elevation Profile
Tutorial 4.6: Creating Property Lines with Coordinates and a Prototype Drawing
Summary
Review
Exercises

SETTING DISPLAY FORMAT AND PRECISION (UNITS AND DDUNITS)

The AutoCAD **units** command and the Units Control dialog box enable you to set the type and precision of units you will use in the drawing. Options within the Units command and Units Control dialog box control two types of unit display: linear and angular. Other options enable you to control the precision with which the unit values appear for linear and angular measurement.

The unit settings affect the following:

- The display of the coordinates on the status bar
- The appearance of the values when dimensioning
- The format of the values when you examine the drawing for an area or distance
- The format for entering coordinates, distances and angles at the `Command:` line

You can set the units by accessing a text box, or through the Units Control dialog box. To access the text box, enter **`units`** at the `Command:` prompt. You can access the Units Control dialog box in the following ways:

- Enter **`ddunits`** at the `Command:` prompt
- Choose Units from Data on the menu bar.

UNITS REPORT FORMATS

AutoCAD has five different measurement report formats: scientific, decimal, engineering, architectural, and fractional. The examples shown in Table 4.1 show how the value of 15.5 drawing units appears in each format.

Each type is designed for a specific purpose. *You* must determine the units in which to create the drawing. Note the five types:

FOR THE PROFESSIONAL

A generic unit can be declared as anything you want: an inch, a mile, a millimeter, or a kilometer.

TABLE 4.1 UNITS OF MEASUREMENT

Report Format	Example
Scientific	1.55E+01
Decimal	15.50
Engineering	1′-3.50″
Architectural	1′-3 1/2″
Fractional	15 1/2

- **Scientific units.** Dimensions are given as a real number raised to a power of 10, such as 125E+02. You can use scientific notation to represent any system of measure. You use scientific notation primarily when working with very large numbers.
- **Decimal units.** Dimensions are given in units, such as 1.75 or 3.625. Decimal units are generally used in mechanical drafting, because ANSI Y14.5M Dimensioning and Tolerancing standards specify that decimal inch or metric units in millimeters be used in engineering drawings. AutoCAD can display a maximum of eight decimal places. Decimal is the default type of unit in AutoCAD.
- **Engineering units.** Dimensions are given in feet, inches, and decimal parts of an inch, such as 6′-5.25″. AutoCAD automatically converts and displays 12 inches as 1 foot. It is important to note that inches is the default unit. If 6 is entered it is assumed to be 6 inches. To enter feet, you must include the (′) symbol. Each engineering unit in AutoCAD represents one inch. Engineering units are used primarily in civil drafting. Detailed construction drawings and topographic maps for planning and constructing highways and harbors are examples of typical civil drafting projects.
- **Architectural units.** Dimensions are given in feet, inches, and fractional parts of an inch, such as $6'\text{-}11\frac{1}{4}''$. Twelve inches is automatically converted to 1 foot. Architectural units are used for residential and commercial planning and construction drawings. The smallest fraction that AutoCAD can display is $\frac{1}{256}''$ It is important to note that inches is the default unit. If 6 is entered, it is assumed to be 6 inches. To enter feet, you must include the (′) symbol.
- **Fractional units.** Dimensions are given in whole units and parts of a unit as a fraction, such as $26\frac{5}{8}$. Fractional units may be any value, such as inches, feet, or miles. You can use fractional representation with any system of measure. As with architectural units, the smallest fraction that AutoCAD can display is $\frac{1}{256}''$.

Display Precision

The display format and entry format of the units selected is determined by the number of decimal places or the smallest fraction. The easiest method of selecting the units and setting the display precision is with the Units Control dialog box (Figure. 4.1). You can access this dialog box in one of two ways:

- Choose Units from Data on the menu bar.
- Enter **`ddunits`** at the `Command:` prompt.

The default precision value is shown in the dialog box. After you have determined the type of units you will use, you must decide on the accuracy of the drawing display. For example, if you are using decimal units, two digits may be shown as 2.88, three digits as 2.875, and four digits as 2.8751. As shown in this example for decimal units, AutoCAD rounds the value of the display.

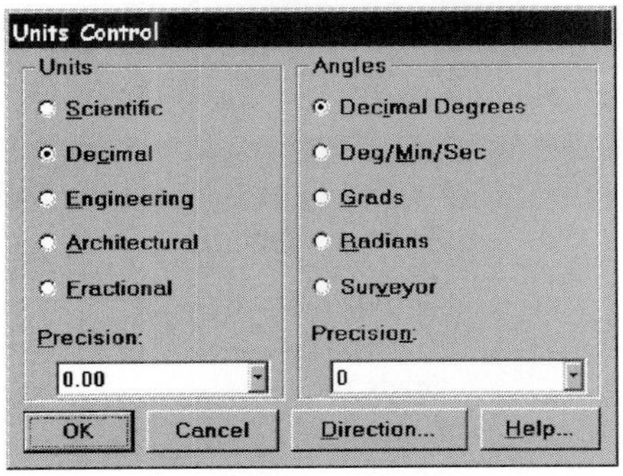

Figure 4.1
Use the Units Control dialog box to set the type of units and the precision.

For the Professional

Regardless of the display precision setting, AutoCAD is accurate to 14 places for all types of units. The only values affected by changing the precision are the display of the coordinates on the status bar and the format of the values when you examine the drawing for an area or distance.

When you are working on mechanical drawings, three to four digits are normally used for inch drawings. For metric drawings, one- or two-place decimals are generally used, such as 16.5 or 16.50. This difference is due to the greater distance represented by inches as opposed to millimeters.

With architectural and fractional units, the precision is determined by the size of the fraction's denominator. Selecting 1/8 results in the values being displayed in 1/8-inch increments (or their least common denominator). For example, the display may read 6′-5$\frac{1}{8}$″. If 1/4 was chosen as the precision, the same dimension would be rounded off to the nearest 1/4-inch increment, or 6′-5$\frac{1}{4}$″.

Angular Measurement

AutoCAD also has five different angular measurement options. The examples in Table 4.2 show how the value of 45.5 degrees appears in each format.

Here are descriptions of the angular measurement options for AutoCAD:

- **Decimal degrees.** Displays angular measurement as real numbers with up to eight decimal places. This is the default type of angular measurement in AutoCAD.
- **Deg/Min/Sec.** Displays angular measurement in degrees, minutes, and seconds. This representation uses ASCII characters, such as 30d12′38″. Measurements of less than 1 second are displayed as decimal places.
- **Grads.** Displays angular measurement as grads. A lowercase *g* appears after the value, such as 37g. Ninety degrees equals 100 grads.
- **Radians.** Displays angular measurement as radians. A lowercase *r* appears after the value, such as 6.2832r. A radian is 180/pi degrees.
- **Surveyor's units.** Displays angular measurement in degrees, minutes, and seconds together with quadrant bearings. An example is N45d12′25″E. Surveyor's units are based on a circle divided into four quadrants, so no angular value can be greater than 90 degrees.

For the Professional

If the status bar doesn't have enough room to display the coordinates normally, AutoCAD sometimes displays them in scientific units. This does not mean that the units have changed, only that AutoCAD must use scientific units to display them.

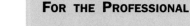

Table 4.2 Units of Angular Measurement

Report Format	Example
Decimal Degrees	42.5000
Deg/Min/Sec	42d30′0″
Grads	47.2222g
Radians	0.7418r
Surveyor's units	N 47d30′0″E

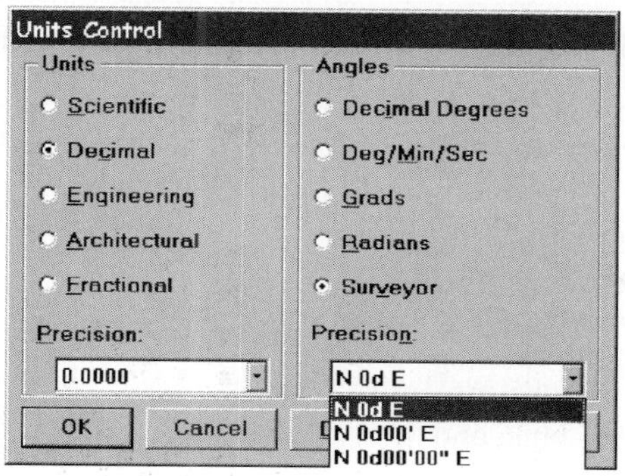

Figure 4.2
Use the Units Control dialog box to set the precision for angles.

Angle Display Precision The degree of accuracy for angles is determined by the drawing requirements. Two-place decimal degrees or degrees and minutes are normally used for mechanical drawings. Mapmaking with civil drawings often requires degrees, minutes, and seconds.

You can easily change the angle display precision in the Units Control dialog box. As noted, you access the Units Control dialog box by entering ddunits at the `Command:` prompt or choosing Data/Units. To change the precision, select the arrow at the right of the Precision text box. The Precision list box appears, as shown in Figure 4.2. Use your pointing device to select the precision you want.

Angle Direction By default, AutoCAD assumes that 0 degrees is toward the right (east, or 3 o'clock). Also by default, angles increase in the counterclockwise direction, as shown in Figure 4.13.

You can change the location of 0 degrees and the direction of angular measurement with the Direction Control dialog box. Surveyors often change these defaults because typically they measure angles clockwise from north rather than counterclockwise from east. To change the angle direction and location of 0 degrees, choose Direction in the Units Control dialog box. The Direction Control dialog box appears, as shown in Figure 4.3.

To change the angle 0 direction, select the appropriate location with the corresponding radio button. If you choose Other, you can enter an angle value in the box, which becomes the new angle 0 direction, or you can choose Pick, which allows you to "show" AutoCAD the direction for angle 0 by picking two points in the drawing window.

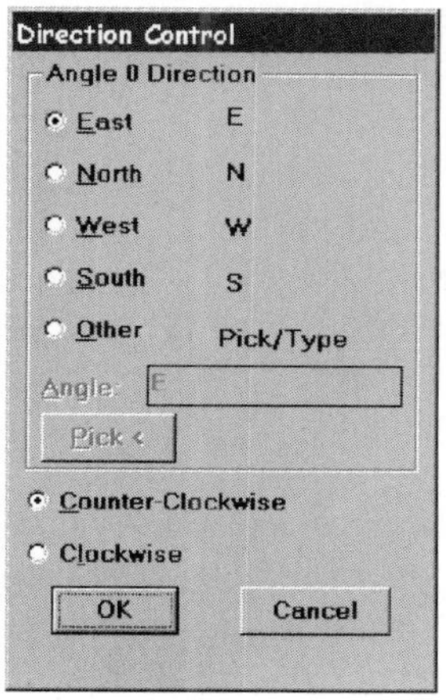

Figure 4.3
Change the angle 0 location and direction of angular measurement in the Direction Control dialog box.

Tutorial 4.1: Drawing Lines Using the Five Different Units

In this tutorial you will create five parallel lines using the different units discussed in the unit. Once all five lines are created you'll be able to compare them.

1.  From the Standard toolbar, select New. If prompted with the Save Changes dialog box, select No. In the Create New Drawing dialog box, enter the proper path, name the drawing Lines, then select OK.
2. Choose Data/Units. Change the units to Scientific and choose OK.
3. Select Tools/Toolbars/Draw to access the Draw toolbar.
4. 
   - From the Draw toolbar, select Line.
   - At the `_line From point:` prompt, type **2e00,2e00** and press Enter.
   - At the `To point:` prompt, type **1.45e01,2e00** and press Enter.
   - At the `To point:` prompt, press Enter.
5. Choose Data/Units. Change the units to Decimal and choose OK.
6. 
   - From the Draw toolbar, select Line.
   - At the `_line From point:` prompt, type **2,3** and press Enter.
   - At the `To point:` prompt, type **14.5,3** and press Enter.
   - At the `To point:` prompt, press Enter.
7. Choose Data/Units.
   Change the units to Engineering and choose OK.
8. 
   - From the Draw toolbar, select Line.
   - At the `_line From point:` prompt, type **0'2",04** and press Enter.
   - For this example we'll use the relative coordinate method to describe the line length.
   - At the `To point:` prompt, type **@1'.5",0** and press Enter.
   - At the `To point:` prompt, press Enter.
9. Choose Data/Units. Change the units to Architectural and choose OK.
10. 
    - From the Draw toolbar, select Line.
    - At the `_line From point:` prompt, type **0'2,0'5** and press Enter.
    - For this example we'll use the relative polar coordinate method to describe the line length.
    - At the `To point:` prompt, type **@1'0-1/2"<0** and press enter.
    - At the `To point:` prompt, press Enter.
11. Choose Data/Units. Change the units to Fractional and choose OK.
12. 
    - From the Draw toolbar, select Line.
    - At the `_line From point:` prompt, type 2,6 and press Enter.
    - For this example we'll use the polar coordinate method to describe the line length.
    - At the `To point:` prompt, type **@12-1/2<0** and press Enter.
    - At the `To point:` prompt, press Enter.
13.  To see all lines fill the screen select the Zoom All icon from the Standard toolbar. All lines are now displayed for your inspection.

For the Professional

Point locations can be entered in architectural units as well as decimal units. When you indicate architectural units, use hyphens only to distinguish fractions from whole inches. Additionally, do not use spaces while giving a dimension. For example, you can specify 6 feet, $5\frac{1}{4}$ inches as $6'5\frac{1}{4}"$ or 6'5.25", but not as $6'\text{-}5\frac{1}{4}"$.

WORKING WITH PROTOTYPE DRAWINGS

AutoCAD comes with a standard prototype drawing named **acad.dwg.** By default, this prototype drawing is used every time you begin a new drawing. If you continually use the default **acad.dwg** prototype drawing, you will soon discover that you frequently make the same drawing aids adjustments over and over. Units, limits, grid, and snap are drawing tools that need to be set every time you begin a new drawing that is at a different size than the prototype.

A prototype drawing may be defined as any drawing file you want to use as the template for the new drawing you are creating. The prototype drawing can contain settings for such variables as the limits, snap increment, and grid spacing. After the prototype drawing is loaded, you can create geometry as before. The advantage of using a prototype drawing is that it frees you from having to change the same settings every time you start a new drawing.

For the Professional

There is nothing different about a drawing that is used as a prototype. Any AutoCAD drawing can be used as a prototype for any other drawing.

When you initially create a prototype drawing in AutoCAD, you set the limits, units, snap, and grid variables to your current specifications. In time, you may want to set up a prototype for each drawing size and type. For example, you might establish different prototype drawings that set the AutoCAD drafting tools and contain a border and title block for A-, B-, and C-size drawings.

You may set up different prototypes for mechanical, electrical, and architectural drawings. Whenever you create several drawings that contain similar settings, consider making and using a prototype drawing. You can select any drawing to be your prototype drawing when you select the New icon from the Standard toolbar, or select New from the File menu.

Creating a New Drawing from a Prototype

When AutoCAD starts, the standard AutoCAD graphics window is displayed. As discussed in Unit 2, you can begin creating geometry immediately, without giving your drawing a name. If you want to use a prototype drawing, you must assign the prototype before you begin working on the new drawing. You can begin a new drawing with one of these methods:

- Select New from the Standard toolbar.
- Enter **`new`** at the `Command:` prompt.
- Choose New from the File menu.

Either method accesses the Create New Drawing dialog box (see Figure 4.4). The text box to the right of the Prototype button is already filled in with the file name **acad.dwg.** This is AutoCAD's default prototype drawing.

When you click the Prototype button, a list of possible prototype drawings appears in the Prototype Drawing File dialog box (Figure 4.5). AutoCAD displays the contents of the c:\r13\com\support subdirectory because this is where the default **acad.dwg** prototype drawing is located. If you change directories and choose a different prototype drawing, that directory becomes the default directory automatically displayed in the Create New Drawing and Prototype Drawing File dialog boxes. The List Files of Type list box at the bottom of the Prototype Drawing File dialog box filters out all file names that do not have the **.dwg** extension.

After you select a new prototype drawing, you are ready to begin working on the drawing. All settings that were part of the prototype drawing are now part of your new drawing. The prototype drawing file will not be changed in any way when you begin creating geometry in the new drawing.

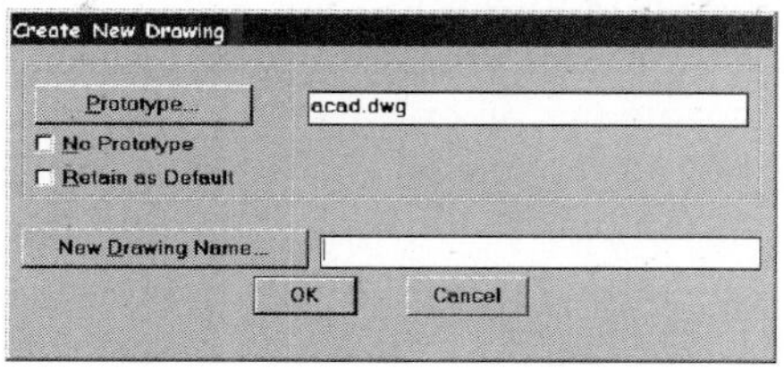

Figure 4.4
The Create New Drawing dialog box with the default AutoCAD prototype drawing acad already provided.

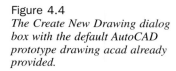

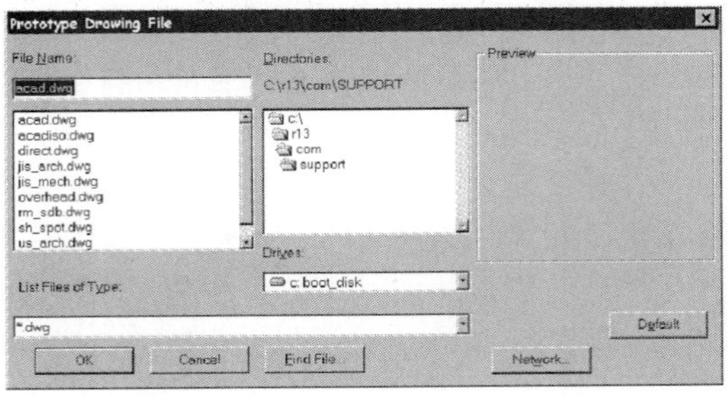

Figure 4.5
In the Prototype Drawing File dialog box, you can select a different prototype drawing.

Skill Builder

After you select a prototype drawing, you do not have to enter a drawing name in the Create New Drawing dialog box. If you press Enter after selecting a prototype drawing, you can create and edit your drawing without giving it a name. You are prompted for a name the first time you save the drawing. Although this is fine for experimental drawings, you should get into the habit of naming your drawings from the beginning.

Setting Prototype Drawing Options

The Create New Drawing dialog box contains two options that can be set regarding prototype drawings. They are the No Prototype and Retain As Default check boxes. The **acad.dwg** drawing remains as the default prototype drawing unless you select the Retain As Default check box and then select a different prototype.

Occasionally, you may need to start a new drawing with AutoCAD's default settings but without any prototype drawing. You usually do this when you import into the drawing editor a **dxf** or **iges** file made by AutoCAD or another graphics program. In this case, you use the No Prototype option. When you use No Prototype, you get only AutoCAD's default settings; any settings or entities you may have in your own prototype will not be set or drawn. The next time you create a new drawing, your prototype will load as usual.

Proper use of prototype drawings can considerably increase the speed at which drawings are created. Many repetitive set-up tasks can be stored in prototype drawings. Remember, a prototype drawing is created like any other drawing. Consequently, any drawing can be used as a prototype drawing.

COORDINATE SYSTEM BASICS

One of the historic landmarks of science and mathematics was the introduction of coordinates into geometry. The key idea behind the coordinate system is how a given set of points is represented. Points are represented as an ordered pair of real numbers, written in such a way that you can distinguish one number as the "first" and the other as "second." The usual notation is (x,y), where x and y are real numbers.

Ordered pairs of real numbers may be associated with points of a coordinate plane. For example, suppose that an ordered pair of numbers (x,y) is given. The first number of the pair is located on horizontal line L1, with the positive direction to the right (the x-axis). The second number of the pair is located on vertical line L2 (the y-axis), with the positive direction upward and the origin the same as that of the x-axis. The point (P) where the two lines intersect is labeled (x,y). The numbers x and y are called the Carte-

TUTORIAL 4.2: CREATING A PROTOTYPE DRAWING

In this tutorial, you create a prototype drawing. This prototype will be used in a later exercise to help you draw a site plan. In this prototype drawing, you will set units, limits, grid, and snap; load a phantom linetype; and set the linetype scale. You begin by creating a new drawing. Follow these steps:

1.  From the Standard toolbar, select New. If prompted with the Save Changes dialog box, select No. In the Create New Drawing dialog box, enter the proper path and name the drawing **aproto** in the text box as shown in Figure 4.6. Because you are creating a prototype drawing and not actually using one, the AutoCAD default **acad.dwg** prototype is used. When you have entered the correct information, select OK.

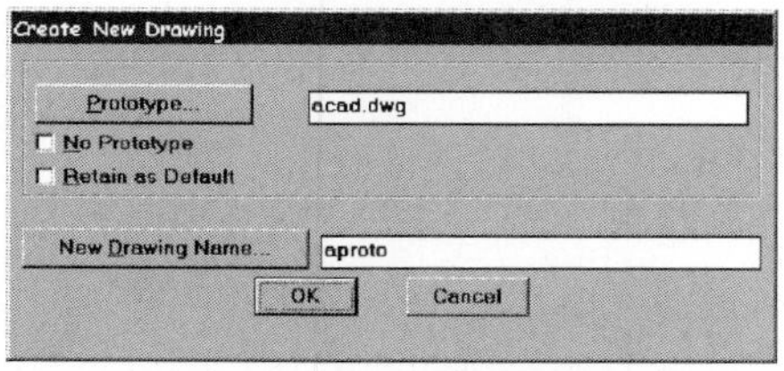

Figure 4.6 *Use the Create New Drawing dialog box to create the prototype file.*

You should now see the standard AutoCAD graphics window. First, you need to set the units. For this exercise, you will be using architectural units with a precision of 0′-0″ and surveyor angles with a precision of N 0d E. Follow these steps:

1. Choose Data/Units. The Units Control dialog box appears.
2. Using the pointing device, adjust the dialog box to reflect the settings shown in Figure 4.7.

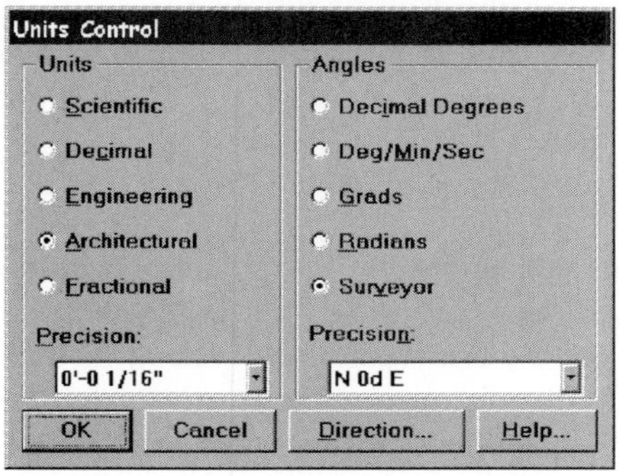

Figure 4.7 *Setting Units to Architectural, Precision to $\frac{1}{16}$″, and Angles to Surveyor.*

Next, set the limits for the prototype drawing. The lower-left limits will remain 0′-0″, and the upper-right limits will be 144′-0″,96′-0″. Follow these steps:

1. Choose Data/Drawing Limits.
2. At the `ON/OFF/<Lower left corner><0′-0″,0′-0″>:` prompt, press Enter.
3. At the `Upper right corner <1′-0″,0′-9″>:` prompt, type **144′-0″,96′-0″** and press Enter.

To show the entire limits within the view window, you issue the Zoom All option:

1.  From the Standard toolbar, choose the Zoom All icon.

After the limits are established, set the grid to 5′ and the snap to 1′:

1. Choose Options/Drawings Aids to access the Drawing Aids dialog box.
2. Enter 5′ for the grid X and Y spacing.
3. Enter 1′ for the snap X and Y spacing.
4. Check the Snap On and Grid On check boxes. Your dialog box should appear as shown in Figure 4.8.

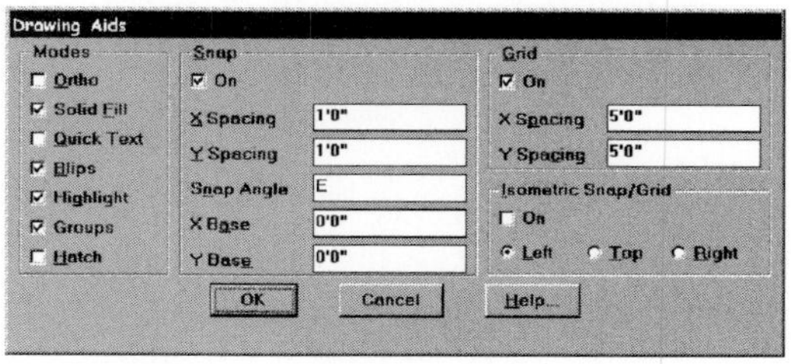

Figure 4.8 *Setting the Grid to 5′ and the Snap to 1′.*

Next, load a phantom line. Up to this point, the only linetypes you have drawn have been continuous lines. To create the site plan, you will need to use a phantom linetype. Although this procedure is introduced here, an in-depth discussion of loading linetypes and modifying linetype scales can be found in Unit 5, "Understanding Layers and Linetypes." Follow these steps:

1. 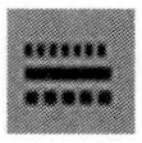 From the Object Properties toolbar, choose the Linetype icon. This displays the Select Linetype dialog box.
2. To load the Phantom linetype, select Load. The Load or Reload Linetype dialog box is displayed. If the linetype has been previously loaded, the Reload Linetype dialog box will appear.
3. Use the scroll bar to display Phantom in the Available Linetype list box and then select Phantom.
4. Press Enter or select OK to accept the Load or Reload Linetypes dialog box and return to the Select Linetype dialog box.
5. In the Select Linetype dialog box, pick the picture of the sample Phantom linetype from the Loaded Linetypes list box to set it as the current linetype.

The next task is to set the linetype scale to 96 so that the line will be scaled correctly when displayed or plotted. A full description of linetype scaling is covered in Unit 5.

6. In the Select Linetype dialog box, move the pointing device into the Linetype Scale edit box and press the Pick button.
7. For the new scale factor, enter 96.
8. Select OK to accept the Select Linetype dialog box. The **phantom** linetype is now loaded and set, and the linetype scale is set.
9.  The aproto.dwg prototype file is now ready to be saved for use later in this unit. To save the drawing, click the **save** icon on the Standard toolbar.

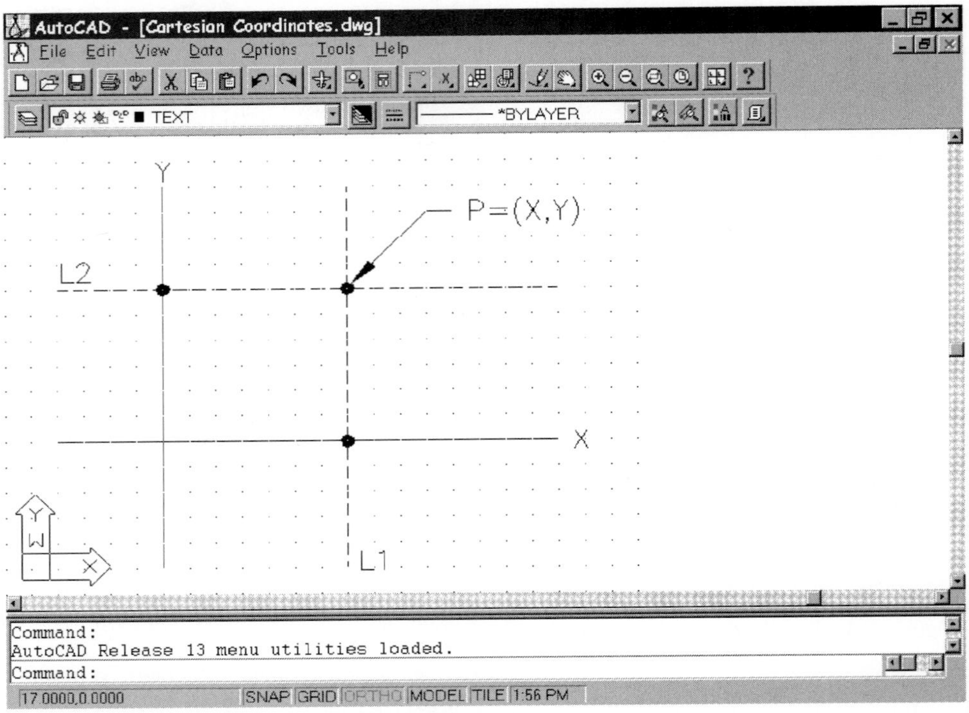

Figure 4.9
The Cartesian coordinate system used to locate point P.

sian coordinates of the point P (Figure 4.9). Cartesian is named in honor of Descartes, a French philosopher who introduced the concept in the seventeenth century.

AutoCAD uses the same Cartesian coordinate system to designate points within a drawing. When you create a 2-D drawing, you can enter points for geometry creation with either the pointing device or the keyboard. The coordinate display in the status bar at the bottom of the screen shows the current location of the crosshairs in the present unit of measure. Note that the readout uses the Cartesian coordinate system. It should also be noted that AutoCAD has full 3-D potential by adding the distance from the origin along the z-axis to the Cartesian coordinates, as in (x,y,z). This concept is used when creating three-dimensional drawings.

Using Coordinates in AutoCAD

At this point, you should be familiar with the standard AutoCAD graphics window. Notice that an icon is shown in the lower-left corner, consisting of two perpendicular arrows. These arrows are directional indicators for the user coordinate system, or UCS. While creating 2-D drawings, the UCS icon shows the direction of the positive values for the x- and y-axes. The UCS is based on the Cartesian coordinate system and divides space into four quadrants. Figure 4.10 shows the UCS icon and the division of space based on Cartesian coordinates. You locate points in these quadrants by specifying their location in horizontal (x) and vertical (y) directions along the plane. It is also possible to change the origin point of the UCS.

Skill Builder

To remove the UCS icon, select Options/UCS/Icon. If Icon has a check next to it, the UCS icon is displayed. If it is not checked, it is not displayed. You can toggle the display of the UCS icon on and off by picking Icon.

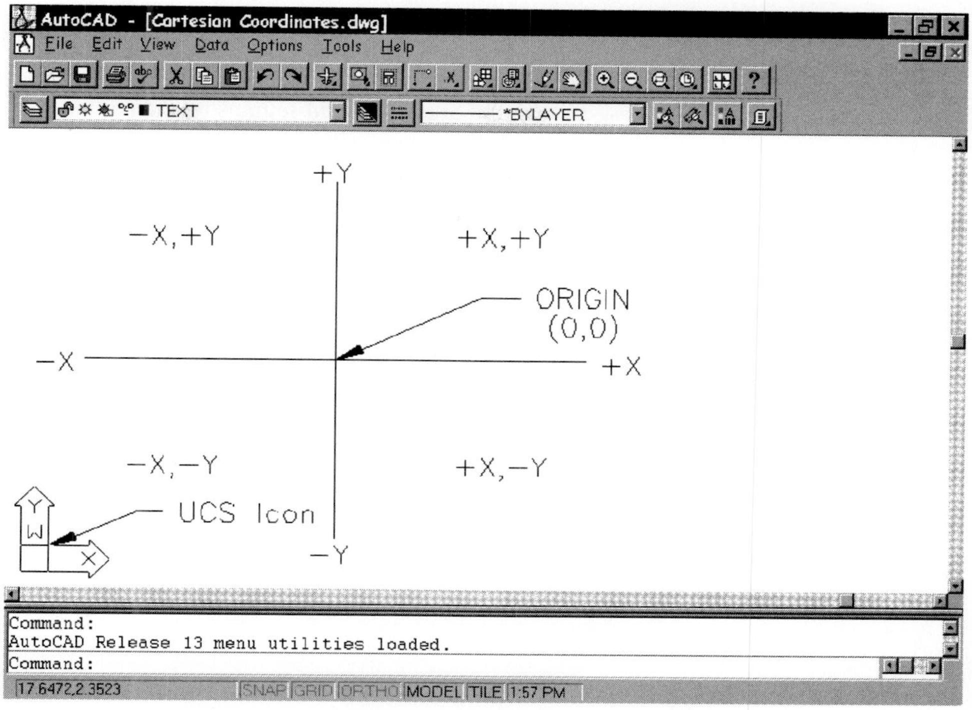

Figure 4.10
The division of space, using the Cartesian coordinate system, with the UCS icon displayed.

The AutoCAD screen has a direct relationship to the Cartesian coordinate system (see Figure 4.11). As you begin creating lines, AutoCAD asks you to specify the `From point:`. In Unit 2, you entered this information, using the pointing device, in association with the snap and grid. You did that by moving the crosshairs to a point on-screen and pressing the Pick button on the pointing device.

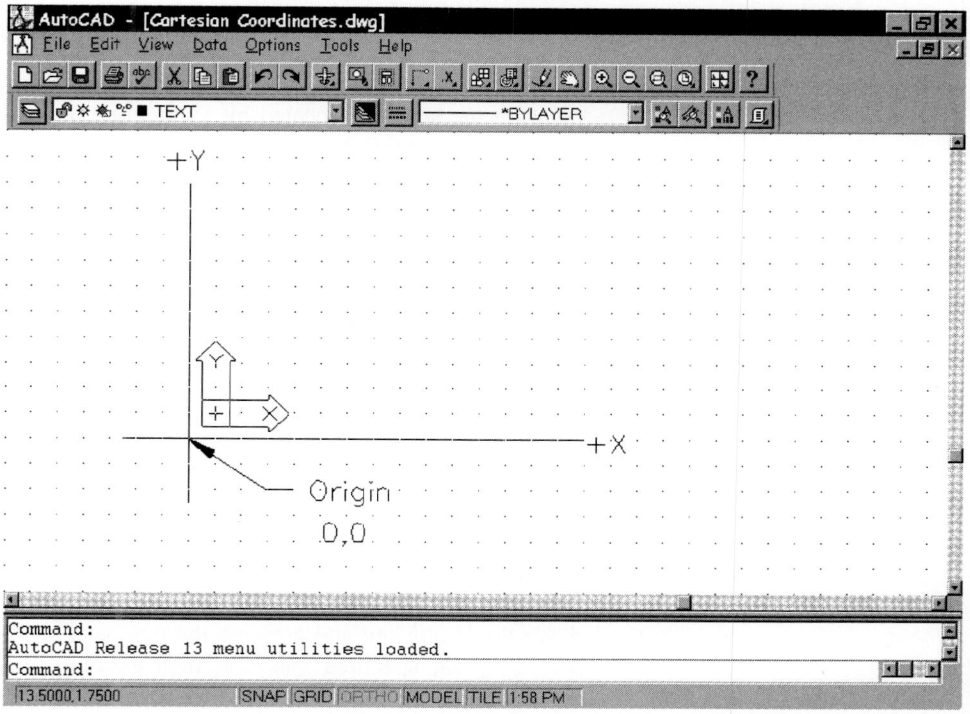

Figure 4.11
The relationship of the drawing screen to the Cartesian coordinate system. Limits are set with the lower-left corner at 0,0 and the upper-right corner at two positive values.

Using the pointing device with the snap and grid is excellent for creating certain types of geometry. Because of constraints imposed by the Snap and Grid, however, very specific locations cannot be made. In an attempt to locate more specific points, you could change the Snap and Grid settings to smaller values. When the grid spacing is too small, AutoCAD responds with the message `Grid too dense to display`. When the snap increment is set very small, it becomes difficult, if not impossible, to pick exact locations. Because many disciplines (such as architecture and engineering) often deal with very specific locations, a more exact means of controlling the "to point" is needed. You can control this point by using absolute, relative, absolute polar, and relative polar coordinates.

For the Professional

Even though the Grid, Snap, and Ortho modes may be activated, any coordinate entered through the keyboard overrides any of these settings. This is true even if the desired point location does not fall on the grid or cannot be snapped to, or if the `To point:` location is at an angle from the previous location with Ortho mode turned on.

Skill Builder

You can switch the coordinate entry method at any time during a command sequence. The first coordinate may be absolute, followed by a relative move, an absolute polar coordinate and then using the pointing device.

Entering Absolute Coordinates The absolute coordinate system locates all points from an origin presumed to be 0,0. The origin point is understood to be the same point on which the limits, snap, and grid are based. The origin is presumed to be 0,0 because the lower-left corner of the display screen may be set at any location other than 0,0. Setting the lower-left corner at 0,0 is the most common and recommended setting, however.

The axes for the x and y coordinates intersect at 0,0 (refer to Figure 4.11). Each point on the screen is located by a numeric coordinate based on the intersection of the x- and y-axes at 0,0. You define points by entering the coordinates of x and y, separated by a comma.

For the Professional

Point locations can be entered in architectural units as well as decimal units. When you indicate architectural units, use hyphens only to distinguish fractions from whole inches. Additionally, do not use spaces while giving a dimension. For example, you can specify 6 feet, $5\frac{1}{4}$ inches as 6′5-$\frac{1}{4}$″ or 6′5.25″, but not as 6′-5$\frac{1}{4}$″.

Entering Relative Coordinates Relative coordinates are used to locate "to points" in relation to the previous point, rather than the origin. You enter relative coordinates in a manner similar to the way you enter absolute coordinates. When you enter relative coordinates, the @ (*at* symbol) must precede your entry. You select this symbol by holding down the ⇧Shift key and pressing the number @/2 key on the keyboard. For example, if the last point specified was 6,4, then entering @3,4 is equivalent to specifying the absolute coordinates 6+3 and 4+4, or 9,8.

Tutorial 4.3: Using Absolute Coordinates to Create a Side Elevation Profile

In this tutorial, you create a side elevation profile (see Figure 4.12) using the Line command and absolute coordinates. Follow these steps:

1.  From the Standard toolbar, select New. If prompted with the Save Changes dialog box, select No.

2.  From the Draw toolbar, select Line. You will draw all five lines continuously, starting at point A and moving counterclockwise to points B, C, D, E, and finally back to point A. All points in this exercise are specified using absolute coordinates.

3. At the `From point:` prompt, type **`2,2`** and press Enter. The line starts at point A. Continue using absolute coordinates to complete the drawing.

4. To locate point B, enter **`8,2`** at the `To point:` prompt.

5. To locate point C, enter **`8,5.5`** at the `To point:` prompt.

6. To locate point D, enter **`5,7`** at the `To point:`.

7. To locate point E, enter **`2,5.5`** at the `To point:` prompt.

8. To close the line on starting point A, enter **`c`** at the `To point:` prompt.

For the Professional

When you are entering the coordinates and notice a mistake, simply type **`u`** at the `To point:` prompt and press Enter. This will undo the last coordinate and allow you to reenter the correct coordinates.

Figure 4.12 *Creating the side elevation profile, using absolute coordinates.*

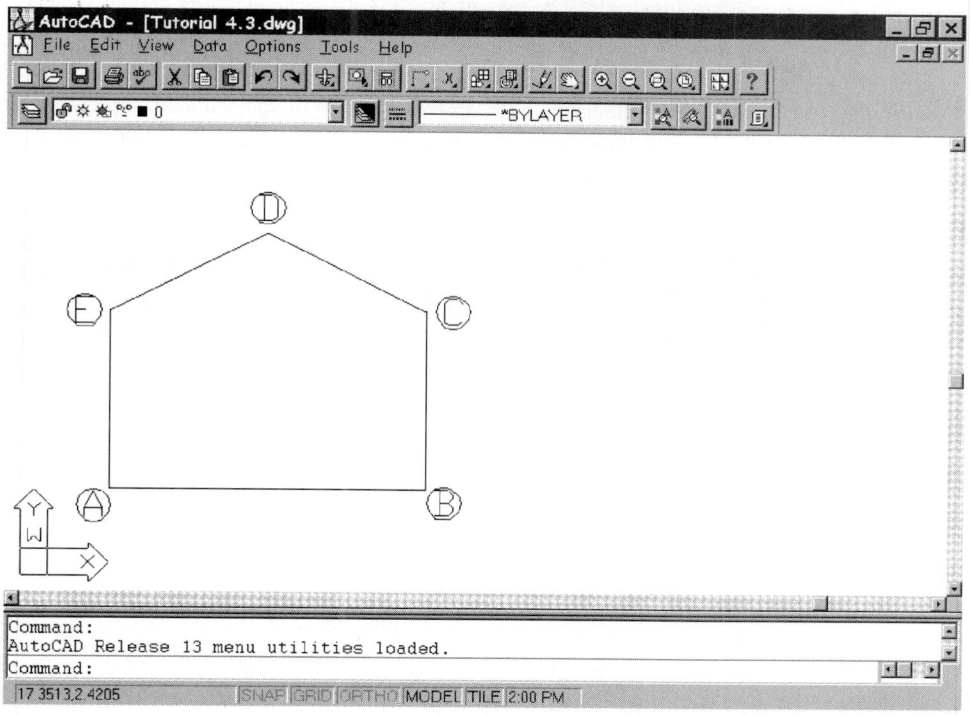

For the Professional

To draw an object from a previous data point, enter @ for the relative specification. This stipulates a zero offset. For example, if the last point entered was 5,7, entering just the @ specifies 5,7 again.

Understanding Polar Coordinates

Polar coordinates can be defined as a distance and angle from a specified point. By default, AutoCAD measures angles in a counterclockwise manner. Zero degrees is toward the positive x-axis, to the right of the point being referenced. This means that 90 degrees is straight up, toward the positive y-axis; 180 degrees is to the left, toward the negative x-axis; and 270 degrees is straight down, toward the negative y-axis. Figure 4.13 shows the default AutoCAD angle measurement in a two-dimensional coordinate system. This direction can be changed using the units command if so desired.

Using Absolute Polar Coordinates You designate an absolute polar coordinate by entering first the distance, then the < sign, and then the angle. For example, to specify a 6-unit-long line at an angle of 45 degrees, you would enter **`6<45`** as the coordinate at the `To point:` prompt. AutoCAD locates the end point of the line 6 units away from the origin 0,0 point at an angle of 45 degrees. All absolute polar coordinates are measured from the origin.

Using Relative Polar Coordinates Relative polar coordinates are measured from the last point entered as a distance followed by an angle. To specify a relative polar coordinate, precede the distance and angle with the @ symbol. To specify a line of 3 units at an angle of 60 degrees from the last point picked, you would enter **`@3<60`** at the `To point:` prompt. AutoCAD locates the end point of the line 3 units away from the last point entered at an angle of 60 degrees.

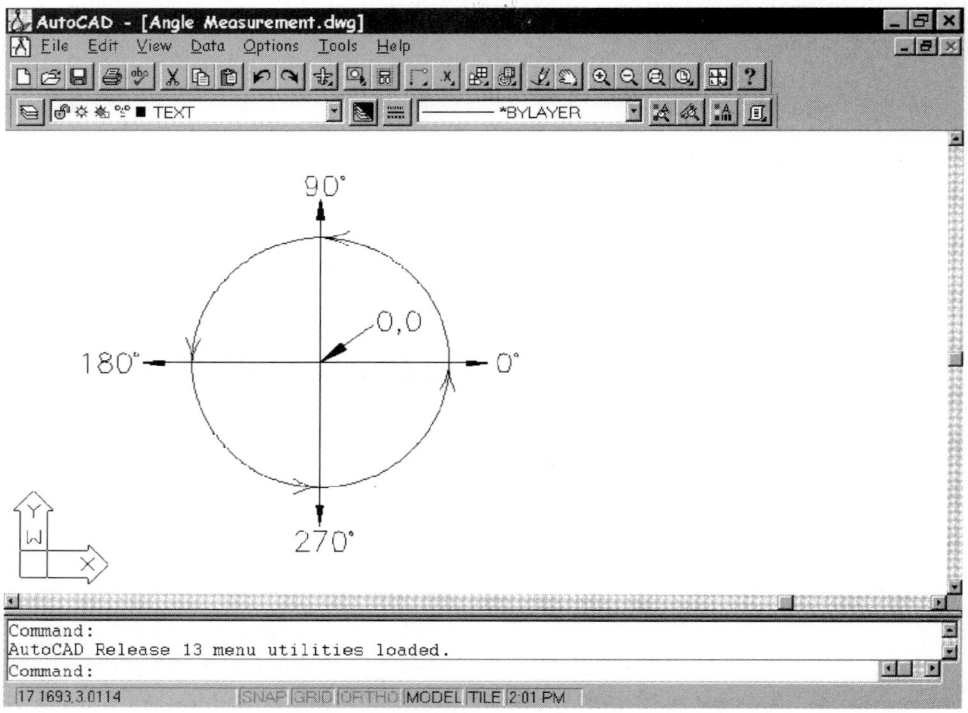

Figure 4.13
The default AutoCAD angle measurement system in a 2-D coordinate system.

TUTORIAL 4.4: USING RELATIVE COORDINATES TO CREATE A SIDE ELEVATION PROFILE

In this tutorial, you create the side elevation profile found in Figure 4.12, using the Line command and relative coordinates. Follow these steps:

1.  From the Standard toolbar, select New. If prompted with the Save Changes dialog box, select No.
2.  From the Draw toolbar, select Line. You will draw all five lines continuously, starting at point A and moving counterclockwise to points B, C, D, E, and finally back to point A. All points in this exercise are specified using relative coordinates except point A, which will be specified using absolute coordinates.
3. At the `From point:` prompt, enter **2,2** for point A.
4. To locate point B, type **@6,0** at the `To point:` prompt.
5. To locate point C, type **@0,3.5** at the `To point:` prompt.
6. To locate point D, type **@-3,1.5** at the `To point:` prompt.
7. To locate point E, type **@-3,-1.5** at the `To point:` prompt.
8. To close the line on starting point A, enter **c** at the `To point:` prompt.

TUTORIAL 4.5: USING RELATIVE AND ABSOLUTE POLAR COORDINATES TO CREATE A SIDE ELEVATION PROFILE

In this tutorial, you create the side elevation profile found in Figure 4.12. You use the Line command and relative and absolute polar coordinates. Follow these steps:

1.  From the Standard toolbar, select New. If prompted with the Save Changes dialog box, select No.
2.  From the Draw toolbar, select Line. As in the preceding tutorials, draw all five lines of the side elevation continuously. You will begin at point A and move counterclockwise to points B, C, D, E, and finally back to point A. Point A is located using absolute polar coordinates. All subsequent points are located using relative polar coordinates.
3. At the `From point:` prompt, enter **2.8284<45** to begin the line at point A.
4. To locate point B, enter **@6<0** at the `To point:` prompt.
5. To locate point C, enter **@3.5<90** at the `To point:` prompt.
6. To locate point D, enter **@3.3541<153** at the `To point:` prompt.
7. To locate point E, enter **@3.3541<207** at the `To point:` prompt.
8. To close the line on starting point A, enter c at the `To point:` prompt.

You may notice that the last line segment does not appear perfectly vertical. This is because the values for the distance and the angle were rounded off.

In the next tutorial you will load the prototype drawing you created earlier and draw a site plan, using several of the coordinate entry methods previously discussed.

Tutorial 4.6: Creating Property Lines with Coordinates and a Prototype Drawing

In this tutorial, you create the property lines shown in Figure 4.14. To begin this drawing, you will need to have completed the prototype drawing exercise at the beginning of Unit 3. That file is used to load default settings for this drawing. After loading this prototype and beginning a new drawing, you will be ready to create the property lines, using a phantom linetype.

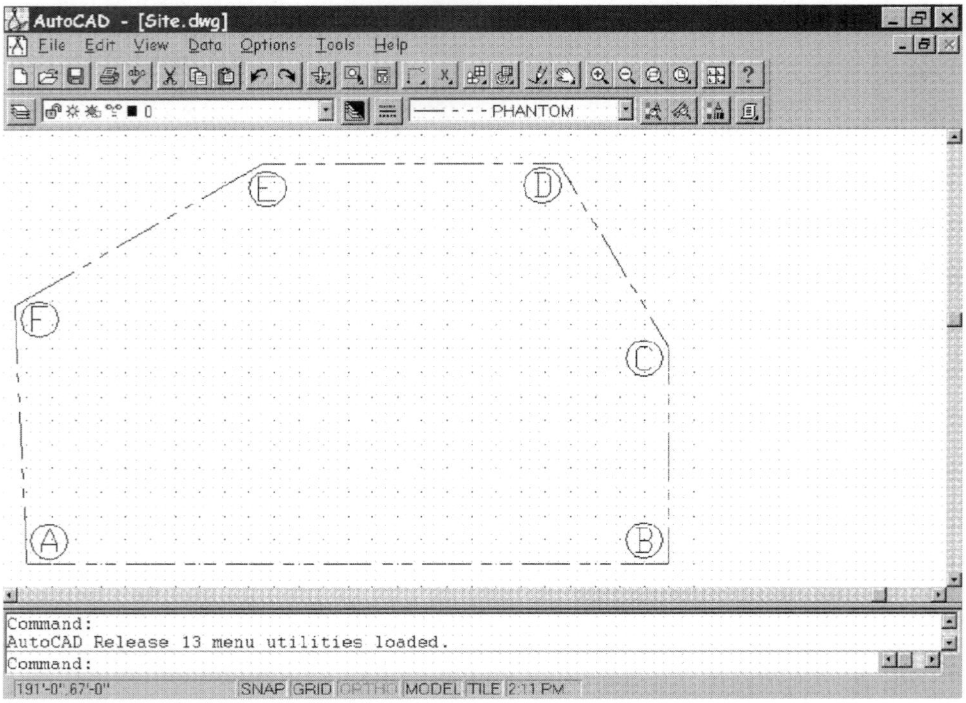

Figure 4.14 *The completed property lines drawing.*

1.  From the Standard toolbar, select New. If prompted with the Save Changes dialog box, select No.
2. When the Create New Drawing dialog box appears, adjust your settings to reflect those found in Figure 4.15.

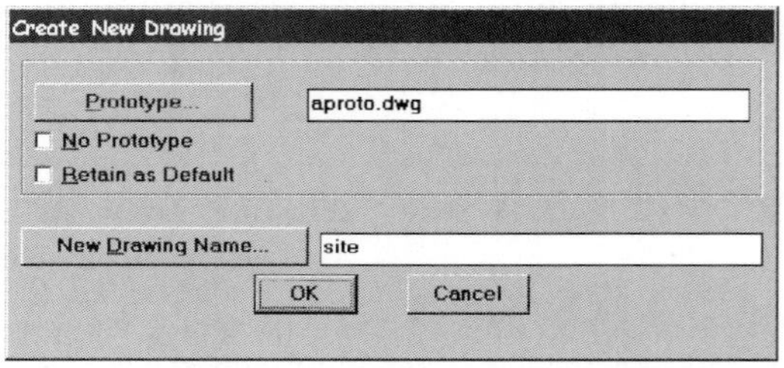

Figure 4.15 *Use the Create New Drawing dialog box to begin the property line drawing.*

Now you begin the drawing, using the Line command and absolute coordinates to specify point A:

1.  From the Draw toolbar, select Line. At the `From point:` prompt, enter **5′,5′**.

To continue the line to points B, C, and D, use relative polar coordinates. Note that you will be using architectural units and the surveyor's units of angle measurements.

2. To locate point B, enter **@130¢<N90E** at the `To point:` prompt.
3. To locate point C, enter **@45¢<N0E** at the `To point:` prompt.
4. To locate point D, enter **@45¢<N30W** at the `To point:` prompt.

To continue the line to points E and F, use relative coordinates, absolute coordinates, and the Close option to complete the property lines. Although you are using different coordinate entry methods in this tutorial, it should be apparent that any method could be used to place the points. You should not limit yourself to only one coordinate entry method. An efficient AutoCAD user will know which coordinate method to use and when to use it.

5. To locate point E, use a relative move. At the `To point:` prompt, enter **@-60′,0′**.
6. To locate point F, you use an absolute move. At the `To point:` prompt, enter **2′,59′**.
7. To close the line on starting point A, enter **c** at the `To point:` prompt.
8.  Save your drawing by selecting Save from the Standard toolbar.

SUMMARY

Selecting the proper units and precision gives AutoCAD the power and versatility to be used in a wide variety of occupations. Remember you are not limited to one setting of units or precision in a drawing, but may change them at any time without affecting objects previously created.

Prototype drawings, if properly used, can save you a considerable amount of time. Including common settings, title blocks, and even geometry in a prototype drawing not only improves drawing standardization but also increases productivity.

It is important that you become proficient with the coordinate entry methods introduced in this unit. Without a mastery of these concepts it is impossible to create difficult drawings accurately. It's very important that the AutoCAD user never "guess" the appropriate points. What may look fine on the AutoCAD screen will probably result in an inaccurate drawing when plotted.

REVIEW

1. List four things the type of units selected affects in your drawing.
2. List and briefly describe the five types of measurement report formats available.
3. Describe the relationship between display precision and accuracy of AutoCAD.
4. Explain prototype drawing and how it is similar to other drawings.
5. Create an illustration to explain the absolute coordinate entry method for locating points in a drawing.
6. Create an illustration to explain the relative coordinate entry method for locating points in a drawing.
7. Create an illustration to explain the absolute polar coordinate entry method for locating points in a drawing.
8. Create an illustration to explain the relative polar coordinate entry method for locating points in a drawing.
9. Explain the advantages of using the coordinate entry method for locating points as opposed to using the Snap, Grid, and Ortho modes.
10. Explain how a drawing that looks correct on the screen, or even on a plot, may not be accurate.

EXERCISE 4

Prepare detail drawings for the Model Glider shown in Figure 4.16.

1. Set the units to Architectural, precision of $\frac{1}{32}''$.
2. Create a detail drawing for each part required to produce the Model Glider. Use Snap, Grid, Ortho and coordinate entry methods to produce an accurate drawing.

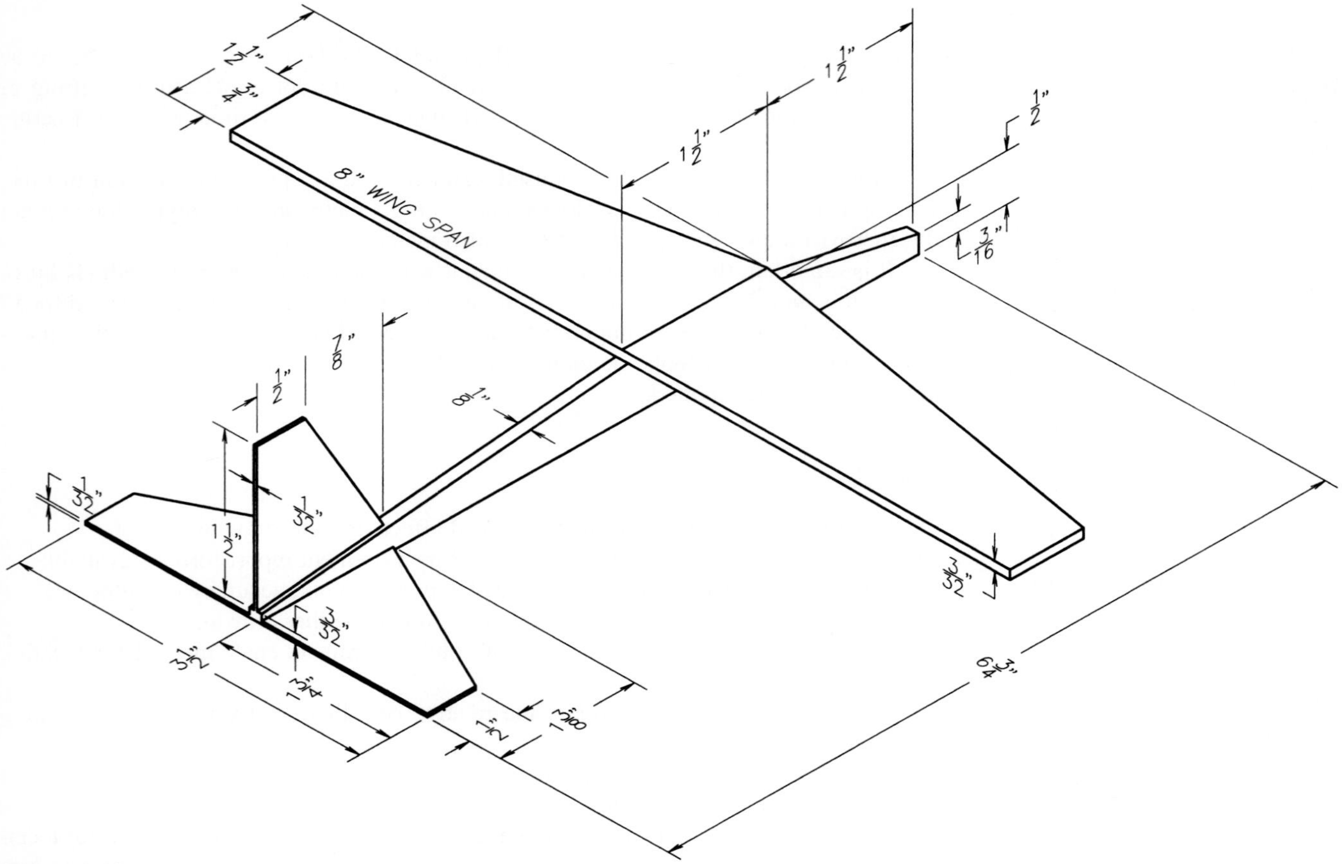

Figure 4.16
Prepare detail drawings for each part of the Model Glider.

UNIT

5 UNDERSTANDING LAYERS AND LINETYPES

OVERVIEW

Working with layers is a fundamental principal of all CAD systems. By using layers, you can group objects together, much the same way a manual drafter may draw groups of objects on separate sheets of transparent paper. You will first learn how to create and work with layers. Next, you will assign different linetypes to your layers.

OBJECTIVES

- Use a dialog box to control layers.
- Create new layers.
- Change the current layer.
- Change a layer's color.
- Control the layer visibility.
- Recognize a linetype.
- List the available linetypes.
- Load a linetype.
- Set a linetype.
- Assign a linetype to a layer.
- Understand the linetype scale.

INTRODUCTION

Layers offer you a means of grouping objects together. Layering is done similarly to the way a manual drafter may draw groups of objects on separate transparent sheets of paper. The final product consists of all the transparent sheets combined in a single stack. Under these circumstances, the manual drafter can draw on only one sheet at a time. The same concept is true for AutoCAD. When using layers in AutoCAD, you can place objects on only the current layer. However, AutoCAD enables you to move objects from one layer to another with the **change,** CHPROP, and DDCHPROP commands, which are covered in Unit 14, "Modifying Object Characteristics and Extracting Information from your Drawing."

Whether creating a drawing manually or on a CAD system, the basis of the drawing is the line. Each line on a technical drawing has a definite meaning and is drawn in a specific way. This can be a tedious and time-consuming process in manual drafting. Creating a hidden line, for example, involves drawing a series of dashes and spaces. Each dash and space must be precisely measured.

Using AutoCAD instead of manual drafting procedures frees you from having to draw different linetypes. AutoCAD contains a predefined alphabet of lines, including several that conform to ISO (International Organization of Standardization) standard linetypes. An alphabet of lines is a set of conventional symbols covering all the lines needed for different purposes on a drawing.

OUTLINE

Working with Layers
Tutorial 5.1: Adding Layers to a Prototype Drawing
Tutorial 5.2: Changing the Current Layer
Tutorial 5.3: Controlling Layer Color
Controlling Layer Visibility
Tutorial 5.4: Controlling Layer Visibility
Tutorial 5.5: Completing the Apartment Complex Front Elevation with Layers
Understanding Linetypes
Tutorial 5.6: Loading a Linetype
Tutorial 5.7: Setting the Linetype
Tutorial 5.8: Adding Hidden and Center Lines and Changing the Linetype Scale
Tutorial 5.9: Creating a Linetype
Summary
Review
Exercises

WORKING WITH LAYERS

In manual drafting, you can separate details of a design by placing them on different sheets of media. This technique is called *pin drafting,* in which accurately spaced holes are punched in the polyester drafting film at the top edge of the sheets. These holes are aligned on pins attached to a metal strip, and the pins match the holes punched in the film. This technique ensures that each overlay is perfectly aligned with the others. To reflect the finished design, the overlays are attached by the alignment pins and run through a reproduction operation to obtain full-size prints.

Using overlays, or layers, as they are called in AutoCAD, is much easier to use in computer-aided design than in the manual pin-drafting technique. Using layers in AutoCAD has many other benefits:

- You can group distinct information on separate layers. In an architectural drawing, the floor plan can be on one layer, the electrical plan on another layer, and the plumbing plan on a third layer.
- Several different drafters can work on a project at the same time to increase productivity. In an architectural project, for example, several drafters may be given the same floor plan. One drafter can complete the electrical plan on one layer, and another drafter can complete the plumbing plan on a different layer. When the different plans come together, they fit because everyone worked from the same floor plan.
- You can assign each layer a different color to improve clarity. A complex floor plan combined with an electrical plan and a plumbing plan can be very difficult to visualize. Separating the different elements by color can greatly improve clarity.
- You can plot each layer in a different color or pen width. Again, this technique can help improve clarity when you visualize the final drawing.
- You can turn off layers, or freeze them, to decrease the information on-screen. Turning off the plumbing layer when viewing the electrical plan, for example, can make the electrical plan much easier to see.
- You can reproduce drawing layers individually or combine the layers in any format. For example, you can reproduce the floor plan and plumbing plan together to send to the plumbing contractor. You can reproduce the floor plan and electrical plan together to send to different electrical contractors for a bid.

Layers are commonly used in all fields of CAD drafting. In electronics drafting, for example, each level of a printed circuit board can be placed on a different layer. Interior designs can have a layer for the floor plan and a layer for each article of furniture. Mechanical designs can have separate layers for each of the views, dimensions, sections, notes, and symbols.

AutoCAD allows an unlimited number of layers on which to create a drawing. You can assign each layer its own name, its own color, and its own linetype. Properly used, layers can improve the clarity of a drawing and improve productivity.

USING THE LAYER CONTROL DIALOG BOX (DDLMODES)

You can create layers and assign a name, color, and linetype at the `Command:` prompt by entering **layer.** All the layer options are shown at the `Command:` prompt if you access the

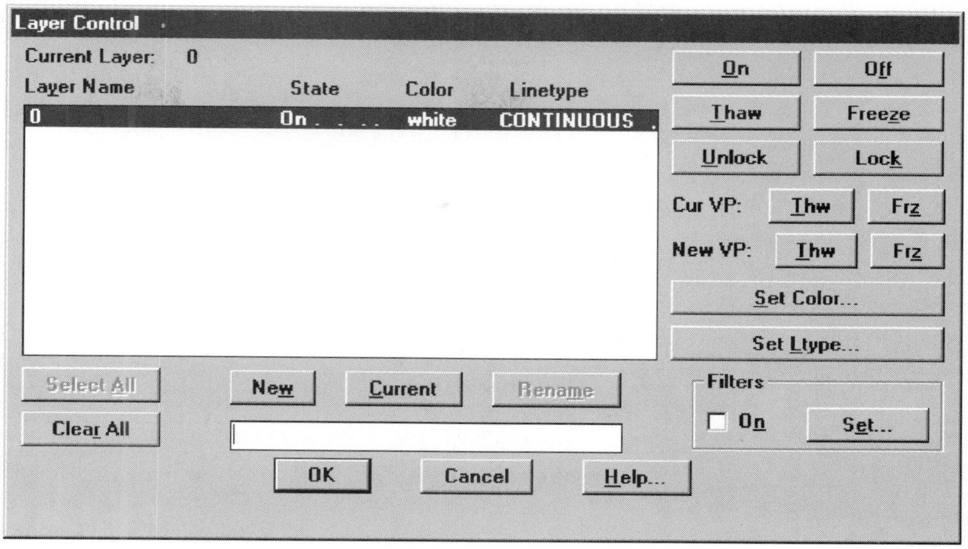

Figure 5.1
Use the Layer Control dialog box to set all the layer variables.

Layer command in this manner. In practice, however, it's more efficient to set the layer options you want by using the Layer Control dialog box (Figure 5.1). You can access the Layer Control dialog box in one of three ways:

- Enter **ddlmodes** at the `Command:` prompt.
- Select Layers from the Data menu.
- Choose the Layers button from the Object Properties floating toolbar.

Naming Layers The structure of AutoCAD drawing layers is normally defined in the drafting standards of a firm. These standards should, at a minimum, specify the names of layers and the type of information to be placed on each layer. Commercial standards are available, such as those defined by the AIA (American Institute of Architects) in their publication, *CAD Layer Guidelines.*

Standardizing layer names and content is an extremely important aspect of CAD drawing. In a typical architectural drawing, you may easily have over 100 layers. You may, for example, have separate layers for the floor, ceiling, foundation, partition layout, electrical, structural, heating, ventilation, air conditioning, and roof drainage.

Without standardization, it becomes virtually impossible to have different people work on a project. Imagine trying to determine which layer contains the plumbing plan from a list containing over 100 layer names. You may even have deviant versions of the same layer names, each created by different people working on the project!

Adding New Layers When working on a drawing, you can add new layers at any time with the Layer Control dialog box. To create a new layer, first type the name in the edit box. Then select the New button. By default, the vertical flashing bar appears in the edit box (Figure 5.2).

Skill Builder

Layer names can consist of 31 characters, including numbers, letters and the special characters dollar sign ($), hyphen (-), and underscore (_). You can't use spaces within the layer name. After entering the name, choose the New button.

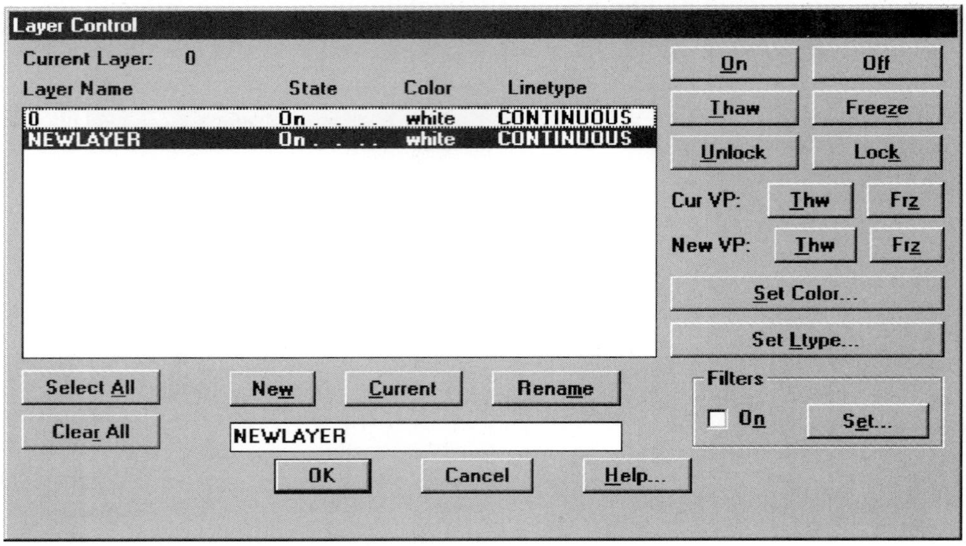

Figure 5.2
To create a new layer, type the new layer name in the edit box and choose New.

Tutorial 5.1: Adding Layers to a Prototype Drawing

In this tutorial, you will create new layers to add to the apartment complex drawing. Follow these steps:

1.  Select the Open button from the Standard toolbar and load 05DWG01.
   Use the file that is displayed to create layers for the completed prototype drawing.
2.  Choose the Layers button from the Object Properties toolbar.
   The Layer Control dialog box appears (Figure 5.3). Notice in the Layer Name column that three layers are already created. The default 0 layer, the FRONT_ELEV layer, and the HATCH layer. You'll add four more layers to this prototype drawing.
3. In the edit box, enter **`windows,doors,vents,constr,`** and then choose New. Four new layers are now listed in the Layer Name column. Notice that at this time the names are not alphabetically listed. Don't close the drawing or dialog box; the next tutorial continues from this point.

Figure 5.3 *Use the Layer Control dialog box to add new layers.*

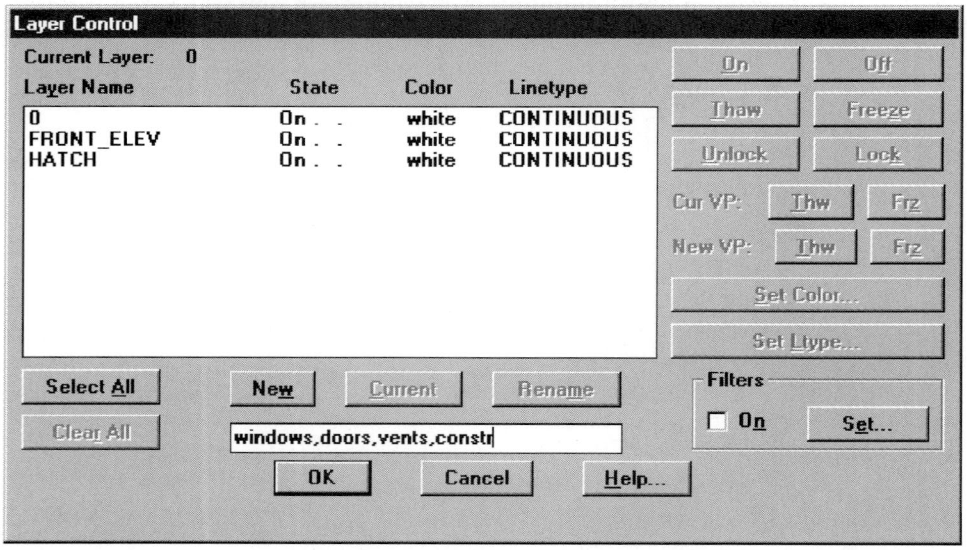

When you initially type the layer names, AutoCAD adds the new names to the bottom of the list. When you reenter the Layer Control dialog box, AutoCAD automatically alphabetizes the layer names. If a layer name doesn't appear on the list, use the scroll bars to move down the list.

Skill Builder

Make sure you choose New and not the OK button after you type the layer name. If you click OK, the layer just named is not created and saved in the Layer Control dialog box.

For the Professional

The list of Layer names in the Layer dialog box is alphabetized provided that the number of layers doesn't exceed the value of the MAXSORT system variable. The default for MAXSORT is 200. This means you can have up to 200 layers and still get the names displayed in order. If you add another layer, AutoCAD will stop trying to sort the layers. This keeps AutoCAD from wasting valuable time on potentially trivial pursuits. If you have more layers than the setting for MAXSORT allows for, you can increase the value of MAXSORT to a number higher than the current number of layers to get the layers displayed in order. To do this, enter **maxsort** at the `Command:` prompt. At the `New value for MAXSORT <200>:` prompt, enter the new number.

Changing the Current Layer (CLAYER) When you set a layer to be current, all geometry created will be on that layer, acquiring all the characteristics assigned to it (color, linetype, state, etc.). The name of the current layer is displayed in the status bar and in the Object Properties toolbar as shown in Figure 5.4. Layer 0 is the default current layer.

The current layer is the one on which objects are drawn. To create objects on a layer that is not current, you must first make the layer current and then create the objects. The following options change the current layer:

Figure 5.4
The current layer name appears in the Standard toolbar.

- At the `Command:` prompt, enter **`clayer.`** AutoCAD displays the prompt `New value for CLAYER <"current layer">:`. Enter the name of the layer you want to make current. The layer name you type must be an existing layer.
- In the Layer Control area of the Object Properties floating toolbar, click the DOWN ARROW. A list of all available layers appears (see Figure 5.5). Move the pointer to

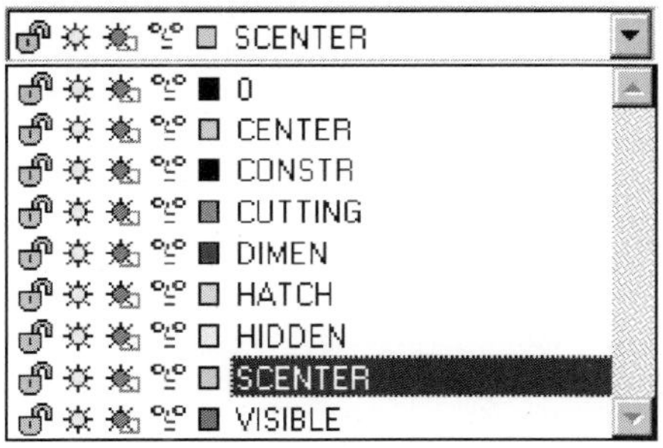

Figure 5.5
Use the Object Properties floating toolbar to change the current layer.

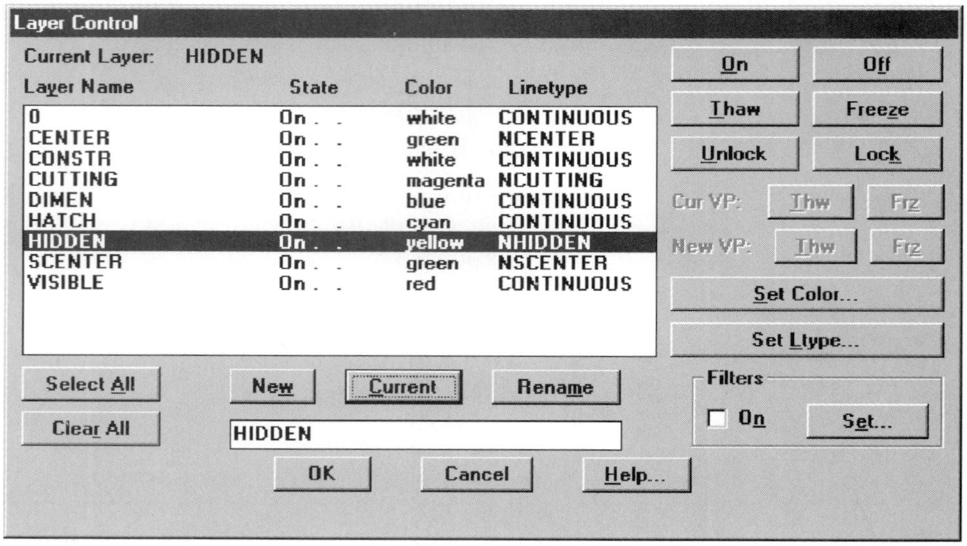

Figure 5.6
To make a layer current by using the Layer Control dialog box, highlight the appropriate layer and choose Current.

the layer you want to make current and then click. The new current layer appears in the Object Properties floating toolbar.

- Use the Layer Control dialog box and highlight the appropriate layer (see Figure 5.6). Then choose Current. The current layer name appears at the top of the Layer Control dialog box after `Current Layer:`. Choose OK.

TUTORIAL 5.2: CHANGING THE CURRENT LAYER

This tutorial continues from the preceding tutorial. The Layer Control dialog box should still be displayed. In the Layer Control dialog box, notice that the current layer is the 0 layer. You want to change that setting so that the Windows layer is the current layer. Follow these steps:

1. Move your cursor to the word Windows in the Layer Name column and select it. Notice that many previously dimmed options become available.
2. Click the Current button. Notice that the `Current Layer:` prompt has now changed to Windows. Click OK to accept the new layers and the current layer setting.

The toolbar now shows the current layer as Windows (Figure 5.7).

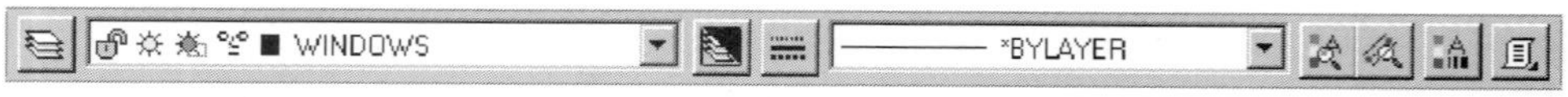

Figure 5.7
The current layer name appears in the toolbar.

Changing the Layer Color When you change a layer's color, all objects drawn on that layer will display the assigned color. To change a layer's color, use the Layer Control dialog box and highlight the layer name, in the layer name list. If you have multiple layers that are to be the same color, you can select those layers as well. If all layers are to receive the same color, you can use the Select All button. To deselect or clear your group of layers, use the Clear All button in the Layer Control dialog box.

By choosing Set Color, you open the Select Color dialog box (Figure 5.8). The number of colors displayed depends on your graphics card and monitor. A monochrome monitor usually displays only one color—white, amber, or green. Color systems generally support 16 or 256 colors. Layer colors are coded by name and number. To change the color, you can select any of the colors that appear in the dialog box.

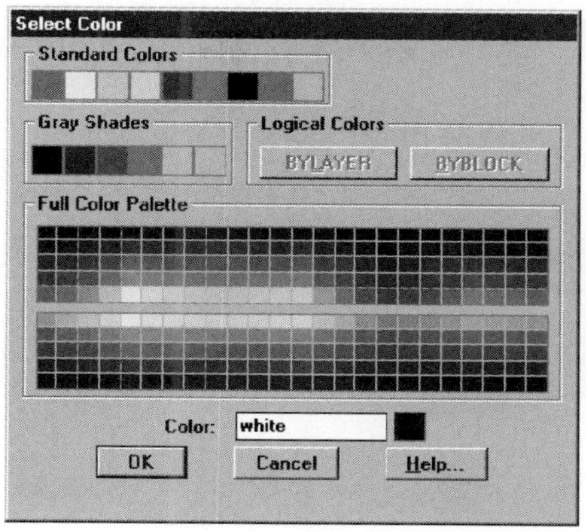

Figure 5.8
To select a layer color, pick any color displayed on-screen.

Tutorial 5.3: Controlling Layer Color

In this tutorial, you will learn how to control a layer's color.

1.  Select the Open button from the Standard toolbar and load 05DWG02. The front elevation of an apartment complex appears (Figure 5.9). You will use this file to adjust layer colors.
2.  Select Layers from the Object Properties toolbar. When the Layer Control dialog box appears, highlight the Doors layer.
3. Choose the Set Color button.
   The Select Color dialog box appears (Figure 5.10).
4. Choose the standard color Red. Notice that the word `Red` appears in the Color edit box. To accept the color, choose OK.
5. You now return to the Layer Control dialog box. Notice that the Color column now says Red for the Doors layer. Click OK. Notice also that the front door on the front elevation of the apartment complex turns red. Any new line drawn with the Doors layer set to current will now be red.
6. Complete this tutorial by assigning cyan to the Windows layer and blue to the Vents layer. Don't close the drawing; the next tutorial continues from this point.

Figure 5.9 *Use the apartment complex file to adjust layer colors.*

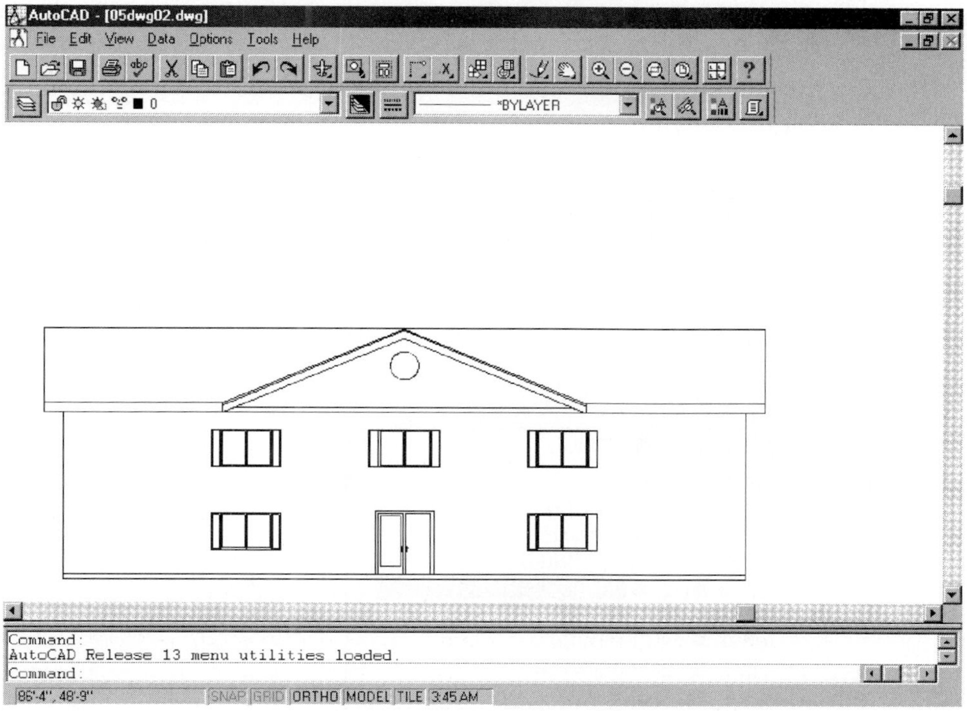

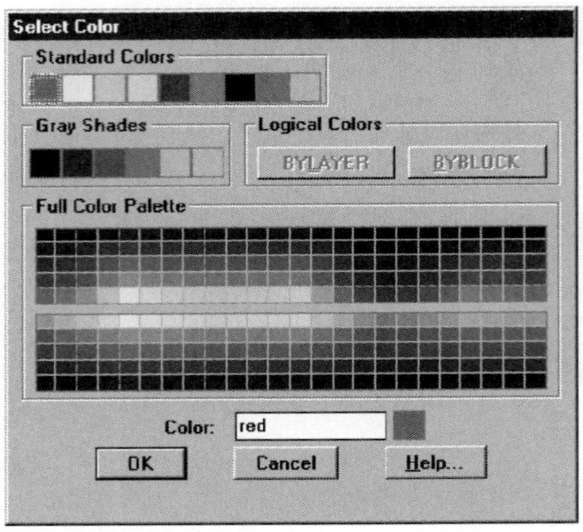

Figure 5.10
Set the layer color with the Select Color dialog box.

CONTROLLING LAYER VISIBILITY

One of the advantages of using layers is the capability to turn them on and off to make viewing the drawing easier. You also can freeze and thaw layers for plotting. You can control layer visibility from the Layer Control dialog box and from the Object Properties floating toolbar.

Turning Layers On and Off

When you turn off a layer, it isn't displayed on-screen or plotted. Often, you may need to turn a layer off to decrease the confusion on your screen. Or you may need to turn layers off to hide dimensions, hatching, or other parts of the drawing. To turn layers off, use one of the following two methods:

- In the Layer Control dialog box, highlight the layer or layers you want to turn off. Then choose Off.

- Select the DOWN ARROW to the right of the Layer Control toolbar. The Layer Control toolbar is located on the Object Properties toolbar. Choose the face icon of the layer you want to turn off (Figure 5.11). When you click the face icon, the eyes close, indicating that the layer is off. In Figure 5.11, the Center and Dimen layers are turned off.

Skill Builder

Layers that are turned off are not plotted. Although turning off a layer will sometimes increase the visibility of a drawing, turning off a layer won't affect AutoCAD's speed because the objects are still calculated.

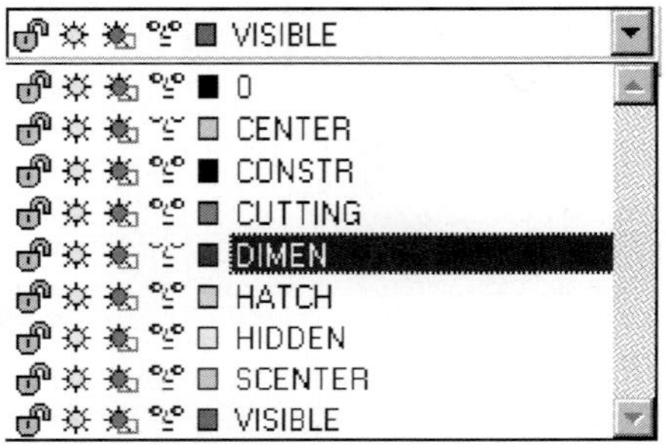

Figure 5.11
Turn layers off by clicking the face icon in the Layer Control toolbar.

FOR THE PROFESSIONAL

If you try to turn the current layer off, AutoCAD displays the error message shown in Figure 5.12. If you turn the current layer off, you cannot see any objects already on it or any new objects you add to it until you turn the layer back on. In most cases, there is no reason to turn the current layer off.

FREEZING AND THAWING LAYERS

Freezing a layer is similar to turning it off. The layer is not displayed on-screen or plotted. When a layer is turned off, however, it is still regenerated during a drawing regeneration. Frozen layers are not regenerated, so freezing layers in a complex drawing is a good way to speed up regeneration time. Freezing a layer makes the objects invisible; the objects are not displayed, regenerated, or plotted. Note that you cannot freeze the current layer. You can freeze layers in these ways:

- In the Layer Control dialog box, highlight the layer or layers you want to freeze. Then choose the Free<u>z</u>e button.
- Select the DOWN ARROW to the right of the Layer Control toolbar. Choose the sun icon of the layer you want to turn off (Figure 5.13). When you click this icon, the sun icon changes to a snowflake, indicating that the layer is frozen. In Figure 5.13, the Constr and Hatch layers are frozen.

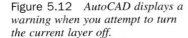

You may notice the other options in the Layer Control toolbar to the right of the sun icon. These features allow you to control the visibility of layers in multiple view ports. This concept will be discussed in a later unit.

LOCKING AND UNLOCKING LAYERS

When different people have access to or are working on a drawing, locking a layer can be beneficial. When a layer is locked, you can't edit or change it. You can lock a layer to make object selection easier. You can see the objects on a locked layer, but you can't select them. That means that you can use the locked layer objects as reference points without selecting them accidentally when you're selecting objects in a complex drawing. The layer is still visible and can be plotted. Note that you can't lock the current layer. Use one of these methods to lock a layer:

- In the Layer Control dialog box, highlight the layer or layers you want to lock. Then click the Lock button.
- Select the DOWN ARROW to the right of the Layer Control toolbar. Choose the lock icon of the layer you want to lock (refer to Figure 5.13). When you choose the Lock (the picture of a lock) icon, the icon changes, indicating that the layer is locked. Notice in Figure 5.13 that the Cutting and Visible layers are locked.

Figure 5.12 *AutoCAD displays a warning when you attempt to turn the current layer off.*

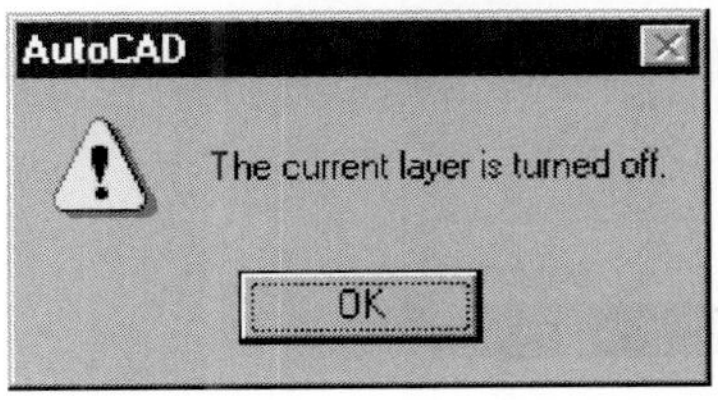

Figure 5.13 *Freeze layers by clicking the sun icon in the Layer Control toolbar.*

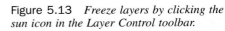

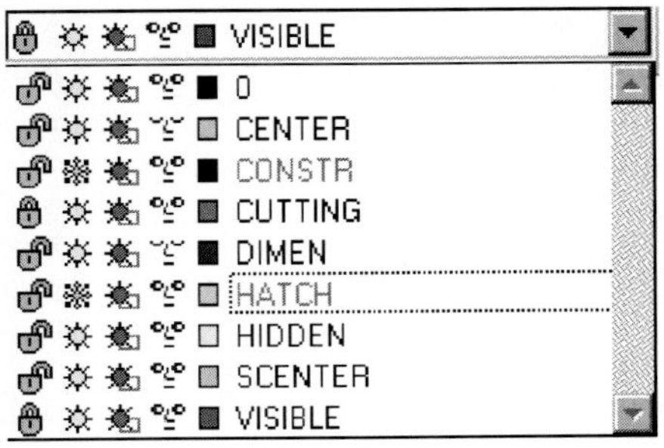

Tutorial 5.4: Controlling Layer Visibility

This tutorial continues from the preceding tutorial. Follow these steps:

1.  Select Layers from the Object Properties toolbar. The Layer Control dialog box appears.
2. Highlight the Doors, Windows, and Vents layers. Now choose the Off button near the upper-right corner of the dialog box.
   Notice that the word On disappears from the State column for each entry.
3. Now choose OK.
   You should notice that the windows, doors, and vents are no longer visible in the drawing. If you check the Layer Control toolbar (Figure 5.14) you should see the face icon with the eyes closed next to the Doors, Windows, and Vents layers.
4.  Select Layers from the Object Properties toolbar. The Layer Control dialog box appears.
5. Select the Doors, Windows, and Vents layers again. Now select the On button near the upper-right of the dialog box.
   Notice that the word *On* reappears in the State column.
6. Choose OK.
   Notice that the windows, doors, and vents are now visible in the drawing. Don't close the drawing; the next tutorial continues from this point.

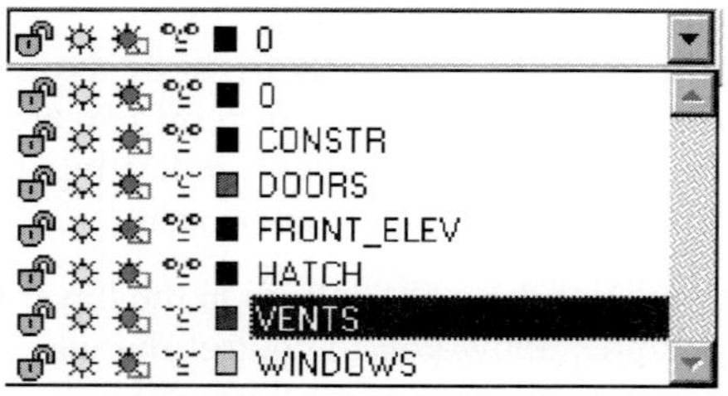

Figure 5.14
Turning off the Doors, Windows, and Vents layers in the apartment complex front elevation drawing.

Renaming Layers

To change the name of a layer, select the layer (only one) in the Layer Control dialog box. Then click in the edit box below the Rename button and edit the name. When you have finished typing the new name in the box, click the Rename button. AutoCAD changes the layer's name.

Using Filters to Limit the Display of Layer Names

Some drawings may contain hundreds of layer names. Because the Layer Control dialog box displays layer names in alphabetical order, you must scroll through all the layer names to find the ones to change. The Filters section of the dialog box enables you to limit the number of layers the Layer Control dialog box displays. Click the Set button under Filters, and the Set Layer Filters dialog box appears (Figure 5.15).

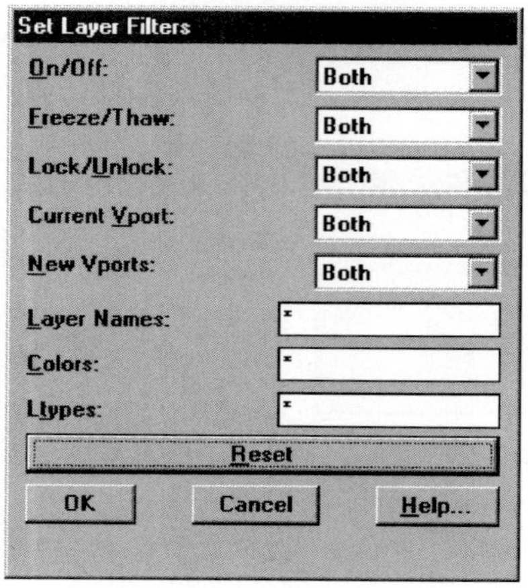

Figure 5.15
Use the Set Layer Filters dialog box to limit the layer names displayed.

In the Set Layer Filters dialog box, you can display layers that are on, off, frozen, thawed, locked, or unlocked (or any combination of these). In the Layer Names edit box, you can use wild cards (*) to specify layer names. For example, if you want to display only layers whose names begin with *H,* type *h** in the Layer Names edit box. Only layers whose names begin with *H* appear in the list of layers. You can also use wild cards to display layers by Colors or Ltypes.

Tutorial 5.5: Completing the Apartment Complex Front Elevation with Layers

This tutorial continues from the preceding tutorial. You may have noticed that the front elevation is incomplete. In this tutorial, you complete the drawing by drawing objects on specific layers. First create the rest of the vent found on the gable of the roof. Use these steps:

1.  Use the Object Properties toolbar and select the Vents layer. To do this, select the DOWN ARROW on the Layer Control box of the Object Properties toolbar. Now select the Vents layer. The Vents layer is now current.
2.  Select Circle from the Draw toolbar. If the Draw toolbar is not displayed, select Tools, Toolbars, Draw.

   `3P/2P/TTR/<Center point>:` **`37'11", 23'1"`**
   `Diameter/<Radius>:` **`1'`**

   The inner portion of the vent should be drawn in blue (You chose blue for this object in an earlier tutorial).
3.  The door is the next section you need to complete. Using the Object Properties toolbar, make the Doors layer the current layer.
4.  Select Rectangle from the Draw toolbar. To access the Rectangle button, first select and hold the Polygon button on the Draw toolbar. This will cause the flyout menu to appear. Continueholding down the select button, and scroll down the flyout menu until Rectangle is highlighted.

   `First corner:` **`38'4",1'6"`**
   `Other corner:` **`40'5",7'`**

   You should now have the inner glass pane for the right door drawn in red.
5.  Now draw the shutter on the lower-right window. Using the Object Properties toolbar, make the Windows layer the current layer.
6.  Select Rectangle from the Draw toolbar.

   `First corner:` **`57'4",3'4"`**
   `Other corner:` **`58'2",7'2"`**

   You should now have the shutter drawn in cyan. Cyan was chosen in a previous tutorial. You also should have the completed front elevation (see Figure 5.16).
7.  Select Save from the Standard toolbar.

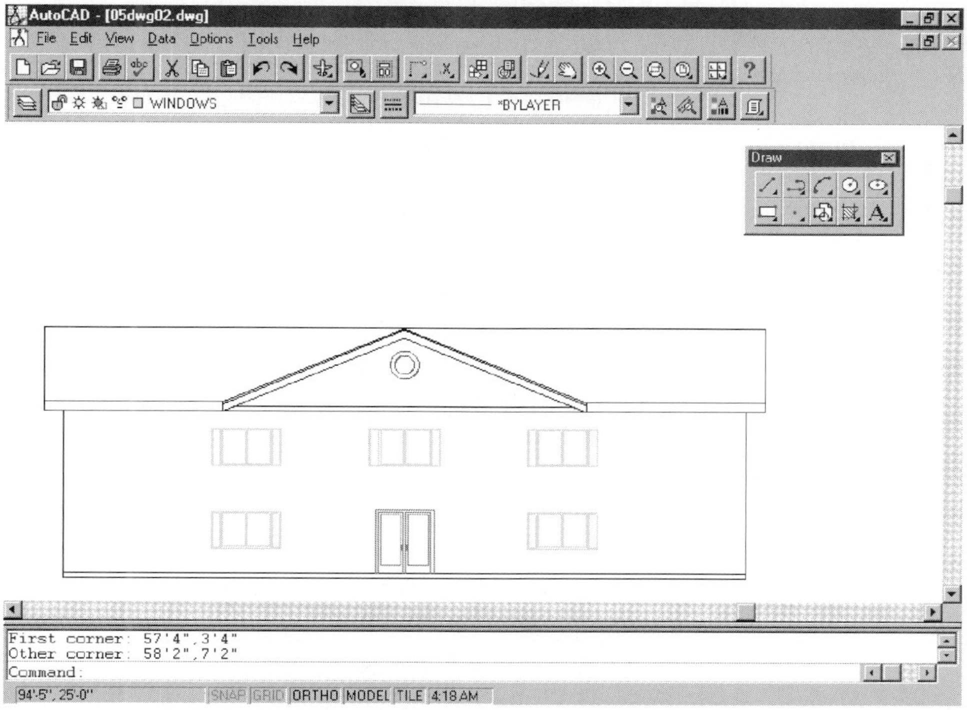

Figure 5.16 *The completed apartment complex front elevation.*

UNDERSTANDING LINETYPES

In the previous section you created layers and assigned colors to them. You also can assign AutoCAD's wide variety of linetypes to the layers you created. This section discusses the use of linetypes in your drawing.

To use a linetype, it must meet two qualifications. First, its definition must exist. It may be a pre-defined AutoCAD linetype, or one you created. Second, the existing linetype must be loaded into the drawing.

WHAT ARE LINETYPES?

A linetype is simply a repeating pattern of dots, dashes, and blank spaces. The linetype name and its corresponding definition determine the specific sequence and relative lengths of dashes, dots, and blank spaces.

A drawing may contain a variety of different linetypes. A certain type of line may be used on a drawing to represent a hidden surface, for example. Other lines may be used to represent the center point of circles or arcs. Figure 5.17 shows examples of several different linetypes available within AutoCAD.

LISTING LINETYPES (LINETYPE, DDLTYPE)

AutoCAD has a wide variety of linetypes available for use in a drawing. There are two methods you can use to obtain a list along with a picture of available linetypes. One method is to type *linetype* at the `Command:` prompt, and respond with a question mark (?) as follows:

```
Command: linetype
?/Create/Load/Set:?
```

This accesses the Select Linetype File dialog box as shown in Figure 5.18. Select acad.lin in the File Name column. Choose OK. You'll see a text screen and a list of AutoCAD's predefined linetypes. Continue to press Enter until you see the `?/Create/`

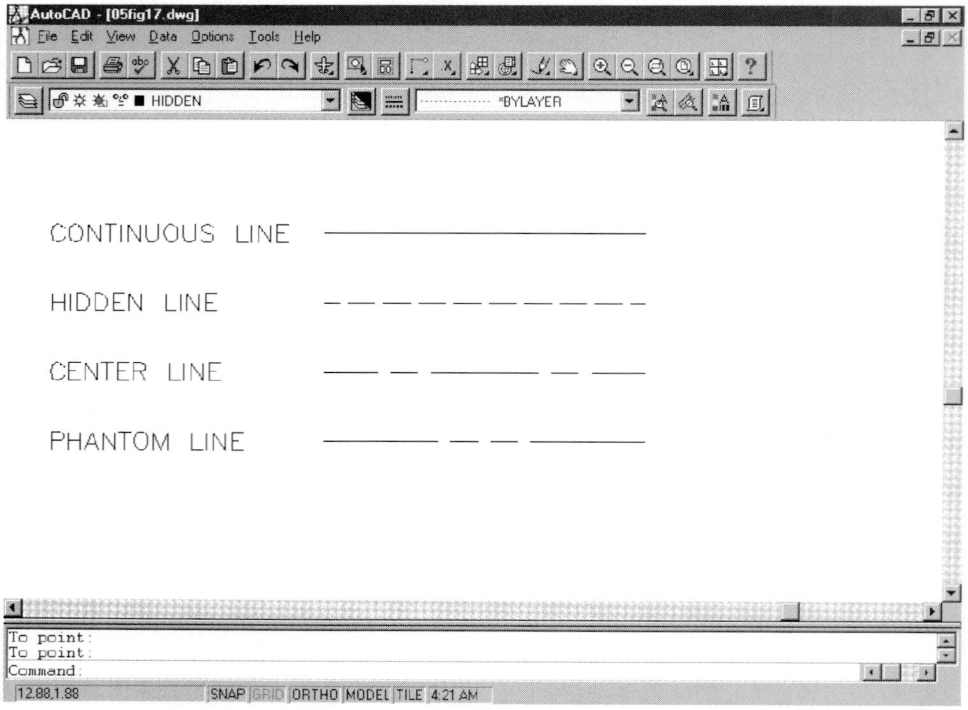

Figure 5.17
The continuous, hidden, center, and phantom lines are examples of linetypes available within AutoCAD.

`Load/Set:` prompt. Pressing Enter at this prompt returns you to the `Command:` prompt. To switch from the text screen to the drawing editor, press F2 key.

You can also see a list of AutoCAD's predefined linetypes and load a linetype by using the Load or Reload Linetype dialog box. This can be done by selecting Load in the Select Linetype dialog box. The following procedures first access the Select Linetype dialog box shown in Figure 5.19. In the Select Linetype dialog box, choose Load and the Load or Reload Linetypes dialog box appears as shown in Figure 5.20.

Each of the following procedures gives you access to the Select Linetype dialog box:

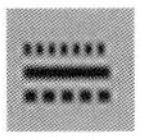

- Select the Linetype button from the Object Properties toolbar.
- Select Linetype from the Data pull-down menu.
- Select the Layers button from the Object Properties toolbar to access the Layer Control dialog box. In the Layer Control dialog box select Set Ltype to access the Select Linetype dialog box. To use this option, you must have a layer highlighted in the Layer Control dialog box.
- Access the Object Creation Modes dialog box by selecting Object Creation from the Data pull-down menu. Select Linetype to display the Select Linetype dialog box.
- Enter **ddltype** at the `Command:` prompt.

AutoCAD has several predefined linetypes available that meet the ISO format. To see a complete listing of all available linetypes, use the arrow keys on the right side of the dialog box to scroll down the list.

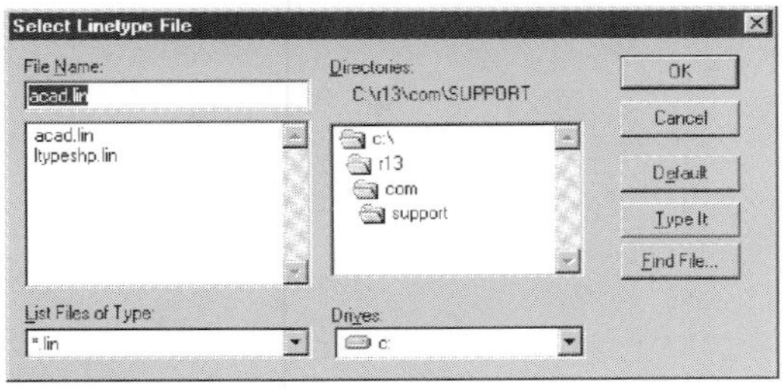

Figure 5.18 *Use the Select Linetype File dialog box to choose from the available linetype files.*

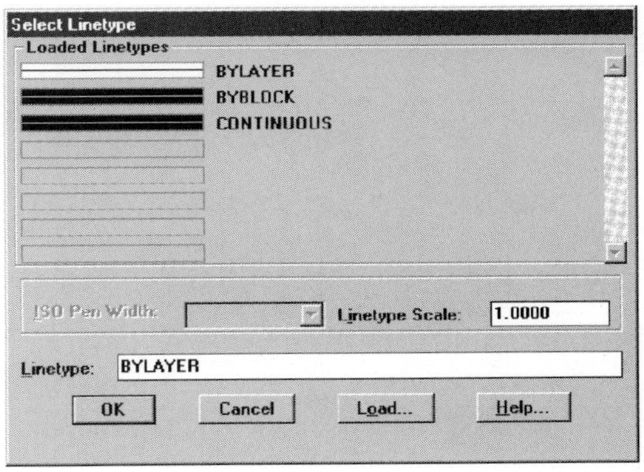

Figure 5.19 *Selecting Load in the Select Linetype dialog box causes the Load or Reload Linetypes dialog box to appear.*

Figure 5.20
Linetypes available within AutoCAD may be viewed in the Load or Reload Linetypes dialog box.

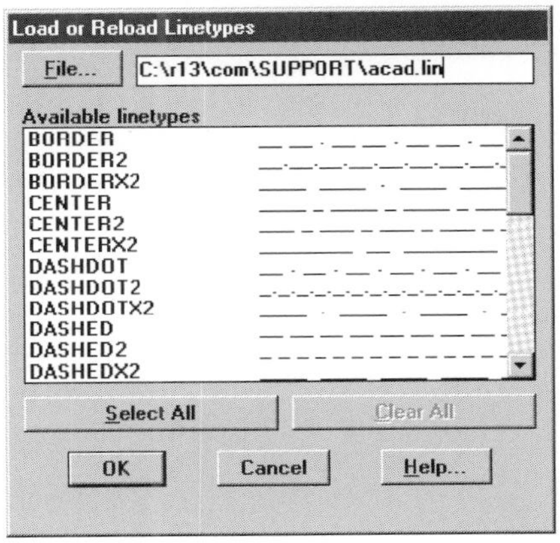

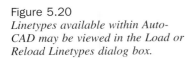

Skill Builder

All linetypes available with AutoCAD are found in the **acad.lin** file. If you have linetypes stored in a different file or location, click the File button in the Load or Reload dialog box and select the appropriate path and filename.

Loading a Linetype

Before you can use a linetype, it must be loaded. A linetype may be loaded from the Load or Reload Linetypes dialog box. To load a linetype, first click any linetype in the Load or Reload Linetype dialog box to highlight it (refer to Figure 5.20). You can highlight as many different linetypes as you like. You also can use the Select All or Clear All buttons.

Skill Builder

By default, AutoCAD has the CONTINUOUS linetype loaded.

When you have selected all the linetypes you want to load, click OK. The linetypes selected for loading appear in the Select Linetype dialog box.

For the Professional

You should limit the number of linetypes loaded to the ones necessary for the current drawing. Limiting the number of linetypes decreases the file size. A convenient alternative is to load all the linetypes and later purge the unneeded ones.

Tutorial 5.6: Loading a Linetype

In this and the following unit tutorials, you complete the drawing of the clamp bracket shown in Figure 5.21. You can start by loading a file from the work disk. Then, you load two linetypes using two different methods. You will finish the clamp bracket drawing later in the unit.

1.  Select the Open button from the Standard toolbar to access the Open Drawing dialog box. Load the 05DWG03 file.
   After the file is loaded, your screen should resemble Figure 5.22.
2. 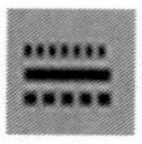 Choose the Linetype button from the Object Properties toolbar. You will use the Select Linetype dialog box to load the hidden linetype.
   The Select Linetype dialog box appears (refer to Figure 5.19).
3. Click the Load Button in the Select Linetype dialog box.
   The Load or Reload Linetypes dialog box appears (refer to Figure 5.20).
4. Use the scroll bar to move down the list and select the HIDDEN linetype. Select OK.
   The hidden linetype now appears in the Select Linetype dialog box under the Loaded Linetypes section.
5. Access the Load or Reload linetypes dialog box again and load the CENTER linetype.
6. Click OK to accept the new loaded linetypes. The next tutorial continues from this point.

Figure 5.21
Use linetypes to complete the clamp bracket drawing.

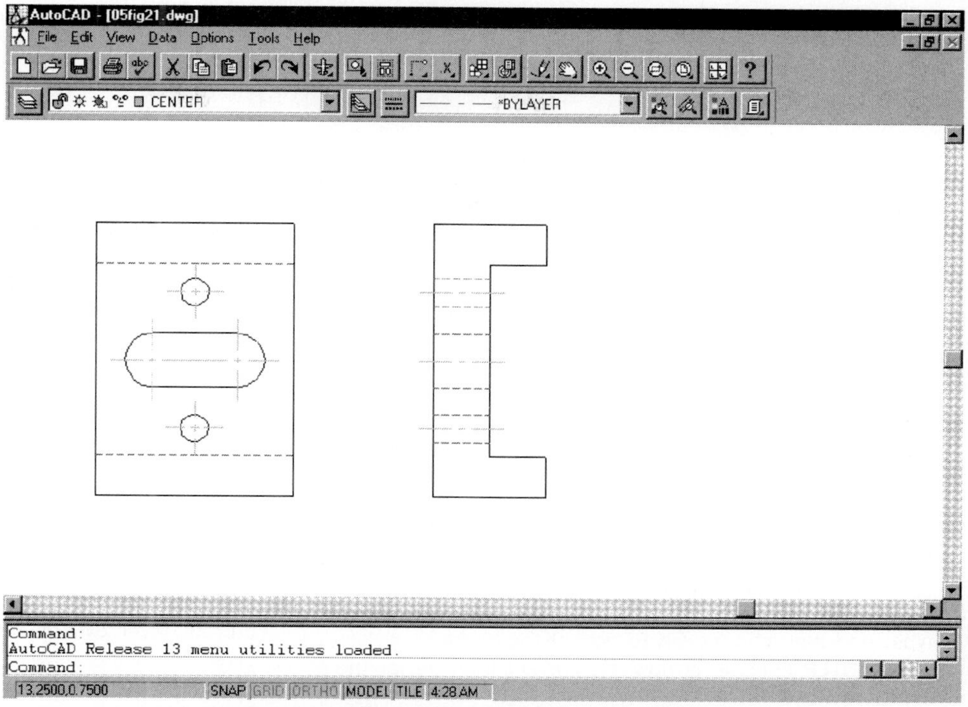

Figure 5.22
Loading the clamp bracket work file.

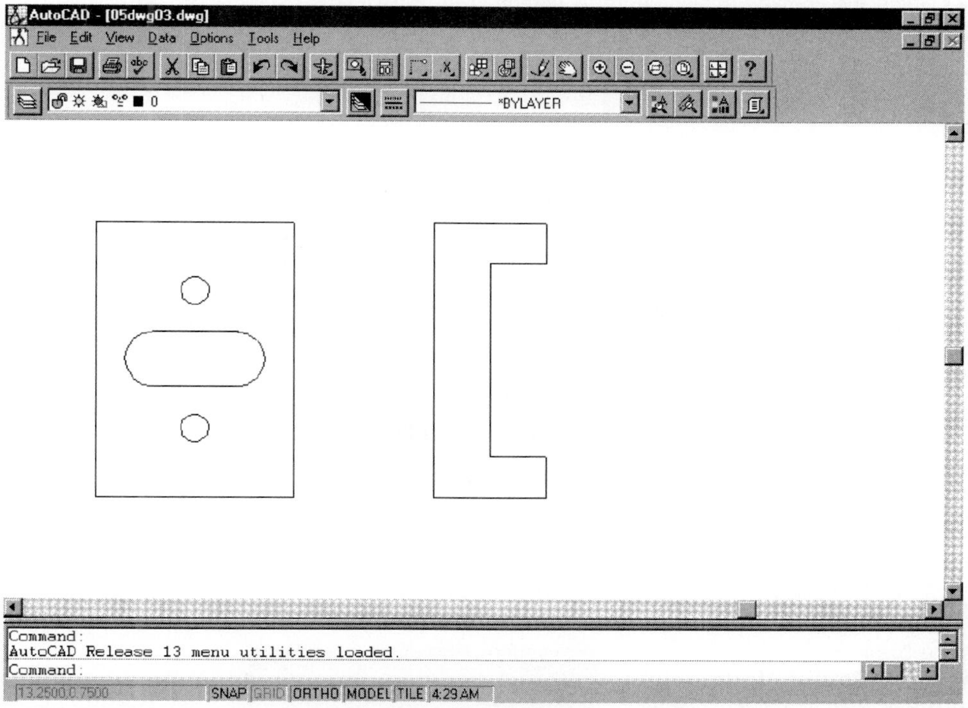

Setting the Linetype

Once a linetype has been loaded, it can be assigned to a layer. This is done within the Layer Control dialog box. The linetype must be loaded before you can assign it to a layer. To assign a linetype to a layer, select the applicable layers and choose Set Ltype. When the Select Linetype dialog box appears, select the linetype you want to assign to the layer and click OK. Linetypes are assigned to a given layer so that all objects drawn on that layer will have that linetype automatically. Linetypes are set to a layer for the same reasons that colors are.

Tutorial 5.7: Setting the Linetype

The Load or Reload Linetype dialog box also can be invoked using the Layer Control dialog box. In this tutorial, you will use the Layer Control dialog box to access the Load or Reload Linetype dialog box and load a center line. You also assign the center line and the hidden line you loaded in the previous tutorial to existing layers.

1.  Continue from the previous tutorial. Choose the Layers button from the Object Properties toolbar. The Layer Control dialog box appears as shown in Figure 5.23.
2. Select the CENTER layer and then choose the Set Ltype button.
   The Select Linetype dialog box appears.
3. In the Select Linetype dialog box, select the CENTER linetype, and then choose OK to accept the changes.
   The CENTER linetype is now the current linetype for the center layer.
4. Finish the linetype assignments by selecting the HIDDEN layer, assigning it to the HIDDEN linetype to it.

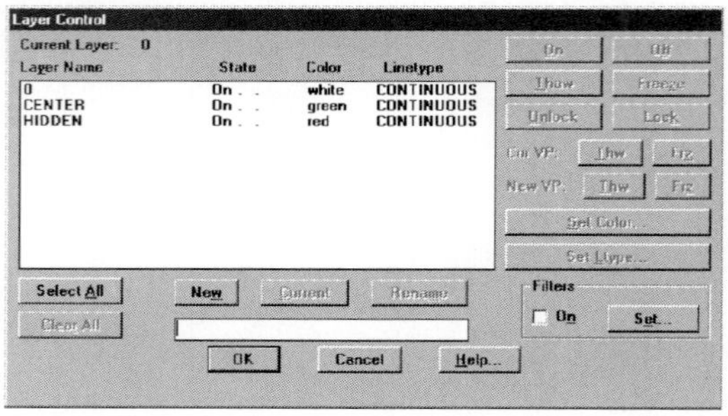

Figure 5.23 *The Layer Control dialog box for the clamp bracket drawing.*

5. Once the selection is made, make the HIDDEN layer the current layer by selecting the Current button and then click OK in the Layer Control dialog box to accept the changes. The next tutorial continues from here.

You are now ready to start drawing with the loaded linetypes.

Setting a Default Linetype

Normally when you assign a linetype to a layer and make it the current layer, any objects you create will have the linetype assigned to that layer. AutoCAD also gives you the option of setting a default linetype for all objects drawn, regardless of what layer you select and what linetype is assigned to it. You can change this setting in the Object Creation Modes dialog box. Access the Object Creation Modes Dialog box by:

- Choosing the Object Creation button from the Object Properties toolbar.
- Selecting Object Creation in the Data pull-down menu.
- Entering **ddemodes** at the `Command:` prompt.

By default, the setting after Linetype reads BYLAYER as shown in Figure 5.24. To assign a default linetype, click the Linetype box. This opens the Select Linetype dialog box. If the desired linetype does not appear, choose the Load button and the appropriate

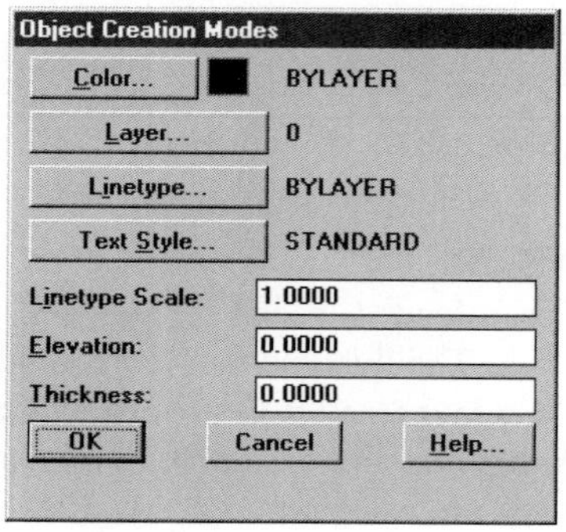

Figure 5.24 *The Object Creation Modes dialog box can be used to assign a default linetype to all entities created.*

linetype and choose OK to return to the Object Creation Modes dialog box. The setting after Linetype should now read the name of the linetype just selected. Choose OK to return to the drawing editor. From this point on, all objects drawn will have the default linetype unless you modify them with the CHANGE, DDCHPROP, CHPROP, or DDMODIFY commands.

SKILL BUILDER

Setting a default linetype can cause confusion. After setting a default linetype, everything you draw has the same linetype even when changing layers. You may have different linetypes assigned to the layers, but it won't matter when you change layers.

Even though you change to a different layer assigned a new linetype, the default setting in the Object Creation Modes dialog box is overriding any linetype you select in the new layer. To have new objects adopt the linetype of the current layer, you need to change the Linetypes setting in the Object Creation Modes dialog box back to BYLAYER.

UNDERSTANDING LINETYPE SCALE (LTSCALE)

A linetype in AutoCAD is defined by a series of dashes and spaces. The LTSCALE command allows you to change the relative scale of the dashes and spaces that define a linetype. As long as the linetype scale is set to 1.0, the length of the spaces and dashes are the same as when the linetype was originally defined.

Most drawings created on AutoCAD are drawn full-size. When the drawing is plotted, it remains full-size while the plot is scaled. The LTSCALE command can be used to achieve the correct linetype scale in the finished drawing. Generally the linetype scale should be proportional to the working scale of the drawing. For example, a drawing that is plotted at 1/8′=1′-0″ is reduced 96 times its actual size when plotted on the paper. For this example the linetype scale for the drawing should be 96.

Setting the Linetype Scale for All Objects The default setting for the linetype scale is 1.0. If the drawing is going to be plotted at full-scale (1 = 1), the default linetype scale setting is fine. If the drawing is going to be plotted at a smaller scale (such as 1 = 96), you need to increase the size of the linetype by increasing the value of the linetype scale (to 96 if the plot scale is 1 = 96). You can change the linetype scale by using any of the following methods:

- From the Options pull-down menu, choose Linetypes, then choose Global Linetype Scale.
- Enter **ltscale** at the `Command:` prompt.

Entering ltscale at the `Command:` prompt displays the following:

```
Command:ltscale
New scale factor <1.0000>: Enter a positive whole number or
decimal
```

Using any method just described will set the linetype scale for all linetypes in the entire drawing. After you set a new linetype scale factor, AutoCAD automatically regenerates the drawing unless you have the automatic regen turned off.

You can also set the linetype scale for newly created objects by using any of the following:

- Choose Object Creation from the Data pull-down menu and enter the new linetype scale in the Linetype Scale edit box.

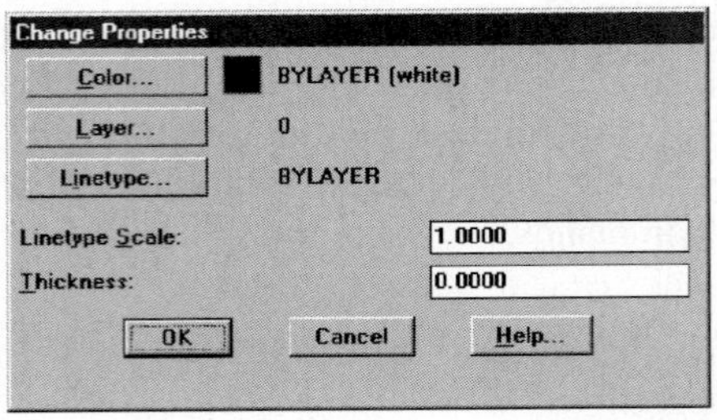

Figure 5.25
The Change Properties dialog box allows you to change the linetype scale of individual entities.

- Choose the Object Creation button from the Object Properties toolbar. Enter the linetype scale in the Linetype Scale edit box.
- Access the Select Linetype dialog box by choosing the Linetype button on the Object Properties toolbar. Enter the new linetype scale in the Linetype Scale edit box.

These procedures will not change the linetype scale of existing objects, only objects created after changing the scale.

Setting the Linetype Scale for Individual Objects You can also assign a different linetype scale to individual objects by using the Change Properties dialog box (see Figure 5.25). Access this dialog box by entering **ddchprop** at the `Command:` prompt.

After entering **ddchprop,** AutoCAD prompts `Select objects:`. After selecting an object and pressing Enter, the Change Properties dialog box appears. Enter the new linetype scale and choose OK. The linetype scale is changed only for the objects selected.

You can also change individual linetype scale with the Modify dialog box. You can access the Modify dialog box in the following way:

- Enter **ddmodify** at the `Command:` prompt. AutoCAD prompts `Select object to modify:`.
-  Select the Properties button from the Object Properties toolbar. You are given the option of selecting one or more objects. If you select one object, you will see the Modify dialog box. If more than one object is selected, you will see the Change Properties dialog box.

The Modify dialog box that appears will depend upon the entity selected. To change the linetype scale for the individual entity selected, enter the new value in the Linetype Scale box.

Tutorial 5.8: Adding Hidden and Center Lines and Changing the Linetype Scale

In this tutorial you will complete the orthographic projection drawing of the clamp bracket. You will add center and hidden lines to the drawing and change the linetype scale.

1. Continue from the previous tutorial.
2. Begin by drawing the hidden lines. Start with the top hidden line in the right side view.
   The hidden line layer is the current layer, so all lines drawn are hidden.
3.  Choose the Line icon from the Draw toolbar.

```
From point: 8,6
To point: 9,6
To point:
```

4. Complete the hidden lines in both views as shown in Figure 5.26. All pickpoints are on **snap** points. If the **snap** is not active, turn it on by double-clicking the word **snap** in the status bar or by pressing F9 key.
5.  Change the current layer to the CENTER layer by choosing the Layer Control button on the Object Properties toolbar.
6.  Draw the center line for the slot first.
   Select the Line icon from the Draw toolbar.

```
From point: 2.25,4.5
To point: 3.75,4.5
To point: 5.25,4.5
To point:
```

   Notice that the lines don't appear as center lines. You must change the linetype scale.
7. From the Options pull-down menu, choose Linetypes, then choose Global Linetype Scale.

```
New scale factor <1.0000>: .75
```

The lines now appear as center lines and all linetypes in the drawing are modified according to the new scale factor.

Skill Builder

Linetypes are defined as a series of dash-dot sequences per drawing unit. Depending on the scale of the drawing, the linetype scale may have to be modified to make the linetype look correct.

The HIDDEN linetype is defined as a sequence of visible segments and open spaces. The visible segments are 0.25 drawing units long and the spaces are 0.125 drawing units long. By setting the LTSCALE to 0.75, objects shown in the HIDDEN linetype appear with visible segments that are 0.1875 (0.25 * 0.75) drawing units in length and open spaces that are 0.09375 (0.125 * 0.75) drawing units long.

8. Complete the drawing by adding the remaining center lines as shown in Figure 5.27.

Notice that the center lines on the two small holes do not appear as center lines. Your first reaction may be to change the linetype scale again. Another change may adversely affect the rest of the drawing. The scale needs to be changed only for those center lines.

To change the linetype scale independently follow these steps:

1.  Choose the Properties button on the Object Properties toolbar.

2. Select the four center lines that are on the smaller holes on the front view and press Enter.
The Change Properties dialog box appears.

3. In the Change Properties dialog box, change the Linetype Scale to .5 and choose OK.
The center lines change scale and the drawing should now be similar to Figure 5.21.

For the Professional

Dashed and dotted linetypes normally take longer to repaint or regenerate. Setting LTSCALE to a large number turns every linetype into a solid line. This could significantly speed up display in large drawings with multiple linetypes. Before plotting however, set the correct LTSCALE number and regenerate the drawing.

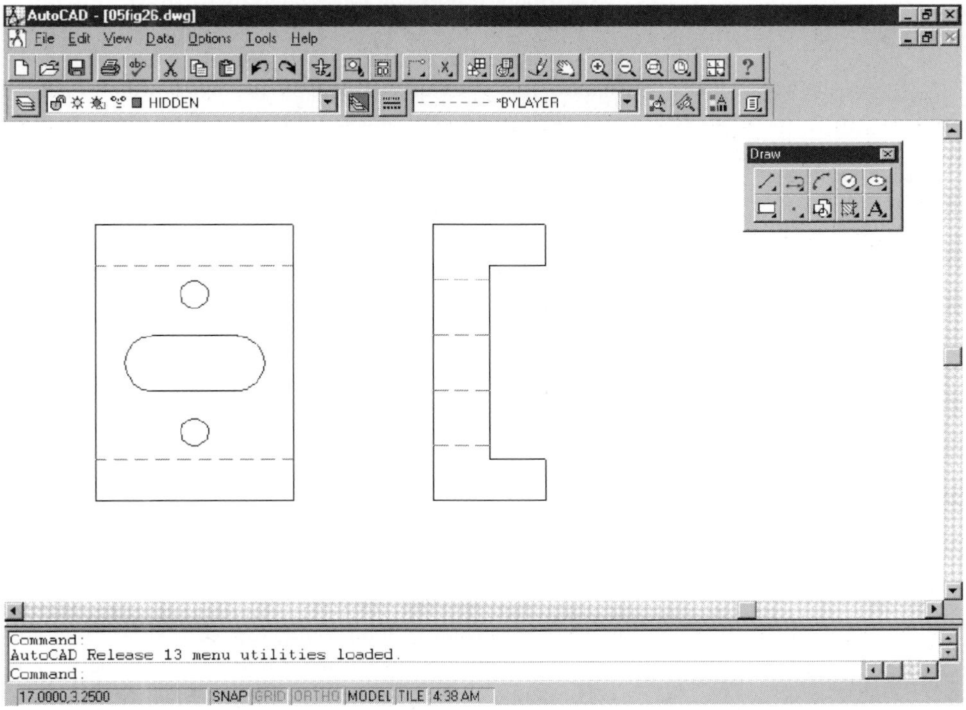

Figure 5.26
Completing the hidden lines of the clamp bracket orthographic drawing.

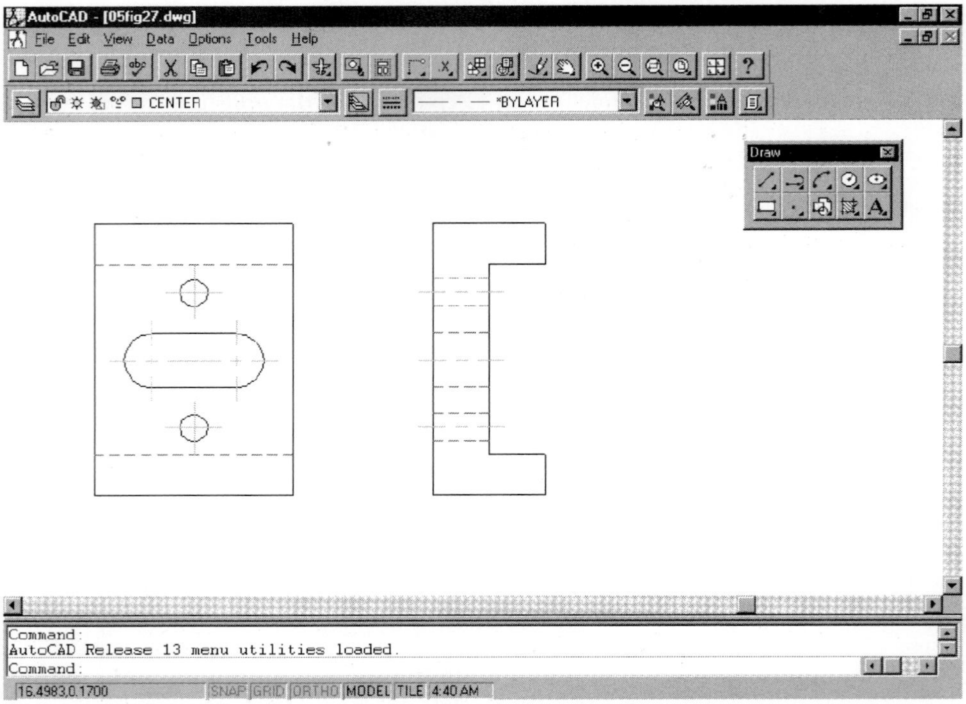

Figure 5.27
Completing the center lines of the clamp bracket orthographic drawing.

Creating Your Own Linetypes (LINETYPE)

AutoCAD has approximately 40 standard linetypes available, including several that conform to ISO conventions. If your drawing requires other linetypes not available in AutoCAD, you can add new ones. The line conventions endorsed by the American National Standards Institute, ANSI Y14.2-M-1979 (R1987) are commonly used in many occupations. Mapping/surveying drawings often have specific linetypes for such things as topography lines, utilities, fences and many other descriptive lines. By using the Create option of the Linetype command you can define your own custom linetype.

Linetype definitions are stored in files with a .LIN extension. The AutoCAD standard linetypes are located in the **acad.lin** file. Simple linetypes consist of a series of dashes, dots, and spaces. Complex linetypes can include repeating out-of-line objects, such as text and shapes, along with optional in-line dashes, dots, and spaces.

Linetype Definition All linetype definitions consist of two parts (see Figure 5.28):

- Header Line
- Pattern Line

Header Line The header line contains an asterisk (*) followed by the name of the linetype and the linetype description. The format for the header line is:

```
*Linetype Name, Description
```

The following example shows the header line for the Border linetype available in AutoCAD:

```
*BORDER,__ __ . __ __ . __ __ .
```

The linetype name is required for all linetype definitions. The linetype name is used when you want to load a linetype, or assign a linetype to an object. When creating your own linetypes, select a name that will help the user recognize the linetype by its name. The name cannot contain spaces.

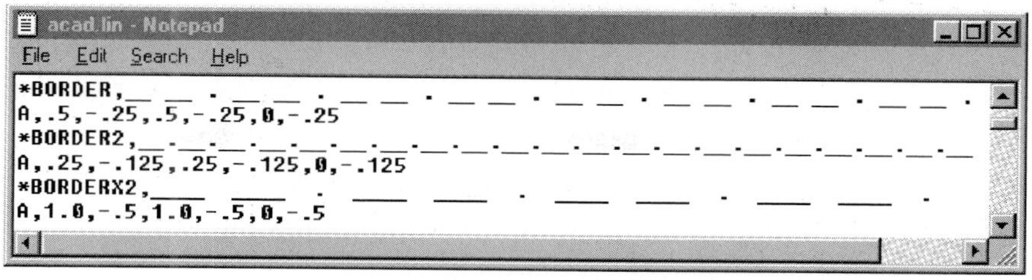

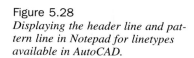

Figure 5.28
Displaying the header line and pattern line in Notepad for linetypes available in AutoCAD.

The description is a graphical representation of the line. This can be generated by using dashes, dots, and spaces from the keyboard. This graphic is used by AutoCAD when you want to display the linetype on-screen, either with the LINETYPE command with the ? option, or by accessing the Load or Reload Linetypes dialog box. The linetype description cannot exceed 47 characters.

Pattern Line The pattern line contains the definition of the line pattern. The format for the pattern line is:

```
Alignment Field Specification, Linetype Specification
```

The following example shows the pattern line for the Border linetype available in AutoCAD:

```
A,.5,-.25,.5,-.25,0,-.25
```

In the above example the alignment field specification is A. This is the only alignment field supported by AutoCAD, therefore every pattern line starts with the letter **A.** Using A-type alignment guarantees that lines and arcs start and end with a dash. The linetype specification defines the dot-dash pattern used to generate the line. The maximum number of linetype specifications is 12.

Creating a Linetype Specification Simple linetypes are created by combining three basic elements into a desired configuration. The three basic elements used to define a linetype specification are dash, dot, and space. A dash is generated by specifying a positive number. Specifying a .5, for example, will generate a line 0.5 units long. Spaces are generated by specifying a negative number. Specifying −.25, for example, generates a space 0.25 units long. A dot is generated by specifying a zero length.

The Border linetype specification was:

```
A,.5,-.25,.5,-.25,0,-.25
```

Examining the Border linetype specification shows it will draw a line 0.5 units, followed by a space of 0.25 units, another line 0.5 units, a 0.25 space, a dot, and finishing up with a 0.25 space. This pattern will repeat for the remainder of the object being drawn.

For the Professional

In certain cases you may draw a line with a loaded and selected linetype that you thought contained dashes and spaces, but the line appears continuous on the screen. In order for the linetype to display the pattern, it must be at least as long as the sum of the parts in its definition. To make the line appear correctly, you can change the LTSCALE for the object, or increase its length until the correct pattern appears.

TUTORIAL 5.9: CREATING A LINETYPE

For this tutorial you will create a simple linetype consisting of a dash and two dots.

1.  Select the New button from the Standard toolbar. If prompted with the Save Changes dialog box, select No. In the Create New Drawing dialog box, enter the proper path and name the drawing **newline** in the text box.
2. Enter `linetype` at the `Command:` prompt.

   At the `?/Create/Load/Set:` prompt enter `c`.
3. At the `Name of linetype to create:` prompt enter `dash_dot`.
4. In the Create or Append Linetype File dialog box, change to the A drive and enter `new` in the File Name: edit box. Choose OK.

   If you select an existing filename, the new linetype is added to the existing linetypes in the file.
5. At the `Descriptive Text:` prompt, enter `_.._.._.._`
6. At the `Enter pattern (on next line):` prompt enter `.250,-.125,0,-.125,0`

   This defines the line segment as having a dash 0.250 units, a .125 space, a dot, a .125 space, and another dot.
7. At the `?/Create/Load/Set:` prompt press enter.
8.  To see what the linetype looks like, select the Linetype button on the Object Properties toolbar. The Select Linetype dialog box appears as shown previously in Figure 5.19.
9. Choose the Load button.

   The Dash_Dot linetype is displayed in the Load or Reload Linetypes dialog box.

SUMMARY

Proper use of layers not only helps organize your drawing's linetypes, colors, and objects, but also helps in visualization and plotting. Standardizing layer names, linetypes, and colors is an essential part of AutoCAD and should be used in all of your drawings.

Drafting requires the proper use of various linetypes such as continuous, hidden, and center. In order for a draftsman to properly present his ideas or drawings, it's imperative that he or she know how to properly use linetypes. Creating different linetypes (such as hidden or center lines) in manual drafting can be a long and tedious process. One of the major advantages of using AutoCAD over manual drafting procedures is the freedom from having to draw different linetypes. AutoCAD contains many predefined linetypes, including several industry standard ISO linetypes.

To use a linetype in a drawing, its definition must exist in a .LIN library file. Once its definition exists, it must be loaded into the drawing. The linetype can then be assigned to layers for use in the drawing.

While most drawings done on AutoCAD are drawn full-size, when the drawing is plotted, the plot is scaled to enable the drawing to fit on a standard size of paper. The LTSCALE command can be used to achieve the correct linetype scale in the finished drawing. In most cases the linetype scale should be set to the working scale of the drawing.

REVIEW

1. List six reasons why using layers is beneficial for CAD drawing.
2. Explain how you would determine how many layers you need and what names you would give them for a typical CAD project.
3. Explain the relationship between layer name, color, and linetype.
4. Clarify the difference between turning layers on and off, and freezing and thawing them.
5. Explain what locking and unlocking a layer does and how it can be used in a drawing.
6. List the two qualifications a linetype must have before it can be used.
7. Define *linetype* and what it is used for.
8. Explain how you can determine what linetypes AutoCAD has available for use.
9. Define linetype scale and what it is used for.
10. Clarify how you would determine the linetype scale for a typical CAD drawing.

EXERCISE 5

Draw the six views of the L-BLOCK shown in Figure 5.29. The grid spacing is .25″.

1. Set your grid and snap to .25″.
2. Create three new layers with the following parameters:

Name	Color	Linetype
Visible	Red	CONTINUOUS
Hidden	Yellow	HIDDEN
Border	Green	HIDDENX2

3. Draw the six views. View and border locations are important.
4. Do not add any text, dimensions, or draw the isometric view.

Figure 5.29 *Draw the six views of the L-BLOCK.*

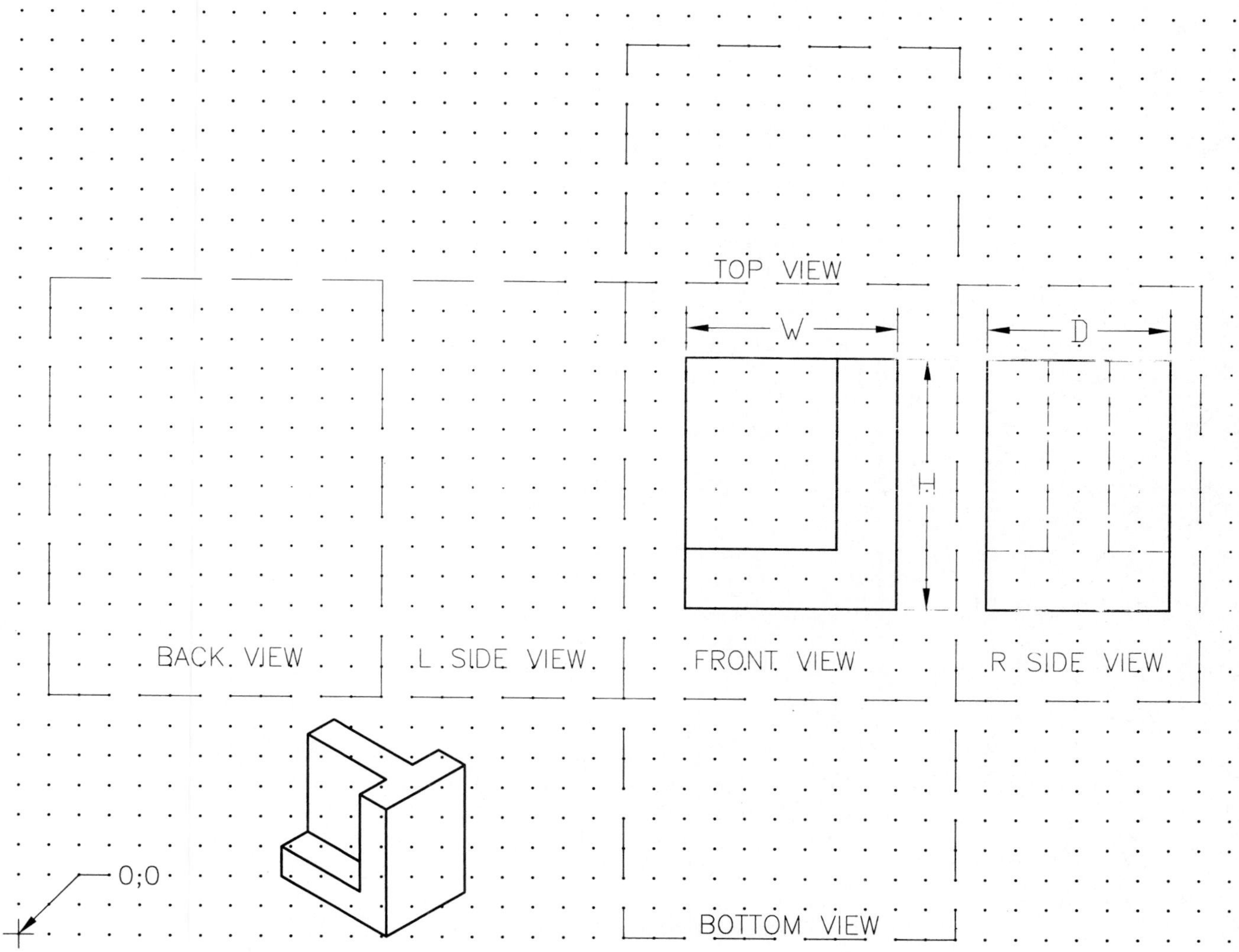

UNIT 6 CREATING BASIC GEOMETRY

OVERVIEW

The AutoCAD basic drawing commands—LINE, ARC, and CIRCLE—usually make up the majority of geometry in a typical drawing. To speed up the drawing process and help create complicated geometry, AutoCAD offers the RECTANG and POLYGON commands.

OBJECTIVES

- Draw a rectangle.
- Draw circles with the **circle** command options.
- Draw arcs with the most common **arc** commands.
- Draw polygons with the **polygon** command options.

INTRODUCTION

This unit describes some basic AutoCAD commands. These commands cast the foundation for almost any geometry you create. The **line** command draws lines, the **circle** command draws circles, and the **arc** command draws arcs. (Most AutoCAD commands have names that describe their function.) When combined with lines, circles and arcs make up the majority of most objects. You will use these basic commands to create a stove, breakfast bar, and hot tub.

OUTLINE

Drawing Rectangles (RECTANG)
Tutorial 6.1: Creating a Rectangle
Drawing Circles (CIRCLE)
Tutorial 6.2: Creating a Circle with Center Radius
Tutorial 6.3: Creating a Circle with Center Diameter
Tutorial 6.4: Creating a Circle with Three Points
Tutorial 6.5: Creating a Circle with Two Points
Tutorial 6.6: Creating Circles with Tangent, Tangent, Radius
Tutorial 6.7: Drawing a Stove/Oven Symbol
Drawing Arcs (ARC)
Tutorial 6.8: Creating an Arc with the 3 Points Option
Tutorial 6.9: Creating an Arc with Start, Center, End
Tutorial 6.10: Creating an Arc with Start, End, Radius
Tutorial 6.11: Continuing an Arc from an Existing Arc
Tutorial 6.12: Drawing a Breakfast Bar Symbol
Tutorial 6.13: Drawing an Inscribed Polygon
Tutorial 6.14: Drawing a Hot Tub Symbol with Polygon, Rectang, and Circle
Summary
Review
Exercises

DRAWING RECTANGLES (RECTANG)

The **rectang** command enables you to draw rectangles easily. AutoCAD asks you to locate the first corner and then the opposite corner, as shown in Figure 6.1. You can mark corner locations with the crosshairs or keyboard coordinate entry. The corners of the rectangle don't have to be selected from left to right or top to bottom. You can also pick two diagonally opposing corners. To locate the corners, you can use any combination of coordinate entry methods, including absolute, relative, absolute polar, and relative polar.

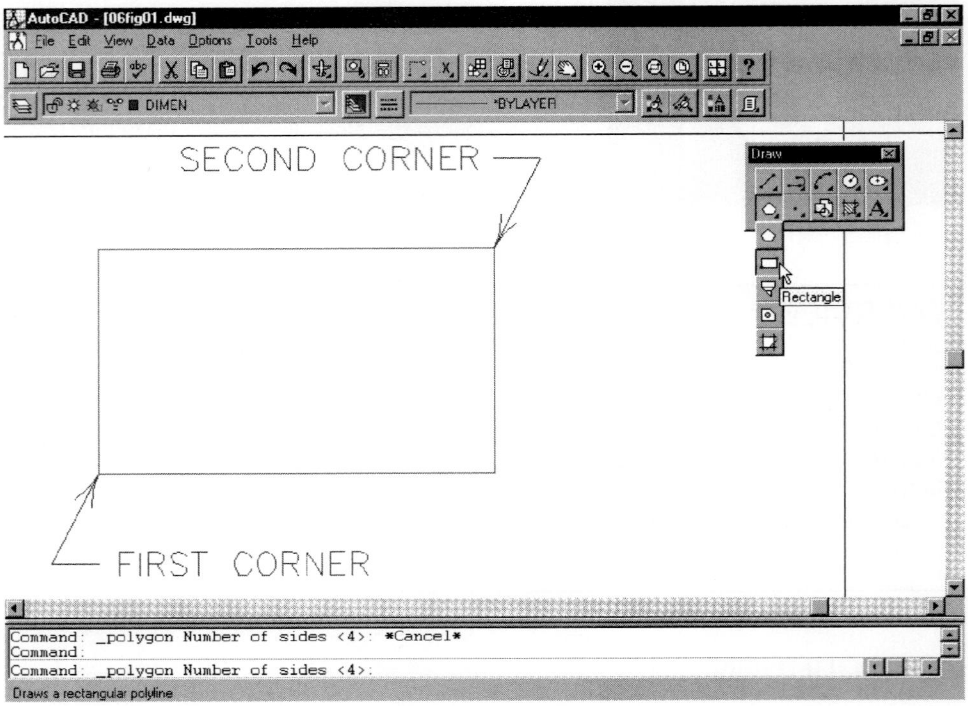

Figure 6.1
Use the mouse or keyboard coordinate entry to locate the first corner and then the opposite corner of a rectangle.

Access the **rectang** command in one of two ways:

- Choose the Polygon button on the Draw floating toolbar. The polygon flyout submenu appears. The second button is Rectangle, as shown in Figure 6.1. To access the Draw floating toolbar, select Tools, Toolbars, Draw from the pull-down menu.
- Enter **rectang** at the `Command:` prompt.

When you create a rectangle, AutoCAD treats it as one entity, called a *polyline.* To edit the individual sides, you must explode the rectangle. First access the **explode** command, then select the object you want to break into individual parts. You can access the **explode** command in the following ways:

- Choose the Explode button on the Modify toolbar as shown in Figure 6.2. To access the Modify floating toolbar, select Tools, Toolbars, Modify from the pull-down menu.
- Enter **`explode`** at the `Command:` prompt.

Tutorial 6.1: Creating a Rectangle

In this tutorial, you will create the simple 3-unit × 5-unit rectangle shown in Figure 6.2. Follow these steps:

1.  Choose New from the Standard toolbar. In the New Drawing dialog box, click OK or press Enter.

2.  Choose Rectangle from the Draw toolbar.

3. Specify the coordinates for the two corners of the rectangle.

```
First corner: 1,1
Other corner: @3,5
```

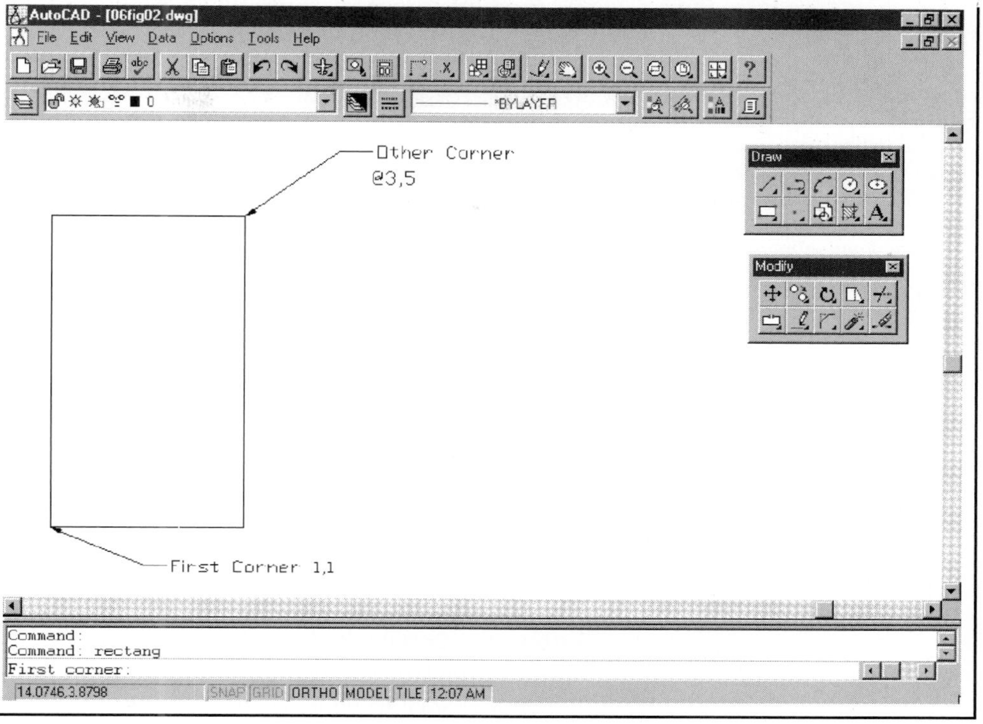

Figure 6.2
You can easily create this 3-unit × 5-unit rectangle.

DRAWING CIRCLES (CIRCLE)

Circles are as much a part of a typical drawing as lines are. AutoCAD gives you five options for drawing a circle:

- **Center, Radius.** You first specify the center point of the circle and then the radius of the circle.
- **Center, Diameter.** You first specify the center point of the circle and then the diameter of the circle.
- **2 Point.** You specify two points that define the diameter of the circle.
- **3 Point.** You specify three points on the circumference of the circle.
- **Tangent, Tangent, Radius.** You specify two entities that will be tangent to the circle and the circle's radius.

You can access the Circle command in one of two ways:

- Click the Circle button on the Draw toolbar. This will bring up a submenu called a flyout menu, showing the five options for creating a circle (see Figure 6.3).
- Enter **circle** at the `Command:` prompt.

Skill Builder

You also can enter **c** at the `Command:` prompt as a shortcut to begin the **circle** command.

Drawing Circles with Center Point and Radius

When you select the Circle, Center, Radius button from the Circle flyout menu, AutoCAD first asks you to select a center point. You can locate the center point with either the crosshairs or coordinate entry. After you select the center point, pick the radius in the

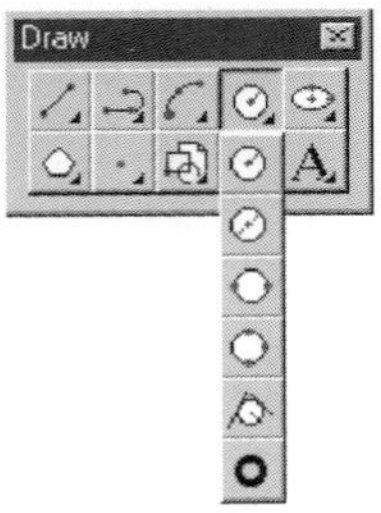

Figure 6.3
The five options for drawing the circle, plus the Donut button, are available on the flyout menu, activated when you select Circle from the Draw floating toolbar.

drawing window or type the radius value (see Figure 6.4). If you are selecting the center point and radius with the crosshairs, you can set and turn on Snap and Grid to aid in locating the center point. Watch the coordinate display window to locate the exact center point and radius. Here's the command sequence for using the Center, Radius option:

```
3P/2P/TTR/<Center point>: Enter the coordinates or pick the center
point.
Diameter/<Radius>: Drag the circle to the desired radius and pick.
Alternately enter the radius size.
```

Setting the Default Radius Radius is the **circle** command's default option. The radius value that you type becomes the default value the next time you use the **circle** command.

If you want to set a default radius for the **circle** command, use the **circlerad** system variable. Then the same default circle radius appears each time you use the **circle** command until you use a different value. The following command sequence sets the **circlerad** value:

```
Command: circlerad
New value for CIRCLERAD<current value>: Set the value you want,
such as .25.
```

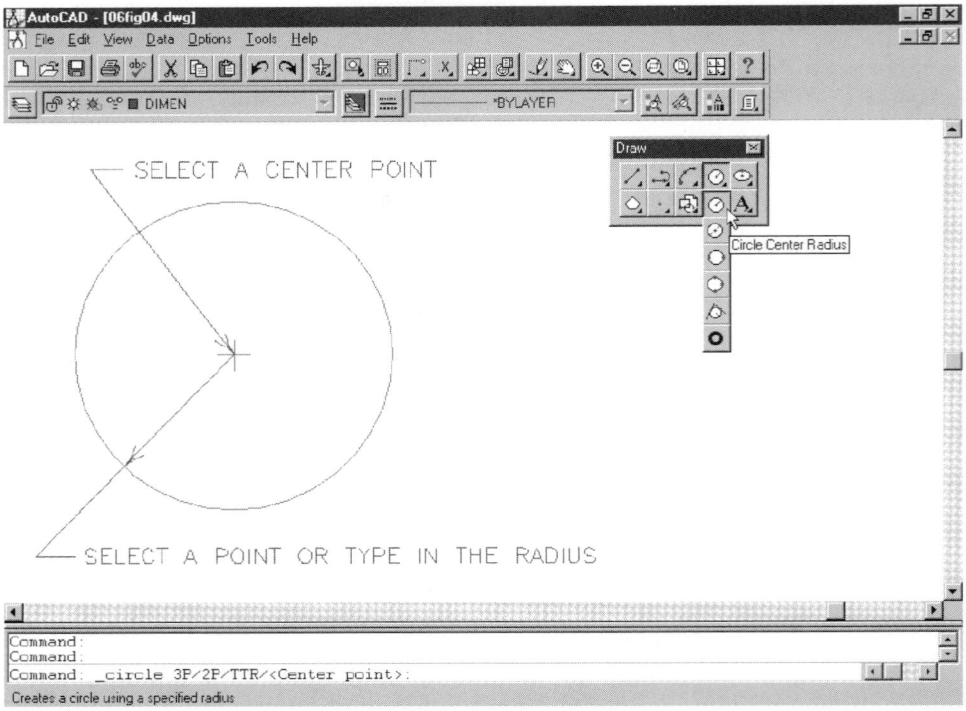

Figure 6.4
First specify a center point, then specify the radius when drawing a circle.

When you use the **circle** command, the sequence now looks like this: Select the Circle, Center, Radius button from the Circle flyout menu.

3P/2P/TTR/<Center point>: *Locate center point.*
Diameter/<Radius><.25>:

This command draws a circle with a radius of .25 at the center location specified. If you set the **circlerad** system variable to a nonzero value and then issue the **circle** command, you simply need to pick the circle's center point as prompted and then press Enter at the Diameter/<Radius>: prompt. You can always enter a different radius or pick a different radius point if you do not want to use the default value you set with **circlerad.** Remember that if you override the default value for the radius by picking a new point or entering a new value, the default value is reset to your new entry.

SKILL BUILDER

When drawing a series of identical circles, once the first circle is drawn, the radius setting is retained as the default by the **circlerad** system variable. As you continue to draw the other identical circles, once the center point is established, press Enter to accept the default radius. This technique can help speed up drafting time.

DRAWING CIRCLES WITH CENTER POINT AND DIAMETER

You can select the Center Diameter option of **circle** as follows:

- Select the Circle, Center, Diameter button from the Circle flyout menu.
- Enter **circle** at the Command: prompt.

TUTORIAL 6.2: CREATING A CIRCLE WITH CENTER RADIUS

This tutorial and the next show you how to create the series of circles shown in Figure 6.5, using the Center Radius and Center Diameter options. Circles A, B, and C are created using the Radius option. Begin by creating a new drawing:

1.  Choose New from the Standard toolbar. In the New Drawing dialog box, click OK or press Enter.
2.  Select the Circle, Center, Radius button from the Circle flyout menu.
3. Enter the absolute coordinates for the center point for circle A.

   3P/2P/TTR/<Center point>: **2,4.25**

4. Enter the value for the radius.

   Diameter/<Radius>: **.75**

5. Next, re-enter the Circle, Center, Radius command. While you select the Circle, Center, Radius button from the Circle flyout menu, pressing Enter will automatically re-enter the last command.
6. Enter the absolute coordinates for the center point for circle B.

   3P/2P/TTR/<Center point>: **3.75,4.25**

7. Since the radius value was entered in the previous circle, pressing Enter will accept the default value and draw the circle.

   Diameter/<Radius><0.7500>:

8. Re-enter the Circle, Center, Radius command and draw circle C. Use the absolute values of **5.5** and **4.25** for the center point and use the default radius value of **.75.** The next tutorial on drawing circles with the Center Point and Diameter will continue from here.

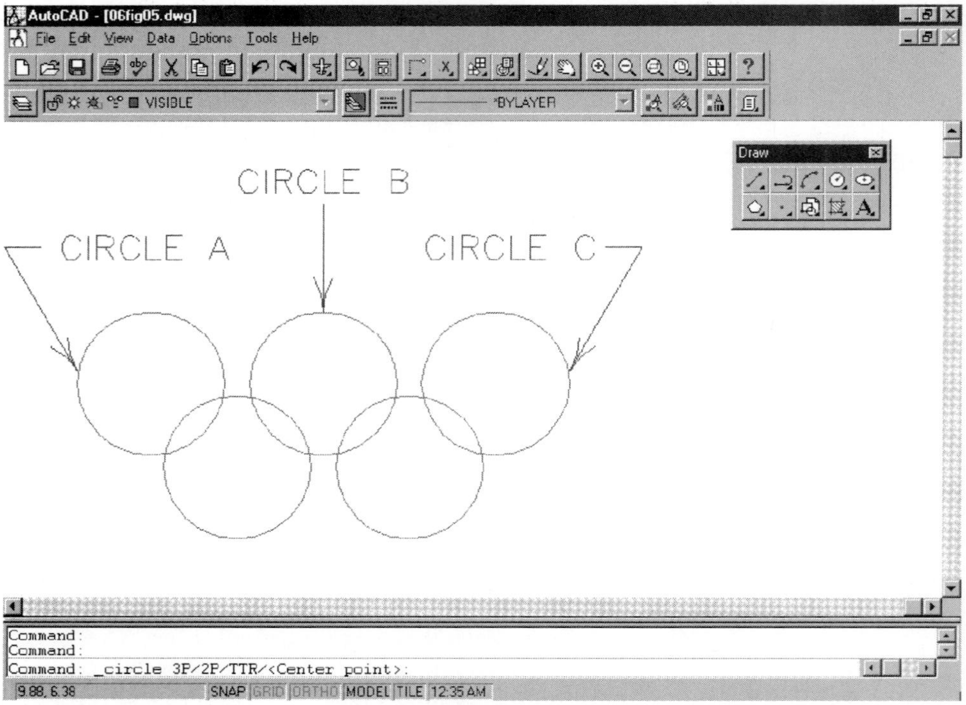

Figure 6.5
Drawing circles using the Center Radius and Center Diameter options.

If you enter **circle** at the `Command:` prompt, you must enter **d** for the diameter option because radius is the default as shown in the following example:

```
Command: circle
3P/2P/TTR/<Center point>: Locate center point.
Diameter/<Radius>: d
Diameter: Enter the diameter size or drag the circle to the
desired diameter size and pick.
```

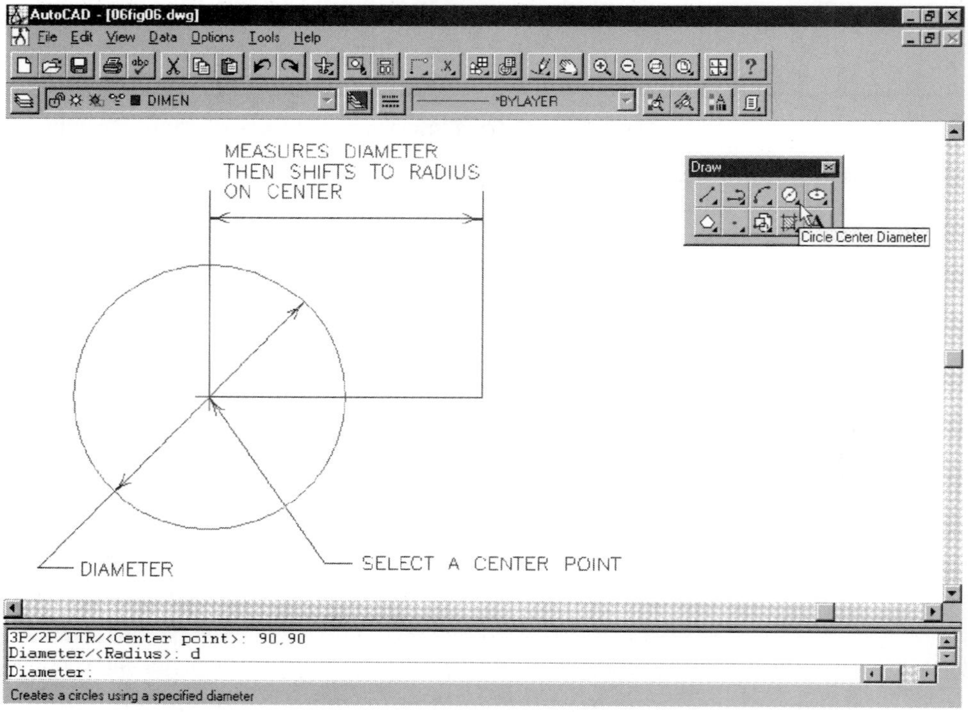

Figure 6.6
When you draw a circle with the Center, Diameter option, the distance from the center of the circle to the crosshairs represents the diameter of the circle.

When using the Center Diameter option, notice that as the pointer measures the diameter of the circle, the circle's edge passes midway between the center and crosshair, as shown in Figure 6.6. The Center, Diameter option is frequently used since most circle dimensions are given as diameters.

When you choose the Circle, Center, Diameter button from the Circle flyout, the initial prompt is for the center point of the circle. After you locate the center point, you are automatically prompted for the diameter.

After you draw a circle with the Diameter option, the previous default setting is converted to a diameter. If your next circle is drawn with the Radius option, AutoCAD changes the default to a radius measurement based on the previous diameter. If the **circlerad** value is set to .75, for example, the default for a circle drawn with the Diameter option is automatically set to 1.50 (twice the radius).

Tutorial 6.3: Creating a Circle with Center Diameter

For this tutorial you will create circles D and E shown in Figure 6.7 using the Center Diameter option.

1. 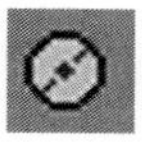 Continue from the previous tutorial. Select the Circle Center Diameter button from the Circle flyout menu.
2. Enter the absolute coordinates for the center point for circle D.

   `3P/2P/TTR/<Center point>:` **`2.875,3.375`**

3. In the previous tutorial you set the circle radius to .75. AutoCAD automatically changes this value to the diameter and displays it in the prompt. Press Enter to accept the default diameter for the circle.

   `Diameter <1.5000>:`

4. Re-enter the Circle, Center, Diameter command and draw circle E. Use the absolute values of **4.625** and **3.375** for the center point and use the default diameter value of **1.5000.**

Figure 6.7 *Draw circles D and E using the Center Diameter option.*

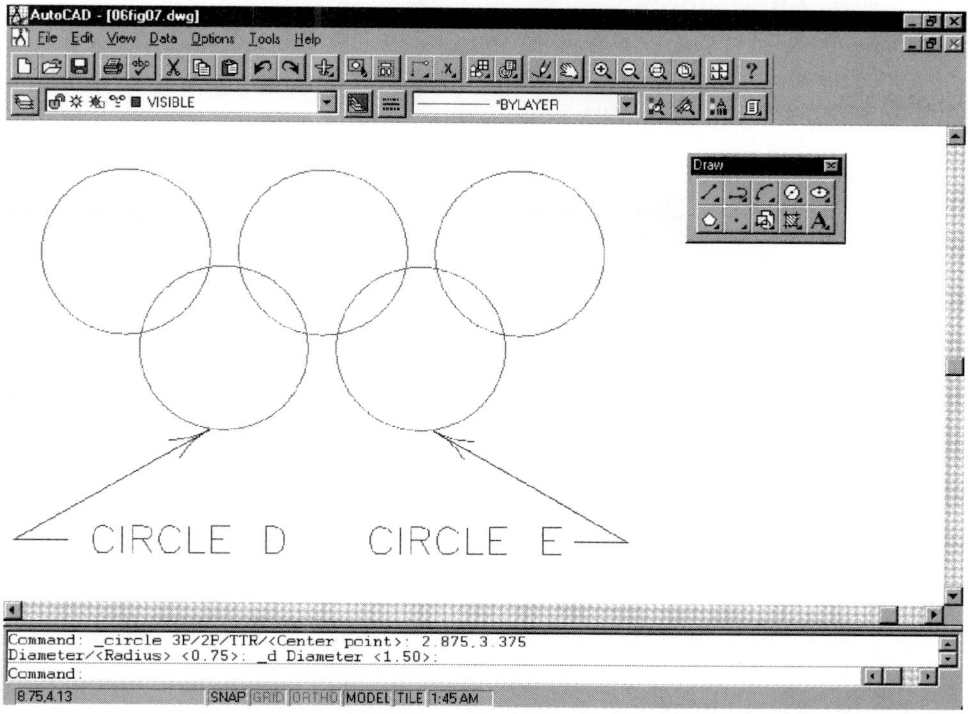

Drawing Circles with Three Points

When you know three points on the perimeter, the three-point option is the best method to use for drawing a circle. You can select the three points in any order, as shown in Figure 6.8. Here is the command sequence for a three-point circle:

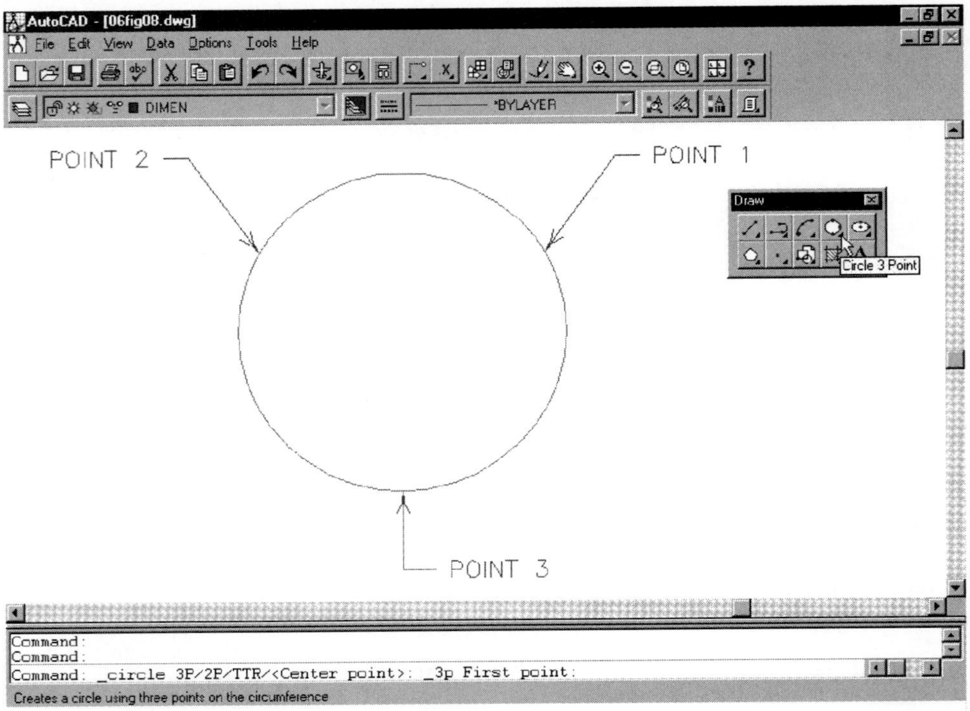

Figure 6.8
Draw a circle by selecting three points on the perimeter.

Tutorial 6.4: Creating a Circle with Three Points

This tutorial and the next two show you how to create the series of circles shown in Figure 6.9, using the different methods available in AutoCAD. Circle A is created using the 3-point option. Begin by creating a new drawing:

1.  Choose New from the Standard toolbar. In the New Drawing dialog box, click OK or press Enter.
2.  Select the Circle 3 Point button from the Circle flyout menu.
3. Enter the absolute coordinates for all three points.

```
First point: 2,2
Second point: 3,3
Third point: 4,2
```

You should now have the circle A shown in Figure 6.9.

Figure 6.9
Drawing circle A using the 3-point option, circle B using the 2-point option, and circle C using the Tan Tan Radius option.

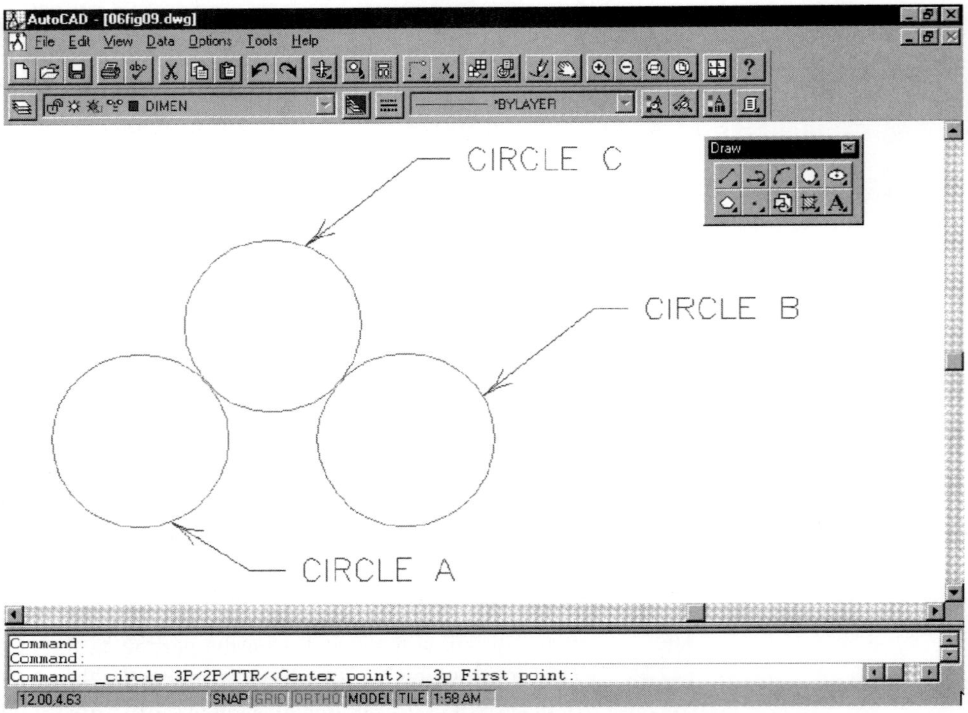

Select the Circle 3 Point button on the Circle flyout menu.

```
3P/2P/TTR/<Center point>:
First point: Select first point.
Second point: Select second point.
Third point: Select third point.
```

AutoCAD automatically calculates the radius of the circle just created and uses this value as the default for the next circle.

Drawing Circles with Two Points

You can draw a 2-point circle by selecting two points that lie on the circle's perimeter, as shown in Figure 6.10. These two points define the circle's diameter. This option can be useful when the diameter of the circle is known but the center point is difficult to locate. Here is the command sequence for a 2-point circle:

```
Select the Circle 2 Point button from the Circle flyout menu.
First point on diameter: Select first point.
Second point on diameter: Select second point.
```

AutoCAD will automatically calculate the radius of the circle just created and use this value as the default for the next circle.

Drawing Circles with Tangent, Tangent, Radius

The Tangent, Tangent, Radius option (TTR) allows you to draw a circle of a specific radius that has two points of tangency with existing objects. The existing objects may be another circle or a line. After selecting the two tangency points, you can specify the circle radius.

Skill Builder

The term *tangent* refers to another circle, line, or arc that comes into contact with another circle or arc at one point. The point where the objects touch is called the *point of tangency.* When two circles are tangent, they touch at only one point. A line drawn between the centers passes through the point of tangency.

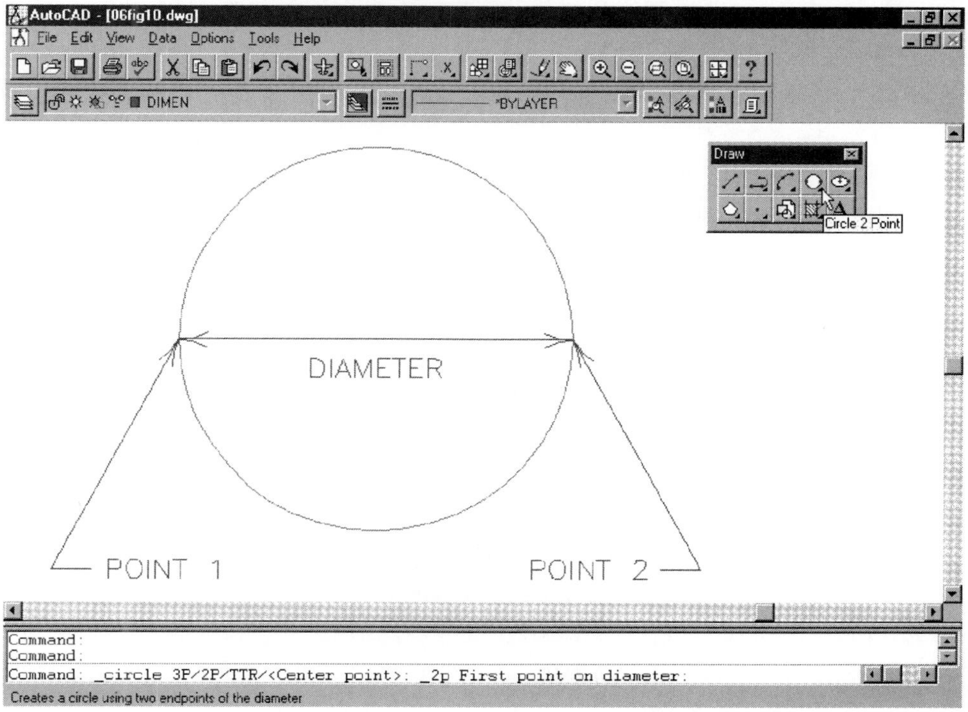

Figure 6.10
Draw a circle by selecting two points on the perimeter.

TUTORIAL 6.5: CREATING A CIRCLE WITH TWO POINTS

Continuing from the preceding tutorial, you can draw circle B with the 2-point option. Follow these steps:

1.  Select the Circle 2 Point button from the Circle flyout menu.

2. Enter the absolute coordinates for the first point and the polar coordinates for the second point.

```
First point: 5,2
Second point: @2<0
```

You should now have the two circles labeled A and B shown in Figure 6.9.

When you need to draw a circle tangent to two given lines, circles, or arcs, choose the Tangent, Tangent, Radius option. Select the lines or line and arc to which the new circle will be tangent. After you select these objects, give the radius. The command sequence for using the Tangent, Tangent, Radius option is as follows:

Select the Circle Tan Tan Radius button from the Circle flyout menu.

```
Enter Tangent spec: Select the first line, circle, or arc.
Enter second Tangent spec: Select the second line, circle, or arc.
Radius <current>: Enter a radius value.
```

SKILL BUILDER

If you enter a radius value that is too small, AutoCAD gives you the message `Circle does not exist.`

The radius you enter for the Tangent, Tangent, Radius option becomes the default value for the next circle. Figure 6.11 shows two examples using the Tangent, Tangent, Radius option.

FOR THE PROFESSIONAL

To locate the center of a circle at the same coordinates as the last selected point on the previously created object, use the @ symbol. The @ symbol retrieves the value stored as the AutoCAD LASTPOINT value. For example, if you want to locate the center of a circle at the endpoint of a previously drawn line, enter the @ symbol at the Circle-Center Point prompt as in the following example:

Select the Line button from the Draw floating toolbar.

```
From point: 2,2
To point: 4,4
To point:
```

Select the Circle, Center, Radius button from the Circle flyout menu.

```
3P/2P/TTR/<Center point>: @
```

Using the @ symbol in this example automatically retrieves the last selected point 4,4 (endpoint of the last drawn line) as the center of the circle.

```
Diameter/<Radius>: Press Enter to accept the default value.
```

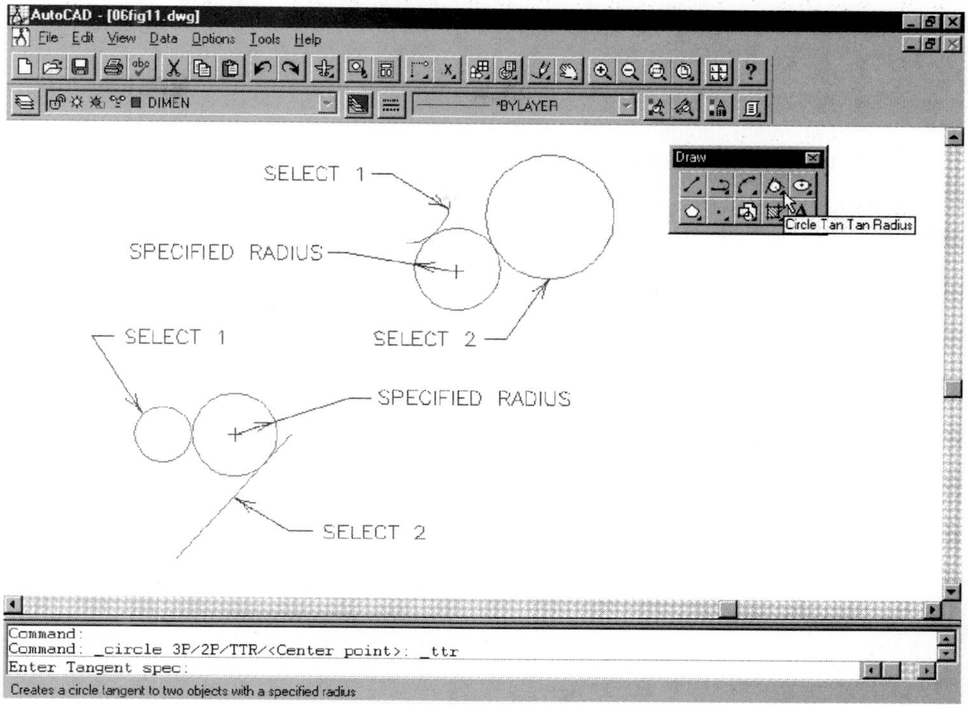

Figure 6.11
Use Tangent, Tangent, Radius to draw circles tangent to two given entities.

Tutorial 6.6: Creating Circles with Tangent, Tangent, Radius

Now create another circle that is tangent to circles A and B drawn in the previous tutorials. The new circle will have a radius of 1 unit. Follow these steps:

1.  Select the Circle Tan, Tan, Radius button from the Circle flyout menu.
2. Specify the first two circles. Depending on the location where you pick the two circles, the new circle may be below the two existing circles. This is because the Tangent, Tangent, Radius option is *position sensitive;* that is, the position of the crosshairs on the circles you select influences the location of the resulting tangent circle. To create a tangent circle above the two existing circles, be sure to pick the top parts of the circles.

   `Enter Tangent spec:` *`Select circle A.`*
   `Enter second Tangent spec:` *`Select circle B.`*
3. At the `Radius:` prompt, enter **1**.

You should now have the three circles shown in Figure 6.9.

Tutorial 6.7: Drawing a Stove/Oven Symbol

This tutorial describes how to create a stove/oven symbol (see Figure 6.12). The symbol is composed of a rectangle and four circles and enables you to practice the commands you used earlier in the unit. Because you will use this symbol in an architectural drawing, you must change the units. After completing the symbol, save it as **stove.** To begin the process, follow these steps:

1.  Select the New button from the Standard toolbar. In the Create New Drawing dialog box, enter **stove** for the new drawing name. If the AutoCAD dialog box appears, select No unless you want to save the current drawing. If you want to save the current drawing, select Yes and enter a path and drawing name.
2. Choose Data, Units. The Units Control dialog box appears. Change the units to architectural with a precision of 0′-0″.
3.  Now begin drawing the symbol. Start by creating the rectangle shown in Figure 6.13. Make sure the Draw floating toolbar appears on the screen. Select the Rectangle button from the Polygon flyout menu.
4. Locate the corners of the rectangle.

   `First corner:` **`1,1`**
   `Other corner:` **`@30,26`**

5.  Notice that you cannot see the complete rectangle. You will need to use the Zoom command to display the rectangle within the drawing area. Select the Zoom Scale button from the zoom flyout menu located on the Standard toolbar. For the scale factor, enter **.2**.

Now you are ready to create the circles that represent the burners on the stove. Two burners will be 8″ diameters; the other two will be 10″ diameters. You begin by drawing the 8″ diameter burners. Follow these steps:

1.  Select the Circle, Center, Radius button from the Circle flyout menu.
2. Specify the absolute coordinates for the center point and give the radius.

```
CIRCLE 3P/2P/TTR/<Center point>: 9,8
Diameter/<Radius>: 4
```

You should now have the lower-left burner drawn.

3. Repeat steps 1 and 2 for the upper-right burner. Pressing Enter at the `Command:` prompt reissues the **circle** command.

```
Command:
CIRCLE 3P/2P/TTR/<Center point>: 2',1'-9"
Diameter/<Radius><0'-4">:
```

Your drawing should now resemble Figure 6.14.

4. To complete the stove/oven symbol, create the two remaining 10″-diameter burners—first the upper-left burner and then the lower-right burner.

```
Command:
CIRCLE 3P/2P/TTR/<Center point>: 9",1'-9"
Diameter/<Radius><0'-4">: 5
Command:
CIRCLE 3P/2P/TTR/<Center point>: 2',8
Diameter/<Radius><0'-5">: Press Enter to accept the default radius value of 5.
```

 The stove symbol is now complete and should resemble the symbol in Figure 6.12. You can save the drawing by selecting the Save button from the Standard toolbar.

Skill Builder

When working with architectural units, it's not necessary to type the inch (″) symbol after a distance value. If a distance value isn't followed by a foot symbol (′), AutoCAD assumes the value to be in inches.

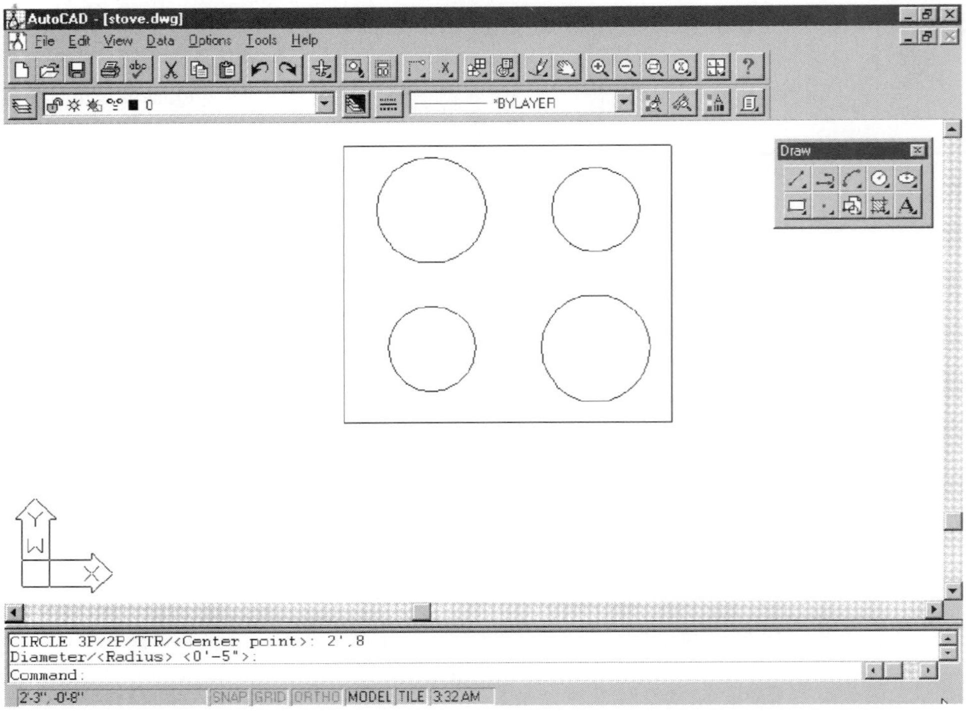

Figure 6.12
Draw this stove/oven symbol, created with the rectangle and circle commands.

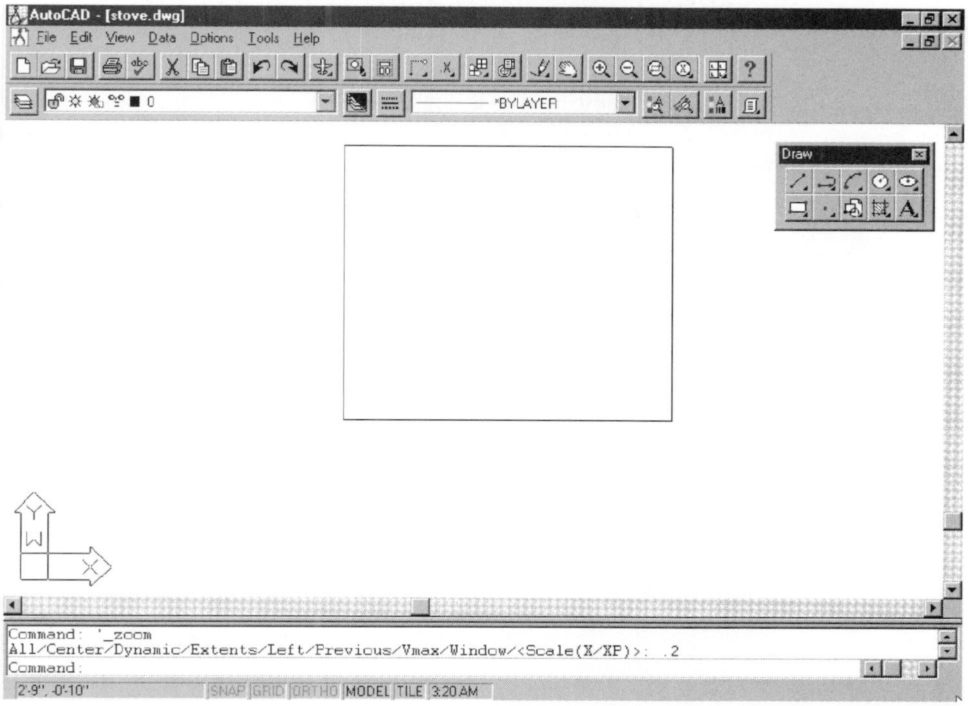

Figure 6.13 *Use the Rectang command to create the stove/oven symbol.*

Figure 6.14 *The stove/oven symbol with the 8″-diameter burners completed.*

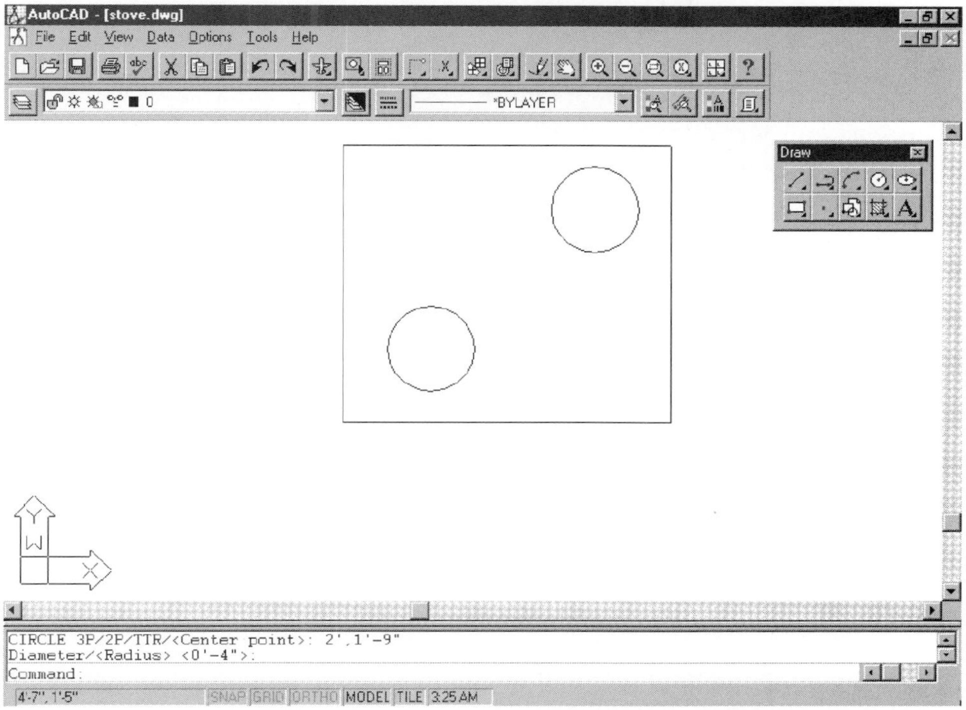

DRAWING ARCS (ARC)

An arc may be defined as a partial circle. AutoCAD offers 11 different methods for drawing an arc. These methods are based on start points, start directions, center points, included angles, endpoints, lengths of chord, and radius. You can access the Arc command in one of several ways:

- Choose the Arc 3 Points button on the Draw floating toolbar. A flyout submenu appears, showing 11 options for creating an arc (see Figure 6.15).
- Enter **arc** at the `Command:` prompt.

SKILL BUILDER

When you select one of the 11 options for creating an arc on the flyout submenu, the information needed to create the particular arc appears at the bottom of the AutoCAD display. For example, when you select the first Arc 3 Point icon, it says "Creates an arc using three points" at the bottom of the AutoCAD display.

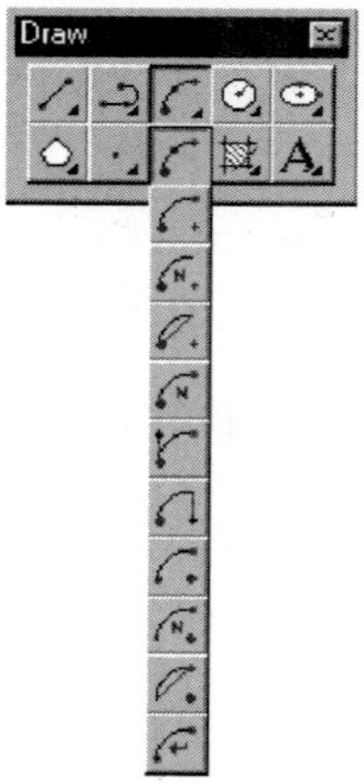

Figure 6.15
Options for creating an arc are available on the Arc flyout menu.

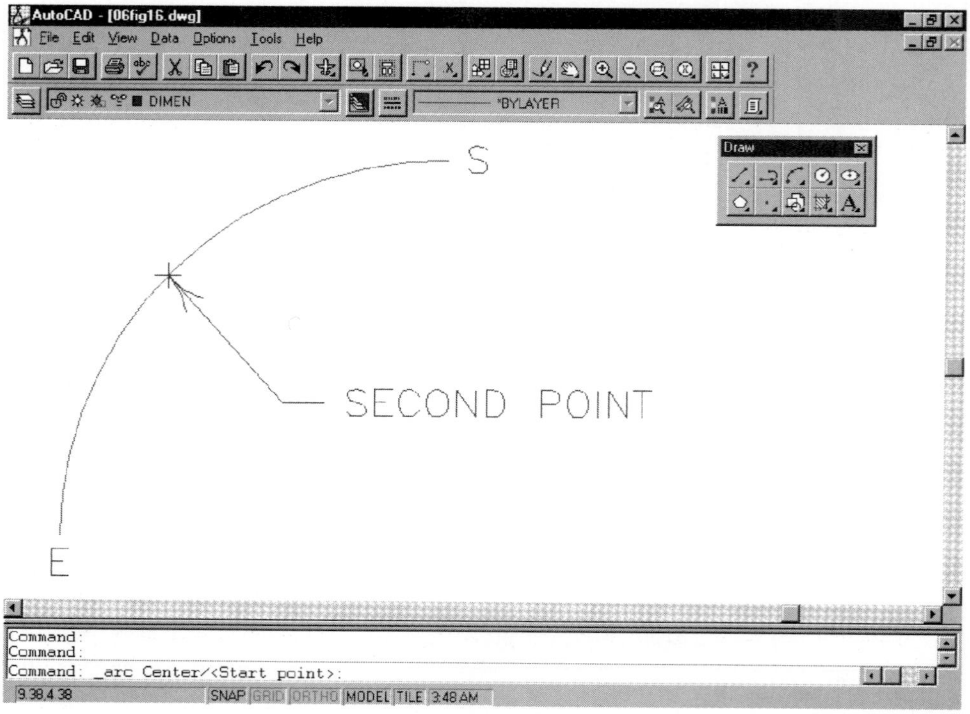

Figure 6.16
Using the 3 Point option to draw an arc.

Drawing Arcs with Three Point

When you draw an arc with the 3 Point option, AutoCAD prompts you for the start point, a second point along the arc, and the endpoint, as shown in Figure 6.16. You can draw the arc clockwise or counterclockwise. Drag the arc into position as you locate the endpoint. AutoCAD uses the following command sequence when you click the Arc 3 Point button on the Arc flyout menu:

Choose the Arc 3 Point button.

Center/<Start point>: *Select the start point (S) on the arc.*
Center/End/<Second point>: *Select the second point on the arc.*
End point: *Select the endpoint (E) of the arc.*

Tutorial 6.8: Creating an Arc with the 3 Point Option

This tutorial describes how to create an arc using the 3 Point option, one of the many options available. Because of the great variety of ways to create arcs, the tutorials provided here cover only four of the most popular methods.

1.  Choose New from the Standard toolbar. In the New Drawing dialog box, click OK or press Enter.

2.  Select the Arc 3 Points option from the Arc flyout menu.

Center/<Start point>: **5,5**
Center/End/<Second point>: **3,3**
End point: *Using the crosshairs, drag the arc into place until your arc looks similar to that found in Figure 6.17.*

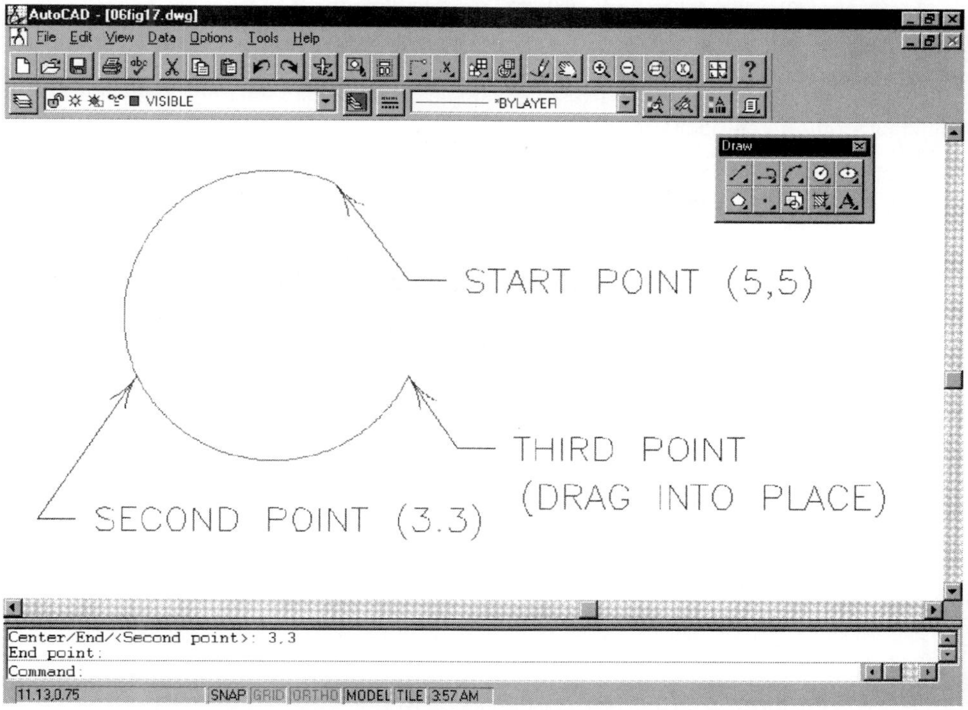

Figure 6.17
Creating an arc with the 3 Point option.

Drawing Arcs with Start, Center, End

You can select the Arc Start, Center, End button when you know the start point, center point, and endpoint of the arc. When you locate the start and center points, you establish the arc's radius. Because the endpoint furnishes the arc length, the arc does not pass through the endpoint unless this point is also on the radius (see Figure 6.18).

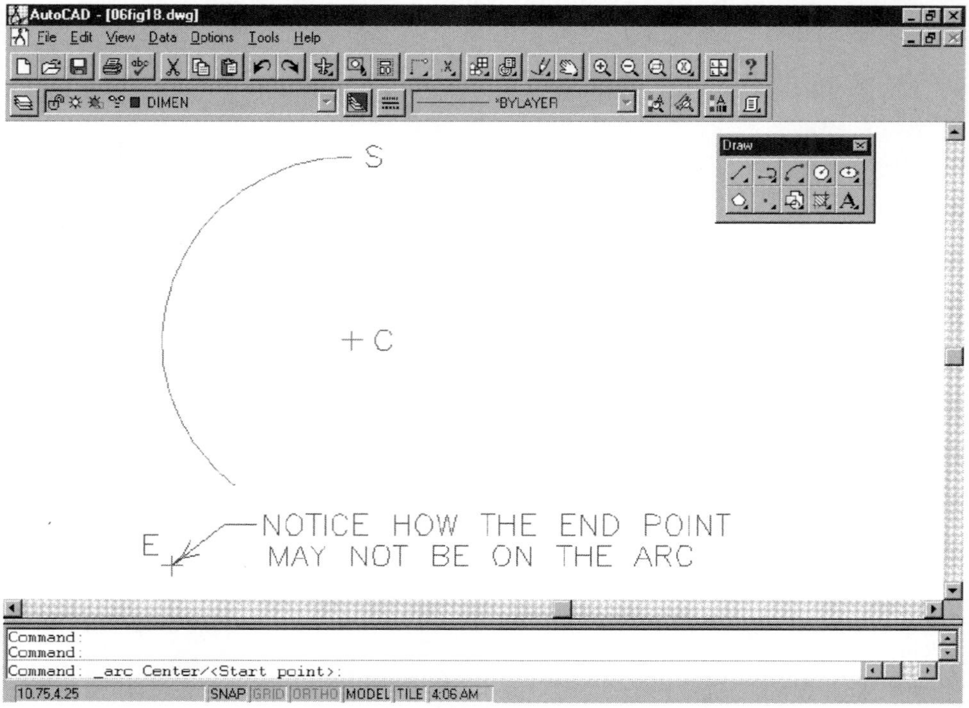

Figure 6.18
Drawing an arc with the Start, Center, End option.

TUTORIAL 6.9: CREATING AN ARC WITH START, CENTER, END

This tutorial describes how to create an arc using the Start, Center, End option:

1. Choose New from the Standard toolbar. In the New Drawing dialog box, click OK or press Enter.
2. Select the Arc Start, Center, End button from the Arc flyout menu.
3. Establish the three points of the arc.

`ARC Center/<Start point>:` *Click near the bottom center of the drawing area.*

`Center/End/<Second point>: _cCenter:` *Select a point approximately five units up and three units to the left of the start point.*

`Angle/Length of chord/<End point>:` *Drag the arc's endpoint until you have an arc similar to that found in Figure 6.19*

Use your coordinates display to help estimate your movement. You may also want to turn **snap** on by double-clicking the **snap** button at the bottom of the screen.

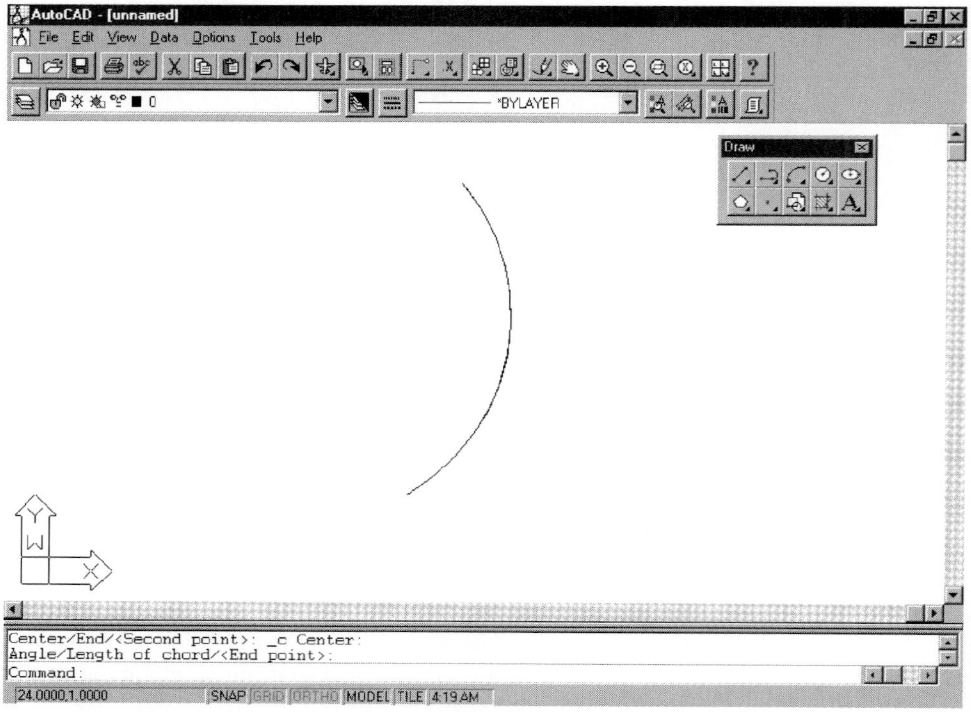

Figure 6.19
Create this arc using the Start, Center, End option.

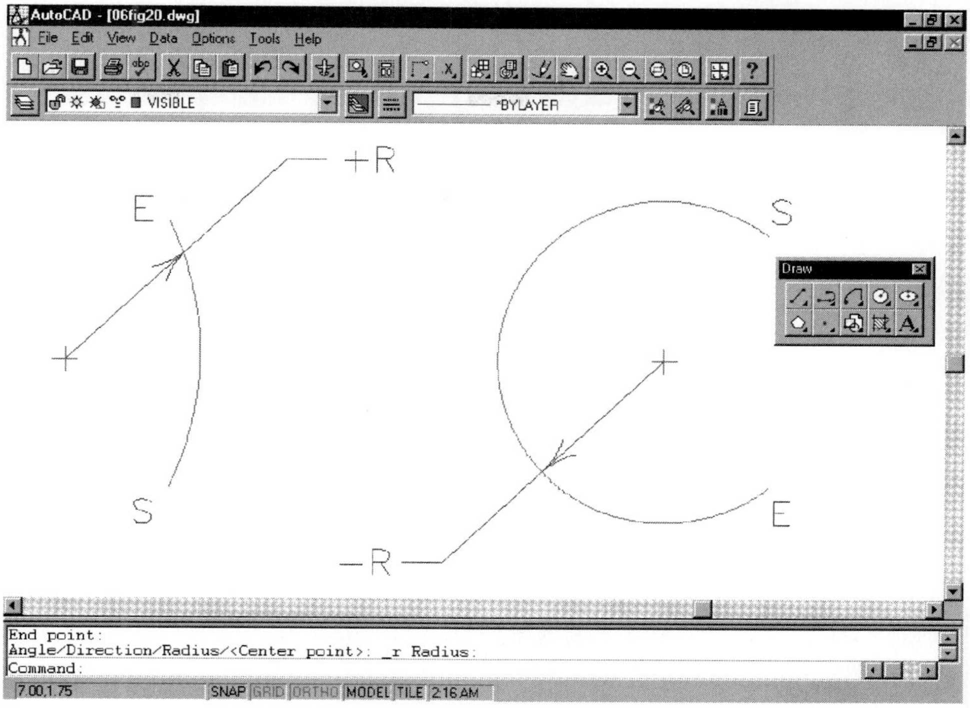

Figure 6.20
Drawing an arc with the Start, End, Radius option.

AutoCAD uses the following command sequence when you select the Arc Start, Center, End button:

`Center/<Start point>:` *`Select the start point (S) on the arc.`*
`Center/End/<Second point>: _cCenter:` *`Select the arc's center point (C).`*
`Angle/Length of chord/<End point>:` *`Select the arc's endpoint (E).`*

Drawing Arcs with Start, End, Radius (SER)

When using the Start, End, Radius option, you can draw an arc only in the counterclockwise direction. A positive radius value results in the shortest arc possible between the start point and the endpoint. A negative radius value results in the longest arc possible, as shown in Figure 6.20. The command sequence which appears when you select the Arc Start, End, Radius button as follows:

`Center/<Start point>:` *`Select the arc's start point.`*
`End point:` *`Select the arc's endpoint.`*
`Angle/Direction/Radius/<Center point>:_r Radius:` *`Pick or type a positive or negative radius.`*

Tutorial 6.10: Creating an Arc with Start, End, Radius

In this tutorial, you will create an arc using the Start, End, Radius option. Follow these steps:

1.  Choose New from the Standard toolbar. In the New Drawing dialog box, click OK or press Enter.
2.  Select the Arc Start, End, Radius button from the Arc flyout menu on the Draw toolbar.
3. Establish the points of the arc.

   `ARC Center/<Start point>:` *`Click near the center of the drawing area.`*
   `End point:` *`Select a point approximately three units to the right of the second point.`*
4. Give the radius.
5. `Angle/Direction/Radius/<Center point>: r_radius:` **`2`**

You should now have an arc similar to the one shown in Figure 6.21.

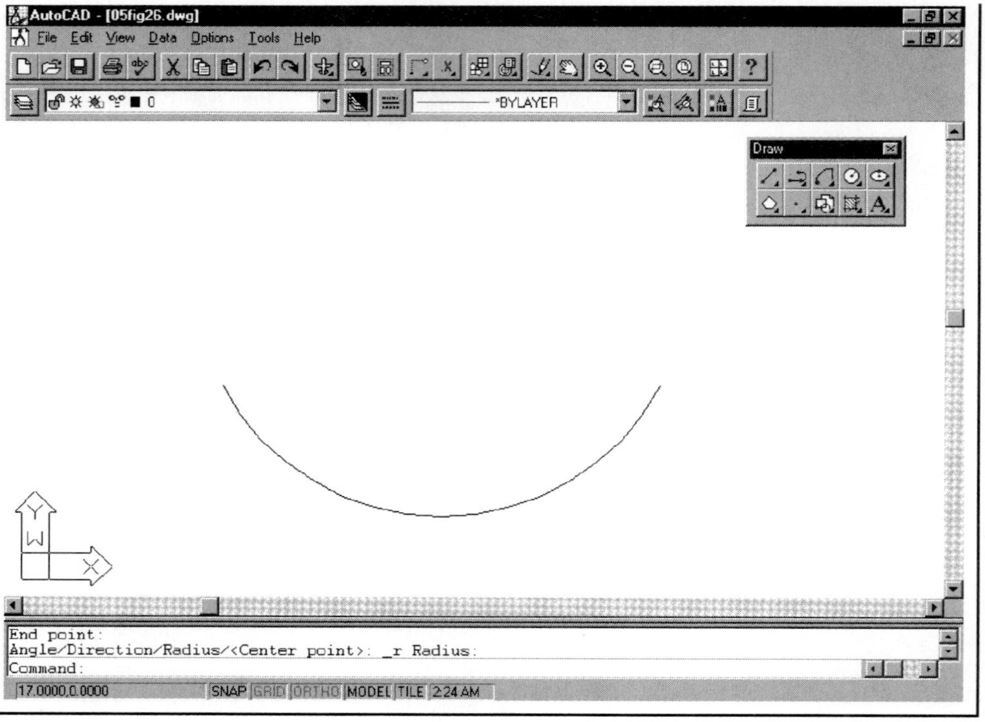

Figure 6.21
An arc drawn with the Start, End, Radius option.

Continuing an Arc from an Existing Arc

The Continue option enables you to continue an arc from the previous arc. When you draw arcs with this method, each consecutive arc is tangent to the previous arc. The start point and direction are taken from the endpoint and direction of the previous arc (see Figure 6.22). Here's the command sequence when you select the Arc Continue button:

`End point:` *`Select or type the distance from the start point.`*

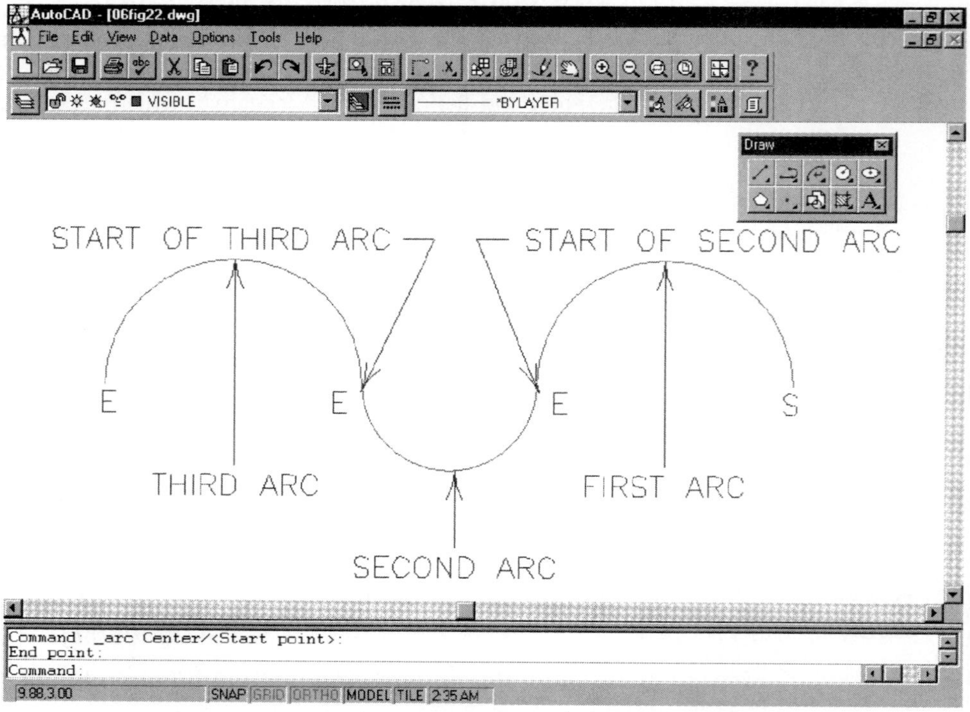

Figure 6.22
Drawing an arc with the Continue option.

Skill Builder

If you draw an arc using the Arc Continue option and then press Enter, AutoCAD reissues the arc command. If you press Enter again (at the first Arc prompt), you accept the last point entered (end of the last arc) as your Start point for the next arc. This is equivalent to selecting the Arc Continue option.

Tutorial 6.11: Continuing an Arc from an Existing Arc

In this tutorial you will create an arc with the Start, Center, End method to create arc A as shown in Figure 6.23. You will then use the Arc Continue option to create arcs B and C.

1.  Choose New from the Standard toolbar. In the New Drawing dialog box, click OK or press Enter.

2.  First, create arc A using the Arc Start, Center, End method. Select the Arc Start, Center, End button from the Arc flyout menu and enter the absolute coordinates of 1,2.75 for the start point of the arc.

```
Center/<Start point>: 1,2.75
```

3. For the center point, enter the absolute coordinates of 2.50,2.75.

```
Center/End/<Second point>: _c Center:
2.50,2.75
```

4. For the endpoint, enter the absolute coordinates of 4,2.75.

Angle/Length of chord/<End point>: **4,2.75**

5.  Next, select the Arc Continue button to create arc B. Notice how the next arc begins at the endpoint of the previous arc, A. Enter the absolute coordinates of 6.75,2.75 for the endpoint of the continued arc.

```
Endpoint: 6.75,2.75
```

6. To create the final arc, press Enter twice. This will re-enter the Arc Continue command and use the endpoint of the previous arc B as the start point for the next arc. Use the absolute coordinates of 8,2.75 as the endpoint of the continued arc.

```
Command:
ARC Center/<Start point>:
End point: 8,2.75
```

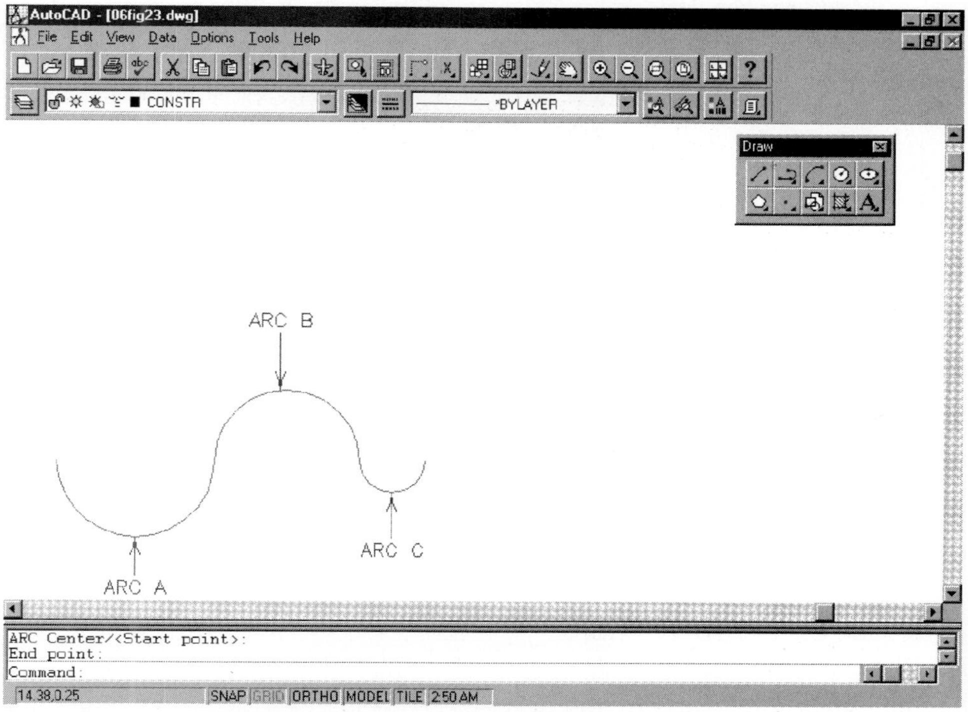

Figure 6.23
Use the Arc Continue option to create several arcs in succession.

TUTORIAL 6.12: DRAWING A BREAKFAST BAR SYMBOL

This tutorial explains how to create the breakfast bar symbol shown in Figure 6.24. You can create this symbol by using the **line, arc,** and **circle** commands. All of the commands are available on the Draw floating toolbar. Because this symbol is for an architectural drawing, you need to change the units. After you have completed the drawing, save the file as **brkbar.**

To draw this symbol, follow these steps:

1.  Select the New button from the Standard toolbar. If the AutoCAD dialog box appears, select No unless you want to save the current drawing. If you want to save the current drawing, select Yes and enter a path and drawing name. In the Create New Drawing dialog box, use **BRKBAR** for the drawing name.
2. From the Data pull-down menu, select Units. The Units Control dialog box appears. Change the units to architectural with a precision of 0′-0″.
3.  Make sure the Draw floating toolbar appears on your screen. Select the Line button from the Draw floating toolbar.

   From point: **1′,1′**
   To point: **@2′6″<90**
   To point:

4.  At this point, you cannot see the line you have just drawn, so use the Zoom command.

   Select the Zoom All button from the Zoom flyout menu. You can access this flyout menu by selecting the Zoom button on the Standard toolbar. This will bring up the flyout menu.
   Your screen should resemble Figure 6.25.

5.  Now draw the next line. Select the Line button from the Draw floating toolbar.

   From point: **1′,1′**
   To point: **@10′6″<0**
   To point:

6.  Notice that you still cannot see the complete drawing, so use **zoom** again. Select the Zoom Scale button from the Zoom flyout menu.

   All/Center/Dynamic/Extents/Left/Previous/Vmax/window/<Scale(X/XP)>: **.05**

   Your screen should now look like Figure 6.26.

7.  Next draw the third line. Select the Line button from the Draw floating toolbar.

   From point: **1′, 3′6″**
   To point: **@10′6″<0**
   To point:

Figure 6.24
The completed breakfast bar symbol.

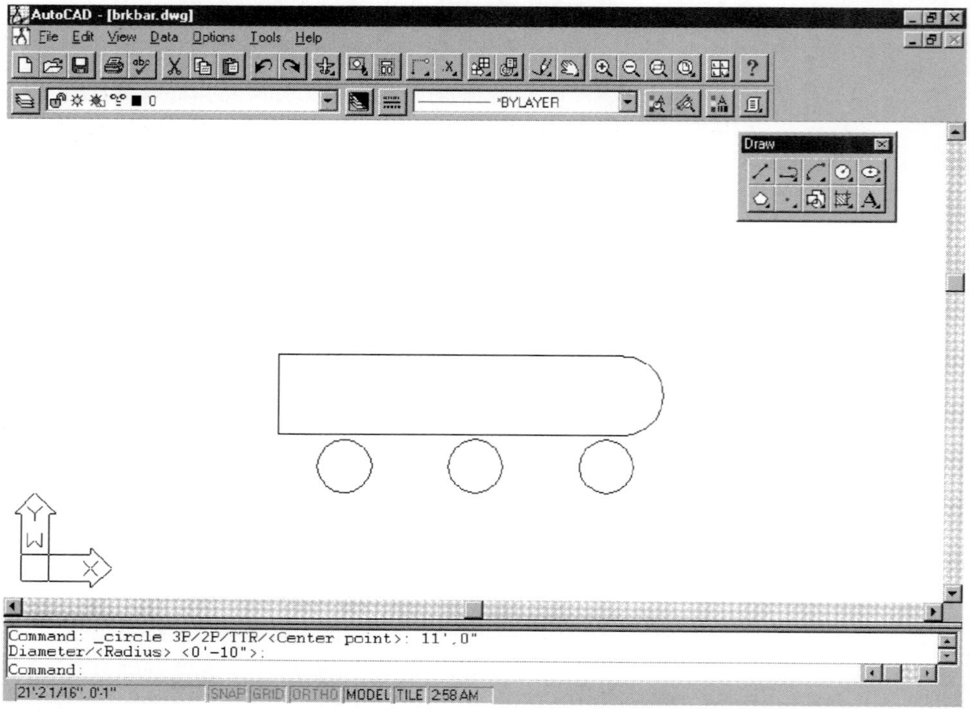

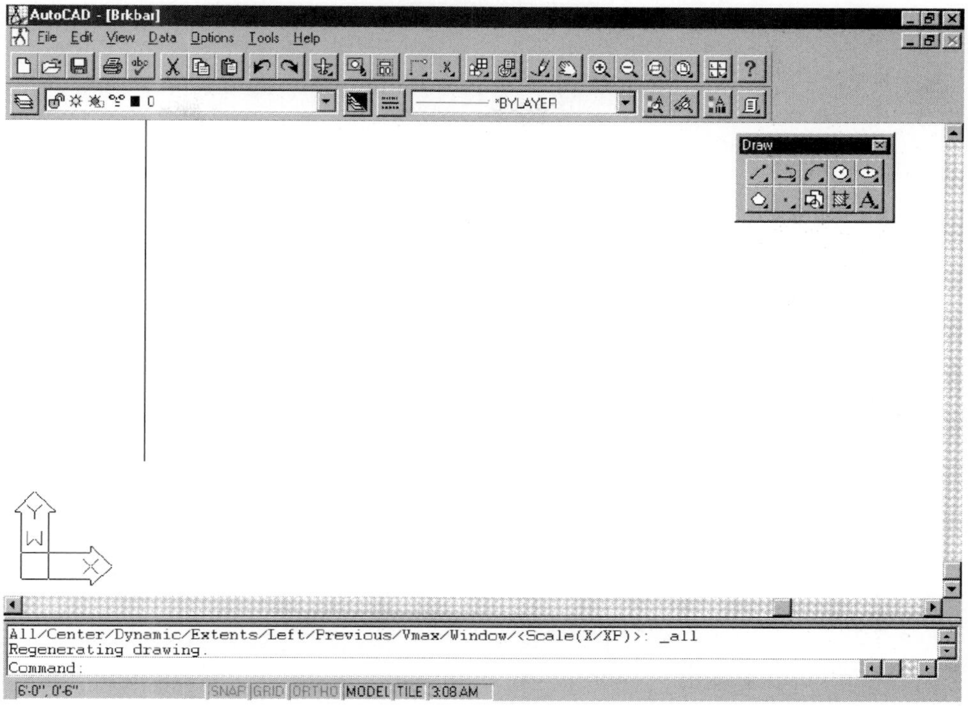

Figure 6.25
Drawing the first line of the breakfast bar symbol.

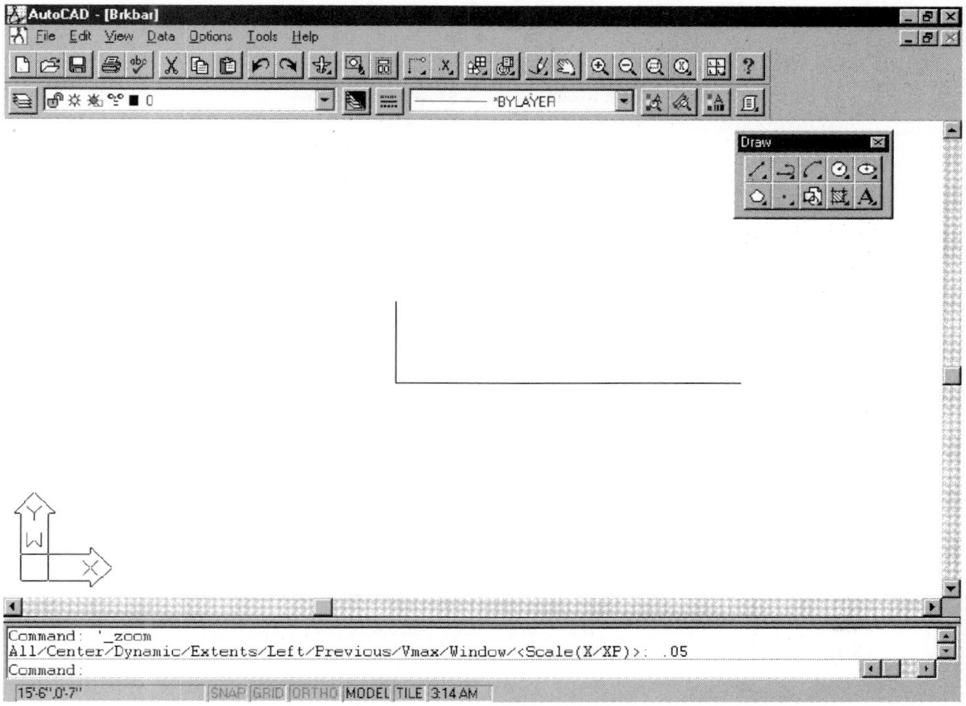

Figure 6.26
*Use the **zoom** command to display the uncompleted breakfast bar symbol.*

8.  Draw an arc, establishing its three points using the Start, Center, End option. Select the Arc Start, Center, End button from the Arc flyout menu.

`Center/<Start point>:` **`11'6",1'`**

`Center/End/<Second point>: _c Center:` **`11'6",2'3"`**

`Angle/Length of chord/<End point>:` **`11'6",3'6"`**

You should have the bar itself drawn as shown in Figure 6.27.

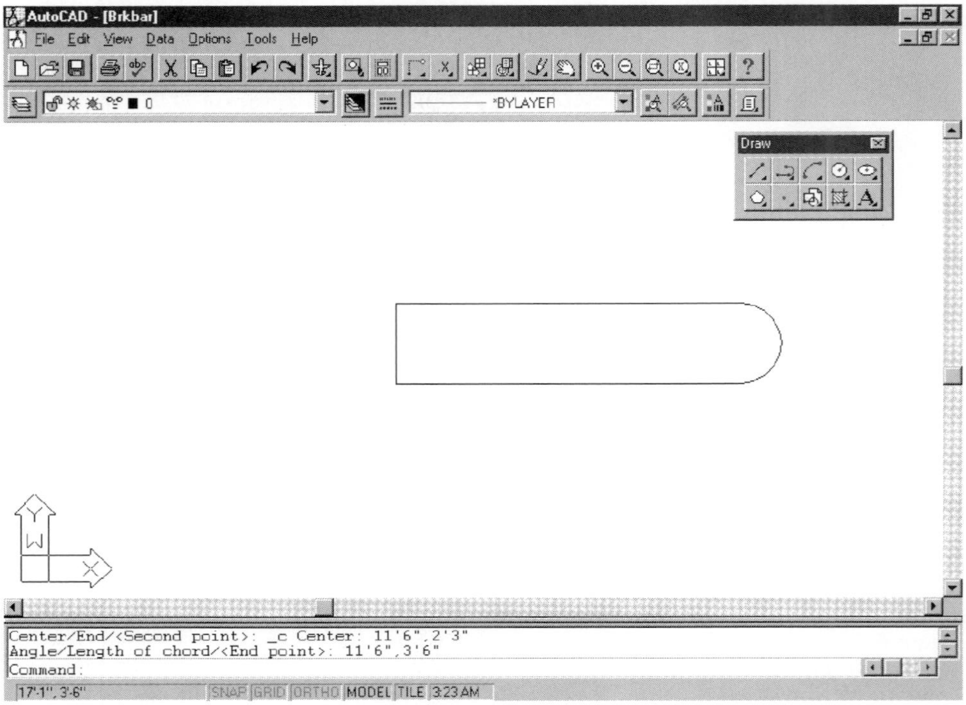

Figure 6.27
The completed breakfast bar without chairs.

9.  You are now ready to add three chairs to the breakfast bar. The chairs are 20″ in diameter. Use the **circle** command to draw three circles to the specifications that follow. Select the Circle-Center-Radius button from the Circle flyout menu.

`3P/2P/TTR/<Center point>:` **`3′,0″`**
`Diameter/<Radius><0′-1″>:` **`10″`**

10.  Select the Circle-Center-Radius button from the Circle flyout menu. Alternately, you could press the Enter key. Pressing the Enter key at the `Command:` prompt will automatically recall the last command executed.

`3P/2P/TTR/<Center point>:` **`7′,0′`**
`Diameter/<Radius><0′-10″>:` *`Press Enter to accept the default value of 10″.`*

11. At the `Command:` prompt, press Enter to return to the Circle command.

`3P/2P/TTR/<Center point>:` **`11′,0′`**
`Diameter/<Radius><0′-10″>:Press Enter to accept the default value of 10″.`

12.  Select the Save button from the Standard toolbar.

Drawing Polygons (POLYGON)

A polygon is a closed figure bounded by three or more line segments. Triangles, squares, and hexagons are examples of polygons commonly found in many drawings. Creating polygons in manual drafting can be difficult and time-consuming. Templates are available for some common polygons, such as triangles and hexagons, but templates are limited in the sizes they offer.

With AutoCAD's polygon command, you can easily draw regular multisided polygons. When you create a polygon in AutoCAD, it is drawn as a closed polyline object. In other words, the polygon is one object, and you cannot edit the individual entities unless you explode the polygon. Polylines are discussed in Unit 12, "Advanced Drawing Techniques." You can access the polygon command in one of these ways:

- Choose the Polygon button from the Draw floating toolbar. A flyout menu appears, displaying the Polygon options (see Figure 6.28).
- Enter **`polygon`** at the `Command:` prompt.

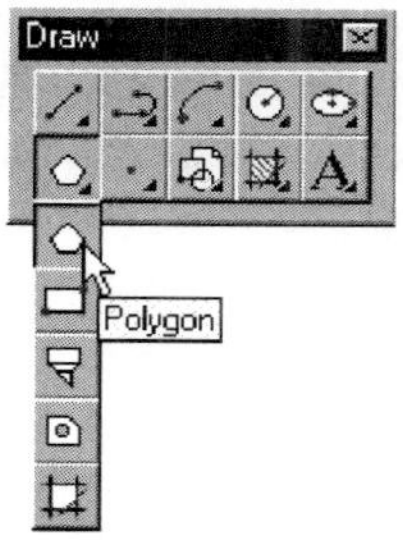

Figure 6.28
The Polygon button on the Draw floating toolbar.

The **polygon** command enables you to create a figure with up to 1,024 sides of the same length. To create a polygon, any of the following three methods may be used.

Creating Inscribed Polygons One method for creating a polygon is to create an inscribed polygon. In an inscribed polygon, the lines making up the polygon are contained totally within an imaginary circle on which the polygon is based. The endpoints of the polygon sides lie on this circle. The circle itself is never actually drawn. Here's the command sequence for the Inscribed polygon option:

Select the Polygon button from the Draw floating toolbar.

`Number of sides <4>:` *Enter the number of sides.*
`Edge/<Center of polygon>:` *Enter or Select the polygon's center point.*
`Inscribed in circle/Circumscribed about circle (I/C) <I>:` *Since Inscribed is the default, press Enter.*
`Radius of circle:` *Enter or Select the polygon's radius.*

Skill Builder

While you are being prompted for the radius, AutoCAD displays a temporary image of the polygon that will be created. You can rotate and re-size the polygon at this time using the crosshairs or by entering a coordinate value.

Creating Circumscribed Polygons In a circumscribed polygon, the polygon's lines are outside the imaginary circle on which the polygon is based. Again, the circle isn't drawn. The Circumscribed option creates a polygon with the polygon edges tangent to an imaginary circle. The following command sequence is used with the Circumscribed polygon option:

Select the Polygon button from the Draw floating toolbar.

`Edge/<Center of polygon>:` *Select the polygon's center point.*
`Inscribed in circle/Circumscribed about circle (I/C) <I>:` **c**
`Radius of circle:` *Enter or select the polygon's radius.*

For the Professional

The **polysides** system variable keeps track of the number of sides specified in the previous **polygon** command. When you re-enter the **polygon** command, the default value in the Number of Sides prompt will be the same as the number of sides you specified in the previous polygon command.

Specifying Polygons by Edge When you need to draw a polygon with one corner passing through a point, the Edge option is very useful. Occasionally, you may know the length of each of the polygon's sides but not the radius of the polygon. By choosing the Edge option, you can specify the length of one of the polygon's sides by selecting two points (or entering coordinates) to determine the endpoints of a side. AutoCAD draws one edge between these points and constructs the rest of the polygon accordingly. Here's the command sequence for the Edge polygon option:

Select the Polygon button from the Draw floating toolbar.

`Number of sides:` *Enter the number of sides.*
`Edge/ <Center of polygon>:` **e**
`First endpoint of edge:` *Indicate first endpoint of edge.*
`Second endpoint of edge:` *Indicate second endpoint of edge.*

Tutorial 6.13: Drawing an Inscribed Polygon

This tutorial covers the basics of drawing polygons in AutoCAD. You will create an 8-sided inscribed polygon with a radius of 4 units. Before you begin to draw the polygon, start a new drawing. Follow these steps:

1.  Choose New from the Standard toolbar. In the New Drawing dialog box, click OK or press Enter.
2.  Select the Polygon button from the Draw floating toolbar.

`Number of sides <4>:` **8**
`Edge/<Center of Polygon>:` *Select a point near the center of the drawing.*
`Inscribed in circle/Circumscribed about circle (I/C)<I>:` **I**
`Radius of circle:` **4**

You should now have an 8-sided polygon similar to the one in Figure 6.29.

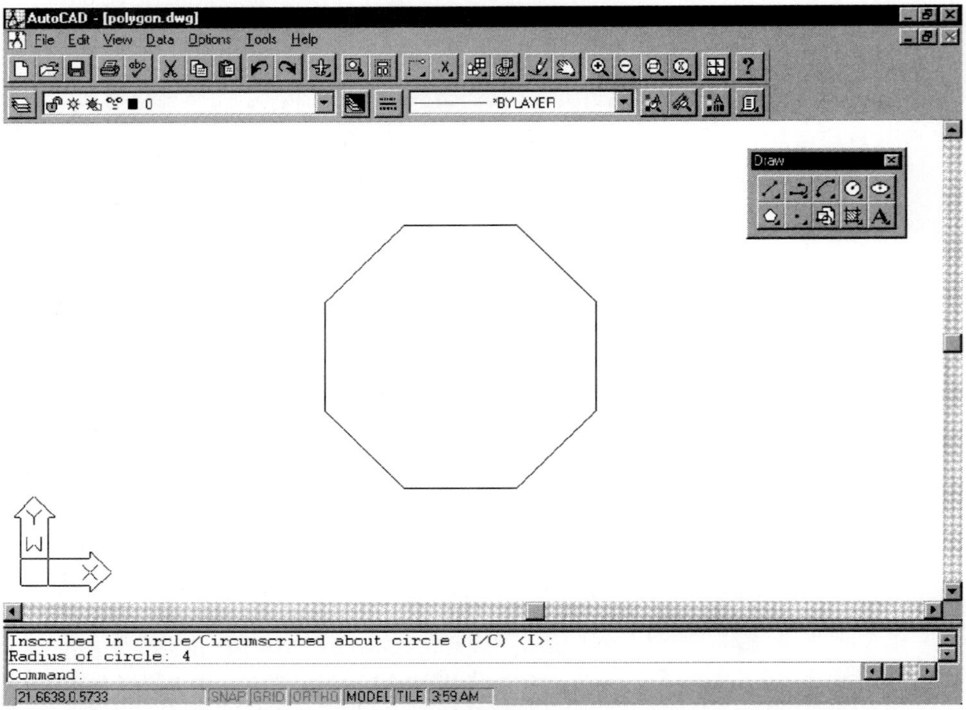

Figure 6.29
Drawing an inscribed polygon.

Tutorial 6.14: Drawing a Hot Tub Symbol with Polygon, Rectang, and Circle

This tutorial explains how to create the hot tub symbol shown in Figure 6.30. This symbol requires use of the **rectang, polygon,** and **circle** commands.

To create the hot tub symbol, follow these steps:

1.  Choose New from the Standard toolbar. In the New Drawing dialog box, click OK or press Enter.
2. Choose Data, Units. In the Units dialog box, change units to architectural with a precision of 0′-0″.
3. Make sure you have the Draw floating toolbar displayed before continuing. First you'll create the rectangle.

    Choose the Rectangle button from the Draw floating toolbar.

   `First corner:` **2″,2″**
   `Other corner:` **@12′,12′**
4. At this point, you cannot see the rectangle you've just drawn, so use the **zoom** command.

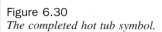

    Select the Zoom All button from the Zoom flyout menu. Your screen should resemble Figure 6.31.
5. Now draw the polygon.

    Choose the Polygon button from the Rectangle flyout menu.

   `Number of sides:<4>:` **8**
   `Edge/<Center of polygon>:` **6′2″,6′2″**
   `Inscribed in circle/Circumscribed about circle(I/C)<I>:`
   `Radius of circle:` **5′6″**
6. Complete the symbol by drawing the drain, using the **circle** command.

    Choose the Circle, Center, Radius button from the Circle flyout menu.

   `3P/2P/TTR/<Center point>:` **6′2″,6′2″**
   `Diameter/<Radius>:` **5″**
7.  To save the file for use at a later time, select the Save button from the Standard toolbar and name it Polygon.

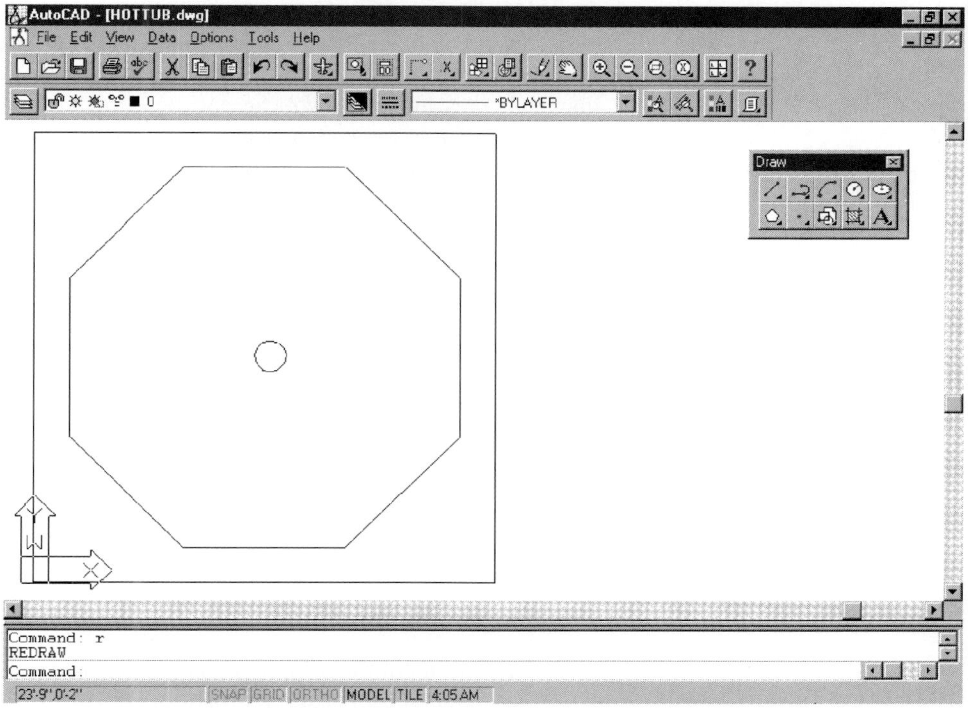

Figure 6.30
The completed hot tub symbol.

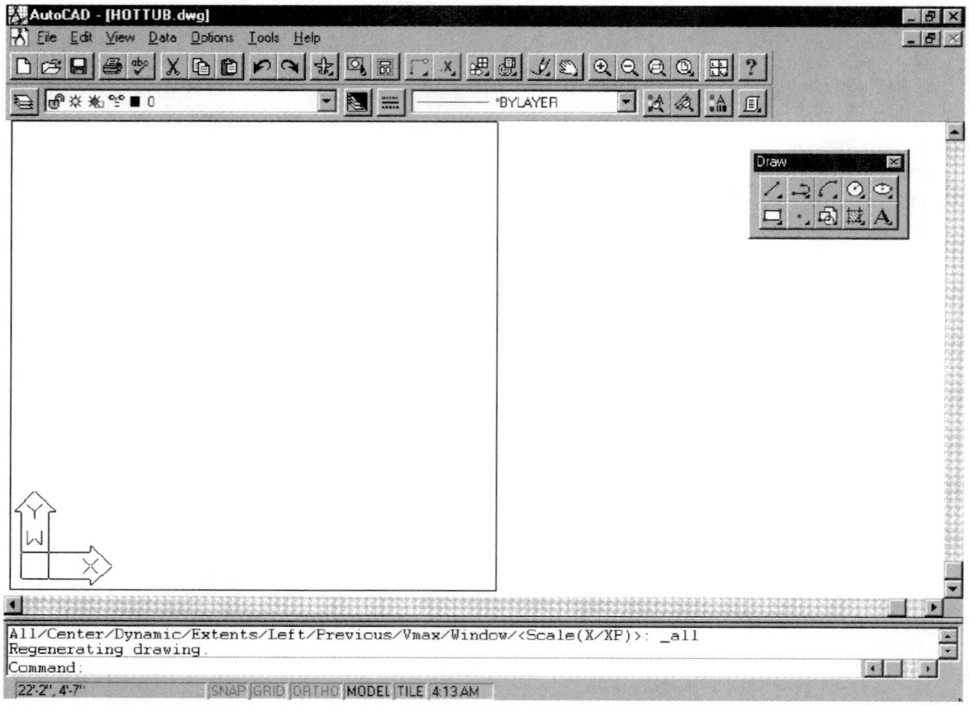

Figure 6.31
Drawing the outside edge of the hot tub symbol.

SUMMARY

The AutoCAD basic drawing commands—**line, arc,** and **circle**—usually make up most of the geometry in a typical drawing. To speed up the drawing process and help create complicated geometry, AutoCAD offers the **rectang** and **polygon** commands.

Once you have created a circle and entered a diameter or radius, the **circlerad** system variable stores that value. If you have to draw several circles with the same radius or diameter, pressing Enter will accept the default value and draw the circle. This is an important point to remember to help you increase your drawing speed. This default value is maintained and updated during the current drawing session only.

While there are many options available to create an **arc,** the most common and the ones you should be familiar with are: Three Points, Start, Center, End; Start, End, Radius; and continuing an arc from an existing arc.

Triangles, squares, and hexagons are examples of polygons commonly found in many drawings. Often difficult and time-consuming to do in manual drafting, AutoCAD's **polygon** command allows you to easily draw multisided polygons.

REVIEW

1. Define the relationship of radius and diameter to an arc and circle.
2. On a blank sheet of paper, sketch a line that is tangent to a circle. Label the point of tangency and show how you determined where the tangency point is.
3. When creating a circle that is tangent to two previously created circles, explain how the location you pick the existing circles influences the location of the resulting tangent circle.
4. Explain the differences between a rectangle created using the **line** command and a rectangle created using the **rectang** command.
5. List and explain three different methods you could use to accurately locate the second point of a rectangle you are creating using the **rectang** command.
6. Describe the difference between inscribed and circumscribed polygons.

7. Explain what the **circlerad** system variable is and how you can use it to speed up drafting time.
8. Illustrate two methods you could use to draw a circle if you know the diameter but have difficulty locating the center point.
9. Clarify how commands like **polygon** can be used to create geometry faster and more accurately than possible with manual drafting methods.
10. Define the **explode** command. What objects discussed in this unit can it be used on?

EXERCISE 6

1. Create the double door swing shown in Figure 6.32. Make the wall sections 6″ thick, and the doors 2′-6″ wide.
2. Create the rocker arm shown in Figure 6.33.

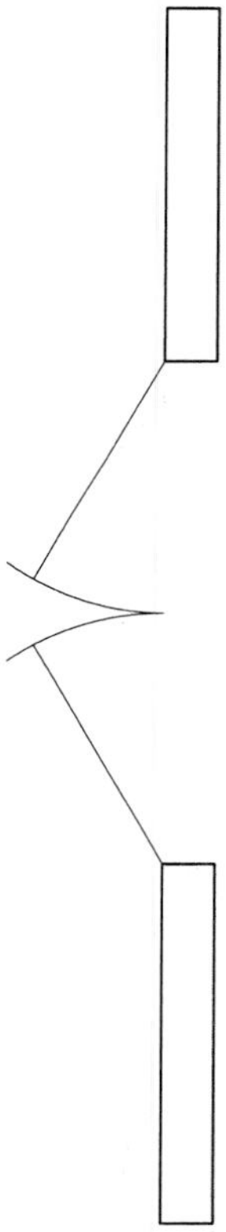

Figure 6.32
Use the Rectangle and Arc commands to create the double door swing.

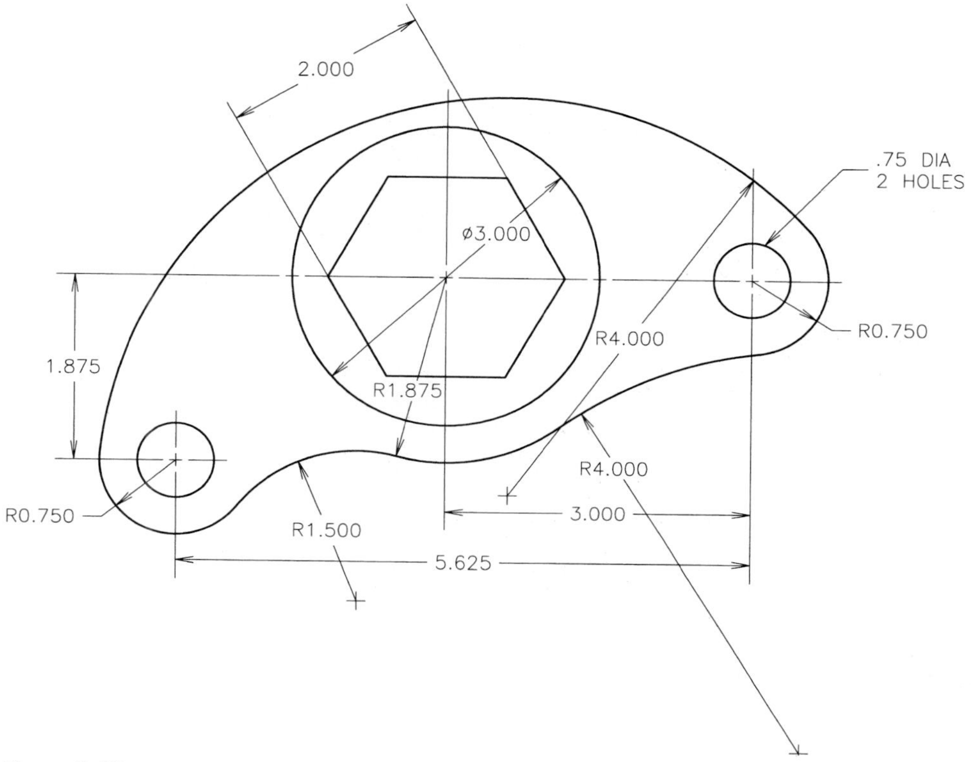

Figure 6.33
Use the Arc, Circle, and Polygon commands to create the rocker arm.

UNIT 7

ANNOTATING A DRAWING WITH TEXT AND HATCHING

OVERVIEW

By using AutoCAD you can communicate your ideas through the creation of different objects into a finished product—a drawing. Even the best design and most skilled draftsperson can't always completely convey all of the necessary information, however. AutoCAD's text tools can help you add and emphasize details about your drawings. In addition to text, AutoCAD provides other tools to enhance the readability of your drawing. One of the most effective two-dimensional tools is AutoCAD's Hatch command.

OBJECTIVES

- Create and edit text styles **(style, ddstyle)**.
- Add text to your drawing **(text, dtext)**.
- Create paragraphs of text in your drawing **(mtext)**.
- Import text into your drawing from other programs.
- Edit your text **(change, ddedit, ddmodify)**.
- Find and correct spelling mistakes in your drawing **(spell)**.
- Create a hatching pattern **(bhatch)**.
- Define the area to hatch.
- Draw associative hatched areas.
- Avoid and troubleshoot hatching problems.

INTRODUCTION

Almost every drawing you create will contain text of some type, even if is only your name. Most drawings will contain a great deal of text. Text in technical drawings is commonly in the form of notes, describing objects contained in the drawing. Text is also commonly used to create a bill of materials and include information in a title block.

A typical engineering drawing may contain dimensions, manufacturing notes, bill of materials, schedule, or revisions. Architectural drawings commonly have written descriptions of rooms, instructions for construction, and notes concerning materials or furnishings. AutoCAD provides several different methods to create and edit text in your drawing. You can also import text created in other programs, such as Notepad, Microsoft Word, or WordPerfect.

While text is often used to include information and clarify drawings, hatching is another tool that can be used to increase the readability of your drawing. Hatching is a way of applying various patterns to certain areas of your drawing. A hatch pattern may be as simple as a pattern of lines, or as complex as a wood shake symbol on an architectural drawing.

OUTLINE

Adding Text to a Drawing
Tutorial 7.1: Creating Your Own Text Style
Tutorial 7.2: Creating Text with TEXT and DTEXT
Tutorial 7.3: Using MTEXT to create and Import Text
Tutorial 7.4: Editing TEXT and MTEXT
Tutorial 7.5: Hiding and SpellChecking Text
Filling Areas with Hatching
Tutorial 7.6: Creating a Hatch Pattern
Tutorial 7.7: Hatching an Area of a Drawing
Tutorial 7.8: Editing a Hatch
Summary
Review
Exercises

ADDING TEXT TO A DRAWING

When you create text in your drawing, it is treated as any other AutoCAD object; that is, a line of text can be erased, moved, rotated, or edited like any other graphical object. The **text, dtext,** and **mtext** commands are used to create text in your drawing. Creating and editing text has evolved over time during the different releases of AutoCAD. The **text** command was included in the earliest versions of the program. It allowed you to enter text one line at a time in the AutoCAD command line. Later versions included the **dtext** command, which allows you to enter the characters dynamically on-screen as you type them in the command line.

mtext is the most recent command used to enter text. The **mtext** command features a full-featured text editing window. In the window you can cut and paste text, as well as assign it different properties (such as color and height). **mtext** offers so much flexibility that you can assign different colors, fonts, and height to different words and even letters right in the middle of your paragraph. You also can easily import text from other programs right into the **mtext** editing window.

In this unit you will be using many different aspects of creating and editing text. The majority of these commands are available on the Draw and Modify toolbars. By default this toolbar is not turned on. Choose Tools, Toolbars, then Draw, and Tools, Toolbars, then Modify to activate them.

DEFINING A TEXT STYLE (STYLE, DDSTYLE)

Before you begin entering your text into a drawing, you must decide how the text will look. What type of font will you use? How big will it be? Should it lean to the left, right, or even backward? Each text style has its own name and contains parameters that define the font, height, width, obliquing angle, and orientation (backwards, forwards, upside-down, or vertical).

Styles are used to customize your text and ensure uniform use of the text. Most of your styles will use the same font, with different text sizes and width factors. Only one style, called Standard, is already loaded in AutoCAD.

A text style is created by selecting a font file as a foundation, then specifying other parameters to define the letters. There are two different methods you can use to create a text style. Typing **style** at the `Command:` prompt allows you to define a text style at the command line. You can also create a text style with the Text Style dialog box. You can access the Text Style dialog box in the following way:

- Select the Object Creation button from the Object Properties toolbar to access the Object Creation Modes dialog box. Select the Text Style button to access the Text Style dialog box.
- Select Text Style from the Data pull-down menu.
- Type **ddstyle** at the `Command:` prompt .

Both the command line and dialog box methods offer the same options for creating a text style. The dialog box option, however, offers a graphical preview of fonts available within AutoCAD, along with a preview of the style you are creating. The dialog box also accesses the Select Font File dialog box, which gives you easy access to the font files included in AutoCAD. For these reasons we will concentrate on defining a text style with the dialog box. The Text Style dialog box is shown in Figure 7.1.

Creating and changing a text style can all be accomplished in the Text Style dialog box, along with giving you a preview of what the style will look like. The procedure for creating a text style is as follows:

1. **Naming the style.** Give your new style a name. This style and any others created will be available for use in many different text and text-related commands.
2. **Select a font.** After naming your new style, select a font. The font file selected becomes a foundation for designing the new style.

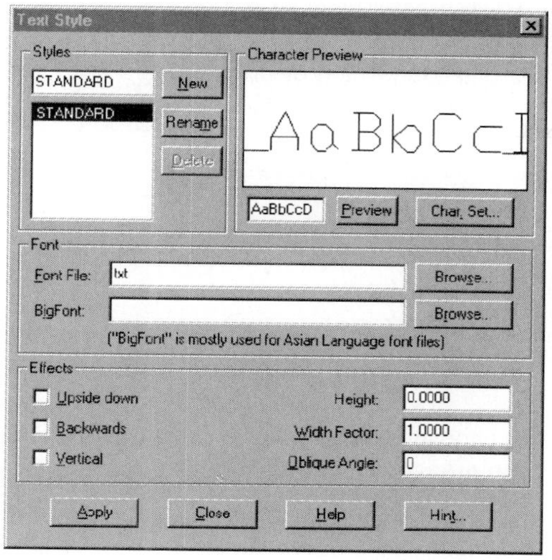

Figure 7.1
The Text Style dialog box gives you a graphical preview of fonts.

3. **Preview the font.** The Character Preview window will provide a graphical picture of your selected font. Also, as you add effects to the font, these will be reflected in the window.
4. **Add effects.** Select the type of effects you want for your style. These include setting a default height, width factor, and special effects such as upside down and backwards.

Naming the Text Style The first step is to give the text style a name. The text style you create automatically becomes the current style when you use the **dtext, mtext,** or **text** commands. To name the style, enter a name in the Styles text box and choose the New button. The new style will appear in the lower styles window. Notice you can also Delete and Rename a style.

Selecting a Font After naming the style, the next step is to select a font. In the Font File text box, enter the path and name of the font file you want to use. Alternately, you can select a font file from a dialog box. Choose the Browse... button to the right of the Font File text box (see Figure 7.2). This will access the Select Font File dialog box shown in Figure 7.3.

The font files supplied by AutoCAD are normally found in the R13\COM\FONTS subdirectory. Additional fonts also may be found on your computer. You can use any AutoCAD font (.SHX), postscript font (.PFA or .PFB), or True Type font (.TTF). For example, many other programs, such as word processors, include additional True Type fonts. Additional True Type fonts are normally stored in the WINDOWS\FONTS subdirectory.

FOR THE PROFESSIONAL

To locate all possible fonts on your computer, you can search your disk and look for files containing .PFA, PFB, SHX, or .TTF extensions. A search function is included in the Windows Explorer. Select Tools, Find, Files or Folders in the Windows Explorer to access the Find All Files dialog box.

Figure 7.2
The Font File text box in the Text Style dialog box is used to enter the name of the font file you want to use.

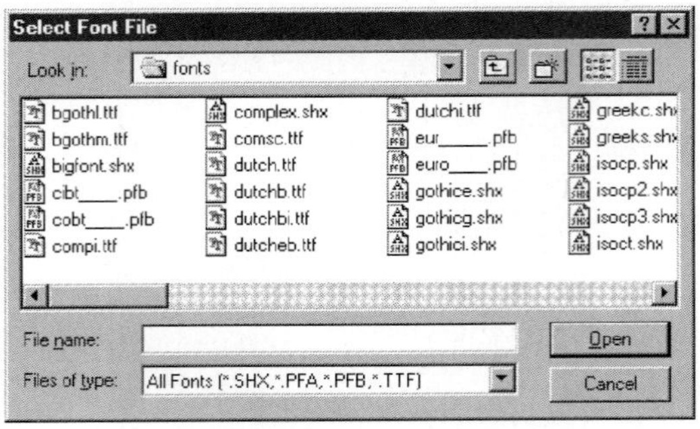

Figure 7.3
Use the Select Font File dialog box to choose the font file you want to use.

After choosing the font file you want and clicking Open in the Select Font File dialog box, you are returned to the Text Style dialog box.

Skill Builder

While there are many interesting and unique fonts available, take care when you select the font to use in your drawing. Complex fonts containing a lot of lines and arcs can significantly slow down your computer. The amount of time it takes to re-draw and re-generate the screen increases, as does the disk space required for the drawing. Another factor is your output device. If you are using a pen plotter for output, each individual line and arc in each letter has to be drawn by the pen, taking a considerable amount of time to plot.

Character Preview After selecting a font file and returning to the Text Style dialog box, you will see a picture of the font you just selected in the Character Preview window. Options in the Character Preview window are Preview and Char. Set. Both of these options can be used to obtain a better view of what your selected font looks like.

- **Preview.** This button is used in conjunction with the small text box immediately to the left of the preview button. By default, the text box contains AaBbCcD. What is entered in this text box appears in the Character Preview window. Enter the text you want to appear in the text box, then press the Preview button (see Figure 7.4). Use this option to experiment with different words and letters to see exactly how they will look in your drawing.
- **Char. Set.** Selecting the Char. Set button accesses the Text Style Standard Symbol Set image window shown in Figure 7.5. This shows the entire character set for the selected font. The question marks in the dialog box represent ASCII characters that AutoCAD doesn't recognize.

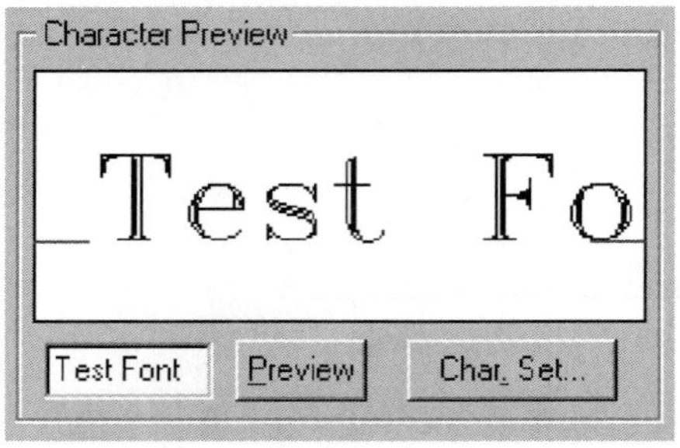

Figure 7.4
Entering text in the Preview text box and choosing the Preview button shows the text in the Character Preview window using the selected font.

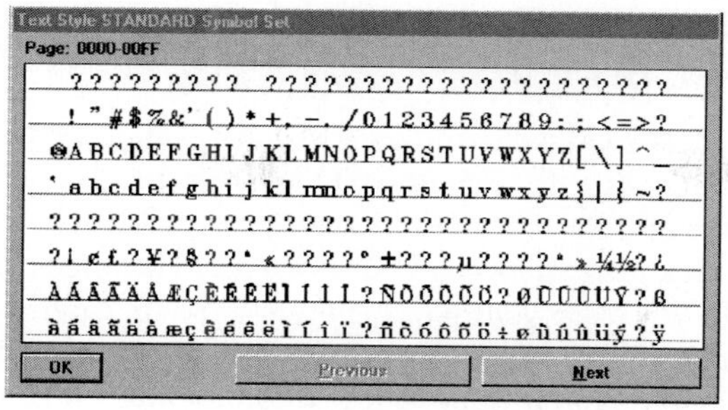

Figure 7.5
The Text Style Standard Symbol Set image window shows the entire character set for the selected font.

Effects The font file you selected now becomes a foundation for the new styles based on your choices for the effects. As you add different effects, click the Apply button to see the changes reflected on the font in the Character Preview window. These effects are explained below and shown in Figure 7.6.

- **Upside down.** The text will appear upside down in the order it is typed.
- **Backwards.** Creates backward characters, which can be useful in certain applications such as the printing industry.
- **Vertical.** Creates letters vertically. Not all fonts will support vertical letters. The font file must support dual orientation for you to make it vertical. After selecting the Vertical effect, check the Character Preview window. If the text does not appear vertical, the font does not support dual orientation.
- **Height.** Entering a text height will supply a constant value to the style when it is used in the **dtext, mtext,** or **text** commands. Setting the height to a specific value will also override the text height for dimensioning **(dimtix).** Setting a default value for the height will ensure standardization throughout your drawing. Changing the Height field does not affect the Character Preview window.

  Accepting the default value of 0 will cause AutoCAD to prompt you for a height whenever you use the **dtext, mtext,** or **text** commands. Using 0 as a height will allow you to vary the height for the style each time you insert text.

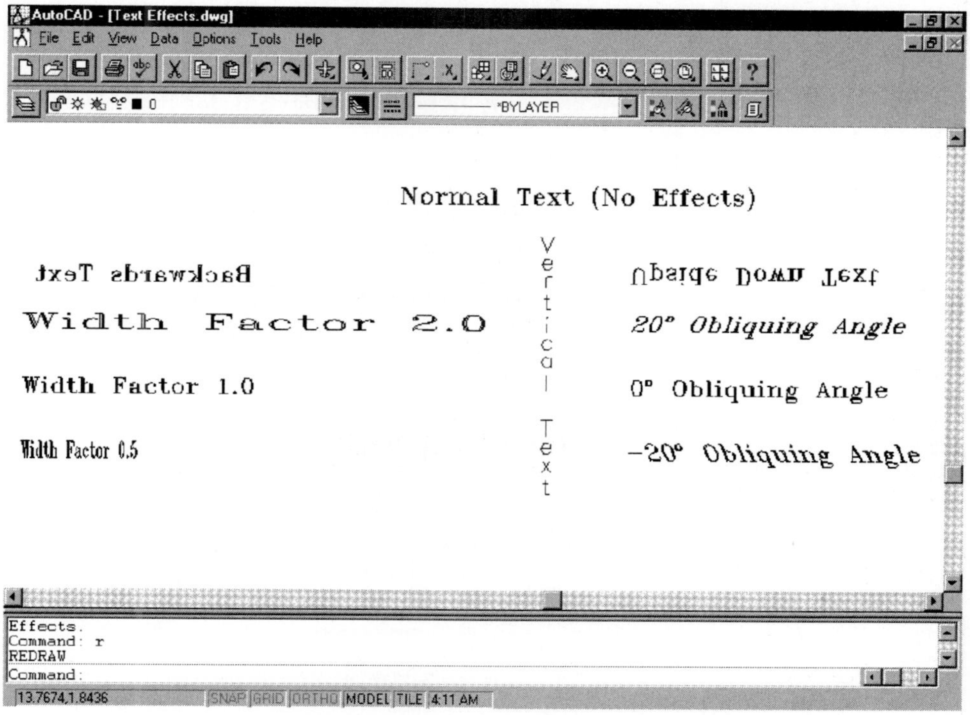

Figure 7.6
A sample of different text effects.

SKILL BUILDER

In most cases you will want to create your text styles with a fixed height instead of accepting the default 0. By using text styles with a predetermined height, you can avoid the extra step of having to supply a height each time you enter text with the **text, dtext,** or **mtext** commands. When determining your text height, make sure you keep your plotting scale in mind. Multiply your desired text height by the drawing scale factor (see Unit 3, "Viewing and Plotting a Drawing"). For example, if you want your text to plot 0.25″ high at a scale of 1/4″=1′, give your text style a height of 12″.

- **Width factor.** The default width factor is 1. This value determines how much AutoCAD will compress or stretch the text along its width. A factor less than 1 compresses the text, while a factor greater than 1 stretches the text.
- **Obliquing angle.** Entering an obliquing angle will cause the text to lean to the left or right. A negative value causes the text to lean left. This is relative to the face of a clock, where an obliquing angle of 0 equals 12 o'clock, and an angle of 90 equals 3 o'clock.

FOR THE PROFESSIONAL

When creating font styles, in most cases it is desirable to use the same font file for all of your different styles, just changing the parameters or effects. For example, when creating lettering for use on isometric planes, use the same font file for all styles, changing only the obliquing angle for the other styles. This can be done by creating different styles, with each style using the same font file but assigning different parameters to each style. This will ensure standardization within your drawing.

SKILL BUILDER

If you make a mistake in naming your style, there are two different ways you can change it. In the Text Style dialog box select the Rename option. Highlight the name of the style you want to rename, type the new name in the Styles text box, and select the Rename button.

You can also rename your styles in the Rename dialog box, shown in Figure 7.7. Select Data, Rename to access the Rename dialog box. Highlight Style in the Named Objects box. The current styles in the drawing will appear in the Items list box. Highlight the style name you want to rename in the Items list box. The name appears in the Old Name box. Enter the new name in the Rename To box and select OK.

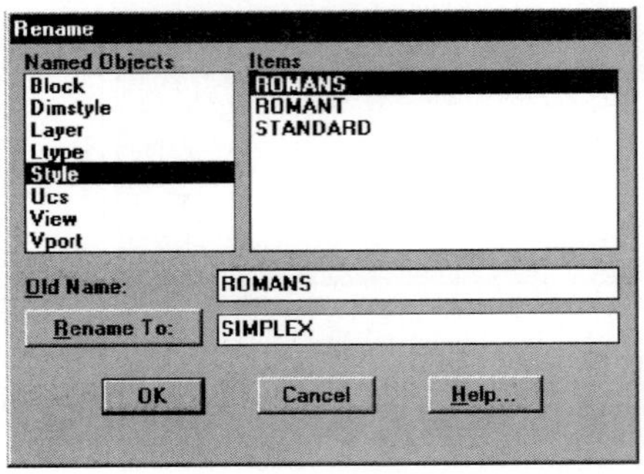

Figure 7.7
Use the Rename dialog box to rename a text style.

TUTORIAL 7.1: CREATING YOUR OWN TEXT STYLE

In this tutorial you will load the title block, as shown in Figure 7.8. You will also create two text styles that you will use later when you insert text into the title block. The title block is used in all subsequent tutorials in this section.

1.  Select the Open button from the Standard toolbar and load 07DWG01. This will open the title block as shown in Figure 7.8.
2. Select Text Style from the Data pull-down menu. The Text Style dialog box appears as shown in Figure 7.9.
3. The first style you will create will use the Roman Simplex font with a height of 0.100.
4. Type `Romans` in the Styles text box, and click the New button.
5. Select the Browse... button to the right of the Font File text box. The Select Font File dialog box appears as shown in Figure 7.10.
6. In the Select Font File dialog box, change to the appropriate drive and directory where your fonts are located. Normally they are in the \R13\COM\FONTS subdirectory. The fonts are listed in alphabetical order, so scroll over and select the romans.shx file. Select Open to open the text file and close the dialog box.

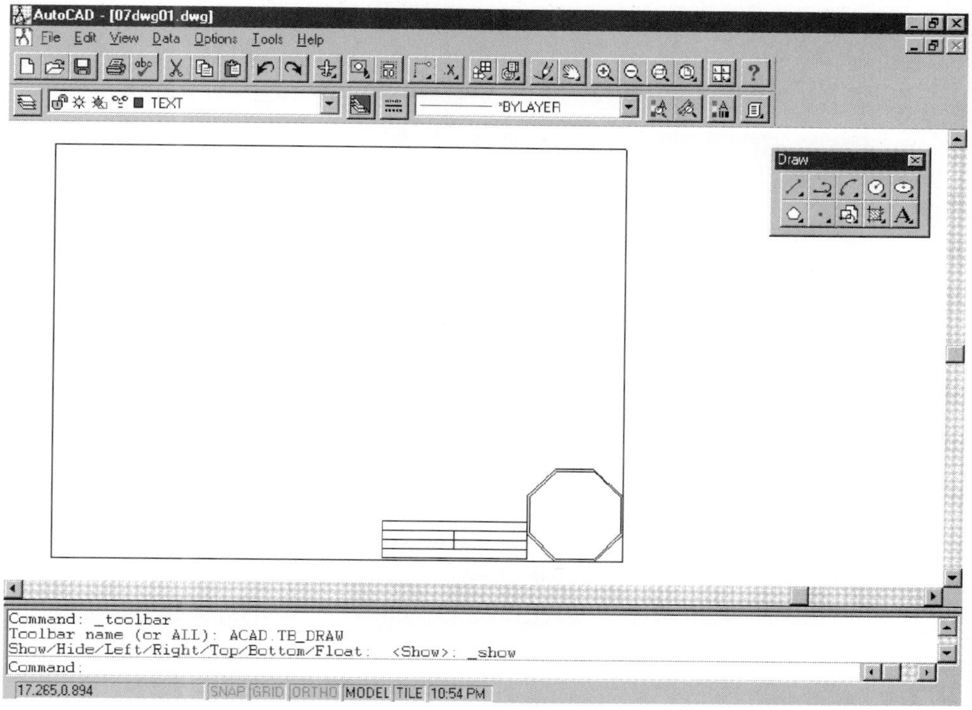

Figure 7.8
Loading the title block.

Figure 7.9 *Use the Text Style dialog box to create your styles.*

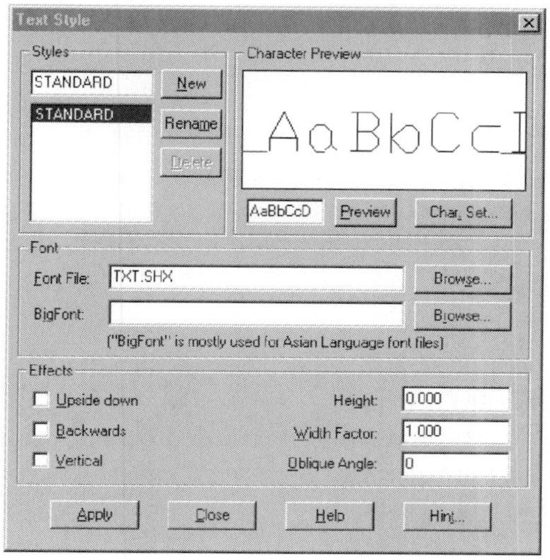

Figure 7.10 *Selecting the romans.shx file in the Select Font File dialog box.*

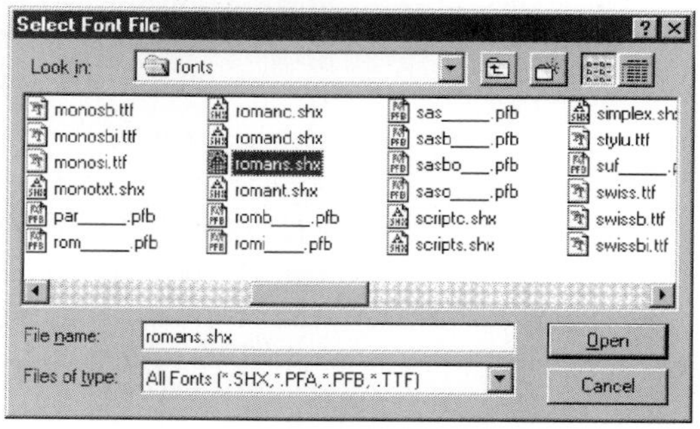

7. Change the Height to `0.100`.
8. Select the Apply button. Your Text Styles dialog box should look like Figure 7.11.
9. Experiment with the Preview and Char. Set buttons to get a better idea of what this font looks like.

   Type `Test` in the text box to the left of the Preview button, then select Preview. The word *Test* appears in the Character Preview window.

   Select the Char. Set button to display the Text Style ROMANS Symbol set. This dialog box shows all characters available with the romans.shx font file. Select OK.
10. Next you will create another style using the romant font, with a height of 0.1875 and an obliquing angle of 10.
11. Type `ROMANT` in the Styles text box, and click the New button.
12. Select the Browse... button to the right of the Font File text box. In the Select Font File dialog box select the romant.shx file and select Open.
13. Change the Height to **0.1875,** and change Oblique Angle to **10.**
14. Select the Apply button. Your Text Style dialog box should look like Figure 7.12.
15. Select the Close button in the Text Style dialog box. This completes your creation of the text styles. In the next tutorial you will use the styles you created to add text to the title block.

Figure 7.11 *The Text Style dialog box with the* ROMANS *style defined.*

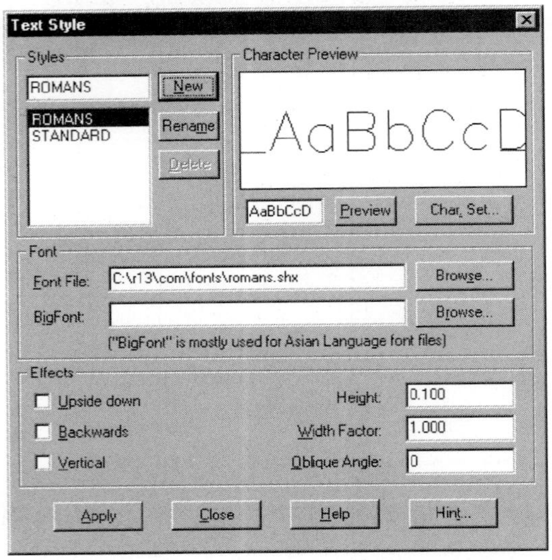

Figure 7.12 *The Text Style dialog box with two new styles defined.*

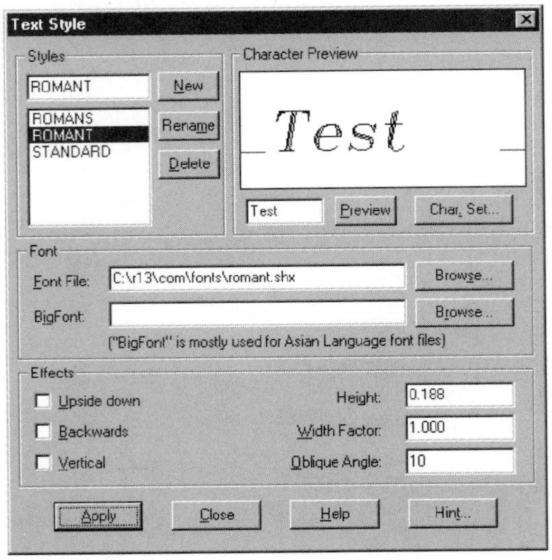

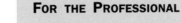

For the Professional

If your drawing is going to be sent to other people or companies, you may want to send the font files along with the drawing if you want your text to display as you originally created it. This is especially true if you use fonts other than the standard AutoCAD ones. If you need to send fonts along with your drawing, keep in mind that some third-party font publishers do not allow people who haven't purchased their fonts to have access to them. If you use third-party fonts and anticipate having to send them out, check the license agreement that came with the fonts to make sure you can freely distribute them.

Entering Text with Text and DText

The two primary commands for entering text are the **text** and **dtext** commands. With the **text** command you can enter single lines of text. The **dtext** command lets you enter multiple lines of text and shows the text on-screen as you type it.

text. You can access the **text** command by:

- Selecting the Single Line Text button from the Draw toolbar. Selecting the Text button on the Draw toolbar will access a flyout menu containing the Single Line Text button.
- At the `Command:` prompt type **text.**

dtext. The **dtext** command will allow you to enter multiple lines of text in column alignment. You can also backspace to the previous line if needed. When you are using the **dtext** command, a box approximately the size of a single character appears on-screen. As you type the text, it appears, character by character, on the screen as well as on the command line. You can access the **dtext** command by:

- Selecting the DText button from the Draw toolbar. Selecting the Text button on the Draw toolbar will access a flyout menu, containing the DText button.
- At the `Command:` prompt type **dtext.**

Both the **text** and **dtext** commands are used at the command line. After accessing either command, AutoCAD prompts:

`Justify/Style/<Start point>:` *Pick a point or enter coordinates.*
`Height <0.200>:` *If you did not enter a height when defining the style, this prompt appears allowing you to set the height. If you did enter a height when defining the style, this prompt will not appear.*
`Rotation angle <0>:` *Press Enter or type a value.*
`Text:` *Type the desired line of text and press Enter.*

If you selected the **text** command, after entering your line of text at the `Text:` line you will be returned to the `Command:` prompt. If you selected the **dtext** command, when you press Enter AutoCAD automatically displays the `Text:` prompt again. Additional lines of text are automatically spaced below the previous line. To end the command, press Enter at a blank `Text:` prompt.

Changing the Style

If you respond by typing `Style` or (`s`) at the initial prompt, you will be given the opportunity to change your current text style. At this prompt you can enter the name of a predefined style, or type `?` to see a list of styles currently available.

`Justify/Style/<Start point>:` **s**
`Style name (or ?) <STANDARD>:` *Press Enter to accept the current style, type in the name of a style, or type ?.*

Typing `?` causes the following prompt to appear:

`Text style(s) to list <*>:` *Press Enter to display a list of currently available styles.*

Justifying Text

AutoCAD provides you with the opportunity to accurately place, or justify text based on a specific point, called the *text insertion point.* The default justification point is the lower-left corner. When you specify text justification, you're telling AutoCAD where to locate the text's insertion point:

`Justify/Style/<Start point>:` **j**
`Align/Fit/Center/Middle/Right/TL/TC/TR/ML/MC/MR/BL/BC/BR:`

AutoCAD recognizes 15 different positions on text strings that you can use to justify text (T = Top, M = Middle, B = Bottom). You'll probably use the following four justifications most (see Figure 7.13). Some possible uses for justifying text include setting up

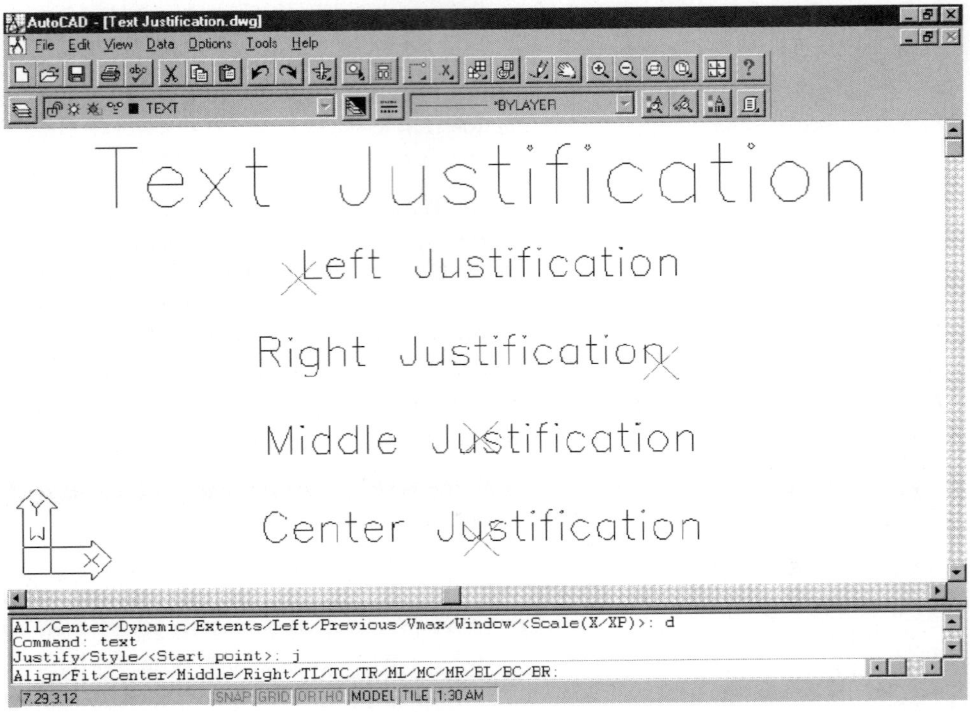

Figure 7.13
The different text justification methods.

a table for a bill of materials, aligning text in your title block, or centering text inside objects.

- **Left.** This is the default response if you don't select another justification option. AutoCAD justifies the text by using the text's lower-left corner of the text for the insertion point.
- **Center.** The baseline of the first line of text is centered at the justification point. If you are using the **dtext** command, additional lines of text are centered below the first line.
- **Middle.** Centers the first line of text both vertically and horizontally about the justification point. This option is useful for centering text in circles and rectangles.
- **Right.** Creates text that is justified using the lower-right corner of the text for the insertion point. This is the opposite of Left justification.

The other justification options (TL, TC, ML, MC, MR, BL, BC and BR) are variations on the justification methods explained above. The difference is that the insertion point is modified to include both vertical and horizontal alignment at the left, center or right justification points.

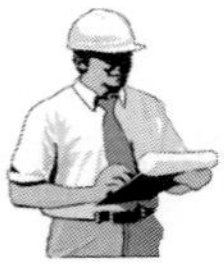

SKILL BUILDER

If you are using the **dtext** command, the characters will appear on-screen as you type the text. The text will not follow any justification options until *after* you press the Enter key at a blank `Text:` prompt to end the command.

ALIGNING TEXT (ALIGN AND FIT)

Occasionally you may want to align text to fill up space between two points. The Align and Fit justify options give you that opportunity. Both options work the same—after you choose either one, you are asked to specify two points between which AutoCAD will generate the text (see Figure 7.14).

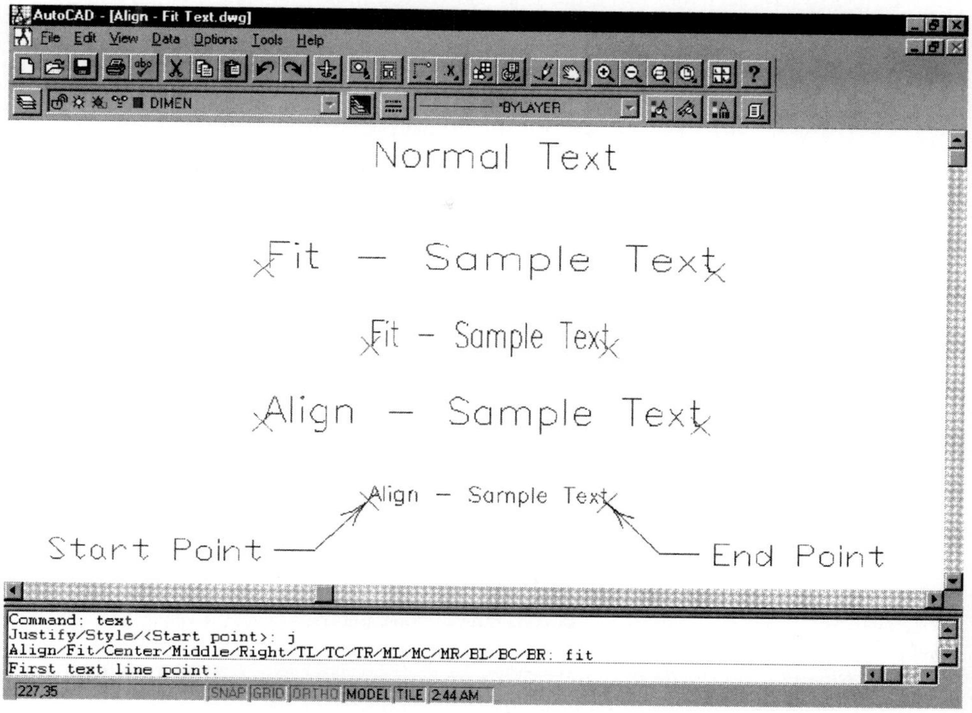

Figure 7.14
The Align and Fit justification options.

- **Fit.** The Fit option stretches or compresses the width of the text to fit, while maintaining a constant height. The height of the last piece of text entered is used as the default.
- **Align.** The Align option adjusts the text's height to maintain a natural-looking ratio between the text's height and length.

Using Special Characters in Text

When creating text, you can generate special characters in text strings by embedding special codes in your text as you type. These codes can be used to show degrees, diameter, and center point. They can also be used to underscore and overscore text, and display subscript, and superscript text. The codes that AutoCAD recognizes are:

%%o	Overscore
%%u	Underscore
%%d	Degree symbol
%%p	Plus/minus symbol
%%c	Diameter symbol
%%%	Percent symbol

For example, typing the following at the `Text:` prompt displays the text shown in Figure 7.15. If you are using the **dtext** command, the characters appear on-screen exactly as you've typed them. The symbols will not appear until after you press Enter at a blank `Text:` prompt.

Select the DText button from the Draw toolbar.

```
Justify/Style/<Start point>: Pick start point.
Text: %%oOverscore%%o text
Text: %%uUnderscore%%u text
Text: Degree Symbol: %%d
Text: Plus-Minus Symbol: %%p
Text: Diameter Symbol: %%c
Text: Percent Symbol: %%%
Text:
```

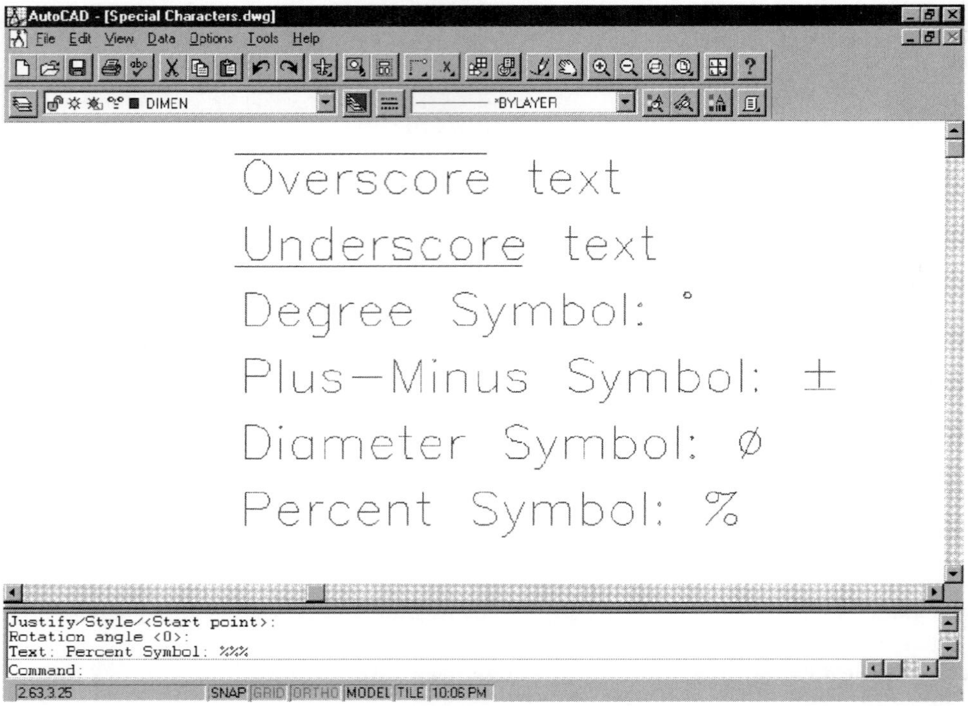

Figure 7.15
Results of using the special character codes.

TUTORIAL 7.2: CREATING TEXT WITH TEXT AND DTEXT

In this tutorial you will enter text into the title block drawing using the styles you created earlier.

1.  Make sure the title block drawing (07DWG01) is displayed on your screen. Select the Named Views button on the Standard toolbar.

   The View Control dialog box appears (Figure 7.16).

2. In the Views window, select TITLE_BLOCK, then select the Restore button.

   `TITLE_BLOCK` will appear after `Restore View:`

   shown in Figure 7.16. Click OK, and the screen zooms in on the title block.

3.  Select the DText button on the Draw toolbar.

4. Confirm that ROMANS is the current style, otherwise select it:

   `Justify/Style/<Start Point>:` **s**
   `Style name (or ?) <ROMANT>:` **romans**

5. Accept the default left justification, and choose the text's start point:

   `Justify/Style/<Start point>:` **7.0,0.7**

6. Accept the default rotation angle:

   `Rotation angle <0>:`

7. Type the first text string. Notice that the text appears on-screen as well as in the command line when you type.

   `Text:` **DRAWN BY:**

8. Before continuing, make sure your **snap** is turned on. At the next `Text:` prompt, *pick* the point **7.000,0.500** *before* you type any text. When you are picking the next point you don't need to press Enter to get to the next prompt. Then type the text string:

   `Text:` **DATE:**

9. Enter the rest of the ROMANS text by picking points at the `Text:` prompts. Then type the text shown here:

At this point:	**Enter this text:**
7.000,0.300	FILE NAME:
7.000,0.100	CLIENT:
8.500,0.500	REVISION:
8.500,0.300	APPROVED:

10.  After typing *APPROVED:* press Enter at the `Text:` prompt to end the command. If you made a mistake, select the Erase button on the Modify toolbar and erase the incorrect text. Access the DText command, select the Start Point, and reenter the text.

11. For the next set of text you will use the ROMANT style and the **text** command.

12.  Select the Single Line Text button from the Draw toolbar.

```
Justify/Style/<Start point>: s
Style name (or ?) <ROMANS>: romant
```

13. Choose Center justification:

```
Justify/Style/<Start point>: j
Align/Fit/Center/Middle/Right/TL/TC/TR/
ML/MC/MR/BL/BC/BR: c
Center point: 10.900,1.100
```

14. Change the rotation angle to 45.

```
Rotation angle <0>: 45
```

15. Type the text string.

```
Text: HOT-TUB
```

16. Use the ROMANT style again, this time using the Align justification.

17.  Select the Single Line Text button from the Draw toolbar.

```
Justify/Style/<Start point>: j
Align/Fit/Center/Middle/Right/
TL/TC/TR/ML/MC/MR/BL/BC/BR: a
First text line point: 10.650,0.250
Second text point line: 11.650,1.250
```

18. Type the text string:

```
Text: DESIGNS
```

After entering the last line of text, your drawing should look similar to Figure 7.17.

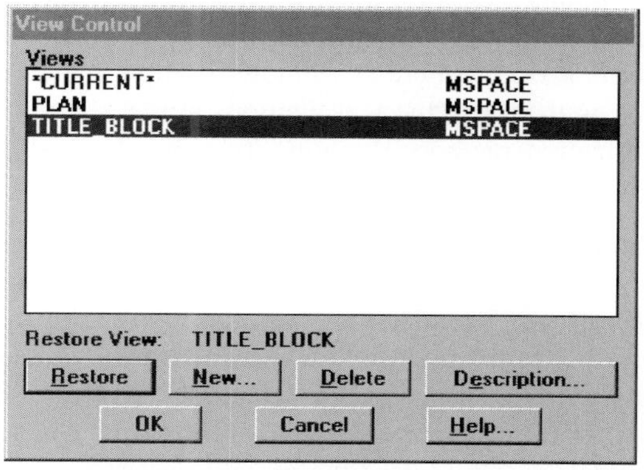

Figure 7.16
The View Control dialog box, used to restore the TITLE_BLOCK view.

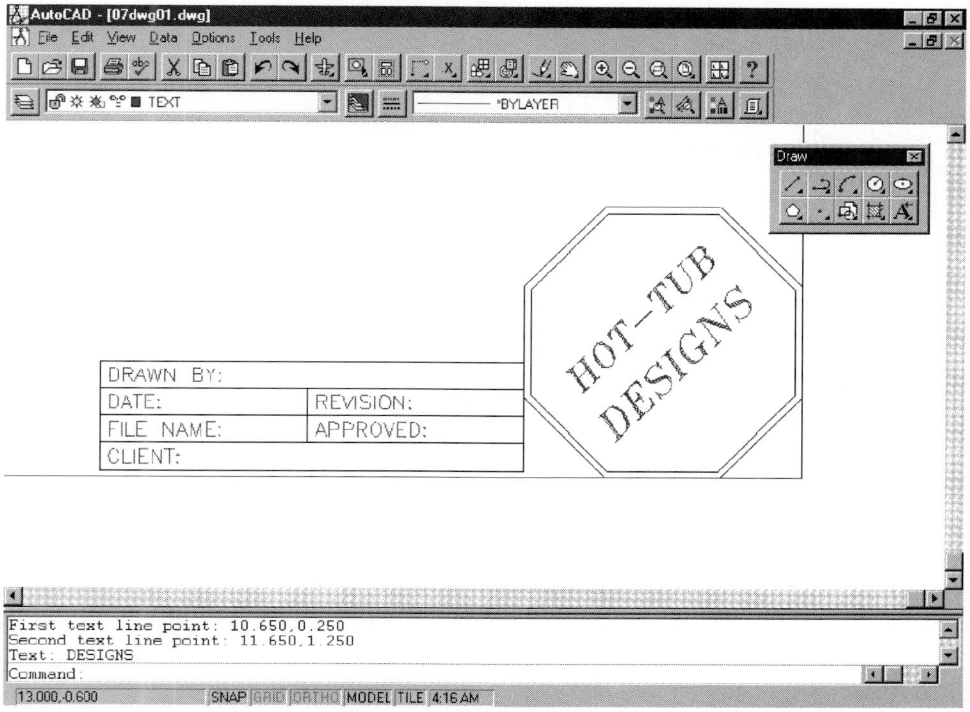

Figure 7.17
The completed title block.

Entering Text with MText

The **mtext** command provides an integrated text editor you can use to create and edit text in Windows. With **mtext** you can create paragraph objects, define a specific area of your drawing for the **mtext** objects, import text, and change properties of your MText objects. A feature that is unique to **mtext** is the ability to intermix font styles and sizes within a single MText object. You invoke the **mtext** command by:

- Select the Text button from the Draw toolbar.
- Type **mtext** at the `Command:` prompt.

When you invoke the **mtext** command, the following prompt appears:

```
Attach/Rotation/Style/Height/Direction/<Insertion point>:
```

When the **mtext** prompt appears, the default option allows you to supply an Insertion point and Other corner representing the diagonal corners of the text boundary, similar to defining a window. After defining the window, the Edit MText dialog box appears.

By default, the first point picked becomes the MText insertion point, and the second point determines the width of the text lines. Looking at Figure 7.18, it appears that the text fits inside of the text window. The text window, however, does not always define the outer boundary of the text. Options at the MText command line allow you to change the justification method, rotation, style, height, and direction. Options available at the command line are as follows:

- **Attach.** The attach option lets you change the justification method. This will determine how the text is justified about the insertion point, or first point picked.
- **Rotation.** This specifies the rotation angle of the text. This is similar to the **dtext** and **text** rotation option, where the text is rotated about the insertion point.
- **Style.** Style lets you set a default style for the MText. This is identical to the Style option for **dtext** or **mtext.** With **mtext,** however, you can alter the style of any letter or word at a later time in the Edit MText dialog box.

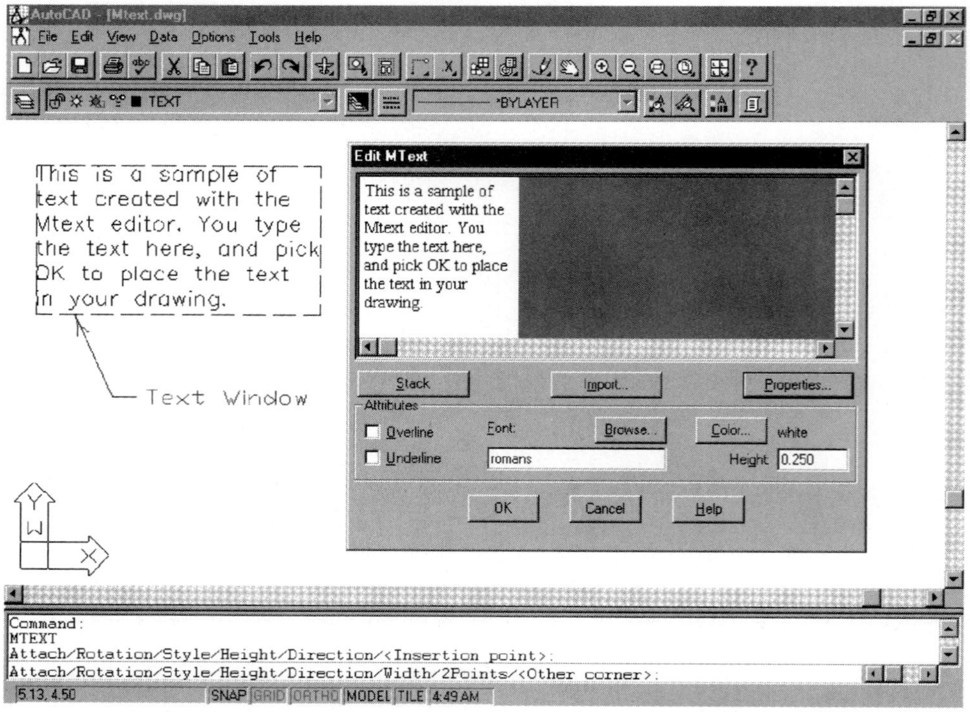

Figure 7.18
Use the Edit MText dialog box to create paragraph objects.

- **Height.** Setting the height specifies a default height for the uppercase text. You can also change the height in the Edit MText dialog box.
- **Direction.** Two options are available for direction—horizontal (left to right) or vertical (top to bottom). If vertical is selected, the text paragraph is anchored to the insertion point and the second point picked defines the paragraph *height,* not width as with horizontal MText.
- **Width/2Points.** These are the two methods that can be used to specify the width of the text window. Width prompts you to enter a value; 2Points prompts you for two points specifying the text box.

After specifying the text boundary, enter the Edit MText dialog box shown in Figure 7.18. There are several ways you can control the text in the dialog box. You can format all of the text by selecting the options before entering any text. You can also format existing text (all text or just a few letters or words) by highlighting it and selecting the desired options. You can highlight text by holding down the Pick button on your pointing device while dragging across the desired letters or words. Figure 7.20 shows various options applied to text with the Edit MText dialog box. Options within the Edit MText dialog box are:

- **Stack.** Using this option lets you stack words, letters, or numbers (such as fractions) in one line of text. Place a slash (/) or caret (^) between the objects you want to stack. A slash (/) creates a horizontal line between the stack, and a caret (^) creates the stack without the line. To stack objects, highlight the words or numbers and pick the Stack button.
- **Import.** This opens the Import Text File dialog box, allowing you to import any text file composed of straight ASCII characters.
- **Properties.** This accesses the MText Properties dialog box, shown in Figure 7.19. Any properties you set using this dialog box will change the entire paragraph. Use the MText Properties dialog box to control paragraph wide formatting. Use options in the Edit MText dialog box to control settings for selected text.
- **Attributes.** Settings in this area allow you to Underline or Overline selected text. You can also change the Color, Height, and Font of the selected text. Use the Browse... button to help you search for a specific font.

IMPORTING TEXT

AutoCAD allows you two different options for importing ASCII files created by other sources. By importing ASCII files from other sources, you can save a great deal of time. For example, you may have several drawings that all need the same type of notes. Instead of typing this information each time you use it, you can import the .TXT file. The imported file creates a text object, like ones created with the MText command. Text that is imported assumes the default formats and font settings used by the current text style. The options for importing a text file into AutoCAD are:

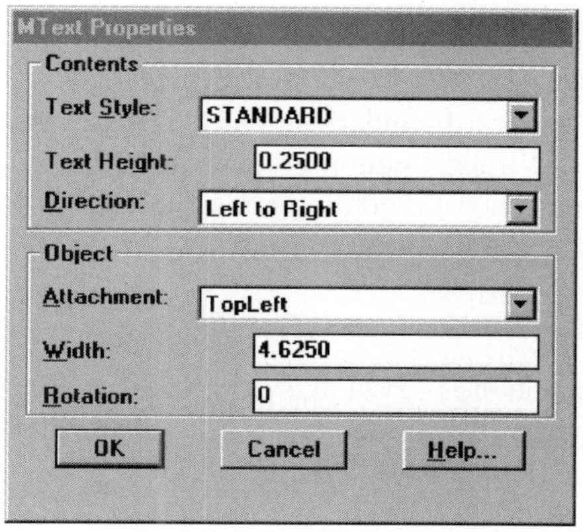

Figure 7.19
The MText Properties dialog box should be used to control paragraph wide formatting.

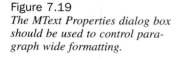

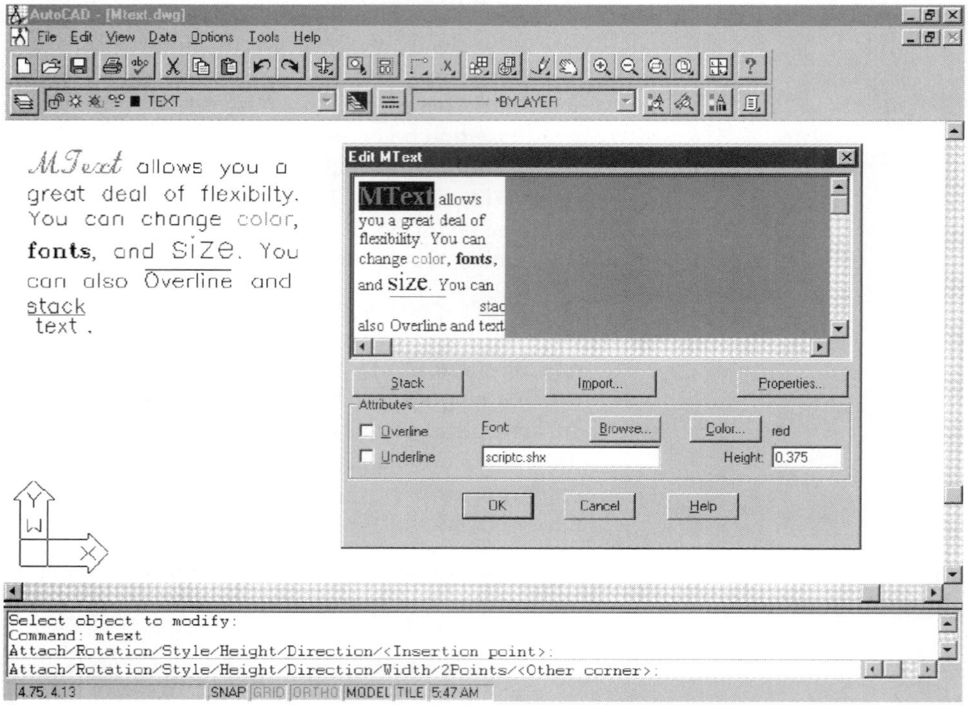

Figure 7.20
Sample text created with the Edit MText dialog box.

- Drag a text file directly into AutoCAD from Windows Explorer.
- Use the Import button in the Edit MText dialog box.

These procedures are explained below:

Dragging a File into AutoCAD To drag a file into AutoCAD, use the following process:

1. Open the Windows Explorer, making sure it doesn't fill the entire screen.
2. Find the file you want to import. It must have a .TXT extension and contain ASCII characters only (no formatting codes). Windows Notepad by default saves files in the correct format with the .TXT extension. If you are using a different program, such as Microsoft Word, save the file as MS-DOS text (.TXT file).
3. Drag the .TXT file into AutoCAD. AutoCAD will draw the text as an MText object at the point you released the button.

Importing a File into the Edit MText Dialog Box To import a file into the Edit MText dialog box, use the following process:

1. Select the Text button on the Draw toolbar.
2. Specify the text boundary and any other properties.
3. Choose the Import button in the Edit MText dialog box. The Import Text File dialog box appears.
4. Select the file you want to import. As with the dragging option, the file must have a .TXT extension.
5. Edit the text in the Edit MText dialog box as needed, and pick OK.

Another option is to cut and paste objects into AutoCAD. In your text editor, highlight and copy the selected text to the clipboard. In AutoCAD, select the Paste button on the Standard toolbar.

Tutorial 7.3: Using MText to Create and Import Text

Using the Edit MText dialog box, you will create your own paragraph of text and import text into your drawing.

1.  Select the Save button from the Standard toolbar to save your drawing.
2. Begin Windows Notepad and turn on the Word Wrap function.
   Select Edit, Word Wrap. A check mark will appear next to Word Wrap.
3. Type the following in Windows Notepad. Do not press Enter at the end of the line, but let Notepad "wrap" the line back.
   Watching the sunset from your contour seat while the therapeutic jets work their magic is the perfect way to end the day.
4. Select File, Save in Notepad and save the file as SPA. Notepad will automatically apply the .TXT extension. Minimize notepad.
5. At this point you should be in AutoCAD, with 07DWG01 displayed and the TITLE_BLOCK view restored.
6.  Select the Text button on the Draw toolbar. Enter the first insertion point:

```
Attach/Rotation/Style/Height/Direction/
Width/2Points/<Insertion point>: 7.0,1.9
```

7. Enter the other corner:

```
Attach/Rotation/Style/Height/Direction/
Width/2Points/<Other Corner>: 10.0,0.9
```

8. In the Edit MText dialog box, select the Properties button.
   The MText Properties dialog box appears. Change the Text Style to ROMANS and the Text Height to 0.100. Your dialog box should look like Figure 7.21. Select OK to close the MText Properties dialog box.
9. Type the following in the Edit MText dialog box. Do not press Enter at the end of the line, but let the dialog box "wrap" the line back.
   HOT-TUB DESIGNS is a leader in the manufacture of quality spas.
10. Leave one space between the flashing cursor and the period at the end of the line. Pick the Import button.
    The Import Text File dialog box appears. Select the SPA.TXT file.
    Pick the Open button to import your file into the Edit MText dialog box.
11. Your Edit MText dialog box should look like Figure 7.22.
12. Pick OK in the Edit MText dialog box to place the text in the drawing. Your completed title block should look like Figure 7.23.

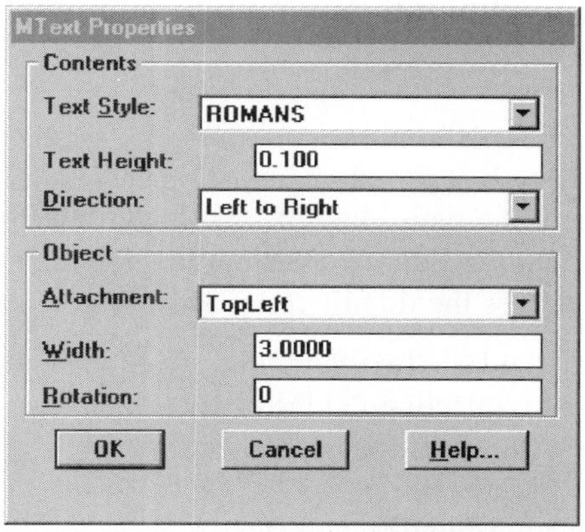

Figure 7.21
The correct settings for the MText Properties dialog box.

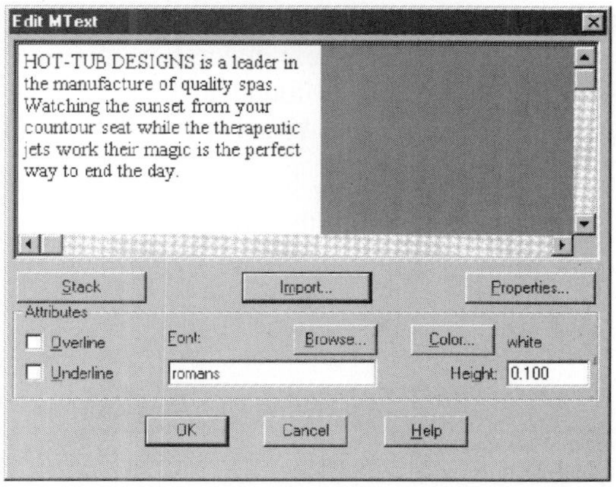

Figure 7.22
The Edit MText dialog box with the imported text.

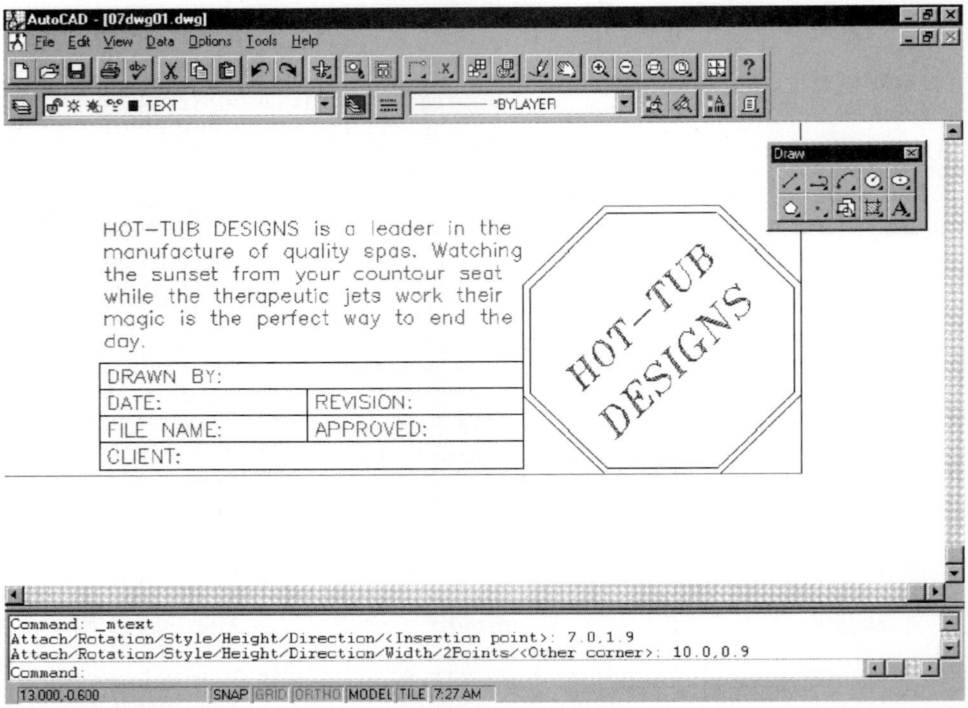

Figure 7.23
The completed title block with the MText inserted.

Editing Text (CHANGE, DDEDIT, and DDMODIFY)

The three AutoCAD commands that are commonly used to edit existing text are **change, ddedit,** and **ddmodify. ddedit** and **ddmodify** both use dialog boxes. **change** works from the command line.

ddedit. The **ddedit** command is the simplest of the text editing commands to use, accessing a dialog box for editing existing characters in a drawing. You can edit individual characters or the entire line of text. If the selected text was created with the **text** or **dtext** commands, the Edit Text dialog box (Figure 7.24) appears displaying one line of text. You can access the **ddedit** command by:

- Selecting the Edit Text button on the Modify toolbar. It's located on a flyout menu, accessed by selecting the Edit Polyline button.
- Type **ddedit** at the `Command:` prompt.

ddmodify. With **ddmodify** you can do any kind of editing to existing text, including an upside down, backwards, width factor, and obliquing angle change. Invoking this command accesses the Modify Text dialog box (Figure 7.25). A thorough explanation of the **ddmodify** command can be found in Unit 14, "Modifying Object Characteristics and Extracting Information From Your Drawing." You can access the **ddmodify** command by:

- Selecting the Properties button on the Object properties toolbar.
- Select Properties from the Edit pull-down menu.
- Type **ddmodify** at the `Command:` prompt.

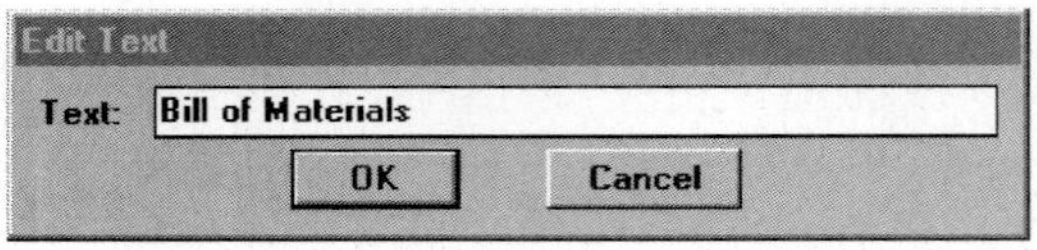

Figure 7.24
The Edit Text dialog box allows you to use standard text editing methods.

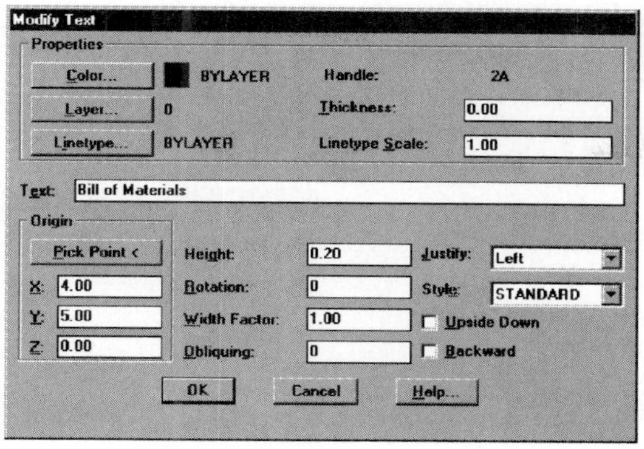

Figure 7.25
The Modify Text dialog box allows you to change every aspect of your text object.

change. The **change** command allows you to edit both text and its properties at the command line. **change** allows you to pick any number of text strings and edit them sequentially. You can access the **change** command by:

- Type **change** at the `Command:` prompt.

The **change** command allows you to change three things: Points, Properties, or Text. Although the word *text* never appears as an option, the **change** command will recognize text if selected and display the following prompt:

`Select objects:` *`Pick one or several lines of text.`*
`Select objects:`
`Properties/<Change point>:`
`Enter text insertion point:` *`Pick a new insertion point, or Enter for no change.`*
`Text style: STANDARD` *`(Indicates the current style)`*
`New style or RETURN for no change:` *`Enter style name, or Enter for no change.`*
`New height <0.20>:` *`Enter a new value for height, or Enter for no change.`*
`New rotation angle <0>:` *`Enter a new value for the rotation angle, or Enter for no change.`*
`New text <old text>:` *`Enter the new complete line of text, or Enter for no change.`*

Editing MText Objects

Multiline text objects created with the **mtext** command are defined differently than other text objects. Fortunately, you can use many of the same commands you used to edit your Text and **dtext** objects. You have two options: **ddedit** and **ddmodify.**

ddedit. If you want to modify the contents only, the quickest way is to use the **ddedit** command. Select the Edit Text button from the Modify toolbar, or type **ddedit** at the `Command:` prompt. At the `<Select an annotation object>/Undo:` prompt, select your MText object, and the Edit MText dialog box appears (see Figure 7.26).

ddmodify. If you need to modify more than the contents, use the **ddmodify** command. **ddmodify** will allow you to modify several of the MText's properties, including insertion point, color, and layer. Select the Properties button on the Object Properties toolbar or choose Edit Properties. Select the MText you wish to modify, and the Modify MText dialog box appears (see Figure 7.27). Selecting the Edit Contents button takes you to the Edit MText dialog box shown earlier in Figure 7.26. Selecting the Edit Properties button brings up the MText Properties dialog box, shown in Figure 7.19.

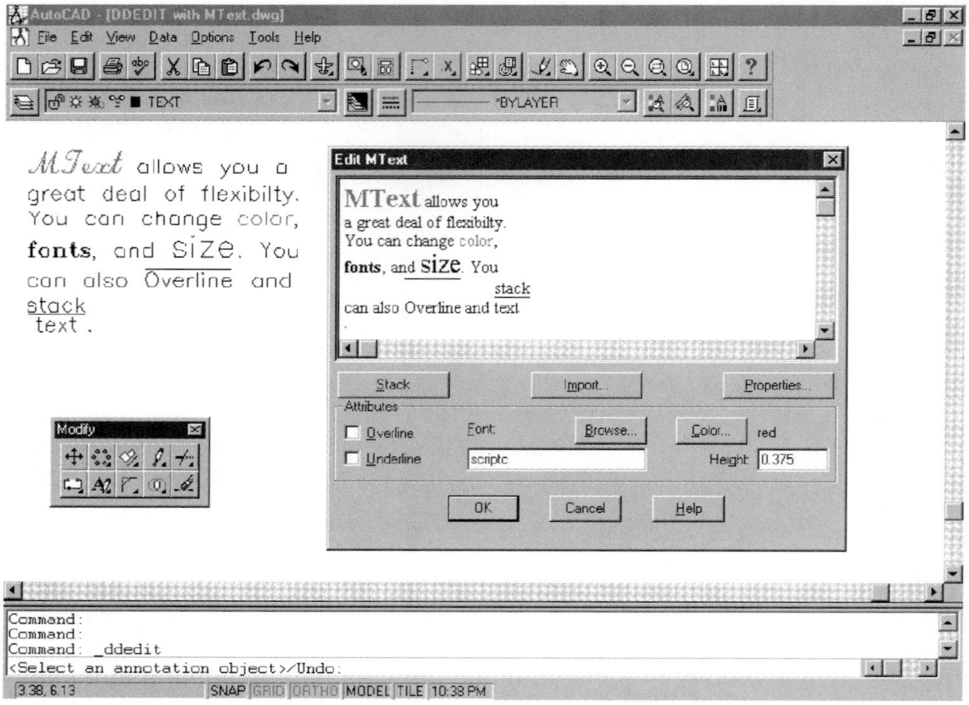

Figure 7.26
Use the ***ddedit*** *command to select MText and modify it in the Edit MText dialog box.*

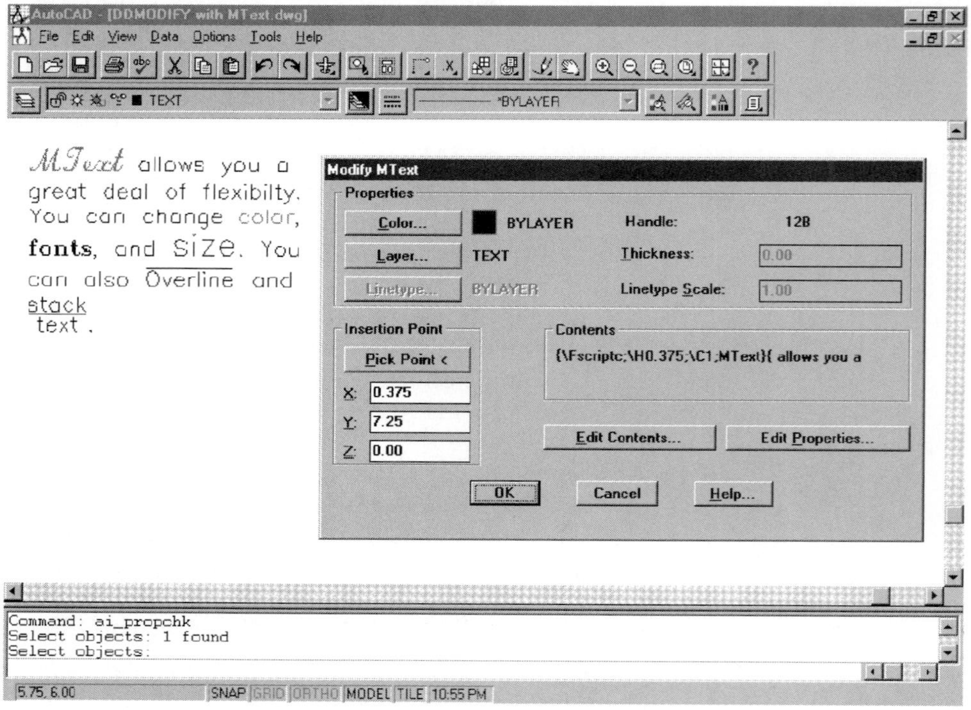

Figure 7.27
The Modify MText dialog box can be used to modify many of the MText's properties.

Tutorial 7.4: Editing Text and MText

The ability to edit your text is essential. Correcting mistakes and changing styles are just two common editing functions you should know if you need to edit your text. In this tutorial you will edit Text and MText you created in your earlier tutorials.

1. To begin the tutorial you should be in AutoCAD, with 07DWG01 displayed, with the TITLE_BLOCK view restored.
2.  Select the Edit Text button on the Modify toolbar.
   At the `Select an annotation object>/ Undo:` prompt, select the DRAWN BY: text. The Edit Text dialog box appears.
3. Change the text in the Edit Text dialog box to include your name, shown in Figure 7.28. Click OK.
4. When the `Select an annotation object>/Undo:` prompt reappears, select the APROVED: text. The Edit Text dialog box appears.
   Change the spelling of APPROVED: to APPRUVED:. (We are purposely misspelling this word for use in the next tutorial). Click OK.
5. Select anywhere on the multiline text you created earlier (HOT-TUB DESIGNS is a, etc.) at the `Select an annotation object>/Undo:` prompt.
   The Edit MText dialog box appears.
6. Hold the Pick button down and drag it over the words *HOT-TUB DESIGNS* to highlight it.
   Change the Height to 0.150, and the Color to red. Your Edit MText dialog box should look like Figure 7.29.
7. Click OK to close the dialog box and press Enter at the `Select an annotation object>/Undo:` prompt to return to the `Command:` line. Your drawing should look like Figure 7.30. This completes the tutorial on editing.

Figure 7.28 *Use the Edit Text dialog box to add your name.*

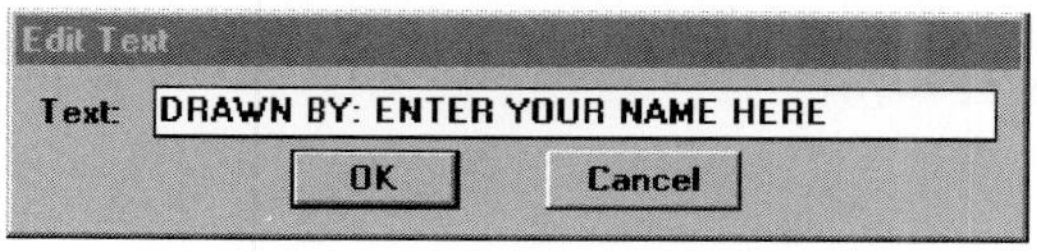

Figure 7.29 *Change the height and color in the Edit MText dialog box.*

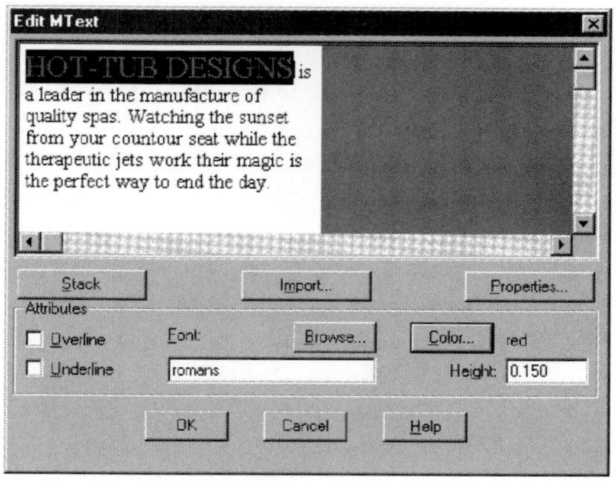

Figure 7.30
The title block after editing the text.

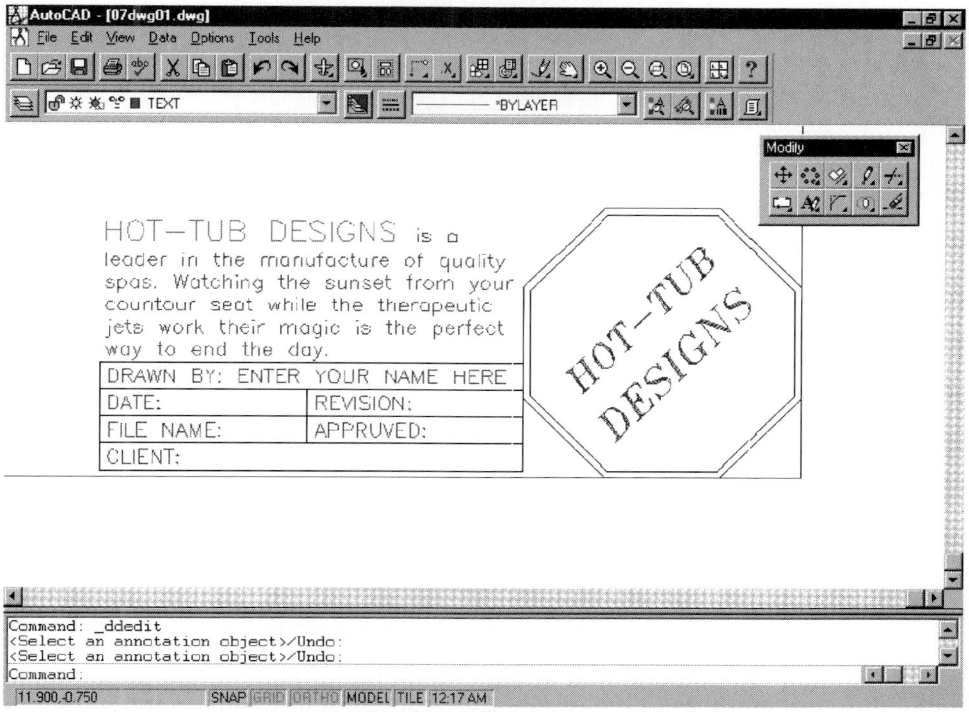

Hiding and Displaying Text (QText, TextQlty, TextFill)

A drawing containing a lot of text can significantly slow down your computer. Redrawing and Regeneration can take a long time because AutoCAD has to redraw all of the text to the screen. AutoCAD offers several commands that can be used to alter the display and appearance of your text.

qtext **qtext** stands for Quick Text, and allows you to display a line of text as a box. Instead of the text, a rectangular box is drawn, outlining the space consumed by the text. Using **qtext** can also speed up plotting of check plots (plots made during the design process used to check the drawing) since text will be plotted as blocks. Access the **qtext** command by:

- Selecting Options, Display, and then Text Frame Only.
- Select Options, Drawing Aids to access the Drawing Aids dialog box. Select the Quick Text box.
- Type **qtext** at the `Command:` prompt.

qtext has two settings—on and off. After **qtext** is turned on, you must regenerate the drawing to display the text as boxes. When you turn **qtext** off, you must again regenerate the drawing to display the text normally.

textqlty The screen display and plotting of TrueType (.TTF) and Post Script fonts (.PFA or .PFB) is determined by the setting of the **textqlty** system variable. The default value for **textqlty** is 50, with acceptable values ranging from 0 to 100. The default value of 50 sets the text resolution to 300 dpi. Decreasing the value makes the text appear more jagged, but regeneration and plot times are reduced. Increasing the value to 100 sets the resolution to 600 dpi, making the text appear smooth, but increasing regeneration and plot times. You can set the **textqlty** variable by:

- Selecting Options, Display, Text Quality.
- Type **textqlty** at the `Command:` prompt.

Skill Builder

Changing the **textqlty** value affects all Post Script and TrueType fonts in your drawing. Fonts other than Post Script and TrueType in your drawing are not affected by the **textqlty** value.

textfill The **textfill** variable affects the appearance of TrueType (.TTF) and Post Script fonts (.PFA or .PFB). By default, text created with these fonts appears as outlines. If you change the **textfill** variable to on, AutoCAD displays and plots the text filled in. Use a Regen after changing the variable to reflect the new setting. You can set the **textfill** variable by:

- Selecting Options, Display, Filled Text.
- Type **textfill** at the `Command:` prompt.

Spell Checking a Drawing

One of the most frequently requested additions to earlier versions of AutoCAD was a spell checker. AutoCAD now has an internal spell checker that you can use to check and correct existing text in your drawing created using the **text, dtext,** or **mtext** commands. If you use a word processor, you are probably already familiar with this feature. With **spell** you can check a single string, or all text objects in your drawing at once. You can access the **spell** function in the following ways:

- Select the Spelling button from the Standard toolbar.
- Choose Tools, Spelling.
- Type **spell** at the `Command:` prompt.

After accessing the **spell** command, AutoCAD prompts:

```
Select objects:
```

Use any of your object selection methods (pick, window, fence, etc.) to select as many text objects as you want to check. You can pick a single line of text, or window your entire drawing. AutoCAD will ignore any non-text objects in your selection set, so you don't need to filter them out.

After creating your selection set, AutoCAD matches the words in your selection set to the words in the current dictionary. If AutoCAD finds a word it thinks is misspelled, the Check Spelling dialog box appears as shown in Figure 7.31.

There are several options available in the Check Spelling dialog box when AutoCAD thinks it has found a misspelled word:

Suggestions. In the suggestions box, AutoCAD lists other words that are similar to the identified misspelled word. To see more suggestions, pick the Lookup button.

Ignore. This occurrence of the word is bypassed, and the spell checker will resume.

Ignore All. All instances of the word are ignored. If the same word appears more than once in the drawing, selecting Ignore will bypass only the first occurrence. The Check Spelling dialog box will appear when the word is found again; however, selecting Ignore All will bypass all other instances of the word.

Change. This will change the spelling of the word identified as misspelled to the word appearing in the top Suggestions box. To show more suggestions, pick the Lookup button.

Change All. This will change the spelling of all instances of the misspelled word to the word appearing in the top Suggestions box.

Lookup. Picking Lookup offers more words with similar spellings to appear in the Suggestions window.

Add. As AutoCAD checks the drawing for misspelled words, it often indicates that a proper name or acronym is misspelled. If you use the word often, you can pick the Add button to add it to a custom dictionary. To use the Add button, a custom dictionary must be specified in the Change Directories dialog box.

Change Directories. Before you can use the Add feature to include words not in the standard dictionary, you must create or specify a custom dictionary in the Change Dictionaries dialog box shown in Figure 7.32. To create a custom dictionary,

Figure 7.31 *The Check Spelling dialog box appears when AutoCAD thinks a word is misspelled.*

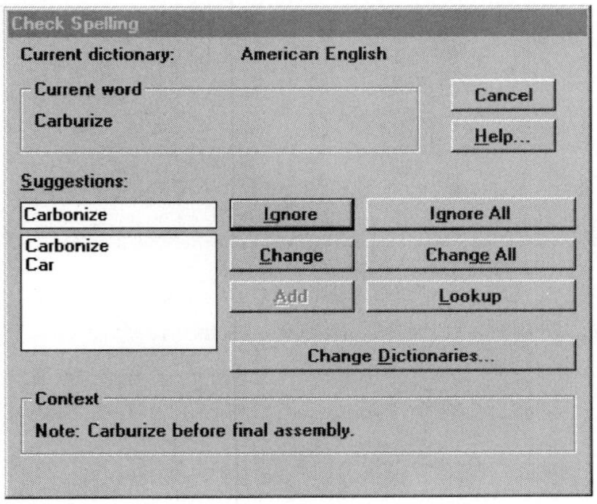

Figure 7.32 *You must specify a custom dictionary before you can add words.*

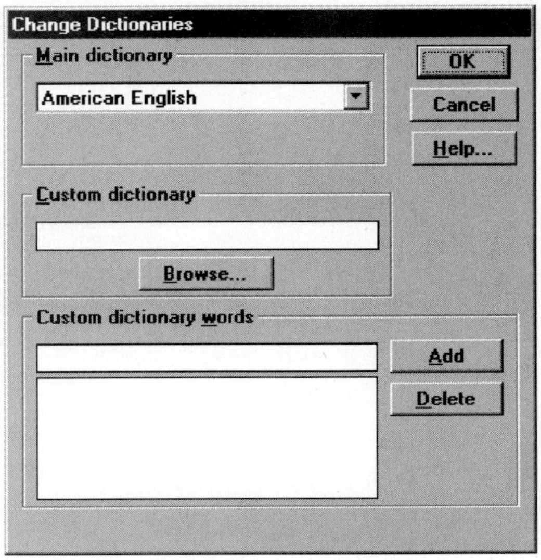

enter the path and name with the .CUS extension. To select from a list of custom dictionaries, select the Browse... button. After creating or specifying a custom dictionary, words can be added by using the Add button in the Check Spelling dialog box, or by entering the word in the Custom dictionary text edit box.

TUTORIAL 7.5: HIDING AND SPELL CHECKING TEXT

In this final tutorial on text, you will hide your text to help speed up drawing regeneration and plotting. You will also check the spelling of your drawing.

1. To complete the final tutorial you should be in AutoCAD, with 07DWG01 displayed and the TITLE_BLOCK view restored.
2.  Select the Spelling button from the Standard toobar.
3. At the `Select objects:` prompt, enter `all`. This will cause **spell** to check all text in your drawing.
4. At the `Select objects:` prompt press Enter. AutoCAD will begin checking the spelling of your drawing.

   As each unrecognized word is displayed with the listed suggestion and possible spellings, select the appropriate action. When the word APPRUVED: that we intentionally misspelled in the previous tutorial appears, select Change to update the spelling. Continue the spell checking until the AutoCAD message `Spelling check complete` appears.
5. Select Options, Display, and then Text Frame Only.
6. At the `Command:` prompt type **regen.**

   The screen regenerates, and all of the text appears as boxes (see Figure 7.33).
7. Select Options, Display, and then Outline Text.
8. At the `Command:` prompt type **regen.**

   The screen regenerates, and all of the text appears as before.
9.  Select the Save button to save your drawing. This concludes the text tutorials.

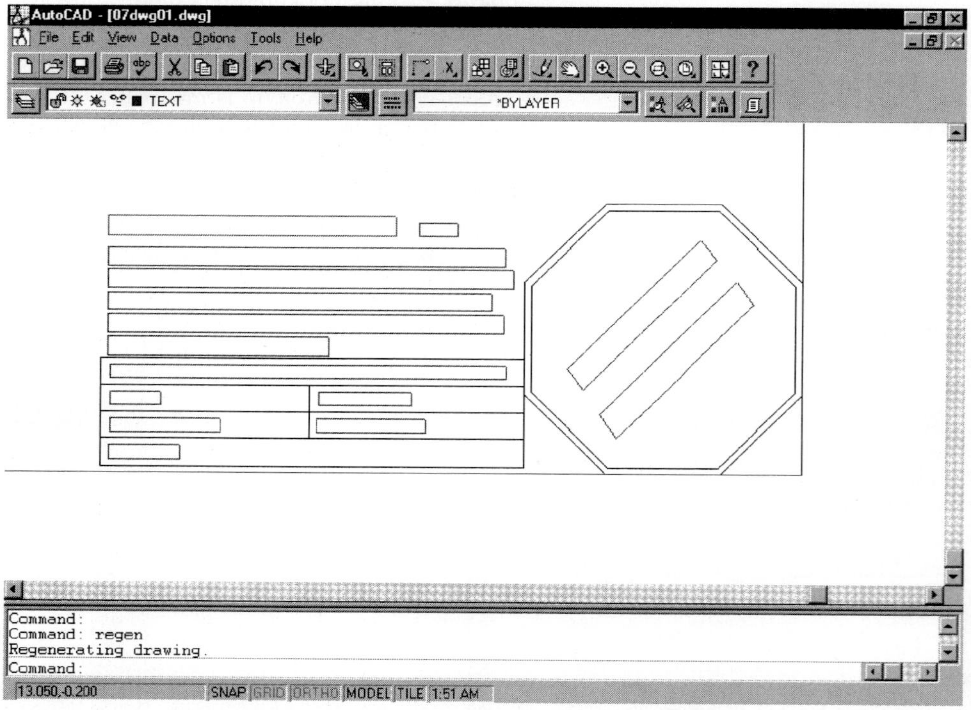

Figure 7.33
*The effects of **qtext** after it's turned on and a regen has occurred.*

FILLING AREAS WITH HATCHING

Text is often used in a drawing to emphasize details about your designs that can't be shown through drawing alone. Hatching is another tool used by the designer to enhance the readability of drawings. Hatching is commonly found in many disciplines, such as on mechanical drawings to indicate a section or interior view of a part. In the architectural discipline, hatching is also known as *poch.* It provides a way of applying various patterns (such as wood, stone, or brick) to certain areas of a drawing.

When you create a hatch, you need to define a boundary. A boundary is simply an area enclosed by AutoCAD objects. These objects can overlap or intersect each other, but cannot contain any openings or gaps between the objects that define the boundary. When you create a hatch, AutoCAD draws a temporary closed polyline boundary over the objects that define the boundary. AutoCAD then applies the hatch pattern to the polyline boundary. You have the option to leave the polyline boundary for future reference and use it for perimeter and area calculations. For a complete discussion of polylines, see Unit 12, "Advanced Drawing Techniques."

CREATING HATCHING PATTERNS (BHATCH)

AutoCAD offers two options for creating a hatch. The original **hatch** command requires you to create your own boundary using objects that close perfectly. Any gaps or overlaps in the objects can cause unexpected results. Defining your own boundaries and using the **hatch** command is often a tedious process, producing tenuous results.

The **hatch** command is still in AutoCAD, but most users will choose to use the **bhatch** command. **bhatch** can fill any area as long as it can find some kind of bounding object. These objects can be small segments of larger objects, and do not even need to be connected. Hatch patterns created with **bhatch** are also associative. This means the hatch pattern is associated with the boundary, so when the boundary changes (by **stretch, scale, move,** etc.) the hatch pattern automatically conforms to the new shape. For these reasons **bhatch** is superior to **hatch** and is recommended in most cases.

You can access the **bhatch** command by using one of the following methods:

- Select the Hatch button from the Draw toolbar.
- Type **bhatch** at the `Command:` prompt.

Accessing the **bhatch** command displays the Boundary Hatch dialog box shown in Figure 7.34. The **bhatch** features are discussed later in this section.

DEFINING THE PATTERN TYPE

Before you can create a hatch, you must first select and define the pattern you want to use. There are three different types of patterns you can choose: predefined, user-defined, and

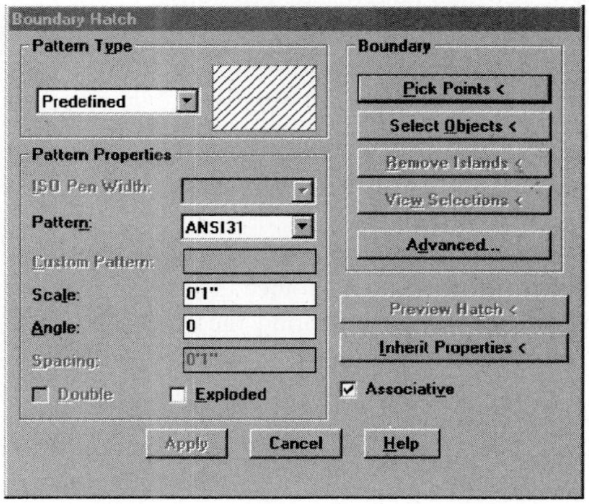

Figure 7.34
The Boundary Hatch dialog box.

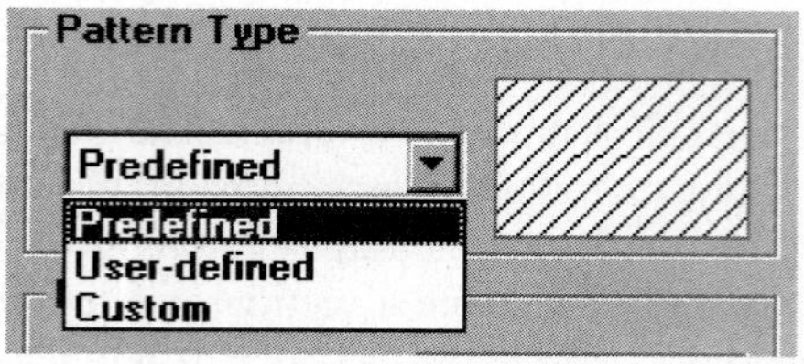

Figure 7.35
The pop-down list, displaying the three pattern type options.

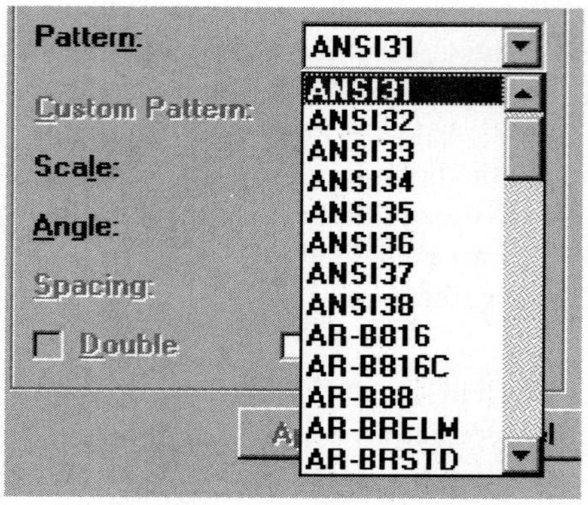

Figure 7.36
Selecting a pattern name from the pop-down list.

custom. Selecting the DOWN ARROW under Pattern Type accesses a pop-down list, displaying the three options shown in Figure 7.35.

Predefined AutoCAD offers a number of predefined hatch patterns stored in the ACAD.PAT file. There are two ways you can select from the predefined patterns. One method is to use the Pattern pop-down list shown in Figure 7.36. Choosing the DOWN ARROW allows you to scroll through the pattern names. When you select a pattern from the pop-down list, the image tile under Pattern Type displays a sample of the pattern.

The other method is to click the image tile. Clicking the image tile causes the display to sequence through the possible selections. The name of the pattern is also updated in the Pattern text box as you cycle through the selections.

User-defined The user-defined option allows you to create a hatch pattern. The pattern uses lines based on the current linetype. When you select the user-defined option, the Pattern and Scale options are disabled and the Spacing and Double options are enabled. To create a user-defined pattern, specify the Angle of the lines, the Spacing between the lines, and select Double if you want perpendicular lines.

Custom Custom patterns are previously created user-defined patterns that are not found in the standard ACAD.PAT file. Custom hatch patterns are offered as third-party add-in packages. You also can create your own custom hatch pattern. Creating your own custom hatch pattern is similar to defining your own custom linetype. For more information, consult the AutoCAD Customization Guide.

PATTERN PROPERTIES

The options in this area are used to specify the type of hatch pattern drawn and the parameters that govern its appearance. These properties help define the size, angle, and pattern of the hatch. After creating the hatch, you can modify several of these properties using the **hatchedit** command.

- **ISO Pen Width.** For this option to be enabled, you must select an ISO hatch pattern. Selecting an ISO Pen Width from the pop-down list automatically sets the pattern scaling in relation to the ISO linetype.

- **Pattern.** If a Predefined hatch pattern is selected under Pattern Type, the names of the available patterns in the ACAD.PAT file are displayed in a pop-down list. After selecting a pattern, set the desired Scale and Angle of the pattern.
- **Custom Pattern.** This option is available only if Custom Pattern is selected under Pattern Type. This option allows you to access patterns not available in the ACAD.PAT file.
- **Scale.** After a predefined or custom pattern has been chosen, you can assign a Scale to the pattern. The default value of 1 is the scale the pattern was originally defined at. A value of 2 is twice the original scale, and .5 is half the original scale.
- **Angle.** The Angle applies to all three pattern types. The pattern angle is set relative to the x-axis. The default angle of 0 represents whatever angle the hatch pattern was created at and is displayed in the image tile. Any angle entered will deflect the existing pattern by the specified value (in degrees).
- **Spacing.** This is applicable only if User-defined is specified under Pattern Type. Spacing is the distance between the lines of a user-defined hatch pattern, measured in the current drawing units.
- **Double.** Like spacing, this option is available only with User-defined patterns. Selecting *double* takes the line definition and repeats it perpendicular to or at 90° from the first set of lines.
- **Exploded.** A hatch pattern is normally drawn as one object. Creating an exploded pattern means that the pattern will be created as individual lines and/or dots when drawn. With exploded hatch patterns, you can edit the hatch lines individually. Patterns drawn in this manner have several drawbacks, however. The pattern is no longer associated with the boundary. If you edit the boundary, the hatch pattern is no longer updated. Also, since the hatch pattern is no longer one object, the drawing file increases considerably.

FOR THE PROFESSIONAL

AutoCAD stores the pattern properties in the following system variables:

Predefined or Custom Pattern Name	**HPNAME**
Scale	HPSCALE
Angle	HPANG
Spacing	HPSPACE
Double	HPDOUBLE

TUTORIAL 7.6: CREATING A HATCH PATTERN

For the first tutorial in this section you will use a predefined pattern. Begin by loading the hot-tub, shown in Figure 7.37. The hot-tub is used in all subsequent tutorials in this section.

1.  Select the Open button from the Standard toolbar and load 07DWG02. This loads the hot-tub as shown in Figure 7.37.
2.  Select the Hatch button from the Draw toolbar.

   The Boundary Hatch dialog box appears (see Figure 7.34).
3. Select the DOWN ARROW to the right of the Pattern text box.

   A pop-down menu appears, showing the predefined hatch patterns.
4. Select the AR-HBONE pattern.

   The pattern appears in the image tile.
5. Leave the rest of the values at their default. Your Boundary Hatch dialog box should look like Figure 7.38. Leave the dialog box open because the next tutorial will continue from here.

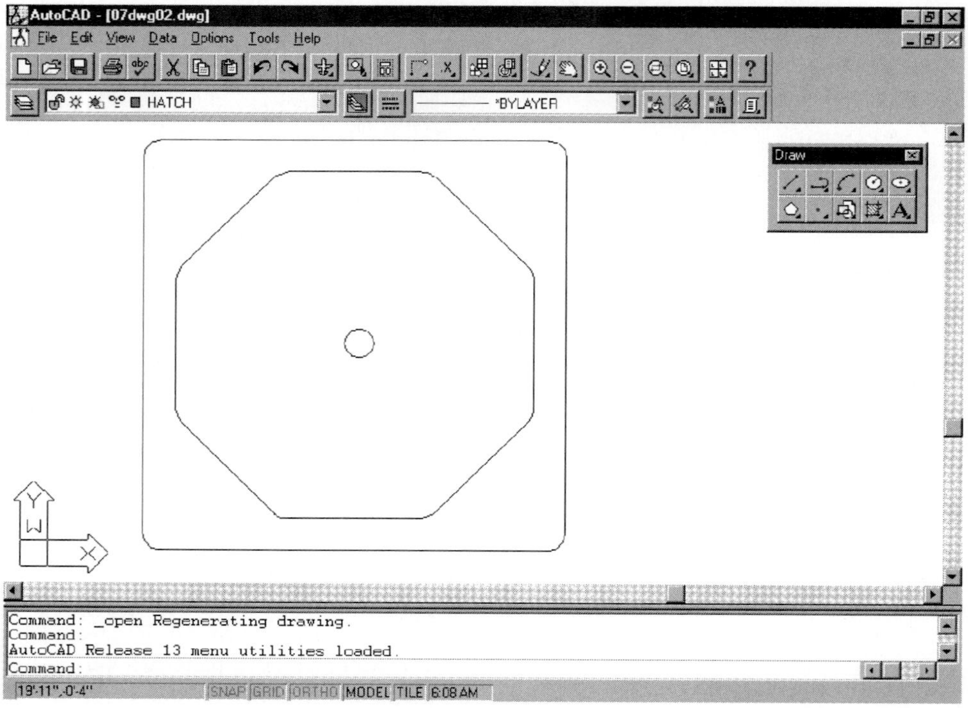

Figure 7.37
Loading the hot-tub.

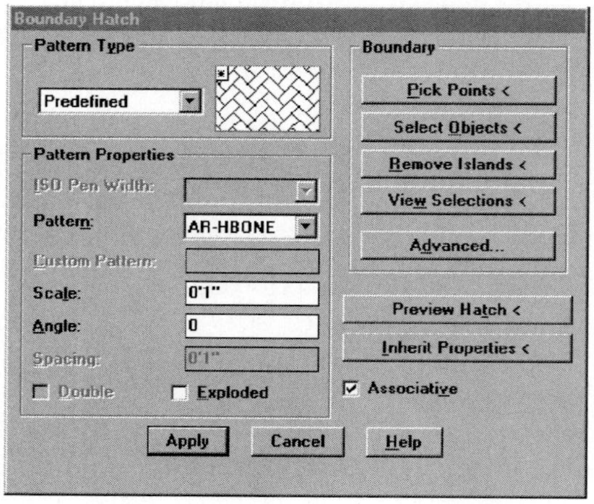

Figure 7.38
The completed hatch pattern.

Defining the Area to Hatch

After selecting and defining the hatch pattern, the next step is to determine what areas you want hatched. The Boundary area of the Boundary Hatch dialog box provides the tools to fine-tune the hatch area.

- **Pick Points.** The Pick Points option is a powerful feature that allows AutoCAD to automatically detect the boundary for you. When you select the Pick Points option, AutoCAD prompts `Select internal point:`. To begin the process, you need only to select a point inside the area to be hatched. After picking an internal point, AutoCAD traces and highlights the boundary. In a large and complex drawing this process can be time-consuming. You can also create multiple boundaries by selecting multiple internal points.

  If you choose a point that does not have a closed boundary, AutoCAD responds `Nothing was found to make a boundary of`. Choosing OK allows you to select another internal point.

- **Select Objects.** Using this option you can specify the boundary with the Select Objects method. The objects you select must form a closed shape with no gaps or overlaps or you can get some undesirable results. This method works best when you have an already closed object, such as a polygon or circle.
- **Remove Islands.** This option is active only if you define the boundary with the Pick Points option. If you remove an island, AutoCAD hatches through the object as though it didn't exist.
- **View Selections.** The View Selections option lets you see the boundary or selection set that AutoCAD has created. Use this option as a check to ensure the desired areas are selected. If this is not the boundary you want, you can redefine it using the Advanced options.
- **Advanced.** This accesses the Advanced Options dialog box, which is discussed in the Advanced Options section later in this unit.
- **Preview Hatch.** This is an easy way to test your hatch pattern and boundary selection visually. Use the Preview Hatch option after specifying the hatch parameters and selecting the boundaries. AutoCAD removes the dialog box and applies your settings to the boundary or objects selected. Choose Continue to go back to the Boundary Hatch dialog box.
- **Inherit Properties.** The Inherit Properties option allows you to take advantage of other pre-existing hatch patterns in your drawing. After selecting the Inherit Properties button, AutoCAD prompts `Select hatch object:`. Picking a previously drawn hatch pattern resets all of the parameters in the Boundary Hatch dialog box to those of the selected pattern. The next hatch pattern drawn should look exactly like the one you chose in the drawing.
- **Associative.** An associative hatch pattern means that all objects that make up the pattern are linked to the boundary that defines it. This link allows the hatch pattern to adopt any changes in the boundary.
- **Apply.** This is normally the last step in the hatching process. Selecting Apply causes AutoCAD to create the hatch pattern using all of the parameters specified in the Boundary Hatch dialog box. After the hatch is created you are returned to the `Command:` prompt for further drawing and editing.

TUTORIAL 7.7: HATCHING AN AREA OF A DRAWING

Using the hatch pattern you defined in the previous tutorial, you will apply the pattern to your drawing. You will also edit the outside boundary of the hot-tub to see the effect of associative hatching.

1. Continue from the previous tutorial. You should have the Boundary Hatch dialog box displayed, with the ARHBONE pattern defined.
2. Select the Pick Points button in the Boundary Hatch dialog box.

   The dialog box disappears, and you are prompted to

   `Select internal point:.`
3. Select a point between the outside deck and the inner wall of the hot-tub as shown in Figure 7.39.
4. After selecting the internal point, the hot-tub symbol appears dashed, indicating the boundary.

   Press Enter at the `Select internal point:` prompt to return to the Boundary Hatch dialog box.
5. Select the Preview Hatch button to see what the pattern and boundary selections look like.

   The dialog box disappears, and you see the hatch pattern displayed within the boundary. Click the Continue button to return to the Boundary Hatch dialog box.
6. If the hatch looked correct in the preview, select the Apply button.
7. The hatch is applied to the hot-tub as shown in Figure 7.40.

Since you applied an associative hatch pattern, you should be able to change the boundary objects, which will automatically update the hatch.

1.  Select the Scale button on the Modify toolbar. Scale is located on a flyout menu accessed by selecting and holding the Point button.
2. To help in the selection of the outside deck, a group was defined using the outside edge. You will use the group option in response to the `Select objects:` prompt. For more information on Groups, see Unit 15, "Using Symbols."

```
Select objects: group
Enter group name: outside
1 found
Select objects:
```

3. Enter 6′-0″,6′-0″ for the base point.

`Base point:` **`6′-0″,6′-0″`**

4. Enter a scale factor of 1.2.

`<Scale factor>/Reference:` **`1.2`**

5. The outside deck is increased in size, and the hatch pattern is automatically updated. Your drawing should look similar to Figure 7.41. Compare the size of the deck to Figure 7.40.

6.  Select the Save button to save your drawing. This completes the hatching tutorial. In the next tutorial you will edit the hatch pattern.

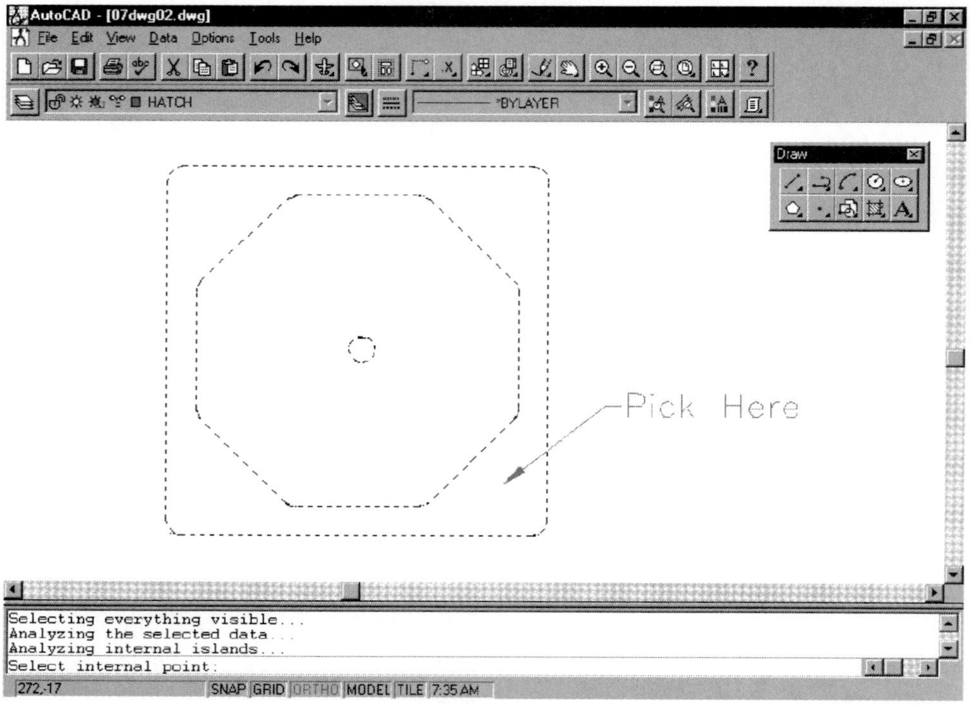

Figure 7.39
Select an internal point in the hot-tub to define the hatch boundary.

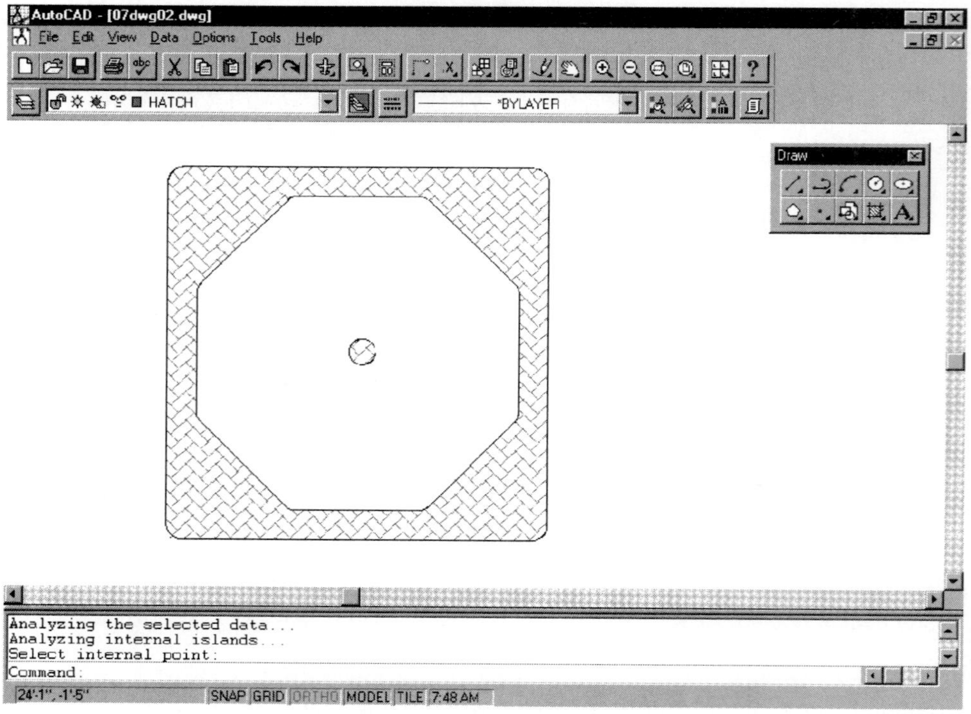

Figure 7.40
The finished hatch pattern.

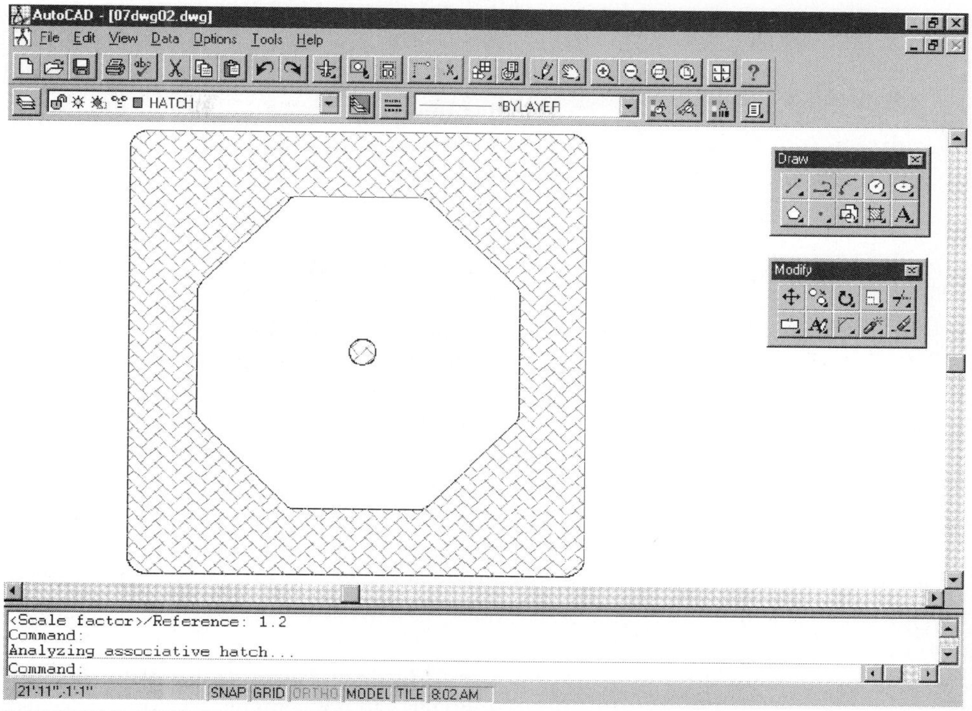

Figure 7.41
After scaling the hot-tub deck, the associative hatch pattern is automatically updated.

Advanced Hatching Options

AutoCAD give you several options if you need to fine-tune your hatch pattern. These options allow you to speed up your boundary search and refine the results of your hatch pattern. The options are available in the Advanced Options dialog box (Figure 7.42). You can access the Advanced Options dialog box by:

- Selecting the Advanced button in the Boundary Hatch dialog box.

  The settings in the Advanced Options dialog box are:

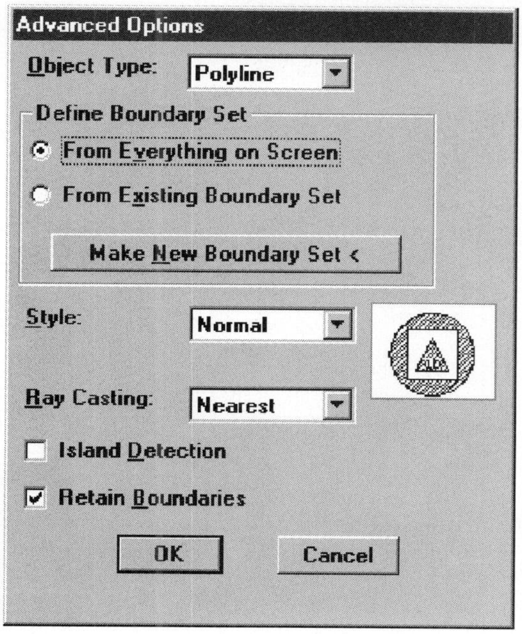

Figure 7.42
The Advanced Options dialog box lets you fine-tune your hatch pattern.

Object Type. This option is enabled only when the Retain Boundaries box is checked. The Object Type pop-down box lists the two object types used to define boundaries in AutoCAD: polylines and regions. Polyline is the default and is most common.

Define Boundary Set. When you use **bhatch** to hatch inside a boundary, AutoCAD evaluates every object currently visible on the screen, even if it is unrelated to the area you want to hatch. In large drawings containing many objects, this search can take a considerable amount of time.

You can speed up this delay by constructing a boundary set made up of a limited number of objects. When you select the Make New Boundary Set button, the dialog box disappears and you are returned to the screen. Use any selection set method (pick, window, fence, etc.) and select objects or a smaller area to define the new boundary set. After selecting the objects to include in the new boundary set, press Enter. The Advanced Options dialog appears, and From Existing Boundary Set is now active and selected. Now when you use the Pick Points option, only objects included in your new boundary set are evaluated to create the hatch boundary.

Style. Three styles available when defining a hatch pattern are Normal, Outer, and Ignore. Each style determines how AutoCAD will evaluate objects within the outer boundary of the hatch pattern (see Figure 7.43). As you select the different options, an example showing the result of each style type is shown in the image tile at the right of the Style list.

Normal. This is the default Style selection and should be used for most applications. Hatching begins at the outer boundary and moves inward, alternately applying and not applying the pattern as interior shapes or text are applied.

Outer. Selecting Outer causes AutoCAD to hatch only the outer closed shape. Hatching is turned off for all interior closed shapes.

Ignore. With Ignore the hatch pattern is drawn from the outer boundary inward, ignoring any interior shapes. The hatch pattern is drawn though all interior shapes.

Ray Casting. The Ray Casting options are available only when Island Detection is turned off. Ray casting is a technique AutoCAD uses to determine the hatch bound-

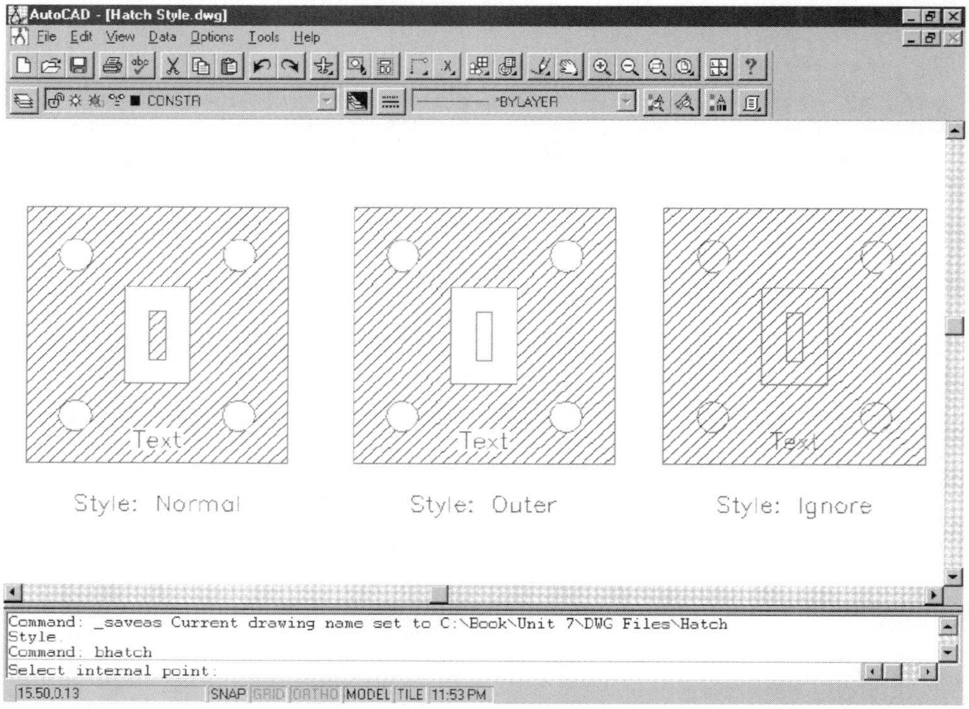

Figure 7.43
Examples of Normal, Outer, and Ignore styles.

ary. When you use the Pick Points option, you first select an internal point inside the completely closed area you want to hatch. From this point, AutoCAD casts rays in four directions to find the nearest object. When a ray hits an object, it traces around it in a counterclockwise direction until it finds a closed boundary.

At times ray tracing can have difficulty finding the closed object, and an error message is displayed such as `Point is outside of boundary` or `Nothing was found to make a boundary out of.` This message indicates AutoCAD didn't find a suitable boundary element when it began to look for objects to construct the hatching. One possible explanation is the nearest object found might not be a boundary, but an island.

When AutoCAD begins to look for boundary objects, it looks at the closest object first. To correct an error message, first try picking your point closer to the object you want to look for a boundary. If that doesn't work you can tell AutoCAD to look in a specific direction. The Ray Casting option lets you tell AutoCAD the direction to look for its first boundary. The default is Nearest. You can change to a specific X or Y direction for ray casting by clicking the Ray Casting pop-down list. Options are +x (right), −x (left), +y (up), or −y (down).

Island Detection. When Island Detection is turned on, it also looks for island areas within the boundary and adds them to the final boundary definition. When Island Detection is turned off, AutoCAD ignores these objects when it creates the boundary definition.

Retain Boundaries. As AutoCAD uses the ray casting method to define a boundary for hatching, it creates a temporary polyline that is discarded after the hatching process. Checking the Retain Boundaries box keeps the boundary. You can specify a Polyline or Region boundary under Object Type in the Advanced Options toolbar. Polyline is the most common choice because it can be used for area and perimeter calculations.

EDITING A HATCH (HATCHEDIT)

If you have an existing associative hatch pattern, you can edit it with the **hatchedit** command. You can use **hatchedit** to fine-tune several hatching parameters on an existing associative hatch. You can access **hatchedit** by:

- Selecting the Edit Hatch button on the Modify toolbar. It's located on a flyout menu, accessed by selecting the Edit Polyline button.
- Type **hatchedit** at the `Command:` prompt.

After accessing the **hatchedit** command by either method, the Hatchedit dialog box appears as shown in Figure 7.44. The Hatchedit dialog box is similar to the Boundary Hatch dialog box (Figure 7.34) with some of the options disabled. The dialog box pro-

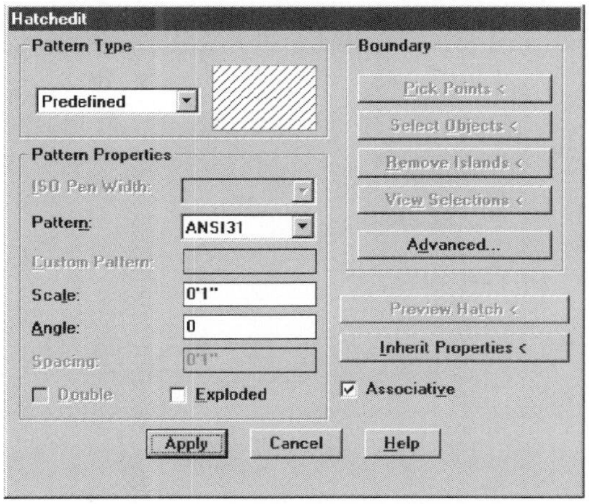

Figure 7.44
The Hatchedit dialog box allows you to edit an existing associative hatch pattern.

vides options for changing the Pattern Type (Predefined, User-defined, or Custom), Pattern, Scale, and Angle of the existing pattern. You can explode the existing hatch and change it to nonassociative. You can also access the Advanced Options dialog box and change the Style.

Tutorial 7.8: Editing a Hatch

In this final hatch tutorial, you will edit the existing associative hatch pattern you defined and applied on the hot-tub symbol.

1. Continue from the previous tutorial. You should have the AR-HBONE pattern applied to the hot-tub symbol. The drain in the middle of the symbol also contains a hatch pattern, which you are going to remove.

2.  Select the Edit Hatch button from the Modify toolbar.

AutoCAD prompts `Edit hatch object:`. Pick the AR-HBONE pattern you applied in the previous tutorial.

3. When the Hatchedit dialog box appears, select the Advanced button.

The Advanced Options dialog box appears. Change the Style to Outer. Your dialog box should look like Figure 7.45.

4. Select OK in the Advanced Options dialog box.

The Hatchedit dialog box appears.

5. Select Apply.

The hot-tub symbol reappears, with the hatch pattern removed from the drain as shown in Figure 7.46.

6.  Select the Save button from the Standard toolbar. This completes the tutorials on hatching.

Figure 7.45 *Change the Style to Outer in the Advanced Options dialog box.*

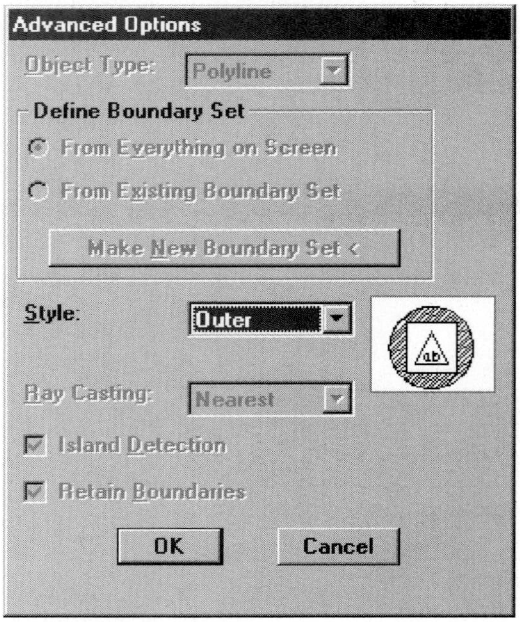

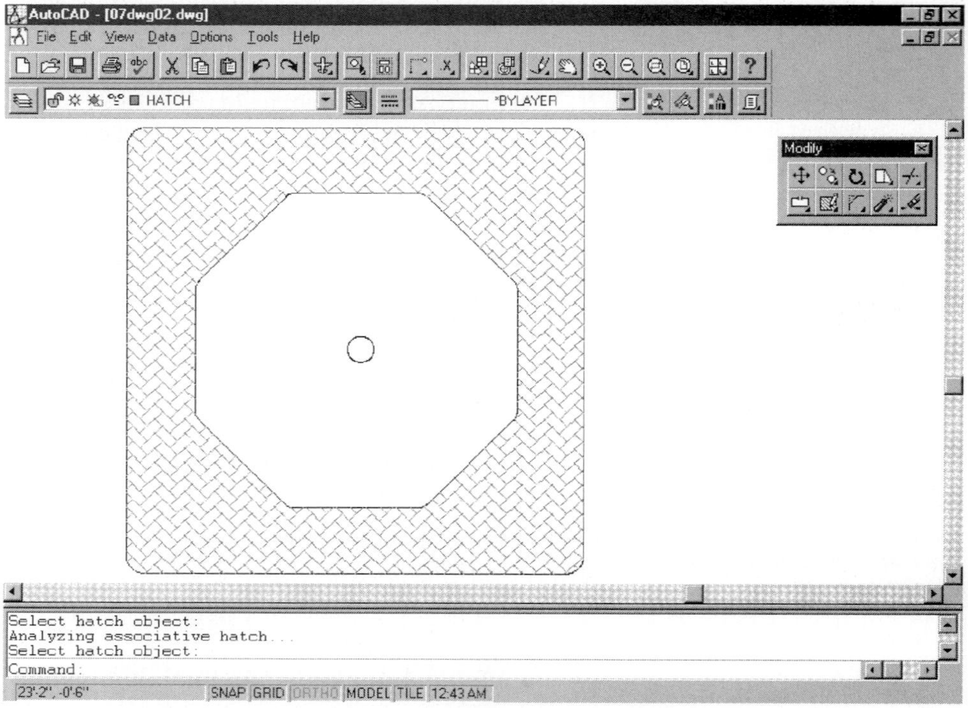

Figure 7.46 *The completed hatching tutorial.*

Understanding Common Hatching Problems

Several problems can occur when attempting to define your boundary for hatching. If you are getting `Point is outside of boundary` or `Nothing was found to make a boundary out of` error messages, there are several things you can try. First make sure you have a completely closed shape. Check the corners of the objects to make sure they meet. If you are sure you have a closed shape, select the Make New Boundary Set option in the Advanced Options dialog box to clear out any previous boundaries. When selecting the objects used to define your boundary, select only the ones directly associated with your hatch.

If you are having trouble with islands in your boundary, try the Select Objects and Remove Islands buttons to further refine the selection set. Use the View Selections button to see what objects are currently selected for the boundary. Then, use the Preview Hatch button to see the results. Continue to use these buttons until the hatch appears as you want it.

Another option has to do with the way AutoCAD creates the preview hatch. Occasionally AutoCAD will not complete the preview hatch pattern. This doesn't always mean your pattern is incorrect. If you have refined your boundary selecting and it looks close, apply it. You can always use **hatchedit** to change it.

SUMMARY

Text and hatching are two of the most effective tools used to enhance the readability of your drawings. When creating text, you first need to define your text styles. In most cases you should use the same or similar fonts, adjusting the effects for different applications. Keep your output device in mind. AutoCAD has many fonts to choose from, including the option of using other third-party fonts. While complex fonts may look impressive, they can significantly increase drawing regeneration and file size. Plotting can also be time-consuming when using complex fonts. If you need complex fonts, consider using the **qtext** command to speed regeneration and check plotting.

For creating text, the **mtext** command gives you a great deal of flexibility when entering text. You can import text from outside sources, and assign different fonts, colors, and sizes to individual letters or words in **mtext.**

Use the **bhatch** command to fill areas of your drawing with a predefined, user-defined, or custom pattern. The **bhatch** command can make hatch boundary definition easy with the Pick Points option.

After creating text or hatching, you also have the ability to edit them. Text can be edited with the **change, ddedit,** and **ddmodify** commands. **mtext** can be edited with the **ddedit** and **ddmodify** commands. You can edit hatch patterns with the **hatchedit** command. Most of the commands for creating text and hatching are available on the Draw toolbar. The editing commands for Text and Hatch are available on the Modify toolbar.

REVIEW

1. List the six effects you can apply to a text style and briefly describe the meaning of each.
2. Explain the difference between the **text** and **dtext** commands.
3. Clarify the difference between the Align and Fit justify options.
4. Describe features that are unique to creating text with the **mtext** command.
5. Recite the three commands that are commonly used to edit existing text and the advantages and disadvantages of each.
6. If you wanted your text on a drawing to plot .375″ high and your drawing scale factor was 3, illustrate how you would determine the correct text style height.
7. List three different steps you could take to speed up redrawing and regeneration time on a drawing that contains a lot of text.

8. Explain associative hatching and its advantages.
9. Explain how you would avoid hatching over text that appears within the boundaries of an area to be hatched.
10. List steps you would take if you get a `Point is outside boundary` error message when attempting to define your boundary for hatching.

EXERCISE 7

1. Load the title block drawing 7-1 shown in Figure 7.47. Create text styles and insert the appropriate text so your completed title block looks like Figure 7.48.
2. Load the lathe gear drawing 7-2 as shown in Figure 7.49. Hatch the appropriate areas so your completed drawing looks like Figure 7.50.

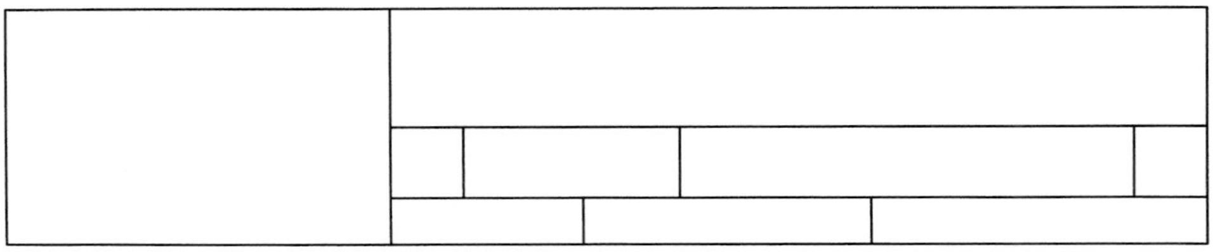

Figure 7.47 *Create the appropriate text styles to complete the title block.*

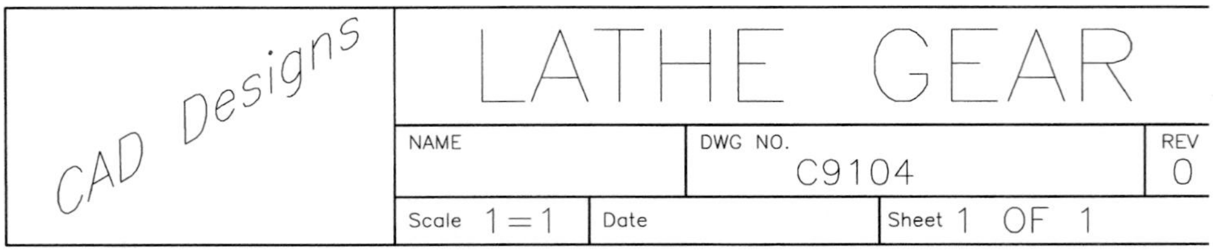

Figure 7.48 *The completed title block with inserted text.*

Figure 7.49 *The lathe gear before hatching.*

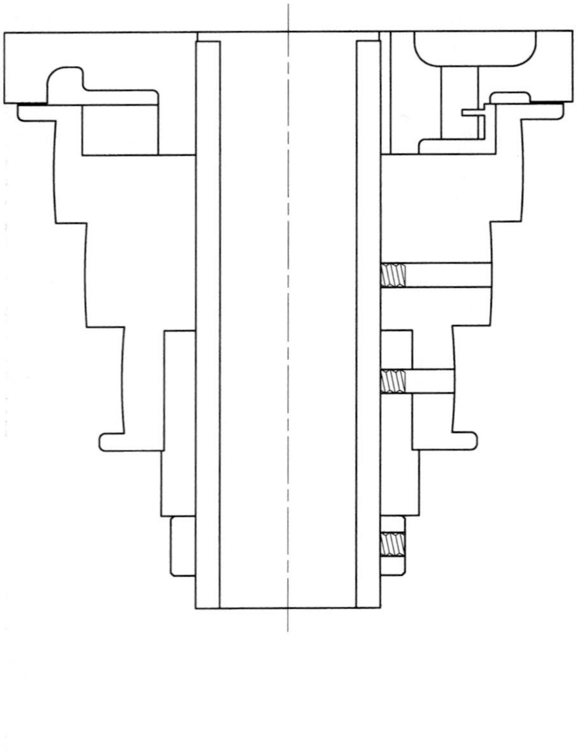

Figure 7.50 *The lathe gear with the appropriate areas hatched.*

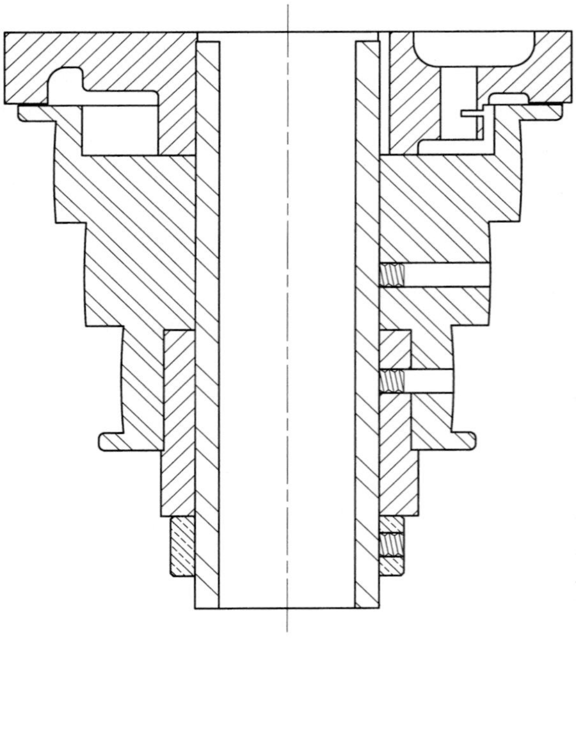

UNIT

8 DRAWING ACCURATELY

OVERVIEW

When you attempt to pick points on-screen, you may have difficulty locating an exact position without some type of help. Typing the point coordinates is one method. AutoCAD has several other methods to help control the movement of the crosshair. Another method is the Snap function introduced in Unit 2, "Creating Your First Drawing." This unit introduces another method for accurately locating precise points: the Object Snap, or OSnap, function. You will also work with point filters, another technique that will help you draw accurately as well as increase your productivity.

OBJECTIVES

- Understand the relationship between Object Points and Object Snap.
- Draw with the temporary Object Snap modes.
- Draw with the running Object Snap modes.
- Control the aperture size for Object Snap.
- Create new points by filtering out the point component you want.

INTRODUCTION

A competent draftsperson can locate a point on a drawing by using a straight edge and rule with a fair amount of accuracy. Using the point as a reference, the draftsperson can draw more objects. One of the first steps in creating accurate drawings is to locate precise points. One method of locating precise points in AutoCAD is to type the coordinates, as you did in Unit 4, "Basic CAD Drawing Techniques." In most cases, however, you do not have such complete information that you can type all the points. Regardless of the information available, typing points is tedious work and prone to typing errors. The Object Snap, or OSnap function is another method of accurately locating precise points.

Object Snap is a very useful tool. The term *Object Snap* refers to a function in which the crosshairs are forced to snap exactly to a specific point or location of an existing object. One of the primary advantages of using Object Snap is that you don't have to pick an exact point. Suppose you want to draw a line beginning at the exact intersection of two previously created lines. If the intersection point of the lines is not on the Snap increment, you may try to guess and pick the intersection point with the crosshairs. Unfortunately, you'll probably miss. With Object Snap, you just pick somewhere near the intersection of the lines. The crosshairs automatically snap to the exact intersection. AutoCAD offers several Object Snap modes to help locate specific points on existing geometry accurately.

OUTLINE

Working with Entity Points and Object Snap
Drawing with Object Snap Modes
Tutorial 8.1: Using Temporary Object Snap Modes to Create a Circle-Top Window
Tutorial 8.2: Using Running Object Snap Modes to Create a Divided Octagon
Tutorial 8.3: Using Multiple Running Object Snap Modes
Tutorial 8.4: Using Point Filters to Locate a Circle in the Center of a Rectangle
Summary
Review
Exercises

WORKING WITH ENTITY POINTS AND OBJECT SNAP

When you create geometry in AutoCAD, vectors are used to display the objects drawn on the graphics screen. A vector may be defined as a quantity completely specified by a magnitude and a direction. Using vectors allows AutoCAD to store a great deal of information about each object. A line, for example, has a starting point, ending point, and specific length; and the line points in a certain direction. Different types of objects have different types of information associated with them. A circle, for example, has a center point and radius.

The vector information stored with each object enables AutoCAD to perform calculations on the object. By accessing the information stored with each object, you can locate endpoints, midpoints, intersections, center points, and other geometric information. The Object Snap function allows you to access this information and select these exact points when creating geometry. It is very important that the new user of AutoCAD understand it is never accurate to just guess, or "eyeball," locations and points. What may appear accurate on-screen will probably be inaccurate when plotted, and it will definitely be inaccurate in the drawing database. Generally, the plotting device has a higher level of precision than the computer display and, therefore, can display mistakes that otherwise seemed fine on the computer display.

FOR THE PROFESSIONAL

It is very important to maintain an accurate computer database for all of your drawings. When you begin creating a drawing on the computer, it is important that information be entered accurately. Lines that don't meet and circles that are not tangent can have grave consequences. If a CAD drawing was to be used later to create a toolpath for a Numerical Control machine, or used to calculate a bill of materials, integrity of the drawing database is essential. Just because a drawing looks good on-screen and plots correctly is no guarantee it is accurate. The professional CAD draftsperson will use the **snap** function, coordinate entry, and Object Snaps to create accurate drawings.

UNDERSTANDING OBJECT POINTS AND OBJECT SNAP

Before discussing the Object Snap modes, you should learn about the objects on which you'll use the Object Snap modes. Figure 8.1 shows the most common graphic objects and their potential snap points.

AutoCAD has 11 different Object Snap modes. The next sections explain each Object Snap mode and provide examples.

Each Object Snap mode can be abbreviated to its first three letters. Notice that the first three letters are capitalized in the following sections. These abbreviations are the only letters you need to enter to access the corresponding Object Snap mode. The following section explains the service performed by each Object Snap mode.

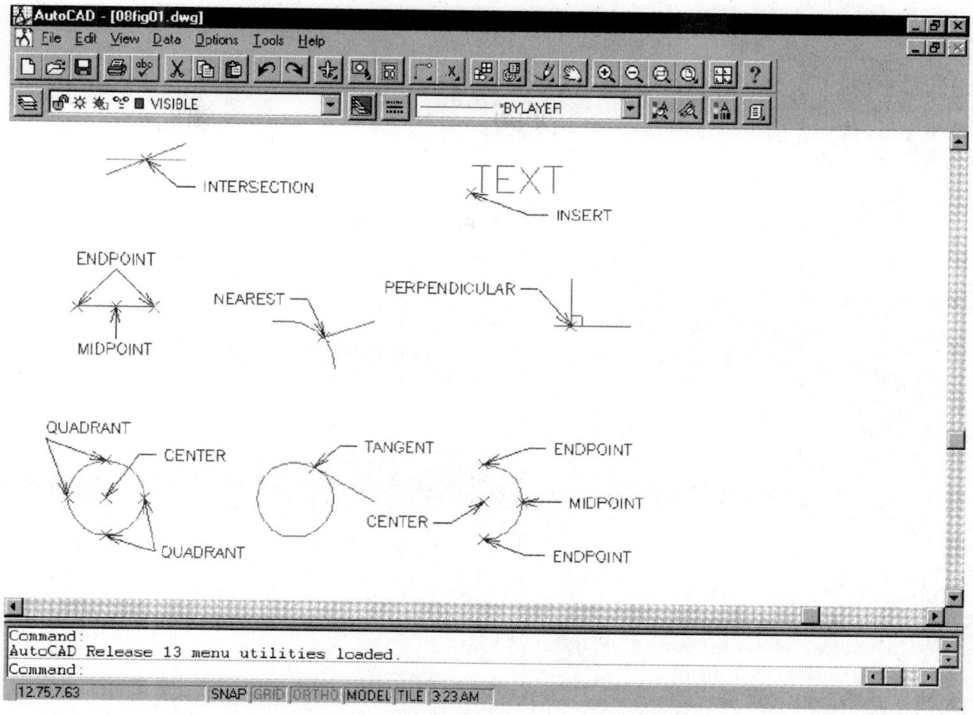

Figure 8.1
Object Snap Points on eight common graphic objects.

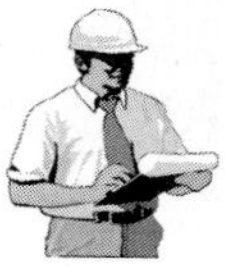

Skill Builder

Object Snaps are not commands but modes used in connection with AutoCAD drawing and editing functions. Entering **int** or **cen** at the `Command:` prompt displays an error message.

For the Professional

Object Snaps can also be picked from the cursor menu, by holding down the ⇧Shift key while using the right button on the pointing device. The cursor menu appears at the location of the crosshairs.

An alternative to typing the first three letters is to select the corresponding Object Snap button. You can find the Object Snap buttons by first selecting the Object Snap button on the Standard toolbar. When you select the Object Snap button, a flyout menu appears, displaying all of the Object Snap modes. The Object Snap button and flyout menu is shown in Figure 8.2.

endpoint A common task when you are creating geometry is to connect a line, arc, or center point of a circle to the endpoint of an existing line or arc. To select the endpoint, move the aperture box past the midpoint of the line or arc toward the end you want to pick and select. Figure 8.3 snaps a new line to the endpoint of an existing arc.

midpoint To find the midpoint of a line or arc, use the **midpoint** Object Snap mode. For example, to connect a line from any point to the midpoint of an arc, place the aperture anywhere on the arc and pick. The line automatically snaps to the midpoint of the arc (see

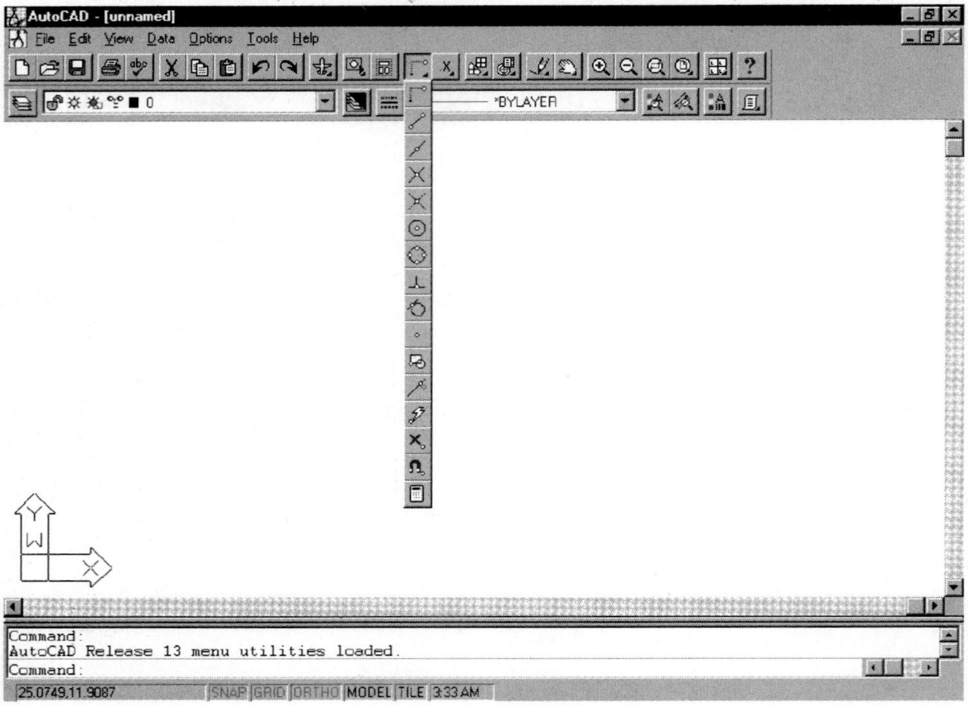

Figure 8.2
The Object Snap button on the Standard toolbar shows all the Object Snap modes in a flyout menu.

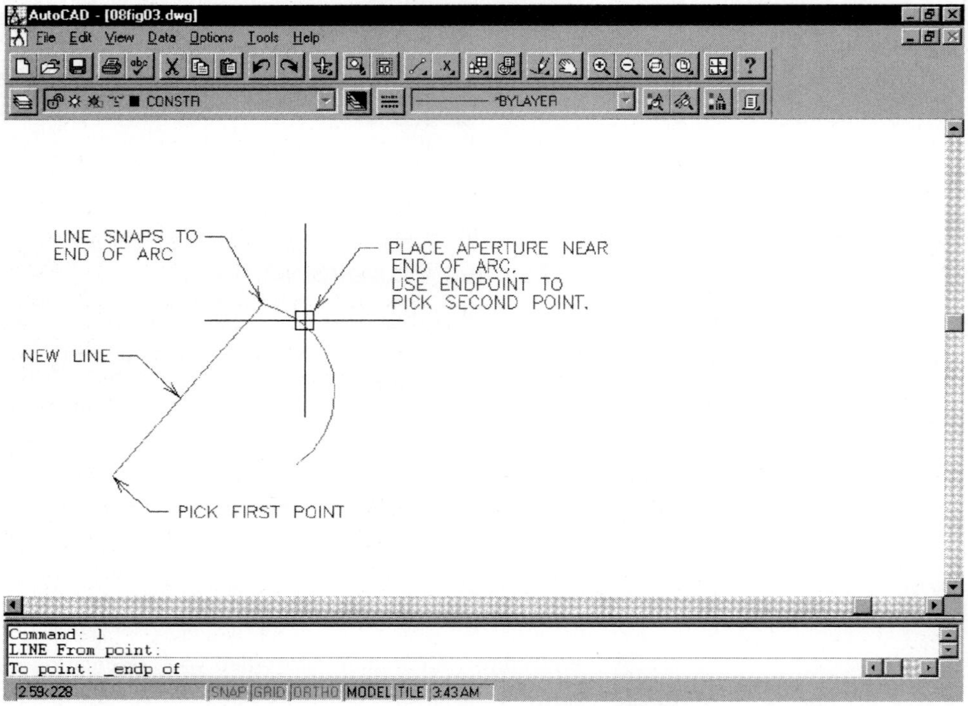

Figure 8.3
Object Snap a new line to the endpoint of an arc.

Figure 8.4). You can also snap to the midpoint of a line (see Figure 8.4). Notice that you don't need to pick anywhere near the midpoint of the arc or line to snap to the midpoint.

center The **center** option enables you to snap to the center point of an arc, circle, or donut. Figure 8.5 shows a line snapped between the center of circle A and the cen-

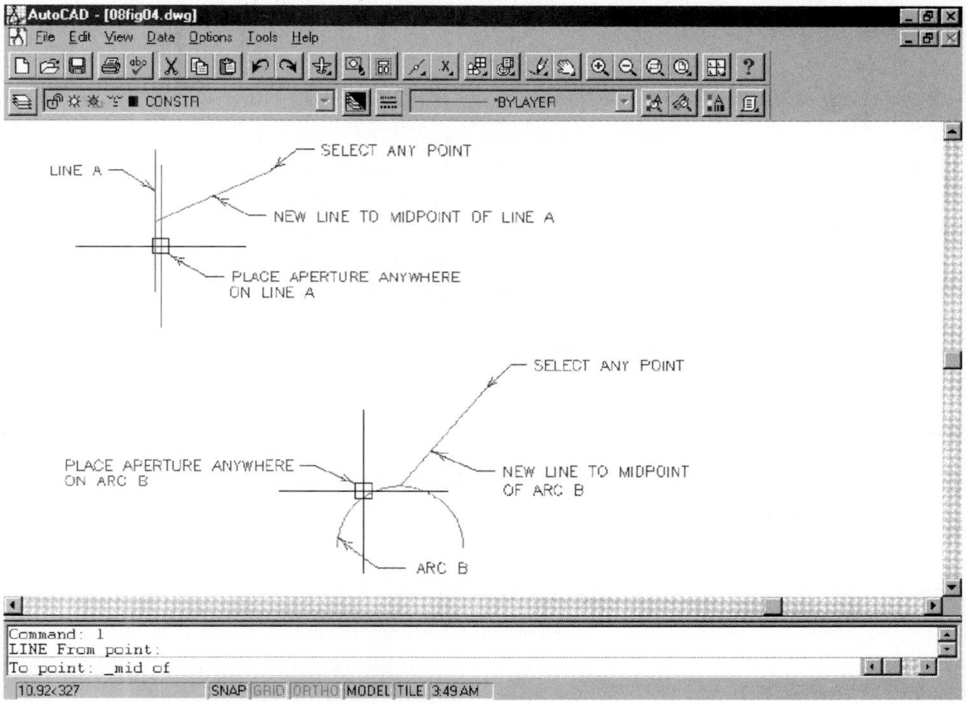

Figure 8.4
Object Snap to the midpoint of a line or arc.

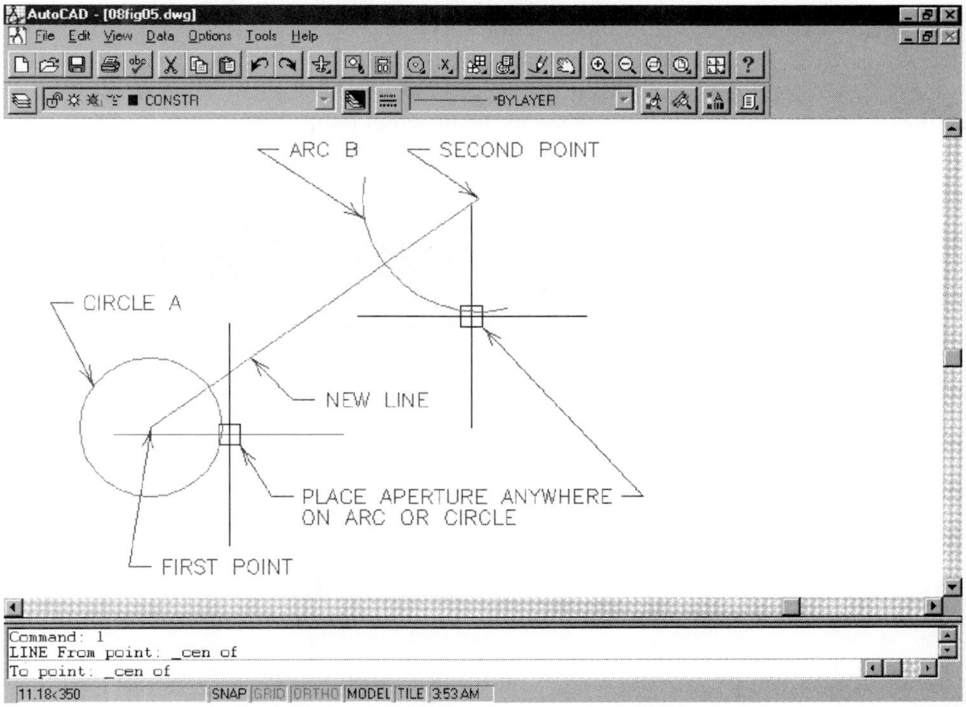

Figure 8.5
Object Snap to the center of a circle or arc.

ter of arc B. To select the center point, you must select the arc or circle itself, not the center.

NODe In addition to drawing geometry such as lines, circles, and arcs, you can define point objects in AutoCAD. A point object is referred to as a *node.* You can use point objects singularly or with other commands such as **divide** and **measure.** Unit 12,

"Advanced Drawing Techniques," covers point creation and the use of points with the **divide** and **measure** commands. Using the **node** Object Snap finds a point object (see Figure 8.6).

quadrant AutoCAD defines a quadrant as a quarter section of a circle, donut, or arc. Using the QUAdrant Object Snap mode, you can find the 0-, 90-, 180-, and 270-degree positions on a circle, donut, or arc (see Figure 8.7).

When snapping to a quadrant, locate the aperture on the circle, donut, or arc closest to the proposed quadrant. Figure 8.7 shows the endpoint of a line located at one of the quadrants in circle A.

intersection The INTersection Object Snap mode snaps to the point where objects cross each other. The INTersection mode also allows you to snap to the imaginary intersection of two objects that do not actually intersect but would if one or both were extended. The **intersection** Object Snap mode requires that there be a point (real or imaginary) in 2-D or 3-D space where an intersection occurs.

To select an intersection point with one pick, the intersection of the two objects must be inside the aperture box. Figure 8.8 shows snapping line C to the intersection point of circle A and arc B.

You can also select the intersection of objects one at a time. This method works well when geometry is crowded together and snapping to an intersection point is difficult. When you use **intersection** and select a single object, AutoCAD prompts you to select the second object. The crosshairs will snap to the intersection of the two objects selected or to the point where they would intersect if one or both were extended.

insertion When you create text in AutoCAD, you must first specify its location. The location point where you initially create the text is the insertion point. Other AutoCAD objects that have insertion points are shapes, blocks, and attributes. Figure 8.9 shows a snap to the insertion point of text.

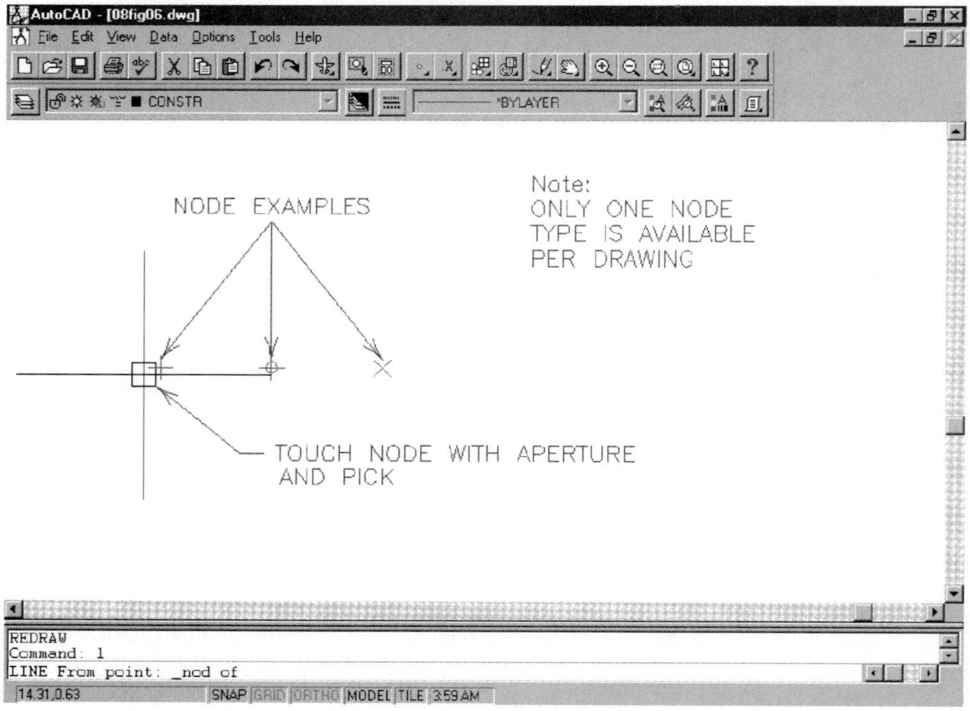

Figure 8.6
Object Snap to a point object, referred to as a node.

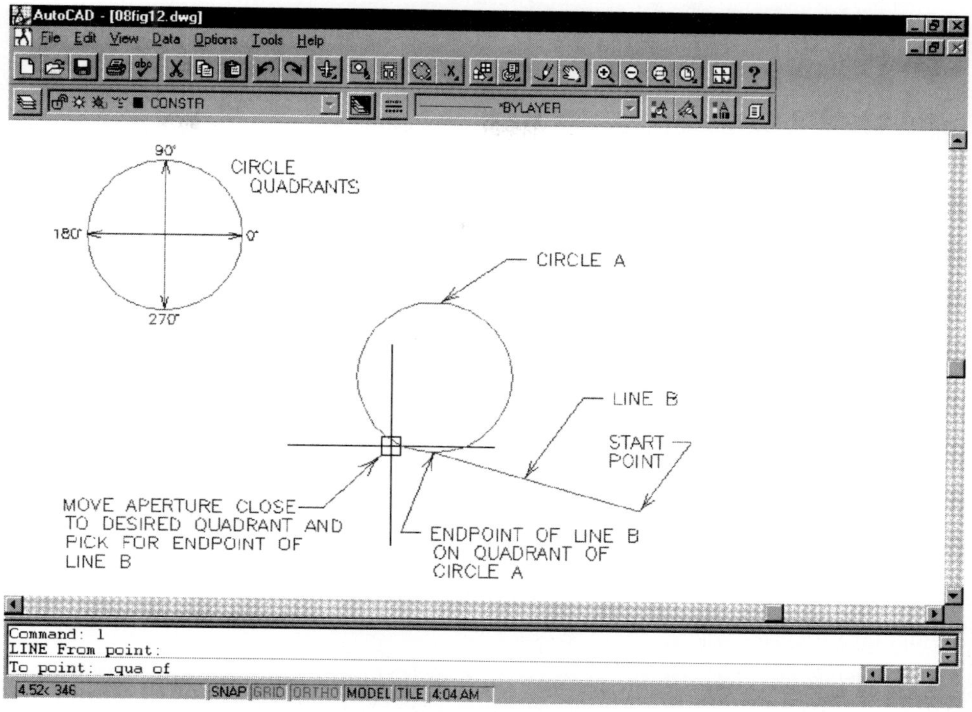

Figure 8.7
Use Object Snap QUAdrant to locate one of the quadrants on a circle.

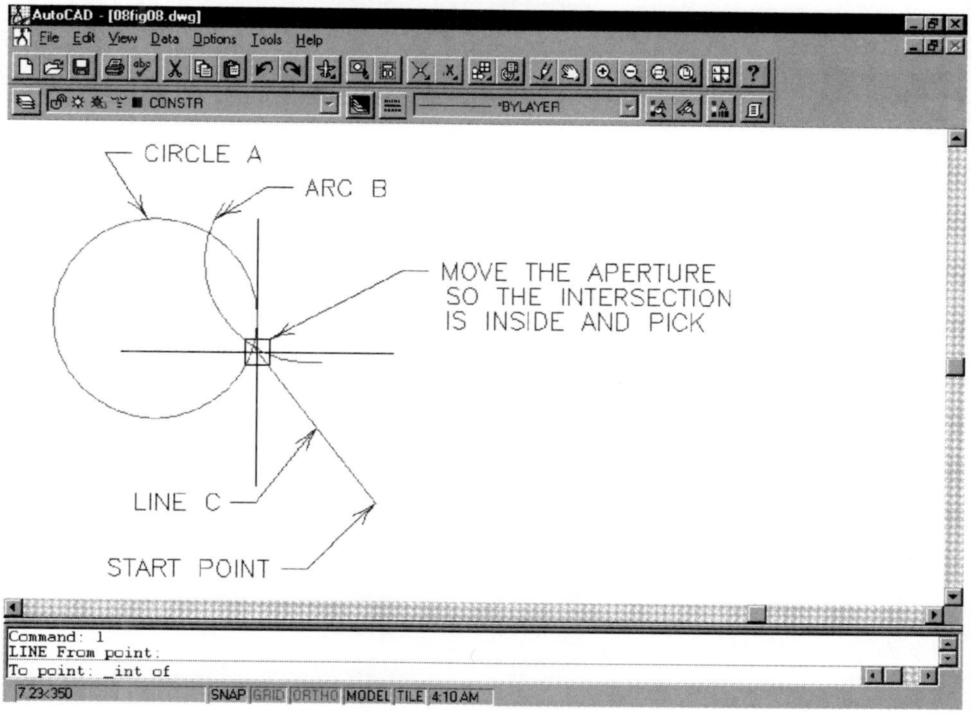

Figure 8.8
Using the **intersection** *Object Snap mode.*

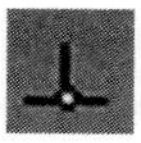

perpendicular A typical geometric construction is to snap a point on a line, arc, or circle that forms a perpendicular from the current point to the selected object. You can perform this step easily, using the **perpendicular** Object Snap. Figure 8.10 shows how the **perpendicular** Object Snap mode is used to create a line perpendicular to line B.

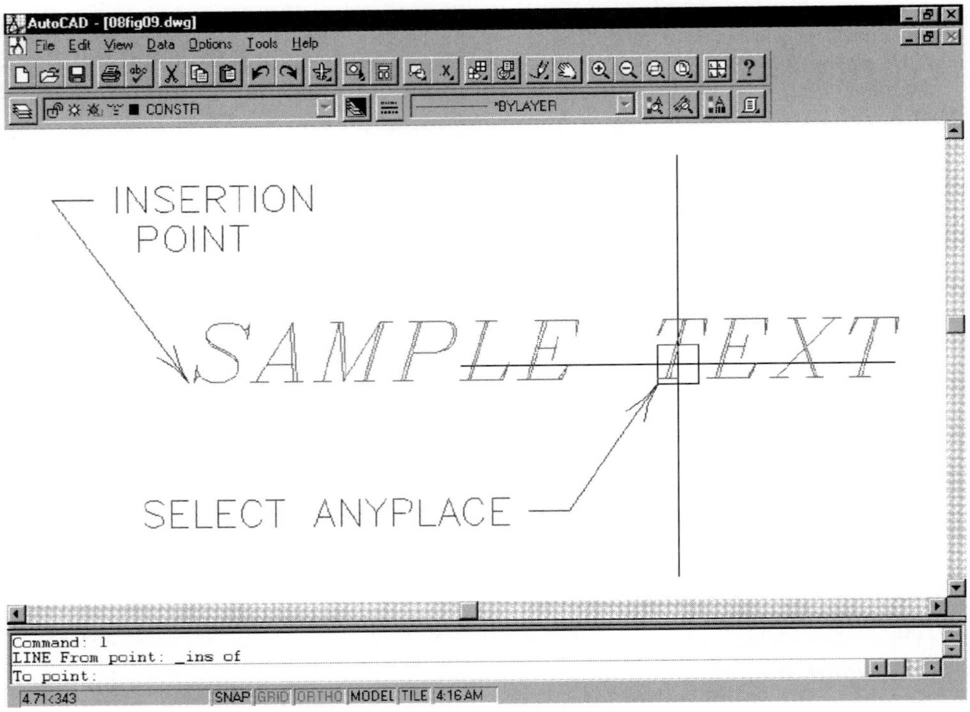

Figure 8.9
Use the **insertion** *Object Snap mode to snap to the insertion point of text.*

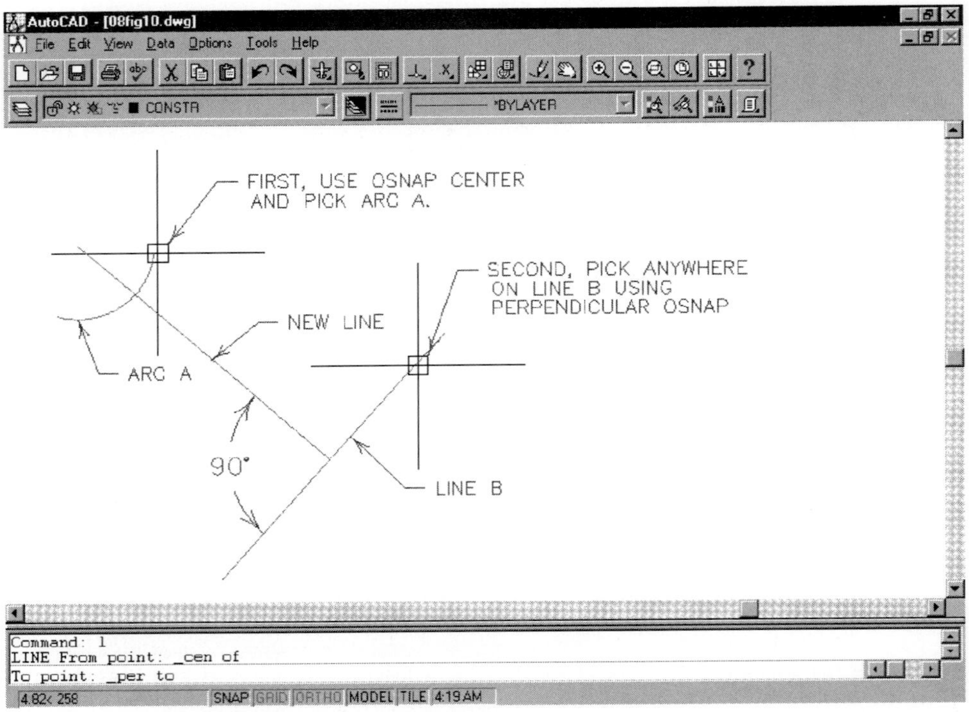

Figure 8.10
Using the **perpendicular** *Object Snap option.*

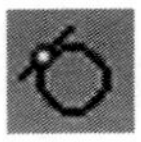

tangent Locating tangent points on arcs and circles can be difficult if you use manual drafting procedures. AutoCAD greatly simplifies this process by providing the **tangent** Object Snap mode. **tangent** enables you to snap to a point on an object that forms a tangent between the object and another point. Figure 8.11 shows a new line tangent to arc A and circle B.

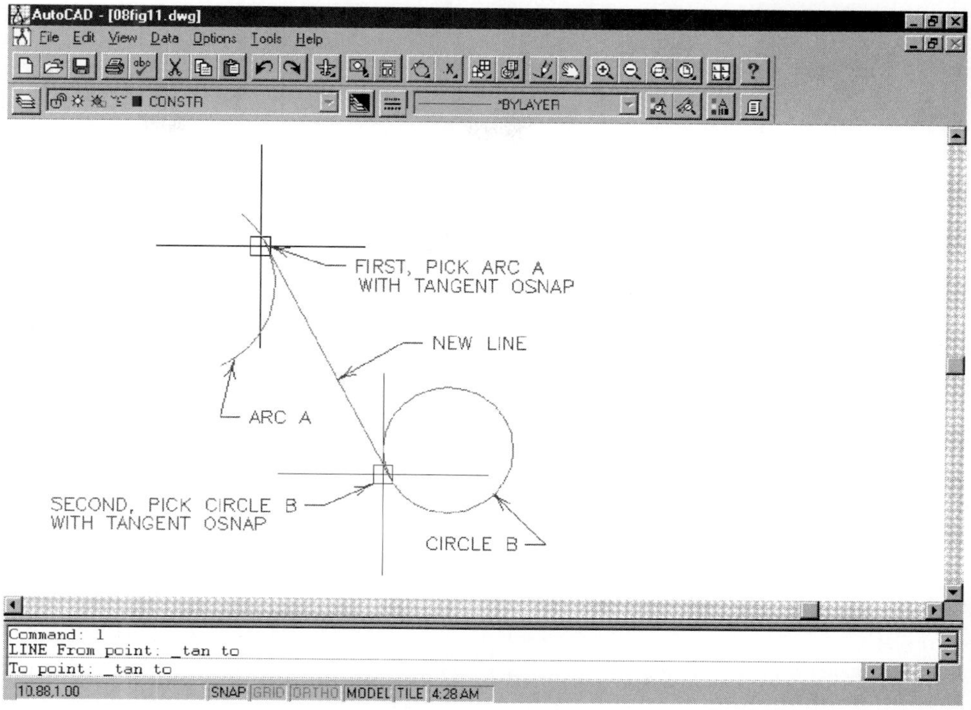

Figure 8.11
Use the **tangent** *Object Snap to draw a line tangent to a circle and arc.*

SKILL BUILDER

AutoCAD sometimes has problems finding a tangent point unless you are zoomed in close to the selected object.

nearest The **nearest** Object Snap mode snaps to a point on a line, circle, arc, or other object that is nearest to the center of the target box, where the crosshairs intersect. Figure 8.12 shows how **nearest** is used to connect a line from a point to a location on an arc.

from Another useful tool for precisely locating points in a drawing is the **from** function. The **from** function allows you to use any position on-screen as a base point for entering relative coordinates. For example, let's say you want to draw an 18″-diameter circular ceiling light fixture in a floor plan that's 5 feet in either direction from the corner of a room. You could use the **from** function to select the corner and then enter relative coordinates to locate the center of the circle. The command sequence in this example would be:

Select **circle** from the draw toolbar.

At the CIRCLE 3P/2P/TTR <Center point>: prompt, type **from** and press Enter.

At the FROM prompt, type **int** and press Enter.

At the of prompt, pick the wall corner and type **@5′,5′** and press Enter.

At the Diameter/<Radius> <default>: prompt, type 18 and press Enter.

If you press Enter at the From point: prompt of the **line** command or the Center/<Start point>: prompt of the **arc** command, the crosshair snaps to the endpoint of the last object created. You also can type a relative coordinate, which begins a new object relative to the last object.

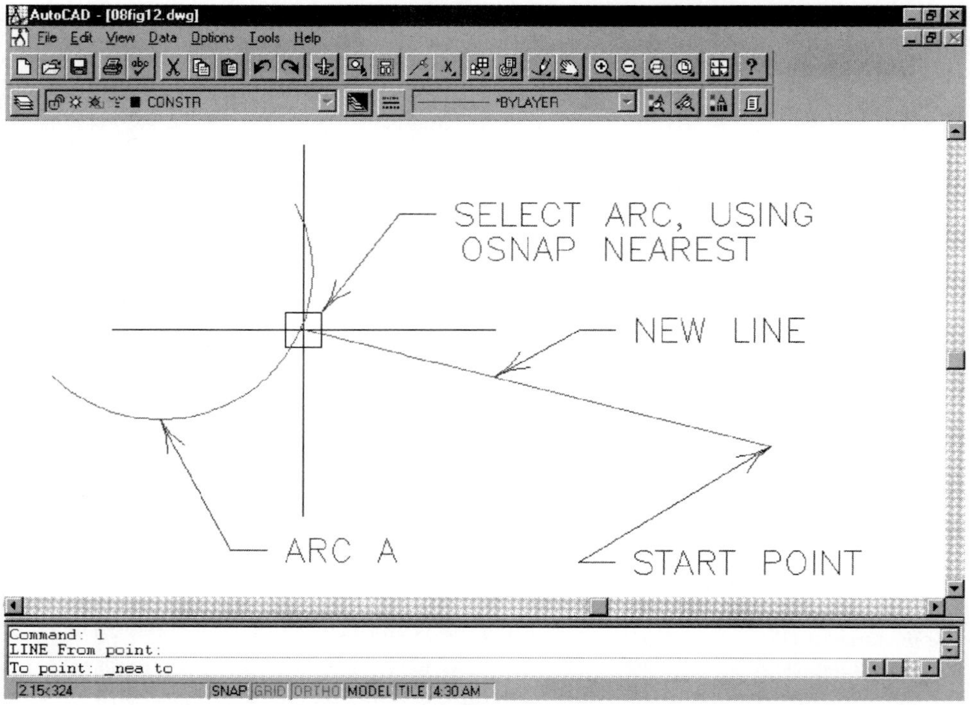

Figure 8.12
Using the **nearest** *Object Snap mode to draw a line to an arc.*

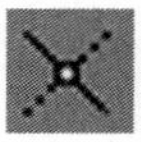

apparent intersection This Object Snap snaps to the **apparent** intersection of two objects which may or may not intersect in 3-D space. For **apparent** intersection to work in 3-D space, the objects must appear to intersect from the current viewpoint.

DRAWING WITH OBJECT SNAP MODES

Object Snap modes can be used in different ways when creating geometry. A temporary Object Snap mode can be used for one selection only. In running Object Snap mode, the selected Snap mode is activated every time you make a selection. You can have multiple running Snap modes, and can override a running Snap mode with a temporary Object Snap mode.

Drawing with Temporary Object Snap Modes

A temporary Object Snap mode is effective for one selection only. An alternative to a temporary Object Snap is the running Object Snap mode, which is discussed in the next section. Use any of the following methods to activate a temporary Object Snap mode:

- Enter an Object Snap mode by typing its first three letters at a prompt line. The following command sequence shows the temporary **endpoint** Object Snap:

Select the Line button from the Draw toolbar.

`From point:` **end**
`of:` *`Select the endpoint of the object you want.`*

Entering **end** at the `From point:` invokes the Object Snap **endpoint** for one command.

Skill Builder

Instead of typing **end** as the abbreviation for endpoint, you might want to type **endp.** If you accidentally enter **end** at the `Command:` prompt rather than at a prompt line, you will save your drawing and exit AutoCAD.

- From the Standard toolbar, select the Object Snap button. The flyout menu shows all of the Object Snap modes. Pick the Object Snap mode you want (refer to Figure 8.2).
- Hold down the ⇧Shift key and click the right mouse button, or the middle button of a three-button mouse. Either of these methods activates the cursor menu of Osnap commands. The cursor menu appears at the location of the screen crosshair. Select the Object Snap you want, and the cursor menu disappears. The selected Object Snap is enabled for one pick (see Figure 8.13).

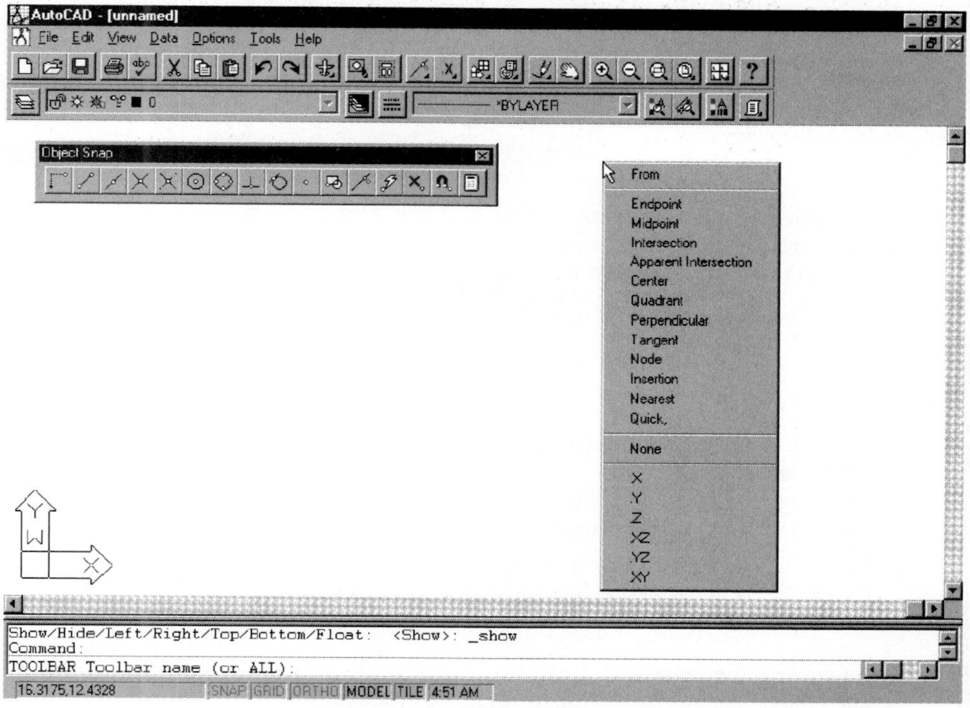

Figure 8.13
The Object Snap flyout menu displays all available Object Snap modes.

Tutorial 8.1: Using Temporary Object Snap Modes to Create a Circle-Top Window

In this tutorial, you will use temporary Object Snaps to create the circle-top window shown in Figure 8.14. Because this symbol is for an architectural drawing, you need to change the units. After you have completed the drawing, save the file as CTWINDOW.

1.  Select the New button from the Standard toolbar. If the AutoCAD dialog box appears, select No unless you want to save the current drawing. If you want to save the current drawing, select Yes and enter a path and drawing name using CTWINDOW for the drawing name.
2. From the Data pull-down menu, select Units. The Units Control dialog box appears. Change the units to architectural with a precision of **0′-0″**.

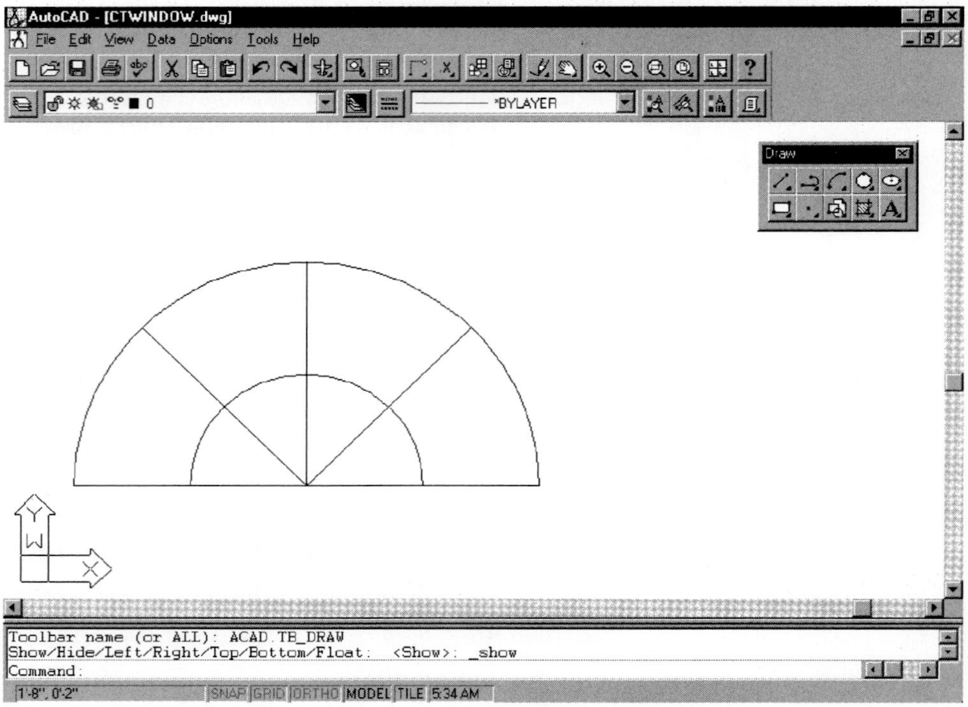

Figure 8.14 *Drawing a circle-top window using temporary Object Snap modes.*

3.  Draw the first horizontal and vertical line. Make sure the Draw toolbar appears on your screen. Select the Line button from the Draw toolbar.

```
From point: 2',3'
To point: 7',3'
To point: 7',8'
To point:
```

Use the **zoom** command to adjust your display to see the lines.

4. Draw the second horizontal line.

 Select Line from the draw toolbar.

```
From point: 7',3"
To point: 12',3"
To point:
```

5. Begin drawing the inner arc.

 Select the Arc Start Center End arc from the Arc flyout on the Draw toolbar.

```
<Start point>: mid
```

AutoCAD is now waiting for the midpoint of an object.

6. Move the aperture box to the middle of line C,D and click the Pick button (see Figure 8.15).

```
Center: int
```

7. Now select point C (see Figure 8.15).

```
<End point>: mid
```

8. Move the aperture box to pick the middle of line A,C (see Figure 8.15).

The drawing should now look like that in Figure 8.16.

9. Begin drawing the outer arc.

10.  Select the Arc Start Center End button from the Arc flyout on the Draw toolbar.

```
<Start point>: end
```

AutoCAD is now waiting for an end of object selection.

11. Pick point D, as shown in Figure 8.15.

```
Center: int
```

12. Pick point C (refer to Figure 8.15).

```
Center/End/<Second Point>: c
<End point>: end
```

Move the target box to point B and pick that point (refer to Figure 8.15).

13. Continue with the outer arc.

```
Command: press enter (this repeats the previous command)
Center/<Start point>: end
```

14. Move the target box to point B and pick that point, as shown in Figure 8.15, and click the Pick button.

```
Center: int
```

15. Pick point C (refer to Figure 8.15).

```
Angle/Length of chord/<End point>: end
```

16. Move the aperture box to point A and pick that point (refer to Figure 8.15).

The drawing should now look like that in Figure 8.17.

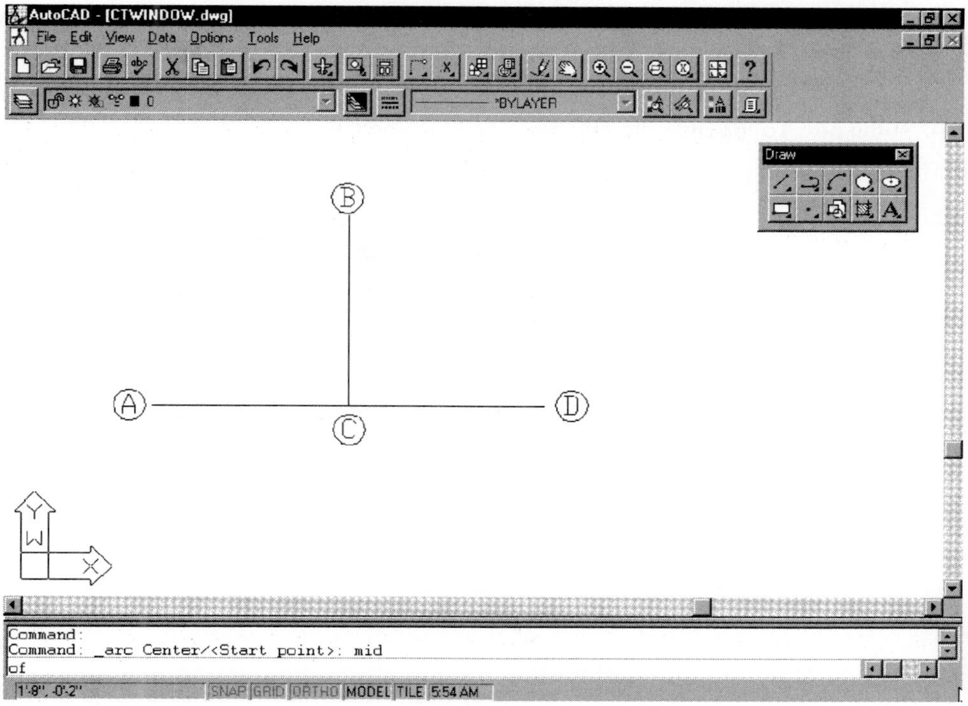

Figure 8.15
Use Object Snap to create the inner arc of the circle-top window.

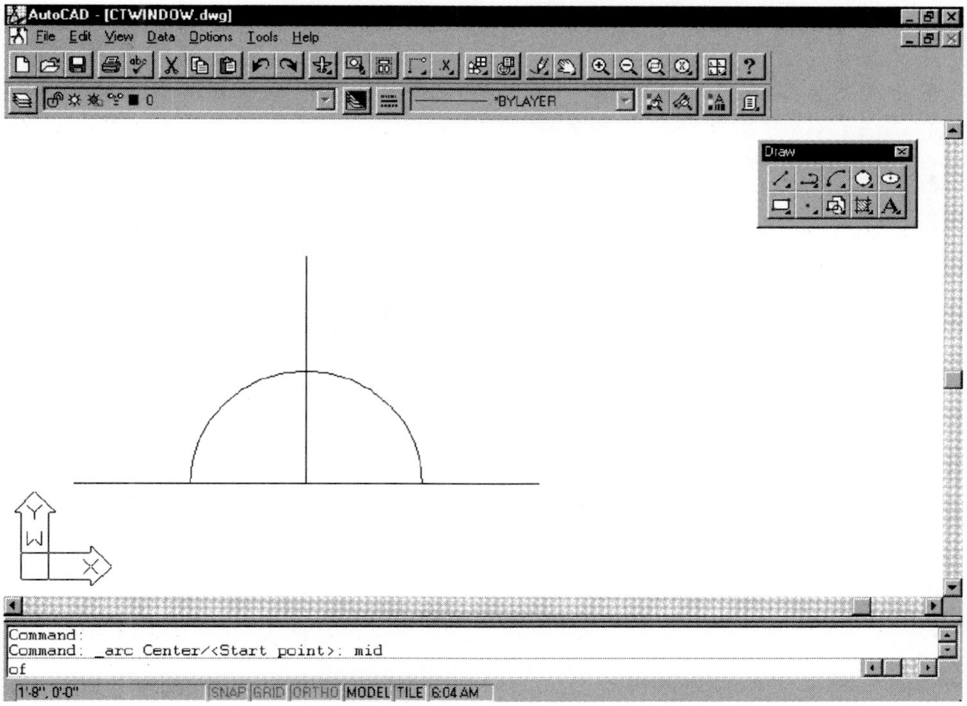

Figure 8.16
The circle-top window with the inner arc complete.

17. Issue the **line** command.

Select Line from the Draw toolbar.

`From point:` **`int`**

18. Move the aperture box to point C, as shown in Figure 8.15, and press the Pick button.

19. At the `To point:` prompt, enter **mid** and select the middle of the outer arc at point E (see Figure 8.18).

20. At the next `To point:` prompt, press Enter to end the command.

21. Issue the **line** command again.

Select Line from the Draw toolbar.

`From point:` **`cen`**

22. Move the aperture box to point F, and pick that point (see Figure 8.18).

23. At the `To point:` prompt, enter **mid** and then pick point F (refer to Figure 8.18).

24. At the next **`To point:`** prompt, press Enter to end the command.

25.  Select the Save button from the Standard toolbar.

You have now completed the circle-top window, as shown in Figure 8.14.

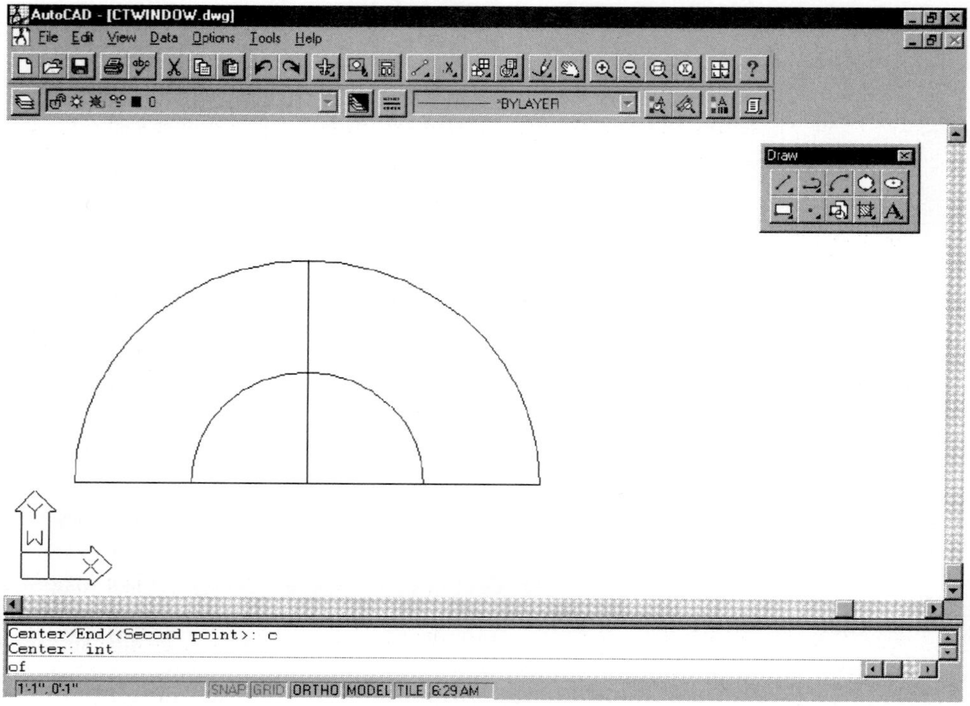

Figure 8.17
The circle-top window with the outer arc complete.

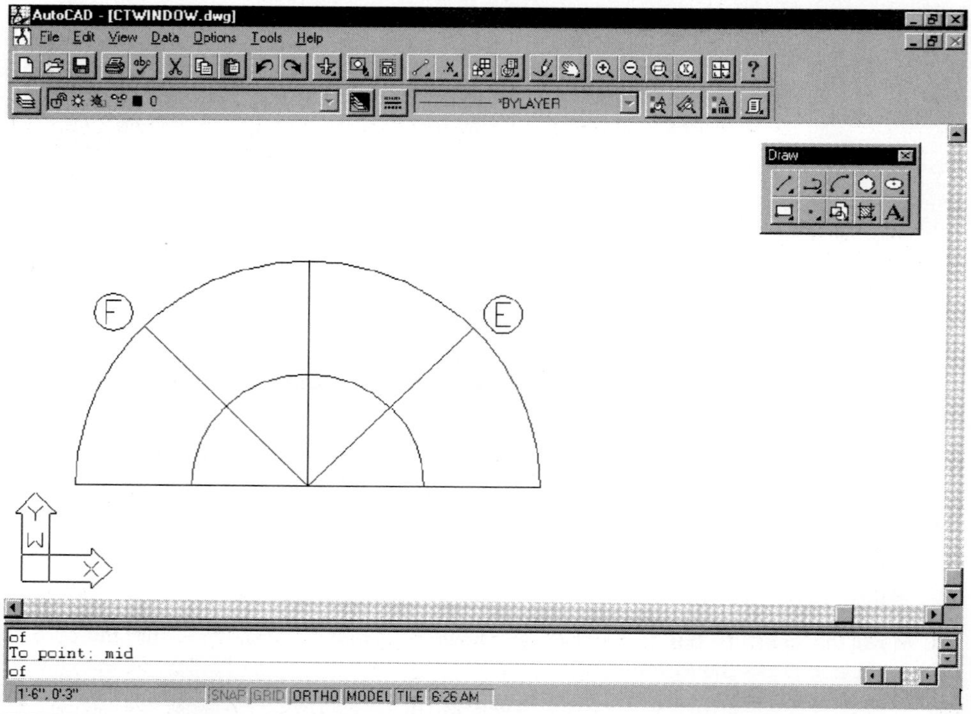

Figure 8.18
Drawing diagonal lines for the circle-top window.

Using Running Object Snap Modes (osnap and ddosnap)

An earlier section explained the use of temporary Object Snap modes. You can access these temporary Osnaps by entering the first three letters at a prompt line during a command sequence, selecting the options from the pull-down menu, floating cursor menu, or clicking the Object Snap icon in the Standard toolbar. When you use one of these methods, the Object Snap mode is activated for one selection only. When AutoCAD prompts you to indicate a point, you can use a temporary Object Snap mode to help you locate that point precisely on existing geometry.

The temporary Object Snap modes work well in many situations. If you plan to use an Object Snap frequently, you can set up a running object snap mode. When you set up a running Object Snap mode, the chosen Object Snap is activated every time you make a selection. Any of the following methods will set a running object snap mode:

- Access the Running Object Snap dialog box (see Figure 8.19). When you have the Running Object Snap dialog box displayed, select the Object Snap modes you want. You can access the Running Object Snap dialog box as follows:
  - Select the Running Osnap button from the Osnap flyout toolbar.
  - From the Options menu, choose Running Object Snap.
- At the `Command:` prompt, enter **ddosnap** to access the Running Object Snap dialog box.
- At the `Command:` prompt, enter **osnap.** AutoCAD prompts with `Object snap modes:`. Enter the first three letters of the Object Snap you want.

AutoCAD lets you know that an Object Snap mode has been selected by automatically displaying the aperture box whenever a command is started. Under normal use the aperture box is not displayed until an Object Snap has been selected.

To discontinue a running Object Snap, enter *none* at the `Object snap modes:` prompt. You can also deselect the Object Snap mode in the Running Object Snap dialog box.

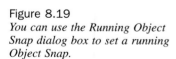

Skill Builder

You can use a temporary Object Snap to supersede the running Object Snap mode for a given selection. As with using temporary Object Snaps, the temporary snap will override any running Object Snap modes for one selection.

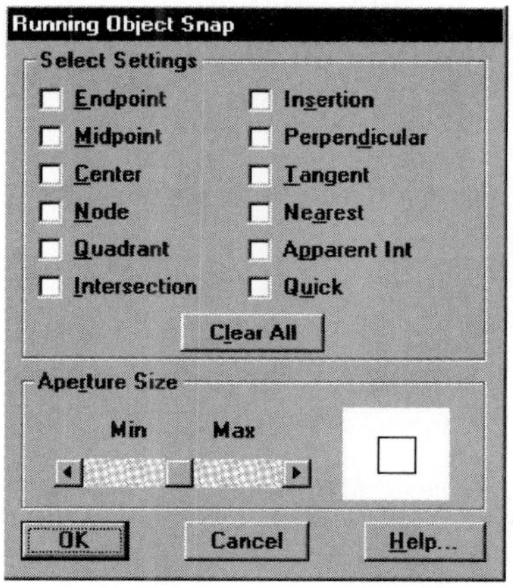

Figure 8.19
You can use the Running Object Snap dialog box to set a running Object Snap.

Tutorial 8.2: Using Running Object Snap Modes to Create a Divided Octagon

In this tutorial, you will use running Object Snaps to create the divided octagon shown in Figure 8.20. To create the octagon, follow these steps:

1.  From the Standard toolbar, select Open. If prompted with the Save Changes dialog box, select Yes and save the previous work.
2. Open drawing 08dwg01.
   You should now have the drawing shown in Figure 8.21 in your drawing area.
3. From the Options menu, choose Running Object Snap.
4. In the Running Object Snaps dialog box, choose Endpoint.

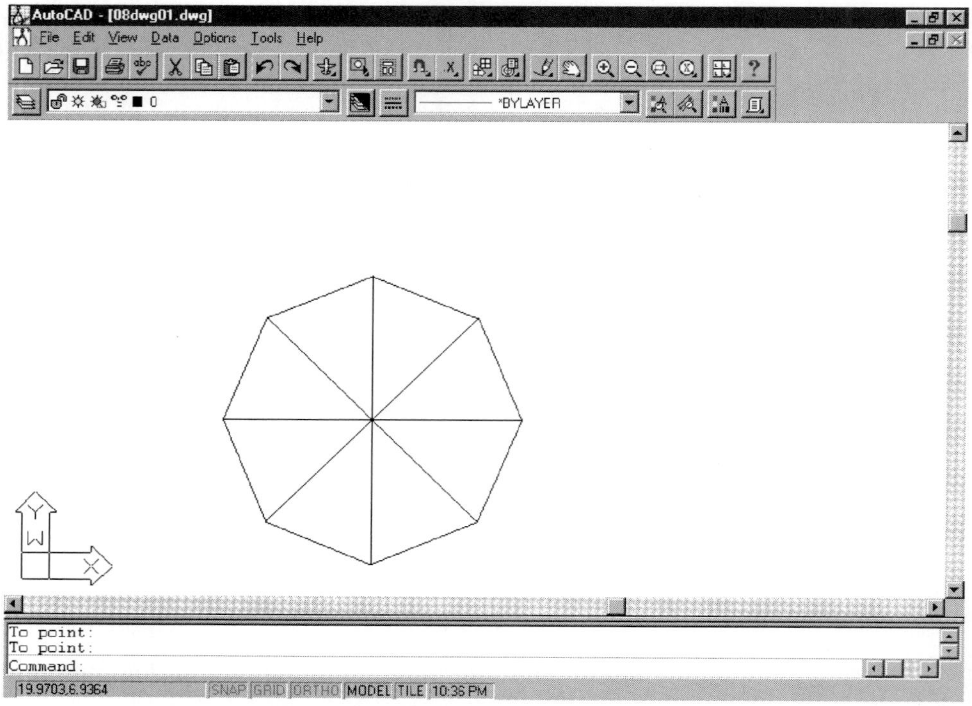

Figure 8.20
Draw a divided octagon using running Object Snap modes.

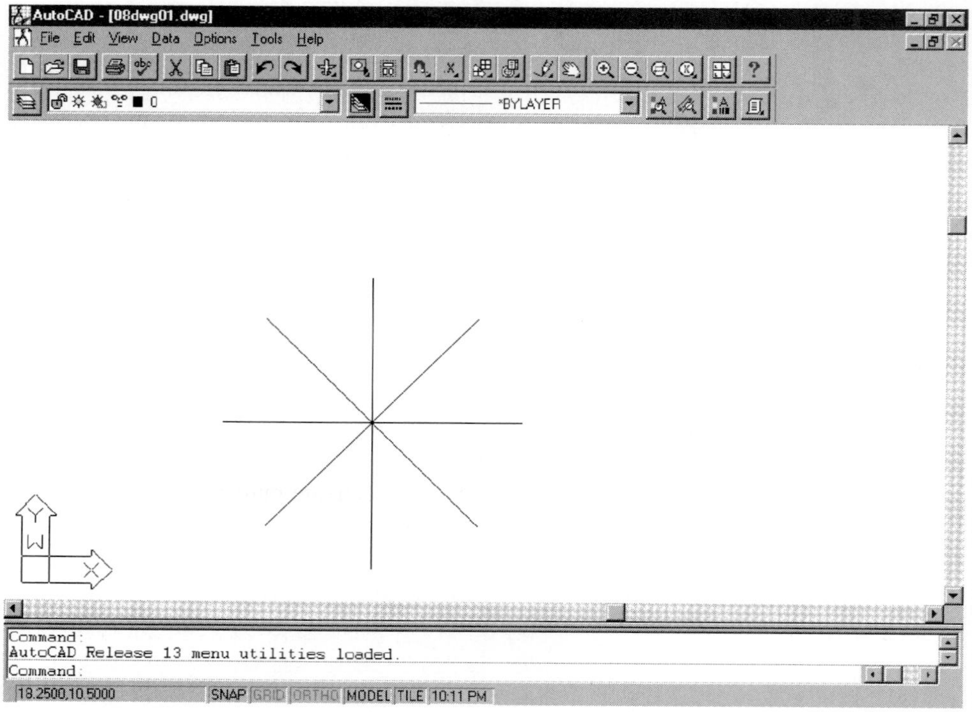

Figure 8.21
Open the 08DWG01 drawing in preparation for creating a divided octagon.

This command sets the running Object Snap to the END of the Object Snap setting.

5.  Choose the Line button from the Draw toolbar.
6. At the `From point:` prompt, move the aperture box and pick point A (see Figure 8.22).
7. At the `To point:` prompt, move the aperture box and pick point B.
8. Continue responding to the `To point:` prompts by moving the aperture box and picking each point (see Figure 8.22).
9. After you finish point H, respond to the next `To point:` prompt by pressing Enter.

You now have the divided octagon shown previously in Figure 8.20.

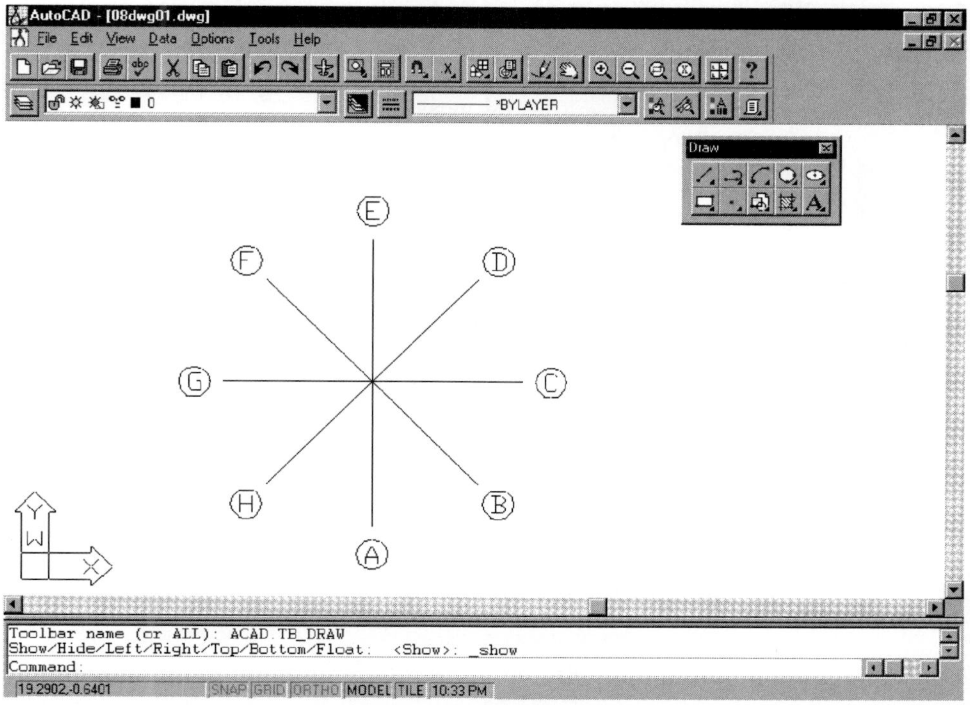

Figure 8.22
Select the endpoints to create the divided polygon.

For the Professional

At times you may encounter situations where you try to select a point and the crosshairs jump to the end of a line that is close by. The problem is most likely that a running Object Snap is still selected. When you try to select a point, you may have the other line within the aperture box. AutoCAD remembers the running Osnap and selects that point. To correct this, turn off the running Object Snap using the Running Object Snap dialog box.

Using Multiple Running Object Snap Modes

In addition to using single Object Snap modes, you can direct AutoCAD to use multiple Object Snap modes. When you use multiple Object Snap modes, AutoCAD chooses the point closest to the center of the pickbox that meets the criteria of one of the set Object Snap modes. You can activate multiple Object Snap modes in one of two ways:

- At the `Command:` prompt, enter **osnap.** When AutoCAD prompts with `Object snap modes:`, enter the first three letters of the Object Snap modes you want, separated by commas.
- Access the Running Object Snap dialog box (see Figure 8.19). When you have the Running Object Snap dialog box displayed, select the Object Snap modes you want. You can access the Running Object Snap dialog box as follows:

- Select the Running Osnap button from the Osnap flyout toolbar.
- From the Options menu, choose Running Object Snap.
- At the `Command:` prompt, enter **ddosnap.**

TUTORIAL 8.3: USING MULTIPLE RUNNING OBJECT SNAP MODES

In this tutorial, you learn how to use multiple running Object Snap modes. Follow these steps:

1.  From the Standard toolbar, select New. If prompted with the Save Changes dialog box, select No. Enter a name for the drawing and accept the dialog box.

2.  Choose the Line button from the Draw toolbar.

3. At the `From point:` prompt, move the crosshair to the lower-left portion of the screen and pick a point near the location of A (see Figure 8.23).

4. At the `To point:` prompt, move the crosshair to the upper-right portion of the drawing area and pick point B.

5. At the `To point:` prompt, press Enter to exit the command.

You should now have a line similar to that in Figure 8.23.

6. From the Options menu, select Running Object Snap. The Running Object Snap dialog box appears.

7. Select the Endpoint and Midpoint options and click OK (see Figure 8.24).

8.  Choose the Line button from the Draw toolbar.

Notice that the aperture box automatically appears on the crosshairs and is waiting for a selection.

9. At the `From point:` prompt, move the crosshairs close to point B (see Figure 8.23). When the line is within the aperture box, pick that point.

Now move your crosshair away from the line. Notice that the line begins at the exact endpoint of the previous line.

10. At the `To point:` prompt, enter **u** to undo your last selection.

11. The `From point:` prompt appears again. This time, instead of selecting the endpoint, move your crosshairs toward the center of the line.

Notice that the aperture box automatically appears. When the middle of the line is within the aperture box, pick the point. Now move your crosshair away from the line. This time, notice that the line begins at the middle of the previous line.

12. At the `To point:` prompt, press Enter to exit the Line command.

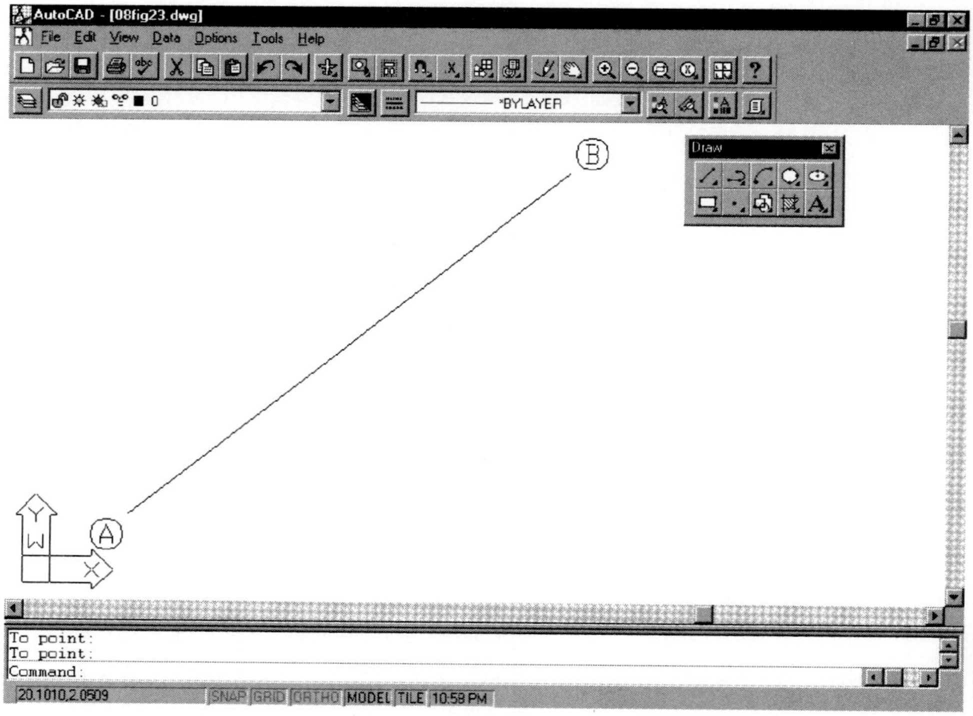

Figure 8.23
Creating line A,B.

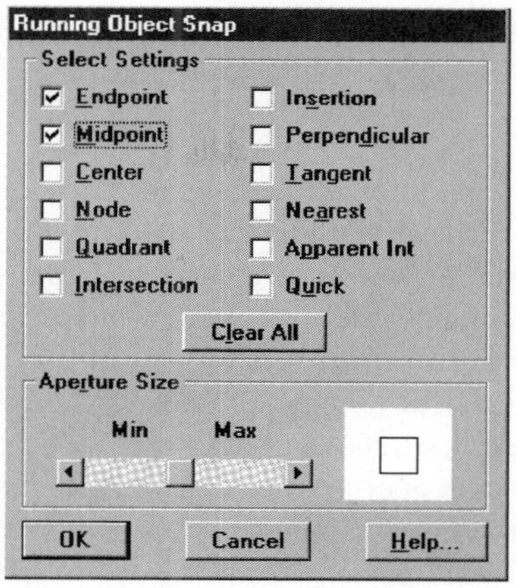

Figure 8.24
Select Endpoint and Midpoint Object Snap modes in the Running Object Snap dialog box.

Using QUIck Object Snap Modes

When you select geometry in AutoCAD by using Object Snap modes, AutoCAD searches for the best solution to your request. In a simple drawing, this process happens very quickly. As drawings become more complex, however, finding the Object Snap may take some time. You can speed up this process by selecting the QUIck modifier for the Object Snap mode.

When you use the QUIck modifier, the method of picking the best point is overridden, and AutoCAD picks the first point that meets the selection criteria set with the running Object Snap mode. The problem you may find with using QUIck Object Snaps is that the first AutoCAD selection may not be the best choice. In most cases, though, the QUIck mode works to your advantage and helps increase productivity. You can access the QUIck mode in one of two ways:

- When you enter Object Snap modes by typing the first three letters at a prompt line, precede them with QUI. The following command sequence shows the QUIck temporary Object Snap:
  Select Line from the Draw toolbar.

  ```
  From point: qui,endp,int
  of: Select the endpoint of the object you want.
  ```

  Entering **qui,endp,int** invokes the QUIck Object Snap for whichever criteria is met first, either end or int.
- Select the Quick check box in the Running Object Snap dialog box.

Turning Running Object Snaps Off

When you are finished using a particular set of running Object Snaps, you can change them to another **snap**, set of snaps, or you can turn the running Object Snaps off. You can turn the Running Object Snaps off with one of three methods:

- Select Clear All from the Running Object Snap dialog box.
- At the `Command:` prompt, enter **osnap.** When AutoCAD prompts with `Object snap modes:`, enter **none.**

You can also turn the Running Object Snaps off for one command with the following method:

- Select the Snap to None button on the Object Snap flyout menu on the Standard toolbar or Object Snap toolbar.

Controlling Aperture Box Size

The aperture box appears on-screen when you enter an Object Snap mode or use the **osnap** command. You can enlarge or reduce the size of the aperture box. Do not confuse the aperture box with the pickbox. The aperture box appears on-screen only when Object Snap modes are used. The pickbox appears on-screen when you issue any command that activates the `Select objects:` prompt. The pickbox is displayed in place of the crosshairs.

Enlarging the aperture box makes it cover a wider area, enabling you to place and pick objects more easily. Enlarging the aperture box also makes it cover more potential pick points. However, these enlargements can force AutoCAD to process the information longer before determining the best point, which can slow down the computer significantly.

Reducing the size of the aperture box makes it cover a narrower area. This lessens the potential pick process, speeding up AutoCAD's selection of the best pick point. The disadvantage to a small aperture box is that you must place it more precisely because it covers less area. Try experimenting on your own to see how changing the target box size affects point selection. You can change the aperture box size with one of two methods:

- At the `Command:` prompt, enter **aperture,** or at any prompt enter **'aperture.** Enter the aperture box size in pixels. You are limited to a number between 1 and 50 pixels.
- In the Running Object Snap dialog box, move the scroll bar between Min and Max, watching the sample target box change size. Choose OK when the target box is the size you want.

Using Point Filters for 2-D Construction

To be a productive user of AutoCAD, you need a good understanding of the coordinate system and the tools used to supply point information to AutoCAD commands. In Unit 4, "Basic CAD Drawing Techniques," you entered point information using absolute, relative, absolute polar, and relative polar coordinates. Another point-related tool is point filters.

A point filter is not a command. A point filter is a method of substituting a known coordinate value into a command, usually a Draw command. For example, when a command asks you to select a point (such as `To point:` when using the Line command), you have several options. You can select the point with the pointing device, enter a coordinate value, or use an Object Snap. Point filters can be used to apply an existing object's coordinates as another response. With a Point Filter you can define or "build" the needed X and Y coordinate by using the known coordinate of an existing X or Y point.

Skill Builder

All AutoCAD point coordinates include a Z coordinate. In 2-D drawings, the Z coordinate is always zero.

Point filters can be used whenever you are prompted for a point, such as the `Circle 3P/2P/TTR/<Center point>:` or the `Arc Center/<Start point>:` prompt. You can access point filters in one of the following methods:

- Select the .X button from the Standard toolbar. This will access a flyout menu, showing all of the different point filter options.
- Specify a point filter at a `point:` prompt by entering a period (.) followed by the letter X,Y, or Z, or a combination of any two letters.

A good example of when you might want to use point filters would be when you have a plan and side view of a part. In Figure 8.25, the object in the plan view has a hole in the middle of the part. The hole needs to be represented accurately on the side view. One method would be to draw construction lines from the top and bottom quadrants of the hole, with **ortho** on, and extend them through the side view. You could later trim the line. While this method works, you can also use point filters to draw the hidden lines.

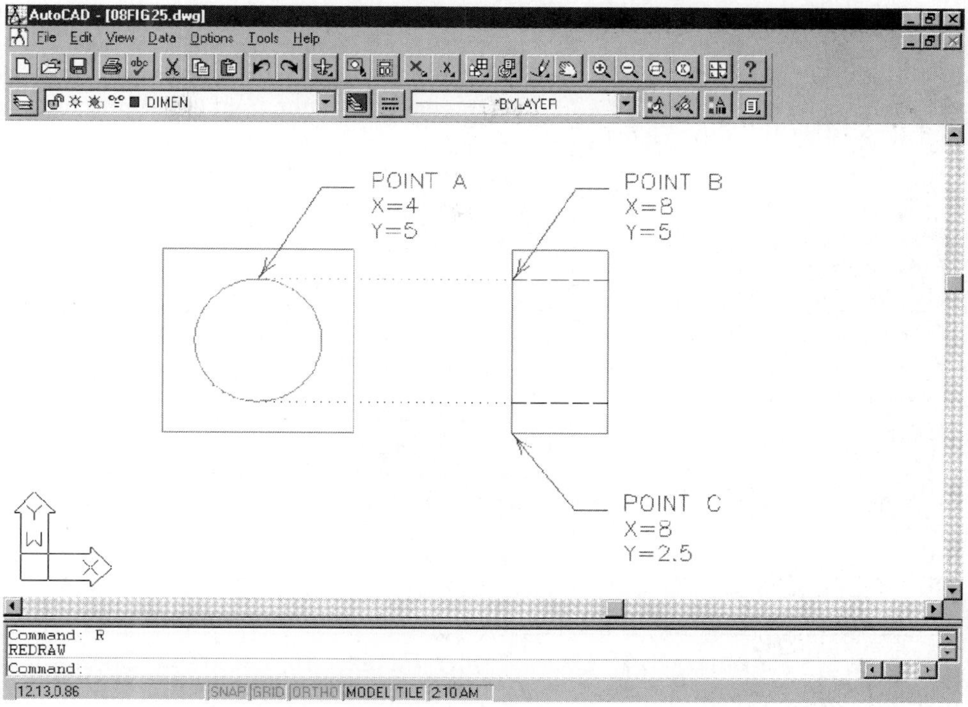

Figure 8.25
Use point filters to obtain the coordinates for the hidden lines.

Construction lines are as important in CAD as they are in manual drafting. If you used a construction line in Figure 8.25 to draw a line representing the hidden hole in the side view, you are really looking for the intersection point, or point B, so you know where to start the hidden line. Point filters can give you the advantages of using construction lines without going through the work of creating extra lines and then having to trim them. Once you learn how to use point filters, they can increase your drawing productivity.

Using the .X Point Filter

Point filters are useful when you need to draw a point that is even with another point in one axis, but has a different ordinate value in the other axis. Looking at Figure 8.25, points B and C have the same value for the x-axis. To draw the hidden line beginning at point B you could use an .X point filter to locate and filter the X coordinate from point C. The command sequence would look like this:

Select the Line button from the Draw toolbar.

```
From point: .X (type .X or select the .X button from the Standard
toolbar)
of
```

After entering the point filter, AutoCAD responds with of. Use the **endpoint** Osnap and select point C. AutoCAD will filter the X component of point C and pass the value to the Line command. AutoCAD responds with:

```
(need YZ):
```

Using the .Y Point Filter

Continuing from the previous example, the prompt `(need YZ):` means you still must provide AutoCAD with the Y and Z values to complete the point. You can pick a point or enter a value from the keyboard. If you enter a YZ value (or an XZ value if you were filtering the Y component) from the keyboard you must also specify a Z value of zero as in the following example:

```
(need YZ): 2,0
```

Referring to Figure 8.25, points A and B have the same value for the y-axis. They also have the same Z value, since Z is always 0 in all 2-D drafting. The complete command sequence for locating the hidden line in the side view is:

Select the Line button from the Draw toolbar.

`From point:` *.X (type .X or select the .X button from the Standard toolbar)*
`of` *end*
`of` *(select point C to filter the X component)*
`(need YZ):` *qua*
`of` *(select the top of the circle, point A)*
`To point:` *per (select the line opposite point B)*
`To point:`

For 2-D drawings such as those used in the previous example, only .X and .Y point filters are needed. The .X and .Y point filters can be specified in any order, depending upon the point you want to filter. Many applications in 3-D drawings use the .XY, .XZ and .YZ point filters.

TUTORIAL 8.4: USING POINT FILTERS TO LOCATE A CIRCLE IN THE CENTER OF A RECTANGLE

In this tutorial you will draw a circle with its center located at the center of an existing rectangle. The coordinate for the center of the circle has an X component equal to the midpoint of a horizontal (top or bottom) line and a Y component equal to the midpoint of a vertical (side) line. You will filter the X component from the midpoint of a horizontal line and filter the Y component from the midpoint of a vertical line. Follow these steps:

1.  From the Standard toolbar, select New. If prompted with the Save Changes dialog box, select No. Enter a name for the drawing and accept the dialog box.
2.  Choose the Line button from the Draw toolbar.

   `From point:` **3,2**
   `To point:` **@5<0**
   `To point:` **@7<90**
   `To point:` **3,9**
   `To point:` **c**
3.  Choose the Circle Center Diameter button from the Draw toolbar.
4.  `3P/2P/TTR/<Center point>:` Choose the .X button from the Standard toolbar.

   `.x of` **mid**
   `select the approximate mid-point of either top or bottom line.`
   `of (need YZ):` **mid**
   `select the approximate midpoint of either vertical (side) line.`
   `Diameter/<Radius>:_d Diameter:` **3.5**

You now see a circle see with its center located at the center of a rectangle.

SUMMARY

Proper use of Object Snaps increases the accuracy of your drawings as well as simplifies the creation of geometry. Object Snaps ensure that no points are "guesses"—all points are precise. When used with coordinates, Object Snaps will help you create drawings that are accurate and useful.

Point filter will also increase the accuracy of your drawings by allowing you to capture or filter points from existing geometry. Used properly, point filters can increase your drawing productivity.

REVIEW

1. Give three reasons why is it important to maintain an accurate computer database for your drawing.
2. Define Object Snap and how it applies to geometry creation.
3. Clarify the QUAdrant Object Snap mode by labeling the quadrants on a circle and explaining how they relate to Object Snap.
4. Explain the difference between running and temporary Object Snaps.
5. When using multiple Object Snap modes, explain how the snap location is determined.
6. Define QUIck Object Snap and how it can be used to speed up object selection.
7. Illustrate the advantages and disadvantages of using a large aperture box when using an Object Snap mode.
8. Explain the difference between the aperture box and the pick box.
9. Illustrate the advantages and disadvantages of using a small aperture box when using an Object Snap mode.
10. Define point filter and how it can be used to increase drawing productivity.

EXERCISE 8

1. Load drawing EX8-1 shown in Figure 8.26. Use the appropriate Object Snap modes to complete the drawing as shown in Figure 8.27.
2. Create the Fireplace mantle drawing shown in Figure 8.28.

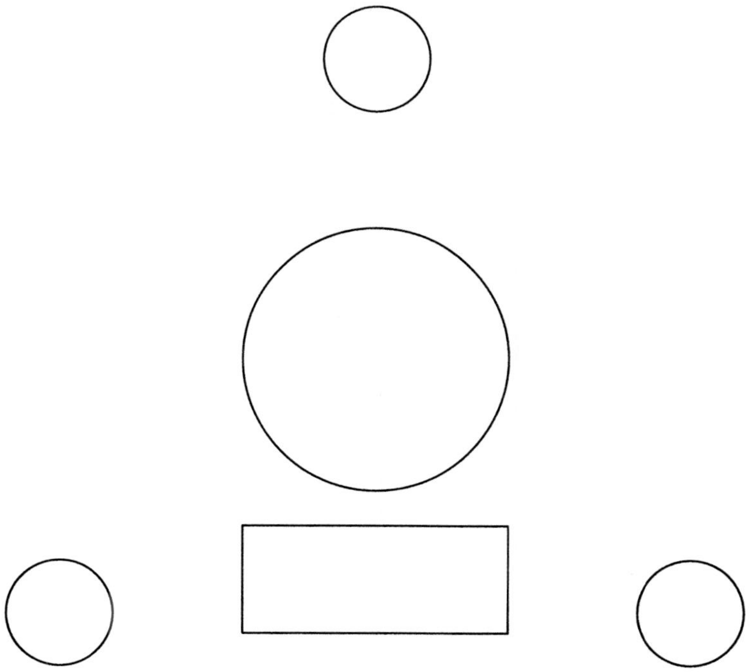

Figure 8.26
Drawing EX8-1.

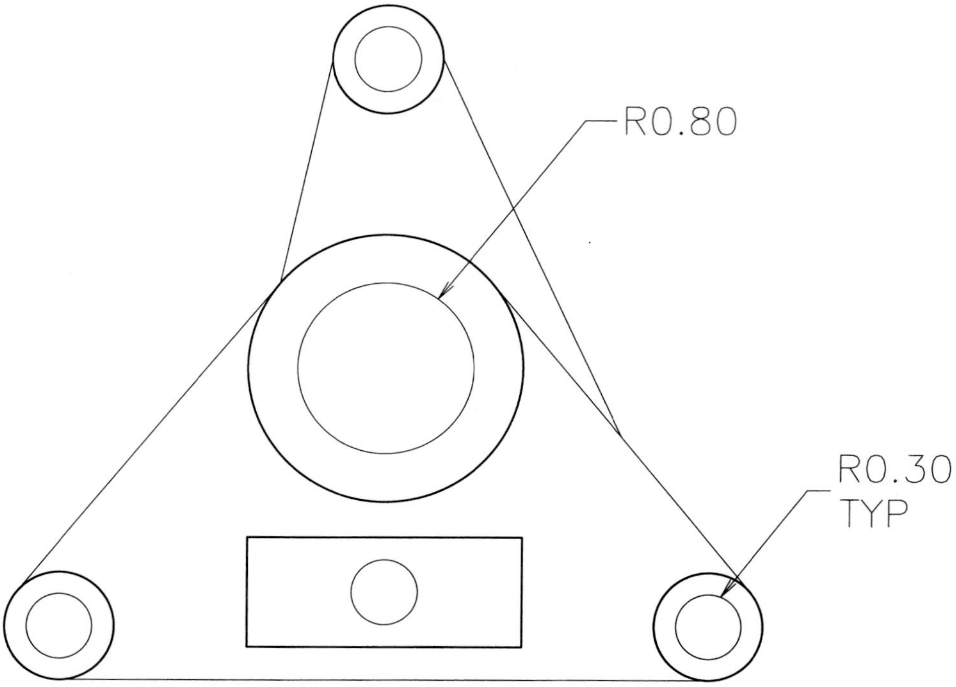

Figure 8.27
Use the appropriate Object Snap modes to complete the drawing.

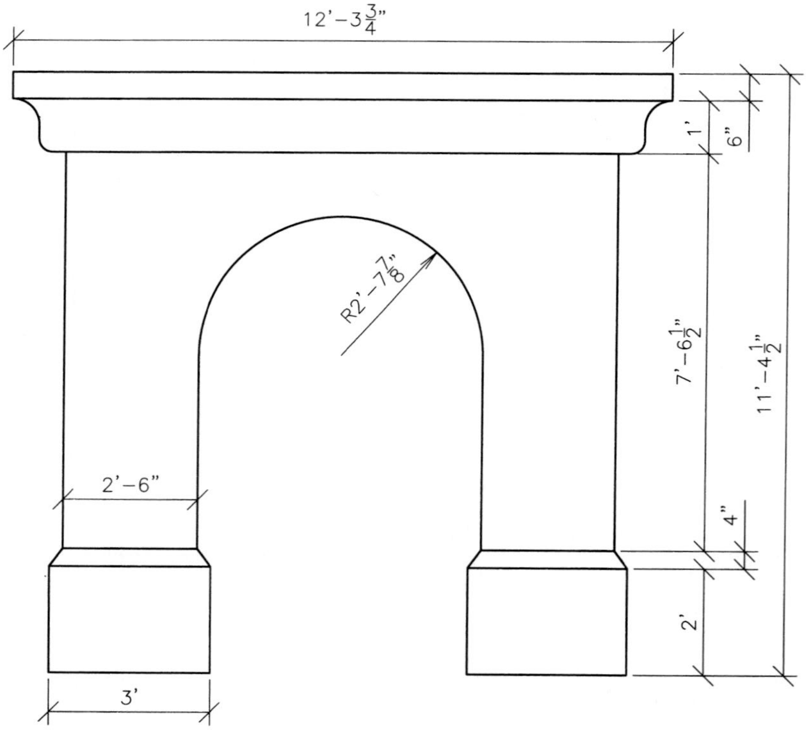

Figure 8.28
Use your knowledge of geometry creation to draw the Fireplace mantle.

UNIT

9

Creating Selection Sets

OVERVIEW

Creating objects in AutoCAD is only a small part of producing a finished drawing. Many times, you will have to edit existing objects. Editing objects includes selecting the objects during one of various editing commands. Erasing objects is one example of an editing command that uses selection sets.

When you perform any editing operations, you must tell AutoCAD what objects you want to edit. When you invoke the **erase** command, for example, AutoCAD prompts you to select the objects to erase. When you select one or more objects, you create a selection set. Before you can use many of the editing commands, you need a thorough understanding of selection sets. During this chapter the various selection methods will be introduced while you perform a series of tutorials.

OBJECTIVES

- Understand the purpose of selection sets.
- Create selection sets with the pick-first method.
- Create selection sets with the pick-after method.
- Control the selection set with 16 different methods.

INTRODUCTION

When you use an editing command, such as **erase**, `Select objects:` is usually the first prompt you see. AutoCAD uses the term *object* as a general reference to any element that can be seen on-screen. When the Select objects: prompt appears, AutoCAD asks you to select the object that you want to edit. When an object is selected, it becomes highlighted on-screen. When an object is highlighted for selection, it typically changes from a solid color to a dashed outline. When you execute the editing command, it affects only the highlighted objects.

OUTLINE

Methods for Creating a Selection Set
Selecting Objects
Tutorial 9.1: Picking Points
Tutorial 9.2: Selecting Objects with a Window
Tutorial 9.3: Selecting the Last Object Created
Tutorial 9.4: Selecting with the Crossing Option
Tutorial 9.5: Selecting Objects with a Box
Tutorial 9.6: Selecting All Objects

Tutorial 9.7: Using the Window Polygon (WPolygon)
Tutorial 9.8: Using the Crossing Polygon (CPolygon)
Tutorial 9.9: Selecting with a Fence
Tutorial 9.10: Selecting a Single Object
Tutorial 9.11: Selecting the Previous Selection Set
Tutorial 9.12: Removing and Adding Objects to the Selection Set
Tutorial 9.13: Undoing a Selection
Tutorial 9.14: Canceling the Selection
Tutorial 9.15: Creating an Object Selection Filter
Summary
Review
Exercises

Skill Builder

The way objects appear when selected is controlled by the **highlight** system variable. When this system variable is set to 0, objects do not appear highlighted when selected. When the variable is set to 1, objects appear highlighted when selected. Set this variable by entering **highlight** at the `Command:` prompt or clicking Highlight in the Drawing Aids dialog box. In most cases, you should leave the **highlight** system variable set to 1 (on), which is the default.

For the Professional

AutoCAD uses both a `Select objects:` prompt and a `Select object:` prompt. AutoCAD displays the `Select objects:` prompt when the current command works for multiple objects (selection sets). AutoCAD displays the `Select object:` prompt when the current command works with only one object.

METHODS FOR CREATING A SELECTION SET

You can use the AutoCAD editing commands on a single object or a group of objects. Editing a single object is simple—just pick the object. Selecting many objects can be tiresome and nonproductive when you pick them one at a time. Fortunately, AutoCAD offers many ways to choose groups of objects to create a selection set. A selection set can consist of anything from a single line to the entire drawing.

Picking Objects

Whenever you enter a command that requires you to select an object, a small box, called the *Pickbox,* become visible where the pointing device is located. The Pickbox sometimes appears at the junction of the crosshairs and always occurs by itself whenever you enter a command that requires you to select objects. Figure 9.1 shows the Pickbox by itself as well as the junction of the crosshairs. Once the object is selected, it is displayed as a dashed line as shown in Figure 9.2.

You can adjust the size of the Pickbox in the Object Selection Settings dialog box, as shown in Figure 9.3. You can access the Object Selection Settings dialog box by:

- From the Options pull-down menu, choose Selection.
- Enter **`ddselect`** at the `Command:` prompt.

Selecting Objects with the Toolbar

Different methods for selecting objects are also available on the Select Objects floating toolbar. The Select Objects floating toolbar is shown in Figure 9.4. You can access the Select Objects floating toolbar by:

- Selecting the Select Window button on the Standard toolbar. This will invoke a flyout menu, showing all of the Select Objects options.
- Choose Toolbars from the Tools menu bar. When the flyout menu appears, pick Select Objects.

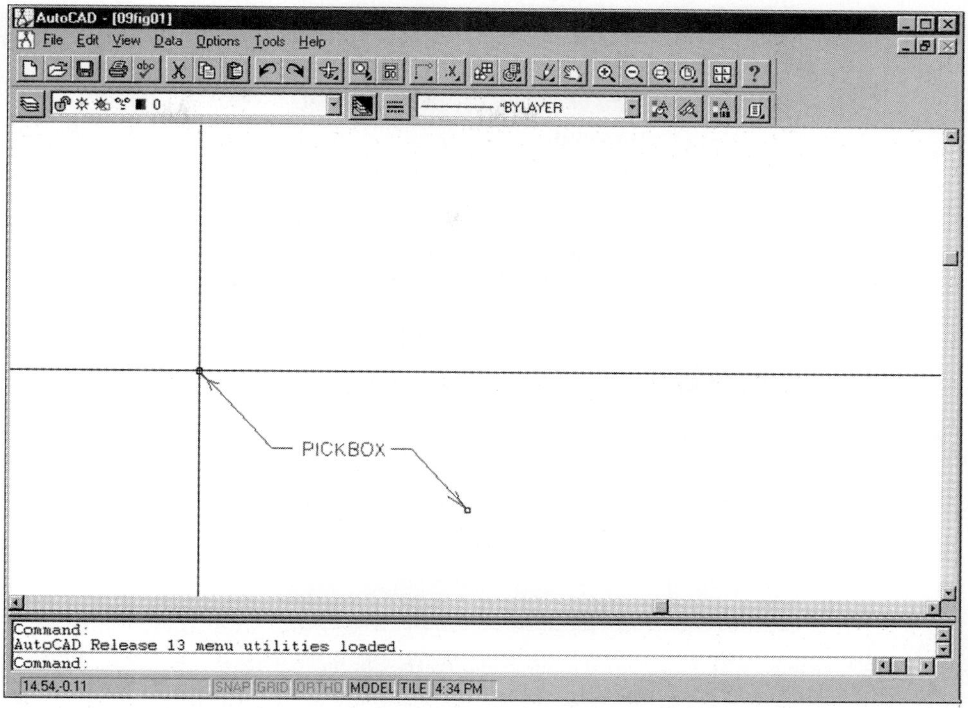

Figure 9.1
The Pickbox indicates when you can select objects.

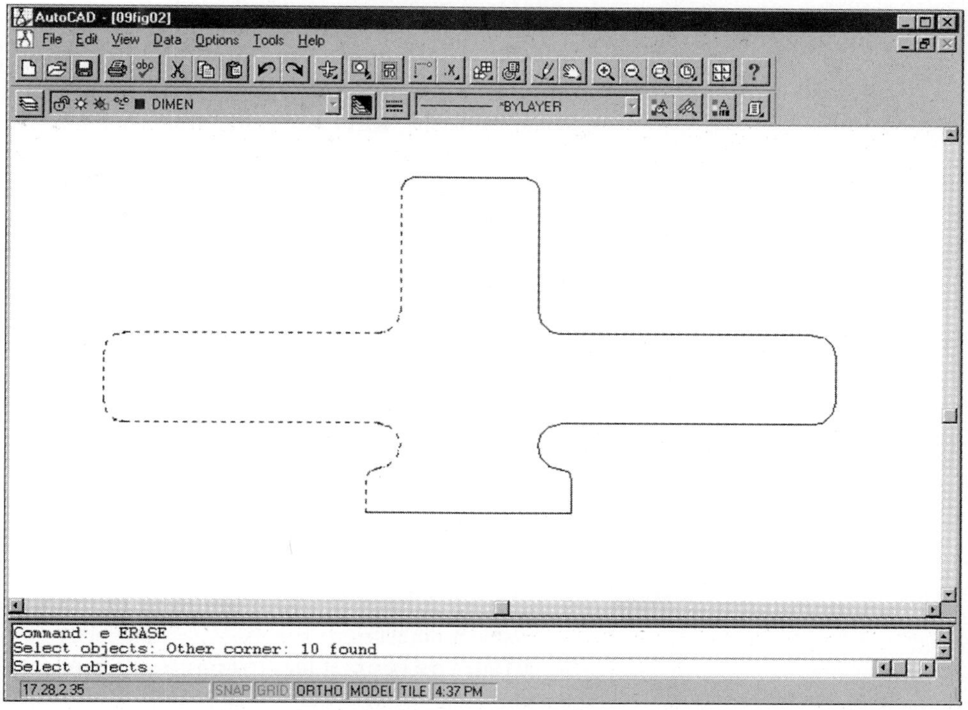

Figure 9.2
Objects in a selection set appear dashed.

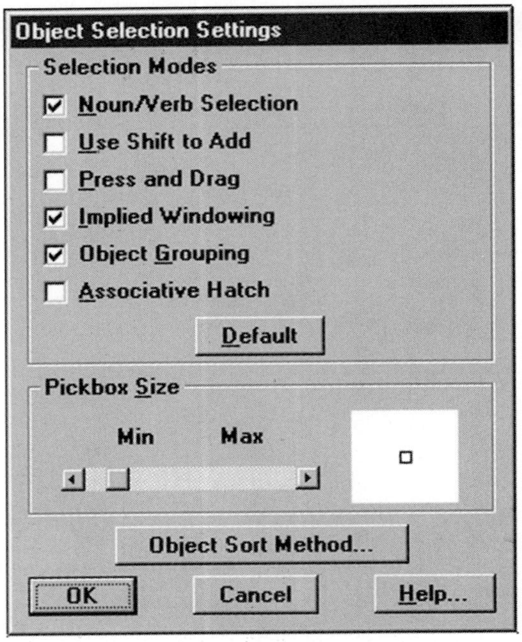

Figure 9.3 *Adjust the size of the Pickbox in the Object Selection Settings dialog box by dragging the Pickbox Size slider bar.*

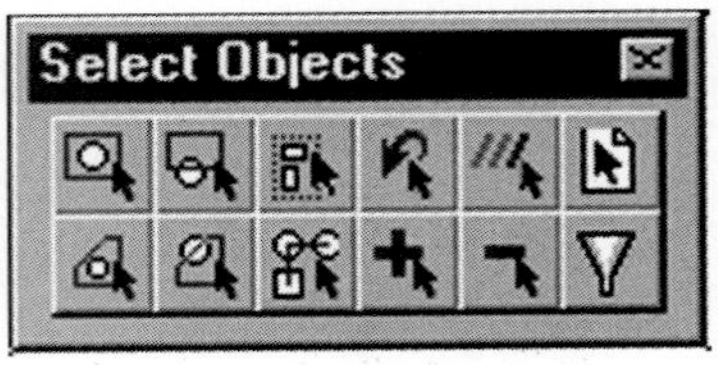

Figure 9.4 *The Select Objects floating toolbar contains various buttons for creating selection sets.*

USING THE **select** COMMAND

Besides providing all the editing commands that prompt you to select objects, AutoCAD offers a separate command called **select**. **select** does nothing but create a selection set. When using the **select** command you can select the objects you want to edit first, then issue the appropriate editing command. At the editing command's `Select objects:` prompt, you can tell the command to use the selection set you created with **select**. This is discussed in greater detail in the following sections.

All the selection options are available with the **select** command. To access the **select** command do one of the following:

- From the Standard toolbar, choose the Select Objects flyout.
- At the `Command:` prompt, enter **`select.`**

The following command sequence is used with this command:

Command: `select`
`Select objects: Use any method for creating a selection set`

You can access the **`select`** command by:

- From the Standard toolbar, choose the Select Window button. This invokes a flyout menu showing the different Select Objects options. You can choose any option to select objects.
- Enter **`select`** at the `Command:` prompt.

SELECTING OBJECTS

AutoCAD offers a variety of ways to select objects, add objects to the selection set, and remove objects from the selection set. Any of the options described in the following sections can be used with the **select** command, pick-first selection (provided the **pickfirst** system variable is set to 1), or pick-after selection. The different ways of selecting objects are summarized in Table 9.1.

TABLE 9.1 SELECTION SET CREATION OPTIONS

ICON	Name	Abbreviation	Description
	Window	W	Selects all objects completely enclosed within a defined window.
	Crossing	C	Selects all objects completely enclosed or touching a defined window.
	Group	G	Selects all objects within a defined group.
	Previous	P	Selects the objects included in the most recent selection set.
	Last	L	Selects the most recently created visible objects.
	All	All	Selects all visible objects on thawed layers.
	WPolygon	WP	Selects all objects completely enclosed within a defined polygon. Similar to a window, but the defined polygon can have more than four sides.
	Crossing	C	Selects all objects completely enclosed or touching a defined window. Similar to a crossing window, but the defined crossing polygon can have more than four sides.
	Fence	F	Selects all objects that cross a selection fence. Creating a selection fence is similar to drawing a line. As the fence is created, any object crossing the fence is selected.
	Add	A	Switches the selection set to the add mode. This is normally used after the Remove option to continue adding objects to the selection set.
	Remove	R	Switches the selection set to the remove mode. This is used to remove objects that were inadvertently included in the selection set. To continue adding more objects to the selection set, use the Add option.

PICK-FIRST SELECTION VERSUS PICK-AFTER SELECTION

AutoCAD offers two methods for building a selection set:

- AutoCAD's default is called pick-first selection. With pick-first selection enabled, you may build the selection set first and then issue the editing command. The editing command performs the appropriate operation on the selection without prompting for any additional selection information. This method of selection is also called *noun/verb selection.*
- With pick-after selection, you can first issue the command and then select the objects to be edited. If you have not established a selection set by using pick-first selection, AutoCAD automatically uses pick-after selection. Pick-after selection is also called *verb/noun selection.*

FOR THE PROFESSIONAL

When attempting to build a selection set before issuing an editing command, you may notice small blue boxes appearing on the objects selected. These are called Grips and are discussed in Unit 11.

TABLE 9.2 PICK-FIRST SELECTION COMMANDS

Commands that Work with Pick-First Selection	Commands that Don't Work with Pick-First Selection
Array	Break
Block	Chamfer
Change	Divide
Copy	Edgesurf
Ddchprop	Extend
Dview	Fillet
Erase	Measure
Explode	Offset
Hatch	Revsurf
List	Rulesurf
Mirror	Tabsurf
Move	Trim
Rotate	
Scale	
Stretch	
Wblock	

When pick-first selection is enabled and no commands are active, the Pickbox appears at the intersection of the crosshairs. With pick-first selection, you may begin selecting objects at any time when you are at the `Command:` prompt. Objects may be selected before you enter any commands.

The pick-first selection method is governed by the **pickfirst** system variable. To disable pick-first selection, use one of the two following methods.

- Enter **pickfirst** at the `Command:` prompt. The default value is 1 (on). To disable Pickfirst, enter 0 as the New value for **pickfirst**.
- Enter **ddselect** at the `Command:` prompt to access the Object Selection Settings dialog box. You can also access the Object Selection Settings dialog box by choosing Selection in the Options pull-down menu. Under Selection Modes, check the Noun/Verb Selection box. By default, this box is checked to turn pick-first selection on. To disable pick-first selection, remove the X in Noun/Verb Selection.

Only certain AutoCAD commands may be used with pick-first selection. Some commands, because they need to know exactly where an object is selected, ignore pick-first selection. Table 9.2 shows which commands work with pick-first selection and which commands do not.

USING ⇧Shift TO SELECT OBJECTS

Microsoft Windows uses a standard of pressing ⇧Shift to add objects in a selection set. By default in AutoCAD, you do not need to use ⇧Shift to add objects in a selection set. If you feel comfortable using the Windows standard of ⇧Shift for object selection, you can enable AutoCAD to use ⇧Shift to add objects in a selection set.

By default, you can add objects to the selection set by picking them with the Pickbox. If you want to remove an object from the selection set, hold down ⇧Shift and pick the object with the Pickbox. The existing selection set remains intact minus the object you just selected with the Pickbox.

Use of ⇧Shift is governed by the **pickadd** system variable. By default, **pickadd** is on and AutoCAD behaves as previously described. When **pickadd** is turned off, each selection replaces the objects in the current selection set with the object you just selected. You must press ⇧Shift to add objects to the selection set. To remove an object from the

Tutorial 9.1: Picking Points

AutoCAD automatically uses the default single object selection method for adding objects to the selection set. Just use the Pickbox to select single objects to add to the selection set. Objects added to the selection set appear dashed, provided the **highlight** system variable is set to 1 (on).

In this tutorial, you will use the default selection option, the Pickbox, to select specific objects found in the apartment floor plan shown in Figure 9.5. This drawing will be used for all tutorials in this chapter. To create a selection set using the default method, follow these steps:

1.  Select the Open button from the Standard toolbar. If the AutoCAD Save Changes dialog box appears, select No unless you want to save the current drawing. If you want to save the current drawing, select Yes and enter a path and drawing name.
2. In the Select File dialog box, change to the appropriate drive and directory and choose file 09fig05. Your screen will resemble Figure 9.5.
3. At the `Command:` prompt, enter **select**. The `Select objects:` prompt appears, and you see the default Pickbox in the drawing area (Figure 9.6).
4. Move your pointing device and notice that the crosshairs are no longer available. All selections are made with this Pickbox.
5. Click the arc at the end of the breakfast bar. Notice that the end of the breakfast bar becomes highlighted as shown in Figure 9.6. The default selection option allows you to enter one object at a time to the selection set.
6. Press ↵Enter to accept the selection.

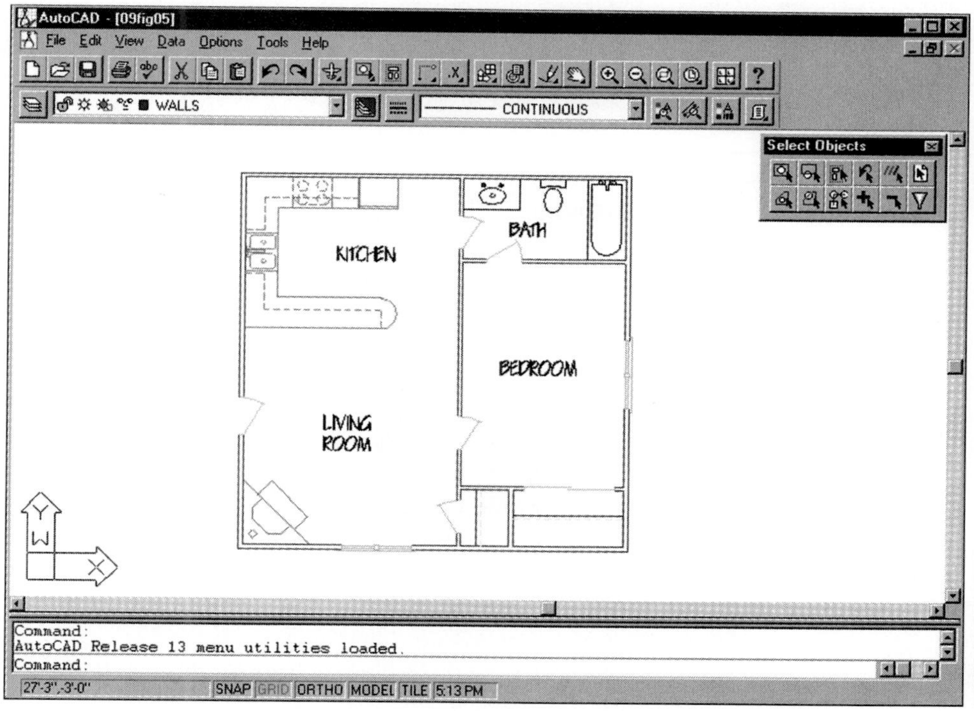

Figure 9.5
Using the apartment floor plan to make selection sets.

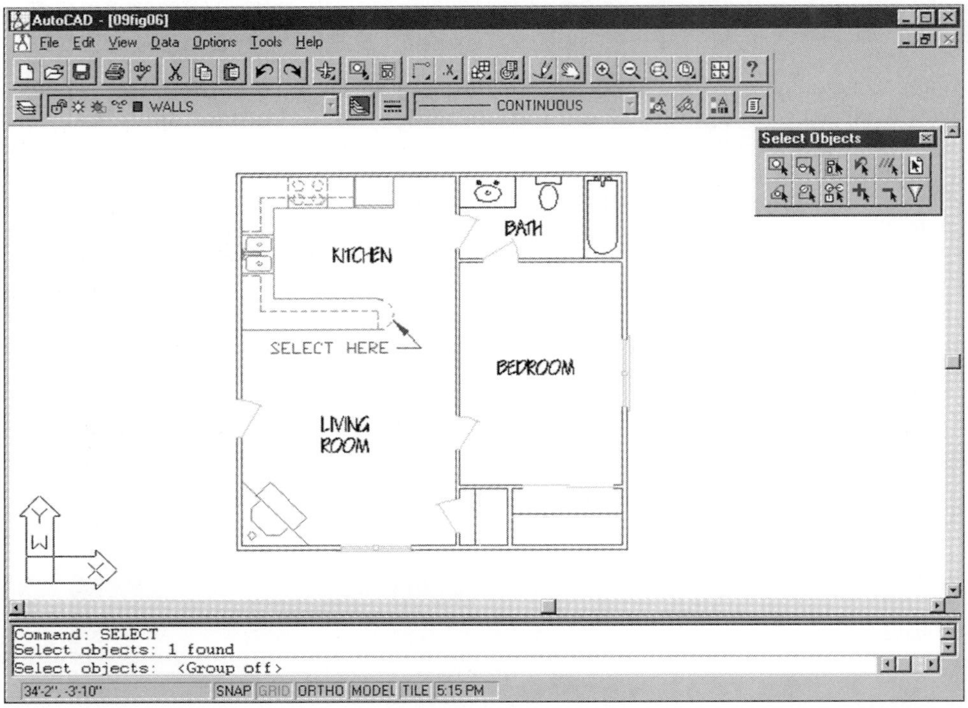

Figure 9.6
Using the Pickbox to select the arc at the end of the breakfast bar.

Tutorial 9.2: Selecting Objects with a Window

When you choose to select objects with a window, AutoCAD asks you to pick the two corners of a rectangle that completely surround the objects you want to edit. After you pick the second corner point, AutoCAD highlights all objects that are completely enclosed within the window.

In this tutorial, you will use the Window selection option to select specific objects found in the apartment floor plan in Figure 9.5. Follow these steps:

1.  Choose the Select Window button in the Select Objects floating toolbar.

Figure 9.7
Defining the upper-left and bottom-right corners needed to create a window selection.

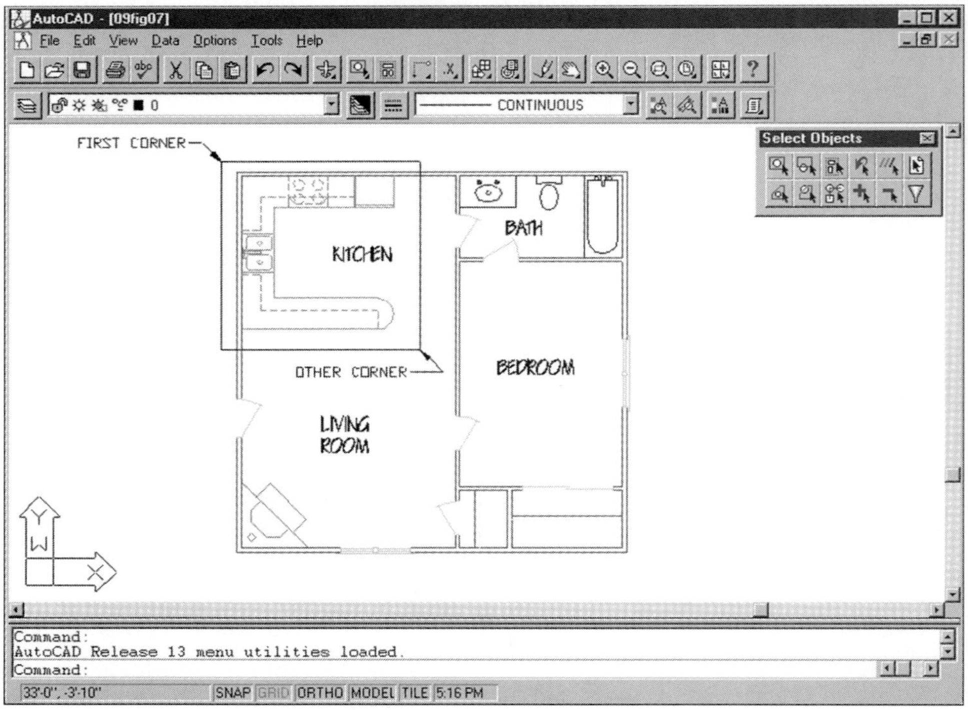

2. At the `First corner:` prompt, move the crosshairs to the upper-left corner of the window as shown in Figure 9.7 and pick the first corner point.
3. At the `Other corner:` prompt, move the crosshairs to the bottom-right corner to create the window shown in Figure 9.7, and pick the second corner point. Notice that all objects within the kitchen are now highlighted as shown in Figure 9.8. Notice also that the walls in the kitchen are not highlighted because those objects are not completely within the window.
4. At the `Select objects:` prompt, press Enter to accept the selection.

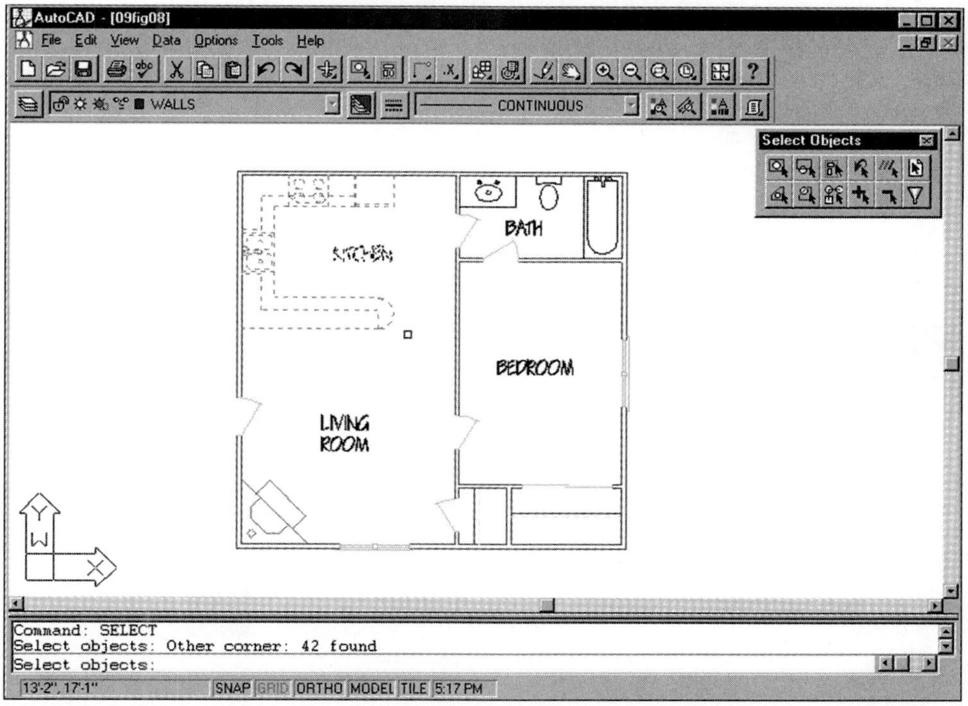

Figure 9.8
Use the Window selection option to select all objects located in the kitchen.

selection set, press Shift when selecting it. If you add an object without pressing Shift with **pickadd** off, any previous objects in the selection set are removed.

You can invoke the **pickadd** system variable by typing **pickadd** at the `Command:` line. You can also turn on the **pickadd** variable in the Object Selection Settings dialog box. The option is labeled Use Shift to Add in the dialog box.

For the Professional

It is not necessary to select the Window button to use it as the selection mode. In the default selection set mode, move the Pickbox directly to the first point of the window on the left side of the objects to be selected and pick the first corner point. Be careful not to pick an object with the Pickbox. When using the window selection mode it is important to select the first point on the left side of the objects being selected. Selecting a point on the right side of the objects being selected has a different function. AutoCAD automatically starts the window selection mode as you move the crosshairs to the right.

Changing the Press and Drag Settings

Certain software packages utilize the click-drag-release method of object selection. This means that a selection window is created by clicking one corner, dragging the window into place, and releasing the pointing device button. If you feel comfortable using the click-drag-release method of object selection, you can enable AutoCAD to use this method also.

The Press and Drag setting governs how boxes are formed. With Press and Drag turned off (default), you create a Pickbox by clicking the Pick button once for each corner. When Press and Drag is turned on, you can create boxes by holding down the Pick button and dragging the crosshairs from the first corner to the second corner of the box, and then releasing. You can change the Press and Drag setting in the Object Selection Settings dialog box. The option is labeled Press and Drag.

You can also set Press and Drag with the **pickdrag** system variable. To change the **pickdrag** variable, enter **pickdrag** at the `Command:` prompt.

Tutorial 9.3: Selecting the Last Object Created

The Last option tells AutoCAD to select the last object that was drawn and is visible on-screen. In this tutorial, you will use the Last selection option to select specific objects found in the apartment floor plan in Figure 9.5.

For this example, you will erase and draw a line on the floor plan. You will draw the line before you use the last selection option. Follow these steps:

1. Erase the top horizontal line on the apartment complex drawing that represents the exterior wall as shown in Figure 9.9.
2. Select the Line button from the Draw toolbar.
3. At the `From point:` prompt, enter 1′,31′.
4. At the `To point:` prompt, enter 31′,31′.
5. At the `To point:` prompt, press Enter to exit the **line** command.

You should now have the completed floor plan, as shown in Figure 9.9.

In this part of the tutorial you will use the Select Last option to select specific objects found in the apartment floor plan.

1. Choose the Select Last button from the Select Objects floating toolbar. Notice that the line you just created is highlighted. The Last selection option always chooses the object that was drawn last as long as that object is visible on-screen.
2. Press Enter to accept the selection set.

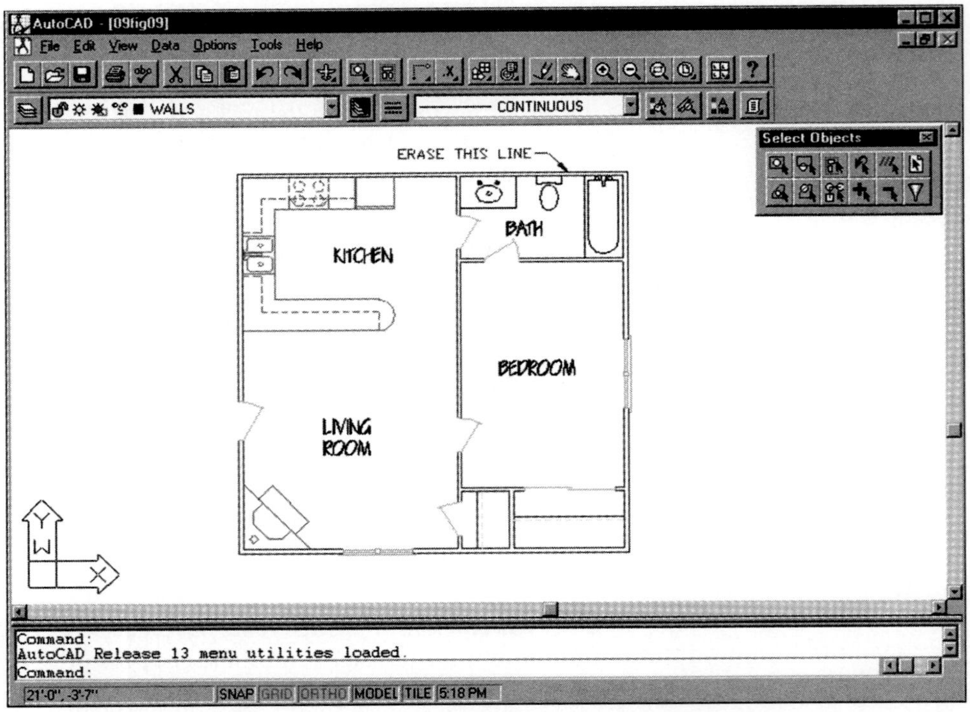

Figure 9.9
Erase and then recreate the top line of the floor plan for use in selecting the Last Object Created tutorial.

Tutorial 9.4: Selecting with the Crossing Option

The Crossing option is similar to the Window option except that Crossing selects any object that touches or crosses the window border, as well as any objects contained inside the window. A crossing window can be identified by a highlighted or dashed border on the window.

Figure 9.10 shows the difference between the crossing window and window selection options. The figure on the left shows a window totally enclosing the box and touching only the circle. Notice that only the box is selected. The figure on the right shows the same geometry with the same-size crossing window. The crossing window is totally enclosing the box and touching only the circle. Notice that with the crossing window, both the box and circle are selected.

In this tutorial, you will use the Crossing selection option to select specific objects found in the apartment floor plan.

Follow these steps:

1.  Choose the Select Crossing button from the Select Objects floating toolbar.
2. At the `First corner:` prompt, move the cursor to the upper-left corner of the window and pick the first corner point as shown in Figure 9.11.
3. At the `Other corner:` prompt, move the crosshairs to the bottom-right corner to create the window shown in Figure 9.11 and pick the other corner point. Notice that all objects within the kitchen are now highlighted and include the walls that were not selected when the Window option was used. The Crossing option selects all objects that the window crosses or encloses.
4. At the `Select objects:` prompt, press Enter to accept the selection set.

For the Professional

It is not necessary to pick the Crossing button to use it as the selection mode. In the default selection set mode, move directly to the first point of the crossing window on the right side of the object and make the selection. Be careful not to pick an object with the Pickbox. AutoCAD automatically starts the crossing selection mode as you move the crosshairs to the left.

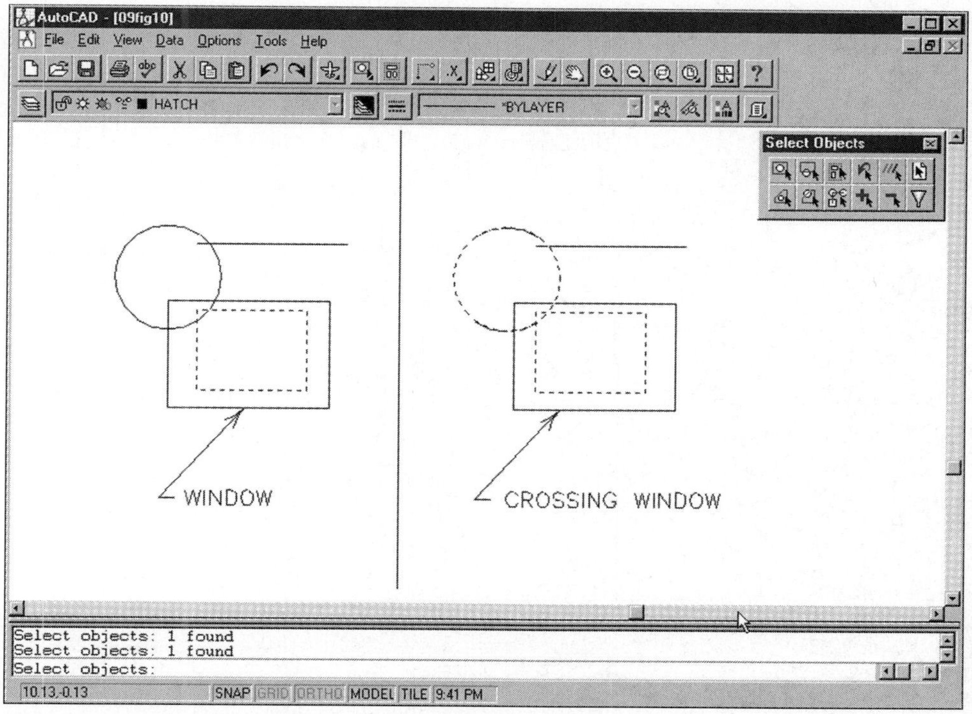

Figure 9.10
A crossing window selects all objects totally enclosing or touching it.

Tutorial 9.5: Selecting Objects with a Box

The Box option combines the Window and Crossing options. If the second point picked is to the right of the first, the box uses window selection. Only objects completely inside the box are selected. If the second point is to the left of the first, the box uses crossing selection. With the crossing selection, any object that touches or crosses the window border, as well as any objects contained inside the window, is selected. As with the Window and Crossing options, the crossing window is identified by a highlighted or dashed border. To use this option, you can enter **box** at the prompt, without abbreviation.

In this tutorial, you will use the Box selection option to select specific objects found in the apartment floor plan in Figure 9.5. Use these steps:

1. At the `Command:` prompt, enter **`select.`**
2. At the `Select objects:` prompt, enter **`box.`**
3. At the `First corner:` prompt, move the crosshairs to the upper-left corner of the window as shown in Figure 9.11 and pick the first point.
4. At the `Other corner:` prompt, move the crosshairs to the bottom-right corner to create the same box shown in Figure 9.11 and pick the other corner point. Notice that the selection is identical to the Window option used previously.
5. Press Enter to accept the selection set.
6. At the `Command:` prompt, press Enter to reissue the **select** command.
7. At the `Select objects:` prompt, enter **`box.`**
8. At the `First corner:` prompt, move the crosshairs to the lower-right other corner of the window as shown in Figure 9.11 and pick the first corner point.
9. At the `Other corner:` prompt, move the crosshairs to the upper-left corner to create the box as shown in Figure 9.11 and make the selection. Notice that the selection is identical to the Crossing option used previously.
10. Press Enter to accept the selection set.

For the Professional

Box is the default selection mode. It is not necessary to type **box** at the prompt to use this option. After completing this tutorial, you should not need to type this option during future drawing sessions.

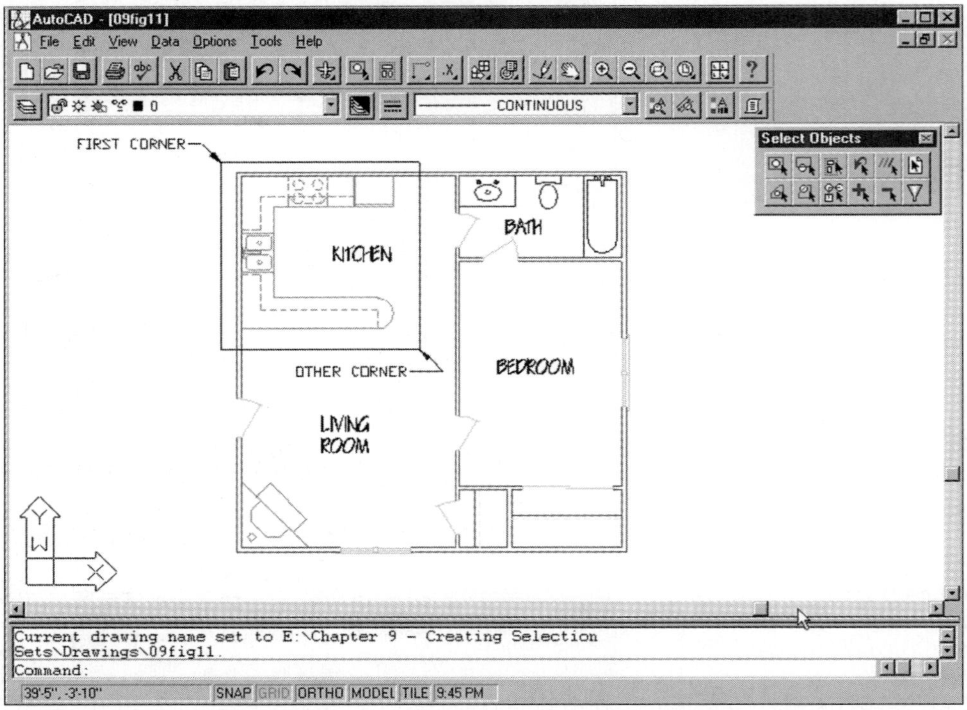

Figure 9.11
Use these points to select objects using the Box option.

Tutorial 9.6: Selecting All Objects

The All option selects all objects in the drawing. Objects on frozen layers are not selected.

In this tutorial, you will use the All selection option to select all objects in the apartment floor plan in Figure 9.5. Follow these steps:

1.  Choose the Select All button from the Select Objects floating toolbar. Notice that all objects in the drawing are highlighted. The All selection option chooses all objects in the drawing that are not on a frozen layer.
2. Press Enter to accept the selection set.

Tutorial 9.7: Using the Window Polygon (WPolygon)

The WPolygon option stands for Window Polygon; it is similar to the Window option in that the polygon you create must totally enclose the objects to be selected. A polygon is defined as a closed plane figure bounded by three or more line segments. You can have any number of sides surrounding the objects you want to include in the selection set. The shape of the polygon is limited to straight line segments that cannot intersect. AutoCAD automatically closes the polygon on the start point after the second point is picked, but you can continue to add sides to it. If you enter an incorrect point on the polygon, enter *U* (for Undo) to remove the last point entered. You can designate the last point by pressing Enter or the space bar.

In this tutorial, you will use the WPolygon selection option to select specific objects found in the apartment floor plan in Figure 9.5. Use these steps:

1.  Choose the Select Window Polygon button from the Select Objects floating toolbar.
2. At the `First polygon point:` prompt, move the crosshair so that it is in approximately the same location as the one found in Figure 9.12 and pick the first point.
3. At the `Undo/<Endpoint of line>:` prompt, move the crosshair so that it is approximately in the same location as the one found in Figure 9.13 and pick the second point.
4. At the `Undo/<Endpoint of line>:` prompt, move the crosshair so it is approximately in the same location as the one found in Figure 9.14 and pick the third point. You now have a triangle as your selection polygon.
5. At the `Undo/<Endpoint of line>:` press Enter to accept the triangle as the polygon selection. The WPolygon option selects all objects that are completely within the polygon.
6. At the `Select objects:` prompt, press Enter to accept the selection set.

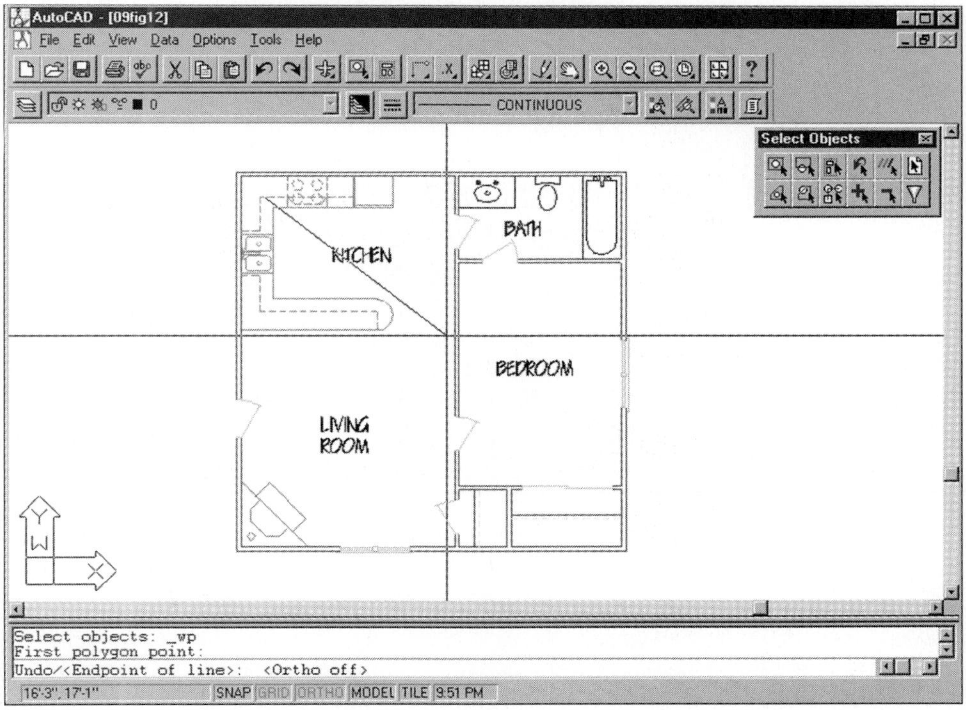

Figure 9.12
Select the first point of the WPolygon selection option.

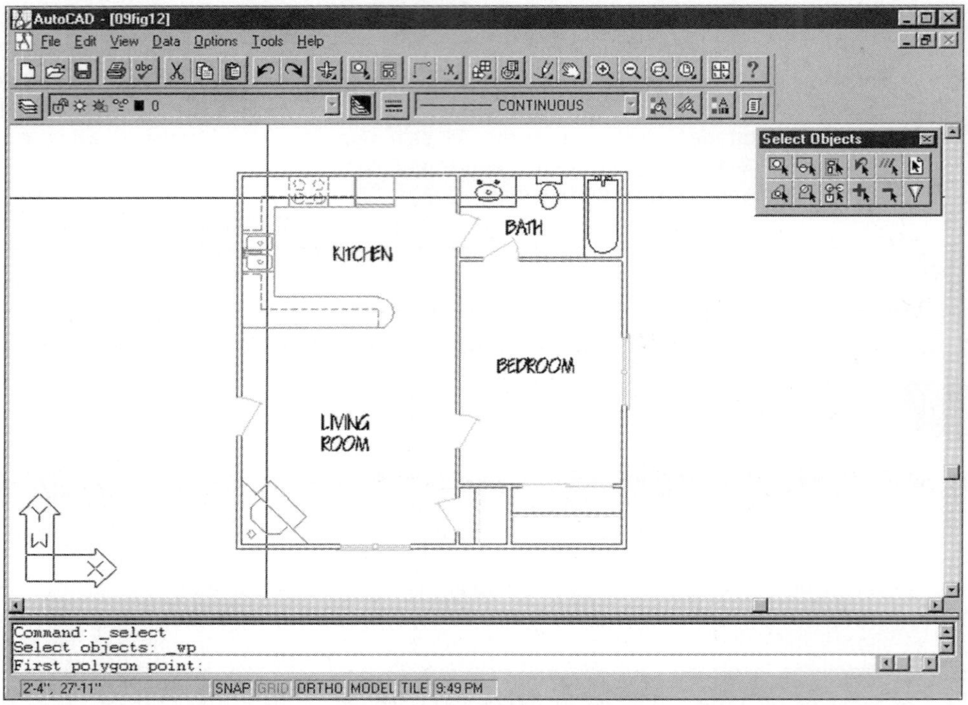

Figure 9.13
When selecting the second point of the WPolygon selection option, remember the completed polygon must totally enclose the objects to be selected.

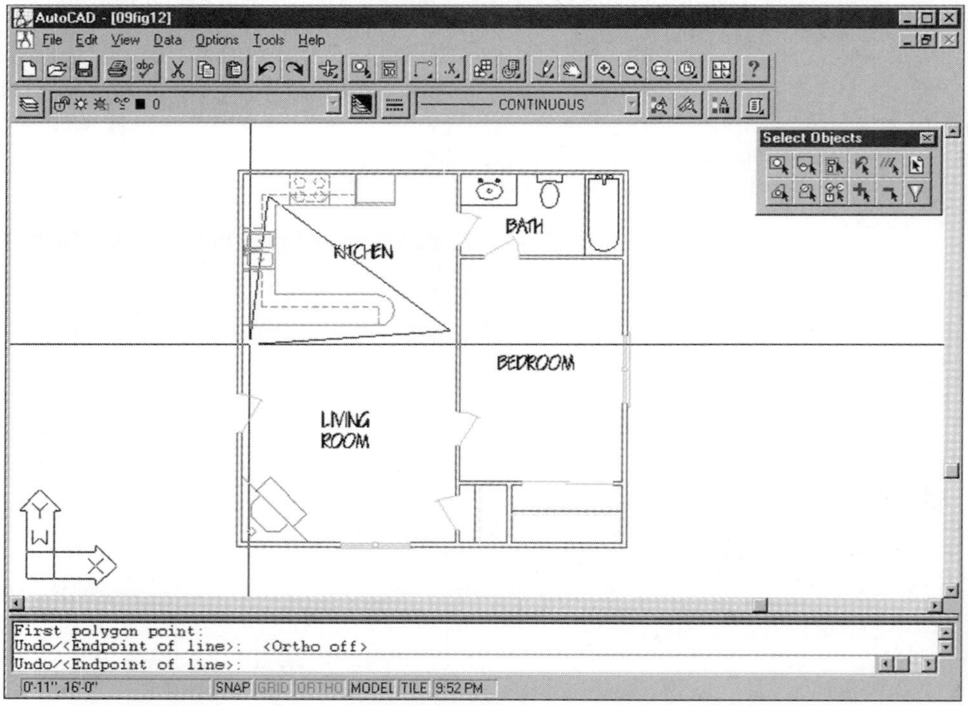

Figure 9.14
When selecting the third point of the WPolygon selection option and pressing Enter*, all objects totally enclosed in the polygon are selected.*

Tutorial 9.8: Using the Crossing Polygon (CPolygon)

The CPolygon option stands for Crossing Polygon and is similar to the Crossing window option in that anything the polygon touches is added to the selection set. As with the WPolygon, the CPolygon can have any number of sides, and the shape of the polygon is limited to straight line segments that cannot cross one another. If you enter an incorrect point on the CPolygon, enter *U* (for Undo) to remove the last point entered. To close the polygon, press ↵Enter or the space bar.

In this tutorial, you will use the CPolygon selection option to select specific objects found in the apartment floor plan in Figure 9.5. Follow these steps:

1.  Choose the Select Crossing Polygon button from the Select Objects floating toolbar.
2. At the `First polygon point:` prompt, move the crosshair so that it is approximately in the same location as the one found in Figure 9.12 and pick the first point.
3. At the `Undo/<Endpoint of line>:` prompt, move the crosshair so that it is approximately in the same location as the one found in Figure 9.13 and pick the second point.
4. At the `Undo/<Endpoint of line>:` prompt, move the crosshair so that it is approximately in the same location as the one found in Figure 9.14 and pick the third point. You should now have a triangle as your selection polygon.
5. At the `Undo/<Endpoint of line>:` prompt, press ↵Enter to accept the triangle as the polygon selection. The CPolygon option will select all objects within the polygon as well at those objects that are crossed over by the polygon (see Figure 9.15).
6. At the `Select objects:` prompt, press ↵Enter to accept the selection set.

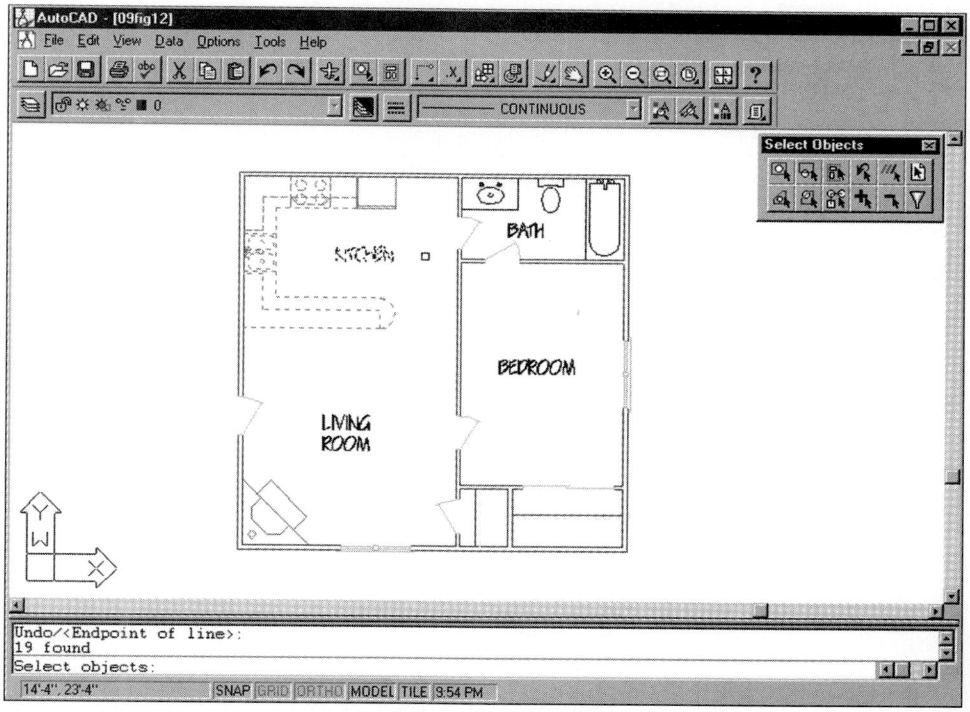

Figure 9.15
The Crossing Polygon selects all objects within the polygon as well as all objects crossed over by the polygon.

Tutorial 9.9: Selecting with a Fence

The Fence option is similar to the CPolygon option, but the polygon is never closed by connecting the first point to the last. Any objects that cross or intersect the fence are included in the selection set. The fence can cross over itself. As with the CPolygon or WPolygon option, you can enter *U* to undo a pick point. With the fence, you do not have to enter the last point; just drag the cursor away from the preceding point. When you press Enter or the space bar, AutoCAD accepts the position of the cursor as the last point on the fence.

In this tutorial, you will use the Fence selection option to select specific objects found in the apartment floor plan in Figure 9.5. Follow these steps:

1.  Choose the Select Fence button from the Select Objects floating toolbar.
2. At the `First Fence point:` prompt, enter **1′7,16′2.**
3. At the `Undo/<Endpoint of Line>:` prompt, enter **1′7,28′5.**
4. At the `Undo/<Endpoint of line 7:` prompt, enter **8′, 28′5.**
5. At the `Undo/<Endpoint of Line>:` prompt, press Enter. Notice that all objects that the fence crossed over were selected, as shown in Figure 9.16.
6. At the `Select objects:` prompt, press Enter to accept the selection set.

Skill Builder

In this example, you typed coordinates to make the selection. It is not necessary to use the coordinates exclusively when creating selection sets. Using the mouse is also a good way to visually select points.

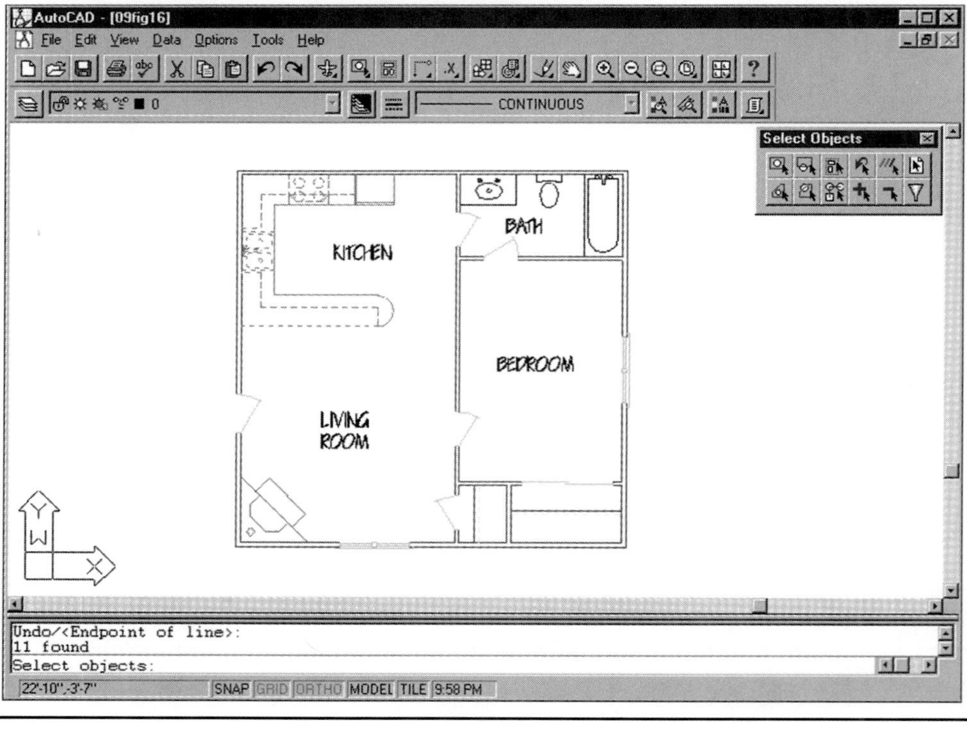

Figure 9.16
When using the Fence selection option, any objects that cross or intersect the fence are included in the selection set.

Selecting Multiple Objects from the Drawing Database

Every time you pick an object to be included in a selection set, AutoCAD immediately scans the entire database of the drawing. This process can be very slow in a complex drawing. Using the Multiple option makes AutoCAD scan the drawing database only once to look for the objects to include in the selection set. This allows you to specify multiple pick points without highlighting the objects. This can increase the selection process for complex objects.

To use the Multiple option, enter *M* at the `Select objects:` prompt. AutoCAD then repeats the `Select objects:` prompt. Continue adding or removing objects from the selection set. All other selection set methods are disabled until you have individually selected the objects to include in the selection set. When you have completed the selection set, press [Enter]. AutoCAD scans the drawing once to look for objects to include in the selection set.

TUTORIAL 9.10: SELECTING A SINGLE OBJECT

With the Single option, you can select only one object rather than continuing to prompt for further selections. This can speed up the editing process when you need to select only one object or a single group of objects.

In this tutorial, you will use the Single selection option to select specific objects found in the apartment floor plan in Figure 9.5. Follow these steps:

1. At the `Command:` prompt, enter **select**.
2. At the `Select objects:` prompt, enter **single**. *Single* can be abbreviated as **si**.
3. Select any object in the apartment floor plan. Notice that after the object is selected you are automatically taken back to the `Command:` prompt. The Single selection option allows only one selection for that selection set.

COMPLETING THE SELECTION SET

In the previous tutorials, you have been using the [Enter] key or the space bar to cause AutoCAD to stop asking for selection set objects. At that point, AutoCAD will continue the editing command based on the current selection set. Pressing [Enter] or the space bar is called a null response, indicating there is nothing more to add to AutoCAD. You will use the null response on a variety of commands. You have used it in the past to stop the **line** command. Be aware of the commands that require the null response. A common error is to begin a new command before a required null response is issued.

TUTORIAL 9.11: SELECTING THE PREVIOUS SELECTION SET

The Previous option enables you to use the preceding selection set as the current selection set. This option is helpful when you want to use several different commands on the same group of objects.

1.  Choose the Select Previous button from the Select Objects floating toolbar. Notice that the selection set from the preceding tutorial is selected. The Previous selection option always recalls the last selection set created—for possible additions or removals to the set.
2. At the `Select objects:` prompt, press [Enter] to accept the selection set.

Changing the Selection When using any of the selection methods to select objects, you may occasionally pick unwanted objects or change your mind about a selection. You can cycle through multiple objects in the Pickbox area, undo a selection, remove objects from the selected group, or even cancel the entire selection.

OBJECT SELECTION CYCLING

When working on a complex drawing, it's often difficult to select the correct object by picking. With several objects falling inside the Pickbox, AutoCAD is likely to grab the wrong one at any given time. You can always make the Pickbox smaller to make it less likely that multiple objects are captured, but that also makes it less likely that you'll be able to easily select what you're trying to get. Another option is to zoom in for a closer look, but that takes time and is distracting.

AutoCAD's solution to the problem is object selection cycling. Go ahead and enlarge that Pickbox to keep from squinting. Then hold down [Ctrl] when you press the

Pick button to select an object. If AutoCAD highlights an object that you don't want, press the Pick button again to move to the next object within the Pickbox range. Repeat until the object needed is included in the selection set.

Tutorial 9.12: Removing and Adding Objects to the Selection Set

In certain instances, it may be more beneficial to use a crossing window than to select individual objects. This allows you to save time by selecting a large group of objects at once. You can then go back with the Remove option and remove objects you don't want included.

You can remove objects from the selection set with the Remove option. When you enter **r**, AutoCAD responds with the `Remove objects:` prompt. To remove objects, you can use any selection option to pick objects to remove from the selection set.

When you are in the Remove mode, the Add option switches you back to the selection mode. The `Select objects:` prompt returns, and you can continue to add objects to the selection set.

In this tutorial, you will use the Remove and Add selection options to select specific objects found in the apartment floor plan in Figure 9.5. Follow these steps:

1.  Choose the Select All button from the Select Objects floating toolbar.
2.  At the `Select objects:` prompt, choose the Select Remove button from the Select Objects floating toolbar.
3. At the `Remove object:` prompt, move the crosshairs to any wall line and select it. Notice that the object is no longer highlighted and is no longer included in the selection set.
4. At the `Remove object:` prompt, select any other wall line. That object is also no longer part of the selection set.
5.  At the `Remove object:` prompt, choose the Select Add button from the Select Objects floating toolbar.
6. Now select the wall lines you just removed. Notice that they are highlighted and added to the selection set.
7. At the `Select objects:` prompt, press [Enter] to accept the selection set.

Skill Builder

Instead of selecting the Remove icon, you can hold down [Shift] and pick the objects that you want to remove from the selection set.

Tutorial 9.13: Undoing a Selection

The Undo option enables you to step back through the object selection process and remove objects in the reverse order in which they were chosen.

In this tutorial, you will use the Undo selection option to deselect specific objects found in the apartment floor plan in Figure 9.5. Use these steps:

1. At the `Command:` prompt, enter **select**.
2. At the `Select objects:` prompt, select any wall line object.
3. The object is highlighted.
4. At the `Select objects:` prompt, enter **undo**.
5. The wall line object is removed from the selection set. The Undo option reverses any selection made in the previous selection attempt.
6. At the `Select objects:` prompt, press [Enter].

Tutorial 9.14: Canceling the Selection

Using [Esc] is the quickest way to cancel the object selection process. Pressing [Esc] immediately returns you to the `Command:` prompt. AutoCAD does not remember any selection set created, and you cannot use the set with the next editing command.

In this tutorial, you will use [Esc] to cancel a selection option of specific objects found in the apartment floor plan in Figure 9.5. Follow these steps:

1.  Choose the Select All button from the Select Objects floating toolbar.
2. At the `Select objects:` prompt, press [Esc]. Notice the message `Select objects: *Cancel*` above the `Command:` prompt. This message verifies that the previous selection set has been canceled.

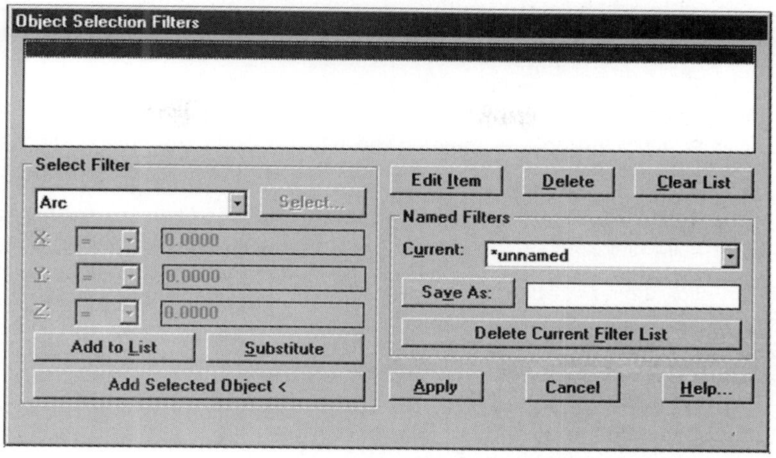

Figure 9.17
The Object Selection Filters dialog box is used to create a list of properties required of an object for it to be selected.

Using the Object Selection Filters

Object selection filters are used to create a list of properties that are required of an object for it to be selected. For example, you could set up an object selection filter for a specific layer. When you used any object selection method, the only objects selected would be the ones included in the selection set and residing on the filtered layer.

You can access the Object Selection Filters dialog box shown in Figure 9.17 by using one of the following methods:

- Select the Selection Filters button on the Select Objects floating toolbar.
- Enter **'filter** at the `Command:` prompt or at the `Select objects:` prompt.

Object selection filters can be useful if you have a complex drawing and want to select specific objects. For example, your drawing contains a large number of 2″-diameter circles residing on different layers, and they all need to be changed to a 2.125″-diameter. By setting up a filter for a 2″-circle, you can use it in conjunction with the Select All option. When the selection process begins, only objects meeting the filter criteria (a 2″-circle) are selected.

Selecting Groups

AutoCAD Release 13 now includes the ability to group a set of objects together in a named selection set. This feature allows you to select a group of objects with one selection.

After you have defined a group, you can select it by choosing the Select Group icon from the Select Objects floating toolbar. When AutoCAD prompts `Enter group name:`, type in the name of a previously defined group. All objects in the defined group are selected.

System Variables That Affect Selecting Objects

System variables are used to store information about the current drawing and AutoCAD configuration. As a reference, this section provides a list of several system variables that are used specifically to control AutoCAD's behavior when selecting objects. By changing the settings of certain variables, you can make AutoCAD behave like previous releases of AutoCAD or other popular CAD systems that you may have worked with in the past. By being allowed to modify these settings, it can in some cases reduce the learning curve for those who have worked on other CAD systems.

Pickfirst The **pickfirst** system variable controls the method of object selection. By default, **pickfirst** is enabled so that you can select an object first and then use an edit or inquiry command.

Tutorial 9.15: Creating an Object Selection Filter

For this tutorial, you will use the apartment floor plan and set up an Object Selection Filter. After the filter is defined, you will select all objects. Only the objects meeting the filter criteria are selected.

1.  Choose the Selection Filters button from the Select Objects floating toolbar.
2. Under Select Filter, click the DOWN ARROW next to Arc. Use the scroll bars to move down to Layer, and select it.
3. Choose the Select button in the Select Filter box. The Select Layer(s) dialog box appears. Choose the Doors layer.
4. In the Select Filter box, choose Add to List. The Object Selection Filters dialog box now looks like Figure 9.18.
5. Select Apply. The Select Filters dialog box disappears and you return to the drawing. The `Select Objects:` prompt appears.
6. At the `Select Objects:` prompt, type **all.** AutoCAD responds with 168 found, 154 were filtered out. Notice only the objects on the Doors layer are selected.
7. Press Enter to accept the selection set.

In addition to specifying specific layers, you can also pick objects from your drawing. The Add Selected Object button in the Object Selection Filters dialog box returns you to the drawing, where you can select an object. After the object is selected, you are returned to the Object Selection Filters dialog box. The information captured from the object selected now appears in the box at the top of the dialog box. You can edit this information or delete it as needed.

You can also save object selection filters you defined for later use. Properly used, object selection filters can greatly speed up the selection process in complicated drawings.

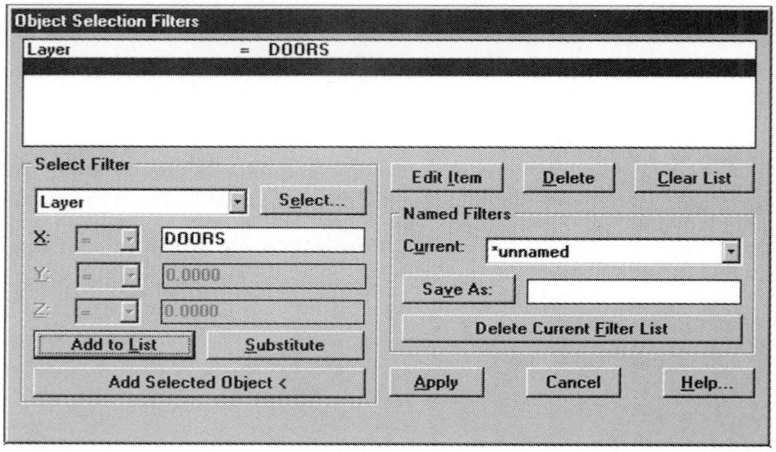

Figure 9.18
The Object Selection Filters dialog box can be used to set a filter to select only objects residing on a specific layer.

Pickadd **pickadd** is used to control how objects are added or removed from the selection set. By default, **pickadd** is enabled. When each object is selected, either by windowing or selected individually, it is added to the current selection set. To remove objects from the selection set with **pickadd** enabled, hold down Shift while selecting.

When **pickadd** is disabled, only the objects most recently selected, either by windowing or selected individually, become the selection set. Any objects previously selected are removed from the selection set. To add more objects to the selection set, hold down Shift while selecting.

Pickdrag **pickdrag** is used to control the method for drawing a selection window. By default, **pickdrag** is set so the selection window is drawn by clicking the pointing device at one corner, and clicking it again at the other corner.

If you set the **pickdrag** system variable to 1, you create the selection window by clicking the selection window at one corner, holding down the button, dragging the window to size, and releasing the button at the other corner.

Pickauto The **pickauto** system variable controls automatic windowing any time the `Select objects:` prompt appears. By default, you can draw a selection window (either window or crossing window) automatically at the `Select objects:` prompt. Turning **pickauto** off disables this function.

SUMMARY

A thorough understanding of selection sets is important because all editing commands utilize them. AutoCAD offers a variety of selection methods designed to cover almost any circumstance and any number of objects. As you begin to create and modify multiple objects, try to employ selection sets with which you have little experience. As you begin to understand their capabilities and functions, you will soon learn how to choose the best selection set method for the task at hand. Remember, there are many ways to properly use selection sets. Use the method or combination of methods best suited to the present task and to your abilities.

REVIEW

1. What is a selection set?
2. Explain the use of the **select** command.
3. How can an object be removed from a selection set?
4. What is the difference between the Window and Crossing Selection methods?
5. How are selections canceled?
6. Explain how to select every object in a drawing database.
7. Describe a situation where the Fence Selection Set option would be beneficial.
8. How is a previous selection set used?
9. What is the purpose of selection filters?
10. Discuss the difference between the Pick-First selection and the Pick-After selection.

EXERCISE 9

In this assignment you will create a drawing containing various shapes, as shown in Figure 9.19, and then create selection sets using the various selection set methods.

1. Create the drawing shown in Figure 9.19.
2. Use Decimal units with a precision of 0.000.

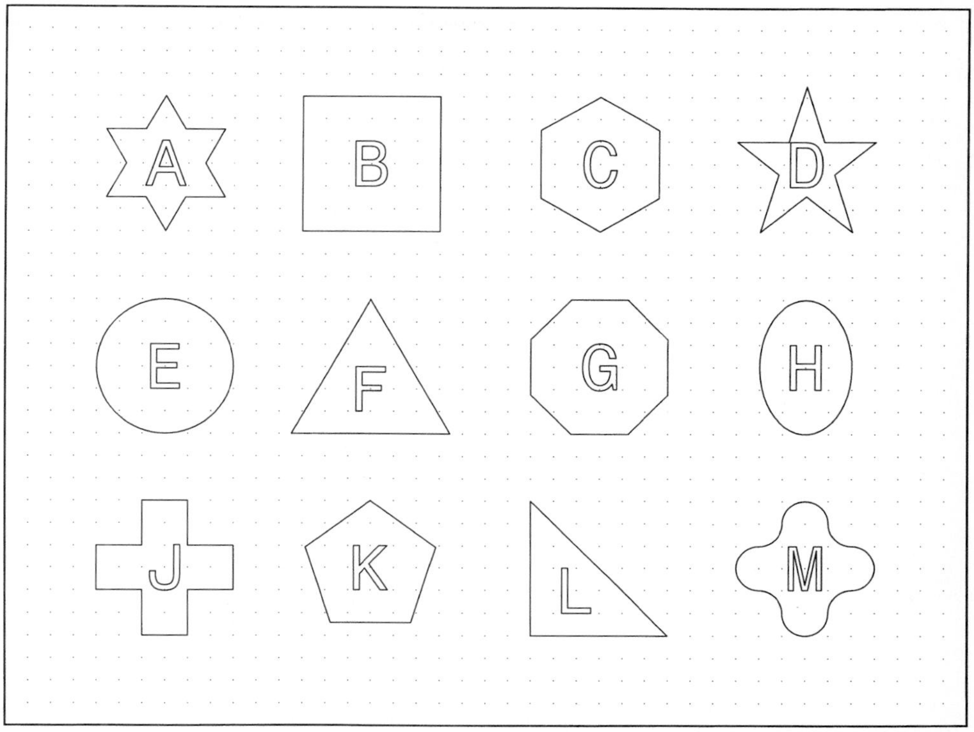

Figure 9.19
Create this drawing and then practice creating selection sets.

3. Use upper-right limits of 10.5,8.
4. **Set grid** equal to .25.
5. Set **snap** equal to .125.
6. Turn the **ucsicon** off.
7. Consider utilizing layers to assist in the grouping of objects.
8. Create a border with a thickness of .02 units.
9. Create letters with a height of .5 units using the MONOS.TTF font file.
10. Using the grid display as a guide, create the shapes shown in their approximate locations. Each shape should be a closed polygon when completed.
11. Save the drawing as Shapes.dwg.
12. Plot the drawing on an A-size sheet of paper.
13. Using the **select** command, create selection sets using the table below. The order listed is not necessarily the order that should be used when selecting objects to be included in the selection set. Once a selection set has been created, cancel the set and then begin the next set. Continue practicing using the selection set procedures until you completely understand their operation.

TABLE 9.3 Selections Set Assignment Table

Selection Method	Set Number	Objects
Single	1	G
	2	M
Multiple	3	A,D,J
	4	B,E,F,L,M - Remove M
Window	5	A,B,C,D,E,F,G,H
	6	B,D,F,G,H,K,L,M - Remove G
Crossing	7	G,H,L,M
Fence	8	C,F,H,J
	9	A,E,F,J,L - Remove E
All	10	A,B,C,D,E,F,G,H,J,K,L,M - Remove the border

UNIT 10

BASIC EDITING SKILLS

OVERVIEW

One of the advantages of using AutoCAD over traditional manual drafting is the ability to quickly edit incorrect or developing design ideas. The basic editing skills discussed in this chapter will not only allow you to edit existing objects, but they will, in many cases, also automate the construction of additional objects that are similar to those already found on the drawing. You will also find commands that help you get out of a jam by allowing you to recover from mistakes. Each of these commands is very useful and will save you many hours of object construction when the full potential of each is utilized.

OBJECTIVES

- Erase and restore objects.
- Use editing commands to move, copy, and offset objects.
- Rotate, Mirror, and Stretch objects.
- Modify line lengths.
- Modify corners.
- Create multiple copies of objects.

INTRODUCTION

Whenever you create a new drawing you will find yourself using both geometry creation and editing commands. You were introduced to geometry creation commands in previous units, and your instructor has probably already introduced you to some of the more basic editing skills—such as erasing objects and undoing the last command—both of which will be described in full in this unit. But there are many others that will make you wonder, "Why weren't we shown that earlier?" You will notice that as these commands are introduced, you will immediately begin to think of situations where the command will be beneficial and make it easier to complete your design or drawing.

As you begin to create lines and circles, you will want a way to quickly correct your mistake. Believe it or not, you will eventually make a mistake. It may not even be a mistake, just a new design feature or enhancement. Either way, AutoCAD provides many commands that will allow you to quickly modify your drawing.

You may have heard the phrase, "Let's not reinvent the wheel." AutoCAD allows you to create other instances of objects that have already been created. For instance, you may be creating a drawing for an auditorium capable of seating 500 people. It would take a lot of time if we had to draw each individual chair. AutoCAD will allow you to copy the chair and move it to another location. If you need multiple copies of the object, there are commands to automate locating these objects as well. Maybe you don't need other copies of objects; you just need to change sizes and locations, or to simply modify a corner so that it is rounded. Whatever editing you need to accomplish, you can be assured that there is a command just right for the task. The first section in this unit will introduce you to deleting and restoring objects.

OUTLINE

Deleting and Restoring Objects
Tutorial 10.1: Erasing and Restoring Objects
Tutorial 10.2: Working with Undo and Redo
Tutorial 10.3: Purging an Unwanted Layer
Moving, Copying, and Offsetting Objects
Tutorial 10.4: Moving Objects
Tutorial 10.5: Copying Objects
Tutorial 10.6: Offsetting Objects
Rotating, Mirroring, Scaling, and Stretching Objects
Tutorial 10.7: Rotating Objects
Tutorial 10 8: Mirroring Objects
Tutorial 10.9: Scaling Objects
Tutorial 10.10: Stretching Objects
Editing Edges and Corners of Objects
Tutorial 10.11: Shortening Objects with the **trim** Command
Tutorial 10.12: Using the **break** Command
Tutorial 10.13: Extending Objects
Tutorial 10.14: Rounding and Cleaning Edges with the **fillet** Command
Tutorial 10.15: Creating Chamfers
Producing Arrays of Objects
Tutorial 10.16: Duplicating Elements in a Grid Format
Tutorial 10.17: Duplicating Elements in a Circular Format
Summary
Review
Exercises

DELETING AND RESTORING OBJECTS

As you progress through your design, you will find many times when you need to erase an object. The object may be incorrect or it may be a construction line that is no longer needed. And unlike the paper and eraser counterpart, when you erase the line in AutoCAD, there is no faint line or erasures to indicate that a line was once located at a certain point. When you erase a line in AutoCAD, it would appear that it is gone forever. But as you will find in this section, there are ways to return a line that has been erased. Let's look at deleting objects first.

DELETING OBJECTS

The first thing you will notice about deleting objects in AutoCAD is that it doesn't work exactly as you would expect. When you use an eraser, you have to move it back and forth over the line you are erasing until you have completely covered the line. AutoCAD requires you to select the object at only one location and it will then erase the entire object. You can use the **erase** command to delete objects. This command can be accessed using one of two methods.

- Select the Erase button from the Modify toolbar.
- Enter `erase` at the `Command:` prompt.

SKILL BUILDER

The hot key for the **erase** command is *E* followed by ↵Enter.

Once the **erase** command is activated, you will be asked to select the object(s) to erase. You can select the object singularly, or you can use selection sets to select multiple objects. Once you have made your selections, the objects will be erased.

SKILL BUILDER

If you are not comfortable with selection sets, it might be wise to review the previous unit. All of the editing skills in this unit require proficient use of selection sets to be properly executed.

It may appear that after the object has been erased, it is gone forever. That is not the case, as you will find after Tutorial 10.1.

Restoring Accidentally Erased Objects

There are occasions when you erase lines and think, "Why did I do that?" Or you may even say softly to yourself "Oops!" Well, believe it or not, you can type just what you say, *oops,* and that command will bring back the last selection set erased. You have to wonder where the programmers of AutoCAD came up with that command name. Even programmers have a sense of humor. Despite the humor behind the **oops** command, it is very useful and needed. There are two ways to access the **oops** command:

- Select the Oops! button from the Miscellaneous toolbar.
- Enter **`oops`** at the `Command:` prompt.

Tutorial 10.1: Erasing and Restoring Objects

The tutorials in this unit serve three purposes: to see if you can create basic geometry, utilize selection sets, and perform basic editing skills as introduced. As you progress through the tutorials in this unit, you will create a proposed office/conference room for a firm know as Graphics Plus. With each successive tutorial, you will add another component of the office. By the end of this unit, you should have the completed office as shown in Figure 10.1.

In this first tutorial, you will create and edit lines that comprise the interior walls of the office. Before creating the drawing, you will load a prototype drawing that will contain all settings and layers necessary to complete this drawing.

1.  Open the OFFICE1.DWG file from the tutorial disk. A blank screen will be loaded, but all necessary settings will be established and all layers will be created.
2. Ensure that Wall is the current layer.
3.  Use the **line** command and create a square that is 15′ × 15′ and whose lower-left corner starts at the coordinates of 6′,3′. For the purpose of this tutorial, make sure you use the **line** command and not the **rectang** command. Do not worry that the square is not centered on the drawing. We will correct that in a later step.
4.  Select Erase from the Modify toolbar. The `Select objects:` prompt will appear.
5. Select the bottom line of the square that you just created. It will be highlighted.
6. The `Select objects:` prompt will appear. Press ↵Enter to erase the line as shown in Figure 10.2. Let's restore the line in the next step.
7. Select Oops! from the Miscellaneous toolbar. The line will reappear.

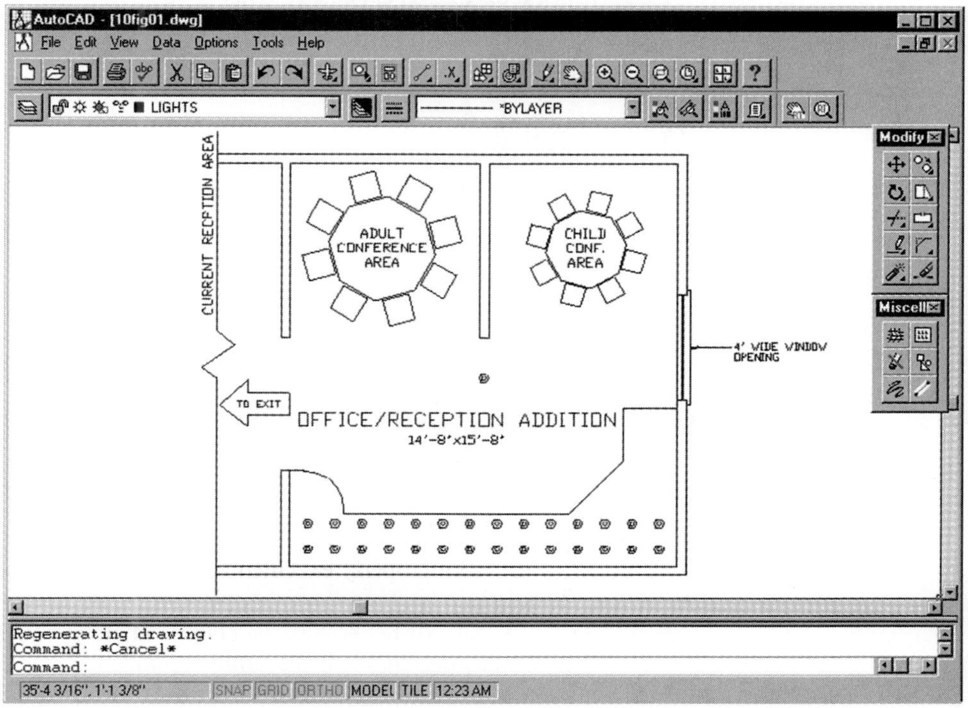

Figure 10.1
The completed office layout.

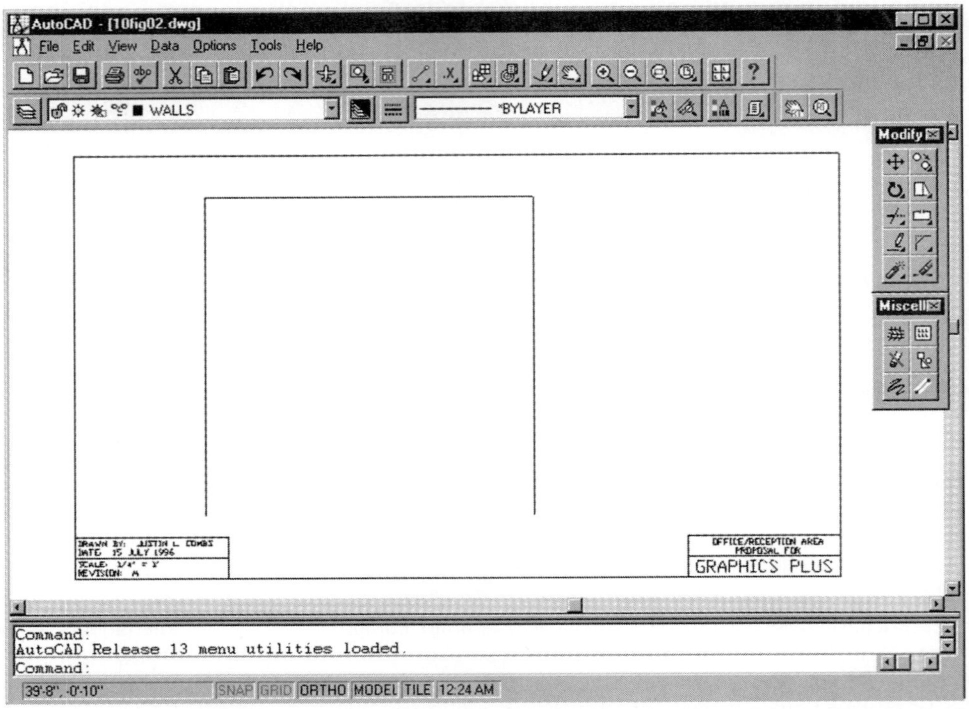

Figure 10.2.
Erasing the bottom line of the square.

Once the command is entered, the last erased selection set will be restored. It is important to note that this command will work only on the last erased selection set, not on prior selection sets.

Undoing Your Work

oops is convenient when you need to recover the last erased selection set, but what do you do if you need to reverse the last five or six drawing and editing commands because it just didn't go as expected? What if you actually needed objects that were erased six or seven **erase** commands ago? There, of course, is a command to cover these instances. The **undo** command allows you to undo the last command executed and any command prior to that within the current drawing session. The current drawing session can be defined as the point where a file was created or opened. Once the file is closed or AutoCAD is exited, the current drawing session is closed. The next time the file is opened begins the new drawing session. Undo is so complete that you could begin a new drawing and, as long as the file hasn't been closed, you can work for five hours and undo back to the beginning command. There are three ways to use this command:

- Select the Undo button from the Standard toolbar. Selecting this button will undo the last command executed.
- Enter **u** at the `Command:` prompt. This option will also undo the last command executed.
- Enter **undo** at the `Command:` prompt. Upon entering this command, the `Auto/Control/BEgin/End/Mark/Back/<Number>:` prompt will appear. Select from one of the following options:
  - **Auto.** Set this option to Off or On. When set to On, will undo a menu selection as a single command.
  - **Control.** Modifies the abilities of the **undo** command. Use one of the following options:
    - **All.** All features of the command are available.
    - **None.** Turns off the **undo** command.
    - **One.** Limits the **undo** command to a single command.

- **BEgin.** Used to mark the beginning of an **undo** group.
- **End.** Used to mark the end of an **undo** group. When this group is reached, Undo will undo all commands located within this group at once instead of its individual commands.
- **Mark.** Used to make a reference point for **undo** for later.
- **Back.** Will undo back to the last mark specified.
- **Number.** Will undo the number of commands entered. An entry of 10 would undo the last 10 commands executed.

- Entering **u** within certain commands will allow you to undo a step within a command. For instance, using this option during the **line** command will allow you to undo the last point selected but to continue with that command.

So, what if you make a mistake and perform an **undo?** If you try to reverse the last **undo** (this is where it gets tricky), you will undo the command prior to the **undo,** not the **undo** itself. The command you need to use in this case is the **redo** command. This command can be entered as follows:

- Select the Redo button from the Standard toolbar.
- Enter `redo` at the `Command:` prompt.

TUTORIAL 10.2: WORKING WITH UNDO AND REDO

This tutorial continues from the previous tutorial. In this tutorial you will use the **undo** and **redo** commands to modify the drawing to include possible design changes.

1. Enter `undo` at the `Command:` prompt. The `Auto/Control/BEgin/End/Mark/Back/<Number>:` prompt will appear.
2. Enter `m` and press Enter to select the Mark option. This mark is created so that if our design changes don't work out, we can undo back to our original design.
3.  Select the Erase button from the Modify toolbar. The `Select objects:` prompt will appear.
4. Select the right and bottom line of the square you created in the previous tutorial and click the right mouse button. The lines will disappear as shown in Figure 10.3. Let's consider making the right wall an angular wall.
5.  Select the **line** command from the Draw toolbar.

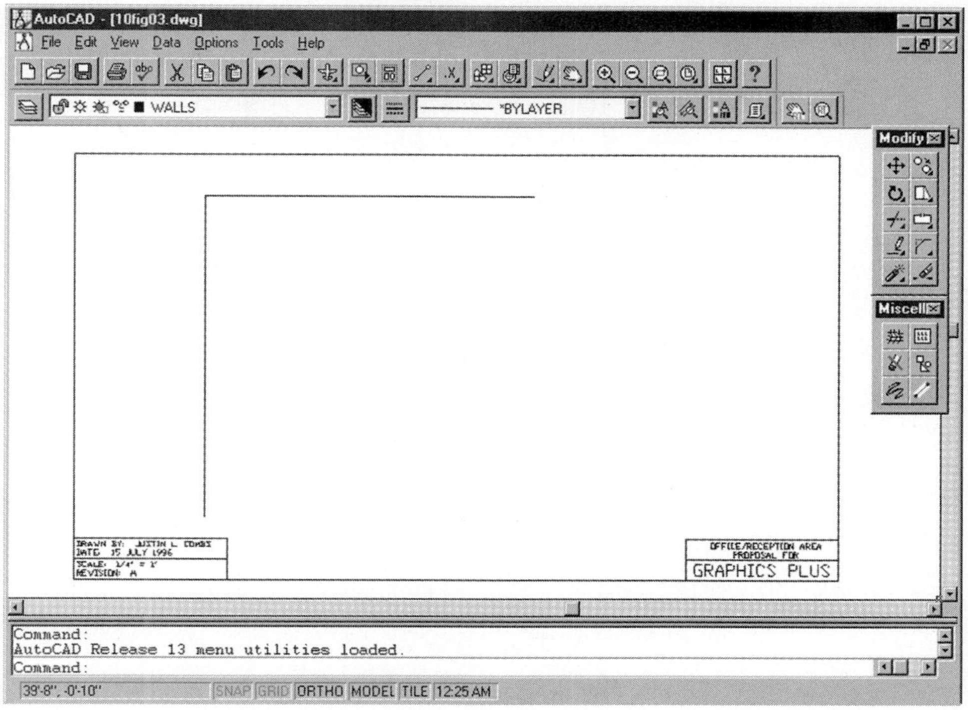

Figure 10.3
Erasing lines on the office complex.

6. At the `From point:` prompt, use the Endpoint object snap and choose the right end of the top line.
7. At the `To point:` prompt, enter @16′<250 and press Enter. A line will be created.
8. At the `To point:` prompt, enter @10′<180 and press Enter. A horizontal line will be created. This line appears to be too long and does not intersect the bottom of the left vertical line. You need to correct this.
9. At the `To point:` prompt, enter **u** and press Enter. This will undo the last point selected in Step 8 so you may correct the mistake.
10. At the `To point:` prompt, enter **endp** and press Enter.
11. At the `of` prompt select the bottom of the left vertical line. The line will connect to the bottom of the left vertical line.
12. At the `To point:` press Enter. This will end the command. You should now have the figure shown in Figure

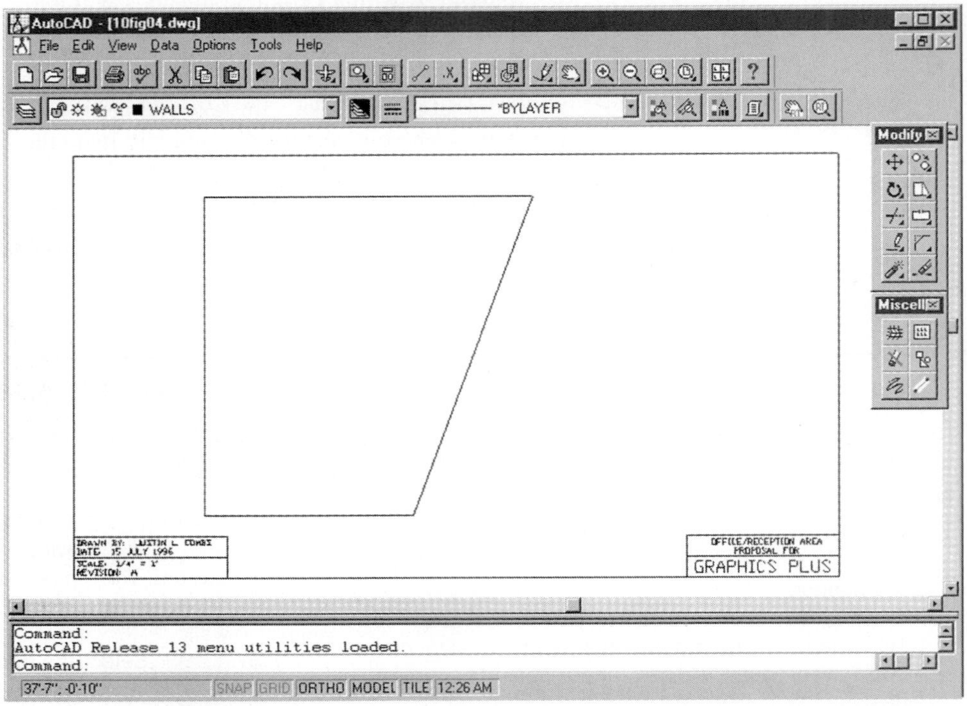

Figure 10.4
The proposed angular wall.

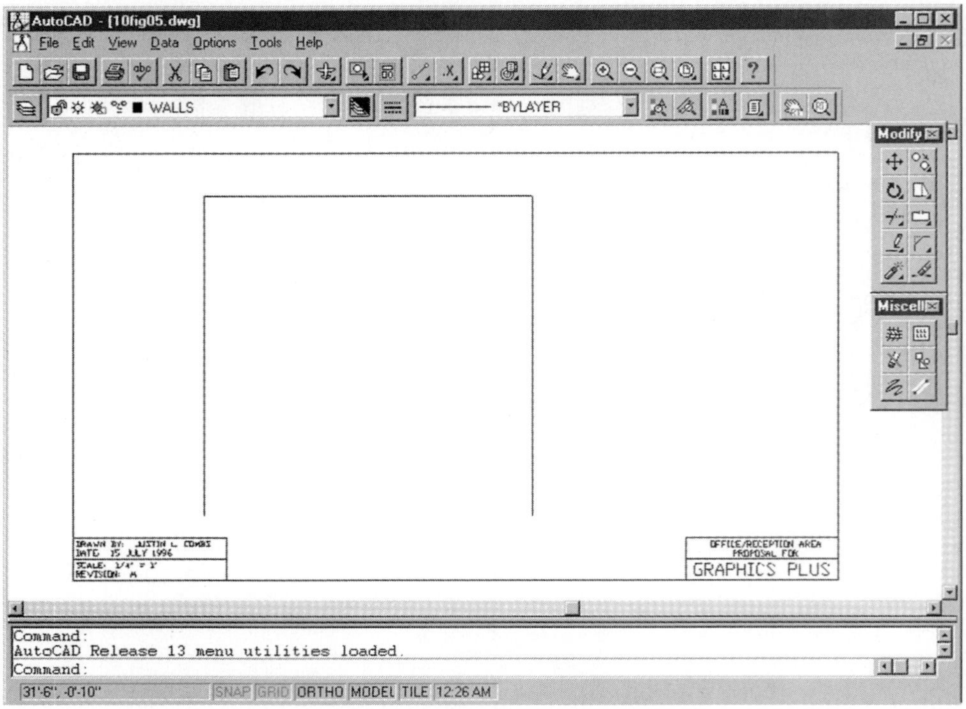

Figure 10.5
Preparing for the next tutorial.

10.4. After viewing the changes, you may notice that this is not quite what you wanted. Maybe the standard square room will work better. Let's return it to the way it was. We could use **undo** and step back to the point where the changes started, but we preplanned and placed an undo mark.

13. Enter `undo` at the `Command:` prompt. The `Auto/Control/BEgin/End/Mark/Back/<Number>:` prompt will appear.

14. Enter `b` and press [Enter]. The drawing will revert back to the original plan. To verify the design again, let's redisplay the angular plan.

15.  Select the **redo** button from the Standard toolbar. This will reverse the last undo and return the angular plan.

16.  Select the **undo** button from the Standard toolbar. This will undo the **redo** and return the square floor plan. Before continuing on to the next tutorial, we need to make a slight change.

17.  Select the Erase button from the Modify toolbar.

18. At the `Select objects:` prompt, select the bottom horizontal line and press the right mouse button. The line will be erased and your drawing should resemble the one shown in Figure 10.5.

TUTORIAL 10.3: PURGING AN UNWANTED LAYER

This tutorial continues from the previous tutorial. In this tutorial you will purge a layer that is not being used.

1. Enter **purge** at the command prompt. The `Purge unused Blocks/Dimstyles/LAyers/LTypes/SHapes/STyles/Mlinestyles/All:` prompt will appear.

2. Enter **la** and press [Enter]. You will be asked one at a time, which layer to purge. Follow the command sequence as it appears below. Notice that you are not asked to purge the Border or Walls layers. Those layers contain objects and cannot be purged.

```
Purge layer COUNTER? <N> n
Purge layer DESK? <N> n
Purge layer FILE? <N> n
Purge layer FLOOR? <N> y
```

3.  Select the Layers button from the Object Properties toolbar. The Layers dialog box appears as shown in Figure 10.6. Notice that the Floor layer has been removed.

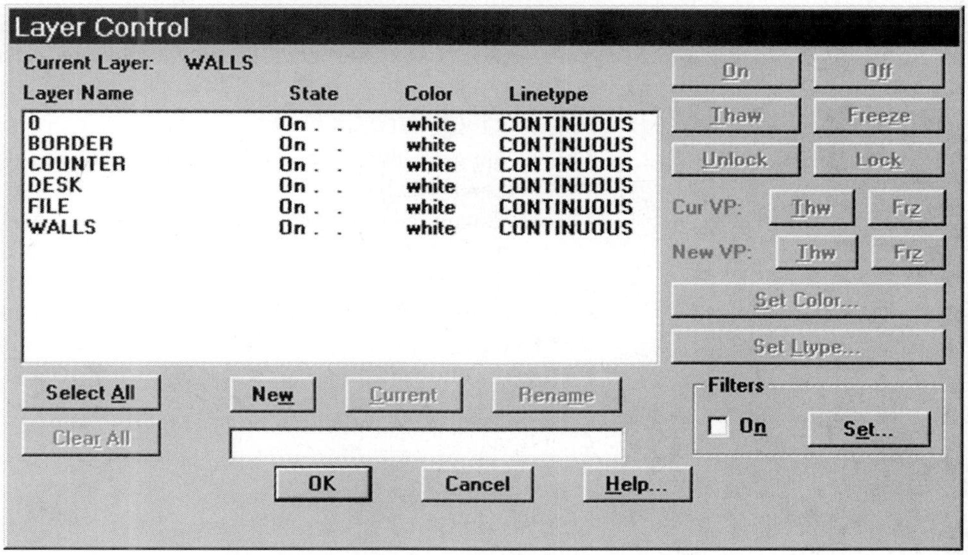

Figure 10.6
Viewing the Layer list to verify that the Floor layer was purged.

Once this command is entered, the last undo performed will be reversed. This command only will work if the last command performed was **undo.** If any other command was executed afterwards, nothing will happen.

Removing Unwanted Objects

As you begin to create complex drawings that contain many linetypes, layers, text styles, and blocks your drawing may become cluttered with unreferenced items. You may have created a layer only to find that you never used it, or loaded a linetype that was not used in the drawing. You can rid yourself of this often confusing clutter by using an advanced command known as **purge**. To access the **purge** command, enter **purge** at the `Command:` prompt. Once entered, the following prompt will appear:

```
Purge unused
Blocks/Dimstyles/LAyers/LTypes/SHapes/STyles/Mlinestyles/All:
```

When this prompt appears, select the objects you wish to purge. The only objects that can be purged are those that are not being used. By purging items, you cut down on the memory requirements and storage requirements for the file.

For the Professional

If you select the All option, you will purge all items that are not being referenced. This is helpful when you are not sure what is being used and what is not.

MOVING, COPYING, AND OFFSETTING OBJECTS

The next three commands presented are easy commands to understand—until you try to apply them. Often, these commands confuse students because of the flexibility they allow. Moving and copying objects are very similar tasks. They each ask for the same information. Offsetting works similarly to the two commands, but requires the user to enter different reference points. Learning each command individually, as presented here, should help you understand its use a little better. The **move** command is the basis for the other two commands.

Moving Objects

One of the great things about AutoCAD is that you never have to worry if a drawing is centered on a title block, if a window is in the exact location, or if the side view of a hole is aligned with the top view. First, worry about the accuracy of the drawing, then you can use the **move** command to place the objects in the correct locations. To perform this same procedure on a paper drawing may require a complete retracing of the drawing or erasing and redrawing a part. Either way, this can take some time. When you use AutoCAD you don't have to worry about redrawing an object that is in the wrong position. You can enter the **move** command with one of the following methods:

- Select the Move button on the Modify toolbar.
- Enter **move** at the `Command:` prompt.

Skill Builder

The hot key for the **move** command is **m** followed by the [Enter].

Once you have entered the command, the following prompt appears:

```
Select objects:
```

At this prompt, select the objects you wish to move. You can select objects individually, or you can use selection sets for multiple objects. Once the objects to be moved have been selected, you will see the following prompt:

```
Base point or displacement:
```

This point defines where the object is to be moved from. It is generally a key location for the object(s) being moved. For instance, you would probably choose the center of a circle as the base point or a corner of a rectangle. The base point does not even have to be on the object. You could select coordinates. Once you have selected the base point, the following prompt will appear.

```
Second point or displacement:
```

This is where the power of the command comes into play. You can move the object with the cursor. The object will be attached to the crosshairs at the point selected as your

Tutorial 10.4: Moving Objects

This tutorial continues from the previous tutorial. In this tutorial you will relocate the lines that represent the wall of the office. By relocating the walls, we will ensure that the office is centered within the border.

1.  Select the Move button from the Modify toolbar. The `Select objects:` prompt appears.
2. Use the Window selection set option and create a window around the three lines that represent the walls. Once the window has been created, click the right mouse button to accept the selection set.
3. At the `Base point or displacement:` prompt, select the bottom end point of the left vertical line.
4. At the `Second point of displacement:` prompt, move the crosshairs to the right of the vertical line. Notice that **ortho** is turned on to ensure that the displacement is exactly horizontal.
5. Enter **4'** at the `Command:` prompt and press ↵Enter. The walls are now moved and are centered within the border as shown in Figure 10.7.

For the Professional

As you continue to use AutoCAD, you will find that the exact placement of the object is not important during the creation of the drawing. It can always be moved so that it is accurately and neatly centered within a given title block.

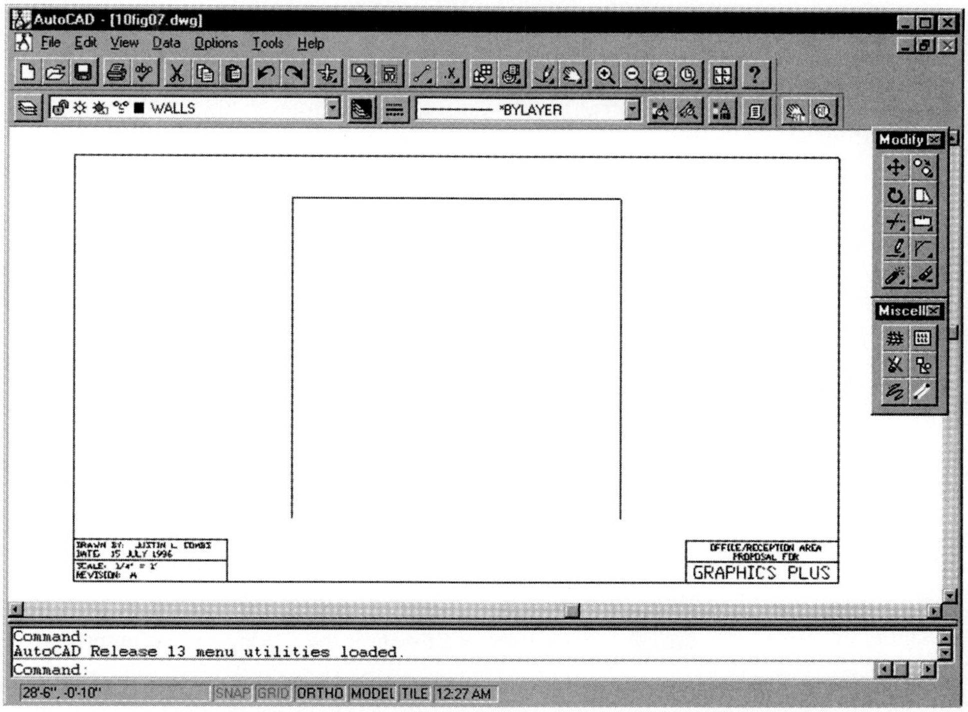

Figure 10.7
Centering the drawing within the border.

base point, or you can use coordinates to place the object. A common method used prior to AutoCAD Release 13c4 was to use polar coordinates. To move the object down two units, you would use @2<270. The object would then be relocated. You can still use this method, but the latest versions of AutoCAD allow you to move your cursor in the direction you want the object to move and type the distance of displacement. For our example, you would just move the cursor down and enter *2*.

Copying Objects

As you create drawings, you will find that many objects are duplicates of others already created. One of the greatest advantages of using AutoCAD is the ability to duplicate these common objects. No longer do you have to redraw objects over and over. You will find that the **copy** command will save you many hours of work. This command is similar in execution to the **move** command. The only difference is that **copy** will leave a copy of the object at the base point, after you specify the second point of displacement. To access the **copy** command, use one of the following methods:

- Select the Copy object button from the Modify toolbar.
- Enter **`copy`** at the `Command:` prompt.

Skill Builder

The hot key for the **copy** command is **cp** followed by the ↵Enter.

Once you have entered the command, the following prompt appears:

`Select objects:`

At this prompt, select the objects that you wish to copy. You can select objects individually or you can use selection sets for multiple objects. Once the objects to be copied have been selected, you will see the following prompt:

`<Base point or displacement>:/Multiple:`

The default selection, Base point or displacement, defines where the object is to be copied from. It is generally a key location for the object(s) being copied. The Multiple option allows you to create multiple copies of the object. To create multiple copies, just specify multiple second points. You can continue creating copies as long as you wish. If you do not choose the Multiple option, you will create only one copy of the object, and the command will conclude. Selecting this option will give you the `Base point or displacement:` prompt. Once you have selected the base point, the following prompt will appear:

`Second point or displacement:`

You can copy the object being moved with the cursor. The object will be attached to the crosshairs at the point selected as your base point, or you can use the coordinates to place the object. To copy the object down two units, move the cursor down and enter *2*.

Creating Objects with **offset**

In the previous tutorial you created a copy of a line that was offset from the original at a distance specified by the use of the Endpoint object snap. If that distance was known, we could use the **offset** command. The **offset** command creates an offset copy of an object at a distance specified. To execute this command, use one of the following options:

- Select the Offset button from the Copy flyout menu on the Modify toolbar.
- Enter **`offset`** at the `Command:` prompt.

Once the **offset** command is entered, the following prompt is displayed.

Tutorial 10.5: Copying Objects

This tutorial continues from the previous tutorial. In this tutorial you will create a copy of the top horizontal line and place it at the bottom of the lines representing the wall.

1.  Select the Copy objects button from the Modify toolbar. The `Select objects:` prompt appears.
2. Select the top horizontal line and click the right mouse button to accept the selection set.
3. At the `<Base point or displacement prompt>/Multiple:` prompt, select the Intersection of the left vertical line and the horizontal line selected in step 2.
4. At the `Second point of displacement:` prompt, select the Endpoint object snap.
5. At the `of` prompt, select the bottom of the left vertical line. You will once again have the complete square outline representing the boundaries of the walls as shown in Figure 10.8.

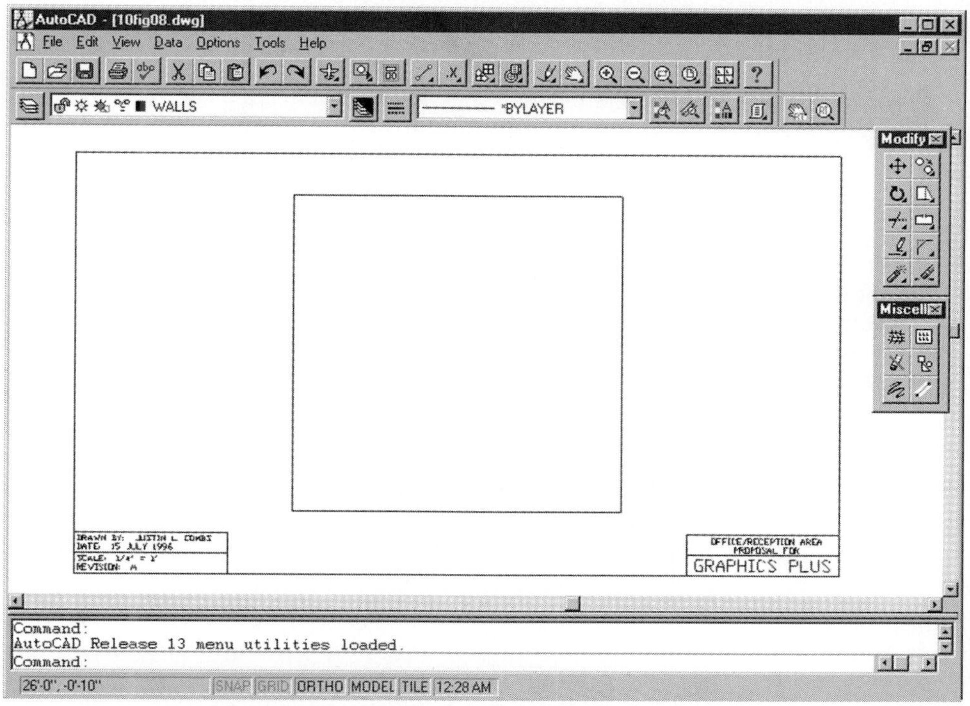

Figure 10.8
The boundaries of the walls.

`Offset distance or Through <Through>:`

Specify the distance using the keyboard, or use the digitizer to specify the starting and ending point for the offset. If you select the Through option, AutoCAD will prompt you to select the object to offset and then ask you to specify the through point or the point at which you want to create a copy of the object. If you do not select the Through option, the following prompt will appear:

`Select object to offset:`

Select the object you wish to offset. Only one object can be selected at a time. Once selected, the next prompt will appear:

`Side to offset?`

Choose the side of the object that specifies the direction for the offset. The offset object will be created. You should be aware of how this command works with certain objects. Figure 10.9 displays the effects of this command on different object types.

When a line is offset, the copy is created on the side specified. If you offset a circle, a new circle will be created that is concentric with the original circle. A polyline that is offset will create a new polyline that follows the profile of the original.

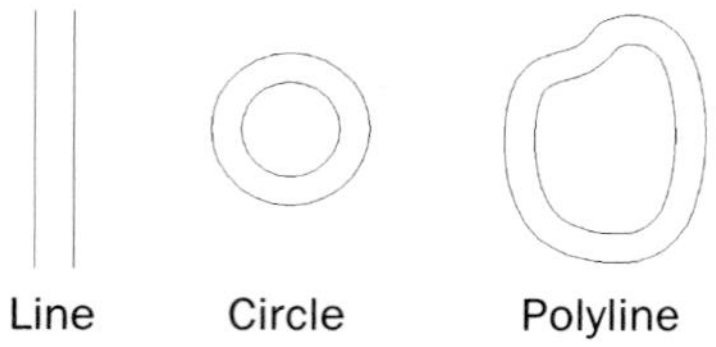

Figure 10.9
Various effects of the Offset line on objects.

Tutorial 10.6: Offsetting Objects

This tutorial continues from the previous tutorial. In this tutorial you will use the **offset** command to add thickness to the walls of the office.

1.  Select the Offset button from the Copy flyout menu on the Modify toolbar. The `Offset distance or Through <Through>:` prompt will be displayed.
2. Enter 4″ and press ↵Enter. The `Select object to offset:` prompt will appear.
3. Select the left vertical line. The `Side to offset?` prompt will appear.
4. Select the right side of the object, or towards the inside of the square. A duplicate will be created to the right of the original as shown in Figure 10.10. The `Select object to offset:` prompt will reappear.
5. Select the top horizontal line. The `Side to offset?` prompt will appear.
6. Select below the top line, or towards the inside of the square. A duplicate line will be created below the original. The `Select object to offset:` prompt will reappear.
7. Continue around the square in the same fashion until the **offset** command has been used on the remaining two lines. When complete, your drawing should resemble Figure 10.11.
8. Once complete, the `Select object to offset:` prompt will reappear. Click the right mouse button to exit the command. You may notice that the corners of the inside box are not correct. We will correct this problem in a later tutorial.

Skill Builder

To enter 4″ you do not need to include the (″) marks. AutoCAD's default unit in the Architectural units style is the inch.

Figure 10.10
The first line to offset.

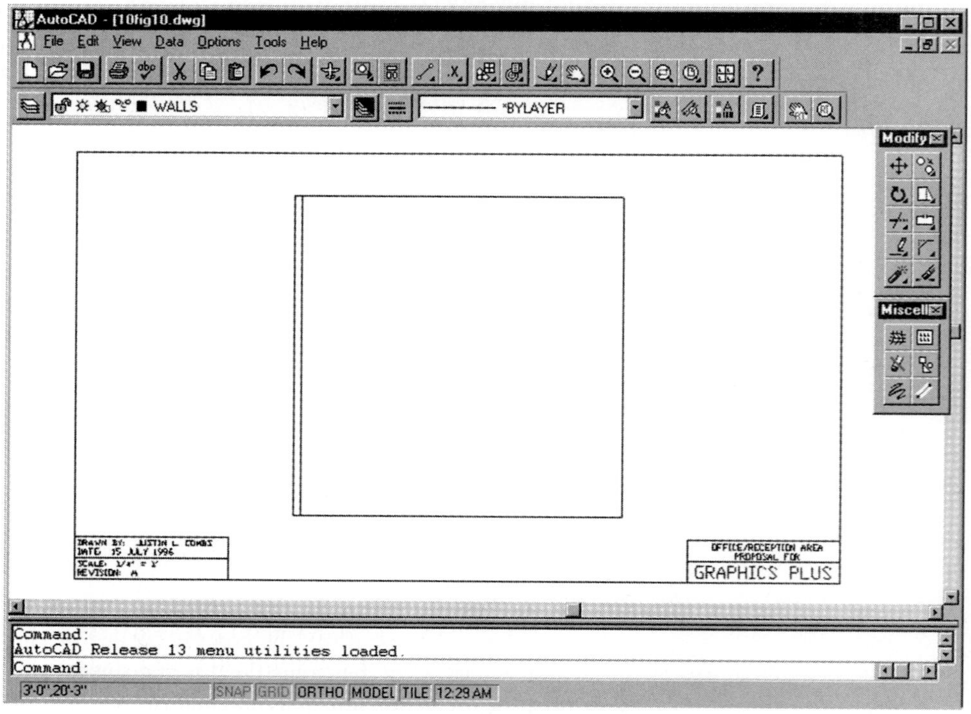

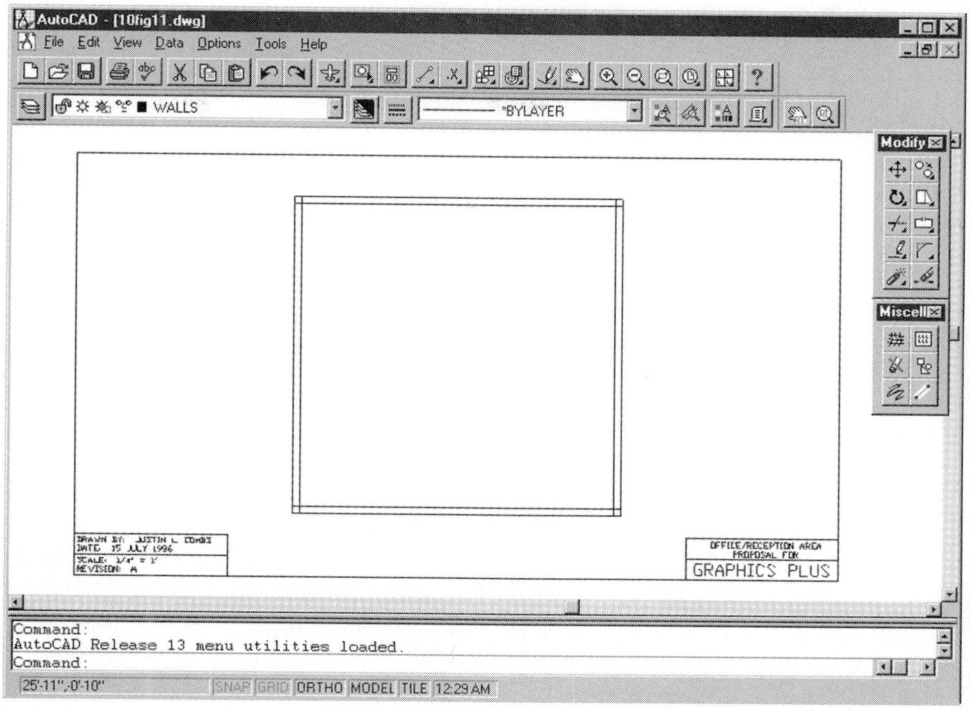

Figure 10.11
*Using the **offset** command to create the interior wall boundaries.*

ROTATING, MIRRORING, SCALING, AND STRETCHING OBJECTS

You may occasionally find that the object you create is correct, but the orientation is wrong. If you have a symmetrical object, you may have discovered that the **copy** command does not provide an easy way to create one-half the object and then copy it to create the other half. Finally, there are occasions when the object you created may be inaccurate in only one direction. It may be too long or too short. Each of these problems is easily corrected using the commands in this section.

Rotating Objects

You will find as you create objects that there are many lines that have to be rotated for the proper orientation. Polar coordinates can be used to assist you in creating lines at a particular angle, but there are occasions when it just may be easier to create the object in a traditional horizontal or vertical orientation and then rotate it into the proper position. A good example of this would be placing a home on a plot plan. While the plot may contain boundaries that are horizontal and vertical, the house may sit on the plot at a 45° angle. You would not want to create every line with the 45° angle adjustment. The easiest way to solve this problem would be to create the house in its traditional orientation and then rotate at the specified angle. AutoCAD provides the **rotate** command for just this purpose. In traditional drawing you would create the plot plan, rotate the drawing paper, create the house, then rotate the drawing back to its horizontal orientation—the opposite procedure from the AutoCAD method. To access the **rotate** command, use one of the following methods:

- Select the Rotate button from the Modify toolbar.
- Enter `rotate` at the `Command:` prompt.

Once the command has been entered, the following prompt will appear:

`Select objects:`

Use selection sets to select the objects you want to rotate and then click the right mouse button.

`Base point:`

Select the rotation point for the objects you wish to rotate. This point is the center of an imaginary arc that is used to rotate the objects. Do not get this confused with the base point for the **move** and **copy** commands. During a rotation, the objects will not be displaced, but rotated. Once the base point has been selected, the next prompt will appear:

`<Rotation angle>/Reference:`

The default rotation angle options allows you to specify the rotation angle. To rotate the objects 45° counterclockwise, you would enter a value of +45. To rotate the objects 45° clockwise, you would use –45.

SKILL BUILDER

The direction of rotation is specified in the **ddunits** command. The clockwise/counterclockwise orientation can be modified using the Direction Control dialog box found in the Units dialog box.

If you choose the Reference option, you will be presented with the following prompt:

`Reference angle <0>:`

This option allows you to specify the starting and ending angles for the object rotation. For instance, say you wanted to rotate an object 30°, not from horizontal but starting at 40° and rotating to 70°. The Reference option allows you to accomplish this. Once you have specified the reference, or starting angle, the last prompt appears:

`New angle:`

This is the ending angle, or in the example, 70°. This can be entered numerically or by selecting a point in the drawing area. Figure 10.12 shows the results of using both of these options.

The first triangle is the original orientation. The second triangle was rotated 30° using the Rotation Angle option. The third triangle was rotated using a starting angle of 10 and an ending angle of 70 for a resultant of 60°.

CREATING MIRROR IMAGES

When you mirror an object, you create objects that are flipped on a specified axis. An exact duplicate is created that is a mirror image of the original based on the mirror line that you specify. The mirror line does not have to be vertical or horizontal. It can be oriented at any angle. There are many times when it is advantageous to mirror objects, such as using this command on symmetrical objects or objects that are identical about a given axis. Figure

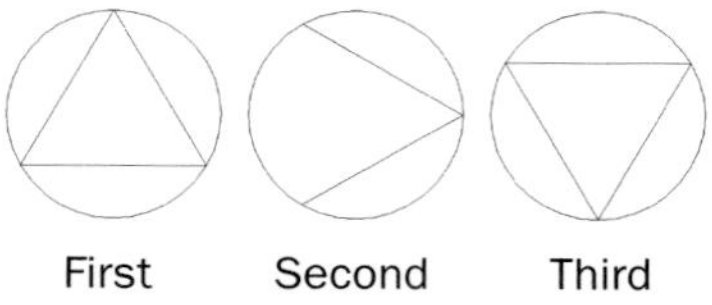

Figure 10.12
*Use the **rotation** command options on the triangle.*

Tutorial 10.7: Rotating Objects

This tutorial continues from the previous tutorial. In this tutorial you will create an octagon that represents a conference table. After the octagon has been created, you will rotate it to the proper orientation. After it has been rotated, you will create a square that represents a chair. In a later tutorial you will create an array of the chair that will create other copies of the chair around the table. Let's begin the tutorial by creating the conference table.

1. Ensure that Table is the current layer.
2.  Select the Polygon button from the Draw toolbar. The `Number of sides <4>:` prompt appears.
3. Enter 8 for the number of sides and press Enter. The `Edge/<Center of polygon>:` prompt appears.
4. Enter **13'9,14'5** for the coordinates for the center of the polygon and press Enter. The `Inscribed in circle/Circumscribed about circle (I/C) <I>:` prompt appears.
5. Press Enter to accept the Inscribed option. The `Radius of circle:` prompt appears.
6. Enter **24** for the radius of the polygon and press Enter. The polygon will be created. Next we will create a square that represents a chair at the head of the table.
7.  Select Rectangle from the Polygon flyout menu on the Draw toolbar. The `First corner:` prompt appears.
8. Enter **13'3,16'4** and press Enter. The `Other corner:` corner prompt appears.
9. Enter **@12,12** and press Enter. A rectangle will be created. Now that both objects have been created as shown in Figure 10.13, we need to rotate them slightly so that the orientation matches the requirements of the customer.
10.  Select the Rotate button from the modify toolbar. The `Select objects:` prompt appears.
11. Select the octagon and rectangle that you created and click the right mouse button. The `Base point:` prompt will appear.
12. Enter **13'9,14'5** and press Enter. The `<Rotation angle>/Reference:` prompt will appear.
13. Enter **−30** and press Enter. The table and chair will rotate clockwise as shown in Figure 10.14.

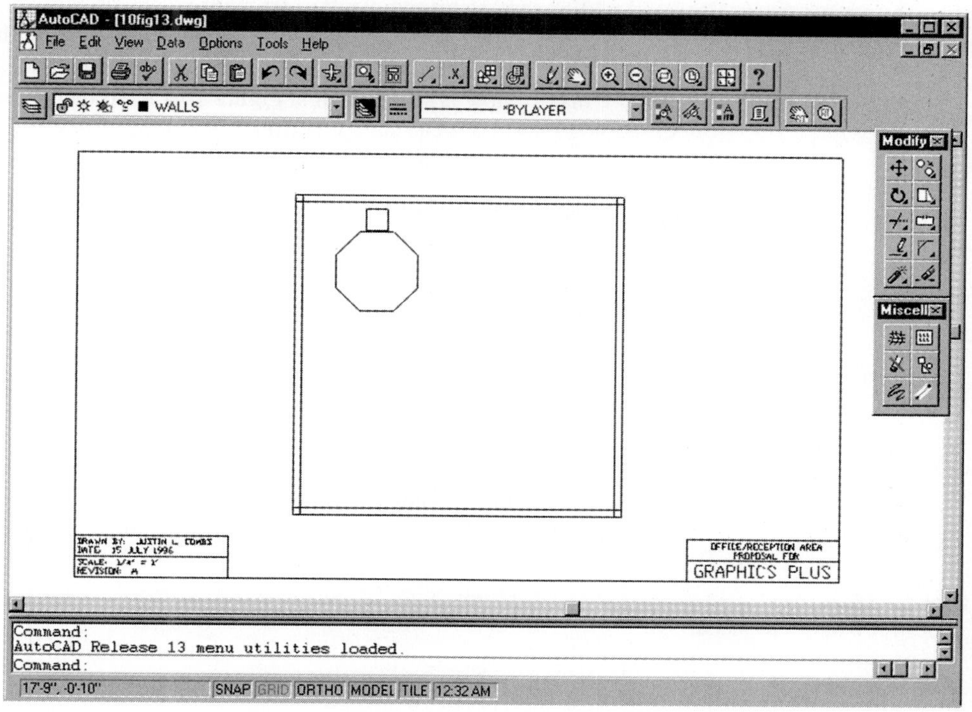

Figure 10.13
The conference table and head chair.

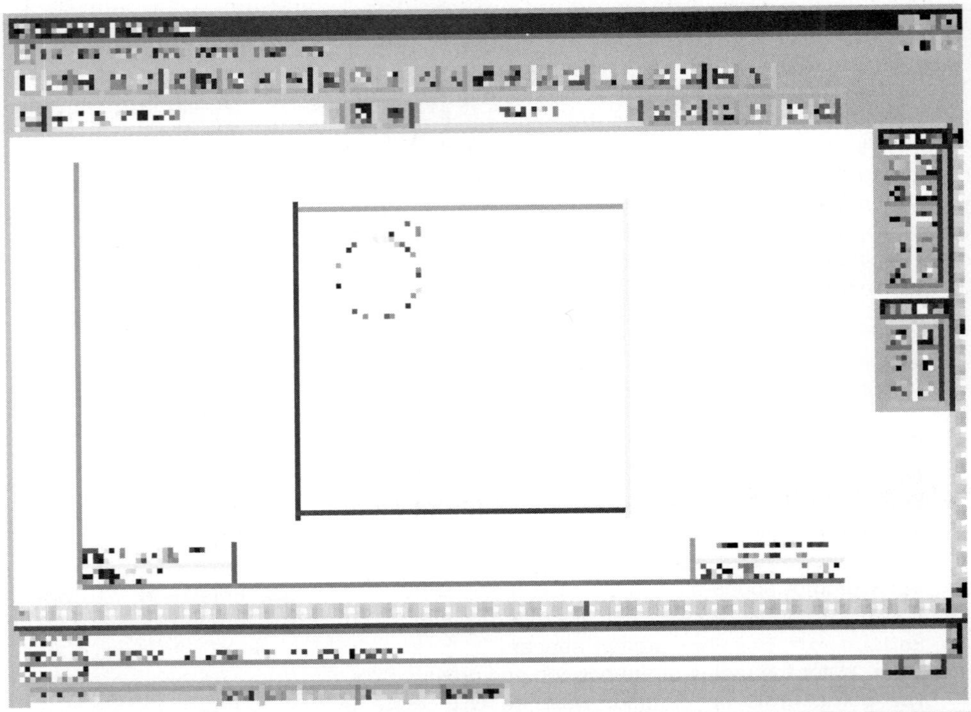

Figure 10.14
The table and chair rotated.

10.15 shows an example of a symmetrical object. It is often easier and more efficient to create half of the object and then mirror that half to create the rest of the object. You can also use the **mirror** command to place a mirrored duplicate of an object at another location. This example is also shown in Figure 10.15. No matter how you use the **mirror** command, you will find it can save you from re-creating a duplicate of an existing object.

To access the **mirror** command, use one of the following methods:

- Select Mirror from the Copy flyout menu on the Modify toolbar.
- Type **`mirror`** at the `Command:` prompt.

Once this command has been entered, the following prompt will appear:

```
Select objects:
```

Use a selection set method to select the objects you wish to mirror. Once the selection set has been created, the next prompt will appear:

```
First point of mirror line:
```

Select a point that represents the beginning point of the mirror line. The mirror line defines the location and distance away from the original object. If the object being mir-

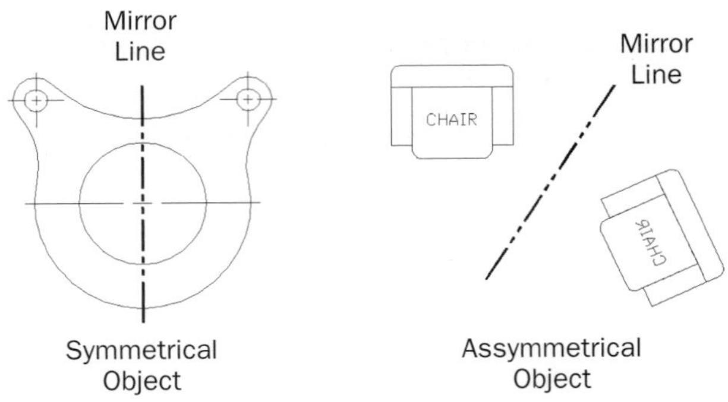

Figure 10.15
*Uses for the **mirror** command.*

rored is to be attached to the copy, then the mirror line should be attached to the original copy as shown on the symmetrical mirror in Figure 10.16. Once this point is selected, the following prompt will appear:

`Second point:`

Select the second point of the mirror line. The next prompt will appear:

`Delete old object(s)? <N>`

This option will delete the original if you need to mirror the object without creating another copy. The default is not to delete the old object.

Tutorial 10.8: Mirroring Objects

This tutorial continues from the previous tutorial. In this tutorial you will mirror the conference table, created in the previous tutorial, to create an exact mirrored duplicate on the right side of the room.

1.  Select Mirror from the Copy flyout menu on the Modify toolbar. The `Select objects:` prompt will appear.
2. Use the Window or Crossing selection set to choose the conference table and the chair that was created in the previous tutorial. Refer to Figure 10.14 to assist in selecting these objects.
3. Once you have selected the objects to be mirrored, click the right mouse button. The `First point of mirror line:` prompt will appear.
4. Use the **mid** object snap and select the top horizontal line. As you drag the mouse, a mirror line will appear. As this mirror line is drawn, a preview of the mirrored image will appear. The `Second point:` prompt appears.
5. Ensure that **ortho** is activated and move the mouse so that a vertical line is traveling down. Click the left mouse button. The second line does not have to end at a specific point. It indicates only the direction of the mirror line. Once the mirror line is created, the `Delete old objects? <N>` prompt appears.
6. Press Enter to prevent AutoCAD from deleting the original object. You will now have two conference tables and two chairs located in the office as shown in Figure 10.16.

Figure 10.16
Two tables and chairs are now located on the office drawing.

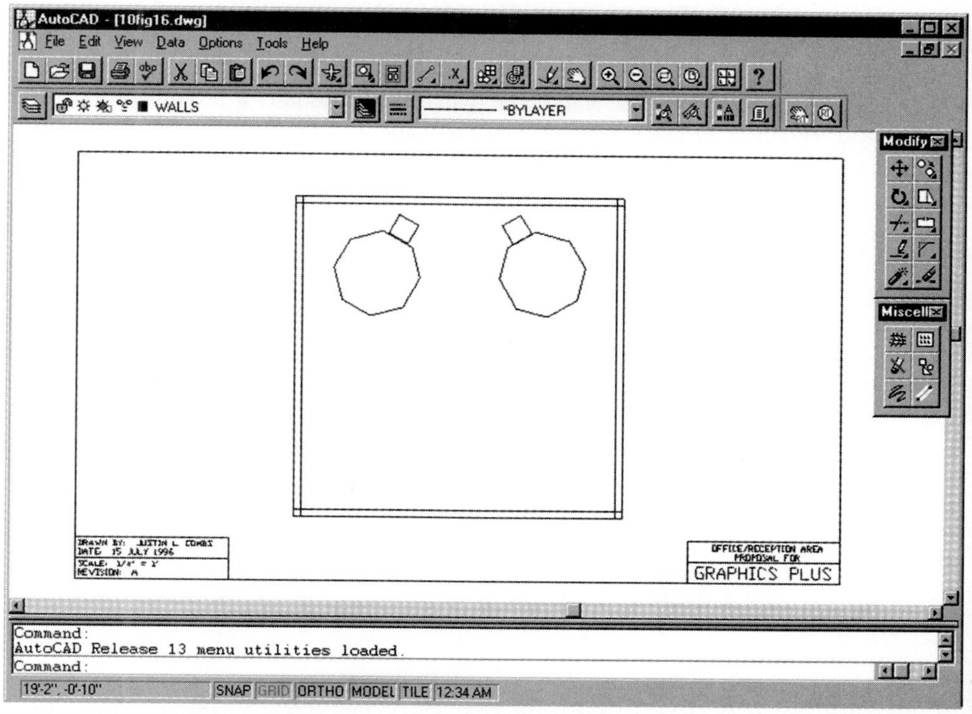

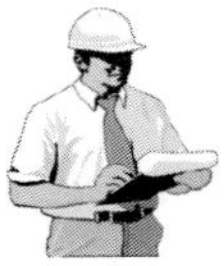

Skill Builder

This command will mirror text in two ways—either by keeping the correct orientation, so that the text can be read, or by mirroring the text as well. You can control how the text is mirrored by using the **mirrtext** system variable. When you enter this variable, you will be asked to enter a value of 1 or 0. 1 will mirror the text, and a setting of 0 will ensure that the text is legible. The default is 1.

Scaling Parts of a Drawing

There are many times when an object that is created may need to be reduced or enlarged in size. This may be because the original design of an object calls for more than one size. An example would be that of a pulley. While the basic shape of the pulley does not change, the size of the pulley may. You would not want to create a brand new drawing of the pulley if the size is the only change. For example, what if you have just been given a change to a floor plan? The change instructs you to double the living room. You can use the **scale** command to accomplish this. To enter the **scale** command, use one of the following methods:

- Select the Scale button from the Stretch flyout menu on the Modify toolbar.
- Type **scale** at the Command: prompt.

Once this command has been entered, the following prompt will appear:

Select objects:

Use a selection set method to select the objects you wish to scale. Once the selection set has been created, the next prompt will appear:

Base point:

Select a point that represents the base point of the object to be scaled. This point can be anywhere but is usually a prominent location on the object being scaled. A base point for a rectangle may be a corner and a base point for a circle may be the center. The base point will be where the object is scaled from. Once this point is selected, the following prompt will appear:

<Scale factor>/Reference:

If you use the default scale factor selection, enter a value and press Enter. Entering a value of .5 would scale the drawing about the base point in half. Using a value of 2 would double the object's size. If you enter a value, the command will be complete and the new scaled object will be created.

Skill Builder

To create a scaled copy of an object, first use the **copy** command to create a duplicate of the object and then use the **scale** command to modify the size of the copy.

If you choose the Reference option, the following prompt appears:

Reference length <1>:

This option allows you to specify the scale factor based on an absolute size used as a reference for a new size.

`New length:`

Enter the new scale length. As an example, a circle with a diameter of 2 is to be scaled. A value of 2 is entered as the reference length prompt, and a value of 3 is entered at the new length prompt. Your object will be enlarged so that the diameter of the circle is now 3.

TUTORIAL 10.9: SCALING OBJECTS

In this tutorial you will modify the scale of one of the conference tables. The conference table on the right is to be used as a table for children that are an average age of 6 years old. A large table would be too big for the children, so we will create a smaller version using the **scale** command.

1.  Select the Scale button from the Stretch flyout menu on the Modify toolbar. The `Select objects:` prompt appears.
2. Use the Window or Crossing selection set to choose the conference table and chair located on the right side of the office. This is the same table and chair that were created by mirroring those on the left side of the office.
3. Once you have selected the objects to be scaled, click the right mouse button. The `Base point:` prompt will appear.
4. Enter **21'3,14'5** and press Enter. The `<Scale factor>/Reference:` prompt will appear. The coordinates specified is the center of the polygon.
5. Enter **.75** and press Enter. The table and chair will be scaled 75 percent of its original size as shown in Figure 10.17.

FOR THE PROFESSIONAL

Although the coordinates for the center of the table are given in this tutorial, you should be able to obtain those coordinates on your own. Consider the different methods that can be used to locate this center point and see if you can use your AutoCAD skills to identify this center point.

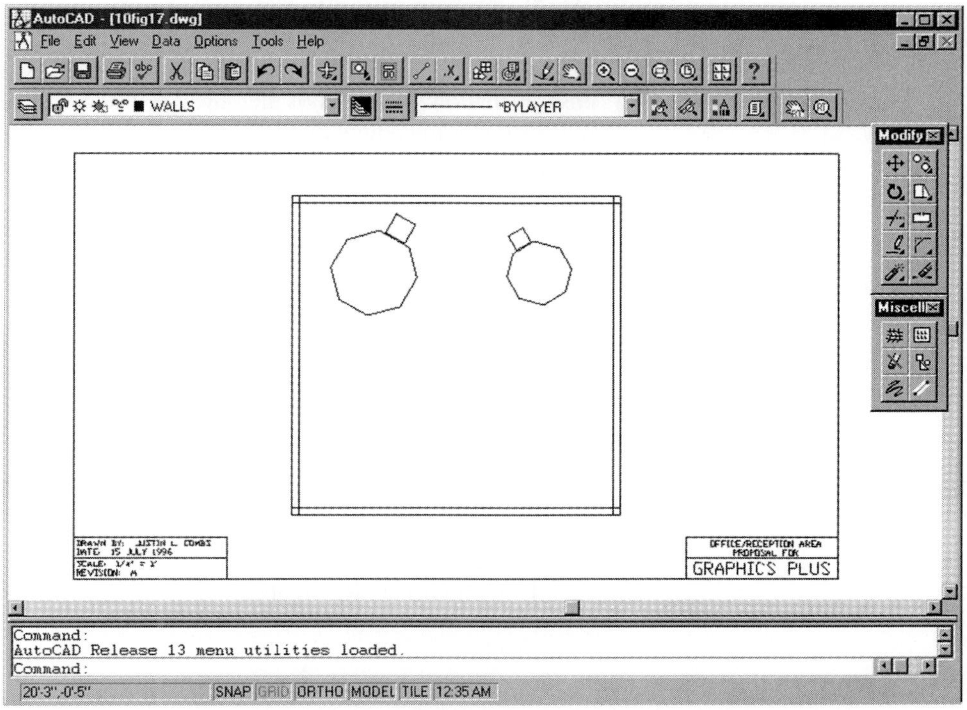

Figure 10.17
Scaling an adult-sized table for the children.

STRETCHING PARTS OF A DRAWING

There are many occasions where the **scale** command may not be appropriate. One such occasion is when you need to scale an object in only one direction. The **scale** command cannot be used because it scales the object about the x- and y-axis. If you use the **stretch** command you can lengthen or shorten an object. This is helpful if you need to change the length of an object but not the height. You will find that this command differs slightly than the others presented in this unit. The selection of the objects plays an important part in the utilization of this command. Before explaining proper selection methods, let's present the ways to enter the command.

- Select the Stretch button on the Modify toolbar.
- Type **`stretch`** at the `Command:` prompt.

Once this command has been entered, the following prompt will appear:

```
Select objects to stretch by crossing-window or -polygon...
Select objects:
```

The prompt displays information on the proper use of the command with the first line. The second line instructs you to select objects as you have done with other commands. The default selection method is the crossing function when this command is chosen from the toolbar. The crossing function provides the most efficient way to use this command. The crossing option ensures that all objects to be stretched are selected. If you have a complex shape you may wish to use the polygon method. When making the selection, ensure that all objects that will be affected by the **stretch** command are selected. Once all objects have been selected the following prompt will appear:

```
Base point or displacement:
```

Choose the point at which the objects will be stretched from. Once selected, the following prompt will appear:

```
Second point of displacement:
```

Select the point that specifies where the objects will be stretched. Once selected, the objects will be stretched to that point specified and the object will be modified.

You need to be aware of the differences of this command when selecting objects to be stretched. Stretch works with a feature known as an *anchor point.* This anchor point ensures that only one end of the object selected will be stretched. As you create a Crossing selection, the points that fall within the crossing are the points that may be stretched. The points not selected during the Crossing selection become the anchor points as shown in Figure 10.18.

In the example in Figure 10.18, the points specified within the window will be stretched, while the points that do not fall within the crossing window will remain in that same location. They are the anchor points.

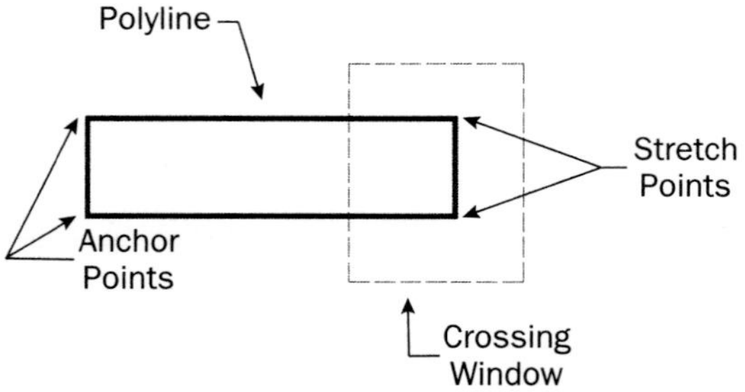

Figure 10.18
The Crossing option is used to specify the anchor point.

Tutorial 10.10: Stretching Objects

This tutorial continues from the previous tutorial. In this tutorial you will stretch the walls 1′ to increase the overall depth of the office.

1. Ensure the Walls is the current layer.
2.  Select the Stretch button on the Modify toolbar. The `Select objects:` prompt will appear.
3. Create a Crossing window similar to the one shown in Figure 10.19 and click the right mouse button. The `Base point or displacement:` prompt will appear.
4. Ensure that Ortho is on and select a point somewhere in the middle of the office. The `Second point of displacement:` prompt appears.
5. Move the crosshairs up and down. Notice that the room size is adjusted based on the crossing point selected. The points within the crossing selection move, while the points that were not included in the crossing selection become the anchor or stationary points.
6. Enter **@1′<270** in the `Command:` prompt. The vertical room dimension will be increased by 1′ as shown in Figure 10.20.

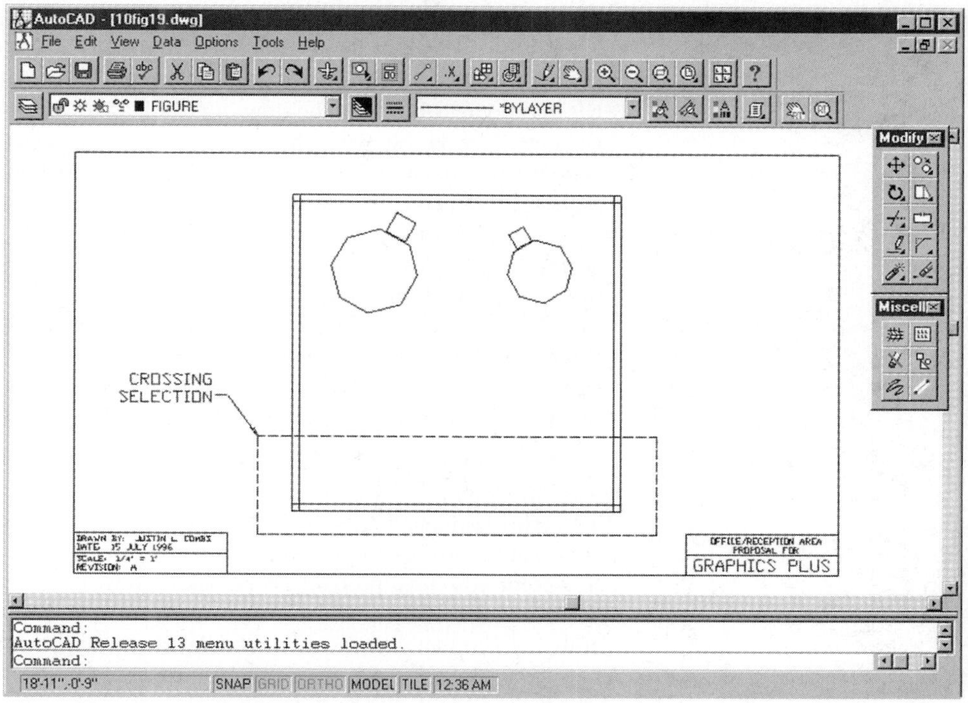

Figure 10.19
Create the Crossing window shown.

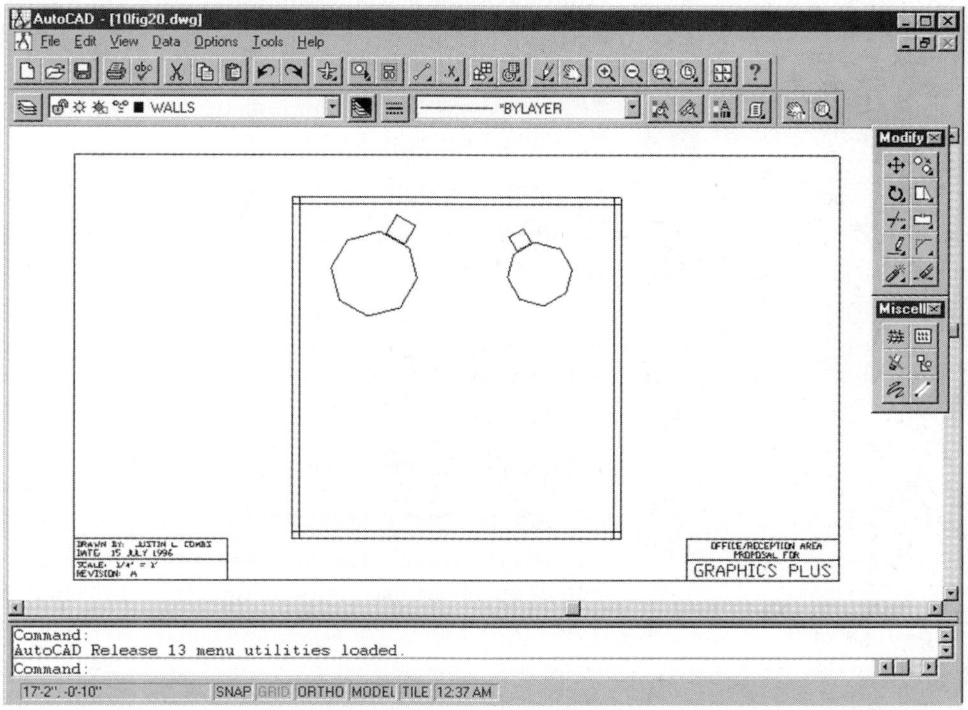

Figure 10.20
The walls after they have been stretched.

Skill Builder

If you use multiple selection sets to select objects to be stretched, only the last objects selected will be stretched.

EDITING EDGES AND CORNERS OF OBJECTS

You may not always create a line that is the correct length. There are many commands available other than **stretch** that allow you to lengthen or shorten these lines without knowing specific size information. There are two commands that allow you to cut an object that is too long, as well as lengthen a line that may be too short. Both of these commands rely on other objects to determine the new length. This ability to shorten and lengthen lines based on other objects in the drawing can lead to some very interesting design techniques as you will soon discover. There will also be times when you find that a single line should actually be broken to form two lines. Once this one line is broken into two, you now have more start and endpoints to use as references for the creation of other objects.

As you work in your specific discipline of study and begin to utilize AutoCAD as a drafting and design tool, you will begin to notice that not all corners are 90°. In the mechanical field, items that are formed by casting have corners that are rounded due to the nature of the manufacturing process. Interior design may incorporate a corner cabinet that is set within a 90° corner of a room. It would be advantageous to have commands that would automatically create the rounded or beveled corners. This section will address the ways to modify the lengths of lines and the appearance of corners.

Trimming Objects

The **trim** command may be the single most valuable AutoCAD editing command. This command is similar to the manual process of erasing only a small portion of a line. Up to this point you have probably been asking how to erase just a portion of the line instead of erasing the whole line and then re-creating it manually. In the design process, it is generally agreed that designs should be developed and modified as they are created. You cannot always develop the final design on the first attempt. The **trim** command will allow you to use AutoCAD as a design tool as well as a drafting tool. Knowing that you can easily adjust the length of a line may make you less anxious about your creation.

This command is very powerful and very easy to use. Enter the **trim** command using one of the following methods:

- Select the Trim button from the Modify toolbar.
- Enter `trim` at the `Command:` prompt.

Once the command has been entered, the following prompt will appear.

```
Select cutting edges: (Projmode = UCS, Edgemode = No extend)
Select objects:
```

Select the objects used as the cutting lines. A good way to think about the cutting lines is to think of a pair of scissors following the cutting line and cutting (trimming) the lines you will select to be shortened. The cutting lines do not have to be lines only; they can be polylines, circles, arcs, or any other object besides text. You can select as many cutting planes as needed during this step. Once the cutting lines have been selected the following prompt will appear:

```
<Select object to trim>/Project/Edge/Undo:
```

At this point, select the object to be trimmed. It is important that you select the portion of the object that you want to discard. Selecting the Undo option will undo the last trim function performed. The Project and Edge functions, while very powerful and use-

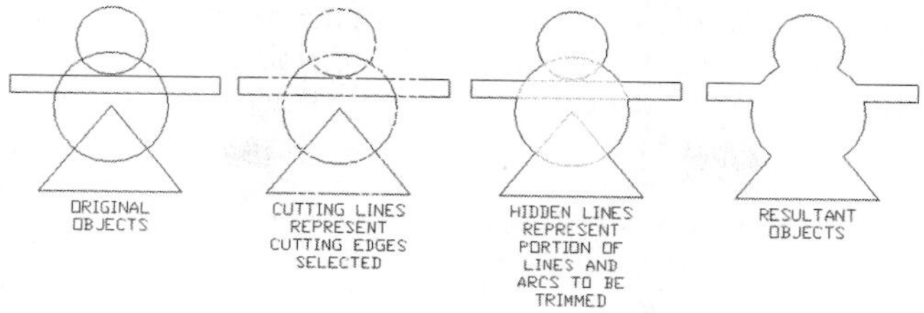

Figure 10.21
Various uses for the **trim** *command.*

ful, will not be discussed in this book. They are both used to assist in the creation of 3-D objects. Those objects are not discussed in this text. Once you have trimmed all objects, click the right mouse button to exit the command. Figure 10.21 displays the use of **trim** with various cutting planes and various objects.

TUTORIAL 10.11: SHORTENING OBJECTS WITH THE TRIM COMMAND

This tutorial continues from the previous tutorial. In this tutorial you will create a wall that will divide the two areas between the conference tables. This will allow some privacy between the adult conference table and the child conference table. You will then use the **trim** command to create a T-intersection between that wall and the upper exterior wall.

1. Ensure that Walls is the current layer.
2.  Select the Line button from the Draw toolbar. The `Line From point:` prompt appears.
3. Press (Enter). The `To point:` prompt appears.
4. Ensure that **ortho** is on and move the crosshairs down.
5. Enter `7'` and press (Enter). A 7′-line is drawn towards the bottom of the drawing. The `To point:` prompt appears.
6. Move the crosshairs to the right, enter **`4,`** and press (Enter). A 4″-line is created traveling to the right of the drawing. The `To point:` prompt appears.
7. Move the crosshairs up, enter `7'`, and press (Enter). A 7″-line is created toward the top of the drawing. The `To point:` prompt appears.
8. Press (Enter). The **line** command exits. A new wall has been created as shown in Figure 10.22. Next, you will use the **trim** command to create a T-intersection between the new wall created and the top exterior wall.
9. Use the **zoom** command to get a better view of the intersection as shown in Figure 10.23.
10.  Select the Trim button from the Modify toolbar. The `Select cutting edges: Select objects:` prompt appears.

Figure 10.22
A new wall has been created on the office plan.

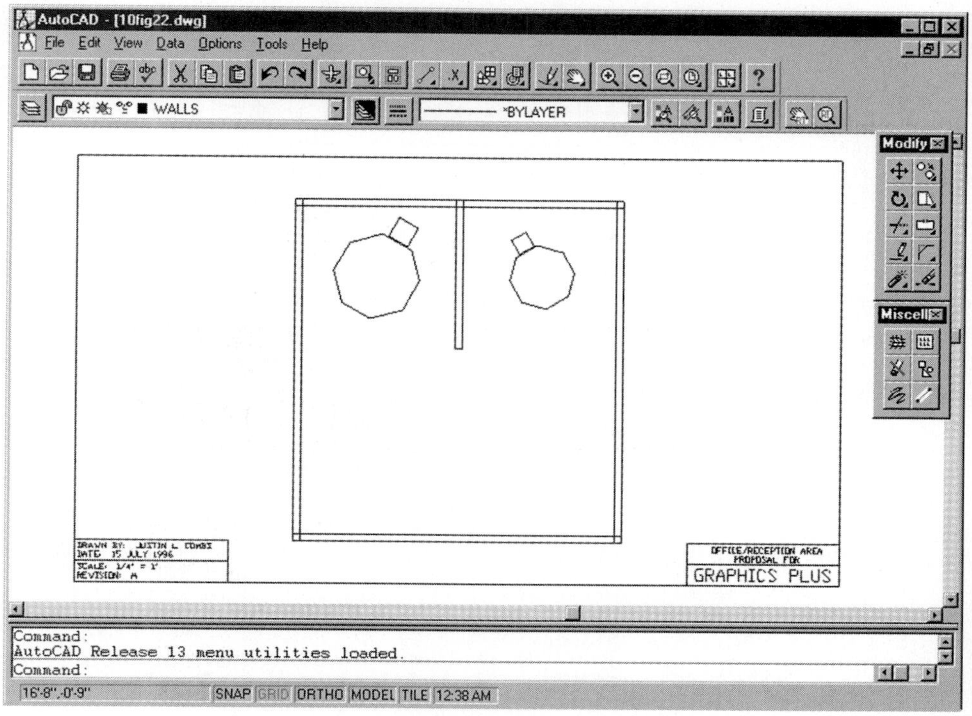

11. Create a Crossing selection set as shown in Figure 10.24 and click the right mouse button. The two walls will be highlighted and the `<Select object to trim>:/Project/Edge/Undo:` prompt will appear.
12. Select the portion of the lines shown in Figure 10.24 to remove. As you select each portion it will immediately be removed. If you make a mistake, use the Undo option and continue.
13. Once all three lines have been selected, click the right mouse button to exit the command. The new T-intersection is created as shown in Figure 10.25.
14. 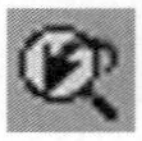 Select Zoom Previous from the Zoom toolbar. The view will return to display all of the office.

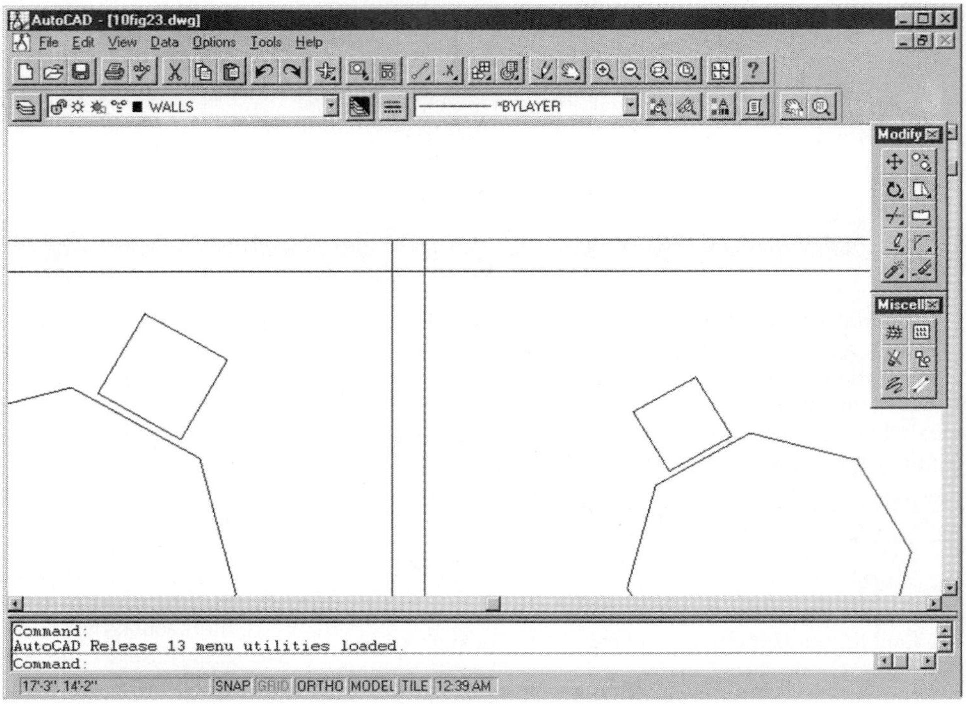

Figure 10.23
*Use the **zoom** command to create a view similar to this one.*

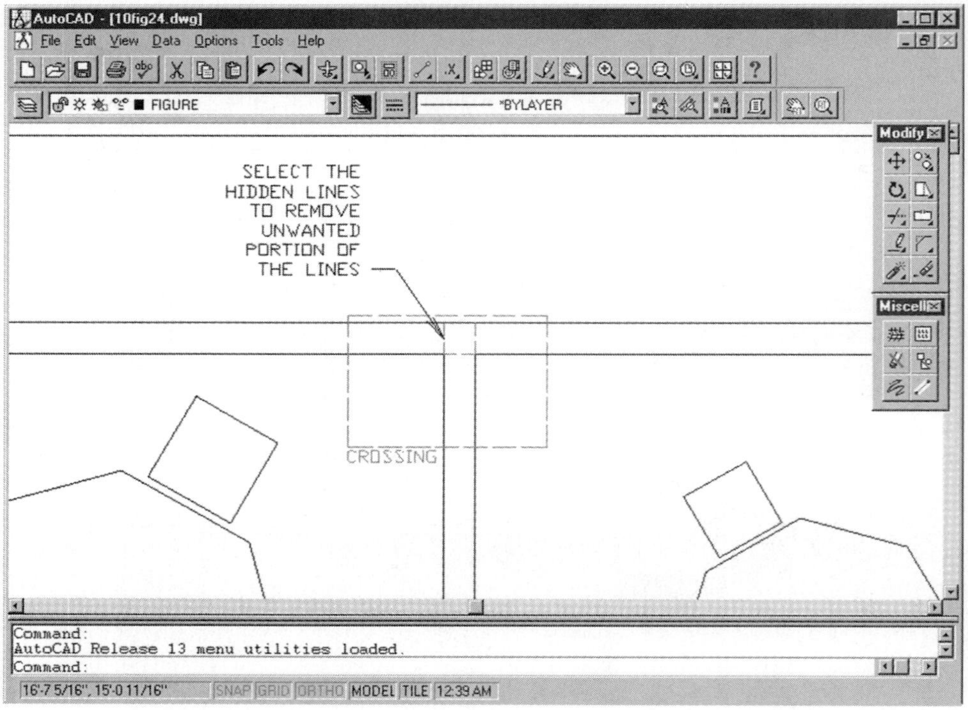

Figure 10.24
Create this Crossing selection and portions of the lines to be removed.

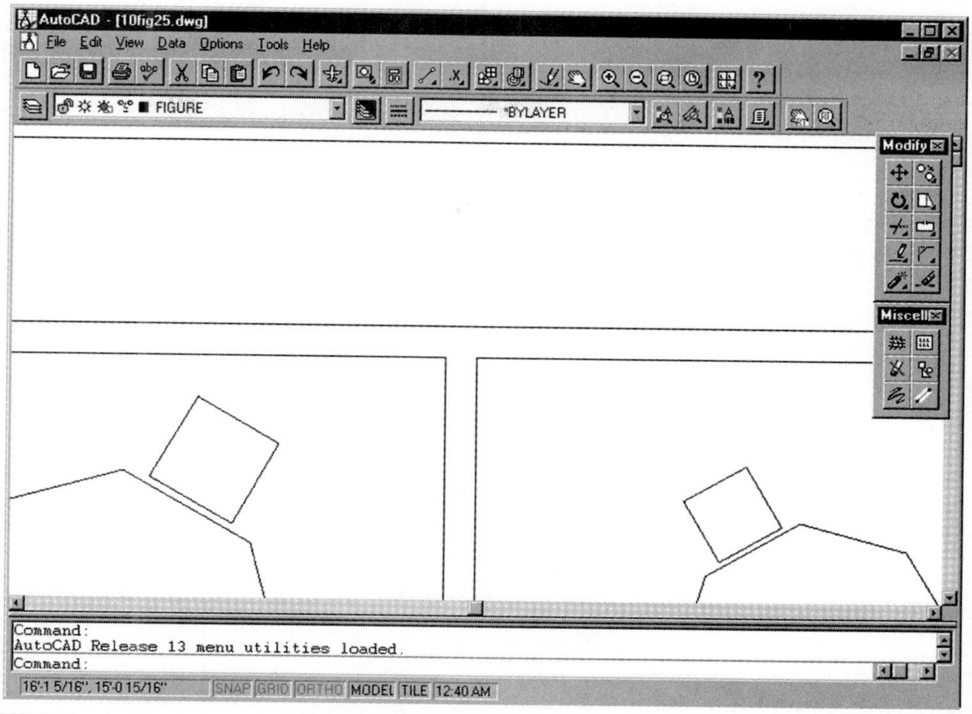

Figure 10.25
The T-intersection.

Erasing Parts of Objects

As you begin to create objects, you will eventually want not only to trim an object, but also to break an object to create other new objects. In the previous tutorial we could have used the **break** command to create the T-intersection, but because reference lines were already included, it was simpler to use the **trim** command. Suppose reference lines are not available. That's where the **break** command comes in handy. You can specify the break points as you use the command. To begin the command use one of the options below:

- Select the 1 Point button from the Modify toolbar.
- Enter **`break`** at the `Command:` prompt.

Using the Break button provides you with four break flyout buttons. Each button function is described below.

- **1 Point.** This option allows you to break an object by selecting a point on the object. Using this option will result in two separate objects. For example, if you use this option and select the middle of a line, the result will be two lines that both have an endpoint located where the middle of the previous single line was located. This option does not function on circles or closed polygons.

- **1 Point Select.** This option allows you to break an object by selecting the object to break first and then by selecting a break point. The break point defines the point at which the object is to be broken.

- **2 Points.** This option allows you to break an object by selecting two points on the object only. The first point you select on the object identifies the object to be broken as well as the first part of the object to be removed. The second point specifies the endpoint of the portion of the object to remove.

- **2 Points Select.** This option allows you to break an object by selecting the object first and then specifying the two points to be removed from the object.

Each of these options provides the following prompts at various times throughout the **break** command. The prompts are displayed below as they would be presented if the

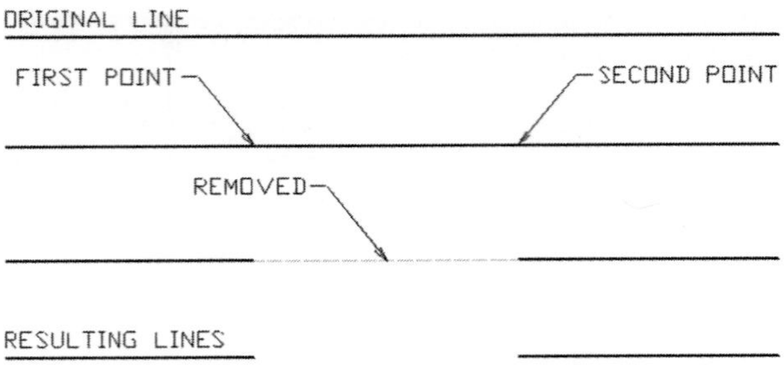

Figure 10.26
Before and after the line has been broken.

break command were entered at the `Command:` prompt. The first prompt to appear is shown below.

`Select object:`

This prompt allows you to select the object to be broken. It also has a second function not mentioned in the prompt. The point at which you pick the object can also be used as the first break point if you are using multiple break points. Once selected, the following prompt appears:

`Enter second point (or F for first point):`

Select the second point that represents the other break point for the object. Entering **f** at the prompt will allow you to specify the first point over if you did not do so correctly at the first prompt. If you choose this option, the following prompt appears:

`Enter first point:`

Select the first point again. When selected, the next prompt appears:

`Second point:`

Select the second point and the object will be broken. Figure 10.26 displays a line that has been broken.

Tutorial 10.12: Using the break Command

This tutorial continues from the previous tutorial. In this tutorial you will use the **break** command to create a 5′-entrance into the office.

1.  Select 2 Points from the 1 Point flyout on the Modify toolbar. The `Select object:` prompt appears.
2. Enter **10′,11′** and press Enter. The first break point is defined and the `Enter second point (or F for first point):` prompt appears. You will now define the second break point.
3. Enter **@5′<270** and press Enter. The second break point will be defined 5′ below the first break point and the command will terminate. To finish the opening to the office, you need to create one more break on the line to the right of the one you just broke.
4.  Select 2 Points from the 1 Point flyout on the Modify toolbar. The `Select object:` prompt appears.
5. Enter **10′4,11′** and press Enter. The first break point is defined and the `Enter second point (or F for first point):` prompt appears. You will now define the second break point.
6. Enter **@5′<270** and press Enter. The second break point will be defined 5′ below the first break point and the command will terminate. You will now have the opening as shown in Figure 10.27.
7. The opening is now created, but two lines need to be created that specify the termination of the two new lines. Use your acquired skills to create the two lines shown in Figure 10.28.

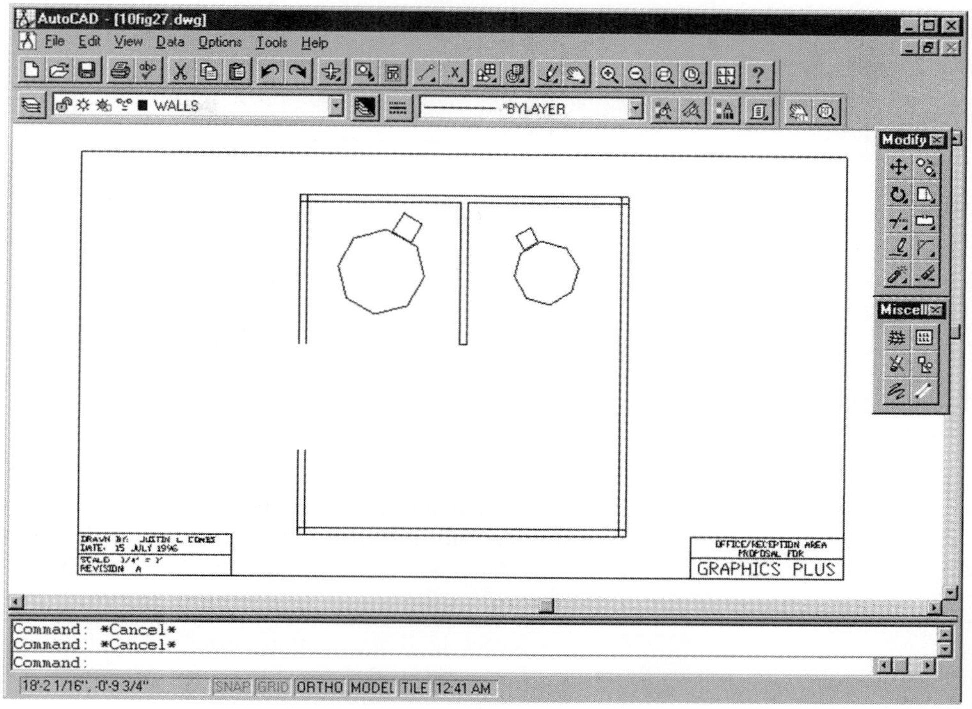

Figure 10.27
The opening is created, but the walls need to be terminated.

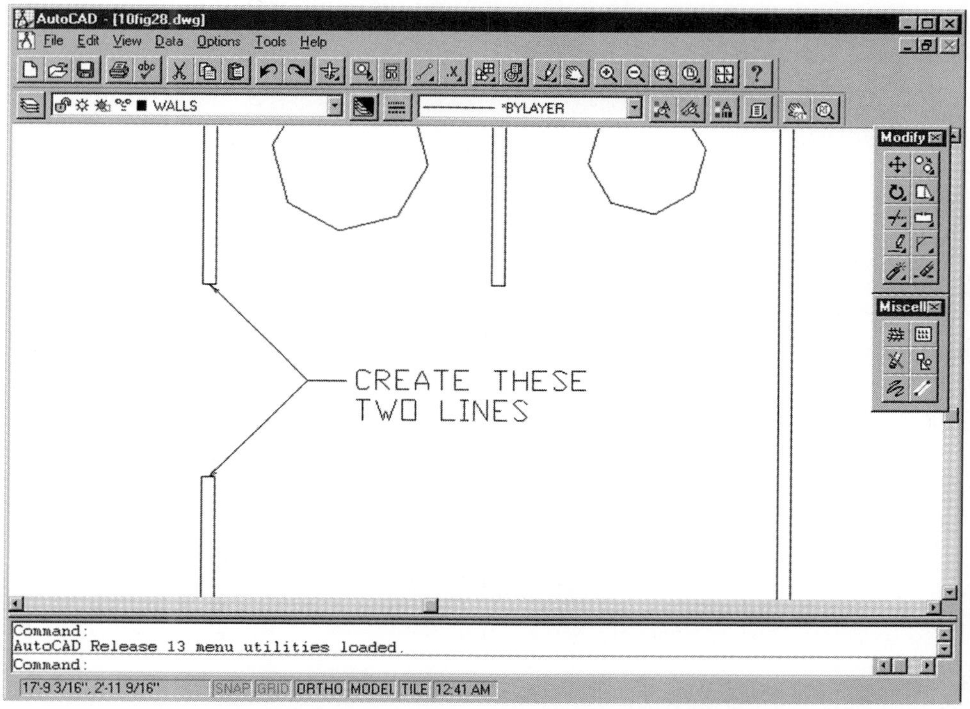

Figure 10.28
Complete the walls by creating these two lines.

Extending Objects

The opposite of trimming an object is to extend the object. This section will describe the procedures needed to extend an object so that it may be lengthened. You will find that this command is very similar to the **trim** command with opposite results. The selection of boundary edges is similar to selecting cutting lines, and the selection of the

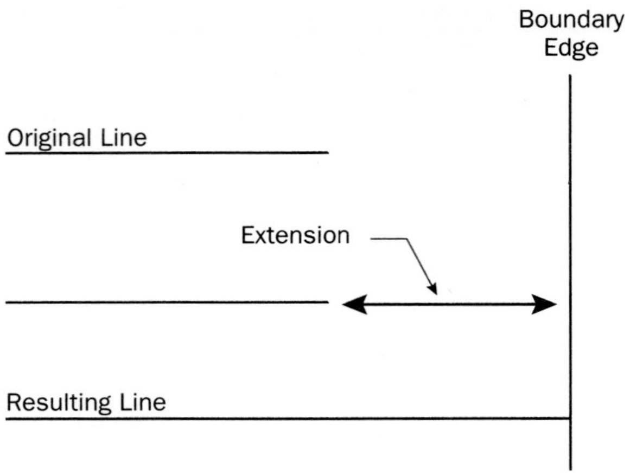

Figure 10.29
Extending a line.

objects to extend identical to the way items to be trimmed are selected. Using the **extend** command with the **trim** command can significantly decrease the number of lines that have to be erased and then redrawn. To access the **extend** command, use one of the two methods described:

- Select the Extend button from the Trim flyout button on the Modify toolbar.
- Enter **`extend`** at the `Command:` prompt.

Once the command has been entered, the following prompt will appear.

```
Select boundary edges: (Projmode = UCS, Edgemode = No extend)
Select objects:
```

Select the objects used as the boundary edges. The boundary edge is where the objects are to extend. You can select as many boundary edges as needed during this step. Once the boundary edges have been selected, the following prompt will appear:

```
<Select object to extend>/Project/Edge/Undo:
```

At this point select the object to be extended. It is important that you select the object on the end that is to be extended toward the boundary edge. Selecting the Undo option will undo the last Extend function performed. Once you have extended all objects, click the right mouse button to exit the command. Figure 10.29 displays the use of extend on a line.

For the Professional

Many AutoCAD users will create rough sketches of objects using **line** commands and will then use the **`trim`** and **`extend`** commands to refine their design. An example of this is shown in Figure 10.30.

Figure 10.30
Use rough lines, and then use **trim** *and* **extend** *to refine your design.*

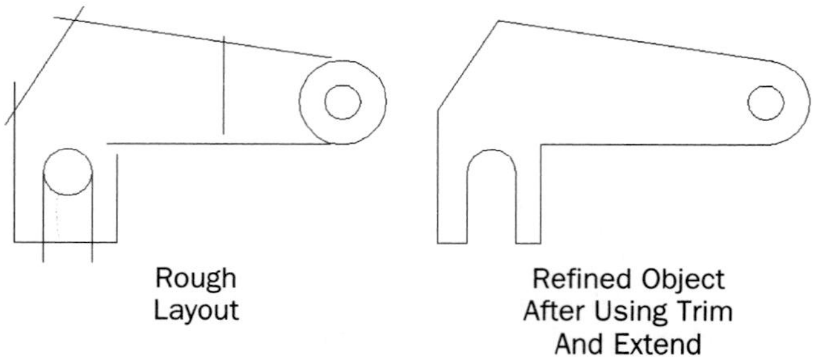

Tutorial 10.13: Extending Objects

This tutorial continues from the previous tutorial. In this tutorial you will use the **extend** command to assist in the creation of a work counter for the office complex.

1. Make Counter the current layer.
2.  Select the Line button from the Draw toolbar. The `From point:` prompt appears.
3. Enter `10'4,6'` and press Enter. The `To point:` prompt appears.
4. Move the crosshairs to the right, enter `2'`, and press Enter. The `To point:` prompt appears.
5. Move the crosshairs down, enter `1'8`, and press Enter. The `To point:` prompt appears.
6. Move the crosshairs to the right, enter `8'`, and press Enter. The `To point:` prompt appears.
7. Move the crosshairs down, enter `2'`, and press Enter. The `To point:` prompt appears.
8. Press Enter to exit the command. The counter is created as shown in Figure 10.31.
9. A change has been made to the counter specifications. Instead of ending short of the wall, the client would like the counter to extend to the wall. To make the changes, begin by selecting Erase from the Modify toolbar.
10. Select the vertical line shown in Figure 10.32 and press Enter. The line will be erased.
11.  Select the Extend button from the Trim flyout button on the Modify toolbar. The `Select boundary edges:` prompt appears.
12. Select the vertical line specified in Figure 10.23 and press Enter. The line will be highlighted and the `<Select object to extend>/Project/Edge/Undo:` prompt will appear.
13. Select the horizontal counter line specified in Figure 10.23 and press Enter. The line will be extended to the boundary line.
14. Right-click to exit the command. The counter will now be modified as shown in Figure 10.33.

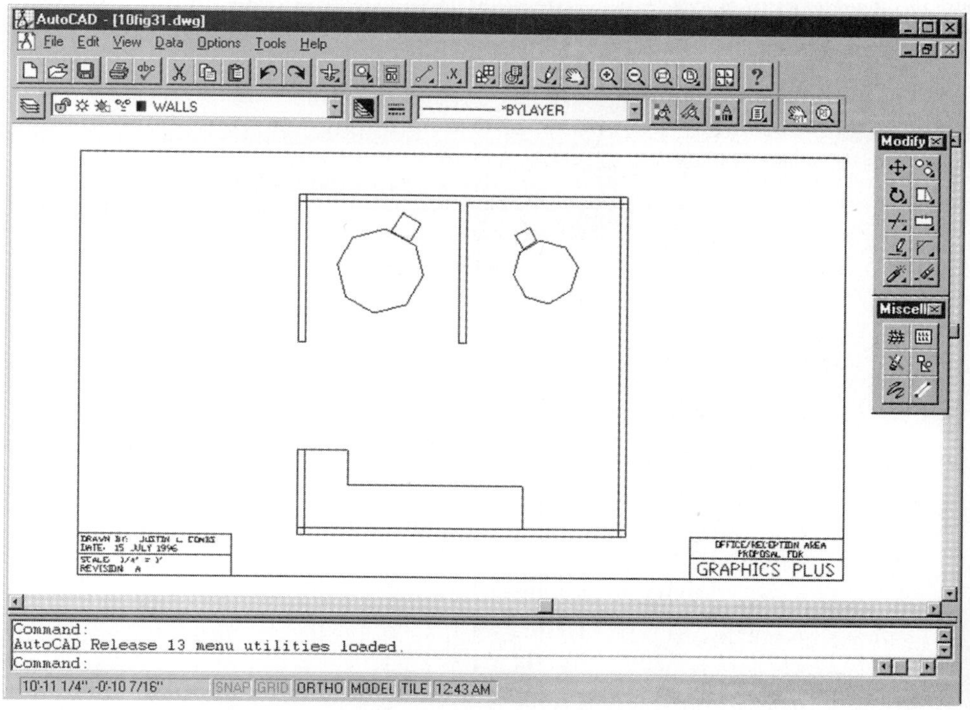

Figure 10.31
Creating the work counter.

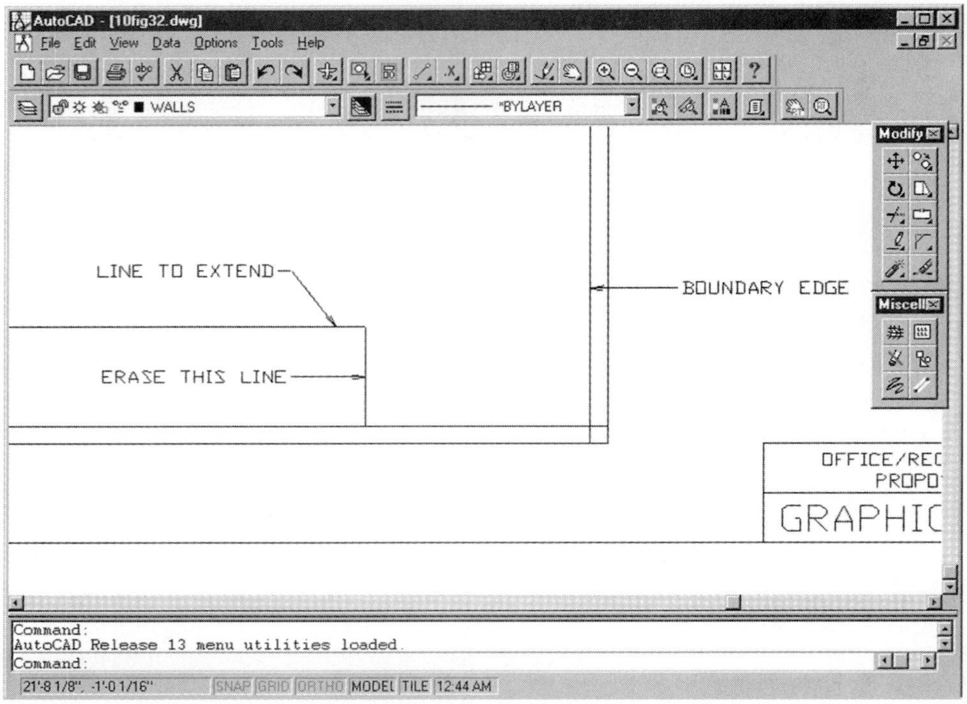

Figure 10.32
Use this figure to assist in making selections for the work counter modifications.

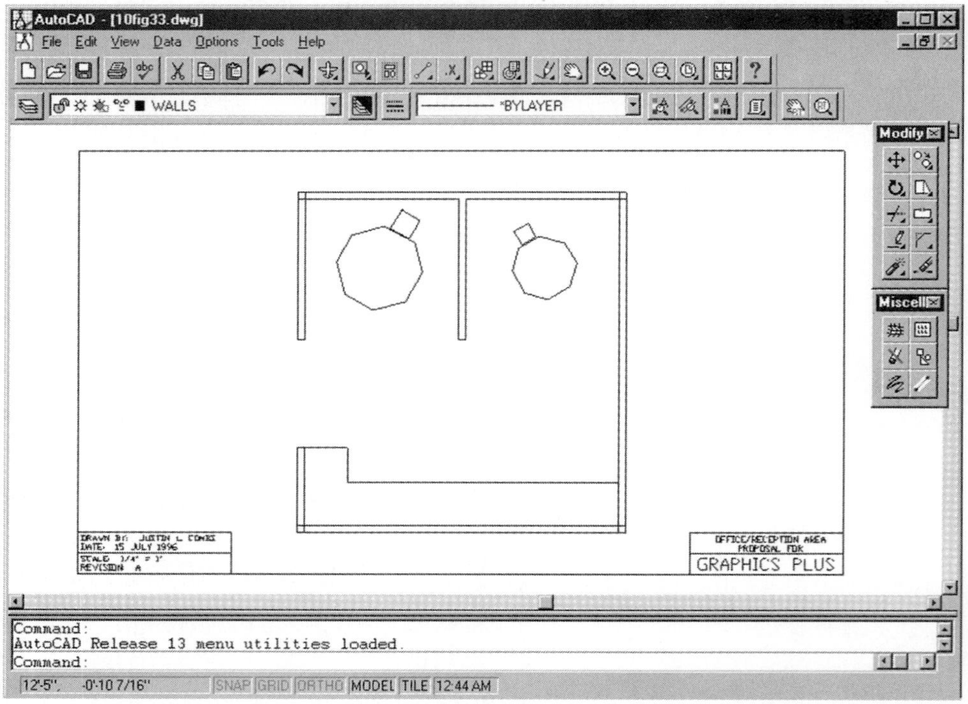

Figure 10.33
Office with the counter modified.

Filleting Objects

The **fillet** command is used to round corners. It is a very simple command that can save much time. Without the **fillet** command, you would have to create arcs or circles in the corner and then trim the lines. This command will automate that process. The **fillet** command can be used not only on lines, but also on circles, arcs, and polylines. To use the **fillet** command you must have two objects, unless you are using this command to modify a closed polygon. In that case you need only the single polyline. If you fillet a polyline, all vertices on the closed polyline will be modified. To begin the command, use one of the following methods:

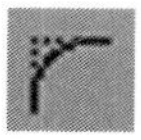

- Select the Fillet button from the Chamfer flyout menu on the Modify toolbar.
- Type `fillet` at the `Command:` prompt.

Once the command has been entered, the following prompt will appear:

`Polyline/Radius/Trim/<Select first object>:`

Each one of the available fillet options is described below:

- `Select polyline:` This option allows you to choose to fillet polylines. In order to do so you must first enter a value other than zero in the Radius option described next. Filleting polylines will fillet each vertice on the polyline.

Skill Builder

When a polyline is selected, the radius can be changed at any time by changing the fillet radius and selecting the polyline again. The fillet will then be updated. This feature is not available for lines and arcs. Those objects must first have the fillet erased and then have the **fillet** command reapplied.

- `Fillet Radius:` Specifies the radius for the fillet. Once this option is specified, the command terminates and the **fillet** command must be reentered to resume a fillet operation. A simple way to do so is to press ↵Enter immediately after the command has been terminated.

Skill Builder

If you specify a radius of zero and choose two objects that do not intersect or that pass through one another, the objects will be connected and a square corner will be created.

- `Trim/No trim <Trim>:` Selects whether the command trims the objects in the fillet set or leaves the objects their original lengths.
- `Select first object:` Selects the first object to be used to create the fillet. When an object has been selected, the `Select second object:` prompt appears. Select the second object in the fillet set and an arc will be created with the radius selected that is tangent to both objects selected.

Figure 10.34 displays various uses for the **fillet** command.

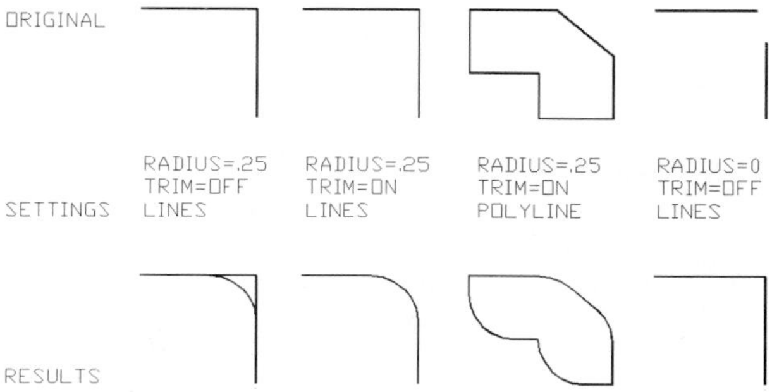

Figure 10.34
*Use the **fillet** command to create these various shapes.*

TUTORIAL 10.14: ROUNDING AND CLEANING EDGES WITH THE FILLET COMMAND

This tutorial continues from the previous tutorial. In this tutorial you will modify the counter so that it is rounded at the entrance into the office. You will then use the **fillet** command to clean up the interior wall corners.

1.  Select the Fillet button from the Chamfer flyout menu on the Modify toolbar. The `Polyline/Radius/Trim/<Select first object>:` prompt appears.

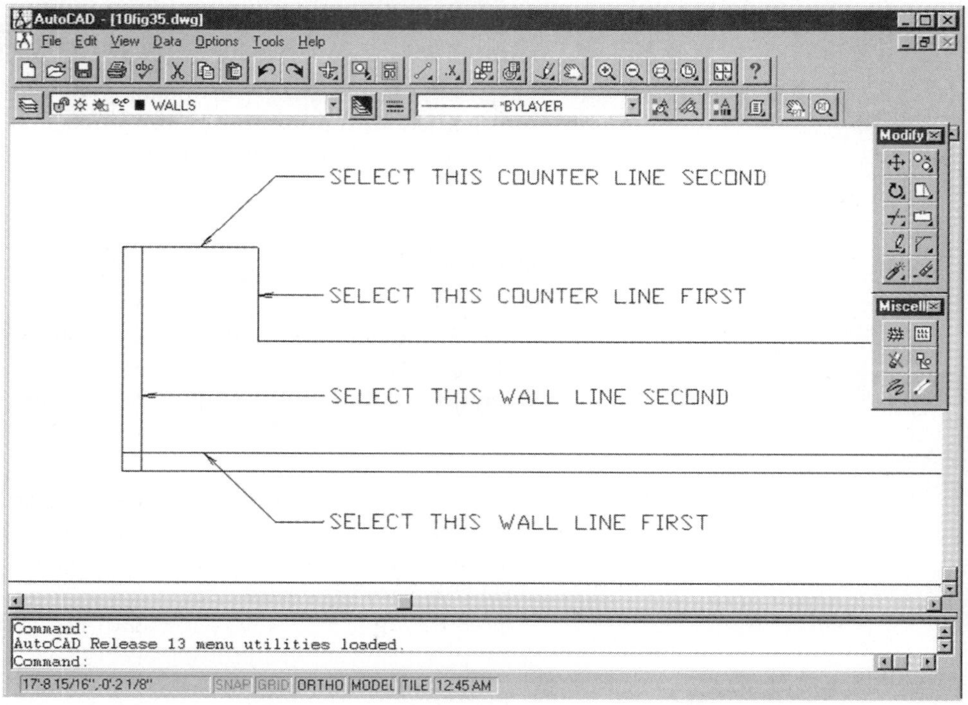

Figure 10.35
Use this figure to assist in selecting the lines to be trimmed.

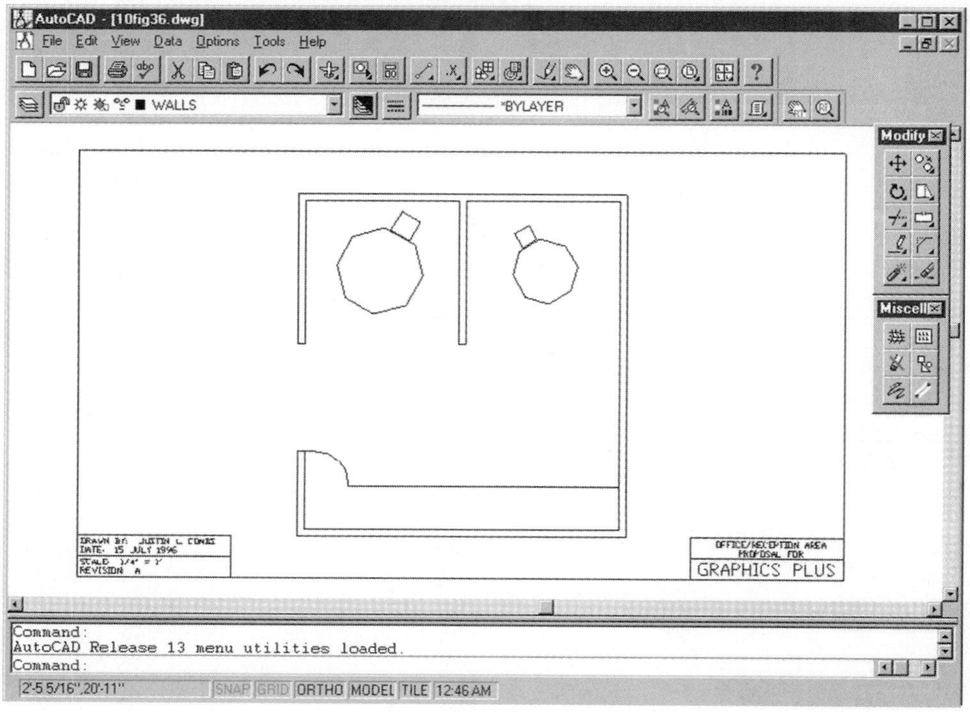

Figure 10.36
*The office project after using the **fillet** command.*

2. Enter `r` and press Enter. The `Fillet radius:` prompt appears.
3. Enter `1'6` and press Enter. The **fillet** command exits.
4. Press Enter to reenter the **fillet** command. Once again the `Polyline/Radius/Trim/<Select first object>:` prompt appears.
5. Select the counter line specified in Figure 10.35. The `Select second object:` prompt appears.
6. Select the second line specified in Figure 10.35. The counter corner will now be rounded. The next step is to use the **fillet** command to clean up the interior wall intersections.
7. Press Enter to reenter the **fillet** command. The `Polyline/Radius/Trim/<Select first object>:` prompt appears.
8. Enter `r` and press Enter. The `Fillet radius:` prompt appears.
9. Enter `0` and press Enter. The **fillet** command exits.
10. Press Enter to reenter the **fillet** command. The `Polyline/Radius/Trim/<Select first object>:` prompt appears.
11. Select the wall line specified in Figure 10.35. The `Select second object:` prompt appears.
12. Select the wall line specified in Figure 10.35. The corner will now be squared and the lines will be trimmed to produce clean wall lines.
13. Repeat steps 10–12 for all corners of the office. Your drawing should now resemble Figure 10.36.

Chamfering Objects

Like the **fillet** command, **chamfer** modifies the intersection of two objects, but not with an arc, with a bevel. This command functions identically to the **fillet** command except for the options that specify the chamfer variables.

To use the **chamfer** command, ensure that two objects will or are intersecting. Polylines need three or more vertices in order for this command to function. To begin the command, use one of the following methods:

- Select the Chamfer button on the Modify toolbar.
- Type **`chamfer`** at the `Command:` prompt.

Once the command has been entered, the following prompt will appear:

`Polyline/Distance/Angle/Trim/Method/<Select first object>:`

Each one of the available fillet options is described below.

- `Select polyline:` This option allows you to choose to chamfer polylines. Chamfering polylines will chamfer each vertice on the polyline.

Skill Builder

When a polyline is selected, the chamfer can be changed at any time by changing the chamfer variables and selecting the polyline again. The chamfer will then be updated. This feature is not available for lines and arcs. Those objects must first have the chamfer erased and then the chamfer command reapplied.

- `Enter first chamfer distance <0.000>:` Specifies the distance from the intersection of the first object selected to the beginning of the chamfer bevel.
- `Enter second chamfer distance <0.000>:` Specifies the distance from the intersection of the second object selected to the beginning of the chamfer bevel.

Skill Builder

If you specify a distance of zero and choose two objects that do not intersect or that pass through one another, the objects will be connected and a square corner will be created.

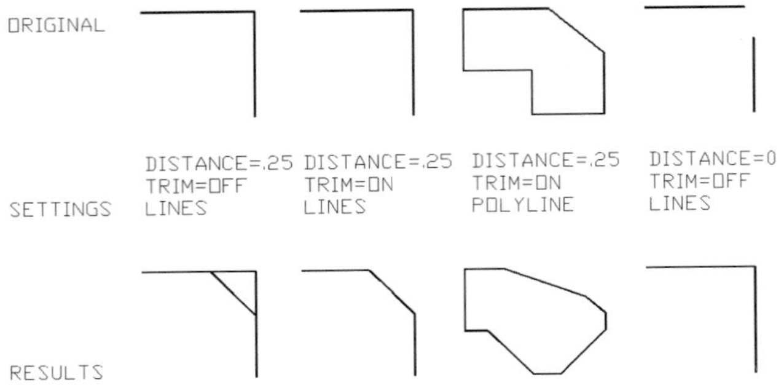

Figure 10.37
Use the **chamfer** *command to create these various shapes.*

- `Enter chamfer length on the first line <0.000>:` When the Angle option is chosen, this prompt defines the chamfer by indicating a starting distance from the intersection point of the line selected. Once this information is entered, the next prompt appears.
- `Enter chamfer angle on the first line <0.000>:` Enter the angle for the chamfer.
- `Trim/No trim <Trim>:` Selects whether the command trims the objects in the fillet set or leaves the objects their original lengths.
- `Distance/Angle:` Specifies the method preferred for entering chamfer values.
- `Select first object:` Selects the first object to be used to create the fillet. When an object has been selected, the `Select second object:` prompt appears. Select the second object in the chamfer set and a chamfer line will be created.

Figure 10.37 displays various uses for the **chamfer** command.

Tutorial 10.15: Creating Chamfers

This tutorial continues from the previous tutorial. In this tutorial you will use the **chamfer** command to create a corner counter on the lower-right corner of the office. The client would like to extend the counter along the right wall to increase work space.

1.  Select the Line button from the Draw toolbar. The `From point:` prompt appears.
2. Enter **22′8,4′4** and press ↵Enter. The `To point:` prompt appears.
3. Move the crosshairs up, enter **4′**, and press ↵Enter. The `To point:` prompt appears.
4. Move the crosshairs to the right, enter **2′**, and press ↵Enter. The `To point:` prompt appears.
5. Press ↵Enter to exit the command. The counter extension is created as shown in Figure 10.38.
6.  Select the Chamfer button from the Modify toolbar. You will now create a corner work center on the counter. The `Polyline/Distance/Angle/Trim/Method/<Select first object>:` prompt appears.
7. Enter **d** to specify the distance of the Chamfer. The `Enter first chamfer distance:` prompt appears.
8. Enter **2′** and press ↵Enter. The `Enter second chamfer distance:` prompt appears.
9. Enter **2′** and press ↵Enter. The command terminates.
10. Press ↵Enter. The **chamfer** command is reissued and the `(TRIM mode) Current chamfer Dist1 = 2′-0″, Dist2 = 2′-0″ Polyline/Distance/Angle/Trim/Method/<Select first object>:` prompt appears.
11. Select the first lines specified in Figure 10.38. The `Select second line:` prompt appears.
12. Select the second lines specified in Figure 10.38. The corner will be chamfered.
13. Click the right mouse button to exit the command. Your counter should resemble the one in Figure 10.39.

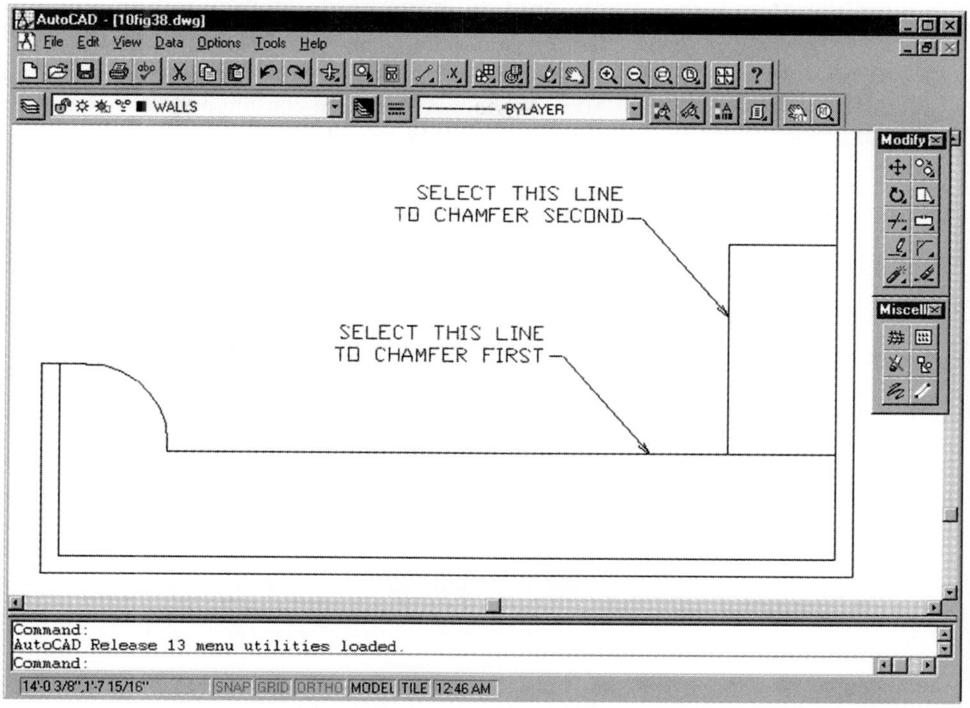

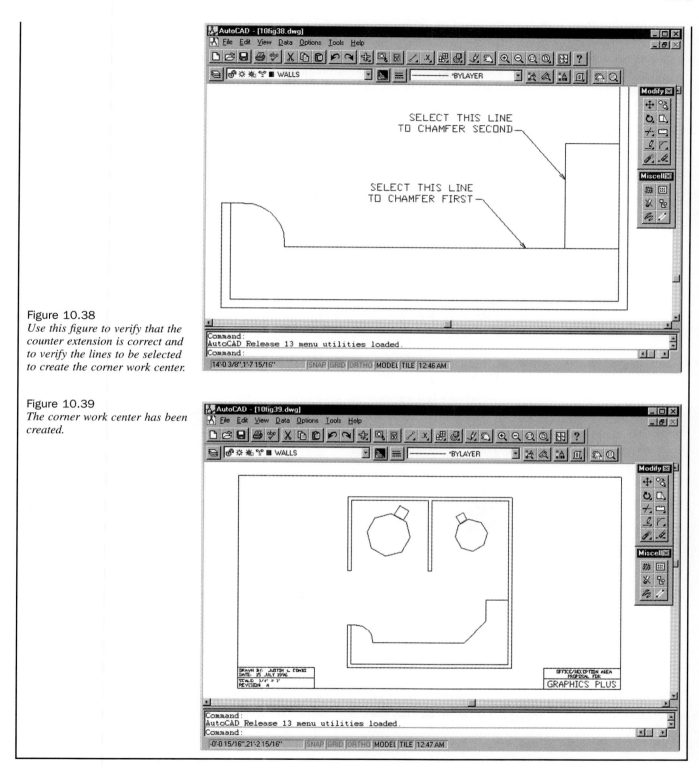

Figure 10.38
Use this figure to verify that the counter extension is correct and to verify the lines to be selected to create the corner work center.

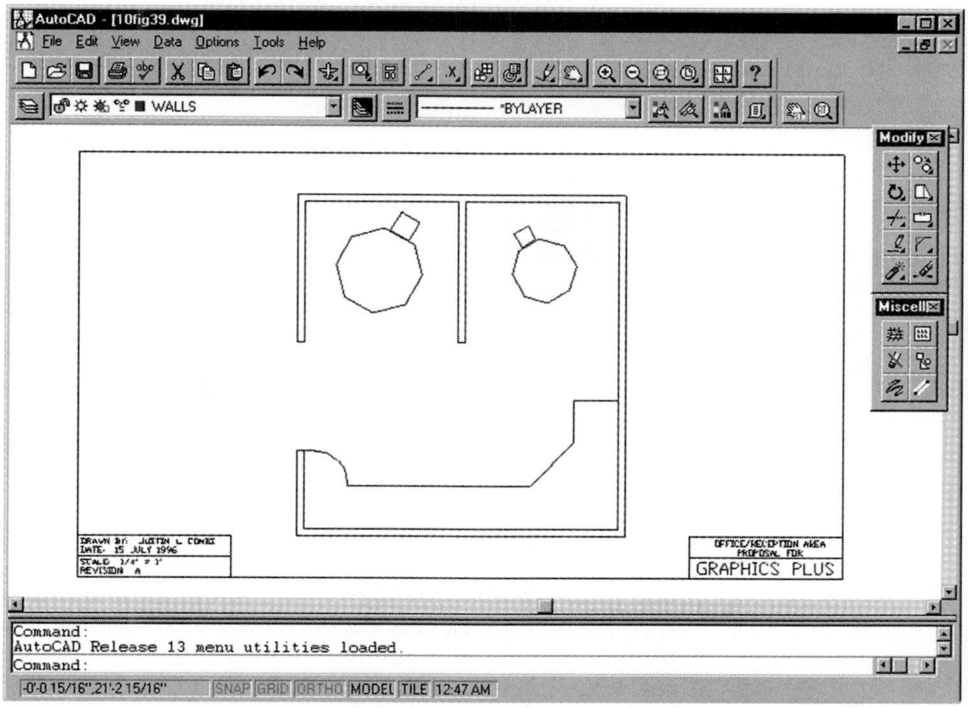

Figure 10.39
The corner work center has been created.

PRODUCING ARRAYS OF OBJECTS

Arrays provide a quick and easy way to create multiple copies of objects in a pattern. Examples would include an auditorium with seats. These seats would be created in rows and columns, or in a rectangular pattern. Another example would be the teeth on a gear. These teeth are rotated and copied around a center point and placed in a circular pattern, or polar pattern. You can probably think of many more examples of each type of array. A rectangular array could be simulated using the **copy** Multiple command, and the polar array could be simulated using the **copy** and **rotate** commands. Using these methods would be tedious and time-consuming, not to mention inaccurate when it comes to polar arrays. AutoCAD provides the **array** command to relieve the frustration of trying to create these patterns manually. While this section of the unit discusses each of these types of arrays separately, the command is the same when entered at the Command: prompt.

- Enter **array** at the Command: prompt.
  Once the command is entered, the following prompt appears:

```
Select objects.
```

At this point select the objects you wish to array and click the right mouse button. Once the selection has been made the following prompt appears:

```
Rectangular or Polar array (R/P) <R>:
```

At this point you can select either the Rectangular or Polar array. From here the command is different for each type of array. Using the buttons on the toolbars automates these first steps and bypasses the need to select the type of array at the Command: prompt. Let's look at arrays with the Rectangular Array.

Rectangular Arrays

Selecting a rectangular array allows you to duplicate objects in a row-and-column pattern. In order to use this command you must know the spacing necessary between the row and columns as well as the number of rows and columns. The objects selected to be arrayed are always located on the first row and column of the rectangular array. The spacing can be entered using the keyboard or by specifying the distance using the crosshairs. Once you have determined all of the necessary information required by the **array** command, you may activate it using the Command: prompt described previously or by selecting the

Rectangular Array button from the Copy flyout menu on the Modify toolbar. Once the command is entered from the toolbar, the following command sequence is presented:

- Select objects: Selects the object(s) to be arrayed.
- Rectangular or Polar array (R/P) <R>: _r: Using the toolbar automatically selects the Rectangular Array option, saving you a keystroke.
- Number of rows (---) <1>: Selects the number of rows to be included in the rectangular array. The (---) symbol is a visual reminder of what constitutes a row.
- Number of columns (|||) <1>: Selects the number of columns to be included in the rectangular array. The (|||) symbol is a visual reminder of what constitutes a column.
- Unit cell or distance between rows (---): Enters the distance between each horizontal object. Be sure to include the width of the object being arrayed. A positive value will create rows above the current object. A negative number will create rows below the current object.
- Distance between columns (|||): Enter the distance between each vertical object. Be sure to include the height of the object being arrayed. A positive value will create columns to the right of the current object. A negative number will create columns to the left of the current object.

Once the command prompts are completed, the array will be created. Figure 10.40 displays a box and the parameters needed to create an array.

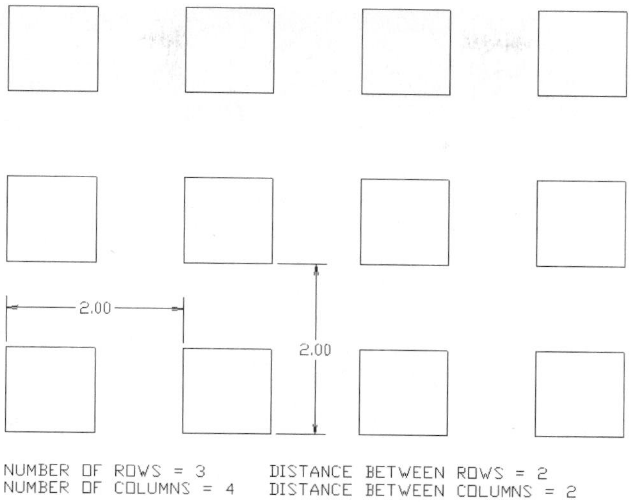

Figure 10.40
Using Rectangular Array to create multiple copies of the square.

Skill Builder

Rectangular arrays are always created parallel to the x- and y-axis unless the Snap angle is changed in the Drawing Aids dialog box that is displayed using the **ddromodes** command.

Tutorial 10.16: Duplicating Elements in a Grid Format

This tutorial continues from the previous tutorial. In this tutorial you will create a series of recessed light symbols in a rectangular pattern above the counter area.

1. Make Lights the current layer.
2.  Select the Circle Center Diameter button on the Circle flyout menu on the Draw toolbar. The `3P/2P/TTR/<Center point>:` prompt appears.
3. Enter **11′,3′** and press Enter. The `Diameter/<Radius>:_d Diameter:` prompt appears.
4. Enter **4** and press Enter. A circle will be created. To complete the symbol, follow the next step.
5. Use the **offset** command and offset the circle 1″. Select the inside of the circle as the side to offset. Next, you will use this symbol and the **array** command to create multiple copies of the symbol in a rectangular pattern.
6.  Select the Rectangular Array button from the Copy flyout menu on the Modify toolbar. The `Select objects:` prompt will appear.
7. Use a Window or Crossing selection set and select the light symbol you created in Steps 1–4, then click the right mouse button. The `Number of rows (---) <1>:` prompt appears.
8. Enter **2** and press Enter. The `Number of columns (|||)<1>:` prompt appears.
9. Enter **14** and press Enter. The `Unit cell or distance between rows (---):` prompt appears.
10. Enter **1′** and press Enter. The `Distance between columns(|||):` prompt appears.
11. Enter **1′** and press Enter. The array of lights will be created as shown in Figure 10.41.

For the Professional

Be careful not to select the 3-D Rectangular Array button 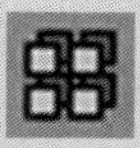 instead of the Rectangular Array button . The two are very similar but are not interchangeable.

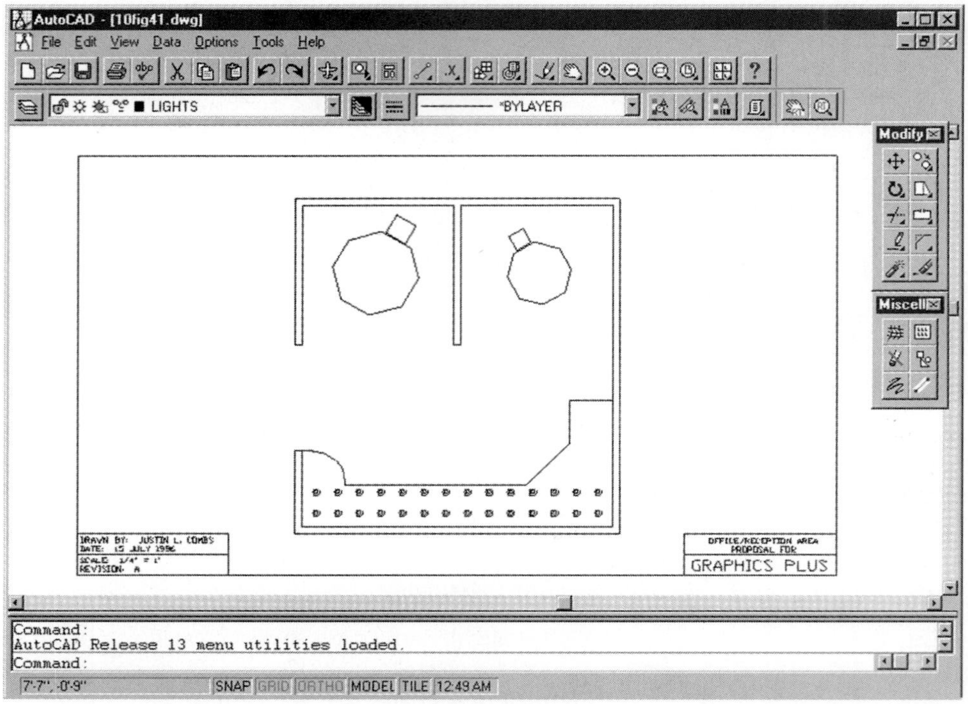

Figure 10.41
Adding a rectangular array of lights.

Polar Arrays

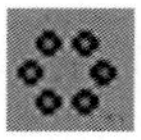

Objects are not always placed in a rectangular pattern. There are many times when a pattern of objects is circular. The **array** command has an option that will allow you to create a series of objects in this circular or polar pattern. To access the command, select the Polar Array button from the Copy flyout menu on the Modify toolbar. Once the command is entered from the toolbar, the following command sequence is presented:

- `Select objects`: Selects the object(s) to be arrayed.
- `Rectangular or Polar array (R/P) <R>: _p`: Using the toolbar automatically selects the Polar Array option, saving you a keystroke.
- `Center point of array`: This point defines the center of the circular pattern as well as the size of the radius around which the array is created.
- `Number of items`: Enters the number of items to be created in the array including the original object.
- `Angle to fill (+=ccw, -=cw)<360>`: This value specifies the angle of inclusion for the placement of the new objects being created. Entering a value of 0 will allow you to supply the amount of separation, in degrees, between each duplicate object created. Using a + or – value will ensure either a counterclockwise or clockwise rotation accordingly.
- `Rotate objects as they are rotate?<Y>`: This option allows you to select whether you want the objects to be rotated around the center point as they are copied. Figure 10.42 shows an example of a polar array with and without objects rotated. It also provides other information that may better explain this command visually.

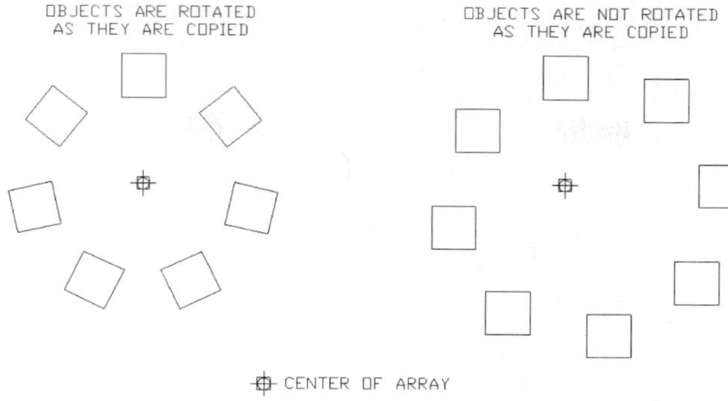

Figure 10.42
*The various options of the **polar array** command.*

Tutorial 10.17: Duplicating Elements in a Circular Format

This tutorial continues from the previous tutorial. In this tutorial you will finish creating the conference table with chairs using a polar array. Since it will be hard to determine the center of the octagon-shaped table, you will create a construction line that will be used to select the center point of the array. Once this point has been found, the construction line will be erased. Before beginning, you may find it useful to use the **zoom** command to zoom in on the left adult conference area.

1.  Draw a line from one corner of the octagon to an opposite corner as shown in Figure 10.43. This line will be used in a later step to find the center of octagon.
2.  Select the Polar Array button from the Copy fly-out menu on the Modify toolbar. The `Select objects:` prompt appears.
3. Select the adult-sized chair located next to the adult-sized table on the left side of the privacy wall and click the right mouse button. The `Center point of array:` prompt appears.
4. Use the **midpoint** Object Snap and select the construction line created in Step 1. The `Number of items:` prompt appears.
5. Enter **8** and press ↵Enter. The `Angle to fill (+=ccw, -=cw) <360>:` prompt appears.
6. Press ↵Enter to accept the default selection of ccw 360°. The `Rotate objects as they are copied? <Y>` prompt appears.
7. Press ↵Enter to accept the default Yes selection. The chairs will be rotated around the conference table.
8.  Erase the construction line created in Step 1.
9. Repeat Steps 1–8 for the chairs on the right conference area. Your drawing should now resemble the one found in Figure 10.44.
10. Add the rest of the objects found in Figure 10.1 to complete this tutorial. Experiment with the commands learned in this and previous units to ensure that your drawing is as similar to Figure 10.1 as possible.
11. Save the file as OFFICE2.DWG.

For the Professional

Be careful not to select the 3-D Polar Array button  instead of the Polar Array button 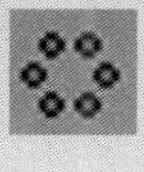. The two are similar but are not interchangeable.

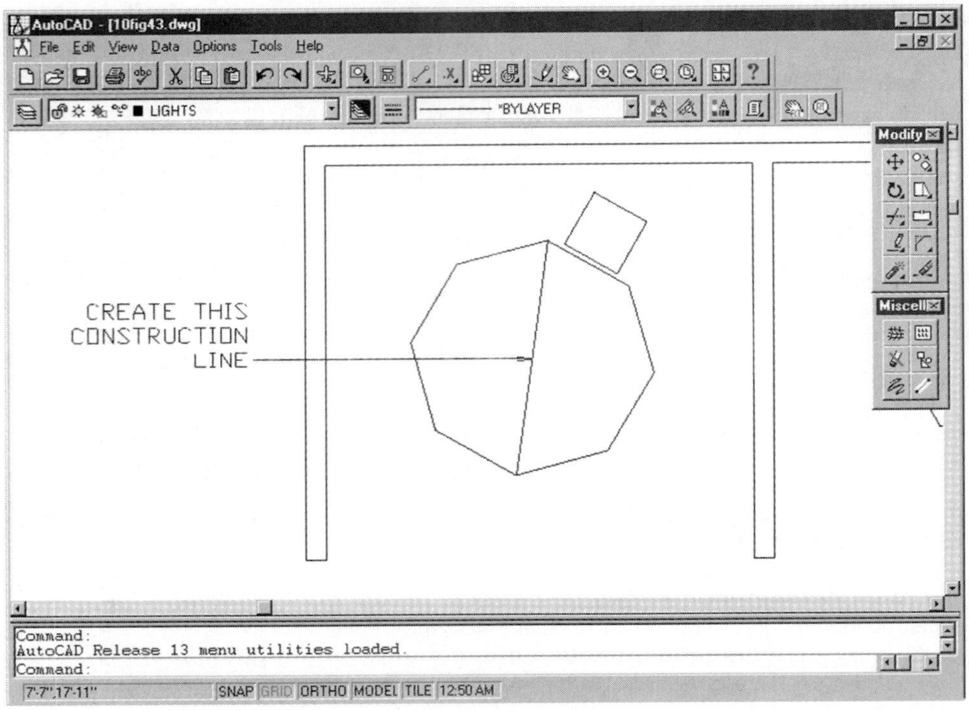

Figure 10.43
Creating a construction line to assist in locating the center of the octagon.

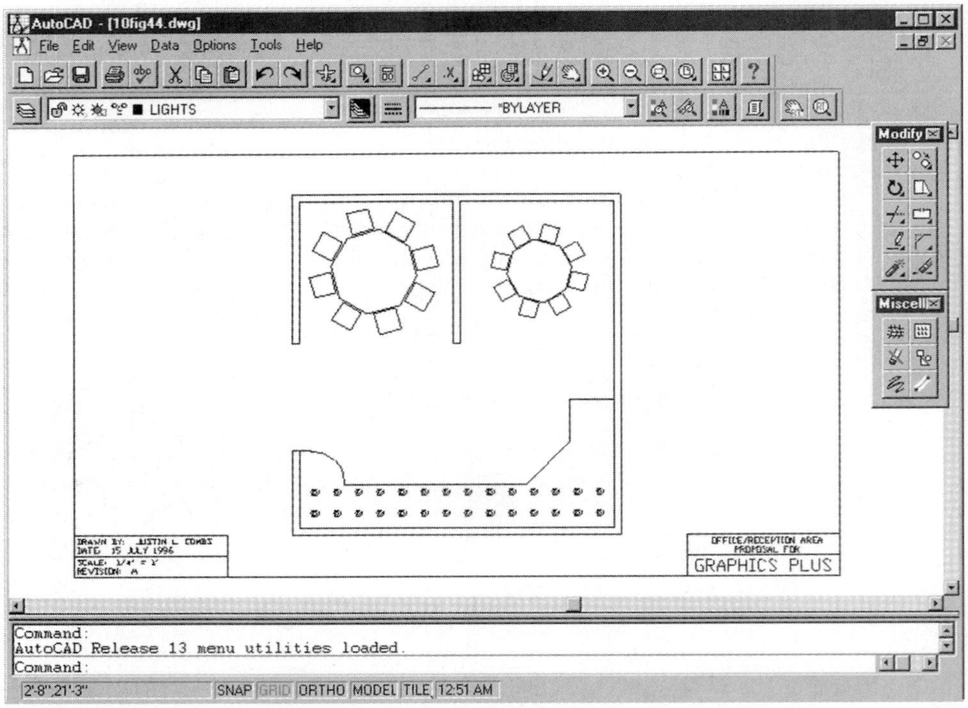

Figure 10.44
The incomplete video game controller design.

SUMMARY

You will find that by using the basic editing skills presented in this unit, you are able to modify and create what may have appeared to be complex drawings. The commands presented will be invaluable to you as you begin to create these complex and time-consuming drawings. Many editing commands modify existing objects, while others will create new geometry based on existing objects. By creating these duplicate objects, the AutoCAD user saves time. The next unit will introduce you to grips, a feature of AutoCAD that incorporates many of the modifications commands described in this unit. Before continuing to the next unit, be sure you have a good grasp on the features and functions of the commands presented in this unit.

REVIEW

1. Explain the association between the **erase** and **oops** commands.
2. How many Undo commands can be performed during a drawing session?
3. Why would a layer be purged?
4. Discuss the difference between the **copy** and **move** commands.
5. Describe a situation where the **mirror** command would be beneficial.
6. What common point is needed for the **move, copy,** and **scale** commands?
7. Explain the difference between the **fillet** and **chamfer** commands.
8. Discuss the similarities between the **trim** and **extend** commands.
9. List the two types of arrays and discuss their use.
10. Why are editing skills important?

EXERCISE 10

In this assignment you will load and complete a partial drawing of a video game controller shown in Figure 10.44 to resemble the drawing shown in Figure 10.45. You will

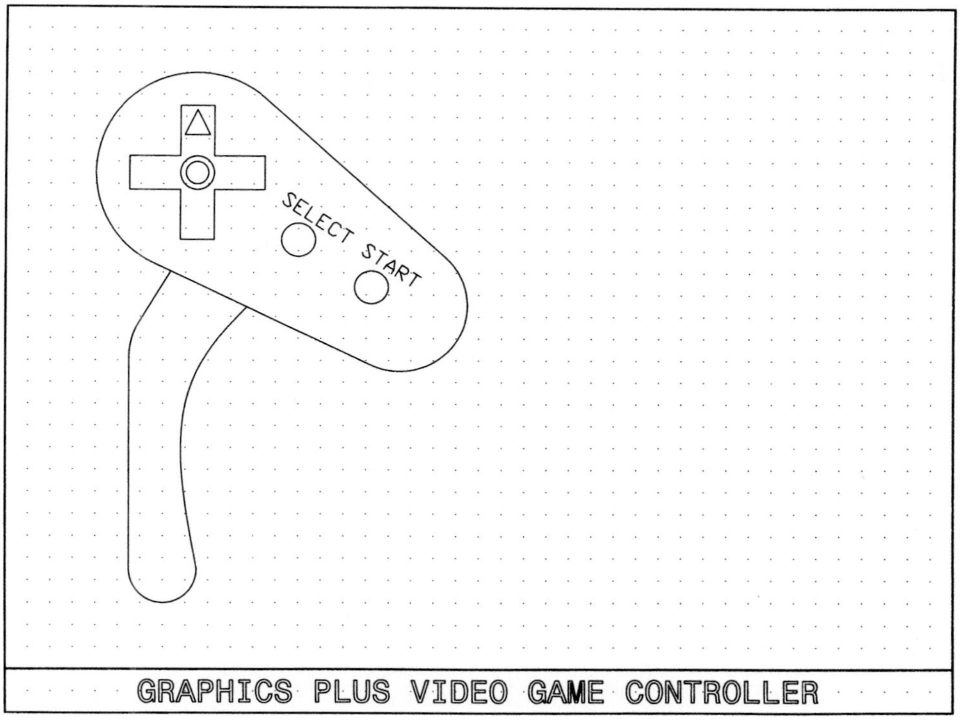

Figure 10.45
The completed video game controller design.

use the editing commands introduced in this unit to complete the drawing, and you should use very few drawing commands. The steps below will assist you in completing the drawing. Not every step needed to complete the drawing is listed; it is up to you to determine what additional steps are necessary. The grid has been displayed to assist you in determining approximate sizes of the objects. Do not worry if you feel you are approximating a dimension. Be more concerned with the editing skills you are developing.

1. Load the Controller.dwg drawing file from the workdisk.
2. Array the directional arrows to complete the thumb pad.
3. Create the grid lines by using the **array** command. *Hint:* you may have to explode some polylines in order to utilize certain objects.
4. Mirror the left side to create the right side.
5. The right side requires that all controls be scaled. Look carefully at the grid to determine an approximate scale.
6. Use the **offset, trim, extend** and **fillet** commands to complete the center.
7. Use the **dtext** command to finish the drawing.
8. Save the file as Video Controller.dwg.
9. Plot the drawing at full-scale.

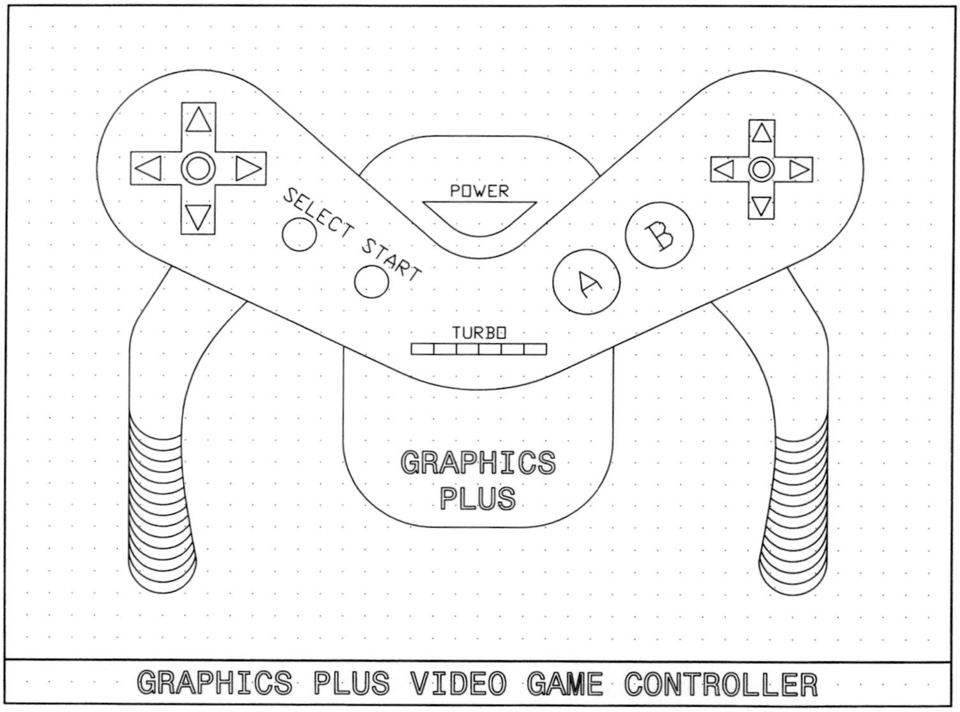

UNIT 11

EDITING WITH GRIPS

OVERVIEW

Editing a drawing is a common practice when using AutoCAD. Moving, copying, and rotating objects are just some of the editing functions you use when working on your drawing. These commands were introduced in the previous unit. The Grips function offers a convenient way to edit objects using the crosshairs, without entering commands.

OBJECTIVES

- Turn on grips and set grip options.
- Stretch objects with grips.
- Move objects with grips.
- Rotate objects with grips.
- Scale objects with grips.
- Mirror objects with grips.
- Copy objects with grips.

INTRODUCTION

If you use manual drafting techniques, it can take hours to modify and edit a drawing. Simply moving a door on a floor plan or modifying a counterbore could require lots of erasing and redrawing. Using AutoCAD makes these same editing tasks simpler and quicker. In Unit 10, "Basic Editing Techniques," you learned how to perform a variety of editing tasks such as Move, Copy, Stretch, Rotate, Mirror, and Scale.

Grips provide one of the quickest methods for performing many editing tasks. Understanding and using grips is an important skill that you need to develop to become proficient with AutoCAD. As you become familiar with grips, you will wonder how you got along without them.

OUTLINE

Working with Grips
Tutorial 11.1: Selecting Single and Multiple Grips
Tutorial 11.2: Setting Grip Options
Using the Grip Modes
Tutorial 11.3: Stretching Objects with Grips
Tutorial 11.4: Moving Objects with Grips
Tutorial 11.5: Rotating Objects with Grips
Tutorial 11.6: Scaling Objects with Grips
Tutorial 11.7: Mirroring Objects with Grips
Tutorial 11.8: Copying Objects with Grips
Implications of Using the Same Grip Point
Summary
Review
Exercises

WORKING WITH GRIPS

Grips are small blue squares or boxes that appear at specific locations on an object after the object is selected using the crosshairs. After an object is selected with grips, you can perform several different grip functions on the object. The grip modes include Stretch, Move, Rotate, Scale, and Mirror.

By default, grips are turned on in AutoCAD. A simple way to check if grips are turned on is to select an object with the crosshairs while the AutoCAD `Command:` prompt is displayed. To do this, move the pickbox over an object and press the Pick button. If small blue squares (grips) appear on the object, grips are enabled.

SKILL BUILDER

The small pickbox on the AutoCAD crosshairs does not necessarily mean that grips are enabled. The cursor pickbox also indicates that the Pick-First, or noun/verb, selection is enabled.

When using grips, you can select the objects first and then issue the appropriate grip mode. This is called noun/verb, or Pick-First selection. For more information, see Unit 9, "Creating Selection Sets," which discusses the two methods for selecting objects in AutoCAD.

In the second method, you can issue a command and then select the objects. The objects are selected in response to the command's prompts. This method is called verb/noun, or Pick-After, selection. It is called verb/noun selection because you specify the verb action or command, such as **erase** before you specify the objects to which you want to apply the action.

Grips can work in conjunction with noun/verb (Pick-First) selection. By default, noun/verb selection is enabled in AutoCAD. The **pickfirst** system variable controls the method of object selection. This is saved as part of the configuration, which means that after it is turned off, it will remain turned off for all subsequent drawings until it is turned on again. You can change the Pickfirst system variable by following these steps:

- Enter **`pickfirst`** at the `Command:` prompt and enter the new value.
- Access the Object Selection Settings dialog box shown in Figure 11.1. This can be done by entering **`ddselect`** at the `Command:` prompt. The Noun/Verb Selection check box will change the setting of the **pickfirst** system variable.
- Access the Object Selection Settings dialog box by choosing Options/Selection... from the pull-down menu.

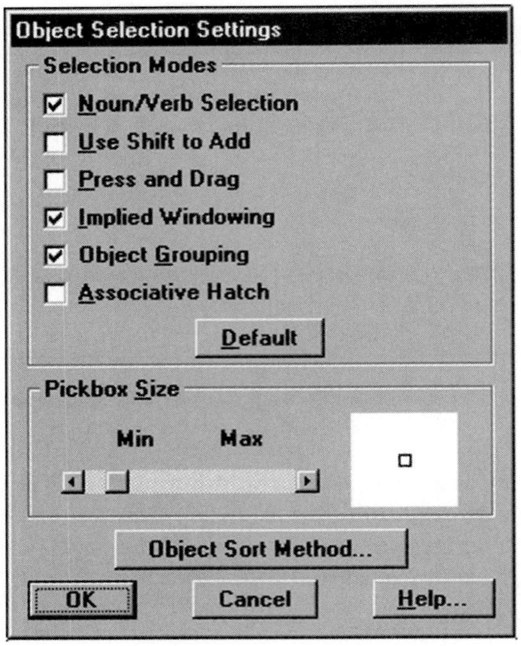

Figure 11.1
The Object Selection Settings dialog box governs the enabling of noun/verb object selection.

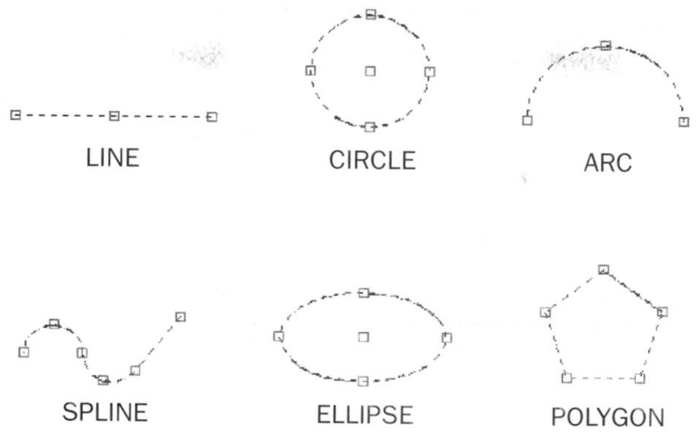

Figure 11.2
Grips displayed on several AutoCAD objects.

Selecting Objects with Grips

With Grips enabled and the `Command:` prompt displayed, you can use any object selection method to make grips appear on the object. One method used to select an object is to place the crosshairs directly on the object.

Alternately, you can invoke the implied selection (Auto selection) method. When using the implied selection method you do not pick directly on the object, but rather you define a window. By specifying the second window point to the left of the first window point, you create a window. Everything totally enclosed by the window is selected. By placing the second window point to the right of the first window point, you create a crossing window. Anything touching the window is selected.

When an object is selected using grips, boxes appear at specific locations on the object, as shown in Figure 11.2. Grips allow the user to modify the selected object by moving one or several grips together, in combination with one of the five grip modes.

Initially, grips appear as hollow blue boxes. This type of grip is called a *warm grip*. Grips are always warm first, with the object's grips displayed in blue (default color) and the object highlighted. After an object is selected and its grips appear, you have two options. One option is to invoke one of the grip modes. The other option is to select multiple grips on the objects. When a grip is selected for editing with the cursor, the grip becomes a solid red box (default color) and is called a *hot grip*. The blue and red colors are defaults, and can be changed. See "Setting Grips Options" later in this unit for more information on how to set the grip colors.

To select a single grip and invoke the grip modes, place the cursor on the grip and click the Pick button. The cursor will automatically snap to the exact center location of the grip and the grip will turn red. The stretch grip mode is the first grip editing mode invoked. You also can enable multiple objects with grips to create a selection set. Creating a selection set and editing objects with multiple grips is a two-step procedure:

1. Select the objects you need to include in the selection set to enable the warm grips. The grips will appear blue and all of the objects selected will appear highlighted.
2. Select a single grip. The selected grip will be changed to hot (default red color). A hot grip is the default base point used for the editing action. The base point may be defined as the reference point that will be used for subsequent grip modes. When a hot grip exists, a different series of prompts appear in place of the `Command:` prompt. A grip must be changed to hot before the editing options appear. Two or more grips can be made hot at the same time by pressing ⇧Shift while selecting each grip.

You also can remove an object from the selection set. This is done by pressing ⇧Shift and selecting a highlighted object that has warm grips. The object's grips are now called *cold grips*. Cold grips are created when you deselect a highlighted object that has warm grips. Even though an object containing cold grips is not included in the selection set, you can still select a grip on the object to use as the base point for the editing action.

TABLE 11.1 Summary of the Hot, Warm, and Cold Grip States

Grip State	Grip Color	Grip Explanation
Cold	Blue grips	The object is not part of the selection set. A cold grip can be snapped to or used as an alternate base point. A grip is made cold by deselecting a highlighted object that has warm grips.
Warm	Blue grips	The object is included in the selection set. A grip is always warm first.
Hot	Red grips	The object is included in the selection set. A hot grip is used as the base point, or control point, for the editing action. A grip is made hot by selecting a warm grip. More than one grip can be hot at one time. This is done by pressing ⇧Shift while selecting each grip.

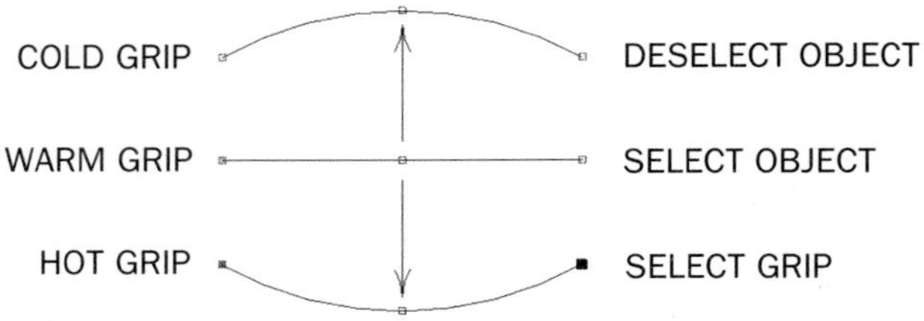

Figure 11.3
Grips have three states: warm, hot, and cold.

Selecting a grip on a deselected (unhighlighted) object to use as a base point does not turn red, however.

Table 11.1 and Figure 11.3 summarize the three grip states.

For the Professional

You can select multiple grips only when AutoCAD is displaying the `Command:` prompt and you hold down ⇧Shift when selecting the first grip. Once the grip mode is active, you can't select any more grips as "hot" grips, although you can select any grip as a response to a grip mode prompt.

To deselect all objects and remove their grips, press Esc twice. The first press removes the objects from the selection set. The second press removes all grips. The **redraw** and **regen** commands do not have any effect on displayed grips.

To change a specific object's grip status, pick the object while holding down ⇧Shift. Picking the same object a second time while holding down ⇧Shift will remove the object's grips.

Which editing method is best to use—grips or the more traditional verb/noun (Pick-After) method? Unfortunately, no hard and fast rules exist to help you choose between the two editing methods. In some situations, grips can provide you with a better editing method. In other situations, the more traditional verb/noun method works best. The more

Tutorial 11.1: Selecting Single and Multiple Grips

In this and the following unit tutorials, you will use grips to modify the drawing of the gear shown in Figure 11.4. You will begin by opening an existing drawing.

1.  Select the Open button from the Standard toolbar. If the AutoCAD Save Changes dialog box appears, select No unless you want to save the current drawing. If you want to save the current drawing, select Yes and enter a path and drawing name.
2. When the Select File dialog box appears, load the 11DWG01 file from the workdisk. After the file is loaded, your screen should resemble Figure 11.4.
3. Select the circle, as shown in Figure 11.5. The circle becomes highlighted and the grips appear (see Figure 11.6). You have just made a single selection.
4. To make a multiple selection, click any other object and notice that the grips will appear on that object as well.

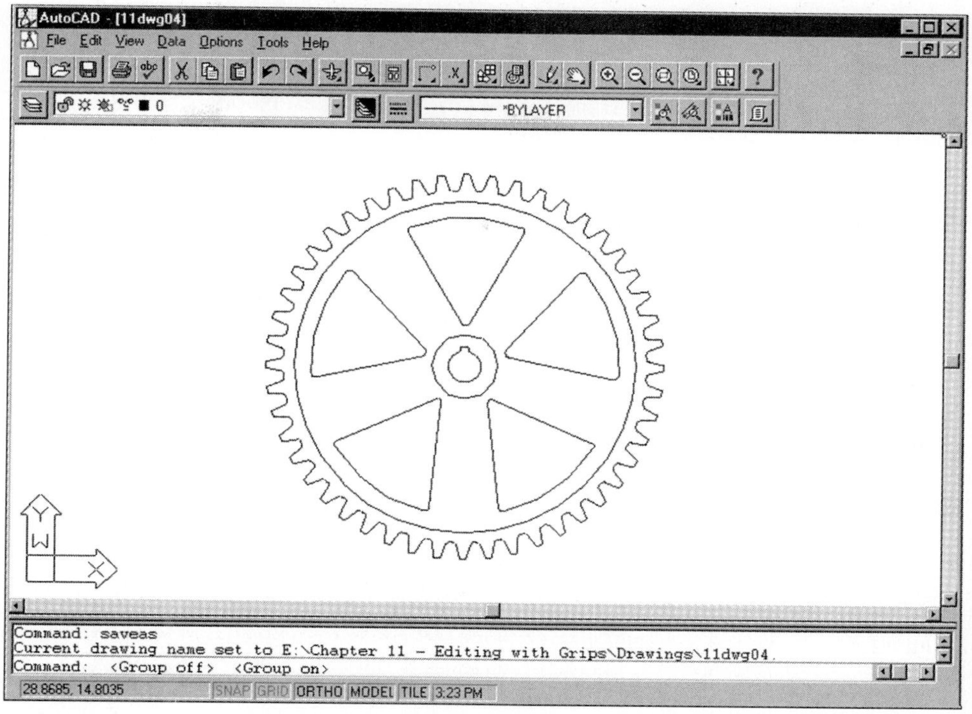

Figure 11.4
Use grips to modify the gear drawing.

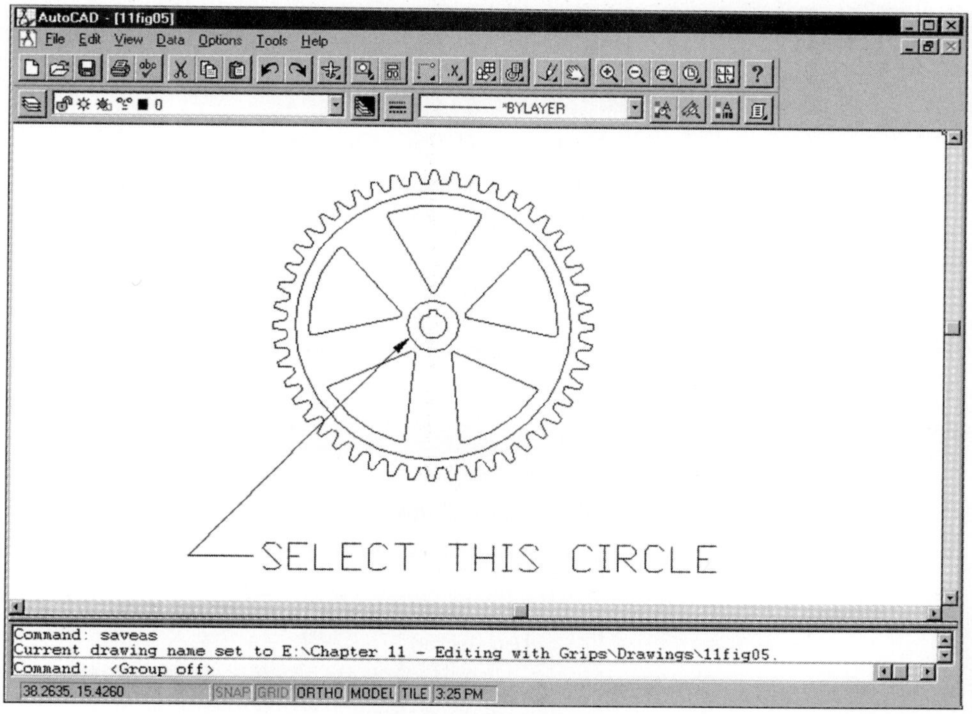

Figure 11.5
Select the inner circle.

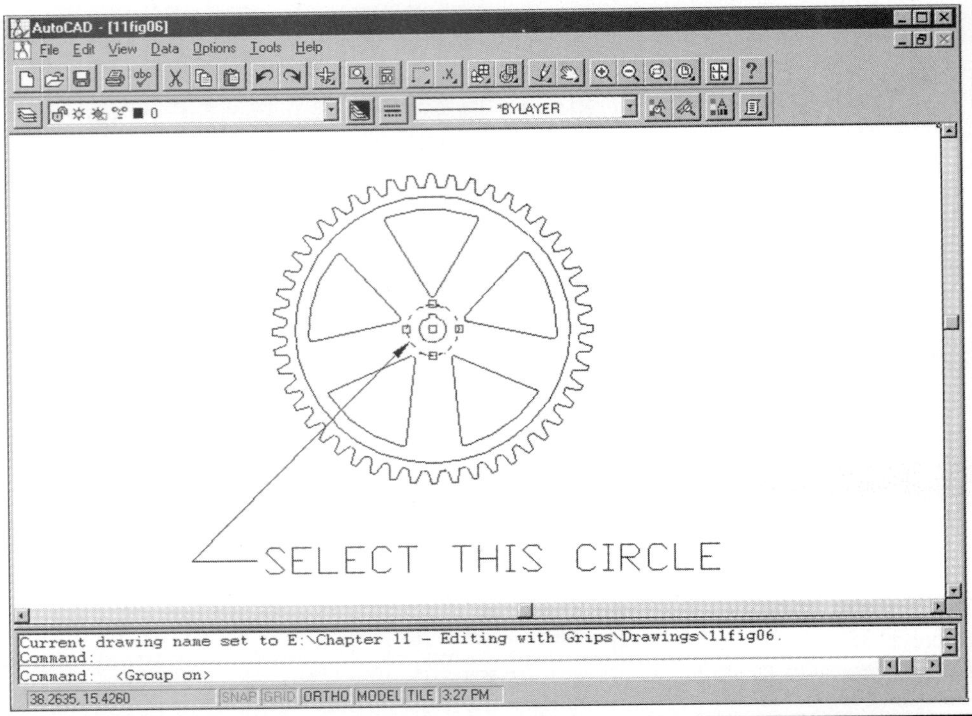

Figure 11.6
The highlighted circle showing the grips.

you work with AutoCAD, the easier it will be to determine which editing method will work best for each application. You will also find that in some situations, it's purely a matter of personnal preference.

Setting Grips Options

The Grips dialog box, shown in Figure 11.7, can be used to change several grip characteristics. In this dialog box, you can turn the grips on and off, set the grip size, and specify the colors to be used for selected and unselected grips. You can access the Grips dialog box as follows:

- Enter **`ddgrips`** at the `Command:` prompt.
- Choose Options/Grips.

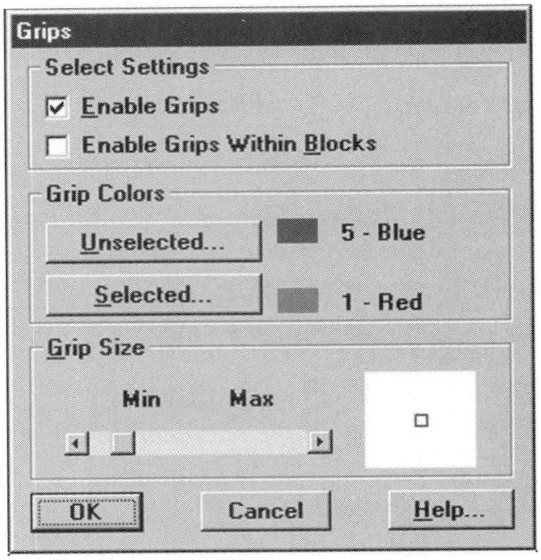

Figure 11.7
The Grips dialog box can be used to change many of the grip features.

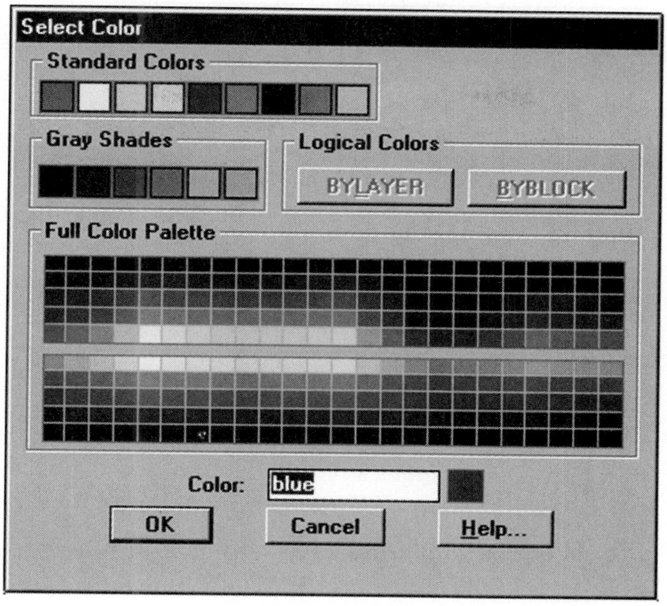

Figure 11.8
The Select Color dialog box can be used to change the unselected and selected grip colors.

If you deselect the Enable Grips check box in the Grips dialog box, grips will not appear when you select objects. This can be useful if you do not want to use the grip modes on the selection set. Grip colors can be changed by selecting the Unselected or Selected buttons. Choosing either box will invoke the Select Color dialog box (see Figure 11.8). This will change the color of the grips on objects.

You also can change grip size in the Grip Size area of the Grips dialog box. This allows you to change the size of the grip located at the intersection of the crosshairs. To change the grip size, move the slider bar back and forth. You can also change the size by changing the **gripsize** system variable.

The settings for grips are stored in several system variables. All of these variables are saved in the configuration—not in the individual drawings. Table 11.2 lists the system variables and their corresponding uses.

Editing Blocks with Grips

AutoCAD has the **block** command that allows you to define a group of objects as a single object. Once defined, these symbols, or blocks, can be inserted into a drawing full-size, scaled, or rotated.

AutoCAD recognizes a block as a single object, regardless of the number of objects it contains. For this reason, blocks usually display only one grip. This single grip is located at the block's insertion point. AutoCAD has the system variable called **gripblock** to control the method of displaying grips within a block. By default, **gripblock** is 0, meaning off. When it is turned on, all objects within the block display grips as if they are individual objects. This is useful when you want to edit a block using a base point other than the block's insertion point. To change the **gripblock** system variable, follow these steps:

TABLE 11.2 Grips System Variables and Their Uses

GRIPBLOCK	By default (color 0), assigns grips only to the insertion point of blocks
GRIPCOLOR	By default, blue (color 5) is assigned to nonselected grips
GRIPHOT	By default, red (color 1) is assigned to selected grips
GRIPS	By default (1), grips are enabled
GRIPSIZE	By default (3), the height of the grip boxes in pixels

TUTORIAL 11.2: SETTING GRIP OPTIONS

This tutorial continues from the previous tutorial. In this tutorial you will use the Grips dialog box to change the Grip options settings.

1. Choose Options/Grips. The Grips dialog box appears (Figure 11.7).
2. Change the unselected grip color to yellow.
3. In the Grip Size area of the Grips dialog box, double-click the right arrow on the slider bar to increase the size of the grips.
4. Choose OK to accept the changes.
5. When bringing up the Grips dialog box, all previously displayed grips are cleared. You must reselect the circle seen earlier in Figure 11.4. Notice that the grip colors and sizes have now been changed.
6. Open the Grips dialog box and change the grip settings back to the defaults (refer to Figure 11.7).

- Enter **gripblock** at the `Command:` prompt. AutoCAD will respond with `New value for GRIPBLOCK <0>:`. The default value is 0, for off. Entering 1 will turn **gripblock** on.
- Invoke the Grips dialog box and select the Enable Grips Within Blocks check box.

USING THE GRIP MODES

When you pick a grip and it becomes active (hot), the grip changes color. If you pick a grip without pressing Shift, AutoCAD enters the Stretch grip mode. The Stretch grip mode can be used to stretch selected objects based on the selected grip. Pressing Shift while selecting your first grip allows you to select multiple grips.

The Stretch mode is one of five grip modes. The grip modes include:

- **Stretch.** This grip mode allows you to stretch objects. It is similar to the **stretch** command.
- **Move.** With this grip mode, you can move objects from one location to another. This grip mode is similar to the **move** command.
- **Rotate.** The Rotate grip mode enables you to rotate objects around a hot grip or selected base point. This is similar to the **rotate** command.
- **Scale.** The Scale grip mode allows you to scale objects larger or smaller. It is similar to the **scale** command.
- **Mirror.** Using the Mirror grip mode enables you to mirror selected objects about an axis. The Mirror grip mode is similar to the **mirror** command.

To cycle through the five grip editing modes in order to select one, use one of the following methods:

- Press Enter.
- Press the space bar.
- Enter the first two letters of the command.

STRETCHING OBJECTS WITH GRIPS

When modifying objects in mechanical drafting, it is common to increase the length of a part. In architectural drafting, room sizes can be stretched to increase the square footage. The **stretch** command will move a selected part of an object without disturbing the connections between the objects.

The stretch mode is similar to the **stretch** command. It allows you to modify the length of an object or group of objects. While stretching objects generally makes them longer or shorter, the effects of stretching certain objects is somewhat different. When a circle is stretched using the Stretch grip mode, its radius becomes larger or smaller.

Stretching objects with grips is a fairly straightforward process. Selecting the grip at the endpoint of a line will change the location of the endpoint, which lengthens or shortens the line. Selecting the grip on the quadrant of a circle will modify its radius. Invoking the Stretch mode displays the following `Command:` prompt:

```
** STRETCH **
<Stretch to point>/Base point/Copy/Undo/eXit:
```

- **Base point.** The Base point option appears with all of the main grip editing options.
- **Copy.** Copy is another suboption of every choice. Its use is discussed in the section, "Copying Objects with Grips."
- **Undo.** You can invoke the Undo option by entering *U*. It will undo the last Copy or Base point selection.
- **eXit.** Entering an *X* will exit the Stretch mode.

Tutorial 11.3: Stretching Objects with Grips

This tutorial continues from the previous tutorial. In this tutorial you will use grips to modify the diameter of the hub on the gear.

1. Using the crosshairs, select the circle shown previously in Figure 11.5. Grips will appear on the center and at the quadrants of the circle.
2. Ensure that the Ortho mode is off by checking the status line at the bottom of the screen. If you see Ortho displayed, double click on the word **ortho.**
3. Click one of the quadrant grips and move the crosshairs left and right. Notice that the diameter of the circle changes as you move the crosshairs.
4. Make the diameter of the circle smaller than it was originally and press the Pick button. Notice that the grips are displayed after the stretch has been performed. AutoCAD is ready to perform another operation on that object.
5. Next, stretch the circle using the Base point option. First, select the outer circle. You should have grips displayed on both circles (see Figure 11.9).
6. Select one of the quadrant grips on the inner circle. AutoCAD prompts:

```
** STRETCH **
<Stretch to point>/Base
point/Copy/Undo/eXit:
```

7. Enter **b** in response to the prompt. This will allow you to use any other grip or point as the base point instead of the hot grip.

```
** STRETCH **
<Stretch to point>/Base
point/Copy/Undo/eXit: b
Base point:
```

8. Select one of the quadrant grips on the outer circle. Notice the diameter of the inner circle changes as you move the crosshairs, using the new base point, but the outer circle does not change because the quadrant grip was not hot.

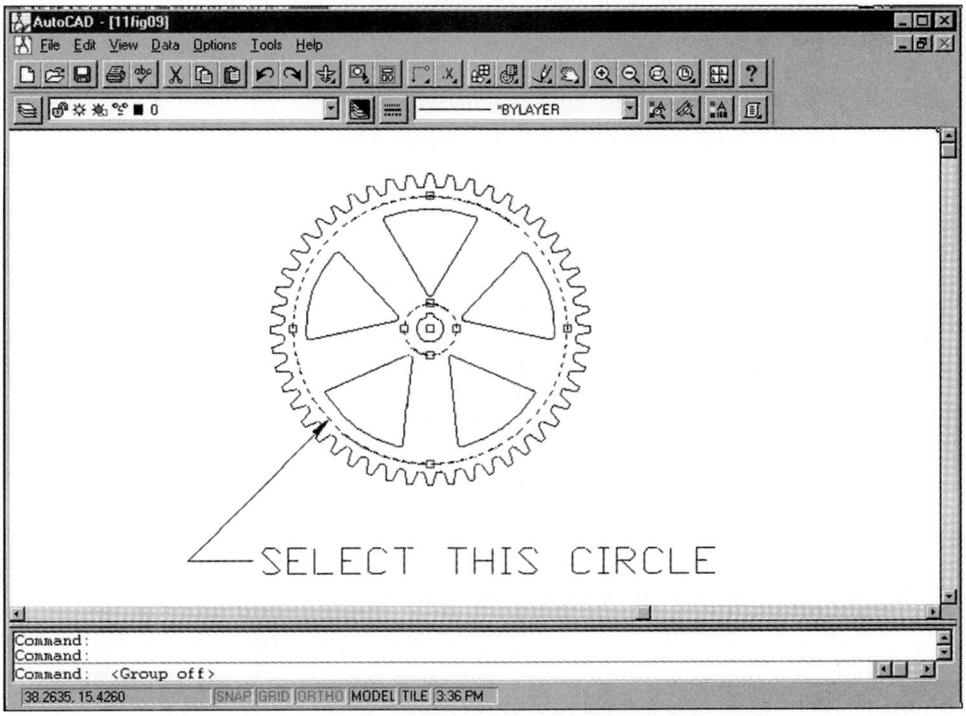

Figure 11.9
Use the Base point on the outer circle to stretch the diameter of the inner circle.

Attempting to stretch certain objects will result in moving the object rather than stretching it. This will happen when you select a grip that does not have a valid stretch modification. Selecting the midpoint of a line, center of a circle, or insertion point of text will move the object rather than stretch it.

Some objects cannot be stretched regardless of which grip is selected. Blocks are an example of such objects. A block may consist of a number of different objects, but AutoCAD recognizes a block as one single object. The objects are locked together and cannot be changed in any way, including stretching. Another example is text. Text can be moved or scaled, but can't be stretched.

Moving Objects with Grips

In the previous section on stretching objects with grips it was noted that you can move certain objects to a new location with the Stretch mode. If you select the midpoint of a line, center of a circle, or insertion point of text you will move the object rather than stretch it.

Moving objects with the Stretch mode does not work in all situations or for all objects. The Move mode is explicitly for moving objects.

AutoCAD also provides the **move** command. The **move** command also can use Pick-First selection. In certain cases, the **move** command is preferred over the Move grip mode. If you need to define and move a complex selection set, the **move** command is generally easier to use. Invoking the Move grip mode displays the following `Command:` prompt:

```
** MOVE **
<Move to point>/Base point/Copy/Undo/eXit:
```

- **Base point.** The Base point option appears with all of the main grip editing options.
- **Copy.** Allows you to create a copy of the object while it is being moved.
- **Undo.** You can invoke the Undo option by typing the letter *U*. It will undo the last copy or base point selection.
- **eXit.** Entering **x** will exit the Move grip mode.

Tutorial 11.4: Moving Objects with Grips

This tutorial continues from the previous tutorial. In this tutorial you will use grips to move the circle that represents the hub on the gear.

1. Grips should still be displayed from the previous tutorial on the inner and outer circles. If grips are not present on the circles, select the circles with the crosshairs.
2. Select the grip located in the center of the circles. This will display the `** STRETCH **` prompt and options.
3. To change to the `** MOVE **` prompt and options, press the space bar. The grip mode prompt will indicate that you will now be performing a Move function. As mentioned in the text, it's not necessary to perform this step if the prompt indicates stretch and the center of a circle is selected.
4. Move the crosshairs around the screen and notice that the circles move with it.
5. Click anywhere on-screen to place the circle.
6. Next, undo the previous move. Use the **undo** command to place the circle back in its original position.

   ```
   Command: u
   ```

7. Next you will move the circle using the Base point option. First, select the inner and outer circles.
8. Remove the outer circle from the selection set. Hold [Shift] and select the outer circle. The outer circle grips are still blue, but the grips are cold and the outer circle object is no longer highlighted.
9. Select one of the quadrant grips on the inner circle. When AutoCAD displays the `** STRETCH **` prompt, press the space bar. AutoCAD will display the `** MOVE **` prompt as follows:

   ```
   ** MOVE **<Move to point>/Base
   point/Copy/Undo/eXit:
   ```

10. Enter **b** in response to the prompt. This will allow you to use any other grip or point as the base point instead of the hot grip.

    ```
    ** MOVE **<Move to point>/Base
    point/Copy/Undo/eXit: b
    Base point:
    ```

11. Select one of the quadrant grips on the outer circle. Notice the inner circle moves as you change the location of the crosshairs, using the new base point.
12. Click anywhere on-screen to move the circle.
13. Use the **undo** command to place the circle back in its original position.

Rotating Objects with Grips

With the Rotate grip mode, you can rotate existing objects on a drawing. The **rotate** command can be very useful if you need a part drawn at a specific angle. Using the Rotate grip mode, you can draw the part in normal x,y coordinates and then place it at any angle in the drawing.

For example, if you need to draw the wing of a building at 80°, you can draw the wing at 0°, and then use the Rotate grip mode to rotate it into place. Rotating an object using the rotate grip mode is a three-step procedure:

1. Select the objects you want to rotate. To select more than one object, hold down ⇧Shift when selecting the first object, or use a window.
2. Select a grip that you want to use for the center of rotation. The selected grip will turn red.
3. Specify the rotation angle. You can either select a point on the screen or type in the rotation angle.

The Rotate grip mode displays the following prompt:

```
** ROTATE **
<Rotation Angle>/Base point/Copy/Undo/Reference/eXit:
```

The following options are listed when using the Rotate grip mode:

- **Base point.** Allows you to use any other grip or point as the base point instead of the hot grip.
- **Copy.** Creates a rotated copy of an object.
- **Undo.** This will undo the last copy or base point selection. It will function only after a Base or Copy option.
- **Reference.** Allows you either to enter an angle to use as a reference, or select two points on an existing object you want to align it with.
- **eXit.** Entering an **x** will exit the Rotate grip mode.

Scaling Objects with Grips

The Scale grip mode can be used to adjust the size of the objects proportionally. The grip initially selected will be the base point for the scaling operation. The Scale grip mode displays the following `Command:` prompt and options:

```
** SCALE **
<Scale factor>/Base point/Copy/Undo/Reference/eXit:
```

Tutorial 11.5: Rotating Objects with Grips

This tutorial continues from the previous tutorial. In this tutorial you will use grips to rotate the drawing of the gear.

1. Create a window by picking the first point to the upper left of the gear and the second point to the lower right of the gear as shown in Figure 11.10.
2. Grips will appear on all objects in the drawing.
3. Click the grip located in the center of the gear.
4. Press the space bar twice to invoke the Rotate option.
5. Rotate the gear 30°, as shown in Figure 11.11. AutoCAD will prompt:

```
** ROTATE **
<Rotation Angle>/Base
point/Copy/Undo/Reference/eXit: 30
```

6. Rotate the gear again using the Reference option. The Reference option will allow you either to enter an angle to use as a reference, or select two points on an existing object you want to align it with.
7. Click the grip located in the center of the gear to make it hot.
8. Press the space bar twice to invoke the Rotate option. At the `** ROTATE **` prompt, enter **R**.

```
** ROTATE **
<Rotation Angle>/Base
point/Copy/Undo/Reference/eXit: r
```

9. AutoCAD will prompt for the reference angle as shown below. Enter 30, which is the angle you originally rotated the gear to.

```
Reference Angle <0>: 30
```

10. You are now prompted for a new angle based on the reference angle you just entered. Entering 0 (zero) will rotate the gear back to its original position.

```
** ROTATE **
<New angle>/Base
point/Copy/Undo/Reference/eXit: 0
```

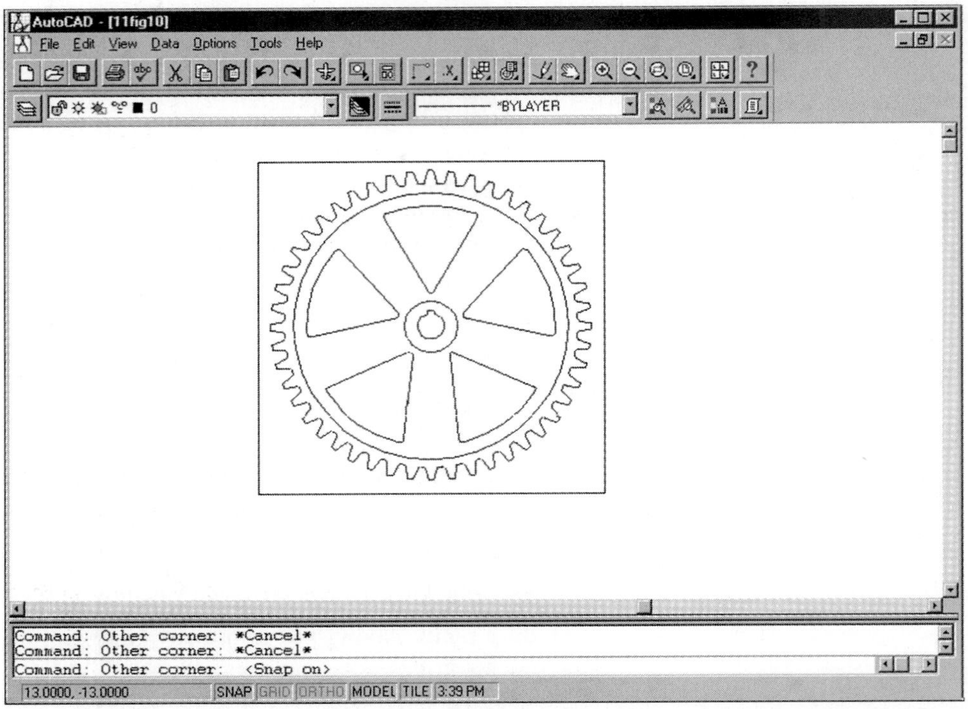

Figure 11.10
Create a window around the gear by selecting the upper-right corner first and the lower-left corner second.

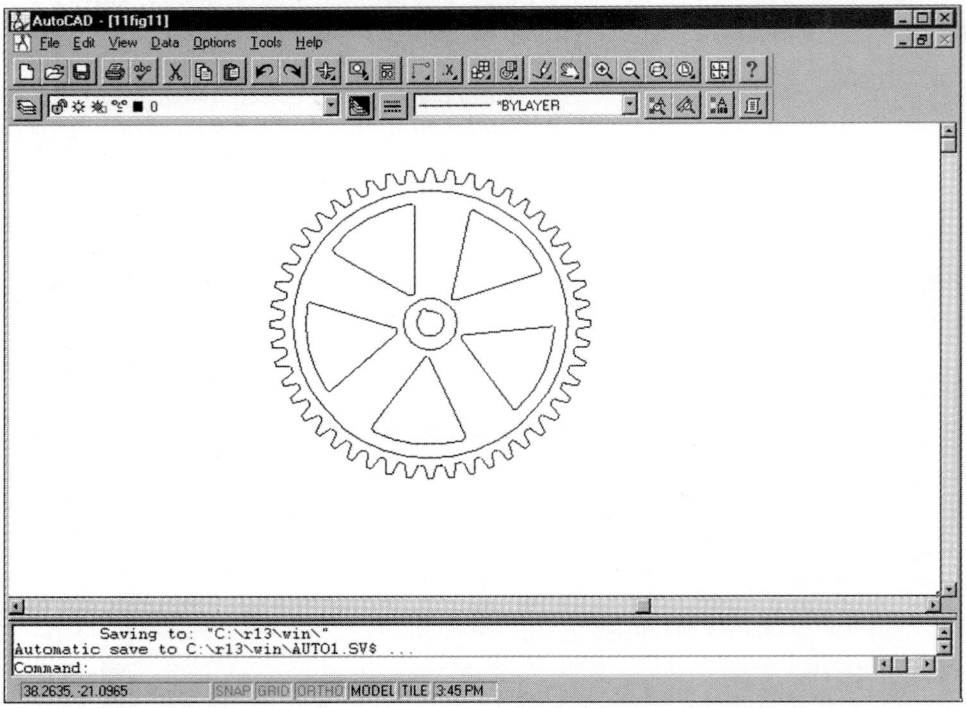

Figure 11.11
Placement of the gear drawing after rotating it 30°.

The following options are available when using the Scale grip mode:

- **Base point.** You can use any other grip or point as the base point instead of the hot grip.
- **Copy.** Allows you to create a scaled copy of the object.
- **Undo.** This undoes the last copy or base point selection.
- **Reference.** Used to calculate a scale factor based on reference units you provide.

- **eXit.** Entering an **x** will exit the Scale grip mode.

Selecting the Reference option will cause AutoCAD to calculate a scale factor based on the reference units you provide. For example, suppose you have a line that is 2.5 units long, and you want it to be 3.375 units long. You can calculate the scale factor on a calculator (1.35), but the scale factor reference allows AutoCAD to do all the work for you.

When you select the Reference option, the following prompt appears:

```
Reference Length <1.0000>:
```

Enter the current length of the line (2.5). When AutoCAD displays the `<New length>:` grip mode prompt, enter the final distance (3.375). AutoCAD will perform the calculation for you.

TUTORIAL 11.6: SCALING OBJECTS WITH GRIPS

This tutorial continues from the previous tutorial. In this tutorial you will use grips to scale the size of the gear.

1. Create a window around the gear, as shown in Figure 11.10. Grips will appear on all objects in the drawing.
2. Select the grip located in the center of the gear.
3. Press the space bar until Scale appears on the `Command:` prompt.
4. Scale the gear to half of its original size by typing **.5**.

```
** SCALE **
<Scale factor>/Base
point/Copy/Undo/Reference/eXit: .5
```

5. Use the **undo** command to return the gear to its original size.

```
Command: u
```

MIRRORING OBJECTS WITH GRIPS

The Mirror grip mode allows you to make a mirror image of the objects selected along a mirror line. The mirror line is a line that shows where the mirror image reflects from the original. When using the Mirror grip mode, AutoCAD assumes the most recent active grip is one endpoint of the mirror line unless you specify a different point. The mirror line can be thought of as a pivot point for the objects being mirrored. The Mirror grip mode displays the following prompt:

```
** MIRROR **
<Second point>/Base point/Copy/Undo/eXit:
```

The following are Mirror grip mode options:

- **Second point.** The point that defines the other endpoint of the mirror line. The first point is the most recent active grip unless specified otherwise.
- **Base point.** Allows you to use any other grip or point as the first point in the mirror line instead of the hot grip.
- **Copy.** Allows you to create a mirrored copy.
- **Undo.** This will undo the last copy or base point selection.
- **eXit.** Entering an **x** will exit the Mirror grip mode.

The Mirror grip mode is ideal for creating symmetrical objects. Symmetrical objects are those objects that are equal shape on each side of a center line. For instance, a circle is symmetrical because it is the same shape, a 180° arc, if a vertical or horizontal line is created through the center of the circle. An equilateral triangle is symmetrical only about a single center line that passes through a point and is perpendicular to the opposite edge. Many designs contain parts that are symmetrical. Before you begin drawing, examine the parts carefully and look at the relationships between the different objects. If the parts contain symmetrical objects, Mirror greatly reduces the amount of geometry creation you need to do in the drawing.

When using the Mirror grip mode, you can leave the original drawing intact and make a mirror duplicate of it, or remove the original object. To leave the original intact, select the Copy option.

Tutorial 11.7: Mirroring Objects with Grips

This tutorial continues from the previous tutorial. In this tutorial you use grips to mirror one of the gear splines.

1. Clear all previous grips by pressing Esc twice.
2. Erase the line shown in Figure 11.12.
3. Select the line and arc shown in Figure 11.13.
4. Deselect the arc to remove it from the selection set. Do this by placing the crosshairs directly on the arc and holding down ⇧Shift while selecting the arc.
5. Select the grip at the bottom of the line.
6. Press the space bar until the Mirror option is displayed as shown:

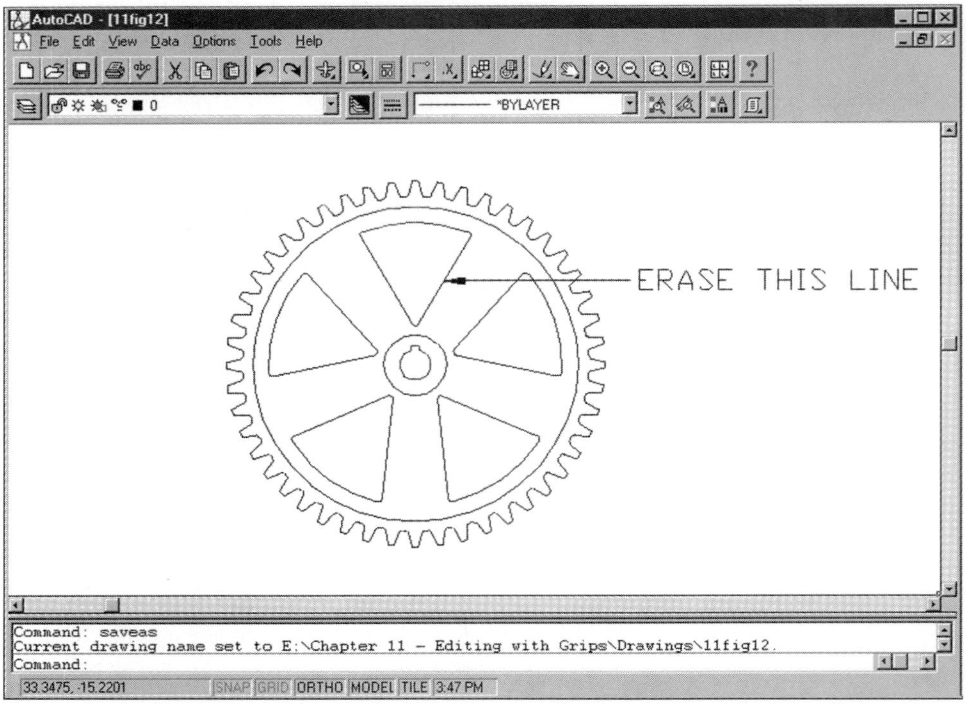

Figure 11.12
Erase the line in the gear drawing.

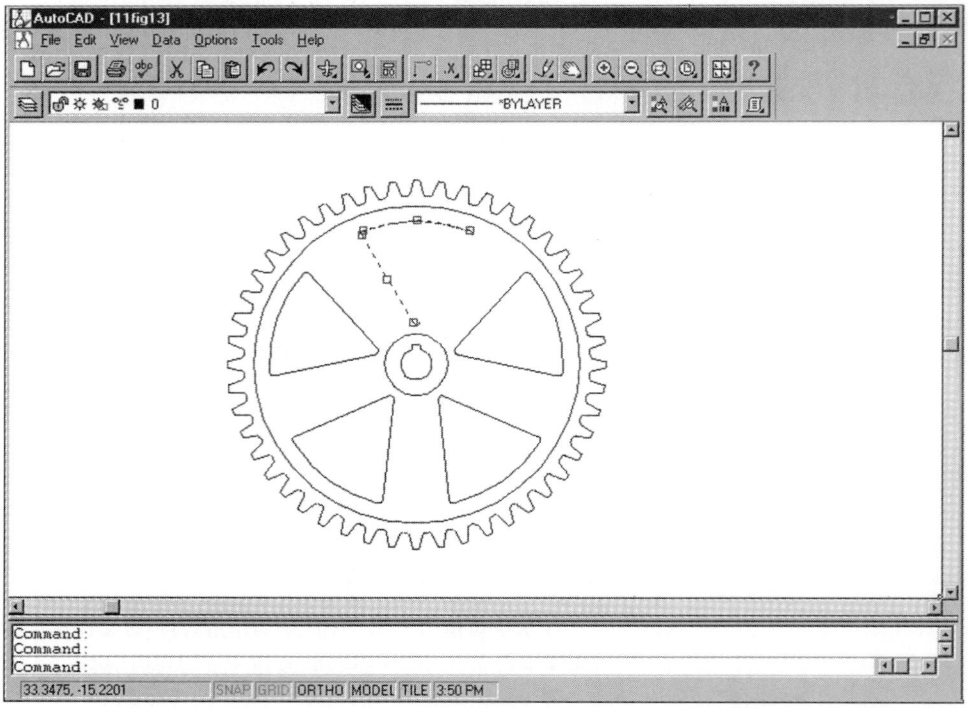

Figure 11.13
Selecting the line and the arc to be mirrored.

```
** MIRROR **
<Second point>/Base point/Copy/Undo/
eXit:
```

7. Check to make sure Ortho is on. If it is not displayed at the top of the screen, press F8.
8. At the `Mirror:` prompt, change the base point by entering a **b**.

```
** MIRROR **
<Second point>/Base point/Copy/Undo/
eXit: b
Base point:
```

9. Select the grip in the midpoint of the arc.
10. Move the crosshairs up; notice how a ghosted mirrored line will appear.
11. In order to keep the original line, enter **c** at the `Mirror:` prompt and press the space bar. This will invoke the Copy option, keeping the original line intact.

```
** MIRROR **
<Second point>/Base point/Copy/Undo/
eXit: c
```

12. When you return to the `Mirror (multiple):` prompt, press the Selection button.

```
** MIRROR (multiple)**
<Second point>/Base point/Copy/Undo/
eXit: Press the Selection button.
```

13. When you return to the `Mirror (multiple):` prompt, press Enter.
14. Press Ctrl C twice to clear all of the grips.

Copying Objects with Grips

Each of the grip modes contains a Copy option. Copy provides a great deal of flexibility when used to edit objects. The Copy option allows you to combine a copy operation with any of the other grip modes. This capability allows you to copy objects while you also stretch, move, rotate, mirror, or scale the objects.

While each of the grip modes includes the Copy option, its usage differs slightly depending on which grip mode you are using. In all cases, however, the original object remains intact and a copy is made of it. The following list describes how the Copy option affects the different grip modes:

- **Stretch.** The object originally selected remains intact and is not stretched. All copies of the object are stretched.
- **Move.** The original object remains intact and in its current location. The copy is moved to its new location.
- **Rotate.** The original object is not rotated and remains in its original location. All duplicate objects are rotated around the selected grip point.
- **Mirror.** Using the Copy option with Mirror causes the original object to remain in its original location. All mirrored objects are mirrored about the defined mirror line.
- **Scale.** The original object is not scaled and remains in its same location. All duplicate objects are scaled.

When the Copy option is selected with any of the other grip modes, it also switches to a multiple mode. This means you can perform the selected grip mode as many times as needed without having to reselect objects or reenter the command. For example, suppose you use the Rotate grip mode with the Copy option. With the Copy option you can create as many copies of the original as needed, all rotated around the same center point, but at different rotation angles.

Skill Builder

Pressing ⇧Shift while in the Move (multiple), or other grip edit options, allows you to move the gripped entities. Holding ⇧Shift during the **move** Grip mode causes the crosshairs to move based on a grid described by the previous point selected.

You also can switch to the Multiple Copy mode by entering **c** (for the Copy option). In Figure 11.14, a rectangle was first drawn using the Rectangle icon from the Draw toolbar. Then the grips on the rectangle are activated by selecting it. The upper-right grip is

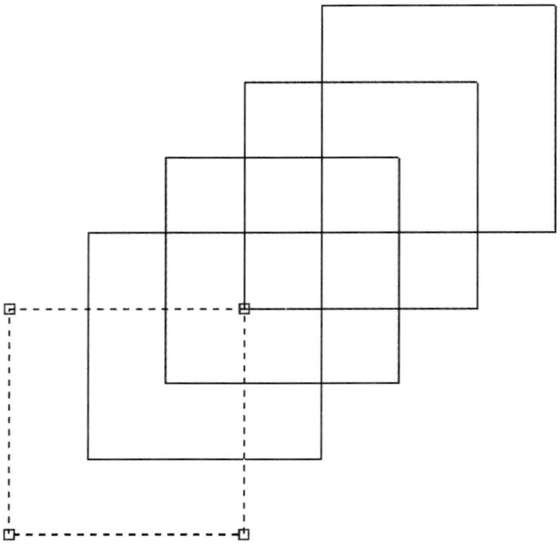

Figure 11.14
Use the Multiple Copy mode by pressing down ⇧Shift.

selected as the grip point. Next, the Move grip mode is activated by pressing the space bar. In the Move grip mode, entering **c** from the command line will let you copy and move multiple times. Pressing down ⇧Shift before picking the point to move fixes the distance to copy. You can make multiple copies of the rectangle with the same offset distance, as shown in Figure 11.14.

TUTORIAL 11.8: COPYING OBJECTS WITH GRIPS

This tutorial continues from the previous tutorial. In this tutorial you will use grips to Copy the gear.

1. Create a window around the gear, as shown in Figure 11.10.
2. Grips appear on all objects in the drawing.
3. Click the grip located in the center of the gear.
4. Press the space bar one time until the Move option is selected.

```
** MOVE **
<Move to point>/Base
point/Copy/Undo/eXit:
```

5. Enter **c** to choose the Copy option and move the cursor to the right of the gear.

```
** MOVE **<Move to point>/Base
point/Copy/Undo/eXit: c
```

6. Notice that a gear appearing in dashed lines is attached to the crosshairs.
7. Click anywhere to the right of the gear to place a copy of the gear in the drawing area.

IMPLICATIONS OF USING THE SAME GRIP POINT

As part of your drafting tasks, you will often find that multiple objects will share the same grip point. This can happen when you create objects using Object Snaps. For example, drawing a line from the midpoint of another line means that the midpoint of the first line and the endpoint of the second line is the same point. When grips are activated, by selecting both of these lines, the common grip point helps to maintain the relationship between the lines. Thus, any command executed with the common grip point affects both objects.

In Figure 11.15, circle A shares its center point with a quadrant point on circle B. Also, the lines shown connect the centers to the respective quadrant point of each circle. If you rotate both circles and lines about a common grip point (the center of circle A) by 45°, both circles and lines will maintain their respective snap points.

However, there are cases where using the common grip point to affect multiple objects may not be desirable. In such cases, objects that should not be affected need to be removed from the selection set by holding ⇧Shift and selecting the object again. Layer

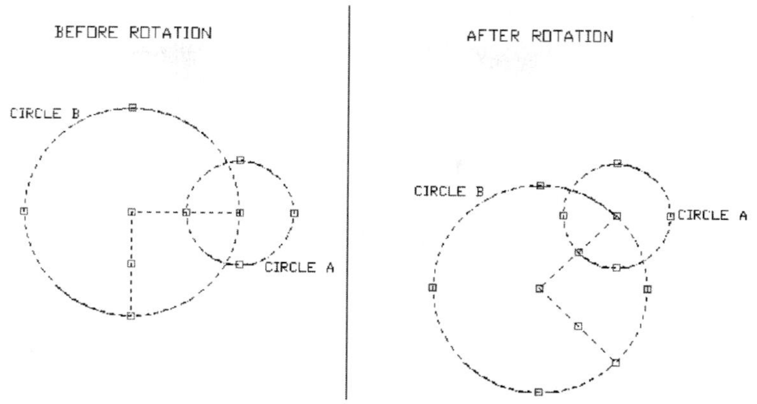

Figure 11.15
Rotating objects with a common grip point maintains their respective snap points.

control also can be used to turn off or freeze layers consisting of objects that you want to remain unaffected. Remember, grip selection applies only to objects on active layers.

SUMMARY

When creating a drawing in AutoCAD, editing your geometry is a common practice. The proper use of grips gives you a fast and efficient method of stretching, moving, rotating, scaling, mirroring, and moving objects.

By default, grips are turned on in AutoCAD. You can change several of the grip settings in the Grips dialog box, including grip size and color. These settings are saved as part of the AutoCAD configuration file, and not with each individual drawing.

After completing this unit, you will have used grips to perform a variety of editing functions. Before continuing, you may want to review the earlier unit on editing techniques. This will give you a chance to compare editing with grips and the more traditional editing methods.

REVIEW

1. How are grips activated?
2. Describe the appearance of grips.
3. Where do grips appear on a line?
4. Where do grips appear on a circle?
5. What are the default colors for grips?
6. What is the default color for a hot grip?
7. How are grip modes selected?
8. List the five grip modes available and describe their uses.
9. Compare the verb-noun selection and the noun-verb selection.
10. List the grip options available in the Grips dialog box.

EXERCISE 11

In this assignment you will modify a Logo design, shown in Figure 11.16, using grips and basic editing skills. For this assignment you should focus on the use of grips for as many modifications as possible. Use the tips and setup procedures listed below to assist you. Use the grid to assist in determining geometry sizes.

1. Use Decimal units with a precision of 0.000.
2. Use upper-right limits of 10.5,8.
3. Set **grid** equal to .25.
4. Set **snap** equal to .125.

5. Turn the **ucsicon** off.
6. Consider utilizing layers to assist in the grouping of objects.
7. Create a border with a thickness of .02 units.
8. The letters were created with a height of .25 units using the MONOS.TTF font file.
9. Using the grid display as a guide, create the shapes shown in their approximate locations. Each shape should be a closed polygon when completed.
10. Create the logo on the left side of the drawing shown in Figure 11.16.
11. Using grips, copy and modify the logo so that it appears as the one shown on the right side of Figure 11.16.
12. Save the drawing as Logo.dwg.
13. Plot the drawing on an A-size sheet of paper.

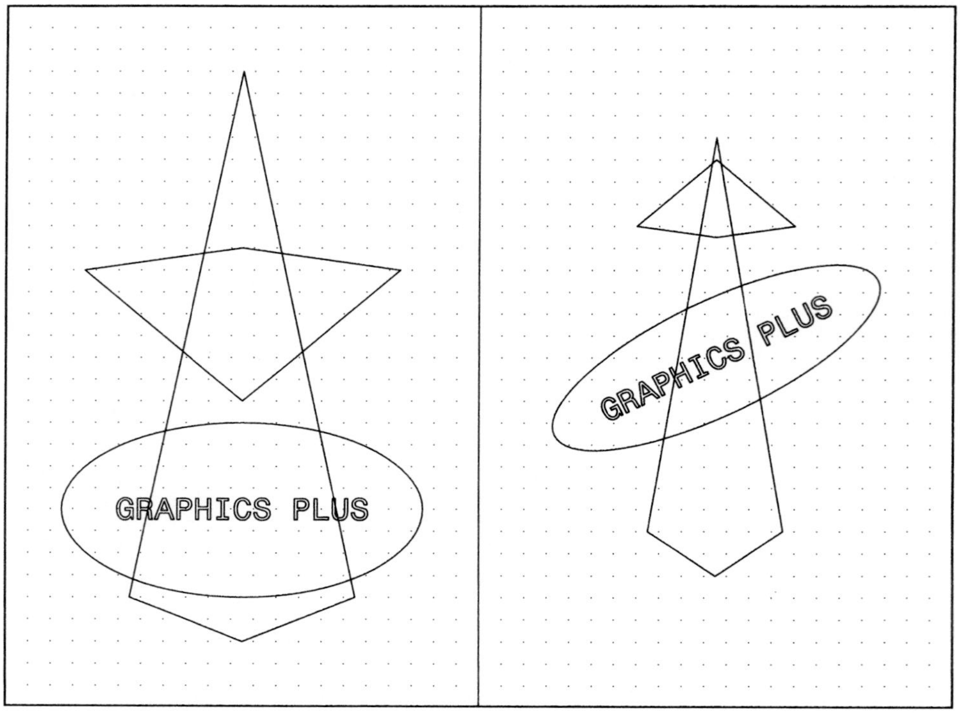

Figure 11.16
Using grips, modify the logo on the left to appear as the logo on the right.

UNIT

12 ADVANCED DRAWING TECHNIQUES

OVERVIEW

In addition to the basic geometry commands you used in Unit 4, "Basic CAD Drawing Techniques," AutoCAD offers several additional commands that can help increase your drawing productivity. This unit introduces several additional drawing techniques. When used with the basic geometry commands, you are on the way to becoming an efficient and accurate CAD draftsperson.

OBJECTIVES

- Use the **point** command to understand and use permanent points.
- Control the display and size of points with **ddtype.**
- Use the **divide** command to divide an object into equal segments.
- Use the **measure** command to measure equal distances along an object.
- Use the **donut** or **doughnut** command to create filled circles.
- Use variations of the **ellipse** command to create ellipses.
- Use the **ray** and **xline** commands to create construction lines.
- Create freehand drawings with the **sketch** command.
- Use the **mlstyle** command to define a multiline style.
- Use the **mline** command to draw a multiline.
- Use the **mledit** command to edit multilines.
- Draw a polyline with **pline.**
- Draw a polyline with **boundary.**
- Edit a polyline with **pedit.**

INTRODUCTION

As you begin creating objects in AutoCAD, information on each object is stored in a database. This information is available in a form that is easily accessed. AutoCAD can calculate the exact length of a given object, regardless of its shape. This greatly simplifies certain procedures, such as dividing an object into an equal number of segments. The **divide** command can divide an object, regardless of its shape, into equal segments. (Dividing an object into equal parts in manual drafting can be accomplished with geometric construction but with a limited degree of accuracy.)

Along with dividing an object in equal segments, another common occurrence in drafting is to place objects at equal distances, such as marking a wall to locate studs. By accessing the database, AutoCAD simplifies the process of marking equal distances along an object. The **measure** command measures equal lengths that you specify along an object, and then places corresponding points on the object.

Certain types of objects, such as ellipses, can be very time-consuming to draw with manual drafting techniques; geometric construction techniques can be slow and cumbersome. Ellipse templates can help speed up the process, but you are limited to the templates available. The **ellipse** command makes drawing ellipses simple. AutoCAD provides a wide variety of techniques for creating ellipses. In addition, the **donut** or **doughnut** (AutoCAD will accept either spelling) command provides an efficient method for producing rings and solid-filled circles.

AutoCAD also offers infinite and semi-infinite lines that can be used as construction lines. A ray **(ray)** is a semi-infinite line that has a finite starting point and extends to infinity. An infinite line **(xline)** has no starting or stopping point. In addition to drawing straight line segments, AutoCAD also offers the **sketch** command. **sketch** allows you to create freehand drawings.

In this unit, you will practice different methods used to divide an object into equal segments and a method for laying out equal distances along an object. You also will learn how to create filled circles and ellipses, create infinite and semi-infinite construction lines, and create freehand drawings.

Most drafting and design drawings have the need to create multiple lines parallel to one another. Electrical engineers draw wiring diagrams and circuit boards that consist of multiple parallel lines. Civil engineers design roadways consisting of multiple parallel lines indicating dividing lines, road edges, and curbs. Architects use parallel lines to represent walls, counters, and trim. Multilines are another powerful feature of AutoCAD that addresses these needs.

Polylines are one of AutoCAD's most versatile objects. Polylines can replace some of AutoCAD's basic objects, such as lines and arcs, and can combine them into a single object. Polylines are so flexible that AutoCAD itself uses them to draw polygons and donuts when you use the **polygon** and **donut** commands.

OUTLINE

Indicating Locations with Point
Dividing and Measuring an Object
Tutorial 12.1: Drawing a Stair Elevation
Drawing Rings, Solid-Filled Circles, and Ellipses
Tutorial 12.2: Creating a Bathroom Sink Symbol
Drawing Infinite Lines and Freehand Drawings
Tutorial 12.3: Sketching Your Initials with the Sketch Command
Working with Mutilines
Tutorial 12.4: Creating Multilne Styles with Mlstyle
Tutorial 12.5: Drawing Multilines
Tutorial 12.6: Adding Vertices to a Multiline
Tutorial 12.7: Removing Multiline Sections
Tutorial 12.8: Making Multiline Corners
Using Polylines
Tutorial 12.9: Drawing Polylines using the Line and Arc Options
Tutorial 12.10: Creating a Boundary
Tutorial 12.11: Modifying a Polyline's Vertices
Summary
Review
Exercises

INDICATING LOCATIONS WITH POINT

In a drawing, you can create points as objects, just as you can create lines, circles, and arcs. Points are used for many different purposes in technical drawings. For example, points can be used to represent the following:

- Intersection location of objects
- Center line of structural beams
- Locations of contact for mechanical parts
- Centers of rotation

Although point objects created with the **point** command are referred to as permanent points, they are no more permanent than any other AutoCAD object. Points can be copied, moved, or erased just like lines or circles. The term *permanent points* is used to distinguish between **point** objects and points that are picked during the course of a command. When you specify a center point for a circle, for example, you designate a coordinate for the circle. You do not create a point object. When using the **point** command, however, you actually create an object. By default, a point appears as a dot on-screen. When the drawing is saved, any points created with the **point** command are saved with the drawing.

While the point is a permanent object saved with the drawing, in most cases the **point** object is used temporarily until another object is laid over it or references it. After an object is placed over the point or references it, the point is normally removed from the drawing screen. You can remove the point by erasing it or freezing the layer where the point is located.

To access the **point** command, use one of these methods:

- Click the Point button on the Draw toolbar. A flyout submenu appears. The Point button displays a flyout toolbar that has Point, Divide, and Measure on it.
- Enter `point` at the `Command:` prompt.

You can enter point locations with the pointing device or any coordinate method (absolute, relative, absolute polar, and relative polar). You can snap to a point location, using temporary or permanent Object Snap modes. The Object Snap mode associated with **point** is Node.

Selecting the Point Style

By default, points appear as dots on-screen. Dots can be difficult to see, especially in a complex drawing. The size and style of the point can be changed by the AutoCAD system variables **pdsize** and **pdmode**. Use **pdmode** to change the point style at the `Command:` prompt. However, because it is difficult to remember the value for each point style, it's easier to use the Point Style dialog box to set the point style.

AutoCAD offers the Point Style dialog box with graphic options. As suggested, this dialog box is much easier to use than the **pdmode** and **pdsize** commands. To change the point style, select the new style from the Point Style dialog box (see Figure 12.1). You can access the Point Style dialog box by using one of these methods:

- Enter **`ddptype`** at the `Command:` prompt.
- Choose Options, Display, and Point Style.

Skill Builder

When the point style is changed in a drawing, all current and previously created points are displayed with the current point style. Although all previously created points are changed, they do not appear changed on-screen until after the drawing regenerates. Changing the point style does not automatically cause the drawing to regenerate.

Setting the Point Size (pdmode)

Besides changing the point style, you can change the size of the point. AutoCAD offers two options for setting the point size: Set Size Relative to Screen and Set Size in Absolute Units. Both options are available in the Point Style dialog box.

Setting Point Size Relative to Screen Size

By default, the Set Size Relative to Screen radio button in the Point Style dialog box is selected. The height of the point symbols are a percentage of the screen height. Thus, the point size remains constant as you zoom in and out of the drawing. The size of the symbols changes only during a drawing regeneration, and a drawing does not automatically regenerate when you zoom in and out. For example, suppose you set the height of a point symbol to a percentage of the screen height and zoom in on the point. Without regener-

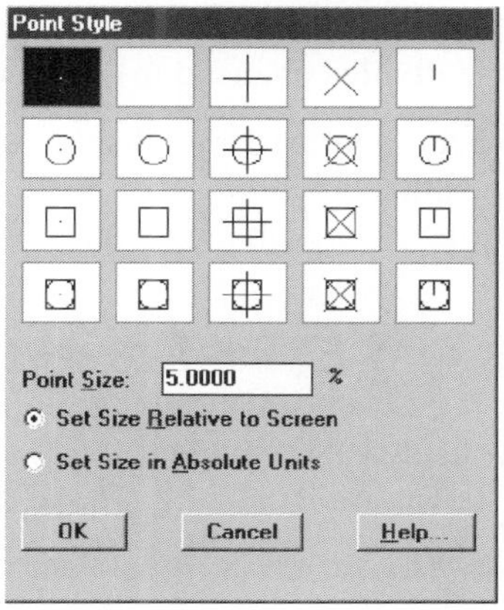

Figure 12.1
The Point Style dialog box is used to change the style and size of a point.

ating the screen, the point will appear much larger. When the screen regenerates, however, the points will appear approximately the same size as before.

Setting Point Size to an Absolute Unit

Selecting the Set Size in Absolute Units radio button in the Point Style dialog box gives the points a set unit size. Selecting this option causes the points to stay the same size as you zoom in and out of the drawing.

Skill Builder

You can also change the point size by entering `pdsize` at the `Command:` prompt. A zero setting generates a point that is 5 percent of the screen height. If **pdsize** is positive, the point is given an absolute unit. Using a negative value sets the point size relative to screen size.

Setting point size to an absolute unit or to a relative-to-screen size depends on personal preference and whether you will be zooming the display in and out to select points. To keep the points at a constant size, even when zooming in and out, set the point size relative to the screen size. To keep the point size consistent with the rest of the drawing, set the point size to an absolute unit.

DIVIDING AND MEASURING AN OBJECT

In manual drafting, you are often called on to divide an object into equal spaces. The divisions may be used to lay out lines or to reference other geometry. Geometric construction techniques make it possible to divide lines, arcs, and circles into equal distances. Geometric construction techniques in manual drafting are often inaccurate, are always time-consuming, and may not work on curves or other objects.

AutoCAD, however, provides a simple method of dividing an object. AutoCAD maintains a mathematical model of every object in the database, so it is possible to calculate the exact length of the object, regardless of its shape. Using this information, you can divide the object into an equal number of segments.

The **divide** command enables you to partition most types of objects into equal-length segments. **divide** works with lines, arcs, circles, donuts, polylines, splines, and ellipses.

Unlike manual methods for dividing objects, AutoCAD's **divide** command calculates division points to the same 14-decimal-place accuracy as all other AutoCAD functions. To divide an object into equal spaces, select the object to be divided and specify the number of segments.

You can access the **divide** command in one of two ways:

- Select the Point button on the Draw floating toolbar. A flyout menu is displayed. Select the Divide button.
- Enter **`divide`** at the `Command:` prompt.

Dividing Objects into Equal Segments

The **divide** command does not actually divide an object into separate segments. The object is unaffected by the division. **divide** places point objects on the object at the exact segment divisions, as shown in Figure 12.2. The **node** Object Snap can be used to snap to the division marks.

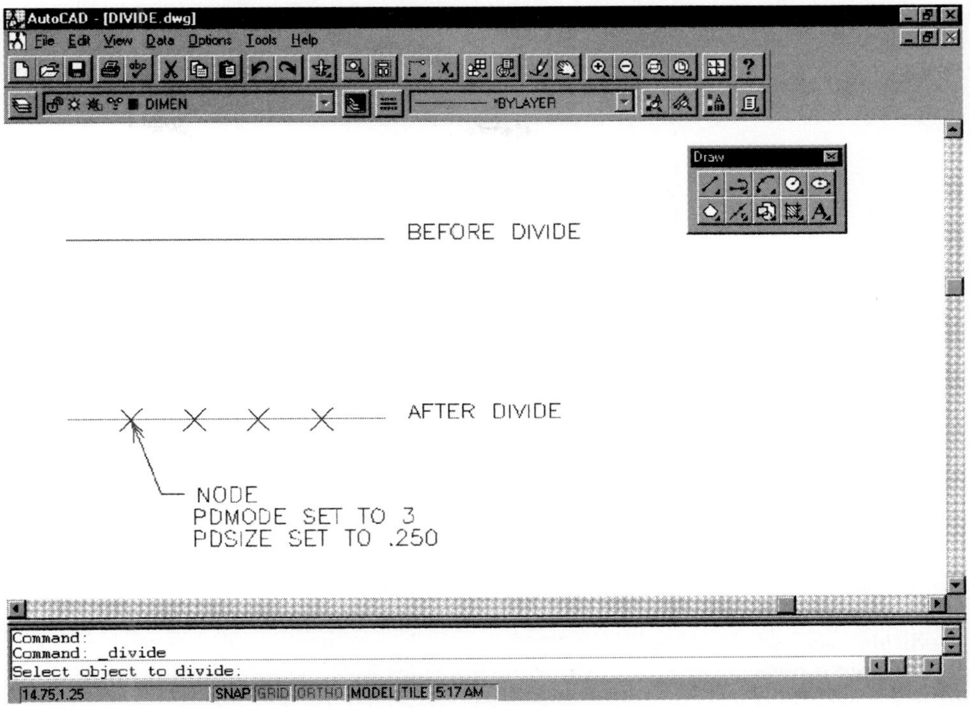

Figure 12.2
The Divide command can be used to place evenly spaced point objects along a line.

Skill Builder

Because **divide** uses points to indicate segment divisions, change the point size and style through the Point Style dialog box **(ddtype)** before issuing **divide**. The segment division points are then easier to see. If you do not change the point size and style before issuing **divide**, a point that cannot be seen is created on top of the object.

To divide an object into equal spaces, first select the object to divide. When the **divide** command is issued, AutoCAD prompts with `Select object to divide:`. You can select any line, arc, circle, donut, ellipse, polyline, or any other object made using polylines (such as a polygon). After the object to divide is selected, AutoCAD displays the prompt `<Number of segments>/Block:`. You can specify the number of segments into which the object should be divided. AutoCAD calculates the distance for each segment and places points on the object.

Using Divide to Insert Objects

The **divide** command also enables you to insert a block at each division point, as shown in Figure 12.3. A block is an object or group of objects that can be used repeatedly in a drawing. Blocks are discussed in Unit 15, "Using Symbols and Attributes." For example, you could use the **divide** command in combination with a block of electrical outlet symbols to space the outlets evenly along a wall. To use a block with the **divide** command, the block must already be defined in the drawing and have a name. To insert a block at each division point, first select the Divide button on the Draw toolbar. The following command sequence appears:

Select Object to Divide: *Select the object to divide.*
<Number of segments>/Block: *b*
Block name to insert: *Enter the name of the block insert.*

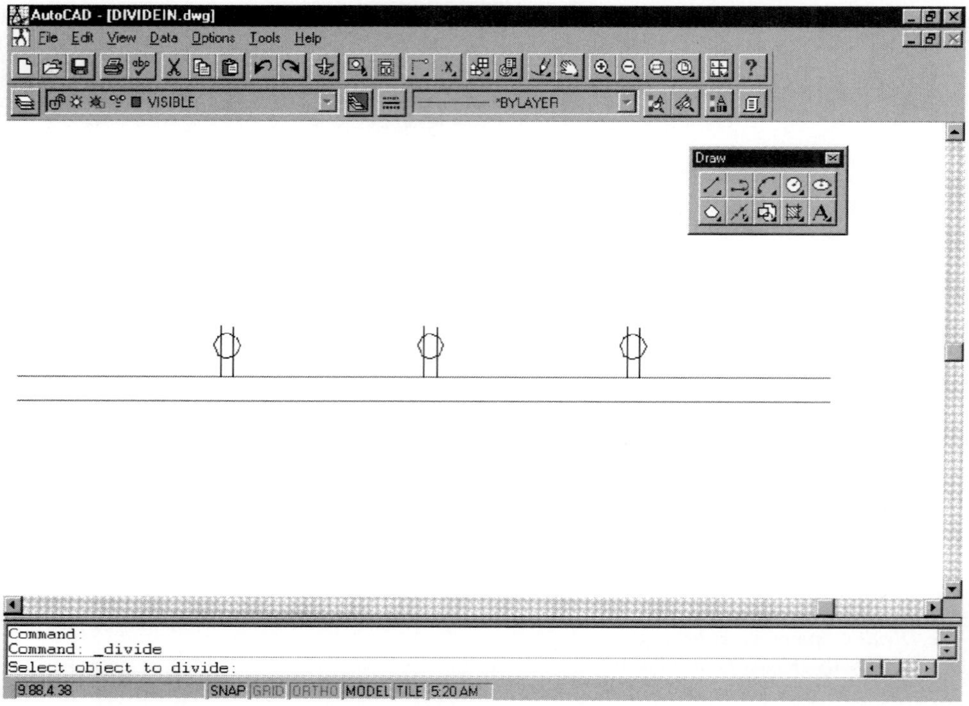

Figure 12.3
The **divide** *command can also be used to insert a symbol at each division point.*

`Align block with object?<Y>:` *If you answer y here, AutoCAD rotates the block to follow the contour of the object. If you answer n, AutoCAD does not rotate the block.*
`Number of Segments:` *Specify the number of segments.*

Using **divide** when inserting blocks can save some of the time required to lay out the location manually. Aligning the blocks with the object depends on the purpose you need to achieve. If all the blocks need to be oriented the same way, do not align them with the object. Figure 12.4 shows a block that is both aligned and not aligned with an object.

Measuring an Object (measure)

In addition to dividing an object into equal spaces, you are often called on to lay out fixed distances along an object. AutoCAD provides another command for this purpose. The **measure** command calibrates equal lengths that you specify. **divide** creates equal lengths as well, but **measure** uses a fixed length. As with the **divide** command, **measure** places points on the object. Figure 12.5 shows the difference between the **divide** and **measure** commands. Notice that the point objects are spaced every 1 inch with the **measure** command, even though the line cannot be equally divided into 1-inch increments.

The **measure** command can be used to locate outlets along a wall, locate pitch points for a thread, or mark specified graduations for a gauge. You can access the **measure** command using one of these methods:

- Click the Point button on the Draw floating toolbar. From the flyout menu that appears, click the Measure button.
- Enter **`measure`** at the `Command:` prompt.

The **measure** command is similar to the **divide** command. When **measure** is invoked, AutoCAD prompts you to select an object. With **measure,** you can partition lines, arcs, circles, donuts, splines, polylines, or other objects made using polylines (such as a polygon or ellipse).

measure and **divide** work similarly. The difference is in the results. **measure** places points or blocks at a spacing you specify. **divide** places points or blocks on an object by dividing it into a specific number of equal segments.

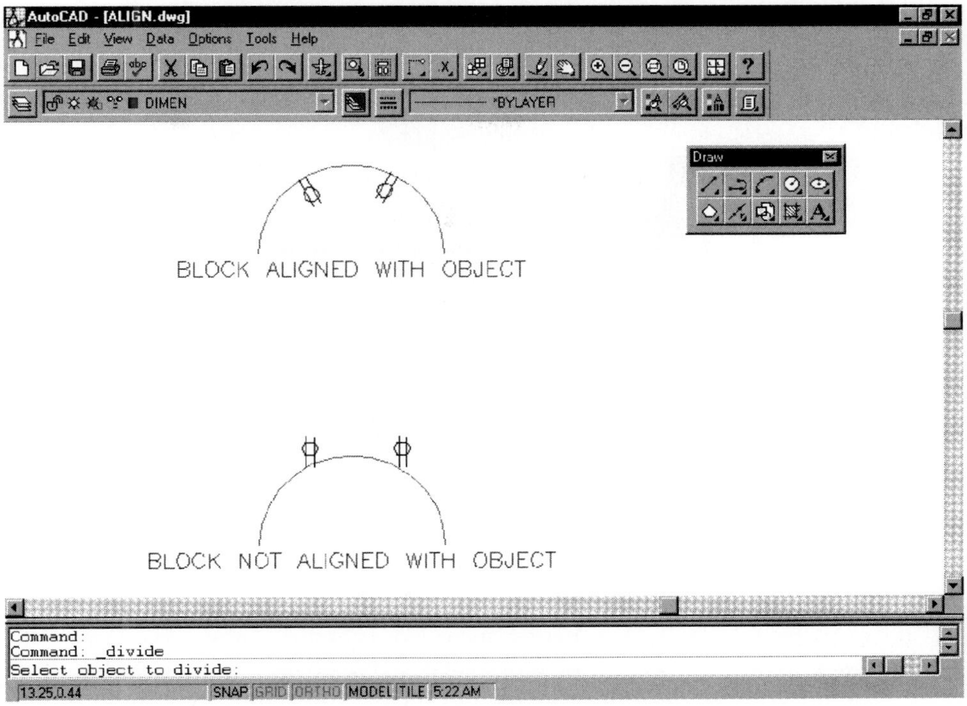

Figure 12.4
Blocks can be aligned with an object using **divide,** *saving some of the time required to lay the block out manually.*

As with the **divide** command, **measure** does not actually separate the object into individual segments. The object is unaffected by the **measure** command. **measure** places point objects at intervals you specify at the exact segment divisions. You can then use the Object Snap **node** to snap to the division marks.

Before using the **measure** command, change the point size and style through the Point Style dialog box **(ddtype).** After you have issued the **measure** command, AutoCAD displays the `Select object to measure:` prompt. After you select the appropri-

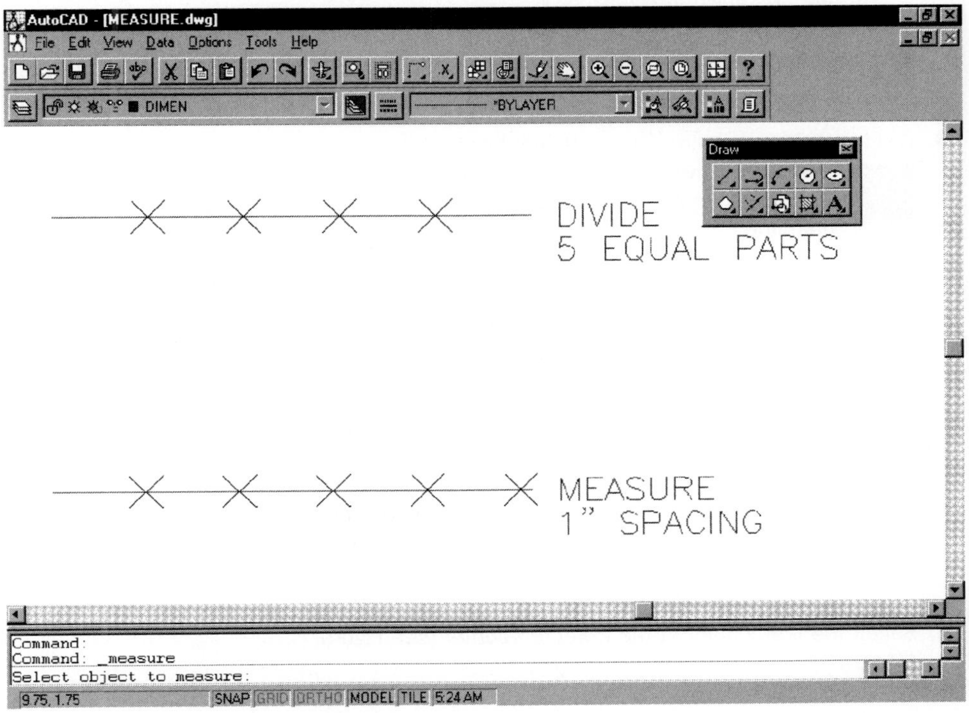

Figure 12.5
The **measure** *command places point objects at 1-inch increments, even though the object selected cannot be equally divided into 1-inch increments.*

ate object, AutoCAD prompts with <Segment length>/Block:. Specify the distance at which you want to place points on the object.

SKILL BUILDER

The location that you initially select on the object is important when you use the **measure** command. The endpoint of the object nearest your selection defines the end of the object from which AutoCAD begins measuring.

USING **measure** TO INSERT OBJECTS

You can also use the **measure** command to automatically insert a block at each point measured on an object. To use a block with **measure,** the block must be previously defined in the drawing and have a name.

First click the Point button on the Draw floating toolbar. From the flyout menu that appears, click the Measure button (the third button). Then use the following command sequence to insert a block at a specified interval on an existing object:

Select object to measure: *Select the object to measure.*
<Segment length>/Block: *b*
Block name to insert: *Enter the name of the block insert.*
Align block with object?<Y>: *If you enter y here, AutoCAD rotates the block to follow the contour of the object. If you enter n, AutoCAD doesn't rotate the block.*
Segment length: *Specify the segment length.*

TUTORIAL 12.1: DRAWING A STAIR ELEVATION

In this tutorial, you will use the **point** and **divide** commands covered thus far to draw a stair elevation (see Figure 12.6).

To begin, follow these steps:

1.  Select the Open button from the Standard toolbar and load 12DWG01. This will open the drawing as shown in Figure 12.7.
2. From the Options menu, select Display, then Point Style. The Point Style dialog box appears.
3. Select the point style that resembles an *x,* which is found in the first row (see Figure 12.8), then click OK.
4. Divide the diagonal line into 14 equal segments.

    Select the Divide button from the Draw toolbar.
   Select object to divide: Click the diagonal line.

   Number of segments>/Block: **14**

   The diagonal line is now divided into 14 equal segments, and those segments are divided using the *x* point style (see Figure 12.9).
5. Issue the **line** command and draw the first stair, using the **node** Object Snap mode to snap to the division.

    Select the Line button from the Draw toolbar.

   From point: **4",6"**
   To point: **@7-11/16"<90**
   To point: **nod**
6. Select the first *x* point at the lower-left corner (see Figure 12.10).

The Node Object Snap always snaps to a point.

To point:

Now that you have drawn one step, complete the stairs by copying the point objects to the top of each step's riser. You will set up an object selection filter to easily select all of the point objects.

Command: **copy**
Select objects: *At this point you will set up an object selection filter.*

1.  Choose the Selection Filters button from the Select Group flyout on the Standard toolbar.
2. In the Object Selection Filters dialog box, choose the DOWN ARROW to the right of Arc. Using the arrows, scroll down until you see *Point* and select it.
3. Click Add to List. Your Object Selection Filters dialog box should look like Figure 12.11.
4. In the Object Selection Filters dialog box, select Apply.

Applying filter to selection.
Select objects: **all**
18 found
5 were filtered out.
Select objects:
Exiting filtered selection. 13 found
Select objects:

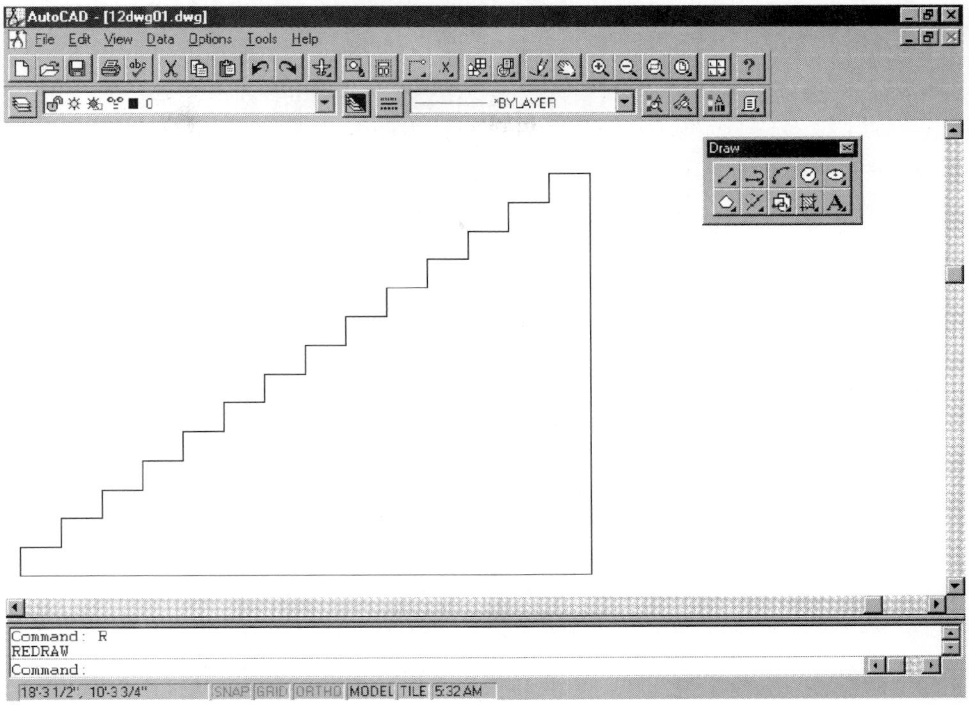

Figure 12.6
Drawing a stair elevation.

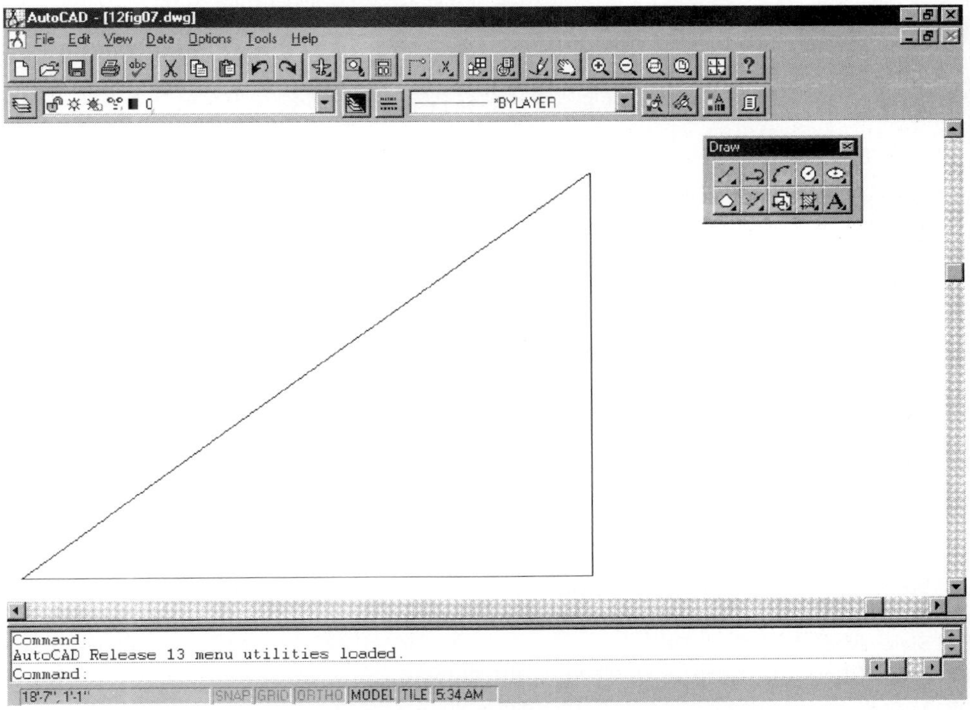

Figure 12.7
Load the prototype drawing to draw the stair elevation.

`<Base point or displacement>/Multiple:` **nod**

5. Select the first *x* point at the lower-left corner (refer to Figure 12.10).

`Second point of displacement:` **@7-11/16<90**

6. Now you have copied the point objects. To complete the stairs, use the Line command to connect the point objects, using the **node** Object Snap.
7. Repeat this procedure until you have drawn all 14 steps in the stairs.

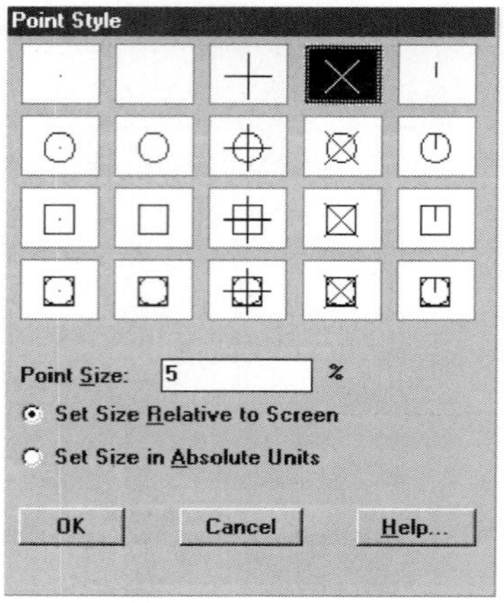

Figure 12.8
Specify the point style.

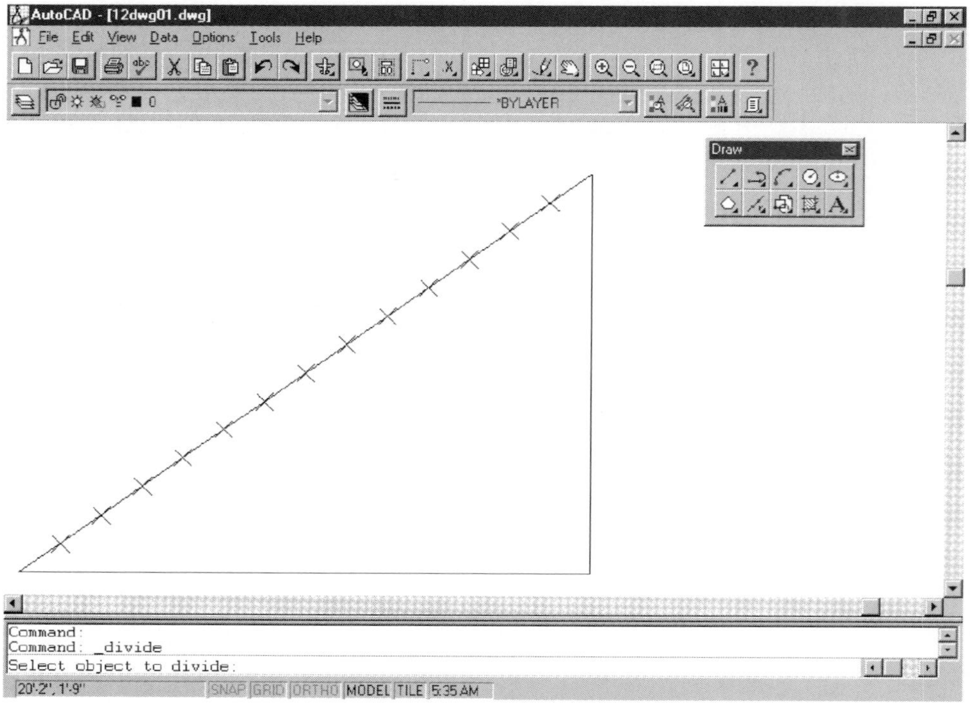

Figure 12.9
The diagonal line is divided into 14 equal segments.

You may have noticed that the drawing looks peculiar with each point represented as an *x*. To correct the situation, follow these steps:

1. Select Options, Display, Point Style...
2. Select the first point style in the first row of the Point Style dialog box. Click OK.
   Notice that no change takes place on the drawing.
3. To change the representation of the points, enter **regen** at the `Command:` prompt.
   The points appear to have been removed. They are still there, but now they are represented as dots that can't be seen because the lines overlap them.

After you have drawn all the stairs, complete the drawing by following these steps:

1. At the `Command:` prompt, enter **e**.
2. At the `Select objects:` prompt, select the diagonal line that you divided earlier. Press Enter.
   The diagonal line is erased.
   You should now have the completed stair elevation (refer to Figure 12.6).

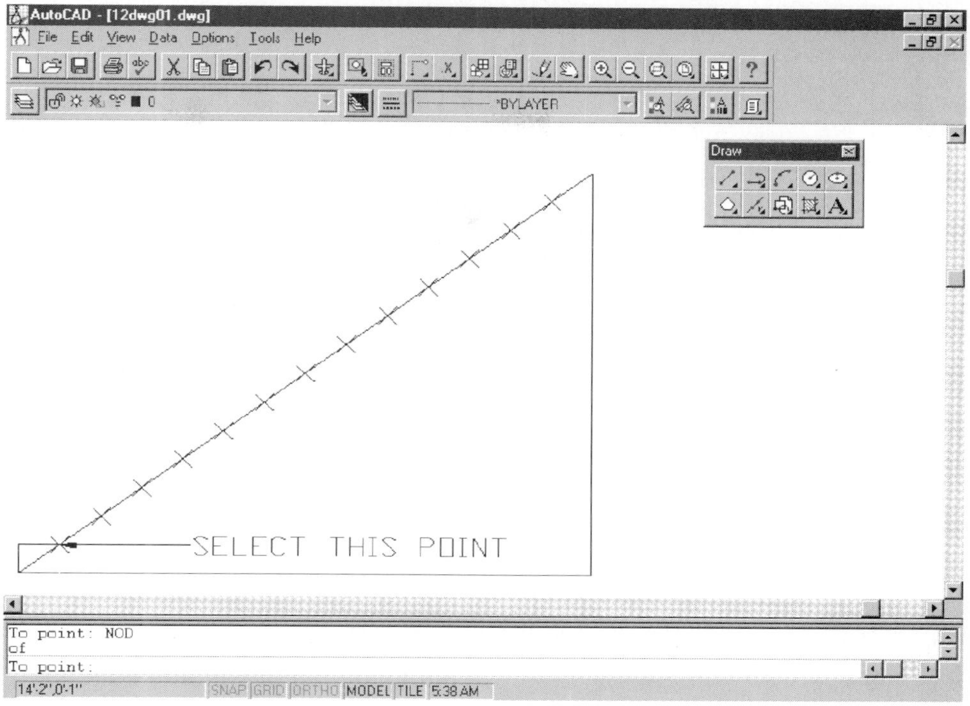

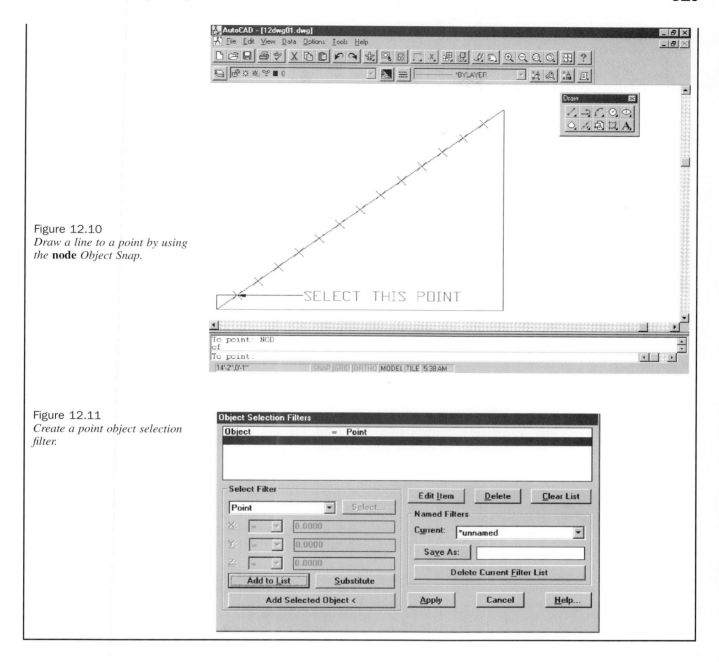

Figure 12.10
Draw a line to a point by using the **node** *Object Snap.*

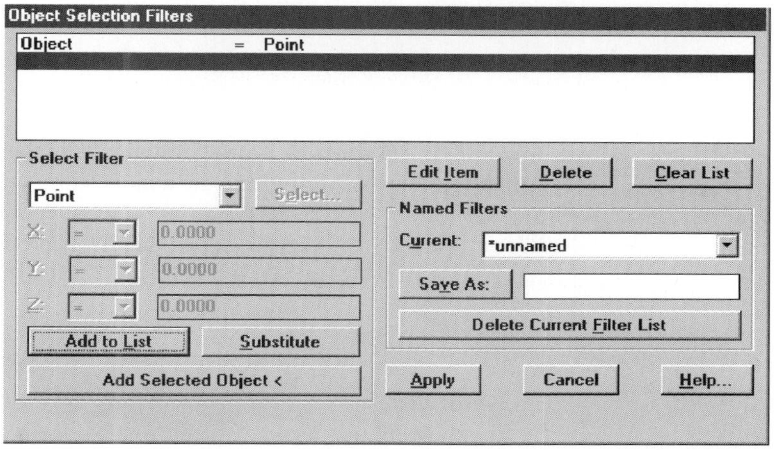

Figure 12.11
Create a point object selection filter.

Both the **divide** and **measure** commands can insert a block at each division point. In the previous tutorial, you could have made a block out of the first step and then used the **divide** command to insert the step along the line. When **divide** prompts you for the number of objects, respond with `b` for **block** and enter the name of the first step block, then specify `14` as the number of segments.

There are many ways to accomplish tasks in AutoCAD, as shown by the preceding example. For the majority of tasks, there is no right or wrong way. The best method is the one that works best for you.

DRAWING RINGS, SOLID-FILLED CIRCLES, AND ELLIPSES

To construct solid circles, AutoCAD offers the **donut** or **doughnut** command. When creating the circles, you can specify both inner and outer diameters. The "donuts" are actually circular polylines.

The **donut** command allows you to draw thick circles. It can have any inside or outside diameter, or be completely filled in. You access the **donut** command with one of two methods:

- From the Draw floating toolbar, select Circle to access the flyout menu. The last button is Donut.
- Enter `donut` or `doughnut` at the `Command:` prompt.

The **donut** command first prompts for the inner and outer diameters and then for the center point. AutoCad then draws the two circles and fills in the space between them. You can use the following command sequence to create a donut:

Select Donut from the Circle flyout menu.

`Inside diameter <current>:` *Specify a new inside diameter or press Enter to accept the current value.*
`Outside diameter <current>:` *Specify a new outside diameter or press Enter to accept the current value.*
`Center of doughnut:` *Select the donut center point with the crosshair or enter the coordinates.*
`Center of doughnut:` *Select the center point for another donut or press Enter to return to the Command: prompt.*

FOR THE PROFESSIONAL

If your drawing contains a lot of donuts, filling them can take a long time. You can temporarily turn off Fill inside the donuts with the **fill** command. When the **fill** mode is turned off, donuts appear as segmented or concentric circles. You can use **fill** transparently by entering `'fill` while inside a command.

With AutoCAD, you can draw three kinds of donuts (see Figure 12.12):

- **Solid-filled.** Set the inside diameter to 0.
- **Regular.** Set the inside diameter to a value greater than 0 and smaller than the outside diameter.
- **Ring.** Set the inside diameter equal to the outside diameter.

The **donutid** and **donutod** system variables control the inside and outside diameters of the donut. These variables are updated whenever you use the **donut** command. These diameters can be set directly when using the **donut** command and remain the same until you change them. Knowing this can save time if you need to draw several donuts with the same inside and outside diameters.

DRAWING ELLIPSES **(ellipse)**

Ellipses are used in many forms of drawing. When you view a circle at an angle, you see an elliptical shape. For example, when you rotate a circle 60° from the line of sight, you see a 30° ellipse.

An ellipse consists of a center point, major axis, and minor axis (see Figure 12.13). The **ellipse** command provides several methods for creating an ellipse based on these three characteristics. You can also create isometric circles with the **ellipse** command. The

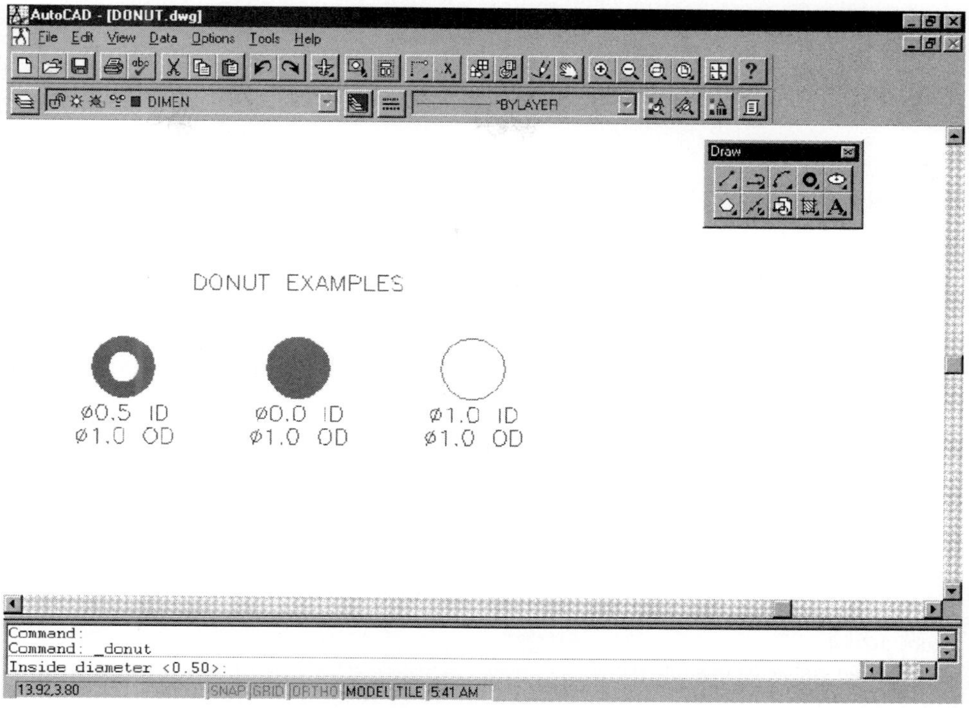

Figure 12.12
Donuts with different inside diameters.

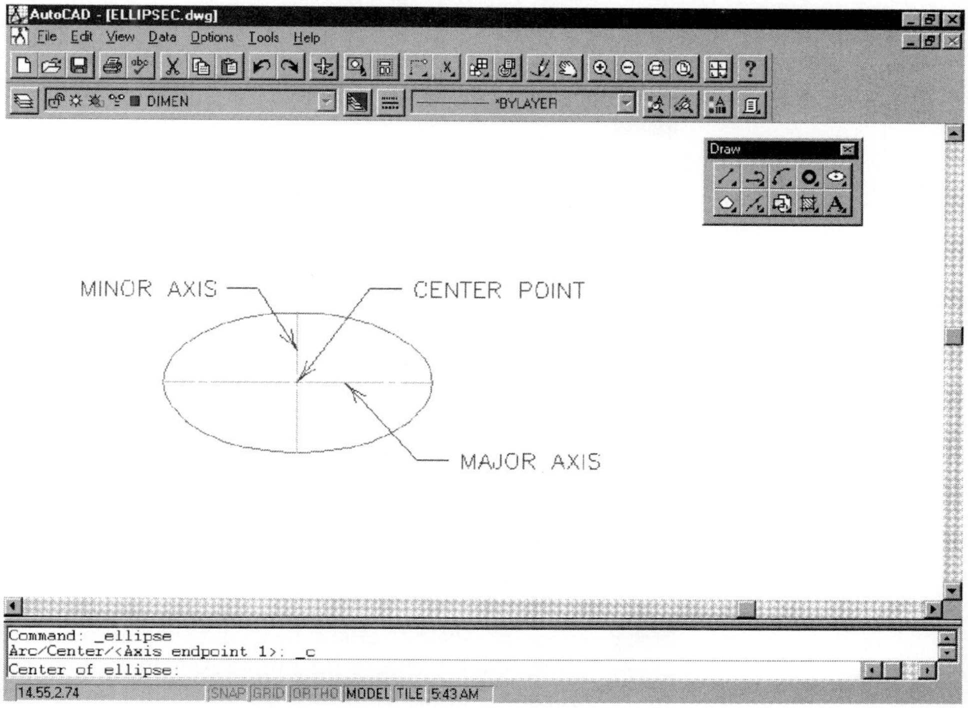

Figure 12.13
The major parts of an ellipse.

method you use to create the ellipse depends on the drawing you are creating. You can access the **ellipse** command in one of these ways:

- Click the Ellipse button on the Draw floating toolbar. This brings up a flyout menu, offering three options for creating an ellipse.
- Enter **`ellipse`** at the `Command:` prompt.

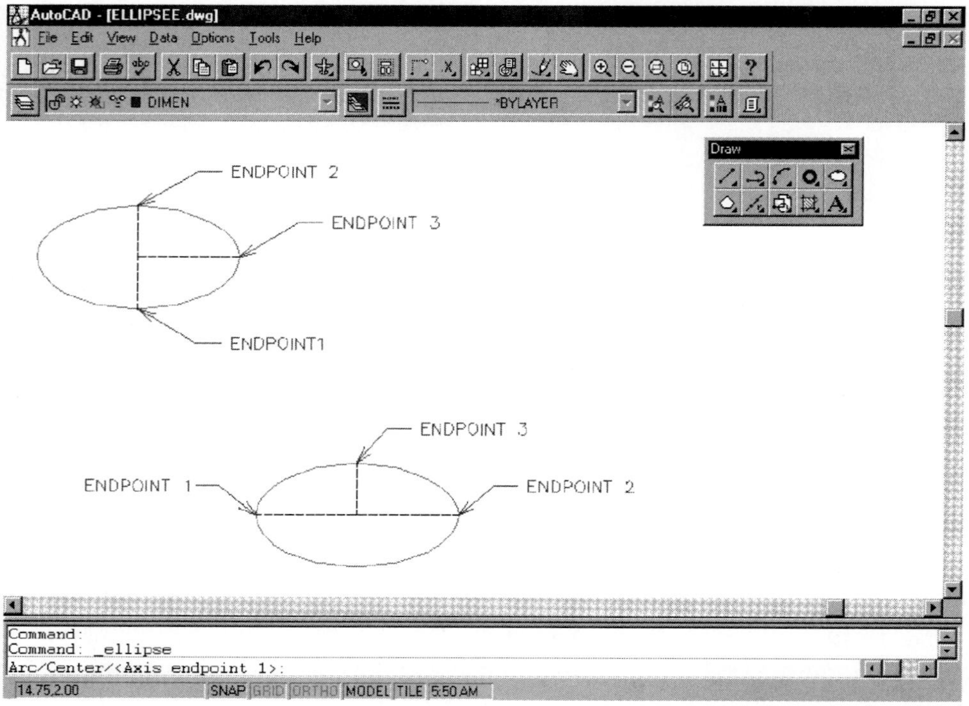

Figure 12.14
Construct an ellipse by defining the axis endpoints.

Defining Endpoints and Distances

To create an ellipse, you can define two endpoints to locate one axis of the ellipse, and then define a third point to determine the boundaries of the radius of the second axis.

To create an ellipse by defining two axis endpoints with a third point, first choose the Ellipse button from the Draw floating toolbar and then choose the Ellipse Axis End button (the second button). Then follow this command sequence:

Arc/Center/<Axis endpoint 1>: *specify endpoint 1 with coordinates or the cursor, as shown in Figure 12.14.*
Axis Endpoint 2: *Specify endpoint 2.*
<Other axis distance>/Rotation: *Specify endpoint 3 for the second axis.*

Defining Endpoints and Rotation

You can also create an ellipse by defining the endpoints of the major axis and the rotation angle of the ellipse. The shape of the ellipse is defined by rotating a circle about the ellipse's axis by the specified angle. A response of 45 draws an ellipse that is 45° from the line of sight. Responding with 0 draws a circle with the circle's diameter equal to both major and minor axes. AutoCAD rejects any angle greater than 89.4° because the ellipse appears as a line. Figure 12.15 shows the relationship between several ellipses having the same major axis length but different angles of rotation.

To create an ellipse by defining the endpoints of the major axis and a rotation angle of the ellipse, choose the Ellipse Axis End button from the Draw toolbar. The following command sequence is then given:

Arc/Center/<Axis endpoint 1>: *Specify endpoint 1 of the major axis with coordinates or the cursor.*
Axis Endpoint 2: *Specify endpoint 2 of the major axis.*
<Other axis distance>/Rotation: *r*
Rotation around major axis: *Enter a rotation angle.*

Notice that you can create an isometric ellipse by using the Rotation option and an angle of 60°. AutoCAD, however, does not rotate the ellipse along the isometric axis the

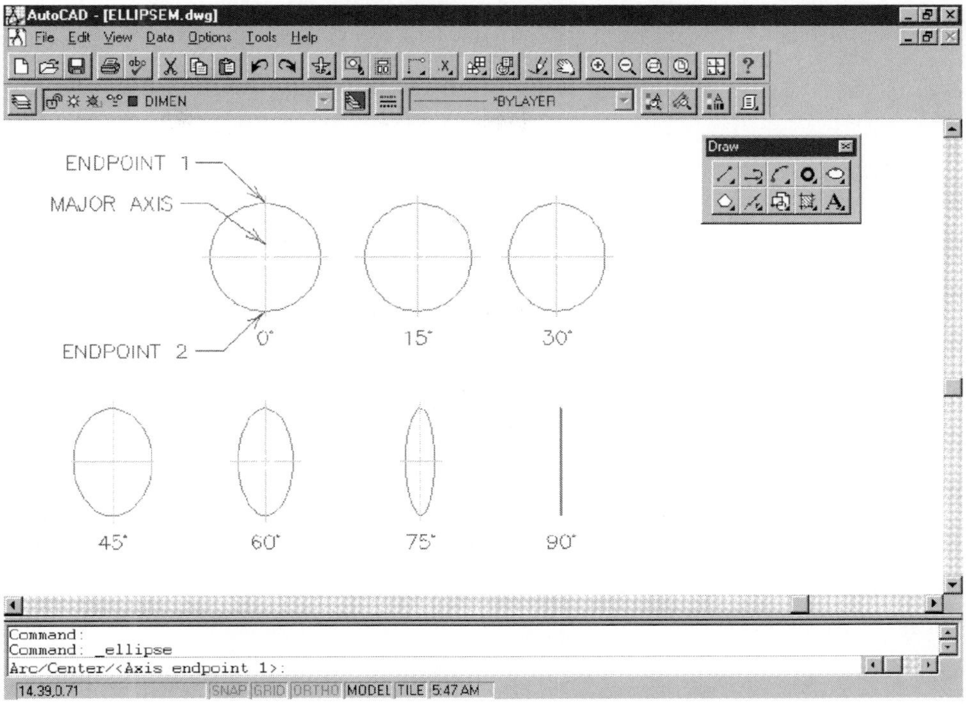

Figure 12.15
Create an ellipse by defining the major axis length with different angles of rotation.

way it needs to be. To create a true isometric ellipse, use the isometric snap and the **iso-circle** option of the **ellipse** command.

Defining Center and Axis Points

In addition to locating the axis endpoints to define an ellipse, you can also locate the center point and two axis points (see Figure 12.16).

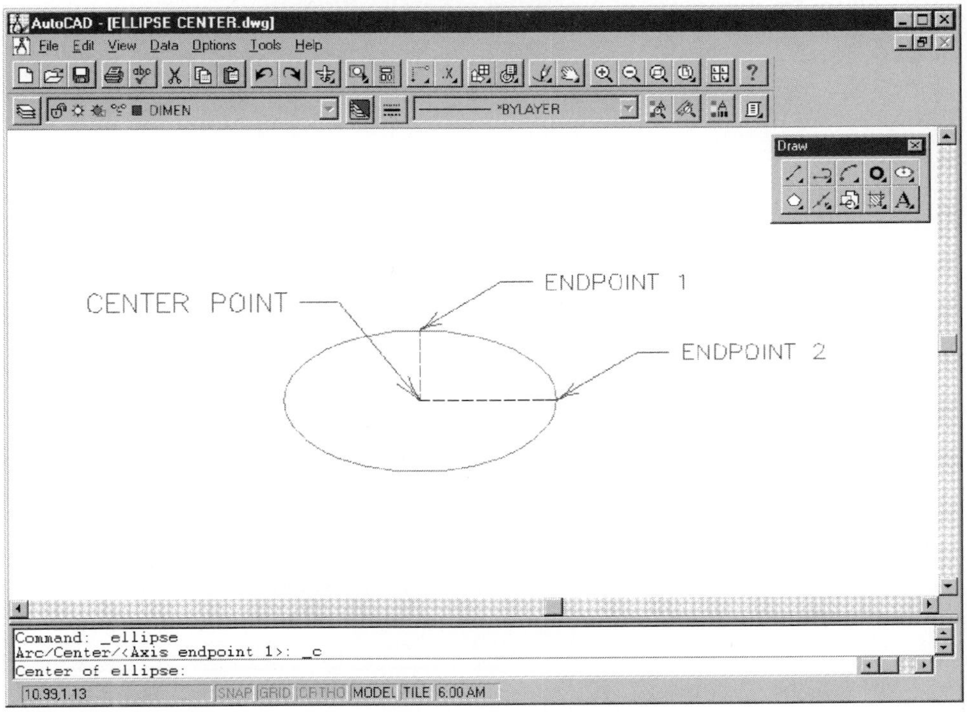

Figure 12.16
You can draw an ellipse by specifying the center and two axis endpoints.

To create an ellipse by defining the center and two axis points, choose the Ellipse Center button on the Draw toolbar. Then use this command sequence:

```
Arc/Center/<Axis endpoint 1>: _c
Center of ellipse: Specify the axis center with coordinates or the cursor, as shown in Figure 12.16.
Axis endpoint: Specify the endpoint of the first axis.
<Other axis distance>/Rotation: Specify the endpoint of the second axis.
```

Notice that you can also specify an axis of rotation after defining the center point and the endpoint of one axis.

Defining an Ellipse Arc

In addition to creating a complete ellipse, you can define a partial ellipse (see Figure 12.17). The Ellipse Arc command begins by creating an ellipse. By selecting the proper options in the Ellipse Arc command, you can use any of the previous methods to create the ellipse. After the ellipse is created, the default prompt asks for start and end angles. These angles determine the start point and endpoint of the ellipse.

To define an ellipse arc, choose the Ellipse Arc button on the Draw toolbar. Then follow this command sequence:

```
Arc/Center/<Axis endpoint 1>: _a
<axis endpoint 1>/center: Specify the axis center with coordinates or the cursor.
Axis endpoint 2: Specify the axis endpoint.
<Other axis distance>/Rotation: Specify the endpoint of the second axis.
Parameter/<start angle>: Specify where you want the ellipse to begin.
Parameter/Included/<end angle>: Specify where you want the ellipse to end.
```

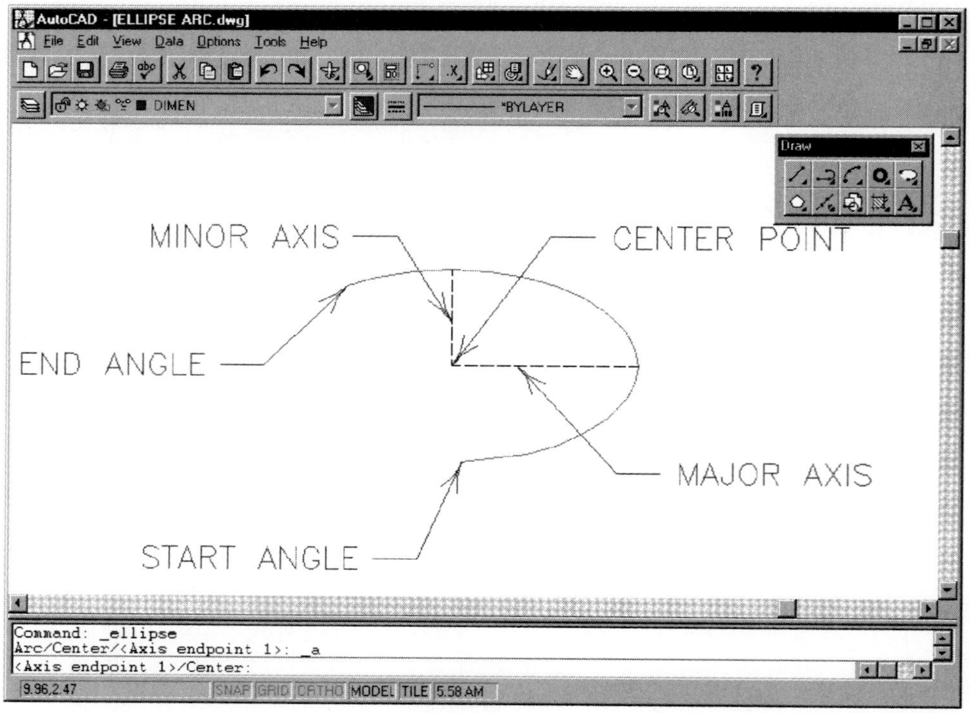

Figure 12.17
Use the Ellipse Arc command to create a partial ellipse.

TUTORIAL 12.2: CREATING A BATHROOM SINK SYMBOL

In this tutorial, you will create the bathroom sink symbol using the **donut** and **ellipse** commands (see Figure 12.18).

To create the bathroom sink symbol, follow these steps:

1.  Select the Open button from the Standard toolbar and load 12DWG02. This will open the drawing needed to begin the bathroom sink symbol as shown in Figure 12.19.

    First you will create the bowl using an ellipse. Select the Ellipse Center button from the Ellipse flyout menu on the Draw floating toolbar.

   `<Axis endpoint 1>/Center:` **`c`**
   `Center of ellipse:` **`cen`**

2. Select the circle in the middle of the drawing that represents the drain of the sink.
3. Next, establish first the length of the ellipse's major axis and then the minor axis.

   `Axis endpoint:` **`@1′<0`**
   `<Other axis distance>/Rotation:` **`@8″]<90`**

Your drawing should now resemble that in Figure 12.20.

Complete the bathroom sink symbol by using the **donut** command to draw the left handle.

4.  Select the Donut button from the Circle flyout menu on the Draw toolbar.

   `Inside diameter<0′-1″>:` **`2″`**
   `Outside diameter<0′-1″>:` **`4″`**

5. At the `Center of doughnut:` prompt, enter `1′7″,2′1″`. At that same prompt, press Enter to finish the command.
6. 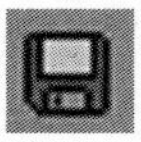 Select the Save button to save your drawing.

You should now have the symbol shown earlier in Figure 12.18.

Figure 12.18 *Create a bathroom sink symbol.*

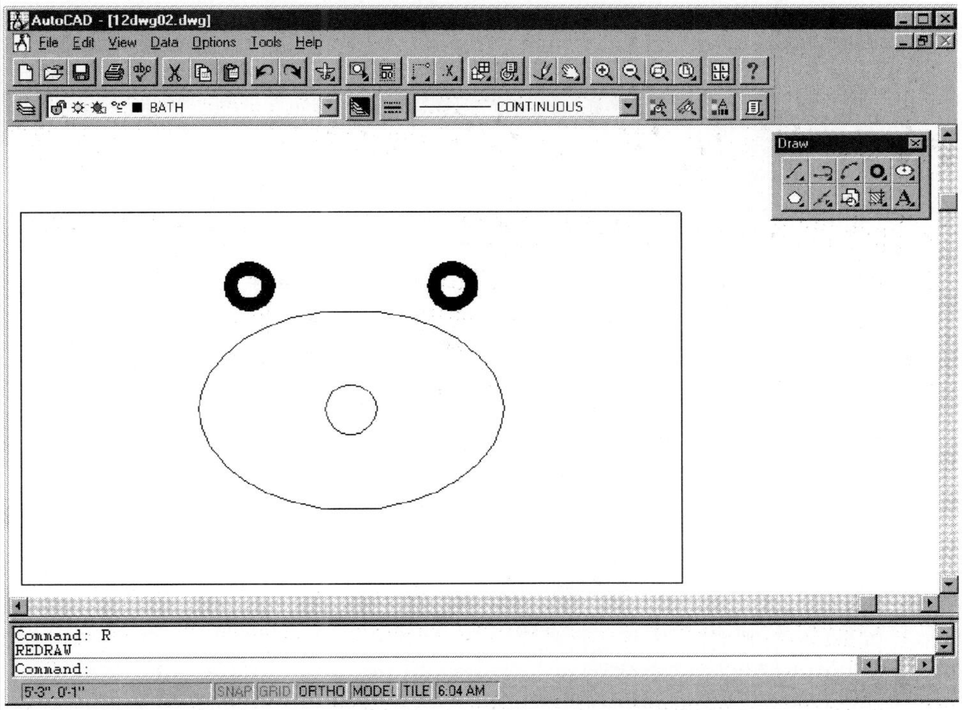

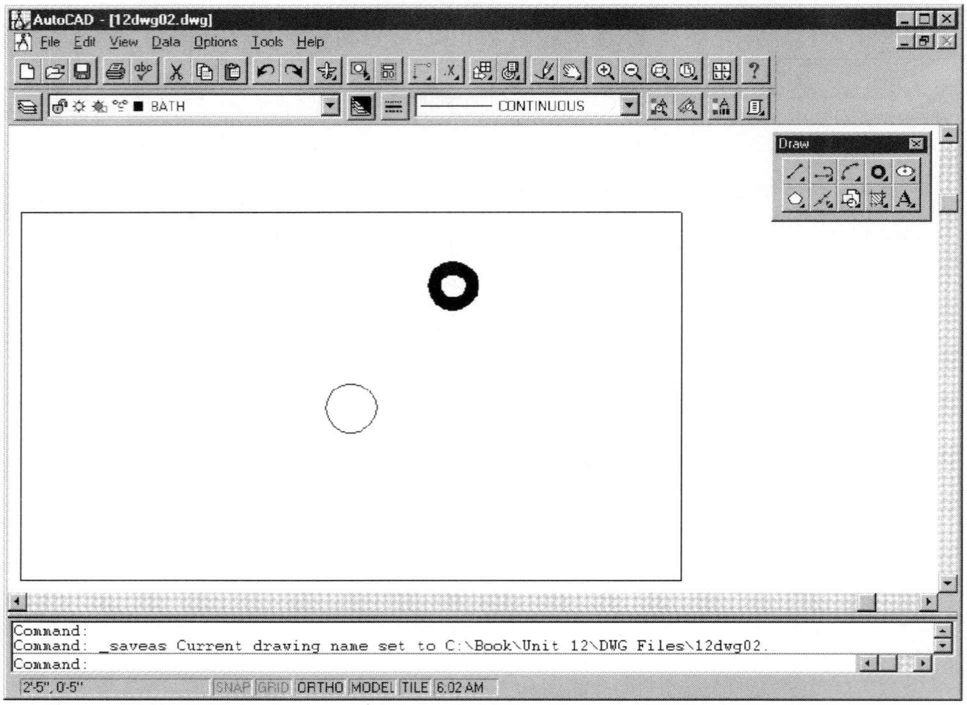

Figure 12.19
Load the prototype drawing to create the bathroom sink symbol.

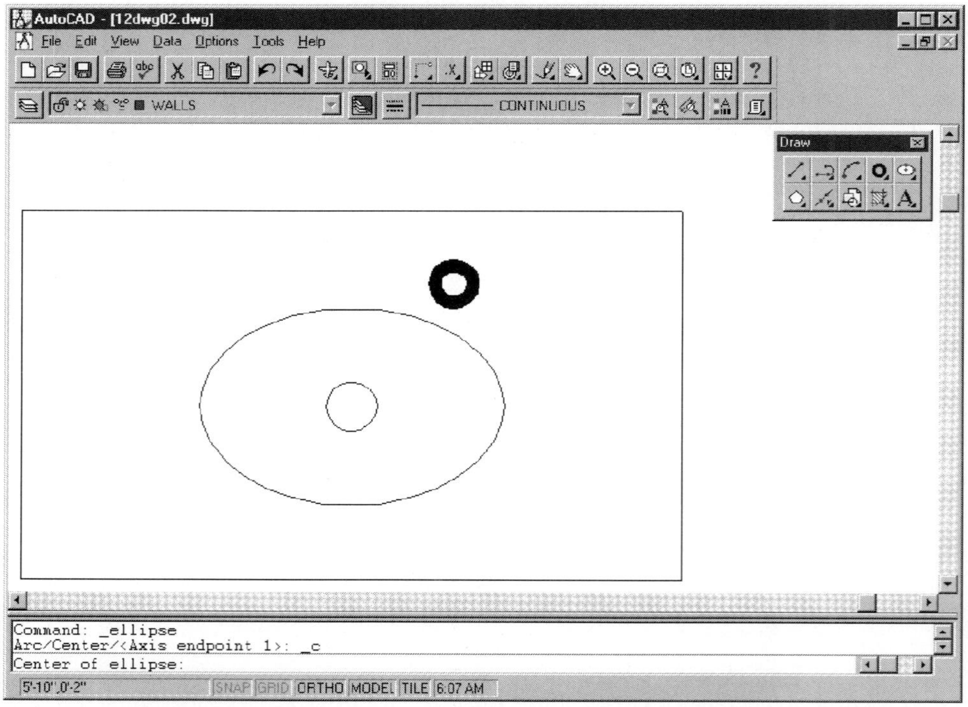

Figure 12.20
Draw the bowl of the bathroom sink symbol with the **ellipse** *command.*

DRAWING INFINITE LINES AND FREEHAND DRAWINGS

The **xline** command creates an infinite construction line. Since the line created by **xline** is infinite, it does not affect the zoom command. An infinite line can be useful in geometry construction. It is also a good way of creating lines that orient you in 2-D and 3-D space. You can access the **xline** command by using one of these two methods:

- From the Draw toolbar, choose the Line button. This causes a flyout menu to appear, showing the Construction Line button.
- Type `xline` at the `Command:` prompt.

After invoking the **xline** command, AutoCAD prompts:

`Hor/Ver/Ang/Bisect/Offset<From point>:`

Drawing Infinite Lines (xline)

The **xline** options are different methods that can be used to create an infinite line. These options are described as follows.

From Point This option is the default that creates an infinite line passing through two points, as shown in Figure 12.21.

`Hor/Ver/Ang/Bisect/Offset<From point>:` *Specify Point 1. This will become the first point the* **xline** *will pass through.*
`Through point:` Specify Point 2. *This will be the second point you want the* **xline** *to pass through.*
`Through point:` *Continue to specify points. All* **xlines** *created will pass through point 1. When you have finished selecting points, press Enter to end the command.*

Hor This option creates a horizontal **xline** passing through a single point, as shown in Figure 12.22.

`Hor/Ver/Ang/Bisect/Offset<From point>:` *hor*
`Through point:` Specify a point (point 1) *through which you want the* **xline** *to pass. This will create an* **xline** *parallel to the*

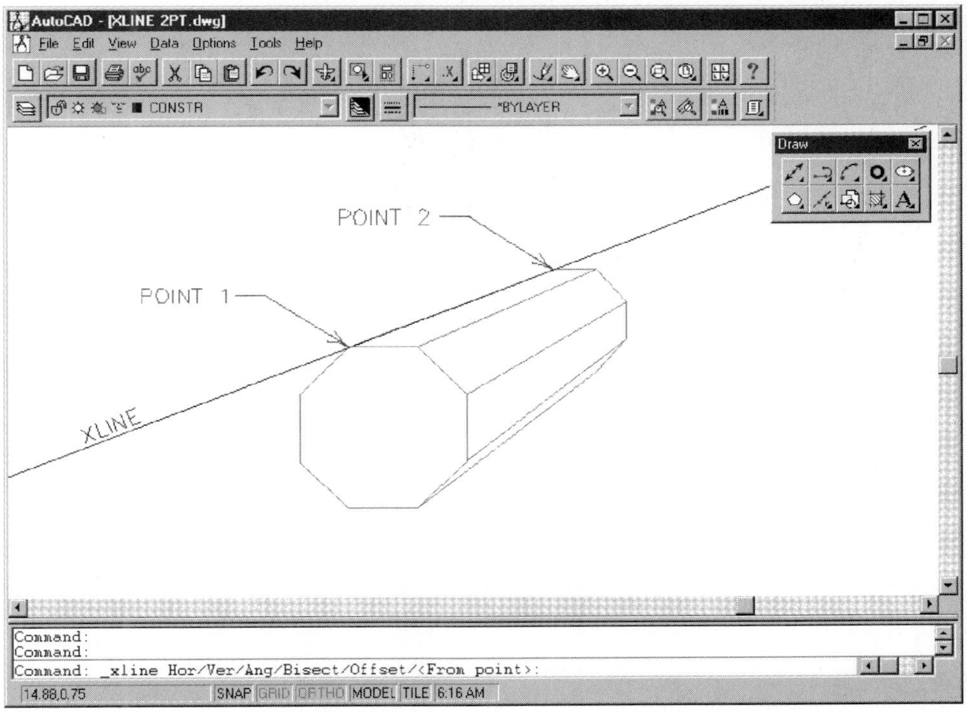

Figure 12.21
An infinite **xline** *can be created by specifying two points.*

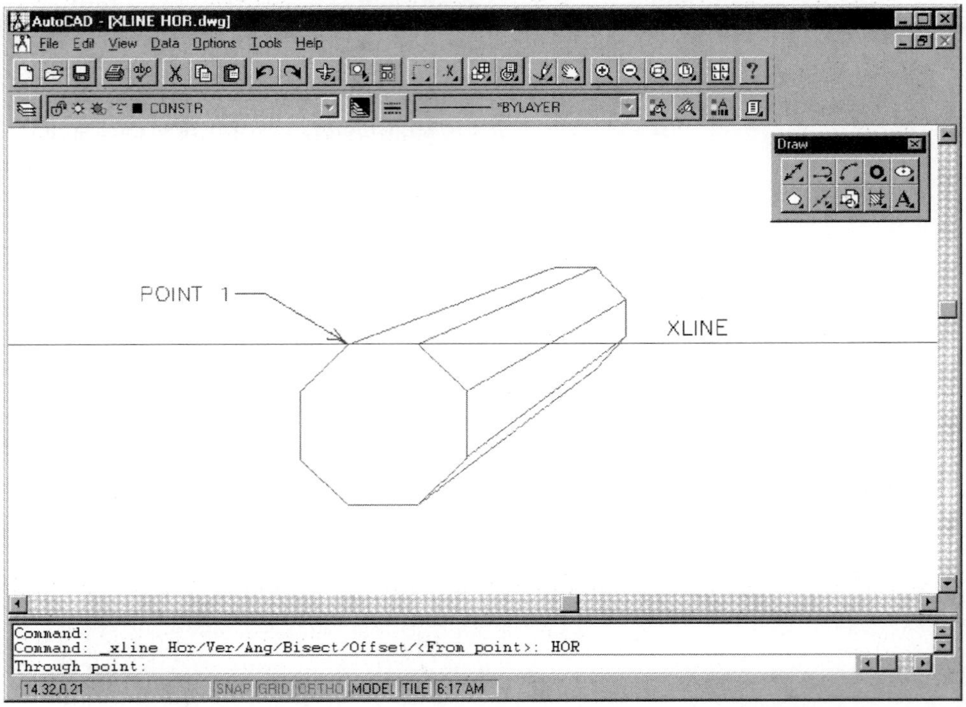

Figure 12.22
The Hor option creates an **xline** *parallel to the x-axis through a specified point.*

x-axis, passing through the selected point. When you have completed selecting points, press Enter to end the command.

Ver This option creates a vertical **xline** passing through a single point, as shown in Figure 12.23.

Hor/Ver/Ang/Bisect/Offset<From point>: *ver*
Through point: *Specify a point (point 1) through which you want the* **xline** *to pass. The* **xline** *created will pass through the selected point and be parallel to the y-axis. When you have completed selecting points, press Enter to end the command.*

Ang This option creates an **xline** at a specified angle. There are two options when creating an angular **xline**. You can specify the angle of the **xline** and a point the **xline** will pass through, or create the **xline** at a specific angle from a reference line.

Specifying the Angle of the xline and a Point This option creates an infinite **xline** at the specified angle going through a point, as shown in Figure 12.24.

Hor/Ver/Ang/Bisect/Offset<From point>: *ang*
Reference/<Enter angle (0.00)>: *Specify the angle of the* **xline.**
Through point: *Specify the point (1) through which you want the angular* **xline** *to pass. When you have completed selecting points, press Enter to end the command.*

Specifying the Angle of the xline from a Selected Reference Line This option creates an angled **xline** by referencing an existing object, as shown in Figure 12.25. The angle is measured in a counterclockwise direction from the reference line.

Hor/Ver/Ang/Bisect/Offset<From point>: *ang*
Reference/<Enter angle (0.00)>: *r*

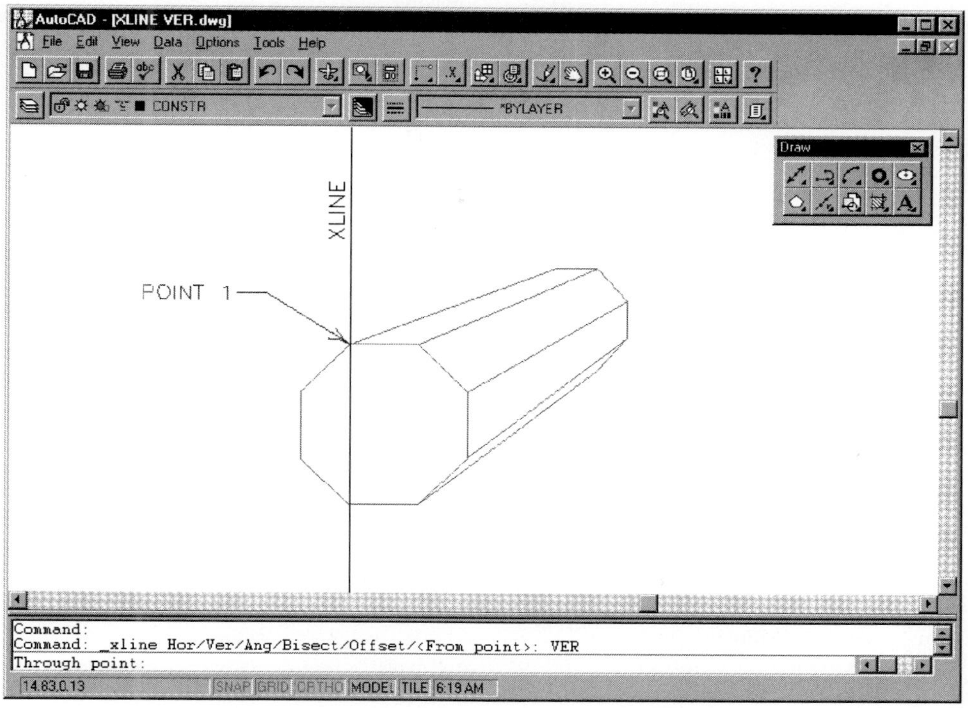

Figure 12.23
Use the Ver option to create an **xline** *parallel to the y-axis passing through a selected point.*

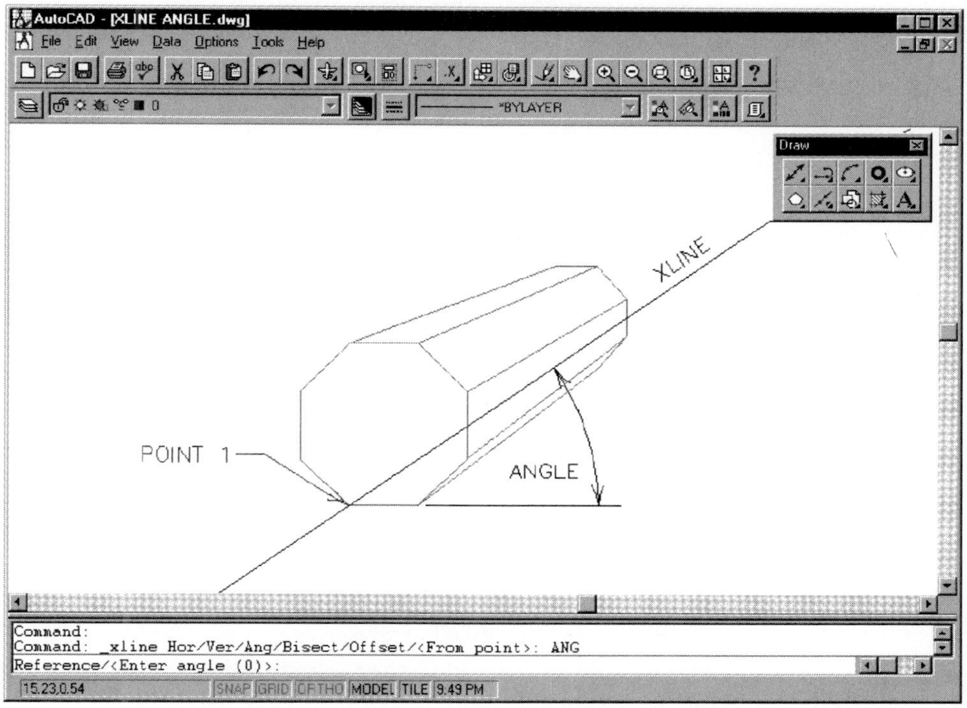

Figure 12.24
Create an angular **xline** *by specifying the angle and a point it passes through.*

Select a line object: *Select another* **xline**, *ray, line, or polyline.*
Enter angle: *Specify the angle.*
Through point: *Specify a point (1) through which you want the* **xline** *to pass. When you have completed selecting points, press Enter to end the command.*

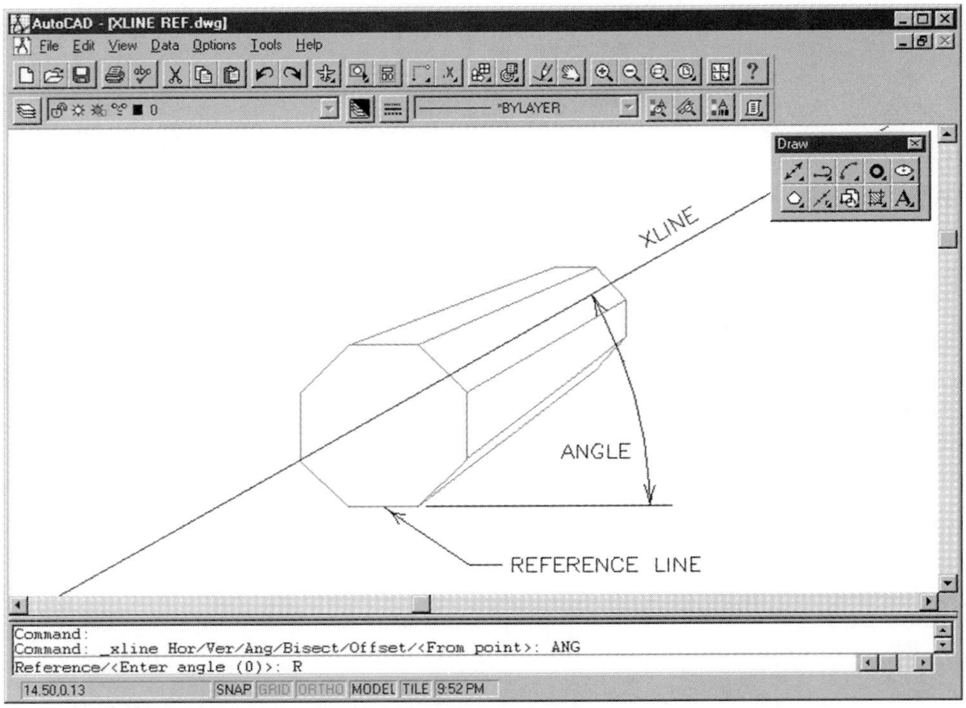

Figure 12.25
Create an angular **xline** *by specifying an angle from a selected reference line.*

Bisect This option creates an **xline** that passes through a selected angle vertex and bisects the angle between two selected points. The **xline** lies in the plane determined by the three points. The Bisect option is shown in Figure 12.26.

```
Hor/Ver/Ang/Bisect/Offset<From point>: bisect
Angle vertex point: Specify a point (1) that will be the vertex of
the angle. The completed xline will pass through this point.
```

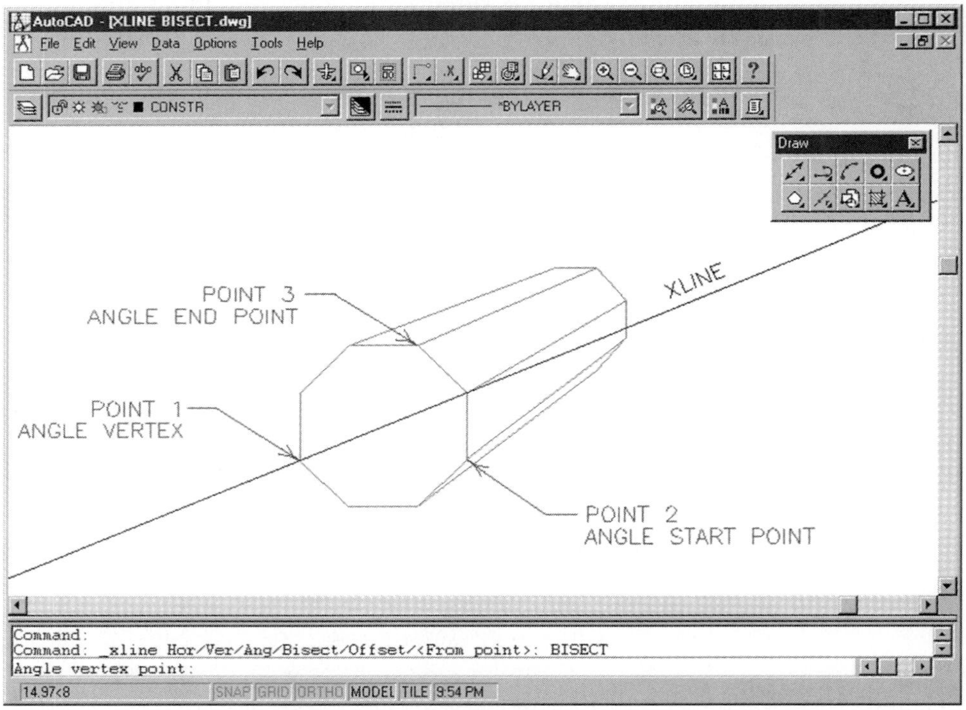

Figure 12.26
Creat an **xline** *that passes through a selected angle vertex, bisecting the angle between the second and third points.*

`Angle start point:` *`Specify a point (2) that will form one side of the angle.`*
`Angle end point:` *`Specify a point (3) that will form the other side of the angle. When you have completed selecting points, press Enter to end the command.`*

Offset This option creates an **xline** that is parallel to another object, as shown in Figure 12.27. This is similar to the **offset** command discussed in Unit 10, except that an infinite **xline** is created.

`Hor/Ver/Ang/Bisect/Offset<From point>:` *`offset`*
`Offset distance or Through <0.00>:` *`Specify an offset distance or T. Selecting T will prompt for a point the`* **`xline`** *`will pass through.`*
`Select a line object:` *`Select another`* **`xline`**, *`line, polyline, or ray.`*
`Side to offset?` *`Specify a point (1). When you have completed selecting points, press Enter to end the command.`*

Drawing Rays (ray)

The **ray** command creates a semi-infinite line. As opposed to an infinite line **(xline),** a ray **(ray)** has a finite starting point and extends to infinity, as shown in Figure 12.28. You can access the **ray** command by using one of these two methods:

- From the Draw floating toolbar, choose the Line button. This causes a flyout menu to appear containing the Ray button.
- Type **`ray`** at the `Command:` prompt.

After invoking the **ray** command, AutoCAD prompts:

`From point:` *`Specify a starting point (1) where you want the ray to begin.`*

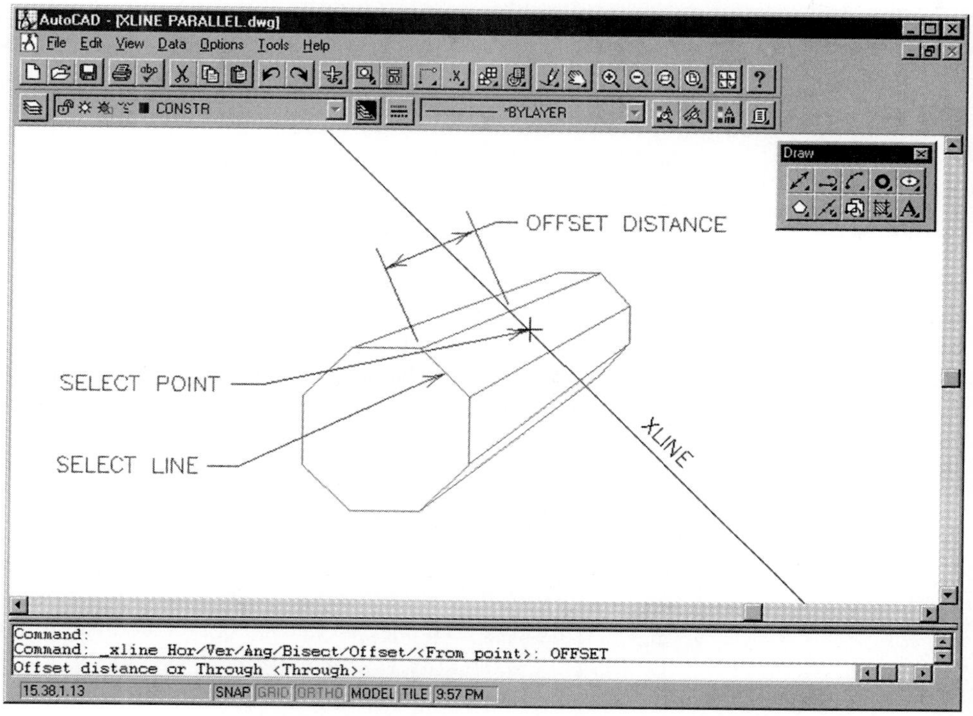

Figure 12.27
Create an **xline** *parallel to another object.*

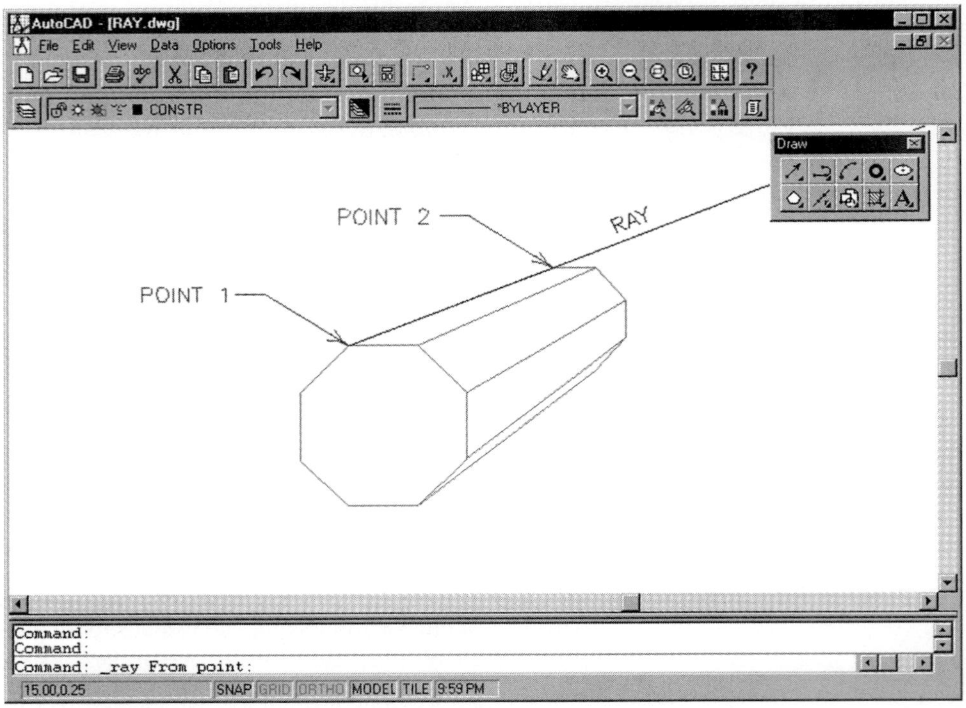

Figure 12.28
A ray is a semi-infinite line, defined by specifying a starting point and a point through which you want the ray to pass.

`Through point:` *Specify a point (2) through which you want the ray to pass. When you have completed selecting points, press Enter to end the command.*

Creating Freehand Drawings (sketch)

The **sketch** command can be used to create freehand drawings in AutoCAD. Common uses of this command include creating map outlines, entering signatures, or creating short break lines in mechanical drawings. When using the **sketch** command, the sketching is captured as a series of short independent lines. The length of these lines is governed by the record increment. You can access the **sketch** command by using one of these two methods:

- Choose the Sketch button from the Miscellaneous toolbar.
- Type **`sketch`** at the `Command:` prompt.

After invoking the **sketch** command, AutoCAD prompts:

`Record increment <0.10>:` *Specify an increment or accept the default.*

The record increment specifies the distance, in drawing units, that you move your drawing device before AutoCAD draws a line on the drawing. The larger the record increment, the farther the drawing device must be moved before it will generate a line.

Skill Builder

If you use a small record increment, you can quickly add hundreds of lines to your drawing, resulting in very large drawing files. You should use **sketch** conservatively, taking care to choose a record increment appropriate to your task so that you can draw accurately while keeping your drawings to a manageable size.

TABLE 12.1 Sketch Command Options

Option	Use
`Pen`	This option raises and lowers the sketching pen. You must raise the pen before you can select any menu items with your pointing device.
`eXit`	AutoCAD ends the **sketch** command and makes your sketch part of the drawing.
`Quit`	AutoCAD exits the command without recording anything.
`Record`	AutoCAD records your sketch without exiting the command or changing your pen's position. You can move the cursor to another position and sketch some more.
`Erase`	AutoCAD lets you erase all or part of your temporary sketch lines and raises the pen if it is down.
`Connect`	This option lowers the pen and continues the sketch from the endpoint of the last sketched line.
`. (period)`	This option is used to draw a straight line segment from the endpoint of the last sketched line to the pen's current location. The pen is automatically lowered at the beginning of the line segment and raised at the end.

After specifying the record increment, AutoCAD displays the following options on the Command: line:

`Sketch. Pen eXit Quit Record Erase Connect.`

At this point you are ready to begin sketching. Select a point on the drawing and begin freehand sketching. The options just displayed apply once you start sketching.

Skill Builder

When you are using the **sketch** command make sure Ortho and Snap are turned off. Sketch is intended to create freehand drawings. Using Snap while sketching can cause the freehand lines to "snap" to specific points. Ortho can cause the sketch to appear blocky, because Ortho is intended to create only horizontal and vertical lines.

When you are sketching, AutoCAD displays the `<Pen down>` prompt. As you move your pointing device, freehand geometry begins to appear on-screen. The appearance of the freehand geometry depends on the record increment setting. When you have completed your sketch, type *p* or pick a point with your drawing device. AutoCAD displays the `<Pen up>` prompt.

At this point, you can select one of the options shown in Table 12.1, or you can lower the pen (press the Pick button or type `P`) and start sketching again. Also, you do not have to pick up the pen (Pick button or `P`) before selecting one of the options.

Tutorial 12.3: Sketching Your Initials with the Sketch Command

Now give **sketch** a try. Use the drawing you've been working on in this unit—12DWG02, the bathroom sink symbol. You'll sketch your initials in the lower right corner of the sink.

1. Make sure you have the Bathroom Sink drawing displayed (12DWG02.DWG).
2.  Choose the Aerial button from the Standard toolbar to invoke the Aerial View dialog box. Use the Aerial View to draw a window around the lower-right corner.
3. Make sure Snap and Ortho are turned off in the toolbar at the bottom of the screen.
4.  Choose Sketch from the Miscellaneous toolbar.
5. Press Enter to accept the default Record increment of 0′-1″. AutoCAD displays the **sketch** options on the `Command:` line.

`Sketch. Pen eXit Quit Record Erase Connect.`

6. Move the crosshairs into the lower-right corner of the windowed section and select a point to begin sketching. AutoCAD prompts with `<Pen down>`.
7. Move your pointing device around (you don't need to hold down the Pick button) to get a feel for how **sketch** works. When you want to stop sketching, press the Pick button again. AutoCAD prompts with `<Pen up>`.
8. Now you can take one of two actions. You can enter `q` to exit from the command and not record your sketched lines, or you can enter `e` to access **sketch** erase mode and erase what you've drawn. If you quit, immediately press Enter to start the **sketch** command again.
9. Experiment with sketching lines and erasing or quitting until you feel comfortable with sketching. Then try sketching your initials. When they look good to you, enter `X` to record what you sketched and exit the command.
10.  Select the Save button on the Standard toolbar to save your drawing.

WORKING WITH MULTILINES

Multilines are useful for creating drawings consisting of many parallel lines. An architectural floor plan, for example, contains many parallel lines representing walls. Instead of constructing the parallel lines individually, only one multiline needs to be drawn to depict the wall.

The multiline feature allows you to draw composite lines that consist of multiple parallel lines. A single multiline can contain up to 16 parallel lines. The lines that make up a multiline are called elements. Each element in a multiline can have a different offset, color, and linetype. The **mlstyle** command is used to create different multiline styles and define the properties of each element within the multiline. To draw multilines based on the style(s) you created, you will use the **mline** command. Since a multiline is one object, with its complex configuration defined by the **mlstyle** command, traditional editing commands such as **trim** and **extend** cannot be used. The **mledit** command provides the necessary editing functions for existing multilines.

DEFINING MULTILINE STYLES (mlstyle)

By default, the multiline style `STANDARD` has two lines that are offset at 0.5 and -0.5. In most cases you will want to create your own multiline style. Each style can have up to 16 parallel elements, with each element containing its own color and linetype. Each element of a multiline is defined by its own offset distance, which you define. You also define the origin point of the multiline, which serves as the offset point.

The **mlstyle** command allows you to set the style of multilines. In addition to specifying the number of elements in the multiline and the properties of each element, you can control its end caps, end lines, and background color. With **mlstyle** you can also display style names, set the current style, load, save, and rename styles, or edit their description.

You can access the **mlstyle** command by any of these methods:

- Click the Multiline Style button on the Object Properties toolbar.
- Choose Data, Multiline Style.
- Enter **`mlstyle`** at the `Command:` prompt.

The Mlstyle command will access the Multiline Styles dialog box, shown in Figure 12.29. The dialog box can be divided into three areas: Multiline Style, Element Properties, and Multiline Properties. Note the Multiline Style dialog box contains a preview window, providing a thumbnail view of the current multiline settings (except for color fill).

Multiline Style The Multiline Style area has the following options:

- **Current.** Choosing the DOWN ARROW in the `Current:` box accesses a pop-up list displaying the current multiline style, along with all styles currently loaded in the drawing. This allows you to select a new style name from the list and make it current.

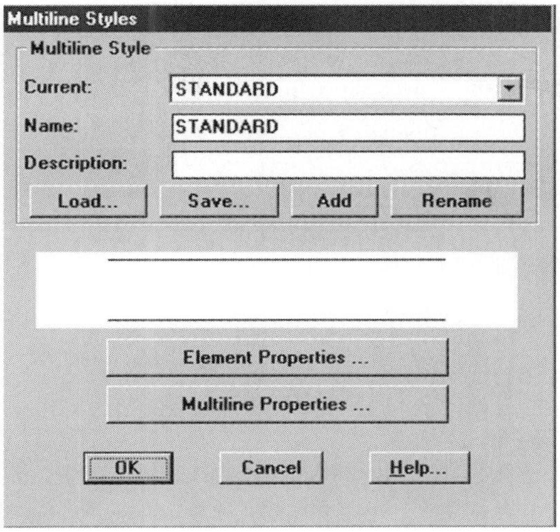

Figure 12.29
The Multiline Styles dialog box.

- **Name.** The `Name:` edit box is used to name a new multiline style or rename an existing one. First define the Element and Multiline properties, enter a style name in the `Name:` edit box, then choose the Save button.

  To rename a style, first make it the current style. Enter the new name in the edit box and choose the Rename button. You can't rename the default STANDARD multiline style. To make a copy of the current style, first make the style you want to copy current. Next enter a new style name in the `Name:` edit box, then choose the Save button.

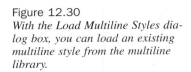

For the Professional

The multiline style definitions are stored in the multiline library file, ACAD.MLN.

- **Description.** The `Description:` edit box allows you to enter up to a 255-character description, including spaces, to the current multiline style.
- **Load...** Choosing the Load... button accesses the Load Multiline Styles dialog box as shown in Figure 12.30. All styles available in the current MLN library file are displayed. To access a different library file, choose the `File`... button to access the Load Multiline Style from File dialog box.
- **Save...** Choose the `Save`... button to save or copy a multiline style. Before you can save a multiline style you must first give it a name in the `Name:` edit box.
- **Add.** This will add the style name listed in the `Name:` edit box to the current list of multiline styles available.
- **Rename.** This will allow you to rename a multiline style. Refer to Name.

Element Properties The Element Properties button accesses the Element Properties dialog box shown in Figure 12.31. This dialog box allows you to define the properties for each element in the current multiline style. Each area is described in more detail:

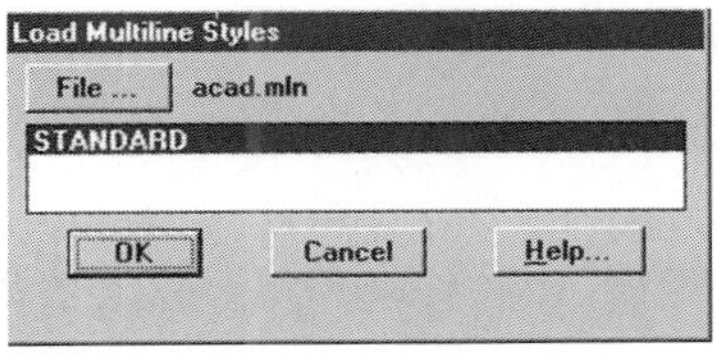

Figure 12.30
With the Load Multiline Styles dialog box, you can load an existing multiline style from the multiline library.

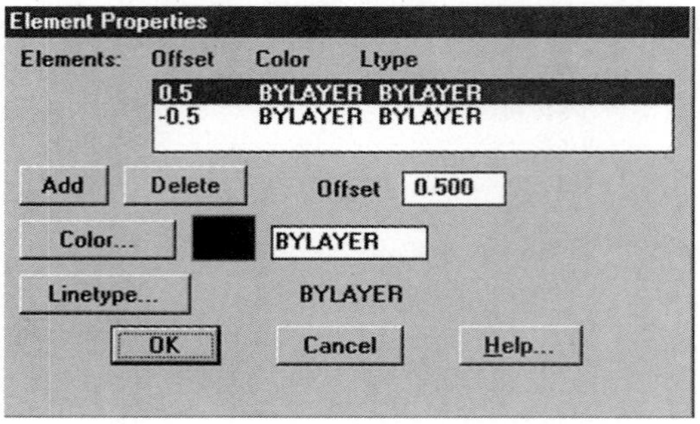

Figure 12.31
In the Element Properties Dialog box you can define the properties for each element in the current multiline style.

- `Elements.` This window displays all of the elements (lines) in the current multiline style.
  - `Offset.` The offset value defines the location of each element from the multiline origin point. The origin point is considered 0,0.
  - `Color.` Displays the color of each element. See Color.
  - `Ltype.` Displays the linetype for each element. See Linetype.
- `Add.` Used to add new elements to the current multiline style.
- `Delete.` Deletes the highlighted element from current multiline style.
- `Offset.` Enter the amount of offset you want for the highlighted element. Offset values can be either positive or negative, as shown in Figure 12.32.
- `Color...` Choose the `Color...` button to access the Select Color dialog box. Select a color to assign to the highlighted element.
- `Linetype...` Choose the `Linetype...` button to access the Select Linetype dialog box. From this dialog box you can select from any linetypes currently loaded or load other linetypes. Select a linetype to assign to the highlighted element. For a review on loading and creating linetypes, refer to Unit 5, "Understanding Layers and Linetypes."

Multiline Properties The Multiline Properties button accesses the Multiline Properties dialog box shown in Figure 12.33. This dialog box allows you to set various properties of the current multiline style.

- `Display joints.` Selecting this check box will display segment joints at the vertices of each multiline segment. Figure 12.34 shows a multiline with and without the segment joints displayed. The joint in a multiline is also referred to as a miter.

The Caps area of the Multiline Properties dialog box has several options for controlling and displaying the start and end of the multiline. Refer to Figure 12.34 for examples.

- `Line.` Caps the starting and/or end segments of a multiline with a line.
- `Arc.` Caps the starting and/or end segments of a multiline with an arc.
- `Inner arcs.` The Inner arcs option will create an arc between the starting and/or end pairs of inner elements. If there is an odd number of inner elements, the center element is not connected.
- `Fill.` Controls the background fill of the current multiline and sets its color.

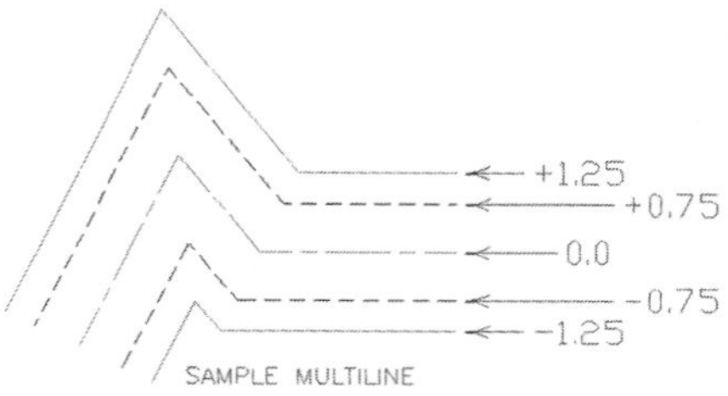

Figure 12.32
A multiline with each element offset from origin 0.0.

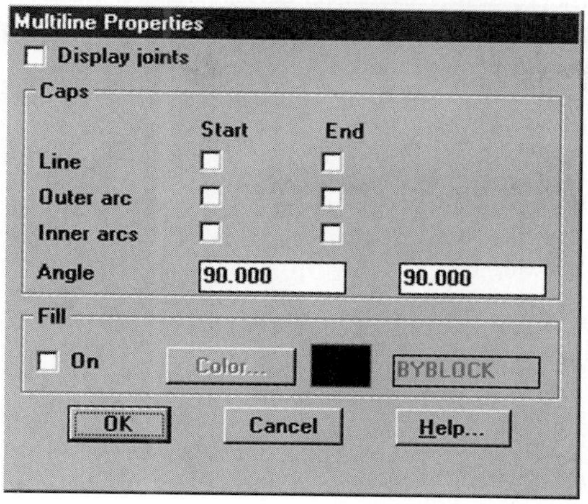

Figure 12.33
The Multiline Properties dialog box.

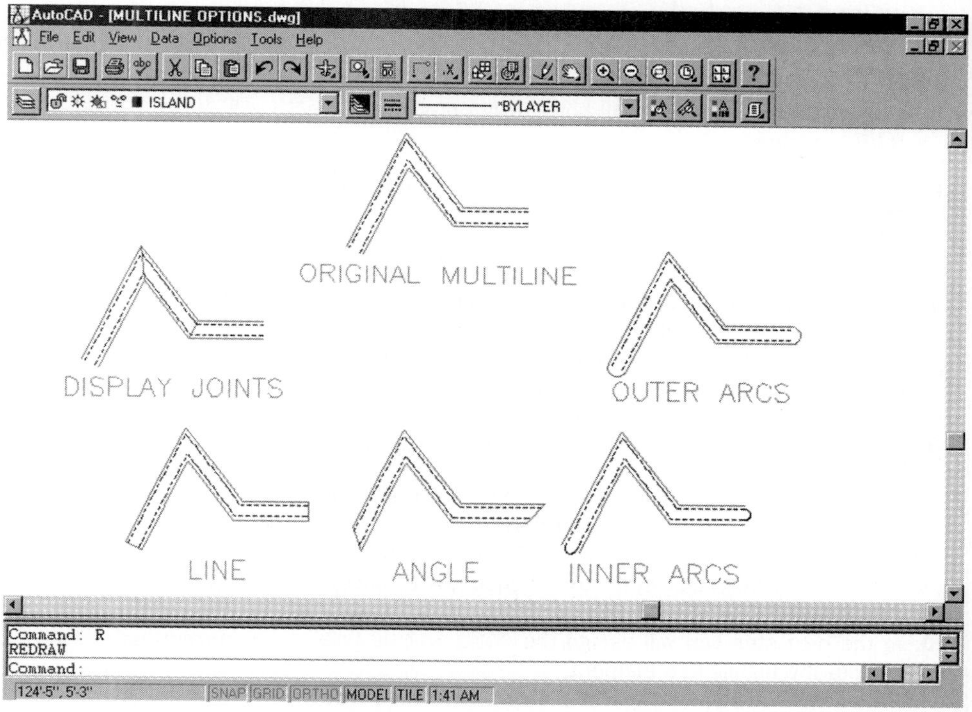

Figure 12.34
Examples of different multiline caps.

- `On`. Selecting this check box will turn on the background fill.
- `Color`. This option is grayed out unless the background fill button is turned on. Selecting the color button will access the Select Color dialog box, allowing you to select a background color for the multiline.

Creating Multilines

The **mline** command is used to draw multilines. Before you can draw a multiline, you must define the individual line elements with the **mlstyle** command. AutoCAD offers one standard multiline. You can access the **mline** command by either of these methods:

- Click and hold the Polyline button on the Draw toolbar. This will access a flyout menu. The third button is Multiline.
- Enter the `Command:` prompt.

Tutorial 12.4: Creating Multiline Styles with Mlstyle

In this tutorial you will use the **mlstyle** command to create two new multilines. These multilines will be used in the next two tutorials to create, and then modify, a kitchen counter. Follow these steps:

1.  Select the New button from the Standard toolbar and use **counter** for the drawing name.
2. From the Data pull-down menu, select Units. The Units Control dialog box appears. Change the units to architectural with a precision of 0′-0″.
3. Select Options, Linetype, Global Linetype Scale. Set the Linetype Scale to 24.
4. From the Data pull-down menu, select Drawing Limits. Leave the lower-left corner at 0′-0″,0′-0″ and change the upper-right corner to 20′-0″, 16′-0″.

```
ON/OFF<Lower left corner> <0'-0",0'-0">:
Upper right corner <1'-0",0'-9">:
20'-0",16'-0"
```

5.  Choose the Zoom All button from the Standard toolbar.
6.  Choose the Multiline Style button from the Object Properties toolbar.
   The Multiline Styles dialog box appears as shown in Figure 12.29.
7. First you will create a new multiline style. Select the Element Properties button.
8. Change the offset value of the highlighted element to **15.00.** This is done by changing the value shown in the Offset edit box.
9. Next you will change the color of the highlighted element.
   Choose either the Color button or the color swatch. This will access the Select Color dialog box.
   Choose the red swatch from the Standard Colors, or type red in the Color edit box. Choose OK to accept your choice.
10. In the next step you will assign the CONTINUOUS linetype to the highlighted element.
    Choose the Linetype button to access the Loaded Linetypes dialog box. Select the CONTINUOUS linetype, then choose OK to accept your choice.
    The settings for the first element should match Figure 12.35.
11. Highlight the element -0.5 and repeat steps 7 through 10. Change the properties of this element to **-15.0,** red, and CONTINUOUS.

The next steps involve adding a new element to the list, setting the Display joints and Caps option, and saving your new multiline style.

1. Choose the Add button in the Element Properties dialog box.
   A new element is added to the list and highlighted.

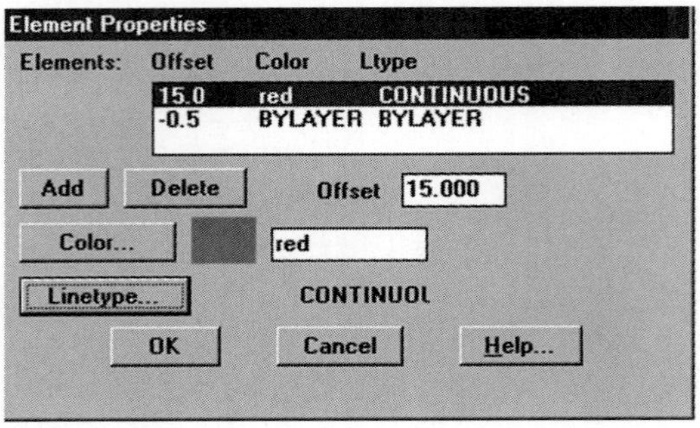

Figure 12.35 *The Element Properties dialog box with the first element properties set.*

2. Change the properties of this element to **-9.0, yellow,** and HIDDEN. Since HIDDEN is not a linetype loaded by default, you will need to load it.
   Choose the Linetype button to access the Loaded Linetypes dialog box.
   In the Select Linetype dialog box, select Load. This will access the Load or Reload Linetypes dialog box.
   Choose the HIDDEN linetype from the scrolling window. Choose OK to accept your choice.
   In the Select Linetype dialog box, select the HIDDEN linetype, then choose OK to accept your choice.
3. Three elements should now be in the list 15.0, -9.0, and -15.0. Choose OK to return to the Multiline Styles dialog box.
4. Choose the Multiline Properties dialog box.
   The Multiline Properties dialog box appears on-screen.
   Select the Display joints option.
   In the Caps area, select both the Start and End caps for the Line option.
5. Your settings should be the same as Figure 12.36.
6. Choose OK to return to the Multiline Styles dialog box.
7. Enter Counter in the Name: edit box, replacing STANDARD.
8. Choose the Add button to include the new style in the current list of styles loaded in the drawing file.

Your Multiline Styles dialog box should now look like Figure 12.37. Notice your new, current multiline style displayed in the preview window.

Now you will use the commands you just covered to create another new multiline style. This style will be similar to the COUNTER style you just defined.

1. Select the Multiline Properties button to access the Multiline Properties dialog box.
2. The Display joints, Line Start and End caps should be checked.

In the Caps area, select both the Start and End caps for the Outer arc option.

3. Name the new style ISLAND, and use the Add button to add it to the current list of loaded multiline styles.

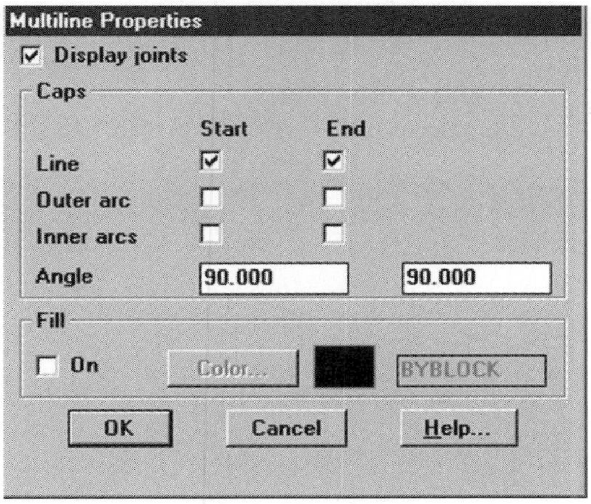

Figure 12.36 *The Multiline Properties dialog box with the options set.*

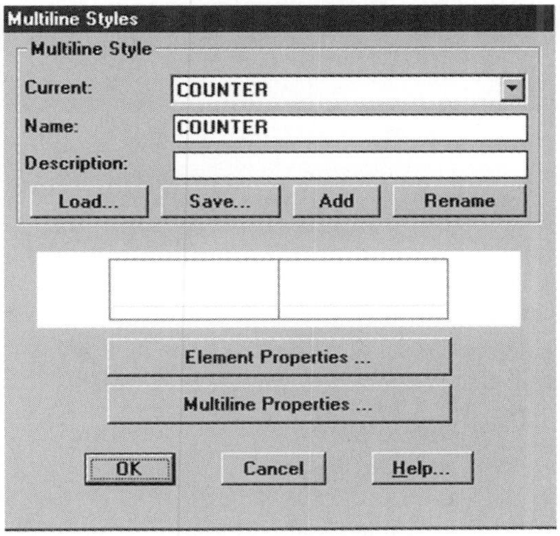

Figure 12.37 *The Multiline Styles dialog box with the new multiline style defined.*

4. Choose the Save button to save the new multiline styles you just defined.
5. The Save Multiline Style dialog box appears. Change to the correct drive and directory, and enter `Counter` in the File Name edit box. AutoCAD will automatically add the MLN extension to the file.

   Your multiline styles dialog box should now look like Figure 12.38.

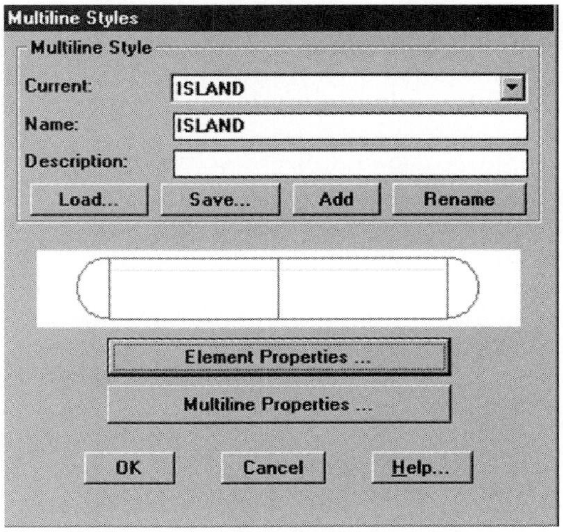

Figure 12.38 *The Multiline Styles dialog box with the ISLAND style defined.*

The following is the command prompt sequence of the **mline** command:

`Justification = Top, Scale = 1.00, Style = STANDARD`
`Justification/Scale/STyle/<From point>:` *`Select a point.`*
`To point:` *`Select the second point.`*
`Undo/<To point>:` *`Select the next point, enter U for undo.`*

If you entered more than two points, the Close option is added as shown:

`Close/Undo/<To point>:` *`Select the next point, enter U for undo, or C for close.`*

When you access the **mline** command, the top line shows the status of the multiline justification, scale, and style name. The next line shows the following prompt: `Justification/Scale/STyle/<From point>:`. Explanations of these options are as follows:

- `Top/Zero/Bottom <top>:` Accessed at the `Justification/Scale/STyle/<From point>:` prompt by entering a `j`. This option determines how a multiline is drawn between the specified points. Three justifications are available for the **mline** command—Top, Zero, and Bottom as shown in Figure 12.39.

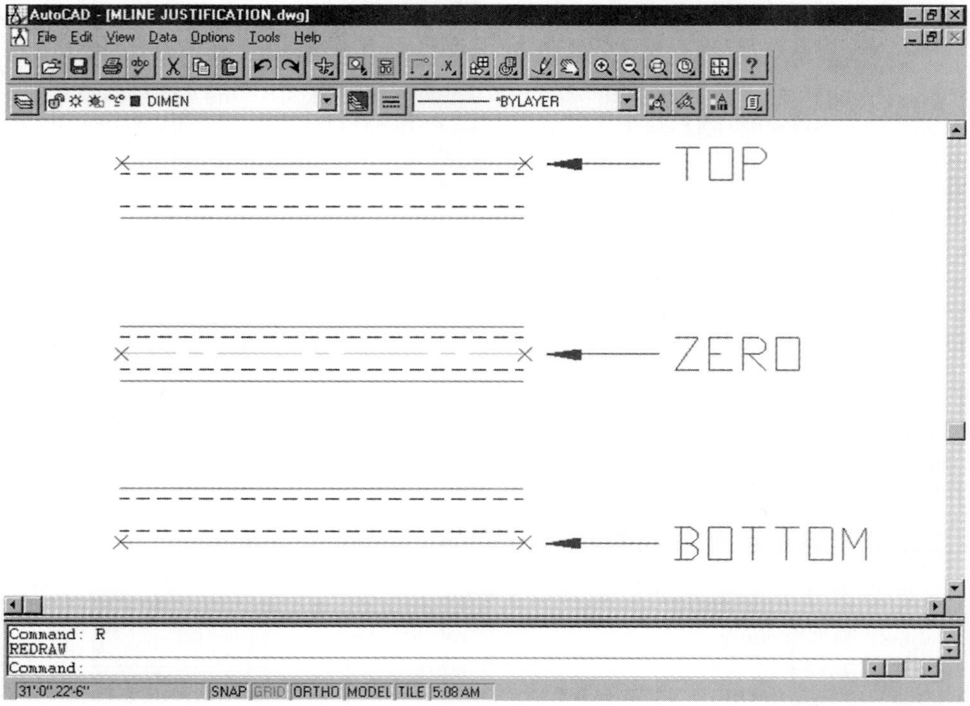

Figure 12.39
Examples of multiline justification.

- `Top.` This is the default setting. This aligns the top of the set of line elements along the points you pick as you draw.
- `Zero.` A zero setting uses the center of the set of elements as the pick point.
- `Bottom.` Bottom aligns the bottom line element between the pick points.

Skill Builder

The justification methods are defined for drawing a multiline from left to right (positive X direction). The top of the multiline (as it is defined in **mlstyle**) is between the pick points when you draw from left to right. If you draw from right to left, the multiline is drawn upside down.

- `Set Mline scale <1.00>:` Accessed by entering an `s` at the `Justification/Scale/STyle/<From point>:` prompt. The scale option controls the overall width of the current multiline style. A scale factor of 2 results in the multiline being twice as wide as the style definition. A scale factor of 0 collapses the multiline into a single line.
  You can also enter a negative scale factor. A negative scale value flips the multline pattern over, with the most negative element placed on top.
- `Mstyle name (or ?):` Accessed by entering `st` from the `Justification/Scale/Style/<From point>:` prompt. This option allows you to load different multiline styles, provided they have been previously created. At the prompt you can enter a multiline style name, type `?` to access a text box showing a list of styles loaded in the current drawing, or press Enter to retain the default style. You can also use the **mlstyle** dialog box to select a current multiline style by a more visible method.

TUTORIAL 12.5: DRAWING MULTILINES

In this tutorial you will use the multiline styles created in the previous tutorial to draw a kitchen layout. Continue from the previous tutorial and follow these steps.

1.  Click the Multiline Style button on the Object Properties toolbar.
   The Multiline Styles dialog box appears.
2. In the Current edit box, click on the DOWN ARROW and make `COUNTER` the current style.
3. Your Multiline Styles dialog box should look like Figure 12.40.

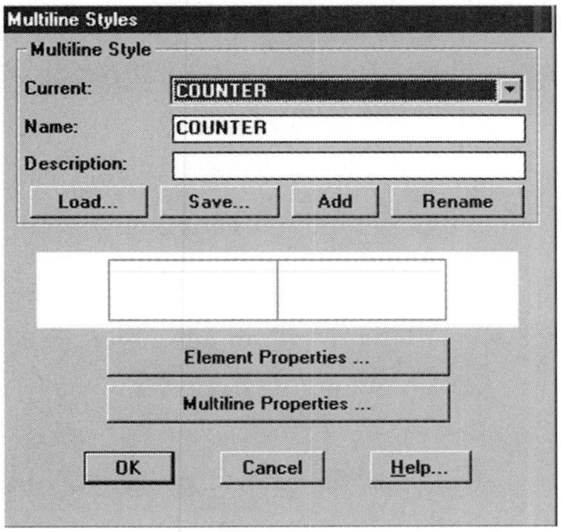

Figure 12.40 *The Multiline Styles dialog box displaying COUNTER as the current style.*

4.  Select the Multiline button from the Draw toolbar.
5. Begin the kitchen counter.

```
Justification = Top, Scale = 1.00, Style = COUNTER
Justification/Scale/STyle/<From point>: 3'-0",5'-6"
```

6. At the `To point>:` prompt enter **@9'-6"<90**
7. At the `Undo/<To point>:` prompt enter **@9'-0",0**
8. At the `Close/Undo/<To point>:` prompt, press Enter to end the **`mline`** command.

This completes the first part of the kitchen layout. The layout on your screen should look like Figure 12.41. Next, you will complete the kitchen layout by adding an island.

Complete the following steps:

1. Press Enter at the `Command:` prompt to start the **mline** command again.
2. Change the current style to ISLAND by entering st at the prompt.

```
Justification = Top, Scale = 1.00, Style = COUNTER
Justification/Scale/STyle/<From point>: st
```

3. Change the current **mline** style to ISLAND.

```
Mstyle name (or ?): island
```

4. Begin the island.

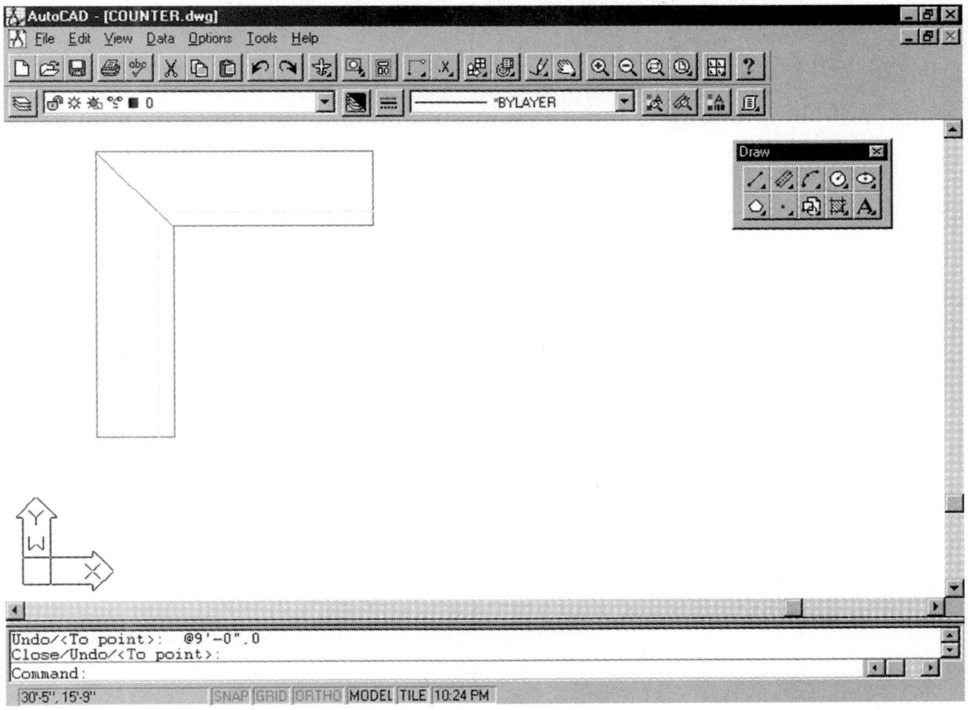

Figure 12.41 *Completing the first section of the kitchen layout.*

`Justification = Top, Scale = 1.00, Style = ISLAND`
`Justification/Scale/STyle/<From point>:` **17′-0″,3′-0″**

5. At the `To point>:` prompt enter **8′-0″,3′-0″**
6. At the `Undo/<To point>:` prompt press Enter to end the **mline** command.

This completes the kitchen layout. Figure 12.42 shows the completed layout. The next tutorial will continue from here, where you will make several design changes in the kitchen.

Figure 12.42 *The completed kitchen layout.*

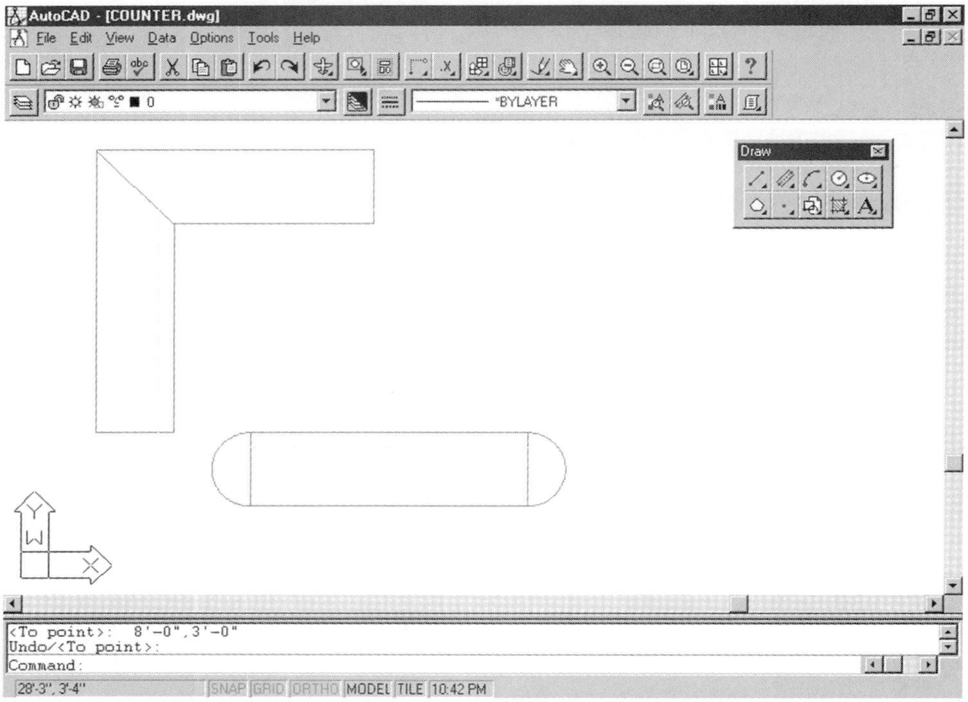

Editing Multilines

A multiline is treated as one object in AutoCAD, with its complex configuration defined by the **mlstyle** command. Because of this standard, editing commands such as **trim, extend, fillet, chamfer, offset** and **break** do not have any effect on multilines. Instead, a different set of editing functions is designed specifically to edit multilines. The **mledit** command (multiline edit) provides the necessary editing functions for existing multilines.

These tools are designed to edit multilines that cross, form a tee, and create corner joints and vertices. You can also cut and weld multilines. AutoCAD displays the multiline editing tools in a dialog box, shown in Figure 12.43. You can access the Multiline Edit Tools dialog box by:

- Click the Edit Polyline button on the Modify toolbar. Continue to hold down the pick button to access the flyout menu. Move the pointer to the second button on the flyout, Edit Multiline.
- Enter **`mledit`** at the `Command:` prompt.

To access the editing commands, click the image tile of your choice. The name of the editing button is displayed in the lower-left corner of the dialog box. Next, choose the OK button to start the command.

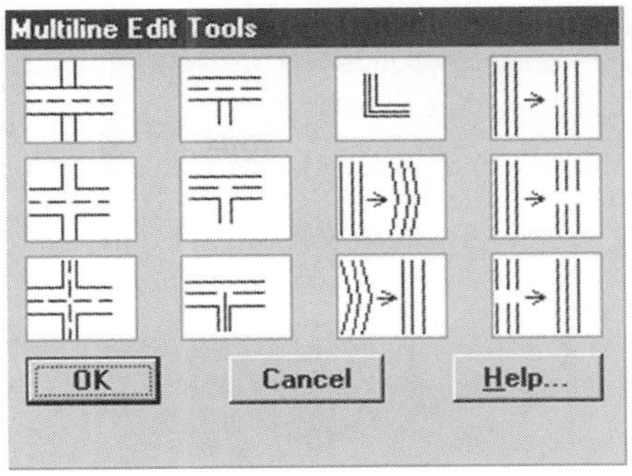

Figure 12.43
The Multiline Edit Tools dialog box.

For the Professional

You can also use the **mledit** in command line format. Use a hyphen (-) symbol as a prefix to the command. The following prompt appears:

```
Command: -mledit
Mline editing option AV/DV/CC/OC/MC/CT/OT/MT/CJ/CS/CA/WA:
```

The Multiline Edit Tools dialog box is organized into four main sets of editing tools, as shown in Table 12.2.

Crossing Tools The first set of tools, Crossing, are for editing crossing multilines. Each of the three commands creates a different type of crossing intersection. These commands work similarly to a combination of the **trim** and **fillet** commands used to edit other AutoCAD objects.

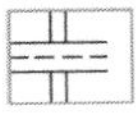

Closed Cross Closed Cross is used to trim one of two intersecting multilines. The first multiline picked is trimmed to the outer edges of the second multiline picked. All elements in the first multiline picked are trimmed (Figure 12.44).

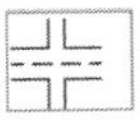

Open Cross Open Cross creates an open intersection between two multilines. All elements of the first multiline picked are trimmed to the outer edges of the second. Only the outer line elements of the second multiline are trimmed, with the inner lines continuing through the middle (Figure 12.45).

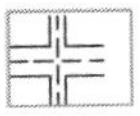

Merged Cross With Merged Cross you can create an open intersection between the outside multiline elements. The inside elements are merged. The inner line elements are merged at the second multilines next set. A full merge (both continue through) occurs only if the second multiline picked has only one inner line element (Figure 12.46).

TABLE 12.2 Multiline Edit Tools

Crossing	Tee	Corner, Vertices	Lines
Closed Cross	Closed Tee	Corner Joint	Cut Single
Open Cross	Open Tee	Vertex Add	Cut All
Merged Cross	Merged Tee	Vertex Delete	Weld

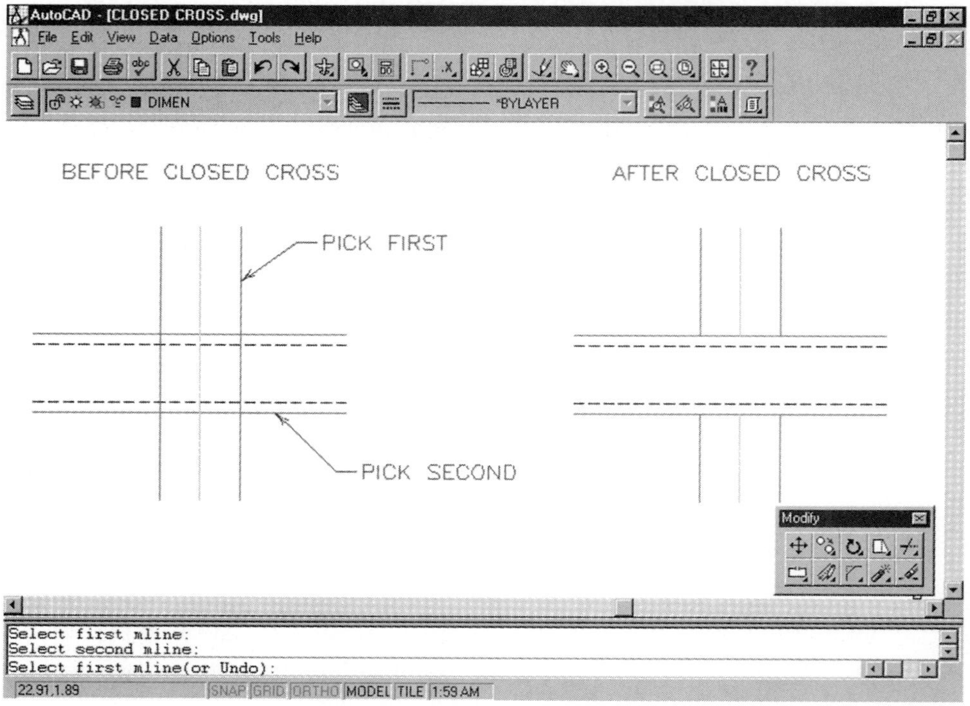

Figure 12.44
An example of closed crossing multilines.

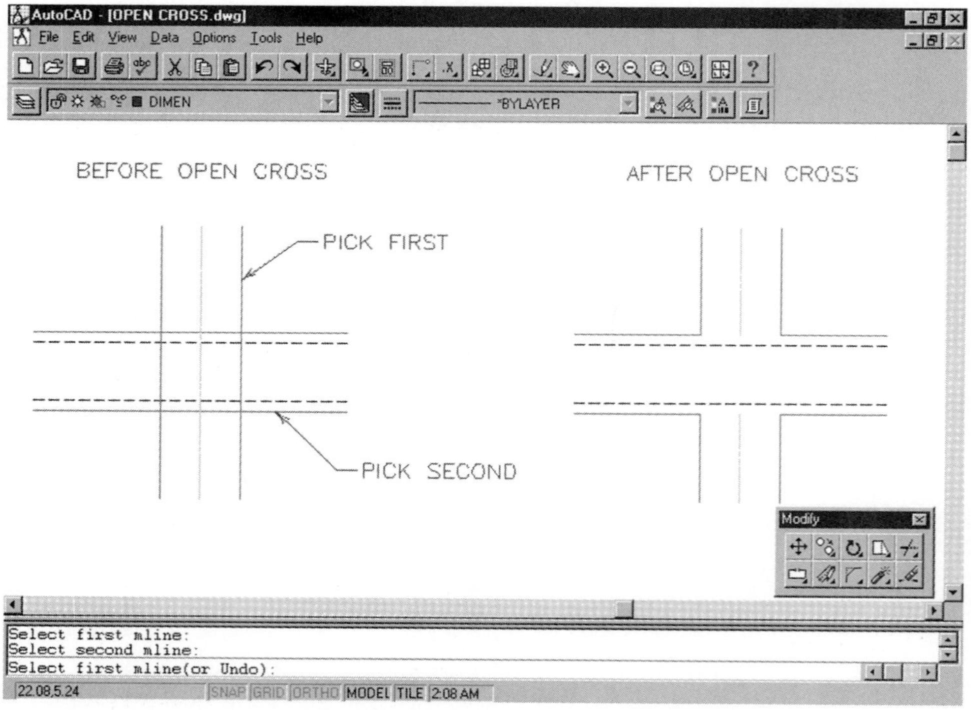

Figure 12.45
An example of open crossing multilines.

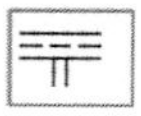

Closed Tee The Closed Tee command creates a closed intersection between two multilines, trimming or extending the first multiline. The first multiline picked is trimmed or extended to the nearest outer edge of the second. Only the side of the first multiline nearest the pick point remains. The second multiline is not affected (Figure 12.47).

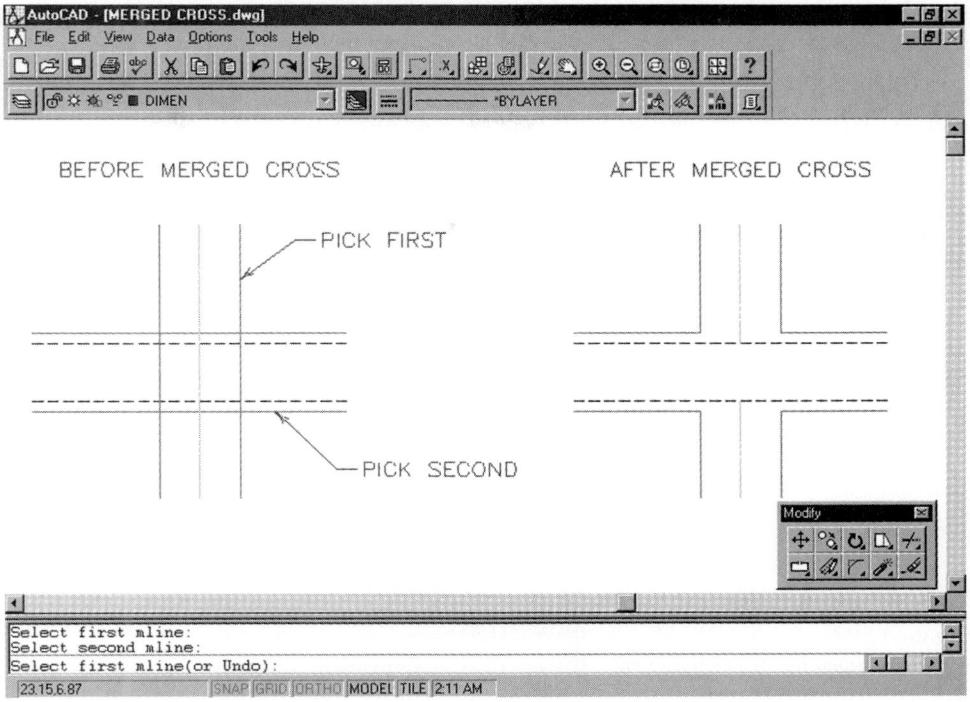

Figure 12.46
An example of merged crossing multilines.

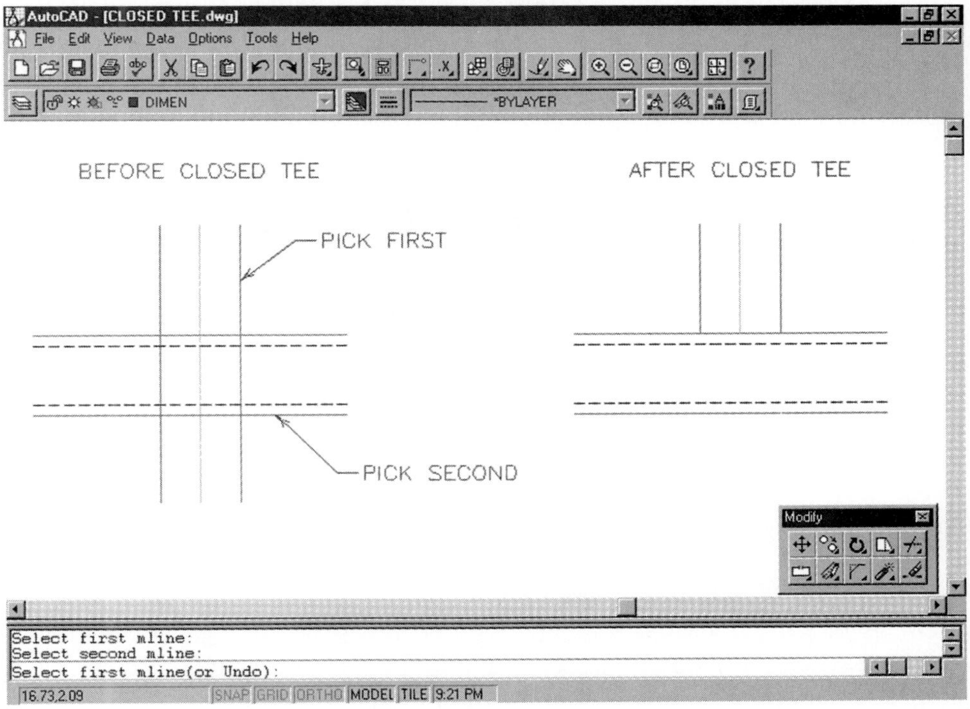

Figure 12.47
You can trim or extend the first multiline selected, creating a closed tee.

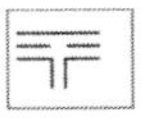

Open Tee Open Tee creates an open intersection between two multilines, also trimming or extending the first multiline. All elements of the first multiline picked are trimmed at the outer edge of the second multiline. Only the outer line element of the second multiline is trimmed (Figure 12.48).

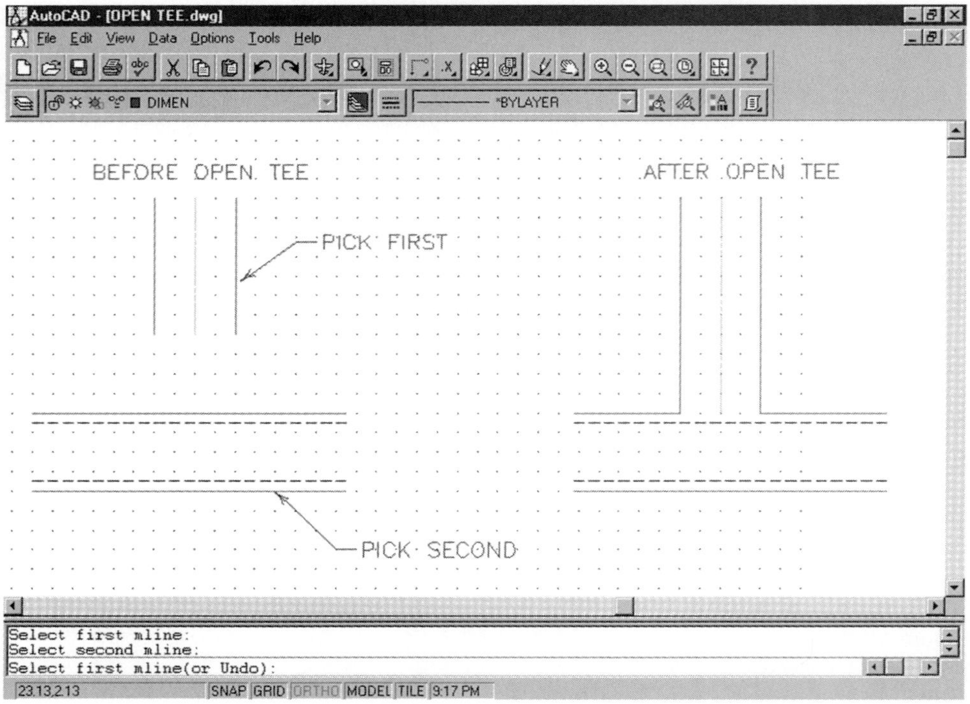

Figure 12.48
Create an open tee by extending the first multiline selected.

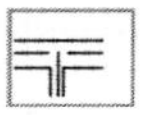

Merged Tee The Merged Tee command creates an open intersection between outside multiline elements and merges the inner elements, either trimming or extending the first multiline. The merge occurs at the second multilines first inner element. Only the side of the first line nearest the pick point remains (Figure 12.49).

Figure 12.49
An example of merged tee multilines.

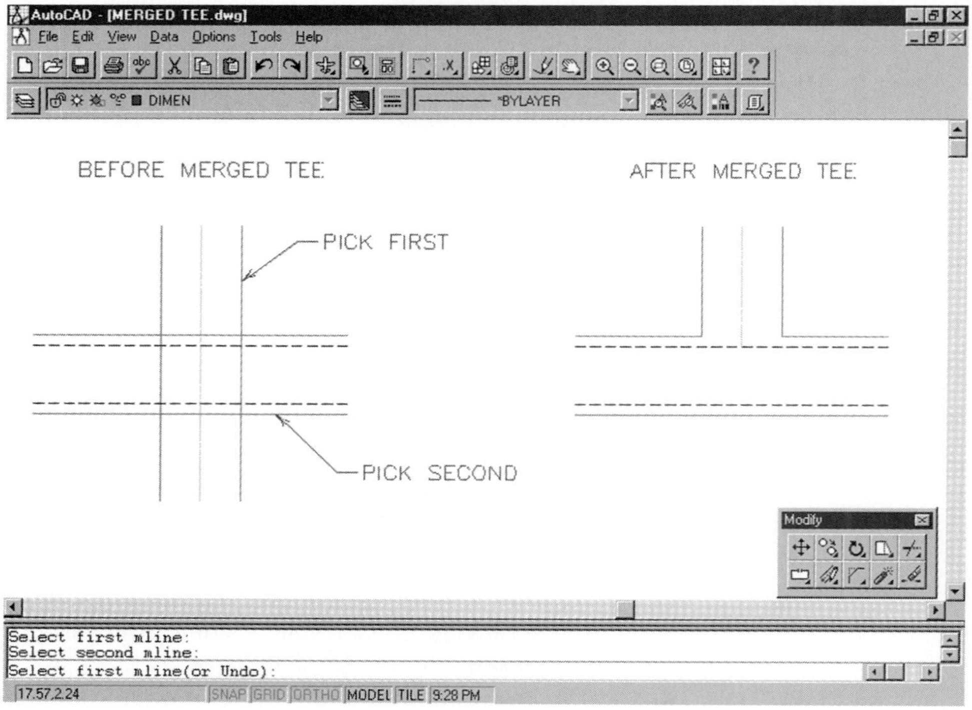

Corner Joint The Corner Joint option trims both multilines selected and creates a corner. Only the picked sides of the multilines remain, with the extending portions of both (if any) trimmed. All of the inner line elements are merged (Figure 12.50).

Add Vertex Use Add Vertex to add a vertex to a selected multiline at the point it was picked. When the vertex is added, it is not readily apparent that a new vertex exists, nor does the multiline visibly change in any way unless you have Display joints turned on in the Multiline Properties dialog box. If Display joints is turned on, a line will appear wherever you add a vertex. By adding the vertex, it is now possible to further edit the multiline with stretch or grips (Figure 12.51).

Delete Vertex Delete Vertex removes the vertex that is selected when picking a multiline. The resulting multiline contains only one straight segment between the adjacent two vertices. The multiline immediately changes when you delete the vertex. No additional editing is necessary (Fig 12.52).

Cut Single This is similar to the BREAK 2 POINTS command. When using Cut Single on a multiline, the break occurs between the two pick points. The break points can be on either side of the multiline (Figure 12.53).

Cut All When using the Cut All option, the line elements are cut at the pick points in a direction perpendicular to the axis of the multiline. Although the resulting multiline appears to be cut into separate multilines, it remains one single object. Using Move or Grips to stretch the multiline causes the cut to close (Figure 12.54).

Weld All Weld All repairs and rejoins sections of a multiline that have been removed. It reverses the action of a cut, causing the multiline to be restored to its original configuration. Pick points on either side of the break (Figure 12.55).

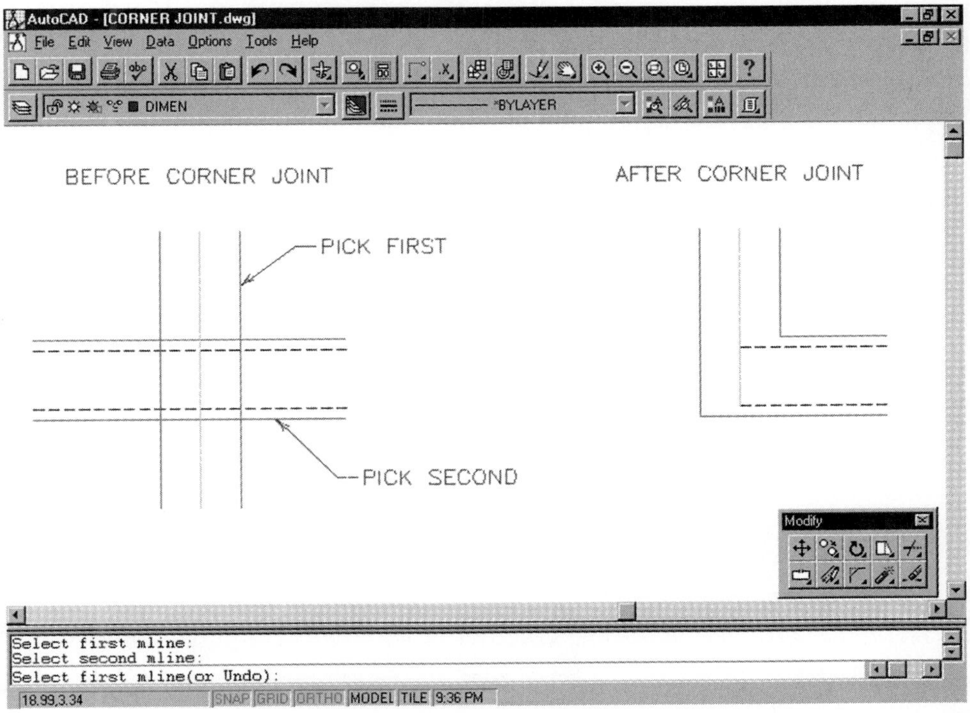

Figure 12.50
Creating a corner joint with two multilines.

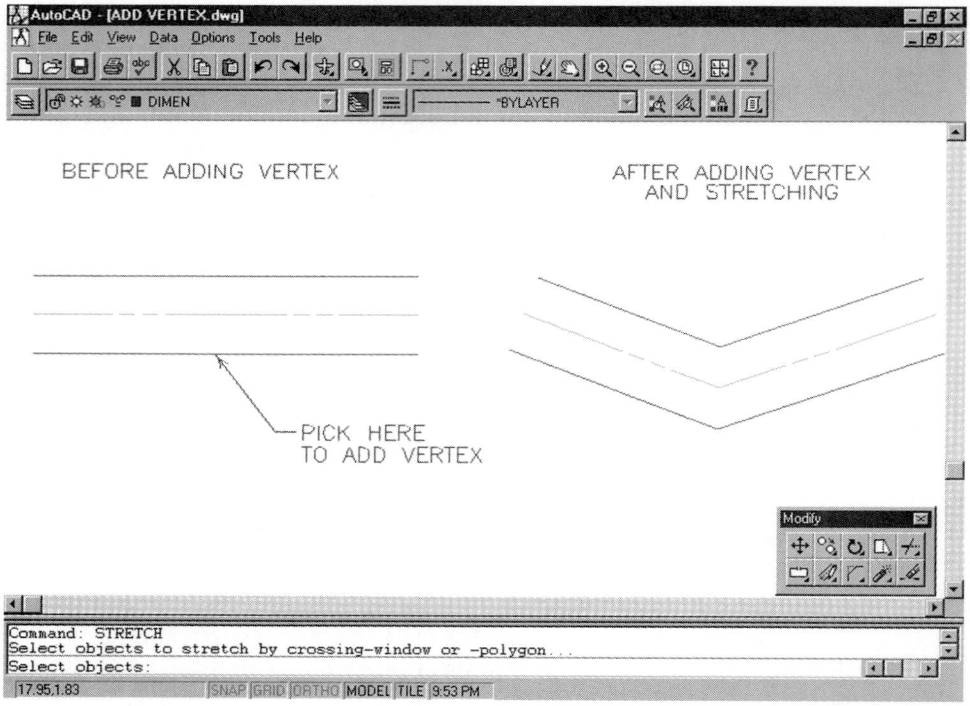

Figure 12.51
A vertex is added to a multiline at the point you pick.

Figure 12.52
Deleting a vertex from an existing multiline.

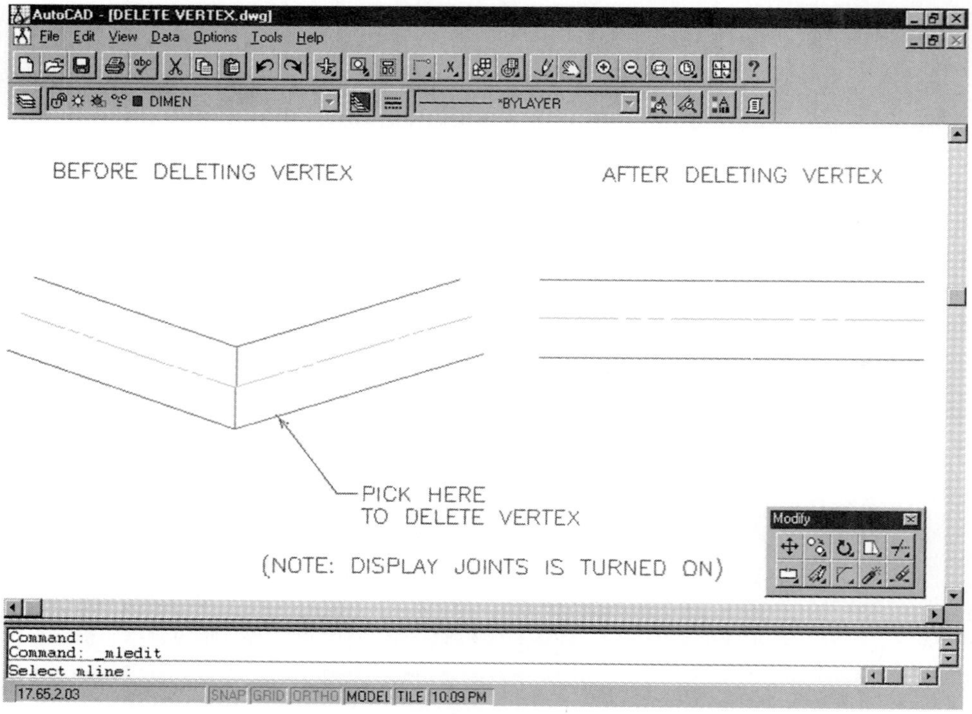

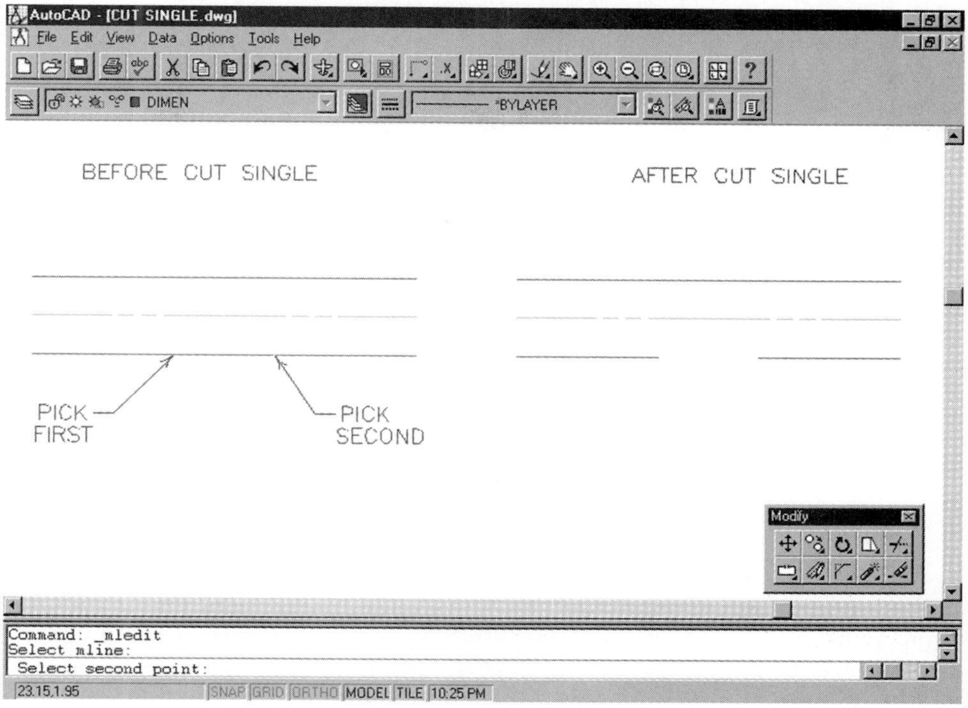

Figure 12.53
An example of a section removed from a single element of a multi-line.

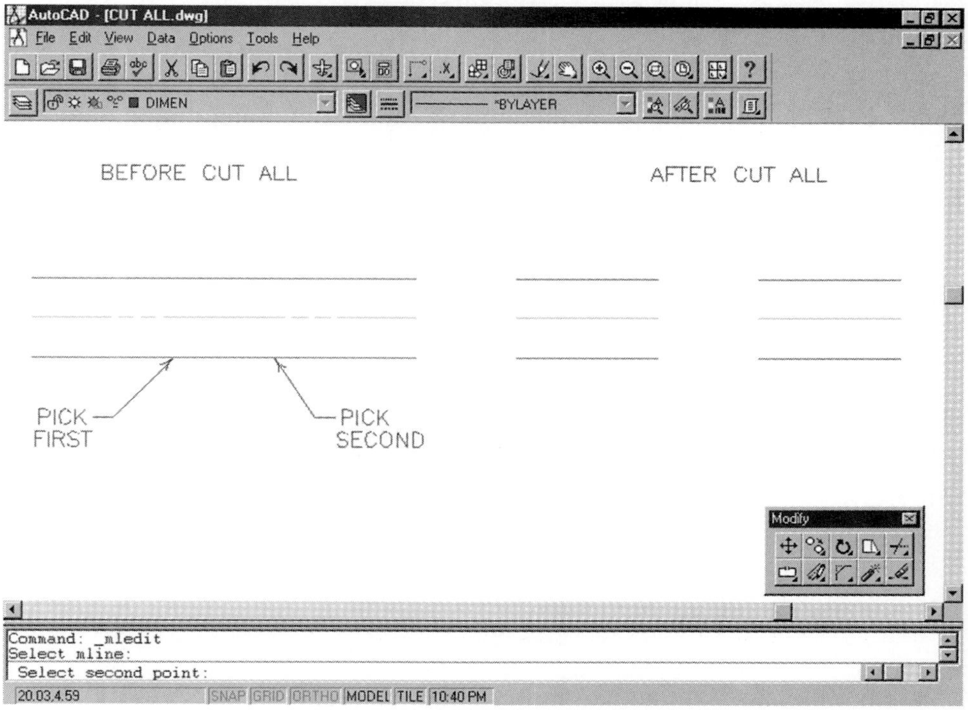

Figure 12.54
An example of a section removed from all the elements of a multiline.

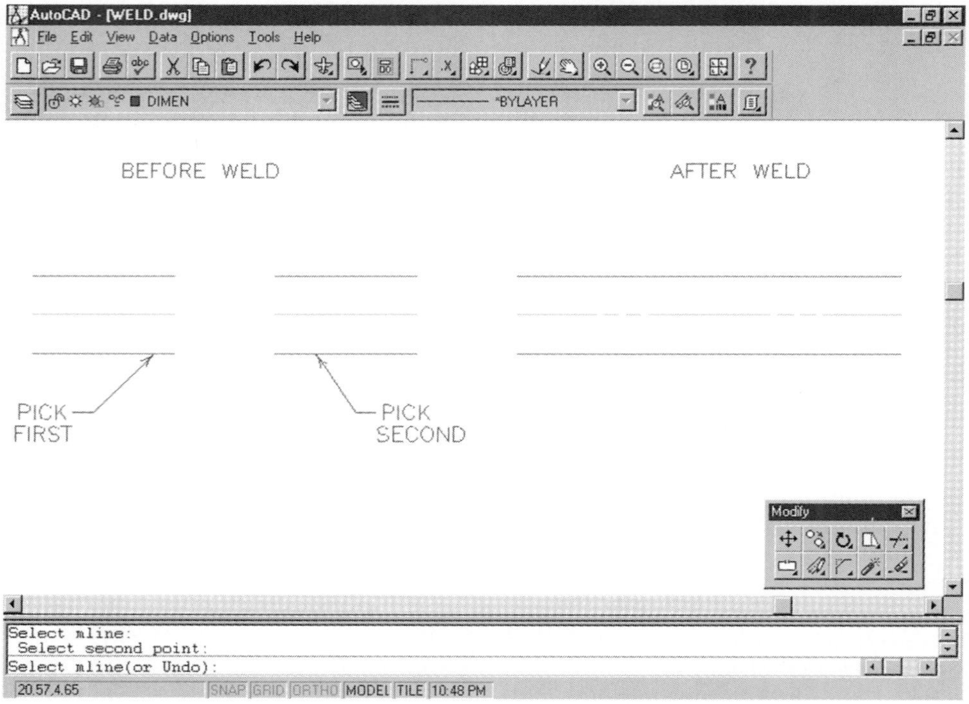

Figure 12.55
Using the Weld All option to repair a cut multiline.

Tutorial 12.6: Adding Vertices to a Multiline

In the next series of tutorials you will modify the kitchen counter you created in the previous tutorials. First you will use the Add Vertex edit command to mark a new opening in the kitchen counter for a stove. To add vertices to the kitchen counter, follow these steps:

1.  Click the Edit Multiline button on the Modify toolbar.
2. 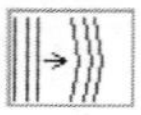 At the Edit Multilines dialog box, select the Add Vertex image tile and choose OK.
3. Add the first vertex.

   `Select mline:` **5′-6″, 8′-0″**

   A vertex is added to the vertical section of the original countertop.
4. Add the second vertex.

   `Select mline(or Undo):` **@32″<90**

   This adds a second vertex 32 inches away, marking a new opening for a stove.
5. At the `Select mline(or Undo):` prompt, press Enter to end the **mledit** command.

Two vertices have been added to the kitchen counter layout. These vertices will represent a new opening for a stove after you complete the next tutorial. Figure 12.56 shows the kitchen counter layout with the new vertices added.

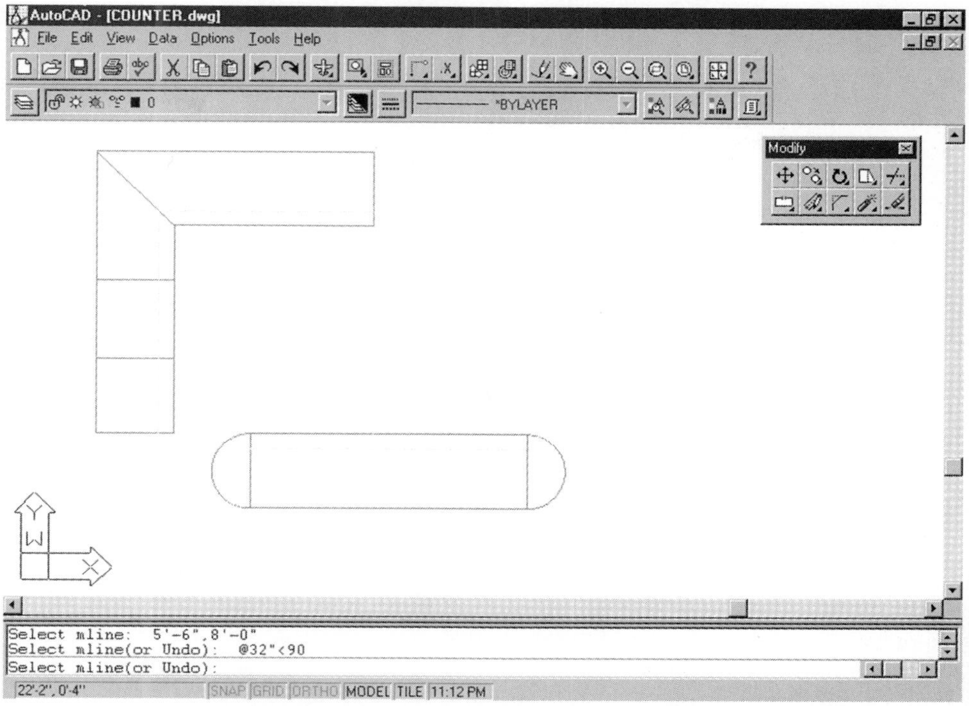

Figure 12.56
Kitchen layout with the vertices added.

Tutorial 12.7: Removing Multiline Sections

In this tutorial you will use the `Cut All` editing option to create an opening in the kitchen counter where the vertices were added in the preceding tutorial. Follow these steps:

1.  Click the Edit Multiline button on the Modify toolbar.
2. 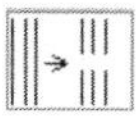 Click the Cut All image tile in the Multiline Edit Tools dialog box.
3. You will use the End Osnap to select the endpoint of the first vertex.

   `Select mline:` **`end`**

   `of` Select the endpoint of the first vertex added. Refer to Figure 12.57.
4. Use End Osnap again to select the endpoint of the second vertex.

   `Select second point:` **`end`**

   `of` Select the endpoint of the second vertex added. Refer to Figure 12.57.
5. At the `Select mline(or Undo):` prompt, press Enter to end the **cut all** command.

You have now added two vertices to the kitchen counter and created a new opening for a stove. In the next tutorial you will remove one of the original counter openings. Figure 12.58 shows the kitchen counter with the opening for the stove.

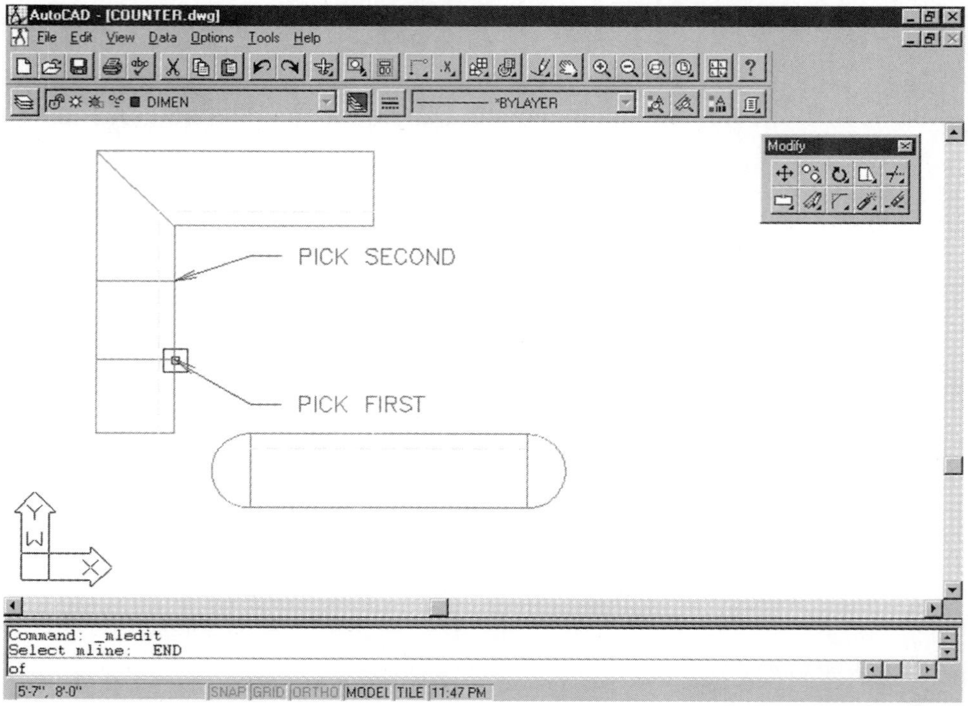

Figure 12.57
Endpoints to select for the Cut All editing command.

Figure 12.58
Kitchen counter layout with the stove opening.

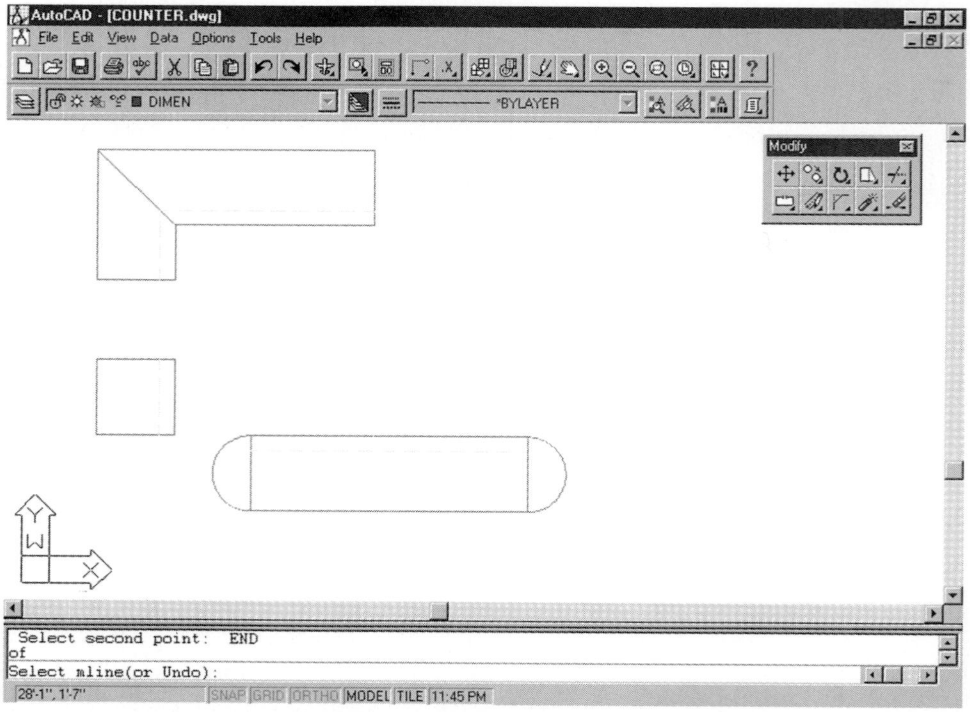

Tutorial 12.8: Making Multiline Corners

To complete the modifications to the kitchen counter you will use the Corner Joint editing command to eliminate one of the original openings in the counter. Follow these steps:

1.  Click the Edit Multiline button on the Modify toolbar.
2. 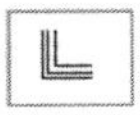 Click the Corner Joint image tile in the Multiline Edit Tools dialog box.
3. At the `Select first mline:` prompt, pick the first multiline shown in Figure 12.59.
4. At the `Select second mline:` prompt, pick the second multiline shown in Figure 12.59.
5. At the `Select first mline(or Undo):` prompt, press Enter to end the Corner Joint command.
6.  Click the Save button to save your work.

   You have now added two vertices to the kitchen counter, cut an opening for the stove, and removed one of the original openings. Figure 12.60 shows the completed kitchen layout. This concludes the tutorials on multilines.

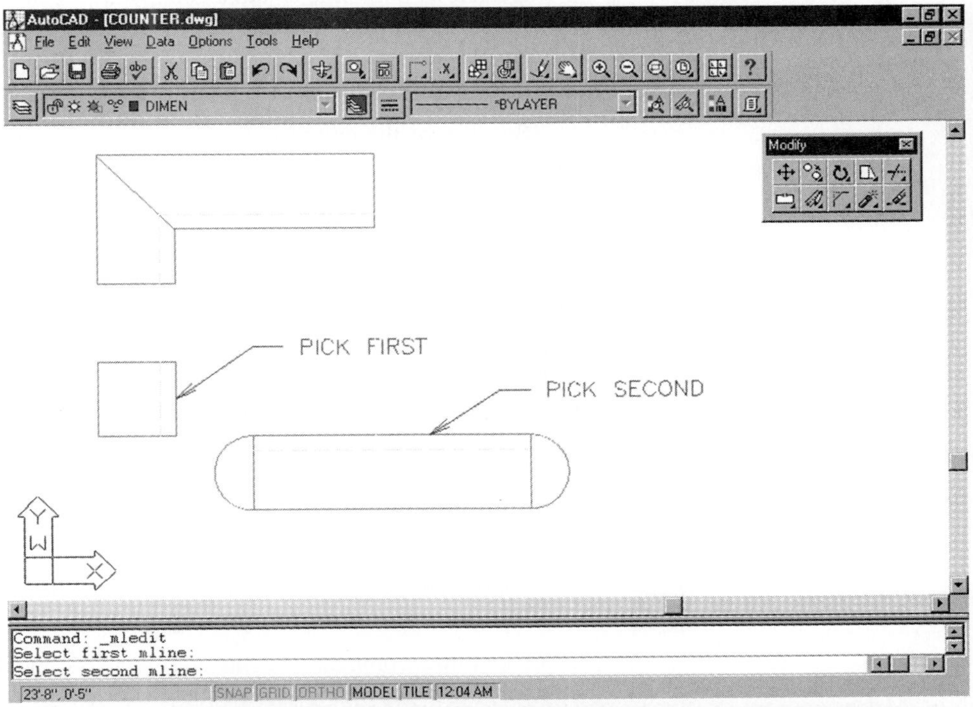

Figure 12.59
Multilines to select for the Corner Joint multiline editing command.

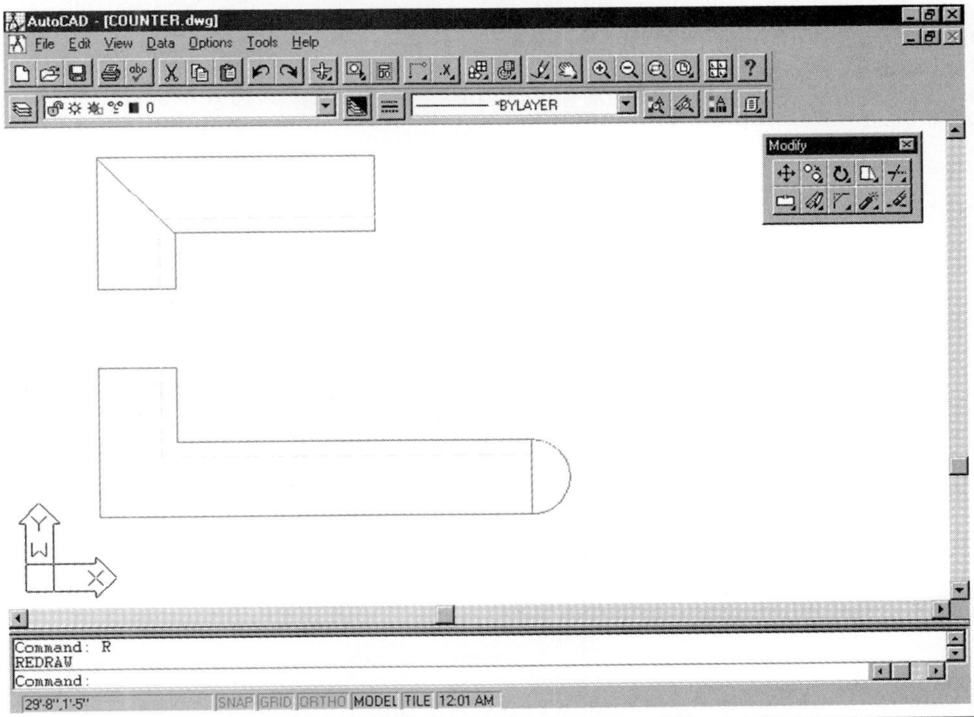

Figure 12.60
The completed kitchen counter layout.

USING POLYLINES

A polyline is a connected sequence of line and arc segments that is treated by AutoCAD as a single entity. A polyline (or **pline**) has several special features that make it more versatile than basic lines or arcs. Several features of a polyline are:

- A **pline** can have a specified width, while arcs and lines have no width.
- **pline** segments can consist of lines and arcs. **pline** segments created with one **pline** command are treated by AutoCAD as one object. Individual line and arc segments created with the **line** and **arc** commands are all individual objects.
- Polylines are very flexible and can be used to draw any shape, such as a filled circle or a donut.
- It is easy to determine the area or perimeter of a polyline.

Because of the complexity of polylines, they require their own command to edit them. You can also draw lines and arcs and later convert them into a polyline. Figure 12.61 shows several examples of polylines.

For the Professional

Polylines can be useful when drawing closed areas or when line width is required. These features, however, do require more space in the drawing database. This additional space can become a factor in large drawings. If this is a concern, polylines can be exploded, returning them to normal lines and arcs.

The following methods can be used to initiate the **pline** command:

- Choose the Polyline button from the Draw floating toolbar.
- Type `pline` at the `Command:` prompt.

The **pline** command begins the same as the **line** command. After the `From point:` is established, the Pline options are accessible.

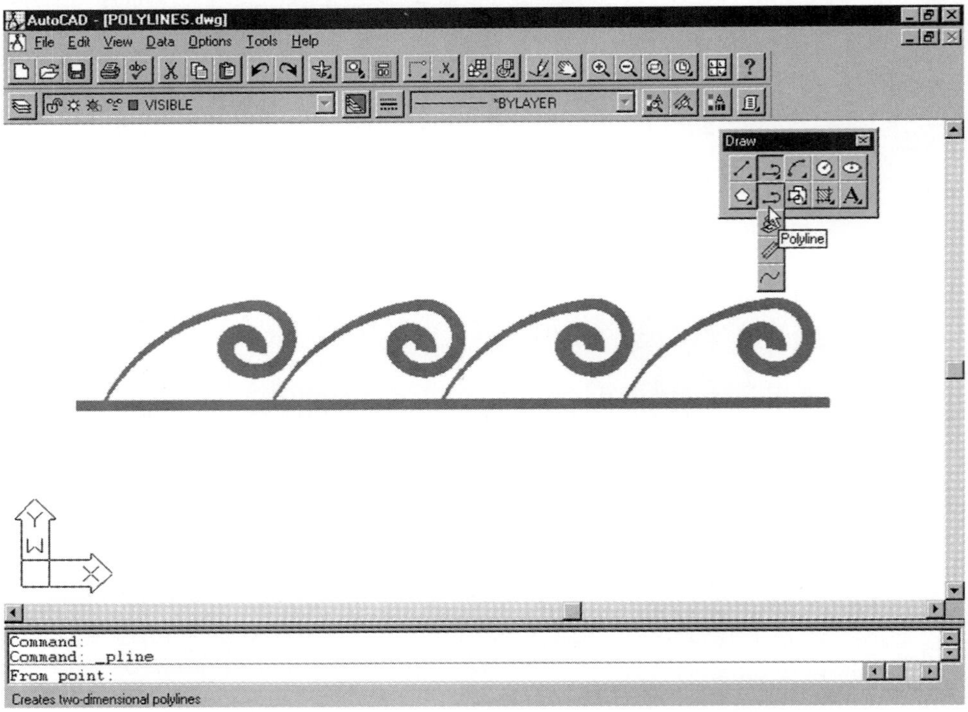

Figure 12.61
Polylines can be composed of line and arc segments, each having different widths.

```
Command: pline
From point: Select a point
Arc/Close/Halfwidth/Length/Undo/Width/<Endpoint of line>:
```

If you enter an a at this prompt, you will see a new set of options used to generate an arc.

```
Angle/Center/Close/Direction/Halfwidth/Line/Radius/Second
pt/Undo/Width/
<Endpoint of arc>:
```

Polyline Options

The **pline** command features several options that you can use when you make polylines. They are in the form of single letter options, which you enter at the command line. The next section describes options that apply to all polylines, whether created with lines, arcs, or both.

Close The Close option creates the closing segment connecting the first and last points specified with the current **pline** command.

Skill Builder

You should always use the Close option to close a polyline that ends where it began. AutoCAD draws a clean corner when the Close option is used. If you end the polygon by picking the endpoint, AutoCAD leaves a notch at the coincident start and endpoint (see Figure 12.62).

Halfwidth With Halfwidth, you specify half the total width of the polyline (default is 0). A **pline** can be tapered by specifying a different starting and ending halfwidth. The next polyline segment is drawn at double the width you entered. If you specified different values for the beginning and ending halfwidth, you will get a tapered line or arc

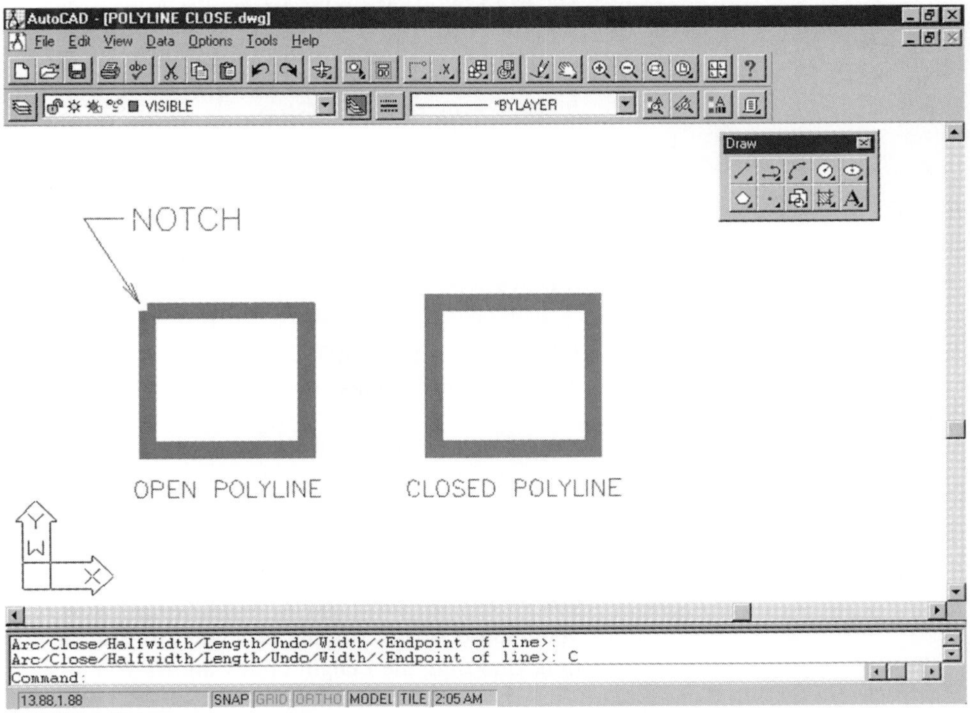

Figure 12.62
Not closing polylines that begin and end at the same point leaves a notch at that point, especially if the polyline has a width greater than 0.

segment. You can change the halfwidth value at any time while you are drawing your polyline.

For the Professional

Polylines with a width or halfwidth greater than 0 are filled in solid. The visibility of this solid is controlled by the **fillmode** system variable. If **fillmode=1** (default), solid fills are visible. If **fillmode=0,** only the outline of the polyline is visible. If you change the **fillmode** system variable, you must **regen** the drawing to see the change.

Length Using Length will draw a polyline segment at the same angle as, and connected to, the previous segment. The Length option prompts you for the length of the next straight line polyline segment. If the previous segment was an arc, Length will draw a straight segment tangent to the previous arc. The Length option does not appear when drawing polyline arc segments. To use the Length option when creating arcs, you must first return to the Line option and then select Length.

Undo Undo will remove the last segment drawn from the polyline. It can be used repeatedly to undo multiple segments, all the way back to the beginning of the polyline.

Width You can use Width to specify the starting and ending widths of a polyline. Width and Halfwidth are very similar, the difference being when Width is selected, the number you entered is not doubled. When the Width option is selected, AutoCAD prompts:

```
Starting width <0.0000>:
```

If you entered 1 for the starting width, the next prompt will read:

```
Ending width <1.0000>:
```

You can enter a different value for the ending width, allowing you to create polyline segments that taper. This can be applied to both straight line and arc segments. Figure 12.61 showed polylines with different starting and ending widths.

For the Professional

The **plinewid** system variable is used to store the default polyline width.

```
Command: plinewid
New value for PLINEWID <0.0000>: Enter a new value.
```

Polyline Arc Options

The following options are used specifically when drawing polyline arc segments.

Angle This option is used to specify the included (inside) angle of an arc segment. A positive value (default) will draw the arc in a counterclockwise manner. A negative value will indicate a clockwise direction for the arc generation.

CEnter CEnter will create a polyline arc segment by specifying the center point. Once you specify the center point, AutoCAD prompts `Angle/Length/<End point>:`. If you choose Angle, you are prompted for the included angle just as in the previous section. Choosing the Length option allows you to specify the length of the coordinates.

Direction With Direction, you can specify an explicit starting direction for the arc by specifying a point in the direction you want the arc to go. This is useful when you don't want a series of tangent arcs, such as drawing a scalloped tree line on a civil engineering plan.

Radius To draw an arc using the Radius option, first enter a radius distance or choose two points representing that distance.

Second pt This specifies a polyline arc using the three-point method similar to the three-point arc described in Unit 6, "Creating Basic Geometry."

TUTORIAL 12.9: DRAWING POLYLINES USING THE LINE AND ARC OPTIONS

In this tutorial you will draw a parking lot using a combination of polyline arc and line segments. You will begin by opening file 12DWG03. When you are finished, your parking lot should look similar to Figure 12.63.

To begin, follow these steps:

1. Select the Open button from the Standard toolbar and load 12DWG03. This will open the drawing needed to begin the parking lot.
2. Choose the Polyline button from the Draw toolbar.

   `From point:` **`440,70`**

   This is the absolute coordinate to start from. Current line width is 0.0
3. `Arc/Close/Halfwidth/Length/Undo/Width/ <Endpoint of Line>:` **`250,70`**
4. `Arc/Close/Halfwidth/Length/Undo/Width/ <Endpoint of Line>:` **`250,240`**
5. `Arc/Close/Halfwidth/Length/Undo/Width/ <Endpoint of Line>:` **`380,240`**
6. `Arc/Close/Halfwidth/Length/Undo/Width/ <Endpoint of Line>:` **`a`**
7. `Angle/CEnter/Close/Direction/Halfwidth/ Line/Radius/Second pt/Undo/Width/ <Endpoint of arc>:` **`ce`**
8. `Center point:` **`380,190`**
9. `Angle/Length/<End point>:` **`a`**
10. `Included angle:` **`-90`**
11. `Angle/CEnter/Close/Direction/Halfwidth/ Line/Radius/Second pt/Undo/Width/ <Endpoint of arc>:` **`385,140`**
12. `Angle/CEnter/Close/Direction/Halfwidth/ Line/Radius/Second pt/Undo/Width/ <Endpoint of arc>:` **`l`**

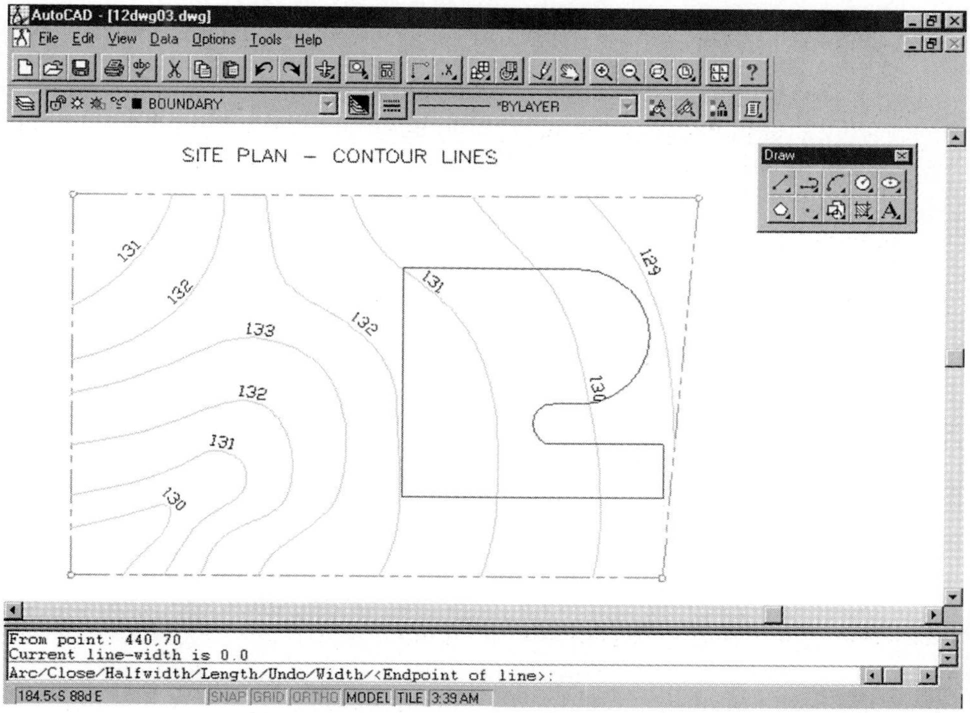

Figure 12.63
The completed parking lot drawn using **pline.**

13. Arc/Close/Halfwidth/Length/Undo/Width/ <Endpoint of Line>: **360,140**
14. Arc/Close/Halfwidth/Length/Undo/Width/ <Endpoint of Line>: **a**
15. Angle/CEnter/Close/Direction/Halfwidth/ Line/Radius/Second pt/Undo/Width/ <Endpoint of arc>: **360,110**
16. Angle/CEnter/Close/Direction/Halfwidth/ Line/Radius/Second pt/Undo/Width/ <Endpoint of arc>: **l**
17. Arc/Close/Halfwidth/Length/Undo/Width/ <Endpoint of Line>: **440,110**
18. Arc/Close/Halfwidth/Length/Undo/Width/ <Endpoint of Line>: **c**

In the upcoming tutorials you will calculate the area of a selected portion of the parking lot, and modify it using the **pedit** command.

Drawing Boundary Polylines

boundary is a powerful command that allows you to create a closed polyline or region from a number of unrelated objects. Boundary is very similar to the **bhatch** command without the hatching. The shapes can be any AutoCAD objects and can be in any configuration. One use for **boundary** is finding the area and perimeter of irregular objects that may include curves. Figure 12.64 shows a successful boundary creation.

boundary creates either a polyline or region object that forms the boundary shape. The resulting polyline may be difficult to see since it is created on top of the other objects. It is a good idea to change the layer and color before using the **boundary** command so it is easier to find the resulting polyline.

You can access the **boundary** command with either of the following methods:

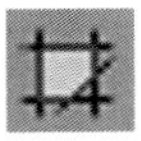

- Choose the Boundary button from the Polygon flyout menu on the Draw toolbar.
- Type `boundary` at the Command: prompt.

Either of these methods will access the Boundary Creation dialog box, shown in Figure 12.65.

To create a new boundary, select the Pick Points button on the Boundary Creation dialog box. Boundary then uses the ray-casting method to find the nearest entity, then

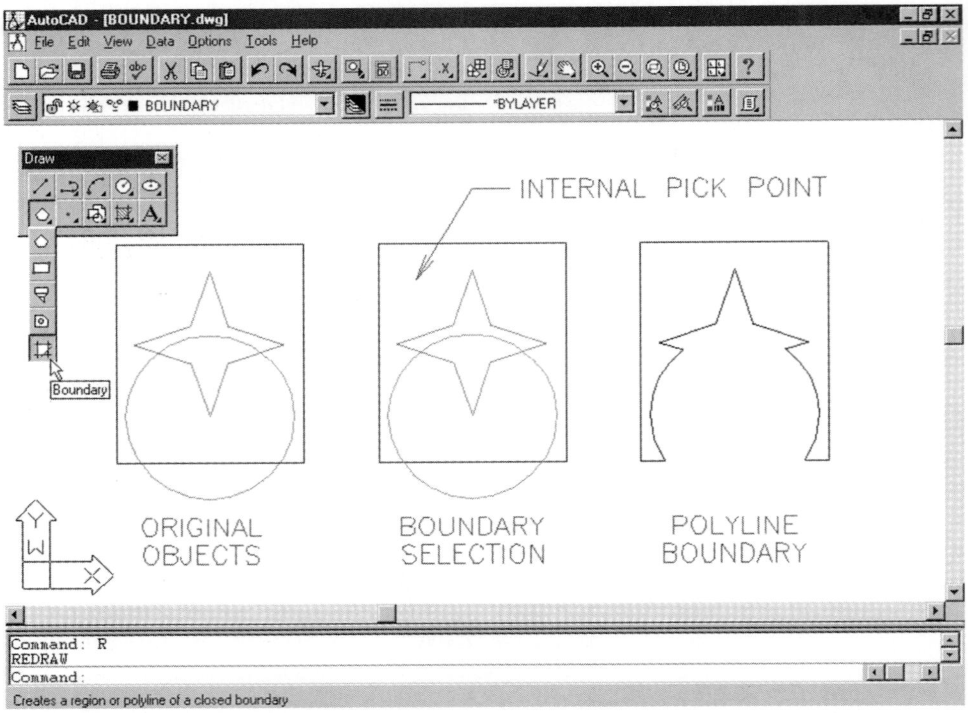

Figure 12.64
Create a finished polyline with the **boundary** *command.*

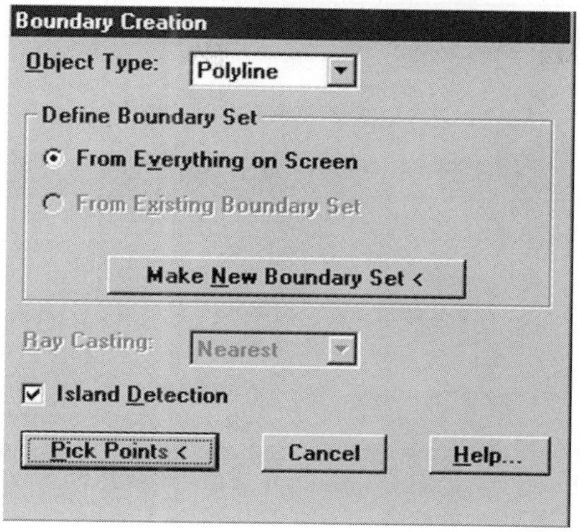

Figure 12.65
Use the Boundary Creation dialog box to define a boundary.

traces around it until the enclosed path is found. Options within the Boundary Creation dialog box are as follows:

Object Type The resulting boundary will be either a Polyline or Region. If islands are found, two or more polylines are formed, but only one Region.

Define Boundary Set By default, AutoCAD considers all visible objects on the drawing when evaluating the boundary. On large drawings this can take a considerable amount of time. To speed up the boundary identification, you can specify which objects should be considered for ray casting. If a boundary set already exists, the From Existing Boundary Set button is active.

To define a new boundary set, select the Make New Boundary Set button in the Boundary Creation dialog box. The dialog box disappears so you can pick the drawing objects you want included for composing the boundary set. After selecting all of the objects for the boundary set, press Enter to return to the Boundary Creation dialog box. Notice the From Existing Boundary Set button is now active and selected. Use your Pick Points button to select the boundary from your defined boundary selection set.

Ray Casting If objects on the screen are too close, or complex, AutoCAD may have difficulty determining the proper boundary. The ray-casting option lets you specify the direction AutoCAD looks for a boundary. Of the five available options, Nearest is most likely to provide the best results. Ray casting is available only when Island Detection is inactive. For more information on Ray Casting, review the Hatching section of Unit 7, "Annotating a Drawing with Text and Hatching."

Island Detection When Island Detection is active, AutoCAD includes interior enclosed objects in the boundary.

Pick Points After setting the appropriate options, select the Pick Points button. AutoCAD prompts `Select internal point:`. Specifying a point inside the surrounding objects starts the process of defining a boundary. After AutoCAD has found what it thinks are the edges, it highlights the sides so you can evaluate the results. You can choose multiple areas before accepting the final boundary.

AutoCAD creates a polyline of the resulting boundary that can be moved, rotated, or copied, like any other object. You can also use the polyline editing (**pedit** commands) to edit the resulting polyline.

Tutorial 12.10: Creating a Boundary

For this tutorial you will create a boundary of one section of the parking lot you created in the previous tutorial. Follow these steps:

1. Select the Layer Control button from the Object Properties toolbar and change the current layer to Boundary.
2. 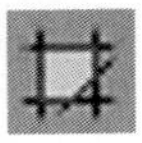 Select the Boundary button from the Polygon toolbar.
   The Boundary Creation dialog box appears.
3. Select the Pick Points button in the Boundary Creation dialog box.
4. `Select internal point`: Select a point in the left side of the parking lot. See Figure 12.66.
5. After selecting the internal point, AutoCAD responds:

```
Analyzing the selected data…
Analyzing internal islands…
Select internal point: Press Enter to end
the boundary definition.
Boundary created 1 polyline
```

6. Select the Layer Control button from the Object Properties toolbar and turn off all layers except Boundary.

You should see the resulting polyline created with the **boundary** command as shown in Figure 12.67.

You can now use the **area** command to calculate the area and perimeter of that section of the parking lot. In the next tutorial you will modify the parking lot using the **pedit** commands.

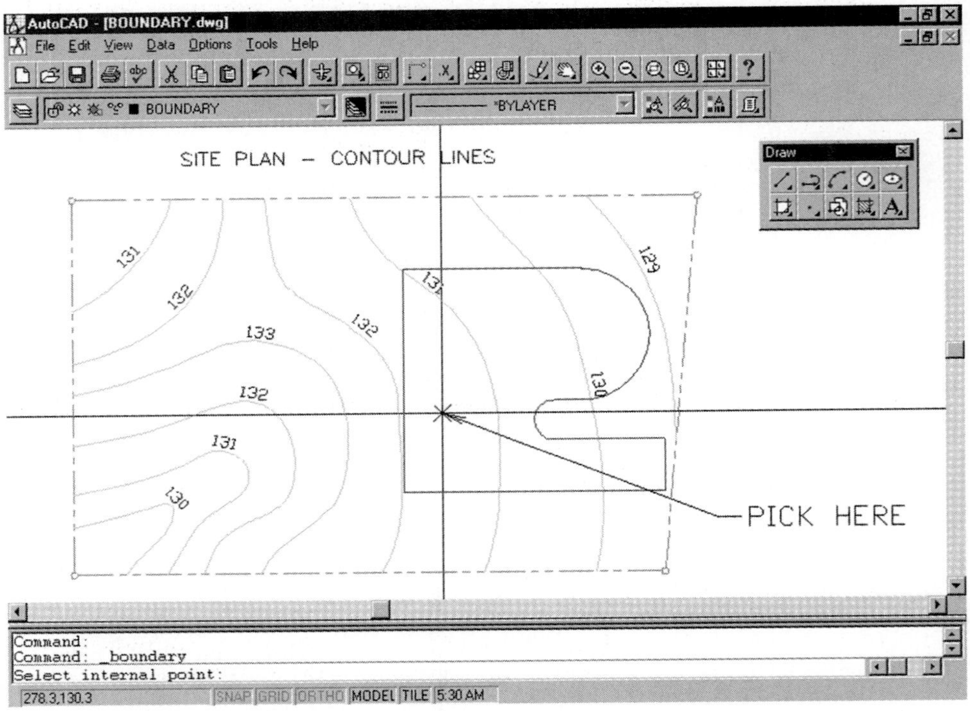

Figure 12.66
Selecting a point to define the boundary of the left side of the parking lot.

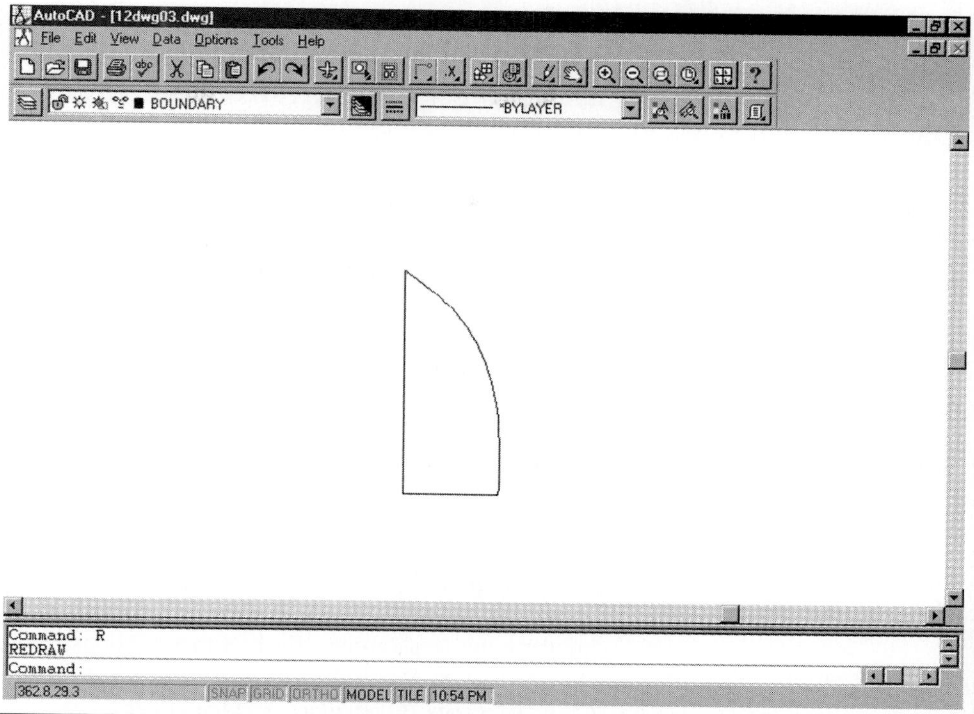

Figure 12.67
The resulting polyline created with the Boundary command.

Editing Polylines

While basic editing commands such as **stretch, copy** and **move** can be used with polylines, they don't give you access to a polyline's unique features. AutoCAD offers the **pedit** command, where you can fine-tune a polyline down to the vertex level. You can use **pedit** to do the following:

- Convert AutoCAD lines and arcs to polylines.
- Open a closed polyline, or close an open polyline.
- Join lines, arcs, or other polylines to the polyline you are editing.
- Change a polyline's width.
- Move, add, or remove vertices.
- Add or remove curves.

Skill Builder

Drawing, and especially editing, polylines can become very involved. An alternative to drawing a polyline would be to create the desired shape normally using **line, arc, circle, trim,** etc., then converting it into a polyline with the **pedit** command. An alternative to editing a polyline would be to break the polyline down into individual objects with the **explode** command.

You can access the **pedit** command by either of the following methods:

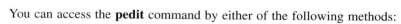

- Select the Edit Polyline button from the Modify toolbar.
- Type **pedit** at the `Command:` prompt.

After starting the **pedit** command, AutoCAD prompts you to `Select polyline:`.

You can pick any polyline, line, or arc. If you pick a polyline, AutoCAD displays the following Pedit options:

```
Open/Join/Width/Edit vertex/Fit/Spline/Decurve/Ltype gen/Undo/eXit
<X>:
```

SKILL BUILDER

If you start the **pedit** command and pick a line or arc instead of a polyline, AutoCAD prompts:

```
Object selected is not a polyline.
Do you want to turn it into one? <Y>
```

If you accept the default (Yes), AutoCAD converts the selected line or arc into a polyline then displays the **pedit** options.

The **pedit** options include adding sections to a polyline, opening or closing them, giving the polyline a new width, fitting a curve through the polyline's vertices, or adjusting the polyline's vertices. Each of these options is discussed in the following sections.

CLOSING OR OPENING A POLYLINE (**pedit** CLOSE AND OPEN)

Using the Close option will connect the last segment created with the first segment of an existing open polygon. An "open" polygon is defined as one that wasn't closed with the **pline** command's Close option when it was created. The closed polyline becomes one continuous object having no start or endpoint, as opposed to one closed by picking points. A closed polyline reacts differently to the Spline option, and to some other commands such as Fillet.

Similarly, you can open a closed polygon with the Open option. Using the Open option will delete the closing segment of the polygon.

JOINING POLYLINES (**pedit** JOIN)

The Join option will join, or connect, other polylines, lines, and arcs to an existing polyline. The objects that you want to join to the polyline must have exact matching endpoints before they can be joined. The inability to join objects to an existing polyline is usually because they have different endpoints. They may appear to be the same on-screen, but in reality they are not. Another common problem with objects failing to join is because they are at a different elevation (Z) levels.

SETTING POLYLINE WIDTH (**pedit** WIDTH)

Width allows you to specify a constant width to the entire polyline. You can't use this option to make tapering segments or assign varying widths to different parts of the polygon. If you want to use **pedit** to create tapers or assign varying widths, use the Width option under Edit Vertex discussed later in this unit.

CURVING AND DECURVING POLYLINES

In addition to creating polylines with line and curve segments, you can fit mathematically calculated curves across an entire polygon. You can also remove curves and arcs. Figure 12.68 compares a regular straight polygon with the three types of curved polygons you can create.

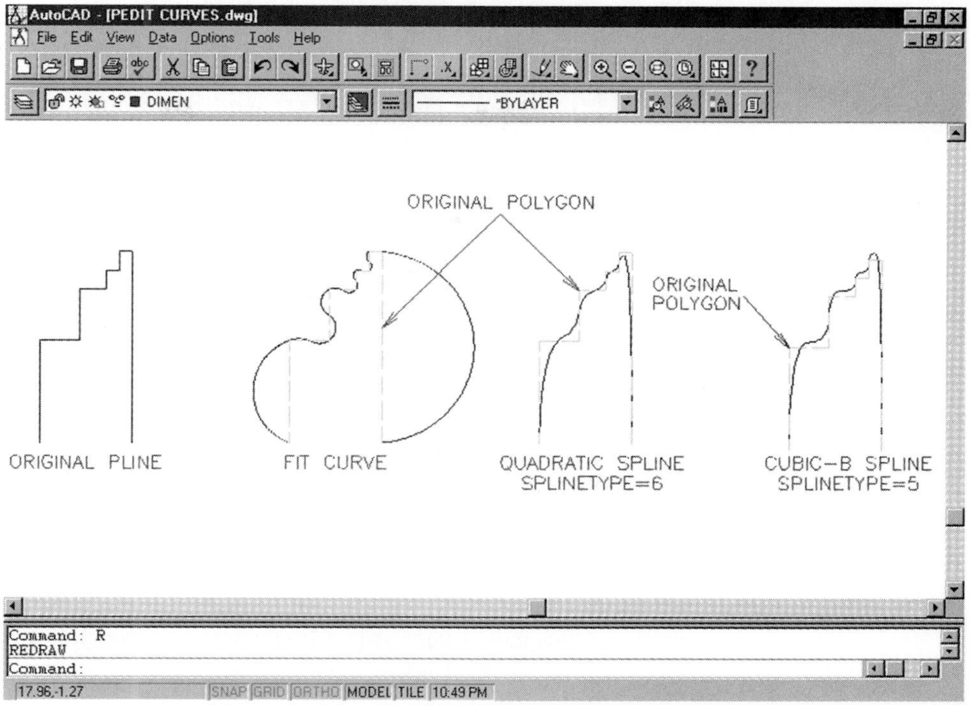

Figure 12.68
The four types of polylines are uncurved, fit curve, quadratic spline, and cubic-b spline.

Fitting a Curve (pedit Fit) The **pedit** Fit option converts the polyline from straight line segments to arcs. At each vertex of the polyline, Fit creates a new arc segment that is tangent, at its start point, to the previous arc (except the first point, since there is no previous arc to be tangent to). The arc's endpoint is then tangent to the next vertex.

The curve consists of two arcs for each pair of vertices. The resulting curve passes through all vertices in the original polyline (Figure 12.68).

Unfitting a Curve (pedit Decurve) Using Decurve will remove all curves from a polyline. This includes curves created with **pline's** arc option as well as those resulting from **pedit's** Fit and Spline options. The polyline is returned to its original straight line segments state.

Creating a Spline Curve (pedit Spline) The history of spline curves can be traced back hundreds of years to ancient shipbuilders. As ship design became more complex, they needed a method to generate complex curves with wood. To create these complex curves, they pounded pegs into the ground and threaded thin strips of wood around them to generate the required complex curves. By altering the placement of the pegs they could fine-tune their design.

This practice eventually found its way into mathematical use. The pegs came to be called control points, which were used to define the curve, also known as a Spline curve. As with many other mathematical principles, this practice was also adapted for use in computer modeling.

Using the **pedit** Spline option, AutoCAD can generate splines from existing polylines, using the vertices of the original, uncurved polyline as the curve's control points. The location of these vertices and their relationship to each other define the path of the resulting spline curve. The appearance and generation of splines can be adjusted by changing the values of three AutoCAD system variables: **splinesegs, splframe,** and **splinetype.** To change the values of these variables, type their names at the `Command:` prompt. A detailed explanation of these variables is as follows:

- **spinesegs.** This variable controls the number of line segments created when the Spline option is used. This value must be set before creating the spline. A higher value means more segments and a better approximation of the spline, but it also slows down AutoCAD and increases the size of the drawing file. The default value is 8. Figure 12.69 shows two different values for the **splineseg** variable—2 and 20.
- **splframe.** SPLFRAME is used to display the spline frame (the original polyline) on-screen. The default value for SPLFRAME is 0, meaning the frame is not displayed. By changing SPLFRAME to 1 and regenerating the drawing, you can see the original polyline displayed along with the resulting spline. If you edit the original polyline with **stretch** or grips, the spline automatically adjusts to the new frame position. You can also access **splframe** through Options, Display, Spline Frame. Figure 12.68 shows the SPLINEFRAME value set to 1 in the resulting splines.
- **splinetype.** This variable controls the type of spline generated. The default value of 6 generates a cubic b-spline. If you set SPLINETYPE to 5, a quadratic b-spline is generated. SPLINETYPE accepts only these two values, 5 or 6. The variable must be set before cerating the spline. The practical difference of these settings is that the cubic b-spline is smoother, but the quadratic b-spline more closely follows the frame. Figure 12.69 shows the difference between the quadratic b-spline and the cubic b-spline.

Spline Linetype Generation (**pedit** Ltype gen)

In Unit 5, "Understanding Layers and Linetypes," you learned how to create, load, and assign linetypes to different objects in your drawing. You can also assign linetypes to polylines. By default, when a linetype is assigned to a polyline, the linetype segments start and stop at each vertex as if each polyline segment was an individual line segment. The Ltype gen option lets you change the default setting by applying the linetype to the polyline as a whole rather than to its individual segments. This is especially effective on splined polylines. When you choose the Ltype gen option, AutoCAD displays the prompt:

```
Full PLINE linetype ON/OFF <Off>:
```

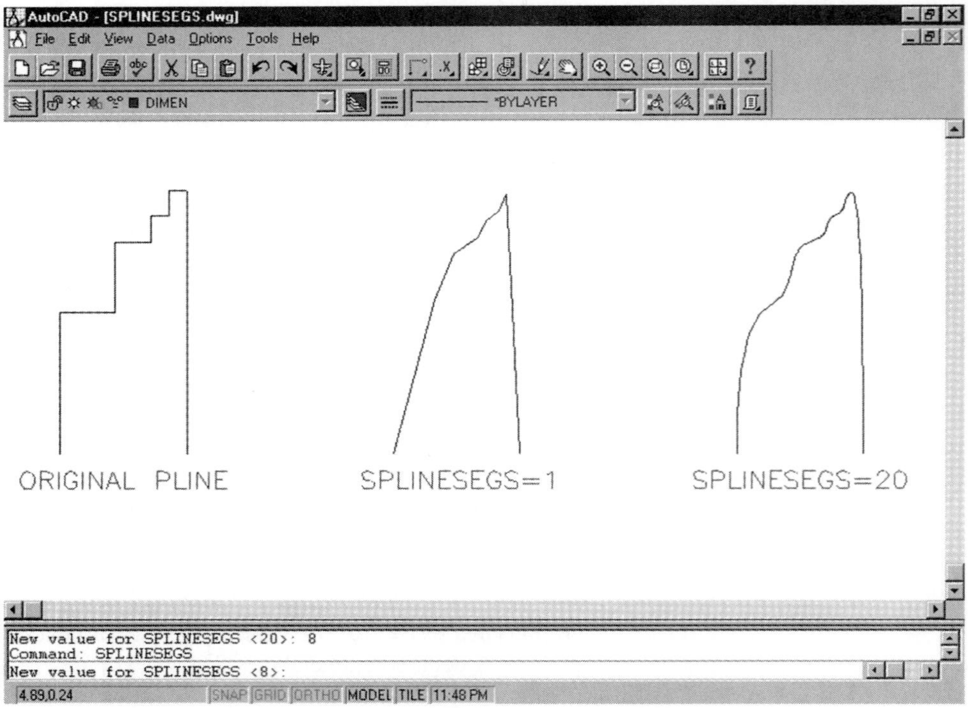

Figure 12.69
A higher **splinesegs** *value means a smoother spline curve, but decreases system performance and increases file size.*

Enter on to generate the linetype over the entire polygon. Using the Ltype gen option retroactively changes polylines that have already been drawn. AutoCAD also offers the **plinegen** system variable that lets you control how new, noncontinuous linetypes are drawn.

- **plinegen.** You can set the **plinegen** system variable by:
  - Select Options, Linetypes, Linetype Generation.
  - Type plinegen at the Command: prompt.

  A setting of 1 (or a check on Linetype Generation in the pull-down menu) creates a consistent linetype pattern for all new polylines. It disregards vertices in the polyline when applying the linetype, like the Ltype gen ON setting. Unlike Ltype gen, **plinegen** is not retroactive; it will only affect new polylines.

Changing the Last **pedit** (**pedit Undo**)

Undo will reverse the most recent **pedit** option. You can undo your edits to the polyline all the way back to when you invoked the **pedit** command, one step at a time.

Editing Polyline Vertices (**pedit** Edit Vertices)

All of the **pedit** options discussed thus far apply to the entire polyline. You can also edit polylines on a vertex-by-vertex basis and apply edits to individual parts of the polygon. When you select the Edit Vertex option from the **pedit** options list, a submenu is displayed listing another series of editing options:

```
Next/Previous/Break/Insert/Move/Regen/Straighten/Tangent/Width/
eXit <N>:
```

After accessing the Edit vertex submenu, you will notice a small X located on the first vertex of the polygon (see Figure 12.70). By pressing the Enter key you can move the vertex on the polyline and begin editing the polyline anywhere along its length. The rest of this unit discusses the vertex editing options.

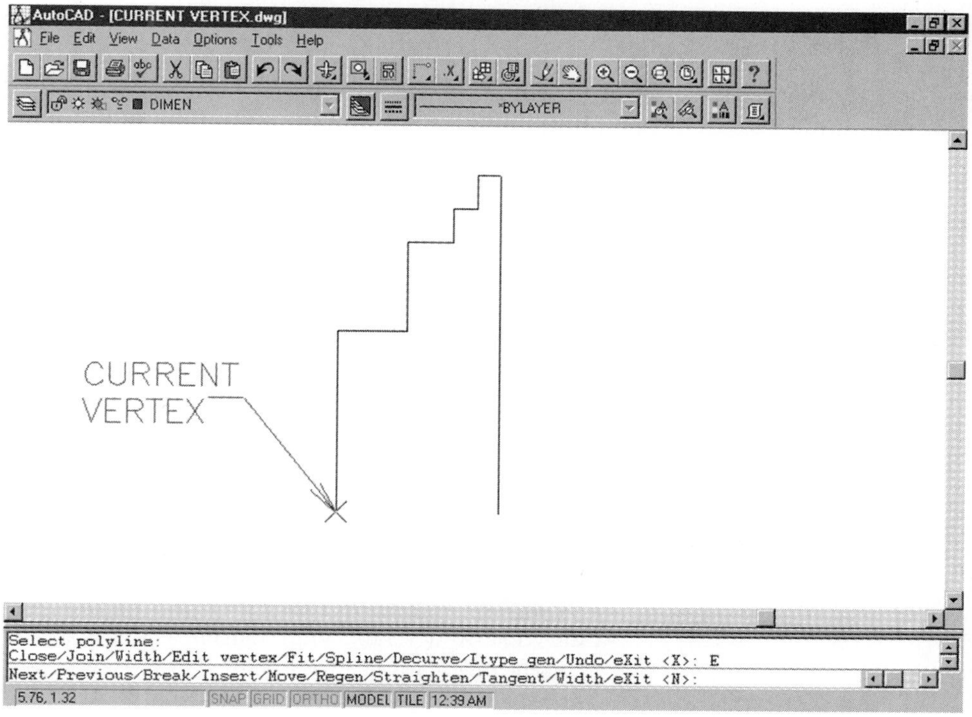

Figure 12.70
Displaying the current vertex, which appears when you access the Edit vertex submenu.

Moving the Place Marker (Next and Previous) As shown in the preceding section, you can move along the polyline by pressing Enter, because the Next option is the default. If you want to go back in the other direction, select the Previous option. Remember you just have to type `p`, not the entire word. When you type `n` or `p`, AutoCAD makes that option the default.

Breaking a Polyline at a Vertex (Break) With the Break option you have two choices:

- `Single Vertex`. You can break the polyline at a single vertex, leaving all the original segments of the polyline intact. In effect, you will end up with two unconnected polylines, starting from the vertex where you began the break.
- `Two Vertices`. This option removes one or more segments of the polyline between the marked vertex and the next one selected by the Next or Previous option.

To Break a polyline, start the **pedit** command, pick a polyline, choose Edit Vertex, and use the Next or Previous options to move to the vertex where you want to start the break. AutoCAD will display the following prompt:

```
Next/Previous/Go/eXit<N>:
```

To break the polygon at the current vertex selected, choose Go.

To break the polyline between two vertices (and remove the segments between them), enter `n` or `p` to move to another vertex. Enter `g` to remove all of the segments between the two vertices. You can't break a polyline at its start or endpoints.

Moving a Vertex (Move) Move allows you to relocate a polyline vertex. Enter `n` or `p` to get to the vertex you want to move, then choose the Move option. AutoCAD prompts:

```
Enter new location:
```

Pick the new location for the vertex, and it is moved there. Any segments connected to the moved vertex are adjusted accordingly.

Adding Vertices (Insert) With Insert, you can insert a new vertex at any location on the polyline after the vertex that is marked with the `X`. First move to a vertex before the location you want to add one. Entering `I` will choose the Insert option and display the following prompt:

```
Enter location of new vertex:
```

Pick a point or use a polar, relative, or absolute point selection to specify the location of the new vertex.

Removing Vertices (Straighten) Used to straighten the polyline segments between two vertices. Use `n` or `p` to move the `X` marker to the vertex that marks the beginning of the segment you want to straighten. Enter `s` to begin the straighten option and display the following prompt:

```
Next/Previous/Go/eXit <N>:
```

Use Next or Previous to move to the vertex that marks the end of the segment you want to straighten, and select Go. AutoCAD will remove all vertices that are between the beginning and ending vertices and draw a single straight segment.

Changing Tangency (Tangent) Tangent allows you to add an angle, or tangent direction, to a vertex. With Tangent you can specify the direction of tangency for the current vertex for use with **pedit** Fit option. The tangent angle has no effect on spline-fit curves.

Changing Segment Width (Width) The Width option can change the width of the polyline segment immediately following the marked vertex. Use Next or Previous to move to the vertex that begins the segment to which you want to assign width. AutoCAD asks for a starting width and an ending width, just like when you applied widths with the **pline** command.

After specifying the new widths, the polyline is not updated immediately showing the new widths. You must either exit the Edit vertex mode or use the Edit vertex Regen option to display your new widths.

Redrawing a Polyline (Regen) Using Regen will update the polyline on screen, restoring sections of the polyline that appear to be missing. It can also be used to see new widths that you've applied to the polyline with the Edit Vertex - Width option. The Regen option regenerates only the polyline, not the entire drawing.

Leaving Edit Vertex and Pedit (eXit) After you've completed editing your polyline's vertices, you need to exit from the Edit vertices mode. Choosing the eXit option takes you back to the **pedit** options. From there, the **pedit** eXit option (the command's default) ends the **pedit** command.

Tutorial 12.11: Modifying a Polyline's Vertices

In this tutorial you will modify the parking lot you created during the earlier tutorials in this section.

1. Select the Layer Control button from the Object Properties toolbar and turn on all layers. Also, turn off the Boundary layer.
   You should see the parking lot you created in an earlier tutorial as shown in Figure 12.63.
2.  Choose the Edit Polyline button on the Modify toobar.

   `Select polyline:` Select the parking lot.
3. Next you will enter the Edit Vertex mode and modify the polyline.

   `Open/Join/Width/Edit vertex/Fit/Spline/`
   `Decurve/Ltype gen/Undo/eXit <X>:` **e**
4. Press the Enter key three times until the `X` marking the current vertex is at "Point 1" as shown in Figure 12.71.
5. You are going to straighten the curved section in the parking lot using the Straighten option and picking vertices on each side of the arc. Follow these prompts:

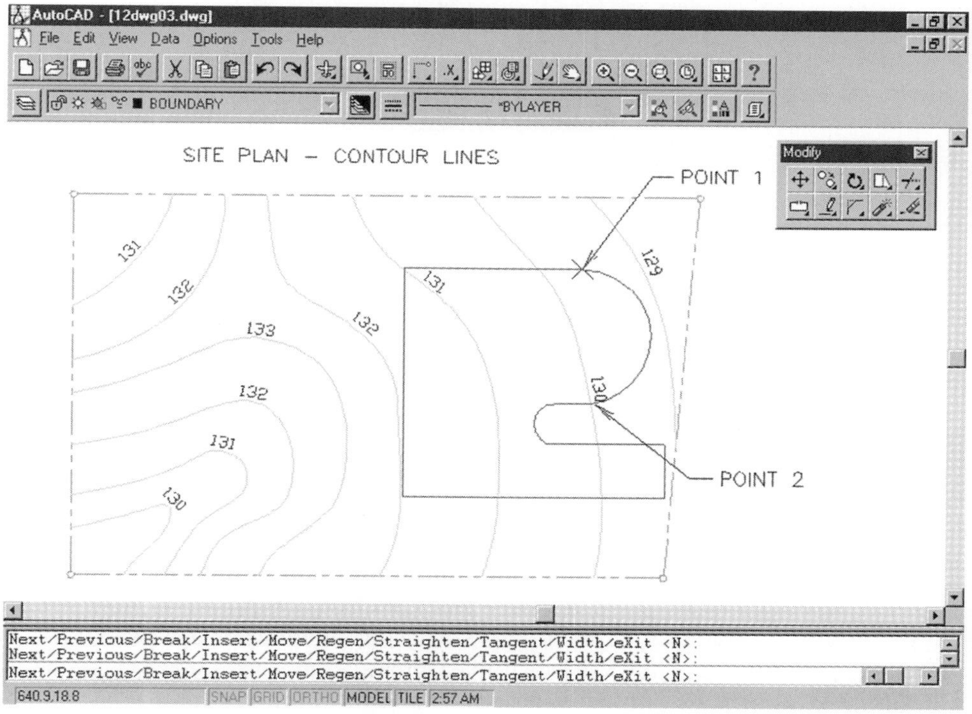

Figure 12.71
Vertex locations in preparation for straightening out the arc section of the parking lot.

6. `Next/Previous/Break/Insert/Move/Regen/Straighten/Tangent/Width/eXit <N>:` **s**
7. `Next/Previous/Go/Exit <N>:` Press Enter twice until the current vertex is at "Point 2" as shown in Figure 12.71.
8. Activate the Straighten option by selecting Go.

   `Next/Previous/Go/eXit <N>:` **G**

9. To complete the parking lot you will move the two Overtices located at Point 1 and Point 2.

   `Next/Previous/Break/Insert/Move/Regen/Straighten/Tangent/Width/eXit <N>:` **m**
   `Enter new location:` **440,240**

10. Move the current vertex to Point 2 by pressing the Enter key once, and re-enter the Move option.

    `Next/Previous/Break/Insert/Move/Regen/Straighten/Tangent/Width/eXit <N>:` Press Enter to move the current vertex to Point 2.
    `Next/Previous/Break/Insert/Move/Regen/Straighten/Tangent/Width/eXit <N>:` **m**
    `Enter new location:` **440,140**

11. Enter `X` to exit the Edit Vertex mode.
12. `Next/Previous/Break/Insert/Move/Regen/Straighten/Tangent/Width/eXit <N>: x`
13.  Press Enter at the **pedit** prompt to exit. Choose the Save button on the Standard toolbar to save your work.

    You have now completed the parking lot, and your drawing should look like Figure 12.72.

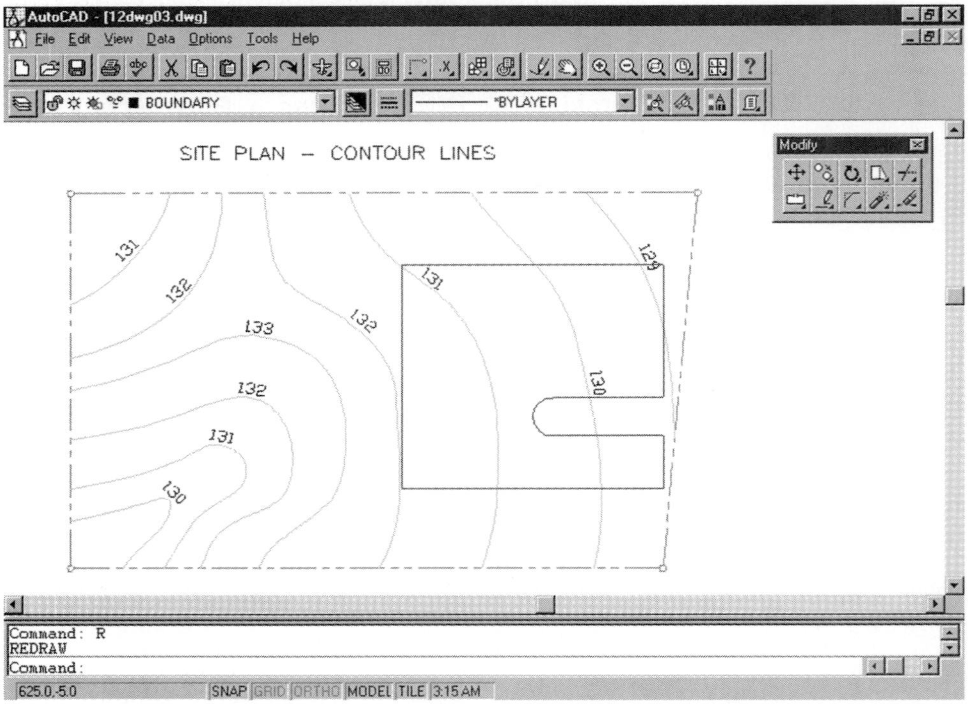

Figure 12.72
The completed parking lot.

SUMMARY

Although the **point** command can be used by itself to locate permanent points on a drawing, it is normally used with the **divide** and **measure** commands. Always set the point size and style in the Point Style dialog box before using either the **divide** or **measure** command.

You can also use the **divide** and **measure** commands to insert groups of objects (blocks). Both commands give you the option of aligning the inserted objects with the object. If used properly, these commands can speed up drawing time immensely.

AutoCAD also offers several other commands for creating specific types of objects that can be time-consuming or difficult to draw. The **ellipse** command makes ellipse creation simple, while the **donut** command provides an excellent method for creating rings and solid-filled circles. Additionally, you can use the **sketch** command to create freehand lines on your drawing.

If you need to create construction lines on a drawing, the **xline** and **ray** commands are excellent choices. The **xline** command creates an infinite construction line, while a **ray** has a finite starting point and extends to infinity. They can be edited just like any other normal AutoCAD object.

Many drafting and design disciplines have the need to create multiple lines parallel to one another. In manual drafting this can be a time-consuming process. Fortunately AutoCAD offers a series of commands specifically designed for this task. The **mlstyle** command allows you to create up to 16 parallel elements, each with its own color and linetype. Once you have designed the style of your multiline, use the **mline** to begin drawing them. Because of their special nature, multilines have their own set of editing tools. To edit multilines, AutoCAD uses the **mledit** command.

Polylines are one of AutoCAD's most versatile objects. A polyline is a single object composed of any number of connected straight (line) and curved (arc) segments. You can also convert existing lines and arcs to polylines. Polylines are edited with several special options, accessed with the **pedit** command.

All of the commands discussed in this unit were designed to increase your productivity and efficiency as a draftsperson. The **boundary** command, for example, makes the process of calculating area and perimeter of complex objects simple. Mastering the commands in this unit will not only make you a better draftsperson, but will make you a highly valued employee as well.

REVIEW

1. Give two examples of when it would be beneficial to set point size relative to screen size as opposed to setting it to an absolute unit.
2. Draw two sample objects and illustrate the difference between the Divide and Measure commands.
3. Explain the relationship between **pdmode** and **pdsize** to the Divide and Measure commands.
4. List the command and procedure you would use to create a completely filled in circle.
5. Create a simple ellipse and label the center point, major axis, and minor axis.
6. Clarify how you would use infinite lines when constructing geometry.
7. Explain how the **sketch** command creates sketched objects and how the record increment affects its file size and appearance.
8. List five examples of when it would be advantageous to use multilines.
9. Define polyline and why AutoCAD creates certain objects using polylines.
10. If you have a polyline object, spell out two different methods you could use to edit the object and the advantages and disadvantages of each.

EXERCISE 12

12-1. Create the Vegetable Garden shown in Figure 12.73 using the following information:

1. Create a multiline style to border the beds. Make the beds 16′ × 4′.
2. Create a Donut to represent the pumpkins. Leave a 3-inch space between each pumpkin.
3. Define a point style to represent the carrots, placing 9 evenly spaced points in the carrot bed.
4. Use the Ellipse and Pline commands to create the symbols at the top of each bed.
5. Sketch a pumpkin and carrot in the appropriate symbols.

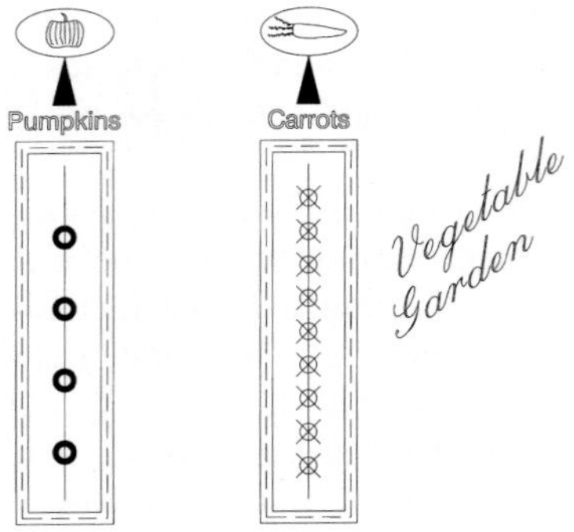

Figure 12.73
The completed vegetable garden.

UNIT

13 DIMENSIONING A DRAWING

OVERVIEW

Dimensioning a drawing is perhaps the most important step in creating a technical drawing. AutoCAD provides numerous commands and variables to assist in the creation of these dimensions. New AutoCAD users typically find dimensioning a drawing a very intimidating process. But with practice and knowledge of dimensioning rules, AutoCAD can assist in creating perfect and accurate dimensions that can even be fun once you understand the commands.

OBJECTIVES

- Understand dimensions and their use.
- Understand the importance of associative dimensioning.
- Create and use dimension styles and style families.
- Modify existing dimensions.
- Create oblique dimensions.
- Create leaders.

INTRODUCTION

As you have progressed through this book, you have seen many drawings and tutorials that included dimensions. These dimensions display measurement information about the object that is being described in the drawing. A sample of a drawing with dimensions can be found in Figure 13.1. Notice that there are enough dimensions to accurately describe the object.

While it is important to have dimensions to assist you in creating drawings, it is even more important that you have dimensions included on the drawing, especially if you are going to manufacture the part or construct the building described on the drawing. If dimensions are not accurate or if they are not placed appropriately, it will be very difficult to read and obtain the information needed from the drawing.

This unit will not only teach you the commands used in AutoCAD to create dimensions, but it will also give you a brief introduction to dimensions themselves. While placement of dimensions is very important, it is beyond the scope of this book to describe how to properly dimension a drawing. Depending on the discipline of study, there may be certain standards that have to be adhered to when locating dimensions on a drawing. Two of these standards, ANSI and AIA, will be discussed. It is important that you learn any standards necessary and apply them to the AutoCAD dimensioning commands.

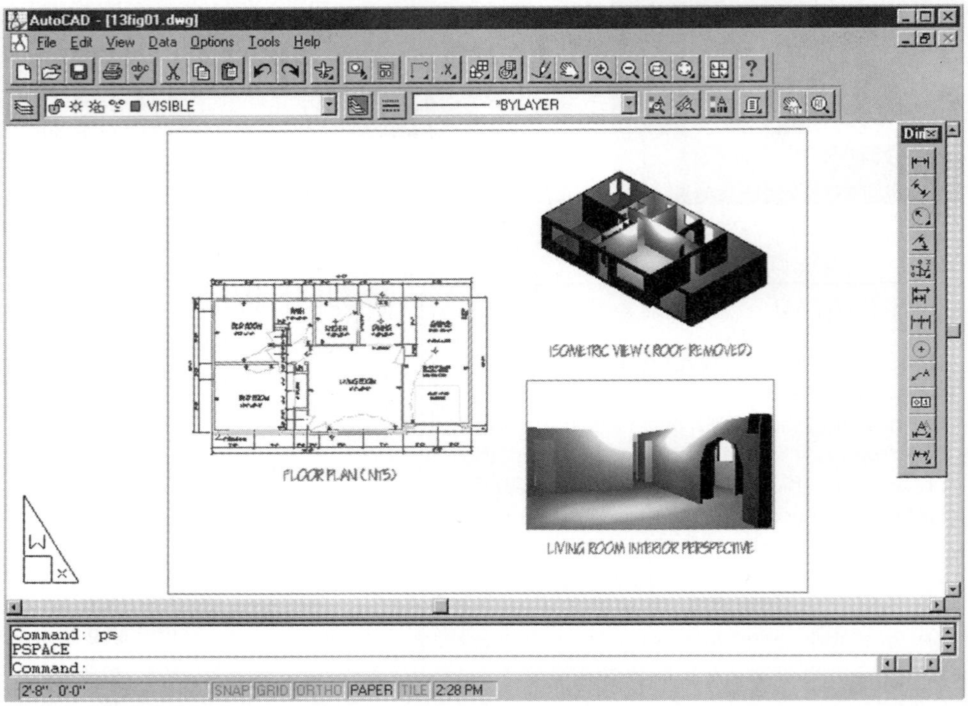

Figure 13.1
Dimensions allow the reader to visualize the size of an object.

OUTLINE

Dimensioning Basics and Dimensioning with Precision
Tutorial 13.1: Creating a Dimension Style and Changing the Dimension Geometry
Tutorial 13.2: Changing the Dimension Line Format
Tutorial 13.3: Changing the Dimension Text Format
Linear and Radial Dimensioning
Tutorial 13.4: Creating Linear Dimensions
Tutorial 13.5: Creating Aligned Dimensions
Tutorial 13.6: Adding Continued and Baseline Dimensions
Tutorial 13.7: Adding Radius and Diameter Dimensions
Angular Dimensioning
Editing Dimensions
Tutorial 13.8: Adding Angular Dimensions
Tutorial 13.9: Modifying Dimensions
Additional Dimensioning Features
Tutorial 13.10: Adding Leaders
Summary
Review
Exercises

DIMENSIONING BASICS AND DIMENSIONING WITH PRECISION

As you begin to create dimensions you will find that they are only as accurate as the drawing you create. If you need a precision of .0001, for example, you must create the object with the same precision before AutoCAD can dimension it accurately. Don't naturally assume that because AutoCAD placed a "wrong" dimension, that it is the software's fault. Operator/Drafter error is probably the culprit. You will also learn how to modify the dimension and its appearance. Avoid just modifying the dimension text. Always correct the object, not the dimension itself. If you attempt to change only the dimension, you will find that your other dimensions will not add up and you will begin a chain reaction that will take you longer to fix than if you had just made the simple correction to the objects themselves.

The creation of the dimension is based on one very important issue, the location of the dimension endpoints. "Eyeballing" the dimensions is not accurate enough. Get into the habit of using Object Snaps with the placement of all dimension start and endpoints. When you begin dimensioning it is often useful to use the **ddosnap** command to select a running Object Snap. Using Object Snaps will ensure that the selection you make is accurate and precise in relation to the object you are dimensioning.

As mentioned in the Introduction, dimensioning can be a very frustrating endeavor for the new student. AutoCAD Release 13 has overcome many of the shortcomings of previous versions. Dimensioning has become much more intuitive. In previous versions, the CAD operator had to learn many cryptic dimension variables. The `Command:` prompt was the primary means by which to modify these dimensioning variables. AutoCAD now includes dialog boxes with image tiles that describe the portions of the dimensions that are being affected by the changes, and which are made in the same dialog box. Toolbars also allow dimensions to be selected, placed, and modified quickly.

Previous versions of AutoCAD required the user to change the `Command:` prompt to a `Dim:` prompt. With AutoCAD Release 13, you no longer need to access this `Dim:` prompt to create dimensions. New `Command:` prompt commands and toolbars have been added to save the user a few more steps when dimensioning a drawing. This unit will mention the `Dim:` prompt occasionally, but it will focus on the new dimensioning commands to make you more productive. AutoCAD even ensures that all dimension commands are located in a single toolbar, called the Dimensioning toolbar. Now, more than ever, is the time to learn how to properly use and apply AutoCAD dimensions. Before you begin creating dimensions, let's review the elements that comprise a dimension.

Parts of a Dimension

In order to make changes to the different features that comprise dimension and affect its appearance, it is important that you know the associated terminology. Figure 13.2 displays the various components that make up a dimension. After reviewing the figure, the rest of this section will explain each feature's use.

- **Dimension Text.** Indicates the measurement of the distance specified by the dimension line. The dimension text can be placed on top of the dimension line or within the dimension line.
- **Dimension Line.** Displays the direction and distance of the measurement.
- **Extension Line.** Extends from the measurement to the dimension line to assist in guiding the eye to the proper dimension.
- **Terminator.** Terminates the dimension line where it intersects with the extension line. Used to assist in the visual display of the dimension. A terminator can be an arrow, tick mark, dot, or custom-made object.
- **Leader.** Used to point to a feature that requires further annotation beyond dimensioning. It is composed of an extension line and a terminator, typically an arrow.
- **Center Lines.** The intersection of the horizontal and vertical line represents the center of a circle or arc.

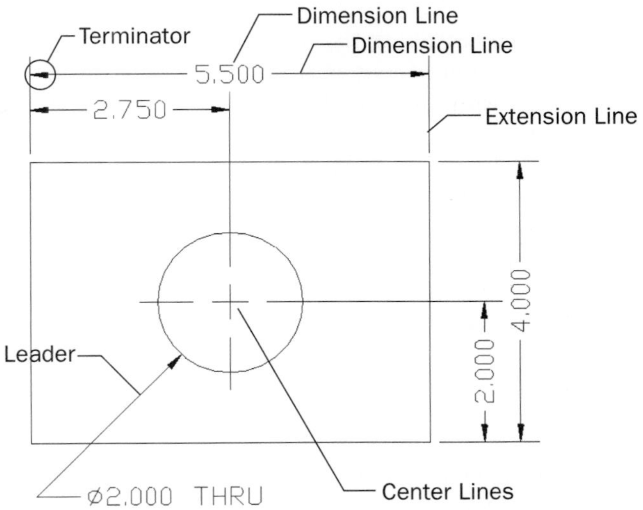

Figure 13.2
The parts of a dimension.

You can modify the sizes of these features by using Dimensioning System Variables. These variables can be modified two ways: by using the variables and the `Command:` prompt, or more efficiently by using the Dimension Styles dialog box. Each of these methods will be discussed later in this unit.

Standards Organizations

So just what size do you create a terminator or dimension text? How far does the dimension line extend away from the object it is dimensioning? Those answers can be found from Standards Organizations. Two popular American associations—the American National Standards Institute (ANSI) and the American Institute of Architects (AIA)—provide guidance on how dimensions are to be used and represented. For an international flare, use the International Standards Organization (ISO). Each of these organizations provides standard guidelines for the creation of technical drawings in their respective field. ANSI and ISO provide guidance for mechanical drawings, and AIA for, of course, architectural and interior design drawings. You will find that by comparing the standards the appearance of the dimension will differ. Figure 13.3 shows the differences between ANSI and AIA dimensions.

Fortunately, the terminology for the parts of the dimensions are the same. Only the appearance changes. Notice that the differences in appearance are the terminators and the location of the dimension text. The extension lines themselves do not change. As you will find later in this unit, it is very easy to modify the dimension so that you can create either ANSI or AIA standard dimensions.

Associative and Non-Associative Dimensions

As you create dimensions you will find that you can create both associative and non-associative dimensions. In the early days of AutoCAD, dimensions came in one standard form, non-associative. This meant that the dimension was created out of a series of lines and text but had no other properties than just the individual objects themselves. The dimensions could not adjust to changes to the object they dimensioned. If the length of a line changed, the dimension would remain the same.

With the inclusion of associative dimensions, the days of the "dumb dimensions" are over. Associative dimensions are complex objects that can change and reflect the new modifications made to the objects they describe. For instance, if you create a line three units long and place a dimension on that object, you can now use the **stretch** command to modify the length of the line to four units, and the dimension will automatically change to reflect the new length of the line as shown in Figure 13.4. No erasing and recreating the dimension is needed.

Associative dimensions also allow other features as listed. Each feature will be discussed later in this unit.

- Dimension styles, similar to text styles, can be created to modify the appearance of the dimensions and to quickly change that appearance.
- Grips can be used to modify the dimension.
- Associative dimensions can be changed to non-associative dimensions but not vice versa.

Let's discuss the last item in the list. To change an associative dimension to a non-associative dimension, use the **explode** command. This will non-associate the dimension

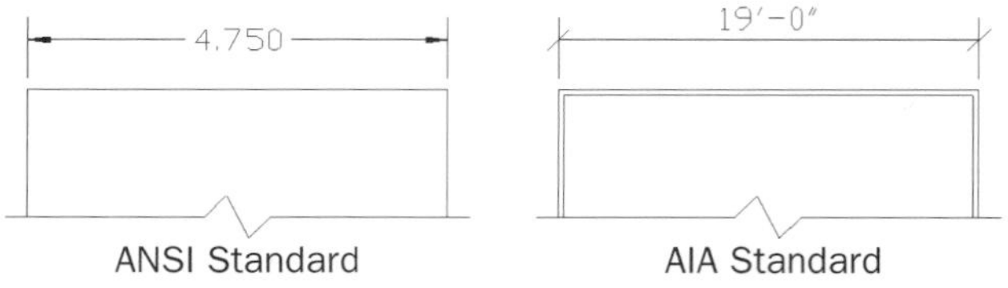

Figure 13.3
ANSI and AIA standard dimensions.

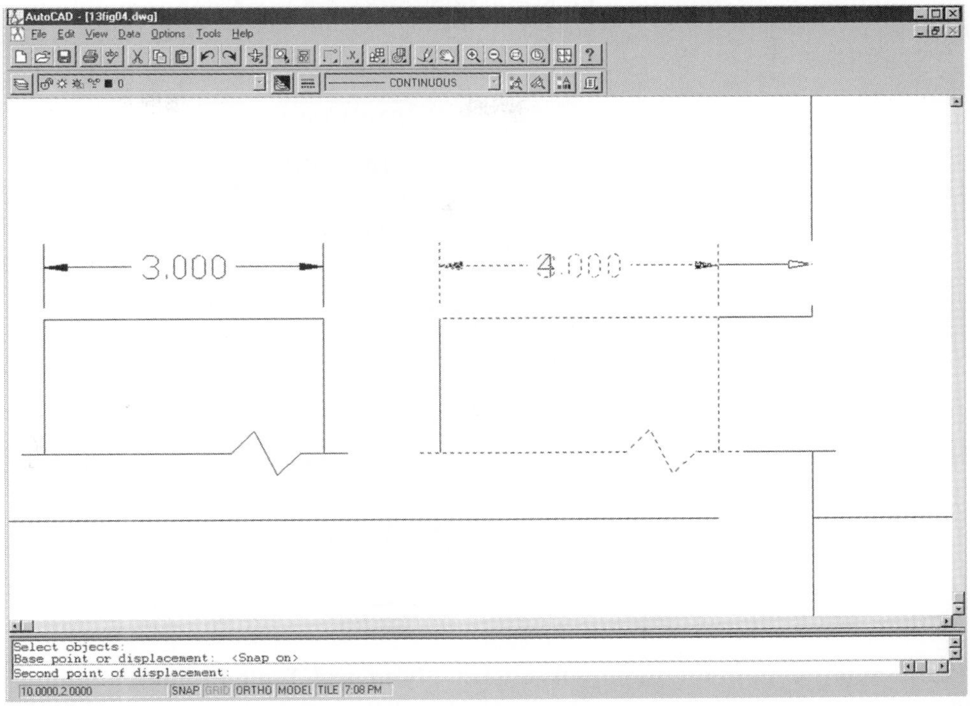

Figure 13.4
Changing an associative dimension from three units to four units.

with an object, as well as break it into its individual components. Instead of one object, you will have six: two lines representing the extension lines, one line representing the dimension line, two polylines representing the arrowheads and a text object that was once the dimension text. Each of these objects will be placed on the 0 layer and its color will be modified to that layer's color.

So why would you ever want to explode a dimension? Believe it or not, AutoCAD is not perfect. Especially when it comes to creating dimensions. Because there are so many different standards, Autodesk (the creators of AutoCAD) had to make some concessions when it came to dimension variable defaults and the way dimensions are created. Do not naturally assume that because AutoCAD created the dimension a certain way, that it is the correct way. Often times, in order to get the dimension "just right," you will need to explode the dimension and modify the objects individually to give the drawing a more professional appearance. Do not be afraid to explode the dimension, but also do not get carried away. Associative dimensions are very useful in later editing of the drawing, whereas non-associative dimensions are not.

Skill Builder

You can force AutoCAD to create all associative or non-associative dimensions by using the **dimaso** system variable at the `Command:` prompt.

Creating Dimension Styles

Before creating a dimension, you must choose a dimension style and then adjust the dimension variables accordingly. A dimension style is a series of dimensions that have been formatted with a consistent appearance. Two popular styles include ANSI and AIA as described earlier. Using styles, you can modify the appearance of the dimension text font, the location and size of the text, the type and size of the terminator, the size of a center mark, as well as other features.

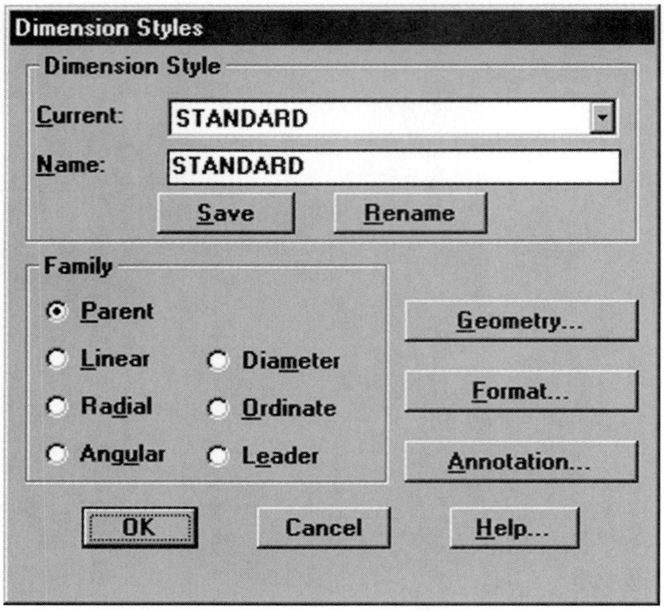

Figure 13.5
The Dimension Styles dialog box.

Dimension Styles and Their Families Modifying the style of a dimension is very easy when the Dimension Styles dialog box is used. To access the dialog box found in Figure 13.5, use the following procedures:

- Select the Dimension Styles button from the Dimensioning toolbar.
- Type **ddim** at the `Command:` prompt.

Once the command is selected, the Dimension Styles dialog box will be displayed. The components of the dialog box are described below.

- **Dimension Style.** Use this dialog box tile to display the name of the current dimension style. To change the dimension style, select the Current list box to display all styles presently defined within the drawing. If you wish to create a new style, type the name of the style to be created in the Name: text edit box. If you select the Save button, you will save the newly named style. Selecting the Rename button will rename the current dimension style with the name in the text edit box. Once you have created or renamed the dimension style, you can begin modifying the settings for the current dimension style using the Geometry, Format, and Annotation buttons. Each will be described later.
- **Family.** This tile is used to modify the dimension settings for dimension subtypes. Each dimension style is composed of a "parent" style and many "children" styles. These children styles are used to modify the current dimension settings to comply with the type of dimension that they represent. For instance, in an architectural drawing, the terminator is typically a tick mark and the dimension text is above the dimension line. Suppose you need to create a leader on the architectural drawing. Leaders require an arrowhead terminator, and the dimension text is centered at the end of the extension line, but the text height is still the same as the normal architectural style. You could create an entirely new style or you could create a child leader style from the parent architectural style. To do so, you would select Leader in the Family tile. All of the settings from the parent architectural style would be applied, but now you can make the specific changes to the style that are different for leaders. AutoCAD provides not only the Leader child, but also Linear, Radial, Angular, Diameter, and Ordinate. All of these options will typically require slight adjustments to the parent family for those types of dimensions to be represented properly.

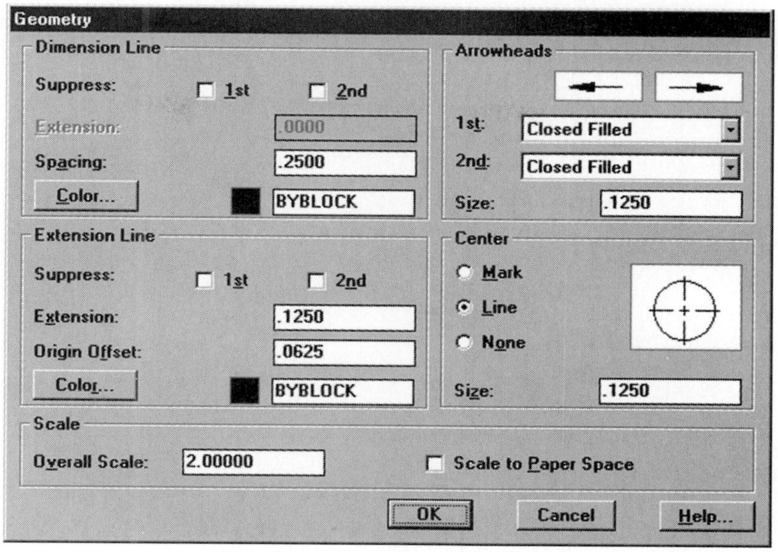

Figure 13.6
Use the Geometry dialog box to modify the dimension appearance.

- **Geometry.** Selecting this button will display the Geometry dialog box. This dialog box is used to modify the basic appearance of the dimension geometry.
- **Format.** Selecting this button will display the Format dialog box. This dialog box is used to modify the dimension text positioning in relationship to the dimension line.
- **Annotation.** Selecting this button will display the Annotation dialog box. This dialog box is used to modify how the dimension text appears within the dimension.

Modifying Dimension Geometry Selecting the Geometry button on the Dimension Styles dialog box will display the Geometry dialog box as shown in Figure 13.6. This dialog box is used to modify the settings that control how dimension lines, extension lines, terminators, and center marks are created. This section will discuss each of these settings.

- **Dimension Line tile.** Use this section to modify the appearance of the dimension line. This tile includes the following options:
  - **Suppress.** Select either 1st or 2nd to suppress the beginning or ending portion of the dimension line. Figure 13.7 shows the effects of suppression.
  - **Extension.** Controls the amount that the dimension line extends past the extension lines. A value of 0 will terminate the dimension line at the intersection of the extension line. Any positive value will extend the dimension line past the extension line the specified amount. It is important to note that this option is available only with oblique terminators selected. This is a common setting for architectural dimensions.
  - **Spacing.** Establishes the amount of spacing between successive dimensions, as shown in Figure 13.8.
  - **Color...** Used to modify the color of the dimension line. Selecting this button will display the Select Color dialog box.

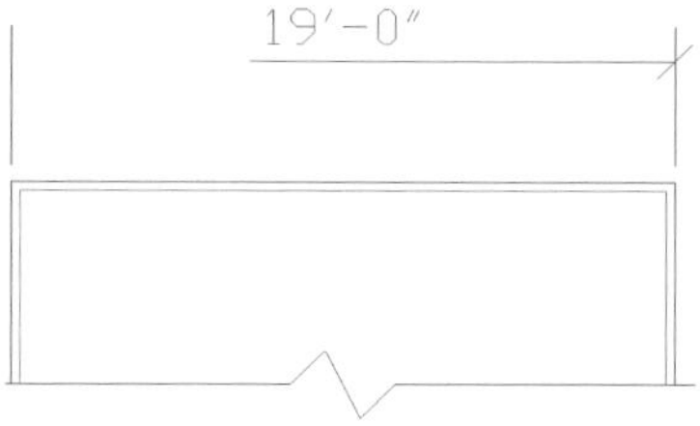

Figure 13.7
The effects of dimension line suppression on a horizontal dimension.

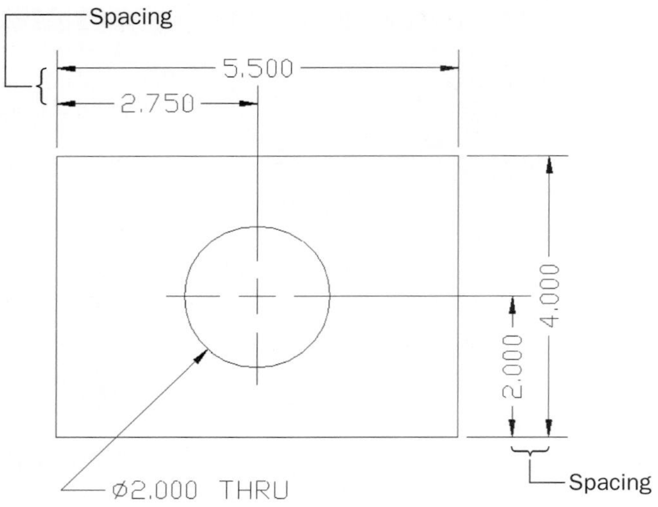

Figure 13.8
Use spacing to automate the distance specified between successive dimensions.

Below the Dimension Line tile is the Extension Line tile. This tile is used to modify the appearance of extension lines. The options are as follows:

- **Suppress.** Select either 1st or 2nd to suppress the beginning or ending extension line. Figure 13.9 shows the effects of extension line suppression on a dimension.
- **Extension.** Controls the amount that the extension line extends past the dimension lines. A value of 0 will terminate the dimension line at the intersection of the dimension line. Any positive value will extend the extension line past the dimension line the specified amount.
- **Origin Offset.** Modifies the extension line offset from the point selected to define the beginning and ending of a measurement. The extension line offset is shown in Figure 13.10.
- **Color. . .** Used to modify the color of the extension line. Selecting this button will display the Select Color dialog box.

The upper-right tile, called the Arrowheads tile, allows you to modify the appearance of the terminator. The options for this tile are defined as follows.

Figure 13.9 *The effects of extension line suppression on a horizontal dimension.*

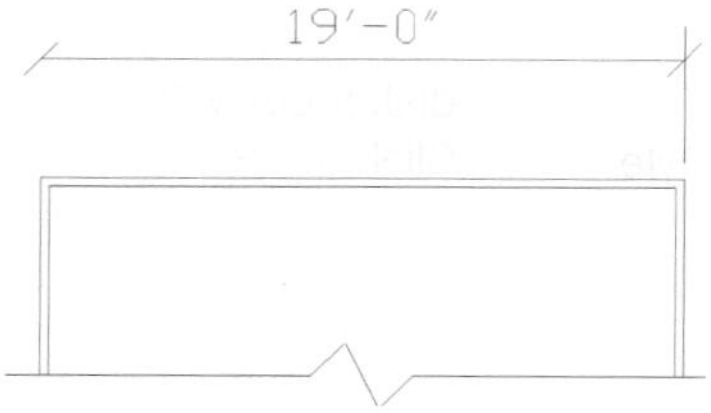

Figure 13.10 *The extension line offset.*

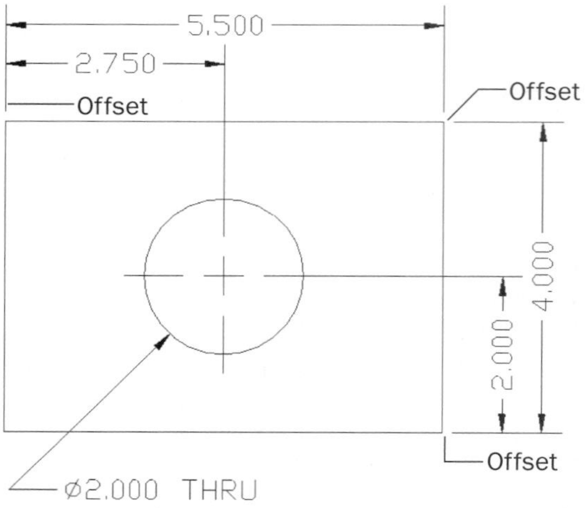

- **Image Tiles.** Selecting the left image tile will cycle both the left and right image tiles through the available terminator selections. Selecting the right image tile will cycle only the right image tile through the available terminator selections. Select the right image tile only if you want to have different terminators on both sides of the dimension (something you don't see every day).
- **1st.** Use this list box to select the type of terminator by name for the first terminator created on a dimension.
- **2nd.** Use this list box to select the type of terminator by name for the second terminator created on a dimension.
- **Size.** Use this edit box to modify the size of the terminator.

Below the Arrowheads tile is the Center tile. This tile is used to modify the appearance of center marks and center lines. Center lines are usually used to show the center of a circle or arc. The options located within the Center tile are described as follows:

- **Mark.** Select this radio button if you wish to have a center mark placed when you create a diameter or radial dimension.
- **Line.** Select this radio button if you wish to have the center mark extend past the circle or arc that is being dimensioned when a diameter or radial dimension is created.
- **None.** Suppresses any center marks or lines on a diameter or radial dimension.
- **Size.** Modifies the size of the center mark created.

The final tile in this dialog box is the Scale tile. This tile is used to modify the scale of the dimension settings.

- **Overall Scale.** Modifies the overall scale of the settings made in the Geometry dialog box. For instance, if you create a drawing that is to be plotted at half scale, you would want to change the value for this text edit box to 2. This will ensure that all of your settings are doubled so that when they are finally plotted at half scale, they will retain their correct plotted value.
- **Scale to Paper Space.** Selecting this check box informs AutoCAD to use the scale factor of the current viewport that has been created in paper space.

Once you have made the changes to the dialog box, you can select OK to accept the changes or Cancel to cancel the changes. If you need further clarification on an option, click the Help button.

TUTORIAL 13.1: CREATING A DIMENSION STYLE AND CHANGING THE DIMENSION GEOMETRY

In this tutorial you will create a new dimension style called TUTORIAL and modify the values in the Geometry dialog box.

1.  Select the Open button on the Standard toolbar. The Select File dialog box will appear.
2. Select the dimensions.dwg file from the tutorial disk. The dimensions drawing will be loaded as shown in Figure 13.11.
3.  Select the Dimension Style button on the Dimension toolbar. The Dimension Styles dialog box shown in Figure 13.12 will be displayed.
4. In the Name text edit box, double click. The current style name will be highlighted. Type *tutorial* in the edit box.
5. Select the Geometry button. The Geometry dialog box will be displayed as shown in Figure 13.13.
6. Make the changes to the dialog box so that they match those changes found in Figure 13.13. The attributes to change include the following:

   Dimension Line Spacing = .25
   Extension Line Extension = .125
   Arrowheads = Open
   Arrowhead Size = .125
   Center Mark = None
   Overall Scale = 2
7. After making the changes, select the OK button. The Geometry dialog box will close and the Dimension Styles dialog box will reappear.
8. Click the Save button. The current settings will be saved to the style named TUTORIAL.
9. Do not close this dialog box. Stop here and continue reading the unit or precede to the next tutorial.

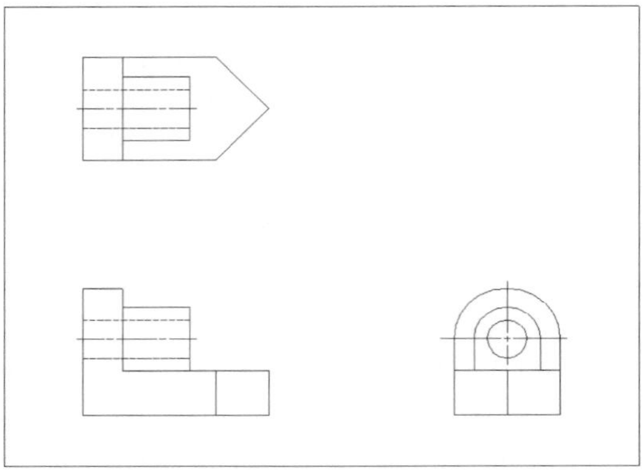

Figure 13.11
Use this drawing file for all tutorials in this unit.

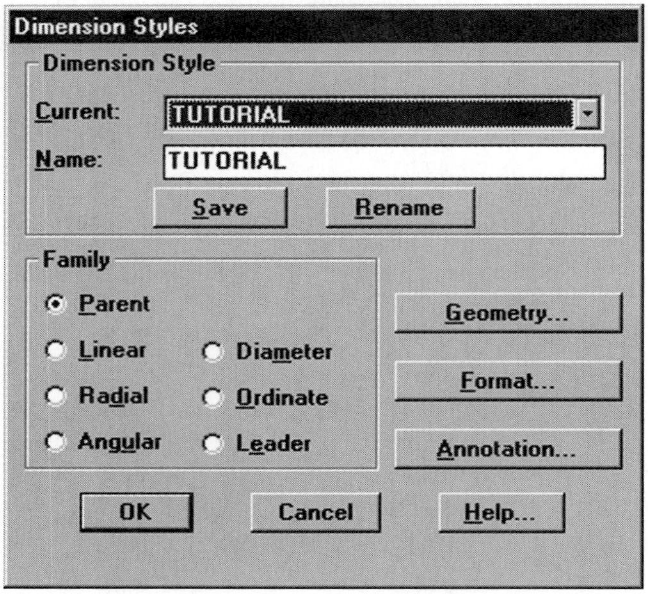

Figure 13.12
The Dimension Styles dialog box.

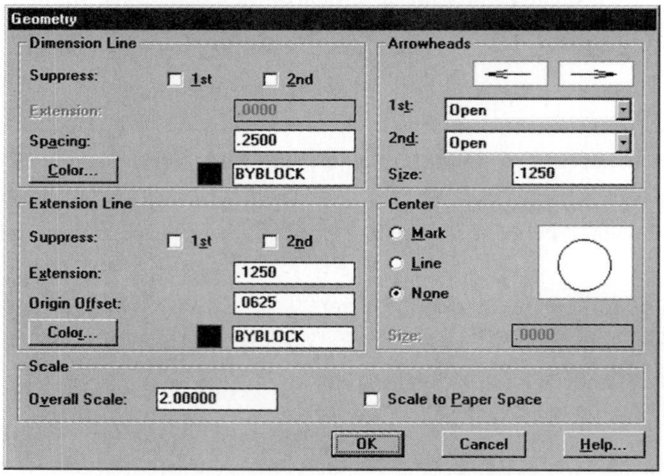

Figure 13.13
The Geometry dialog box. Use this figure to assist you in creating the TUTORIAL dimension style.

Formatting Dimension Lines Selecting the Format button on the Dimension Styles dialog box will display the Format dialog box as shown in Figure 13.14. This dialog box is used to modify the settings that control how dimension text is represented and its location in relation to the actual dimension. This section will discuss each of these settings.

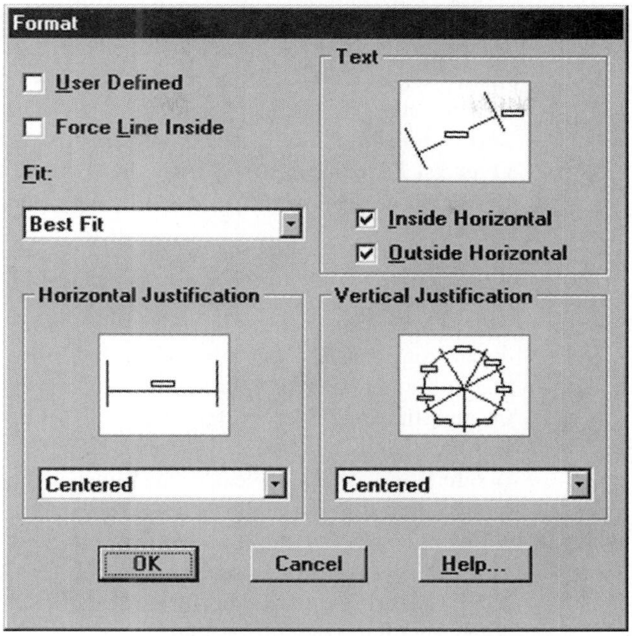

Figure 13.14
Use the Format dialog box to modify the location of the dimension line.

- **User Defined.** Asks the operator to specify the location of the dimension text each time a dimension is created. The operator has to physically move the dimension text into place before the dimension is created. When this option is selected, Horizontal Justification is disabled.
- **Force Line Inside.** In many instances, AutoCAD will not place dimension lines between the extension lines if there is not the prerequisite space available. This option will force a dimension line to be created between the extension lines no matter how much distance is between them.

Underneath these two options is the Horizontal Justification tile. The following options are available:

- **Fit.** Used in a similar fashion to the previous option, this drop-down menu allows you to specify whether to force terminators and text between extension lines—regardless of the distance.
- **Horizontal Justification.** Use this option to specify the horizontal location of the text on the dimension. There are two ways to select the options available for this tile: by selecting the option from the drop-down menu or by clicking on the image tile and cycling through the options visually. The options available are listed as follows. Figure 13.15 shows the effects of each setting on a horizontal dimension.

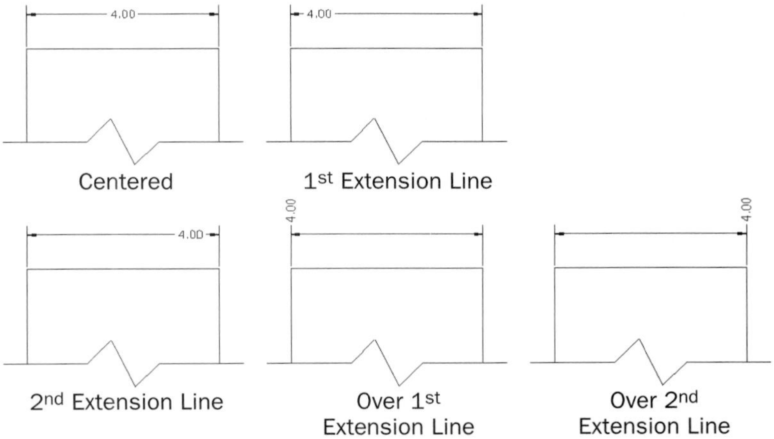

Figure 13.15
The various horizontal justification options for dimension text.

- **Centered.** Centers the dimension text on the dimension line.
- **1st Extension Line.** Places the dimension text next to the first extension line. The first extension line is established as the first point that is selected when creating a dimension.
- **2nd Extension Line.** Places the dimension text next to the second extension line.
- **Over 1st Extension Line.** Places the dimension text over the first extension line.
- **Over 2nd Extension Line.** Places the dimension text over the second extension line.

Once you have finished selecting the Horizontal Justifications options, use the Text tile to select how the dimension text is aligned. A list of the options follows.

- **Text.** This option controls the orientation of the dimension text in relationship to the dimension line. The two options available are described below. You can mix and match the options using the check box, or you can click on the image tile to cycle through the available options. Figure 13.16 displays a vertical dimension with the various options available.
- **Inside Horizontal.** If selected, the dimension text that is located inside a dimension will be placed horizontally, or the text can be read from the bottom of the drawing. If this option is not selected, the text will be aligned with the dimension line.
- **Outside Horizontal.** If selected, the dimension text that is located outside of a dimension will be placed horizontally. If this option is not selected, the text will be aligned with the dimension line.

Just as there is Horizontal Justification, there is a way to modify the dimension text's Vertical Justification. That tile's options are as follows:

- **Vertical Justification.** Use this option to specify the vertical location of the text on the dimension. There are two ways to select the options available for this tile: by selecting the option from the drop-down menu or by clicking on the image tile and cycling through the options visually. The options available are listed below. Figure 13.17 shows the effects of each setting on a horizontal dimension.
  - **Centered.** Places the text centered in the dimension line.
  - **Above.** Places the text above the dimension line.
  - **Below.** Places the text below the dimension line.
  - **JIS.** Japanese Industrial Standards. Places the text according to JIS. Though not represented in Figure 13.17, this standard is used on a series of angular dimensions to ensure that the dimension text is always aligned to be on top of the dimension line, no matter what angle the dimension is created.

Once you have made the changes to the dialog box, you can select OK to accept the changes or Cancel to cancel the changes. If you need further clarification on an option, click the Help button.

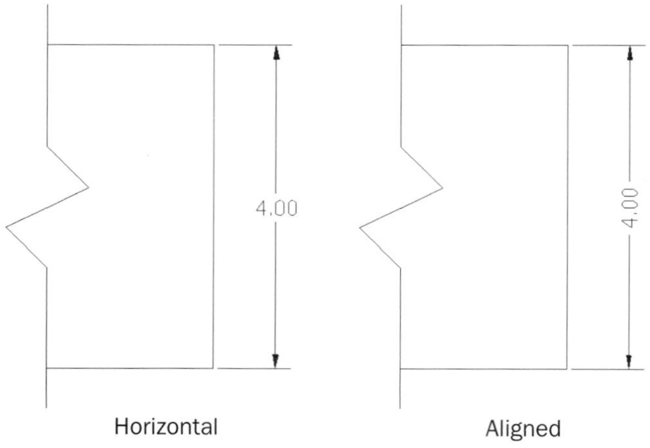

Figure 13.16
Text can be aligned or horizontal with the dimension line or horizontal.

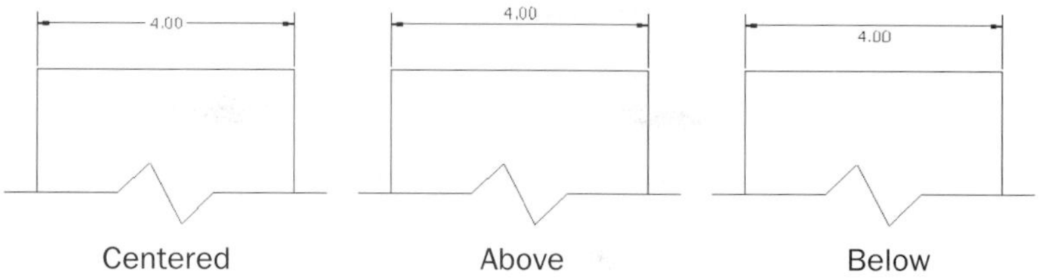

Figure 13.17
The various vertical justification options for dimension text.

TUTORIAL 13.2: CHANGING THE DIMENSION LINE FORMAT

This tutorial continues from the previous tutorial. In this tutorial you will modify the dimension line format.

1. Select the Format button. The Format dialog box will be displayed as shown in Figure 13.18.
2. The only change to the defaults in this dialog box is to deselect the Inside Horizontal check box. Verify your settings with those in Figure 13.18.
3. After making the changes, select the OK button. The Format dialog box will close, and the Dimension Styles dialog box will reappear.
4. Click the Save button. The current settings will be saved to the style named TUTORIAL. It is not necessary to complete this step, but it does enforce good practice to save at every available step.
5. Do not close this dialog box. Stop here and continue reading the unit or precede to the next tutorial.

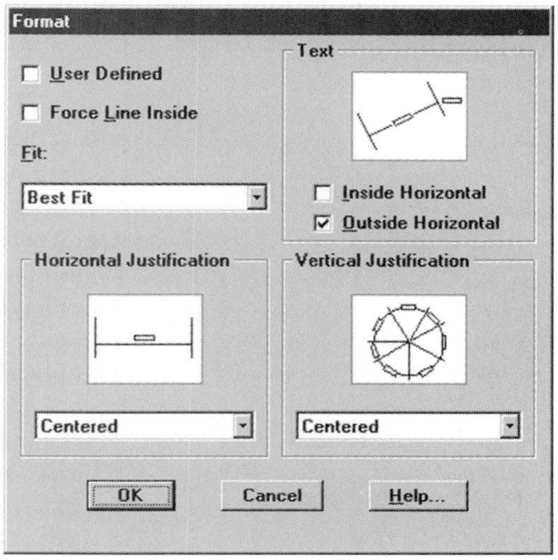

Figure 13.18 *The Format dialog box.*

Establishing Dimension Text Format Selecting the Annotation button on the Dimension Styles dialog box will display the Annotation dialog box as shown in Figure 13.19. This dialog box is used to modify the settings that control how the appearance, tolerance, and values of the dimension are represented. Each of the tiles of this dialog box are discussed below.

The Primary Units tile is a very important part of this dialog box. It specifies the type of units to be represented within the dimension.

Figure 13.19
Use the Annotation dialog box to modify the appearance of the annotation in a dimension.

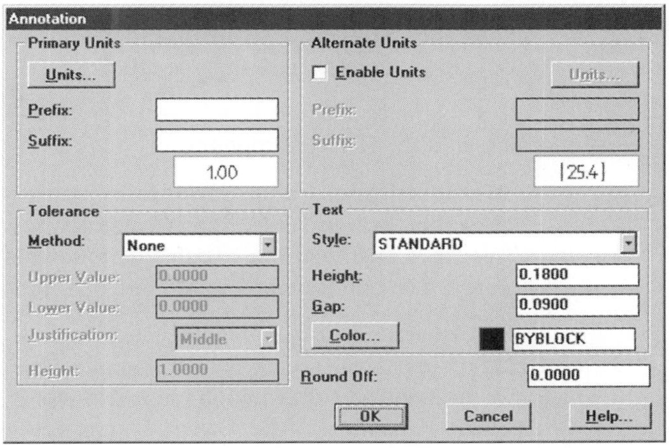

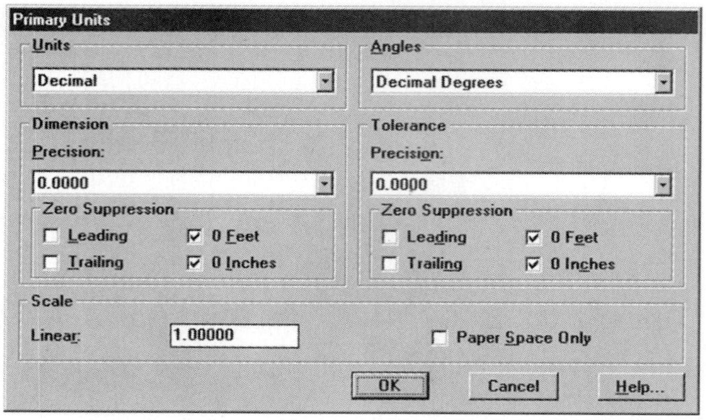

Figure 13.20
Use this dialog box to control the type of dimensioning units.

- **Units...** Selecting this button will display the Primary Units dialog box as shown in Figure 13.20. This dialog box is similar to the Units Control dialog box. Its options are discussed below.
  - **Units.** Use this drop-down menu to select the type of units to be represented within the dimension.
  - **Dimension Precision.** Use this drop-down menu to specify the precision for the units.
  - **Dimension Zero Suppression.** Select the appropriate check box to suppress a Leading, Trailing, 0 Feet, and 0 Inches of a dimension. The last two options are available only if you have selected architectural units.
  - **Angles.** Use the drop-down menu to select the type of angular measurement needed.
  - **Tolerance Precision.** Use this drop-down menu to specify the precision for angular measurements.
  - **Tolerance Zero Suppression.** Select the appropriate check box to suppress a Leading, Trailing, 0 Feet, and 0 Inches of a dimension.
  - **Scale Linear.** Modifies the scale of the dimension. Using a value of 2, for instance, would increase each dimension text value by a factor of 2. A measurement that is actually 3 units would be displayed as 6 units.
  - **Scale Paper Space Only.** Paper space is not covered in this book, but selecting this option will allow the dimension units to be scaled based on the current scale factor of the viewport in which it is created in.

Once you have selected the type of units to be used in the dimension, you can begin to specify whether you need tolerance dimensioning. Used primarily in mechanical drawing, tolerancing theory will not be covered in this book and only a brief discussion of each option's use will be presented.

- **Tolerance Method.** Use the drop-down menu to select either None, Symmetrical, Deviation, Limits, or Basic type tolerances.

If a tolerance method is selected, you will need to provide additional tolerance information in the following options:

- **Tolerance Upper Value.** Specifies the upper tolerance value.
- **Tolerance Lower Value.** Specifies the lower tolerance value.
- **Tolerance Justification.** Use this drop-down menu to select the location of the tolerance. The options are Top, Middle, and Bottom.

The Alternate Units tile allows you to include two different units of measurement on a single dimension. A very common application would be to have both standard and metric dimensions on a drawing of a part that was to be produced in the United States as well as in other countries. The Alternate Units options are described as follows.

- **Enable Units.** Turns on Alternate Units. If selected, the Units... button in this tile will be made available. It is identical to the Units button found in the Primary Units tile. Refer to that section for more details.
- **Prefix.** Allows you to specify an Alternate Units prefix.
- **Suffix.** Allows you to specify an Alternate Units suffix.

The last tile to be considered in this dialog box is the Text tile. This tile will specify how the text is represented within the dimension. Its options are described below.

- **Text Style.** Allows you to select the style of text to be used for the dimension text from a drop-down menu. A style must have been previously defined using the **ddstyle** command in order for styles other than STANDARD to be available.
- **Text Height.** Specifies the height of the dimension text.
- **Text Gap.** Specifies the distance between the dimension line and the text.
- **Text Color...** Selecting this button displays the Color dialog box. Use this dialog box to specify the color that the text will be within a dimension.

The last option available on this dialog box is Round Off.

- **Round Off.** Used in conjunction with the Units Precision, this option will change the dimension text to match the nearest round-off value that you enter.

TUTORIAL 13.3: CHANGING THE DIMENSION TEXT FORMAT

This tutorial continues from the previous tutorial. In this tutorial you will modify the dimension line format.

1. Select the Annotation button. The Annotation dialog box will be displayed as shown in Figure 13.21.
2. Select the Units... button. The Primary Units dialog box will be displayed as shown in Figure 13.22.
3. Make the changes to the Primary Units dialog box to match those shown in Figure 13.22. The changes include the following:

   Dimension Precision = 0.000
   Zero Suppression Leading = On
   Tolerance Precision = 0
   Tolerance Zero Suppression
     Leading = On
     Trailing = On

4. After making the changes, select the OK button. The Primary Units dialog box will close and the Annotation dialog box will reappear.
5. Change the Text Height to .125 and the Text Gap to .0625.
6. After making the changes, select the OK button. The Annotation dialog box will close and the Dimension Styles dialog box will reappear.
7. Click the Save button. The current settings will be saved to the style named TUTORIAL.
8. Select the OK button. The Dimension Styles dialog box will close.

These settings will be used to create dimensions on the tutorial drawing that was loaded from the tutorial disk. If you wish to complete the dimensioning chapter tutorials, leave this file open and continue reading. If you would like to finish at a later time, save the file.

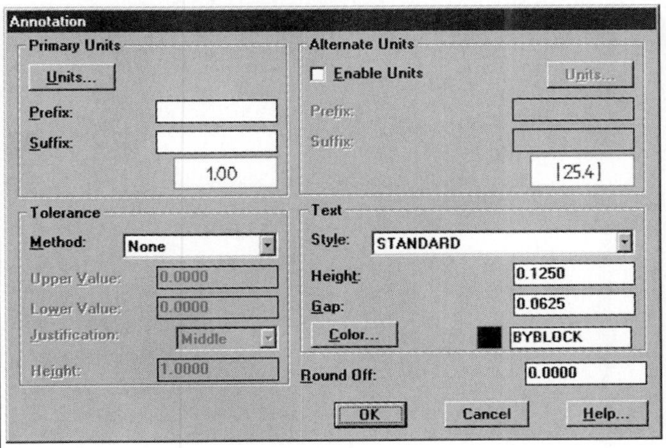

Figure 13.21 *The Annotation dialog box.*

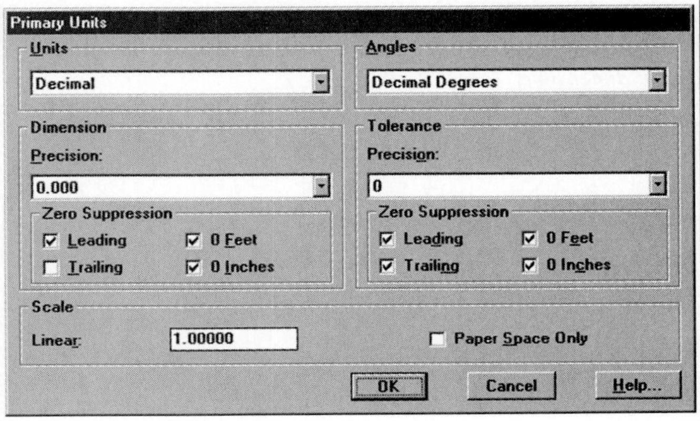

Figure 13.22 *The Primary Units dialog box is used to control the format of the units displayed in a dimension.*

Once you have made the changes to the dialog box, you can select OK to accept the changes or Cancel to cancel the changes. If you need further clarification on an option, click the Help button.

LINEAR AND RADIAL DIMENSIONING

After you have adjusted your dimension settings and styles, it is time to begin creating dimensions. Linear and radial dimensions are the most common dimensions created. With the inclusion of new AutoCAD commands and toolbars in Release 13 for Windows, they have become very easy to create. Linear dimensions consist both of vertical and horizontal dimensions, as shown in Figure 13.23.

Very similar to linear dimensions are aligned dimensions. These are dimensions that are not vertical or horizontal. They are also shown in Figure 13.23.

Not all geometry on a drawing will be linear. Many drawings include arcs and circles to describe fillets or holes or even a curved wall. These objects need to be dimensioned if the object is going to be manufactured or constructed. Because of this, AutoCAD provides Radial dimensions. A radial dimension is shown in Figure 13.23. Let's begin this section with a study of basic horizontal and vertical, or linear, dimensions.

LINEAR DIMENSIONS

In a previous version of AutoCAD, you would need two commands and a different `Command:` prompt to create simple horizontal dimensions. The command sequence would be as follows:

```
Command: dim
Dim: hor
First extension line origin or RETURN to select:
Second extension line origin:
Dimension line location (Text/Angle):
Dimension text <5.0795>:
```

You will notice that the `Command:` prompt had to first be changed to a Dim prompt and then the command could be executed. If you needed to create a new object, you would have to exit the `Dim:` prompt by using the **exit** command or pressing Esc twice. This would return you to the `Command:` prompt, where you could once again create basic geometry. This is a lengthy process that would frustrate even the best AutoCAD users. While this method of creating dimensions is still available to the hard-to-upgrade user, a new way of creating dimensions was included in Release 13. No longer is the

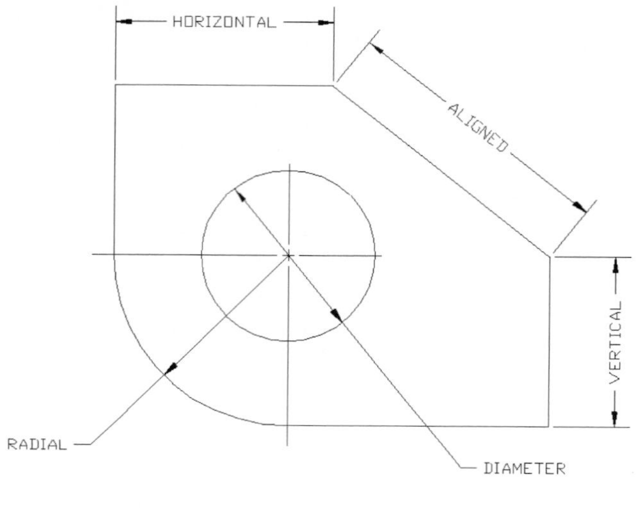

Figure 13.23
Vertical, Horizontal, Aligned, and Radial dimensions.

`Dim:` prompt needed. All dimensions can be created from the `Command:` prompt and through the use of toolbars.

The command to create horizontal and vertical dimensions can be accessed using one of the two methods described here:

- Select the Linear Dimension button from the Dimension toolbar.
- Typing **dimlinear** at the `Command:` prompt.

Once activated, you will see the following string of options. Each option is discussed after the option is presented.

```
Command: _dimlinear
```

This is the text that is entered if you select the command from the dimension toolbar.

```
First extension line origin or RETURN to select:
```

At this point you can select the first extension line origin or press Enter to select a line. If you choose to select a line, the first and second extension line origin will be selected for you automatically based on the start and endpoint of the line. You would not use the object selection method if the total length of a distance to be dimensioned is broken by two or more objects.

```
Second extension line origin:
```

If you select a first extension line origin, you will be presented with this option. Select the second extension line origin to specify the overall length of the linear dimension.

```
Dimension line location (Text/Angle/Horizontal/Vertical/Rotated):
```

There are many choices for you to make now. You can move the mouse to define the location of the dimension line. Moving the mouse left or right will cause the dimension to be horizontal; moving the mouse up and down will cause the dimension to be vertical. If you would like, you can use one of the following options presented at the `Command:` prompt.

SKILL BUILDER

It is not necessary to type the entire option name—just the first letter of the options you wish to modify.

- **Text.** Modifies the default text.
- **Angle.** Rotates the text.
- **Horizontal.** Forces the text to be horizontal.
- **Vertical.** Forces the text to be vertical.
- **Rotated.** Rotates the dimension line at an angle you specify.

```
Dimension text <4.8516>:
```

You are given this prompt to verify that the dimension text that is going to be created is correct. At this point you can modify the text if you wish.

ALIGNED DIMENSIONS

Aligned dimensions are identical to linear dimensions in appearance. The only difference is the dimension line orientation. Aligned dimensions are typically slanted at an angle.

TUTORIAL 13.4: CREATING LINEAR DIMENSIONS

In this tutorial, you will create a horizontal and vertical linear dimension on the *dimension.dwg* file that was loaded from the tutorial disk. In order for this tutorial to work correctly, you must first have completed the tutorials prior to this one. That will ensure that the styles are scaled and created properly to match those of this tutorial.

1. Ensure that the Dimensions layer is the current layer.
2.  Select the Linear Dimension button from the dimension toolbar. First extension line origin or RETURN to select: appears in the Command: prompt window.
3. Press (Enter). Select object to dimension: appears in the Command: prompt window.
4. Select the line specified in Figure 13.24.
5. At the Dimension line location (Text/Angle/Horizontal/Vertical/Rotated): prompt, move the dimension line above the line approximately .75 units; .75 units is used because this drawing will be plotted at half scale. Typically, a dimension line is placed at .375 inches away from the object in a mechanical drawing such as this one. Use Snap to assist in placing the dimension line location. The Snap increment for this tutorial drawing is set to .25.
6. At the Dimension text <5.000>: prompt, press (Enter). A horizontal dimension will be placed as shown in Figure 13.25. Next, create a vertical dimension.
7. 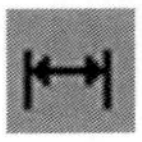 Select the Linear Dimension button from the dimension toolbar. First extension line origin or RETURN to select: appears in the Command: prompt window. Select the point specified in Figure 13.24. Use the Endpoint Object Snap to ensure that you select the point accurately.

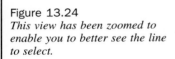

SKILL BUILDER

You could also use polar coordinates to specify the dimension line location. To place a dimension line exactly .75 units away from a line, use @.75<90.

FOR THE PROFESSIONAL

When specifying dimensions, you should always use Object Snap to attach the dimension accurately on the object or distance being dimensioned.

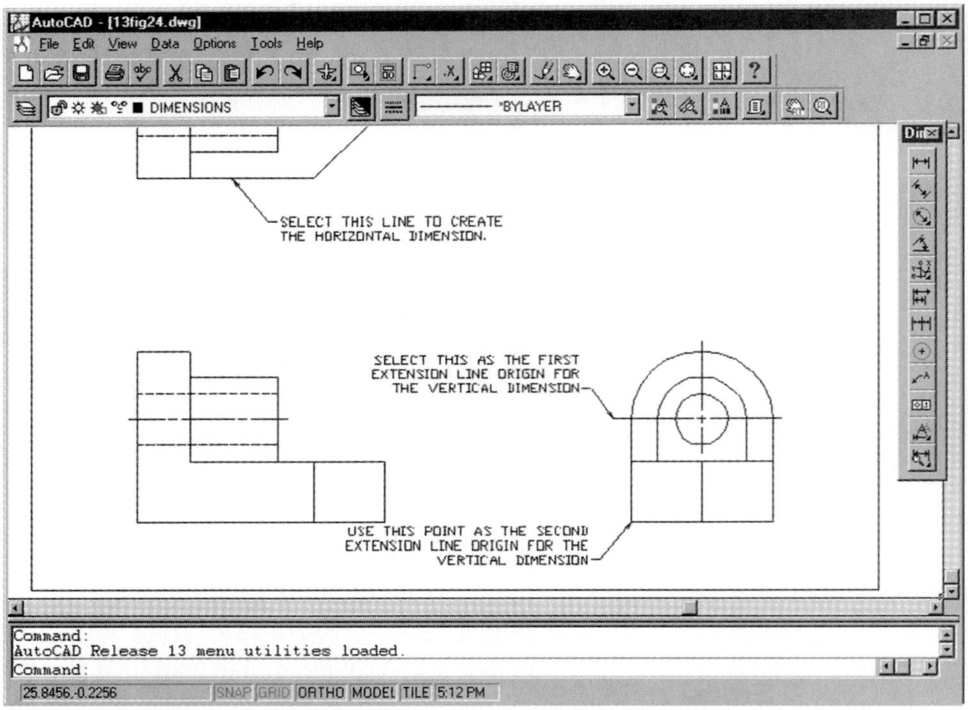

Figure 13.24
This view has been zoomed to enable you to better see the line to select.

8. At the `Second extension line origin:` prompt, select the point specified in Figure 13.25.
9. At the `Dimension line location (Text/Angle/Horizontal/Vertical/Rotated):` prompt, move the dimension line .75 units to the left of the vertical line the dimension is describing.
10. At the `Dimension text <3.000>:` prompt, press Enter. The vertical dimension will be placed. You should now have a horizontal and vertical dimension as shown in Figure 13.25.

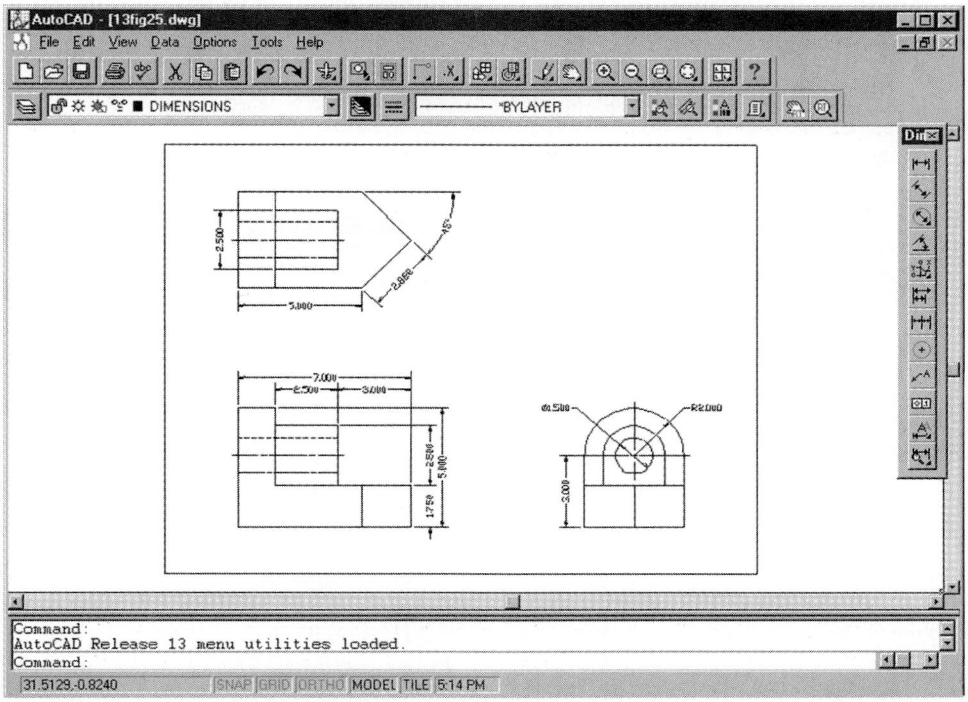

Figure 13.25
A horizontal and vertical dimension has been created on the tutorial drawing file.

Creating aligned dimensions is very similar to creating linear dimensions. Use one of the following two methods to execute the command:

- Select the Aligned Dimension button from the Dimension toolbar.
- Type **dimaligned** at the `Command:` prompt.

Once the command is entered, the procedure for creating the aligned dimension is the same as for creating a linear dimension.

Skill Builder

You can use the **dimaligned** command to create linear dimensions. To ensure a horizontal or vertical dimension, turn **ortho** on. Instead of having to select the **dimlinear** command after a **dimaligned,** you could simply press the space bar to execute the previous command, **dimaligned,** and create a linear dimension.

Continued Dimension Strings

More often than not, you will find a string of continued dimensions on a drawing. It is very rare that a single dimension will be able to describe the complete profile of an object. AutoCAD provides two commands that allow you to continue your dimensions using pre-

Tutorial 13.5: Creating Aligned Dimensions

This tutorial continues from the previous tutorial. In this tutorial, you will create an aligned dimension on the top view of the object displayed in the tutorial drawing.

1. Ensure that **ortho** is off.
2. 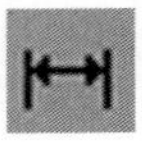 Select the Aligned Dimension button from the dimension toolbar. `First extension line origin or RETURN to select:` appears in the `Command:` prompt window.
3. Press Enter. `Select object to dimension:` appears in the `Command:` prompt window.
4. Select the line specified in Figure 13.26.
5. At the `Dimension line location (Text/Angle/Horizontal/Vertical/Rotated):` prompt, move the dimension line away from the line approximately .75 units. Use **snap** to assist in placing the dimension line location.
6. At the `Dimension text <2.828>:` prompt, press Enter. An aligned dimension will be placed as shown in Figure 13.25.

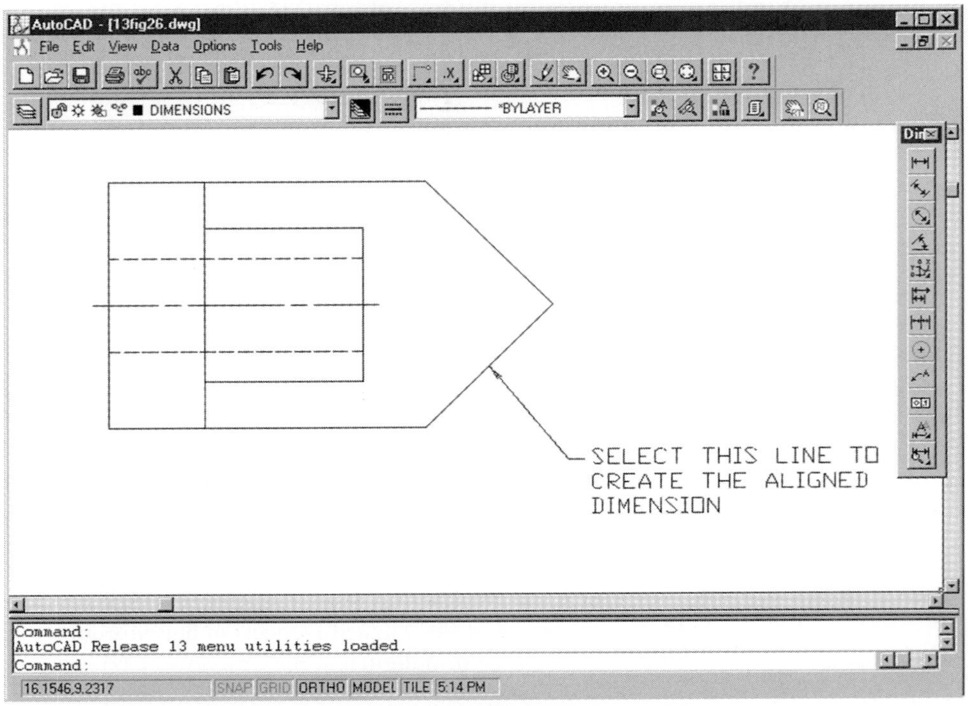

Figure 13.26
This view has been zoomed to enable you to better see the line to select.

vious dimensions as the base point, **dimcontinued** and **dimbaseline.** An example of each command is presented in Figure 13.27.

You should use these two commands whenever you have continued dimension strings. A bad technique to develop is creating continued dimension strings with the **dimlinear** and **dimaligned** commands. If you use these two commands to create con-

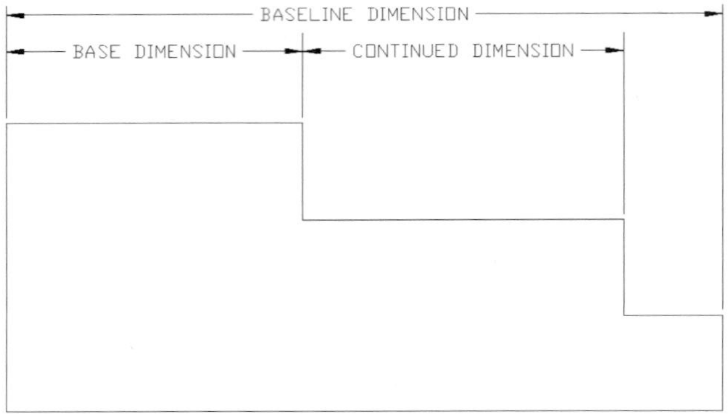

Figure 13.27
These two commands rely on previously created dimensions.

tinued dimensions strings, you will find overlapping objects. Overlapping objects cause a plot to appear darker where the objects overlap. You will also find that by using the incorrect commands, you will force yourself to do a lot more work creating and editing dimensions. These two continued dimension string commands are very easy to use once you understand their operation. Let's take a look at the **dimcontinue** command first.

The **dimcontinue** command will create a continued dimension string from the last linear or aligned dimension you created. The dimension lines of the previous and the new dimension will be aligned. You can also continue dimensioning from other linear or aligned dimensions by selecting the right options. Before beginning the **dimcontinue** command, ensure that a previous dimension has been created that requires a continued dimension string. Enter the command using one of the following two procedures:

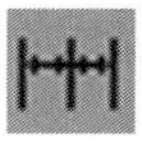

- Select the Continued Dimension button from the Dimension toolbar.
- Type **`dimcontinue`** at the **`Command:`** prompt.

Like the continued dimension, baseline dimensions do not align their dimension lines. Instead, the dimension line of the baseline dimension is placed away from the previous dimension at the distance specified in the Dimension Line Spacing text edit box of the Geometry dialog box located as an option of the Dimension Styles dialog box. To invoke the **dimbaseline** command, use one of the following procedures:

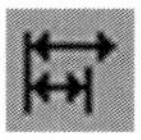

- Select the Baseline Dimension button from the Dimension toolbar.
- Type **`dimbaseline`** at the **`Command:`** prompt.

When either of these dimension commands is entered, the following will appear in the `Command:` prompt:

`Second extension line origin or RETURN to select:`

Select the next point for the continued dimension string to continue to. If you would like to create a continued dimension string from a dimension that was not the last dimension created, press Enter. The following will appear in the `Command:` prompt.

`Select continued dimension:`

Tutorial 13.6: Adding Continued and Baseline Dimensions

This tutorial continues from the preceding tutorial. In this tutorial you will create the horizontal continued and baseline dimensions shown in Figure 13.25. After completing those dimensions, you will be given the opportunity to create the vertical continued string of dimensions on your own.

1. 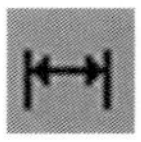 Select the Linear Dimension button from the dimension toolbar. `First extension line origin or RETURN to select:` appears in the `Command:` prompt window.
2. Press Enter. `Select object to dimension:` appears in the `Command:` prompt window.
3. Select the line specified in Figure 13.28.
4. At the `Dimension line location (Text/Angle/Horizontal/Vertical/Rotated):` prompt, move the dimension line above the line approximately .75 units. This dimension will become the base for the continued dimension you will now create.
5.  Select the Continued Dimension button from the Dimension toolbar.
6. At the `Second extension line origin or RETURN to select:` prompt, select the point identified in Figure 13.28. The continued dimension will be created. Next, we need to create a baseline dimension.
7. 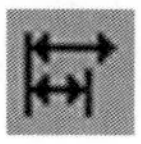 Select the Baseline Dimension button from the Dimension toolbar.
8. At the `Second extension line origin or RETURN to select:` prompt, press Enter.
9. At the `Select continued dimension:` prompt, select the extension line specified in Figure 13.29.
10. The `Second extension line origin or RETURN to select:` prompt will appear again. Select the point specified in Figure 13.29 to finish creating the baseline dimension.
11. You have now created both continued and baseline dimensions. Now try and recreate the vertical continued dimension string on your own. If you are having problems, erase the horizontal dimensions and repeat steps 1–10.

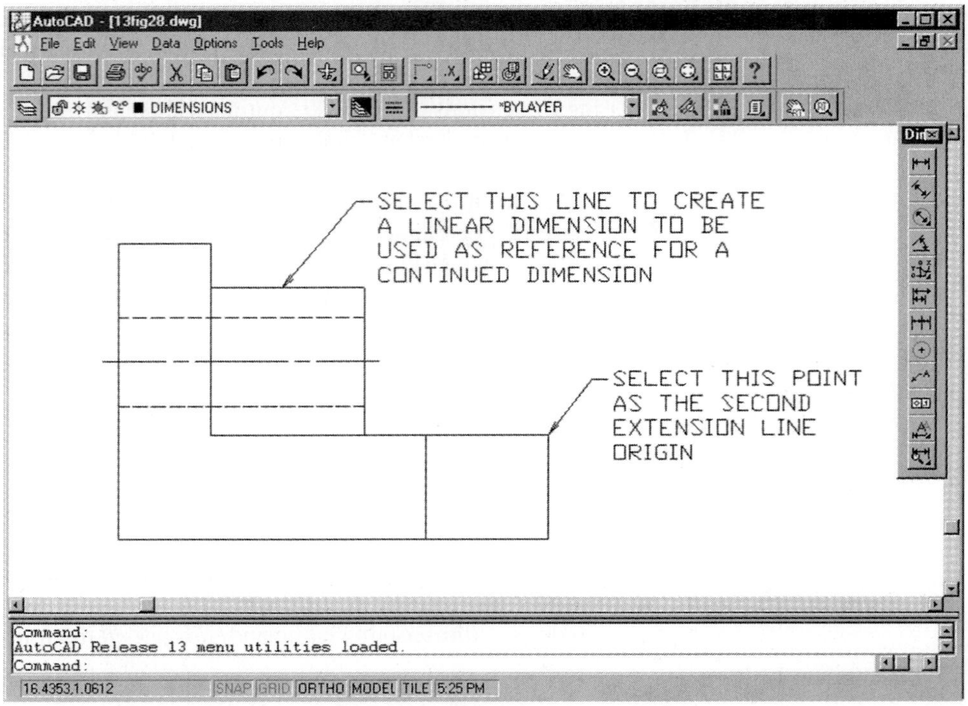

Figure 13.28
This view has been zoomed to enable you to better see the line to select.

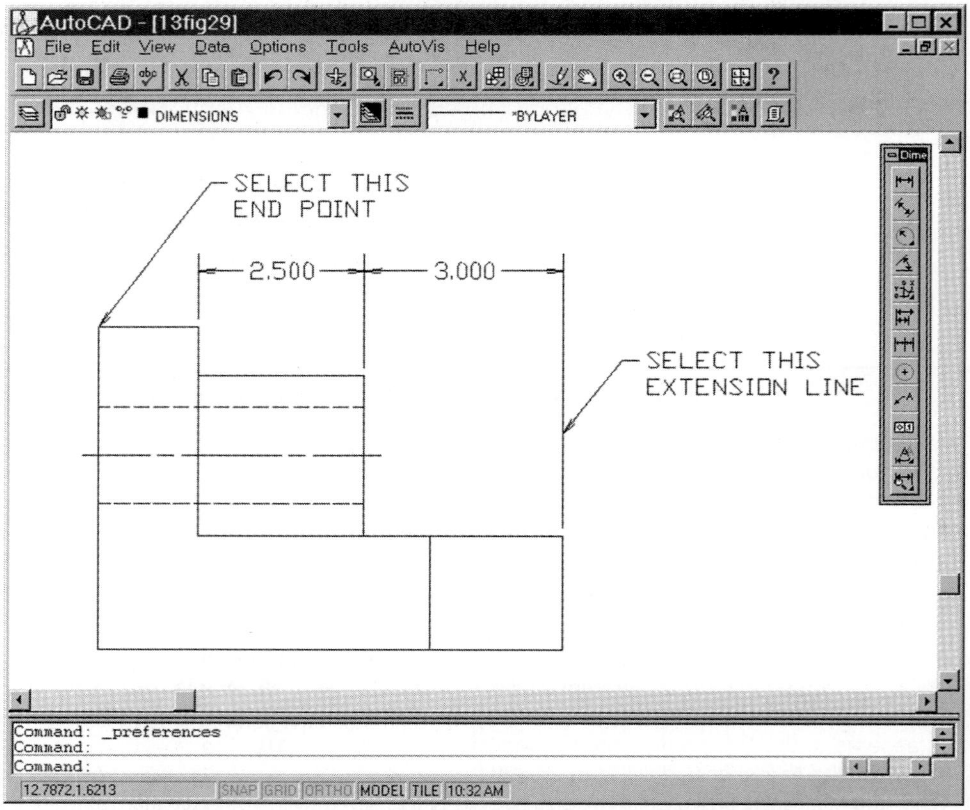

Figure 13.29
Select this extension line to ensure a correct baseline dimension is created.

Select the first extension line created on the dimension to be used as the reference dimension for the continued string. Once that extension line has been chosen, you will once again be asked to select the second extension line origin. Select that point and the continued dimension will be created.

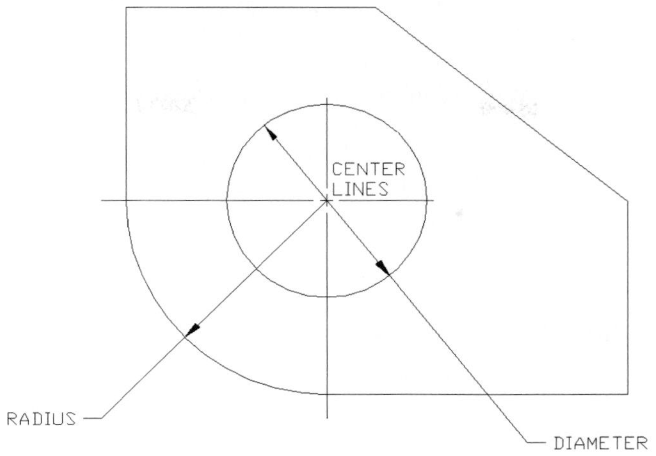

Figure 13.30
This object has Radius, Diameter, and Center lines.

RADIAL DIMENSIONS

Not every object located on a drawing is linear. Many objects you find on a drawing are circular. The world would be a pretty square place if there were no curves. It would also be slower traveling from point A to point B without circular wheels. If we are going to create these items, we need good detailed drawings that contain both radius and diameter dimensions. In most cases, we can use a diameter to describe a circle. A circle on a drawing can represent a cylinder or hole. The term *radius* is used to describe a partial circle or an arc. An arc may represent a fillet or a curve in a driveway on a site plan. Be sure you always use the correct terminology when describing one of these objects or when dimensioning them on a drawing. AutoCAD provides the **dimradius** and the **dimdiameter** commands to create these dimensions. These commands will even add the radius and diameter symbol for you. Figure 13.30 shows both radius and diameter dimensions.

To enter the **dimradius** command, use one of the two procedures listed:

- Select the Radius Dimension button from the Dimension toolbar.
- At the `Command:` prompt, type **dimradius.**

To enter the **dimdiameter** command:

- Select the Diameter Dimension button from the Dimension toolbar. The Diameter button is located on the Radial Dimension flyout.
- At the `Command:` prompt, type **dimdiameter.**

Once either command has been selected, you must choose an arc or a circle. Depending on your dimension style settings, you may or may not have to place the location of the dimension text.

Whenever you have a circle or arc, you will most likely find center lines or a center mark. Center lines are used to locate the center of a circle or arc. Unless you are specifying a fillet radius on a mechanical drawing, you should try and provide these lines as a guide for the manufacturer. AutoCAD can automate creating center lines with the **dimcenter** command. You can specify whether AutoCAD creates a center mark or center line in the dimension style that you establish. Sample center lines are shown in Figure 13.30.

To create a center mark or centerline,

- Select the Center Mark button on the Dimension toolbar.
- Type **dimcenter** at the `Command:` prompt. The Center Mark button is located on the Radial Dimension flyout.

Once the command is entered, simply select the circle or arc to receive the center line or center mark.

For the Professional

The center lines created with the **dimcenter** command are not always correct or complete. You should not rely only on this command to create proper center lines. Many skilled AutoCAD users will forgo this command and create the center lines manually to ensure that they are drawn correctly and to appropriate standards.

Tutorial 13.7: Adding Radius and Diameter Dimensions

In this tutorial you will create a radius and diameter dimension on the right-side view of the tutorial drawing as shown in Figure 13.25. Before creating these dimensions, you will first modify the tutorial dimension style by adding two family settings, Radial and Diameter, to allow you to place the dimension text instead of having AutoCAD automatically place the dimension text for you.

1.  Select Dimension Styles from the Dimension toolbar. The Dimension Styles dialog box will appear.
2. Select the Radial option in the Family tile.
3. Select the Format button. The Format dialog box appears.
4. Select the User Defined check box. This allows you to place the dimension text at any location you specify instead of the AutoCAD default location.
5. Select the OK button. The Format dialog box will close and the Dimension Styles Dialog box will reappear.
6. Select the Save button to save the style changes to the TUTORIAL dimension style. A Radial family style has now been created. Whenever a radial dimension is needed, simply display the Dimension Styles dialog box and select the Radial radio button to activate this style family. Now let's create a diameter style.
7. Select the Diameter option in the Family tile.
8. Select the Format button. The Format dialog box appears.
9. Select the User Defined check box.
10. Select the OK button. The Format dialog box will close and the Dimension Styles dialog box will reappear.
11. Select the Save button to save the style changes to the TUTORIAL dimension style. A Diameter family style has now been created. Whenever a diameter dimension is needed, simply display the Dimension Styles dialog box and select the Diameter radio button to activate this style family.
12. Since the next dimension to be created is a radius dimension, select the Radial family radio button.

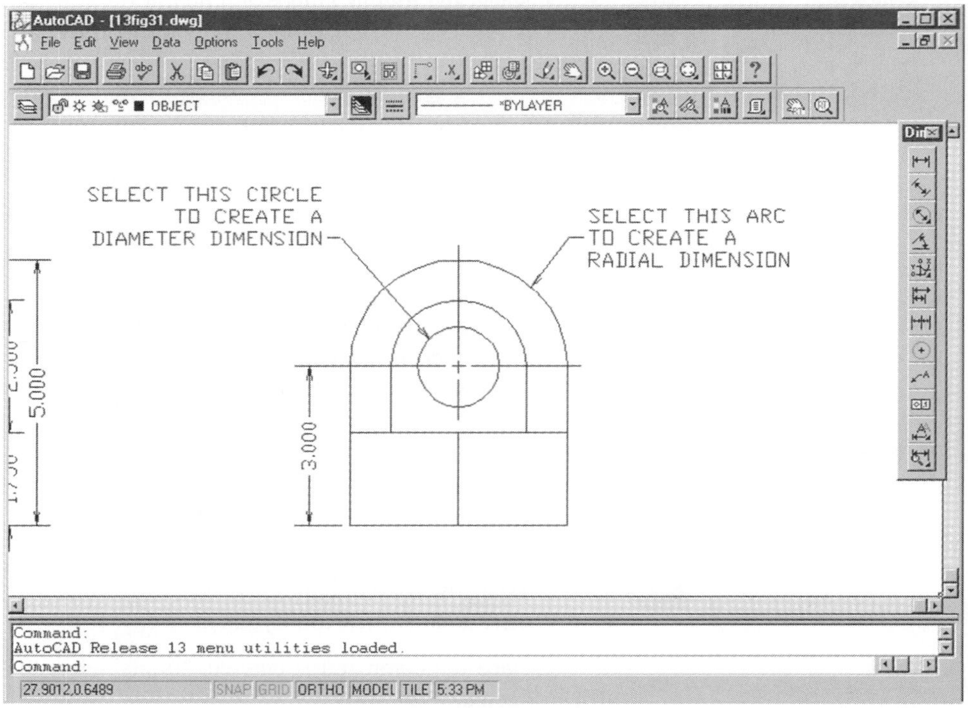

Figure 13.31
Use these objects to create radius and diameter dimensions.

13. Select OK to close the Dimension Styles dialog box.
14.  Select Radius Dimension from the Dimension toolbar. The `Select arc or circle:` prompt appears.
15. Select the Arc specified in Figure 13.31. The `Dimension text <2.000>:` prompt appears in the `Command:` prompt, press the right mouse button to accept the value.
16. The `Dimension line location (Text/Angle):` prompt appears. Move the cursor to place the Radial dimension at approximately the same location as the one found in Figure 13.25 and then press the left mouse button. The radius dimension will be created. Note that an *R* is placed before the dimension. This is the standard mechanical notation for radius dimensions.
17.  Select Dimension Styles from the Dimension toolbar. The Dimension Styles dialog box will appear.
18. Select the Diameter option in the Family tile.
19. Click OK to accept the style family.
20.  Select Diameter Dimension from the Dimension toolbar. The `Select arc or circle:` prompt appears.
21. Select the circle specified in Figure 13.31. The `Dimension text <2.000>:` prompt appears in the `Command:` prompt. Press the right mouse button to accept the value.
22. The `Dimension line location (Text/Angle):` prompt appears. Move the cursor to place the Diameter dimension at approximately the same location as the one found in Figure 13.25 and then press the left mouse button. The Diameter dimension will be created. Note that a diameter symbol is placed before the dimension. This is the standard mechanical notation for diameter dimensions.

ANGULAR DIMENSIONING

Just as the world is not composed of straight lines. It is also not composed of 90° angles. Many objects contain angles that are more or less than the familiar right angle. Consider an octagonal gazebo or a pyramid. Each of these objects contains angles other than right. This section will show you how to create dimensions that specify an angular dimension.

ANGULAR DIMENSIONS

A key to remember before creating angular dimensions is that you need an angle defined in a drawing before you need to use this command. You will typically not create an angular dimension on a right angle. If no angular dimension is created, the angle is assumed to be a right angle. To create angular dimensions, use the **dimangular** command. Use one of the following procedures for starting the command:

- Select the Angular Dimension button from the Dimension toolbar.
- Type **dimangular** at the `Command:` prompt.

Once the command is entered, you will be asked to select the arc, circle, or line that defines the angle to receive the dimension. There are four ways to define angles using AutoCAD. They are discussed here:

- **Two non-parallel lines.** Select any two lines that are not parallel. Once selected, you will need to place the dimension text. It will generally fall within the angular dimension unless there is not enough room for the text. Moving the text to different areas can lead to completely different angular measurements. Experiment with this command on two non-parallel lines to see the different values and orientations that this selection will create.
- **Arcs.** Selecting an arc will cause the angular measurement to measure the angle between the start and ending points of the arc. The placement of the text will once again affect the appearance of the angular dimension.
- **Circle and a defined point.** The point at which you select the circle becomes the start point for the arc that is going to be defined. Next, pick a point on the circle to define the ending point for the arc. This option is identical to the arc, except that you are starting with a circle and specifying a portion of that circle to be an arc.

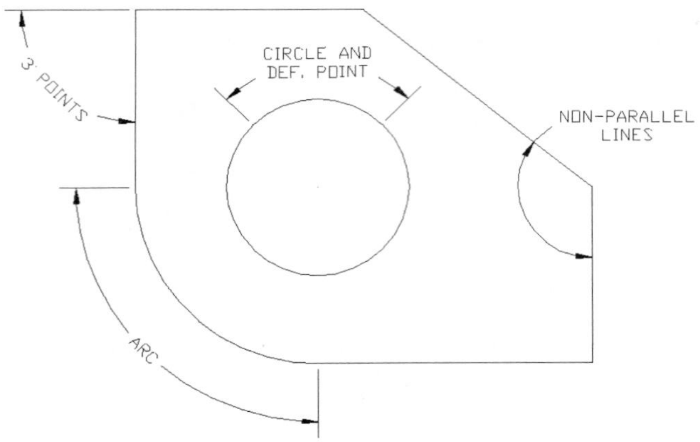

Figure 13.32
Use these options to create an angular dimension.

- **Three defined points.** Use this method to select three points that define an angle. To use this option, press Enter at the `Select arc, circle, line, or RETURN:` prompt. Then select the first point to define the start point of the angle. The next point you select will be the vertex of the arc and, finally, the third point will be the end point for the arc. Figure 13.32 displays this and the previous three options for selecting objects to create an Angular Dimension.

EDITING DIMENSIONS

Creating dimensions is one of the advantages of using CAD software over the traditional manual drawing method. And while it may seem that this one feature alone is worth the price, where AutoCAD really shines is in the way it can modify the dimensions. There are many times when you will want to change the dimension text or its location, suppress extension lines, or even change the type of terminator. You do not need to erase the dimension and then recreate it. You can simply modify it. This section will discuss two commands used to modify dimensions, the **dimtedit** and **ddmodify** command. You will also find that Grips are very useful when modifying dimension.

Relocating and Rotating Dimension Text

What do you do if you have inadvertently selected a location for the dimension text that is not what you wanted? Do you erase the dimension and try it again? Probably not. With AutoCAD you can easily modify the location of the dimension text by using the **dimtedit** command. Let's take a brief look at this command and its features. You will find that this command differs from others in the use of its button on the toolbar. Unlike other sections, let's first take a look at the command prompt method and then discuss the use of the toolbar. We will discuss the options step by step.

1. Type **`dimtedit`** at the `Command:` prompt.
2. The `Select dimension:` prompt will appear. Select the dimension that contains the text to be modified.
3. The `Enter text location (Left/Right/Home/Angle):` prompt appears. You can now move the mouse to modify the location of the dimension line. You can also select from one of four options described below:
   - **Left.** Moves the text to the left of the dimension line.
   - **Right.** Moves the text to the right of the dimension line.
   - **Home.** Moves the text to its original position that the text was placed when the dimension was created.
   - **Angle.** Changes the angle of the text.
4. Once the dimension has been modified to your liking, press the right mouse button to exit the command.

Tutorial 13.8: Adding Angular Dimensions

This tutorial continues from the previous tutorial. In this tutorial you will create an angular dimension on the top view of tutorial drawing. When created, the angular dimension will be in line with the existing horizontal dimension. You will use the two non-parallel method to create this angular dimension.

1. Ensure that **snap** is turned off.
2.  Select the Angular Dimension button from the Dimension toolbar. The `Select arc, circle, line, or RETURN:` prompt will appear in the `Command:` prompt.
3. Select the line shown in Figure 13.33.
4. At the `Second line:` prompt, select the second line specified in Figure 13.33.
5. At the `Dimension arc line location:` prompt, move the dimension line to the right and visually line it up with the existing aligned dimension, with the dimension text of 2.828. Refer to Figure 13.25. Once it is aligned, select that point.
6. It may not appear immediately, but the angular dimension has an extension line that is sitting on top of the aligned dimension line. If we were to plot the drawing, that extension line would appear thicker. We need to modify the dimension so that it suppresses the second extension line. We will make the correction in a later tutorial.

Figure 13.33
Select these two lines to create the angular dimension.

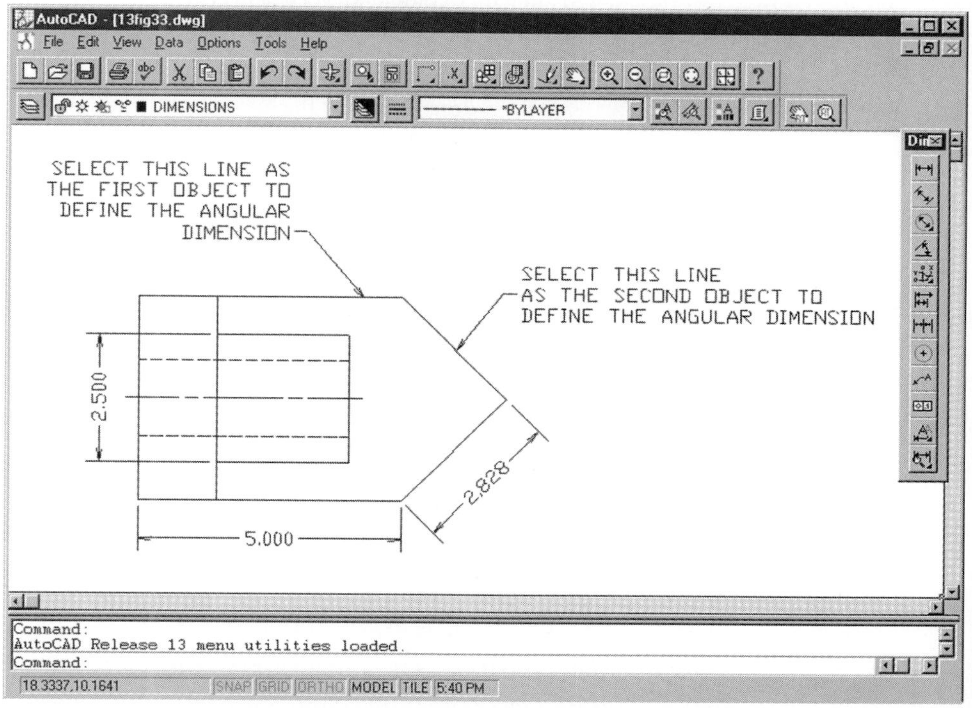

You can also use the toolbars to modify the location of the dimension text within the dimension. AutoCAD has six buttons on the dimension toolbar that perform many of the same functions as the **dimtedit** command. You use the flyout feature of the Home button to display the options available. Figure 13.34 displays these buttons and their location on the Dimension toolbar as well as defining their use. Once a button is selected, select the dimension to be modified.

Skill Builder

If you want to modify the text, not the text position, use the **ddedit** command and then select the dimension to modify. You can also use the **ddmodify** command described in the next section, but that will require an extra step.

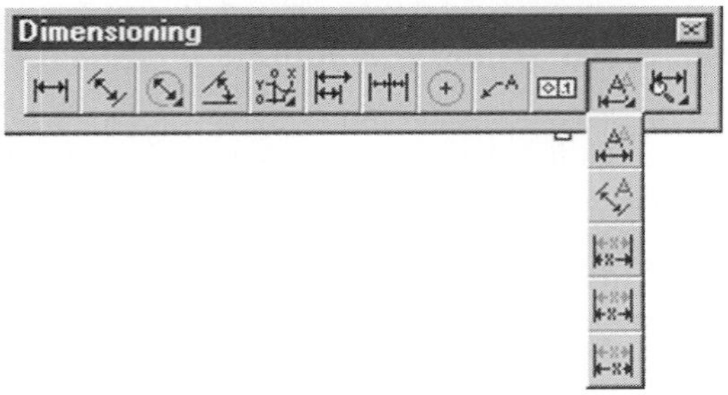

Figure 13.34
Use these buttons to modify the text location.

Modifying Dimensions and Dimension Text

While you can modify the dimension text location, there are many other parts of the dimension that can be modified as well. The command to modify a dimension is the same as the command to modify any other object, **ddmodify. ddmodify** was discussed in a previous unit, but we should look at how it is specifically used to modify a dimension. You will find this command very powerful once you become familiar with the plethora of options. To invoke the **ddmodify** command you can use one of two options:

- Select the Properties button on the Object Properties toolbar.
- Type `ddmodify` at the `Command:` prompt.

Once the command has been entered, select the dimension to be modified. When the dimension is selected, a dialog box similar to the one in Figure 13.35 will be displayed.

Let's take a brief look at the options available in this dialog box.

- The Properties tile contains the same options as those found in the **ddchprop** command. This command is discussed in Unit 7.
- The Edit button will display the Edit Mtext dialog box. This is the same dialog box that was discussed with the **ddedit** command.
- The Style drop-down menu allows you to change the style of the dimension. It can be changed to any predefined style.
- The Geometry, Format, and Annotation buttons display the same dialog boxes that appear when these same buttons are chosen from the Dimension Styles dialog box. Make the changes to the appropriate dialog box and close the dialog box. That will return you to the Modify Dimension dialog box. Select OK to accept the changes and the dimension will be modified.

Modifying the Dimension Object Using Object Grips

Like other objects, dimensions can be moved, copied, rotated, and stretched. A previous unit was completely devoted to grips and their operations. Grips provide an additional way to modify dimensions. Each type of dimension will have different grip points that

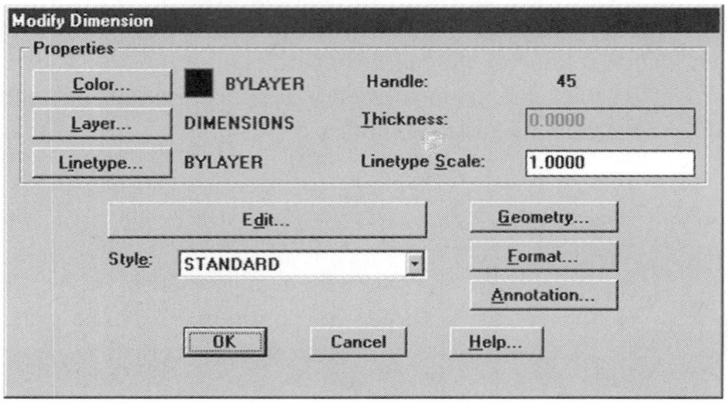

Figure 13.35
The Modify Dimension dialog box.

can be used to modify specific attributes of a dimension. Using grips on dimensions is not unlike using them for other objects. At the `Command:` prompt, select a dimension. Grips will appear at key locations that affect the dimension. Select the grip point to modify and move, copy, rotate, or stretch it to another location. Using grips is beneficial for the following situations:

- Change the location of the dimension text. While **dimtedit** will accomplish this, it is sometimes quicker to use grips to perform this function.
- Modify the location of the dimension line.
- Rotate the dimension text.
- Close the gap between extension line and centerline.

You may find many other uses other than the ones listed above. Experiment with grips and you may find that it is much faster and more convenient than using the **ddmodify** command.

TUTORIAL 13.9: MODIFYING DIMENSIONS

This tutorial continues from the previous tutorial. In this tutorial you will modify the diameter dimension found in the right-side view of the tutorial drawing. You will add a note to the dimension as well as changing the terminator from an open arrow to a closed arrow.

1.  Select the Properties button from the Object Properties toolbar. The `Select objects:` prompt appears.
2. Select the diameter dimension shown in Figure 13.36 and click the right mouse button. The Modify Dimension dialog box appears as shown in Figure 13.37.
3. Select the Edit button. The Edit Mtext dialog box appears as shown in Figure 13.38. Notice that no text is entered, only a <>. The <> is the equivalent of a variable. AutoCAD will place the appropriate dimension based on the object, in this case, a circle to which it is attached.
4. Move the cursor so that it is located after <>.
5. Add one space and the word *THRU* capitalized.
6. Click the OK button. The Modify Dimension dialog box appears.
7. Select the Geometry button. The Geometry dialog box appears.
8. Change the open arrows to closed filled arrows.
9. Click the OK button. The Modify Dimension dialog box appears.
10. Click the OK button. The changes to the diameter dimension will be displayed as shown in Figure 13.39.
11. Complete the tutorial for this object by changing the terminator back to the open arrowheads.

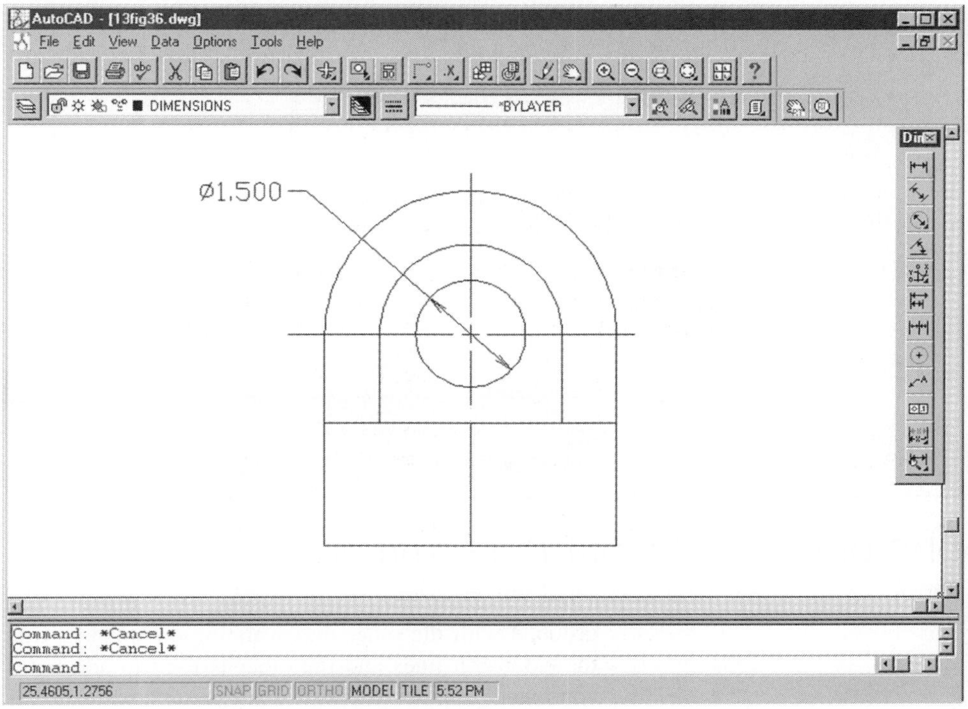

Figure 13.36
Select this diameter dimension to modify.

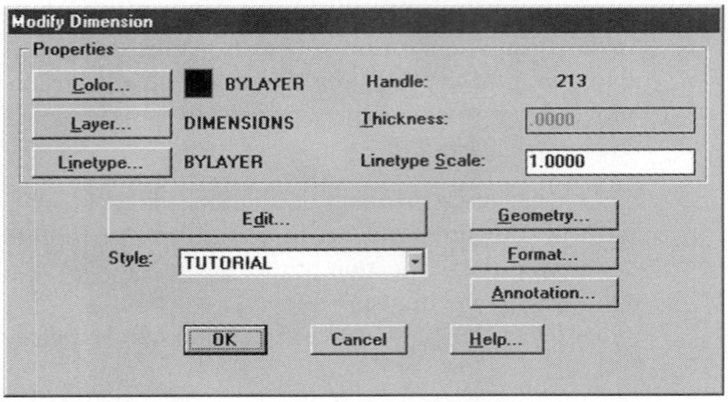

Figure 13.37
Use this dialog box as the "jump-off" point for modifying dimension properties.

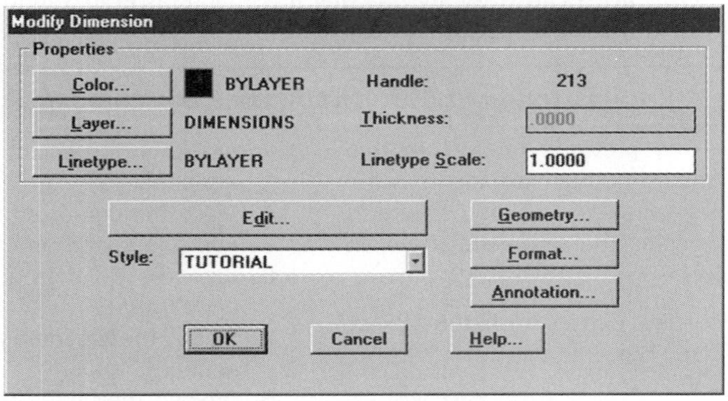

Figure 13.38
The Mtext dialog box is used to modify the dimension text.

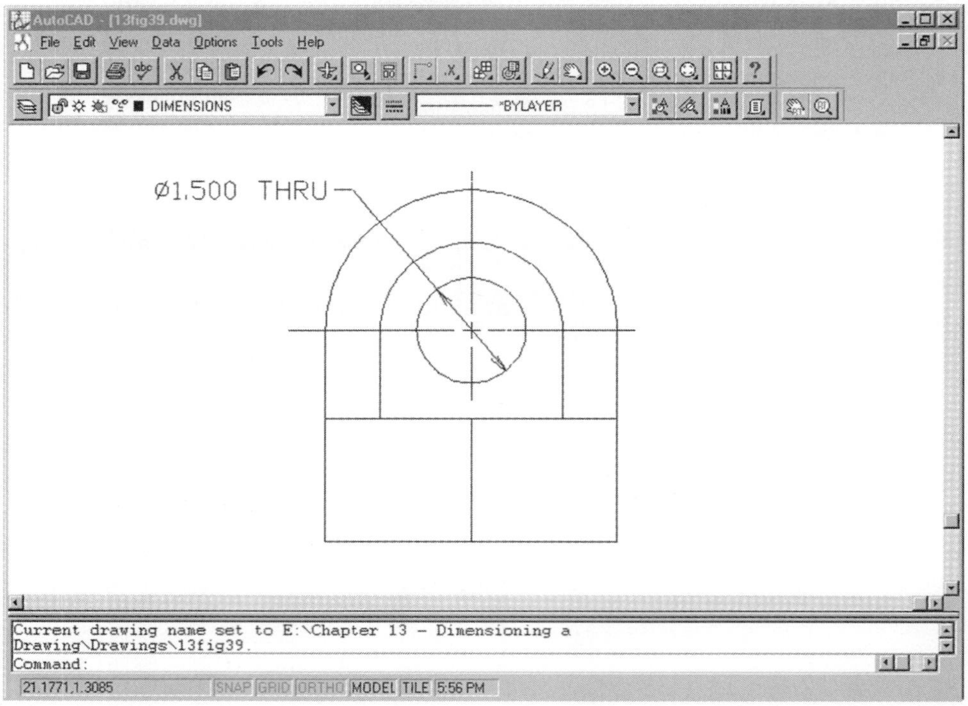

Figure 13.39
The diameter dimension after it has been modified.

ADDITIONAL DIMENSIONING FEATURES

The last section of this unit discusses two dimensioning commands that cannot be easily grouped with the other dimensioning commands. One will modify the oblique angle of the extension lines and the other is used to add notes to a drawing. Both of these new commands can be very useful in special circumstances.

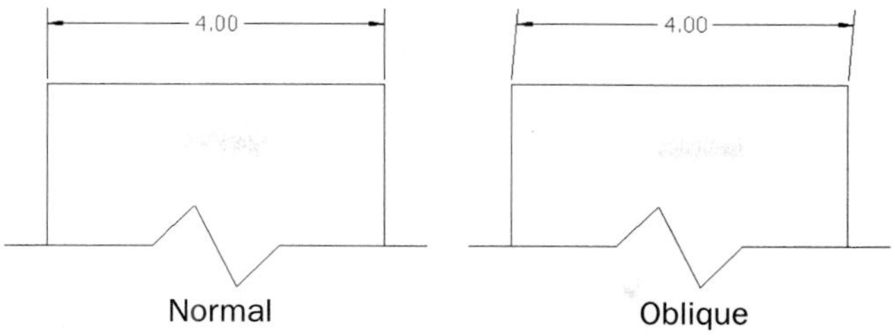

Figure 13.40
Modifying a horizontal dimension to an obliquing dimension.

Oblique Dimensions

Oblique dimensions are used very rarely but their use can be very beneficial if you are trying to dimension pictorial drawings such as isometrics. Isometric drawings are discussed in the last unit of this book. Since their use is quite rare for general drawings, we will look at this command very briefly. Use the following command sequence to create oblique dimensions:

1. Ensure that a linear or aligned dimension has been created.
2. To begin the command, select the Dimension Styles flyout menu and select the Oblique button.
3. Select the dimension or dimensions you wish to oblique and click the right mouse button.
4. At the `Enter obliquing angle (RETURN for none):` prompt, enter the value that represents the obliquing angle. AutoCAD assumes the angle you enter to be an absolute obliquing angle. For instance, if you want to apply an obliquing angle to vertical extension lines (90°) 5° to the right, you would enter 85°. This example is shown in Figure 13.40.

Leaders

Leaders are used to place notes on a drawing. These notes can be used to describe an object or feature in a way that dimensions may not be able to describe. Leaders are composed of a terminator, usually an arrowhead, a leader line, and the leader text as shown in Figure 13.41.

If you were to try and create the leader manually you would have to use the pline command to create the arrowhead, followed by a pline for the leader line, and finally use the **mtext** command to create the leader text. A fairly lengthy procedure. AutoCAD automates leader creation with the **leader** command. You can enter the **leader** command in two ways:

- Select Leader from the Dimension toolbar.
- Enter **`leader`** at the **`Command:`** prompt.

Once the command has been entered, you will continue to create the leader using the following steps:

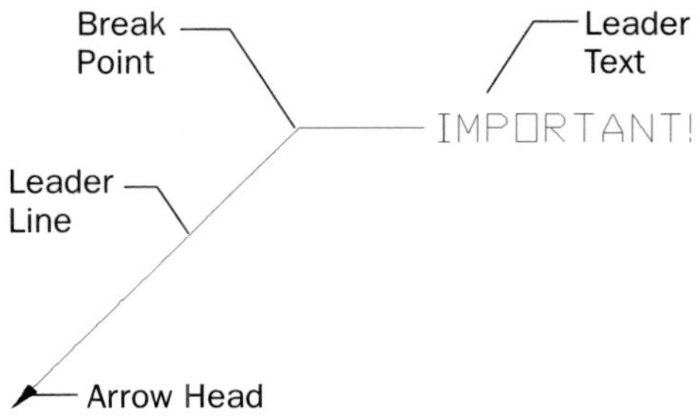

Figure 13.41
An example of a leader with all components annotated.

1. At the `From point:` prompt, enter the location to which the leader will be pointing.
2. At the `To point:` prompt, enter the point that is the break point of the leader line.
3. At the `To point (Format/Annotation/Undo)<Annotation>:` prompt, select from one of the options described below.
   - **Format.** Further options for this selection include the following:
     - **Spline.** Creates the leader line as a spline, or curved shape.
     - **Straight.** Creates the leader line as a series of straight lines.
     - **Arrow.** Creates the leader line with an arrow on the end of the start point.
     - **None.** Omits the creation of an arrow on the end of the start point of the leader line.
   - **Annotation.** Begins the creation of the annotation text string.
   - **Undo.** Use the option to undo the last sequence of this command.
4. At the `Annotation (or RETURN for options):` prompt, begin typing the annotation or press [Enter] for more annotation options.
5. At the `Tolerance/Copy/Block/None/<Mtext>:` prompt, select from one of the options described below.
   - **Tolerance.** Use this option if you wish to incorporate tolerances with your leader.
   - **Copy.** Copies the note from another text string located on the drawing.
   - **Block.** Inserts a block at the end of the leader line instead of an annotation.
   - **None.** Will not place any annotation on the leader.
   - **Mtext.** Displays the Mtext dialog box. Use the dialog box to create the annotation.
6. Once all steps have been completed, the leader will be created and the text will be placed.

For the Professional

The **leader** command does always place the text properly. You should know that the leader line should always start at the top left of the annotation or at the bottom right of the annotation. The leader line should be aligned with the middle of the text as shown in Figure 13.41.

Tutorial 13.10: Adding Leaders

In this tutorial you will add a lengthy note to an object on a drawing. The note will be imported from an existing text file that was created using the Windows 95 Notepad application.

1.  Open the Leader drawing file from the tutorial disk.
2.  Select the Leader button from the Dimension toolbar.
3. At the `From point:` prompt, enter **12.5,9.75.**
4. At the `To point:` prompt, enter **14,12.75.**
5. At the `To point (Format/Annotation/Undo) <Annotation>:` prompt, press [Enter].
6. At the `Annotation (or RETURN for options):` prompt press [Enter].
7. At the `Tolerance/Copy/Block/None/<Mtext>:` prompt, press [Enter]. The Mtext dialog box appears.
8. Select the Import button. The Import Text File dialog box appears.
9. Select the Clock Info.txt file from the tutorial disk.
10. Select the OK button. The dialog box closes and the Mtext dialog box reappears.
11. Select the OK button. The leader will be created with the imported text.
12. Since AutoCAD centered the text block on the leader line, we will need to move it manually to make it correct.
13. Move the text so that the middle of the first line of the leader note is aligned with the leader line as shown in Figure 13.42.

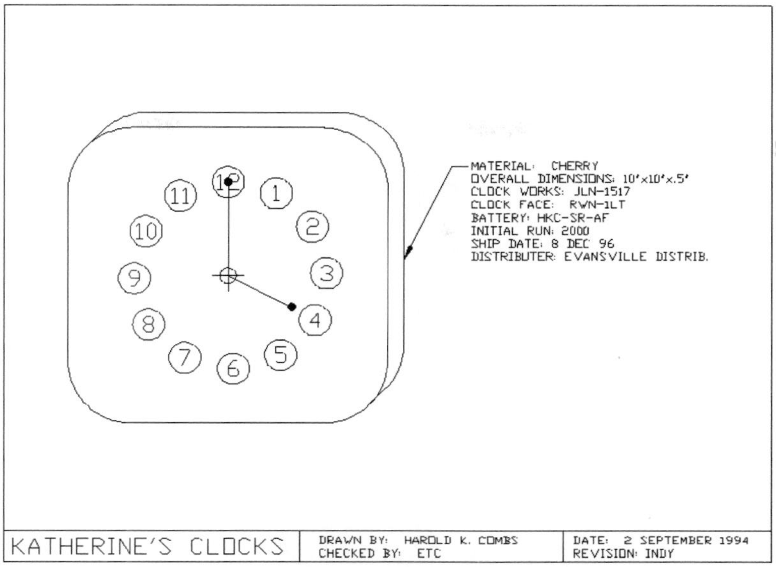

Figure 13.42
The completed drawing with the leader and text placed.

SUMMARY

Dimensions are very important to technical drawings. They are needed so that the part or building can be manufactured correctly. Without them, drawings are just that, drawings. They do not contain necessary information and just become works of art instead of legal manufacturing documents. Creating dimensions manually was a very time-consuming procedure. And if you ever needed to modify the dimensions, you would find that it was no easy task. AutoCAD allows you to create and modify dimensions quickly and correctly. Release 13 increases performance by getting rid of the `Dim:` prompt requirement, placing all dimensioning commands on the Dimensions toolbar, and by increasing the capabilities of the Modify Dimension dialog box. Even the use of leaders has been improved with the implementation of Mtext and the ability to insert text files created with other software. No longer should AutoCAD students dread or even fear drawings that contain numerous and complicated dimensions. With AutoCAD in their drawing arsenal, they can create any dimension needed quickly and with ease.

REVIEW

1. Explain the advantages of associative dimensions.
2. What is the purpose of standards organizations such as ANSI and AIA?
3. Why are dimension styles important?
4. What are the two types of linear dimensions?
5. Discuss the difference between continued and baseline dimensions.
6. When are diameter dimensions used?
7. Explain the purpose of the Dimension Styles dialog box.
8. Explain the difference between drawing units and dimension units.
9. What command allows you to easily modify an existing dimension? List three common attributes that can be made to all dimensions.
10. When are leaders used?

EXERCISE 13

In this assignment you will create and dimension the drawing of a metal plate found in Figure 13.43. Use the directions below to assist you in creating this drawing as accurately

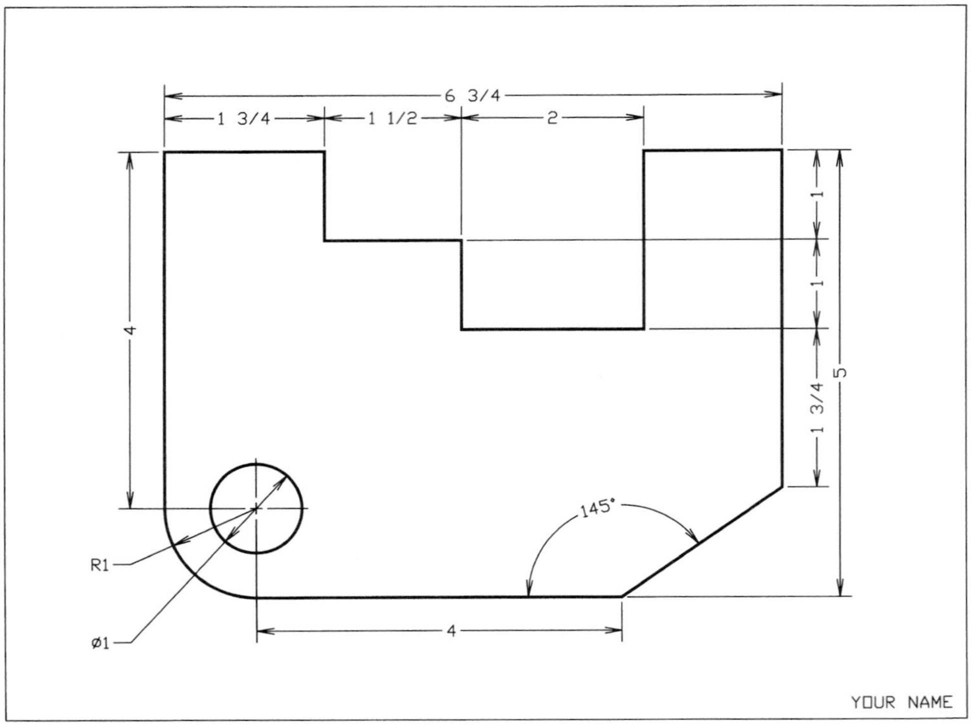

Figure 13.43
The completed drawing of the metal plate with dimensions.

as possible. Although this assignment is a very simplistic one, it will familiarize you with the commands necessary to start creating dimensions.

1. Determine the type of units necessary by analyzing Figure 13.43.
2. Set the upper-right limit at 10.5,8.
3. Set **grid** and **snap** to your preferences.
4. Create necessary and appropriate layers. A copy of the layers created for this assignment is shown in Figure 13.44.
5. Create the object lines using a polyline with a thickness of .03.
6. Create a dimension style called DIMENSIONS and use the settings found in the dialog boxes shown in Figure 13.45.
7. Save the drawing as metal plate.dwg.
8. Plot the drawing at full scale.

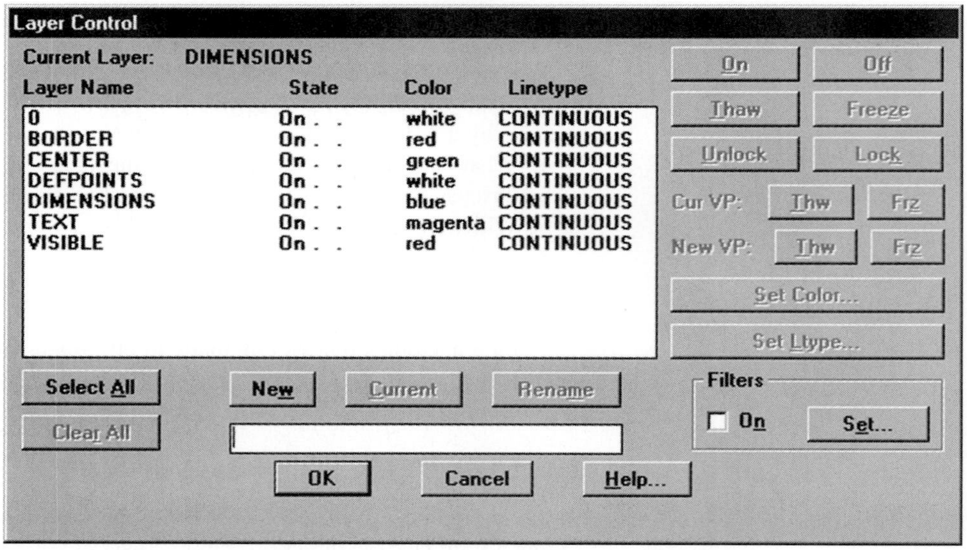

Figure 13.44
A list of the layers used for the metal plate drawing.

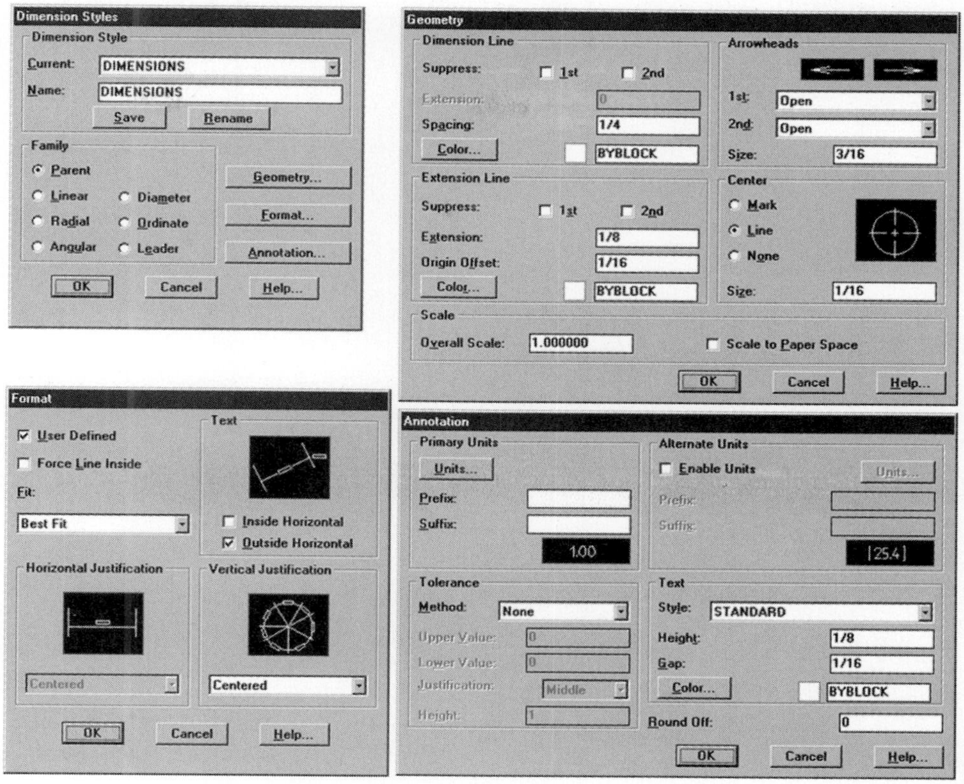

Figure 13.45
Use these settings to assist in the creation of a dimension style to be used for this assignment.

UNIT 14

MODIFYING OBJECT CHARACTERISTICS AND EXTRACTING INFORMATION FROM YOUR DRAWING

OVERVIEW

When you create objects within AutoCAD, a great deal of information is stored about each individual object. You can access this database in a variety of different ways. In this unit you will learn how to modify an object's characteristics, such as how to move an existing object from one layer to another. You will also learn how to extract information from AutoCAD's database regarding the drawing as a whole, or on specific objects in the drawing.

OBJECTIVES

- Change the properties of drawing objects.
- Change the geometric characteristics of drawing objects.
- Set default object properties.
- Edit text with a dialog box.
- Rename object traits.
- Remove unwanted objects.
- List the current status of AutoCAD **(status).**
- List the information stored for drawing objects **(list** and **dblist).**
- Determine a distance and angle **(dist).**
- Locate the coordinates of a point on-screen **(id).**
- Calculate the area of a given shape **(area).**
- Keep track of the time spent on a drawing **(time).**

INTRODUCTION

AutoCAD's major advantage over manual drafting techniques is its capacity to modify existing drawings quickly and easily. To change the linetype of a line on a manually created drawing, you must erase the line and then draw it again. With AutoCAD, you simply select the line and assign it a new linetype.

Every time an object is created in a drawing, AutoCAD stores information in a database for that specific object. For example, the information stored for a linetype includes starting point, ending point, specific length, and direction, but it isn't limited to just those items. The information in the database may be accessed through a variety of commands. In this unit, you'll learn how to extract information from AutoCAD's database.

AutoCAD also offers several commands that allow you to modify the database information for each particular object. There are times when it's advantageous to change certain properties. AutoCAD gives you the ability to easily change the layer an object is on, along with the linetype.

Changing text, including dimensions, is another easy task. Instead of retyping a line of text to change one word, you can invoke a dialog box showing the existing text. To edit the text, use the cursor, backspace, and arrow keys to make the necessary changes in the dialog box. When you press Enter, the updated text appears on-screen, in the same location with the same style.

You can also rename object traits, such as layer names, linetype names, or text style names through a dialog box. Finally, you can purge or remove unwanted objects, such as layers or linetypes, from your drawing at any time.

OUTLINE

Modifying Object Properties
Tutorial 14.1: Using the Change Properties Dialog Box
Tutorial 14.2: Using the Modify Dialog Box
Tutorial 14.3: Modifying Object Characteristics
Extracting Information from your Drawing
Tutorial 14.4: Listing the Status of a File
Tutorial 14.5: Listing the Objects of a File
Tutorial 14.6: Using the Dist Command
Tutorial 14.7: Using the ID Command
Tutorial 14.8: Using the Area Command
Tutorial 14.9: Using the Area Command
Tutorial 14.10: Using the Time Command
Summary
Review
Exercises

MODIFYING OBJECT PROPERTIES

AutoCAD allows you to make a variety of changes to an existing object. The **change** and **chprop** commands allow you to change the layer, linetype, color, and thickness properties. Neither of these commands provide a dialog box, however. **change** allows you to edit properties or point information. The Properties option of **change** includes **elevation** and **ltscale** in the list of properties. The Change Point option of **change** allows you to change start points, endpoints, insertion points, text styles, text wording, and so on, of the object selected. The exact options depend on the type of object selected. **chprop** includes an **ltscale** option.

The **ddchprop** command will access the Change Properties dialog box that allows you to modify several object properties available with the `Command:` line options (**change**, **chprop**) in a user-friendly dialog box (see Figure 14.1). The Change Properties dialog box can be accessed as follows:

- Select the Properties button from the Object Properties toolbar.
- Select Properties from the Edit pull-down menu.
- Type **ddchprop** at the `Command:` prompt.

The Change Properties dialog box displays the existing color, layer, linetype, linetype scale, and thickness of the object. The following sections describe how to use the dialog box to change the properties of the selected object.

SELECTING MULTIPLE OBJECTS FOR MODIFICATION

By using the Change Properties dialog box, you can modify object properties of more than one object at a time. When the **ddchprop** command is invoked, AutoCAD prompts `Select Objects:`. At this point you can use any method for creating a selection set, such as window, fence, and so on. When you have finished creating the selection set, press Enter. The Change Properties dialog box appears.

SKILL BUILDER

You can also use pick-first selection to create the selection set of objects to be changed. If a selection set exists when you invoke the **ddchprop** command, AutoCAD performs the changes specified on the existing selection set.

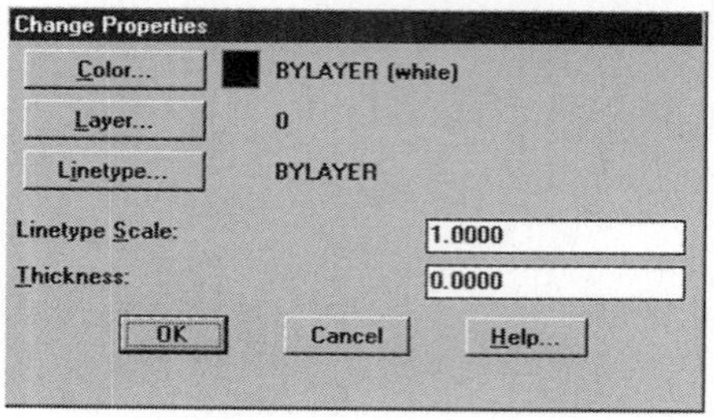

Figure 14.1
Use the Change Properties dialog box to modify many object characteristics.

When selecting more than one object to modify, you can select any combination of objects. A selection set could consist of a line, arc, and circle, each on a different layer with a different linetype. When the Change Properties dialog box appears, Varies will appear after the Layer button, indicating the selected objects are on different layers. The **ddchprop** dialog box will give all selected objects the same settings. When you click OK, all selected objects will be on the same layer with the same **ltscale.**

Changing Color and Linetype

If you want to change the object color from the Change Properties dialog box, pick the Color button. The Select Color dialog box appears. Picking the Linetype button will display the Select Linetype dialog box.

Skill Builder

In the Change Properties dialog box, you can change color and linetypes for objects regardless of the layer the object is on. For example, you can have a green object with a hidden linetype on a layer that is red with a continuous linetype. Modifying individual object characteristics (color and linetype) without regard to layer settings can cause confusion in a drawing. It's recommended that you leave the default `bylayer` setting for the color and linetype so that is it is not always necessary to change color and linetypes before creating new entities.

Moving the Object to a Different Layer

To change the layer an object is currently on, pick the Layer button from the Change Properties dialog box. This will bring up the Select Layer dialog box as shown in Figure 14.2. When a different layer is chosen, either by typing the name of the layer in the edit box or selecting the layer from the list, the setting for the new layer will appear in the Change Properties dialog box. The object selected will now be on the layer selected, and it will have the corresponding color and linetype for that layer.

Adjusting the Linetype Scale

The Change Properties dialog box will also allow you to individually change the Linetype Scale for selected objects. The **ltscale** variable changes the linetype scale for all objects. Proper use of the Change Properties dialog box allows you to have objects with different linetype scales within a drawing.

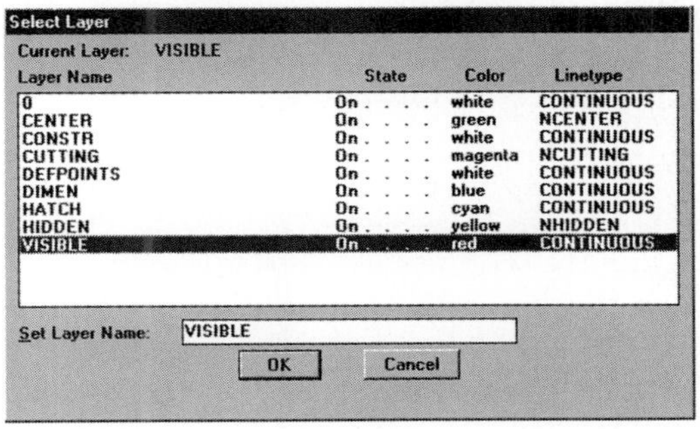

Figure 14.2
The Select Layer dialog box is used to change the layer the selected objects are on.

Tutorial 14.1: Using the Change Properties Dialog Box

In this tutorial, you'll use the **ddchprop** dialog box to change the properties of a circle and a line.

1.  Select New from the Standard toolbar. If prompted by the AutoCAD Save Changes dialog box, select the appropriate response.

When the Create New Drawing dialog box appears, press Enter.

2. 
   - Select Line from the Draw toolbar.
   - At the `_line From point:` prompt, type **2,2** and press Enter.
   - At the `To point:` prompt, type **7,7** and press Enter.
3. 
   - Select the Circle Center Radius button from the Draw toolbar.
   - At the `_circle 3P/2P/TTR/<Center point>:` prompt, type **10,4** and press Enter.
   - At the `Diameter/<Radius>:` prompt, type **2** and press Enter.
4. 
   - Select the Layers button from the Object Properties toolbar and create a new layer called Objects in the Layer Control dialog box.
   - Make the color of the layer blue. Select OK.
5. 
   - Select the Properties button from the Object Properties toobar.
6. At the `Select objects:` prompt, select the line and the circle and press Enter.
7. Click the Layer button in the Change Properties dialog box. The Select Layer dialog box appears.
8.
   - Select the Objects layer and click OK.
   - Select OK at the Change Properties dialog box.
   - Both the line and the circle change to blue and are placed on the Objects layer.

Changing Object Characteristics (ddmodify)

AutoCAD allows you to edit an object by modifying the information stored for the object in a dialog box. AutoCAD also lists various properties of the selected object.

The **ddmodify** command displays the Modify dialog box.

Skill Builder

The title of the dialog box changes, depending on the object selected. For a line, the title bar displays Modify Line. For an arc, the title bar displays Modify Arc.

The information that appears in the Modify dialog box changes according to the type of object selected (see Figure 14.3). The dialog box may display current properties or object characteristics without giving you the option of changing all of them. The Modify dialog box can be accessed by using any of these methods:

- Click the Properties button on the Object Properties toolbar.
- Select Properties from the Edit pull-down menu.
- Type **ddmodify** at the `Command:` prompt.

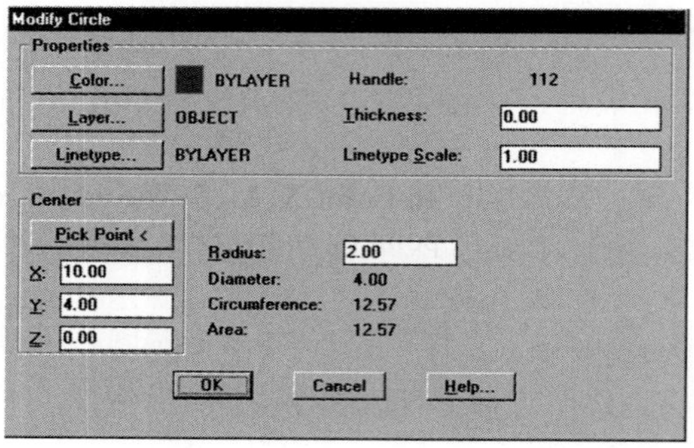

Figure 14.3
The information displayed in the Modify dialog box depends upon the object selected.

For the Professional

The professional may notice the methods for accessing the Modify dialog box are the same as the methods for accessing the Change Properties dialog box. The dialog box that appears and the options you are able to change depend on what you select when the `Select objects:` prompt appears. If you select multiple objects (line, arc, etc.) the Change Properties dialog box appears, allowing you to change the Color, Layer, Linetype, Linetype Scale and Thickness for all of the objects selected.

If you select one object, the Modify object dialog box appears, allowing you to change a variety of characteristics for the selected object. While the Modify object dialog box allows you more flexibility to change multiple characteristics of the selected object, you have to select each object you want to change independently.

The information that can be changed with the Modify dialog box varies depending on the object selected. Regardless of the type of object selected, the top portion of the Modify dialog box will display the same information. This information includes Color, Layer, Linetype, Linetype Scale, and Thickness. This is the same information that appears in the Change Properties dialog box.

In the Properties section of the Modify dialog box, the Color and Linetype should both be set to BYLAYER unless the color or linetype has been changed. Selecting the Layer button will bring up the Select Layer dialog box shown earlier in Figure 14.2. Depending upon the type of object selected, you may or may not be able to change the Thickness and Linetype Scale. The Thickness edit box allows you to change the thickness of an object. Thickness is used primarily in 3-D drawings.

Skill Builder

The **ddmodify** command allows you to change the layer an object is on, but it won't let you create new layers or rename existing layers.

The Modify dialog box also displays the handle for the object. The object handle is a unique identifier that AutoCAD assigns to the object. The handle is permanently assigned throughout the object's lifetime in the drawing. The handle is saved with the object in the drawing file and never changes. If the object is deleted from the drawing, the handle is also deleted and not used again in that drawing.

Changing a Line When you choose the Properties button on the Object Properties toolbar and select a single line, the following attributes can be modified:

- **From Point and To Point-Pick Point.** The dialog box disappears and you return to the drawing editor. The `From pt:` or `To point:` prompt appears allowing you to pick a new start point or endpoint with the cursor, or enter coordinates for a new endpoint.
- **From Point and To Point-X, Y, Z.** The edit boxes change the X, Y, and Z coordinates for the start point or endpoint of the line. The endpoints automatically change when you click the OK button.

When a line is picked, the Modify Line dialog box appears as shown in Figure 14.4. The Modify Line dialog box contains information about the line from the two endpoints, with edit boxes to change the endpoint coordinates. Selecting the Pick Point< button

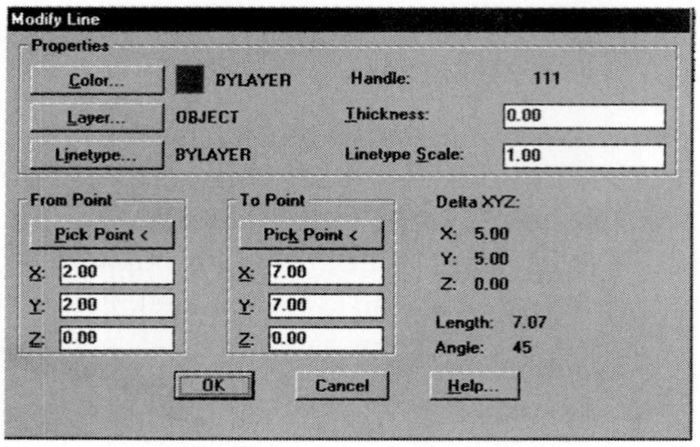

Figure 14.4
The Modify Line dialog box can change the two endpoints of a line.

returns you to the drawing editor. In the drawing editor you can select a new point with the cursor. You can also type a coordinate, using an absolute, relative, absolute polar, or relative polar coordinate entry method in response to the `From pt:` or `To point:` prompt.

Changing an Arc When you choose the Properties button on the Object Properties toolbar and select a single arc, the following attributes can be modified (see Figure 14.5):

- **Pick Point.** The dialog box disappears and you are returned to the drawing editor. The `Center point:` prompt appears, where you can pick a new center point with the cursor, or enter coordinates for a new center point.
- **X, Y, Z.** The edit boxes change the X, Y, and Z coordinates for the center point of the arc. The center point automatically changes when you click the OK button.
- **Radius.** To change the radius, double-click the Radius edit box. Enter a new value and the arc will change to the new value as reflected in the Arc Length value edit box.
- **Start Angle.** Double-clicking in the Start Angle edit box changes the start angle of the arc. Arcs are drawn in a counterclockwise manner. Pressing Enter after changing the Start Angle updates the Arc Length and Total Angle values.
- **End Angle.** The edit box is used to change the End Angle of the arc. Pressing Enter after changing the End Angle also updates the Arc Length and Total Angle values.

Changing a Circle When choosing the Properties button on the Object Properties toolbar and selecting a single circle, the following attributes can be modified:

- **Center Pick Point.** The dialog box disappears and you return to the drawing editor. The Center option allows you to pick a new center point with the cursor, or enter coordinates for a new endpoint.

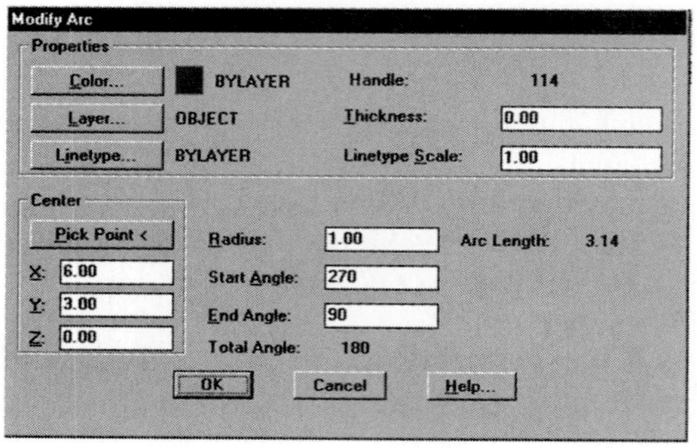

Figure 14.5
The center point, radius, start angle, and end angle of an arc can be edited in the Modify Arc dialog box.

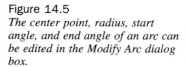

- **X, Y, Z.** The edit boxes change the X, Y, and Z coordinates for the center point of the circle. The center point automatically changes when you click the OK button.
- **Radius.** Changing the value will change the size of the radius of the circle.

When changing circular objects, related information for the Diameter, Circumference, and area appear (Figure 14.6). Typing a new value in the Radius edit box and pressing Enter updates the Diameter, Circumference, and Area values.

Changing Text Use the Modify Text dialog box to easily and quickly change text created with the **text** or **dtext** command. To open the Modify Text dialog box as shown in Figure 14.7, choose the Properties button on the Object Properties toolbar and select the text to modify. After selecting the text, the following information is displayed:

- **Text.** To edit the text wording, move the cursor to the Text edit box and remove, add, or change the text as necessary.
- **Origin.** To change the text origin, select the Pick Point< button and select a new point on the screen. You can also enter new coordinates in the X , Y, and Z edit boxes.
- **Height.** To automatically change the text height, enter a new value in the Height edit box.
- **Rotation.** Use this to change the Rotation angle of the selected text.
- **Width Factor.** Alters the Width (expansion/compression) factor of the selected text.
- **Obliquing Angle.** The obliquing angle is an offset from 90°. A positive offset results in characters that lean to the right, and a negative value causes the characters to slant to the left. The maximum angle you can enter is 85°.
- **Justify.** Selecting the arrow to the right of the Justify: box brings up the justification pop-up list. Select the desired justification from the list.
- **Style.** To change the text to a new style, select the arrow to the right of the Style box. All text styles that have been previously created appear in the pop-up list. Select the desired style from the list.
- **Upside Down and Backward.** Checking the Upside Down and Backward boxes causes the text to appear upside down or backward.

Changing an Xline When you choose the Properties button on the Object Properties toolbar and a single xline is selected, the following attributes can be modified:

- **Root Point.** The Root Point of an xline is the initial point that was used to define the xline. The Root Point can be changed with the Pick Point< button or by entering the coordinates in the X, Y, or Z edit boxes. If you select the Pick Point< but-

Figure 14.6 *Using the Modify Circle dialog box to change the size of a circle.*

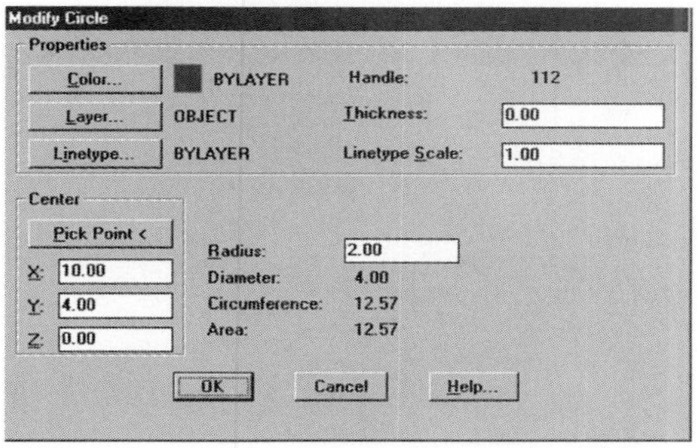

Figure 14.7 *The Modify Text dialog box offers a simple means of editing text.*

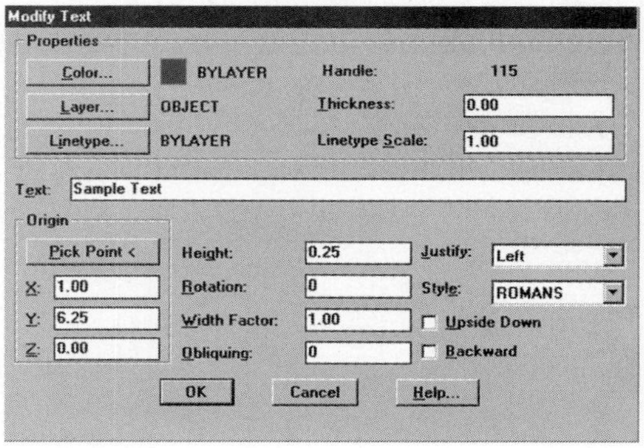

ton the dialog box disappears and you are returned to the drawing editor. The `Root point:` prompt allows you to pick a new conceptual midpoint of the xline by using the cursor, or by entering coordinates.

- **Second Point.** Modifying the Second Point allows you to change the Direction Vector of the xline. The Modify Xline dialog box is shown in Figure 14.8.The edit boxes change the X, Y, and Z coordinates for the direction vector. The direction vector automatically changes when you pick the OK button. If you select the Pick Point< button, the dialog box disappears and you are returned to the drawing editor. The `Second point:` prompt allows you to pick a new direction vector by using the cursor, or by entering coordinates.
- **Direction Vector.** The Direction Vector area displays the change in coordinates from the root point to the second point. This is updated automatically whenever you change the Root Point or the Second Point for the xline. Note you cannot change the Direction Vector by using this option.

Changing a Ray The Modify Ray dialog box shown in Figure 14.9 is similar to the Modify Xline dialog box. The Start Point is the point where the ray begins. As with the Xline, modifying the Second Point allows you to change the Direction Vector of the ray. When you choose the Properties button on the Object Properties toolbar and a single ray is selected, the following attributes can be modified:

- **Start Point.** The initial point where the ray began. The Start Point can be changed with the Pick Point< button or by entering the coordinates in the X, Y, or Z edit boxes. If you select the Pick Point< button, the dialog box disappears and you are returned to the drawing editor. The `From pt:` prompt allows you to pick a new start point for the ray by using the cursor, or by entering coordinates.
- **To Point.** The second point that the ray passes through. The To Point can also be changed with a Pick Point< button or by entering coordinates in the X, Y, or Z edit boxes. If you select the Pick Point< button, the dialog box disappears and you are returned to the drawing editor. The `To point:` prompt allows you to pick a new point the ray will pass through using the cursor, or by entering coordinates.
- **Direction Vector.** The Direction Vector area displays the change in coordinates from the start point to the second point of the ray. This is updated automatically whenever you change the Start Point or the Second Point. Note you cannot change the Direction Vector by using this option.

Changing an Mline When you choose the Properties button on the Object Properties toolbar and select an mline, no attributes can be changed. The Modify Multiline dialog box is displayed, and you can change only the Layer and Linetype Scale. The dialog box also displays the Mline Style of the selected multiline. To modify the Mline, see **mledit** in Unit 12, "Advanced Drawing Techniques."

Figure 14.8 *With the Modify Xline dialog box, you can change the Root Point and Second Point, automatically updating the Direction Vector.*

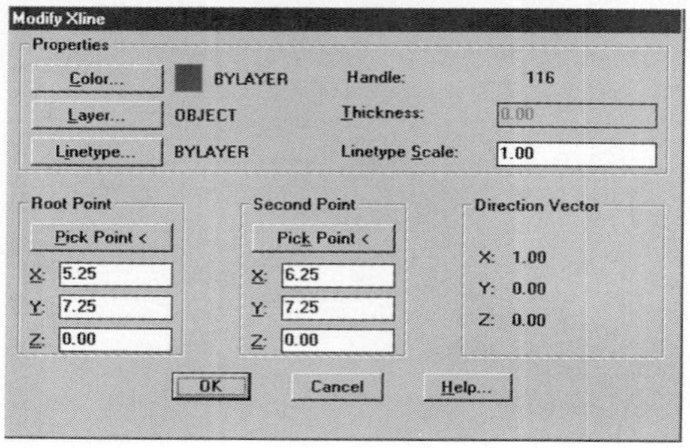

Figure 14.9 *In the Modify Ray dialog box, you can change the Start Point and Second Point of a ray.*

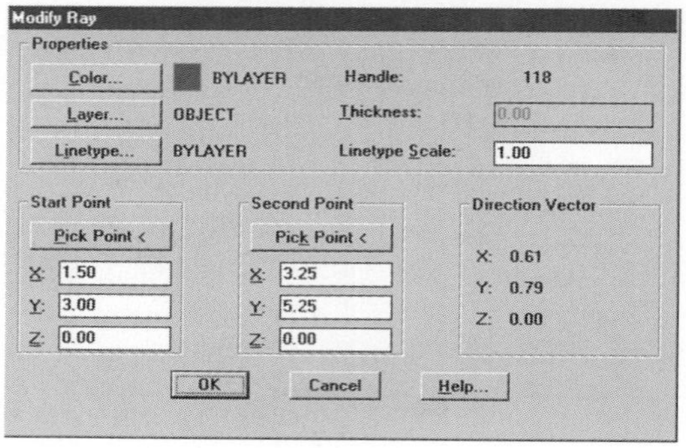

Changing a Hatch If you choose the Properties button on the Object Properties toolbar and pick a hatch, you get the Modify Associative Hatch dialog box as shown in Figure 14.10. Selecting Hatch Edit from the Modify Associative Hatch dialog box opens the Hatch edit dialog box as shown in Figure 14.11. This is the same dialog box that appears when you use the **bhatch** command. When editing a hatch, you are limited to certain selections in the Hatch edit dialog box.

Changing a Dimension When you choose the Properties button on the Object Properties toolbar and select a dimension, the Modify Dimension dialog box appears. This dialog box offers several options to change an existing dimension as shown in Figure 14.12. The following attributes can be modified:

- **Edit.** To change the existing text, select the Edit button and enter a new value in the Edit Mtext dialog box.
- **Style.** Allows you to quickly change the style of the dimension. To change the dimension to a new style, select the down arrow to the right of the Style text box to access a pop-up list. All previously created dimension styles appear in the pop-up list. Select the desired style from the list and press Enter.
- **Geometry.** Selecting the Geometry button in the Modify Dimension dialog box brings up the Geometry dialog box as shown in Figure 14.13. You can modify the

Figure 14.10 *To modify a hatch, choose the Properties button on the Object Properties toolbar and select the hatch, then select Hatch Edit in the Modify Associative Hatch dialog box.*

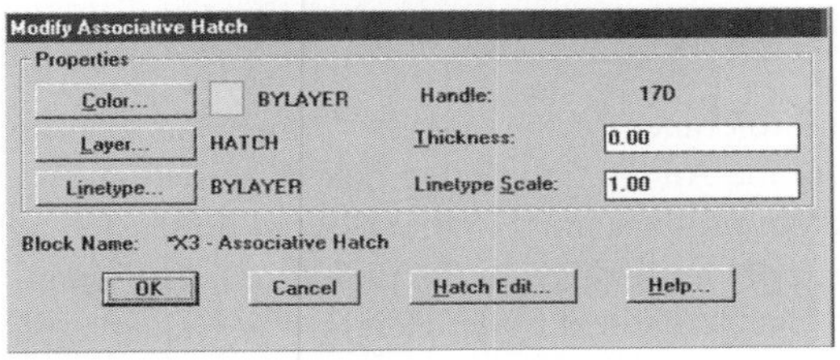

Figure 14.11 *The Hatch edit dialog box is displayed when Hatch Edit is selected from the Modify Associative Hatch dialog box.*

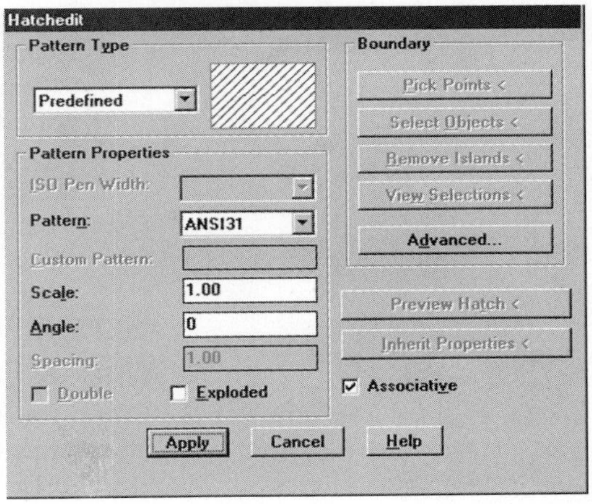

Figure 14.12 *In the Modify Dimension dialog box, you can change the text and text style.*

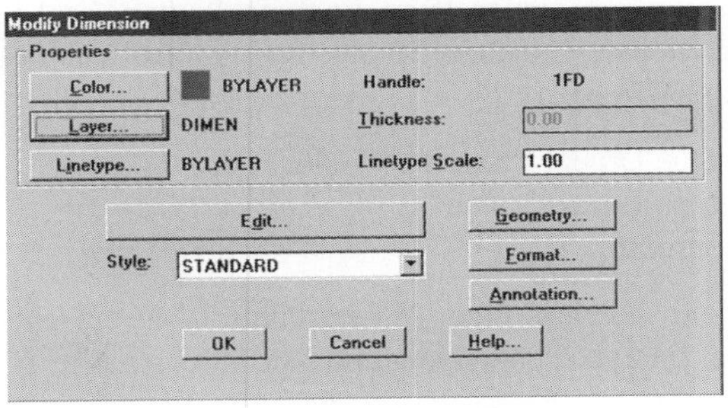

Figure 14.13 *Selecting the Geometry button in the Modify Dimension dialog box opens the Geometry dialog box.*

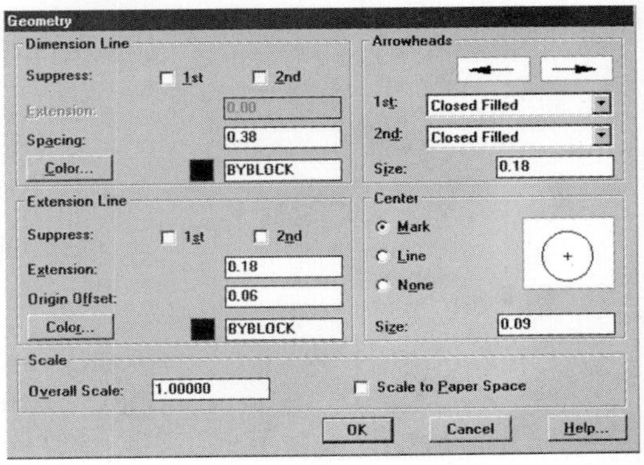

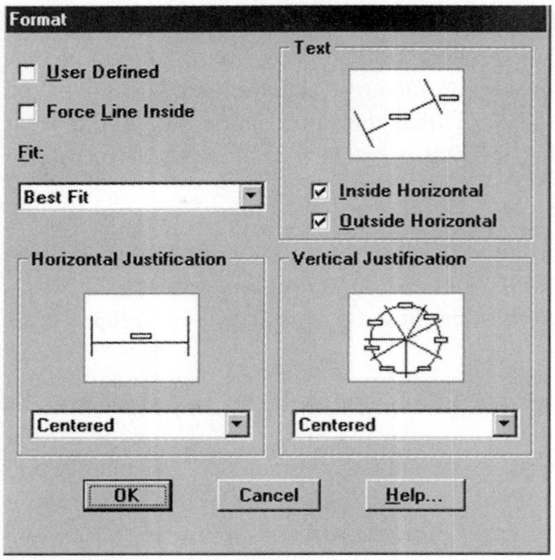

Figure 14.14 *Fit and justification changes to the selected dimension text can be made in the Format dialog box.*

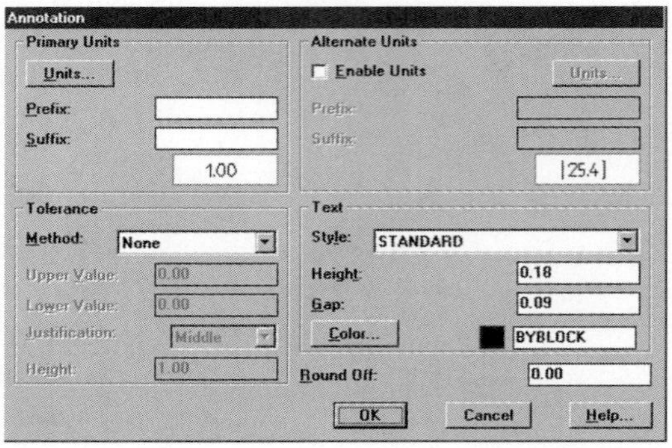

Figure 14.15 *In the Annotation dialog box, a Tolerance can be applied or changed and units can be assigned to the selected dimension.*

Dimension line, Extension Line, Arrowheads, and Center (if applicable to the dimension selected). You can also change the Overall Scale for the dimension selected.

- **Format.** The Format button in the Modify Dimension dialog box allows you to change the fit and justification of the text in the selected dimension, as shown in Figure 14.14.
- **Annotation.** To change the units and tolerance of the selected dimension, choose the Annotation button. This brings up the Annotation dialog box as shown in Figure 14.15. Here you can assign different primary units to the selected dimension as well as alternate units. You can also apply a tolerance to the dimension. The Annotation dialog box also enables you to change the text Style, Height, and Gap as well.

Setting Default Object Properties with a Dialog Box

Every object created within AutoCAD has color, linetype, thickness, linetype scale, and layer properties. Normally the object receives the current setting at the time the object is created. The Object Creation Modes dialog box allows object creation with specific settings regardless of the layer. It's important to note at this point that the ltscale is independent of the layer.

You can set the default properties when creating objects in the Object Creation Modes dialog box. The dialog box shows settings for color, layer, linetype, linetype scale, text style, elevation, and thickness. The Object Creation Modes dialog box can be accessed by using the following methods:

- Select the Object Creation button on the Object Properties toolbar.
- Select Object Creation from the Data pull-down menu.
- Type **`ddemodes`** at the `Command:` prompt.

The Object Creation Modes dialog box, shown in Figure 14.16, controls the current settings for color, layer, linetype, text style, linetype scale, elevation, and thickness.

Setting the Default Object Color and Linetype Selecting a Color or Linetype in the Object Creation Modes dialog box overrides the current layer color and linetype. Selecting a specific color or linetype in the Object Creation Modes dialog box enables objects

TUTORIAL 14.2: USING THE MODIFY DIALOG BOX

In this tutorial you will use the Modify dialog box to change attributes of the line and circle you created in the previous tutorial.

1. Continue from the previous tutorial.
2.  Select the Properties button from the Object Properties toolbar.
3. Select the line that you created in the previous tutorial. The Modify Line dialog box appears. Change the `From Point X` value to 3 and click OK.

    If the change was not apparent and you would like to see the difference, select the Undo button from the Standard toolbar. Watch the screen closely to see the change.
4.  Select the Properties button from the Object Properties toolbar.
5. This time, select the circle that was created in the previous tutorial. The Modify Circle dialog box appears.
6.  Change the Radius from 2 to 3 and click OK. Again, if the changes were not apparent, use Undo to see the changes made.

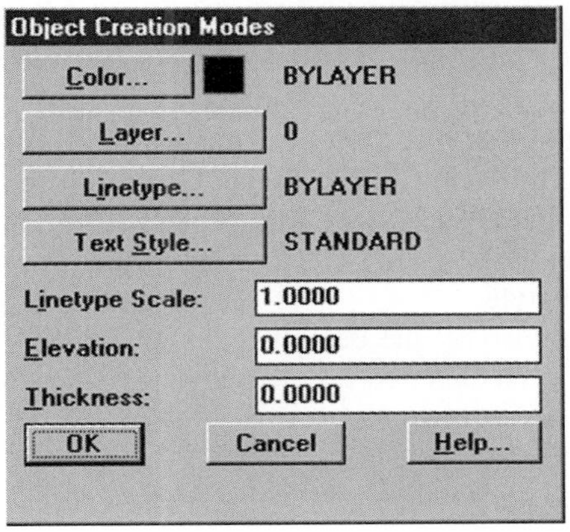

Figure 14.16
The Object Creation Modes dialog box controls current object settings.

with various colors or linetypes to reside on the same layer. For example you could draw a line on one part of the object in yellow with a hidden line. A different line could have a continuous linetype with a red color. Both objects could reside on the same layer, so when the layer is frozen or turned off, neither of the lines appear on screen. Options for the Color and Linetype buttons are as follows:

- **Color.** Selecting the Color button in the Object Creation Modes dialog box opens the Select Color dialog box. This is the same dialog box displayed when selecting Color from the Layer Control dialog box. Click any of the displayed colors to set the color you want. You can also select the BYLAYER or BYBLOCK buttons under Logical Colors.
- **Linetype.** The Linetype button opens the Select Linetype dialog box. This dialog box is identical to the one displayed in the Layer Control dialog box. You can also select the Bylayer or Byblock options.

SKILL BUILDER

Changing the color or linetype in the Object Creation Modes dialog box causes all future objects to be drawn in that color or linetype regardless of the layer on which they reside.

In certain cases it may be easier to change the current color and linetype setting as you work. Initially this may seem easier than planning ahead and creating a well-organized set of layers, complete with preset colors and linetypes. Creating a prototype drawing involves careful planning, and is more advantageous. It can be very difficult to reset objects to a specific layer at a later time, especially in a complex drawing.

SKILL BUILDER

If you begin creating new geometry and everything is drawn on the same layer with the same color, even when you change layers, check the Change Properties dialog box (**ddchprop**). Make sure Color and Linetype both say `BYLAYER`. Also, check the Object Creation Modes dialog box **(ddemodes)**, making sure Color and Linetype each say `BYLAYER`. When `BYLAYER` is selected, objects inherit the linetype and color properties assigned to their respective layer.

To avoid problems and confusion, don't use explicit settings for color and linetype in the Object Creation Modes dialog box. Leave the Color and Linetype settings to the default values of BYLAYER unless you need to mix color and linetypes on the same layer.

Setting Other Default Object Properties Selecting Layer in the Object Creation Modes dialog box brings up the Layer Control dialog box. You can create new layers, or make an existing layer current. The Text Style button activates the Select Text Style dialog box. Although you can't create a new text style, you can select any existing text style as the current style.

You can also set the default Linetype Scale by entering the value in the edit box. When working on standard 2-D drawings, use the following settings in the Object Creation Modes dialog box:

Color:	BYLAYER
Linetype:	BYLAYER
Elevation:	0.00
Thickness:	0.00

EDITING TEXT

To edit your text, you can choose the Properties button on the Object Properties toolbar and select a single line of text. This will access the Modify Text dialog box. Another option if you only want to edit individual characters or the entire line of text is to use the **ddedit** command. This will bring up a dialog box. You can access the **ddedit** dialog box by:

- Choose the Edit Text button from the Modify toolbar. The Edit Text button is on the Edit Polyline flyout menu.
- Type **ddedit** at the `Command:` prompt.

Either option will display the following prompt:

`<Select an annotation object>/Undo:`

The screen cursor takes the shape of the square pick box, where you move to the desired text and pick. If the text was created with the **text** or **dtext** commands the Edit Text dialog box will appear as shown in Figure 14.17. The line of text you picked will appear in the dialog box, ready for editing.

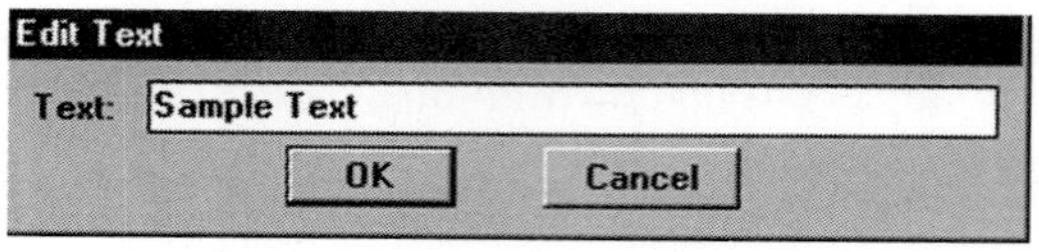

Figure 14.17
The Edit Text dialog box displays the selected text, ready for editing.

If the text you selected was created by Mtext, the Edit Mtext dialog box appears. This is the same dialog box that was used to create the text. For an explanation on how to use the Edit Mtext dialog box, see Unit 7, "Annotating a Drawing with Text and Hatching."

Renaming Object Traits

When working within AutoCAD you can assign names to several different components. Two of these components are layers and text styles. The **ddrename** command may be used to change the name of any of the following objects:

- Layer
- Linetype (Ltype)
- Text Style (Style)
- View
- Dimension Style (Dimstyle)
- Block
- User Coordinate System (UCS)
- Viewpoint Configurations (Vport)

To rename an object, you must have previously defined the object and given it a name. The Rename dialog box may be accessed by typing **ddrename** at the `Command:` prompt.

The **ddrename** command brings up the Rename dialog box shown in Figure 14.18. The options within the dialog box enable you to select the type of object you want to rename. For example, selecting Layer from the Named Objects list displays all current layer names in the Items box. To change the name of a layer, select the name you want to change from the Items box. AutoCAD will display the name of the layer selected in the Old Name edit box. Type the new name in the Rename To edit box, and click the Rename To button. When you have completed renaming objects, click OK to return to the drawing editor.

For the Professional

There is also a rename command available, which you can access by typing `rename` at the `Command:` prompt. If you use this command you can change the same items as **ddrename** but AutoCAD won't display a dialog box and the command is less interactive. Because dialog boxes are a large part of the AutoCAD user interface, the professional should use the dialog boxes whenever possible.

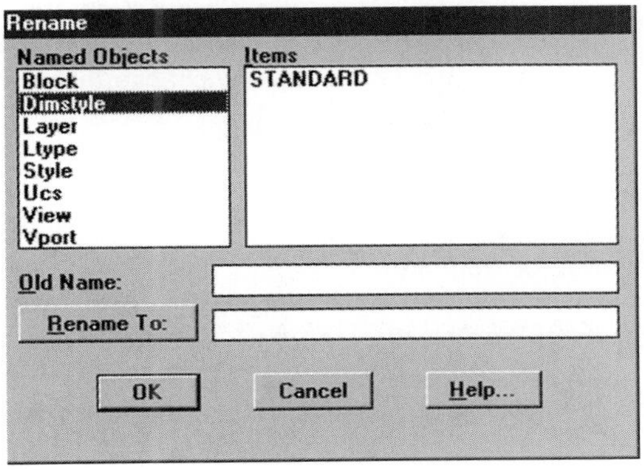

Figure 14.18
The Rename dialog box is used to rename existing named objects, such as layers and linetypes.

Removing Unwanted Objects

As you continue working on a drawing, it can become cluttered with extra layers, linetypes, and text styles that you no longer need. Having extra objects in the drawing enlarges the size of the drawing file, increasing the time needed to load the drawing into AutoCAD. The **purge** command can be used to remove unwanted named objects from a drawing.

Skill Builder

You can purge the drawing at any time during the drawing session.

The **purge** command removes the following objects from a drawing:

- Blocks (Blocks)
- Dimension Styles (Dimstyles)
- Layers (LAyers)
- Linetypes (LTypes)
- Shapes (SHapes)
- Text Styles (STyles)
- APPID Table (APPOD)
- Multiple Lines Styles (Mline)
- All

To access the **purge** command, type `purge` at the `Command:` prompt. AutoCAD allows you to specify the type of objects you want to delete. Normally, you should select the All option to clear everything you don't need. **purge** removes only named objects that aren't used in the drawing. AutoCAD also prompts you for confirmation before deleting any objects.

Tutorial 14.3: Modifying Object Characteristics

In this tutorial, you'll use the commands introduced in this unit to modify the hot-tub symbol.

1.  From the Standard toolbar, select Open. If prompted with the Save Changes dialog box, select Yes and save the previous work.
2. In the Open Drawing dialog box, change to the proper drive and diredtory and enter 14dwg01 in the File Name edit box. Choose OK.
3. You should now have the drawing shown in Figure 14.19 in your drawing area.
4. 
   - First create a new layer called HOTTUB.
   - Select the Layers button from the Object Properties toolbar. The Layer Control dialog box appears.
   - Create a new layer called HOTTUB, color red, then click OK to close the dialog box.
5. The hot-tub symbol is currently on layer 0. You are going to move it to the HOTTUB layer.
6. 
   - Select the Properties button from the Object Properties toolbar.
   - At the `Select objects:` prompt, type all and press Enter.
   - At the `Select objects:` prompt, press Enter.

The Change Properties dialog box appears as shown in Figure 14.20.

7.
   - Click the Layer button. The Select Layer dialog box appears.
   - Select the HOTTUB layer and click OK. The Select Layer dialog box will close.
   - Click OK in the Change Properties dialog box to accept the changes.
8. Now change the size of the drain in the hot-tub symbol.
9.  Select the Properties button from the Object Properties toolbar. At the `Select objects:` prompt, select the circle in the middle of the symbol that represents the drain and press Enter.

The Modify Circle dialog box appears as shown in Figure 14.21.

In the Radius edit Box, change the 6″ to 8″ and click OK. Notice that the size of the drain is now larger.

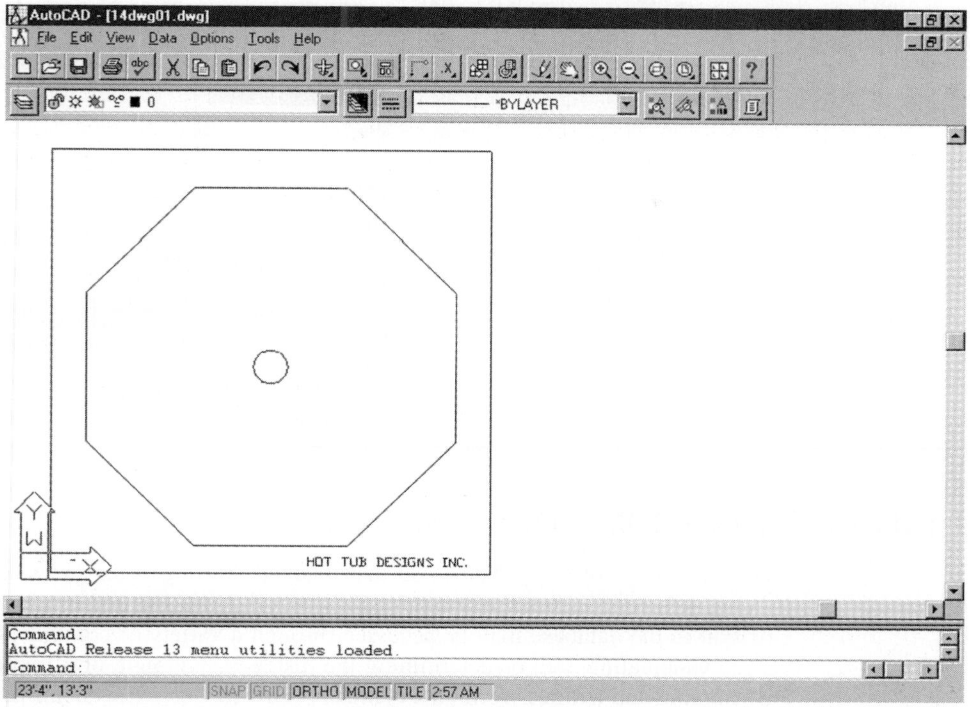

Figure 14.19 *Modifying object characteristics of the hot-tub symbol.*

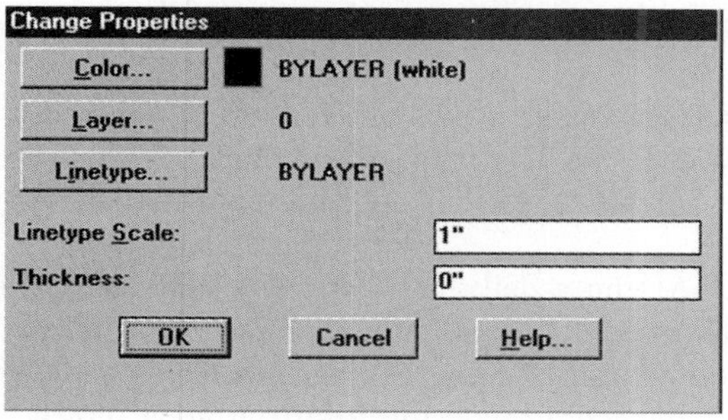

Figure 14.20 *Using the Change Properties Dialog Box to change the layer of the hot-tub symbol.*

10. The text on the lower right of the symbol needs to be larger.

11.  Select the Properties button from the Object Properties toolbar.

Figure 14.21 *Change the size of the hot-tub drain using the Modify Circle dialog box.*

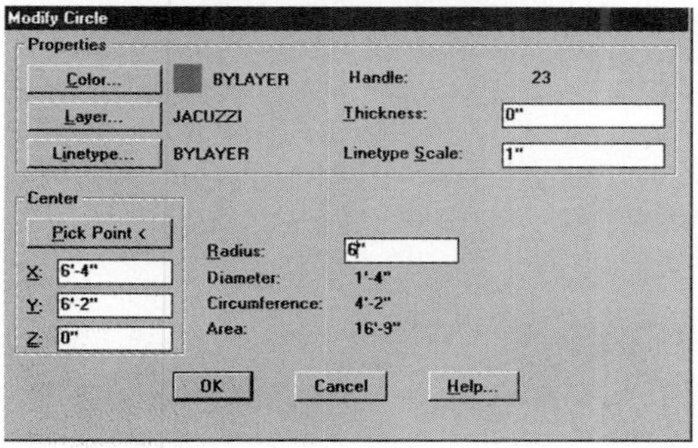

12. At the `Select objects:` prompt, select the text and press Enter. The Modify Text dialog box appears.

13. In the Height edit box, change 3″ to 5″. Change the X origin to 4′. Your Modify Text dialog box should look like Figure 14.22.

14. Finally, change the name of the HOTTUB layer to JACUZZI.

Select Data, Rename. The Rename dialog box appears.

Select Layer in the Named Objects column.

Then select HOTTUB in the Items column.

HOTTUB will appear in the Old Name input box as shown in Figure 14.23.

In the `Rename To:` input box, type `JACUZZI` and click the `Rename To` button.

Click OK to accept the renaming of the layer.

Figure 14.22 *Changing the size and origin of the text in the hot-tub symbol.*

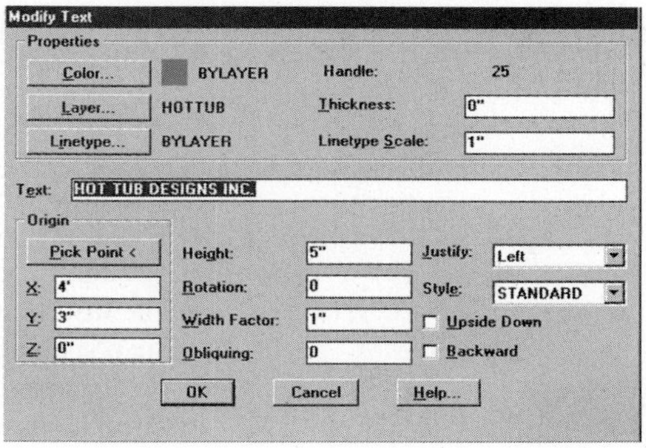

15.  Select the Save button on the Standard toolbar to save your changes.

You have now completed the Modifying Object Characteristics tutorial.

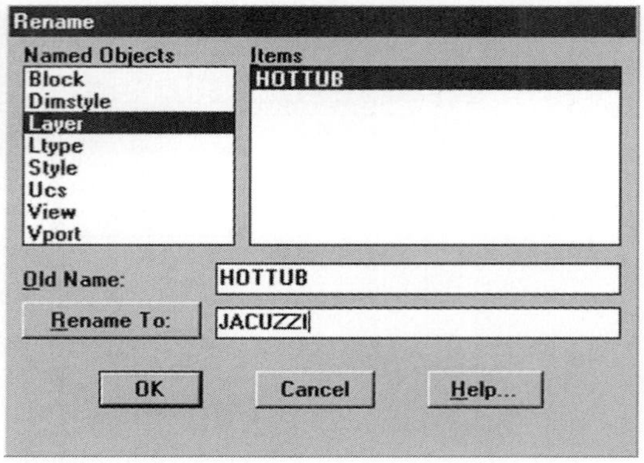

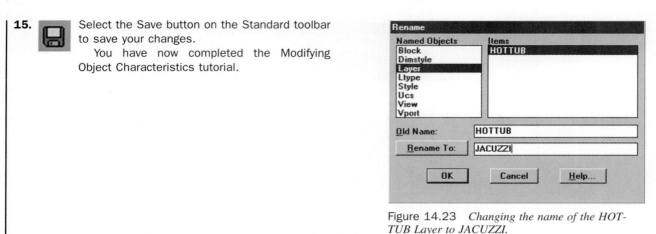

Figure 14.23 *Changing the name of the HOTTUB Layer to JACUZZI.*

EXTRACTING INFORMATION FROM YOUR DRAWING

One advantage of using AutoCAD over manual drafting is the great deal of information AutoCAD stores about the drawing. This information is stored in a database. The information in the database may be accessed through a variety of commands.

Calculating area or determining the distance and angle of a line can be very time-consuming and tedious work on a manually drawn object. The database AutoCAD creates is in a form that is easy to access and manipulate. By simply entering **list** and selecting a line, AutoCAD displays the line's distance and angle in the current units. Commands such as **list, dblist** and **status** display all the information stored for a specific object or for the entire drawing database.

AutoCAD also offers additional commands which are very useful when determining the area and perimeter of an object. By picking points on an object, AutoCAD calculates the object's area and perimeter. You also can easily add and subtract objects, such as an island, from the area.

Many individuals using AutoCAD on a daily basis are very concerned with the amount of time it takes to create and revise drawings. This information is often essential for billing purposes. AutoCAD automatically begins a timer whenever a drawing is started or revised. Issuing the **time** command displays this information on-screen.

LISTING THE STATUS OF AUTOCAD (status)

To obtain current information about your drawing, AutoCAD provides the **status** command. The **status** command may be accessed by:

- Choosing Data, Status.
- Entering `status` at the `Command:` prompt.

When the **status** command is invoked, AutoCAD switches to a text window and generates a report based on the current drawing. The **status** command reports information on the following:

- Name of the drawing
- Number of objects in the drawing
- The limits setting for current space (model space or paper space)
- The drawing's actual extents (model space or paper space)
- The limits of the current display
- The insertion base point
- Snap spacing
- Grid spacing
- Current space (model space or paper space)

- Object snap modes: (endpoint, intersection, etc.)
- Current layer, color, linetype, thickness, and elevation
- The on/off settings for Fill, Ortho, Snap, Grid, Qtext, and Tablet
- Available disk space and swap file size, physical memory, swap file space

When reporting the Drawing Limits, AutoCAD compares the physical limits of the drawing to the actual limits you set. The space is either model space or paper space. If any objects are located outside the limits, AutoCAD responds with `***OVER` in the Model space uses section. All coordinates and distances displayed with the **status** command are in the format specified in the most recent **units** command. Entering `status` at the `Dim:` prompt reports the values and descriptions of all dimension variables.

AutoCAD also reports the amount of disk space available at the `Free disk:` line. As you continue creating geometry and the file size grows, you should maintain enough free space available at the `Free disk:` line at least equal to the size of the drawing. When working on a drawing, AutoCAD creates a variety of temporary files that are not saved with your drawing file. Because the temporary files are not saved as part of the drawing but are necessary when working on the drawing, you need extra disk space available when the drawing file is open.

For the Professional

If you are working on a large drawing, the computer may seem really slow. Several factors can cause your computer to slow down when running AutoCAD. The number of programs you currently have running in Windows is one factor. Look at the programs running in your taskbar. Close everything but AutoCAD. This helps free up some system resources. If the computer consistently seems to access the hard drive when using AutoCAD, consider adding more memory to the computer. Adding more memory improves not only AutoCAD's performance, but other programs' performance as well.

Tutorial 14.4: Listing the Status of a File

In this tutorial you will load the hot-tub symbol and list the status of the file. This file should remain open for all subsequent tutorials in this unit.

1.  Choose the Open button from the Standard toolbar. If the AutoCAD dialog box appears, choose No unless you want to save the current drawing. If you want to save the current drawing, choose Yes and enter a path and drawing name.
2. In the Select File dialog box, change to the appropriate drive and directory and choose file 14DWG01. This is the hot-tub drawing you were working on earlier.
3. Choose Data, Status.

   The AutoCAD text screen appears and the status information for the hot-tub symbol file appears as shown in Figure 14.24. The information on your screen may vary from that of Figure 14.24 because of the difference in your computer's configuration.
4. To return to the drawing area, press the F2 function key. The screen should now revert back to the hot-tub symbol. The next tutorial in this unit will continue from here.

Figure 14.24
Listing the status of the hot-tub symbol file.

```
AutoCAD Text Window
Edit
Command:
Command: _status 53 objects in A:\14dwg01
Model space limits are X:      0'-0"   Y:      0'-0"  (Off)
                       X:      1'-0"   Y:      0'-9"
Model space uses       X:      0'-0"   Y:      0'-0"
                       X:     12'-8"   Y:     12'-8" **Over
Display shows          X:     -1'-4"   Y:     -0'-8"
                       X:     25'-9"   Y:     13'-6"
Insertion base is      X:      0'-0"   Y:      0'-0"   Z:      0'-0"
Snap resolution is     X:      0'-1"   Y:      0'-1"
Grid spacing is        X:      0'-0"   Y:      0'-0"

Current space:        Model space
Current layer:        0
Current color:        BYLAYER -- 7 (white)
Current linetype:     BYLAYER -- CONTINUOUS
Current elevation:     0'-0"  thickness:      0'-0"
Fill on  Grid off  Ortho on  Qtext off  Snap off  Tablet off
Object snap modes:    None
Free disk (dwg+temp=A:): 241664 bytes
Free physical memory: 0.7 Mbytes (out of 15.5M).
Free swap file space: 27.6 Mbytes (out of 55.6M).
Press RETURN to continue:
Virtual address space: 36.9 Mbytes.

Command:
```

LISTING OBJECT INFORMATION

To obtain information about selected objects in your drawing, use the **list** command. The **list** command displays information about any selected objects within the drawing. The **list** command may be accessed as follows:

- Choose the List button on the Standard toolbar.
- Type **list** at the `Command:` prompt.

To use the List command, select the objects you want information about at the `Select objects:` prompt. When you have completed selecting objects, press Enter. AutoCAD displays the information on the selected objects in a text screen.

The **dblist** command refers to Database List. This command displays all information about every object in the current drawing. The information provided with the **dblist** command is in the same format as the **list** command. As soon as you enter `dblist` at the `Command:` prompt, the data begins scrolling on-screen. The scrolling automatically stops when a complete page has been filled with information. To continue scrolling to the next page, press Enter.

SKILL BUILDER

Using the **dblist** command on a large drawing can take a long time to display all of the information. To display database information, it is usually more beneficial to select individual objects with the **list** command. To stop the **dblist** command, press the Escape key. This ends the scrolling and returns you to the drawing editor.

Reporting Distances and Angles To find the distance and angle between two points, use the **dist** command. The **dist** command is accessed as follows:

- Choose the Distance button on the Object Properties toolbar. It is located on a flyout menu, accessed by choosing the List button.
- Entering **`dist`** at the `Command:` prompt,

To use the **dist** command, select two points on the screen. The **dist** command displays the distance and angle of the line. It also gives the delta x, y, and z dimensions.

Tutorial 14.5: Listing the Objects of a File

In this tutorial you will list the object properties in the hot-tub symbol using both the **list** and **dblist** commands.

1.  Continue from the previous tutorial. Begin this tutorial by first listing object properties singularly. Choose the List button from the Object Properties toolbar.
2. At the `Select objects:` prompt, select the outside edge of the hot-tub symbol as shown in Figure 14.25 and press Enter.

   The AutoCAD text screen appears as shown in Figure 14.26.

   AutoCAD displays a `Press RETURN to continue:` prompt at the bottom of the screen. Press Enter to view the remaining information. Review the information in the AutoCAD text screen.
3. Press the F2 function key to return to the drawing area.
4. Next list all of the objects found in the hot-tub drawing symbol file.

   `Command:` **`dblist`**
5. The AutoCAD text screen appears and you notice that AutoCAD begins a list of all objects found in the hot-tub drawing file. The list is similar to the list produced in step #1 of this tutorial. Review the list.
6. When the `Press RETURN to continue:` prompt appears, press Enter to continue the list. If you don't want to review the complete list, the **dblist** command can be canceled by pressing the Escape key. Press the F2 function key to return to the drawing area.

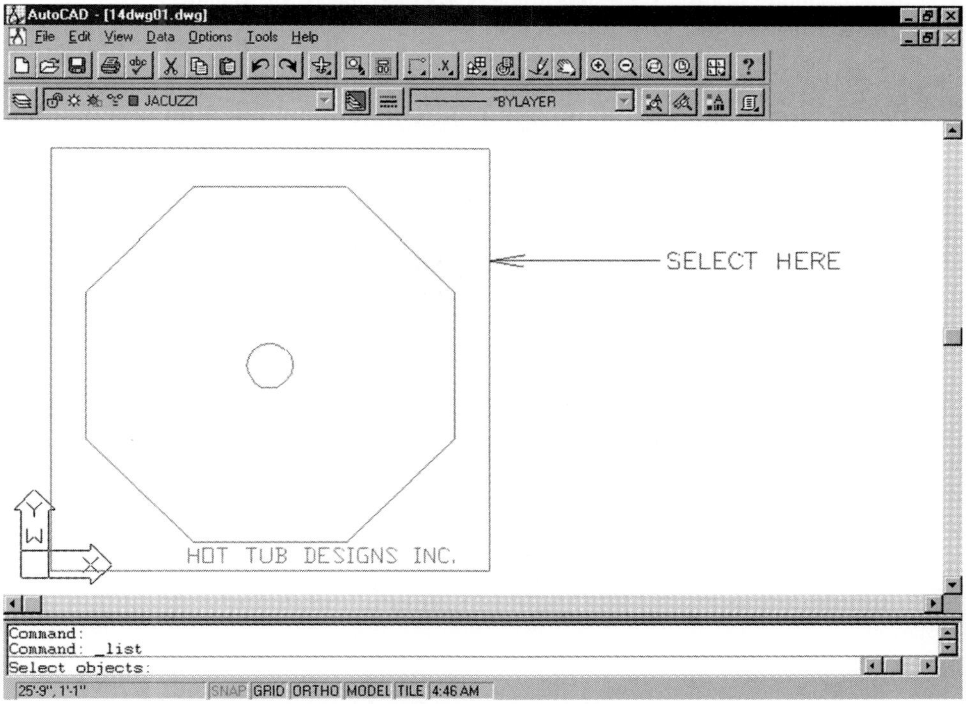

Figure 14.25
Selecting the outside edge of the hot-tub symbol.

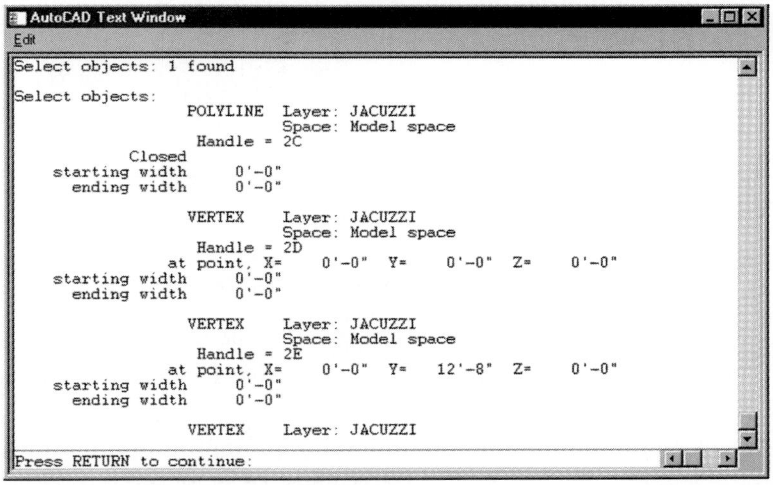

Figure 14.26
Viewing the AutoCAD text screen list of the information for the outside edge of the hot-tub symbol.

Skill Builder

To ensure accuracy when using the **dist** command, always use **osnap** commands to accurately pick locations. Alternatively, make sure the point locations lie on Snap points and that Snap is turned on.

Tutorial 14.6: Using the Dist Command

In this tutorial you will use the Dist command to determine the diagonal distance across the corners of the hot-tub symbol.

1.  Continue from the previous tutorial. Choose the Distance button from the List flyout menu.
2. First, select the upper-right corner of the hot-tub symbol as shown in Figure 14.27. Use the INTersection Osnap to ensure that your selection is exactly on the corner.

`First point:` **`int`**

3. Next, select the lower-left corner of the hot-tub symbol as shown in Figure 14.27. Again, use the **intersection** Osnap.

`Second point:` **`int`**

4. Unlike the **list** command, the AutoCAD text screen does not appear. This information for the **dist** command appears in the command prompt area as shown in Figure 14.27.

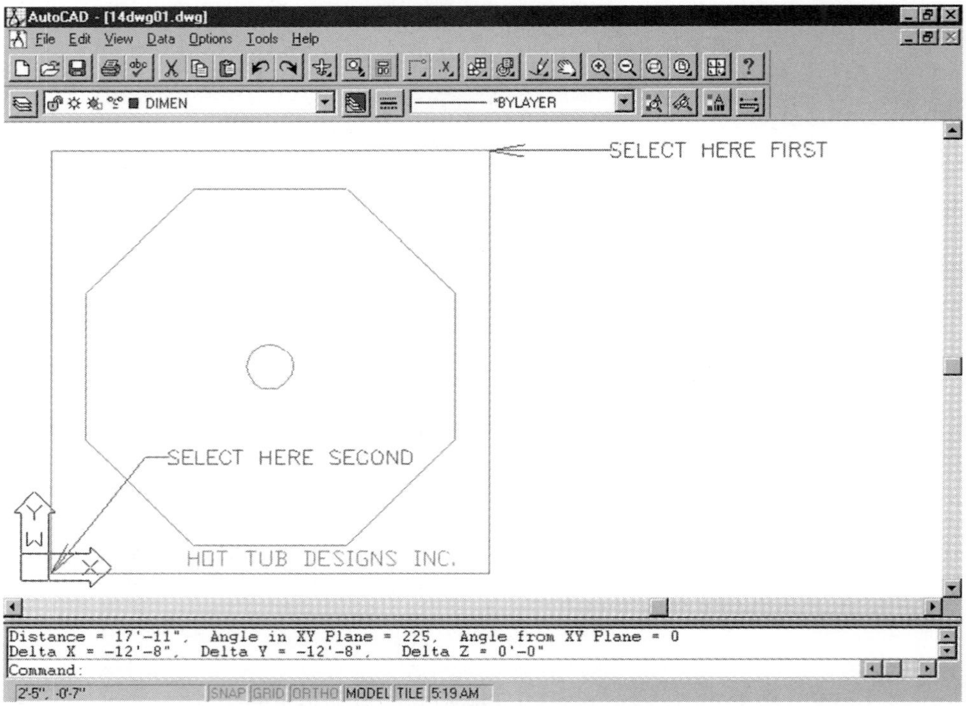

Figure 14.27
Selecting the upper-right and lower-left corners of the hot-tub symbol.

Locating Points (ID) As you are working on a new drawing or editing an existing drawing, it is often necessary to determine the coordinates for a specific location. The ID command is used to display information about a point location, giving its coordinates. The ID command may be accessed as follows:

- Choose the List button on the Object Properties toolbar to bring up a flyout menu containing the Locate Point button.
- Enter **`id`** at the `Command:` prompt.

To use the ID command, pick the point to be identified. Use the proper Osnap mode to ensure accuracy.

The ID command also performs another important function. As you use ID to locate a point, the coordinates of the last point entered are stored in the **lastpoint** system variable. This is very useful when you want to begin drawing at a set distance from a specific point rather than a point you pick.

For example, to locate the center of a circle located .38 on the x- and y-axis from the corner of an object, select ID and pick the corner as shown in Figure 14.28. Next, select **circle** and enter a relative coordinate. The command sequence is shown in the following example:

```
Command: id
Point: int Use the OSNAP-INTersection of (select the corner)
Command: circle
3P/2P/TTR/<Center point>: @-.38,.38
```

This uses the **lastpoint** variable found with the ID command, locating the center of the circle with a Relative coordinate.

```
Diameter/<Radius>: d
Diameter: .38
Command:
```

Whenever you use the ID command, it automatically resets the **lastpoint** system variable to the value of the ID point. Using the @ sign tells AutoCAD to use the **lastpoint** value.

The From Object Snap also can be used to begin drawing at a set distance from a specific point. The From Object Snap makes a temporary reference point as the basis for locating subsequent points.

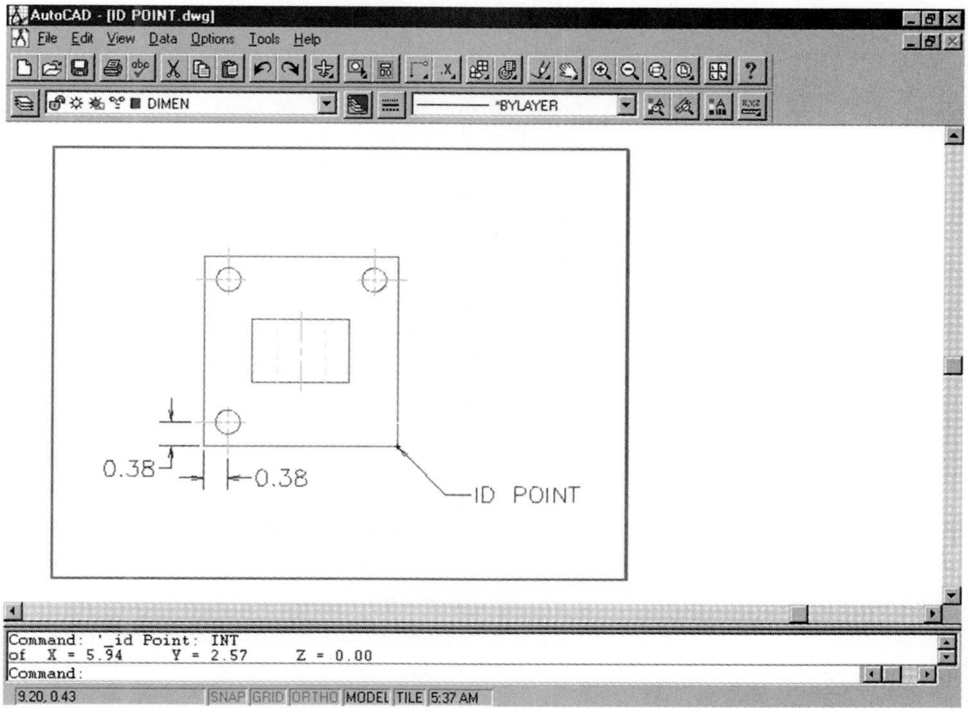

Figure 14.28
Locating the center of a circle using the ID command to set the **lastpoint** *system variable.*

Tutorial 14.7: Using the ID Command

In this tutorial, you will use the ID command to determine the location of the upper-right corner of the hot-tub symbol.

1. 

Continue from the previous tutorial. Choose the Locate Point button from the Object Properties toolbar.
2. Select the upper-right corner of the hot-tub symbol as shown in Figure 14.27. Use the INTersection Osnap to ensure your selection is exactly on the corner.

```
Point: int
of Select the Select Here First point as
in Figure 14.27.
```

3. The point ID information appears in the `Command:` prompt area. This information gives us the x, y, and z coordinates of the upper-right hand corner of the hot-tub symbol.

Calculating Area

Calculating boundary area is required in many disciplines. A contractor may need to determine the square footage in a building or room to estimate building costs. A machinist may need to calculate the surface area of a part to determine the amount of protective coating needed.

One advantage of working with AutoCAD is the ease in which the drawing database may be used to make area calculations on a given drawing. The **area** command may be accessed by:

- Choosing the Inquiry button on the Object Properties toolbar brings up a flyout menu, showing the Area button.
- Typing **area** at the `Command:` prompt.

The basic function of the Area command is to find the area of any predefined circle or polyline. The following command sequence calculates the area for a selected object:

Choose the Area button on the Object Properties toolbar.

```
<First point>/Object/Add/Subtract: o
Select objects: Select object
Area=(x.xx), Circumference=(x.xx)
```

Finding Area

In addition to finding the area of any predefined circle or polyline, you can also pick points to find the area of an object that is not a predefined circle or polyline. With the **area** First point option, you can pick points to define a boundary and AutoCAD calculates the area and perimeter of the boundary. When you pick two points, AutoCAD calculates the distance between them as the perimeter. If you pick three or more points, AutoCAD connects all of the points to create an imaginary polygon. AutoCAD reports the area and perimeter of the polygon. Pressing Enter at the `Next point:` prompt ends the pick point process. The following command sequence calculates the area for a selected object as shown in Figure 14.30:

Select the Area button from the Object Properties toolbar.

```
<First point>/Object/Add/Subtract: Select the first point (1)
Next point: Select the second point (2)
Next point: Select the third point (3)
Next point: Select the fourth point (4)
Next point: Select the fifth point (5)
Next point: Enter
```

When calculating area with the First point option, shapes or lines do not have to be closed for AutoCAD to calculate their area. If the shape is not closed, AutoCAD calculates the area as if a line connected the first and last points. Specifically, AutoCAD automatically closes the area back to the starting point.

Tutorial 14.8: Using the area Command

In this tutorial, you will use the **area** command to determine the area of the drain in the hot-tub symbol.

1.  Continue from the previous tutorial. Choose the Area button from the Object Properties toolbar.

2. Use the Object option and select the circle that represents the drain as in Figure 14.29.

   `<First point>/Object/Add/Subtract: o`
   `Select objects:` **`Select the drain as shown in Figure 14.29.`**

3. The area of the circle appears in the `Command:` prompt area as shown in Figure 14.29.

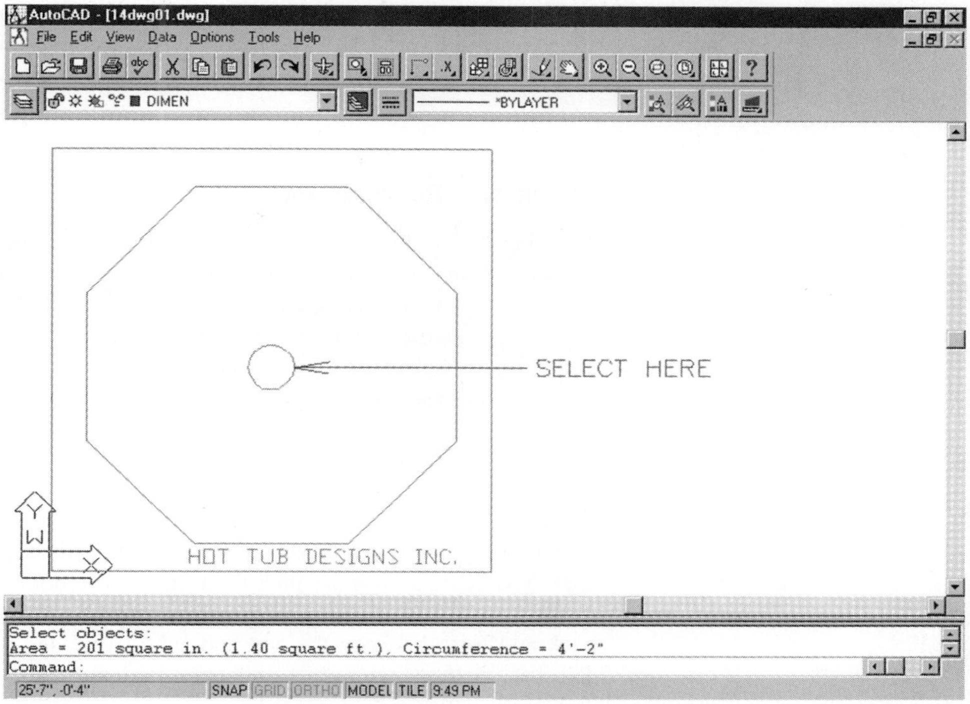

Figure 14.29
Using the Object option of area to calculate the area of the hot tub drain. The area information appars in the `Command:` *prompt section.*

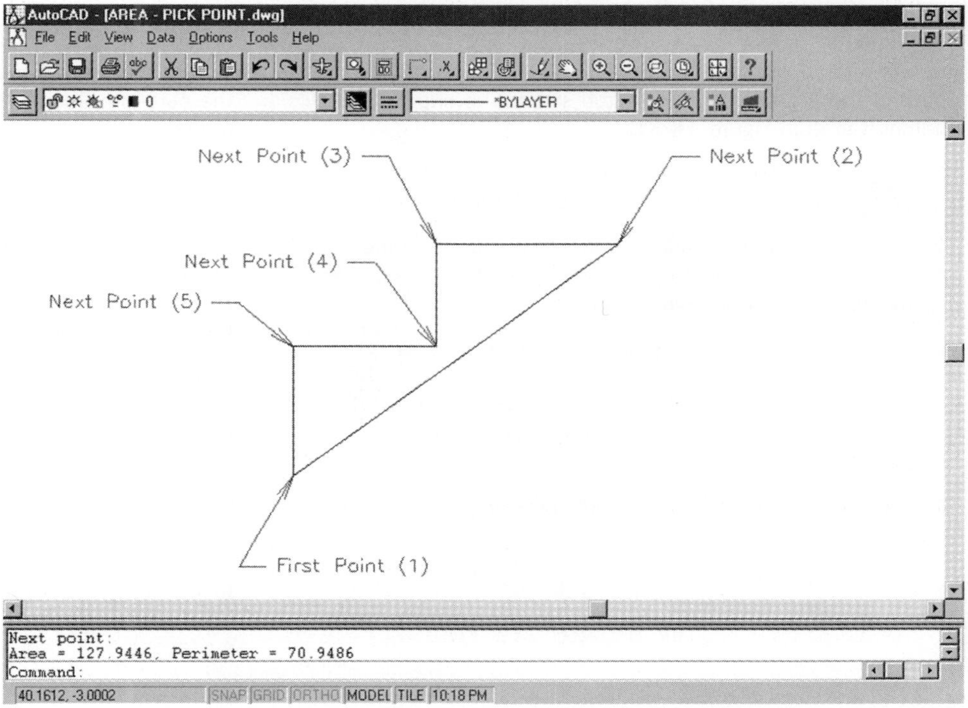

Figure 14.30
Using the Pick Point option of area to calculate the area and perimeter of an object.

SKILL BUILDER

When using the Area First point option, always use an Object Snap when picking the points. To increase speed and accuracy, set a running **osnap** to INTersection or ENDpoint to help pick the vertices.

First point is the default mode of the **area** command. To calculate the area of a shape, pick all vertices of the shape. Note the First point option works only with shapes created with straight lines.

FOR THE PROFESSIONAL

Using the **area** First point option to calculate area can be time-consuming since you must pick every vertex on the object. If you know you are going to calculate areas on an object, consider creating the geometry with the **pline** command. You could also change the geometry to a polyline with **pedit.** Then you can use the Object option and select the entire object. Another option is to use the **boundary** command discussed in Unit 12, "Advanced Drawing Techniques."

ADDING AND SUBTRACTING FEATURES

The **area** command also allows you to add and subtract closed objects from the calculated area. You also can use the pick point method to define an area to add or subtract. AutoCAD keeps a running total of the area, based on the objects you select. You can switch back and forth between the add and subtract modes as needed. You can also mix point selection methods with object selection to define the boundary you want calculated.

TUTORIAL 14.9: USING THE AREA COMMAND

In this tutorial, you use the **area** command to determine the area of the top face of the hot-tub symbol as shown by the hatched area in Figure 14.31.

1.  Continue from the previous tutorial. Choose the Area button from the Object Properties toolbar.
2. You will first use the Add option. Once you are in the add mode, use the Object option and select the outside rectangle as shown in Figure 14.32.

```
<First point>/Object/Add/Subtract: a
<First point>/Object/Subtract: o
(ADD mode) Select objects: Select the outside rectangle as shown in Figure 14.32.
```

3. The area of the rectangle is displayed in the `Command:` prompt area.

```
Area = 23104 square in. (160.44 square ft.), Perimeter = 50'-8"
Total area = 23104 square in. (160.44 square ft.)
```

4. To find the area required, you must subtract the area of the octagon. Change from the add mode to the subtract mode.

```
(ADD mode) Select objects: Press Enter
<First point>/Object/Subtract: s
```

5. Select the octagon as shown in Figure 14.32. After you enter the object mode, the prompt shows that you are in the subtract mode. When you select the octagon, its area is subtracted from the area of the rectangle.

```
<First point>/Object/Add: o
(SUBTRACT mode) Select objects: Select the octagon as shown in Figure 14.32.
```

6. The area of the octagon is displayed in the `Command:` prompt area and it is equal to 13573 square inches (94.26 sq. ft.).

   Notice that this time the total area is no longer equal to the area of the octagon, but is the area of the rectangle minus the area of the octagon. So the area of the surface is 9531 square inches (66.19 sq. ft.).

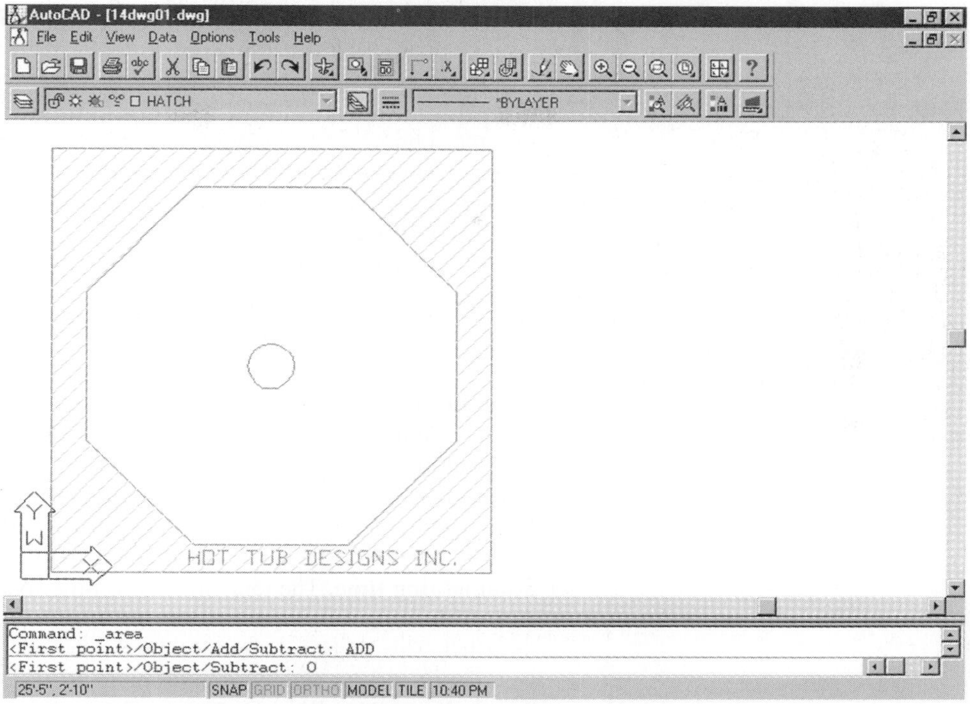

Figure 14.31
Determining the area of the top face of the hot-tub symbol.

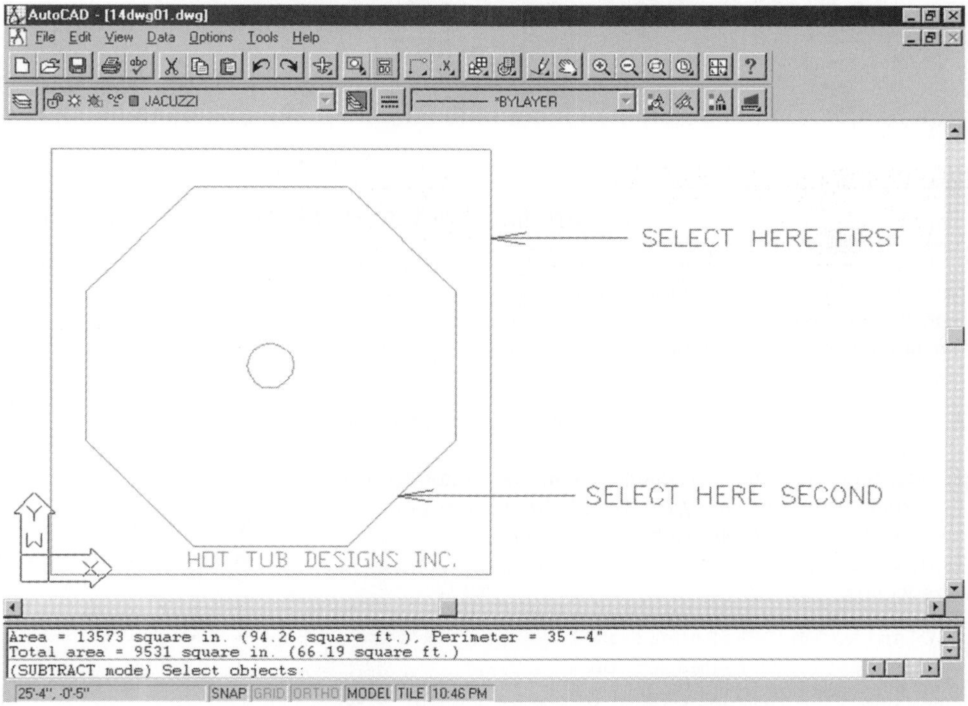

Figure 14.32
Using the Area-Subtract option to determine the area of the top face of the hot-tub symbol.

Keeping Track of Time

The clock within your computer automatically keeps track of the current date and time. AutoCAD uses this clock to maintain accurate time information about your drawing. The **time** command may be accessed by the following methods:

- Choose Time from the Data pull-down menu.
- At the `Command:` prompt, enter **`time`**.

When the **time** command is issued, AutoCAD displays the time information on-screen and responds with the following prompt:

`Display/ON/OFF/Reset:`

The four options affect only the elapsed timer. This allows the timer to be used as a stopwatch. Time is not updated with the **quit** command because Quit does not indicate that anything has been done in the drawing and that any time needs to be recorded. If you **save** and then **quit**, the **save** updates the timer.

The Reset option resets the elapsed timer to 0 and turns the clock back on. To view the display again after resetting the clock, choose the Display option. Off turns off the elapsed timer; On turns the timer back on. The time display contains the following information:

- **Current time.** Displays the current time and date according to the computer. Because AutoCAD uses the computer's clock, you must make sure the computer's date and time are set properly.
- **Created.** This is the date and time the current drawing was started.
- **Last updated.** The time the current drawing file was last updated. This time is updated whenever the **save** or **end** command is issued.
- **Total editing time.** The total amount of time spent in all drawing sessions with the current drawing. If you end a drawing session with **quit,** the session's time is not recorded. This time includes all time the drawing file was open, whether you were working on the drawing or doing something else, like going to the gym. As long as the file is open, time is added to the Total editing time.
- **Elapsed timer (on).** This timer is affected by the Reset option. It can be turned On, Off, or Reset.
- **Next automatic save in.** Indicates the next time the drawing will be automatically saved by AutoCAD. The system variable **savetime** determines this time.

TUTORIAL 14.10: USING THE TIME COMMAND

In this tutorial you will use the **time** command to determine when the hot-tub symbol file was created. You also will learn how to use the Elapsed Timer to record and measure the amount of elapsed time you are working on a drawing for.

1. Continue from the previous tutorial. Choose Time from the Data pull-down menu.
2. The time summary is displayed in the AutoCAD text screen as shown in Figure 14.33. Notice the time and date that the hot-tub symbol was created.
3. Reset the timer, turn it on, and wait approximately 15 seconds.

   `Display/ON/OFF/Reset:` **r**
   `Display/ON/OFF/Reset:` **on**

4. After waiting approximately 15 seconds, turn the timer off.

   `Display/ON/OFF/Reset:` **off**

5. Display the time and note the elapsed time.

   `Display/ON/OFF/Reset:` **d**

6. The time summary is displayed once again in the AutoCAD text screen. Look at the Elapsed timer section. Notice that the timer is off and the elapsed time is approximately 15 seconds. Press the F2 function key to return to the drawing area.

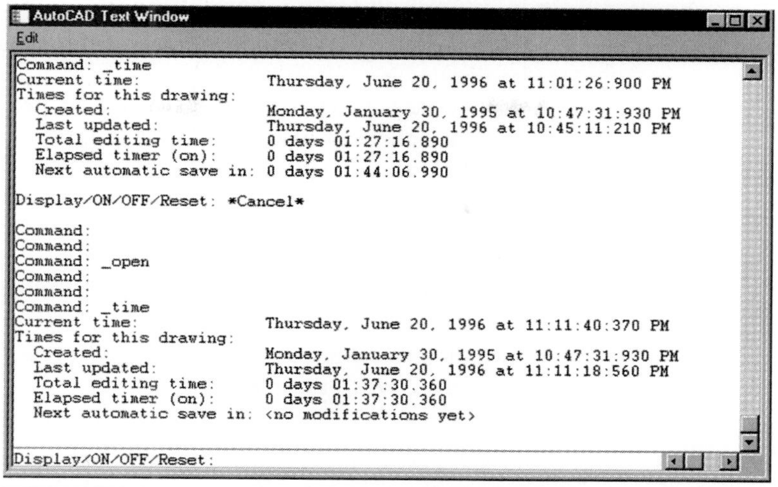
AutoCAD Text Window
Edit
Command: _time
Current time: Thursday, June 20, 1996 at 11:01:26:900 PM
Times for this drawing:
Created: Monday, January 30, 1995 at 10:47:31:930 PM
Last updated: Thursday, June 20, 1996 at 10:45:11:210 PM
Total editing time: 0 days 01:27:16.890
Elapsed timer (on): 0 days 01:27:16.890
Next automatic save in: 0 days 01:44:06.990
Display/ON/OFF/Reset: *Cancel*
Command:
Command:
Command: _open
Command:
Command:
Command: _time
Current time: Thursday, June 20, 1996 at 11:11:40:370 PM
Times for this drawing:
Created: Monday, January 30, 1995 at 10:47:31:930 PM
Last updated: Thursday, June 20, 1996 at 11:11:18:560 PM
Total editing time: 0 days 01:37:30.360
Elapsed timer (on): 0 days 01:37:30.360
Next automatic save in: <no modifications yet>
Display/ON/OFF/Reset:

Figure 14.33
Viewing the time information for the hot-tub symbol file in the AutoCAD text screen.

SUMMARY

Besides geometry creation, AutoCAD offers several powerful commands to change an existing object. The **ddchprop** command allows you to easily move several objects to a different layer. For more in-depth changes, the **ddmodify** command lists not only the current database information for an existing object, but also allows you to change the information.

Text can be edited with either the **ddmodify** or **ddedit** command. Rename existing objects with the **ddrename** command. Purging your drawing of unwanted objects is a good file management practice. Proper use of the **purge** command reduces file size, creating more space on your storage media for additional files.

The ability to easily access the drawing database is an important part of using AutoCAD. While the **status, list,** and **dblist** commands give complete information on selected objects, this information cannot be changed.

The ID command can be very useful to locate points in a drawing and set the **lastpoint** system variable. Properly used, ID can greatly speed up drawing time. Setting the **lastpoint** variable can be used to begin drawing at a set distance from a given point rather than at a point you pick.

Calculating **area** is also easily accomplished using AutoCAD. Used in conjunction with the **boundary** command, area calculations on complex geometry is greatly simplified. Keeping track of time is another feature that can be very useful, especially in billing situations. Since AutoCAD automatically starts the clock each time you open a drawing file, you will always have accurate information on when the drawing was started, edited, and how much time you spent working on it. The amount of time spent working on a drawing is usually a major consideration when using AutoCAD. Using the **time** function can help you keep track of how much time is spent working on a drawing.

The commands discussed in this unit depend upon the database for the drawing. Maintaining the integrity of your drawing database is essential. Always create objects using the proper AutoCAD commands you have been introduced to. **Never** guess at a point location. Make sure your objects do not contain multiple instances, such as several lines on top of one another. While they may not be evident on the screen or a plot, they will definitely affect the drawing database.

REVIEW

1. List the type of information that is stored in a drawing database for a line, arc, and circle.

2. Explain the importance of maintaining the integrity of a drawing's database.
3. Explain the advantages of modifying an existing object as opposed to deleting and re-creating it.
4. List the steps you would take to change the **ltscale** for a single object on a drawing.
5. List the options available if you want to change the spelling of a word contained in a single line of text on a drawing.
6. Explain the options you have if you want to rename a layer.
7. Describe the use of the **purge** command, its advantages, and when it should be used.
8. Clarify the difference between the **list** and **dblist** commands and when they should be used.
9. List the procedure you would follow to locate the center of a circle which is .875″ from the corner of an object.
10. List and explain three different methods that are available for determining area.

EXERCISE 14

14.1 Load a prototype of drawing 8.2, the fireplace mantle that you created in Unit 8. Lengthen the mantle 1′ as shown in Figure 14.34 using the following information:

1. Before beginning, set the timer to keep track of how long it took you to make the modifications.
2. Use the **ddchprop** command to increase the length of the lines and radius of the arc.
3. Use the **move** command to move the remaining geometry to the new location.
4. After extending the mantle 1′, calculate the area of brick needed to construct the mantle as shown in Figure 14.35.

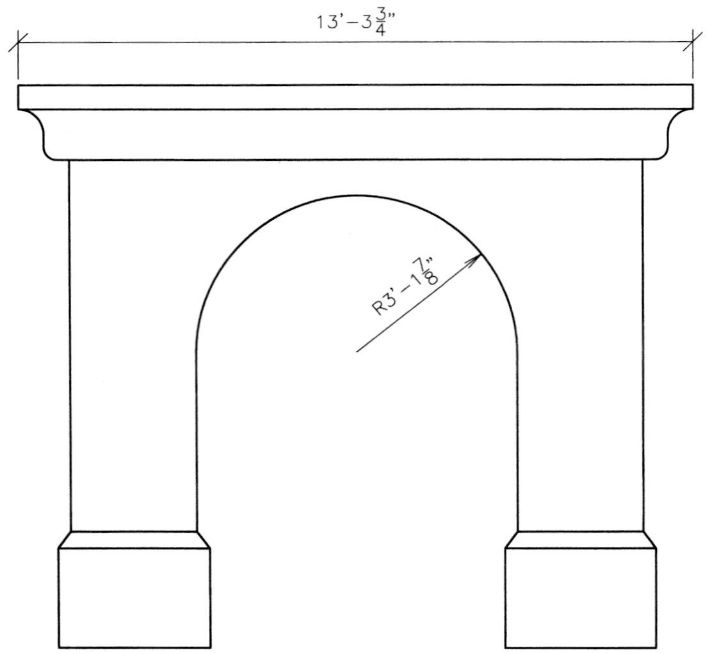

Figure 14.34
Extend the length of the fireplace mantle 1′.

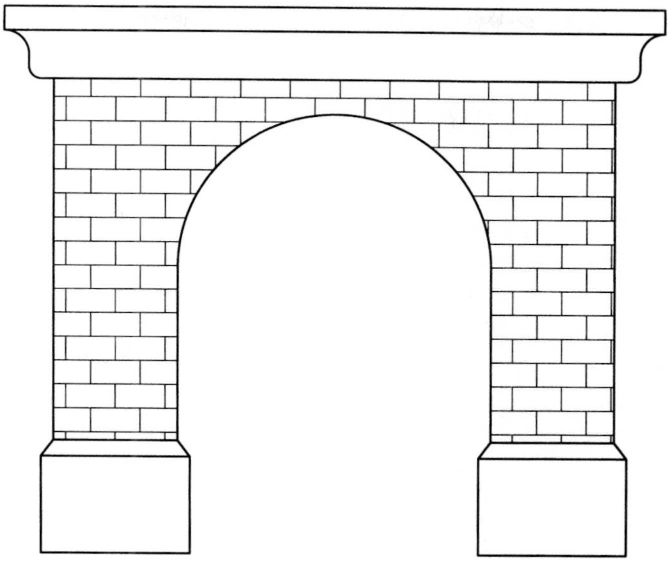

Figure 14.35
Determine the area of brick needed to construct the mantle.

UNIT

15 Using Symbols and Attributes

OVERVIEW

One advantage of using AutoCAD over manual drafting techniques is the ability to copy existing geometry to other locations in the drawing. AutoCAD also lets you copy existing geometry between drawings. For example, you could use the symbol for a water closet created in one drawing in several other drawings. You can also attach text strings that label or describe each symbol you create. This unit discusses AutoCAD's ability to use geometry created in one drawing in one or several other drawings, and how to attach text strings to that geometry.

OBJECTIVES

- Use the Object Grouping function to group objects.
- Create a symbol library with the Block command.
- Write a section of a drawing to a file with the Wblock command.
- Insert a symbol into a drawing.
- Insert multiple symbols into a drawing.
- Specify a new insertion point of a symbol with the Base command.
- Break a block apart into separate objects.
- Define attributes and attach them to a block.
- Edit attribute definitions.
- Extract attribute information.
- Redefine a block and update its attributes.

INTRODUCTION

Many drawings contain common geometric elements called symbols. In architecture, symbols are often used for door openings and kitchen appliances. Mechanical drawings may use a symbol for a nut or bolt. In manual drafting, these symbols may be placed in the drawing with a template.

AutoCAD can store these symbols for later use. AutoCAD has a feature called **block** that allows you to define a group of objects as a single object. Once defined, these symbols, or blocks, can be inserted into a drawing full-size, scaled, or rotated.

The **group** feature allows you to create a series of named selection sets. One of the major differences between this command and the **block** command is the ability to select a series of objects based on its group association. As you explore the group command you will no doubt find it a much more convenient method of grouping objects within a drawing than using the block command.

Blocks can be improved by adding a line of text to them, known as an attribute. Attributes allow you to attach text information to your blocks, which can be later extracted into database and spreadsheet programs. Attributes can also be used for entering text that changes with each insertion of a block. For example, you could define attributes in your title block drawing that prompt for the drafter's name, current date, and project ID each time the title block is inserted into a drawing.

OUTLINE

Using Groups
Tutorial 15.1: Creating a Bathtub Symbol
Tutorial 15.2: Using Block with the ? Option
Tutorial 15.3: Using WBlock to Create a Door Symbol
Tutorial 15.4: Inserting Symbols into a Drawing
Adding Information to Blocks with Attributes
Tutorial 15.5: Defining and Inserting an Attribute
Tutorial 15.6: Changing the Attribute's Display Setting
Tutorial 15.7: Redefining Attributes with **attredef**
Tutorial 15.8: Extracting Attribute Data
Summary
Review
Exercises

USING GROUPS

Often there may be several objects in your drawing that are related in some way and require some type of editing action. For example, all objects representing an electrical outlet in a floorplan may need to be selected for copying, changing color, or changing layer. In complex drawings containing a large number of objects, the process of creating a selection set (with pick box, window, etc.) can take a considerable amount of time. A floor plan of a large building may have literally thousands of electrical outlet symbols.

Similar to blocks, groups allow you to group objects together in a named selection set. A group is a set of objects that you can assign a name and description to. One of the key differences between **group** and **block** is that an object can be assigned to more than one group. Once a group is created, it can be assigned a selectable status. If the group is defined as selectable, you can pick the entire group at any `Select objects:` prompt by picking any individual member. You can also type `group` or the letter `g` at the `Select Objects:` prompt and enter the group name. You will find this command useful if you have a large number of objects that you want to modify at one time. For example, if all the objects in an architectural drawing representing electrical outlets were assigned to a group named "outlets," the entire group could be selected during the **move** command as follows:

```
Command: move
Select objects: g
Enter group name: outlets
450 found
Base point or displacement:
```

You access the **group** command by doing either of the following:

- Select the Object Group button on the Standard toolbar.
- Type **`group`** at the `Command:` prompt.

When you access the **group** command, the Object Grouping dialog box appears as shown in Figure 15.1, and you are presented with the following options:

- **Group Name.** Enter a group name here. The group name convention is the same as the layer naming conventions and can be up to 31 characters long. AutoCAD converts the name to uppercase. Once a name has been given to the group, that name appears in the Group Name listing.
- **Description.** Enter a descriptive phrase for the group. The description can be up to 64 characters in length and is optional.
- **Find Name.** Allows you to select an object and then list the name of the group or groups that the object is associated with.
- **Highlight.** Shows all objects within a group. The group objects are shown in the drawing area.
- **Include Unnamed.** Allows you to view unnamed groups in the dialog box.
- **New.** Creates a new group from the objects you have selected.

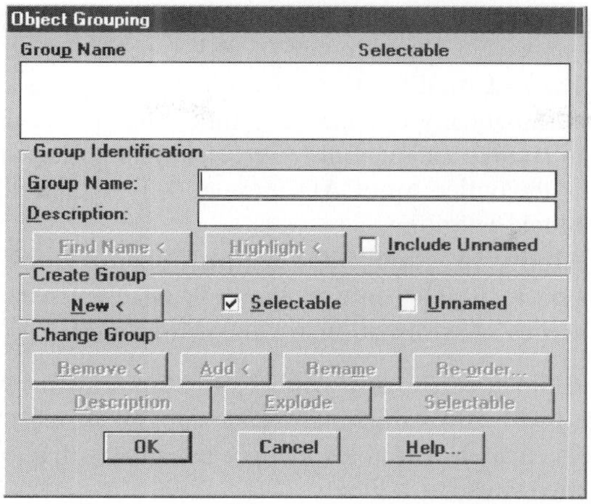

Figure 15.1
The Object Grouping dialog box.

- **Selectable.** Determines whether a group can be selected when a single object within the group is picked. If a group is unselectable, selecting any object within the group only selects that single object.
- **Unnamed.** Creates a group without a given name. AutoCAD assigns an anonymous name, *AN where N is a sequential number that indicates the new number of unnamed groups as they are created.
- **Remove.** Removes objects from a group. You can remove all objects within a group, but the group is still defined. Removing objects from a group doesn't remove them from the drawing.
- **Add.** Adds objects to a group.
- **Rename.** Renames a selected group to the name found in the Group Name edit box. Select the group first, type the new group name in the Group Name edit box, and then click the Rename button.
- **Re-order.** Selecting this button immediately displays the Order Group dialog box. In this dialog box you can change the order of the objects in a group. Objects are numbered as they are selected into the group. Re-ordering allows you to reverse the numbering scheme or change the scheme one by one.
- **Description.** Changes the existing description of a group. Uses the same procedure as Rename.
- **Explode.** Deletes a group. Select the group you want to delete from the list, then click the Explode button. The group definition is deleted but the objects remain in the drawing.
- **Selectable.** Allows you to change whether or not an existing group is selectable.

Using Blocks to Represent Symbols

Drawing an object once, with the ability to insert it into several other drawings, is one of the greatest time-saving features of AutoCAD. A block may be defined as a single object that is composed of many other objects. You can create objects as you normally would, using any of AutoCAD's drawing and editing tools. These objects can then be compiled into a block for use as a symbol in your drawing. Several advantages to using blocks are:

- **Ability to share blocks.** A copy of a block can be stored on disk for use in other drawings. If you work with a standard set of symbols, for example, one person can draw the symbols and then share them with everyone else. This collection of standardized symbols can be called a symbol library.
- **Reduction in file size.** When the **copy** command is used, all of the objects are duplicated. For example, you have a symbol in a drawing that consists of 100 objects. When you **copy** the objects, you duplicate the objects. If you **copy** it 10 times, you have added 1000 new objects to the drawing file. If you make the objects a block and insert it 10 times, you only create 110 objects. 100 objects are for the

original block, with 10 for each block. When you use blocks in your drawing, you can save a great amount of disk space.

- **Ease of modification.** If a block is updated or changed in a drawing, AutoCAD automatically updates all symbols based on that block. For example, if you decide to change the symbol for an electrical outlet, you first redefine the **block** definition of the outlet. AutoCAD automatically updates all electrical outlets based on the new **block** definition.
- **Ability to attach information.** When a block is created, you can attach information to it. This information can be extracted and used in other programs. These pieces of information are called attributes.

A block can be any symbol or entire drawing that you need to use more than once. Before you begin a drawing, create a rough sketch of the drawing. Look for assemblies, symbols, shapes, and notes that are used more than once. This information can be drawn once, then saved as a block.

Creating Symbol Libraries To make a block, begin creating geometry using any AutoCAD commands. When you've finished creating the geometry, determine the best place on the symbol to use as an insertion point. When the block is inserted into the drawing, the symbol is placed with its insertion point on the screen crosshairs.

Once the symbol is created and the insertion point determined, use the **block** command. Either of the following gives you access to the **block** command:

- Select the Insert Block button on the Draw toolbar to bring up a fly-out menu showing the different options for the **block** command.
- Type `block` at the `Command:` prompt.

Once you've invoked the **block** command, AutoCAD prompts for the name and insertion point. The block name may not exceed 31 characters. Additionally, use the appropriate Osnap command or coordinate values when specifying the insertion point. You can use any selection set method such as Window, Fence, or crossing to pick the objects that make up the block. The following command sequence is used when defining a block:

Select the Block button from the Draw toolbar.

`Block name (or ?):` *Type in the block name.*
`Insertion base point:` *Pick the insertion point using OSNAP or by entering coordinates.*
`Select Objects:` *Select the objects comprising the symbol, using any selection set method.*
`Select Objects:` *Press Enter.*

When you have completed the **block** command sequence, the original defining objects are erased from the screen. The defined block is now part of the current drawing file. It may not be used in any other drawing—only the one it was created in. Saving the block to be used in another file is discussed in "Writing Blocks to a File" later on in this unit.

A block can be created from any objects that are already in your drawing. If you create a symbol for a door, for example, you can use the **block** command to create a block from its objects. The block definition is now stored with the drawing, and the original objects disappear from the screen. Once the block is created, it may be inserted into the drawing as many times as needed.

SKILL BUILDER

After creating the block, the original defining objects are erased from the screen. To restore the objects that defined the block, type `oops` at the `Command:` prompt or select the Oops button from the Miscellaneous toolbar.

Tutorial 15.1: Creating a Bathtub Symbol

In this tutorial you load the apartment floor plan, as shown in Figure 15.2, and create a bathtub symbol to be used in the apartment floor plan. The apartment floor plan drawing is used in all subsequent tutorials in this unit.

1.  Select the Open button from the Standard toolbar and load 15DWG01. This will open the title block as shown in Figure 15.2.

2. Change the view to display the left bathroom.

 Select the Named Views button from the Standard toolbar.

The View Control dialog box appears as shown in Figure 15.3. Select the Leftbath view, click the Restore button, and thenclick OK to select the new view. The screen zooms into the left bathroom as shown in Figure 15.4.

3.  Now create the bathtub symbol block. Select the Block button from the Draw toolbar.

```
Block name (or ?): bathtub
Insertion base point: 1'-10", 29'-8"
Select objects: Window around the bathtub as shown in Figure 15.5.
Select objects:
```

The bathtub disappears. Note the WALLS layer was locked, so they were not selected when you windowed around the bathtub. Since the symbol is needed in this location, it may be helpful to bring it back.

4. Return the bathtub drawing to its original position.

 Select the Oops button from the Miscellaneous toolbar.

The bathtub drawing is redisplayed within the drawing area in its original position.

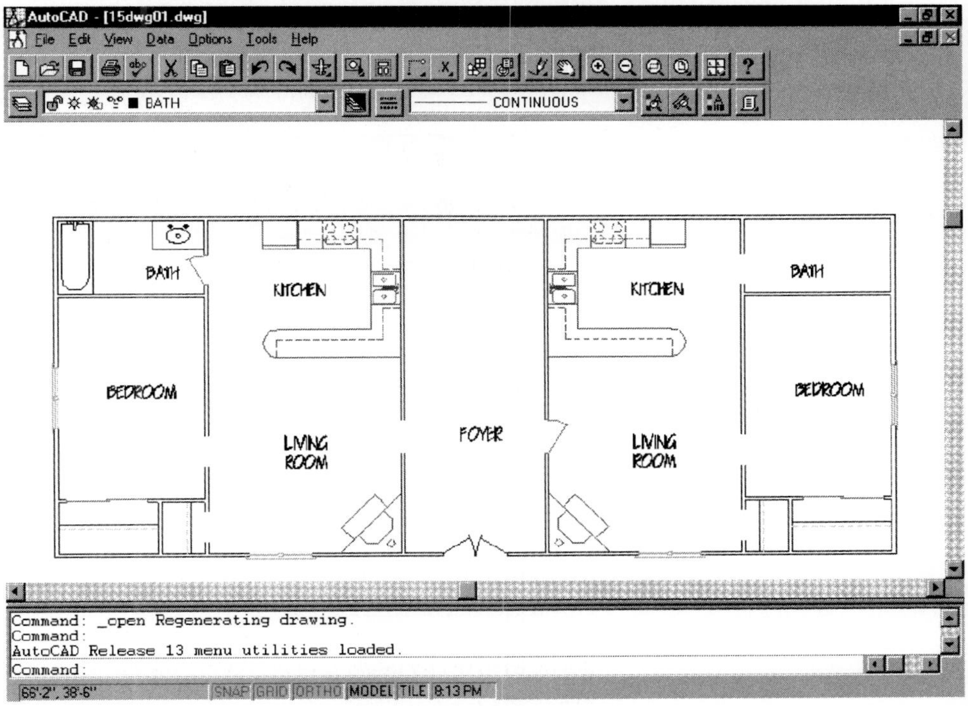

Figure 15.2
Loading the apartment floor plan.

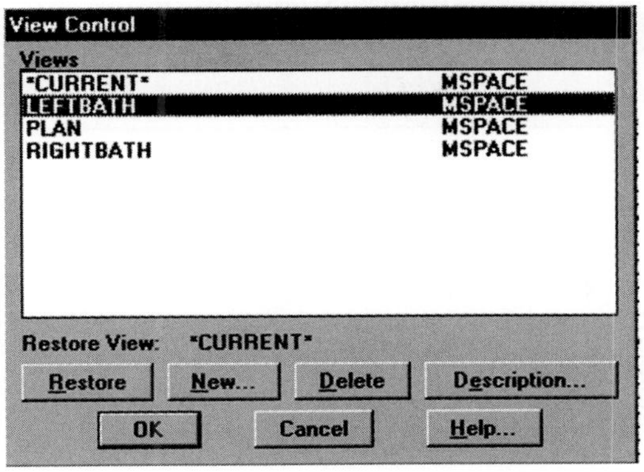

Figure 15.3
Using the View Control dialog box to select the Leftbath predefined view.

Figure 15.4
Viewing the left bathroom to create a bathtub symbol.

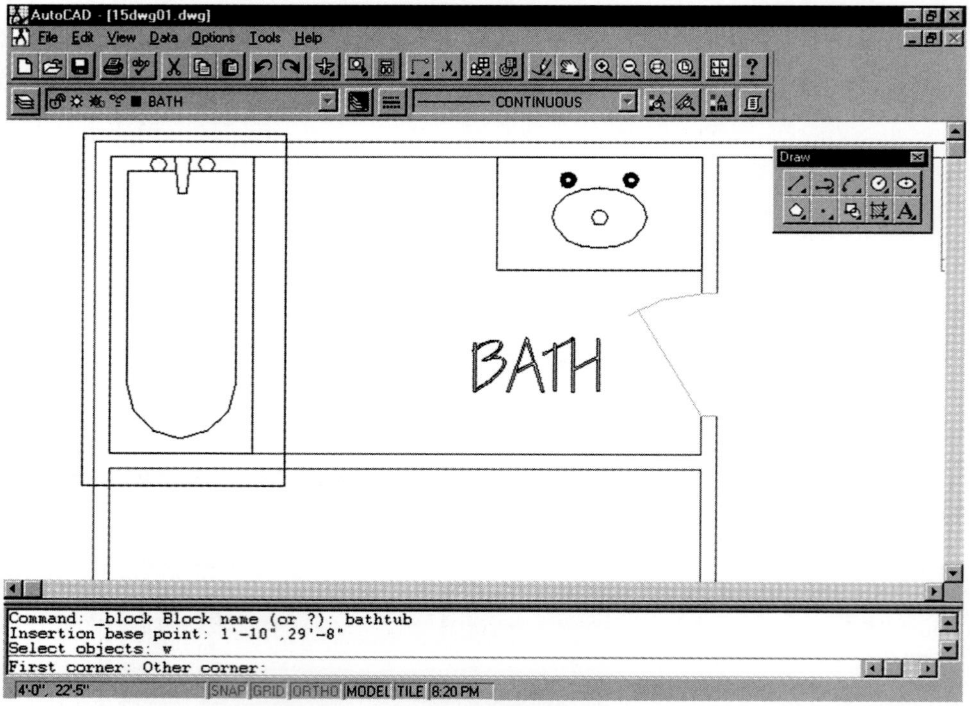

Figure 15.5
Use Window to select the objects to be included in the bathtub symbol.

Listing Blocks in the Current Drawing

To list the blocks defined in the current drawing, first enter the **block** command. At the `Block name (or ?):` prompt, enter a question mark as follows:

Select the Block button from the Draw toolbar.

```
Block name (or ?): ?
Block(s) to list<*>:
```

This brings up a list of all blocks currently defined in the drawing. The following information is displayed in the text window:

```
Defined Blocks
```

(This area lists all blocks, alphabetically by name, defined in the drawing.)

User Blocks	External References	Dependent Blocks	Unnamed Blocks
0	0	0	0

User Blocks are blocks you created. External Reference are other drawings referenced from your drawing. Dependent Blocks are blocks that reside in an externally referenced drawing. Unnamed Blocks are certain types of objects, such as associative dimensions or hatch patterns.

Tutorial 15.2: Using Block with the ? Option

1. Continue from the previous tutorial.
2.  Select the Block button from the Draw toolbar.

```
Block name (or ?): ?
Block(s) to list<*>:
```

Notice that the bathtub is now listed as a block within our tutorial file.

Creating Blocks on Layer 0

When objects are created on specific layers and blocked, they retain their original characteristics when inserted back into the drawing. To have a block adopt the characteristics of the current layer, create the original objects on layer 0.

When objects are created on layer 0 and blocked, the objects "float through" to the current layer and inherit the color and linetype of the current layer. The following list summarizes block creation, layers, and layer 0:

Block maintains original object color and linetype when inserted. To maintain the color and linetype the objects were originally created with, draw the initial objects with the color, linetype, and layer you want. After creating the objects, block them. When the block is inserted back into the drawing, they retain their original color and linetype regardless of the current color, linetype, or layer.

Block adopts characteristics of the current color and linetype when inserted. To have objects adopt the current color and linetype, initially create the objects on layer 0. After creating the objects on layer 0, block them. When the block is inserted back into the original drawing, they adopt the current color and linetype.

Using Layers to Create Blocks

When blocks are created, the objects used to define the block may be drawn on various layers. When you insert a block, the objects are placed in the drawing as well as the layers in which they were created. Creating the objects used to define a block on specific layers is an easy way to help assist in the standardization of layers. For example, create blocks such as doors on a layer called doors; when that block is inserted by anyone, the layer is automatically created. It's important to note that the block can be inserted on any layer and the new layers are still created unless there are duplicate layer names.

If the layer that the block is inserted on is frozen or turned off, that block won't be displayed. Also, the layers that are newly created by inserting blocks can be manipulated individually, but the layer setting that the block was inserted on has precedence. If the block is exploded, the objects of the former block are no longer associated with the layer that the block was placed on. The block objects are now separate objects on their predefined layers.

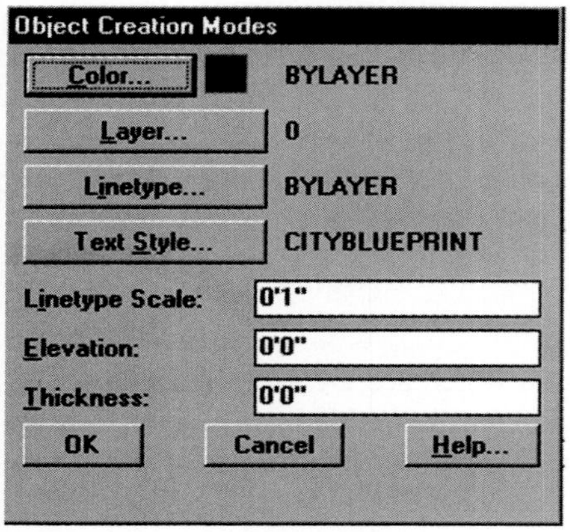

Figure 15.6 *The default color and linetype can be set with the Object Creation Modes dialog box.*

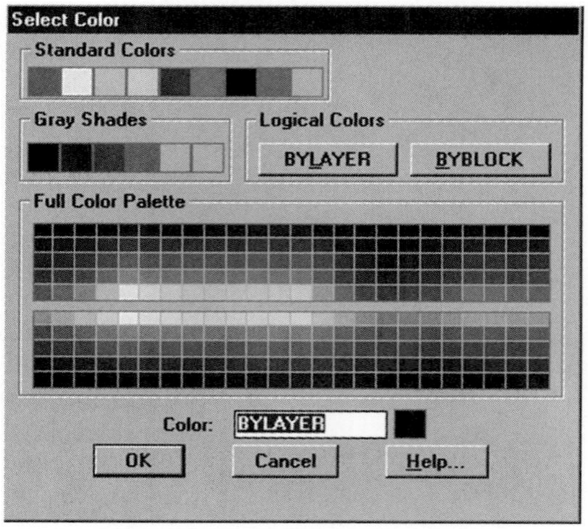

Figure 15.7 *The default object color can be set to Byblock in the Select Color dialog box.*

Using **byblock** with Blocks

The Object Creation Modes dialog box **(ddemodes),** shown in Figure 15.6, controls the current settings for Color and Linetype. Selecting the Color option in the Object Creation Modes dialog box brings up the Select Color dialog box. One option in the Select Color dialog box is to set the Logical Colors Byblock (see Figure 15.7).

Set the Color and Linetype to `BYLAYER` if you want to control the color and linetype of each incident of a block by using the color and linetype of the current layer. Draw all of the block's objects on layer 0 with color and linetype set to `BYLAYER`.

Set the Color and Linetype to `BYBLOCK` if you want to control the color and linetype of each incident of a block by using the current explicit color and linetype. Draw each of the block's objects with color and linetype set to `BYBLOCK`. After creating the objects, you can change the layer, color, and linetype using **ddchprop** before creating the block.

Writing Blocks to a File

A block created from a group of objects can only be used in the current drawing. The **wblock** command writes all or part of a drawing to a file. When you **wblock** a group of objects, you essentially create a block and copy it to a new drawing file on the disk. This drawing file is no different than any other drawing file you create and save.

Once the **wblock** definition is written to a file, it can be used outside of the current drawing. The **wblock** command enables you to export symbols created in a drawing to use in other drawings. The **wblock** command may be accessed by:

- Typing **`wblock`** at the `Command:` prompt.
- Select Export from the File pull-down menu. This will access the Export Data dialog box. Make sure you select drawing (*.DWG) as the type of file you want to export.

When you enter the **wblock** command, the Create Drawing File dialog box appears. Select the drive, path and name of the **wblock** file to create. Don't include a file extension, since AutoCAD assumes you are creating a DWG file and automatically adds it.

Skill Builder

Proper file management techniques are very important when using blocks. One of the greatest benefits of AutoCAD is the capability to store common symbols for future use. The ability to easily locate a symbol after it has been stored on the disk is just as important as how it was created.

After entering the drive, path and name, AutoCAD prompts you for a block name. Enter the name of the block you wish to write to the disk. The following list summarizes responses to the `Block name:` prompt:

- `Block name:` (Specify the name of the block to write to disk.) This option writes an existing block file to disk.
- `Block name:` = The = (equal) sign means that you want to create a **wblock** of an existing block and that the existing block has the same name as the file name you already entered for the wblock in the Create Drawing File dialog box.
- `Block name:` * Typing the * writes the entire drawing to disk. Using the * option with the **wblock** command doesn't write unreferenced symbols (layers, blocks, linetypes, text styles, and dimension styles) to the drawing file. Using this technique is similar to applying the **purge** command to your drawing. By dropping unused symbols from the drawing, the drawing file is reduced in size.
- `Block name:` (Press spacebar or Enter) Pressing the Spacebar or Enter key causes AutoCAD to prompt for the `Insertion base point:`. After selecting the Insertion base point, you are prompted to `Select objects:`. Using this method allows you to write a group of objects to disk without first making them into a block with the **block** command.

Skill Builder

Using the **wblock** command creates a standard AutoCAD DWG drawing file which can be edited. It's also important to note that the insertion point of the block drawing file is now the origin for the drawing file.

Tutorial 15.3: Using WBlock to Create a Door Symbol

In this tutorial you create a **wblock** of the 2′8″ door symbol found in the bathroom.

1. Continue from the previous tutorial. You should still see the left bathroom displayed.
2. Create a **wblock** of the door symbol.

   `Command: wblock`

   The Create Drawing File dialog box appears as shown in Figure 15.8. Change to the A:\ drive and in the File Name input box type 2-8DOOR. Click OK.

   `Block name:` **`press`** `Enter`
   `Insertion base point:` **`13'-2",24'-0"`**
   `Select objects:`

   Create a window around the door as shown in Figure 15.9.

   `Select objects:`

   The door drawing disappears and is saved as a drawing file for later use in this or another drawing.
3. Now return the door drawing back to its original position.

   `Command:` **`oops`**

   The door drawing is restored back to its original location on the apartment floor plan drawing.

Figure 15.8 *Using the Create Drawing File dialog box to name the Wblock.*

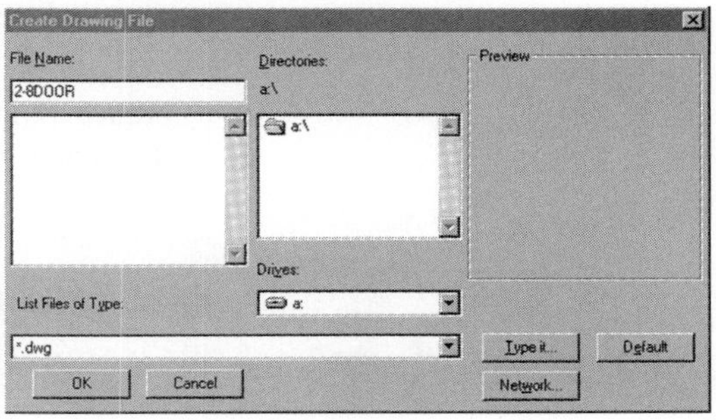

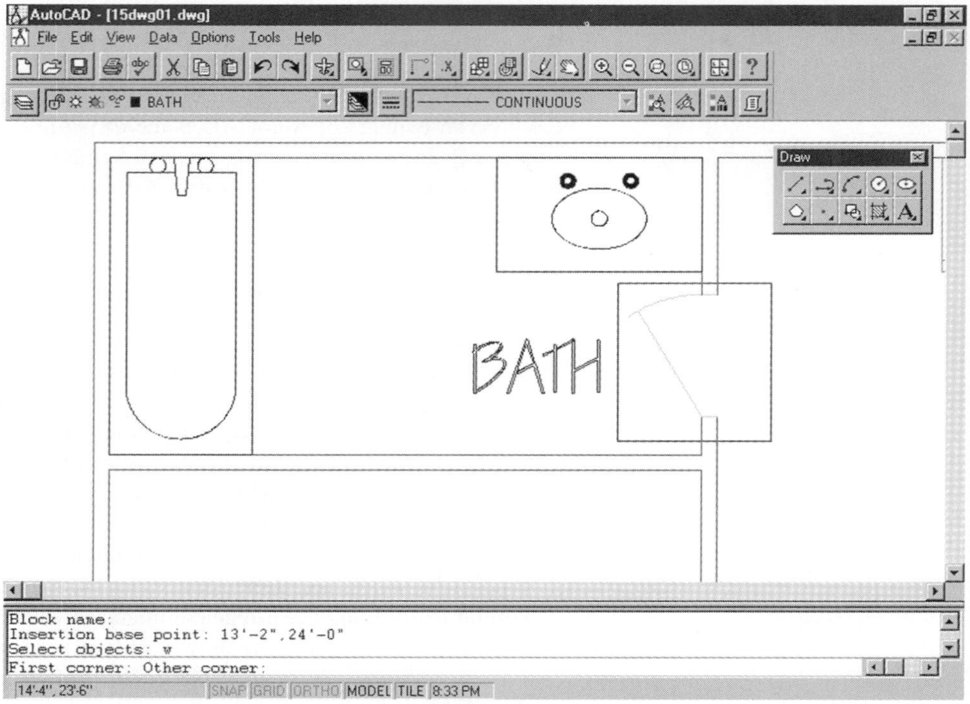

Figure 15.9
Using the Window Selection method to select the bathroom door in the apartment floor plan.

Points to Consider when Creating a Block or WBlock When creating a block or wblock, several factors affect your ability to use the block. The layer, color, linetype, insertion point, and size the block was drawn at all affect the block when you try to use it. Following are tips that help in the creation of blocks and avoid confusion when creating and later inserting blocks.

- **Layer, color, and linetype.** To have the block take on the characteristics of the layer it is inserted on, all the block's objects must be on layer 0 when you create the block and the color and linetype variables must be set to bylayer.

  If the block was created from objects on any layer other than layer 0, the block retains the characteristics of that layer. If the block objects were created on several layers, the block's objects remain on the original layers when inserted. If the block was created on a layer that doesn't exist in the current drawing, AutoCAD recreates that layer when the block is inserted.
- **Drawing a block to scale.** When creating a block, draw all the objects that comprise the block to unit (full) size. For example, suppose you draw an electrical outlet symbol 1 unit wide. When inserting the block in a different drawing, AutoCAD automatically prompts you to specify a scale factor for the block. If you want the electrical outlet symbol to be 2 units across in the new drawing, specify a scale factor of 2. If the block should be half a unit, use a scale factor of .5.
- **Defining the insertion base point.** The **block** and **wblock** command's `Insertion base point:` prompt asks you to define a reference point on the block. This reference point is used when inserting the block into the drawing. Select a reference point that is convenient for future reference. For example, the center or lower-left corner are commonly used as reference points.

SKILL BUILDER

Existing block names can be changed with the Rename dialog box **(ddrename).**

Inserting Symbols into a Drawing After defining a block in a drawing, the block can be inserted into the drawing. Additionally, you can insert any drawing file (including files created with the **wblock** command) into a drawing as a block. AutoCAD provides the **insert, ddinsert,** and **minsert** commands for inserting a block into a drawing.

When inserting a block into drawing, you must specify four things:

- The name of the block or file to insert.
- The point where you want the block inserted.
- The rotation of the block.
- The block scale in the X-, Y-, and Z-axis.

If you type `insert` at the `Command:` line, AutoCAD prompts you for this information. The **ddinsert** command is similar to the **insert** command in the way it inserts blocks or files into a drawing. The **ddinsert** command opens the Insert dialog box that can be used to locate the block or file name and specify the insertion parameters. In most cases the **ddinsert** command is easier to use. The Insert dialog box can be accessed by:

- Selecting the Insert Block button on the Draw toolbar.
- Type **`ddinsert`** at the `Command:` prompt.

The Insert dialog box is shown in Figure 15.10. To select a block that is already defined in the drawing, select the Block button. This causes the Defined Blocks dialog box to appear as shown in Figure 15.11.

To insert a file into the drawing as a block, select the File button. This causes the Select Drawing File dialog box to appear as shown in Figure 15.12. Change to the appropriate drive and directory and choose the desired file.

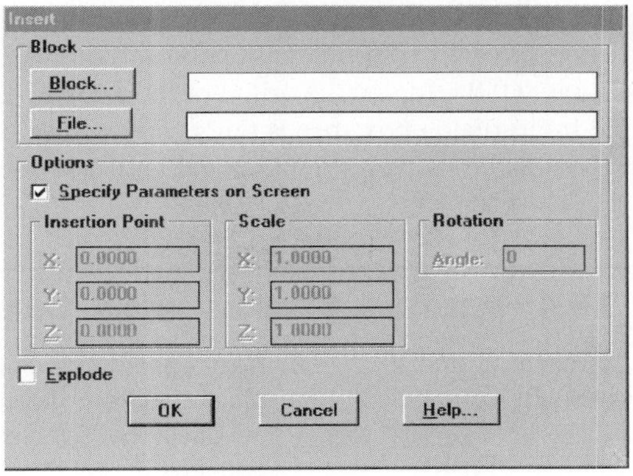

Figure 15.10
Use the Insert dialog box to insert blocks easily.

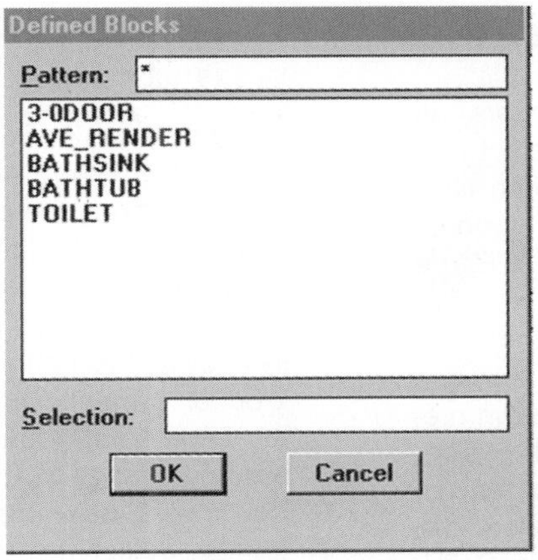

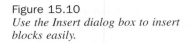

Figure 15.11 *The Defined Blocks dialog box lists all blocks currently defined in the drawing.*

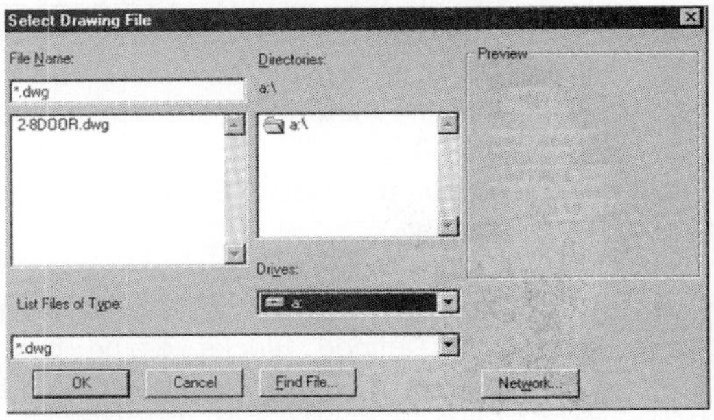

Figure 15.12 *The Select Drawing File dialog box allows you to select a file to insert into the current drawing as a block.*

The insertion point, scale, and rotation of the block can be set in the edit boxes in the Insert dialog box. By default, the Specify Parameters on Screen box is checked. If this option is used, you are returned to the drawing editor after selecting the appropriate block or file and selecting OK. You are then prompted to specify the insertion point, scale, and rotation parameters at the `Command:` prompt. AutoCAD dynamically changes the appearance of the block as you specify the rotation and scale values.

Skill Builder

The insertion base point specified when the block was created is the point at which the block is now inserted. If you're inserting a drawing file where you didn't specify a base point, the origin (0,0,0) becomes the insertion base point by default.

To change the parameters in the Insert dialog box, remove the check in the Specify Parameters on Screen checkbox. Type the appropriate values in the edit boxes. Setting the parameters in the Insert dialog box doesn't allow you to see the size and orientation of the block prior to insertion however.

Skill Builder

When inserting entire drawings it's often easier to remove the check in the Specify Parameters on Screen box and set the values in the Insert dialog box. Since entire drawings have the insertion base point set to 0,0,0, this option can speed up block insertion. 0,0,0 refers to the origin of the drawing being inserted. Setting the values in the Insert dialog box speeds things up because AutoCAD doesn't have to try and represent the drawing as you alter the insertion point, scale, and rotation on screen.

Tutorial 15.4: Inserting Symbols into a Drawing

In this tutorial you learn how to insert the bathtub and 2-8door symbols that you created in the previous tutorials. Begin by first inserting the bathtub symbol.

1. Continue from the previous tutorial. Change the view to display the right bathroom.

Select the Named Views button from the Standard toolbar.

The View Control dialog box appears as shown previously in Figure 15.3. Select the RIGHTBATH view, click Restore, and then click OK to select the new view. The screen zooms into the right bathroom view as shown in Figure 15.13.

2.  Select the Insert Block button from the Draw toolbar.

The Insert dialog box appears as shown previously in Figure 15.10. Click the Block button. The Defined Blocks dialog box appears as shown previously in Figure 15.11. Select the bathtub symbol and click the OK button. BATHTUB appears in the Block input box of the Insert dialog box.

3. Next specify the parameters for inserting the bathtub block into your drawing.

Click the Specify Parameters on Screen button to uncheck it.

Change the values for the Insertion Point to:

X: 70'-2"
Y: 29'-8"

Leave the Z, Scale, and Rotation values to their default. Your dialog box should look like Figure 15.14.

4. After specifying the correct parameters for inserting the bathtub symbol, click OK. The bathtub symbol is inserted into the bathroom as shown in Figure 15.15.

5.  You're now ready to add the 2-8door symbol to the bathroom drawing. Before inserting the 2-8door symbol, change to the DOORS layer. Choose the Layer Control button on the Object Properties toolbar and change to the DOORS layer.

6. Now insert the 2-8door Symbol.

7.  Select the Insert Block button from the Draw toolbar.

The Insert dialog box appears. Click the File

button. The Select Drawing File dialog box appears as shown previously in Figure 15.12. Change to the A:\ drive and select the 2-8DOOR.dwg. A picture of the 2-8door symbol will appear in the Preview window. Click OK to continue.

8. Next specify the parameters for inserting the 2-8door into your drawing.

Click the Specify Parameters on Screen button to uncheck it.

Change the values for the Insertion Point to:

```
X: 58'-10"
Y: 26'-8"
```

Change the Rotation to:

```
Angle: 180
```

9. Leave the Z and Scale values to their default. Your dialog box should look like Figure 15.16.

10.  After specifying the correct parameters for inserting the 2-8door symbol, click OK. The 2-8door symbol is inserted into the bathroom as shown in Figure 15.17. Select the Save button from the Standard toolbar to save your drawing.

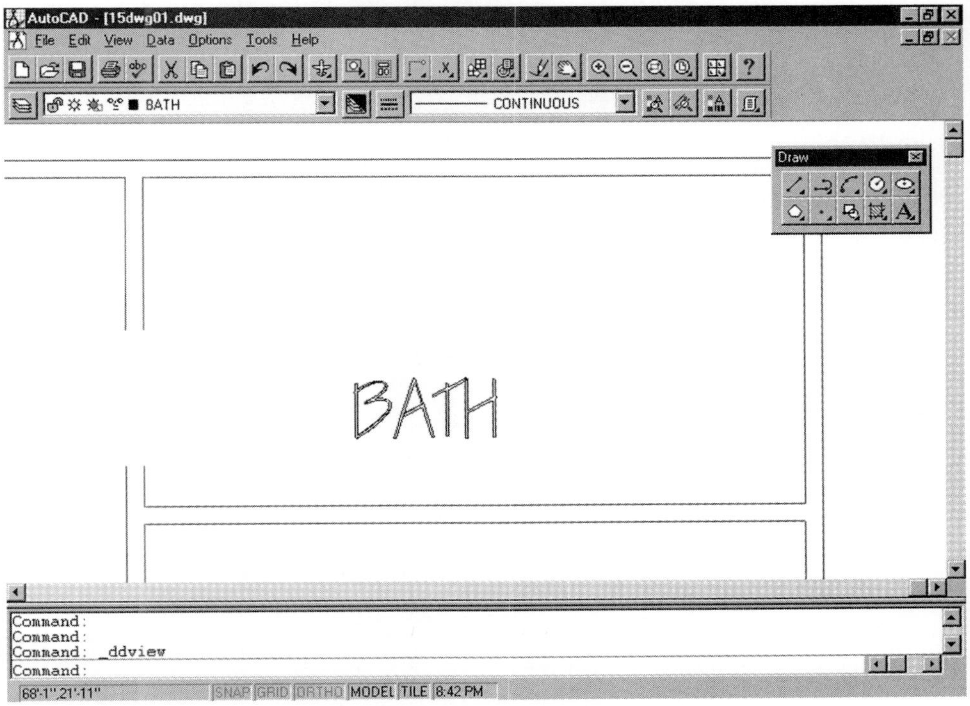

Figure 15.13
The RIGHTBATH predefined view, displayed by using the View Control dialog box.

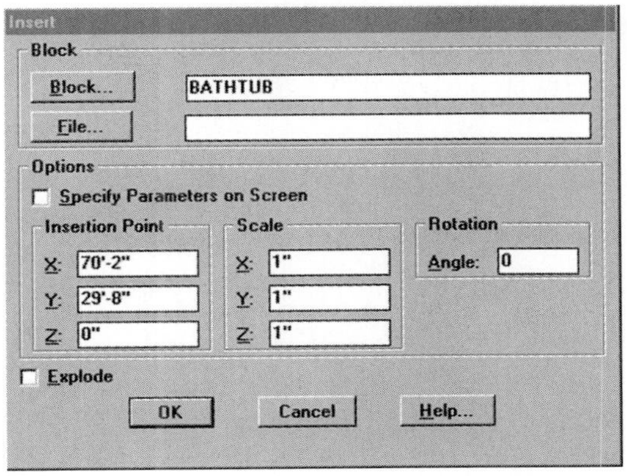

Figure 15.14
Using the Insert dialog box to insert the bathtub symbol.

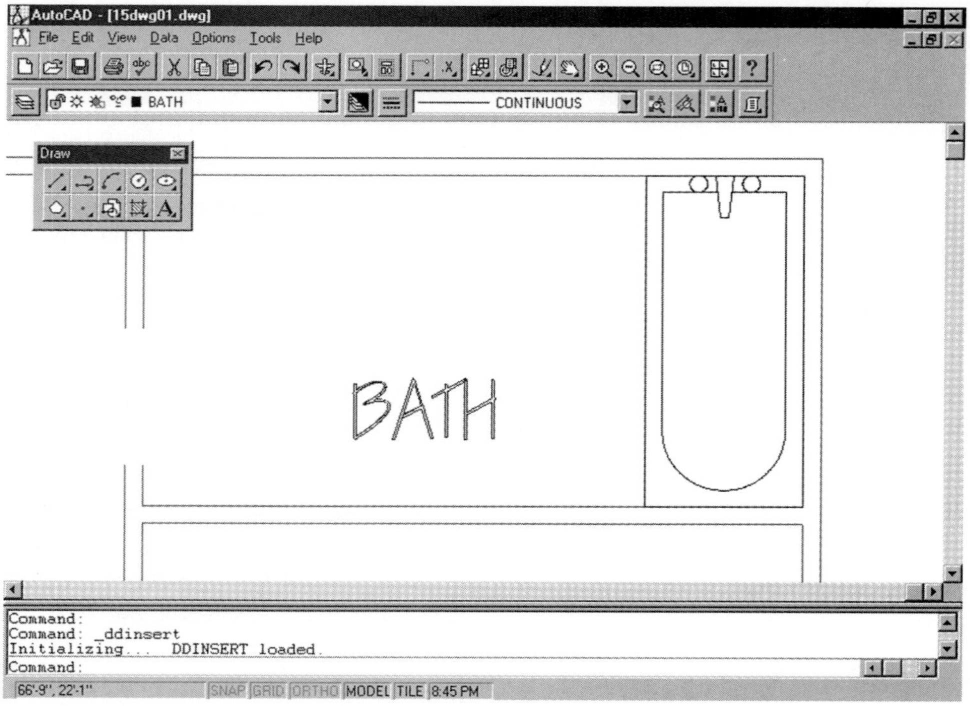

Figure 15.15
The right bathroom with the bathtub symbol inserted.

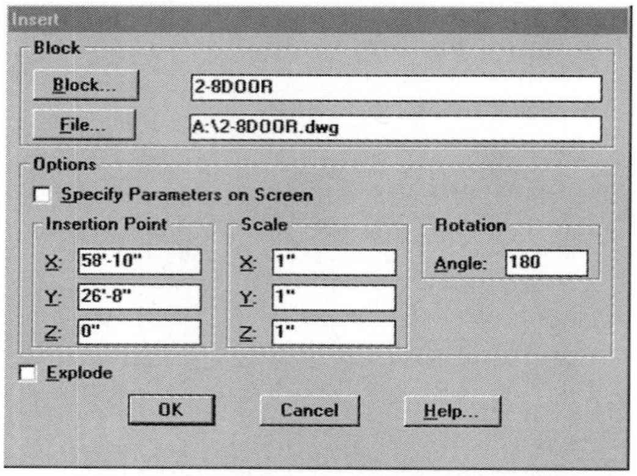

Figure 15.16
Using the Insert dialog box to insert the 2-8door symbol.

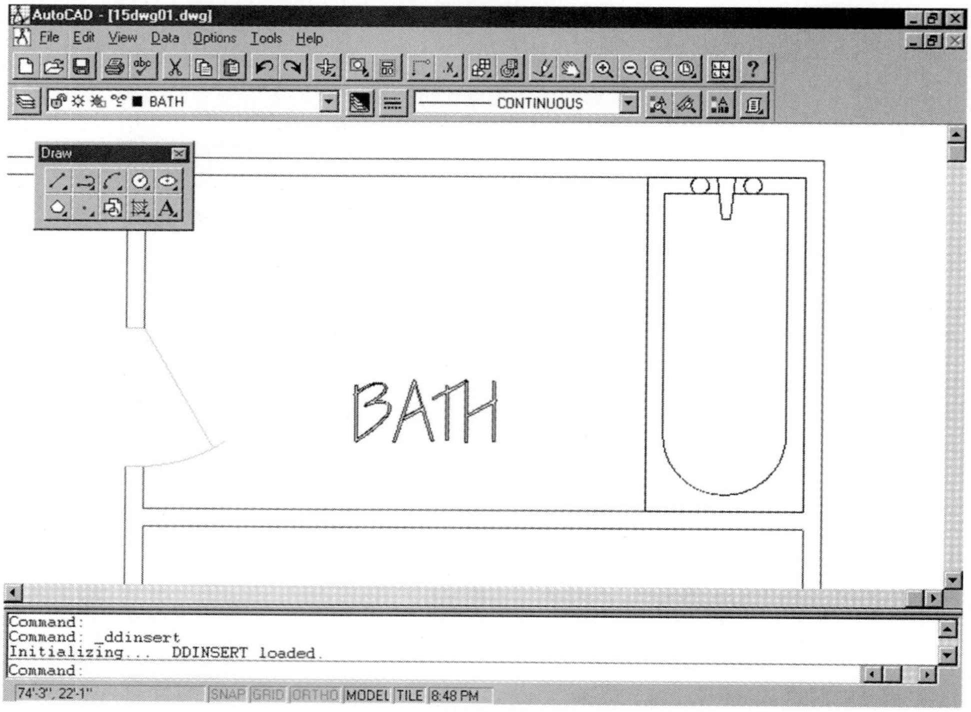

Figure 15.17
The bathroom after the bathtub and 2-8door symbols have been inserted.

Specifying a New Insertion Point (BASE) The **`insert`** or **`ddinsert`** command can be used to insert an entire drawing into the existing drawing. By default, the drawing being inserted has a base insertion point of 0,0,0. The **`base`** command can be used to change the insertion point for the new drawing. The **`base`** command can be accessed by:

- Typing **`base`** at the `Command:` prompt.

To determine the best location for the base point, examine the drawing view and the location of the inserted drawing. After you redefine the base point, all subsequent drawings are inserted at that point.

Breaking Blocks Apart (EXPLODE) When you create a block from a group of objects in AutoCAD, it's defined as a single object. The individual objects in the block definition can't be edited.

When a block is exploded, the block definition is removed and the block is broken down into its individual objects. Exploding a block creates a drawing database entry for each object in the block. Exploding a block can have a significant effect on the size of a drawing. The **explode** command is used to explode an existing block. The **explode** command can be accessed as follows:

- Select the Explode button from the Modify toolbar.
- Type **`explode`** at the `Command:` prompt.

After the block is exploded, the individual objects that were part of the block can now be edited. Exploding a block only affects the selected block and doesn't affect any other blocks with the same name.

SKILL BUILDER

You can use the Insert dialog box **(ddinsert)** to explode a block before it's inserted. Simply place a check in the Explode checkbox.

Inserting More than One Block The **minsert** (Multiple **insert**) command combines the features of the **insert** and **array** commands for block insertion. All blocks in the array are recognized as a single object. Using the **minsert** command for inserting and arranging blocks not only saves time but disk space as well. The **minsert** command can be accessed by:

- Choose the Insert Multiple Blocks from the Miscellaneous toolbar.
- Type **`minsert`** at the `Command:` prompt.

After accessing the **minsert** command, AutoCAD prompts:

```
Block name (or ?): enter name of block.
Insertion point: type in or select coordinates to insert block.
X scale factor <1> / Corner / XYZ: press Enter or change scale.
Y scale factor (default=X): press Enter or change scale.
Rotation angle <0>: enter angle.
Number of rows (--) <1>: enter number of rows.
Number of columns (|||) <1>: enter number of columns.
```

SKILL BUILDER

All blocks included in the **minsert** array have the same scale and rotation. Additionally, blocks inserted with **minsert** can't be exploded.

Updating a Symbol To edit a block, it first must be broken down into its original objects. This is especially important when an entire drawing is inserted. The **explode** command is used to break the block apart into its individual objects. To make sure the block was exploded properly, select any object that was formally part of the block. Only that object should be highlighted.

Occasionally situations arise when a block must be edited. AutoCAD allows you to redefine an existing block, even if it has been placed on the drawing many times. To update a symbol defined as a block, use the following procedure:

1. Insert the block you want redefined anywhere on the drawing.
2. Explode the block just inserted with the **explode** command.
3. Edit the block using any of AutoCAD's editing commands.
4. Begin the **block** command.
5. When prompted for the name, give the edited block the same name it had before. Answer `Yes` when AutoCAD prompts `Redefine it? <N>`.
6. Specify the same insertion point on the edited block as the original.
7. All blocks that were inserted are updated when the **block** command is completed.

If you try to redefine the block without using the **explode** command, the following error message is displayed and the command is aborted:

```
Block <name> references itself
*Invalid*
```

The error message is alerting you to the fact that you're trying to recreate a block that already exists. Use the **explode** command on the block and redefine it.

Editing Blocks with Grips Because AutoCAD defines blocks as a single object, a block normally displays one grip. This single grip is located at the insertion point of the block. This grip can be used to perform all the Grip auto edit functions such as move and copy on the block.

The **gripblock** system variable is used to control the display of grips within a block. The easiest way to control the gripblock variable is with the Grips dialog box. The Grips dialog box can be accessed by:

- Selecting Grips from the Options pull-down menu.
- Type **`ddgrips`** at the `Command:` prompt.

To enable the **gripblock** variable, check the box labeled Enable Grips Within Blocks in the Grips dialog box.

The default setting for the **gripblock** variable is 0 or off. When **gripblock** is off, the block displays a single grip. When **gripblock** is set to 1 or on, all individual objects within the block display grips as if they were single objects. This can be useful if you need to edit the basepoint in the block.

Even though each individual object displays its grips when **gripblock** is set to 1, you can't use the grips to edit the individual objects within the block—only the basepoint. The block must first be exploded to edit the individual objects.

Nesting Blocks Nested blocks are simply blocks that contain other blocks. You can create a block that contains another block by just selecting the block as the object to include in the new block. If you explode a block that contains a block, it converts both blocks to all the individual objects.

ADDING INFORMATION TO BLOCKS WITH ATTRIBUTES

In the last section you used blocks to represent symbols in your drawing. You created symbols for a bathtub and a door. Attributes are text strings that can be used to label or describe each block. The associated attributes can give you the related description of each block, such as the manufacturer, cost, model number, part number, etc.

An attribute can be thought of as a label or description of a block. The attribute is included with the objects when you define the block (using the **block** or **wblock** commands). When the block is inserted **(ddinsert)** into a drawing, the attributes associated with it are also inserted. Creating an attribute to associate with a block is a four-step process.

1. Create the objects that will comprise the block using your geometry creation and editing commands.
2. Define the attribute using the **attdef** or **ddattdef** commands.
3. Use the **block** or **wblock** commands to convert the drawing objects and attributes into a named block. When the `Select objects:` prompt appears, select all of the drawing objects and attributes.
4. Use the **insert** or **ddinsert** commands to insert the block and associated attributes into a drawing.

DEFINING AN ATTRIBUTE

Commands that create attributes are available in both Command: line and dialog box versions. To create an attribute you can do any of the following:

- Select the Define Attribute button from the Attribute toolbar. This will access the Attribute Definition dialog box.
- Type **`ddattdef`** at the `Command:` prompt. This will also access the Attribute Definition dialog box.
- Type **`attdef`** at the `Command:` prompt. This method will allow you to define an attribute at the command line.

Choosing the Define Attribute button or typing `ddattdef` at the `Command:` prompt provides a dialog box where you can enter an attribute's settings. Using the dialog box is more convenient than using the Command line options because it is like a one-stop shopping center—you can make all of your selections at one time. The Attribute Definition dialog box is displayed in Figure 15.18. The procedure for defining an attribute and the parts of the dialog box are described in the following sections.

ATTRIBUTE TAG, PROMPT, AND VALUE

The most basic attribute consists of a tag, prompt, and value. You can enter up to 256 characters in each one of the text boxes.

- **Tag.** The tag is the name or description of the attribute, such as MANUFACTURER, MODEL_NO, etc. The tag can contain any characters except spaces. AutoCAD automatically changes any lowercase letters to uppercase.
- **Prompt.** When inserting the block with the attribute into a drawing, AutoCAD will display the prompt, asking you what value the attribute will have when it is inserted. For example, your prompt might be "Enter the item's cost:" When you

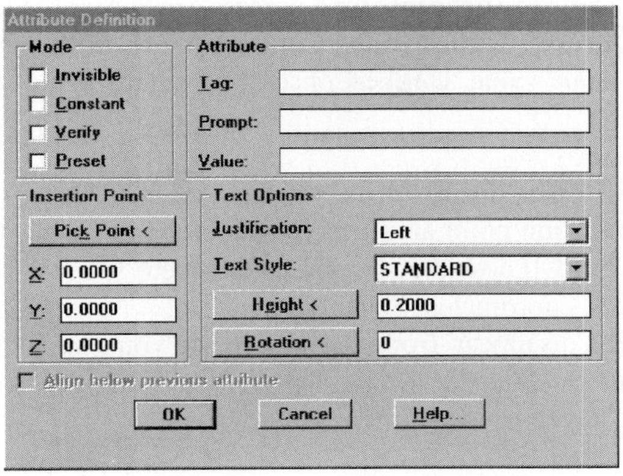

Figure 15.18
The Attribute Definition dialog box can be used to enter all of your attribute definitions at one time.

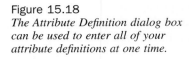

insert the block with the attribute, the prompt will appear on screen, and you will enter the cost. The cost information is then included in the block.

The **attdia** system variable controls the use of the Enter Attributes dialog box. If set to (1)ON, the Enter Attributes dialog box will appear, displaying your prompt and allowing you to enter your attribute values in an easy to use dialog box. If **attdia** is set to 0 (the default), your prompt will appear in the command box, where you must enter your attribute values.

- **Value.** When you define an attribute you can assign a default value that AutoCAD uses if you do not supply a value when you insert the attribute. The default value will usually be set to the most common value.

SKILL BUILDER

If you make a mistake when defining the attribute, you can use **ddedit** to edit the Tag, Prompt, and Value fields before you make it into a block.

ATTRIBUTE MODE SETTINGS

Attributes can be defined that exhibit any combination of four modes: Invisible, Constant, Verify, and Preset. The exception is with the Constant mode. When Constant is selected, you cannot select the Verify or Preset modes. Each mode has a specific effect on the attribute when it is inserted into the drawing:

- **Invisible.** An attribute with the invisible mode selected will not appear in the drawing when it is inserted.

SKILL BUILDER

Defining an attribute as invisible can be used to prevent unnecessary information from cluttering up your drawing. Even though an attribute is defined as invisible, you can still make AutoCAD display it on screen with the **attdisp** command.

- **Constant.** A constant attribute always has a fixed value when inserted. You are not prompted for a value when you insert it, and you cannot edit it.
- **Verify.** This will prompt you to verify the value so you can change your answer before it is inserted into the drawing. Using the Verify mode is a good idea when you're creating attributes that can be easily misspelled or mistakenly typed. It does, however, slow down the insertion process, since AutoCAD will prompt you twice for the value.
- **Preset.** Similar to the Constant mode, in that Preset attributes will always have the same value. Unlike Constant variables, you can edit Preset variables later.

ATTRIBUTE INSERTION POINT SETTINGS

The insertion point area lets you specify where the attribute will appear on the screen. If you already know the specific point where you want the attribute to appear, enter the X, Y, and Z coordinates. Selecting the `Pick Point<` option causes the dialog box to temporarily disappear from the screen so you can pick a point on your drawing. If the attribute ends up in the wrong location for some reason, you can always use the **move** command to re-locate the attribute.

Attribute Text Options

In the Text Options area of the Attribute Definition dialog box, you can set the justification, style, height, and rotation of the attribute text.

- **Justification.** Choosing the down arrow to the right of the text box accesses a pop-up list, showing the justification options. For a complete explanation of these options, review Unit 7, "Annotating a Drawing with Text and Hatching."
- **Text Style.** Allows you to choose a pre-defined text style from a pop-up menu that appears by choosing the down arrow at the right of the text box. For information on creating and using text styles, review Unit 7, "Annotating a Drawing with Text and Hatching."
- **Height.** Used to specify the height of the attribute text. If you selected Align from the Justification list, the Height option is not available.
- **Rotation.** Enter a rotation angle for the attribute text, or choose the Rotation< button to specify the rotation angle on the screen. The Rotation option is not available if you selected Align or Fit from the Justification list.

Editing Attribute Definitions Before making the attribute into a block you can edit the attribute's tag, prompt, or value. The **ddedit** command provides an easy way to edit attribute definitions in a user-friendly dialog box. You can access the Edit Attribute Definition Dialog box by:

- Type `ddedit` at the `Command:` prompt.

  AutoCAD then prompts:

`<Select a TEXT or ATTDEF object>/Undo:`

Select the attribute definition that you want to edit. The Edit Attribute Definition dialog box appears (Figure 15.19), where you can edit the attribute's tag, prompt, or value. Use your standard Windows text editing options in these fields.

Skill Builder

After the attribute definition is made into a block, it becomes an attribute and you can no longer edit it with **ddedit.** You can, however, explode the block, so the attribute will revert back to an attribute definition and you can use **ddedit** on it.

Although you can only edit one attribute definition at a time, the command will stay active until you press Enter at the `<Select a TEXT or ATTDEF object>/Undo:` prompt. That way you can continue to edit your attributes without having to re-start the command between edits.

Making a Block of Your Attributes To create a block of attributes, follow the same procedures introduced earlier in this unit. You can also create a block of nothing in it but attributes. This can be useful for adding a Bill of Materials, Change Orders, or other required text information to your drawing.

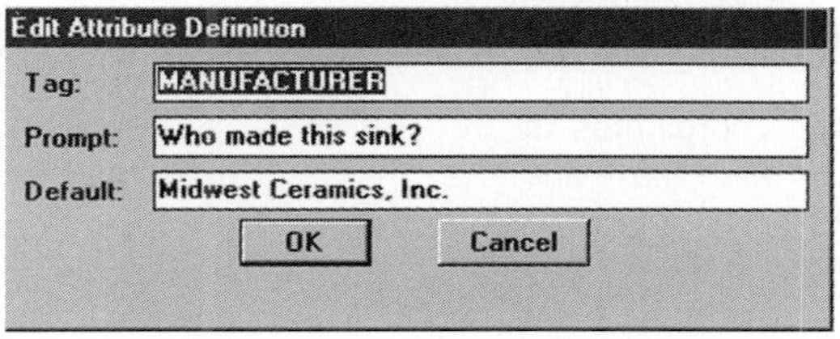

Figure 15.19
The Edit Attribute Definition dialog box lets you edit attribute definitions before they are made part of a block.

For the Professional

When you create a block with attributes, the order of attribute selection is important. The order in which AutoCAD inserts a block is last to first. This means that the last object created in the block will be the first object inserted, including the attributes. If you want your attributes to prompt you in a specific order, select them in that order when making the block. Doing so overrides the standard way in which AutoCAD inserts a block with respect to the attributes. The first attribute you select at the `Select objects:` prompt will be the first attribute you receive a prompt for. Conversely, the last attribute you select will be the last one you are prompted for.

Tutorial 15.5: Defining and Inserting an Attribute

In this tutorial you will define several attributes for the bathroom sink in the apartment complex bathroom. This is the same drawing you were working on earlier in this unit. Before you begin, make sure the ATTDIA system variable is set to 1, and you have the Draw and Attribute toolbars displayed.

1.  Select the Open button from the Standard toolbar and open the apartment complex (15DWG01).
2.  Select the Named Views button from the Standard toolbar, and restore the LEFTBATH view. You are going to make some attributes for the sink, and then make the sink and its attributes into a block.
3.  Select the Define Attribute button from the Attribute toolbar.
   AutoCAD displays the Attribute Definition dialog box.
4. Enter the following values into the Attribute section:

   `Tag:` **`MANUFACTURER`**
   `Prompt:` **`Who made this sink?`**
   `Value:` **`Midwest Ceramics, Inc.`**

5. Select the DOWN ARROW in the `Text Style:` box to access the pop-up list. Change the style to STANDARD.
6. In the `Height<` text box, change the value to **2″**.
7. Click the `Pick Point<` button in the Insertion Point area.
   The dialog box closes and you are returned to the drawing editor.
8. Double click on the Snap button on the status bar at the bottom of the screen to turn on the snap mode. Pick the point **`8′-7″,29′-5″`**.
   The dialog box reappears. You see the coordinates of the point you picked automatically entered in the X and Y edit boxes of the Intersection Point area. Your Attribute Definition dialog box should reflect the setting shown in Figure 15.20.

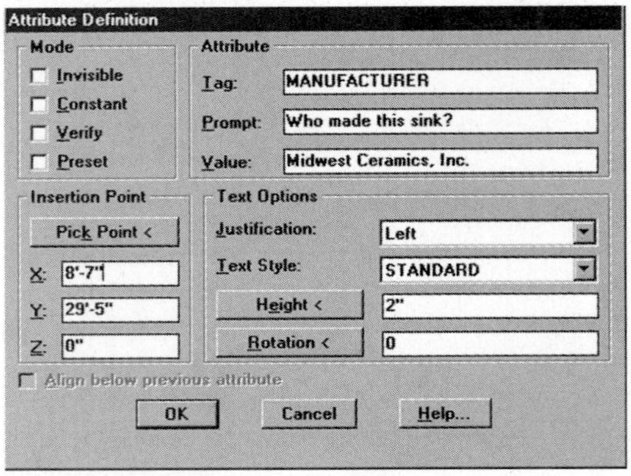

Figure 15.20 *The completed Attribute Definition dialog box.*

9. Select OK.
   You should see the word MANUFACTURER written across the sink's upper left corner (see Figure 15.21).
10. Press Enter to repeat the **ddattdef** command and create another attribute. For the `Tag:` enter **`PRICE`**. For the `Prompt:`, enter `How much does it cost?` For the `Value:` enter **`$175.00.`** Instead of picking or entering an insertion point, select the `Align below previous attribute` check box. Your Attribute Definition dialog box should reflect the settings shown in Figure 15.22. Then select OK.

Now that you have completed two attribute definitions, you will block the sink symbol and the two attributes and insert it into your drawing. Follow these steps:

1.  Select the Block button from the Draw toolbar and name the block SINK. Make the insertion base point the intersection of the two cabinet lines (8′-6″, 27′-2″). Select your two attributes, the lines that form the cabinet, the ellipse that represents the sink, the drain circle, and the donuts.

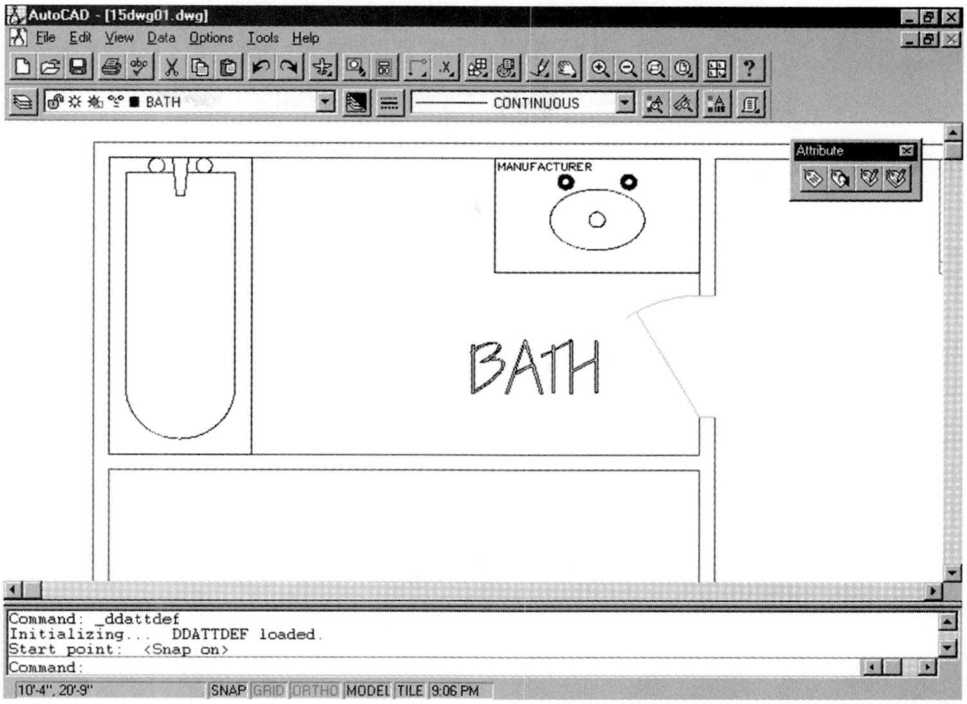

Figure 15.21 *The sink with the attribute definition in place.*

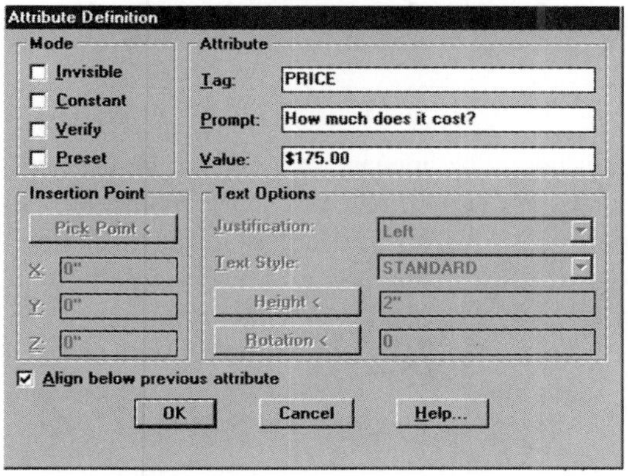

Figure 15.22 *The completed Attribute Definition dialog box with Align below previous attribute check box selected.*

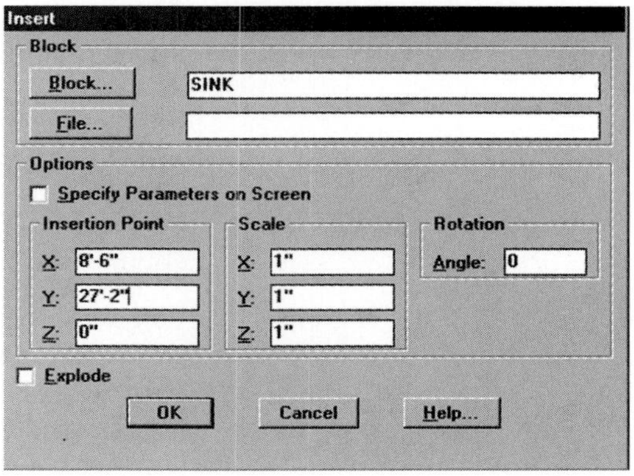

Figure 15.23 *The Insert dialog box, with the proper setting for insertion of the SINK block.*

For the Professional

Select your attributes first when creating the block. This will insure you are prompted for the attribute values in order.

2.  Select the Insert Block button from the Draw toolbar. Select the block SINK, and use an X value of 8′-6″ and a Y value of 27′-2″ for the Insertion Point. Your Insert dialog box should look like Figure 15.23.
3. After you select OK in the Insert dialog box, the Enter Attributes dialog box appears. This dialog box will only appear if you set your ATTDIA system variable to 1. Note that the order for the attributes is consistent with the order in which you selected them when creating the block. Change `How much does it cost?` to **`$185.00`**, then select OK.

Now that you have successfully created a block with attributes, save your drawing for later use. You will be modifying the attributes later in this section.

Editing Attributes in a Block After defining your attributes, placed them in blocks, and inserted the blocks into your drawing, there may be times when you need to edit your attribute values. AutoCAD provides the **attedit** and **ddatte** commands to edit attributes in a block, and **attredef** is used to add or modify attributes in an existing block definition.

SKILL BUILDER

Before an attribute is blocked and inserted into a drawing, you can modify it with the **change** command, as well as **ddedit, modify,** and **ddmodify**. After a block with an attribute is inserted, the attribute can only be modified with the **attedit, ddatte,** and **attredf** commands.

USING **ddatte** TO EDIT ATTRIBUTES IN A BLOCK

The **ddatte** (Dialog Attribute Edit) command allows you to edit attributes of existing blocks in the drawing using the Edit Attributes dialog box. You can access the Edit Attributes dialog box in the following ways:

- Select the Edit Attribute button from the Attribute toolbar.
- Type `ddatte` at the `Command:` prompt.

After selecting the Edit Attribute button or typing `ddatte`, AutoCAD responds with the following prompt:

`Select block:` *`Select any attributed block for attribute editing.`*

At this point the Edit Attributes dialog box appears, as shown in Figure 15.24. Each line in the box contains an attribute prompt and an edit box that contains the attribute's current value. Use any of the standard Windows text editing methods to change the text in the edit boxes. Press the Tab key to cycle among the edit fields and dialog box buttons at the bottom of the dialog box.

After you have completed editing, select the OK button to exit the command, update the attributes, and close the dialog box.

EDITING ATTRIBUTES WITH **attedit**

If you need to edit more than one attribute's value or you want to edit attributes globally, AutoCAD provides the **attedit** command. You can access **attedit** as follows:

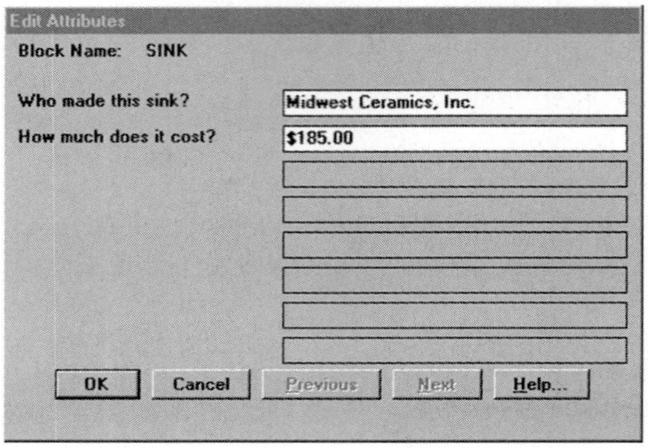

Figure 15.24
The Edit Attributes dialog box allows you to edit the attributes of a single block's variable attributes.

- Select the Edit Attribute Globally button from the Attribute toolbar.
- Type **`attedit`** at the `Command:` prompt.

After accessing **attedit,** AutoCAD responds with the following prompt:

```
Edit attributes one at a time? <Y>
```

You have two possible responses—YES or NO. Your response to this prompt determines what will happen next.

Editing Attributes One at a Time with **attedit**

If you respond Yes to the `Edit attributes one at a time?` prompt, you will edit the attributes one at a time, allowing you to pick each attribute individually. Attributes must be visible to be edited one at a time. You can first narrow the selection set of attributes to edit. Answering Yes causes AutoCAD to display the following three prompts sequentially:

```
Block name specification <*>:
Attribute tag specification <*>:
Attribute value specification <*>:
```

During these prompts you have the option of creating a selection set of names, tags, and values you want to filter. You can use commas and wildcard characters in your specification. Attribute values are case sensitive—the upper and lowercase letters must be specified exactly.

After you've narrowed your search, AutoCAD prompts `Select attribute:`. You can use any of AutoCAD's object selection methods—window, crossing, fence, etc., to select attributes you want to edit.

Skill Builder

The `Select attribute:` prompt works differently from AutoCAD's standard `Select objects:` prompt. When you select an object at the `Select objects:` prompt and press Enter, AutoCAD displays another `Select objects:` prompt, allowing you to add or remove objects from your selection set.

AutoCAD only issues one `Select attribute:` prompt, however. Make sure you select all the attributes you want to edit at that prompt, because as soon as you press Enter, AutoCAD continues with the command.

For the Professional

Using the **attedit** command and filtering the selection set of attributes can be a very powerful option if your drawing has a large number of attributes. For example, your task might involve editing a few attributes out of perhaps hundreds on a large floor plan. Continually zooming in and out and editing the attributes individually could be a long and tedious process. Using the **attedit** command with the proper filters can speed up this process considerably.

First, start the command and select Yes to edit the attributes individually. Set up a block name specification filter which contains the blocks you want to edit, then window the entire drawing at the `Select attribute:` prompt. AutoCAD searches the entire drawing database, and selects only those attributes associated with the particular block you specified. AutoCAD saves you the trouble of zooming around the drawing and individually picking the attributes you want to edit.

After filtering your selection set and selecting the attributes you want to edit, AutoCAD confirms the number of attributes selected and prompts:

```
Value/Position/Height/Angle/Style/Layer/Color/Next <N>:
```

AutoCAD places a small X at the head of the first attribute. The default response is Next. Pressing the Enter key will move the X to the next attribute in the selection set. This procedure is very similar to the **pedit** command's Edit vertex options. Unlike the `Edit vertex` prompt, the **attedit** command does not offer a Previous option. As you continue to press Enter, AutoCAD will cycle you through the attributes. After the last attribute, AutoCAD ends the command.

The X designator gives you one last chance to select the attributes you really want to edit. When the X designator is positioned on an attribute you want to edit, type the first letter or entire word of the editing option you want to use.

EDITING ATTRIBUTES GLOBALLY WITH **attedit**

If you respond `No` to the `Edit attributes one at a time?` prompt, you can globally edit all attribute values. Attributes can be visible or invisible to edit globally. In global editing, you can only edit attribute's values; you cannot change other characteristics such as height or color. Global editing, however, saves you the trouble of having to type the same old and new text strings over and over as you would need to do if you were individually editing attributes. Answering No causes AutoCAD to display the following prompt:

```
Global edit of attribute values.
Edit only attributes visible on screen? <Y>
```

Selecting the default Yes AutoCAD will only find the chosen attributes that are visible on the screen. If you are zoomed in on a particular section of the drawing, only the attributes you can see in the zoomed area will be used. If you select No at this prompt AutoCAD will find all of the chosen attributes in the drawing, including attributes that were defined as invisible. Using No can save you the time of having to do a Zoom All or Zoom Extents.

After choosing between all chosen attributes or visible chosen attributes, AutoCAD displays the search narrowing options that you saw when you edited attributes one at a time:

```
Block name specification <*>:
Attribute tag specification <*>:
Attribute value specification <*>:
```

Once you have narrowed your selection set using the above parameters, AutoCAD prompts: `Select attribute:`. Just when you edited variables individually, you can use any of AutoCAD's object selection methods to pick the attributes you want to edit. After you've chosen them all, press Enter. If you choose any Constant attributes, AutoCAD casts them out of the selection set. AutoCAD then prompts:

```
String to change: Enter the text string you want to change.
New string: Enter the new value.
```

At this point AutoCAD searches for the string you wanted to change, and replaces all occurrences of the string with the new string. No changes are made if the string is not found. The string can be any number of characters, and can be embedded within an attribute text.

If you're editing only visible attributes, AutoCAD dynamically replaces the text; you watch it happen on screen. If you're editing all attributes, AutoCAD replaces the text internally, and then regenerates the drawing when it's done to update the attribute values.

For the Professional

When you edit attributes globally and choose to edit attributes not visible on the screen, you should narrow your selection set. If you accept the <*> defaults, AutoCAD will evaluate every attribute in the drawing to see if it contains the text string you want to change. If you have a lot of attributes in your drawing, this evaluation could take a considerable amount of time. By not limiting your search parameters you also run the risk of inadvertently changing values you don't want changed, as AutoCAD will replace any occurrence in any attribute of the old text string with the new one.

Changing the Default Display Setting The **attdisp** (ATTribute DISPlay) command lets you control the visibility of all inserted attributes in the drawing. You can access the **attdisp** command by:

- Select Attribute Display from the Options, Display pull-down menu.
- Type **`attdisp`** at the `Command:` prompt.

The ATTDISP prompt has the following three options:

```
Normal/ON/OFF <Normal>:
```

- **Normal.** This is the default setting, with normal attributes displayed, and invisible attributes not displayed.
- **ON.** All attributes (normal and invisible) are displayed. This is a good choice if you want to select and edit invisible attributes with the **ddatte** and **attedit** commands.
- **OFF.** No attributes in the drawing are displayed. If the drawing appears cluttered with attributes displayed, or if you need to create a plot without attributes, selecting OFF will make them temporarily invisible.

Tutorial 15.6: Changing the Attribute's Display Setting

In this tutorial you will add an attribute that will be invisible to the SINK block.

1. This tutorial continues from the previous one. You should have 15DWG01 displayed, with the LEFTBATH view restored.
2.  Select the Explode button from the Modify toolbar and explode the SINK block created earlier. The attributes in the block revert to attribute definitions, and the objects are separate again.
3.  Select the Define Attribute button from the Attribute toolbar.
   In the Attribute Definition dialog box, enter the following information:

   ```
   Mode: Check the Invisible box.
   Tag: PART_NO
   Prompt: What is the manufacturer's
   part number?
   Value: MS1228WT
   ```

4. Select the following Text Options:

   ```
   Text Style: STANDARD
   Height: 2"
   Insertion point: X: 8'-7" Y: 27'-3"
   ```

   Compare your screen to Figure 15.25.
5. Click the OK button.
   You should see the word PART_NO written across the sink's lower-left corner.
6.  Select the Block button from the Draw toolbar. Enter the name `sink` and answer the prompt.

   ```
   Block name (or ?): sink
   Block SINK already exists.
   Redefine it? <N> y
   ```

7. Make the insertion base point the intersection of the two cabinet lines `(8'-6", 27'-2")`. Select your three attributes, the lines that form the cabinet, the ellipse that represents the sink, the drain circle, and the donuts.
8.  Select the Insert Block button from the Draw toolbar. Insert the SINK at coordinates `8'-6", 27'-2"` with a scale factor of 1 and a rotation angle of 0. The Enter Attributes dialog box, shown in Figure 15.26, will appear. Select OK to accept the default values and close the dialog box.

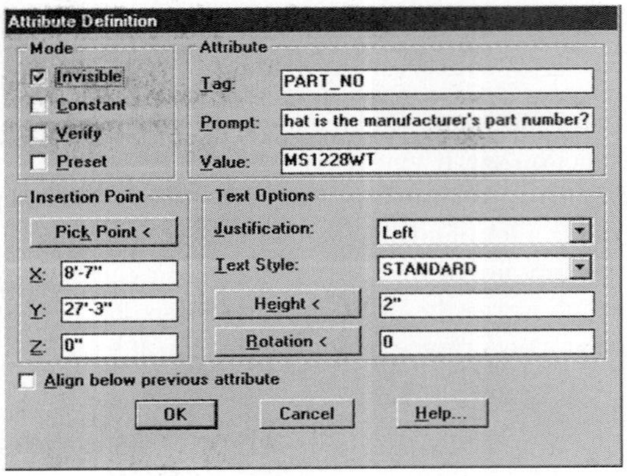

Figure 15.25 *The completed Attribute Definition dialog box.*

9. At the `Command:` prompt enter the following:

```
Command: attdisp
Normal/ON/OFF <Normal>: on
Regenerating drawing.
```

Look at the SINK block and count the number of visible attributes. You should have three attributes (see Figure 15.27).

10. Now turn off all of the attributes.

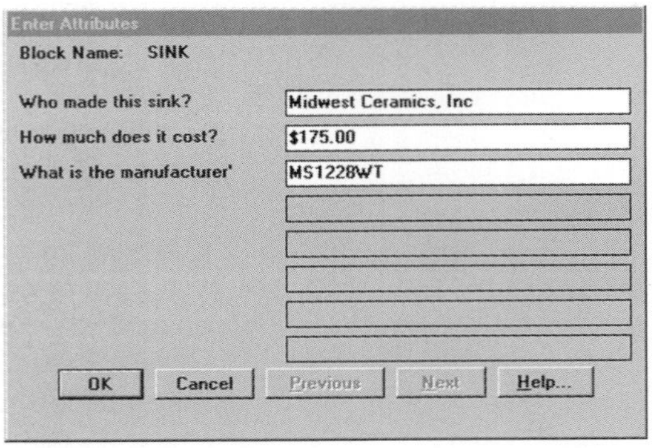

Figure 15.26 *The Enter Attributes dialog box.*

```
Command: attdisp
Normal/ON/OFF <ON>: off
Regenerating drawing.
```

11. Now count the visible attributes in the SINK (see Figure 15.28). You shouldn't see any attributes.

12. Use the **attdisp** command to set the attribute display back to normal.
The SINK block is now displayed normally, with only two visible attributes.

Figure 15.27 *Both the visible and invisible attributes appear in the SINK block with* ***attdisp*** *set to ON.*

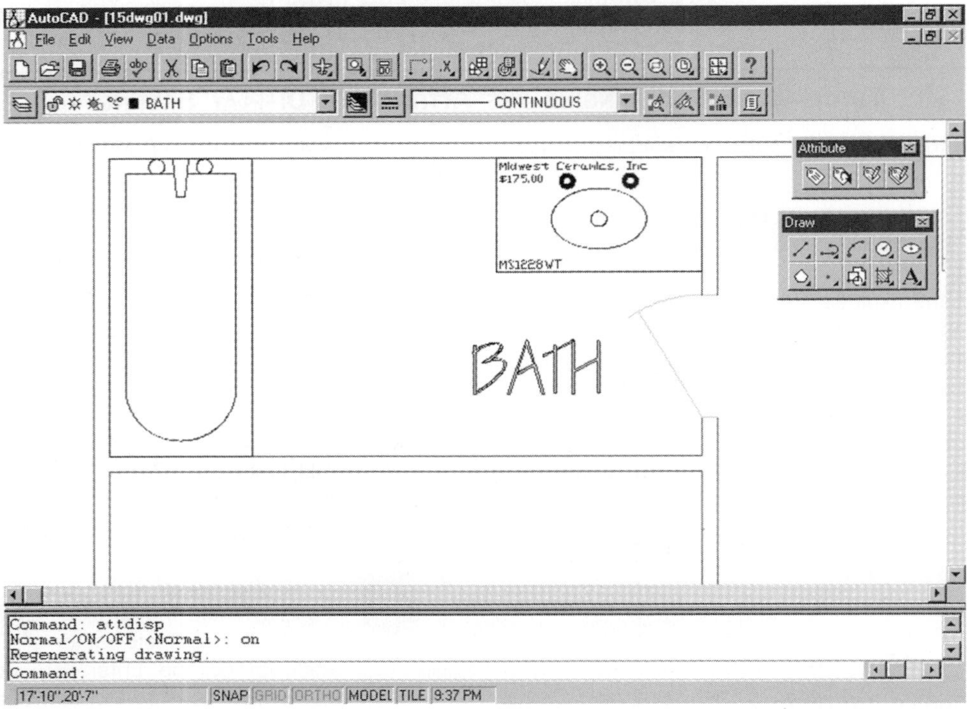

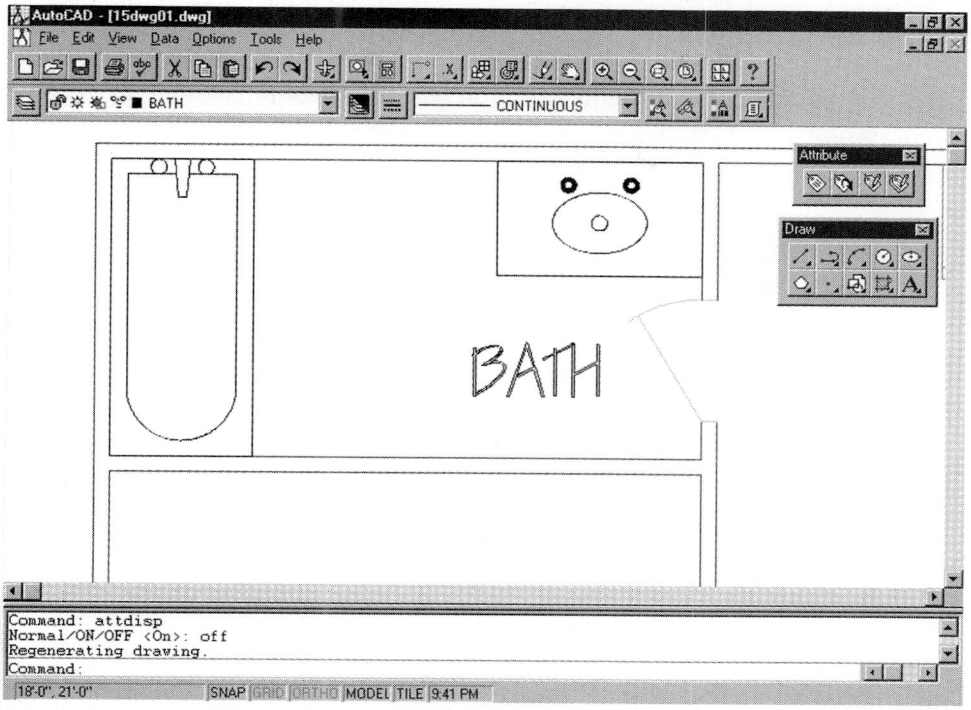

Figure 15.28 *Neither visible nor invisible attributes are displayed when* **attdisp** *is set to OFF.*

Using the attredef Command to Edit Attributes **attredef** is used to redefine a block and update all of its associated attributes. You can edit, remove, rename, or add an attribute to an inserted block. With **attredef,** however, you can update every insertion of that block with the new changes. To use this command, use the following procedure:

1. Copy or reinsert the block you want to update.
2. Explode the block with the attributes you want to define.
3. Create, edit, or delete attributes as needed. After exploding the block there are three different methods you can use: **ddedit, ddmodify,** or **attdef. ddedit** is the dialog box used to edit existing text. It will recognize text as attributes, but only allows you to change the attribute tags.

   You can also use the **ddmodify** command. **ddmodify** not only recognizes the text as attributes, but you can also modify the Tag, Prompt, default Value, and attribute modes. Figure 15.29 shows the Modify Attribute Definition dialog box accessed by the **ddmodify** command used on the Manufacturer tag.

   The **ddedit** and **ddmodify** commands will edit existing attributes. To create a new attribute from scratch, use the **attdef** command.

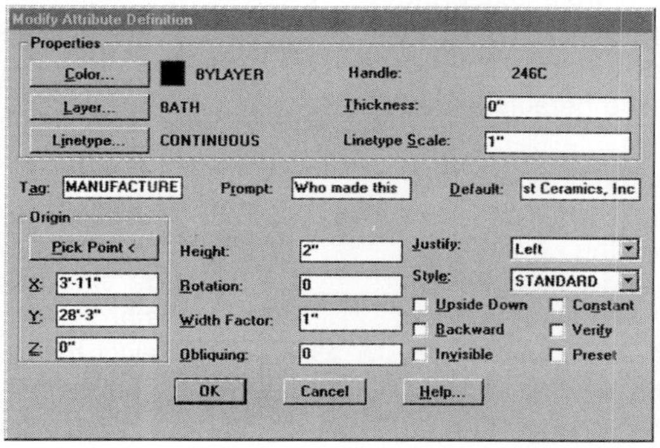

Figure 15.29
The Modify Attribute Definition dialog box can be used to edit an existing attribute.

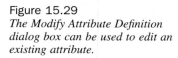

4. Invoke the **attredef** command.
You can access the **attredef** command by any of the following methods:

- Select the Redefine Attribute from the Attribute toolbar.
- Type `attredef` at the `Command:` prompt.

After accessing the **attredef** command, AutoCAD responds with the following prompt:

`Name of Block you wish to redefine:` *Enter the name of the block.*
`Select objects for new Block...`
`Select objects:` *Pick your attributes in order.*
`Select objects:` *Pick your objects.*
`Select objects:`
`Insertion base point of new Block:` *Select point.*

After completing the command, the new block definition is updated, and all instances of the block automatically and globally changed to reflect the new settings. If you need to make any corrections to the individual attributes you can use the **ddatte** command.

TUTORIAL 15.7: REDEFINING ATTRIBUTES WITH attredef

For this tutorial you will edit the SINK block, and update it throughout the drawing with the **attredef** command. Make sure you have completed the previous tutorials in this section, and have 15DWG01 displayed on your screen with the LEFTBATH view restored. Follow these steps:

1. Select the Named Views button from the Standard toolbar and restore the RIGHTBATH view.
2. You will insert two `SINK` blocks into your drawing. One will go in the bathroom on the right, and the other one you will edit.
3. Select the Insert Block button from the Draw toolbar. Select the `SINK` block, insertion point `59'-2", 27'-2"`. In the Enter Attributes dialog box, accept the default values and click OK.
4. Select the Named Views button from the Standard toolbar and restore the LEFTBATH view.
5. Select the Insert Block button from the Draw toolbar. Again select the `SINK` block, using an insertion point of `3'-10", 26'-0"`. In the Enter Attributes dialog box, accept the default values and click OK.
6. Select the Explode button from the Modify toolbar, select the block you just inserted, and press Enter until you see the `Command:` prompt. The block explodes and looks like Figure 15.30.
7. Select the Properties button from the Object Properties toolbar, select the text `MANUFACTURER`, and press Enter. The Modify Attribute Definition dialog box appears. Select the Invisible check box.
Select OK.
8. Press Enter to reaccess the last command and select the text `PRICE`. In the modify Attribute Definition Dialog Box select the Invisible check box. Select OK.
9. Select the Redefine Attribute from the Attribute toolbar.

`Name of Block you wish to redefine:` **`sink`**
`Select objects for new Block...`
`Select objects:` **`pick your attributes, in order`**
`Select objects:` **`select the objects comprising the sink symbol`**
`Select objects:`
`Insertion base point of new Block:` **`pick the lower left corner of the sink symbol (3'-10',26'-0").`**

At this point the drawing regenerates, and the inserted block you just redefined disappears from the screen. Notice the sink attributes are not visible.

10. Select the Named Views button from the Standard toolbar and restore the RIGHTBATH view. The sink attributes are not visible in the right bathroom.
11. Select the Save button on the Standard toolbar to save your drawing.

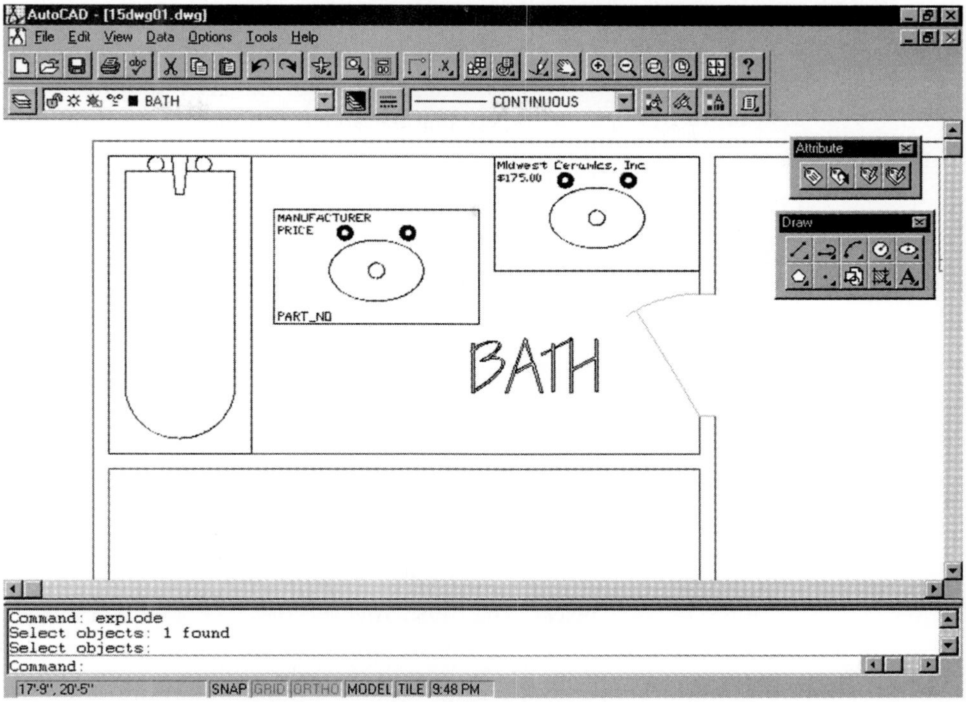

Figure 15.30
The inserted SINK block, exploded and ready for editing.

Extracting Attribute Information In the first part of this section you used attributes to assign text strings that can be used to label or describe blocks within your drawing. The associated attributes can give you the related description of each block, such as the manufacturer, cost, model number, part number, etc.

Another important function of attributes is the ability to extract the attribute information from a drawing into a format suitable for import into a database or spreadsheet program. You can use this extracted attribute information to perform tasks such as assembling bills of materials, parts lists, cost estimates, and inventories. The following steps are used to extract attribute information from your drawing:

1. **Save your drawing.** Before saving, make sure you have inserted all of your blocks and related attributes into your drawing.
2. **Create a Template file.** Using a word processor or a text editor, create a template file. The template file tells AutoCAD which attributes' data will be included in the extract file.
3. **Extract the information.** In AutoCAD, use the **attext** or **ddattext** commands to specify the file to extract the information to.
4. **Use the information.** Examine the extract file in your text editor, or import the extracted file into a database or spreadsheet program.

Creating a Template File

The template file tells AutoCAD what format the extracted data will assume and which attribute's data will be included in the extract file. The template file must be an ASCII file, and it must have a file extension of TXT. You can create the template file in a text editor (such as Windows Notepad) or word processor (Microsoft Word or WordPerfect, in non-document mode). Your template file should look similar to the following example:

```
BL:NAME        C009000
BL:X           N060004
BL:Y           N060004
```

MANUFACTURER	C012000
COST	N005002
PART_NO	C007000

Examining the above example, the first column contains the field name. The first three lines (with the BL: prefix) are called the Block Characteristics and Predefined Field Names. They contain information about the blocks from which you extracted the data from. The BL: defines the fields as special, and in this example NAME is the block name, X is the block's X insertion point, and Y is the Y insertion point. The remaining three lines in the first column contain the attribute tags, MANUFACTURER, COST and PART_NO.

Leave a single space between the first and second columns. The second column contains a code that tells AutoCAD the attribute data's type. This specifies whether the information is numeric or character, the database or spreadsheet field's width, and the number of decimal places (applicable to numeric data only). In the second column, the first letter must be N or C. The C indicates the information contains characters. An N indicates the information is numeric. The second three fields specify the field width of C or N. The last three fields specify the decimal places of N.

The MANUFACTURER row specifies C012000. This means the data extracted from the MANUFACTURER attribute tag contains characters, and has a field width of 12 places. The COST row specifies N005002. For this attribute field, the tag contains numbers, with a field width of 5, carried to two decimal places. These are only a sample of some of the more commonly used fields. For a complete listing refer to the AutoCAD manuals.

SKILL BUILDER

When you are creating your template file, you must keep several important points in mind. First, make sure there are no decimal place entries for character fields. Also, make sure your attributes do not contain characters for fields you specify as numeric in your template file. Second, do not use the Tab key, add extra spaces (single spaces between columns only), or insert an additional line or carriage return at the end of the template. If you are having trouble with your attribute extraction, the problem is usually in your template file.

EXTRACTING INFORMATION

After you have created the template file, the next step is to extract the data. You can use the **attext** command (for command line format), or use the Attribute Extraction dialog box. You can access the Attribute Extraction dialog box by:

- Type `ddattext` at the `Command:` prompt.

The **attext** command accomplishes the same thing as the Attribute Extraction dialog box, shown in Figure 15.31.

Let's look in detail at the options offered by the Attribute Extraction dialog box.

- **File Format.** Specifies the structure of the extract file. CDF and SDF are common formats used by data and spreadsheet programs. You need to determine ahead of time what format your program uses so you can extract the data in the proper format.
  - **Comma Delimited Format.** In the CDF format, the extract's fields are separated by a character you specify. The default character for CDF is a comma (,).
  - **Space Delimited Format.** The SDF format uses spaces to separate the fields. The fields are fixed lengths that are padded with spaces so the columns align evenly,

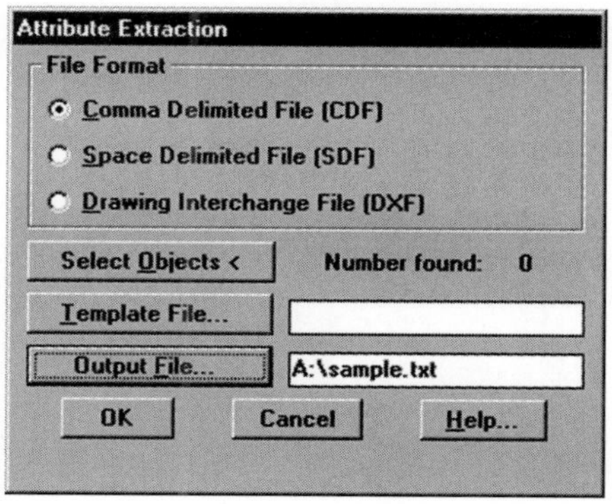

Figure 15.31
The Attribute Extraction dialog box.

with numerical fields being right-justified. SDF files are normally the easiest to read format.

- **Drawing Interchange File.** This exports the data in a variation of the standard AutoCAD DXF format. This format contains more information than the CDF or SDF formats, but is generally harder to read. Since DXF is a standard format, it does not require a template file. You would probably only use the DXF format if you wanted to import attributes into another CAD program.
- **Select Objects<.** You can use the Select Objects option if you want to choose specific blocks to extract data from.
- **Template File.** Accesses the Template File dialog box, where you can select your previously created template file.
- **Output File.** Accesses the Output File dialog box, where you select the name of the extract file to create. The default extraction file name is the same as the drawing name with the TXT extension.

After you've entered this information, click OK, and AutoCAD will extract the data for you.

Tutorial 15.8: Extracting Attribute Data

The first step in extracting attributes is to create a template file. You will use Notepad included with Windows. After creating your template file you will use the Attribute Extraction dialog box to extract the attributes from your SINK block to a SDF format.

1. Start Notepad and type the following information exactly as it appears here. Do not use the Tab key or add any line returns before or after the text. Be sure to place a space between the attribute tag and the character or numeric data, and press Enter at the end of each line, including the last line.

BL:NAME	C008000
BL:X	N008004
BL:Y	N008004
MANUFACTURER	C035000
PRICE	C010000
PART_NO	C015000

   Your notepad should look like Figure 15.32 when completed.
2. Save the file as SINK.TXT.
3. If you aren't in AutoCAD, start AutoCAD and open the drawing 15DWG01 that you were working on earlier in this section. Restore the PLAN view.
4. At the `Command:` prompt enter **`ddattext.`** The Attribute Extraction dialog box appears (see Figure 15.33).
5. Select the Space Delimited File radio button.
6. Pick the Template File button and select the template file you created in step 2, SINK.TXT.
7. Accept the default name, 15DWG01.TXT in the Output File dialog box. Your completed Attribute Extraction dialog box should look like Figure 15.33.
8. Select OK in the Attribute Extraction dialog box. AutoCAD creates the text file containing the data specified in the Template file.
9. Open Notepad and open the text file you just created (15DWG01.TXT). It should look like Figure 15.34, with the information arranged into even columns. The space delimited files are good for a quick, unformatted text printout. Comma delimited files are particularly useful for importing into spreadsheets and databases.
10. Close Notepad and AutoCAD. This ends your tutorials on Attributes.

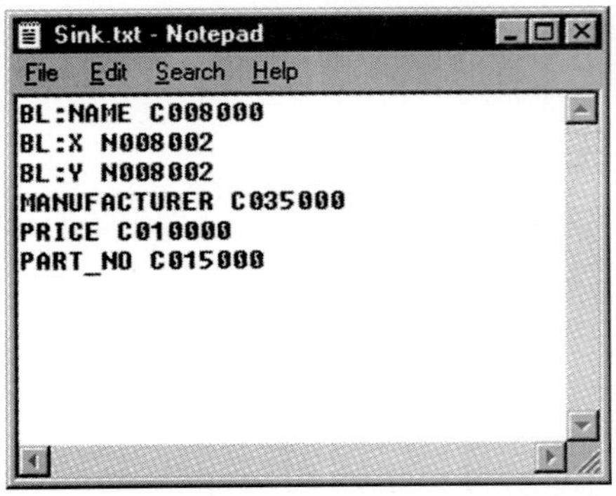

Figure 15.32 *Using Notepad to create the template file.*

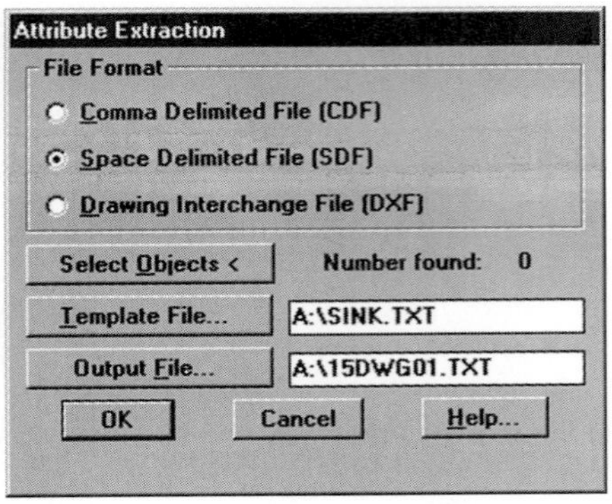

Figure 15.33 *The Attribute Extraction dialog box with the correct information.*

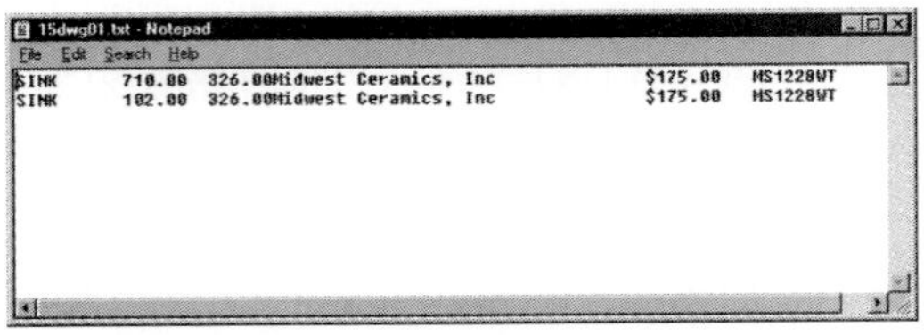

Figure 15.34 *The attribute information extracted into a space delimited format.*

The AutoCAD SQL Extension With attributes you added data in the form of text to your symbols and created a block. You could extract this data in a variety of different formats, suitable for use in spreadsheets and databases. AutoCAD also offers a far more sophisticated method of extracting and manipulating information from your entire drawing. The AutoCAD SQL (Structured Query Language) was introduced in AutoCAD Release 12, and is commonly referred to as ASE. With ASE you can extract and manipulate data from your entire drawing, not just attributes.

A drawing is actually a complex database. A database is a collection of related data, typically organized to serve a specific purpose—in our case, to create a drawing. A demand exists to be able to use data within a drawing for external or non-graphical purposes, such as creating a report or to estimate manufacturing cost. It is also desirable to link data within a drawing to data that resides outside the drawing.

All drawing objects can be linked to an external database with ASE. These linked objects, or attributes, will automatically update the database if the drawing is changed. An interesting point of ASE is the link works both ways, so any changes in the database are imported back to the drawing. For example changing the X value for the length of a line in the database changes the length of the line within AutoCAD. Any information linked to the external database can be manipulated externally to change the drawing itself. For more information on ASE, consult the AutoCAD reference manuals.

SUMMARY

The ability to use information from other drawings is a great benefit of using AutoCAD. Many drawings contain geometric elements called symbols. After creating a symbol, you can use the **block** command to store it for later use. Once defined, these blocks can be inserted into a drawing full-size, scaled, or rotated. One advantage of using the **block** command is the small amount of space required in your drawing to save the blocks. Used properly, the **block** command can actually decrease the size of your drawing file. The **block** command is available at the command line, or through the **block** button on the Draw toolbar.

With the **block** command your symbols are only available for use in the current drawing. If you want to use the symbols in more than one drawing, AutoCAD offers the **wblock** command. With **wblock** you actually create a distinct drawing file for each symbol. Using **wblock** to store your symbols requires more disk space, however, since each symbol you **wblock** creates an additional file.

Once defined, these symbols can be inserted into your drawing. AutoCAD offers the **insert** command, which works at the command line. Using **ddinsert** accesses the Insert dialog box which you can use to insert a **block** or **wblock.** You can access the Insert dialog box by selecting the Block Insert button on the Draw toolbar.

Attributes allow you to attach text information to your blocks. This information can later be extracted for analysis in database or spreadsheet programs. The most common attribute commands are available on the Attribute toolbar. From the toolbar you can define an attribute as well as modify it. Selecting the Define Attribute button accesses the Attribute Definition dialog box. For editing you can select the Redefine Attribute button, Edit Attribute, or Edit Attribute Globally buttons.

After completing this unit you are well on your way to harnessing the power of Computer Aided Drafting. The ability to easily use geometry in more than one place, and in more than one drawing, are just some of the reasons for the popularity of CAD.

REVIEW

1. Describe the **group** command and how you could use it to increase drawing speed and efficiency.
2. List four advantages for using Blocks to represent symbols in a drawing.
3. Explain the variance between creating a block on layer 0 and creating it on a previously defined layer.
4. Explain the difference between the **block** and **wblock** commands.
5. List and explain three points to consider when creating a **block** or **wblock.**
6. List the four things you must specify when inserting a block into a drawing.
7. Explain what the base point of a block is and how you can change it.
8. List the steps of procedure you would take if you needed to change a block.
9. Define attribute and how it relates to blocks.
10. List and explain the methods you could use to change the attribute definitions of a block that was already inserted into a drawing.

EXERCISE 15

Load the Computer Lab drawing EX15-1 shown in Figure 15.35.

1. Create a block of the Table symbol. Define the following attributes:

TAG	VALUE	PROMPT
User (visible)	(Variable Name)	User Name
Descrip (inv, constant)	Table	
Model (inv, constant)	Drafting	
Cost (inv, constant)	$350.00	

2. Create a block of the Computer symbol. Define the following attributes:

TAG	VALUE
Descrip (inv, constant)	Computer
Model (inv, constant)	Pentium Pro
Cost (inv, constant)	$2000.00

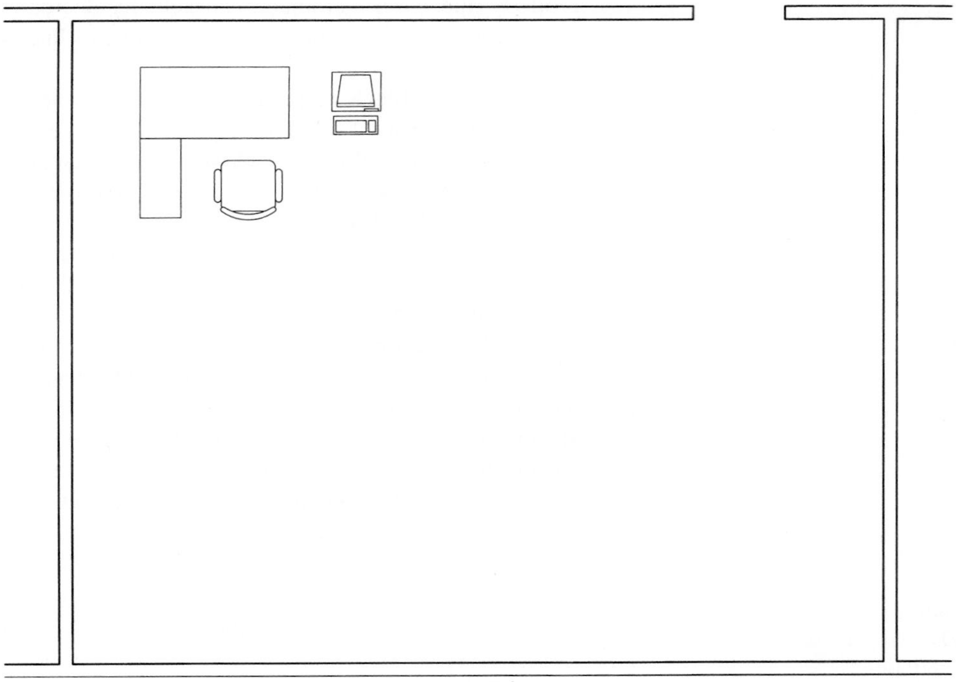

Figure 15.35
Define attributes for the Table, Computer, and Chair symbols.

3. Create a block of the Chair symbol. Define the following attributes:

TAG	VALUE
Descrip (inv, constant)	Chair
Cost (inv, constant)	$175.00

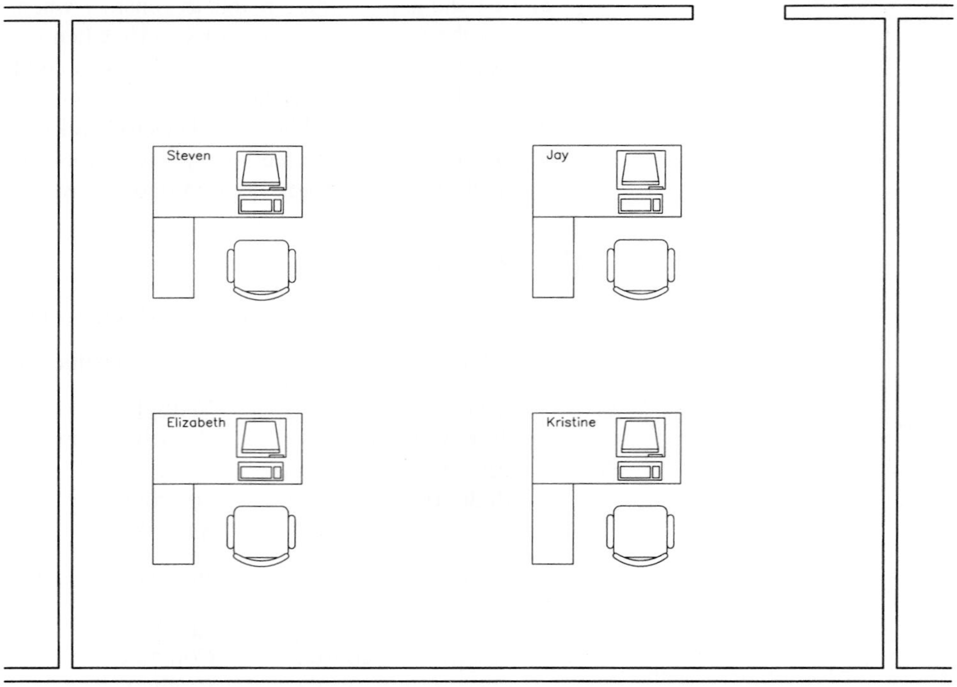

Figure 15.36
The inserted symbols with **attdisp** *set to* **normal.**

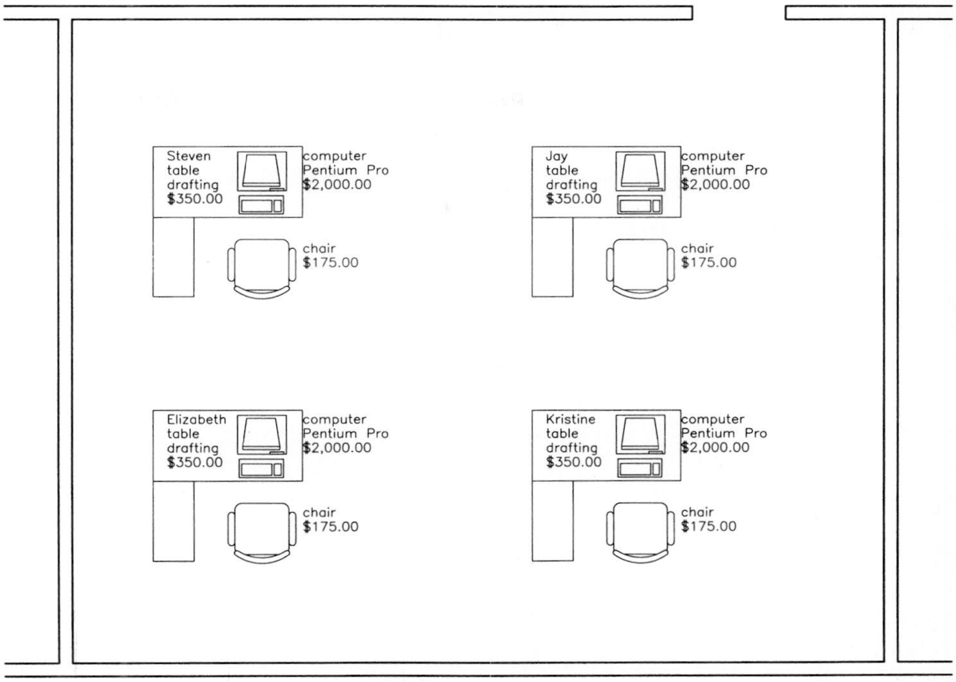

Figure 15.37
The inserted symbols with **attdisp** *set to* **on.**

4. Insert 4 tables, computers, and chairs into the room. Figure 15.36 shows the completed room with **attdisp** set to **normal.** Figure 15.37 has **attdisp** set to **on**.

UNIT 16

CREATING ISOMETRIC DRAWINGS

OVERVIEW

Creating pictorial drawings can significantly enhance the understanding of a technical drawing or presentation. A common type of pictorial drawing is the isometric drawing. Creating isometric drawings using manual drafting tools can be a time-consuming and laborious process. AutoCAD includes many tools that will allow you to create accurate isometric drawings with ease.

OBJECTIVES

- Understand isometric drawings.
- Understand isoplanes.
- Identify the isometric grid.
- Utilize the isometric snap.
- Create isometric geometric shapes and drawings.

INTRODUCTION

Before the advent of computers, isometric drawings were used by draftsmen to allow the layman to be able to visualize what was being represented by a technical orthographic drawing. In order to read a technical drawing, many hours of training was required. With the inclusion of an isometric drawing, anyone can visualize how the object will look when manufactured and, subsequently, this can enhance the understanding of the technical drawings. Figure 16.1 shows a technical drawing of a simple part with an isometric drawing included. Notice that by first viewing the isometric, the technical drawing becomes significantly easier to read.

Today, the computer is used to create sophisticated 3-D computer models. These computer models can be used not only to assist in visualization, but also to analyze the part before it is constructed. Using solid models allows the designer to determine the weight of the object, the center of gravity, how the object will react to stress, and other engineering analyses. While the creation of 3-D models is not covered in this book, it would be advantageous for you to learn how to create and manipulate 3-D models once you have mastered basic 2-D skills. Until you have mastered 3-D concepts, and you may find that you don't need to, use isometric drawings to increase the understanding of your designs.

In order to create isometric drawings, it is important that you first understand how they are created manually and what makes them unique.

OUTLINE

Understanding Isometric and Pictorial Drawings
Setting up an Isometric Drawing
Tutorial 16.1: Setting Up to Create an Isometric Drawing
Creating an Isometric Drawing
Tutorial 16.2: Creating an Isometric Drawing
Summary
Review
Exercises

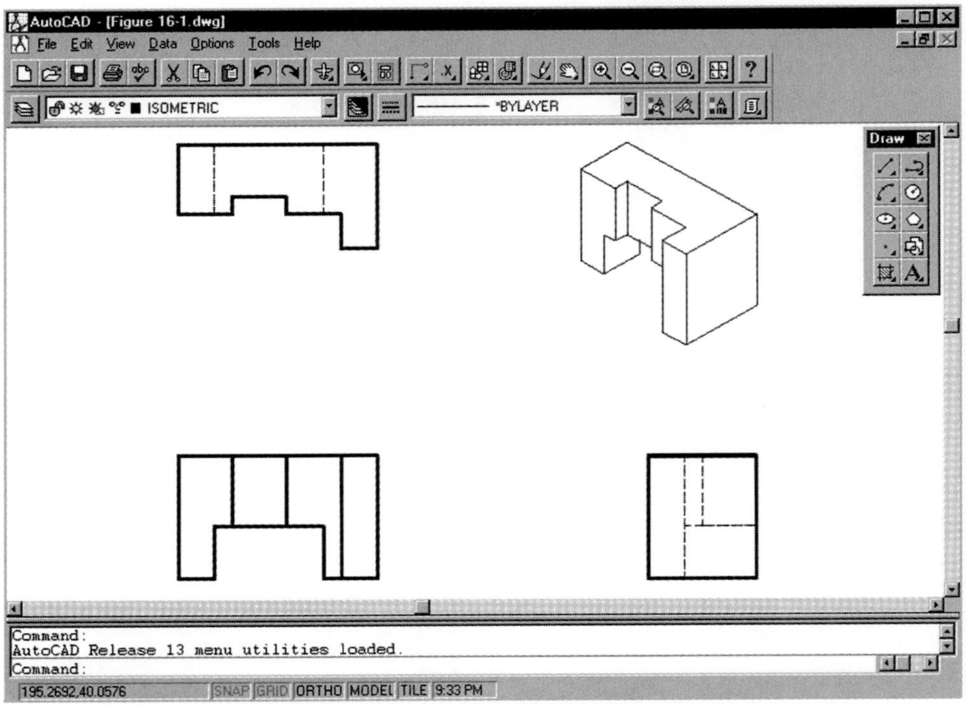

Figure 16.1
Including an isometric drawing makes this technical drawing easier to understand.

UNDERSTANDING ISOMETRIC AND PICTORIAL DRAWINGS

Isometric drawings are a type of pictorial drawing used by drafting professionals to enhance the visualization of an object. There are various types of pictorial drawings and they are grouped in three categories: axonometric, oblique, and perspective. An example of each type of pictorial drawing is shown in Figure 16. 2.

Axonometric drawings are used to allow the viewer to picture the entire object in one view. These drawings are usually used for more technical drawings, such as mechanical drawings and product designs. Oblique drawings are used to emphasize a face that is perpendicular to a line of sight, as well as the depth of an object. It is the least frequently used because it provides the least amount of realism. Typical uses include construction and cabinet drawings. The last and most accurate representation is the perspective drawing. This is the most realistic because, like real life, all lines appear to converge to a set vanishing point. Perspectives are commonly used in architecture and interior design. Figure 16.3 shows a tree listing all of the different types of pictorial drawings and their classifications.

Isometrics are the easiest pictorial drawings to create; they are a type of axonometric drawing. There are two other types of axonometric drawings: the dimetric and trimetric. The prefix *iso* means "equal." *Equal* refers to the scale that is used to create the objects. The same scale is used on all three axes of the drawing. This scale determines the amount of foreshortening that occurs on a given line or plane. Foreshortening causes a

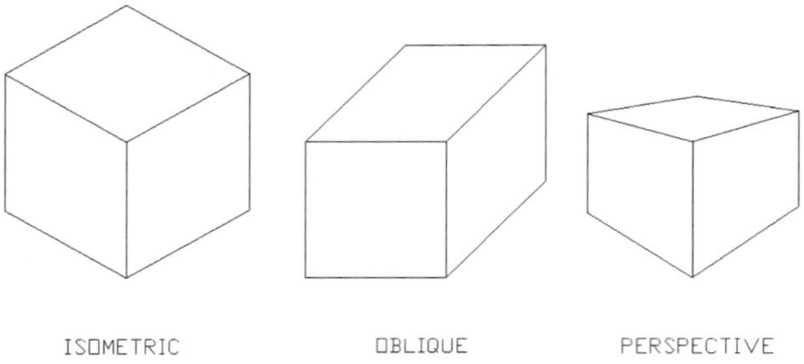

Figure 16.2
The three types of pictorial drawings: axonometric, oblique, and perspective.

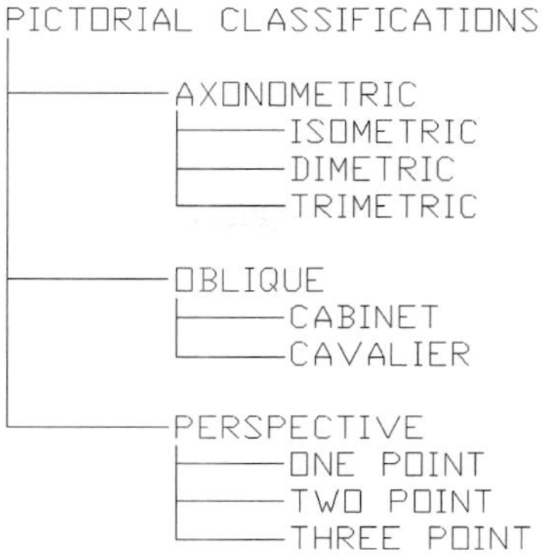

Figure 16.3
The pictorial drawing tree.

line or plane to appear shorter as it travels away from your line of sight at a given angle. As we continue to introduce the creation of isometric drawings, you will see how this scale is used. Dimetric and trimetric drawings have different scales. Dimetric utilizes two different scales—one for the horizontal axis and one for the vertical axis. Trimetric drawings utilize three different scales—a different scale for each axis. These scales are not chosen at random but are produced using graphical methods based on the placement and view of the object. Figure 16.4 displays a box and how it appears using the three types of axonometric drawings.

All of these pictorial drawings are 2-D representations of a 3-D object(s). In other words, to create these drawings, you would use the familiar 2-D AutoCAD commands you have learned. Because isometric drawings are the easiest and fastest to create, they are used most often. While all of these different types of pictorial drawings can be created using AutoCAD, there are specific tools in AutoCAD that assist in the creation of isometric drawings. Each will be introduced in this unit.

The basic tool for creating an isometric drawing is the isometric axis, as shown in Figure 16.5. Each axis is labeled. The x-axis is the width axis, the y-axis is the height axis, and the z-axis is the depth axis. All vertical lines will be parallel to the y-axis, while all horizontal lines will be parallel to either the x- or z-axis. Before creating an isometric drawing you should start with this axis. This axis is created in manual drafting using the 30-degree angle on a 30/60-degree triangle. While the y-axis was drawn using the right corner of the triangle, the x- and z-axis was drawn offset by 30 degrees from horizontal. By offsetting the x- and z-axis, the isometric drawing allows the viewer to see all three dimensions associated with the object.

A discussion of isometric drawings would not be complete without an introduction as to how circles and arcs are represented on isometric drawings. Very rarely will a circle or arc be created on an isometric drawing. To represent a circle, the isometric ellipse is used. To create an arc, a portion of the isometric ellipse is used. Figure 16.6 shows how these circles and arcs are used on an isometric drawing.

In manual drafting, isometric ellipse templates are used to create these shapes. These templates are often confusing to use and to align with the drawing. AutoCAD provides tools that make it easier to create isometric ellipses.

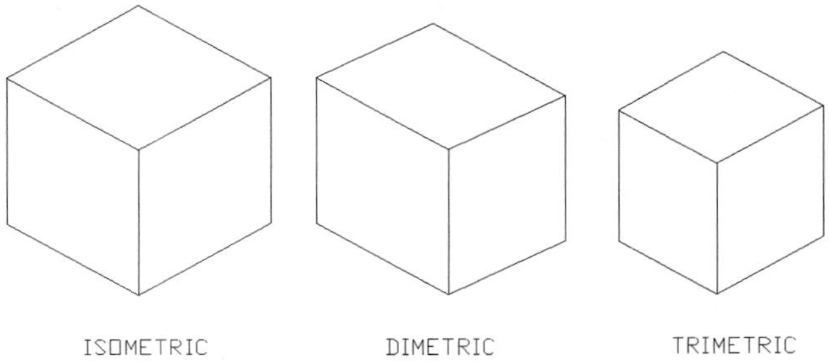

Figure 16.4
The three types of axonometric drawings—isometric, dimetric, and trimetric.

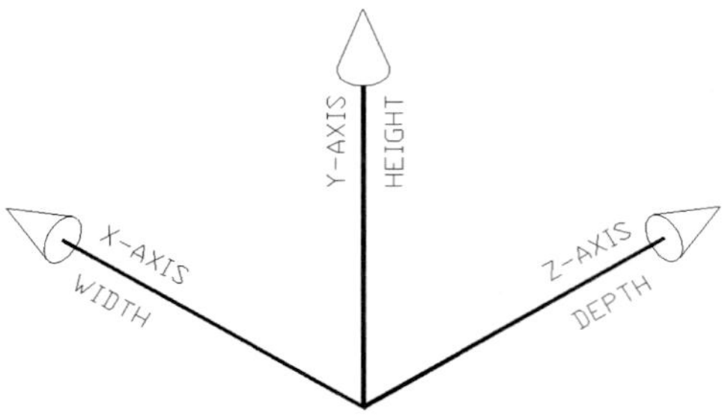

Figure 16.5 *The isometric axis.*

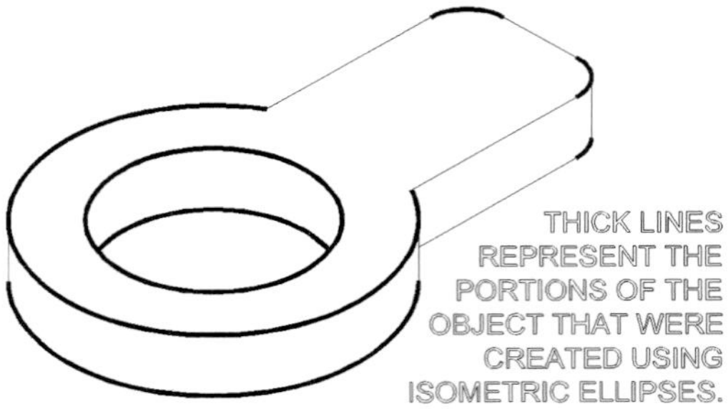

Figure 16.6 *Use isometric ellipses to represent circles and arcs.*

SETTING UP AN ISOMETRIC DRAWING

In order to begin creating an isometric drawing, you need to first modify some settings that will allow the drawing to be created without creating complex construction lines. AutoCAD provides three tools for assisting in the creation of isometric drawings: the isometric grid, the isometric snap, and the isometric plane toggle. Let's take a look at the isometric snap and grid first.

Setting Isometric Snap and Grid

At this point, you are pros at using Grid and Snap to assist in the creation of drawings. What you may not be aware of is that there is another type of Snap and Grid that assists in the creation of isometric drawings. To make changes to the default Grid and Snap, use the Drawing Aids dialog box as shown in Figure 16.7.

To display the dialog box, use one of the following methods:

- Select Options/Drawing Aids from the pull-down menus.
- Type **`ddrmodes`** at the `Command:` prompt.

Notice in the dialog box that there is a tile labeled Isometric Snap/Grid. Within that tile is the On check box. You must select this check box in order to view and use the Isometric Snap and Grid. Once that is done and you select OK, the grid will change to the one shown in Figure 16.8.

Once activated, the isometric snap and grid are used in much the same manner as the regular snap and grid. The difference is that the horizontal grid and snap spacing is now rotated 30° from horizontal. If you redisplay the Drawing Aids dialog box, you will notice that you cannot make any modifications to the X spacing. The horizontal grid and snap settings will now be calculated using the Y settings. You may have also noticed that the crosshairs have changed. The crosshairs now represent the present isometric plane orientation.

Figure 16.7 *Use the Drawing Aids dialog box to begin creating isometric drawings.*

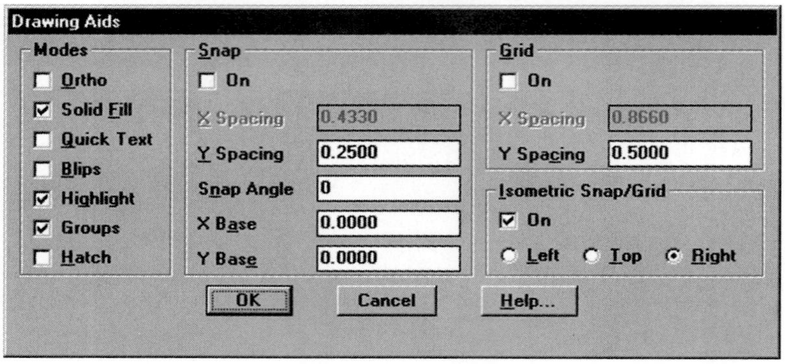

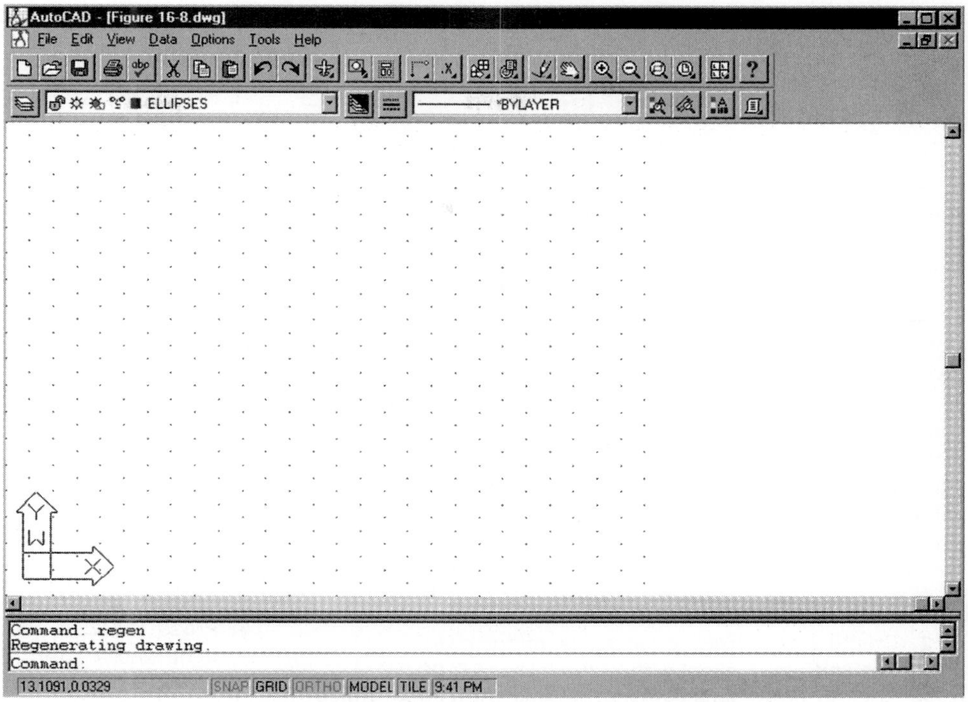

Figure 16.8
Turning on the isometric snap and grid.

Setting and Using the Isometric Plane

Once the isometric snap and grid is activated, the crosshairs will reflect the present isometric plane (isoplane) orientation. All objects will be created on one of three isoplanes. It is important that you have the proper isoplane selected before you create objects. If the proper plane is not selected, you will not be able to create correct lines or orient ellipses properly. There are three isoplanes: left, top, and right. The isoplanes are shown in Figure 16.9.

To change the isoplane you can use one of the following options:

- Select the desired plane in the Drawing Aids dialog box.
- Use the Ctrl E keystroke combination.

If you use the keystroke combination, you will find that the crosshairs will cycle through the available isometric planes. As you cycle through the isoplanes, they will be identified in the `Command:` prompt as shown in Figure 16.10. The crosshairs orientation will also be an indication of the current isoplane. Once you become familiar with this concept, you will be able to quickly identify the isoplane setting from the crosshairs only.

Skill Builder

Train yourself to use the keystroke combination for isoplane toggle. It is much quicker than displaying the dialog box and then selecting the appropriate isoplane.

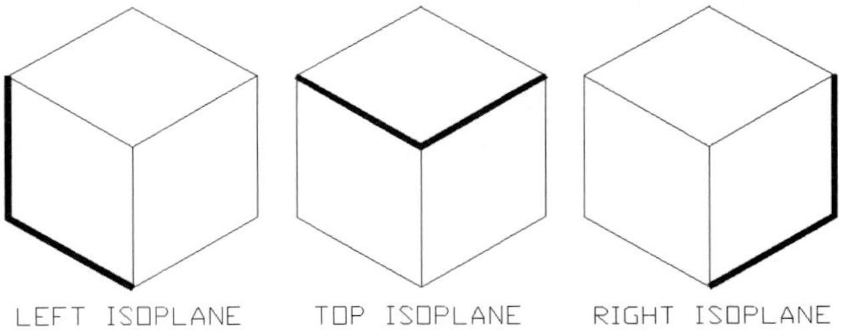

Figure 16.9
The three isometric planes.

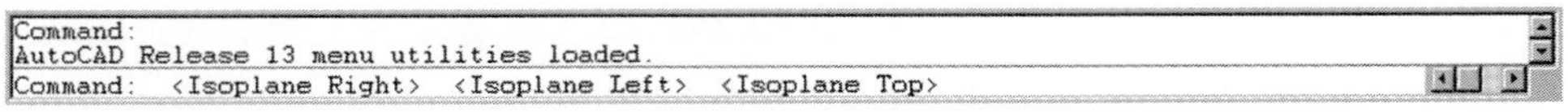
Command:
AutoCAD Release 13 menu utilities loaded.
Command: <Isoplane Right> <Isoplane Left> <Isoplane Top>

Figure 16.10
Identifying the current isoplane in the `Command:` *prompt window.*

In the next section, you will learn how to cycle through the isoplanes.

Tutorial 16.1: Setting Up to Create an Isometric Drawing

In this tutorial you will make the appropriate settings to complete the isometric drawing tutorial located at the end of this unit. You will find as you progress through this tutorial that there will be less information on how to accomplish certain commands than in previous tutorials. You should be able to complete all tasks without the aid of step-by-step instructions. If there is a command or procedure that you do not remember or understand, return to the unit where that command was presented and try to locate the answer to your question.

The procedures outlined in this tutorial can be used to begin any standard isometric drawing.

1. Create a new drawing named *Isometric.dwg.*
2. Set **units** to decimal with a precision of 0.00.
3. Set the upper limits of the drawing to 10.5,8. These limits will be used to create an A-size drawing that can be plotted on a laser or ink jet printer.
4. Select Zoom All from the Standard toolbar. The entire limits will be displayed in the AutoCAD drawing area.
5. Create a layer named OBJECT and make it the current layer. This layer is used to group the drawing objects on a single layer.
6. Display the Drawing Aids dialog box.
7. Turn Snap on.
8. Set the snap Y Spacing to .25.
9. Turn the Grid on.
10. Set the grid Y Spacing to .5.
11. Turn on the Isometric Snap/Grid. Notice that the snap X Spacing is ghosted out. Because there is no absolute X spacing on an isometric grid, you cannot set this value.
12. Select the Top Isoplane.
13. Select OK to accept the values and close the dialog box.
14. Press Ctrl E. The isoplane will change from top to right and `<Isoplane Right>` will appear in the `Command:` prompt.
15. Repeat step 12. The isoplane will change from right to left and `<Isoplane Left>` will appear in the `Command:` prompt.
16. Use **qsave** to save the drawing for use in the next tutorial.

For the Professional

A good AutoCAD operator will be able to find answers for themselves and not have to rely on others. Researching answers to questions oftentimes leads to the discovery of new commands or techniques that may have been forgotten or never introduced. The AutoCAD documentation is a good place to look for answers.

Skill Builder

Because you cannot set the X spacing on an isometric grid, you may find that your drawing is not precise enough to perform a Trim function while cleaning up an isometric drawing. If you find that you cannot trim an object using another isometric object, simply erase the object and then recreate the portion of the object that you need.

CREATING AN ISOMETRIC DRAWING

Once you have made the necessary settings to assist in creating isometric drawings, you may now begin creating the drawing. Once again, the tools you use to create an isometric drawing are the same as those you have learned throughout this book. The only difference is that they will now be used to create a pictorial drawing. The most frequently

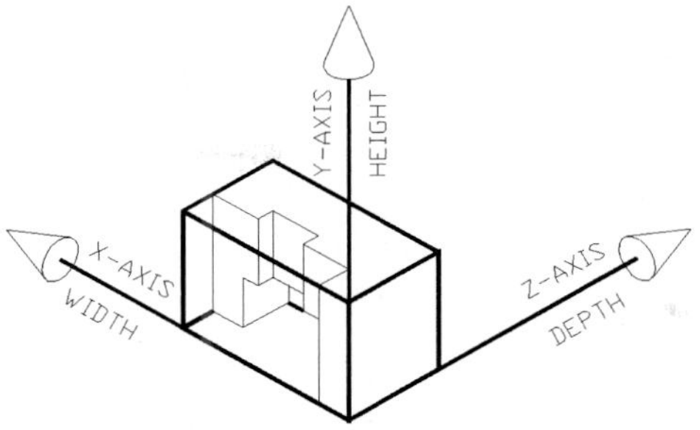

Figure 16.11
The isometric bounding box and lines are parallel to the top isoplane.

used command to create an isometric drawing is the **line** command. It is appropriate that we should begin our discussion of isometric drawing creation with the first object creation command discussed in this book.

Drawing Lines on the Isometric Grid

Drawing lines on the isometric grid will seem a little unusual until you have completed a few isometric drawings and understand how they are created. You will notice as you begin creating lines on the grid, that you can actually place them anywhere and in any direction. To assist in easy creation of isometric drawings, consider using Ortho to constrain the lines—not to vertical or horizontal, but to the isoplane. In other words, if you use Ortho, the lines you draw will be parallel to the isoplane crosshairs orientation. This is an excellent way to begin an isometric drawing. First, create the isometric bounding box of the object, which will include the isometric axis discussed earlier in the unit, and then begin cutting away at the object as shown in Figure 16.11.

If you need to create lines that are not parallel to the isoplane, you simply turn Ortho off and continue drawing. Lines that are not parallel to the isoplane are called non-isometric objects. They are usually drawn to represent an inclined or oblique plane as shown in Figure 16.12.

Typically, when an oblique or inclined plane is represented, it is foreshortened. Therefore, it is necessary to obtain the start and endpoint of the line as opposed to the length of the line since this cannot be easily established. In the last tutorial of this unit, you will learn the steps necessary to create an inclined plane.

Drawing Isometric Ellipses and Arcs

Whenever holes, cylinders, and fillets are to be represented on an isometric drawing you should use an isometric ellipse.

For the Professional

You should never use the **fillet** command to create isometric fillets on a drawing. Since the **fillet** command uses true arcs, not isometric arcs, your representation will always be incorrect.

Figure 16.12
An inclined and oblique plane.

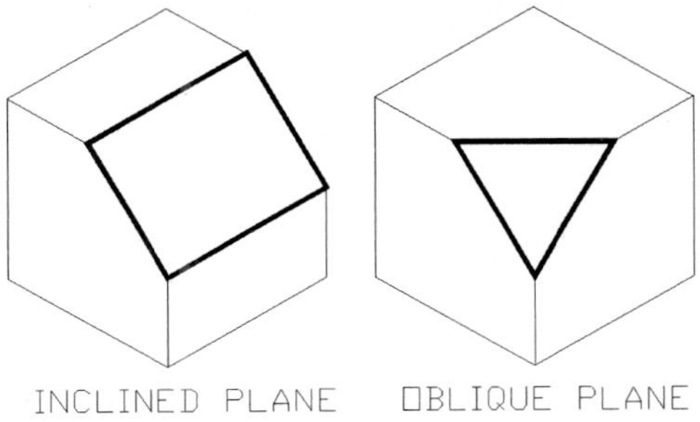

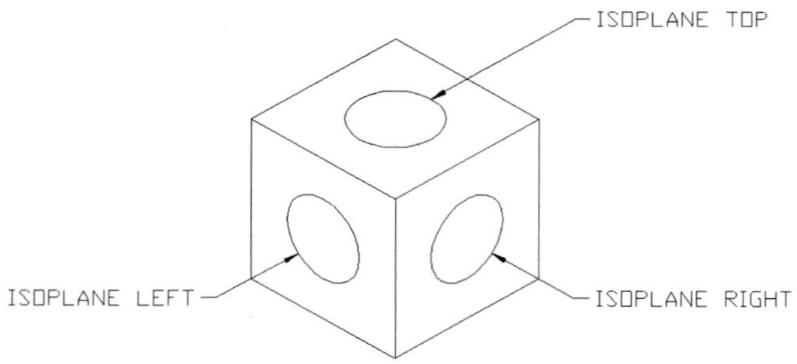

Figure 16.13
Proper alignment of isometric ellipses on isoplanes.

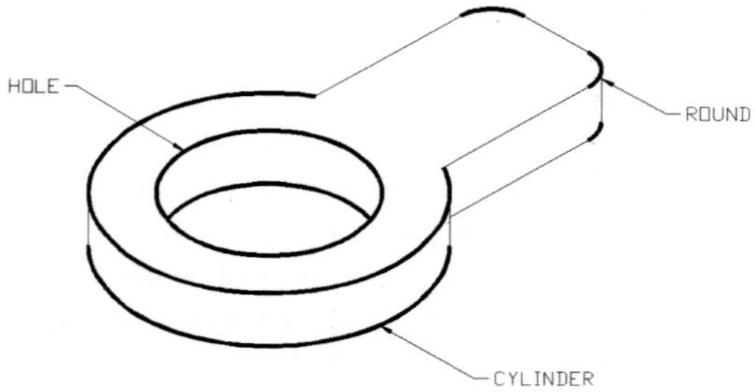

Figure 16.14
Using the isometric ellipse to represent a hole, cylinder, and a rounded corner.

Not only do you have to be sure and use isometric ellipses, you must also become aware of their proper orientation on an isometric drawing. Figure 16.13 shows how ellipses should be aligned on all isoplanes where holes are to be represented. Figure 16.14 shows how isometric ellipses are used to represent a hole, cylinder, and a rounded corner.

To create isometric ellipses, use the **ellipse** command. Isometric ellipses are known as isocircles in AutoCAD. Use the following procedure to create isocircles:

1. Select Ellipse Axis End from the Ellipse flyout on the Draw toolbar.
2. At the `Arc/Center/Isocircle/<Axis endpoint 1>:` prompt, enter **i** and press Enter.
3. At the `Center of Circle:` prompt, place the center of the isocircle using the mouse or coordinates.
4. At the `<Circle radius>/Diameter:` prompt, enter either the radius or diameter of the isocircle.

To create an isometric arc, you must create the complete isocircle and then trim the portion of the isocircle that you do not need. While this may seem time-consuming, it is the only way to correctly and accurately portray the arcs in the pictorial drawing. Figure 16.15 shows a before and after view of a corner that has been rounded using an isocircle. Notice the construction lines used to ensure that the corner is accurately portrayed.

In the tutorial that follows, you will have an opportunity to use isocircles in the creation of an isometric drawing.

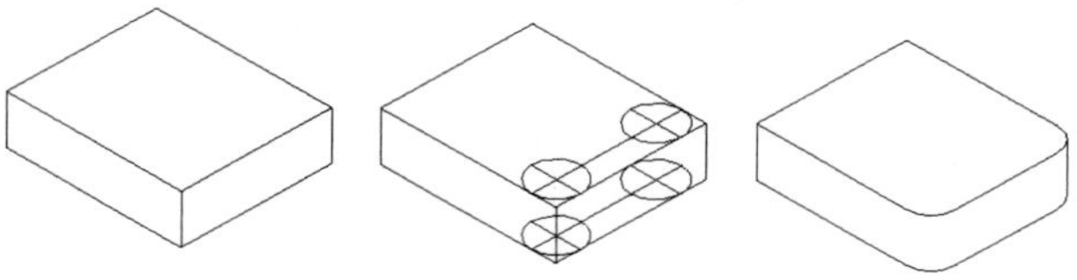

Figure 16.15
Rounding a corner using the isocircle.

TUTORIAL 16.2: CREATING AN ISOMETRIC DRAWING

In this tutorial, you will create the isometric drawing found in Figure 16.16. You will notice that this figure has no dimensions. Typically, isometric drawings are not dimensioned. They are pictorial representations that should never be used as a manufacturing tool. You will normally find only dimensioned isometric drawings in the educational setting. This tutorial will provide you with coordinates so you may create the drawing. Before beginning this tutorial, ensure that you have completed the previous tutorial.

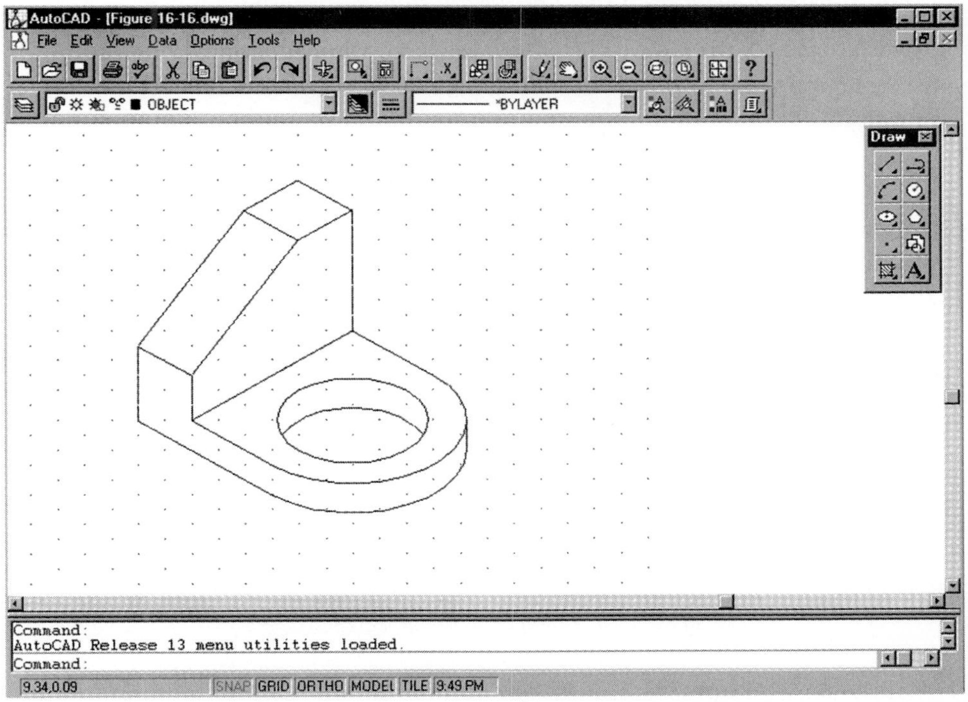

Figure 16.16
Use this Figure to assist in the completion of this tutorial.

1. If you are starting from the present tutorial, skip to step 3.
2. If the settings from the previous tutorial are not loaded, load the *Isometric.dwg* drawing file.
3. Your screen should resemble Figure 16.17. This isometric grid should be displayed.
4. Ensure that **snap** is on. This will allow accurate placement of the objects you create in this tutorial.
5. Turn **ortho** on. This will ensure that your lines will be parallel to the current isoplane orientation.
6. Press Ctrl E until the isoplane is set to left. You may have to press Ctrl E several times.
7. Select the **line** command. Do this from the Draw toolbar or by typing the command at the `Command:` prompt. As a reminder, the hot key for the **line** command is L.
8. At the `Line from point:` prompt, move the crosshairs until it snaps to coordinates 2.17,3. You will use this snap technique to choose all points in this tutorial. Do not enter the coordinates using the keyboard.
9. At the `To point:` prompt, select the coordinates 5.63,1.

Figure 16.17
You are now ready to create your first AutoCAD isometric drawing.

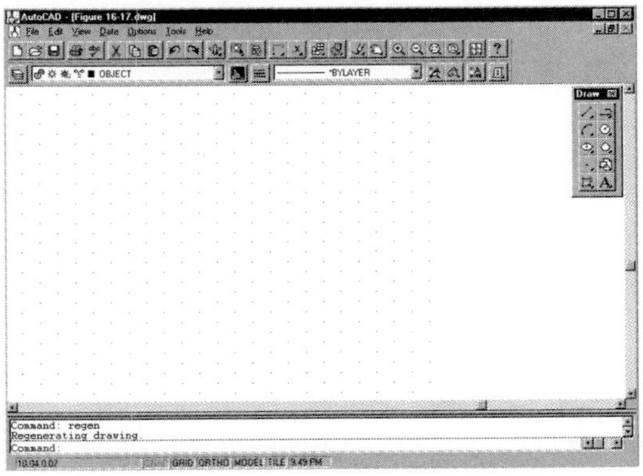

10. At the `To point:` prompt, select the coordinates 8.23,2.5.
11. At the `To point:` prompt, select the coordinates 8.23,5.

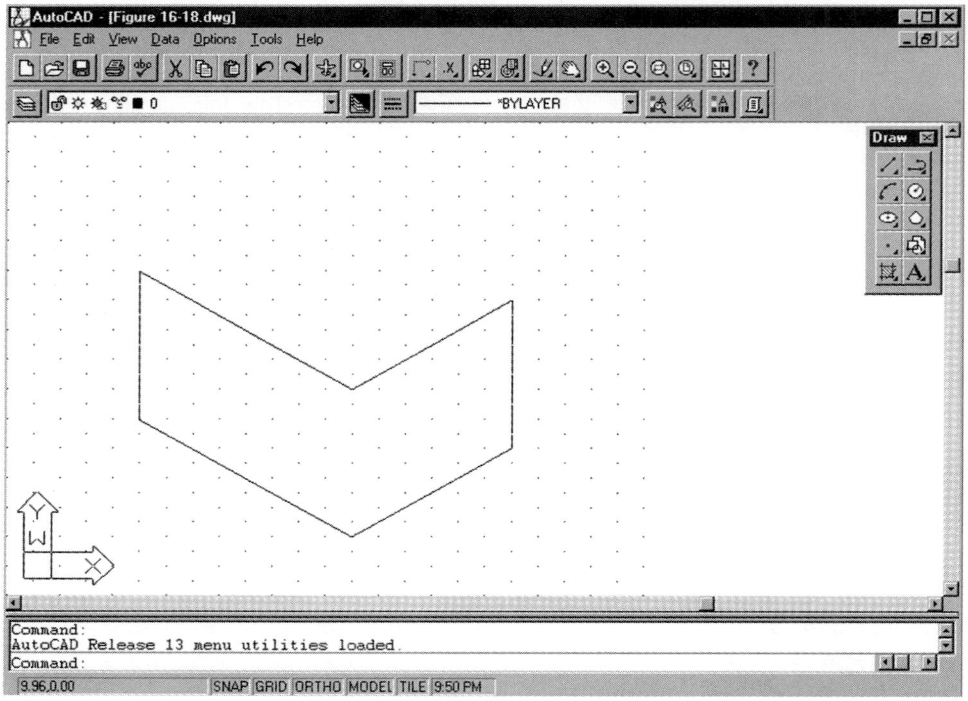

Figure 16.18
Use steps 4 through 13 to create this beginning shape.

12. At the `To point:` prompt, select the coordinates 5.63,3.5.
13. At the `To point:` prompt, select the coordinates 2.17,5.5.
14. At the `To point:` prompt, use the Close option. Your screen should resemble Figure 16.18.
15. Select Isoplane Top.
16. Select the **line** command.
17. At the `Line from point:` prompt, select the coordinates 2.17,5.5.
18. At the `To point:` prompt, select the coordinates 4.76,7.
19. At the `To point:` prompt, select the coordinates 8.23,5.
20. At the `To point:` prompt, press Enter.
21. Select Isoplane Right.
22. Select the **line** command.
23. At the `Line from point:` prompt, select the coordinates 5.63,3.5.
24. At the `To point:` prompt, select the coordinates 5.63,1.
25. At the `To point:` prompt, press Enter. Your screen should now resemble Figure 16.19. What you have drawn is the isometric extents of the object. By drawing this isometric box first, you can verify that the layout of the object is centered on the page, as well as provide necessary guidelines to assist in the later creation of ellipses. The bottom corner also becomes an isometric axis as shown in Figure 16.19.
26. Let's continue our drawing. Select the **line** command.
27. At the `Line from point:` prompt, select the coordinates 5.63,1.5.
28. At the `To point:` prompt, select the coordinates 8.23,3.
29. Select Isoplane Left.
30. At the `To point:` prompt, select the coordinates 5.63,4.5.
31. At the `To point:` prompt, select the coordinates 5.63,6.5.
32. Select Isoplane Top.
33. At the `To point:` prompt, select the coordinates 3.03,5.
34. Select Isoplane Right.
35. At the `To point:` prompt, select the coordinates 3.03,3.
36. At the `To point:` prompt, use the close option.
37. Select Isoplane Top.
38. Select the **line** command.
39. At the `Line from point:` prompt, select the coordinates 3.03,3.
40. At the `To point:` prompt, select the coordinates 5.63,4.5.
41. At the `To point:` prompt, press Enter. Your Figure should resemble Figure 16.20.
42. Use the **trim** and **erase** commands to modify your Figure to resemble the one shown in Figure 16.21. It may be helpful to turn **snap** off while using the **trim** and **erase** commands. If you find that a line cannot be trimmed, consider erasing it and then just redrawing the portion of the line you need. Object snaps will help you ensure that the location of the lines are accurate.

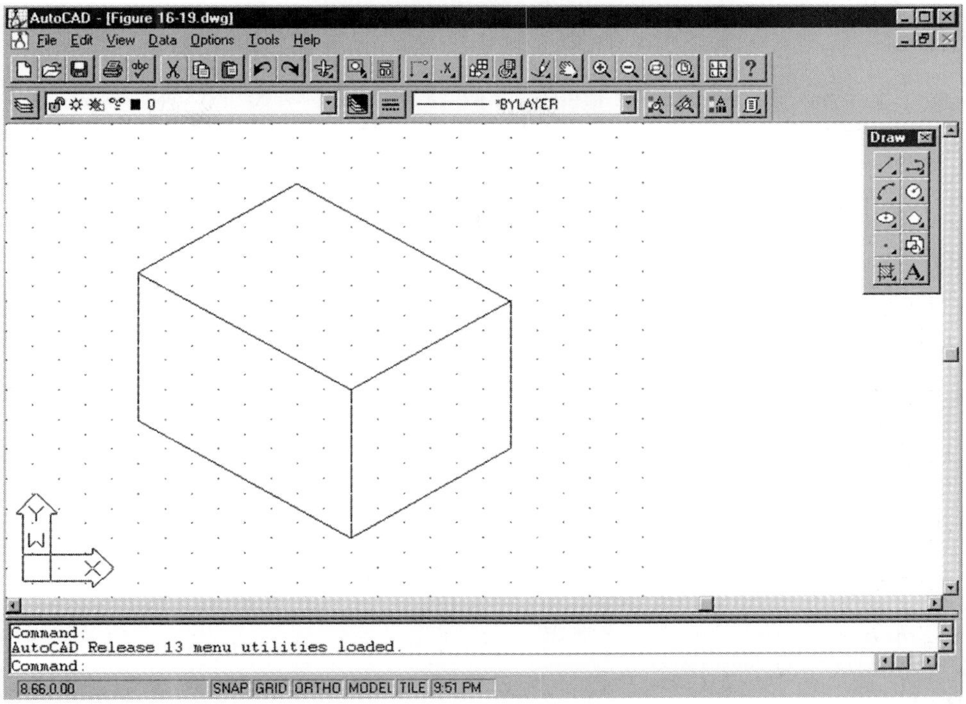

Figure 16.19
The Isometric Box. Notice the corner that represents our isometric axis as described earlier in the unit.

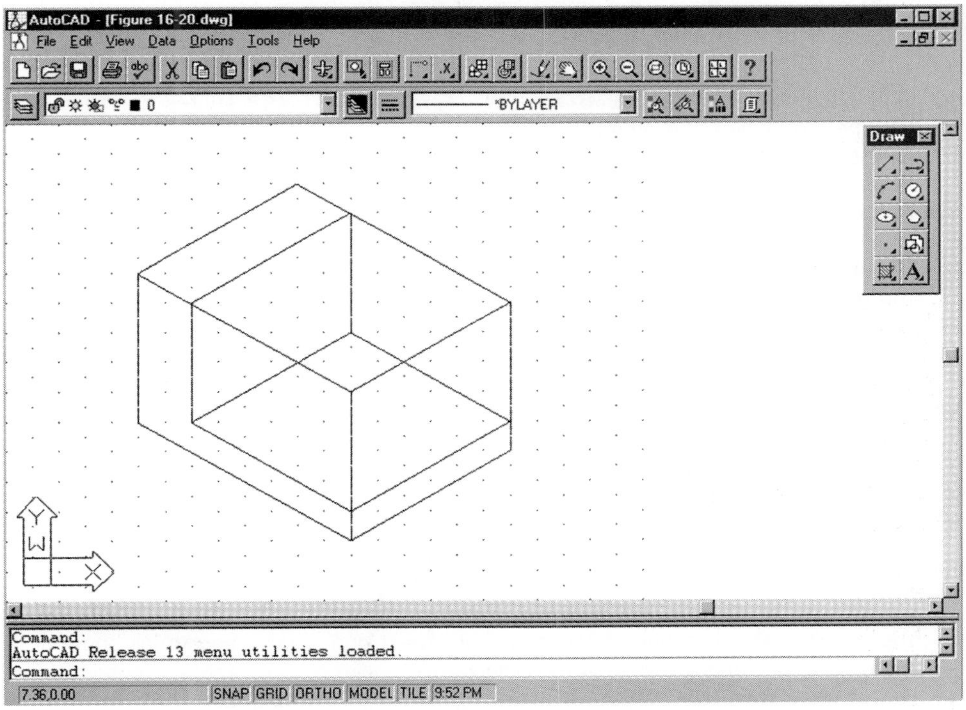

Figure 16.20
You should now start to see the basic shape of the object.

43. Let's get rid of the box look and add some curves to the object. Select the Ellipse Axis End command from the Ellipse flyout menu on the Draw Toolbar. You must select this option if you choose the command from the toolbar, or you could type **ellipse** at the `Command:` prompt. For the rest of this tutorial, if you are asked to select the **ellipse** command, ensure that you use one of these two methods.

44. Verify that the Isoplane is set to Top since you will be creating isometric ellipses that are parallel to the top surface.

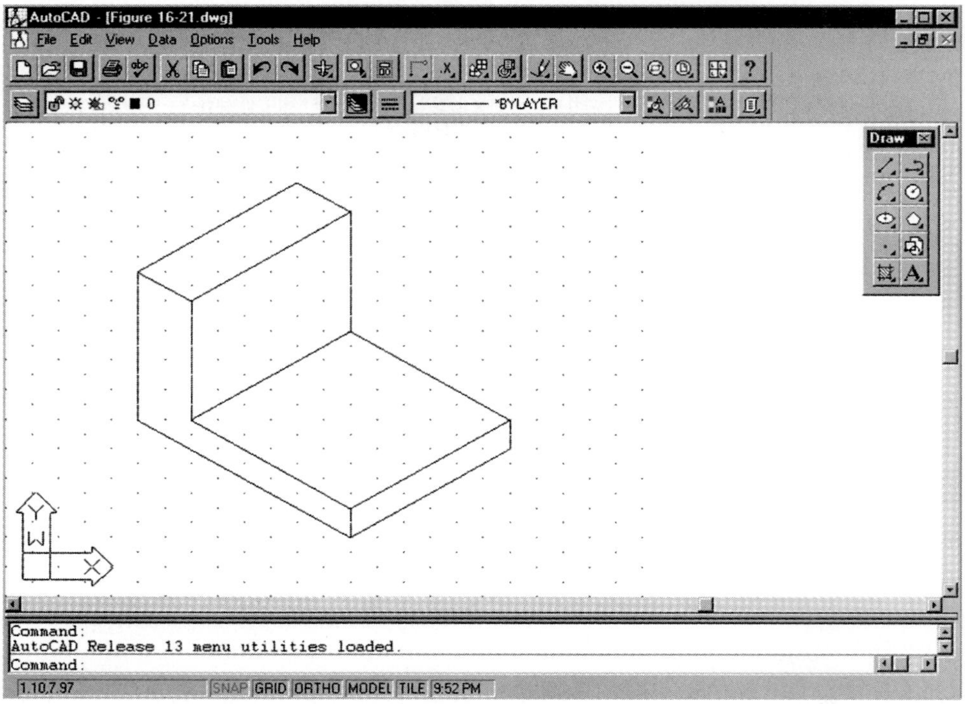

Figure 16.21
Use the trim and erase commands to get rid of unnecessary objects.

45. At the `Arc/Center/Isocircle/<Axis endpoint 1>:` prompt, type **i** and press Enter.
46. At the `Center of circle:` prompt, select coordinates 5.63,3.
47. At the `<Circle radius>/Diameter:` prompt, enter 1.5. A large isometric ellipse will be placed on the drawing. This will be used to round the front portion of the object.
48. Select the **copy** command.
49. At the `Select objects:` prompt, select the ellipse created in step 45 and press Enter.
50. At the `<Base point or displacement>/Multiple:` prompt, select anywhere on the screen. The actual point is not important, because we are going to use polar coordinates to place the copy.
51. At the `Second point of displacement:` prompt, enter @.5<270. A copy of the ellipse will be drawn below the one created in step 45. A value of .5 was used because this was the thickness of the bottom of the object. Let's see how these steps are used one more time by creating a hole in the object.
52. Select the **ellipse** command.
53. At the `Arc/Center/Isocircle/<Axis endpoint 1>:` prompt, type **i** and press Enter.
54. At the `Center of circle:` prompt, use the CENter object snap and select the ellipse created in step 45. This will be the upper ellipse.
55. At the `<Circle radius>/Diameter:` prompt, enter 1. An isometric ellipse that will represent a hole in the object will be created. This ellipse is concentric, shares the same center, as the upper ellipse created in step 45.
56. Select the **copy** command.
57. At the `Select objects:` prompt, select the ellipse created in step 45 and press Enter.
58. At the `<Base point or displacement>/Multiple:` prompt, select anywhere on the screen.
59. At the `Second point of displacement:` prompt, enter @.5<270. A copy of the ellipse will be drawn below the one created in step 50. This will represent the bottom of the hole.
60. Use the **trim** and **erase** commands and modify your drawing so that it looks like the one found in Figure 16.22.
61. Create a line connecting the two outer ellipses.
62. Select the start and end point of the line using the quadrant object snap on the ellipses specified in Figure 16.23.
63. Use the **trim** command and clean up the ellipse connection as shown in Figure 16.24. You may have to use zoom to obtain an acceptable view to work with.
64. Let's complete the object by creating an inclined surface on the object. Set the Isoplane to right.
65. Select the **line** command.
66. At the `Line from point:` prompt, select the coordinates 4.76,6.
67. At the `To point:` prompt, select the coordinates 3.03,3.75.
68. At the `To point:` prompt, select the coordinates 2.17,4.25.

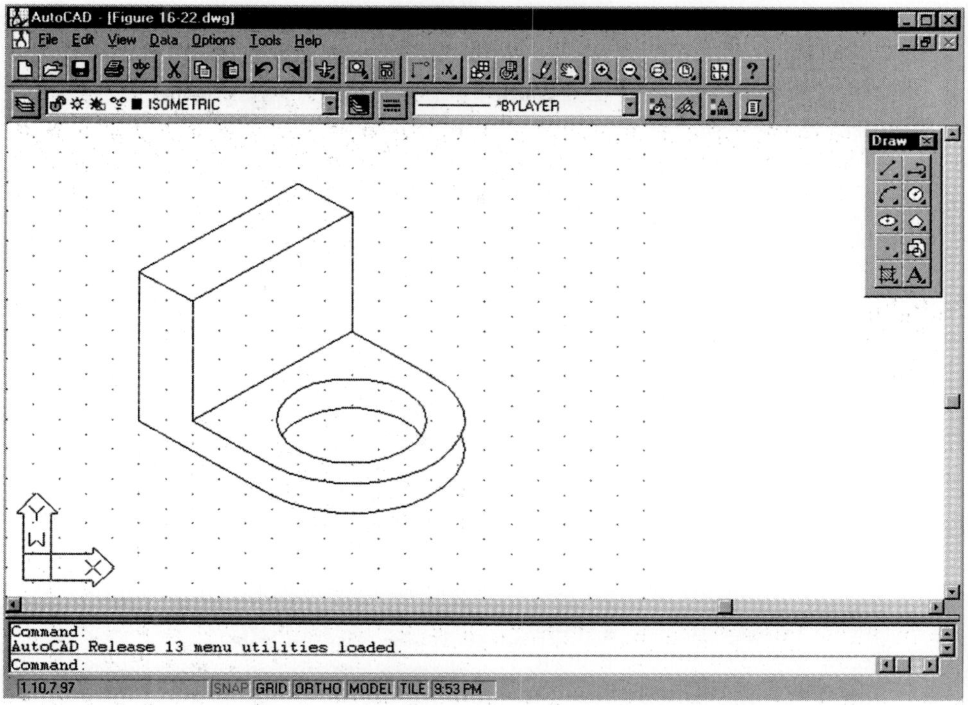

Figure 16.22
The end of the object has been rounded and a hole has been placed through it.

Figure 16.23
Create a line using these two quadrant points.

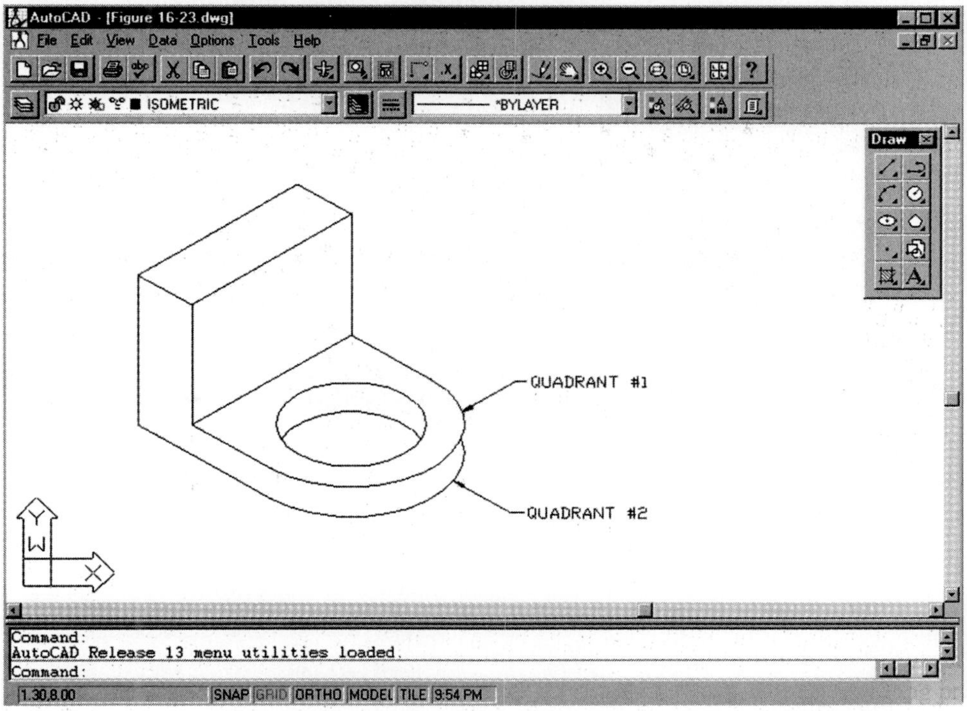

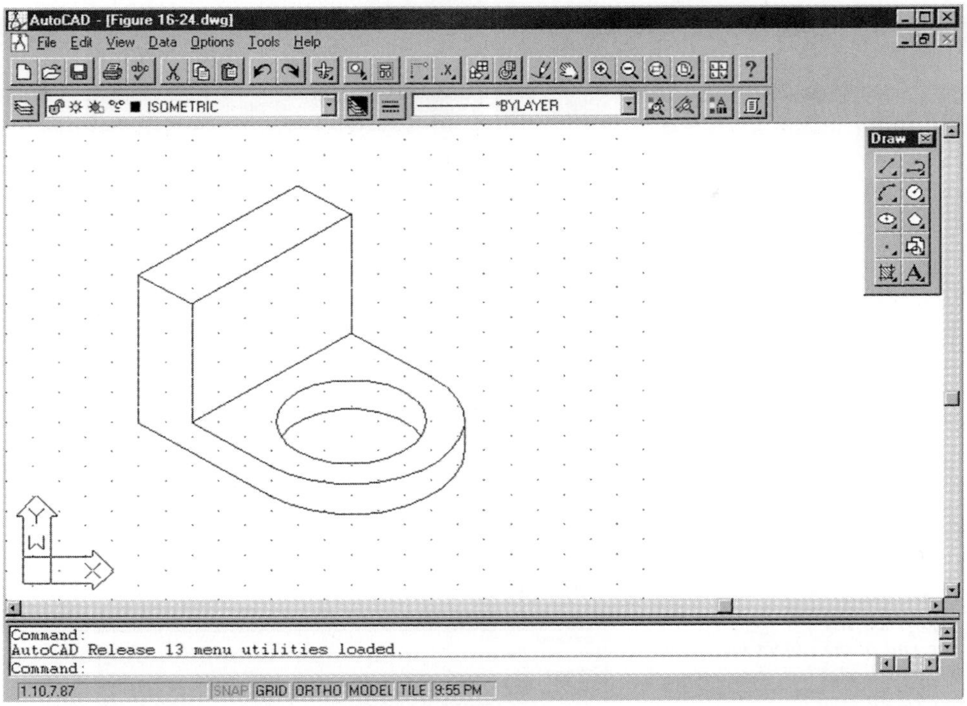

Figure 16.24
Trim the object.

69. At the `To point:` prompt, select the coordinates 3.9,6.5.

70. At the `To point:` prompt, use the close option. You now have the inclined surface in place. All that is left to complete the object is to use the **trim** and **erase** commands to modify the object so that it resembles Figure 16.25.

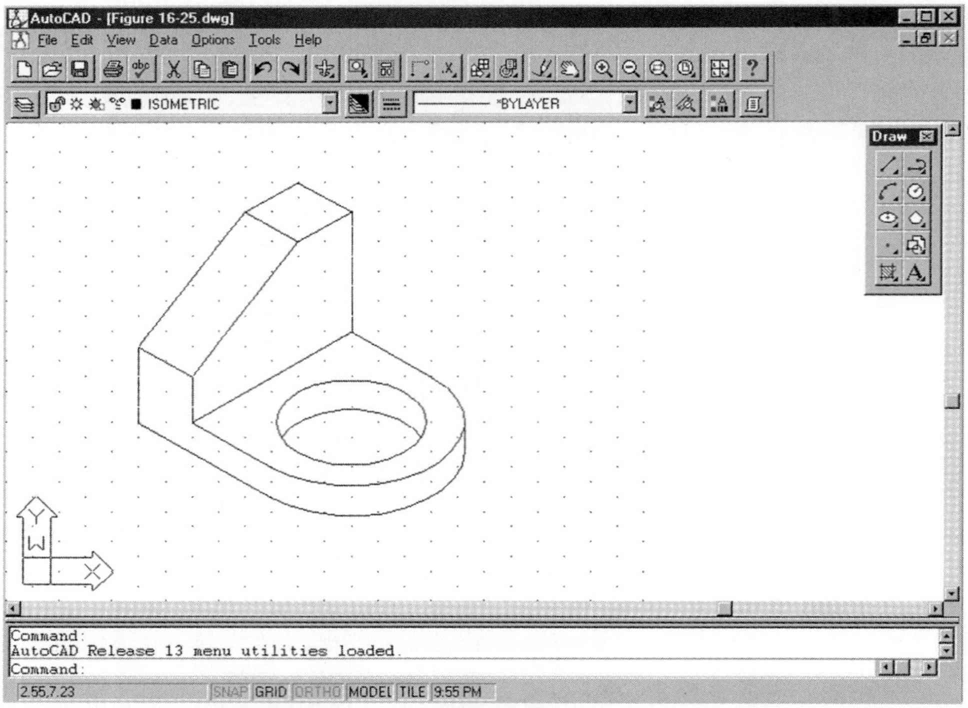

Figure 16.25
Once the lines have been trimmed and erased, the object is complete.

SUMMARY

As you become more familiar with creating isometric drawings in AutoCAD, you will find that you can create some stunning pictorial drawings using very familiar commands such as **line** and **ellipse**. You will also find that creating isometric drawings in AutoCAD is much easier and much more precise than using paper, pen, and template. But remember that the key to a good isometric drawing is isoplane orientation—not only for lines but especially for ellipses. If ellipses are not oriented properly, the drawing will have a bizarre, almost surrealistic look. While this may be fine for the art world, it has no place for technical pictorial drawings.

FOR THE PROFESSIONAL

For more information on isometric drawings, consult Technical Drawing or Technical Illustration books. Also, consider taking a course in technical drawing. Learning the background theory associated with isometric drawings will help you create more accurate AutoCAD isometric drawings.

REVIEW

1. Describe Isometric drawings and their use in technical drawings.
2. List the three types of pictorial drawings.
3. Explain the meaning of the term *isometric*.
4. List the three isometric axes.
5. How are circles represented in isometric drawings?
6. How does isometric snap differ from snap?
7. What effect does the isometric snap have on ORTHO mode?
8. List the settings that need to be modified in the Drawing Aids dialog box in order to create an isometric drawing.
9. Explain the use of the isometric planes.
10. What must be done before the isocircle option is enabled in the **ellipse** command?

EXERCISE 16

In this assignment you will create the dimensioned orthographic view, section and isometric representation of a Roller Mount found in Figure 16.26. This assignment will require you to utilize many of the skills learned in this course to include isometric drawings, orthographic drawings, dimensioning, hatching, viewing, and plotting. Very little guidance is given in this assignment. It is up to you to recreate this assignment as closely and as accurately as possible utilizing all of the AutoCAD skills you have learned. Some basic set-up information is included below. GOOD LUCK!

1. Create the drawing to be plotted on an A-size sheet of paper at half scale. Do not create the scale that is located on the lower left corner of the drawing; use that scale to help you determine the dimensions of the title block.
2. Establish appropriate layers and ensure that you utilize them.
3. Use the *monos.ttf* font and create a TITLE text style. This style is to be used for the large text in the title block.
4. Be sure to include all of the dimensions shown in Figure 16.26. To ensure that you have included all of the dimensions, try and recreate the isometric drawing from your dimensions alone. If you find that you cannot complete the isometric drawing from your dimensions, you will most likely find that you have forgotten one. Locate

the missing dimension, place it on the appropriate view and then continue completing the isometric drawing.

5. Completely fill out the title block using Figure 16.26 as a guide.
6. Save the drawing file using the name Roller Mount.dwg found in Figure 16.26.
7. Plot the drawing.

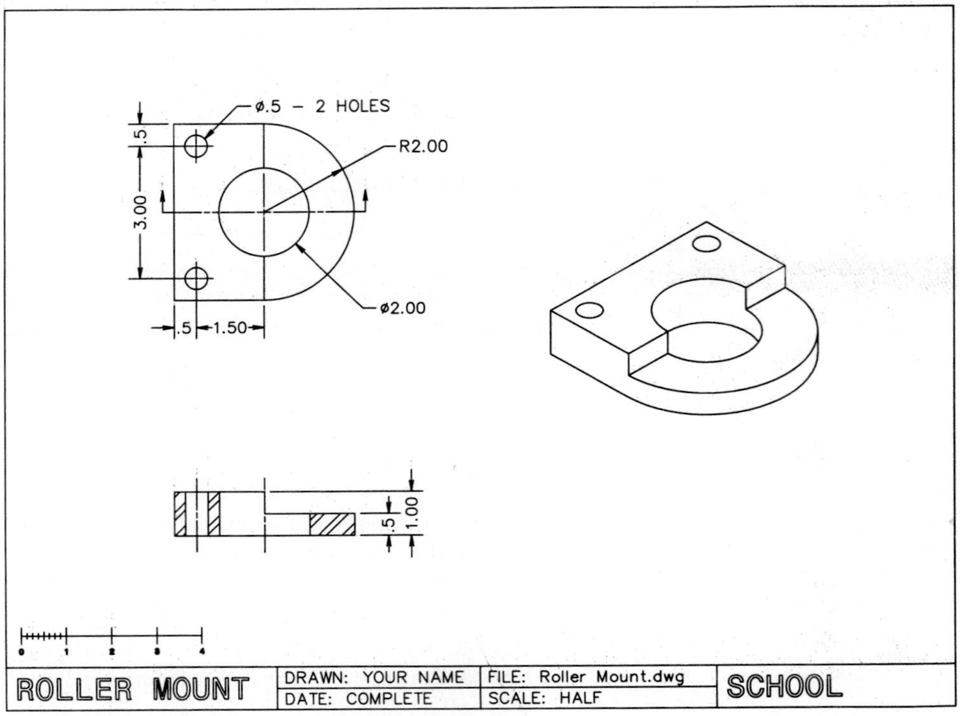

Figure 16.26
Recreate this Roller Mount drawing as accurately as possible.

INDEX

.BAK, 36
.CDF File Format, 466
.CUS Dictionary file, 190
.DWG, 29, 30, 36
.DXF Drawing Interchange File, 104, 467
.PFA Postscript font, 169
.PFB Postscript font, 169
.SDF File Format, 466
.SHX Font, 169
.TTF True Type Font, 169
.Y Point Filter, 223

2 Point
  Circle, 141, 147

3 Point
  Arc, 153
  Circle, 141, 145

Absolute Coordinates, 108
Absolute Polar Coordinates, 110
ACAD.DWG, 102
ACAD.LIN, 134
ACAD.PAT, 193
Accelerator key, 14
Aerial View Window, 77, 80
  Global, 78
  Locator, 78
  Menu Options, 79
  Pan, 78
  Statisitcs, 78
  Zoom, 78
  Zoom In, 78
  Zoom Out, 78
AIA, See American Institute of Architects
American Institute of Architects, 117, 374, 375
American National Standards Institute, 99, 134, 374, 375
Anchor point, 268
Angle Direction, 101
Angular measurement, 100
  Angle Direction, 101
  Decimal Degrees, 100
  Deg/Min/Sec, 100
  display precision, 101
  Grads, 100
  Radians, 100
  Surveyor's units, 100
ANSI, See American National Standards Institute
Aperture Box, 221
APParent, 212
ARC Command, 139, 152, 211, 354
  3 Point, 153
  CENter, 206
  Continue, 156
  DDMODIFY, 412
  ENDPoint, 205
  MIDpoint, 205
  QUAdrant, 208
  Start, Center, End, 153
  Start, End, Radius, 155
  TANgent, 210
Architectural units, 99
AREA Command, 428, 430
ARRAY Command, 284, 286, 451
  polar array, 284, 286
  rectangular arrray, 284, 285
ASE, See structured query language
ATTDEF Command, 453
ATTDIA system variable, 454
ATTDISP Command, 454, 461
ATTEDIT Command, 458, 459
ATTEXT Command, 466
ATTREDEF Command, 458, 463
Attributes, 453
  ATTDEF, 453
  ATTDIA, 454
  ATTDISP, 461
  ATTEXT, 466
  ATTREDEF, 463
  BLOCK, 453
  DDATTDEF, 453
  DDATTE, 458
  DDATTEXT, 466
  Extracting information, 465
  WBLOCK, 453
AutoCAD
  Display, 11
  font (.SHX), 169
  Help, 19
  Release 12, 29, 30
Auxiliary view, 46, 47

BASE, 451
BHATCH Command, 191, 358, 415
BLIPMODE Command, 41
Blips, 41, 43, 52, 59, 61
BLOCK Command, 437, 439-47, 453
  DDEMODES, 444
  DDINSERT, 447
  DDRENAME, 419
  EXPLODE, 451
  Grips, 452
  INSERT, 447
  Layer 0, 443
  MINSERT, 451
  Points to consider, 446
  PURGE, 420
  Updating, 452
BOUNDARY Command, 358, 430
BREAK Command, 273, 274
  1 Point, 273
  1 Point Select, 273
  2 Points, 273
  2 Points Select, 273
BYBLOCK, 444
BYLAYER, 131

Cartesian coordinate, 106
CENter, 206
Center Diameter
  Circle, 143
Center lines, 132, 373
Center, Diameter Circle, 141
Center, Radius Circle, 141
CHAMFER Command, 281, 282
CHANGE Command, 131, 184
CHPROP Command, 131
CIRCLE Command, 139, 141, 142, 143
  2 Point, 141, 147
  3 Point, 141, 145
  CENter, 206
  Center, Diameter, 141
  Center, Radius, 141
  CIRCLERAD variable, 142
  DDMODIFY, 412
  Default radius, 142
  QUAdrant, 208
  TANgent, 210
  Tangent, Tangent, Radius, 141, 147
CIRCLERAD system variable, 142, 143
Circumscribed Polygons, 161
CLAYER Command, 119

Close option, 51
Cold grip, 293, 294
Command History, 12
Command Prompt, 12, 13
Command Window, 12
Commands
ARC, 139, 152, 211, 354
AREA, 428, 430
ARRAY, 284, 286, 451
ATTDISP, 454, 461
BHATCH, 191, 358, 415
BLIPMODE, 41
BLOCK, 437, 439-47, 453
BOUNDARY, 358, 430
BREAK, 273, 274
CHAMFER, 281, 282
CHANGE, 131
CHPROP, 131
CIRCLE, 139, 141, 142, 143
CLAYER, 119
COORDS, 41, 47, 48
COPY, 22, 258, 266, 439
DBLIST, 424, 434
DDCHPROP, 115, 131, 398, 408
DDEDIT, 184
Attributes, 455
Dimension Text, 397
Editing Text, 184, 418
Modifying Contents, 185
MTEXT, 398
DDEMODES, 130, 418, 444
DDGRIPS, 296
DDIM, 376
DDINSERT, 447, 451, 453
DDLTYPE, 127
DDMODIFY, 410, 411
attributes, 463
dimensions, 396, 397, 398
Linetypes, 131
MTEXT, 185
Text, 184
DDOSNAP, 372
DDRENAME, 419
DDRMODES, 41, 42, 476
DDSELECT, 228, 232, 292
DDUNITS, 37, 98, 99, 101, 262
DDVIEW, 82, 83, 84
DIMALIGNED, 389, 390
DIMBASELINE, 391
DIMCENTER, 393, 394
DIMCONTINUE, 391
DIMDIAMETER, 393
DIMLINEAR, 387, 389, 390
DIMRADIUS, 393
DIMTEDIT, 396, 397
DIST, 424, 426
DIVIDE, 309, 312-15
Blocks, 319
DONUT, 310, 320
DOUGHNUT, 320
DSVIEWER, 59, 78
DTEXT, 168, 169-77
Editing Text, 184, 413, 418
ELLIPSE, 309, 320, 321, 323, 479
END, 31
Entering, 13
ERASE, 227, 250, 252
EXPLODE, 140, 361, 374, 451, 452
EXTEND, 276
FILLET, 278, 279, 281, 343
GRID, 41, 42, 44, 46, 49
GROUP, 438
HATCH, 191, 415
HATCHEDIT, 192, 198
ID, 49, 426, 427
LAYER, 117
LEADER, 401
LIMITS, 37, 40, 41, 64, 90
LIMMAX, 40
LIMMIN, 40
LINE, 50
LINETYPE, 126, 134, 135, 363
LIST, 424, 434
LTSCALE, 131
MEASURE, 309, 314-16, 319
MINSERT, 447, 451
MIRROR, 264, 298
MLEDIT, 334, 342
MLSTYLE, 334, 337, 342
MOVE, 256, 258, 298, 300
MTEXT, 168
Editing Text, 185
Entering Text, 180
Leader Text, 401
Spell Checking, 188
Text Height, 172
NEW, 24
OFFSET, 258, 331
OOPS, 251
OPEN, 25, 36
ORTHO, 41
OSNAP, 221, 426, 440
PAN, 59, 75, 76
PEDIT, 359, 361, 362, 365, 367
PLINE, 354, 355, 362, 367, 430
PLOT, 86, 88
POINT, 310
POLYGON, 139, 160, 161
PURGE, 256, 420, 434, 445
QSAVE, 28
QTEXT, 188
QUIT, 31
RAY, 284, 286, 331
RECTANG, 139, 140
REDO, 253
REDRAW, 52, 59, 61, 294
REGEN, 59, 61, 62, 63, 67, 294
REGENAUTO, 62
ROTATE, 261, 298, 301
SAVE, 28
SAVEAS, 29
SAVEASR12, 29
SAVETIME, 30
SCALE, 266, 268
SELECT, 230, 232
SKETCH, 309, 332, 333
SNAP, 41-47
STATUS, 422, 423
STRETCH, 268, 298
STYLE, 168, 419
TEXT, 174
TIME, 422, 431, 432
TRIM, 270
UNDO, 56, 252
VIEW, 60, 76, 82, 84, 90
VIEWRES, 62
WBLOCK, 437, 444, 445, 447, 453
XLINE, 326, 327
ZOOM, 59, 63, 73, 75
Coordinate display, 47, 48, 49
absolute mode, 48
relative mode, 48
Coordinate System, 104
Coordinates, 13
Coords, 41
COPY Command, 22, 258, 266, 439
Crosshairs, 12
C-size, 39
Cursor, 13
Cursor keys, 14

Database, 204
DBLIST Command, 424, 434
DDATTDEF Command, 453
DDATTE Command, 458
DDATTEXT Command, 466
DDCHPROP Command, 115, 131, 398, 408
DDEDIT Command
Attributes, 455
Dimension Text, 397
Editing Text, 184, 418
Modifying Contents, 185
MTEXT, 398
DDEMODES Command, 130, 416, 418, 444
DDGRIPS Command, 296
DDIM Command, 376
DDINSERT Command, 447, 451, 453
DDLTYPE Command, 126, 127
DDMODIFY Command, 410, 411
attributes, 463
dimensions, 396, 397, 398
Linetypes, 131
MTEXT, 185
Text, 184
DDOSNAP Command, 217, 372
DDRENAME Command, 419
DDRMODES Command, 41, 42, 476
DDSELECT Command, 228, 232, 292

DDUNITS Command, 37, 98, 99, 101, 262
DDVIEW Command, 82, 83, 84
Decimal degrees., 100
Decimal units, 99
Deg/Min/Sec, 100
Dialog boxes, 6
  Buttons, 7, 19
  Check boxes, 7, 19
  Edit boxes, 6, 18
  Image tiles, 7, 19
  List boxes, 7, 19
  Radio buttons, 7, 19
  Scroll bars, 7, 19
Dim prompt, 373
DIMALIGNED Command, 389, 390
DIMASO system variable, 375
DIMBASELINE Command, 391
DIMCENTER Command, 393, 394
DIMCONTINUE Command, 391
DIMDIAMTER Command, 393
Dimension style, 375
Dimension styles dialog box, 376-86
  Annotation, 383-86
  Annotation, 377
  dimesion style, 376
  family, 376
  Format, 380-83
  Format, 377
  Geometry, 377-79
  Geometry, 377
Dimensioning, 371-405
  aligned dimensions, 386, 391
  angular dimensions, 382, 395
    arcs, 395
    circle and defined point, 395
    three defined points, 396
    two non-parallel lines, 395
  associative dimensions, 374, 375
  center lines, 132, 373
  DDMODIFY, 415
  dimension line, 373, 377, 378, 380, 383, 391
  dimension styles dialog box, 376-86
  dimension text, 373, 383, 386, 396, 398
  extension line, 373, 378, 382, 416
  leader, 376, 401, 402
  linear dimensions, 386, 387
  modifying with grips, 398-99
  oblique dimensions, 401
  radial dimensions, 386
  terminator, 373
DIMLINEAR Command, 387, 389, 390
DIMRADIUS Command, 393
Dimstyle
  DDRENAME, 419
  PURGE, 420
DIMTEDIT Command, 396, 397
Display list driver, 61
Display precision, 99
DIST Command, 424, 426
DIVIDE Command, 309, 312-15
  Blocks, 319
  Inserting objects, 313
  NODe, 207
DONUT Command, 310, 320
  QUAdrant, 208
DOUGHNUT Command, 320
Drafting equipment, 33
Drawing Area, 12
Drawing database, 56, 57, 60, 61, 89, 90, 242
Drawing editor, 31, 34, 35, 43, 53
DSVIEWER Command, 59, 78
DTEXT Command, 168, 169-77
  Editing Text, 184, 413, 418

ELLIPSE Command, 309, 320, 321, 323, 479
  Arc, 324
END command, 31, 36, 276
ENDPoint, 205
Engineering units, 99
Entering Text
  Aligning, 176
  DTEXT, 174
  MTEXT, 180
  Special Characters, 177
  TEXT, 174
ERASE Command, 227, 250, 252
EXPLODE Command, 140, 361, 374, 451, 452
  Rectangle, 140
EXTEND Command, 276
EXTENTS
  STATUS, 422

Fast zoom, 62
FILLET Command, 278, 279, 281, 343
  options, 279, 281
FILLMODE system variable, 41, 356
Floating-point values, 60, 61
Floppy disk
  limitations, 22
Folders, 24
  Creating, 22
Font
  .PFA Postscript, 169
  .PFB Postscript, 169
  .SHX AutoCAD font, 169
  .TTF True Type, 169
Foreshortening, 474
Fractional units, 99
Freezing, 123
FROm, 211
Function keys, 13

Grads, 100
Graphical user interfaces (GUIs), 1
Grid, 12, 41-44, 285, 479
  STATUS, 422
GRID Command, 42, 44, 46, 49
Grid too dense to display, 42, 108
GRIPBLOCK system variable, 297, 452
Gripmodes, 291, 298
  copy option, 305
  mirror, 298, 303
  move, 298, 300
  rotate, 298, 301
  scale, 298, 301
  stretch, 298
Grips, 291-308
  BLOCK, 452
  WBLOCK, 452
GRIPSIZE system variable, 297
GROUP Command, 438

HATCH Command, 191, 415
  DDMODIFY, 415
HATCHEDIT Command, 192, 198
Hatching, 191
  Advanced options, 197
  Defining the Area, 194
  Editing, 198
  Patterns, 191
  Problems, 201
  Ray Casting, 197
Highlight system variable, 228
Hot grip, 293, 298, 301, 302, 303
Hot keys, 50
HPANGsystem variable, 193
HPDOUBLE system variable, 193
HPNAME sytem variable, 193
HPSCALE system variable, 193
HPSPACE system variable, 193

ID Command, 49, 426, 427
IGES file, 104
Implied selection, 293
Inscribed Polygons, 161
INSertion, 208
International Standards Organization, 374
INTersection, 208
ISO, See International Standards Organization
Isocircle, See isometric ellipse
Isometric axis, 322, 475, 479, 484
Isometric bounding box, 479
Isometric drawings, 47, 401, 474, 473-88
Isometric ellipse, 322, 475, 479
Isometric grid, 43, 476, 478, 479
Isometric plane toggle, 476, 477, 478, 479
Isometric snap, 323, 476, 477
Isoplane, See isometric plane toggle

Justifying Text, 175

LASTPOINT, 148, 427
LAYER Command, 117
Layer Control dialog box, 117
  DDLMODES, 117
Layers, 62
  Adding New Layers, 117
  advantages, 115

Layers, (*cont.*)
  Changing the Current Layer, 119
  Color, 120
  DDLMODES, 116
  DDRENAME, 419
  Filters, 124
  Freezing and Thawing, 123
  frozen, 62
  Layer Control dialog box, 117
  Layer Control toolbar, 123
  Layer names, 117
  Locking and Unlocking, 123
  Naming Layers, 117
  PURGE, 420
  Renaming, 124
  Turning On and Off, 122
Leader, 373
LEADER Command, 401
Limits, 37-41, 67
  grid, 44
  plotting, 92
  rotating snap, 46
  STATUS, 422
  virtual screen, 72
  ZOOM All, 64
  Zoom Dynamic, 67
  Zoom Scale, 74
LIMITS Command, 37, 40, 41, 64, 90
LIMMAX Command, 40
LIMMIN Command, 40
LINE Command, 50, 51, 52, 479
  DDMODIFY, 411
  ENDPoint, 205
  MIDpoint, 205
  Undo option, 51
LINETYPE Command, 126, 134, 135, 363
  Header Line, 134
  Pattern Line, 135
  PURGE, 420
Linetypes, 126
  Creating your own, 134
  DDLTYPE, 126
  DDRENAME, 419
  default, 130
  Definition, 134
  loading, 128
  predefined, 127
  Scale for All Objects, 131
  Scale for Individual Objects, 132
LIST Command, 424, 434
Locking, 123
LTSCALE Command, 131

Magnification power, 65
Manual drafting, 24, 33, 37, 60, 475
MAXSORT, 119
MEASURE Command, 309, 314-16, 319
  Inserting Blocks, 316
  NODe, 207, 315
MIDpoint, 205
MINSERT Command, 447, 451
MIRROR Command, 264, 298
Mirror line, 262, 264, 265, 303, 305
MIRRTEXT system variable, 266
MLEDIT Command, 334, 342
MLINE Command
  DDMODIFY, 414
  PURGE, 420
MLSTYLE Command, 334, 337, 342
MOVE Command, 256, 258, 298, 300
MS/DOS, 1
MTEXT Command, 168
  Editing Text, 185
  Entering Text, 180
  Importing Text, 181
  Leader Text, 401
  Spell Checking, 188
  Text Height, 172
Multilines, 334
  Editing, 342
  MLEDIT, 342
  MLSTYLE, 334
  Properties, 336

Naming Layers, 117
NEArest, 211
NEW command, 24, 29
NODe, 207, 312
Noun/verb selection, See pick-first selection
Null response, 243

Object, 56
Object selection cycling, 243
Object selection filters, 245
Object Snap, 12, 204, 217, 372
  Aperture Box, 221
  APParent, 212
  CENter, 206
  ENDPoint, 205
  FROm, 211
  INSertion, 208
  INTersection, 208
  MIDpoint, 205
  Multiple running modes, 219
  NEArest, 211
  NODe, 207
  PERpendicular, 209
  QUAdrant, 208
  QUIck, 221
  STATUS, 423
  TANgent, 210
  Temporary modes, 212
  Turning Object Snaps Off, 221
Object snaps, 221
OFFSET Command, 258, 331
OOPS Command, 251, 440
OPEN command, 25, 36
Orientation, 262, 477
  crosshairs, 479
  dimension text, 382
  isocircles and arcs, 479
  isometric plane, 476, 477
  mirrored text, 266
  paper, 39
  UCS Icon, 12
  when rotating objects, 261
    cw and ccw, 262
Ortho, 12, 41, 49
  STATUS, 423
Orthographic projection, 49
Orthographic views, 46, 49
OSNAP Command, 217, 221, 426, 440

PAN command, 59, 75, 76
Pan displacement, 76
Paper size, 37, 91, 93
PDMODE Command, 311
PDSIZE Command, 311
PEDIT Command, 359, 361, 362, 365, 367
Pen assignments, 89
Pen parameters, 89
PERpendicular, 209
Pickadd system variable, 232, 235, 246
Pickauto system variable, 246
Pickbox, 12, 228, 232, 243
  aperture box, 222
  crossing window, 237
  object selection cycling, 243, 244
  pick-first selection, 232
  press and drag, 236
  window selection, 235
Pickdrag system variable, 236, 246
Pick-first selection, 231, 232
Pickfirst system variable, 232, 245, 292
Pictorial drawings, 401, 474, 475, 478, 479
  axonometric drawings, 474
    dimetric, 475
    trimetric, 475
  oblique drawings, 474
  perspective drawings, 474
Pixel, 60
PLINE Command, 354, 355, 362, 367, 430
PLOT command, 86, 88
Plot Configuration, 86, 89, 90, 91, 92, 93
  Adjusting the Area Fill, 90
  Display, 90
  Extents, 90
  Hide Lines, 90
  Limits, 90
  Plot to File, 91
  View, 90
  Window, 90
Plot devices, 85
  plotters, 85, 86, 87, 88, 89, 92
    configuring, 87
  printers, 85, 86, 92
Plot origin, 92
Plot preview, 93
Plot rotation, 92
Plot scale, 92

Plotting, 85, 88, 89, 90, 91, 94, 95
Poch, 191
POINT Command, 310
NODe, 207
PDMODE, 311
PDSIZE, 311
Style, 311
Point Filters, 222
.X Point Filter, 223
.Y Point Filter, 223
Polar Coordinates, 110
Absolute, 110
Polygon, 51, 239, 240, 268, 273, 279
POLYGON Command, 139, 160, 161
Circumscribed, 161
Inscribed, 161
POLYSIDES, 161
Specifying by Edge, 162
Polylines, 354, 361
PEDIT, 361
PLINE, 354
SPLFRAME, 364
Spline, 363
SPLINESEGS, 364
SPLINETYPE, 364
POLYSIDES system variable, 161
Postscript font (.PFA or .PFB), 169
Prototype drawing, 24, 102
ACAD.DWG, 102
new, 103
No Prototype option, 104
Options, 104
Pull-Down Menus, 11, 16
PURGE Command, 256, 420, 434, 445

QSAVE Command, 28, 29
QTEXT Command, 188
STATUS, 423
QUAdrant, 208
QUIck, 221
QUIT Command, 30, 31, 53

Radians, 100
Ray Casting, 197, 359
RAY Command, 284, 286, 331
DDMODIFY, 414
Read-Only, 26
RECTANG Command, 139, 140
Explode, 140
REDO Command, 253
REDRAW Command, 52, 59, 61, 294
REGEN Command, 59, 61, 62, 63, 67, 294
REGENAUTO Command, 62
Relative Coordinates, 108
Relative Polar Coordinates, 110
Renaming
Layers, 124
ROTATE Command, 261, 298, 301

SAVE Command, 28, 29, 34
SAVEAS Command, 28, 29, 30
SAVEASR12 Command, 29
SAVETIME variable, 30
Saving, 24, 27, 28, 36, 84
SCALE Command, 266, 268
Scale factor, 266, 302, 303, 340
Scientific units, 99
Screen menus, 12, 18
SELECT Command, 230, 232
Select Linetype dialog box, 127
Selection set, 228
Selection window, 235, 246
Shapes
PURGE, 420
SKETCH Command, 309, 332, 333
Snap, 12, 41-47
STATUS, 422
SPLFRAME system variable, 364
SPLINESEG system variable, 364
SPLINETYPE system varaible, 364
SQL, See structured query language
Status Bar, 12
STATUS Command, 422, 423
STRETCH Command, 268, 298
Structured Query Language, 468
STYLE Command, 168
DDRENAME, 419
PURGE, 420
Surveyor's units, 100

Tangent, 148, 210
Tangent, Tangent, Radius
Circle, 141, 147
Taskbar, 2
Programs, 3
Shut Down, 3
Start button, 3
TEXT Command, 168, 174
DDEDIT, 418
DDMODIFY, 413
Hiding, 188
INSertion, 208
Spell Checking, 188
Text Editing
CHANGE, 185
DDEDIT, 184
DDMODIFY, 184
Text Entering
Changing the Style, 175
Justifying Text, 175
Text Style
Character Preview, 170
DDSTYLE, 168
Effects, 171
Naming the Text Style, 169
Renaming, 172
Selecting a Font, 169
STYLE, 168
TEXTFILL system variable, 188
TEXTQLTY system variable, 188
Thawing, 123
Thumbnails, 25, 26
TIME Command, 422, 431, 432
Toolbars, 12, 15
docked, 15
floating, 15
Tool Windows icon, 16
Transparent, 52, 61, 62, 63, 76
TRIM Command, 270, 276
True Type font (.TTF), 169

UCS, See user coordinate system
UNDO Command, 56, 252
Units, 24, 37, 258, 384
Alternate Units dimensioning, 384
Architectural, 99
architectural default, 260
Decimal, 99
dimensioning precision, 384
dimensioning units, 384
drawing units, 92
Enable Units, 385
Engineering, 99
Fractional, 99
moving objects, 258
polar coordinates, 388
reference units, 302, 303
Scientific, 99
Units Control dialog box, 37, 99, 101
ZOOM, 65, 70
UNITS Command, 98
UNIX, 1
Unlocking, 123
User coordinate system, 106
DDRENAME, 419
icon, 12, 106

Vector graphics information, 60
Vectors, 204
Verb/noun selection, See pick-after selection
View box, 66
VIEW command, 60, 76, 82, 84, 90
DDRENAME, 419
VIEWRES Command, 62
Views, 46, 49, 60, 71, 75, 82, 83, 84
deleting, 83
listing, 83
restoring, 83
saving, 83
VIEWSIZE system variable, 76
Virtual screen, 60, 61, 62, 67, 72, 75
Vport
DDRENAME, 419

Warm grip, 293
WBLOCK Command, 437, 444, 445, 447, 453
EXPLODE, 451
Grips, 452
MINSERT, 451
Points to consider, 446
Updating, 452

Windows
  maximizing, 6
  minimizing, 5
  restoring, 6
Windows 95, 1
  Closing applications, 5
  Help, 8
    Contents, 9
    Find, 9
    Index, 9
  shortcut, 9
  Taskbar, 2
Windows NT 4.0, 1

XLINE Command, 326, 327
  DDMODIFY, 413

ZOOM Command, 59, 63, 73, 75
  ZOOM All, 64
  ZOOM Center, 65
  ZOOM Dynamic, 66
    Current View, 67
    Drawing Extents, 67
    Generated area, 67
    Panning View Box, 67
    White Hourglass, 67
    Zooming View Box, 67
  ZOOM Extents, 70
  ZOOM In, 75
  ZOOM Left, 70
  ZOOM Out, 75
  ZOOM Previous, 71
  ZOOM Scale, 74
  ZOOM Vmax, 72
  ZOOM Window, 73

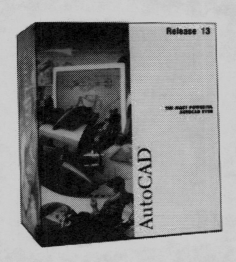